# ICCA
# CONGRESS SERIES

INTERNATIONAL ARBITRATION CONFERENCE
DUBLIN, 8 - 10 JUNE 2008

**Wolters Kluwer**
Law & Business

AUSTIN   BOSTON   CHICAGO   NEW YORK · THE NETHERLANDS

INTERNATIONAL COUNCIL
FOR COMMERCIAL ARBITRATION


50 YEARS OF
THE NEW YORK CONVENTION


GENERAL EDITOR:
ALBERT JAN VAN DEN BERG


with the assistance of the
Permanent Court of Arbitration
Peace Palace, The Hague

ISBN 978-90-411-3212-3

---

*Published by:*
Kluwer Law International
PO Box 316
2400 AH Alphen aan den Rijn
The Netherlands
www.kluwerlaw.com

*Sold and distributed in North, Central and South America by:*
Aspen Publishers, Inc.
7201 McKinney Circle
Frederick, MD 21704
United States of America

*Sold and distributed in all other countries by:*
Turpin Distribution Services Ltd.
Stratton Business Park
Pegasus Drive
Biggleswade
Bedfordshire SG18 8TQ
United Kingdom

Printed on acid-free paper.

© 2009 Kluwer Law International BV, The Netherlands

All Rights Reserved. No part of this publication may be reproduced, stored in a retrieval system, or transmitted in any form or by any means, mechanical, photocopying, recording or otherwise, without prior written permission of the publishers.

Permissions to use this content must be obtained from the copyright owner. Please apply to: Permissions Department, Wolters Kluwer Law & Business, 76 Ninth Avenue, Seventh Floor, New York, NY 10011, United States of America. E-mail: permissions@kluwerlaw.com.

# Preface

ICCA Congress Series no. 14 comprises the proceedings of the 19th ICCA Conference hosted by the Bar Council of Ireland in Dublin on 8-10 June 2008. Delegates from more than fifty countries attended the Conference during which we celebrated a major milestone: the fiftieth anniversary of the New York Convention on the Recognition and Enforcement of Foreign Arbitral Awards, concluded on 10 June 1958. We are grateful to our hosts for their tireless efforts in welcoming us and helping to mark the occasion. We would also like to express our appreciation of the honor of being addressed at the Opening Ceremony by the Prime Minister of Ireland, Mr. Brian Cowen, and during the Conference by the Attorney General of Ireland, Paul Gallagher.

The Conference consisted of two simultaneous Working Groups. Working Group A focused on Arbitration Treaties/Treaty Arbitration and Working Group B focused on Rules-based Solutions to Procedural Issues. Most of the sessions in both Working Groups followed the format of a Reporter who presented a Report on the topic of the session followed by Commentators who then addressed specific aspects of that topic, based on their backgrounds and experiences. Working Goup B also included panel discussions on Assessing the Revision of the UNCITRAL Rules on International Arbitration and Conciliation and on Recent Developments in International Commercial Arbitration. Edited transcripts of them can be found in this volume at pp. 615-632 and 635-645, respectively. The Conference closed with a Plenary Session on the New York Convention at 50, in which proposed revisions to the Convention were presented and debated by the speakers.

I would like to extend my gratitude to the Chairs of the Sessions for their efforts. They are as follows:

*Working Group A: Arbitration Treaties/Treaty Arbitration: Identifying the Expectations, Testing the Assumptions*
– The Impact of Investment Treaty Arbitration: Identifying the Expectations, Testing the Assumptions, chaired by Gabrielle Kaufmann-Kohler
– Investment Treaty Arbitration and Commercial Arbitration: Are They Different Ball Games?, chaired by V.V. Veeder
– Remedies in Investment Treaty Arbitration: The Bottom Line, chaired by Karl-Heinz Böckstiegel
– The Enforcement of Investment Treaty Awards: Getting to Judgment, chaired by Yves Fortier

*Working Group B: Rules-Based Solutions to Procedural Issues*
– Multi-party Disputes, chaired by Carlos Nehring Netto
– Consolidation of Claims, chaired by Iván Szász
– Summary Disposition, chaired by Werner Melis
– Provisional Measures, chaired by Tinuade Oyekunle
– The UNCITRAL Rules Revision: An Assessment, chaired by David D. Caron
– Recent Developments in International Arbitration, chaired by Catherine Kessedjian and William W. Park

PREFACE

*Working Group C: The New York Convention at 50*
— Plenary Session, chaired by Donald Francis Donovan.

Thanks also to those who served with me on the Conference Program Committee: Donald Francis Donovan, chair; Nael G. Bunni; Gabrielle Kaufmann-Kohler; Carlos Nehring Netto; and Jan Paulsson.

A further expression of gratitude goes to Queen Mary University of London and PricewaterhouseCoopers for the luncheon presentation of the results of their fascinating study, *International Arbitration: Corporate Attitudes and Practices 2008*. The study is available at <www.pwc.co.uk/arbitration>.

The next ICCA Congress will be held in Rio, Brazil on 23-26 May 2010. It will be hosted by the Brazilian Arbitration Committee (*Comitê Brasileiro de Arbitragem* — CBAr). Information on the Congress, as it becomes available, will be posted on the ICCA website at <www.arbitration-icca.org> and on the Rio Congress website at <www.iccario2010.org>.

Once again I would like to extend my thanks to the International Bureau of the Permanent Court of Arbitration, and its Secretary-General Mr. Christiaan Kröner, for providing a seat for ICCA's publication activities and supporting us with its facilities.

A final word of thanks goes to the editorial staff of ICCA Publications, in particular Ms. Alice Siegel, assistant managing editor, and Ms. Mary Kendrick, sub-editor, for their invaluable assistance in compiling and editing this volume.


Albert Jan van den Berg
General Editor

# TABLE OF CONTENTS

PREFACE
Albert Jan van den Berg, General Editor     v

TABLE OF CONTENTS     vii

## WORKING GROUP A: ARBITRATION TREATIES/TREATY ARBITRATION

### The Impact of Investment Treaty Arbitration: Identifying the Expectations, Testing the Assumptions

*Moderator:*    Gabrielle Kaufmann-Kohler

#### 1. Origins and Theory

**Report:**    Benedict Kingsbury and Stephan Schill
Investor-State Arbitration as Governance: Fair and Equitable Treatment, Proportionality and the Emerging Global Administrative Law     5

Comment: Margrete Stevens
The ICSID Convention and the Origins of Investment Treaty Arbitration     69

#### 2. Present Expectations and Realities

Comment: Charles N. Brower
Present Expectations and Realities – Comments from the Perspective of an Arbitrator     75

Comment: Brigitte Stern
Present Expectation and Realities     82

### Investment Treaty Arbitration and Commercial Arbitration: Are They Different Ball Games?

*Moderator:*    *V. V. Veeder QC*
Introduction to Investment Treaty Arbitration and Commercial Arbitration: Are They Different Ball Games?     91

TABLE OF CONTENTS

## 3. The Legal Framework

**Report**: Campbell McLachlan
Investment Treaty Arbitration: The Legal Framework      95

Comment: Bernard Hanotiau
Investment Treaty Arbitration and Commercial Arbitration:
Are They Different Ball Games? The Legal Regime/Framework      146

Comment: Brooks W. Daly and Fedelma Claire Smith
Comment on the Differing Legal Frameworks of Investment
Treaty Arbitration and Commercial Arbitration as Seen
Through Precedent, Annulment, and Procedural Rules      151

## 4. The Actual Conduct

**Report:** Abby Cohen Smutny
Investment Treaty Arbitration and Commercial Arbitration:
Are They Different Ballgames? The Actual Conduct      167

Comment: Sarah François-Poncet and Caline Mouawad
So You Want to Start an Investment Treaty Arbitration?
Getting the Notice of Dispute Right      178

Comment: Toby T. Landau QC
Reasons for Reasons: The Tribunal's Duty in Investor-State
Arbitration      187

## 5. Remedies in Investment Treaty Arbitration: The Bottom Line

*Moderator:* Karl-Heinz Böckstiegel

**Report:** Carole Malinvaud
Non-pecuniary Remedies in Investment Treaty and
Commercial Arbitration      209

**Report**: Pierre Bienvenu and Martin J. Valasek
Compensation for Unlawful Expropriation, and Other
Recent Manifestations of the Principle of Full Reparation in
International Investment Law      231

TABLE OF CONTENTS

## 6. The Enforcement of Investment Treaty Awards: Getting to Judgment

*Moderator:* Yves Fortier C.C., O.Q., Q.C., LLD

**Report:** Gaëtan Verhoosel
Annulment and Enforcement Review of Treaty Awards:
To ICSID or Not to ICSID? ........ 285

Comment: Yas Banifatemi
Defending Investment Treaty Awards: Is There an
ICSID Advantage? ........ 318

Comment: Guido Santiago Tawil
Binding Force and Enforcement of ICSID Awards:
Untying Articles 53 and 54 of the ICSID Convention ........ 327

## WORKING GROUP B: RULES-BASED SOLUTIONS TO PROCEDURAL ISSUES

### 1. Multi-Party Disputes

*Moderator:* Carlos Nehring Netto

**Report:** Nathalie Voser
Multi-party Disputes and Joinder of Third Parties ........ 343

Comment: Cristián Conejero Roos
Multi-party Arbitration and Rule-making: Same Issues,
Contrasting Approaches ........ 411

### 2. Consolidation of Claims

*Moderator:* Iván Száz

**Report:** Michael Pryles and Jeffrey Waincymer
Multiple Claims in Arbitration Between the Same Parties ........ 437

Comment: Nayla Comair-Obeid
Consolidation and Joinder in Arbitration –
The Arab Middle Eastern Approach ........ 500

TABLE OF CONTENTS

## 3. Summary Disposition

*Moderator:* Werner Melis

**Report**: Judith Gill QC
Applications for the Early Disposition of Claims in
Arbitration Proceedings     513

Comment: Teresa Giovannini
Comments on Judith Gill's Report on Applications for the
Early Disposition of Arbitration Proceedings     526

Comment: Michael M. Collins SC
Summary Disposition in International Arbitration     532

## 4. Provisional Measures

*Moderator:* Tinuade Oyekunle

**Report:** Luis Enrique Graham
Interim Measures – Ongoing Regulation and Practices
(A View from the UNCITRAL Arbitration Regime)     539
Annex I: Status of the Working Group Regarding the Revision
of the UNCITRAL Arbitration Rules     570
Annex II: Examples of Interim Measures Issued by an Arbitral
Tribunal     575
Annex III: Anti-suit Injunctions     578
Annex IV: Provisions in Rules, Legislation and Case Law that
Balance Convenience and the Likelihood of Success
by the Requesting Party     580

Comment: Nael G. Bunni
Interim Measures in International Commercial Arbitration:
A Commentary on the Report by Luis Enrique Graham     583

Comment: Yang Ing Loong
Provisional Measures     606

## 5. The UNCITRAL Rules Revision: An Assessment

*Moderator:* David D. Caron

**Round Table**:
Round Table on the Assessment of the Revision of the UNCITRAL
Rules on International Commercial Arbitration     615

## 6. Recent Developments in International Arbitration

*Moderators:* Catherine Kessedjian and William W. Park

**Open Discussion**:
Quo Vadis Arbitration?     635

## PLENARY SESSION: THE NEW YORK CONVENTION AT 50

### The New York Convention at 50

*Moderator:* Donald Francis Donovan

**Keynote Address: Albert Jan van den Berg**
Hypothetical Draft Convention on the International Enforcement of Arbitration Agreements and Awards:
Explanatory Note     649
Annex I: Text of the Hypothetical Draft Convention on the International Enforcement of Arbitration Agreements and Awards     667
Annex II: Comparison of Texts: Proposal for Revisions to the 1958 New York Convention     670

Comment: Teresa Cheng BBS, SC, JP
Celebrating the Fiftieth Anniversary of the New York Convention     679

Comment: Emmanuel Gaillard
The Urgency of Not Revising the New York Convention     689

Comment: Carolyn B. Lamm
Comments on the Proposal to Amend the New York Convention     697

Comment: Rory Brady SC
Comments on a New York Convention for the Next Fifty Years     708

LIST OF PARTICIPANTS     713

LIST OF ICCA OFFICERS AND MEMBERS     757

# Working Group A

# Arbitration Treaties/Treaty Arbitration

# Working Group A

## The Impact of Investment Treaty Arbitration: Identifying the Expectations, Testing the Assumptions

### 1. Origins and Theory

# Investor-State Arbitration as Governance: Fair and Equitable Treatment, Proportionality and the Emerging Global Administrative Law

*Benedict Kingsbury* and Stephan Schill***

TABLE OF CONTENTS | Page
---|---
I. Introduction: Investor-State Arbitration and the Emerging Administrative Law of Global Governance | 5
II. Investment Arbitration as Regulation of State Action: "Fair and Equitable Treatment" Jurisprudence | 14
III. Proportionality in International Investment Treaty Arbitrations: Arbitral Tribunals as Review Agencies of the Host State's Exercise of Regulatory Powers | 30
IV. Addressing Demands for Legitimacy in the Investor-State Arbitration System: Roles of Global Administrative Law | 52
V. Conclusion: Problems in Operationalizing the Normative Justifications of the Public-Regarding and Governance-Regarding Dimensions of the Investor-State Arbitration System | 64

## I. INTRODUCTION: INVESTOR-STATE ARBITRATION AND THE EMERGING ADMINISTRATIVE LAW OF GLOBAL GOVERNANCE

Investor-State arbitration, and in particular arbitration based on international investment treaties, is not simply dispute resolution.[1] It is also a structure of global governance.

---

* Murry and Ida Becker Professor of Law, Director of the Institute for International Law and Justice and Co-Director of the Global Administrative Law Project, New York University School of Law. Benedict Kingsbury has written expert opinions in several cases, under ICSID and UNCITRAL Rules, at the request of the Government of Argentina.
** International Arbitration Law Clerk to the Hon. Charles N. Brower, 20 Essex Street Chambers, London; Rechtsanwalt (admitted to the bar in Germany); Attorney-at-Law, New York; Dr. iur., Johann Wolfgang Goethe-Universität. Frankfurt am Main, 2008; LLM International Legal Studies, New York University, 2006; LLM Europäisches und Internationales Wirtschaftsrecht, Universität Augsburg, 2002. We would like to thank José Alvarez, Robert Howse, Jürgen Kurtz and ICCA Dublin conference commentators and participants for helpful comments on earlier drafts of this Report.
1. This Report is concerned primarily with treaty-based investor-State arbitration, arising under one or other of more than 2,500 bilateral, regional and sectoral investment treaties, including the North American Free Trade Agreement (NAFTA) and the Energy Charter Treaty (ECT). For general accounts of investment treaties and related instruments of investment protection see, for example, Rudolf DOLZER and Margrete STEVENS, *Bilateral Investment Treaties* (1995); Giorgio SACERDOTI, *Bilateral Treaties and Multilateral Instruments on Investment Protection*, 269 Recueil des Cours (1997) 251; M. SORNARAJAH, *The International Law of Foreign Investment*, 2nd edn. (2004)

Through publicly available and widely studied awards, investor-State arbitral tribunals are helping to define specific principles of global administrative law and set standards for States in their internal administrative processes.[2] Similarly, investor-State arbitration functions as a review mechanism to assess the balance a government has struck in a particular situation between investor protection and other important public purposes, for example by using proportionality analysis. In addition, decisions made *ex post* by tribunals with regard to such balances may influence what later tribunals will do, and may influence *ex ante* the behavior of States and investors.

Most arbitrators understandably write their awards and their other public remarks within the framework of the primary and immediate function of these arbitrations as being to settle specific individual disputes between investors and States arising out of foreign investment activities. But investor-State arbitral awards have important effects going beyond those who appear before them in individual disputes. Investor-State

---

pp. 204-314; Campbell MCLACHLAN, Laurence SHORE and Matthew WEINIGER, *International Investment Arbitration – Substantive Principles* (2007); Andreas LOWENFELD, *International Economic Law*, 2nd edn., (2008) pp. 467-591; Rudolf DOLZER and Christoph SCHREUER, *Principles of International Investment Law* (2008); Peter MUCHLINSKI, Federico ORTINO and Christoph SCHREUER, eds., *The Oxford Handbook of International Investment Law* (2008); Campbell MCLACHLAN, "Investment Treaty Arbitration: The Legal Framework", this volume, pp. 95-145. This type of arbitration differs from purely contract-based arbitration, in which the governing law, the host State's consent to arbitration, and the rules of the arbitration are dependent on an investor-State contract, not on an international treaty. Although the focus in this Report is on investment treaty arbitration, many of the observations made may apply, subject to modifications, to contract-based investor-State arbitration that is entirely independent of the application of an international treaty. Whether and how the observations made also apply to purely investor-State contract arbitration is not dealt with in this Report. However, the existence of an applicable investor-State contract may have a modifying effect on the treaty analysis and institutional analysis in the Report. Thus, questions of how investor-State tribunals should deal with the public law implications of investment treaty arbitration, such as proportionality analysis or implications of fair and equitable treatment, may potentially be considered differently to the extent that a contractual relationship between host State and investor is involved. For example, investor-State contracts often contain more precise and elaborate rules on the parties' mutual rights and obligations, and applicable contracts may have implications for the specific application of treaty rules and of customary international law. No comment is made on these matters in this Report.

2. New York University School of Law Institute for International Law and Justice's (IILJ) research project on global administrative law includes a website with a substantial series of working papers and extensive bibliographies as well as links to papers from other scholars around the world <www.iilj.org/GAL>. Among the first sets of papers from this project were three journal symposia: Benedict KINGSBURY, Nico KRISCH, Richard STEWART and Jonathan WIENER, eds., *The Emergence of Global Administrative Law*, 68 Law and Contemporary Problems (Summer-Autumn 2005, nos. 3-4), pp. 1-385; Nico KRISCH and Benedict KINGSBURY, eds., *Global Governance and Global Administrative Law in the International Legal Order*, 17 Eur. J. Int'l L. (2006) pp. 1-278; and the Global Administrative Law symposium in 37 NYU Journal of International Law and Politics (2005, no. 4). Subsequent publications include sets of papers from conferences convened by the IILJ with partner institutions: San Andres University in Buenos Aires, *Res Public Argentina* (2007-3), 7-141; University of Cape Town, *Acta Juridica* (2009); the Centre for Policy Research in New Delhi (forthcoming); Tsinghua Law School in Beijing (forthcoming); and the University of Geneva, *International Organizations Law Review* (forthcoming).

arbitral tribunals implement broadly phrased international standards set out in very similar terms in many investment treaties, and concretize and expand or restrict their meaning and reach through interpretation, so that they increasingly define for the majority of States of the world standards of good governance and of the rule of law that are enforceable against them by foreign investors.[3] And they review State action in ways that can have implications for much wider public interests and public policies, and for the legitimacy and methodological justifiability of the tribunals themselves.

The standards thus reinforced or created by arbitral tribunals reflect general principles for the exercise of public power that are applicable not only to State conduct, but likely will be applied over time, mutatis mutandis, to the activities of arbitral tribunals themselves. Investor-State arbitration is thus developing into a form of global governance. These tribunals exercise power in the global administrative space. Individual tribunals exercise power directly through the substantive awards they make in favor of investors or States, as well as through their findings of fact and through their decisions on matters such as amicus briefs, the awarding of costs and interest, or decisions as to timing, to the suspension of proceedings to allow for settlement negotiations, etc. More fundamentally, the tribunals as an aggregate exercise power through influencing the development of a body of global administrative law that guides State behavior, through influencing both customary international law and approaches taken in other sub-fields such as trade law or human rights, and through their approaches to balancing different investor and public interests, in ways that affect public policy and the future conduct of States and investors alike. Any significant exercise of power in the public or administrative sphere raises demands that the exercise of power be legitimate. This applies not only to what is done (or not done) by individual tribunals and arbitrators, and by individual appointing authorities and annulment committees, but also to the system of investor-State arbitration as a whole. The application of global administrative law to, and by, the investor-State arbitration system may be a key future element in helping to address these legitimacy concerns.

Investor-State arbitration, particularly under the more than 2,500 bilateral investment treaties (BITs) and several important regional treaties, including NAFTA and the ASEAN investment treaty, is a burgeoning field, with more than 300 investment treaty-based disputes publicly known and many new arbitrations being initiated each year.[4] At the same time, investor-State arbitration may also be a brittle field. Some States are becoming increasingly wary with respect to investment treaty arbitration and investment treaty protection. The cases related to the Argentine economic emergency,[5] and the

---

3. See David SCHNEIDERMAN, *Constitutionalizing Economic Globalization* (2008).
4. See UNCTAD, *Latest Developments in Investor-State Dispute Settlement, Dispute Settlement* (2008) pp. 1-2, available at <www.unctad.org/en/docs/iteiia20083_en.pdf> (recording 290 investment-treaty-based arbitrations by the end of 2007).
5. Argentina's Minister of Justice Rosatti, for example, was quoted after Argentina lost its first case relating to the emergency measures it took in reaction to the 2001/2002 economic crises (*CMS Gas v. Argentina*, 2005): "We have been insisting that this tribunal is out of its depth here, that it is not prepared to handle such a quantity of cases involving a single country, that it has a pro-business bias, and that it is not qualified to judge a country's economic policy." (see BBC Monitoring Latin America – Political, supplied by BBC Worldwide Monitoring, 17 May 2005).

stance taken by several other Latin American governments,[6] highlight obvious concerns about the suitability and indeed the legitimacy of the existing system for dealing with certain situations.[7] But also traditional capital-exporting countries, like the United States, are becoming increasingly concerned about restrictions investment treaties and investment treaty arbitration impose on their regulatory powers. The United States' experience with NAFTA Chapter 11, for example, has had a direct influence on the attitudes of the United States in more recent free trade agreement and BIT negotiations, and led to modifications to the US model BIT.[8]

---

6. On 30 April 2008, Venezuela communicated to the Netherlands its intention to terminate the Dutch-Venezuelan Bilateral Investment Treaty as of 1 November 2008. Luke Eric PETERSON, ed., Investment Arbitration Reporter (16 May 2008), available online at <www.iareporter.com/Archive/IAR-05-16-08.pdf> (reporting that Venezuela had chosen to end the treaty citing reasons of "national policy"). Bolivia withdrew from the ICSID Convention as of 3 November 2007. See "Bolivia Denounces ICSID Convention", 46 ILM (2007) p. 973. On 12 June 2009, Ecuador's Congress voted to withdraw from the ICSID Convention. Discussion of withdrawal from the ICSID Convention has also been reported with respect to Nicaragua, Venezuela, and Cuba. See Marco E. SCHNABL and Julie BÉDARD, "The Wrong Kind of 'Interesting'", Nat'l L. J. (30 July 2007).

7. Numerous works in the field argue that there is, or may soon develop, a "legitimacy crisis" in investor-State arbitration, variously referring to problems such as the design of the dispute settlement mechanism based on ad hoc arbitration with the ensuing risk of inconsistent decisions, the vagueness and ambiguity of many of the core rights conferred on investors, and the perceived blindness of arbitral tribunals to matters which they do not see as related to investment. See Charles N. BROWER, "A Crisis of Legitimacy", Nat'l L. J. (7 Oct 2002); Charles H. BROWER II, "Structure, Legitimacy, and NAFTA's Investment Chapter", 36 Vand. J. Transnat'l L. (2003) p. 37; Charles N. BROWER, Charles H. BROWER II and Jeremy K. SHARPE, "The Coming Crisis in the Global Adjudication System", 19 Arb. Int'l (2003) p. 415; Ari AFILALO, "Towards a Common Law of International Investment: How NAFTA Chapter 11 Panels Should Solve Their Legitimacy Crisis", 17 Georgetown Int'l Envt'l L. Rev. (2004) p. 51; Ari AFILALO, "Meaning, Ambiguity and Legitimacy: Judicial (Re-)construction of NAFTA Chapter 11", 25 Nw. J. Int'l L. & Bus. (2005) p. 279 at p. 282; M. SORNARAJAH, "A Coming Crisis: Expansionary Trends in Investment Treaty Arbitration" in Karl P. SAUVANT, ed., Appeals Mechanism in International Investment Disputes (2008) pp. 39-45; Gus VAN HARTEN, Investment Treaty Arbitration and Public Law (Oxford 2007); Olivia CHUNG, "The Lopsided International Investment Law Regime and Its Effect on the Future of Investor-State Arbitration", 47 Va. J. Int'l L. (2007) p. 953 (arguing that existing bilateral investment treaties strongly favor investors and that these inequalities will eventually lead to greater difficulties in enforcement of such treaties); Naveen GURUDEVAN, "An Evaluation of Current Legitimacy-based Objections to NAFTA's Chapter 11 Investment Dispute Resolution Process", 6 San Diego Int'l L. J. (2005) p. 399.

8. See Kenneth VANDEVELDE, "A Comparison of the 2004 and 1994 U.S. Model BITs: Rebalancing Investor and Host Country Interests" in Karl P. SAUVANT, ed.,1 Yearbook on International Investment Law and Policy 2008/2009, p. 283; Gilbert GAGNÉ and Jean-Frédéric MORIN, "The Evolving American Policy on Investment Protection: Evidence from Recent FTAs and the 2004 Model BIT", 9 J Intl Econ L (2006) p. 357 at p. 363; Mark KANTOR, "The New Draft Model U.S. BIT: Noteworthy Developments", 21 J. Int'l Arb. (2004) p. 383 at p. 385; Stephen SCHWEBEL, "The United States 2004 Model Bilateral Investment Treaty: An Exercise in the Regressive Development of International Law", 3 TDM (April 2006). See generally Guillermo AGUILAR ALVAREZ and William W. PARK, "The New Face of Investment Arbitration: NAFTA Chapter 11", 28 Yale J Intl L (2003) p. 365 (discussing the phenomenon of developed countries as

Criticism of the system of investor-State arbitration may grow further, as traditional capital-exporting States increasingly see prospects that they will become respondents in investment treaty cases. It is conceivable that in special situations some companies may begin to structure their investments in sensitive sectors of Western economies so as to come under BITs, in the same way as they already take account of trade rules in situating factories, and of tax rules in structuring their transnational operations. Using BITs skillfully and drawing on some expansive interpretations tribunals have given of what is covered as an investment by particular BITs,[9] it would be possible to structure many assets in Western economies through offshore companies in ways that would bring them under BIT protection and thus enable investors to challenge measures taken by traditionally capital-exporting countries. BIT protection and investor-State arbitration could thus become increasingly attractive for private economic actors as a valuable safeguard against possible policy choices by Western governments. A further consideration is the dynamic in which some traditional capital-importing States, like China, are now also major sources of outward investments, including investments in Western States, some of which could be detrimentally affected by some flux in the national politics of traditional capital-exporting countries. Actions taken by Western governments in response to the 2008-2009 financial crisis, for instance, have prompted more serious consideration of investment treaty issues.

Furthermore, although the case law is developing in sophisticated ways, there is a painful unevenness in the quality of reasoning in some awards and decisions, and in any event individual tribunals cannot easily have regard to system-level concerns given their mandate and primary responsibilities to solving an individual dispute submitted by the disputing parties in any single case. Inconsistent and conflicting decisions have resulted from various arbitrations, a factor which is precipitated by the ad hoc nature of arbitral panels and the lack of an appellate or other supervisory body that could ensure more consistency in the jurisprudence and hence increase predictability in investment treaty arbitration.[10] Finally, the architecture of the institutional system, with a myriad of bilateral treaties linked by most-favored-nation clauses, and unanimity required to alter most of the key multilateral conventions, does not make it easy for other actors to

---

respondents in investment treaty arbitration).

9. Cf. also Anthony SINCLAIR, "The Substance of Nationality Requirements in Investment Treaty Arbitration", ICSID Rev. – For. Inv. L. J. (2005) p. 357; Markus BURGSTALLER, "Nationality of Corporate Investors and International Claims against the Investor's Own State", 7 J. World Inv. & Trade (2006) p. 857. Consider, for example, the holding in *Aguas del Tunari, S.A. v. Republic of Bolivia* (ICSID Case No. ARB/02/3), Decision on Respondent's Objections to Jurisdiction of 21 October 2005, paras. 206 et seq., where the tribunal accepted that the device of holding the water assets in Cochabamba through a company incorporated in the Netherlands was enough to trigger the operation of the Netherlands-Bolivia BIT, even though there were no material connections to the Netherlands apart from the incorporation of an investment vehicle. See generally also Stephan SCHILL, *The Multilateralization of International Investment: Law*, Chapter V (Cambridge University Press, forthcoming 2009).

10. See on inconsistencies in investment treaty arbitration and their institutional and procedural reasons Stephan SCHILL, *ibid.*, pp. 281 et seq. See also Susan D. FRANCK, "The Legitimacy Crisis in Investment Treaty Arbitration: Privatizing Public International Law through Inconsistent Decisions", 73 Fordham L. Rev. (2005) p. 1521 at p. 1523.

reform it either. In any event, the political conditions enabling that to happen are not yet present.[11]

Within the severe constraints imposed by the existing architecture of the investor-State arbitration system, several doctrinal approaches for improvement have considerable currency. These include the comprehensive application of general international law methods or treaty interpretation as instantiated in the Vienna Convention on the Law of Treaties (VCLT), deeper analysis and use of the customary international law which underpins or complements central investment treaty provisions, greater reference to "general principles of law" distilled through robust methodologies, and the use of principles of systemic integration and techniques of defragmentation identified by the United Nations International Law Commission and others concerned with the "fragmentation" of international law.

This Report does not seek to reprise the substantial literature on these approaches. Rather, it addresses the complementary but neglected idea that the brittleness of the investor-State arbitration system reflects not only the lack of "system" in the design and planning of its development, but also the failure to embed it in theories of governance which take States and public interests seriously. As the theory and practice of the exercise of public power and expression of public interests have moved along, critics of the investor-State arbitration system regard it as more and more out of step. This Report argues that the theory and practice of the global administrative space, in which global administrative law and ideas of publicness in law play an important part, offers a potentially far-reaching way to conceptualize what investor-State arbitration can be and to bring it more into harmony with current needs and future directions, while not abruptly attempting a complete paradigm change for the currently existing system. Whatever its merits, any attempt to radically change the existing paradigm is bound to confront major politico-economic difficulties unless precipitated by a widely shared sense of crisis.[12]

The concept of global administrative law assumes that much of global governance can usefully be analyzed as administration. Instead of neatly separated levels of regulation (private, local, national, inter-State), a congeries of different actors and different layers together form a variegated "global administrative space" that includes international institutions and transnational networks, as well as domestic administrative bodies that operate within international regimes or cause transboundary regulatory effects.[13] The idea of a "global administrative space" differs from those orthodox understandings of international law in which the international is largely inter-governmental, and there is

---

11. Thus a proposal for change presented by the ICSID Secretariat got very little traction. See ICSID Secretariat, *Possible Improvements of the Framework for ICSID Arbitration*, paras. 20 et seq., available at <www.worldbank.org/icsid/highlights/improve-arb.pdf>. See also Christian TAMS, "An Appealing Option? The Debate about an ICSID Appellate Mechanism", 57 Beiträge zum Transnationalen Wirtschaftsrecht (2006).
12. Cf. also VAN HARTEN, supra fn. 7; Gus VAN HARTEN, "The Public-Private Distinction in the International Arbitration of Individual Claims Against the State", 56 Int'l & Comp. L. Q. (2007) p. 371.
13. Benedict KINGSBURY, et al., "Foreword: Global Governance as Administration", 68 Law & Contemp. Probs. (2005, nos. 3-4) p. 1.

a reasonably sharp separation of the domestic and the international. In the practice of global governance, transnational networks of rule-generators, interpreters and appliers cause such strict barriers to break down.

This global administrative space is increasingly occupied by transnational private regulators, hybrid bodies such as public-private partnerships involving States or inter-State organizations, national public regulators whose actions have external effects but may not be controlled by the central executive authority, informal inter-State bodies with no treaty basis (including "coalitions of the willing"), and formal inter-State institutions (such as those of the United Nations) affecting third parties through administrative-type actions. A lot of the administration of global governance is highly decentralized and not very systematic. Some entities are given roles in global regulatory governance which they may not wish for or be particularly designed or prepared for: some arbitrators in investor-State tribunals may well place these tribunals in this category.

Global administrative law is emerging as the evolving regulatory structures are each confronted with demands for transparency, consultation, participation, reasoned decisions and review mechanisms to promote accountability. These demands, and responses to them, are increasingly framed in terms that have a common normative character, specifically an administrative law character. The sense that there is some unity of proper principles and practices across these issue areas is of growing importance to the strengthening, or eroding, of legitimacy and effectiveness in these different governance regimes. Endeavoring to take account of these phenomena, one approach understands global administrative law as the legal mechanisms, principles and practices, along with supporting social understandings, that promote or otherwise affect the accountability of global administrative bodies, in particular by ensuring that these bodies meet adequate standards of transparency, consultation, participation, rationality and legality, and by providing effective review of the rules and decisions these bodies make.[14]

Global administrative law is concerned with the exercise of public authority by bodies outside the State, and by States in ways that reach beyond the State and its law.[15] It thus imports, at least as an ideal, an aspiration to publicness.[16] Publicness is a necessary element in the concept of law under modern democratic conditions. The claim is that the quality of publicness, and the related quality of generality, are necessary to the concept of law in an era of democratic jurisprudence.[17] Publicness, in this context, refers to the claim that law must be wrought by the whole society, by the public, and the connected claim that law addresses matters of concern to the society as such. It is

---

14. Benedict KINGSBURY, Nico KRISCH and Richard STEWART, "The Emergence of Global Administrative Law", 68 Law & Contemp. Probs. 15 (2005, nos. 3-4).
15. Armin von BOGDANDY, "General Principles of International Public Authority: Sketching a Research Field", 9 German L. J. (2008) p. 1909.
16. Benedict KINGSBURY, "The Concept of 'Law' in Global Administrative Law", 20 Eur. J. Int'l L. (2009) p. 23. This paragraph and the three preceding paragraphs draw from the article cited here.
17. Jeremy WALDRON, "Can There Be a Democratic Jurisprudence?", NYU School of Law, Public Law Research Paper 08-35 (2008) available at <http://papers.ssrn.com/sol3/papers.cfm?abstract_id=1280923&rec=1&srcabs=1299017>.

described as "global" rather than "international" to avoid implying that this is part of the recognized *lex lata* or indeed *lex ferenda*, and to include more diverse legal sources than those encompassed within standard conceptions of "international law".

This Report explores three legal implications of understanding investor-State arbitration as being embedded in the emerging global administrative law and its ideas of publicness (Parts II-IV). Part II of the Report makes the case that arbitral tribunals in investor-State cases are rapidly crafting a set of general standards, and illustrative applications of these standards, for the conduct of States when exercising administrative powers in ways that affect foreign investors. Tribunals are thereby helping to define standards of good administration by States. This is an important development. This Report responds to two particular concerns about it. First, where do the tribunals get these more detailed standards from? Insofar as they are interpreting broad treaty standards (such as fair and equitable treatment), ordinary principles of treaty interpretation and legal analysis may call for, and should be buttressed by, the use of comparative administrative law, and systematic study of how States can and should conduct good administration. Instead, many awards fill the gap with references to other awards (which may themselves be thinly reasoned) and loose subjective views and experiences of the arbitrators. This leads to a second concern, that the standards are being crafted (or invented) in the limited context of investor claims, without adequate engagement with other bodies or material on what good administration by States could and should realistically be in different contexts, and in particular without any coordination with standards of good administration imposed on States by the World Trade Organization (WTO) for trade-related governmental actions, or by international human rights tribunals, or by international financial and aid institutions in loan conditions or in their technical advice to developing countries.

Part III of the Report addresses the challenges that arise as investor-State arbitration proceedings and awards increasingly have to address, and face criticism concerning their lack of responsiveness to, environmental considerations, labour and social standards, and governmental management of economic crises or other fundamental issues for entire populations. Argentina's emergency suspension of tariff increases and of peso convertibility, Bolivia's cancellation of the Bechtel water contract after riots, Ontario's refusal to proceed with a scheme to dump Toronto's refuse into a lake, or Costa Rica's prohibition of development on a foreign-owned ranch because of its proclamation of a nature reserve, are among numerous examples of conflicts between investment protection and competing public concerns. Bailouts, subsidies and other emergency measures taken in response to the global financial crisis that developed in 2008-2009 raise similar issues. In such situations investor-State arbitral tribunals are called upon to weigh a measure taken by a State in exercise of its regulatory power, against the damage done to a foreign investor by that measure. Yet, the methods used by investment tribunals in dealing with such issues are often very different from, and less sophisticated than, methods used in various international and national courts. While many international human rights courts, and indeed many national courts, often conduct a proportionality analysis in order to balance rights and rights-limiting policy choices, in investor-State arbitration only a few tribunals have taken such an approach. Instead, the complexity and polyvalent nature of the issues involved is analyzed and weighed only weakly in a range of cases where a stronger methodology seems called for, including some cases dealing with legislative measures of general application that affect existing foreign investors along with domestic actors, and others dealing with discretionary functions assigned to administrative agencies under local law, but exercised in ways that impose regulatory constraints and thus result in particular harm to foreign investors. Part III examines approaches taken in different dispute settlement bodies to such conflicts of rights and principles. It assesses the recourse made by a few investment tribunals to proportionality analysis when faced with cases of conflict between the protection of investments and the furtherance of a non-investment interest, and argues that this may be a permitted and even necessary element of international law treaty interpretation and application in certain cases. It suggests that arbitral tribunals may indeed have little choice but to adopt approaches that are similar to those adopted by domestic courts and other international courts and tribunals when faced with comparable conflicts between important interests that must all be weighed in the legal appraisal. While use of a proportionality approach may have significant problems – in particular because it risks reposing more governance powers in such tribunals and making more demands on them than may be sustainable – in the long run, the application of proportionality analysis is also congruent with an emerging set of public law principles for global regulatory governance.

Part IV of the Report responds to the observation that, as a form of global governance, investor-State arbitration is increasingly subject to criticism as regards its legitimacy and to demands to meet normative standards of the emerging global administrative law. In similar ways as other institutions that exercise power in global governance, investor-State arbitration is facing demands for accountability on such matters as design of institutions and appointment and recusal of arbitrators, transparency in making materials publicly available, receiving submissions from groups affected by a possible decision, holding public hearings, giving reasons for decisions, becoming amenable to effective review proceedings, and so forth. The first section of Part IV of the Report argues that the normative considerations and legal principles applicable to various transnational governance structures, even though each institution is different, overlap. All of these involve the exercise of public power beyond the State, and most are potentially generators of and subjects of global administrative law. Many are connected also through the unities of a public international legal order.[18] Consequently, it is a mistake to debate these issues in the investor-State arbitration field as if they were wholly isolated from norms and practices of other areas of global governance. Adherence to these wider norms, particularly customary international law and the norms of treaty interpretation along with the norms of the emerging global administrative law and related norms of international public authority, is highly relevant to addressing concerns about legitimacy in investor-State arbitration. The second section of Part IV of the Report takes up one element of this broad agenda, making the specific argument that investor-State arbitration tribunals can themselves help to meet such legitimacy

---

18. Cf. Armin von BOGDANDY, Philipp DANN, Matthias GOLDMANN, "Developing the Publicness of Public International Law: Towards a Legal Framework for Global Governance Activities", 9 German L. J. (2008) p. 1375; and Benedict KINGSBURY, "The International Legal Order" in P. CANE and M. TUSHNET, eds., *The Oxford Handbook of Legal Studies* (2003) p. 271.

demands, even without any fundamental change in the current system, by improving the quality of their reasoning and their engagement with prior decisions.

The conclusion of this Report (Part V) links the discussion to the fundamental question of what the possible normative justifications of an investor-State arbitration system might be, beyond standard but insufficient (and contestable) arguments that it promotes optimal investment and efficient use of resources. Among such deeper justifications might be the promotion of democratic accountability and participation, the promotion of good and orderly State administration, and the protection of rights and other deserving interests. The currently existing system of investor-State arbitration is undoubtedly limited in its ability to fully vindicate any of the normative justifications of the public-regarding and governance-regarding dimensions of investor-State arbitration. Vindication of these values is a public good that for structural reasons is likely to be under-supplied. Major reform may well be needed. But even incremental reforms may be valuable, and some such reforms are already under way. The emerging global administrative law provides important normative and practical guidance in this respect.

II.   INVESTMENT ARBITRATION AS REGULATION OF STATE ACTION: "FAIR AND EQUITABLE TREATMENT" JURISPRUDENCE

The obligation of States to provide "fair and equitable treatment" to foreign investors is a standard provision in modern BITs and multilateral treaties concerning investment, as well as in some friendship, commerce and navigation treaties.[19] As such, it has become the textual basis for a rapidly growing body of interpretive pronouncements and decisions by arbitral tribunals. In many respects this jurisprudence draws upon, or continues deep seams of, customary international law materials and analysis going back many decades. Thus, contemporary controversies over the alleged separation between treaty standards and customary international law, particularly in relation to Art. 1105(1) of the North American Free Trade Agreement (NAFTA), should not obscure the fundamental connections between the treaty standards and mechanisms and the customary international law standards and mechanisms.[20]

However, the traditional structures of State responsibility and diplomatic protection, and the long-established customary international law standards on matters such as denial of justice and due process, are probably not currently effective enough or fine-grained enough for many of the specific questions arising in relation to foreign investment issues

---

19. See on the history of the fair and equitable treatment standard Stephen VASCIANNIE, "The Fair and Equitable Treatment Standard in International Investment Law and Practice", 70 Brit. Yb. Int'l Law (1999) p. 99.
20. On the debate about the relationship between fair and equitable treatment and the international minimum standard under customary international law see Rudolf DOLZER and Christoph SCHREUER, *Principles of International Investment Law* (2008) pp. 124-128; Andrew NEWCOMBE and Lluís PARADELL. *Law and Practice of Investment Treaties: Standards of Treatment* (2009) pp. 263-275; Campbell MCLACHLAN, "Investment Treaties and General International Law", 57 Int'l & Comp. L. Q. (2008) p. 361.

in the modern regulatory practice of States. Instead, customary international law, State treaty practice, and the burgeoning interpretive jurisprudence of investor-State arbitral tribunals, together elaborate an important set of criteria for State conduct, including in the context of purely national administration which in some way affects foreign investors. These standards are inevitably linked to good administrative governance for States more generally, as especially in open economies much administrative practice is applied to everyone and is not special to foreign investors. The jurisprudence of fair and equitable treatment is thus in part a jurisprudence of modern public administration.

Yet, some of the more sweeping dicta about what "fair and equitable treatment" means, misleadingly suggest that it establishes a uniform global standard for State administration that is fully equivalent to the administrative law (or in some respects the constitutional law) of developed countries without regard to specificities of the emerging global economy or national interests and circumstances. There are, of course, longstanding and evolving customary international law standards that are broadly conducive to achieve the object and purpose of investment treaties, in particular to promote foreign investment flows, and to contribute to furnishing a legal framework for the functioning of a global economy. Egregious cases, including flagrant State interferences for opportunistic or corrupt reasons with a foreign investor's assets or operation, clearly violate such a global standard. Many such cases are classic denial of justice or denial of due process situations, and can be addressed without elaborate interpretative structures or underlying governance analysis.

Yet, abstract principles of international investment law, such as "fair and equitable treatment", can under ordinary principles of treaty interpretation be interpreted as going beyond a uniform (but modest) traditional minimum, so that they encompass more demanding standards. At the same time, such demanding standards may need to take into account the context and the specific situation of the host State in question, as well as the circumstances of the investor and the arrangements made in respect of the investment. In this respect, investment treaty tribunals are part of and share the challenge that is being faced by global administrative law generally, i.e., to develop effective techniques of comparative and principled analysis that generate both a robust set of sources for giving content to very general principles, and a methodology for applying them to specific local contexts in line with the requirement of the emerging global society. This makes it possible to deal with situations where a very demanding standard of what is fair and equitable would simply fail to recognize enduring capacity and resource problems in a particular developing country's administration and which should not have surprised a sophisticated investor. A starting point in such situations might be a crude distinction between cases in which a State actively interferes with foreign investments, and cases that concern certain kinds of failures to act, or inadequate responsiveness by the host State's administrative apparatus to a request by the investor.

Interpreting and applying the abstract fair and equitable treatment standard involves a particular hermeneutics grounded in the international law of treaty interpretation expressed in the Vienna Convention on the Law of Treaties, including reference to other applicable rules of international law. This hermeneutics is necessarily customized to the institutions, actors and issues involved. It may – at least as regards less egregious cases and the development of more fine-tuned standards of good governance and good administration – call for the use of a comparative method that attempts to extract general principles from domestic legal systems and from other international legal regimes that prescribe standards for the exercise of governmental or other public powers in administrative processes, in judicial proceedings, and in legislation. Part III of the Report will examine the use of proportionality analysis and related methods of application of such principles. This Part, in contrast, seeks to provide a sketch of elements of "fair and equitable treatment" that find support in general principles of national law, in emerging practices of global administrative bodies in non-investment fields, and above all in the practice of investment tribunals. The aim is to sketch some specific elements of the fair and equitable treatment requirement that have particular applicability to State administration, but also have implications for the further concretization of global administrative law principles.

Five clusters of normative principles recur in the more detailed specification by arbitral tribunals of elements of fair and equitable treatment.[21] These principles are (1) the requirement of stability, predictability and consistency of the legal framework, (2) the protection of legitimate expectations, (3) the requirement to grant procedural and administrative due process and the prohibition of denial of justice, (4) the requirement of transparency, and (5) the requirement of reasonableness and proportionality. These principles also figure prominently as sub-elements or expressions of the broader concept of the rule of law in many domestic legal systems. They may be connected also to, and may come further to influence, cognate principles enunciated by other international bodies for the exercise of public power within and beyond the State. Such connections are drawn in some analyses of customary international law, and in some important decisions of international courts and mixed claims commissions. However, the wider comparative and normative bases for these principles have not yet been explored fully in modern investor-State arbitration. The following sections discuss some of the modern awards on each of the five clusters of principles in order to indicate ways in which this gap might be filled.

*1. Stability, Predictability, Consistency*

International investment treaty tribunals have repeatedly associated fair and equitable treatment with stability, predictability and consistency of the host State's legal framework. The tribunal in *CMS v. Argentina*, for example, stated that "there can be no doubt ... that a stable legal and business environment is an essential element of fair and equitable treatment".[22] Predictability of the legal framework governing the activity of foreign investors has received comparable emphasis. The tribunal in *Metalclad v. Mexico*, for example, based its finding of a violation of Art. 1105(1) NAFTA, inter alia, on the argument that Mexico "failed to ensure a ... predictable framework for Metalclad's

---

21. What follows draws on Stephan SCHILL, "Fair and Equitable Treatment under Investment Treaties as an Embodiment of the Rule of Law", IILJ Working Paper 2006/6 (Global Administrative Law Series), available at <www.iilj.org/publications/2006-6Schill.asp>.
22. *CMS Gas Transmission Company v. The Republic of Argentina* (ICSID Case No. ARB/01/8), Award of 12 May 2005, para. 274. Similarly, *Occidental Exploration and Production Company (OEPC) v. The Republic of Ecuador* (UNCITRAL, LCIA Case No. UN3467), Final Award of 1 July 2004, para. 183.

business planning and investment".[23] Similarly, the tribunal in *Tecmed v. Mexico* explicated that the foreign investor needs to "know beforehand any and all rules and regulations that will govern its investments, as well as the goals of the relevant policies and administrative practices and directives, to be able to plan its investment and comply with such regulations".[24] Some tribunals have added that a lack of clarity of the legal framework or excessively vague rules can violate fair and equitable treatment.[25] Equally, consistency in the government's conduct has received strong emphasis in the jurisprudence. Thus, the tribunal in *Tecmed* emphasized the need for consistency in the decision-making of a national agency in order to conform to fair and equitable treatment.[26] Likewise, in *MTD v. Chile*, the tribunal found a violation of fair and equitable treatment due to "the inconsistency of action between two arms of the same Government vis-à-vis the same investor".[27]

Taken together, these dicta embody several elements of the basic requirements for law as adumbrated in Lon Fuller's "inner morality of law".[28] Many national legal systems place similar emphasis on legal certainty and legal security, perhaps most firmly instantiated in the German *Rechtssicherheit*.[29] This core aspect of normativity of law allows individuals and entities to adapt their behavior to the requirements of the legal order and form stable social and economic relationships. It is an aspiration of most legal systems, certainly under democratic conditions of advanced capitalism. International law and the legal institutions of global governance may well be directed toward promoting and helping realize this aspiration.

Yet, stability and predictability cannot and should not mean that the legal framework will never be able to change, nor do they in themselves provide a business guarantee to investment projects.[30] Similarly, domestic regulatory frameworks are seldom completely

---

23. See *Metalclad Corporation v. The United Mexican States* (ICSID Case No. ARB(AF)/97/1 (NAFTA)), Award of 30 August 2000, para. 99.
24. *Tecnicas Medioambientales Tecmed S.A. v. The United Mexican States* (ICSID CASE No. ARB (AF)/00/2), Award of 29 May 2003, para. 154.
25. See for example *OEPC v. Ecuador*, supra fn. 22, para. 184 (criticizing the vagueness of a change in the domestic tax law that did not "provid[e] any clarity about its meaning and extent").
26. *Tecmed v. Mexico*, supra fn. 24, paras. 154, 162 et seq. See also, *OEPC v. Ecuador*, supra fn. 22, para. 184. Similarly, *Ronald S. Lauder v. Czech Republic*, Final Award of 3 September 2001, paras. 292 et seq.
27. *MTD Equity Sdn. Bhd. and MTD Chile S.A. v. Republic of Chile* (ICSID Case No. Arb/01/7), Award of 25 May 2004, para. 163.
28. Lon FULLER, *The Morality of Law* (1969). See KINGSBURY, supra fn. 16, p. 23.
29. This aspect of the rule of law is recognized, mostly as a constitutional standard, in many domestic legal systems. See for its implementation in the German Constitution Helmuth SCHULZE-FIELITZ in: Horst DREIER, ed., *Grundgesetz – Kommentar*, Vol. II (1998) Art. 20, paras. 117 et seq.; see Richard H. FALLON, "'The Rule of Law' as a Concept in Constitutional Discourse", 97 Columb. L. Rev. (1997, no. 1) pp. 14 et seq. with references to US constitutional practice; more generally, see also Joseph RAZ, "The Rule of Law and its Virtue", 93 L. Quart. Rev. (1977) p. 195, at p. 198.
30. See *Emilio Agustín Maffezini v. The Kingdom of Spain* (ICSID Case No. ARB/97/7), Award of 13 November 2000, para. 64 ("emphasiz[ing] that Bilateral Investment Treaties are not insurance policies against bad business judgments"); *Marvin Roy Feldman Karpa v. The United Mexican States*

free of inconsistencies.[31] In addition, the degree of stability in each legal order will vary with the circumstances the State is facing, and the nature of inconsistencies may vary. Likewise, a serious crisis or even an emergency situation may call for different reactions than the deployment of public power in the normal course of things.[32] Stability, predictability and consistency will thus have to be implemented in view of the circumstances of the case at hand.

2. *The Protection of Confidence and Legitimate Expectations*

The tribunal in *Saluka v. Czech Republic* referred to the concept of legitimate expectations as "the dominant element of that [fair and equitable treatment] standard".[33] The concept is found, in different forms, in many national legal systems[34] and perhaps in general international law.[35] Its main thrust is the protection of confidence against some kinds of administrative and legislative conduct. Thus, the tribunal in *Tecmed v. Mexico* held that fair and equitable treatment requires "provid[ing] to international investments treatment that does not affect the basic expectations that were taken into account by the foreign investors to make the investment".[36] Similarly, the tribunal in *International Thunderbird*

---

(ICSID Case No. ARB(AF)/99/1), Award of 16 December 2002, para. 112 (noting "that not every business problem experienced by a foreign investor is an indirect or creeping expropriation under Article 1110, or a denial of due process or fair and equitable treatment under Article 1110(1)(c)").

31. Cf. FRANCK, supra fn. 10, p. 675 at p. 678.
32. See, for example, *Elettronica Sicula SpA (ELSI) Case (United States of America v. Italy)*, Judgment, 20 July 1989, I.C.J. Reports 1989, p. 15, para. 74: "Clearly the right [to control and manage a company] cannot be interpreted as a sort of warranty that the normal exercise of control and management shall never be disturbed. Every system of law must provide, for example, for interferences with the normal exercise of rights during public emergencies and the like."
33. *Saluka Investments BV v. The Czech Republic* (UNCITRAL), Partial Award of 17 March 2006, para. 302. See also Elizabeth SNODGRASS, "Protecting Investors' Legitimate Expectations", 21 ICSID Rev. – For. Inv. L. J. 1 (2006, no. 1) pp. 1-58.
34. See David DYZENHAUS, "The Rule of (Administrative) Law in International Law", 68 Law & Contemp. Probs. (2005) p. 127 at pp. 133 et seq. with reference to case law in Australia and the United Kingdom; SCHULZE-FIELITZ (supra fn. 29), Art. 20 paras. 134 et seq. concerning German Constitutional Law; Søren SCHØNBERG, *Legitimate Expectations in Administrative Law* (2000) on English, French and EC/EU law; Bruce DYER, "Legitimate Expectations in Procedural Fairness after *Lam*" in Matthew GROVES, ed., *Law and Government in Australia* (2005) pp. 184 et seq. on Australian law; see also Jean-Marie WOEHRLING, "*Le Principe de Confiance Légitime dans la Jurisprudence des Tribunaux*" in John W. BRIDGE, ed., *Comparative Law Facing the 21st Century* (1998) pp. 815 et seq. summarizing a comparative study by the XVth International Congress of Comparative Law, Bristol/UK in 1998.
35. See Jörg P. MÜLLER, *Vertrauensschutz im Völkerrecht* (1971). See more specifically in the context of the law of expropriation of aliens Rudolf DOLZER, "New Foundations of the Law of Expropriation of Alien Property", 75 A.J.I.L. (1981) p. 553, at pp. 579 et seq..
36. *Tecmed v. Mexico*, supra fn. 24, para. 154. The tribunal's approach was also taken up in a number of other cases. See *ADF v. United States*, Award of 9 January 2003, para. 189; *MTD v. Chile*, supra fn. 27, paras. 114 et seq.; *OEPC v. Ecuador*, supra fn. 22, para. 185; *CMS v. Argentina*, supra fn. 22, para. 279; *Eureko B.V. v. Republic of Poland*, Partial Award of 19 August 2005, paras. 235, 241.

*Gaming Corporation v. Mexico* explained that "the concept of 'legitimate expectations' relates ... to a situation where a Contracting Party's conduct creates reasonable and justifiable expectations on the part of an investor (or investment) to act in reliance on said conduct, such that a failure by the NAFTA Party to honour those expectations could cause the investor (or investment) to suffer damages".[37]

Various limitations in the scope and applicability of this doctrine require further honing. Ordinarily, such expectations can arise only through explicit or implicit representations made by the host State (potentially including agency, ratification and other structures of connection to the State, but subject then also to limiting rules).[38] Moreover the investor's expectations about the State's future conduct in ordinary circumstances cannot necessarily be transposed into a "legitimate expectation" about State action in extraordinary circumstances, and expectations ought in many cases to encompass the possibility that the State may take some regulatory actions. States are regulators with public responsibilities. Some such views may be reflected in the suggestion by the tribunal in *Eureko v. Poland* that a breach of basic expectations may not be a violation of fair and equitable treatment if good reasons existed why the expectations of the investor could not be met.[39] Similarly, the tribunal in *Saluka v. Czech Republic* specifically warned of the danger of taking the idea of the investor's expectation too literally since this would "impose upon host States' [sic] obligations which would be inappropriate and unrealistic".[40] Instead, the tribunal considered departing from legitimate expectations of an investor as possible and legitimate to the extent such departures are proportional as "[t]he determination of a breach of [fair and equitable treatment] requires a weighing of the Claimant's legitimate and reasonable expectations on the one hand and the Respondent's legitimate regulatory interests on the other".[41] Against this background, the concept of legitimate expectations requires careful comparative law analysis, and a sophisticated methodology of application. Although the jurisprudential process towards these ends has begun, much further work is required.

3. *Administrative Due Process and Denial of Justice*

As long-standing customary international law recognizes, and as many tribunals applying investment treaties have decided, fair and equitable treatment embraces elements of due

---

37. *International Thunderbird Gaming Corporation v. The United Mexican States* (UNCITRAL/NAFTA), Award of 26 Jan. 2006, para. 147 (internal citation omitted).
38. See on the connection between the expectations and government conduct *ADF v. United States*, supra fn. 36, para. 189, where the tribunal declined to find a violation of Art. 1105(1) NAFTA in a case where the claimant argued that existing case law suggested that an agency would have to grant a waiver from a statutory local content requirement, noting that "any expectations that the Investor had with respect to the relevancy or applicability of the case law it cited were not created by any misleading representations made by authorized officials of the U.S. Federal Government but rather, it appears probable, by legal advice received by the Investor from private U.S. counsel".
39. See *Eureko v. Poland*, supra fn. 36, paras. 232 et seq.
40. *Saluka v. Czech Republic*, supra fn. 33, para. 304.
41. *Saluka v. Czech Republic*, supra fn. 33, para. 306.

process: specifically, administrative and judicial due process.[42] Fair and equitable treatment is thus closely connected to the proper administration of civil and criminal justice.[43] Thus, the tribunal in *Waste Management v. Mexico* defined a violation of fair and equitable treatment as "involv[ing] a lack of due process leading to an outcome which offends judicial propriety – as might be the case with a manifest failure of natural justice in judicial proceedings or a complete lack of transparency and candour in an administrative process".[44] Similarly, for the tribunal in *S.D. Myers v. Canada* fair and equitable treatment, among other elements, included "the international law requirements of due process".[45] The tribunal in *International Thunderbird Gaming v. Mexico* held that the proceedings of a government agency "should be tested against the standards of due process and procedural fairness applicable to administrative officials".[46]

Issues closely connected to due process are also reflected in the jurisprudence linking fair and equitable treatment to the prohibition of arbitrariness[47] and of discrimination. The tribunal in *Loewen v. United States*, for example, stated (obiter) that fair and equitable treatment is violated by "[a] decision which is in breach of municipal law and is discriminatory against the foreign litigant".[48] Similarly, the tribunal in *Waste Management v. Mexico* suggested that "fair and equitable treatment is infringed by conduct attributable to the State and harmful to the claimant if the conduct is arbitrary, grossly unfair, unjust or idiosyncratic, is discriminatory and exposes the claimant to sectional or racial prejudice".[49]

---

42. The national legislator, so far, has not been subjected to any due process notions in investment arbitration. This could, however, be conceivable in the context of legislative expropriations since most BITs explicitly require host States to grant affected investors due process. See Rudolf DOLZER and Margrete STEVENS, *Bilateral Investment Treaties* (1995) pp. 106 et seq.
43. See comprehensively on the closely related concept of denial of justice in international law Jan PAULSSON, *Denial of Justice in International Law* (2005). Recently, both an explicit reference to due process and the concept of denial of justice as part of fair and equitable treatment have been included in the treaty practice of the United States. See, for example, Art. 10.5(2)(a) of the Dominican Republic – Central America – United States Free Trade Agreement, which stipulates that "fair and equitable treatment includes the obligation not to deny justice in criminal, civil, or administrative adjudicatory proceedings in accordance with the principle of due process embodied in the principal legal systems of the world". The Dominican Republic – Central America – United States Free Trade Agreement, signed 5 August 2004, is available at <www.ustr.gov/Trade_Agreements/Bilateral/CAFTA/Section_Index.html>.
44. *Waste Management v. Mexico* (ICSID Case No. ARB(AF)/00/3), Award of 30 April 2004, para. 98.
45. *S.D. Myers v. Canada* (UNCITRAL/NAFTA), Partial Award of 13 November 2000, para. 134.
46. *International Thunderbird Gaming v. Mexico*, supra fn. 37, para. 200.
47. See, in particular, *Elettronica Sicula S.p.A. (ELSI) (United States v. Italy)*, supra fn. 32, p. 76, para. 128 (stating that "[a]rbitrariness is not so much something opposed to a rule of law, as something opposed to the rule of law. This idea was expressed by the Court in the *Asylum* case, when it spoke of 'arbitrary action' being 'substituted for the rule of law'. It is wilful disregard of due process of law, an act which shocks, or at least surprises, a sense of juridical propriety." (internal citations omitted)).
48. *Loewen v. United States*, para. 135.
49. *Waste Management v. Mexico*, supra fn. 44, para. 98; similarly *Eureko v. Poland*, para. 233 (finding that the State "acted not for cause but for purely arbitrary reasons linked to the interplay of Polish politics and nationalistic reasons of a discriminatory character" and therefore breached fair and

What is not yet fully defined, however, is how exactly the requirements of due process blend an international law standard with the controlling local law. State violation of local law can be a significant datum, as several cases illustrate. Thus, in *Metalclad v. Mexico*, for instance, the tribunal focused on the apparent misapplication of a construction law by a local municipality as one element for finding a violation of fair and equitable treatment.[50] Similarly, in *Pope & Talbot v. Canada* the tribunal referred to a lack of competence of a particular agency under national law to initiate administrative proceedings against the investment. Instead of relying "on naked assertions of authority and on threats that the Investment's allocation could be cancelled, reduced or suspended for failure to accept verification", the tribunal said, "before seeking to bludgeon the Investment into compliance, the SLD [i.e., the Canadian administrative agency involved] should have resolved any doubts on the issue and should have advised the Investment of the legal basis for its actions".[51] Similarly, the tribunal in *GAMI Investments, Inc. v. Mexico* deduced from fair and equitable treatment an obligation not only to abide by, but also to enforce existing provisions of national law.[52] In *Tecmed v. Mexico* the tribunal underscored that host States have to make use of "the legal instruments that govern the actions of the investor or the investment in conformity with the function usually assigned to such instruments".[53]

Conversely, the conformity of a State administrative measure with the relevant domestic legal rules has in some cases been referred to by tribunals as indicative that there has not been a violation of the fair and equitable treatment standard. In *Noble Ventures v. Romania*, for example, the tribunal observed that certain bankruptcy proceedings "were initiated and conducted according to the law and not against it"[54] and accordingly denied a violation of fair and equitable treatment. Similarly, in *Lauder v. Czech Republic* the tribunal emphasized that a violation of fair and equitable treatment was usually excluded in case of a "regulatory body taking the necessary actions to enforce the law".[55] This set of cases broadly aligns with the democratic requirement that public power derive its authority from a legal basis and be exercised along the lines of pre-established procedural and substantive rules. As such, the violation of domestic law can

---

    equitable treatment). *S.D. Myers v. Canada*, supra fn. 45, para. 266, also draws a parallel between national treatment and the fair and equitable treatment standard when stating: "Although ... the Tribunal does not rule out the possibility that there could be circumstances in which a denial of the national treatment provisions of the NAFTA would not necessarily offend the minimum standard provisions, a majority of the Tribunal determines that on the facts of this particular case the breach of Article 1102 essentially establishes a breach of Article 1105 as well."

50. *Metalclad v. Mexico*, supra fn. 23, para. 93.
51. *Pope & Talbot, Inc. v. The Government of Canada* (UNCITRAL/NAFTA), Award on the Merits of Phase 2 of 10 April 2001, paras. 174 et seq.
52. *GAMI Investments, Inc. v. The Government of the United Mexican States* (UNCITRAL/NAFTA), Final Award of 15 November 2004, para. 91: "It is in this sense that a government's failure to implement or abide by its own law in a manner adversely affecting a foreign investor may but will not necessarily lead to a violation of Article 1105."
53. *Tecmed v. Mexico*, supra fn. 24, para. 154.
54. *Noble Ventures v. Romania*, Award of 12 October 2005, para. 178.
55. *Lauder v. Czech Republic*, supra fn. 26, para. 297.

translate into a violation of the fair and equitable treatment standard; but the international law standard of fair and equitable treatment is not, of course, simply a mirror of whatever the national law provides.

4.  Transparency

Traditional customary international law on treatment of foreigners and of foreign investments is quite underdeveloped with regard to transparency of governmental information and decision processes. In international law more broadly, the crafting and application of international legal standards for national governmental transparency has been an important direction of legal development. However, it remains a challenging branch of international legal practice, whether in the WTO, the international environmental law-inspired Aarhus Convention model, or international human rights jurisprudence. Many countries, particularly transitional and developing countries, struggle to meet their existing obligation in this respect, and some have adopted constitutional amendments (as in Chile) or legislation to try to hasten both the change of bureaucratic culture and the practical processes of making information available. Furthermore, defining the proper limits on transparency requirements, such as the protection of privacy interests, of commercial confidentiality, or of national security, is complex.

Accordingly, for investment tribunals to pursue such an intricate agenda through the very underspecified fair and equitable treatment standard is far from easy, even though several tribunals have done so. Thus, the tribunal in *Metalclad v. Mexico* concluded that Mexico breached Art. 1105 NAFTA because "Mexico failed to ensure a *transparent* and predictable framework for Metalclad's business planning and investment".[56] The reference in this holding to a transparency requirement was set aside by the Supreme Court of British Columbia exercising jurisdiction under the British Columbia International Arbitration Act.[57] While the British Columbia decision can be contested in some respects, it does indeed seem justified to cast doubt on the breadth for the arbitral tribunal's statements "that all relevant legal requirements for the purpose of initiating, completing and successfully operating investments ... should be capable of being readily known to all affected investors" and that the host State is required "to ensure that the correct position is promptly determined and clearly stated so that investors can proceed with all appropriate expedition in the confident belief that they are acting in accordance with all relevant laws".[58] Statements of such breadth indeed could result in redefining the position and function of administrative agencies by obliging them to reorient their priorities and national missions so as to act as authoritative consultative units and even as de facto insurers in the implementation of foreign investment projects.[59]

---

56. *Metalclad v. Mexico*, supra fn. 23, para. 99 (emphasis added).
57. See Supreme Court of British Columbia, *The United Mexican States v. Metalclad Corporation*, 2001 BCSC 644.
58. *Metalclad v. Mexico*, supra fn. 23, para. 76 (for both citations).
59. Stephan SCHILL, "Revisiting a Landmark: Indirect Expropriation and Fair and Equitable Treatment in the ICSID Case *Tecmed*", 3 TDM (April 2006) p. 15.

Similar concerns could be expressed about the dictum in *Tecmed v. Mexico* that connected the element of legitimate expectations to the requirement of transparency in reasoning:

> "The foreign investor expects the host State to act in a consistent manner, free from ambiguity and totally transparently in its relations with the foreign investor, so that it may know beforehand any and all rules and regulations that will govern its investments, as well as the goals of the relevant policies and administrative practices or directives, to be able to plan its investment and comply with such regulations."[60]

Yet, a more restrictive reading of a transparency requirement under the "fair and equitable treatment" standard seems possible and more readily defensible. In the *Tecmed* case, in fact, transparency was mainly applied to procedural aspects of administrative law, such as the requirement to give sufficient reasons[61] and the obligation to act in a comprehensible and predictable way.[62] These framings buttress the reasonable procedural position of foreign investors in administrative proceedings. Transparency can thus be important even if it is not yet a well-developed additional substantive requirement. Furthermore, it has significant specific functions, such as in assisting procedurally to resolve uncertainty in the domestic law, in which connection it interacts closely with the burden of proof. Comparative law methodology, and the sophisticated analysis and use of normative standards from other areas of international law, potentially has much to contribute in this area.

5.  *Reasonableness and Proportionality*

Finally, investment arbitration tribunals link fair and equitable treatment to the concepts of reasonableness and proportionality. Like proportionality, but with much less methodological precision, reasonableness can be used to control the extent to which interferences of host States with foreign investments are permitted. Thus the tribunal in

---

60. *Tecmed v. Mexico*, supra fn. 24, para. 154; similarly *Maffezini v. Spain*, para. 83.
61. See *Tecmed v. Mexico*, supra fn. 24, para. 123 (stating that "administrative decisions must be duly grounded in order to have, among other things, the transparency required so that persons that disagree with such decisions may challenge them through all the available legal remedies"). Similarly, *Tecmed v. Mexico*, para. 164.
62. See *Tecmed v. Mexico*, supra fn. 24, para. 160 (stating that

> "[t]he incidental Statements as to the Landfill's relocation in the correspondence exchanged between INE and Cytrar or Tecmed ... cannot be considered to be a clear and unequivocal expression of the will of the Mexican authorities to change their position as to the extension of the Permit so long as Cytrar's business was not relocated, nor can it be considered an explicit, transparent and clear warning addressed to Cytrar from the Mexican authorities that rejected conditioning the revocation of the Permit to the relocation of Cytrar's operations at the Landfill to another place").

*Pope & Talbot v. Canada* repeatedly referred to the reasonableness of the conduct of an administrative agency in declining to find a violation of fair and equitable treatment.[63] The element of reasonableness can also be incorporated into a proportionality test, as in *Tecmed v. Mexico*'s dictum that "[t]here must be a reasonable relationship of proportionality between the charge or weight imposed to the foreign investor and the aim sought to be realized by any expropriatory measure".[64]

6. *Implications of the "Fair and Equitable Treatment" Requirement for National Law and Administration*

The five dimensions of fair and equitable treatment mentioned above relate to the exercise of public power by governmental agencies, as well as by national courts and legislatures. They are used as a standard of evaluation of national governmental action (a classic administrative law function), but conducted not by national tribunals, but by tribunals established under international treaties. "Fair and equitable treatment" is not itself a legal standard of direct application in the administrative or constitutional law of most countries, although the five dimensions outlined above have counterparts in much national law. Nevertheless, different processes of diffusion or influence may lead this international standard, with its specific components, to have effects over time on specific laws and administrative practices within states.

This happens where other international institutions (such as the World Bank, or the United Nations Conference on Trade and Development (UNCTAD)) refer to investment treaty standards and jurisprudence, in giving advice to particular countries about legal and institutional reform. Likewise, government agencies in States that have lost arbitral cases may seek to influence the structure and process of administrative decision-making. These processes, and a general normative seepage as more people become familiar with developments in arbitral jurisprudence and in other areas of international law on similar topics, may have effects for the future on the procedural rights and consideration accorded to foreign investors or indeed to others under national law, and even on the exercise and review of administrative discretion.

With respect to administrative procedure, in particular concerning the granting, renunciation or renewal of operating licenses, fair and equitable treatment typically requires national administrations to grant foreign investors a fair opportunity to put forward their case, conduct proceedings in a rational and comprehensible fashion, and give reasons for their decisions. A right to a fair hearing and a right to participation in administrative proceedings, for example, played a role in the NAFTA case *Metalclad v. Mexico* where the tribunal found a breach of fair and equitable treatment because the investor was not properly involved. According to the tribunal the investor should have

---

63. See *Pope & Talbot v. Canada*, supra fn. 51, paras. 123, 125, 128, 155; see also *MTD v. Chile*, supra fn. 27, para. 109 with a reference to an expert opinion by Schwebel.
64. *Tecmed v. Mexico*, supra fn. 24, para. 122. It is possible that an independent jurisprudence of reasonableness can be established and given detailed content. See Olivier CORTEN, *L'utilisation du raisonnable par le juge international: discours juridique, raison et contradictions* (1997). The focus in this Report, however, will be on proportionality, which is discussed extensively in Part III.

been given the chance to participate in a meeting of a local town council that discussed whether a construction permit was to be given for the investor's waste landfill.[65] Similarly, the tribunal in *Tecmed v. Mexico* emphasized fairness in hearings as part of fair and equitable treatment in the context of an administrative proceeding that concerned the non-prolongation of an operating license for a waste landfill. It also stated that the standard required the national administration to take decisions about the requests of a foreign investor.[66]

Fair and equitable treatment requirements may prompt national administrative agencies to give reasons for their decisions and to base these decisions on sufficient factual evidence. This is a potential effect in the NAFTA context of decisions such as *Metalclad v. Mexico*, in which the tribunal determined that Mexico had breached the fair and equitable treatment standard because the decision of a town council to deny the construction permit was not grounded in considerations concerning "construction aspects or flaws of the physical facility",[67] but was mainly motivated by the opposition of the local population to the landfill in question. In the tribunal's view, the decision was therefore not supported by evidence pertaining to legitimate criteria under the municipal construction law. The requirement to supply sufficient evidence also results in a duty to conduct fact-finding and to verify evidence before a final decision is taken. Furthermore, the requirement to give reasons aims at facilitating the legal review of an administrative decision.[68]

Exercises of discretionary powers may also be tempered by requirements of fair and equitable treatment. If, for example, the national administration has consistently tolerated a specific unlawful conduct, fair and equitable treatment may impose restrictions on it intervening only against a foreign investor who engaged in the same conduct.[69] Similarly, legitimate expectations of the investor can set bounds to the administration's discretionary power. Acting contrary to representations made by government officials, for instance, can in certain circumstances constitute a breach of fair and equitable treatment.[70]

Some of these requirements also have implications for national judicial practice. In *Mondev v. United States* the tribunal, for example, entertained the possibility that "the conferral of a general immunity from suit for conduct of a public authority affecting a

---

65. The tribunal particularly pointed out that "the permit was denied at a meeting of the Municipal Town Council of which Metalclad received no notice, to which it received no invitation, and at which it was given no opportunity to appear"; see *Metalclad v. Mexico*, supra fn. 23, para. 91.
66. See *Tecmed v. Mexico*, supra fn. 24, paras. 161 et seq. More specifically on the elements of a fair hearing required under fair and equitable treatment Todd G. WEILER, "NAFTA Article 1105 and the Principles of International Economic Law", 42 Columbia J. Transnat'l L. (2003) p. 35 at pp. 79 et seq.
67. *Metalclad v. Mexico*, supra fn. 23, para. 93.
68. See *Tecmed v. Mexico*, supra fn. 24, para. 123.
69. Cf. Steffen HINDELANG, "'No Equals in Wrong?' The Issue of Equality in a State of Illegality – Some Thoughts to Encourage Discussion", 7 J. World Inv. & Trade (2006) p. 883.
70. See *International Thunderbird Gaming v. Mexico*, supra fn. 37, paras. 137 et seq.; *Metalclad v. Mexico*, paras. 85 et seq.

NAFTA investment could amount to a breach of Article 1105(1) of NAFTA".[71] In *Azinian v. Mexico* the tribunal pointed out that "a denial of justice could be pleaded if the relevant courts refused to entertain a suit, if they subject it to undue delay, or if they administer justice in a seriously inadequate way".[72] Access to domestic courts for foreign investors may also be required, providing an opening for wider global and national arguments about obligations to ensure access to justice. Courts must generally entertain suits in a timely fashion, give a fair hearing to the foreign investor on all essential questions, and base decisions on legal grounds explained by reasons.[73] The standards for judicial proceedings are broadly comparable to those already set under human rights instruments, such as Art. 6 of the European Convention on Human Rights.[74] The distinctive impact on administrative proceedings, however, may be greater.

Overall, fair and equitable treatment requires that domestic administrative proceedings, like judicial proceedings, conform to standards that are derived from a process-oriented understanding of legality and good governance.[75] What is almost completely unknown at present, is how far this developing investment treaty jurisprudence, and the set of global administrative norms that are developing contemporaneously with it, are in fact having an impact prospectively on national practices. It is obvious, however, that the "fair and equitable treatment" standard now included in so many treaties, as interpreted by tribunals in recent years, ought (from a standpoint of government lawyers' advice) to influence the ways in which a State goes about considering any changes to their regulatory frameworks after an investment was made,[76] and more broadly ought to prompt States to adapt their domestic legal orders to standards that are internationally accepted as conforming to the concept of the rule of law.

Although as regards good administration and treatment of foreign investors, some expert guidance and nudging to reform is supplied by the World Bank and comparable bodies in relations with poor or transitional States, there is less of an organized international institutional push for *ex ante* reform in this area than comes from human rights bodies, the EU for accession countries, or the WTO. The risk of *ex post* arbitration

---

71. See *Mondev v. United States* (ICSID Case No. ARB(AF)/99/2 (NAFTA)), Award of 11 October 2002, para. 151 (concluding, however, that the immunity granted to a municipal authority in the case at hand was not a violation of fair and equitable treatment).
72. *Robert Azinian, Kenneth Davitian, & Ellen Baca v. The United Mexican States* (ICSID Case No. ARB (AF)/97/2 (NAFTA)), Award of 1 November 1999, para. 102.
73. See *Azinian*, *ibid.*, para. 102.
74. European Convention for the Protection of Human Rights and Fundamental Freedoms and its protocols, 4 November 1950, 213 U.N.T.S. 222. For this analogy see *Mondev v. United States*, supra fn. 71, para. 144. See also Andrea BJORKLUND, "Reconciling State Sovereignty and Investor Protection in Denial of Justice Claims", 45 Va. J. Int'l L. (2005) p. 809.
75. See for parallel developments of transnational administrative law in the context of administrative proceedings in the EU/EC and similar developments under WTO law Giacinto DELLA CANANEA, "Beyond the State: the Europeanization and Globalization of Procedural Administrative Law", 9 Eur. Publ. L. (2003) p. 563.
76. In this sense Rudolf DOLZER, "Fair and Equitable Treatment: A Key Standard in Investment Treaties", 39 Int'l Law (2005) p. 87 at pp. 100 et seq.

losses seems not readily to seep back into *ex ante* administrative reform.[77] There are of course some obvious exceptions. Chinese scholars point to the implications of episodes in which foreign investors might have considered bringing cases against China, as having had salutary reform effects.[78] A Namibian court referred to the Germany-Namibia BIT in ruling unlawful, on grounds of inadequate consultation and other procedural grounds, the expropriation of absentee German-owned farms in the way the government had proposed to do it. Systematic research on this issue is needed, and is likely to affect practice and policy. In any event, the public and widely analyzed jurisprudence of arbitral tribunals can have effects on future governance; and this reality imposes a responsibility on those constructing this jurisprudence to base it on a sophisticated understanding of the issues and fine-grained analysis of specific problems.

8.  *Reforming the Methodology for Applying the Fair and Equitable Treatment Standard*

The vagueness of the fair and equitable treatment standard has contributed to significant problems in its interpretation and construction by arbitral tribunals. The arbitral jurisprudence meanders without any very thought-out conceptual vision of the principle's function in relation to State administrative conduct. The reasoning in arbitral awards is therefore often weak, at times even unconvincing, in its legal analysis. Often arbitral tribunals restrict themselves to invoking equally weakly reasoned precedent or referring in an inconclusive manner to the object and purpose of BITs without any deeper justification of how the specific construction is grounded in a sophisticated international law approach to treaty interpretation. Ultimately, these shortcomings endanger the suitability of fair and equitable treatment as a concept against which the conduct of host States can be measured in a predictable way.

Furthermore, the jurisprudence has produced some results and dicta that are not generally accepted (and almost certainly are not embraced for prospective internal application) by aggrieved States, and some of the awards not only endorse but perhaps even celebrate a broad *ex post facto* "I will know it when I see it" control of host State conduct.[79] Predictability in its application is, however, essential for host States and foreign investors alike who need to know beforehand what kind of measures entail the international responsibility of the State and, accordingly, against which kind of political and administrative risk the fair and equitable treatment standard protects (and, conversely, what risks the investor takes or should separately insure against).

Specifying what "fair and equitable treatment" actually requires of State administrative agencies necessitates an approach to interpretation and application of "fair and equitable

---

77. Cf. Tom GINSBURG, "International Substitutes for Domestic Institutions", 25 Int'l Rev. L. & Econ. (2005) p. 107; Susan D. FRANCK, "Foreign Direct Investment, Investment Treaty Arbitration and the Rule of Law", 19 McGeorge Global Bus. & Dev. L. J. (2007) p. 337.
78. Xiuli HAN, "The Application of the Principle of Proportionality in *Tecmed v. Mexico*", 6 Chinese J. Int'l L. (2007) p. 635, provides such indications, mainly with regard to indirect expropriation.
79. Cf. in the context of defining the concept of indirect expropriation Yves FORTIER and Stephen L. DRYMER, "Indirect Expropriation in the Law of International Investment: I Know It When I See It, or Caveat Investor", 19 ICSID Rev. – For. Inv. L. J. (2004) p. 293.

treatment" clauses that is much more ambitious than arbitral tribunals have typically undertaken. Instead of relying on a string of abstract quotations from prior arbitral decisions (an approach that is of little help, especially when disputes concern novel circumstances), or positing the content of fair and equitable treatment in an abstract way without sufficient justification, tribunals should use, as part of the hermeneutics of international law treaty interpretation and legal decision-making, a comparative method that draws on domestic and international law regarding good administration. Arbitral tribunals should therefore engage in a comparative analysis of the major domestic legal systems, and of major approaches in international law and institutions, in order to grasp common features those legal systems establish for the exercise of public power.

Such a comparative analysis of national law may influence tribunal jurisprudence in at least two respects. First, it may enable investment tribunals to positively deduce institutional and procedural requirements from the domestic rule of law standards for a context-specific interpretation of fair and equitable treatment. A comparative analysis of domestic legal systems and their understanding of the rule of law may, for example, be used to justify the standards administrative proceedings affecting foreign investors have to live up to.[80] Second, a comparative analysis of the implications of the rule of law under domestic law may be used to justify the conduct of a State vis-à-vis a foreign investor under the fair and equitable treatment standard. If similar conduct, for instance the State-ordered modification of foreclosure provisions in private mortgage contracts in an emergency situation, is generally accepted by domestic legal systems as being in conformity with their understanding of the (national) rule of law, investment tribunals can transpose such findings to the level of international investment treaties as an expression of a general principle of law.

The analysis should not, however, be limited to national legal systems. Cross-regime comparison with other international law regimes is also proving increasingly fruitful. The example of European Court of Human Rights (ECHR) jurisprudence concerning Art. 6 of the European Convention on Human Rights has already been mentioned, and the emerging principles of European administrative law are now also the subject of considerable academic and policy work.[81] The jurisprudence of the WTO Appellate Body is also an important source concerning requirements with respect to the exercise of public power. For example, in its first decision in the *Shrimp-Turtle* case, the Appellate Body held that shrimp from India, Thailand and other countries had been improperly excluded from US markets. The administrative procedures followed by the United States, in applying its turtle-protecting legislation, constituted "arbitrary and unjustifiable discrimination between Members", and hence the United States was precluded from

---

80. See also della CANANEA, supra fn. 75, p. 563 at p. 575 (explaining that the WTO Appellate Body in the *Shrimp-Turtle* Case has "subsumed from national legal orders some general or 'global' principles of administrative law" in order to impose procedural rule of law elements on the exercise of public power by WTO Member States).
81. See, for example, Paul CRAIG, *EU Administrative Law* (2006); Carol HARLOW, *Accountability in the European Union* (2003); Francesca BIGNAMI and Sabino CASSESE, eds., "The Administrative Law of the European Union", 68, Law & Contemp. Probs. (2004) p. 1; Sabino CASSESE, ed., *Trattato di Diritto Amministrativo*, 2nd edn. (2003); Jürgen SCHWARZE, *Europäisches Verwaltungsrecht*, 2nd edn. (2005).

defending its turtle-protecting measures under the GATT Art. XX exceptions. The Appellate Body pointed out that the US procedure for certifying the shrimp industries of particular States as meeting turtle-protecting standards provided:

> "– no formal opportunity for an applicant country to be heard, or to respond to any arguments that may be made against it...
> – no formal written, reasoned decision, whether of acceptance or rejection...
> – no notification of such decisions, and
> – no procedure for review of, or appeal from, a denial".

Comparison involves recognizing differences as well as similarities. International investment treaties have distinct substantive features, and the institutional features and roles of arbitral tribunals under treaties are also distinctive. The mechanisms for the protection and promotion of foreign investment are, however, not an end in themselves. They are rather closely related to the goals of economic growth and development, in particular in developing countries. This was explicitly mentioned as an objective of the ICSID Convention that recognized "the need for international cooperation for economic development, and the role of private international investment therein".[82] The link between the inflow of foreign investment and economic development is further reinforced by the character of the World Bank as a development institution.[83] The implementation of an investor-State dispute settlement mechanism under the ICSID Convention aimed at reducing the political risk connected with investing in a developing country with weaker domestic institutions and a less stable legal and political infrastructure in the interest of growth and development.[84] Whether these objectives have in fact been met by the system as it currently operates, and whether new and more complex goals and limitations may now be part of the purpose of individual treaties and of the system as a whole, are also considerations of central importance. Constructing a jurisprudence that takes adequate account of the full set of relevant considerations is an enterprise that must be connected, at least at the level of ideals, with the underlying normative justifications for the system of investor-State investment arbitration. These

---

82. See the preamble of the ICSID Convention.
83. Aron BROCHES, *The Convention on the Settlement of Investment Disputes between States and Nationals of Other States*, 136 Recueil des Cours (1972-II) p. 331 at pp. 342 et seq.; Burkhard SCHÖBENER and Lars MARKERT, "*Das International Centre for Settlement of Investment Disputes (ICSID)*", 105 ZVglRWiss (2006) p. 65 at p. 67.
84. For debate on the link between institutions and economic growth, see: Edgardo BUSCAGLIA, William RATCLIFF and Robert COOTER, *The Law and Economics of Development* (1997); Jean-Philippe PLATTEAU, *Institutions, Social Norms, and Economic Development* (2000); Dani RODRIK, Arvind SUBRAMANIAN and Francesco TREBBI, "Institutions Rule: The Primacy of Institutions Over Geography and Integration in Economic Development", 9 J. Econ. Growth (2004) p. 131; Daron ACEMOGLU, Simon JOHNSON and James ROBINSON, "Institutions as the Fundamental Cause of Long-Run Growth" in Philippe AGHION and Stephen DURLAUF, eds., *Handbook of Economic Growth* (2005). For a sceptical view on causality between political institutions and economic growth see Edward L. GLAESER, Rafael LA PORTA, Florencio LOPEZ-DE-SILANES and Andrei SHLEIFER, "Do Institutions Cause Growth?", 9 J. Econ. Growth (2004) p. 271.

underlying normative justifications will be discussed in Part V of this Report. The Report turns now to issues concerning the actual conduct by tribunals of their governance task of review of State action, and in particular to comparative study of established governance techniques for courts and tribunals exercising such review functions, such as proportionality analysis.

III. PROPORTIONALITY IN INTERNATIONAL INVESTMENT TREATY ARBITRATIONS: ARBITRAL TRIBUNALS AS REVIEW AGENCIES OF THE HOST STATE'S EXERCISE OF REGULATORY POWERS

Challenges to the legitimacy of investment tribunals exercising power over States also frequently involve some critique of the open-ended language of the investors' rights provisions and concerns that these empower tribunals to abridge the role of States as regulators to protect the public interest, whether for environmental protection, human rights, or to meet emergencies, in the sole interest of protecting property rights and economic interests. This is particularly the case as regards the State's function as a regulator by means of abstract and general regulation. This Part therefore responds to the observation that investment treaty tribunals considering such situations increasingly feel the need to deploy a proportionality analysis where investment treaties frame the duties of the States in relation to investors and investments, without establishing clear textual criteria for permitted departures from or limits to these duties for public regulatory purposes to protect other important interests.

Proportionality analysis is a method of legal interpretation and decision-making in situations of collisions or conflicts of different principles and legitimate public objectives. It is characteristic of this approach to distinguish principles on the basis that they do not work in an "all-or-nothing fashion", but allow for a "more or less".[85] Rules "contain fixed points in the field of the factually and legally possible", that is, a rule is a norm that is either "fulfilled or not".[86] Principles, by contrast, operate differently in that they aim at "commanding that something be realized to the highest degree that is actually and legally possible".[87] As one of the great German exponents of proportionality commented: "Conflicts of rules are played out at the level of validity," whereas "competitions between principles are played out in the dimension of weight."[88] There is, by contrast, tempered enthusiasm for proportionality analysis among US judges,[89] and historically also in

---

85. Ronald DWORKIN, *Takings Rights Seriously* (1978) p. 24.
86. Robert ALEXY, *A Theory of Constitutional Rights* (1986; transl. Julian Rivers, OUP 2002) pp. 47-48.
87. Robert ALEXY, *On the Structure of Legal Principles*, 13 Ratio Juris (2000) p. 294 at p. 295. See also ALEXY, supra fn. 86, p. 47, stating that principles are norms that "require that something be realized to the greatest extent possible given the legal and factual possibilities".
88. ALEXY, *ibid.*, p. 50.
89. Concerning the scope of the proportionality requirement in US constitutional law in particular concerning criminal law in the context of the Eighth Amendment see Alice RISTROPH, "Proportionality as a Principle of Limited Government", 55 Duke L. J. (2005) p. 263 with further references; see also on the hesitance in US constitutional law to accept proportionality as a general

systems influenced by English law, although the process of European integration is having its effects on approaches in the United Kingdom.

There are significant problems, however, in such an enterprise, but also good reasons for it. Proportionality analysis facilitates application of standard concepts of investment protection, and can be accommodated to a certain extent within the concepts of indirect expropriation and fair and equitable treatment, whenever the restriction of the State's regulatory leeway is at play.[90] It thus operationalizes balancing between interests of foreign investors, or more generally property rights, and conflicting public interests. While proportionality analysis no doubt can be susceptible to use as a means to justify particular judicial preferences, when deployed by sophisticated courts and tribunals in national and international jurisprudence to deal with open-ended concepts and difficult balancing, it has proven to be methodologically workable and more coherent and generalizable than the kinds of reasoning applied by many tribunals to "fair and equitable treatment" clauses or the concept of indirect expropriation. The diversity of existing uses of proportionality analysis means that it is possible to undertake wide-ranging and instructive comparative law research and analysis as to what is considered as proportional in various national legal systems and transnational or international tribunals.

In addition, the principle of proportionality may in some respects provide a stricter framework for decisions in investor-State disputes than does the current jurisprudence. It requires arbitrators to engage in a method of assessing the competing legal claims, weighing them, considering alternatives, etc. and provides rational arguments for their decisions. Certainly, proportionality analysis can be criticized as legitimating judicial law-making and as generating a *gouvernement des juges*. But it is more robust than some of the alternative methods for dealing with these difficult assessments currently employed in international investment law. Without the proportionality analysis the concept of indirect expropriation, for example, risks degrading to an analysis without rationalization: "I know it when I see it."[91] Similarly, some subsets of the standard of fair and equitable treatment would, instead of following a structured analysis about the relationship between the investor's expectations of favorable treatment and competing public interests in the application of rule of law standards and the balance between the two, become open to subjective assessments of arbitrators about what they consider fair

---

principle Vicki C. JACKSON, "Ambivalent Resistance and Comparative Constitutionalism: Opening up the Conversation on 'Proportionality', Rights And Federalism", 1 U. Pa. J. Const. L. (1999) p. 583.

90. This limits the scope or application of proportionality analysis as a legal instrument. Thus, cases were the State acts as a party to an investor-State contract will usually not be covered. But see on limitations to the power of States in their capacity as a party to a contract Stephan SCHILL, "Enabling Private Ordering – Function, Scope and Effect of Umbrella Clauses in International Investment Treaties", 18 Minn. J. Int'l L. (2009) p. 1. Furthermore, situations in which decisive controlling rules of priority between property interests and competing non-property interests are already clearly established are usually not subject to the proposed proportionality reasoning and analysis. Proportionality analysis rather finds application in cases where the State itself redistributes or interferes with property rights in the interest of protecting some non-economic interest by means of general legislation or administrative regulation.

91. FORTIER and DRYMER, supra fn. 79, p. 293.

and equitable – a standard of equity, not a legal standard that has normative content. Proportionality, in this respect, may provide more predictability than the lack of any intelligible standard of weighing and balancing, in particular if the procedural aspect or version of proportionality analysis is emphasized, instead of the more substantive versions undertaken under this heading by some domestic courts.

Fundamental to the application of proportionality analysis (and comparable techniques of balancing) in investment treaty arbitration is the question of the relationship of proportionality analysis to the applicable law, and in particular to the applicable international law.[92] The starting point is the good faith interpretation of the applicable treaty. A particular feature of most investment treaties is that they make provisions for investor rights without addressing in a comprehensive fashion the relationship of these to continuing powers of State regulation. It is likely that States parties typically did not intend a severe occlusion of these regulatory powers, and a good faith reading of the text of the applicable treaty in context and in light of the object and purpose of the treaty may well indicate that interpretation calls for a balance to be struck between investor protection and State regulatory powers. In interpreting the text of the treaty in order to be able to apply it to a specific dispute, the interpreter may well have recourse to other relevant rules of international law applicable between the treaty parties (VCLT Art. 31(3)(c)), potentially including general principles of law. In this way, application of the principle of proportionality can be consistent with, and a form of, the interpretation and application of the substantive provisions of investment treaties.

Investment treaty tribunals also engage, at least tacitly, in interpretation and application of the institutional provisions of treaties: the provisions under which the tribunals are established and operate. These provisions cover not only the institutional design of the tribunals and the scope of their work, they also provide the foundation for the governance functions which, as shown in Parts I and II of this Report, are inescapable dimensions of their work. The texts of these treaty provisions are typically sparse in relation to the tribunals' governance roles, and their interpretation also calls for consideration of their context, their object and purpose, and other relevant materials. General principles of law concerning the roles and functions of such juridical decision-making institutions may become relevant. Global administrative law principles on the proper conduct of tribunal processes have obvious relevance, but legal principles of broader ambit, such as proportionality, may also help to give substance to the proper roles and functions of these tribunals in their assessment of State conduct, based on their constitutive treaties. The relationship between hermeneutic functions (i.e., interpretation of texts) and governance functions for any particular tribunal involves complex questions that are not examined in detail in this Report. The essential point is that conflicts between investment protection and other legitimate public interests may have to be fully and fairly weighed in tribunal processes, given that the State parties did not necessarily subordinate all of these other public interests by entering into a particular international investment treaty. Proportionality analysis, in turn, provides a rational

---

92. Where a tribunal analyzes or applies national law, the use of proportionality analysis or other balancing techniques in a particular area of national law may of course be directly relevant, but that is not the focus of the discussion here.

process for weighing and balancing that can itself be grounded in the proper interpretation of investment treaties.[93] Against this background, this section introduces in brief outline the development and diffusion of proportionality analysis in national and international adjudication and dispute settlement, analyzes its methodological structure and examines the use of such reasoning by arbitral tribunals in some specific investor-State disputes.

*1. The Development and Diffusion of Proportionality Analysis*

This section provides basic illustrations of national and international juridical institutions applying proportionality analysis to State action impinging on other rights. The aim is simply to show that the emergence of a general principle may be involved. It is fundamental to emphasize that there are essential differences between the institutional settings, and between the underlying texts, so the precise analysis and background assumptions cannot be transposed even from one international treaty body to another.

At its origin in the domestic law context, proportionality entails a method of defining the relationship between the State and its citizens. It helps resolve conflicts between, on the one hand, the rights of individuals and the interest of the State and, on the other, between conflicting rights of individuals. Proportionality "sets material limits to the interference of public authorities into the private sphere of the citizen"[94] and "provide[s] a tool to define and restrain the regulatory freedom of governments".[95] It helps to define and to balance the public, represented by the interference and its underlying interest of the State or the community concerned, and the private, represented by the interests of the individuals affected.

Proportionality balancing is a concept stemming from German administrative and constitutional law and has migrated from these roots as a mode of balancing between competing rights and interests to numerous jurisdictions in South America, Central and Eastern Europe, as well as various common law jurisdictions.[96] At the outset, the German Constitutional Court (*Bundesverfassungsgericht*) formulated the test of proportionality for the first time in its seminal *Apothekenurteil*, a case concerning the interference with the freedom of profession of pharmacists by a licensing system that limited the number of pharmacy licenses in order to secure the supply of the population with pharmaceuticals. In solving the underlying conflict of rights, the German Constitutional Court stated that the individual right and the public purpose of the law had to be balanced:

---

93. See *MTD v. Chile*, supra fn. 27, para. 113; *Saluka v. Czech Republic*, supra fn. 33, para. 297.
94. Jürgen SCHWARZE, "The Principle of Proportionality and the Principle of Impartiality in European Administrative Law", 1 Rivista Trimestrale di Diritto Pubblico (2003) p. 53.
95. Mads ANDENAS and Stefan ZLEPTNIG, "Proportionality: WTO Law in Comparative Perspective", 42 Tex. Int'l L. J. (2007) p. 371 at p. 383.
96. See on this and the following Alec STONE SWEET and Jud MATHEWS, *Proportionality Balancing and Global Constitutionalism*, Yale Law School Faculty Scholarship Series No. 14 (2008). This paper is also published in 47 Columbia J. Transnat'l L. (2008) p. 72, but page references in this article are to the Yale version.

"The [purpose of] the constitutional right should be to protect the freedom of the individual [while the purpose of] the regulation should be to ensure sufficient protection of societal interests. The individual's claim to freedom will have a stronger effect ... the more his right to free choice of a profession is put into question; the protection of the public will become more urgent, the greater the disadvantages that arise from the free practicing of professions. When one seeks to maximize both ... demands in the most effective way, then the solution can only lie in a careful balancing [*Abwägung*] of the meaning of the two opposed and perhaps conflicting interests."[97]

The Supreme Court of Canada applies a very similar proportionality test since *Regina v. Oakes*, a case that concerned the question whether a provision of the Narcotics Act was in conformity with Canada's Charter of Rights and Freedoms in establishing a rebuttable presumption that a person found to be in possession of drugs was trafficking drugs and thus criminally liable. The Court struck down this provision as violating the presumption of innocence enshrined in the Charter and based its analysis on a three-step "proportionality test":

"First, the measures adopted must be carefully designed to achieve the objective in question. They must not be arbitrary, unfair or based on irrational considerations. In short, they must be rationally connected to the objective. Second, the means, even if rationally connected to the objective in this first sense, should impair 'as little as possible' the right or freedom in question. Third, there must be a proportionality between the effects of the measures which are responsible for limiting the Charter right or freedom, and the objective which has been identified as of 'sufficient importance'."[98]

To give one further example, the Constitutional Court of South Africa also applies a test of proportionality in balancing individual rights and government purposes. In *State v. Makwanyane*, the Court was faced with a challenge against the death penalty as violating the constitutional right against cruel, inhuman and degrading punishments. The Court, through its leading opinion by President Chaskalson, decided to solve the conflict based on a proportionality analysis: "The limitation of constitutional rights for a purpose that is reasonable and necessary in a democratic society involves the weighing up of competing values, and ultimately an assessment based on proportionality."[99] The Court considered that the following factors would need to be taken into account:

"In the balancing process, the relevant considerations will include the nature of the right that is limited, and its importance to an open and democratic society based on freedom and equality; the purpose for which the right is limited and the importance of that purpose to such a society; the extent of the limitation, its

---

97. BVerfGE 7, 377, 404-405.
98. *R. v. Oakes*, [1986] 1 S.C.R. 103, 139.
99. *State v. Makwanyane & Another*, 1995 (3) SA 391, 436 (CC).

efficacy, and particularly where the limitation has to be necessary, whether the desired ends could reasonably be achieved through other means less damaging to the right in question."[100]

Proportionality has also been routinely applied in the context of international legal regimes as a technique for delineating and balancing the conflicting interests of the international legal order and domestic public policy. In the context of the EC/EU, for example, the concept of proportionality has been used by the European Court of Justice (ECJ) to balance the Community's fundamental freedoms – the free movement of goods, services, labor and capital – with conflicting legitimate interests of the Member States.[101] For example, in the *Cassis de Dijon* case the ECJ decided that the free movement of goods, guaranteed in Art. 28 EC, could be violated not only by discriminatory regulations of a Member State, but also through non-discriminatory regulations that limited intra-Community trade. At the same time, however, and as a corollary to this broad understanding of the fundamental freedom, the Court recognized that Member States could limit the free movement of goods in the public interest if this interest constituted a so-called "mandatory requirement". The Court held that

> "[o]bstacles to movement within the community resulting from disparities between the national laws relating to the marketing of the products in question must be accepted in so far as those provisions may be recognized as being necessary in order to satisfy mandatory requirements relating in particular to the effectiveness of fiscal supervision, the protection of public health, the fairness of commercial transactions and the defence of the consumer".[102]

Even though this test is formulated as a necessity test focusing on less restrictive alternatives, the Court applies it very similarly to the proportionality tests described earlier on with respect to the domestic courts.

Similarly, the ECJ and the Court of First Instance require that measures of the Community vis-à-vis Member States, and those affecting individuals subject to the Community legal order, are to be evaluated against the standard of proportionality. The Court of First Instance, for example, explained in a case concerning the review of a Community act that

> "the principle of proportionality, which is one of the general principles of Community law, requires that measures adopted by Community institutions

---

100. *State v Makwanyane & Another*, ibid.
101. See also Evelyn ELLIS, ed., *The Principle of Proportionality in the Laws of Europe* (1999); on proportionality as a principle in EU/EC law Nicholas EMILIOU, *The Principle of Proportionality in European Law: A Comparative Study* (1996) pp. 23 et seq.; Georg NOLTE, "General Principles of German and European Administrative Law – A Comparison in Historic Perspective", 191 Mod. L. Rev. (1994) p. 191; see also T. Jeremy GUNN, "Deconstructing Proportionality in Limitations Analysis", 19 Emory Int'l L. Rev. (2005) p. 465.
102. *Cassis de Dijon*, ECJ 120/78, Judgment of 20 Feb., 1979 – see [1979] ECR 649, para. 8.

should not exceed the limits of what is appropriate and necessary in order to attain the legitimate objectives pursued by the legislation in question, and where there is a choice between several appropriate measures, recourse must be had to the least onerous, and the disadvantages caused must not be disproportionate to the aims pursued".[103]

In the jurisprudence of the ECJ, proportionality is thus used to "manag[e] tensions and conflicts between rights and freedoms, on the one hand, and the power of the EC/EU and of Member States, on the other".[104] It therefore not only constitutes a method for delimiting individual rights and the Member State's right to limit such rights, but also "a mechanism of coordination between the supranational legal order and national legal orders".[105]

In other areas of public international law proportionality plays a similar role in resolving conflicts in the relationships between equal sovereigns. In the law of countermeasures, proportionality is used to limit the reaction against a State breach of international law by another State.[106] Here, proportionality limits both the means and scope of the countermeasures applied.[107] In particular, the countermeasure must not be tailored so as to permanently deprive the State in breach of its fair shares of benefits. As the International Court of Justice (ICJ) stated in the *Gabcíkovo-Nagymaros Case*: "the effects of a countermeasure must be commensurate with the injury suffered, taking account of the rights in question".[108] Likewise, proportionality is an element of the legality of the use of force in the context of the right to self-defence. Even though not appearing explicitly in Art. 51 of the UN Charter, it has been held by the ICJ to constitute part of customary international law according to which "self-defence would warrant only measures which are proportional to the armed attack and necessary to respond to it".[109]

Under WTO law, proportionality analysis also plays an increasing role in balancing the objectives of the international trade regime, notably trade liberalization, non-discrimination in the trade context and the limitation and careful assessment of non-tariff barriers to trade, with conflicting and legitimate government purposes, such as the

---

103. Case T-13/99, Judgment of 23 November 2002 – *Pfizer Animal Health SA v. Commission*, [2002] ECR II-3305, paras. 411 (citing [1990] ECR I-4023, para. 13).
104. STONE SWEET and MATHEWS, supra fn. 96, p. 48.
105. *Ibid.*
106. Thomas M. FRANCK, "On Proportionality of Countermeasures in International Law", 102 A.J.I.L. (2008) p. 715.
107. Enzo CANNIZZARO, "The Role of Proportionality in the Law of International Countermeasures", 12 Eur. J. Int'l L. (2001) p. 889, at p. 897.
108. *Gabcíkovo-Nagymaros Project (Hungary/Slovakia)*, Judgment of 25 September 1997, I.C.J. Reports 1997, p. 7, para. 85.
109. *Military and Paramilitary Activities in and against Nicaragua*, Judgment of 27 June 1986, I.C.J. Reports 1986, p. 14, paras. 176, 194; see also *Legality of the Threat or Use of Nuclear Weapons*, Advisory Opinion of 8 July 1996, I.C.J. Reports 1996, p. 226, paras. 41-42 (stating more generally that "the exercise of the right of self-defence to the conditions of *necessity* and *proportionality* is a rule of customary international law").

protection of public health, public morals or the environment, many but not all of which are enumerated in Art. XX GATT. Even though WTO scholars maintain that no uniform proportionality analysis has developed in the jurisprudence of the Dispute Settlement Body to balance trade and non-trade interests,[110] the various balancing tests applied in this context can nevertheless be framed, on an abstract level, as a type of proportionality analysis.

In *Korea Beef*, for example, a case concerning the labeling and sale of beef depending on its origins as Korean or non-Korean beef in order to protect public health, the Appellate Body explained that

> "[t]he more vital or important ... common interests or values are, the easier it would be to accept as 'necessary' a measure designed as an enforcement instrument. There are other aspects of the enforcement measure to be considered in evaluating that measure as 'necessary'. One is the extent to which the measure contributes to the realization of the end pursued, the securing of compliance with the law or regulation at issue. The greater the contribution, the more easily a measure might be considered to be 'necessary'.... [The] [d]etermination of whether a measure, which is not 'indispensable', may nevertheless be 'necessary' within the contemplation of Article XX(d), involves in every case a process of weighing and balancing a series of factors which prominently include the contribution made by the compliance measure to the enforcement of the law or regulation at issue, the importance of the common interests or values protected by that law or regulation, and the accompanying impact of the law or regulation on imports or exports."[111]

Finally, proportionality plays a crucial role in the jurisprudence of the ECHR in its application of the European Convention on Human Rights and Fundamental Freedoms, notably as regards the resolution of conflicts between individual rights granted under the Convention and public policy of the Member States. Even though the Convention requires, for example, with respect to restrictions of the freedom of expression that a State measure be "necessary in a democratic society", the Court developed this into a proportionality analysis that is similar to the one found in German constitutional law. In its leading case of *Handyside v. the United Kingdom*, a case involving censorship of a book based on violations of public morals, the Court stated that "the adjective 'necessary', within the meaning of Article 10 para. 2 is not synonymous with 'indispensable' [and] neither has it the flexibility of such expressions as ... 'admissible', ... 'useful', 'reasonable', or 'desirable'".[112] Later on, in *Dudgeon v. the United Kingdom*, the Court declared a State measure that criminalized certain homosexual conducts to be "disproportionate" in interfering with the right to privacy.[113] Meanwhile, the Court has

---

110. See Axel DESMEDT, "Proportionality in WTO Law", 4 J. Int'l Econ. L. (2001) p. 441.
111. Appellate Body Report, *Korea – Measures Affecting Imports of Fresh, Chilled and Frozen Beef*, para. 164, WT/DS161/AB/R (11 December 2000).
112. *Handyside v. United Kingdom*, App. No. 5493/72 (Eur. Ct. H.R. December 7, 1976), para. 48.
113. *Dudgeon v. United Kingdom*, App. No. 7525/76 (Eur. Ct. H.R. 22 October 1981).

engaged in proportionality-style balancing with respect to almost every right enshrined in the Convention.[114]

At the same time, however, the Court grants, as stated in the *Handyside* case, a margin of appreciation to the Member States in "mak[ing] the initial assessment of the pressing social need implied by the notion of 'necessity' in this context".[115] It is for them to determine in the first place what they consider necessary for a democratic society and it is this choice that the ECHR subjects to scrutiny. The margin varies depending on the right involved, the government purpose pursued and the degree of interference. Similar to the function of proportionality in the EC/EU-context, proportionality analysis by the Strasbourg Court has to be seen not only in balancing individual rights and public interests, but also as "a basic mechanism of coordinating between the ECHR and national legal systems, and among diverse national systems".[116]

## 2. The Structure of Proportionality Analysis

Proportionality implies a means-ends relationship between the aims pursued by a specific government action and the means employed to achieve this end.[117] Certainly, major differences exist between various versions and methodologies of proportionality analysis, including differences between full-fledged proportionality that involves a substantive review by the adjudicator of the balance struck by the political decision under scrutiny and a more procedural type of review, such as less- or least-restrictive-measure tests.[118] The balancing between conflicting rights and interests will be dependent upon the cultural socializations and values connected to a specific institution, its hermeneutics, and the core legal texts, other legal materials, and the purposes of the specific legal regime. Notwithstanding such variance, as a general matter proportionality analysis provides a guiding structure for decision-makers that requires them to address certain issues and to determine whether measures taken by a State have sufficiently taken into account the rights or interests they interfere with. As developed in the jurisprudence of various domestic and international courts, proportionality analysis can be described as comprising three sub-elements: (1) the principle of suitability, (2) the principle of necessity and (3) the principle of proportionality *stricto sensu*.

### a. Suitability for a legitimate government purpose

The first step in proportionality reasoning is the analysis of whether the measure adopted by the State or government agency serves a legitimate government purpose and is generally suitable to achieve this purpose. The task the decision-maker has to achieve is

---

114. Julian RIVERS, "Proportionality and Variable Intensity of Review", 65 Cambridge L. J. (2006) p. 174, at p. 182. It particularly engaged in a heavy critique of the more lenient reasonableness standards initially applied by the courts in the United Kingdom, see STONE SWEET and MATHEWS, supra fn. 96, pp. 51-53.
115. *Ibid.*
116. *Ibid.*, p. 53.
117. See EMILIOU, supra fn. 101, pp. 23-24.
118. ANDENAS and ZLEPTNIG, supra fn. 95, p. 388.

thus two-fold, but both elements of this first step set a relatively undemanding standard for the State measure to meet, certainly in the context of investor-State arbitration. The first element of the task is to ascertain whether the measure adopted purports to aim at a legitimate purpose. Consequently, illegitimate purposes can be filtered out at this early stage. They constitute *per definitionem* a disproportionate interference with the right or interest protected.

In Investor-State arbitration, most ordinary public purposes of State action will be legitimate purposes, and only in marginal cases will it be necessary to assess the legitimacy of the purpose based on a comparative approach or from its recognition in international treaties. A State action that is manifestly corrupt for the purely private benefit of a crony, or that is a manifest jus cogens violation such as crimes against humanity is obviously not for a legitimate purpose. Overall, however, very few State measures will fail to aim at a legitimate government purpose.

After establishing the legitimacy of the purpose pursued, the decision-maker will have to determine, in the second element of its task, whether the measure taken is suitable to achieve the stated aim. This requires establishing "a causal relationship between the measure and its object".[119] The decision-maker will thus have to determine whether the measure taken furthers the stated purpose in any way. Again, only very few measures will not pass the suitability test, as good faith actions by governments will usually not involve the use of means that are wholly ineffective in pursuing the stated purpose.

b.  *Necessity*

In a second step, proportionality analysis involves a test of necessity. This covers the question of whether there are other, less intrusive means with regard to the right or interest affected that are equally able to achieve the stated goal (without infringing other protected interests). Necessity requires that there is no less restrictive measure that is equally effective.[120] This step requires answering two questions: first, is there a less restrictive measure, and secondly, is this measure equally effective (and reasonably feasible)? The background to this test can again be seen in the optimization the decision-maker has to achieve when balancing conflicting principles.[121] If the right affected is protected in principle, there is no justification for the State to be allowed to infringe upon such rights more than necessary, since there are other equally effective alternatives to achieve the same aim.

c.  *Proportionality Stricto Sensu*

In a final step, proportionality analysis involves a balancing between the effects of the State measure on the affected right or interests and the importance of the government purpose. Proportionality *stricto sensu* requires that the measure is not excessive with regard to the objective pursued and that relative weight is given to each principle.[122] "The

---

119. Jan H. JANS, "Proportionality Revisited", 27 Legal Issues of Econ. Integration (2000) p. 239 at p. 240.
120. *Ibid.*
121. Cf. Robert ALEXY, *A Theory of Constitutional Rights*, p. 399.
122. ALEXY, supra fn. 87, 13 Ratio Juris p. 294, at p. 298.

greater the degree of non-satisfaction of, or detriment to, one principle, the greater must be the importance of satisfying the other."[123] Proportionality *stricto sensu* requires taking into account all available factors such as cost-benefit analysis, the importance of the right affected, the importance of the right or interest protected, the degree of interference (minor v. major interference), the length of interference (permanent v. temporary), the availability of alternative measures that might be less effective, but also proportionally less restrictive for the right affected, and so on.

This third step is apposite because an analysis that stops at the necessity-stage would allow restricting a right severely in order to protect a negligible public interest.[124] In addition, the major advantage of this type of reasoning compared to more deferential standards is that the judge or decision-maker is required to go through an exercise in creative problem-solving that attempts to relate the purpose pursued and the importance of the rights affected. It requires the adjudicator to actively consider alternative policies which could have resulted in a better optimization of the two conflicting rights or interests involved, instead of just assessing their reasonableness, a standard that would necessarily be more deferential to government policy-making, but also accord less protection to the rights protected.

This does not mean, however, that the adjudicator should substitute its own preferences for those of the government, but merely that it should consider whether the reasoning and policy objectives of the State or Government stay within a framework that is based on the recognition of various, eventually conflicting rights or interests which the State tries to generally protect and thus minimize interferences. Depending on the interpretive issues and legal norms involved, all the adjudicator might be allowed to do, for example, is verify whether the State has stayed within an outer framework that is spanned by the recognition of property and investment protection on the one hand and the legitimate public interest on the other.

3. *Applying Proportionality Analysis in Investor-State Arbitration*

Investment tribunals are beginning to adopt (albeit not frequently yet) proportionality analysis when faced with the question whether a regulatory measure stays within the framework set up by the requirement under investment treaties to respect the interests of foreign investors through the concepts of fair and equitable treatment and indirect expropriation. This is particularly evident in two sets of cases which will be discussed in this section. One concerns the question of how to delineate between indirect expropriations that require compensation (depending on the applicable treaty or customary international law) and non-compensable regulation. Another concerns the issue, dealt with in the context of the fair and equitable treatment standard, of the extent to which the investor's legitimate expectations can constitute a bar to regulations that

---

123. ALEXY, supra fn. 86, p. 102.
124. Rupprecht von KRAUSS, *Der Grundsatz der Verhältnismäßigkeit in seiner Bedeutung für die Notwendigkeit des Mittels im Verwaltungsrecht* (1955) p. 15 (stating that "if the measure [of legality] is only necessity" (i.e., the least restrictive means test), then "a quite negligible public interest could lead to a severe right infringement, without being unlawful".).

further a non-investment related interest and adversely affect the expectations an investor had when making its investments.

a. *Proportionality analysis and the concept of indirect expropriation*
International takings law is one field where the tension between investment protection and conflicting rights and interests crystallizes. Virtually all investment treaties contain prohibition on expropriations without compensation. A typical provision is contained, for example, in the BIT between Germany and China that provides:

> "Investments by investors of either Contracting Party shall not directly or indirectly be expropriated, nationalized or subjected to any other measure the effects of which would be tantamount to expropriation or nationalization in the territory of the other Contracting Party (hereinafter referred to as expropriation) except for the public benefit and against compensation."[125]

Expropriation is not necessarily confined to direct expropriations or nationalizations that involve the transfer of title from the foreign investor to the State or a third-party. Depending on the treaty provision or other controlling standard (such as customary international law) it may also cover so-called indirect, creeping or de facto expropriations, involving State measures that do not interfere with the owner's title, but negatively affect the property's substance or void the owner's control over it.[126] Thus one NAFTA tribunal opined that the concept of expropriation

> "includes not only open, deliberate and acknowledged takings of property, such as outright seizure or formal or obligatory transfer of title in favour of the host State, but also covert or incidental interference with the use of property which has

---

125. Art. 4(2) of the China-Germany BIT.
126. See on the concept of indirect expropriation George C. CHRISTIE, "What Constitutes a Taking of Property Under International Law?", 38 Brit. Yb. Int'l L. (1962) p. 307; Burns H. WESTON, "'Constructive Takings' under International Law: A Modest Foray into the Problem of 'Creeping Expropriation'", 16 Va. J. Int'l L. (1975) p. 103; Rosalyn HIGGINS, *The Taking of Property by the State: Recent Developments in International Law*, 176 Recueil des Cours (1982) p. 259 at pp. 322 et seq.; Rudolf DOLZER, "Indirect Expropriation of Alien Property", 1 ICSID Rev. – For. Inv. L. J. (1986) p. 41; Thomas W. WÄLDE and Abba KOLO, "Environmental Regulation, Investment Protection and 'Regulatory Taking' in International Law", 50 Int'l & Comp. L. Q. (2001) p. 811; Catherine YANNACA-SMALL, "'Indirect Expropriation' and the 'Right to Regulate' in International Investment Law", OECD Working Paper on International Investment, No. 2004/4, available at <www.oecd.org/dataoecd/22/54/33776546.pdf>; Jan PAULSSON and Zachary DOUGLAS, "Indirect Expropriation in Investment Treaty Arbitrations" in Norbert HORN and Stefan KRÖLL, eds., *Arbitrating Foreign Investment Disputes* (2004) pp. 145-158; FORTIER and DRYMER, supra fn. 79, p. 293; Andrew NEWCOMBE, "The Boundaries of Regulatory Expropriation", 20 ICSID Rev. – For. Inv. L. J. (2005) p. 1; Bjørn KUNOY, "Developments in Indirect Expropriation Case Law in ICSID Transnational Arbitration", 6 J. World Inv. & Trade. (2005) p. 467; Charles LEBEN, *"La liberté normative de l'etat et la question de l'expropriation indirecte"* in Charles LEBEN, ed., *Le contentieux arbitral transnational relatif a l'investissement international: nouveaux développements* (2006) p. 163.

the effect of depriving the owner, in whole or in significant part, of the use or reasonably-to-be-expected economic benefit of property even if not necessarily to the obvious benefit of the host State".[127]

Classical customary international law and treaty jurisprudence typically hold that covered direct and indirect expropriations are only lawful under international investment treaties if they fulfill a public purpose, are implemented in a non-discriminatory manner and observe due process of law. Finally and most importantly, both direct and indirect expropriations regularly require compensation.[128]

Indirect expropriation can also occur based on regulatory acts of the host State. In arbitral jurisprudence, tribunals vary in basic approaches to the issue of how to distinguish between compensable expropriation and non-compensable regulation of property.[129] Some tribunals solely look at the effects the host State's measure has, thus finding a compensable indirect expropriation either because the impact of the measure reaches a certain intensity, owing either to the permanent interference with fundamental components of the right to property,[130] or to the substantial diminution in or destruction of the value of the property in question.[131] The majority of the tribunals, however, take into account the purpose of a State's measure and adopt the so-called police power doctrine in deciding whether a general measure entitles an investor to compensation under the concept of indirect expropriation.[132] The police powers doctrine recognizes

---

127. *Metalclad v. Mexico*, supra fn. 23, para. 103.
128. For the question of whether the level of compensation differs for indirect expropriation see Yves NOUVEL, "*L'indemnisation d'une expropriation indirecte*", 5 Int'l L. FORUM du droit int. (2003) p. 198; Thomas W. MERRILL, "Incomplete Compensation for Takings", 11 N.Y.U. Envt'l L. J. (2002-2003) p. 110. Cf. also W. Michael REISMAN and Robert D. SLOANE, "Indirect Expropriation and Its Valuation in the BIT Generation", 74 Brit. Yb. Int'l L. (2003) p. 115.
129. See Rudolf DOLZER, *Eigentum, Enteignung und Entschädigung im geltenden Völkerrecht* (1985) pp. 186 et seq.; Rudolf DOLZER, "Indirect Expropriation: New Developments?", 11 N.Y.U. Envt'l L. J. (2002-2003) p. 64 with further references.
130. See *Starrett Housing Corp. v. Iran*, AWD ITL 32-24-1, 19 December 1983, 4 Iran-U.S. Claims Tribunal Reports 122, 154; *Tippetts, Abbett, McCarthy, Stratton v. TAMS-AFFA et al*, AWD 141-7-2, 22 June 1984, 6 Iran-U.S. Claims Tribunal Reports 219, 225 et seq.; on the jurisprudence of the Iran-United States Claims Tribunal on expropriations see George ALDRICH, "What Constitutes a Compensable Taking of Property? The Decisions of the Iran-United States Claims Tribunal", 88 A.J.I.L. (1994) p. 585.
131. *Phelps Dodge Corp. v. Iran*, AWD 217-99-2, 19 March 1986, 10 Iran-U.S. Claims Tribunal Reports 121, 130; see also SWANSON, "Iran-U.S. Claims Tribunal: A Policy Analysis of the Expropriation Cases", 18 Case W. Res. J. Int'l L. (1986) p. 307 at pp. 325 et seq.; WESTON, supra fn. 126, p. 103 at pp. 119 et seq.
132. Maurizio BRUNETTI, "Indirect Expropriation in International Law", 5 Int'l L. FORUM du droit int. (2003) p. 150; DOLZER, "Indirect Expropriation: New Developments?", supra fn. 129, p. 64 at pp. 79 et seq. (2002-2003); Rudolf DOLZER and Felix BLOCH, "Indirect Expropriation: Conceptual Realignments?", 5 Int'l L. FORUM du droit int. (2003) p. 155 at pp. 158 et seq.; Allen S. WEINER, "Indirect Expropriation: The Need for a Taxonomy of 'Legitimate' Regulatory Purposes", 5 Int'l L. FORUM du droit int. (2003) p. 166; *Sea-Land Service Inc. v. Iran*, AWD 135-33-1, 22 June 1984, 6 Iran-U.S. Claims Tribunal Reports 149, 165; *Sedco Inc. v. NIOC and Iran*, AWD ITL 55-129-3, 24 October 1985, 9 Iran-U.S. Claims Tribunal Reports 248, 275

that a State has the power to restrict private property rights without compensation in pursuance of a legitimate purpose. Under this approach, it is not sufficient to determine the effect of a State measure; instead, the measure's effect has to be balanced in relation to the object and purpose of the interference.

Even though most investment treaties do not explicitly contain such exceptions to the protection of property,[133] tribunals acknowledge that host States have the power to restrict private property rights without compensation in pursuance of a legitimate purpose, so long as this purpose is reasonably balanced in relation to the regulation's effect on the investment. Thus, the tribunal in *Tecmed v. Mexico* held that a police power exception formed part of the international law of expropriation: "[t]he principle that the State's exercise of its sovereign powers within the framework of its police power may cause economic damage to those subject to its powers as administrator without entitling them to any compensation whatsoever is undisputable".[134] Similarly, the tribunal in *Methanex v. United States* stressed that

> "as a matter of general international law, a non-discriminatory regulation for a public purpose, which is enacted in accordance with due process and, which affects, inter alios, a foreign investor or investment is not deemed expropriatory and compensable unless specific commitments had been given by the regulating government to the then putative foreign investor contemplating investment that the government would refrain from such regulation".[135]

---

et seq.; *Too v. Greater Modesto Insurance Associates and The United States of America*, AWD 460-880-2, 29 December 1989, 23 Iran-U.S. Claims Tribunal Reports 378, 387 et seq.

133. Security exceptions or similar non-precluded measures provisions, such as those often included in US bilateral investment treaties, raise special issues and are not addressed in this Report. See, for example, Art. 10(1) of the Treaty Between the United States of America and the Arab Republic of Egypt Concerning the Reciprocal Encouragement and Protection of Investments, signed 11 March 1986, entry into force 27 June 1992 (stating that "[t]his Treaty shall not preclude the application by either Party or any subdivision thereof of any and all measures necessary for the maintenance of public order and morals, the fulfillment of its existing international obligations, the protection of its own security interests, or such measures deemed appropriate by the Parties to fulfill future international obligations"). For one view of these clauses, see José E. ALVAREZ and Kathryn KHAMSI, "The Argentine Crisis and Foreign Investors: A Glimpse into the Heart of the Investment Regime" in Karl P. SAUVANT, ed., supra fn. 8, p. 379. For a different view see William BURKE-WHITE and Andreas von STADEN, "Investment Protection in Extraordinary Times: The Interpretation and Application of Non-Precluded Measures Provisions in Bilateral Investment Treaties", 48 Va. J. Int'l L. (2008) p. 307.

134. *Tecmed v. Mexico*, supra fn. 24, para. 119.

135. *Methanex Corporation v. United States of America* (UNCITRAL/NAFTA) Final Award of 3 August 2005, Part IV - Chapt. D - para. 7. Similarly, *International Thunderbird Gaming v. Mexico* (UNCITRAL/NAFTA), supra fn. 37, para. 127; *Saluka v. Czech Republic*, supra fn. 33, para. 254-262; *LG&E Energy Corp., LG&E Capital Corp., LG&E International Inc. v. Argentine Republic* (ICSID Case No. ARB/02/1), Decision on Liability of 3 October 2006, paras. 194-197; *Feldman v. Mexico*, supra fn. 30, paras. 103-106.

How the balancing itself is to be done, however, is not always explained in depth by arbitral tribunals. Yet, the approach of the tribunal in *Tecmed v. Mexico* illustrates well the use of a proportionality analysis to manage tensions between investment protection and competing public policies. In the case at hand, Mexican authorities had not renewed the temporary operating license for a waste landfill that was essential to the business of the Mexican subsidiary of a Spanish investor. For the tribunal this constituted a compensable indirect expropriation. In its argumentation concerning the distinction between indirect expropriation and regulation, the tribunal drew on the jurisprudence on Art. 1 of the First Additional Protocol to the European Convention on Human Rights, and weighed the conflicting interests using a proportionality test familiar from the European Court of Human Rights jurisprudence.

While the agency had justified non-renewal of the landfill license on the basis of the operator's lack of reliability, inter alia owing to its having processed biological and other toxic waste in violation of the operating license and having exceeded the landfill's capacity,[136] the tribunal concluded that political considerations had been decisive.[137] It pointed out that only after massive protests by the local population had occurred in late 1997, did the agency intend to accelerate the relocation of the landfill by refusing to renew the license.[138] Although the investor had already agreed to relocate the landfill, its request to renew the operating license for another five months until the relocation could take place was refused. Moreover, the agency ordered the investor to cease its activities immediately.[139]

In applying the concept of indirect expropriation to the facts at hand, the tribunal followed a two-step analysis. In a first step, it determined whether the State's measure itself was sufficiently intense in order for a non-compensable regulation to turn into a compensable indirect expropriation. This, the tribunal considered, depended on two factors: a temporal and a substantive one. First, the interference with the property interest in question must not be of a transitional nature only; second, the interference must lead to a complete destruction of the property's value. Since the landfill facility could not be used for a different purpose, and could not be sold because of the existing contamination,[140] the effect of the non-renewal of the license potentially amounted to an expropriation.

The tribunal, however, did not conclude the analysis there. Instead, in a second step, it considered the effects of the non-renewal of the operating license only as one factor among others in distinguishing between regulation and indirect expropriation. The reason for this approach, according to the tribunal, is that "[t]he principle that the State's exercise of its sovereign powers within the framework of its police power may cause economic damage to those subject to its powers as administrator without entitling them to any compensation whatsoever is undisputable".[141] In this way, the tribunal accepted

---

136. *Tecmed*, supra fn. 24, paras. 99 et seq.
137. *Tecmed, ibid.*, paras. 127 et seq.
138. *Tecmed, ibid.*, paras. 106 et seq.
139. See *Tecmed, ibid.*, paras. 45, 110 et seq.
140. *Tecmed, ibid.*, para. 117.
141. *Tecmed, ibid.*, paras. 118 et seq.

that bilateral investment treaties in principle do not exclude a State's regulatory power, even if the treaty text did not explicitly provide for the continuous existence of such power. Consequently, the tribunal posited that the BIT requires only that the effects of a specific State measure on private property have to be proportional to the exercise of the State's police power. In essence, the tribunal therefore considered property to be inherently bound and restricted by the police power of the State even if the wording of the Treaty does not explicitly mention a police power exception.

Following the doctrinal structure of fundamental rights reasoning, the tribunal then engaged in a comprehensive proportionality test that weighed and balanced the competing interests in order to determine when legitimate regulation flips over into indirect expropriation. In doing so, the tribunal essentially aimed at achieving "*Konkordanz*" of the various rights and interests affected.[142] From this perspective, a compensable indirect expropriation occurs only when State measures lead to disproportional restrictions of the right to property. Thus, the tribunal stated:

> "[T]he Arbitral Tribunal will consider, in order to determine if they are to be characterized as expropriatory, whether such actions or measures are proportional to the public interest presumably protected thereby and to the protection legally granted to investments, taking into account that the significance of such impact has a key role upon deciding the proportionality. Although the analysis starts at the due deference owing to the State when defining the issues that affect its public policy or the interests of society as a whole, as well as the actions that will be implemented to protect such values, such situation does not prevent the Arbitral Tribunal, without thereby questioning such due deference, from examining the actions of the State in light of Article 5(1) of the Agreement to determine whether measures are reasonable with respect to their goals, the deprivation of economic rights and the legitimate expectations of who suffered such deprivation. There must be a reasonable relationship of proportionality between the charge or weight imposed to the foreign investor and the aim sought to be realized by any expropriatory measure. To value such charge or weight, it is very important to

---

142. The term "*Konkordanz*" or "*praktische Konkordanz*" was coined by the German constitutional law scholar Konrad Hesse and refers to a concept or method of reconciliation and balance of competing fundamental rights. In case two fundamental rights collide, "*Konkordanz*" requires that both rights be reconciled without giving up neither one of them. What this concept primarily excludes is perceiving one of the fundamental rights as superior to any other such right. Instead both rights have to be reconciled in a differentiated manner, a task that is achieved in the fundamental rights context by balancing the different rights and interests on proportionality grounds while aiming at a solution that gives both rights effective protection to the best possible extent. See Konrad HESSE, *Grundzüge des Verfassungsrechts der Bundesrepublik Deutschland*, no. 72, 20th edn. (1995). The concept has been recognized as a governing principle by the German Constitutional Court, see BVerfGE 41, 29; BVerfGE 77, 240; BVerfGE 81, 298; BVerfGE 83, 130; BVerfGE 108, 282. The concept can also be found in the constitutional jurisprudence of the French *Conseil Constitutionnel*, CC *décision* no. 94-352 DC, 18 Jan. 1995, available at <www.conseil-constitutionnel.fr/decision/1994/94352dc.htm>.

measure the size of the ownership deprivation caused by the actions of the State and whether such deprivation was compensated or not."[143]

The concrete aspects the tribunal considered in its balancing approach were the legitimate expectations of the investor, the importance of the regulatory interest pursued by the host State, the weight and the effect of the restriction and other circumstances concerning the investor's position (such as the prior violations of the terms of the operating license by the operating company).[144] Apart from that, the tribunal, in assessing proportionality, also accorded importance to the question whether an investor has been especially and unequally affected by the adoption of a measure.[145] In conclusion, the tribunal held that the non-renewal of the license restricted the claimant's property rights disproportionally and therefore constituted an indirect expropriation. The tribunal placed particular emphasis on the fact that the degree of the operating company's breaches were marginal and that they could not be invoked to justify the refusal to renew the license as a consequence.

In addition, the tribunal also fleshed out its general approach to proportionality reasoning by enumerating certain restrictions on the right to property that it considered proportional, such as police measures taken to eliminate threats to public safety, that is, measures addressed either to the person directly threatening public safety or, in case of an emergency, even against a third party that does not itself constitute a threat to public safety.[146] Interferences with the right to property which are aimed at the prevention of danger are therefore in conformity with international law and do not necessarily give rise to a claim for compensation.

A similar proportionality analysis was also adopted by the tribunal in *LG&E v. Argentina*, a case that concerned the emergency measures Argentina passed in the context of its economic crisis in 2001/2002. These included the pesification of dollar-denominated debts and claims and affected tariff guarantees that were given to foreign investors in the gas and electricity sectors. LG&E brought a claim under the United States-Argentina BIT and argued that the effect of these measures significantly affected the value of its shareholding in an Argentine subsidiary that operated in the gas sector and thus constituted an indirect expropriation.[147]

However, the tribunal denied a finding of indirect expropriation partly because it required a high threshold for interferences with investments in order for them to constitute indirect expropriations. In the tribunal's view, indirect expropriation in the case of shareholder claims presupposed that "governmental measures have 'effectively

---

143. *Tecmed*, supra fn. 24, para. 122.
144. *Tecmed*, ibid., paras. 149 et seq.
145. *Tecmed*, ibid., para. 122. This idea is conveyed in an important strain of takings jurisprudence in Germany that relies on whether property owners had to suffer a special sacrifice to the benefit of the general public ("*Sonderopfer*"). See on this WÄLDE and KOLO, supra fn. 126, p. 811 at pp. 845 et seq.
146. *Tecmed*, supra fn. 24, para. 136.
147. See *LG&E v. Argentina*, supra fn. 135, para. 177. See on the decision, also in comparison to the earlier *CMS v. Argentina* Award, Stephan SCHILL, "International Investment Law and the Host State's Power to Handle Economic Crises", 24 J. Int'l Arb. (2007) p. 265.

neutralize[d] the benefit of property of the foreign owner'. Ownership or enjoyment can be said to be 'neutralized' where a party no longer is in control of the investment, or where it cannot direct the day-to-day operations of the investment."[148] In addition, the tribunal emphasized that interferences that amount to indirect expropriation ordinarily are akin to permanent measures.[149]

In addition, the tribunal endorsed the approach taken by the tribunal in *Tecmed v. Mexico* and incorporated that tribunal's reasoning on a proportionality or balancing test for distinguishing between legitimate non-compensable regulation and compensable indirect expropriation. The tribunal in *LG&E* noted:

> "The question remains as to whether one should only take into account the effects produced by the measure or if one should consider also the context within which a measure was adopted and the host State's purpose. It is this Tribunal's opinion that there must be a balance in the analysis both of the causes and the effects of a measure in order that one may qualify a measure as being of an expropriatory nature. It is important not to confound the State's right to adopt policies with its power to take an expropriatory measure. 'This determination is important because it is one of the main elements to distinguish, from the perspective of an international tribunal between a regulatory measure, which is an ordinary expression of the exercise of the State's police power that entails a decrease in assets or rights, and a *de facto* expropriation that deprives those assets and rights of any real substance.'"[150]

The tribunal in *LG&E* thus suggested that international investment treaties ordinarily do not exclude a host State's power to regulate in the public interest. Instead, it emphasizes that the "State has the right to adopt measures having a social or general welfare purpose".[151] This position is in line with the view of several international courts and tribunals, i.e., that a State is, in general, not internationally liable for bona-fide regulation.[152] Yet, at the same time, the tribunal in *LG&E* suggests that in exceptional

---

148. *LG&E v. Argentina*, supra fn. 135, para. 188 (citing *CME Czech Republic B.V. v. The Czech Republic* (UNCITRAL), Partial Award of 13 September 2001, para. 604 and *Pope & Talbot, Inc. v. The Government of Canada* (UNCITRAL), Interim Award of 26 June 2000, para. 100).
149. *LG&E v. Argentina*, supra fn. 135, para. 193. See also *LG&E v. Argentina*, para. 191 (citing *Pope & Talbot*, supra fn. 148, paras. 101 et seq.) (stating that "[i]nterference with the investment's ability to carry on its business is not satisfied where the investment continues to operate, even if profits are diminished. The impact must be substantial in order that compensation may be claimed for the expropriation.").
150. *LG&E v. Argentina*, supra fn. 135, para. 194 (quoting from *Tecmed v. Mexico*, supra fn. 24, para. 115).
151. *LG&E*, supra fn. 135, para. 195.
152. *LG&E*, ibid., para. 196 (citing American Law Institute, *Restatement (Third) of the Foreign Relations Law of the United States*, Vol. I (1987) Sect. 712, Commentary g, *Too v. Greater Modesto Insurance Associates and The United States of America*, supra fn. 132, 23 Iran-U.S. Claims Tribunal Reports 378, 387 et seq. and *The Oscar Chinn Case (United Kingdom v. Belgium)*, Judgment No. 23 of 12 December 1934, PCIJ Series A/B, Case No. 63, 1934). Similarly, *Sea-Land Service Inc. v. Iran*,

cases even generally applicable regulation in the public interest requires compensation if the measure are "obviously disproportionate".[153]

An approach like this is also reflected in recent State treaty practice, such as recent US agreements which include an interpretation of the concept of indirect expropriation that states: "[e]xcept in rare circumstances, nondiscriminatory regulatory actions by a Party that are designed and applied to protect legitimate public welfare objectives, such as public health, safety, and the environment, do not constitute indirect expropriations".[154] This essentially incorporates a proportionality test into the application of the concept of indirect expropriation and thereby helps balancing investment protection and competing public policy purposes.

*b.    Proportionality analysis and fair and equitable treatment clauses*

Proportionality analysis can also apply in some contexts and with regard to some sub-elements of the fair and equitable treatment standard. As shown in Part II of this Report, the "fair and equitable treatment" standard has been interpreted by different tribunals as encompassing stability and predictability of the legal framework, consistency in the host State's decision-making, the protection of investor confidence or "legitimate expectations", procedural due process and the prohibition of denial of justice, the requirement of transparency, and the concepts of reasonableness and proportionality.[155] Actually applying many of these general propositions often entails weighing competing interests, as well as establishing a standard of review, burdens of proof, and whatever degrees of deference may be appropriate.

For example, the protection of the investor's legitimate expectations does not make the domestic legal framework unchangeable or subject every change to a compensation requirement. Rather a balancing test is sometimes needed in order actually to apply this, and potentially other, aspects of fair and equitable treatment.[156] Thus, the tribunal in *Saluka v. Czech Republic* specifically warned of the danger of taking the idea of the investor's expectation too literally since this would "impose upon host States' [sic]

---

supra fn. 132, 6 Iran-U.S. Claims Tribunal Reports 149, 165; *Sedco Inc. v. NIOC and Iran,* supra fn. 132, 9 Iran-U.S. Claims Tribunal Reports 248, 275 et seq.; *Methanex v. United States,* supra fn. 135, Part IV Chap. D, para. 7; *International Thunderbird Gaming v. Mexico,* supra fn. 37, paras. 123 et seq.; *Saluka v. Czech Republic,* supra fn. 33, paras. 253 et seq.

153. *LG&E v. Argentina,* supra fn. 135, para. 195 (citing *Tecmed v. Mexico,* supra fn. 24, para. 122).

154. See, for example, Art. 15.6, of the United States – Singapore Free Trade Agreement, signed 15 Jan. 2003, entry into force 1 January 2004, in connection with an exchange of letters on the scope of the concept of indirect expropriation, available at <www.ustr.gov/Trade_Agreements/Bilateral/Singapore_FTA/Final_Texts/Section_Index.html>.

155. See supra Sects. II.*1.*-*5*.

156. The main difference between the concept of indirect expropriation and the protection of legitimate expectations under fair and equitable treatment is that indirect expropriation requires interference with a property interest or entitlement, whereas the protection of legitimate expectations under fair and equitable treatment is broader and can encompass the expectation in the continuous existence and operation of a certain regulatory or legislative framework. Balancing tests of different sorts are also beginning to be used in the jurisprudence of investment tribunals on other issues, including in the interpretation of umbrella clauses.

obligations which would be inappropriate and unrealistic".[157] Instead, the tribunal set out to balance the investor's legitimate expectations and the host State's interests within a broader proportionality test. It reasoned:

> "No investor may reasonably expect that the circumstances prevailing at the time the investment is made remain totally unchanged. In order to determine whether frustration of the foreign investor's expectations was justified and reasonable, the host State's legitimate right subsequently to regulate domestic matters in the public interest must be taken into consideration as well. [...]
> The determination of a breach of Article 3.1 by the Czech Republic therefore requires a weighing of the Claimant's legitimate and reasonable expectations on the one hand and the Respondent's legitimate regulatory interests on the other.
> A foreign investor protected by the Treaty may in any case properly expect that the Czech Republic implements its policies *bona fide* by conduct that is, as far as it affects the investors' investment, reasonably justifiable by public policies and that such conduct does not manifestly violate the requirements of consistency, transparency, even-handedness and non-discrimination. In particular, any differential treatment of a foreign investor must not be based on unreasonable distinctions and demands, and must be justified by showing that it bears a reasonable relationship to rational policies not motivated by a preference for other investments over the foreign-owned investment."[158]

The general approach of the tribunal in *Saluka* has also been endorsed by various other tribunals.[159] More broadly, however, arbitral tribunals increasingly link fair and equitable treatment to the concepts of reasonableness and proportionality, controlling the extent to which interferences of host States with foreign investments are permitted. The assessment by the tribunal in *Pope & Talbot v. Canada* of the reasonableness of the conduct

---

157. *Saluka v. Czech Republic*, supra fn. 33, para. 304.
158. *Saluka*, ibid., paras. 305 et seq.
159. See e.g. *BG Group Plc. v. The Republic of Argentina* (UNCITRAL), Final Award of 24 December 2007, para. 298:

> "The duties of the host State must be examined in the light of the legal and business framework as represented to the investor at the time that it decides to invest. This does not imply a freezing of the legal system, as suggested by Argentina. Rather, in order to adapt to changing economic, political and legal circumstances the State's regulatory power still remains in place. As previously held by tribunals addressing similar considerations, '... the host State's legitimate right subsequently to regulate domestic matters in the public interest must be taken into consideration as well'."

(citing *Saluka v. Czech Republic*, supra fn. 33, para. 304). See also *Feldman v. Mexico*, supra fn. 30, para. 112 (stating that "[g]overnments, in their exercise of regulatory power, frequently change their laws and regulations in response to changing economic circumstances or changing political, economic or social considerations. Those changes may well make certain activities less profitable or even uneconomic to continue.").

of an administrative agency[160] and the comments by the tribunal in *Eureko v. Poland* concerning the adequacy of the reasons why the expectations of the investor could not be met, can be seen as importing a general concept of reasonableness into specific interpretations and applications of the fair and equitable treatment standard.[161]

Proportionality-related analysis likewise can potentially play a role when arbitral tribunals scrutinize whether the exercise of administrative discretion conforms to the standard of fair and equitable treatment. The case in *Middle East Cement Shipping and Handling Co S.A. v. Egypt*[162] involved the seizure and auctioning of the Claimant's vessel in order to recover debts the investor had incurred in relation to a State entity. A key question was whether the procedural implementation of the auction was valid, in particular whether sufficient notice of the seizure was given.[163] Arguably in conformity with Egyptian law, the notice was given by attaching a copy of a distraint report to the vessel, because the Claimant could not be found onboard the ship. The tribunal, however, considered that the authority had wrongly exercised its discretion by using this *in absentia* notification instead of notifying the Claimant directly at his local address. Relying on the principle of fair and equitable treatment in interpreting the due process requirement in the expropriation provision of the Greek-Egyptian BIT, the tribunal reasoned that "a matter as important as the seizure and auctioning of a ship of the Claimant should have been notified by a direct communication ... irrespective of whether there was a legal duty or practice to do so by registered mail with return receipt".[164]

This reasoning implies, without formulating it explicitly, a proportionality-type analysis, weighing the importance of investment protection, the legitimate government interest pursued, and the fact that less restrictive but equally effective ways were available to put the claimant on notice of the impending seizure of his ship.

4.   *Proportionality Analysis and Reasoning in Investment Arbitration*

Proportionality analysis is increasingly applied by investment tribunals, in ways that are similar to those in many domestic legal orders and other international dispute settlement systems, including the EC/EU, the ECHR or the WTO dispute settlement system. This concerns, above all, the determination of whether a host State's measures constitutes an indirect expropriation or a violation of some aspects of fair and equitable treatment. Proportionality analysis, however, is open to the criticisms that it confers power on

---

160. See *Pope & Talbot v. Canada*, supra fn. 51, paras. 123, 125, 128, 155; see also *MTD v. Chile*, supra fn. 27, para. 109 with a reference to an expert opinion by Schwebel.
161. See *Eureko v. Poland*, supra fn. 36, paras. 232 et seq. See also discussion at supra fn. 39 and accompanying text.
162. *Middle East Cement Shipping and Handling Co S.A. v. Arab Republic of Egypt* (ICSID Case No. ARB/99/6), Award of 12 April 2002.
163. The issue turned on the question whether the seizure breached the requirement of due process in the provision prohibiting direct and indirect expropriations without compensation in the Egyptian-Greek BIT, and the principle of fair and equitable treatment.
164. *Middle East Cement Shipping v. Egypt*, supra fn. 162, para. 143.

judges to take policy-driven decisions about the proper balance between conflicting rights and interests, and that it encourages a focus on principles above rules.

This criticism may be less problematic in the domestic context as the legislature there has power to reverse court decisions on administrative and legislative standards, at least with regard to future cases. Yet, in the investment treaty context, the revision of BITs is a slow and slow-acting process requiring consent of both contracting State parties. Furthermore, most investment treaties do not provide for an institutional procedure that can be triggered in order to adapt the treaty in response to interpretations by investment tribunals, for example along the lines of the NAFTA Free Trade Commission, an organ through which the State parties can jointly issue authoritative interpretations of the rules and standards applicable to investor-State disputes.[165] While the application of proportionality analysis to constitutional rights has some parallels with its application in the context of interpreting investor rights under investment treaties, national constitutional courts and international treaty-based courts, such as the ECJ and the ECHR, may well be in a better institutional position to bear this weight than are ad hoc and evanescent investment treaty tribunals.

Yet, as shown in this Report, investment treaty tribunals are already exercising governance functions and applying very open-textured standards, in situations where important public interests are involved. Given that reality, and the possibilities of at least a loose structure of control through institutional supervision and checking by other tribunals, as well as critical scrutiny by the academic community, think-tanks and NGOs, the adoption of a proportionality methodology at a minimum establishes criteria and a framework to ensure that tribunals consider the relevant interests under the applicable principles, and weigh or balance them under an established framework. This may produce better and more convincing reasoning, and enable clearer assessment, critique and accountability of tribunals, because each decision must be rationalized under the proportionality framework and methodology. A proportionality analysis certainly seems preferable as a rational process for balancing investment protection and competing interests, by comparison with approaches in which an extensive summary of the facts of the case at hand is followed by the abrupt determination with little intelligible legal reasoning that a State's measure does or does not violate fair and equitable treatment or constitutes a measures tantamount to expropriation based on "I-know-it-when-I-see-it"–type of reasoning.

Proportionality analysis also has the advantage that it is open towards different strands of political theory and different substantive preferences on investment protection.[166] It

---

165. See Art. 1131(2) NAFTA. For such an interpretation, see, for example, NAFTA Free Trade Commission, *Notes of Interpretation of Certain Chapter 11 Provisions*, 31 July 2001, available at <www.international.gc.ca/trade-agreements-accords-commerciaux/disp-diff/NAFTA-Interpr.aspx?lang=en>. Likewise, the new US Model BIT provides for a similar treaty-based body. See Art. 30(3) US Model BIT 2004: "A joint declaration of the Parties, each acting through its representative designated for purposes of this Article declaring their interpretation of a provision of this Treaty shall be binding on a tribunal, and any decision or award issued by a tribunal must be consistent with that joint decision."
166. Cf. ANDENAS and ZLEPTNIG, supra fn. 95, p. 371 at p. 387, drawing on the work of Paul Craig on judicial review of agency decisions in the United Kingdom.

is potentially attractive both to those stressing that tribunals should more broadly take into account non-investment related interests of non-represented parties that are affected by the outcome of a tribunal's decision, and to those seeking to tighten the legal framework of State interferences with foreign investment. Furthermore, the methodological structure of proportionality analysis may have the effect that arbitrators become more accountable since they also have to justify their decisions in a detailed fashion. Proportionality analysis thus has the potential to become a tool to enhance accountability and justification for governmental action and the activity of arbitral tribunals alike.

In summary, while reasons for hesitation must be acknowledged, the principle of proportionality has the potential to help structure both the relationships between States and foreign investors and between States and investment tribunals. Proportionality analysis potentially enhances the legitimacy of rule-governed legal institutions that undertake it. As a study of the adoption of proportionality analysis by more and more national and international courts concludes: "In adopting the proportionality framework, constitutional judges acquire a coherent, practical means of responding to these basic legitimacy questions."[167] Intense concerns about legitimacy in the system of international investment treaty law should drive a rapid adoption of proportionality analysis as a standard technique. This is one step toward investment treaty tribunals recognizing and meeting the demands that their place in global regulatory governance now requires of them.

IV.  ADDRESSING DEMANDS FOR LEGITIMACY IN THE INVESTOR-STATE ARBITRATION SYSTEM: ROLES OF GLOBAL ADMINISTRATIVE LAW

Arbitral tribunals exercise significant power in formulating standards for host State conduct vis-à-vis foreign investors and in reviewing State conduct against these standards. As shown in Parts II and III of this Report, this power is magnified by being part of a system of governance. Numerous scholars and practitioners have pointed to concerns about the legitimacy of these exercises of power, with some asserting that there is or soon will be a veritable "legitimacy crisis".[168] This Part focuses in Sect. *1* on the connection between demands for increased legitimacy and what has been described above as the governance function of investor-State arbitration, and suggests reforms largely capable of implementation by the decision-makers themselves, which will enhance legitimacy through bringing the practices of tribunals and other agencies more into line with applicable principles of the emerging global administrative law. Sect. *2* argues that one particularly important element in doing this is for tribunals and appointing and supervisory agencies to ensure the quality and depth of the tribunals' legal interpretation, analysis and reasoning.

---

167. STONE SWEET and MATHEWS, supra fn. 96, p. 5.
168. See the literature cited supra fn. 7.

1. *Investor-State Tribunals as Regulators Beyond the State: Distinguishing the Different Problems of Legitimacy*

People in democratic societies are accustomed to the idea that exercises of power on public issues, particularly power exercised by public bodies or by bodies authorized by the State to act on public issues, should be legitimate. This applies to investor-State arbitration tribunals which exercise power in the public sphere: they review past actions of States, they in effect help set limits to States' future actions and they take positions on matters affecting entire populations and the way these populations are governed. The tribunals operate and exercise power in the global administrative space, which is created in large part by States through their agreements, including investment treaties and the ICSID and 1958 New York Conventions. The demands for public legitimacy and justification in relation to these investor-State tribunals are thus different, often dramatically different, from those applying to commercial arbitration.

Ordinary transnational commercial arbitration between corporations is a different form of dispute resolution in terms of the legitimacy demands it faces. Whereas investment treaty arbitration faces legitimacy demands stemming from the fact that investment tribunals exercise control over the host State's conduct which operates in a public rather than a private sphere, commercial arbitration cases ordinarily are significant only for the disputing parties and their stakeholders, although on occasion these cases can have some precedential and even systemic implications.[169]

Legitimacy can be approached and understood in Weberian terms, or in democratic terms through the use of democratic electoral processes or plausible substitutes for such processes. These two different approaches to legitimacy will be briefly addressed in turn. Max Weber analyzed the legitimacy (and hence the claim to authority outside the power to coerce obedience) of laws and institutions as coming from one or more of three sources: tradition (i.e., a long-accepted way of conducting matters), charismatic

---

169. On the differences between investment arbitration and regular commercial arbitration see Gus VAN HARTEN and Martin LOUGHLIN, "Investment Treaty Arbitration as a Species of Global Administrative Law", 17 Eur. J. Int'l L. (2006) p. 121 at pp. 139 et seq.; Stephan SCHILL, "Arbitration Risk and Effective Compliance: Cost-Shifting in Investment Treaty Arbitration", 7 J. World Inv. & Trade (2006) p. 653, at pp. 676-679. Experience with commercial arbitration has systemic effects in shaping the judgment of economic actors about whether to include arbitration clauses in future contracts and about which arbitral institutions and rules to use. Loukas MISTELIS, Crina BALTAG, Stavros BREKOULAKIS, *Corporate Attitudes and Practice: Recognition and Enforcement of Foreign Awards* (2008); Loukas MISTELIS, "International Arbitration: Corporate Attitudes and Practices", 15 Am. Rev. Int'l Arb. (2004) p. 525; Theodore EISENBERG, Geoffrey MILLER and Emily SHERWIN, "Arbitration's Summer Soldiers: An Empirical Study of Arbitration Clauses in Consumer and Nonconsumer Contracts", 41 U. Mich. J. L. Ref. (2008) p. 871. With regard to investor-State arbitration based on contracts, or in which a contract is central to the substantive issues, the public legitimacy issues for tribunals are often much the same as where an investment treaty provides the whole basis for the claim. See José ALVAREZ, "Book review", 102 AJIL (2008) p. 909 at pp. 911-912.

leadership or bureaucratic rationality.[170] Investor-State tribunals are hardly traditional from the standpoint of the lay public, and they seldom rely on the public persona and charisma of their individual members. So, in Weberian terms, investor-State arbitration depends, at least in part, on the legality and rationality of its design, its processes, and the technical quality and persuasiveness of the reasons tribunals give in explaining and justifying their decisions. This theme will be discussed in Sect. 2 below.

Electoral democracy provides a different and more elaborate means of legitimation.[171] A particular feature of democratic elections by secret ballot is that they allow for the special democratic freedom of the voters to engage in political expression by allowing them to act arbitrarily. Voters are not required to give reasons for their choice. They are free to throw out the current government because they simply are tired of it.[172] The basic legitimacy of democratic forms of government thus comes through their election by arbitrary voters. Elected leaders, in turn, may also bring legitimacy to the international institutions they establish, control or support, as founders and funders, and to institutions over which they themselves can exercise what might be arbitrary political authority, for example by removing a cabinet minister or the head of a government agency. Extending this democratic legitimation to formal transnational institutions, however, is very difficult, especially for relatively weak States whose influence on these institutions is necessarily limited.[173]

Accordingly, the direct democratic legitimation of investor-State tribunals is tenuous. They are, of course, based on the consent of the relevant States, either in a measured inter-public way through consent to a BIT or regional agreement or to the ICSID Convention, or, more privately and raising special issues, in a State agency's contract with the investor. However, this delegation of decision-making power to arbitral tribunals, without more, is often too thin to provide much democratic legitimacy. The treaty commitments last a long time, they are not supervised through institutions with regular processes of democratic political participation, and the electoral processes which give the basic legitimation to governmental institutions in democratic States can seldom come into play when an investor's arbitral claim is actually made and an arbitral tribunal comes into operation. Furthermore, the host State itself usually only determines the appointment of one of the three arbitrators without needing to compromise with the investor-claimant.

What then are the non-electoral mechanisms of legitimation of transnational institutions that exercise public power, including investor-State arbitral tribunals? This question of non-electoral legitimation is fundamental in all kinds of transnational institutions, especially where they have real powers of governance affecting the rights

---

170. Max WEBER, *Economy and Society: An Outline of Interpretive Sociology* (Guenther Roth and Claus Wittich eds., 1968).
171. See John FEREJOHN, "Accountability in a Global Context", IILJ Working Paper 2007/5 (Global Administrative Law Series) available at <http://iilj.org/publications/documents/2007-5.GAL.Ferejohn.web.pdf>.
172. See *ibid.*, pp. 20 et seq. (discussing the ancient Greek story of a peasant voting to ostracize Aristides the Just, simply because the peasant had enough of him being called "the Just").
173. Grainne de BURCA, "Developing Democracy Beyond the State", 46 Columbia J. Transnat'l L. (2008) p. 221.

and responsibilities of individuals, corporations, States and other groups. In fact, concerns about legitimacy, effectiveness and acting justly, combined with political pressure and protests, have led many transnational institutions to change their practices and their views as to what the applicable norms conferring legitimacy are and indeed what their roles are as regulative institutions and public actors in relation to public issues. For example, the Basle Committee of central bankers now publishes drafts on the internet and invites comments before it adopts new policies on the supervision of commercial banks;[174] the World Bank follows a similar consultation procedure in setting its social safeguards policies, and has an Inspection Panel to which individuals claiming to be victims of a breach of the Bank's own policies can complain;[175] the ICSID Convention now contemplates transparency of documents and hearings during investment arbitrations that would have been unimaginable just a few years ago.[176]

Moreover, these developments, while not universal, are not simply isolated reforms. They are part of the general if uneven emergence of norms of global administrative law, dealing with matters such as participation, transparency, due process, reason-giving, the existence of review mechanisms, accountability and respect for basic public law values including the rule of law.[177] These norms of global administrative law may be applicable

---

174. Michael BARR and Geoffrey MILLER, "Global Administrative Law: The View from Base", 17 Eur. J. Int'l L. (2006) p. 15.
175. Benedict KINGSBURY, "Operational Policies of International Institutions as Part of the Law-Making Process: The World Bank and Indigenous Peoples" in Guy S. GOODWIN-GILL and Stefan TALMON, eds., *The Reality of International Law* (1999) p. 323; David SZABLOWSKI, *Transnational Law and Local Struggles: Mining Communities and the World Bank* (2007).
176. See the amended ICSID Rules: Rule 48(4) (concerning the publication of the legal reasoning of the tribunals); Rule 37(2) (providing for third-party participation as amicus curiae); Rule 32(2) (providing for the possibility to hold public hearings). See on the recent changes to the ICSID Rules Aurélia ANTONIETTI, "The 2006 Amendments of the ICSID Rules and Regulations and the Additional Facility Rules", 21 ICSID Rev. – For. Inv. L. J. (2007) p. 427. See further on issues of transparency and third-party participation in investor-State arbitration Jack J. COE, "Transparency in the Resolution of Investor-State Disputes – Adoption, Adaptation, and NAFTA Leadership", 54 U. Kan. L. Rev. (2006) p. 1339; Carl-Sebastian ZOELLNER, "Third-Party Participation (NGO's and Private Persons) and Transparency in ICSID Proceedings" in Rainer HOFMANN and Christian J. TAMS, eds., *The International Convention for the Settlement of Investment Disputes (ICSID) – Taking Stock After 40 Years* (2007) p. 179; Christian J. TAMS and Carl-Sebastian ZOELLNER, "Amici Curiae im internationalen Investitionsschutzrecht", 45 Archiv des Völkerrechts (2007) p. 217; Christina KNAHR, "Transparency, Third Party Participation and Access to Documents in International Investment Arbitration", 23 Arb. Int'l (2007) p. 327. It is notable, however, that UNCITRAL Rules have been much slower to change, and some prospective parties to arbitrations may strongly prefer fora which have not moved toward "publicness" in these ways.
177. For substantive discussion of specific principles of global administrative law, see the materials cited supra fns. 2 and 12-16, as well as works of Jean-Bernard AUBY, Armin von BOGDANDY, Sabino CASSESE, Richard STEWART, and other leading scholars in this field. An extensive bibliography is available at <www.iilj.org/GAL>. See also the valuable analysis of Robert HOWSE, "Adjudicative Legitimacy and Treaty Interpretation in International Trade Law: The Early Years of WTO Jurisprudence" in Joseph WEILER, ed., *The EU, The WTO and the NAFTA: Towards a Common Law of International Trade* (2000) p. 35, focusing on fair procedures, coherence

as positive law in specific instances. Often, however, they will be influential in determining what weight another decision-making body, such as a national court, will give to the rule or decision issued by the transnational body in question. More generally, they are markers in the framing of debates about the legitimacy of the exercise of power by transnational bodies that affect the lives and well-being of human beings.

In investor-State arbitration, participation by the defending State, and its public, in the actual arbitral proceedings can help somewhat with democratic legitimation, as the elected government engages in appointing a member of the arbitral tribunal it consented to establish, and argues its case. This, however, is hardly enough in cases where tribunals are interpreting provisions, such as the "fair and equitable treatment" standard or the concept of indirect expropriation, that are not precise and thus inescapably confer on tribunals a wide margin in their decision-making. This is compounded because a tribunal's decision on how to interpret and apply one of these open-ended provisions can have implications for non-participants, including dozens of other States and innumerable specific investments around the world, because identical or similar standards are obligatory in virtually every investment treaty relationship. The interpretation of such a provision by arbitral tribunals potentially shapes the future behavior of States and their legislatures and agencies, as well as the expectations and choices of investors and perhaps of other actors affected by investment-related issues. In other words, the effects of public decisions of investment tribunals are not limited to the investment treaty governing the dispute at hand. This can be seen in particular through examination of the importance of precedent, and the prevalence of references to precedent, in investment treaty arbitrations and indeed in the phrasing of treaties.[178]

Adherence by tribunals to global administrative law principles (where these principles are applicable to the work of such tribunals) can play a role in generating and/or enhancing the legitimacy of investment treaty arbitration. Conversely, ignoring these principles provides grounds for serious criticism of the work of tribunals. Part II of this Report examined what the jurisprudence of tribunals has contributed in defining for States a framework based on standards of good governance and the rule of law, mainly through interpretation of the obligation to accord foreign investors fair and equitable treatment. The examination of some of the requirements of good administrative conduct that tribunals derive from fair and equitable treatment, and use as a yardstick for measuring the appropriateness of State conduct, provides a gentle reminder that arbitral tribunals themselves on occasion do not meet the requirements of transparency, predictability, reason-giving and participation of affected interests that they consider fair and equitable treatment entails for States. The tribunals are, of course, not States and are not formally bound to the same standards under the treaties they apply. However, as global administrative law develops, the kinds of requirements investment treaty tribunals apply to States will more and more become an indicator of the legal measure applicable also to their own operations.

---

and integrity in legal interpretation, and sensitivity to other relevant international legal regimes (e.g., international environmental law and institutions), as elements used by the WTO Appellate Body in building its legitimacy.

178. See infra fn. 183 and accompanying text.

Key global administrative law principles for investor-State tribunals obviously include good process, legality and freedom from bias or arbitrariness in the decision-making process. More difficult to attain, because they introduce delay and higher costs, but probably inevitable in the future, are provisions for adequate review of the work of tribunals by a trusted independent mechanism. Independent reasoned review of decisions by arbitrators or by an appointing authority seems essential, and already exists to some extent, where the appointment of an arbitrator is challenged on proper grounds, or where it is alleged that an arbitrator has a direct conflict of interest. Of independent significance for legitimacy, but also relevant if there is substantive review of tribunal awards, is the requirement that arbitral tribunals address the issues and give reasons for their decisions and awards. Courts in democratic States are expected to give convincing legal reasons for their decisions partly because courts are not themselves directly accountable to the public. Certainly, arbitrations can rest on trust – if people trust the third party enough, they may be willing to hand over the decision-making power to the third party even without specifying many rules to be applied nor requiring much reasoning. But this is rare in situations where investor-State relations have deteriorated to the point where arbitration is sought. Where there is little such trust or more concern about legitimacy, the applicable legal rules will usually be more tightly specified through the political process, and reason-giving by the dispute settlement body takes on greater significance as the justification of the body's actions in accordance with the pre-specified law. The next section of this Report examines the norms and practices of reason-giving, and of consideration of awards by other investor-State tribunals, in recent investment arbitration jurisprudence.

2. *Adequate Reasoning and Consideration of Other Awards as Elements of Systemic Legitimacy*

Reason-giving is important as a response to the arguments made, and facts asserted, by the disputants. Reason-giving is also important for the State as a potential repeat defendant, and for non-litigants more generally, as it is the part of the arbitral award which guides future conduct and shapes the normative expectations of a wider audience as tribunals increasingly follow common-law type rationalities and apply structures of reasoning that heavily use and rely on investment arbitration precedent. It is this prospective effect or shaping impact that lies at the heart of the view of investment arbitration tribunals as regulators.

The reasoning of arbitral awards is thus of considerable importance both for the non-electoral legitimacy of the tribunals, and with regard to its regulatory impact on future State administrative and regulatory behavior. Art. 48(3) ICSID Convention does of course provide that an award "shall State the reasons upon which it is based".[179] It does not, however, really explain the purpose of the reason-giving requirement. Furthermore, recent annulment committee decisions, in setting a rather modest standard

---

179. A failure to state reasons also constitutes one of the grounds for the annulment of an ICSID award under Art. 52(1)(e) ICSID Convention. Similarly, other arbitration rules specify that awards have to be reasoned, see, for example, Art. 32(3) UNCITRAL Arbitration Rules (providing, however, that the parties can agree that no reasons shall be required).

for the quality or cogency of the reason-giving needed to avoid annulment, do not put the reason-giving requirement into a wider context of public reason, deliberative democracy, and legitimacy. Instead, they focus primarily on the question whether the reasoning is intelligible to the parties, not necessarily whether the reasons given are adequate for the wider audience of the tribunal, including the legislatures, courts and publics of affected States and of unrelated States potentially affected by investment awards, and also unrelated investors, insurers and other stakeholders.[180]

An implication of the global administrative law approach to global governance, as noted in the opening section of this Report, is that the reasoning of awards and indeed of judicial decisions in investment arbitration disputes should reflect a quality of publicness in law – it should speak not only to the parties to enable them to understand the *ratio decidendi* of the award, but also to the interests and engagements of non-represented and non-participating stakeholders. In particular, to the extent that it affects general principles of international investment law and arbitration, the reasoning should engage with these wider and systemic issues. This does not mean that affirmative statements necessarily must be made on each such issue – prudence, circumspection and minimalism can all be highly desirable arbitral and judicial virtues. Yet, the reasoning should nonetheless be transparent and accessible not only from the point of view of the parties to the proceeding, but to the tribunals' wider audience, including non-participating States, the investment community at large and those groups that may be impacted by specific decisions in the context of foreign investment activities. This is particularly true because of the precedential effect investment awards have in practice.

It is sometimes asserted that because investment tribunals typically do not have precedential authority – that is, they only decide the case before them and each case is a new case – they do not need to worry about having *ex ante* regulative effects on future behavior of the defendant State, let alone other States.[181] Whatever the merits of this as

---

180. While providing reasons does not mean that there are no lacunae, the reasoning has to enable "the reader to follow the reasoning"; see *CMS Gas Transmission Company v. Argentine Republic* (ICSID Case No. ARB/01/8), Decision of the Ad Hoc Committee on the Application for Annulment of the Argentine Republic of 25 September 2007, para. 97; see also *Wena Hotels Ltd. v. Arab Republic of Egypt* (ICSID Case No. ARB/98/4), the Application by the Arab Republic of Egypt for Annulment of the Arbitral Award of 28 January 2002, para. 81.
181. This strategy was, for example, chosen by the tribunal in *RosInvestCo v. Russia* in regard of its non-acceptance of earlier precedent with respect to the issue of whether most-favored-nation (MFN) clauses can import the broader jurisdictional consent host States have given under investment treaties with third countries. See *RosInvestCo UK Ltd. v. The Russian Federation* (SCC Case No. V 079/2005), Award on Jurisdiction, October 2007, para. 137 (observing in a case of open dissent with regard to the interpretation of MFN clauses:

"After having examined them [i.e. decision of arbitral tribunals regarding MFN-clauses and arbitration submissions in other treaties], the Tribunal feels there is no need to enter into a detailed discussion of these decisions. The Tribunal agrees with the Parties that different conclusions can indeed be drawn from them depending on how one evaluates their various wordings both of the arbitration clause and the MFN-clauses and their similarities in allowing generalisations. However, since it is the primary function of this Tribunal to decide the case before it rather than developing further the general discussion on the applicability of MFN clauses

a jurisprudential position, and indeed as a theoretical mechanism for reducing the reach and impact of the decision of each tribunal and hence assuaging the legitimacy problems, it is not the current practice. States, and their legal advisors, would be rash not to consider the arbitral jurisprudence on a specific issue in deciding how to deal with a particular foreign investment. Regard to investment treaty awards is evident also in changes in State practice as States come to draft new investment treaties or revise existing ones. For example, broad interpretations of fair and equitable treatment and the concept of indirect expropriation have led the United States to introduce more restrictive wording in some recently concluded BITs and Free Trade Agreements.[182] In a certain sense, prior jurisprudence thus has been treated by States as de facto regulative.

References to ICSID decisions can be found in nearly all of the more recent ICSID and NAFTA decisions on jurisdiction and awards on the merits. A recent quantitative study of citations investment tribunals make to prior decisions[183] confirms the strong qualitative impression derived by reading recent awards in investment treaty cases, namely that "citations to supposedly subsidiary sources, such as judicial decisions, including arbitral awards, predominate".[184] That the citation of earlier awards carries weight and that earlier awards have an impact on subsequent awards, is also suggested by statements that some investment tribunals have made with regard to the value of earlier arbitral decisions. Although they emphasize the lack of *de iure stare decisis*, they nevertheless have an irresistible urge to turn to earlier decisions for guidance.[185] The

---

to dispute-settlement-provisions, the Tribunal notes that the combined wording in [the MFN clause] and [the arbitration clause] of the [applicable] BIT is not identical to that in any of such other treaties considered in these other decisions.").

182. Art. 10.5(2)(a) of the Dominican Republic – Central America – United States Free Trade Agreement, available at <www.ustr.gov/Trade_Agreements/Bilateral/CAFTA/Section_Index.html>, for instance, stipulates – in departing from the more general treaty language in earlier treaties – that "fair and equitable treatment includes the obligation not to deny justice in criminal, civil, or administrative adjudicatory proceedings in accordance with the principle of due process embodied in the principal legal systems of the world". See further Art. 15.6 of the United States – Singapore Free Trade Agreement, signed 15 January 2003, entered into force 1 Jan. 2004, in connection with an exchange of letters on the scope of the concept of indirect expropriation which clarifies that bona fide general regulation did not regularly constitute a compensable indirect expropriation. More generally on the interaction between investment arbitration and investment treaty practice see UNCTAD, *Investor-State Dispute Settlement and Impact on Investment Rulemaking* (2007) pp. 71-89.
183. Jeffrey P. COMMISSION, "Precedent in Investment Treaty Arbitration – A Citation Analysis of a Developing Jurisprudence", 24 J. Int'l Arb. (2007) p. 129 at pp. 142-154.
184. *Ibid.*, at p. 148. In particular, his results show a "marked increase of citation to ICSID decisions by ICSID tribunals" (*ibid.*, at. p. 149). While ICSID tribunals between 1990 and 2001 cited on average approximately two earlier ICSID decisions and awards, this number increased to an average of more than seven within the period between 2002 and 2006. ICSID decisions on jurisdiction even cited to an average of nine earlier ICSID decisions or awards. Similar trends are also present with regard to decisions under the ICSID Additional Facility and non-ICSID investment treaty awards (see Tables 3-5, at pp. 149-150).
185. See also Gabriele KAUFMANN-KOHLER, "Arbitral Precedent: Dream, Necessity or Excuse?", 23 Arb. Int'l (2007) p. 357.

tribunal in *El Paso v. Argentina*, for example, stated that it would "follow the same line [as earlier awards], especially since both parties, in their written pleadings and oral arguments, have heavily relied on precedent".[186] The way the parties to the disputes rely on precedent therefore suggests the emergence of expectations that tribunals will decide cases not by abstractly interpreting the governing BIT, but by embedding it into the pre-existing structure and content of the discourse among investment treaty awards.[187]

The significance of precedent is particularly evident in the NAFTA award in *Waste Management v. Mexico*, which having itself purported to aggregate and synthesize NAFTA precedents, has now become a *locus classicus* not only on NAFTA's fair and equitable treatment standard but on the parallel standards in BITs. Similar in style to a system of *stare decisis*, the tribunal defined the standard of fair and equitable treatment by referring to earlier NAFTA decisions and stated:

> "Taken together, the *S.D. Myers*, *Mondev*, *ADF* and *Loewen* cases suggest that the minimum standard of treatment of fair and equitable treatment is infringed by conduct attributable to the State and harmful to the claimant if the conduct is arbitrary, grossly unfair, unjust or idiosyncratic, is discriminatory and exposes the

---

186. *El Paso Energy International Company v. The Argentine Republic* (ICSID Case No. ARB/03/15), Decision on Jurisdiction of 27 April 2006, para. 39. See also *AES Corporation v. The Argentine Republic* (ICSID Case No. ARB/02/17), Decision on Jurisdiction of 26 April 2005, para. 18 (observing that the investor relied on earlier investment awards "more or less as if they were precedent [tending] to say that Argentina's objections to the jurisdiction of this Tribunal are moot if not even useless since these tribunals have already determined the answer to be given to identical or similar objections to jurisdiction").

187. Cf. on the emergence of expectations in the reference to, application of and justified departure from precedent Appellate Body Report, *Japan – Taxes on Alcoholic Beverages* WT/DS8/AB/R, WT/DS10/AB/R, WT/DS11/AB/R, adopted 4 October 1996, p. 14 (observing that "[a]dopted panel reports are an important part of the GATT *acquis*. They are often considered by subsequent panels. They create legitimate expectations among WTO Members, and, therefore, should be taken into account where they are relevant to any dispute. However, they are not binding, except with respect to resolving the particular dispute between the parties to that dispute."). Similarly *Saipem S.p.A. v. The People's Republic of Bangladesh* (ICSID Case No. ARB/05/07), Decision on Jurisdiction and Recommendation on Provisional Measures of 21 March 2007, para. 67

> "The Tribunal considers that it is not bound by previous decisions. At the same time, it is of the opinion that it must pay due consideration to earlier decisions of international tribunals. It believes that, subject to compelling contrary grounds, it has a duty to adopt solutions established in a series of consistent cases. It also believes that, subject to the specifics of a given treaty and of the circumstances of the actual case, it has a duty to seek to contribute to the harmonious development of investment law and thereby to meet the legitimate expectations of the community of States and investors towards certainty of the rule of law."

See also *International Thunderbird Gaming v. Mexico*, supra fn. 37, Separate Opinion by Thomas Wälde, para. 16 (observing that "while ... arbitral awards by themselves do not as yet constitute a binding precedent, [footnote omitted] a consistent line of reasoning developing a principle and a particular interpretation of specific treaty obligations should be respected; if an authoritative jurisprudence evolves, it will acquire the character of customary international law and must be respected"). See further *ibid.*, paras. 129-130.

claimant to sectional or racial prejudice, or involves a lack of due process leading to an outcome which offends judicial propriety – as might be the case with a manifest failure of natural justice in judicial proceedings or a complete lack of transparency and candour in an administrative process."[188]

The tribunal thus derived the meaning of fair and equitable treatment primarily from earlier decisions and defined it accordingly, not from its own interpretation of the text of NAFTA. Consequently, the tribunal in *Waste Management* itself focused more on applying the standard thus derived to the facts of the specific case.[189]

Once it is accepted that the legal interpretation and reasoning of tribunals is important as a practical matter for future tribunals, for States, and for the legitimacy of awards among parties and non-parties, some problematic practices of reasoning can be discerned. One problematic pattern is simply to posit in the abstract the normative content of vague standards of investment protection, such as fair and equitable treatment, perhaps supported by some quotations of equally abstract dicta by prior tribunals without further explanations or justifications, and then to assert that the facts of the case meet or do not meet this standard.[190] While this may meet the minimum requirements of reasoning of the sort set by recent ICSID annulment committees,[191] tribunals in this pattern may fail to show how they ground these abstract explications of fair and equitable treatment in a legal fashion capable of assessment and deliberative contestation. They thus also fail to counter the reproach that their content is simply determined based on the subjective standards and preferences of individual arbitrators.

A second problematic pattern consists in a failure to spell out the normative assumptions tribunals are making when interpreting abstract standards, such as fair and equitable treatment, and instead limiting themselves to extensively presenting the facts of a case, with legal issues treated briefly and by assertion more than by legal argumentation and reasoning. One such example is the Partial Award in *Eastern Sugar B.V. v. Czech Republic*, which involved a dispute about breaches of the Netherlands-Czech Republic BIT in view of changes in the domestic law relating to the allocation of sugar quotas.[192] The award extensively recounted the facts relevant to a claim based on a violation of fair and equitable treatment in over 100 paragraphs,[193] and found a violation of that standard, without, however, clearly identifying the standard's legal meaning and normative content, and without even making reference to arbitral "precedent" and relevant sources for treaty interpretation, including international law scholarship on this point. Instead, the award in question simply set out an extremely broad framework within which the normative content of fair and equitable treatment was situated. Thus, the tribunal considered that a violation of fair and equitable treatment, at one end, "does

---

188. *Waste Management, Inc. v. Mexico*, supra fn. 44, para. 98.
189. *Waste Management*, ibid., paras. 99 et seq.
190. See, for example, *S.D. Myers v. Canada*, supra fn. 45, para. 134.
191. See supra fn. 180.
192. *Eastern Sugar B.V. v. The Czech Republic* (SCC Case No. 88/2004), Partial Award of 27 March 2007.
193. *Eastern Sugar*, ibid., paras. 222-343.

not only occur through blatant and outrageous interference", and, at the other, "may also not be invoked each time the law is flawed or not fully and properly implemented by a State".[194] Basing a decision on such a broad framework, however, is inadequate in view of the consensus existing today that fair and equitable treatment is a legal standard with independent normative content[195] and in view of the concretization this standard has already received in arbitral jurisprudence and academic writing.[196]

The type of reasoning in *Eastern Sugar* might be sufficient in settings where a dispute concerns only the parties to a proceeding. Such reasoning, however, does not satisfy the quality demanded of reasoning of dispute settlement bodies in public governance contexts. Although an argument elegantly reviewing every possible precedent on international law issues raised by the parties is not to be expected, and tribunals are inevitably constrained both by the quality of the legal submissions they receive and by resources and costs, it seems plainly insufficient in this field to posit the content of a certain legal standard of investment protection without any careful inquiry into international law sources and without the use of a convincing interpretive methodology. This is an essential responsibility toward the system of arbitration based on international law and to those arguing or arbitrating later investment treaty cases which will properly seek to take account of earlier arbitral awards. More generally, weak reasoning and inadequate assessment of prior jurisprudence fuels concerns that investment tribunals are unaccountable, and apply legal standards that are not only vague and unpredictable, but essentially are made subordinate to the inclinations of investment tribunal members.

Similarly, although investment tribunals are not bound by earlier decisions and can thus diverge without committing an error of law, they nevertheless ought ordinarily to explain why they diverge from the reasoning of well-known prior decisions on the same point.[197] In most cases of "inconsistent decisions" arbitral tribunals do this. The tribunal in *SGS v. Philippines*, for example, extensively engaged in a discussion of the earlier award in *SGS v. Pakistan* that suggested a contrary interpretation and application of umbrella clauses.[198] Likewise, the tribunal in *El Paso Energy v. Argentina* that preferred the solution in *SGS v. Pakistan*, and disapproved of the ruling in *SGS v. Philippines*, engaged in an extensive discussion of why it followed one rather than the other approach.[199] Similarly,

---

194. *Eastern Sugar, ibid.*, para. 272.
195. See only *Oil Platforms (Islamic Republic of Iran v. United States of America)*, Preliminary Objection, Judgment of 12 December 1996, Separate Opinion by Judge Higgins, I.C.J. Reports 1996, 803, 858, para. 39 (noting that fair and equitable treatment constitutes "legal terms of art well known in the field of overseas investment protection" and having a "well-known meaning given to these terms").
196. See Barnali CHOUDHURY, "Evolution or Devolution? – Defining Fair and Equitable Treatment in International Investment Law", 6 J. World Inv. & Trade (2005) p. 297; Christoph SCHREUER, "Fair and Equitable Treatment in Arbitral Practice", 6 J. World Inv. & Trade (2005) p. 357; DOLZER, supra fn. 76, p. 87; SCHILL, supra fn. 21.
197. See FRANCK, supra fn. 10, p. 1521.
198. *SGS Société Générale de Surveillance S.A. v. Republic of the Philippines* (ICSID Case No. ARB/02/6), Decision of the Tribunal on Objections to Jurisdiction of 29 January 2004, paras. 119-126.
199. *El Paso Energy v. Argentina*, supra fn. 186, paras. 71-82.

decisions on the interpretation of most-favored-nation clauses usually discuss in a well-reasoned way inconsistent decisions by other investment tribunals.[200]

*LG&E v. Argentina* and *Enron v. Argentina*, both decisions concerning the lawfulness of Argentina's emergency legislation under the U.S.-Argentina BIT, may raise concerns in this respect. While the decision in *LG&E* largely followed the earlier award in *CMS v. Argentina* concerning the assessment of Argentina's conduct under the substantive BIT obligations, it departed from the *CMS* decision with respect to the plea of necessity.[201] However, while it frequently concurred with the award in the *CMS* case and even cited this award as support for its interpretation of the substantive BIT obligations, including fair and equitable treatment and the concept of indirect expropriation,[202] it did not mention that the *CMS* award fundamentally differed concerning the concept of necessity under international law. Instead, the tribunal in *LG&E* delivered its own decision without rebutting the arguments provided in the *CMS* award against the operation of necessity. The tribunal in *Enron*, in turn, invoked the decision in *LG&E* affirmatively as regards the interpretation of substantive standards of treatment,[203] but largely followed the award in *CMS* concerning the plea of necessity, without engaging, or merely noting, that the tribunal in *LG&E* had adopted a conflicting position.[204] The best way, however, to arrive at a *jurisprudence constante*, which is accepted by investors and States alike, is for the tribunals to set out clearly the arguments for their approach and refute existing counterarguments in order to reach, in a deliberative fashion, convincing results about the proper interpretation of investment law and international law principles.

---

200. See, for example, *Plama Consortium Ltd. v Bulgaria* (ICSID Case No. ARB/03/24), Decision on Jurisdiction of 8 February 2005, paras. 210-226. The same, however, does not hold true as regards the reasoning of the tribunal in *RosInvestCo* (see supra fn. 181), even though the result of this decision may be more convincing. See generally Stephan SCHILL, "Most-Favored-Nation Clauses as a Basis of Jurisdiction in Investment Treaty Arbitration: Arbitral Jurisprudence at a Crossroads", 10 J. World Inv. & Trade (2009) p. 189; and Martins PAPARINSKIS, "MFN Clauses in Investment Arbitration between Maffezini and Plama – A Third Way?" ICSID Review – Foreign Investment Law Journal (forthcoming).
201. *LG&E v. Argentina*, supra fn. 135, paras. 226-266. Compare *CMS v. Argentina*, supra fn. 22, paras. 323-331, 353-394. See for a more detailed comparison of both decisions SCHILL, supra fn. 147, p. 265; see also August REINISCH, "Necessity in International Investment Arbitration – An Unnecessary Split of Opinions in Recent ICSID Cases? Comments on *CMS v. Argentina* and *LG&E v. Argentina*", 8 J. World Inv. & Trade (2007) p. 191; Michael WAIBEL, "Two Worlds of Necessity in ICSID Arbitration: *CMS* and *LG&E*", 20 Leiden J. Int'l L. (2007) p. 637.
202. *LG&E v. Argentina*, supra fn. 135, paras. 125, 128, 171.
203. *Enron Corporation and Ponderosa Assets, L.P. v. Argentine Republic* (ICSID Case No. ARB/01/3), Award of 22 May 2007, paras. 260, 262, 263, 274.
204. *Enron, ibid.*, paras. 288-345. On these cases see Jürgen KURTZ, "Adjudging the Exceptional at International Law: Security, Public Order and Financial Crisis", IILJ Working Paper 2008/6 available at <http://iilj.org/publications/documents/2008-6.Kurtz.pdf>.

V. CONCLUSION: PROBLEMS IN OPERATIONALIZING THE NORMATIVE JUSTIFICATIONS OF THE PUBLIC-REGARDING AND GOVERNANCE-REGARDING DIMENSIONS OF THE INVESTOR-STATE ARBITRATION SYSTEM

This Report has argued that investor-State arbitration is a form of global governance. The case has been made that these arbitral tribunals help define proper standards for State conduct toward investors, and serve as review agencies to assess balances governments have struck between investor interests and public interests. These tribunals are, of course, constrained by the law under which they operate, including treaties under which they are established, and the terms of national law, contracts and other legal instruments. They are also part of a normative legal framework which includes the wider structure of customary international law, general principles of law, and other treaties and international decisions. All of these inform their work. But these observations do not give an exhaustive account of how these tribunals function, nor of what is normatively relevant in appraising the whole system of investor-State arbitration.

Instead, it is essential to reflect on a topic which receives rather less sustained consideration than it merits: on what basis, if any, can the current system of investor-State arbitration be normatively justified? The common proposition that it is justified because it vindicates State aspirations to promote investment flows, if it does indeed do that, addresses only the ordinary functional conception of the tribunals as enforcing commitments and resolving disputes. It is a tenuous justification at best for the more far-reaching governance functions exercised by tribunals. Rather, the normative justifications for the current investor-State arbitration system, *as a form of governance*, which produces and is subject to global administrative law, are very likely to be aligned with one or another of the basic normative conceptions of the role of global administrative law as a whole. Considerations of regulatory efficacy, social welfare, democracy and justice may all come into this. It may be debated whether global administrative law should or realistically can embody robust commitments to promote overall social welfare, or equity and just treatment of marginalized and disregarded economic and social interests, or should instead be concerned more modestly with promoting orderly administration and accountability. Bracketing these far-reaching issues, three basic normative conceptions can be identified for an administrative law of global governance, with potential relevance also to investor-State arbitration as a form of governance: (1) promotion of democracy, (2) promotion of internal administrative accountability and (3) protection of private rights and the rights of States.[205]

The first of these normative conceptions, which views the role of global administrative law as promoting democracy, is probably too demanding to be a systematic objective for investor-State arbitration given the realistic limits to the possibilities of this dispute settlement mechanism, but in special cases particular democratic issues may be highly relevant. Clearly, national administrative law in many countries has a democratic

---

205. On similar normative conceptions behind domestic administrative law, see Eberhard SCHMIDT-ASSMANN, *Das Allgemeine Verwaltungsrecht als Ordnungsidee*, 2nd edn. (2004). The following passages draw from joint work of Benedict Kingsbury and Richard Stewart on global administrative law.

component: it ensures the accountability of administrators to parliament by ensuring their compliance with statutes, and to broader economic and social constituencies through public participation in administrative decision-making procedures. The development of a global administrative law, including through the work of investor-State arbitral tribunals, could potentially strengthen representative democracy at the national level by making global regulatory decisions and institutions more visible and subject to effective scrutiny and review within domestic political systems, thereby also promoting more accountability of global regulatory decision-makers through those systems.[206] This could involve requiring such administrative transparency and accountability processes within the State as part of the standards of treatment required under investment treaties.

The second of these normative conceptions, internal administrative accountability, focuses on securing the accountability of the subordinate or peripheral components of an administrative regime to the legitimating center (whether legislative or executive), especially through ensuring the legality of administrative action. This conception emphasizes organizational and political functions and regime integrity rather than any specific substantive normativity, making it a potential model for an international order, particularly a pluralist one that lacks a strong consensus on substantive norms. This conception provides a strong basis for arguments that global administrative law should be applicable (where apposite) to the work of the institutions of the investor-State arbitral system.

The third normative conception is liberal and rights-oriented: administrative law protects the rights of individuals and other civil society actors, mainly through their participation in administrative procedures and through the availability of review to ensure the legality of a decision. Protection of foreign investors is one instantiation of this conception. This conception may also be extended to the protection of the rights of States; this idea may help to protect publics and public interests even within powerful States, but it is likely to be especially valuable for many developing countries and other weak states that lack political and economic bargaining power and influence. This conception may also overlap with the notion that global administrative law can promote the rule of law by ensuring the public character of regulatory norms, their reasoned elaboration, and their impartial and predictable application.

These three normative conceptions inform quests for legitimacy and accountability in the work of international institutions. They have a direct bearing on the design and functioning of the system of investor-State arbitral tribunals, and on their legitimacy as they exercise the governance functions which are an ineluctable part of their current mandates.

It is fruitful to consider the possible implications of these normative conceptions as justifying the investor-State arbitration system: in particular, they set specific conditions

---

206. Systems of global administrative law might also support the development of deliberative democracy at the level of global regulatory regimes, although the elements of such a conception as well as the conditions of its effective realization have yet to be resolved. See Robert HOWSE, "Transatlantic Regulatory Cooperation and the Problem of Democracy" in George A. BERMANN, Matthias HERDEGEN and Peter L. LINDSETH, eds., *Transatlantic Regulatory Cooperation: Legal Problems and Political Prospects* (2000) p. 469.

or require certain features in its institutional design and institutional practices. At the same time, it must be recognized that problems of structure and of institutional design may currently be an insuperable obstacle to making investment treaty arbitration a totally effective and wholly legitimate means of exercising power for the multiple set of functions which these arbitral institutions are now called on to perform. They are regulatory institutions which must at once: (1) arbitrate and settle actual disputes between specific parties (usually *ex post*, though in some cases the positive economic relations between the disputants may be continuing at the time of the arbitration); (2) adjudicate these same disputes in ways that articulate public power to all concerned with this specific political-economic issue, and with the substantive legal standards involved, by embodying the idea of publicness in law; and (3) regulate by interpreting applicable standards in ways that have prospective effects for States and other actors. This leads to proposals for radical reform, such as Gus Van Harten's argument for abandoning the current model of what he regards as privatized governance and instead creating a public institution with tenured judges, a permanent International Investment Court.[207] As a practical matter, however, proposals for such an institution, or for an appellate structure, seem unlikely to be realized in the near term. Consequently, it seems both imperative and more feasible for those involved in the current system to try to achieve more legitimacy within it, rather than outside of it. This has been the focus of the analysis and relatively modest set of recommendations made in this Report.

One fundamental structural problem with the aspiration to public-regarding and governance-regarding institutional design and arbitral reasoning is that the parties, and particularly the investor, may have little interest in making the effort, and especially in paying the costs of providing this public good, i.e., prospective governance of State behavior, and of the sophisticated balancing of public and investor interests, through retrospective arbitration. Not surprisingly, therefore, this public good is under-supplied. Furthermore, there is no tax and no general system of State contributions to finance most of the system. Even the system-level problems of overextension or weak legitimacy in investor-State arbitration that may threaten its viability, are collective action problems that no single investor, and probably few individual defendant States, want to pay to fix.[208]

Some individual arbitrators or panels of arbitrators may be particularly skilled in this area, and motivated to put extra work into a particular award even without financial recompense. But many arbitrators do not necessarily want to assume large responsibilities without additional compensation, one or both of the parties may indeed be apprehensive about arbitrators who might embed the case into some wider set of

---

207. VAN HARTEN, supra fn. 7, pp. 180 et seq. Similarly questioning the suitability of investor-State arbitration as a mechanism to review sovereign acts of host States, see, for example, Vicki L. BEEN and Joel C. BEAUVAIS, "The Global Fifth Amendment? NAFTA's Investment Protections and the Misguided Quest for an International 'Regulatory Takings' Doctrine", 78 N.Y.U. L. Rev. (2003) p. 30; Marc R. POIRIER, "The NAFTA Chapter 11 Expropriation Debate Through the Eyes of a Property Theorist", 33 Envt'l L. (2003) p. 851.
208. One way of financing the bringing of certain kinds of cases having general importance may be to shift costs to the State party to the arbitration in case the investor's claim was brought in good faith. See SCHILL, supra fn. 169, p. 653.

considerations, and the appointments process in any case can produce mismatches and idiosyncratic combinations. Institutional support, such as is provided by the ICSID Secretariat or other arbitral institutions, could conceivably help in the supply of reasoning addressed to more expansive concerns, particularly if its officials play a significant role and have a system-level view. Yet, the availability of such support varies greatly with the institution and other factors.

This problem is exacerbated by the uneven range of cases brought to investor-State tribunals. Except in very unusual circumstances, States are the only targets of these cases. Public interest organizations do not bring these cases against States – or not yet, although, if they find means to manage the costs, it is possible to imagine NGOs becoming investors to challenge State action through arbitration in the same way as some of them bring suits against foreign States in national courts, or others have for many years purchased shares in corporations to try to influence the corporation's conduct.[209] Thus, it is usually only investors with high economic stakes in the outcome who initiate these cases, and they usually do so to receive a direct economic benefit, not to generate jurisprudence on new issues or raise the quality of reasoning. Furthermore, in some cases investors with meritorious and important claims do not bring them at all, often because they may not want to be shut out of the relevant market. Smaller investors, by contrast, may be discouraged from bringing claims because of the significant costs involved in investor-State arbitration.[210]

The institutional design of the investor-State dispute settlement structures and its capacity to generate an international public good thus contrasts sharply with, for example, international human rights tribunals. These set some limits on *locus standi*, and typically require prior exhaustion of reasonably available local remedies, but are open to persons claiming to be victims of substantive human rights violations at relatively modest cost.[211] The Inspection Panels of the World Bank and other international development banks are similar. In the World Trade Organization, the absence of a direct right to litigate for corporations or other private actors limits the range of cases, but within the inter-State process, a structural problem of undersupply of the public good of law development in ad hoc GATT Panels was in part addressed through the establishment of the more precedent-creating standing seven-member Appellate Body in 1994.[212]

Under the current system the investment arbitration tribunals are a highly decentralized and fragmented regulator. They are usually not well embedded in a unifying institution, although some loose monitoring occurs through multiple

---

209. But see Luke PETERSEN and Nick GALLUS, "International Investment Treaty Protection of Not-for-Profit Organizations", 10 Int'l J. of Not-for-Profit Law (December 2007) p. 47, available at <www.icnl.org/knowledge/ijnl/vol10iss1/ijnl_vol10iss1.pdf> (discussing the protection of investment treaties of NGOs and their activities on foreign territory).

210. Again, cost-shifting techniques may provide a solution to the deterrent effect of high costs. See SCHILL, supra fn. 169, p. 653.

211. Usually they pay nothing toward the costs of the institution itself, or the State's defense, and there may be NGOs or public interest lawyers able and keen to represent them *ex gratia*.

212. For an overview see Joel TRACHTMAN, "The Domain of WTO Dispute Resolution", 40 Harv. Int'l L. J. (1999) p. 333.

appointments of individuals to tribunals. Furthermore, institutions such as the Organisation for Economic Co-operation and Development (OECD), UNCTAD, the World Bank and the WTO Committee on Trade Related Investment Measures all provide some institutional supervision and expert enunciation of foreign investment theories and policies. In addition, some intellectual unity is built by the tribunals themselves in their use of precedents and common methodologies, by inter-governmental institutions distilling and disseminating their work through publications and training in investment law (like UNCTAD, or the OECD), and by unofficial actors such as the arbitration congresses or academic commentators who analyze jurisprudence and existing or proposed treaty clauses. Altogether, however, the tribunals are much less embedded in political institutions capable of helping deliver on governance objectives than are the WTO dispute settlement organs, or even OECD supervisory bodies such as the Bribery Working Group under the OECD's Convention against transnational bribery of government officials. The combination of the strong regulatory effects the investment tribunals have on States, and the lack of political inter-governmental institutions in which the tribunals are effectively embedded, intensifies the premium on high-quality reasoning and knowledgeable shaping of standards for good State administration. The recognition by investor-State tribunals that they are both producers and subjects of global administrative law seems inevitable and is beginning to proceed apace.

# The ICSID Convention and the Origins of Investment Treaty Arbitration

*Margrete Stevens**

| TABLE OF CONTENTS | Page |
|---|---|
| I. Paving the Way for Investment Treaty Arbitration | 69 |
| II. Thicker or Thinner Concepts of the Rule of Law | 70 |
| III. Conclusion | 72 |

I. PAVING THE WAY FOR INVESTMENT TREATY ARBITRATION

Benedict Kingsbury and Stephan Schill have given us a very interesting and thought-provoking Report that raises many legitimacy issues for contemporary investment treaty arbitration. In my comments I will take up some of the problems and recommendations that Professor Kingsbury and Mr. Schill have identified as having an impact on the continued credible operation of the investor-State arbitration system. Bearing in mind this panel's task to identify expectations and test assumptions in the origin and theory of investment treaty arbitration, I will focus particularly on the ICSID Convention because the system established under the Convention paved the way for investment treaty arbitration as we know it today.

Professor Kingsbury and Mr. Schill note that the investor-State mechanism reflects a lack of system in "the design and planning of its development" and that it has failed "to embed in it theories of governance which would take States and public interests seriously".[1] Professor Kingsbury and Mr. Schill further argue that the investor-State arbitration system has fallen out of step with the way the exercise of public power has been moving.

Let me recall the circumstances under which the negotiation of the ICSID Convention came under way in 1961, and consider how the exercise of public power in areas affecting investment has moved along since then and also whether the investor-State dispute settlement mechanism, in its current incarnation, in fact has stepped off the train.

As you may recall, it was in 1961 that the then General Counsel of the World Bank, Aron Broches, first presented his idea to the Bank's Board suggesting that it establish an institution which would offer the services of qualified persons willing to act as arbitrators in specific investment disputes. In promoting this Mr. Broches observed that such a facility would constitute an important step towards the removal of what was one of the impediments to the flow of international capital. The impediment referred to was "the fear of investors that their investment would be exposed to political risks such as outright

---

* Consultant, King & Spalding, Washington, DC.
1. Benedict Kingsbury and Stephan Schill, "Investor-State Arbitration as Governance: Fair and Equitable Treatment, Proportionality and the Emerging Global Administrative Law", this volume, pp. 5-68 at p. 10.

expropriation, government interference and non-observance by the host government of contractual undertakings on the basis of which the investment had been made".[2]

The seventy-four countries that were members of the Bank at the time agreed to pursue Mr. Broches' proposal and proceeded to negotiate the ICSID Convention which was opened for signature in 1965.

II.   THICKER OR THINNER CONCEPTS OF THE RULE OF LAW

As many of you know, the drafting of the Convention included four regional meetings held in 1963 and 1964 in Addis Ababa, Santiago, Geneva and Bangkok. World Bank support for the Convention was explained by Mr. Broches, in similar terms, at each one of the four meetings:

> "The fact that the World Bank has taken the initiative in promoting an international agreement in a field which might not be regarded as falling directly within its sphere of activity was due to the fact that the Bank was not merely a financing mechanism but above all, a development institution. While its activities did consist in large part in the provision of finance, much of its energy and resources were devoted to technical assistance and advice directed towards the promotion of conditions conducive to rapid economic growth, and *the creation of a favorable investment climate in the broadest sense of the term*. To that end sound technical and administrative foundations were essential, *but no less indispensable was the firm establishment of the Rule of Law*."[3] (Emphasis added)

This statement sounds very contemporary to us today, especially the references to the importance of a favorable investment climate and the establishment of the rule of law. However, with the benefit of hindsight, one might say that Aron Broches was a long way ahead of the rest of the Bank. In those days the institution saw growth in terms of public investment in roads, railways, power and agriculture and later health and education. Private sector development did not become a part of the Bank's development strategy until the mid 1980s.

Nowadays, everyone acknowledges the role played by the rule of law concept in economic development, including its role in promoting foreign investment, has turned out to be a much more controversial topic than what might have been anticipated in the 1960s. There is today no uniform agreement as to what "rule of law" means. Instead, scholarly writings often break the concept down into thin (or thinner) and thick (or

---

2. Statement by A. BROCHES, General Counsel, International Bank for Reconstruction and Development, made at Consultative Meetings of Legal Experts, Addis Ababa, December 1963; Santiago, February 1964; Geneva, February 1964; and Bangkok, April 1964. See *History of the ICSID Convention*, Vol. II-1 at pp. 240, 302, 370 and 463.
3. *Ibid.*, at pp. 240, 370 and 462. A similar statement was made at the Santiago meeting. See *ibid.*, at p. 301.

thicker) categories. Concepts are referred to as "thinner" when they do not include broad ideals as to the substance of the law, including human rights law. The thinner concepts of the rule of law have four main purposes:

First, the rule of law should generate predictability or certainty;
Second, the rule of law should preclude the arbitrary exercise of power;
Third, the rule of law should ensure that similar cases are dealt with in similar ways; and
Fourth, the rule of law should provide order, and foster law abiding conduct among people.

A review of investment treaty jurisprudence shows that investor-State tribunals have generally operated within the thinner rule of law concepts in their elaboration of the meaning of the fair and equitable treatment standard. In my view this has been prudent and consistent with the powers given to ICSID tribunals under the Convention. This tradition is now being challenged by Professor Kingsbury and Mr. Schill who encourage tribunals to be more ambitious in their interpretation and application of the fair and equitable treatment standard, arguing that tribunals "should use a comparative method that draws on domestic and international law regarding good administration". In particular, Professor Kingsbury and Mr. Schill suggest that "arbitral tribunals should ... engage in a comparative analysis of the major domestic legal systems in order to grasp common features those legal systems establish for the exercise of public power".[4] This suggestion, I think, poses certain problems, first of all because – as Professor Kingsbury and Mr. Schill acknowledge – tribunals cannot easily have regard to system-level concerns given their responsibilities to the disputing parties in one particular case. But secondly, because the objective of identifying what good administration amounts to would involve the application of thicker rule of law concepts which I do not think States would view as appropriate, and which I believe investor-State tribunals would be ill-equipped to deal with. In the case of transparency, for example, such a review might include the new European draft Convention on access to information as well as the new international standards set by the Inter-American Court of Human Rights. Both instruments are based on historic developments in certain countries which are not shared by countries in other parts of the world.

This recommendation and the problems I think it points to – that is, the relative unevenness in the development of global administrative law – bring me to my second reference to Mr. Broches' observations on the objectives of the World Bank when negotiating the ICSID Convention. This was the Bank's concern to create "a favorable investment climate in the broadest sense of the word". Similar to what can be said with regard to the rule of law concept it can be argued that the World Bank had much less understanding and far fewer tools available forty-five years ago to identify what then constituted a favorable investment climate. As a matter of fact, it is only in the last fifteen years that the Bank has embarked on comprehensive research and analysis to provide evidence as to what kind of conditions are necessary for a country to attract and retain

---

4. KINGSBURY and SCHILL, supra fn. 2, p. 28.

investment. This work includes the World Bank Governance Indicators which measures six dimensions of governance including government effectiveness, regulatory quality and rule of law; the 2005 World Development Report on A Better Investment Climate; and the Doing Business publications – a series of annual surveys covering 178 countries which for the last five years has been produced jointly by the International Finance Corporation and the World Bank.

There is no time here to go into details regarding these publications. Suffice it to say that there is evidence that this particular time is a period when many countries are open to change and active in reforming their normative framework for business regulations. This work is for the first time supported by indicators that can analyze economic outcomes and identify what reforms have worked, where, and why.

III. CONCLUSION

We had been asked for this Panel to identify expectations and to test assumptions. Certainly there was strong belief on the part of the drafters of the ICSID Convention that the creation of a dispute resolution mechanism would materially improve the investment climate and encourage higher flows of foreign direct investment.

Perhaps the fourteen African countries which ratified the ICSID Convention in order for it to come into force in 1966 believed that as well. But foreign direct investment did not greatly increase, at least not until the 1990s, when it began to outstrip foreign aid as the greatest source of external capital for developing countries.

What we can take from this experience and also from the outpouring of research into, on the one hand, governance, and on the other, the investment climate, enables us to put the Convention into perspective.

We now know:

1. That the investment climate has many facets – governance is one;
2. That there is great variation in the quality of governance between countries;
3. That there are many components of governance – one of which is the rule of law (thickly or thinly defined as to your taste); another is the credibility of economic policies; and
4. That within the investment climate a commitment to legal undertakings by host countries and to the enforceability of contracts remain key components.

To conclude I would suggest that the expectations motivating the framing of the ICSID Convention forty years ago were legitimate in regard to the objectives that the negotiators pursued. However, there is far greater understanding today of the complexity of the concept of the rule of law and of what constitutes a sound investment climate, and therefore a different appreciation of what creates legal impediments to the flow of international capital.

# Working Group A

## The Impact of Investment Treaty Arbitration: Identifying the Expectations, Testing the Assumptions

### 2. Present Expectations and Realities

# Present Expectations and Realities – Comments from the Perspective of an Arbitrator

*Charles N. Brower[*]*

TABLE OF CONTENTS | Page
---|---
I. Introduction | 75
II. Shared Expectations? | 75
III. What Nobody Expected | 77
IV. Is Arbitration Suited to the Resolution of Investment Disputes? | 80
V. Closing Thought | 81

## I. INTRODUCTION

I would like to supplement the discussion of expectations and realities in investment arbitration with some observations from the perspective of an arbitrator on three points: (1) the existence of shared expectations of States vis-à-vis international investment law and arbitration; (2) States' expectations concerning the jurisprudence resulting from investor-State arbitration; and (3) the suitability of arbitration as an investment dispute resolution mechanism.

## II. SHARED EXPECTATIONS?

Why is it that we have 2,500-plus bilateral investment treaties (BITs),[1] but that successive efforts over some decades to complete a broad multilateral investment treaty all have failed,[2] leaving only a very few narrower, regional multi-party investment

---

[*] Judge, Iran-United States Claims Tribunal, The Hague; Judge Ad Hoc, Inter-American Court of Human Rights, San Jose, Costa Rica; Arbitrator Member, 20 Essex Street Chambers, London; formerly Acting Legal Adviser, United States Department of State, Deputy Special Counselor to the President of the United States, President, American Society of International Law, and Chairman, Institute for Transnational Arbitration. The author wishes to express his appreciation for the assistance provided in the research for and preparation of this paper by Dr. Stephan Schill.

[1] On the statistical increase of investment treaties see UNCTAD, *Bilateral Investment Treaties in the Mid-1990s* (1998) p. 9; see further UNCTAD, *Recent Developments in International Investment Agreements (2006-June 2007)* (2007) p. 2, available at <www.unctad.org/en/docs/webiteiia20076_en.pdf> (recording an aggregate of 2,573 BITs at the end of 2006).

[2] On the various failed attempts at concluding multilateral investment treaties, such as the 1947 Havana Charter, the 1967 OECD Draft Convention on the Protection of Foreign Property and the 1998 Multilateral Agreement on Investment see Riyaz DATTU, "A Journey from Havana to Paris: The Fifty-Year Quest for the Elusive Multilateral Agreement on Investment", 24 Fordham Int'l L. J. (2000) p. 275. Most recently, attempts to conclude a multilateral investment treaty failed in the Doha Round of the World Trade Organization (WTO). Cf. Sebastian WOLF, "*Welthandelsrechtliche*

treaties such as the North-American Free Trade Agreement (NAFTA),[3] the Central America-Dominican Republic-United States Free Trade Agreement[4] and the notoriously imperfect Energy Charter Treaty?[5] The reason, I submit, is very simple: when two (or a very few) States negotiate an investment treaty, the concrete realities of trade lead them to agree on terms that will facilitate in-bound investment in return for substantive and procedural protections for such investment.[6] In other words, the parties are, in the vernacular, "cutting a deal". By contrast, the greater the number of negotiating parties involved, the more abstract will be the treaty provisions discussed; and the so-called "negotiations" inevitably will morph from "abstract" into "abstruse", in direct proportion to the number and the consequent diversity of the negotiating parties.

This is exactly the reason that the New International Economic Order (N.I.E.O.), to which so much hot air, smoke, bluster and posturing were devoted in the United Nations General Assembly in the 1970s,[7] was, in the end, washed away by the ensuing tsunami of BITs;[8] and it is precisely the reason that Mexico, as an example, became party to a NAFTA containing provisions at odds with, if not indeed diametrically opposed to, the

---

*Rahmenbedingungen für die Liberalisierung ausländischer Direktinvestitionen*", 61 Beiträge zum Transnationalen Wirtschaftsrecht (2006); Kevin C. KENNEDY, "A WTO Agreement on Investment: A Solution in Search of a Problem?", 24 U. Pa. J. Int'l Econ. L. (2003) p. 77.

3. North-American Free Trade Agreement (NAFTA), signed 17 December 1992, entered into force 1 January 1994, 32 I.L.M. (1993) 289 and 605.
4. Central America-Dominican Republic-United States Free Trade Agreement, signed 5 Aug. 2004, available at <www.ustr.gov/Trade_Agreements/Bilateral/CAFTA/CAFTA-DR_Final_Texts/Section_Index.html>.
5. Energy Charter Treaty (Annex I of the Final Act of the European Energy Charter Conference), signed 17 Dec. 1994, 34 I.L.M. (1995) 373.
6. While the question of whether investment treaties actually attract additional investment originally was contentious, most recent studies actually find a positive empirical link between the conclusion of an investment treaty and actual investment flows. For an earlier critical study see Jennifer TOBIN and Susan ROSE-ACKERMAN, "When BITs Have Some Bite: The Political-Economic Environment for Bilateral Investment Treaties" (2006) available at <www.law.yale.edu/documents/pdf/When_BITs_Have_Some_Bite.doc>. For more recent positive studies see Eric NEUMAYER and Laura SPESS, "Do Bilateral Investment Treaties Increase Foreign Direct Investment to Developing Countries?", 33 World Development (2005) p. 1567; Jeswald W. SALACUSE and Nicholas P. SULLIVAN, "Do BITs Really Work? An Evaluation of Bilateral Investment Treaties and Their Grand Bargain", 46 Harv. Int'l L. J. (2005) p. 67; Tim BÜTHE and Helen V. MILNER, "The Politics of Foreign Direct Investment into Developing Countries: Increasing FDI through International Trade Agreements?", 52 Am. J. Pol. Sc. (October 2008, no. 4) p. 741.
7. See "Declaration on the Establishment of a New International Economic Order", UN General Assembly Resolution 3201, UN Doc. A/RES/3201(S-VI) (1 May 1974), reprinted in 13 I.L.M. (1974) 715, and "Charter of Economic Rights and Duties of States", UN General Assembly Resolution Res. 3281 (XXIX), UN Doc. A/RES/3281(XXIX) (12 Dec. 1974), reprinted in 14 I.L.M. (1975) 251.
8. Cf. Thomas W. WÄLDE, "A Requiem for the 'New International Economic Order' – The Rise and Fall of Paradigms in International Economic Law and a Post-mortem with Timeless Significance" in Gerhard HAFNER and Gerhard LOIBL, eds., *Liber Amicorum: Professor Ignaz Seidl-Hohenveldern in Honour of his 80th Birthday* (1998) p. 771.

expropriation provisions of the United Nations General Assembly's N.I.E.O.-inspired Charter of Economic Rights and Duties of States,[9] which had been a pet project of then-President Echevarría of Mexico. In other words, in the end, States put their *mouth* where their *money* is, not vice versa. The bottom line therefore is that BIT parties got what all parties wanted and expected.

III. WHAT NOBODY EXPECTED

What *no* party foresaw was the explosion of arbitrations under these treaties,[10] bringing with them two phenomena:

– Repeat respondents under the same treaty or nearly identical treaties, e.g., Argentina, Canada, the Czech Republic, Ecuador, Mexico, the United States and Venezuela, giving rise to multiple decisions and awards, sometimes conflicting,[11] raising issues of "precedent",[12] with no supreme instance available to impose a consistent and coherent jurisprudence.
– Challenging issues of interpretation such as "What is fair and equitable treatment?";[13]

---

9. See Charles N. BROWER and John B. TEPE, "The Charter of Economic Rights and Duties of States: A Reflection or a Rejection of International Law?", 9 Int'l Law. (1975) p. 295.
10. On the rise of investment treaty arbitrations see UNCTAD, *Investor-State Disputes Arising from Investment Treaties: A Review* (2005) pp. 3-8, available at <www.unctad.org/en/docs/iteiit20054_en.pdf>.
11. Cf. Susan D. FRANCK, "The Legitimacy Crisis in Investment Treaty Arbitration: Privatizing Public International Law Through Inconsistent Decisions", 73 Fordham L. Rev. (2005) p. 1521.
12. See, for example, Jeffrey P. COMMISSION, "Precedent in Investment Treaty Arbitration – A Citation Analysis of a Developing Jurisprudence", 24 J. Int'l Arb. (2007) p. 129; Gabrielle KAUFMANN-KOHLER, "Arbitral Precedent: Dream, Necessity or Excuse?", 23 Arb. Int'l (2007) p. 357.
13. Christoph SCHREUER, "Fair and Equitable Treatment in Arbitral Practice", 6 J. World Inv. & Trade (2005) p. 357; Barnali CHOUDHURY, "Evolution or Devolution? – Defining Fair and Equitable Treatment in International Investment Law", 6 J. World Inv. & Trade (2005) p. 297; Rudolf DOLZER, "Fair and Equitable Treatment: A Key Standard in Investment Treaties", 39 Int'l Law. (2005) p. 87; Stephan SCHILL, "Fair and Equitable Treatment under Investment Treaties as an Embodiment of the Rule of Law", IILJ Working Paper, Global Administrative Law Series, (2006, no. 6    available at <www.iilj.org/publications/2006-6Schill.asp>; Campbell MCLACHLAN, Laurence SHORE and Matthew WEINIGER, *Investment Treaty Arbitration – Substantive Principles* (2007) pp. 226-247; Graham MAYEDA, "Playing Fair: The Meaning of Fair and Equitable Treatment in Bilateral Investment Treaties", 41 J. World Trade (2007) p. 273; Ioana TUDOR, *The Fair and Equitable Treatment Standard in the International Law of Foreign Investment Law* (2008).

"What is the scope of an umbrella clause?";[14] "Can otherwise unagreed dispute settlement provisions be accessed via most-favored-nation clauses?"[15]

The result of these phenomena has been, apart from generating whole new worlds for publications, arbitral institutions, doctoral dissertations and academic discourse, to make Canada and the United States suddenly hunker down in the bunker of defense, overlooking the fact that protection of their investors abroad is far more significant economically than is the need to insulate the national treasury to the point of impregnability from the odd attempt by a foreign investor to nick it, however slightly.[16] And if the capital-exporting treaty parties have reacted badly, certain host countries appear in part to be moving towards the door, by seeking to address ICSID awards in

---

14. For the more recent debate surrounding the application of umbrella clauses see Christoph SCHREUER, "Travelling the BIT Route – Of Waiting Periods, Umbrella Clauses and Forks in the Road", 5 J. World Inv. & Trade (2004) p. 231 at pp. 249-255; Anthony C. SINCLAIR, "The Origins of the Umbrella Clause in the International Law of Investment Protection", 4 Arb. Int'l (2004) p. 411; Thomas W. WÄLDE, "The 'Umbrella Clause' in Investment Arbitration: A Comment on Original Intentions and Recent Cases", 6 J. World Inv. & Trade (2005) p. 183; Bjørn KUNOY, "Singing in the Rain – Developments in the Interpretation of Umbrella Clauses", 7 J. World Inv. & Trade (2006) p. 275; Jarrod WONG, "Umbrella Clauses in Bilateral Investment Treaties: Of Breaches of Contract, Treaty Violations, and the Divide between Developing and Developed Countries in Foreign Investment Disputes", 14 Geo. Mason L. Rev. (2006) p. 135; John P. GAFFNEY and James L. LOFTIS, "The 'Effective Ordinary Meaning' of BITs and the Jurisdiction of Treaty-Based Tribunals to Hear Contract Claims", 8 J. World Inv. & Trade (2007) p. 5; Nick GALLUS, "An Umbrella Just for Two? BIT Obligations Observance Clauses and the Parties to a Contract", 24 Arb. Int'l (2008) p. 157; Stephan SCHILL, "Enabling Private Ordering – Function, Scope and Effect of Umbrella Clauses in International Investment Treaties", 18 Minn. J. Int'l L. (2009) p. 1.
15. On this debate see Rudolf DOLZER and Terry MYERS, "After *Tecmed*: Most-Favoured-Nation Clauses in International Investment Protection Agreements", 19 ICSID Rev. – For. Inv. L. J. (2004) p. 49; Dan H. FREYER and David HERLIHY, "Most-Favoured-Nation Treatment and Dispute Settlement in Investment Arbitration: Just How 'Favoured' is 'Most-Favoured'?", 20 ICSID Rev. – For. Inv. L. J. (2005) p. 58; Locknie HSU, "MFN and Dispute Settlement – When the Twain Meet", 7 J. World Inv. & Trade (2006) p. 25; Jürgen KURTZ, "The MFN Standard and Foreign Investment: An Uneasy Fit?", 6 J. World Inv. & Trade (2004) p. 861; Ruth TEITELBAUM, "Who's Afraid of *Maffezini*? Recent Developments in the Interpretation of Most Favored Nation Clauses", 22 J. Int'l Arb. (2005) p. 225; Alejandro FAYA RODRIGUEZ, "The Most-Favored-Nation Clause in International Investment Agreements", 25 J. Int' Arb. (2008, no. 1) p. 89; Yannick RADI, "The Application of the Most-Favoured-Nation Clause to the Dispute Settlement Provisions of Bilateral Investment Treaties: Domesticating the Trojan Horse", 18 E.J.I.L. (2008) p. 757; Okezie CHUCKWUMERIJE, "Interpreting Most-Favoured-Nation Clauses in Investment Treaty Arbitration", 8 J. Word Inv. & Trade (2007, no. 5) p. 597; see also most recently *RosInvestCo UK Ltd. v. The Russian Federation* (SCC Case No. V 079/2005), Award on Jurisdiction of Oct. 2007, paras. 124-139 (accepting that most-favored-nation clauses can import more favorable consent to arbitration from the third-country BITs).
16. On the phenomenon of traditional capital-exporting countries becoming respondents in investment treaty arbitrations see Guillermo AGUILAR ALVAREZ and William PARK, "The New Face of Investment Arbitration: NAFTA Chapter 11", 28 Yale J. Int'l L. (2003) p. 365.

national courts,[17] or by denouncing the ICSID Convention,[18] or by limiting its application[19] or by dealing similarly with their BITs.[20]

My own view is that the relative lack of success of NAFTA claimants will have the effect – indeed *is* having the effect – of decelerating, if not stemming, the North American preoccupation with defense of the national treasury, and that over time the economic realities of life and associated political events will convince those now yearning

---

17. Reportedly, Argentina has considered opposing the enforcement of ICSID awards in its courts based on the argument that the Argentine Constitution prevails over international treaties and thus allows constitutional review of an ICSID award. A second basis of such considerations has been the alleged invalidity of Argentina's ratification of the ICSID Convention in that it did not conform with newly introduced procedural requirements under the country's Constitution. See Carlos E. ALFARO and Pedro M. LORENTI, "The Growing Opposition of Argentina to ICSID Arbitration Tribunals – A Conflict between International and Domestic Law?", 6 J. World Inv. & Trade (2005) p. 417. Such attempts are, however, contrary to the finality of awards under Arts. 53 and 54 of the ICSID Convention and violate the principle enshrined in Art. 46 of the Vienna Convention on the Law of Treaties that States, in general, cannot invoke a violation of domestic law in order to invalidate their consent to an international treaty. See Stephan SCHILL, "From *Calvo* to *CMS*: Burying an International Law Legacy – Argentina's Currency Reform in the Face of Investment Protection: The ICSID Case – *CMS v. Argentina*", 3 Zeitschrift für Schiedsverfahren/German Arb. J. (2005) p. 285 at p. 292. Less dramatically, and in conformity with the law governing ICSID Additional Facility arbitrations and UNCITRAL arbitrations, respondent States also sometimes attempt to challenge investment treaty awards. See, for example, *The United Mexican States v. Metalclad Corporation*, Supreme Court of British Columbia, Decision of 2 May 2001, 2001 BCSC 644 (concerning the partial set-aside of an ICSID Additional Facility Award by a Canadian court). See further on this Charles H. BROWER, "Investor-State Disputes Under NAFTA: The Empire Strikes Back", 40 Colum. J. Transnat'l L. (2001) p. 43.
18. As of 3 Nov. 2007, Bolivia has withdrawn from the ICSID Convention. See "Bolivia Denounces ICSID Convention", 46 I.L.M. (2007) p. 973. Rhetoric about withdrawal from the ICSID Convention also has been heard in respect of Cuba, Nicaragua and Venezuela. See Marco E. SCHNABL and Julie BÉDARD, "The Wrong Kind of 'Interesting'", Nat'l L. J. (30 July 2007).
19. On 4 Dec. 2007, Ecuador notified the ICSID Secretariat pursuant to Art. 25(4) of the ICSID Convention of a limitation of its consent to ICSID arbitration with regard to disputes arising out of investment in natural resources sector. See <http://icsid.worldbank.org/ICSID/FrontServlet?requestType=ICSIDPublicationsRH&actionVal=ViewAnnouncePDF&AnnouncementType=regular&AnnounceNo=9.pdf>.
20. On 30 April 2008, Venezuela communicated to the Netherlands its intention to terminate the Dutch-Venezuelan Bilateral Investment Treaty as of 1 Nov. 2008. See 1 Investment Treaty Reporter (16 May 2008, no. 1) available at via <www.iareporter.com>. Less radically, other countries, like the United States, have adapted their investment treaty practice and introduced limiting language restating standards such as fair and equitable treatment and the concept of indirect expropriation. See on the new U.S. 2004 Model BIT Gilbert GAGNÉ and Jean-Frédéric MORIN, "The Evolving American Policy on Investment Protection: Evidence from Recent FTAs and the 2004 Model BIT", 9 J. Int'l Econ. L. (2006) p. 357; Mark KANTOR, "The New Draft Model U.S. BIT: Noteworthy Developments", 21 J. Int'l Arb. (2004) p. 383; Stephen SCHWEBEL, "The United States 2004 Model Bilateral Investment Treaty: An Exercise in the Regressive Development of International Law", 3 TDM (April 2006).

for the resurrection of Carlos Calvo and his famous clause,[21] propounded in 1868, that both must remain as dead as dead can be, otherwise investment will dry up to the point of desiccation. One caveat, however: the critical path of this latter event will be affected by how much *we* need *their* oil and gas, and when!

IV.   IS ARBITRATION SUITED TO THE RESOLUTION OF INVESTMENT DISPUTES?

Some, including, in particular, single-issue non-governmental organizations, claim that arbitration is not a legitimate means of resolving issues that undeniably are infused with the public interest, prominent examples being "trade versus health, or environment, or human rights", and, in the case of Argentina, "a sovereign's right to exercise emergency powers in a crisis".[22]

The first objection made is that arbitrators, unlike judges, do not hold public office.[23] Certainly, the arbitrators are usually party-appointed.[24] Yet, this does not mean that the basis of jurisdiction in investment treaty cases is solely party consent. Rather, the appointment mechanism is contained in the rules of the respective arbitration institutions and the ICSID Convention itself. The consent to arbitration by host States, in turn, is contained in their respective investment treaties and is itself a sovereign act of the State.[25] Consequently, the basis of the arbitrators' authority in investment treaty cases is founded

---

21. Cf. Oscar M. GARIBALDI, "Carlos Calvo Redivivus: The Rediscovery of the Calvo Doctrine in the Era of Investment Treaties", 3 TDM (2006, no. 5 ). On the Calvo Doctrine and Calvo Clauses generally see Donald R. SHEA, *The Calvo Clause, A Problem of Inter-American and International Law and Diplomacy* (1955); Friedrich OSCHMANN, *Calvo-Doktrin und Calvo-Klauseln* (1993); Kurt LIPSTEIN, "The Place of the Calvo-Clause in International Law", 22 Brit. Yb. Int'l L. (1945) p. 139.
22. See Vicki L. BEEN and Joel C. BEAUVAIS, "The Global Fifth Amendment? NAFTA's Investment Protections and the Misguided Quest for an International 'Regulatory Takings' Doctrine, 78 N.Y.U. L. Rev. (2003) p. 30; Marc R. POIRIER, "The NAFTA Chapter 11 Expropriation Debate Through the Eyes of a Property Theorist", 33 Envt'l L. (2003) p. 851.
23. See Gus VAN HARTEN, *Investment Treaty Arbitration and Public Law* (2007) pp. 180 et seq.
24. See, for example, Art. 37(2) of the ICSID Convention:

"(a) The Tribunal shall consist of a sole arbitrator or any uneven number of arbitrators appointed as the parties shall agree.
(b) Where the parties do not agree upon the number of arbitrators and the method of their appointment, the Tribunal shall consist of three arbitrators, one arbitrator appointed by each party and the third, who shall be the president of the Tribunal, appointed by agreement of the parties."

25. Jan PAULSSON, "Arbitration Without Privity", 10 ICSID Rev. – For. Inv. L. J. (1995) p. 232; Bernardo CREMADES, "Arbitration in Investment Treaties: Public Offer of Arbitration in Investment-Protection Treaties" in: Robert BRINER, ed., *Law of International Business and Dispute Settlement in the 21st Century* (2001) p. 149 (pointing out that consent to arbitration under investment treaties constitutes a standing offer to initiate arbitration which can be accepted by covered investors by initiating arbitration).

in a public office which is conferred upon them based on international treaties.[26] Their position is thus approved, ipso facto and ipso jure, by the States involved.

A second, closely related objection is that arbitrators are appointed case-by-case to one-off tribunals, hence it is inferred that they will, or may, trim their sails when deciding a case in hopes of securing further appointments.[27] Nothing, however – I repeat: nothing – could be further from the truth! The real and effective control system here is that every second of every minute of every day of the year *someone, somewhere* is judging whatever is our reputation at that moment for deciding fairly, independently, without bias, and wisely.[28] It is that reputation that *will*, or will *not*, result in future employment. And, by the way, who says that national judges, unless installed for life by a wholly non-political process and constitutionally guaranteed no reduction in salary during office, are inherently more "reliable" (whatever *that* means!) or even as "reliable" as "the usual suspects"?

Finally, it has been objected that investment arbitration proceedings are "secret", not exposed to public view. While that was, to me, a legitimate point in the still recent past, it has been greatly alleviated by the progressive, now widespread opening of the proceedings to public view in all respects, which in my view *must* continue and expand.[29]

V.  CLOSING THOUGHT

I submit that what objecting States really dislike about treaty investment arbitration is that they no longer are the exclusive ultimate deciders of what is in the public interest of their people. The concept that NAFTA Chapter 11 tribunals could sit as a "Supreme Court of The North American Continent", for example, potentially overruling even the United States Supreme Court, certainly rattled a lot of cages on the Potomac. Thus, in the end, the ultimate issue is, "How far will States accept external regulatory controls?" This until now intensely European issue now becomes one for the world at large.

---

26. Van Harten himself considers the host State's consent to constitute a sovereign act, see Gus VAN HARTEN, "The Public-Private Distinction in the International Arbitration of Individual Claims Against the State", 56 Int'l & Comp. L. Quart. (2007) p. 371 at p. 378 et seq.
27. See VAN HARTEN, supra fn. 23, pp. 180 et seq.
28. Arbitrators and their decision-making not only are subject to scrutiny by the arbitration community, but also increasingly become the focus of academic and even public discussion in law review articles, internet blogs, discussion fora, newspaper articles, etc.
29. On issues of transparency in investment treaty arbitration see Christina KNAHR and August REINISCH, "Transparency Versus Confidentiality in International Investment Arbitration – The *Biwater Gauff* Compromise", 6 L. & Prac. Int'l Courts & Tribs. (2007) p. 97; Carl-Sebastian ZOELLNER, "Third-Party Participation (NGO's and Private Persons) and Transparency in ICSID Proceedings" in Rainer HOFMANN and Christian J. TAMS (eds.), *The International Convention for the Settlement of Investment Disputes (ICSID) – Taking Stock After 40 Years* (2007) p. 179.

# Comments on Present Expectations and Realities

*Brigitte Stern*[*]

| TABLE OF CONTENTS | Page |
| --- | --- |
| I. The Discrepancy | 82 |
| II. The Past Expectations at the Time of Entering into the BITs | 83 |
| III. The Current Expectations | 85 |

I.   THE DISCREPANCY

This session deals with treaty investment arbitration and our panel is entitled – as you have all seen – Present Expectations and Realities.

My first comment is that such a title strongly suggests that there are on the one side expectations and on the other realities, which do not match; that you have on the one side the dreams at night and on the other the world as it is in full day light. This discrepancy between the desirable and the existing was illustrated last night, when I told a lawyer involved in investment arbitration that I will be speaking in this Panel today. He said – and I am authorized to quote him – "Oh, it's very simple: the expectation is a quick, efficient procedure with an award of damage in which you can understand how the arbitrator decided it. The reality is a lengthy, inefficient procedure whose result is a completely incomprehensible decision on awarded damages."

More seriously, the fact that there is a discrepancy between expectations and reality is an impression I have been getting in several of the last academic colloquia I attended. Last autumn in October 2007, at Columbia University during a colloquium entitled "What's Next in International Investment Law and Policy? Improving the International Investment Law and Policy System", the theme running through the whole meeting was "the need for rebalancing the system". More recently, in April 2008, at the Harvard Law School in Boston, another colloquium had as a self explanatory title "The Backlash Against Investment Arbitration". If so many feel there is a problem, there must be one. *Il n'y a pas de fumée sans feu.* So, I guess we can presume that the real world does not meet the expectations, but I will say a little more on this later.

My second comment is that my colleague and friend Christopher Greenwood has taken some liberties with the title of our Panel – which he was of course fully entitled to do – and has in fact concentrated on past expectations and present realities, while I think our theme was more on the confrontation of the expectations and realities in our contemporaneous time. However, I will follow his example, by defining my topic myself: as I am not sure I have much to say on realities, I prefer to utilize the short time allotted to me to deal with expectations.

---

[*] Professor, University of Paris I – Panthéon-Sorbonne; Member, United Nations Administrative Tribunal (UNAT).

I will first comment briefly on Christopher Greenwood's presentation of past expectations – this topic has also been addressed by Margrete Stevens this morning[1] – and then turn to the present expectations and say a few words on how I see these current expectations, these being of course based on today's realities.

II.   THE PAST EXPECTATIONS AT THE TIME OF ENTERING INTO THE BITS

Quite rightly, the expectations of the capital-exporting countries were distinguished from those of the capital-importing countries.

*1.   The Expectations of the Capital-exporting Countries*

As far as the expectations of the capital-exporting countries were concerned, I naturally agree that their main purpose was to protect the investors from the North investing in the South. Two points made by Christopher Greenwood seem to me particularly interesting. The first point concerns the way the British government saw the content of the bilateral investment treaties (BITs), as not going – and I am quoting – "beyond what was thought to reflect international law". This might have some bearing on the ongoing debate on whether the fair and equitable treatment (FET) or the full protection and security (FPS) standards are similar to the international standards or are different from them.

It is well know that as far as the relation between the FET standard and the minimum standard of international law is concerned, there are two main approaches adopted by ICSID tribunals.

The first approach considers that FET has to be equated with the minimum standard of treatment provided for by general international law. This has been the position adopted by, for example, the *CMS* tribunal:

> "In fact, the Treaty standard of fair and equitable treatment and its connection with the required stability and predictability of the business environment, founded on solemn legal and contractual commitments, is not different from the international law minimum standard and its evolution under customary law."[2]

The second approach deals with FET as an autonomous standard, considered in general as more demanding and more protective of the investor's rights than the minimum standard of treatment provided for by general international law. The *Azurix* tribunal, for example, adopted this position:

---

1. "The ICSID Convention and the Origins of Investment Treaty Arbitration", this volume, pp. 69-72.
2. *CMS Gas Transmission Company v. The Argentine Republic* (ICSID Case No. ARB/01/8), Award of 12 May 2005, para. 284.

"The clause, as drafted, permits to interpret fair and equitable treatment and full protection and security as higher standards than required by international law."[3]

The same duality can be found in the analysis of the FPS standard, as illustrated by this last citation.

The British position clearly gives some support to the first approach. Now, of course, the question remains, whether due to the British "exceptionalism" mentioned by my colleague, this position can be deemed to be the general position of the main exporting countries.

Personally, I would add that I consider this discussion somewhat futile, as the scope and content of the minimum standard of international law is as little defined as the BITs' FET or FPS standard, and as the true question in my view is to know what substantive protection is granted to foreign investors through the FET or the FPS standard: in other words to determine the true content and scope of these standards, rather than try to compare them with other vague international standards.

The second point made by the panellist which I wanted to underscore is the perfectly correct statement that the main capital-exporting countries, although they entered into BITs with reciprocal language, "have had little if any expectations that they would themselves ever be the respondents" in case of investment state arbitration. It is clear that the fact that these countries are now in the position of respondents more and more frequently has a clear impact on the overall balance of the system, as I will mention in a minute.

*2.   The Expectations of the Capital-importing Countries*

As far as the expectations of the capital-importing countries were concerned, I must say I was less convinced by Christopher Greenwood's presentation than by the one concerning the capital-importing countries. May be this is because you know best the place where you come from and Christopher Greenwood clearly comes from an old capital-exporting country!

I am, for example, not sure that it can be abruptly said that "for many of those States the implications of what they were accepting were not clearly understood". I think they knew what they were doing, not more and not less than the developed countries. Not more, because as rightly said by our speaker, most governments of the developed countries had not foreseen, either, the potential that was lying in the BITs. Not less either: just as the capital-exporting countries wanted to protect their investors, the capital-importing countries wanted to attract foreign investments. The signing of a BIT was a symbol of openness to foreign investors, and they thought it was only a symbol and not a strong legal tool. This was also mentioned by Beth Simmons this morning. Nobody was really expecting that consent to arbitration could be given generally just in signing a BIT incorporating a reference to international arbitration, before international arbitrators said so, although it must also be acknowledged that the idea of separate consents was mentioned in the Board of Directors comments on the Washington Convention at the time of its adoption. But I must say that developing States that were

---

3. *Azurix v. Argentine Republic* (ICSID Case No. ARB/01/12), Award of 14 July 2006, para. 361.

somewhat hesitant to enter into the Washington Convention were strongly convinced by Aron Broches, through several continental conferences, that they will always be able to give their consent *specifically*. And, before the landmark decision in *SPP*[4] and *APPL*,[5] nobody really thought that "specifically" could mean unilaterally in a law or bilaterally/multilaterally in a treaty. Charles Brower indeed acknowledged in his Comments that there were some evolutions that nobody expected.[6]

III. THE CURRENT EXPECTATIONS

Here it is less a comment on what has been said than a presentation of how I see the current expectations. I haven't really gone deep enough in psychoanalysis (of my speaker's life) to know whether the expectations I will comment on are indeed the true expectations of the stakeholders of the system or the expectations of the evolution of the investment arbitration system as I see it, as a teaching academic and practicing arbitrator.

In fact, I will try to see *what is expected from the system* more than what is expected by the stakeholders – as there might be contradictory expectations of the investors on one side and the States on the other. In my view, the current expectations are – or should be – that the system of investment arbitration satisfies two criteria that I consider necessary for any system to survive (unless it's a dictatorship), which are to balance the interest of its stakeholders and to be predictable. I will therefore say a few – a very few – words on the necessary balance of interest and the necessary predictability.

*1.    The Necessary Balance of Interest*

In my view, any system can only survive if it satisfies its constituents more or less equally. It cannot lastingly survive if it is too unbalanced.

So, I think that one of the current expectations is certainly a balancing of interest, as stated for example in the decisions on jurisdiction in *El Paso* or *Pan Am*. And I quote:

> "The Tribunal considers that a balanced interpretation is needed, taking into account both State's sovereignty and its responsibility to create an adapted and evolutionary framework for the development of economic activities, and the necessity to protect foreign investment and its continuing flow."[7]

---

4. *Southern Pacific Properties Ltd v. Arab Republic of Egypt* (ICSID Case No. ARB/84/3), Decision on Jurisdiction of 14 April 1988, ICCA *Yearbook Commercial Arbitration* XVI (1991).
5. *Asian Agricultural Products Ltd v. Sri Lanka* (ICSID Case No. ARB/87/3), Award of 27 June 1990, ICSID Review – Foreign Investment Law Journal (1991) p. 514, with a commentary by Nassib G. ZIADÉ, ILM (1990) p. 580
6. See "Comments from the Perspective of an Arbitrator", this volume, pp. 75-81.
7. *El Paso Energy International Company v. The Argentine Republic* (ICSID Case No. ARB/03/15), Decision on Jurisdiction of 27 April 2006, para. 70; *Pan American Energy LLC and BP Argentina Exploration Company v. Argentine Republic* (ICSID Case No. ARB/03/13), Decision on Preliminary Objections of 27 July 2006, para. 99.

As a matter of fact, I think that this rebalancing of the system is at work today, with more capital-exporting countries being sued as respondents. They suddenly realize that the State cannot be held responsible for any change in its legislation required by changing circumstances. What is at stake here is a clarification of the utmost difficult distinction between legitimate regulatory measures which do not call for compensation and illegitimate regulatory measures that amount to indirect expropriation and must therefore give rise to compensation of the foreign investor. I cannot, of course, present here the different trends in the arbitral decisions showing that there are tensions, and implying that there is room for evolution. Let me just quote, as an important symptom of this evolution, the new model American BIT:

> "*Except in rare circumstances*, non-discriminatory regulatory actions by a Party that are designed and applied to protect legitimate public welfare objectives, such as public health, safety, and the environment, do not constitute indirect expropriations."[8] (Emphasis added)

Another example was given by Benedict Kingsbury and Stephan Schill when they stated that: "Norway's latest model BIT is much more explicitly solicitous of public and regulating interest than Norway's earlier more traditionally drafted investment treaties."[9]

So the trend might go towards an approach in which:

– as a matter of principle, general regulations do not amount to indirect expropriation;
– by exception unreasonable general regulation can amount to indirect expropriation if this neutralizes the use of the investment.

2.  *The Necessary Predictability*

The necessary predictability of the content of the standards of treatment and protection of the foreign investor is also of crucial importance.

I firmly believe that there is an absolute necessity for a clarification in the standards of treatment provided for in the BITs.

First of all, I think the different standards have to be distinguished. FET is not FPS, FET is not indirect expropriation. If different standards exist, they have to be differentiated and must play a diversified role.

The fact is that they are not always clearly distinguished. For example, there is not always a clear distinction between indirect expropriation and violation of the legitimate

---

8. The U.S. Model BIT is available at <www.ustr.gov/TradeSectors/Investment/Model BIT/Section Index.html>, Annex B, para. 4b.
9. "Investor-State Arbitration as Governance: Fair and Equitable Treatment, Proportionality and the Emerging Administrative Law", this volume, pp. 5-68.

expectations giving rise to a violation of the FET standard.[10] Sometimes there is a complete assimilation between the FET standard and the FSP standard.

Secondly, I think the FET standard – which plays a central role in today's case law – has to be given a more predictable and less encompassing content. Predictability is important both for the investors and for the States. I salute here the very interesting Report by Benedict Kingsbury and Stephan Schill in this direction. And I remember Lucy Reed, in the Fordham Colloquium organized by Arthur Rovine in June 2007, explaining quite convincingly that the FET standard was more or less used as a replacement for the standard against expropriation.[11]

It is therefore of the utmost importance that this central standard of treatment receives a more or less generally accepted content, which is clearly not the case.

There are very different conceptions, although most of them are quite broad. I can mention the duty to adopt a proactive behaviour in favour of the foreign investor, stated in the *MTD* case, where the tribunal said:

> "In terms of the BIT, fair and equitable treatment should be understood to be treatment in an even-handed and just manner, conducive to fostering the promotion of foreign investment. Its terms are framed as a proactive statement – 'to promote', 'to create', 'to stimulate' – rather than prescriptions for a passive behavior of the State or avoidance of prejudicial conduct to the investors."[12]

I can also mention the program of good governance that no State in the world is capable of guaranteeing detailed in *Tecmed*.[13] Another only slightly less demanding but still far-reaching conception implies that the State is under an obligation to stabilize the legal and business framework in which the foreign investment was made. For example, in the case of *Occidental Exploration and Production Co. v. Ecuador*, the tribunal stated this expressly:

> "Although fair and equitable treatment is not defined in the Treaty, the Preamble clearly records the agreement of the parties that such treatment 'is desirable in order to maintain a stable framework for investment and maximum effective

---

10. For a similar assimilation in doctrine between indirect expropriation and FET, see the following citation; "The major innovation of the 'tantamount' clause, found in substance in almost all BITs, therefore consists in extending the concept of indirect expropriation to an egregious failure to create or maintain the normative favourable conditions' in the host state". W. Michael REISMAN and Robert SLOANE, "Indirect Expropriation and Its Valuation in the BIT Generation", 74 Brit. Y.B. Int'l Law (2003) at p. 15.
11. Lucy REED and Daina BRAY, "Fair and Equitable Treatment: Fairly and Equitably Applied in Lieu of Unlawful Indirect Expropriation?" in Arthur Rovine, ed., *Contemporary Issues in International Arbitration and Mediation* (Martinus Nijhoff 2008) pp. 13-28.
12. *MTD Equity Sdn. Bhd. and MTD Chile S.A. v. Republic of Chile* (ICSID Case No. ARB/01/7), Award of 25 May 2004, para. 113.
13. *Técnicas Medioambientales Tecmed v. México* (ICSID Case No. ARB(AF)/00/2), Decision of 29 May 2003, para. 114.

utilization of economic resources'. The stability of the legal and business framework is thus an essential element of fair and equitable treatment."[14]

It is clear that different tribunals do not have a uniform interpretation of the FET standard, and I think it would be desirable to arrive at a more or less generally accepted concept. Saying that a more or less generally accepted concept should be arrived at does not, however, necessarily mean a content that cannot be adapted to circumstances.

The suggestion made this morning to link FET to the concept of reasonableness and proportionality seems to me very promising. I consider that the repeated statements of arbitral tribunals – which are important for the protection of foreign investors – that "the stability of the legal and business framework is an essential element of fair and equitable treatment" should be understood not as implying an obligation never to change this framework, but as meaning that no unreasonable or unjustified modification of the legal framework should be made.

In conclusion, I will agree with our speaker and accept that "we are where we are". But I also think we have to go forward and improve the system, on the basis of the idea that "*qui n'avance pas recule*", which I might translate by saying that "he or she who does not go forward, steps backward". Let's be optimistic and go forward!

---

14. *Occidental Exploration and Production Co. v. Ecuador* (LCIA Case No. UN 3467), Final Award of 1 July 2004 (UNCITRAL) para. 183.

# Working Group A

# Investment Treaty Arbitration and Commercial Arbitration:

# Are They Different Ball Games?

# Introduction to Investment Treaty Arbitration and Commercial Arbitration: Are They Different Ball Games?

*V.V. Veeder QC[*]*

| TABLE OF CONTENTS | Page |
|---|---|
| I. Two Tribal Traditions | 91 |
| II. The Legal Regime | 91 |
| III. The Practical Conduct | 92 |

## I. TWO TRIBAL TRADITIONS

Over the last forty years, as bilateral investment treaties proliferated exponentially and treaty-based arbitrations ballooned between private investors and states, arbitrators and practitioners entered this new field both from the world of international commercial arbitration and the world of public international law. Today, these two tribes of "privatistes" and "publicistes" work behind the same plough in peaceful co-existence, more or less. Yet the question arises whether such apparent co-existence obscures fundamental differences between the two tribal traditions to which we should now pay greater attention for the future of treaty-based investment arbitration. This ICCA panel examined that question from two separate viewpoints: (i) the legal regime governing treaty-based arbitrations between investors and states; and (ii) the practical conduct of such arbitrations by arbitrators and legal practitioners.

## II. THE LEGAL REGIME

International commercial arbitration is the creature of a private law agrement resulting from the consent of the parties, although its effectiveness also rests upon a patchwork of national and international laws. The applicable legal norms will usually be drawn from a wide variety of national legal systems. Treaty-based arbitration between an investor and a state is a creature of international law; and its applicable norms will usually be drawn from both conventional and customary international law but rarely from a national law (although the resulting award may rely on national laws to ensure its ultimate effectiveness). The question here arises whether these different characteristics require different juridical treatment in principle, or whether the only material difference arises from the involvement of a state as a disputant party. Whatever the answer, is it still appropriate to conduct treaty-based arbitrations under procedures designed for international commercial arbitration; or do we now need to generate specialist procedures (other than ICSID) expressly designed for investor-state disputes under treaty-based arbitrations, such as a modified form of the UNCITRAL Arbitration Rules?

---

[*] Essex Court Chambers, London; Member of ICCA.

Campbell McLachlan addresses these issues in his report below (pp. 95-145), to which Bernard Hanotiau and Brooks Daly (with Fedelma Claire Smith) respond from their different perspectives (pp. 146-150 and 151-164, respectively).

III. PRACTICAL CONDUCT

There are distinct challenges for practitioners and arbitrators in conducting a treaty-based arbitration involving a state as compared to an international commercial arbitration involving private parties only. For example, what are the different strategic and tactical choices for the legal practitioner advising the investor or the state? And what different problems await the unwary, beginning with the choice of arbitral procedure, the forum, waiting-periods, the selection of arbitrators, the pursuit of contract-based claims (as distinct from a breach of treaty), the resort to domestic courts, the exhaustion of local remedies, the distinctions between jurisdiction, admissibility, liabilty, causation and quantum, together with all the practical issues involving a state as a party, including legal representation, document production, interim measures, counterclaims, testimony by officials etc. The list is almost endless.

Abby Cohen Smutny addresses many of these issues in her report below (pp. 167-177), to which Sarah François-Poncet (with Caline Mouawad) and Toby Landau respond in their own particular ways (pp. 178-186 and 187-205, respectively).

It is regrettable that it has not been possible here to reproduce the many observations from the floor: delegates attending this session provided a rich variety of interesting and contrasting comments. As was apparent then and confirmed by the papers below, it is evident that this particular topic does not lend itself to any easy or comprehensive solutions – at least not yet.

# Working Group A

# Investment Treaty Arbitration and Commercial Arbitration:

# Are They Different Ball Games?

# 3. The Legal Framework

# Investment Treaty Arbitration: The Legal Framework

*Campbell McLachlan QC**

TABLE OF CONTENTS | Page
--- | ---
I. The Investment Dispute Conundrum | 95
II. Rationale and Context for Investment Treaty Arbitration | 103
III. Lex Causae | 108
IV. Lex Arbitri | 123
V. Conclusions | 142

I. THE INVESTMENT DISPUTE CONUNDRUM

*1. The Perennial Problem of Investment Protection*

In 1910, just under a century ago, Elihu Root, the founding President of the American Society of International Law, devoted his address to the Society to the subject of the legal protection of foreign investment. He said this:[1]

> "The great accumulation of capital in the money centers of the world, far in excess of the opportunities for home investment, has lead to a great increase of international investment extending over the entire surface of the earth.... All these forms of peaceful interpenetration among the nations of the earth naturally contribute their instances of citizens justly or unjustly dissatisfied with the treatment they receive in foreign countries."

Four years previously in 1906, John Salmond, who is remembered today principally for his works on Jurisprudence and Torts, chose to devote his inaugural lecture in New Zealand to the subject of international law. He closed his remarks with a comment on the potential of arbitration:[2]

> "Few people realised how often arbitration has been employed in international disputes.... It was an impressive thing to see nations with great armies and navies at command, voluntarily submitting their right and lawful claims to a tribunal and

---

* LL B (Hons) (Well), Ph D (Lond), Dip (c.l.) Hag Acad Int'l Law; Professor of Law, Victoria University of Wellington; Bankside Chambers (Auckland) and Essex Court Chambers (London); Member, ICSID Panel of Arbitrators and ICC Court of Arbitration. The writer acknowledges with thanks the research assistance of Jack Wass in the preparation of this Report.
1. Elihu ROOT, "The Basis of Protection to Citizens Residing Abroad", 4 AJIL (1910) p. 517 at pp. 518-519.
2. John SALMOND, "If Germany Came to New Zealand", reprinted in 30 VUWLR (1999) p. 489 at p. 492.

faithfully and honourably performing the judgments given against them. The fact that this had actually taken place in so many cases was full of hope and promise for the future."

There is nothing new in the phenomenon of international investment; or in the problems posed by it for international law; or even in the use of international arbitration as a means of resolving investment disputes.

Indeed, international law has remained at the heart of the law applicable to the resolution of such disputes, despite the obvious relevance (and sometimes express choice) of host state law to govern the parties' contractual relations. Thus, in the *cause célèbre* of the *Lena Goldfields* arbitration,[3] an international arbitral tribunal sitting in 1930 held the Soviet Government liable to pay a massive £13 million (worth some £350 million in modern terms) for the expropriation of the Lena Goldfields concession. Although the concession contract was governed by Russian law, the tribunal held that it would apply both Russian law and, in any difference of interpretation, international law, to the determination of the parties' rights and liabilities. This in turn led it into an enquiry as to the "general principles of law common to civilized nations".[4]

But *Lena Goldfields* also stands as a reminder of what has changed in the intervening period. The Soviet Government would have disappointed Sir John Salmond's hopes. It never honoured the award. Whatever its contribution to jurisprudence, *Lena Goldfields* remains, in Veeder's atmospheric words, a "baleful monument to the absolute power of the State to thwart the consensual process of international arbitration".[5]

2. *The Distinctive Nature of the Investment Treaty Arbitration Solution*

The great achievement, then, of the latter half of the twentieth century in this field has been to provide two procedural innovations, which in combination have proved of great potency in transforming the landscape of investment arbitration. Both of these developments will be so well known as not to need lengthy explanation.

First, the conclusion in 1965 of the ICSID Convention,[6] which created the International Centre for Settlement of Investment Disputes, provided for the first time a dedicated forum for the arbitration of such disputes. Two factors ensured its success as a forum. First, it had been created by states by treaty as a self-contained and specialist system for the resolution of investment disputes. At a stroke, this took investment disputes outside the sometimes messy context of national courts, and created an international law obligation upon states to comply with awards, an obligation which was helpfully underscored by the active oversight of the World Bank. But secondly, however, it committed states to nothing in terms of resolution of actual disputes, since (just as in

---

3. *Lena Goldfields Ltd v. Soviet Union*, The Times, 3 September 1930 (1950-1951) 36 Cornell LQ p. 42.
4. Statute of the Permanent Court of International Justice, Series D- No. 1 (1926) Art. 38(3).
5. V.V. VEEDER, "The *Lena Goldfields* Arbitration: The Historical Roots of Three Ideas", 47 ICLQ (1998) p. 747.
6. Convention on the Settlement of Investment Disputes between States and Nationals of Other States (ICSID Convention) (signed 18 March 1965, entered into force 14 October 1966) 575 UNTS 159.

the case of the International Court of Justice (ICJ)) mere ratification of the Convention did not confer any jurisdiction upon the Centre or its arbitral tribunals. ICSID tribunals were to have no jurisdiction save by the consent of the parties, under Art. 25 of the Convention.[7]

Thus ICSID could have remained a Sleeping Beauty of international arbitration (as indeed it largely was for the first thirty years of its life), had it not been for a second parallel development, namely the conclusion since 1959 of some 2,500 bilateral investment treaties (BITs) (joined now also by free trade agreements and a growing number of regional multilateral agreements) which enshrined basic investment rights, and conferred upon investors for the first time a direct right to enforce those rights by arbitration. It was the realization some two decades later of the practical potential of those treaties to provide the basis for state consent to arbitration for the purpose of the ICSID Convention's Art. 25, which unleashed the peculiar power of investment treaty arbitration. The tribunal in the very first such case, *Asian Agricultural Products v. Sri Lanka*, was constituted just twenty years ago in 1988.[8]

Undoubtedly, investment treaty arbitration has unique features which set it apart from commercial arbitration. The first, memorably described by Jan Paulsson in his seminal article as "Arbitration Without Privity",[9] stems from the fact that the parties' consent to arbitrate is not formed by the *consensus ad idem* of a contract. On the contrary, the state makes a standing offer to arbitrate by treaty, which is accepted by the investor when his claim is filed. Secondly, investment treaty arbitration always consists in the prosecution of a private claim against the state. The foreign investor is always the claimant, and the host state is always the respondent.[10] This follows from the very nature of the rights being enforced, which are conferred by the state on investors as a result of an international agreement between states. The nature of the claim thus bears at least as many parallels, as Professor Geneviève Burdeau has suggested,[11] to a human rights complaint before the European or Inter-American Court of Human Rights as it does to a commercial arbitration.

Investment treaty arbitration was conceived in part as a response to the shortcomings of the public international law process of diplomatic protection. Indeed, it has grown to such an extent that the ICJ commented in its decision of June 2007 in the *Diallo* case that:[12]

---

7. See MCLACHLAN, SHORE and WEINIGER, *International Investment Arbitration: Substantive Principles* (Oxford University Press 2007) [1.05].
8. *Asian Agricultural Products [AAPL] v. Democratic Socialist Republic of Sri Lanka*, Award (ICSID, 1990, El-Kosheri P, Goldman and Adante) 4 ICSID Rep 245.
9. Jan PAULSSON, "Arbitration Without Privity", 10 ICSID Rev–FILJ (1995) p. 232.
10. Although it may be a counter-claimant, where the counterclaim has a sufficiently close connection with the claim: *Saluka Investments BV v. Czech Republic*, Decision on Jurisdiction over the Czech Republic's Counterclaim (UNICTRAL, 2004, Watts C, Behrens and Fortier).
11. G. BURDEAU, "*Nouvelles Perspectives pour l'Arbitrage dans le Contentieux Economique intéressant l'État*", Revue de l'Arbitrage (1995) p. 3.
12. *Case concerning Ahmadou Sadio Diallo (Guinea v. Congo)*, Preliminary Objections, ICJ General List No. 103, 24 May 2007 (the *Diallo* case), [88].

"... in contemporary international law, the protection of the rights of companies and the rights of their shareholders, and the settlement of the associated disputes, are essentially governed by bilateral or multilateral agreements.... In that context, the role of diplomatic protection somewhat faded...."

But it also represents a conscious move away from a contract model to a treaty model for the resolution of fundamental investment disputes. Only a minority of investors ever had concession contracts with the host state. There were in any event, as those who remember the great oil nationalization arbitrations of the 1970s will recall, considerable practical and legal difficulties in dealing with the misuse of sovereign power within a contractual framework.

3.   *A Fragmented System of Dispute Resolution*

*a.   ICSID's deliberate adoption of arbitration as dispute settlement mechanism*
Yet, despite the treaty context, investment treaty dispute settlement uses the forms and procedures of commercial arbitration. This was axiomatic in the formation of the ICSID Convention. The account given by Aron Broches (General Counsel of the World Bank at the time and principal architect of the Convention) of the thinking which led to the creation of the ICSID Convention is illuminating. Broches casts the reasoning process in three steps. First, absent an agreement, the investor's only direct recourse against the host state was governed by local law. Second, if no redress could be found through the exercise of local remedies, the investor would have to petition his own government for diplomatic protection. Yet there may be many political reasons why the home state would not wish to intervene. Third, some large investors had negotiated arbitration agreements with host states, but these might be repudiated by the host state, or otherwise prove ineffective. He concludes:

"The analysis of the problem pointed the way to the solution, namely arrangements, embodied in a treaty, which would ensure that arbitration agreements voluntarily entered into would be implemented."[13]

Such arbitration proceedings would be ones

"... to which the host country and investors would be parties on an equal procedural footing, without either requiring or permitting the intervention of the investor's national State".[14]

In this way, then, the ICSID dispute settlement system represented the conscious adoption of the forms and procedures of contractual arbitration which preceded it, with its emphasis on *direct* rights of action by private claimants to the exclusion of the home

---

13. Aron BROCHES, "The Convention on the Settlement of Investment Disputes between States and Nationals of other States", 136 *Recueil des Cours* (1972) p. 331 at p. 335.
14. *Ibid.* p. 334.

state;[15] on the specific consent of both parties as the prerequisite to the jurisdiction of the arbitrators;[16] and on party autonomy in the selection of the applicable law[17] and the arbitral procedure.[18]

*b.    Contrast with the settlement of trade disputes*
In all of these respects, the system for the resolution of investment disputes which has emerged today is entirely unlike that which applies in the closely related field of trade law. The settlement of trade disputes under the procedures of the Dispute Settlement Understanding of the World Trade Organization (WTO) admits only State parties as litigants, however close may be the interests of private corporations behind the claim. It involves a standing Appellate Body, with a full right of appeal on matters of law.[19] The law and procedures applied are those specified by the Covered Agreements, which are not matters of choice by the parties.[20]

*c.    Influence of public international arbitration*
Yet, of course, the notion of arbitration as a means of resolving disputes was never the sole preserve of commerce. States had known arbitration as a means of resolving inter-state disputes, including claims of diplomatic protection relating to the property of aliens at least since the Jay Treaty in 1794 and probably before.[21] Indeed, arbitration was the classical means of resolving inter-state disputes, which long pre-dates the existence of standing international courts. Thus, when states first turned to establish a standing dispute settlement institution under the Hague Convention for the Pacific Settlement of International Disputes 1899,[22] it was an arbitration institution, the Permanent Court of Arbitration (PCA), which they established. By contrast, it was only after World War I that it proved possible to establish a Permanent Court of International Justice (PCIJ), the predecessor of the ICJ. Thus, the concept of arbitration as a consensual means of resolving disputes was as much a part of the landscape of *public* international law as it was of *private* international law at the time the ICSID Convention was concluded. As will be seen, in some of its procedures, notably the annulment of awards,[23] the ICSID

---

15. Art. 27 ICSID Convention.
16. Art. 25 ICSID Convention.
17. Art. 42 ICSID Convention.
18. Art. 44 ICSID Convention.
19. Art. 17 Understanding on Rules and Procedures governing the Settlement of Disputes (DSU), signed 15 April 1994, Annex 2 to Marrakesh Agreement establishing the World Trade Organization 1868 UNTS 186.
20. *Ibid.*, Arts. 1 and 12.
21. See Alexander STUYT, *Survey of International Arbitrations 1794-1989*, 3rd edn. (Kluwer, Boston 1990); John COLLIER and Vaughan LOWE, *The Settlement of Disputes in International Law* (OUP, Oxford 1999) pp. 31-39; John MERRILLS, *International Dispute Settlement*, 3rd edn., (Cambridge UP, Cambridge) Chap. 5; Christine GRAY and Benedict KINGSBURY, "Developments in Dispute Settlement: Inter-state Arbitration Since 1945", BYIL (1992) p. 97.
22. UKTS 9 (1901), Cd 798; 1 Bevans 230; 187 Con TS 429.
23. Art. 52 ICSID Convention.

Convention consciously borrows from public international arbitration, as well as from international commercial arbitration.

### d. Influence of commercial arbitration in non-ICSID arbitration

Yet, if the influence of the approach and procedures of commercial arbitration has shaped ICSID, such an influence is even more marked in the significant number of investment cases which continue to be decided by arbitral tribunals outside the ICSID system. Many bilateral investment treaties and some significant multilateral instruments, such as the Energy Charter Treaty,[24] designedly offer a "cafeteria-style" choice to investors of a range of dispute resolution options, including arbitration under the aegis of commercial arbitration institutions and ad hoc arbitration under UNCITRAL Rules.[25] Indeed the most recent statistics from UNCTAD suggest that some thirty-eight per cent of known investment arbitrations to date have been held outside the ICSID system.[26]

### e. The perils of fragmentation

So what this leads to is a highly fragmented form of dispute resolution. There is no International Court of Justice, or WTO Appellate Body, to supervise, on a standing basis, the operation of the system as a whole. Further, the very bilateral source of the obligations being enforced offers the prospect of infinitely various treaty provisions. Even differing interpretations of the same provision may be justified, where the object and purpose of the treaty is different, or the *travaux* or subsequent practice of the parties suggests a different result. This has led a number of tribunals to conclude that:[27] "Each tribunal is sovereign, and may retain ... a different solution for resolving the same problem."

The potential difficulties of such a highly fragmented system of adjudication are not to be underestimated. In the short history of investment treaty arbitration to date, there have already been cases where two tribunals, sitting under different treaties, have come to diametrically opposite conclusions on the same facts;[28] or where different tribunals have come to diametrically opposite conclusions on the same issue, even where they share members in common.[29]

---

24. Energy Charter Treaty (signed 17 December 1994, entered into force 16 April 1988) 2080 UNTS 100.
25. MCLACHLAN, SHORE and WEINIGER, supra fn. 7, [3.09].
26. United Nations Conference on Trade and Development (UNCTAD) IIA Monitor No. 1 (2008) "Latest developments in investor-State dispute Settlement", UN Doc. UNCTAD/WEB/ITE/IIA/2008/3.
27. *AES Corp v. Argentine Republic* (ICSID Case No. ARB/02/17), Jurisdiction (ICSID, 2005, Dupuy P, Böckstiegel and Janeiro) para. 30.
28. *Lauder v. Czech Republic*, Final Award (UNCITRAL, 2001, Briner C, Cutler and Klein) 9 ICSID Rep 62; cf. *CME Czech Republic BV (The Netherlands) v. Czech Republic*, Partial Award (UNCITRAL, 2001, Kühn C, Schwebel and Hàndl) 9 ICSID Rep 121.
29. *L G & E Energy Corp v. Argentine Republic*, Decision on Liability (ICSID, 2006, de Maekelt P, Rezek and van den Berg) 18 World Trade & Arb Mat (2006, no. 6) p. 199; cf. *Enron Corp v. Argentine Republic* (ICSID Case No. ARB/01/3), Award (ICSID, 2007, Orrego Vicuña P, van den Berg and Tschanz).

The fragmented nature of the system has also given rise to serious debates about the applicable law and procedure. There have been doctrinal disagreements within tribunals, and with State parties, about the extent to which the treaty standards are autonomous or rather restate customary international law.[30] Within civil society, investment arbitration has become, on occasion, an issue of great political moment, giving rise to calls for a new balance to be struck between host state rights and those of investors;[31] as well as demands for greater transparency and public participation in the process. Some have suggested that the time has come for a Court of Appeals for investment arbitration cases.[32] Others have called for more radical measures. It is not without significance that, just a year ago, the State of Bolivia chose to denounce the ICSID Convention and thus become the first state to withdraw from the system which now encompasses some 143 states.

After two decades of experience with the first wave of investment treaty jurisprudence, it is important, therefore to take the time to take stock of what has been accomplished and where the system should go from here. The task of this Report is the less ambitious (but perhaps no less difficult) one of seeking to frame that debate by teasing out what is really different about investment treaty arbitration in terms of the applicable law, both as to substance (the lex causae) and procedure (the lex arbitri).

4.  *International Law Solutions to the Balance of Private and Public Interests*

The central proposition of this Report is that the core task of investment arbitration is the enduring one of finding a proper balance between two equally valid and important interests: the protection of the private rights of the investor and the legitimate public interest of the host state. As the late Sir Robert Jennings and Sir Arthur Watts put it:[33] "The requirements of international law in this field ... represent an attempt at an accommodation between the conflicting interests involved."

This task is not an easy one. It never has been. But it is not to be solved by the creation of a unified monolithic system *à la* the WTO. There does not appear to be any realistic prospect of this either in procedural terms, given the difficulties in revising a multilateral convention with as many State parties as the ICSID Convention, or in substantive terms, given the fate of the Multilateral Agreement on Investment a decade ago.[34]

---

30. See generally MCLACHLAN, "Investment Treaties and General International Law", 57 ICLQ (2008) p. 361.
31. See examples discussed in Guillermo AGUILAR ALVAREZ and William W. PARK, "The New Face of Investment Arbitration: NAFTA Chapter 11", 28 Yale JIL (2003) p. 365.
32. See the debates reported in Federico ORTINO, Audley SHEPPARD and Hugo WARNER, *Investment Treaty Law: Current Issues*, Volume 1 (British Institute of Comparative and International Law 2006) and Karl SAUVANT, *Appeals Mechanism in International Investment Disputes* (OUP, NY 2008).
33. Robert JENNINGS and Arthur WATTS, eds., *Oppenheim's International Law*, 9th edn. (Longman, London 1992) p. 933. See also MCLACHLAN, SHORE and WEINIGER, supra fn. 7, [1.61].
34. Multilateral Agreement on Investment – Final Unadopted Negotiating Draft, OECD, 22 April 1998 DAFFE/MAI (98) &/REV 1. See also MCLACHLAN, SHORE and WEINIGER, supra fn. 7, [7.58].

But the fragmented system of investment arbitration is not a recipe for anarchy. It is necessary to take a much more rigorous approach to the application of a consistent approach by way of legal method and legal reasoning to the application of the law in investment treaty cases; and identifying the common general principles of international law which underpin this field. In short, this Report advocates taking the "international" in international investment arbitration seriously. This will not make the hard choices go away. But it might provide a more coherent and predictable way of dealing with them.

There is a parallel to be drawn here with the field of international commercial arbitration itself. After all, commercial arbitration has always had to deal with a high degree of fragmentation. The possible applicable leges causae and leges arbitri in international commercial arbitration are at least as various as there are states in the world. Yet the field of international commercial arbitration (beginning with its own master treaty, the 1958 New York Convention)[35] has found an increasing degree of convergence around common principles, especially through the promulgation of model laws and rules which have in turn driven the reform of national laws and the rules of arbitral institutions. It is probably no longer an exaggeration to say that international commercial arbitration has become its own legal system, albeit one which ultimately depends for enforcement upon the cooperation of national courts. While such a contention has long been championed by some scholars,[36] it has now also received judicial recognition at the highest level. Thus the Supreme Court of Canada has held that "Arbitration is part of no state's judicial system.... The arbitrator has no allegiance or connection to any single country.... In short, arbitration is a creature that owes its existence to the will of the parties alone."[37] So, too, the French *Cour de Cassation* held that "... an international arbitral award – which is not anchored to any national legal order – is an international judicial decision...".[38] These observations have considerable implications for the process of arbitration generally. But investment treaty arbitration faces an additional challenge which is quite unlike that of commercial arbitration: that of finding a convergence of approach on substantive law, as well as on procedure.

The overall theme of this Report will be developed by reference to five general points:

(1) *Rationale:* Investment treaty arbitration was born out of an awareness of the limitations of existing methods of resolving disputes between commercial parties and sovereigns. Understanding the problem which investment arbitration was intended to solve may shed light on the distinctive natures of its solutions.

(2) *Context:* However much the ICSID Convention and investment treaties may have sought to insulate investment disputes, they nevertheless take place within a wider set

---

35. Convention on the Recognition and Enforcement of Foreign Arbitral Awards (New York Convention) (adopted 10 June 1958, entered into force 7 June 1959) 330 UNTS 38.
36. Emmanuel GAILLARD, *Aspects Philosophiques du Droit de l'Arbitrage International* (Martinus Nijhoff Publishers, Leiden 2007).
37. *Dell Computer Corp v. Union des consommateurs* (2007) 284 DLR (4th) 577, at [51].
38. *PT Putrabali Adyamulia v. Est Epices*, 29 June 2007, 24 Arb Int (2008) p. 293 at p. 295 (noted PINSOLLE, 24 Arb Int (2008) p. 277).

of legal relationships between investor and host state. To use James Crawford's suggestive phrase "there is no such *place* as the 'international plane'".[39]

(3) *Lex causae:* Tribunals may owe their jurisdiction to the terms of a particular bilateral investment treaty. But that does not mean that the law applicable to determination of the merits is so limited. Treaty rights are located within a matrix of applicable law, which includes a role for host state law, as well as a broader set of international law principles beyond the specific terms of the treaty. The question of the law applicable to the substance turns out, on examination, to require a more sophisticated legal reasoning approach, which combines choice of law analysis with techniques of interpretation.

(4) *Lex arbitri:* There are still substantial conceptual differences in the lex arbitri depending upon whether an investment treaty dispute is to be resolved within or outside the ICSID system. But these may be reducing in a process of convergence on common principles for investment arbitration generally.

(5) *Conclusions:* Finally, the Report concludes with a statement of principles, which may be derived from the foregoing analysis, as to the distinctive characteristics of the law applicable to investment treaty arbitration.

II. RATIONALE AND CONTEXT FOR INVESTMENT TREATY ARBITRATION

The development of investment treaty arbitration was spurred by a widely held view that the existing methods of resolving investment disputes had significant shortcomings, for states as well as for investors, and that a new solution was needed. This point may be made good both as to procedure, and as regards substance.

*1. Procedure*

Before the advent of investment treaty arbitration, disputes between foreign investors and host states could only be resolved: (a) by litigation in the courts of the host state itself; (b) failing satisfaction there, by the pursuit by the home state of an international law claim of diplomatic protection; or exceptionally, where the investor had a concession contract with the host state; (c) by contractual arbitration.

The shortcomings of diplomatic protection are well known:[40] the need to exhaust local remedies before resort could be made to an international claim;[41] the restrictive rules on nationality of corporations – the nemesis of Belgium's claim against Spain in

---

39. James CRAWFORD, "Treaty and Contract in Investment Arbitration: The 22nd Freshfields Lecture on International Arbitration", 29 November 2007, p. 2. Available online at <www.lcil.cam.ac.uk>.
40. The International Law Commission (ILC) has recently completed its codification of the principles of the customary international law of diplomatic protection: ILC "Diplomatic Protection: Text of the Draft Articles with Commentaries Thereto" (DUGARD, Special Rapporteur) in *Report of the International Law Commission on its Fifty-Eighth Session (1 May – 9 June, 3 July – 11 August 2006)*, Official Records of the General Assembly Sixty-First Session, Supplement No. 10, UN Doc. A/61/10, pp. 22-100.
41. *Elettronica Sicula SpA (ELSI) Case (United States of America v. Italy)* 1989 ICJ Rep 15.

*Barcelona Traction*;[42] the absence of an enforceable obligation on the part of the home state to pursue such a claim, and the built-in deterrents in terms of the potential for collateral diplomatic fallout in doing so; and the fact that the existence of a claim to diplomatic protection did not necessarily mean that a forum would be available in which the dispute could be resolved, still less did it ensure that any award which was rendered would be enforceable.

But it should also be recalled that commercial arbitration was seen as an uncertain home for investment claims:

(a) In the first place, only a small minority of investors would have a concession contract with the state, providing for arbitration.

(b) Even in those cases, negotiation of the issues of governing law and forum could quickly become highly sensitive – as the investor's wish to secure an independent forum came up against the state's demands of national sovereignty.

(c) The experience of investors and states on choice of governing law had been uncertain at best. As Professor El-Kosheri has recently recalled,[43] decisions such as the *Abu Dhabi* oil concession arbitration of 1951, in which Lord Asquith dismissed the application of the *Shari'a* law because he regarded it as primitive,[44] were rightly regarded as deeply offensive in non-Western countries. By the same token, techniques employed by investors in order to seek to limit the ability of host states to change the law to their benefit, such as stabilization clauses, were of doubtful effect.

(d) Finally, there were significant doubts about enforcement, in particular in view of the plea of sovereign immunity in national courts. The actual experience of enforcing awards in national courts against sovereigns was highly variable, as witnessed by the range of conflicting decisions reached in the *LIAMCO v. Libya* affair.[45]

For all of these reasons, the advent of the ICSID Convention was seen as a breakthrough, providing a secure and self-contained method of resolving such disputes, in which some of the awesome relics of the past could finally be laid to rest. At the heart of the new regime was a series of provisions which confirmed the self-contained nature of its procedures:

(a) *Exclusion of other remedies:* Art. 26 provides that "Consent of the parties to arbitration under this Convention shall, unless otherwise stated, be deemed consent to such arbitration to the exclusion of any other remedy." This provision is reinforced by the exclusion of diplomatic protection under Art. 27.

---

42. *Barcelona Traction, Light and Power Co Ltd Case* (New Application: 1962) (*Belgium v. Spain*) (second Phase)1970 ICJ Rep 3.
43. Nadia DARWAZEH and Professor Ahmed Sadek EL-KOSHERI, "Arbitration in the Arab World: An Interview with Professor Ahmed Sadek EL-KOSHERI", 25 J Intl Arb (2008) p. 203 at p. 205.
44. *Petroleum Dev. (Trucial Coast) Ltd v. Sheikh of Abu Dhabi*, (1953) 18 ILR 149.
45. *Libyan American Oil Co (LIAMCO) v. Libyan Arab Republic*, (Ad Hoc Arb, 1977, Mahmassani) 62 ILR (1982) 140. The enforcement cases are discussed in W. Laurence CRAIG, William W. PARK and Jan PAULSSON, *International Chamber of Commerce Arbitration*, 3rd edn. (Oceana, Dobbs Ferry, New York 2004) [36.03].

(b) *Self-contained procedure*: Art. 44 creates a self-contained regime for the lex arbitri, consisting (save as the parties otherwise agree) of the Convention and the Arbitration Rules which leaves no room for the application of the national law at the seat of the arbitration, which would otherwise be applicable.[46]

(c) *Self-contained review of awards:* Art. 52 creates an internal procedure for the review and annulment of awards by an ad hoc Committee established under the provisions of the Convention. Contracting States agree, by Art. 53, to exclude any appeal or other remedy against an award. By contrast, outside ICSID, an arbitral award, including one rendered under an investment treaty, is potentially subject to review in the courts of the seat,[47] and also, upon an application for enforcement, by the court from which enforcement is sought under the provisions of Art. V of the 1958 New York Convention.

(d) *Enforcement obligation:* Under Art. 53, the parties to an ICSID arbitration award assume a specific obligation to comply with it. This is reinforced by the obligation on all Contracting States under Art. 54 to "recognize an award rendered pursuant to this Convention as binding and enforce the pecuniary obligations imposed by that award within its territories as if it were a final judgment of a court in that State". This obligation is independent of the provisions for the enforcement of non-ICSID arbitration awards under the New York Convention.

2.   *Law*

If the ICSID Convention was significant in shifting the context for investment disputes procedurally beyond the shortcomings of what had gone before, the advent of investment treaties sought to do the same thing for the applicable substantive standards. It should not be forgotten that, even before World War II, the "High Noon" era for the application of customary law rules on the treatment of aliens in diplomatic protection claims, there was widespread dissent amongst states as to the applicable rules. Latin American states in particular opposed the imposition of any standard beyond that of national treatment.[48]

This sensitivity has remained. Thus, the International Law Commission (ILC) in its work on both state responsibility and diplomatic protection took the view that there was no realistic prospect of securing a consensus of states on the primary rules on the treatment of aliens.[49] There has also been a repeated failure to find multilateral

---

46. Christoph SCHREUER, *The ICSID Convention: A Commentary* (Cambridge UP, Cambridge 2001) p. 666.
47. As in *Occidental Exploration & Production Co v. Republic of Ecuador* [2005] EWCA Civ 1116, [2006] 2 WLR 70 and *Czech Republic v. European Media Ventures SA* [2007] EWHC 2851 (Comm.), [2008] 1 Lloyd's Rep 186.
48. For discussion see: MCLACHLAN SHORE and WEINIGER, supra fn. 7, [7.37]-[7.63].
49. International Law Commission "Responsibilities of States for Internationally Wrongful Acts: Text of the Draft Articles with Commentaries Thereto" (CRAWFORD, Special Rapporteur) in *Report of the International Law Commission of its Fifty-third Session (23 April - 1 June and 2 July - 10 August 2001)*, Official Records of the General Assembly Fifty-sixth Session, Supplement No. 10, UN Doc. A/56/10, 59, 61. For an historical explanation of the reasons which led the ILC to abandon work on the wider codification of the law on the treatment of aliens, as had been proposed by the First Rapporteur, Amador, see: CRAWFORD *The International Law Commission's Articles on State*

agreement on investment standards, most recently with the demise of the Multilateral Agreement on Investment in 1998.[50]

Against that background, both capital-exporting and capital-importing states sought a new beginning by way of treaty provision. Yet – and this is the paradox at the heart of investment treaty law – they did so often in terms which were linked to general international law, either because:

(a) The terms used were a codification of what the rule of custom was said to be – as in the case of expropriation; or
(b) Because the test was expressly stated to be in accordance with international law (or, to use the language of the French model BIT *"conformément aux principes du Droit international"*);[51] or,
(c) Because, as in the case of the new standard of "fair and equitable treatment" the rule performed the *function* of the old minimum standard of treatment, but dressed in new and more progressive garb, and without the baggage which the old law had carried.

Further, despite the huge number of bilateral agreements, with all of the attendant possibility of diversity of language, there is a striking degree of similarity in the text of the core substantive protections. For all of these reasons, the resort to bilateralism does not serve to isolate each treaty regime from the hinterland of common principles and of general international law.

3.  *Party Autonomy*

The second general point is that, both on substance and procedure, the system of investment arbitration necessarily operates within a matrix of other applicable laws and dispute resolution options. Indeed, these alternatives are often hard-wired into the treaty framework, either respecting the role of party autonomy or respecting the complementary functions of national and international law.

The principle of party autonomy finds expression within investment arbitration both in choice of forum and in choice of law:

(a) *Choice of Forum:* Many investment treaties offer to investors a choice of fora in which to bring a claim of breach of treaty. Art. 26 of the Energy Charter Treaty represents a high water mark in this approach, offering a choice between host state courts, contractually agreed methods of dispute resolution, and arbitration under ICSID, the ICSID Additional Facility, the UNCITRAL Rules or the Arbitration Rules of the Stockholm Chamber of Commerce. Even within the ICSID system, where the ICSID Arbitration Rules provide a detailed set of procedural provisions, Art. 44 expressly preserves the autonomy of the parties to agree upon procedural rules.

---

*Responsibility: Introduction, Text and Commentaries* (Cambridge UP, 2002) Chap 1.
50. Supra fn. 34.
51. Reprinted in MCLACHLAN, SHORE and WEINIGER, supra fn. 7, appendix 10, Art. 4.

(b) *Choice of Law:* Party autonomy in choice of applicable law is the point of departure for arbitrations between investors and host states, whether under UNICTRAL Arbitration Rules[52] or other sets of general arbitration rules,[53] or under Art. 42 of the ICSID Convention. Recent reported decisions have highlighted just how imaginative parties to concession contracts continue to be in crafting choice of law provisions: from a straight choice of host state law in *Lesotho Highlands v. Impregilo*[54] to the much more complex amalgam of international law and national law considered in the *Channel Tunnel* case,[55] and the combination of national law and principles of international commercial law referred to in *Svenska Petroleum v. Lithuania.*[56]

4.   *Complementary Roles of National and International Law*

In any event, investment arbitration takes place against a background of parallel application of both the national legal system of the host state and the international legal system:

(a) *Applicable Law:* International law does not purport to regulate numerous aspects of the ongoing relationship between the investor and the host state, which will properly be regulated by host state law. For ordinary working purposes, the investor's relationship with host state law will inevitably be primarily determined by host state law. The function of the international law standards enshrined in investment treaties is not to replace host state law. Rather it is to provide the fundamental protections of international law, in cases where the host state legal system has failed to secure such protections itself.

(b) *Dispute Resolution:* A similar point may be made about the fora for dispute resolution. Many disputes between investors and host states will continue to be resolved in other fora, including host state courts and commercial arbitration. Indeed, *contractual* as opposed to treaty disputes will primarily continue to be resolved in this way. That is why, following the distinction drawn as to applicable law between treaty and contract claims by the Annulment Committee in *Vivendi,* the Committee went on to hold that an investment tribunal "will give effect to any valid choice of forum clause in the contract" in relation to contractual claims.[57] This is not to say that contractual claims are necessarily outside the jurisdiction of an investment tribunal. After all, concession contracts were the paradigm case for ICSID jurisdiction when the ICSID Convention was

---

52. Art. 33(1) (first sentence).
53. E.g., Art. 17(1) (first sentence) International Chamber of Commerce (ICC) Rules of Arbitration.
54. *Lesotho Highlands Development Authority v. Impregilo SpA and others* [2005] UKHL 43, [2006] 1 AC 221.
55. *Channel Tunnel Group Ltd v. United Kingdom and France,* Partial Award (PCA, 30 January 2007) (Crawford P, Fortier, Guillaume, Millett and Paulsson) available at <www.pca-cpa.org> (accessed 30 July 2008).
56. *Svenska Petroleum Exploration AB v. Lithuania (No 2)* [2006] EWCA Civ 1529, [2007] 2 WLR 876.
57. *Compañia de Aguas del Aconquija SA and Vivendi Universal v. Argentina ("Vivendi"),* Decision on Annulment (ICSID, 2002, Fortier P, Crawford and Fernándex Rosas) 6 ICSID Rep 327 [98].

first drafted. Jurisdiction over contract claims may be conferred by treaty. But this does not relieve the tribunal of the responsibility, in upholding the contractual terms, to give effect to a more specific choice of forum for contractual claims, if the parties have made such a choice.

III.  LEX CAUSAE

The question of the law applicable to the substance of an investment treaty arbitration is a question of applicable law at two levels: (a) the identification, as a matter of choice of law, of the legal system or systems applicable to the issues before the tribunal; and (b) the determination, within any such system so designated as applicable, of the relevant rules necessary to decide the issue.

*1.  Choice of Law*

*a.  Art. 42(1) ICSID Convention*
The starting-point for any consideration of choice of law in investment treaty arbitration is Art. 42(1) of the ICSID Convention, which provides:

> "The Tribunal shall decide a dispute in accordance with such rules of law as may be agreed by the parties. In the absence of such agreement, the Tribunal shall apply the law of the Contracting State party to the dispute (including its rules on the conflict of laws) and such rules of international law as may be applicable."

The Report of the World Bank Directors on the conclusion of the Convention reminds us that: "The term 'international law' as used in this context should be understood in the sense given to it by Article 38(1) of the Statute of the International Court of Justice, allowance being made for the fact that Art. 38 was designed to apply to inter-State disputes."[58]

Discussion of choice of law has been somewhat limited in the context of *treaty* claims.[59] At first blush, this is surprising in view of the intense controversy which the formulation of Art. 42(1) of the ICSID Convention aroused during the drafting process, and the diversity of views expressed as to its meaning in the doctrine since its adoption.[60]

---

58. Report of the Executive Directors on the Convention on the Settlement of Investment Disputes between States and Nationals of other States (1993) 1 ICSID Rep 23, [40].
59. But see the excellent Report submitted by Meg KINNEAR, to the Montréal Congress of this Council: "Treaties as Agreements to Arbitrate: International Law as the Governing Law" in *International Arbitration 2006: Back to Basics?*, ICCA Congress Series no. 13 (2007) p. 401; as well as ANTONIO PARRA "Applicable Law in Investor-State Arbitration" in Arthur ROVINE, ed., *Contemporary Issues in International Arbitration and Mediation: the Fordham Papers I* (Martinus Nijhoff, Leiden 2008) and Ole SPIERMANN, "Applicable Law" in Peter MUCHLINSKI, Federico ORTINO and Christoph SCHREUER, *The Oxford Handbook of International Investment Law* (Oxford UP, Oxford 2008) p. 89.
60. See generally SCHREUER, *The ICSID Convention; A Commentary*, supra fn. 46, pp. 549-643.

Some analysts of applicable law in ICSID arbitration generally have endorsed a limited, supplemental and corrective role for international law under Art. 42(1). As Reisman put it: "... the intention of the majority was one of a default choice of law of the host State, unless the parties agreed otherwise. The legislative history certainly does not demonstrate an intent for a disguised superordination of international law in all cases".[61]

On the other hand, Gaillard and Banifatemi contend that international law need not be relegated to a corrective function. Instead, they envisage Art. 42(1) as giving the arbitrators the choice to apply international law, which: "... constitutes a body of substantive rules directly accessible to the tribunal without initial scrutiny into the law of the host State...".[62]

Sacerdoti has argued in the context of investment treaty arbitration that, since investment treaty tribunals are international tribunals applying rights under treaty, international law must always prevail and "... municipal laws are merely 'facts' to be ascertained".[63]

Consideration of the role of Art. 42 in investment treaty cases is complicated by the fact that, when the Convention was prepared, the dominant paradigm for investment arbitration was the concession contract claim. In that context, the Convention's provision for complete party autonomy in cases of agreement between the parties, with a default rule providing for a combination of host state law and international law in the absence of such agreement, makes sense, both as a practical matter and in principle. The negotiation of a contract provides both the investor and the host state with an opportunity to negotiate and agree upon applicable rules of law. In the absence of such agreement, the two natural candidates are host state law (which will, as has been seen, govern many aspects of the investment in any event) and international law. Broches commented in 1967 that: "From the standpoint of the effectiveness of the Convention, the most important thing was clearly to preserve the freedom of the tribunal to apply international law."[64]

What, then, is to be made of the choice of law process within investment treaty arbitration when the tribunal's jurisdiction depends not upon a contract, but upon a treaty, which is itself a creature of international law?

---

61. W. Michael REISMAN, "The Regime for *Lacunae* in the ICSID Choice of Law Provision and the Question of its Threshold", 15 ICSID Rev – FILJ (2000) p. 362 at p. 363.
62. GAILLARD and BANIFATEMI, "The Meaning of 'And' in Art. 42(1), Second Sentence, of the Washington Convention: The Role of International Law in the ICSID Choice of Law Process", 18 ICSID Rev – FILJ (2003) p. 375 at p. 403, relying upon *Wena Hotels Ltd v. Egypt* (ICSID Case No. ARB/98/4), Annulment Decision (ICSID, 2002, Kerameus P, Bucher, Orrego Vicuña) 41 ILM (2002) p. 433.
63. SACERDOTI, "Investment Arbitration Under ICSID and UNICTRAL Rules: Prerequisites, Applicable Law, Review of Awards", 19 ICSID Rev – FILJ (2004, no. 1) pp. 25-26.
64. BROCHES, "The Convention on the Settlement of Investment Disputes between States and Nationals of Other States: Applicable Law and Default Procedure" reprinted in *Selected Essays: World Bank, ICSID, and Other Subjects of Public and Private International Law* (Springer 1995) p. 183.

*b.   Express choice of law by treaty*
In some cases, the treaty itself will provide its own choice of law rule, which would in that event apply as an express choice of law for the purpose of the first sentence of Art. 42(1).[65] Thus, Art. 1131(1) of NAFTA expressly provides: "[A] Tribunal established under this Section shall decide the issues in dispute in accordance with this Agreement and applicable rules of international law." Art. 26(6) of the Energy Charter Treaty does the same.

But sometimes, the choice of law clause in the Treaty merely replicates, in one form or another, the essential tension between host state law and international law reflected in Art. 42(1) of the ICSID Convention. This was the case, for example in the Benelux-Burundi Treaty at issue in *Goetz v. Burundi*.[66] Art. 8(5) of that Treaty, following the Benelux model, provides:

> "The arbitral body decides on the basis of:
> – the domestic law of the contracting party to the dispute, on the territory of which the investment is located, including its rules relating to the conflict of laws;
> – the provisions of the present Treaty;
> – the terms of the particular agreement which might have taken place regarding the investment;
> – the generally admitted rules and principles of international law."

This type of provision is also found in the model treaties of China,[67] and of a number of developing countries.

The 2004 US Model BIT adopts a hybrid approach. It provides that claims for breach of the treaty's substantive provisions are to be decided "in accordance with this Treaty and applicable rules of international law".[68] However, claims for breach of investment agreements and investment authorizations also fall within the subject matter jurisdiction of an investor-state arbitral tribunal under the US model. In the case of such claims, Art. 30(2) of the model applies in substance the choice of law rule in Art. 42 of the ICSID Convention.

But many BITs contain no express applicable law clause. This is the case, for example, for the UK, French and German models. The Dutch model merely comments, somewhat laconically: "The Tribunal shall decide on the basis of respect for the law."[69]

Analysis by Antonio Parra in 2007 has shown that, of the twenty ICSID cases under BITs which had been decided on the merits by that date, fifteen were concerned with treaties which contained no express applicable law provision, while the remaining five had proceeded under treaties which contained a clause of the Benelux type, which

---

65. ICSID *Documents Concerning the Origin and Formation of the Convention* (ICSID, 1968) II, p. 267 (hereinafter *History*).
66. *Goetz v. Burundi,* Award Pt 1 (ICSID, 1999, Weil P, Bedjaoui and Bredin) 6 ICSID Rep 3.
67. China Model BIT, Art. 9(7).
68. US Model BIT 2004, Art. 30(1).
69. Netherlands Model BIT, Art. 12(5), reproduced in MCLACHLAN SHORE and WEINIGER, supra fn. 7, App. 8.

broadly replicates the second sentence of Art. 42(1) of the ICSID Convention with its parallel reference to host state law and international law.[70]

In *Goetz v. Burundi*,[71] as has been seen, the tribunal was confronted with an express applicable law clause in the BIT. It did regard this clause as bringing the case within the framework of the first sentence of Art. 42(1).[72] The tribunal observed:

> "Without doubt the determination of the applicable law is not, in its true sense, made by the parties to the present dispute (Burundi and the claimant investors) but by the parties to the investment treaty (Burundi and Belgium). As that was a case for the parties' consent, the Tribunal considers however that the Republic of Burundi decided in favour of the applicable law as it is determined in the already cited provision of the Belgium-Burundi investment treaty in becoming a party to this treaty and that the claimant investors have effected a similar choice in lodging their claim for arbitration based on the said treaty."[73]

The tribunal decided that the effect of the clause was that it must apply each of Burundi law and the BIT *seriatim*. It concluded:

> "... the Belgium-Burundi investment treaty obliges the Tribunal to examine the legal situation created in the wake of the measure of 29 May 1995 in the context of both: each must reign in its own sphere of application, and in case of conflict between the two it is, by common accord of the parties, the provisions which are more favourable to the investors which must be applied".[74]

This approach of considering every issue in terms respectively of host state law and international law has not gained traction in subsequent investment treaty arbitrations. Despite some distinguished support,[75] it is submitted that it cannot be accepted either as required by the clause in the treaty or, more generally, by the logical methodology necessary to resolve such cases. Instead, as developed further below, the tribunal must undertake a *choice of law* analysis in order to determine which of the range of designated rules of law is applicable to the issue in question.

c.  *Applicable law in the absence of express choice*

i.  Art. 42(1) first sentence

Where there is no such express clause, tribunals have adopted a variety of approaches. Schreuer considers it an open question whether the first sentence of Art. 42(1) permits

---

70. Antonio PARRA, "Applicable Law in Investor-State Arbitration", supra fn. 59.
71. Supra fn. 66, [69], [94]-[99].
72. *Ibid.* [94].
73. *Ibid.*
74. *Ibid.* [99].
75. Christoph SCHREUER "Failure to Apply the Governing Law in International Investment Arbitration", 7 Austrian Rev Int'l & Eur L (2004) p. 147 at p. 160.

an implied choice of law, making the point that too broad a reading of that sentence would be "likely to undermine the residual rule of its second sentence".[76]

In the first-ever investment treaty case, *AAPL v. Sri Lanka*,[77] there was no governing law clause in the BIT itself. Nevertheless, the tribunal considered that the parties could be said to have made an implied choice of international law by reason of the fact that their pleadings focussed on arguments relating to the substantive provisions of the BIT.[78] Asante, who dissented, pointed out that this was to elevate to an express choice of law a process which may in fact amount to no more than the natural tendency of the pleader to respond to the arguments raised by his opponent.[79]

*Wena Hotels v. Egypt* was, like *AAPL v. Sri Lanka*, concerned with a BIT (between Egypt and the United Kingdom) which had no applicable law clause. The tribunal approached the matter on the basis that the second sentence of Art. 42(1) was applicable, but that "the provisions of the IPPA would in any event be the first rules of law to be applied by the tribunal, both on the basis of the agreement of the parties and as mandated by Egyptian law as well as international law".[80] This aspect of the award was the subject of an annulment application.[81]

The ad hoc Committee considered an argument by Egypt that the tribunal had manifestly exceeded its powers by failing to apply Egyptian law, which had been expressly chosen to govern the hotel lease between the investor and Egyptian Hotels Co (EHC), which was the subject matter of the investment. The Committee dismissed this argument by making a distinction between the law applicable to the contract and that applicable to a claim of breach of treaty. The conclusion which it then drew was that: "It follows that it cannot be held that the Parties to the instant case have made a choice of law under the first sentence of Article 42(1) of the ICSID Convention."[82]

ii. Art. 42(1) second sentence

If the better view, then, is that an express choice of law clause in the treaty is necessary for the application of the first sentence of Art. 42(1), how should the second sentence be applied in treaty cases? The *Wena Hotels* ad hoc Committee noted the great controversy that had surrounded the balance to be struck between host state law and international law under this sentence in earlier jurisprudence and doctrine, but decided that:

---

76. SCHREUER, supra fn. 46, p. 573.
77. *AAPL v. Sri Lanka*, supra fn. 8.
78. *Ibid.* [18]-[24].
79. See also the summary of the criticisms of the majority's approach on this issue in SCHREUER, supra fn. 46, pp. 579-580.
80. *Wena Hotels Ltd v. Egypt*, Award (ICSID, 2000, Leigh P, Fadlallah and Wallace) 6 ICSID Rep 68, 112 [79].
81. *Wena Hotels Ltd v. Egypt*, Decision on Annulment (ICSID, 2002, Kerameus P, Bucher and Orrego Vicuña) 6 ICSID Rep 129.
82. *Ibid.*, p. 137 [36].

"What is clear is that the sense and meaning of the negotiations leading to the second sentence of Art. 42(1) allowed for both legal orders to have a role. The law of the host state can indeed be applied in conjunction with international law if this is justified. So too international law can be applied by itself if the appropriate rule is found in this other ambit."[83]

Thus, the Committee concluded that the tribunal had not manifestly exceeded its powers by applying the BIT, rather than Egyptian law, to the dispute. Gaillard and Banifatemi deploy this dictum in order to support an argument that the tribunal thus has freedom of action to choose whether to apply host state law or international law.[84]

iii.   Choice of law between host state law and international law

It is doubtless correct, as the ad hoc Committee observed, that the second sentence of Art. 42(1) "does not draw a sharp line for the distinction of the respective scope of international and of domestic law and, correspondingly, that this has the effect to confer on to the Tribunal a certain *margin and power for interpretation*".[85] (Emphasis added) But, it is submitted that the rule nevertheless still requires the tribunal to undertake a choice of law enquiry. The starting-point for the analysis, as in private international law, is the identification and characterization of the particular *issue* to which the legal rule is to be applied, and the selection of the legal system which properly applies to the determination of that issue.[86]

This will not, without more, necessarily indicate a choice of law rule for all issues. But in many cases, the respective roles of international law and host state law may well be determined by the very nature of the different functions of national and international law. The Annulment Committee in *MTD v. Chile* explained the respective spheres of operation of host state law and international law in this way:

"As noted above, the *lex causae* in this case based on a breach of the BIT is international law. However it will often be necessary for BIT tribunals to apply the law of the host State, and this necessity is reinforced for ICSID tribunals by Art. 42(1) of the ICSID Convention. Whether the applicable law here derived from the first or second sentence of Art. 42(1) does not matter: the Tribunal should have applied Chilean law to those questions which were necessary for its determination and of which Chilean law was the governing law. At the same time,

---

83. *Ibid.*, p. 138 [40], but see the criticism of this approach, as giving insufficient attention to the role of Egyptian law in determining the existence and extent of Wena's investment under the lease agreements at the time of the seizure of the hotels, in DOUGLAS "The Hybrid Foundations of Investment Treaty Arbitration", 74 BYIL (2003) p. 151 at p. 206.
84. GAILLARD and BANIFATEMI, supra fn. 62, pp. 409-410.
85. *Wena Hotels*, supra fn. 81, [39].
86. *MacMillan Inc v. Bishopsgate Investment Trust plc et al. (no 3)*, [1996] 1 WLR 387, 391-392, per Staughton LJ.

the *implications* of some issue of Chilean law for a claim under the BIT were for international law to determine. In short, both laws were relevant."[87]

In this respect, the choice of law question which arises in investment treaty cases is affected by a fundamentally different context from that which applies in the ordinary context of choice of law in private international law. In private international law, the two potentially applicable legal systems stand in a horizontal relationship to each other, being both national legal systems. Each such system deals with the same or similar subject matter, namely private law rights and duties. The task of the court is to choose which of these two systems applies to the resolution of the issue before it. However, the relationship of national law and international law is vertical, and not horizontal. This means that each legal system deals with different types of rights and duties, each of which may be applicable to different issues arising within the same dispute. Thus:

(a) International law does not, for example, *create* private property rights, or rights in contract.[88] Nor does it determine how nationality may be acquired and lost.[89] Those are matters referred to national law. The Annulment Committee held in *Vivendi v. Argentina,* that each of a claim for breach of international law and a claim for breach of national law "will be determined by its own proper law".[90] Returning to the same theme in *CMS v. Argentina,* the Annulment Committee pointed out, in relation to the construction of umbrella clauses, that: "The effect of the umbrella clause is not to transform the obligation which is relied on into something else; the content of the obligation is unaffected, as is its proper law."[91]
(b) On the other hand, the substantive treaty standards themselves have an independent operation as international law standards. In determining their meaning and operation, the second sentence of Art. 42(1) positively requires the tribunal to apply international law. Thus, Broches gives as one of his four examples of where an ICSID tribunal will have occasion to apply international law: "…where the subject-matter or issue is directly regulated by international law, for instance a treaty between the State party to the dispute and the State whose national is the other party to the dispute".[92]

For this purpose, lawfulness or unlawfulness under national law does not per se determine whether there has been a breach of treaty – a principle confirmed by Art. 27

---

87. *MTD Equity Sdn Bhd v. Chile* (ICSID Case No. ARB/01/7), Decision on Annulment (ICSID, 2007, Guillaume P, Crawford and Ondóñez Noriega) [72].
88. DOUGLAS, supra fn. 83, pp. 211-213.
89. *Soufraki v. United Arab Emirates* (ICSID Case No. ARB/02/7), Decision on Annulment (ICSID, 2007, Feliciano P, Nabulsi and Stern); JENNINGS and WATTS, supra fn. 33, [38].
90. *Vivendi,* supra fn. 57, [96].
91. *CMS Gas Transmission Co v. Argentine Republic* (ICSID Case No. ARB/01/8), Decision on Annulment (ICSID, 25 September 2007, Guillaume P, Elaraby and Crawford), [95(c)].
92. BROCHES, supra fn. 13, p. 392.

of the Vienna Convention on the Law of Treaties[93] and Art. 3 of the ILC Draft Articles on State Responsibility,[94] and, in the specific context of investment law, by the ICJ in *ELSI*.[95] Thus, in *Vivendi* the ad hoc Committee held that the claim of breach of treaty had to be governed by international law:

> "In such a case, the inquiry which the ICSID tribunal is required to undertake is one governed by the ICSID Convention, by the BIT and by applicable international law. Such an inquiry is neither in principle determined, nor precluded, by any issue of municipal law, including any municipal law agreement of the parties."[96]

### d. Choice of law outside the ICSID Convention

Is there a difference in the approach to choice of law where the arbitration is conducted outside the ICSID Convention, and Art. 42(1) does not apply? The choice of law rules provided in non-ICSID arbitration rules typically follow the same approach as the first sentence of Art. 42(1) in respecting party autonomy in express choice of rules of law. But they differ markedly from the second sentence of Art. 42(1) in providing a choice of law rule in the absence of choice. Thus, the second sentence of Art. 33 of the UNCITRAL Rules provides: "Failing such designation by the parties, the arbitral tribunal shall apply the law determined by the conflict of laws rules which it considers applicable."

This formulation leaves a wide margin to the arbitral tribunal in the selection of the applicable conflict of laws rules, in contrast to the restriction to host state law and international law in Art. 42(1) of the ICSID Convention.[97] But it is unlikely to have been the intent of the states party to an investment treaty which allows for a choice of ICSID and non-ICSID arbitration that different choice of law approaches (possibly affecting the interpretation and application of the treaty itself) might be applied, depending upon the system of arbitration chosen.[98] This would be contrary to common sense. Host state law provides the only national legal system likely to be relevant to the investment, and the treaty rights themselves are rights under international law.

Is there, then, a difference in approach in the delimitation of the respective roles of host state and international law in non-ICSID cases? This question arose in the controversial *CME v. Czech Republic* case, which was the subject of review proceedings

---

93. Vienna Convention on the Law of Treaties (signed 23 May 1969, entered into force 27 January 1980) 1155 UNTS 331 (Vienna Convention).
94. International Law Commission, *Draft Articles on Responsibility of States for Internationally Wrongful Acts with Commentaries, 2001* (ILC 2005) <www.un.org/law/ilc/>.
95. *ELSI* case, supra fn. 41, p. 51.
96. *Vivendi,* supra fn. 57, [102].
97. For discussion of the various techniques used in its application see COLLINS, BRIGGS, HARRIS, MCCLEAN, MCLACHLAN and MORSE, eds., *Dicey Morris & Collins on the Conflict of Laws* (Sweet & Maxwell, London 2006) (hereinafter *Dicey*) [16-055]-[16-060].
98. A point made in *ADC Affiliate Ltd v. Hungary* (ICSID Case No. ARB/03/16), Award (ICSID, 2006, Kaplan P, Brower, van den Berg) [291].

before the Svea Court of Appeals in Sweden.[99] The Dutch-Czech BIT in question contained an express choice of law clause, similar to that in the Benelux-Burundi Treaty applied in *Goetz*. The tribunal had proceeded under UNCITRAL Rules, and the seat of the arbitration was Stockholm. One of the arguments advanced by the Czech Republic was that the tribunal had exceeded its mandate by failing to apply the law designated by the choice of law provision in the Treaty, and in particular by failing to give adequate consideration to Czech law.[100] The Court declined to accept this argument. The Swedish legislature had sought to reduce the possibilities than an award rendered in Sweden could be set aside on the basis that the tribunal had applied the wrong law,[101] and the Court should therefore only intervene if "the arbitrators' interpretation of the choice of law clause proves to be baseless such that their assessment may be equated with the arbitrators almost having ignored a provision regarding applicable law".[102] The *chapeau* of the choice of law clause itself confirmed that the enumerated sources applied "in particular though not exclusively".[103] The Court did not consider that the clause required consideration of host state law first, even though it appeared first in the list. Rather if the case concerned an alleged violation of the investment treaty, "it might be relevant first of all to apply international law, in light of the Investment Treaty's purpose of affording protection to foreign investors by prescribing norms in accordance with international law".[104]

The Court's decision sheds less light on the choice of law question than might have been hoped. It turned principally on the Swedish arbitration law, which does not even contain a provision on the law applicable in arbitration equivalent to Art. 28 of the UNICTRAL Model Law on International Commercial Arbitration (the Model Law); and the choice of law clause in question had a particularly flexible character, leaving a wide margin of appreciation for the tribunal. The Court did accept that, in principle, failure by an arbitral tribunal to abide by an express choice of law clause in an investment treaty could entitle the award to be set aside on the ground that the arbitrators have exceeded their mandate. But it then set the standard of review at a high threshold, suggesting that it would have only intervened if the tribunal had not applied any of the sources listed in the choice of law clause at all.

From the point of view of methodology, it is submitted that the task of a tribunal in a non-ICSID investment treaty arbitration is in substance the same as in an ICSID case. Subject to the express terms of the treaty itself, including any applicable law provision, it must consider which issues are properly governed by host state law, and which by international law. It is understandable that a court of review might not think it

---

99. *Czech Republic v. CME Czech Republic BV*, 9 ICSID Rep 439 (Svea Court of Appeal, 2003).
100. See in particular the arguments developed by Schreuer and Reinisch, as expert witnesses, in their opinion, available at <www.univie.ac.at/intlaw/pdf/cmeopin_1.pdf>, and in SCHREUER, supra fn. 75, pp. 182-195.
101. *Czech Republic v. CME Czech Republic BV*, supra fn. 99, p. 497.
102. *Ibid.*, p. 498, criticized by BALAŠ, "Review of Awards" in MUCHLINSKI, et al., supra fn. 59, p. 1125 at p. 1142.
103. Cited *ibid*.
104. *Ibid.*, p. 4.

appropriate to dissect choices of law made by the arbitrators under a clause which provides for such choice. That might lead to review on grounds of error of law. But it is regrettable that, in concluding its discussion of this question, the Svea Court appeared to require no more than that one of the sources in the treaty list should have been applied. Such an approach fails to give adequate weight to the express terms of the balance struck in the treaty, which, it is submitted, requires the tribunal to make a reasoned choice as to which of the nominated sources is applicable to the particular issue.

2.   *The Investment Treaty in the Context of International Law*

Where the law applicable to the particular issue is international law, the starting point in any investment treaty case will be the express provisions of the treaty itself. It is those standards which will, applying the reasoning of the tribunal in the *Channel Tunnel* case, constitute the "source of the Parties' respective rights and obligations", furnishing the cause of action which gives rise to the treaty claim, and delimiting the scope of the arbitrators' powers.[105]

Thus, it will be primarily through the techniques of treaty interpretation that the relationship between the treaty and wider international law will be mediated. Such a process of interpretation must start with the treaty text itself, since, Art. 31(1) of the Vienna Convention on the Law of Treaties requires that: "A treaty shall be interpreted in good faith in accordance with the ordinary meaning to be given to the terms of the treaty in their context and in the light of its object and purpose."

The point that Arts. 31 and 32 provide an approach to interpretation which is binding upon investment tribunals bears emphasis, since one recent comprehensive empirical analysis of legal reasoning techniques employed by ICSID tribunals concludes that: "The way in which ICSID tribunals use interpretative arguments in practice is often quite far removed from the structures set out in Arts. 31–32 of the VCLT."[106]

But the fact that one must start with the treaty text does not mean that the treaty is to be applied in isolation. Indeed, the whole structure of Arts. 31 and 32 supports an approach to interpretation in which the text is set against a series of progressively wider fields of reference.[107] In the very first investment treaty arbitration, *AAPL v. Sri Lanka*, the tribunal observed that a BIT:[108]

> "... is not a self-contained closed legal system limited to provide for substantive material rules of direct applicability, but it has to be envisaged within a wider juridical context in which rules from other sources are integrated through implied

---

105. *Channel Tunnel Group Ltd v. United Kingdom and France*, supra fn. 55, [98].
106. Ole Kristian FAUCHALD, "The Legal Reasoning of ICSID Tribunals – an Empirical Analysis", 19 EJIL (2008) p. 301 at pp. 358-359.
107. Campbell MCLACHLAN, "The Principle of Systemic Integration and Art. 31(3)(c) of the Vienna Convention", 54 ICLQ (2005) p. 279 at pp. 310-311, relying upon HUBER, *Annuaire* (1952-I) pp. 200-201.
108. *Asian Agricultural Products v. Sri Lanka*, Award, supra fn. 8, at 265-266, Rule D.

incorporation methods, or by direct reference to certain supplementary rules, whether of international law character or of domestic law nature".

The Annulment Committee in *MTD v. Chile* put it more pithily in stating: "... the Tribunal had to apply international law *as a whole* to the claim, and not the provisions of the BIT in isolation".[109] (Emphasis added) The new draft model Norwegian BIT makes this relationship between the BIT and general international law express by providing: "A Tribunal established under this Section shall make its award based on the provisions of this Agreement *interpreted and applied in accordance with the rules of interpretation of international law.*"[110] (Emphasis added)

But what does this really mean? Simply to determine that international law is the law applicable to the issue reveals little about how the particular rules of a treaty are to be construed and applied. In order to do this, it is necessary to engage in a process of interpretation, which in two respects looks beyond the terms of the treaty: first, through a process of the elaboration of common principles of investment law, being developed through the comparative jurisprudence of tribunals; and, second, by means of the incorporation of other rules of international law applicable in the relations between the parties. It is necessary to say a word about each.

3. *Common Principles of Investment Law*

Despite the potential for conflicts between tribunals on substantive law, in fact the evidence to date indicates that most tribunals do make a conscious effort to consider prior awards, and to develop what one tribunal suggestively called "a body of concordant practice".[111] It has recently been suggested that tribunals may have:

> "... a duty to adopt solutions established in a consistent series of cases.... [and] a duty to seek to contribute to the harmonious development of investment law and thereby to meet the legitimate expectations of the community of States and investors towards the certainty of the rule of law".[112]

But this process is not, as is sometimes argued in the literature, a matter of creating a kind of doctrine of binding precedent in investment arbitration.[113] That would be to mistake the nature of the investment treaty arbitration system, in which tribunals stand in a horizontal, and not a vertical relationship to one another. Seen in this light, it is submitted that the real question is the degree of consistency which any particular award

---

109. *MTD Equity Sdn Bhd v. Chile*, supra fn. 87, para. 61.
110. Art. 14(1) Norway draft Model BIT (December 2007).
111. *Mondev International Ltd v. United States of America*, Award (NAFTA/ICSID(AF), 2002, Stephen P, Crawford and Schwebel) 6 ICSID Rep 181, 222.
112. *Saipem SpA v. Bangladesh* (ICSID Case No. ARB/05/07), Jurisdiction (ICSID, 2007, Kaufmann-Kohler P, Schreuer and Otton).
113. See Christoph SCHREUER and Matthew WEINIGER, "A Doctrine of Precedent?" in MUCHLINSKI, et al., supra fn. 59, p. 1188.

achieves with the overarching rules and principles of international law, rather than merely with prior awards.

In any event, an investigation of the jurisprudence for the purpose of analyzing the substantive principles applicable in international investment arbitration reveals a process much closer to what will be familiar to many lawyers in other legal settings. Tribunals have not been engaged in adding new binding rules to limit the generality of the treaty text – they have no power to do that. No one doubts that the legal rule remains that which is stated shortly in terms of great generality. But the case law sheds the considerable light of experience upon how the general rule applies, by isolating the factors which may be relevant in different fact situations. In this way, the operationalization of the general test in its application to the modern fact patterns presented to tribunals may be compared to the development of the law of civil wrongs, whether in the common law after *Donoghue v. Stevenson*[114] or under the very general provisions of the civil codes.[115] The law is not simply applied. It is elucidated in ways which assist the work of subsequent tribunals.

Thus it is possible to state a series of factors, for example in the application of the fair and equitable treatment standard, which have been relied upon by tribunals as indicating both situations when the standard had been breached, and also situations when it has not.[116] The general principle informing this standard flows from its character as an instrument of supervision at the international law level of the many and various processes of decision-making at national level. The standard is concerned with due process in decision-making, and not with substantive outcomes. It requires the application of fundamental rule of law values in decision-making: predictability; accessibility; impartiality; and natural justice, as contrasted with arbitrary action, a point made by the ICJ in *ELSI*.[117] The standard shares these concerns with international human rights law. The addition of the concept of equity also requires due weight to be given to the proper public purposes of the host state – performing a similar function to that of proportionality in the application of human rights standards.[118]

The central concept of due process may be seen at work in the cases which have applied fair and equitable treatment to administrative decision-making: in prohibiting discrimination between foreign and local investors;[119] the use of powers for improper

---

114. *Donoghue v. Stevenson*, [1932] AC 562.
115. E.g., Art. 1382 French Civil Code.
116. These cases are analysed in MCLACHLAN, SHORE and WEINIGER, supra fn. 7, [7.115]-[7.140].
117. *ELSI* Case, supra fn. 41.
118. A point made in MCLACHLAN, SHORE and WEINIGER, supra fn. 7 at [7.188(2)] and well developed by KINGSBURY and SCHILL in their Report for this Conference: "Investor-State Arbitration, Fair and Equitable Treatment, Proportionality, and the Emerging Administrative Law of Global Governance", this volume, pp. 5-68.
119. *S D Myers Inc v. Canada*, (NAFTA/UNCITRAL, 2000, Hunter P, Schwartz and Chiasson) 8 ICSID Rep 3.

purposes;[120] inconsistency of treatment by different government agencies;[121] coercion and harassment by State authorities;[122] bad faith;[123] and in requiring some degree of transparency.[124] The notion of "legitimate expectations" is also a specific application of this same enquiry into process, and, as the Annulment Committee in *MTD v. Chile* has reminded us, not an independent standard.[125] It is concerned not with proscribing the content of host state law,[126] but rather with ensuring its consistent application, and with enforcing representations by the host state only where these were made specifically enough to the particular investor to justify reliance.[127]

By the same token, the cases have begun to identify factors where balancing equitably the legitimate public interests of the state may indicate that the standard has not been breached: in preserving a legitimate scope for regulatory flexibility;[128] in denying claims where the alleged right is not found in either host state law or international law;[129] and in upholding administrative decisions which have an objective basis[130] and do not have a disproportionate impact on the foreign investor.[131] Tribunals have recognized that they must take the investor's conduct into account as well: BITs "are not insurance policies against bad business decisions",[132] and the investor has its own duty to investigate the host state's applicable law.[133]

Thus far, the jurisprudence of investment protection may be envisaged as an elaborative enterprise: the working out of the application of the general test in the myriad of different specific contexts which the cases have presented to tribunals. The development of such a common law of a legislative text is a familiar one to lawyers – albeit that in the case of BITs the concern is rather with the common language of

---

120. *Técnicas Medioambientales Tecmed SA v. United Mexican States*, Award (ICSID, Grigera Naón P, Fernández Rozas and Bernal Verea) 10 ICSID Rep 130.
121. *MTD v. Chile*, supra fn. 87.
122. *Pope & Talbot Inc v. Canada*, Award (ICSID/UNCITRAL, 2002, Dervaird P, Greenberg and Belman) 7 ICSID Rep 43 *sed quaere* whether that was such a case.
123. *Waste Management Inc v. United Mexican States*, Award (*Waste Management II*)(NAFTA/ICSID (AF), 2004, Crawford P, Civiletti and Gómez) 43 ILM (2004) p. 967 at p. 994.
124. *S D Myers*, supra fn. 119, Separate Opinion of Schwartz, p. 66 at p. 114.
125. *MTD Equity Sdn Bhd v. Chile,* supra fn. 87, [67]-[71].
126. *GAMI Investments Inc v. United Mexican States*, Award (NAFTA/UNCITRAL, 2004, Paulsson P, Muró and Reisman) 44 ILM (2005) p. 545 at p. 560.
127. *International Thunderbird Gaming Corp v. United Mexican States*, Award (NAFTA/UNCITRAL, 2006, van den Berg P, Ariosa and Wälde) [147].
128. *Saluka Investments BV (The Netherlands) v. Czech Republic*, Partial Award (UNCITRAL, 2006, Watts C, Fortier and Behrens) [305].
129. *United Parcel Service of America Inc v. Canada*, Award on Jurisdiction (NAFTA/UNCITRAL, 2002, Keith P, Cass and Fortier) 7 ICSID Rep 285.
130. *Genin v. Estonia*, Award (ICSID, 2001, Fortier P, Heth and van den Berg) 6 ICSID Rep 236.
131. *Pope and Talbot Inc v. Canada*, Award on the Merits of Phase 2 (NAFTA/UNCITRAL, 2001, Dervaird P, Greenberg and Belman) 7 ICSID Rep 43, 102, 130-138 [119]-[155].
132. *Maffezini v. Spain* (Award), 5 ICSID Rep. 419 (ICSID, 2000, Orrego Vicuña P, Buergenthal and Wolf) [64].
133. *MTD v. Chile*, supra fn. 87, [107].

numerous separate texts. This is *not* to say that every award is reconcilable. Plainly, there are still major doctrinal differences in approach between tribunals.[134] But treaty arbitration has on the whole resisted the temptation of extreme compartmentalization. Instead, tribunals have regularly borrowed reasoning and interpretations adopted by tribunals hearing cases under different treaties, but with similar language. Schreuer observes: "Fortunately the problem of inconsistency is not pervasive. Most tribunals carefully examine earlier decisions and accept these as authority most of the time."[135] In the result, an increasingly detailed body of jurisprudence is developing.

This may be seen as the elaboration of a set of common principles or *jurisprudence constante*[136] in the application of the legislative text. The result may be, as Judge Higgins suggested in the *Oil Platforms* case, the emergence of a "special meaning" of a treaty's terms as contemplated by Art. 31(4) of the Vienna Convention, since the key terms "are legal terms of art well known in the field of overseas investment protection".[137]

*4. Systemic Integration in the Interpretation of Investment Treaties*

The second element of the process is the incorporation of other rules of international law by the application of what the author has previously termed the principle of systemic integration in the interpretation of a treaty text. This principle finds reflection in Art. 31(3)(c) of the Vienna Convention on the Law of Treaties, which requires the interpreter to take account of "other rules of international law applicable in the relations between the parties." Recently, in *Djibouti v. France*, the ICJ has again confirmed that this rule codifies a customary rule of interpretation, and its application has been the subject of detailed consideration by a Study Group of the International Law Commission, in the work of which the author collaborated.[138]

The principle may be stated as a presumption with both a positive and a negative aspect:

---

134. See, e.g., the discussion of the doctrine of necessity cases against Argentina in MCLACHLAN, supra fn. 30, pp. 385-391.
135. SCHREUER, "Diversity and Harmonization of Treaty Interpretation in Investment Arbitration", 3 TDM (April 2006, no. 2) p. 1 at p. 17.
136. James CRAWFORD, "Similarity of Issues in Disputes Arising under the Same or Similarly Drafted Investment Treaties" in BANIFATEMI, ed., *Precedent in International Arbitration* (Juris Publishing, 2007) p. 97 at p. 102.
137. *Oil Platforms Case (Islamic Republic of Iran v. United States of America)* (Preliminary Objections) (Separate Opinion of Judge Higgins) 1996 ICJ Rep 847 [39].
138. *Certain Questions of Mutual Assistance in Criminal Matters (Djibouti v. France)* ICJ (4 June 2008); and see generally MCLACHLAN, supra fn. 107 and International Law Commission, "Fragmentation of International Law: Difficulties Arising from the Diversification and Expansion of International Law", Report of the Study Group (Koskenniemi, C) UN Doc. A/CN.4/L682 (13 April 2006), Conclusions of the Study Group, UN Doc. A/CN.4/L.702 (18 July 2006).

(a) *positively* that the parties are taken "to refer to general principles of international law for all questions which [the treaty] does not itself resolve in express terms or in a different way";[139] and,
(b) *negatively* that, in entering into treaty obligations, the parties intend not to act inconsistently with generally recognized principles of international law or with previous treaty obligations towards third states.[140]

The potential importance of this binding rule of interpretation is only now beginning to be fully realized by investment treaty tribunals. Yet it could be of great practical assistance. BITs are often short instruments, incorporating standards expressly in very broad, open-textured language, and with little in the way of *travaux*. Three overall points may be made about what systemic integration may involve in this context.

First, the requirement to consider other applicable rules of international law will have particular application to rules of *customary* international law. There are at least three contexts in which custom may be relevant:

(a) Within the field of investment law, in the interpretation of provisions, such as the protection from expropriation without compensation, which owe an explicit debt to custom;
(b) By applying general international law to issues which the treaty does not itself resolve expressly, such as the rules of state responsibility – the full significance of which, especially as regards circumstances precluding wrongfulness, are only now coming to be realized;[141] and,
(c) By using principles developed in other related areas of international law as a means of giving greater content to the general standards. Thus, for example, the concepts of fair trial and of protection of property have both been developed considerably by human rights courts in the last fifty years. This jurisprudence could assist tribunals in the application of the standards of fair and equitable treatment and protection against expropriation.

Secondly, the principle of systemic interpretation also requires consideration of other treaties applicable between the parties – as made by the ILC in its Fragmentation Conclusions,[142] and also by the ICJ in *Djibouti v. France*.[143] The new model bilateral treaties of the United States and Canada both contain explicit references to international environmental and labour standards, as do both NAFTA and the Energy Charter Treaty.

---

139. *Georges Pinson (France) v. United Mexican States* (1928), V. RIAA, p. 327 (Original French text) (1927-1928) AD Case No. 292 (English Note) (French-Mexican Claims Commission, Verzijl P).
140. *Rights of Passage over Indian Territory (Preliminary Objections) (Portugal v. India) Case* [1957] ICJ Rep. p. 142.
141. See further CRAWFORD, supra fn. 39; Andrea K. BJORKLUND, "Emergency Exceptions: State of Necessity and *Force Majeure*" in MUCHLINSKI, supra fn. 59, p. 459; Kaj Hobér "State Responsibility and Attribution" in *ibid.*, p. 549.
142. Supra fn. 138, ILC Conclusions UN Doc. A/CN.4/L.702, [21].
143. Supra fn. 138, [112]-[114].

Yet, the explicit weighing of the relevance of other public international law commitments of states is still rare in the investment jurisprudence.[144]

Finally, however, the principle of systemic integration remains a principle of treaty interpretation. As such it must take its place within the overall framework of the approach to treaty interpretation in Arts. 31 and 32 of the Vienna Convention. This requires the tribunal to start with the ordinary meaning of its terms, in its context, and in the light of its object and purpose, as Art. 31(1) has it. Thus, reference to other rules of international law will yield to the express terms of the treaty, where they clearly mandate a different approach. As the Annulment Committee in *CMS v. Argentina*[145] has reminded us recently in the context of the doctrine of necessity, this means, for example, that one has to be careful about conflating a primary rule in the treaty itself, with the secondary rules of state responsibility, which apply only if the tribunal has already determined that a primary rule has been breached.[146]

In both of these aspects of the *lex causae*, the development of common principles of substantive law and the use of the public international law rules of interpretation, investment treaty tribunals perform a task which flows from the role of the treaties themselves as creatures of public international law. This central relevance of public international law in every case sets them apart from other arbitral tribunals.

IV.  LEX ARBITRI

*1.  Choice of International Law or the Law of the Seat as the Lex Arbitri*

At first sight, the fragmented nature of the available fora in investment arbitration makes it more difficult to find common principles as to the law applicable to the conduct of the arbitration, the lex arbitri. Everything depends upon the arbitration clause in the treaty. Many bilateral treaties, as well as the Energy Charter Treaty, offer investors a cafeteria-style choice of ICSID or arbitration either under the aegis of a commercial arbitration body or ad hoc applying UNCITRAL Rules. This means that there is a fundamental distinction in principle to be drawn as to the lex arbitri between:

(a) Arbitrations conducted under the ICSID Convention itself, where the lex arbitri is the provisions of the ICSID Convention and Arbitration Rules; and,
(b) Arbitrations conducted outside the ICSID system, where the lex arbitri is, in principle, the general law of arbitration at the tribunal's seat,[147] and where the applicable

---

144. For a recent critique of the jurisprudence in this context see: Moshe HIRSCH, "Interactions between Investment and Non-investment Obligations" in MUCHLINSKI, et al., supra fn. 59, p. 154.
145. *CMS Gas Transmission Co v. Argentina*, Decision on Annulment, supra fn. 91.
146. For further analysis of the significance of the distinction between primary and secondary rules in this context see: Jürgen KURTZ, "Adjudging the Exceptional at International Law: Security, Public Order and Financial Crisis", Institute for International Law and Justice, NYU School of Law, IIJS Working Paper 2008/6.
147. *Dicey*, supra fn. 97, [16-182].

procedural framework will typically be a set of rules, such as the UNCITRAL Arbitration Rules, which were designed with the arbitration of commercial contracts in mind.

*a. Limitations on party autonomy*

But party autonomy does not necessarily mean that there is always a free choice between ICSID and non-ICSID arbitration. Many investment treaties only offer ICSID arbitration – this remains the preferred clause in the British, French, German and Dutch model BITs, provided both states are parties to the Convention. However, despite the widespread ratification of the ICSID Convention, there are still some prominent states which are not party to it. In that event, the Convention cannot supply the *lex arbitri*. States which are not parties to ICSID include Russia, as well as Canada and Mexico. The absence of these last two states means that arbitrations under NAFTA[148] have to be conducted under the ICSID Additional Facility or UNCITRAL Rules. In either of these contexts, the arbitral process is no longer self-contained. The lex arbitri remains the national law of the tribunal's seat.

It is necessary to develop the point about the difference in lex arbitri a little further, by reference to the structures and procedures of both ICSID and non-ICSID investment arbitration, against the background of the functions of the lex arbitri.

*b. Functions of the lex arbitri*[149]

In essence, the procedural law of an arbitration deals with two sets of issues: (a) the *internal* procedure of the arbitration itself: commencement of the arbitration, appointment of arbitrators, pleadings, provisional measures, evidence, hearings and awards; and (b) *external* intervention in the arbitral process. Such intervention may itself have one of three distinct functions: (a) *directory*: it may provide a source of arbitral rules which may be applied to the extent that the parties have not expressly chosen their own rules of procedure; (b) *mandatory*: external law may also, however, place mandatory limits on the autonomy of the parties in arbitration, by prescribing certain matters of arbitral procedure from which no contracting out is permitted; and (c) *supportive*: external intervention may extend the support of processes external to those of the arbitral tribunal, by making available to the parties procedures to deal with matters which are outside the scope of the arbitrators' authority. This arises especially where the procedural measures affect the position of third parties, who are not subject to the jurisdiction of the arbitrators, such as, for example, in the taking of evidence under compulsion or the ordering of provisional measures. It also arises after an award has been rendered and enforcement is sought.

In modern international commercial arbitration, the internal procedures of arbitration are, for most purposes, provided by the procedural rules of an arbitral institution or by a standard set of ad hoc rules, such as the UNCITRAL Rules. However, the external function, to the extent that it is necessary, is provided by the national law at the seat of

---

148. North American Free Trade Agreement (NAFTA), (adopted 17 December 1992, entered into force 1 January 1994) (1993) 32 ILM p. 289.
149. See *Dicey*, supra fn. 97, [16-029]-[16-031].

the arbitration.[150] But in the case of ICSID arbitration, the ICSID Arbitration Rules supply the internal procedure, and the external function is, to the greatest extent possible, provided within the structures of the ICSID Convention on the plane of international law.

*c. ICSID arbitration*

The master rule of the Convention which deals with procedure is Art. 44, which provides:

> "Any arbitration proceeding shall be conducted in accordance with the provisions of this Section and, except as the parties otherwise agree, in accordance with the Arbitration Rules in effect on the date on which the parties consented to arbitration. If any question of procedure arises which is not covered by this Section or the Arbitration Rules or any rules agreed by the parties, the Tribunal shall decide the question."

This article is designed to insulate the procedure of ICSID arbitration from any provisions of national law. As Schreuer puts it: "… Art. 44 creates a comprehensive and self-contained system that is insulated from national rules of procedure. In particular, the place of proceedings has no influence on procedure before an ICSID tribunal."[151]

Three practical factors serve to support this system:

(a) *Detailed nature of ICSID Arbitration Rules:* First, the Arbitration Rules themselves make detailed provision for the majority of issues which are likely to arise in the course of ICSID arbitration. Consisting of fifty-six rules in eight chapters, the Rules deal with: the establishment of the tribunal; its working; general procedural provisions; written and oral procedures (a section which includes rules as to evidence); particular procedures; the award; and its interpretation, revision and annulment. The interpretation of these Rules is assisted by the increasing practice of reporting the procedural decisions of ICSID tribunals, as well as their awards.

(b) *Institutional support:* The operation of the procedural rules is further supported by the existence of the ICSID Secretariat, which maintains an overall institutional knowledge of the operation of ICSID arbitration. In the context of particular cases, this is reinforced by the provision made under Regulation 25 of the Centre's Administrative and Financial Regulations for a Secretary, drawn from the Secretariat, to be appointed for each tribunal (and ad hoc Committee). In practical terms, the Secretary can assist the tribunal members as a resource on matters of procedure.

(c) *Review of Arbitration Rules:* Thirdly, the Arbitration Rules are not a static instrument. On the contrary, the framers of the Convention envisaged that they might be the subject of amendment by the Administrative Council.[152] Revised Rules were adopted in 1984,[153]

---

150. *Ibid.*, Rule 57(2).
151. SCHREUER, supra fn. 46, p. 666.
152. Art. 6(1)(c) ICSID Convention, SCHREUER, supra fn. 46, p. 26.
153. 1 ICSID Rep 157, 181.

and in 2003.[154] There was a further important process of revision from 2004-2006,[155] which resulted in the adoption of Revised Rules effective 10 April 2006. Thus, although the Convention itself would be extremely difficult to amend, given the very large number of State parties, the Rules have proved to be a responsive instrument to perceived needs for change in arbitral procedure. Pertinent examples of this may be found in two of the specific topics examined further below: transparency (which was the subject of important amendments in 2006); and provisional measures (where the practice was changed in 1984).

If, then, ICSID procedure is a product of its own rules, created under the ICSID Convention on the plane of international law, to what extent do they form a completely self-contained regime within international law?[156] Alternatively, to what extent may, or should, an ICSID arbitral tribunal refer to rules and principles of procedure found elsewhere in international law, either in the interpretation of the Rules, or where the Rules are silent? Art. 42(1) of the ICSID Convention, with its general reference to both host state law and international law, applies to the lex causae but not to the lex arbitri, where Art. 44 supplies the rule.[157] Art. 44 gives a measure of autonomy to the parties to agree on matters of procedure (save those governed directly by mandatory rules of the Convention itself). It then confers discretion upon the tribunal to decide for itself matters which are not covered by the Rules. This may be seen as declaratory of the inherent power of any international tribunal to resolve questions of procedure which are not expressly dealt with in its governing rules.[158]

Outside this framework, as the ad hoc Committee put it in *AMCO v. Indonesia*: "Problems of interpretation or lacunae which emerge have to be solved or filled in accordance with the principles and rules of treaty interpretation generally recognized in international law."[159]

Insofar as this may actually require reference outside the context of the ICSID Convention and Rules itself, pursuant to the approach under Art. 31(3)(c) of the Vienna Convention outlined above, two countervailing points may be noted:

(a) *Exclusion of diplomatic protection:* The first is that reference to rules of procedure developed in the context of the espousal of claims to diplomatic protection by states,

---

154. Antonio PARRA, "The Development of the Regulations and Rules of the International Centre for Settlement of Investment Disputes", 22 ICSID Rev – FILJ (2007) p. 55.
155. ICSID Secretariat "Possible Improvements of the Framework for ICSID Arbitration" (22 October 2004), "Suggested Changes to the ICSID Rules and Regulations" (12 May 2005), "Proposed Amendments to the ICSID Rules and Regulations" (2 January 2006), "Amendments to the ICSID Rules and Regulations" (5 April 2006), all available at <http://icsid.worldbank.org/ICSID/ICSID/ViewNewsReleases.jsp>.
156. See the general discussion of self-contained regimes in international law in the ILC Study Group Report on Fragmentation UN Doc. A/CN.4/L.682, 13 April 2006 [123]-[190].
157. SCHREUER, supra fn. 46, p. 666.
158. Introductory Note D to 1968 Arbitration Rules (1993) 1 ICSID Rep 63, 65.
159. *AMCO Asia Corp v. Indonesia* (Decision on Annulment), (ICSID, 1990, Higgins P, Lalonde and Magid) 1 ICSID Rep 509, 514.

even where these have been exercised in relation to the protection of investments, is most unlikely to be appropriate. The point was well made by the International Law Commission in its Report on Diplomatic Protection in distinguishing the procedures under investment treaties:

> "Such treaties abandon or relax the conditions relating to the exercise of diplomatic protection, particularly the rules relating to the nationality of claims and the exhaustion of local remedies.... The dispute settlement procedures provided for in BITs and ICSID offer greater advantages to the investor than the customary international law system of diplomatic protection, as they give the investor direct access to international arbitration, avoid the political uncertainty inherent in the very nature of diplomatic protection and dispense with the conditions necessary for the exercise of diplomatic protection."[160]

For this reason, Art. 17 of the ILC's Draft Articles on Diplomatic Protection provides: "The present draft articles do not apply to the extent that they are inconsistent with special rules of international law, such as treaty provisions for the protection of investments."[161]

(b) *Guidance as to internal procedure of international tribunals:* However, on matters of procedure on which the Rules are silent, it is permissible, even necessary, for an investment tribunal to have regard to practice on the same issue in other comparable international tribunals. For one thing, the tribunal's award may be the subject of an application for annulment if there has been a "serious departure from a fundamental rule of procedure".[162] This expression is not coterminous simply with the text of the ICSID Arbitration Rules themselves. Indeed, in *MINE v. Guinea,* the ad hoc Committee referred to an external example of what was meant by fundamental stating:

> "The Committee considers that a clear example of such a fundamental rule is to be found in Article 18 of the UNCITRAL Model Law on International Commercial Arbitration which provides:
>
> 'The parties shall be treated with equality and each party shall be given full opportunity of presenting his case.'
>
> The term 'fundamental rule of procedure' is not to be understood as necessarily including all of the Arbitration Rules adopted by the Centre."[163]

Elucidation of this term therefore does require some consideration of fundamental rules of procedure at the level of "general principles of law common to civilized

---

160. Supra fn. 39, pp. 89-90.
161. Accord DOUGLAS, supra fn. 83, pp. 213-226.
162. Art. 52(1)(d).
163. *MINE v. Guinea,* Decision on Annulment(Sucharitkul P, Broches and Mbaye) 4 ICSID Rep 85, 97.

nations",[164] and applications for annulment made under this head have normally proceeded on this basis, arguing lack of impartiality, violation of the right to be heard (*audi alteram partem*), absence or abuse of deliberation amongst the arbitrators and violation of the rules of evidence.[165]

Reference to external principles is not restricted to fundamental rules of this kind, but may also be made in cases where the Rules are silent. Thus, for example, ICSID tribunals first had to consider applications for the submission of amicus curiae briefs prior to the inclusion in the 2006 Rules of express provision for this.[166] In so doing, they made reference to the practice of NAFTA tribunals deciding the same question under UNCITRAL Rules.[167] So, too, tribunals have referred to the practice of other international tribunals in deciding whether to stay their proceedings pending the conclusion of other closely related proceedings.[168] That said, to date reported reference to general principles on procedural matters appears to have been limited.[169] This may be partly because the detailed character of the ICSID Rules themselves has reduced the number of questions left unaddressed.

The unique character of ICSID's self-contained lex arbitri really makes itself felt in the extent to which the Convention itself supplies the *external* as well as the internal procedural law. Of course, this self-contained character cannot be complete. In the last resort, as Art. 54 of the Convention makes plain, the assistance of national courts may still be required for the enforcement of ICSID awards. But for almost all other purposes national courts have no role to play. Thus the grant of provisional measures, an area where national courts still have a large role to play in support of other arbitral proceedings, is in ICSID procedure left entirely to the arbitral tribunal, unless the parties specifically agree otherwise.[170] Even more fundamentally, the review of an ICSID award is left exclusively to the annulment procedure provided under Art. 52 of the Convention and is carried out by an ad hoc Committee constituted by the Council under the Convention, and not by a national court.

*d.     Non-ICSID arbitration*

Outside the ICSID system, the position in principle is that investment treaty arbitration is in the same position as any other arbitration. So far as the internal procedure is concerned, the UNCITRAL Rules, which are those most commonly used for non-ICSID investment treaty arbitrations, betray the hallmarks of their origins as rules for

---

164. Art. 38(1)(d) ICJ Statute.
165. SCHREUER, supra fn. 46, pp. 972-982.
166. Rule 37(2) ICSID Arbitration Rules 2006.
167. *Aguas Provinciales de Santa Fe SA v. Argentina* (ICSID Case No. ARB/03/17), Order in Response to a Petition for Participation as Amicus Curiae (ICSID, 2006, Salacuse P, Kaufmann-Kohler and Nikken).
168. *SGS Société Générale de Surveillance v. Philippines*, Jurisdiction (ICSID, 2004, El-Kosheri P, Crawford and Crivillaro) 8 ICSID Rep 515 [171], relying on *MOX Plant Case (Ireland v. United Kingdom)* (PCA, Order No. 3, 24 June 2003) 42 ILM (2003) p. 1187.
169. FAUCHALD, supra fn. 106, p. 312.
170. Rule 39(6), as amended from 1986.

commercial cases. In particular, they assume that the basis for the arbitration will be a commercial contract, rather than a treaty. Thus, by the first sentence of the Preamble, the UN General Assembly states that it is: "Recognizing the value of arbitration as a method of settling disputes arising in the context of international commercial relations."[171] The jurisdictional provision (Art. 1) opens with the words: "Where the parties to a contract have agreed in writing that disputes in relation to that contract shall be referred to arbitration under the UNCITRAL Arbitration Rules...." The choice of law provision (Art. 33) includes, by para. 3, a provision that: "In all cases, the arbitral tribunal shall decide in accordance with the terms of the contract and shall take into account the usages of the trade applicable to the transaction."

However, the fact that the rules have commercial origins should not lead one to underestimate their utility in investment disputes. Comparatively soon after the Rules had been adopted in 1976, they were chosen by the negotiating parties to the Algiers Accords (in adapted form) as the procedural rules for the Iran-U.S. Claims Tribunal.[172] Since this Tribunal has decided many hundreds of disputes between American investors and Iran arising out of the Iranian Revolution, and its decisions have been publicly reported, there is in fact a highly sophisticated body of knowledge about the operation of the Rules in investment cases.[173] Moreover, the fact that the parties select arbitration under UNICTRAL Rules does not necessarily deprive them of the benefits of the administrative support of an institution. In particular, the Permanent Court of Arbitration in The Hague, the world's oldest standing arbitral institution, has considerable institutional expertise in handling claims involving sovereign states and is being chosen to administer an increasing number of investment treaty cases under UNCITRAL Rules.

So far as concerns external supervision of non-ICSID investment treaty arbitration, the lex arbitri will be simply the national law of the seat of the arbitration. Thus, both the English and Swedish Courts of Appeal have specifically rejected submissions that the fact that the arbitral award was rendered pursuant to the provisions of an international treaty affects the applicable standards of review under their national law of arbitration.[174] By definition, the equation will be different depending upon the particular national law in force at the seat of the arbitration. But it might fairly be concluded that there has been a convergence of arbitration law in the major jurisdictions which commonly provide the seat for investment treaty arbitrations in favour of allowing a large measure of party autonomy in arbitration, with a correspondingly limited scope of court intervention.

Where might this really make a difference? Three issues may be selected as providing a basis for a comparison of process: (a) the public transparency of the arbitral process itself; (b) the scope for the grant of provisional measures, both by the arbitral tribunal

---

171. UNGA Resolution 31/98 (15 December 1976).
172. Art. 3(2) Declaration of Algeria concerning the Settlement of Claims by the United States and Iran, 20 ILM (1981) p. 223.
173. David CARON, Lee CAPLAN and Matti PELLONPÄÄ, *The UNCITRAL Arbitration Rules: A Commentary* (Oxford UP, Oxford, 2006).
174. *Czech Republic v. CME Czech Republic BV,* supra fn. 99, at 493 (Svea Court of Appeal, 2003); *Occidental Exploration and Production Co v. Ecuador*, supra fn. 47, [2006] QB 432.

and by national courts in support; and (c) the scope of review of awards. These issues have been selected because they demonstrate, on a conceptual level, a stark difference between the lex arbitri in ICSID arbitration, and outside the ICSID procedure. Yet, it is submitted that, starting from a very different apparent point of departure, analysis of the practice supports an ongoing convergence of approach as a result of the inherent nature of investment treaty arbitration. This is warranted by the *nature* of the public interest in such cases (in the case of transparency); the *character* of the state as a party (in the case of provisional measures); and the *scope* of the arbitration agreement or *compromis*, as being defined by treaty (in the case of review).

2.  *Transparency*

The notion that any part of the arbitral process should be exposed to public view runs directly counter to a deeply ingrained perceived advantage of international commercial arbitration, which is that it exists for the *confidential* resolution of the dispute, as between the parties to it.[175] The extent to which the lex arbitri actually supports a legal obligation of confidence varies widely.[176] But nevertheless, parties to international commercial disputes continue to choose arbitration in part because it is not exposed to public view.

In investment treaty arbitration, however, precisely the opposite principle has developed. Thus, in 2005, the OECD Investment Committee commented that:

> "There is a general understanding amongst the Members of the Investment Committee that additional transparency, in particular in relation to the publication of arbitral awards, subject to the necessary safeguards for the protection of confidential business and governmental information, is desirable to enhance effectiveness and public acceptance of international investment arbitration, as well as contributing to the further development of a public body of jurisprudence. Members of the Investment Committee generally share the view that, especially insofar as proceedings raise important issues of public interest, it may also be desirable to allow third party participation, subject however to clear and specific guidelines."[177]

The same conclusion in principle was reached in the UNCITRAL Arbitration Working Group in 2008:

---

175. See generally Alan REDFERN and Martin HUNTER, *Law and Practice of International Commercial Arbitration*, 4th edn. (Sweet & Maxwell, 2004) [1-53]-[1-68].
176. Even between neighbouring states: cf. *Esso Australia Resources Ltd v. Plowman*, (1995) 183 CLR 10 (HCA) (on which see generally, 11 Arb Int (1995, no. 3)) and Sect. 6 Arbitration Amendment Act 2007 (NZ), noted KAWHARU, 24 Arb Int (2008) p. 405.
177. Organisation for Economic Cooperation and Development, *Transparency and Third Party Participation in Investor-State Dispute Settlement Procedures: Statement by the OECD Investment Committee* (2005) p. 1, available at <www.oecd.org>.

"It was generally recognized that arbitration proceedings in treaty-based arbitration raised issues that, in some respects, differed from ordinary commercial arbitration and a large number of delegations expressed the view that they required, on certain points, distinct regulation. The most frequently mentioned matter for such distinct regulation concerned transparency of the proceedings and the resulting award, an objective which received wide support in principle."[178]

Thus, the fact that investment treaty arbitration deals with matters of public interest is perceived as fundamentally changing the nature of the equation from the commercial arbitration paradigm – from confidentiality to transparency. But, for the moment at least, this recognition in principle is not matched by a consistency of approach in practice. The actual degree of transparency does (absent specific treaty provision) depend upon whether the arbitration proceeds under ICSID Rules, or outside the ICSID system. This is true of both the publication of awards, and the participation of non-parties in the arbitral process.

*a. Publication of awards*

The filing of all ICSID cases is a matter of public record. Although the Centre may not publish awards without the consent of the parties, the practice which has developed, in recognition of the important public interest involved in investment cases, has been that consent has been actively sought and usually provided. In the most recent revision of the Rules, it is in any event provided that the Centre has an obligation to "promptly include in its publications excerpts of the legal reasoning of the Tribunal".[179] This is of considerable benefit to the arbitral community, in that it makes it possible for a real jurisprudence of investment treaty law to develop.

There is no similar provision outside ICSID, and the record of publication of awards (or even disclosure of the existence of proceedings) in non-ICSID investment treaty cases is much more patchy. It generally depends upon the consent of both parties. There may well be reasons why investors, or even those states which are not under the same degree of public pressure at home, may prefer not to disclose the outcome of investment treaty arbitrations. It is important to ensure that the operation of the ICSID system is not subjected to more critical scrutiny simply because ICSID awards are published, when those produced outside ICSID may not be.

*b. Non-party participation*

Further, the new 2006 ICSID Rules now permit a tribunal to admit non-parties to the arbitration proceedings (Rule 32(2)) and to receive and consider written amicus curiae briefs from non-disputing parties (Rule 37(2)). In the former case, a party is given a right to object. In the latter, the tribunal is simply required to consult both parties on any

---

178. "Report of the Working Group on Arbitration and Conciliation on the work of its forty-eighth session" (New York, 4-8 February 2008), UNCITRAL, 41st Sess., UN Doc. A/CN.9/646, para. 69 (available at <www.uncitral.org>) (accessed 30 July 2008).
179. UNCITRAL Arbitration Rules (28 April 1976) <www.uncitral.org>.

decision to allow such a filing, and to hear the parties' observations on any such submission.[180]

The question whether such provisions should also be extended to investment treaty arbitrations conducted under UNCITRAL Arbitration Rules (the UNCITRAL Rules) was the subject of wide-ranging discussion in the Working Group on Arbitration in the course of its current work on the revision of the UNCITRAL Rules. However, despite agreement in principle, the Working Group expressed concern that this issue could delay completion of the revision of the generic Arbitration Rules.[181] The Commission itself agreed by consensus on the importance of ensuring transparency in investor-state arbitration, but decided to defer consideration of how that could best be achieved until after completion of the current revision of the UNCITRAL Rules.[182] For the moment, then, an arbitration proceeding under UNCITRAL Rules need not be the subject of public scrutiny, unless the parties agree, or there is provision for transparency under the applicable investment treaty.

c.   *Specific provision for transparency in investment treaties*
In the case of NAFTA, the Treaty establishes a Free Trade Commission with power to issue interpretative decisions. The Commission first exercised this power in 2001 to record that the Treaty did not impose a general duty of confidentiality, and that the State parties proposed to make tribunal documents publicly available.[183] Public access to the record having been provided, it then became possible for interested non-parties to follow NAFTA arbitral proceedings, and to apply to file their own submissions. Thereafter two NAFTA tribunals applying UNCITRAL Rules decided that Art. 15 of those Rules was sufficiently broad to permit them to receive non-disputing party amicus curiae submissions.[184] This practice was then codified by a further decision of the Commission.[185] Specific provision for transparency is now also found in the US Model BIT 2004[186] and in a number of new-model Free Trade Agreements concluded by the

---

180. For practice under the new Rules see: *Biwater Gauff (Tanzania) Ltd v. Tanzania* (ICSID Case No. ARB/05/22), Procedural Order No. 3 (2006) and Procedural Order No. 5 (2007) (ICSID, Hanotiau P, Born and Landau).
181. Supra fn. 178.
182. Report of the United Nations Commission on International Trade Law, Forty-first session (16 June - 3 July 2008) UNGA Official Records 63rd Session, Supp. No. 17, UN Doc. A/63/17, [314].
183. NAFTA FTA Decision of 31 July 2001, available at <www.naftaclaims.com>.
184. *Methanex Corp v. United States of America*, Award (NAFTA/UNCITRAL, 2005, Veeder P, Rowley and Reisman) 44 ILM (2005) p. 1345 ; *United Parcel Service of America Inc v. Government of Canada*, Decision of the Tribunal on Petitions for Intervention and Participation as Amici Curiae (NAFTA/UNCITRAL, 2001, Keith C, Fortier and Cass).
185. NAFTA FTA Decision of 7 October 2004, available at <www.naftaclaims.com>.
186. Arts. 28(3) and 29, reproduced in MCLACHLAN, SHORE and WEINIGER, supra fn. 7, App. 6.

United States,[187] as well as in the model investment treaties of Canada[188] and Norway,[189] and in other recent agreements.[190]

Thus, in summary, the position thus far reached is that the distinctive public features of investment treaty arbitration do in principle justify a complete reversal of the approach to transparency of proceedings and non-party participation than would ordinarily apply in an international commercial arbitration. But this principle has yet to be realized in practice, where there is now a wide difference between ICSID and most non-ICSID procedure.

3. *Provisional Measures*

In the case of the grant of provisional measures, in theory, ICSID and non-ICSID arbitration also differ considerably. In ICSID arbitration, provisional measures play a limited, non-binding role, with minimal scope for national court intervention; whereas in non-ICSID arbitration, especially under the regime of the UNICTRAL Rules and Model Law, both the arbitral tribunal and national courts have considerable scope to grant provisional measures.

But, on analysis, this difference may often be more apparent than real, at least in the paradigm case of provisional measures designed to freeze assets to secure payment of an award. The combined effect of the law on state immunity from measures of constraint, and jurisdictional limitations means that provisional measures will normally not be enforceable by national courts against state assets without the state's specific consent. Here, then, it is the distinctive consequence of the participation of the state which dictates the procedural consequences, and not the difference in the lex arbitri.

*a. Provisional measures in ICSID arbitration*

Art. 47 of the ICSID Convention provides: "Except as the parties otherwise agree, the Tribunal may, if it considers the circumstances so require, *recommend* any provisional measures which should be taken to preserve the respective rights of either party." (Emphasis added)

Arbitration Rule 39 deals with the procedure for provisional measures. In 2006, these Rules were strengthened to deal with the common situation of provisional measures which are required before the tribunal has been constituted.[191]

---

187. These are available at <www.ustr.gov/assets/Trade_Agreements/Regiona>. See, e.g., Arts. 10.20(3) and 10.21 Central America-Dominican Republic-United States Free Trade Agreement (signed 5 August 2004).
188. Arts. 38 and 39 Canada Model Investment Treaty 2004, available at <www.naftaclaims.com/files/Canada_Model_BIT.pdf>.
189. Arts. 18 and 19 Draft Norway Model BIT (December 2007).
190. E.g., Art. 157(1) of the New Zealand-China Free Trade Agreement 2008 (available at <New Zealand China Free Trade Agreement>), which provides for publication of tribunal documents.
191. Rule 39(1) now makes clear that a request for provisional measures may be made at any time after the institution of the proceeding. A new Rule 39(5) deals with applications made before the tribunal has been constituted. It permits the Secretary-General to set a timetable for the exchange of observations on the request, so that it may be considered by the tribunal "promptly upon its

Reference to the *travaux* of the Convention shows that the word "recommend" was substituted for "prescribe" as a result of the concerns of states at being subjected to binding provisional measures.[192] But, despite this, and in reliance on the jurisprudence of the ICJ resolving a similar issue, tribunals have held that provisional measures are binding on the parties.[193] After all, the PCIJ has held it to be a general principle of international adjudication "to abstain from any measure capable of exercising a prejudicial effect in regard to the execution of the decision to be given...".[194] In any event, the tribunal may take the consequences of non-compliance with a recommendation as to provisional measures into account in its award.[195] This creates a strong incentive to comply with a provisional measure, lest the failure to comply affects the ultimate outcome. However, since the final award itself is directly binding upon the parties by virtue of Art. 53 of the Convention, it is doubtful whether provisional measures simply designed to secure assets out of which an eventual award may be satisfied (a classic reason for granting provisional measures in commercial cases) would, save in exceptional circumstances, be granted against states in ICSID arbitration.[196]

*b. ICSID arbitration and national courts*
As has been seen, Art. 26 of the ICSID Convention provides that consent to ICSID arbitration operates "to the exclusion of any other remedy". One consequence of that provision for a self-contained procedure is to exclude the possibility of resort to national courts for provisional measures. Doubts about this, created as a result of an unfortunate decision of the French *Cour de Cassation*,[197] were put to rest by the addition in 1984 of a new paragraph in the Arbitration Rules. This now appears as Rule 39(6), and provides:

> "Nothing in this Rule shall prevent the parties, *provided that they have so stipulated in the agreement recording their consent*, from requesting any judicial or other authority to order provisional measures, prior to or after the institution of the proceeding, for the preservation of their respective rights and interests." (Emphasis added)

---

constitution".
192. SCHREUER, supra fn. 46, pp. 757-758; *History* supra fn. 65, II, p. 814 et seq.
193. *Casado v. Chile* (2001) (ICSID, 2001, Lalive P, Bedjaoui and Laoro Franco) 6 ICSID Rep 373 [17]-[21], applying *La Grand Case (Germany v. USA)* 2001 ICJ Rep 3, [98] et seq.
194. *Electricity Co of Sofia and Bulgaria Case*, Interim Measures Order (1939) PCIJ Ser A/B No. 79, 199.
195. BROCHES, *History*, supra fn. 65, II, p. 815.
196. *Tanzania Electric Supply Co v. Independent Power Tanzania Ltd* (2005), 8 ICSID Rep 226 (Rokison P, Brower and Rogers), accord SCHREUER, supra fn. 46, p. 777.
197. *Guinea v. Atlantic Triton*, Cass civ I (18 Nov 1986), Rev crit (1987) p. 760 note AUDIT, 26 ILM (1987) p. 373, 82 ILR 76, COLLINS, 234 *Recueil des Cours* (1992, no. 9), pp. 101-105.

The effect of this provision is to require the state's specific agreement in the *compromis* for the grant of provisional measures against it in national courts.[198] Otherwise, no such measures may be sought. This was recently confirmed by the English Court of Appeal in *ETI v. Bolivia,* upholding the setting aside of an ex parte order against Bolivia obtained in connection with ICSID arbitration proceedings.[199] Lawrence Collins LJ held that "the effect of Rule 39(6) is that provisional measures may be sought only from the ICSID tribunal itself, and not from national courts, unless the parties agree otherwise".[200] He held this provision enforceable in the English courts, since it constituted an agreement between the parties not to seek interim measures in a national court.[201]

c.   *Provisional measures in non-ICSID arbitration*

Outside ICSID, the position in principle is that provisional measures are available, both from the arbitral tribunal, and, in support from national courts. This has long been the position under the UNCITRAL Rules[202] and Model Law.[203] Recent (and controversial) amendments to the Model Law have further widened the powers of the tribunal to grant ex parte interim relief.[204] The new amendments also provide for court enforcement of interim measures.[205]

Provision for interim measures of protection, both by arbitral tribunals, and, in support, by national courts, is an important way of securing the efficacy of international commercial arbitration. But there are at least two reasons why it may be doubted whether there will be a considerable practical difference in investment treaty cases, at least as regards obtaining security from national courts over state assets prior to award:

(a) *Jurisdiction:* In the first place, a court will be unlikely to act absent some real connection with the forum. The point is well illustrated by the recent decision of the

---

198. Art. 26(3) 2004 US Model BIT (reproduced in MCLACHLAN SHORE and WEINIGER, supra fn. 7, App. 6, p. 393 at p. 408) makes such an express provision. It now appears in the investment chapters of a number of US Free Trade Agreements. But it is doubtful whether, in view of the current state of US law, it has effective bilateral operation. Since the decision of the US Supreme Court in *Grupo Mexicano de Desarollo SA v. Alliance Bond Fund Inc,* 527 US 308 (1999), a US federal court has no power under federal law to order an interim injunction restraining the disposal of assets pending final judgment or award. Its power is limited to ordering the attachment of assets under state law, a power which is normally limited to assets within the particular state: *Karaha Bodas Co LLC v. Perusahaan Pertambangan Minyak Dam Gas Bumi Negara,* 313 F 3d 70 (2d Cir 2002), cert den 539 US 904 (2003). It was just such a limitation which led to the unsuccessful attempt of the claimant in *ETI* to reinforce its attachment in New York with injunctive relief in England: infra [77]-[78].
199. *ETI Euro Telecom International BV v. Republic of Bolivia* [2008] EWCA Civ 880.
200. *Ibid.* [108].
201. *Ibid.* [109].
202. Art. 26.
203. Art. 17.
204. Art. 17B-C, adopted by the Commission in 2006, available at <www.uncitral.org>.
205. Art. 17H-I.

English High Court in *Mobil Cerro Negro v. Petroleos de Venezuela ("PdV")*[206] The claimant had parallel ICSID and ICC arbitration claims against, respectively, Venezuela, and PdV, the state-owned national oil company of Venezuela. The ICC arbitration had not been commenced, but the clause provided for arbitration in New York. Mobil sought a worldwide freezing order from the English court in support of the contemplated ICC proceedings. There was no evidence that the Respondent had any assets in England or other connection to the forum. Walker J held that:

> "… this court will only be prepared to exercise discretion to grant an application in aid of foreign litigation for a freezing order affecting assets not located here if the respondent or the dispute has a sufficiently strong link here or … there is some other factor of sufficient strength to justify proceeding in the absence of such link".[207]

Where the claim is against the state itself, it has been argued that "the mere presence of the property of the State is insufficient to found jurisdiction, even if it is commercial property",[208] although it cannot be said that this view has been unanimously followed by national courts.

(b) *Immunity:* Further, the law of state immunity is likely to operate as a bar upon pre-award attachment of assets. This was the unequivocal position taken by states in adopting the text of the UN Convention on the Jurisdictional Immunities of States and their Property 2004,[209] Art. 18 of which provides:

> "No pre-judgment measures of constraint, such as attachment or arrest, against property of a State may be taken in connection with a proceeding before a court of another State unless and except to the extent that:
> (a) the State has expressly consented to the taking of such measures as indicated:
> (i) by international agreement;
> (ii) by an arbitration agreement or in a written contract; or
> (iii) by a declaration before the court or by a written communication after a dispute between the parties has arisen; or
> (b) the State has allocated or earmarked property for the satisfaction of the claim which is the object of that proceeding."[210]

---

206. [2008] EWHC 532.
207. *Ibid.* [119]. The orders made in the related New York proceedings were limited to an attachment of funds held by PdV with the Bank of New York in New York: *Mobil Cerro Negro Ltd v. PDVSA Cerro Negro SA,* Civil Action No. 07 Civ 11590-DAB (Bates J, 27 December 2007 and 8 January 2008).
208. COLLINS, supra fn. 197, p. 167; James CRAWFORD, "Execution of Judgments and Foreign Sovereign Immunity", 75 AJIL (1981) p. 820 at pp. 857-858.
209. UNGA Res 38 (2 December 2004) UN Doc. A/Res/59/38.
210. See Hazel FOX, *The Law of State Immunity,* 2nd edn. (Oxford UP, Oxford 2008) pp. 616-631.

The confirmation of immunity of state assets from pre-judgment measures of constraint found in the UN Convention reflects existing state practice. Thus, in the United Kingdom, Sect. 13(2)(a) of the State Immunity Act 1978 prohibits the grant of relief by way of injunction against a state. The only exception is where the State has given its specific written consent.[211] This applies with equal force to injunctions in aid of arbitration.[212] The same position is taken under the US Foreign Sovereign Immunities Act.[213]

Thus, the special position of the state at international law is likely in any event to limit the extent to which a provisional measure freezing assets is available, irrespective of whether the proceedings are brought within the self-contained framework of ICSID or outside that system.

## 4. Review

The third respect in which there is an apparently considerable difference between ICSID and non-ICSID cases is in the approach to review of arbitral awards.[214] A central plank of the ICSID Convention was to insulate awards from review by national courts. In its place, the Contracting States substituted a mechanism for review by an Annulment Committee on five specific grounds enumerated in Art. 52(1). By contrast, investment arbitrations which take place outside the ICSID system are subject to review by the national courts at the seat of the arbitration and according to the standards of review provided for arbitral awards generally under national law, which may vary considerably from state to state. Here, however, analysis suggests a degree of convergence, reflecting both the inherent function of the arbitration agreement or *compromis* as delimiting the scope of the arbitral process and its specific application to investment treaty claims. In order to make this point good, it is necessary to say a little more about the historical origins of the modern standards.[215]

### a. Review under the ICSID Convention

Art. 52 of the ICSID Convention specifies an exhaustive list of five grounds on which an ICSID award may be annulled:

"(a) that the Tribunal was not properly constituted;
(b) that the Tribunal has manifestly exceeded its powers;

---

211. Sect. 13(3).
212. *ETI v. Bolivia*, supra fn. 199, [113].
213. Sect. 1610(d).
214. Analyzed in detail for this Conference by Gaëtan VERHOOSEL in his Report: "Annulment and Enforcement Review of Treaty Awards: To ICSID or Not to ICSID", this volume pp. 285-317.
215. The author is greatly indebted to research undertaken by Jack WASS (under the author's supervision) in the preparation of a research paper for the LL B (Hons) degree at Victoria University of Wellington on "The Meaning of 'Manifest Excess of Powers' in the Convention on the Settlement of Investment Disputes between States and Nationals of other States" (2008), which, it is hoped, will shortly be published in full.

(c) that there was corruption on the part of a member of the Tribunal;
(d) that there has been a serious departure from a fundamental rule of procedure; or
(e) that the award has failed to state the reasons on which it is based".

These grounds were borrowed directly from the International Law Commission's Model Rules on Arbitral Procedure, which had been finalized in 1958.[216] The *procedure* for the review of inter-state arbitral awards proposed by the ILC (a general power of review by the International Court of Justice) had found little favour with states. But the *grounds* for review were much closer to a codification of international law. Thus, when it came to the adoption in the ICSID Convention of a system of internal review (as opposed to review by national courts), the ILC Rules proved entirely apposite, and occasioned almost no amendment or dissent throughout the drafting process.[217]

Of the five specified grounds, it is Art. 52(1)(b), manifest excess of powers, which has since occasioned the most controversy.[218] Yet the principle of *excès de pouvoir*, which this key paragraph enshrines, was already long established as the prime basis for the nullity of an award in public international law. It played an important function in a system which was premised upon the finality of awards without appeal.[219] Thus, when the *Institut* finally completed its codification of arbitration law in 1929, it had emerged as one of only two grounds for the nullity of an award. Fauchille neatly encapsulates the concept as based upon the scope of the *compromis*. "*Les pouvoirs des arbitres sont déterminés par le compromis qui les investit. Ils doivent s'en tenir aux points mêmes qu'ils ont été chargés de trancher.*"[220]

Failure to abide by the *compromis* would thus be, "*un excès de pouvoir*".[221]

Hersch Lauterpacht explained what is meant by the scope of this *compromis*:

"... the remedy can easily be supplied by the exercise of a simple and strictly judicial function, namely, that of interpreting the *compromis*. Excess of jurisdiction may, of course, assume a variety of forms: the arbitrator may have adjudged on a matter not submitted to him, or he may have disregarded the sources of law which he was instructed to apply."[222]

---

216. Art. 35, International Law Commission "Model Rules on Arbitral Procedure with a General Commentary 1958" in *Yearbook* (1958) II, p. 83.
217. SCHREUER, supra fn. 46, pp. 888-889; *History* supra fn. 65, II, pp. 849-850.
218. See generally GAILLARD and BANIFATEMI, eds., *Annulment of ICSID Awards* (Juris Publishing, Huntington, NY 2004).
219. Art. 54 Hague Convention on the Pacific Settlement of Disputes 1899.
220. Paul FAUCHILLE, *Traité de droit international public*, I (Rousseau, Paris 1921) p. 548, and see the other references given by J. L. BRIERLY, "The Hague Conventions and the Nullity of Arbitral Awards", 9 BYIL (1928) p. 114.
221. *Ibid.*
222. H. LAUTERPACHT, "The Legal Remedy in Case of Excess of Jurisdiction", 9 BYIL (1928) p. 117 at p. 118.

The same point was made by a tribunal established under the Permanent Court of Arbitration in the *Orinoco Steamship* case in 1910, when it held that:

> "... excessive exercise of jurisdiction may consist, not only in deciding a question not submitted to the arbitrators, but also in disregarding the imperative provisions of the agreement as to the path along which they are to reach their decisions, notably with regard to the law or the legal principles to be applied".[223]

Seen in this light, it is unsurprising that Broches would have confirmed during the drafting of the ICSID Convention "that the drafters had intended by the words *excès de pouvoir* to refer to the case where a decision of the tribunal went beyond the terms of the *compromis*"[224] and that this included a failure to apply the proper law "if the parties had instructed the Tribunal to apply a particular law".[225] All that the framers of the Convention added to this classical test was the requirement that the excess of powers be "manifest".

The concept that a system of arbitration which set its face against appeal must nevertheless retain a concept of the nullity of an award which exceeds the scope of the parties" *compromis* is not, however, unique to public international law. On the contrary, it owes its origins to the very notion of the supervision of arbitration in Roman Law which was a question of review, not appeal.[226] As it was put by Paulus:

> "... the whole discussion must be founded on the particular terms of the submission, as the arbitrator cannot legally do anything but what was provided by the agreement that he should be able to do; accordingly he cannot decide just as he pleases, nor on whatever question he pleases, but only on the question which it was agreed to refer and in conformity with the agreement".[227]

The notion of a *compromis* applies relatively easily to an arbitration agreement between parties contained in a single document – whether a commercial contract or an inter-state agreement. In an investment treaty arbitration, the written consent of the parties to arbitrate consists in the agreement achieved by the state's standing consent given in the investment treaty itself, subject to the terms and conditions there set out, coupled with the investor's consent given on submission of the claim to arbitration.[228] This arbitration agreement is itself governed by international law.[229] Thus, the terms of the investment treaty itself define the scope of the *compromis*.

---

223. *Orinoco Steamship Co Case, United States v. Venezuela* (PCA, 1910) XI RIAA 227, 239.
224. *History*, supra fn. 65, II, p. 517.
225. *Ibid.*, p. 851.
226. A point recognized by GOLDSCHMIDT in the first work of the *Institut* on the topic in 1875: SCOTT, ed., *Resolutions of the Institute of International Law* (Oxford UP, NY 1916) p. 236.
227. MONRO, ed., *Digest* IV.8.32 (Cambridge UP, Cambridge 1904).
228. *Goetz v. Burundi*, supra fn. 66, at [67]; *American Manufacturing & Trading Ltd v. Zaire*, 5 ICSID Rep (1997) 11, 25-26; *Olguin v. Paraguay*, Jurisdiction, 6 ICSID Rep (2000) 154, [26].
229. *Occidental Exploration & Production Co v. Ecuador*, supra fn. 47, [2006] QB 432, [33].

### b. UNCITRAL arbitration

Outside the framework of ICSID, the review of arbitral awards by national courts may be subject to the vagaries of national laws and judicial approaches at the seat of the arbitration. But excess of the arbitrator's authority, as defined by the scope of the *compromis,* remains a core ground for the setting aside of awards. This may be seen in the provisions of the UNCITRAL Model Law,[230] which have had a considerable impact on the progressive harmonization of the law relating to the review of international arbitral awards, at least amongst states commonly chosen as arbitral seats because of their supportive attitude to arbitration. Art. 34 of the Model Law provides an exclusive list of grounds upon which recourse against an award may be made. It excludes appeal on a point of law. Art. 34(2)(a)(iii) provides for setting aside where:

> "the award deals with a dispute not contemplated by or not falling within the terms of the submission to arbitration, or contains decisions on matters beyond the scope of the submission to arbitration...."

In the equally authoritative French text, this reads:

> "*Que la sentence porte sur un différend non visé dans le compromis ou n'entrant pas dans les prévisions de la clause compromissoire, ou qu'elle contient des décisions qui dépassent les termes du compromis ou de la clause compromissoire....*"

The content of Art. 34 was greatly influenced by the closed list of grounds upon which recognition and enforcement of an award may be refused under Art. V of the New York Convention.[231] Art. 34(2)(a)(iii) is in identical terms (*mutatis mutandis*) to Art. V(1)(c) of the New York Convention. Van den Berg concluded that this provision: "... concerns those cases where the arbitrator has given decisions in excess of his authority due to a transgression of the scope of the arbitration agreement and the questions submitted to him by the parties".[232]

Van den Berg noted that this ground has seldom been relied upon as an objection to enforcement. But it has assumed a particular importance in the context of investment treaty arbitration, in view of the precise definition of the arbitrators' authority achieved by the fact that the investment treaty itself delimits the scope of the *compromis.* The English courts have recently decided two challenges to investment treaty arbitral awards, rendered under UNCITRAL Rules in London, where the principal ground of objection

---

230. UN Docs. A/40/17 (1985) and A/61/17, Annex 1 (2006).
231. Howard HOLTZMANN and Joseph NEUHAUS, *A Guide to the UNCITRAL Model Law on International Commercial Arbitration: Legislative History and Commentary* (1989) p. 1055.
232. Albert Jan VAN DEN BERG, *The New York Arbitration Convention of 1958: Towards a Uniform Interpretation* (Kluwer, Deventer 1981) p. 321.

was excess of jurisdiction[233] or power[234] by the arbitral tribunal.[235] Each case involved a careful interpretation of the treaty, applying Arts. 31-32 of the Vienna Convention, in order to determine whether the decision of the tribunal fell within its scope.

Three concluding observations may be made from this comparison of the basis for review in investment treaty cases as to: (a) the *central function* of review as opposed to appeal; (b) the *nature* of the arbitration agreement; and (c) the *composition* of the review tribunal.

*First*, the central issue in each case is *not* appeal on error of law, but rather the power of the arbitrators as determined by the scope of the arbitration agreement. A general right of appeal is not part of the public international law concept of arbitration. The States parties to the ICSID Convention followed this model by adopting a system of review not appeal. It is difficult to imagine circumstances in which states would wish to revisit that choice and to substitute an appeals court. Such a suggestion was mooted early in the recent review of the ICSID Arbitration Rules, but subsequently abandoned.[236] The possibility of an appellate system has found its way into US treaty practice,[237] but has yet to be actually introduced even on a bilateral basis. Its introduction on a multilateral basis would face formidable hurdles. Within the ICSID system, it would require an amendment to Art. 26 of the Convention, which in turn would require the agreement of all of the Convention's 143 Member States.[238] At the same time, the *general* trend in national arbitration law, confirmed by Art. 34 of the UNCITRAL Model Law, has been to limit the grounds for recourse against awards, by excluding error of law, whilst at the same time continuing to provide for the setting aside of awards where the arbitrator has gone beyond the *compromis*.

*Second*, it is the investment treaty itself which (together with the investor's consent upon institution of proceedings) constitutes the arbitration agreement or *compromis*. Thus, the rights and duties created by the treaty delimit the scope of the powers of the arbitral tribunal. This agreement is governed by international law, and construed in accordance with international law principles of interpretation. The fact that the tribunal's jurisdiction and powers are derived from a treaty between states only underscores the need to retain, whether within or outside the ICSID system, an effective procedure for review, where the parties' agreement to arbitrate has been exceeded by the tribunal.

---

233. Sect. 67(1)(a) Arbitration Act 1996 (UK).
234. *Ibid.*, Sect. 68(2)(b). The House of Lords in *Lesotho Highlands Development Authority v. Impregilo SpA*, supra fn. 54 (a concession contract arbitration, not an investment treaty case) emphasized that an excess of power (otherwise than by excess of substantive jurisdiction) under this clause did not include an error of law, and was derived from the same concept as Art. V(1)(c) of the New York Convention: [30]. However, in view of the foregoing analysis, it may be doubted whether their Lordships gave adequate weight to the significance of the parties' express choice of Lesotho law as an element of the *compromis*.
235. *Occidental Exploration & Production Co v. Ecuador (No 2)* [2006] EWHC 345 (Comm), [2006] 1 Lloyd's Rep 773, affd. [2007] EWCA Civ 656; *Czech Republic v. European Media Ventures SA*, [2008] 1 Lloyd's Rep 186.
236. ICSID Secretariat Papers, supra fn. 155.
237. Annex D, US 2004 Model BIT.
238. Art. 66 ICSID Convention.

*Third*, it is particularly important to develop a *jurisprudence constante* of the principles applicable the grounds for review, as much in ICSID as in any national lex arbitri. One potential way of promoting such an approach may be to move towards a degree of specialization within the ICSID Panel of Arbitrators, so that a specific panel of arbitrators would serve only on annulment committees. That would not be a step which required amendment of the Convention. But, to be fully effective, it would have to be done in a transparent and structured manner. Such a measure might go further than any more far-reaching proposal in facilitating a greater degree of certainty about standards of review. The practical effect would be comparable to what may be achieved over time by a specific national court whose members are regularly engaged in hearing applications for review of arbitral awards.

V.   CONCLUSIONS

The conclusions reached in this Report may therefore be summarized in the following ten points:

*Nature of Investment Treaty Arbitration*

(1) *Distinctive character of investment treaty arbitration:* Investment treaty arbitration derives its unique character from the investment treaty itself: as the basis for state consent to arbitration, and as the principal source of the rights giving rise to the investor's cause of action. This inserts questions of international law into the law applicable to the arbitration agreement, the merits and the procedure, which are not the same as those which arise in an international commercial arbitration based upon an agreement to arbitrate by contract.

(2) *Adoption of arbitration model:* Yet the character of investment treaty arbitration has also been shaped by the conscious adoption, both in the framing of the ICSID Convention and in the drafting of dispute settlement provisions in investment treaties, of arbitration as the means of dispute settlement. The resulting system shares hallmarks of both international commercial arbitration and inter-state arbitration. But it is quite unlike systems of adjudication adopted in other fields of international law, notably in the Dispute Settlement Understanding of the WTO. Of its nature, the arbitration model is a fragmented form of decision-making, since arbitral tribunals are not standing courts, and their jurisdiction depends upon the scope of the parties' agreement to arbitrate or *compromis*.

(3) *International law as means of balancing private and public rights:* The central task of investment treaty arbitration is to find an appropriate balance between the protection of private rights and the recognition of legitimate public interests. This is a function of international law itself, and is to be achieved by the adoption of a consistent approach to legal reasoning in investment treaty cases; and the identification of common general principles of international law which underpin this field.

*Lex causae*

(4) *Choice of applicable law:* Of its nature, the law applicable to the substance in investment treaty arbitration will be: (a) international law and (b) host state law. This is likely to be so whether there is an express choice of law clause in the treaty, or where the matter is left to the provisions of Art. 42(1) of the ICSID Convention (second sentence), or where the tribunal is sitting outside the ICSID framework. The choice of which of these two legal systems applies to a particular issue is a matter of characterizing the issue, and selecting the legal system which properly applies to that issue. Yet this choice of law process may be distinguished from that undertaken in private international litigation or arbitration, since national and international law stand in a vertical, and not horizontal, relationship to each other.

(5) *Investment treaty as a creature of international law:* An investment treaty is not a self-contained regime. It is a creature of international law. Thus:

(a) where international law is applicable to the question in issue, international law as a whole will be applicable, and not simply the treaty in isolation; and

(b) the treaty must be interpreted in accordance with the principles of interpretation (now codified in Arts. 31-32 of the Vienna Convention), which are applicable to all treaties.

(6) *Common principles of international investment law:* Although consistency is still far from being achieved, there is a much stronger movement towards the identification of common principles of law, or a *jurisprudence constante,* in investment treaty cases than in international commercial arbitration. This is not a question of the application of a doctrine of precedent. Rather, it flows from the essentially common questions of law raised by investment treaties.

(7) *Systemic interpretation of investment treaties:* The interpretation of an investment treaty provision begins with the ordinary meaning of its terms in their context and in the light of its object and purpose: Art. 31 Vienna Convention. But it does not end there. A particularly important element in the interpretation of investment treaties is the requirement to have regard to "other rules of international law applicable in the relations between the parties": Art. 31(3)(c) Vienna Convention. This rule embodies a principle of systemic interpretation, requiring the interpreter to consider other rules of international law whether found in other treaties to which both states are parties, or in custom, or in general principles of law common to civilized nations.

*Lex arbitri*

(8) *Party autonomy:* The general principle of party autonomy in arbitration finds recognition in investment treaty arbitration in the widespread (though not universal) existence of a choice between arbitral fora. In particular many investment treaties offer the claimant a choice between (a) ICSID arbitration and (b) ad hoc arbitration under UNCITRAL Rules. Under both systems, the parties may vary the applicable procedure by express agreement.

(9) *Contrast between ICSID and non-ICSID procedural law:* Conceptually, the choice between ICSID arbitration and non-ICSID arbitration represents a major difference in principle:

(a) The ICSID system is designed to operate in a self-contained manner. This is not simply as regards the internal arbitral procedure. It also applies to the exclusion of external intervention by national courts, save only for the ultimate enforcement of an unsatisfied award.
(b) Non-ICSID investment treaty arbitration is in general governed by rules designed for application to international commercial arbitration, and is in principle subject to the national law, and the control of the national courts, at the seat of the arbitration.

(10) *Convergence on common principles:* Important practical differences may still flow from a choice between ICSID and non-ICSID procedures. But analysis of the major areas where differences are commonly identified demonstrates a process of convergence upon common principles, which reflect the distinctive character of investment treaty arbitration: in developing a common understanding (not yet fully realized in practice) that investment treaty arbitration normally requires transparency and not confidentiality; in limiting the availability of provisional measures as a means of securing state assets prior to award; and in framing by reference to the scope of the investment treaty itself the essential question on the review of the award as whether the scope of the parties' *compromis* has been exceeded.

After some twenty years of experience with investment treaty arbitration, it will be tempting for many to conclude that such a fragmented system of dispute resolution risks producing again for the twenty-first century what Tennyson described two centuries ago as:

"... the lawless science of our law,
That codeless myriad of precedent,
That wilderness of single instances".[239]

Yet this Report has sought to demonstrate that the debates over precedent and the development of appellate structures fundamentally mistake the inherent nature of this system. This field of law does not need the creation of a new Tower of Babel.[240] Indeed the fate of the Tower of Babel serves to remind us that, in designing modern systems of international dispute settlement, a plurality of solutions is not a vice or imperfection in the system. But rather it is a necessary, even essential, part of it. The design of solutions to deal, for example, with decisional fragmentation may positively accept plural sites of decision-making and law-making, whilst still searching for just solutions to conflicts of jurisdiction or law which arise.[241] In this task, general international law has a vital role

---

239. Alfred Lord TENNYSON, "Aylmer's Field" (1793) in *The Collected Poems of Alfred Lord Tennyson* (Wordsworth Ed, 1994) p. 581.
240. *Genesis* 11, 1-9.
241. Campbell MCLACHLAN, *Lis Pendens in International Litigation* (Nijhoff, Leiden 2009).

to play. It supplies the reasoning processes which build systemic relationships between rules.[242] It also supplies the general principles, which explain the operation of the system as a whole and help to solve the conflict of opposing rights and interests, which it is the enduring function of jurisprudence to resolve.[243] It will be the successful elucidation and application by arbitral tribunals of consistent processes of reasoning, recognizing the distinctive character of investment treaty arbitration, which will ultimately determine the enduring success of arbitration as an effective means of resolving investment disputes.

---

242. ILC Study Group Fragmentation Report, supra fn. 138, [35].
243. *Eastern Extension, Australasia and China Telegraph Co Ltd Case* (British-United States Claims Arbitral Tribunal) (1923) VI RIAA 112, 114.

# Investment Treaty Arbitration and Commercial Arbitration: Are They Different Ball Games? The Legal Regime/Framework

*Bernard Hanotiau*[*]

| TABLE OF CONTENTS | Page |
| --- | --- |
| I. Introduction | 146 |
| II. Commercial Cases | 146 |
| III. BIT Arbitration | 148 |
| IV. Publicists and Privatists | 149 |

## I. INTRODUCTION

The topic of this afternoon session is to determine whether investment treaty arbitration and commercial arbitration are different ball games. And we are asked to reflect and comment on this issue in light of the legal regimes governing each of these areas.

We have just heard a very elaborate report on this topic by Professor McLachlan (this volume, pp. 95-145). I would like within the very short time frame that I am allocated, to comment from the point of view of an international commercial arbitrator who, after twenty-five years of practice in international commercial arbitration, has stepped into the world of bilateral investment treaty (BIT) arbitration in a number of ICSID and UNCITRAL cases.

In my experience, arbitrating a BIT dispute or drafting a BIT award is a much more difficult exercise than deciding a commercial dispute, whatever its nature. This can be explained for many reasons. Let us start with commercial arbitration.

## II. COMMERCIAL CASES

In commercial arbitration, the arbitrator has a much broader discretionary power in the decision process, whether the parties have agreed on the applicable law or not.

If the parties have not determined the applicable law, arbitration rules often provide that the arbitral tribunal shall make its award in accordance with the rules of law which it considers appropriate. This gives a lot of flexibility to the arbitral tribunal and, very often, it will determine the applicable rules of law by application of what is called "*la voie directe*". In other words, it will choose the law of the State which, in its opinion, has the closest connection to the facts of the case.

In any case, even if the parties have chosen the applicable law or rules of law, most arbitration rules provide that in all cases, the arbitral tribunal shall take into account any

---

[*] Professor of International Dispute Resolution, University of Louvain; Vice-President, London Court of International Arbitration, Institute of Transnational Arbitration and CEPANI (Belgium); Member of ICCA.

applicable trade usages. And we know that the term "trade usages" is not a restrictive term. It applies not only to the usages of a particular trade, but also extends to general principles of international commercial law. And indeed, most modern arbitration rules do not require an arbitral tribunal to apply a legal system as a whole, but rather to apply "rules of law" more generally. This means that arbitrators may, when appropriate, decide to apply transnational rules.

Moreover, in some cases, arbitrators are authorized to decide in equity, "*en amiable composition*", such that they are under no obligation to apply the rules of the otherwise applicable law except if they pertain to public policy.

But in practice, whether the parties have chosen the applicable law, whether it is determined by the arbitral tribunal, whether the arbitral tribunal is authorized to decide in equity, very often in commercial cases the role of the rule of law is extremely limited. There are many awards in which you will not find any substantial legal developments beyond the application of general principles of law such as *pacta sunt servanda*, good faith, full compensation, mitigation of damages. In other words, the parties' agreement is often self-containing, self-sufficient. It embodies all the relevant provisions, the application of which will be sufficient to decide the dispute.

In preparing this paper, I reviewed a number of awards rendered in cases, some of which I was involved with, where there was in parallel a BIT case and a contractual case on the basis of the same facts. I was struck to see that in the contractual awards, written by prominent arbitrators, there was not a single legal argument. The award was devoted in totality to contract interpretation and factual assessment. There was not even a single reference to a rule of interpretation.

So, in commercial arbitration, in many cases, the law will play a secondary role; the dispute will be mainly decided on the basis of the provisions contained in the agreement of the parties, taking into consideration the facts of the case as they appear from the documents submitted by counsel and the witness hearing.

I would also venture to add that in many commercial cases, the equitable impression of the arbitral tribunal, in other words, the way he perceives the equities of the case, will play an important role in the decision of the panel.

Does an arbitral tribunal sitting in a commercial arbitration refer to previous awards in its decision-making process? In my experience, this is very rare, except in relation to very specific substantive or procedural issues which have been dealt with on a regular basis by a number of arbitral tribunals. Commercial arbitration awards are not systematically published and, in any case, they have no binding force. Moreover, very often, even if the general context of two cases is similar, the contractual provisions are different, the facts are different and it is therefore extremely difficult to transpose to one commercial dispute what has been decided in another one.

So much for commercial arbitration.

III. BIT ARBITRATION

How does the situation compare in BIT arbitration? The situation is totally different.

The role of an arbitral tribunal in BIT arbitration is also to adjudicate a dispute. But beyond an assessment of the facts, here, the arbitral panel will also have to perform very substantial, multi-step, legal work before reaching its final decision.

It starts with jurisdiction. It is true that it is becoming common in commercial arbitration to have the procedure bifurcated between jurisdiction and quantum. But in many cases, the issue of jurisdiction is still very factual; for example the panel will have to determine whether the conduct of a non-signatory in the negotiation, performance and/or termination of an agreement amounts to an adhesion to the arbitration clause. In investment arbitration, the issue of jurisdiction is nearly invariably raised by the respondent. It leads the arbitral tribunal to determine whether claimant has standing under the ICSID Convention, for example, but also whether it qualifies for protection under the applicable BIT; whether it is a protected investor for the purposes of the treaty; whether there is an investment; whether the investment is protected under the relevant treaty; and whether the causes of action arise under the BIT. Determining whether the arbitral tribunal has jurisdiction is definitely a much more complex legal task than in commercial arbitration.

The situation is also quite different when it comes to the merits. As opposed to commercial arbitration, where the contract concluded by the parties is often self-containing, investment treaties are not self-contained regimes. International law is a legal system and investment treaties are creatures of it and governed by it. When, by virtue of Art. 42 of the ICSID Convention or otherwise, tribunals are directed that the applicable law to the particular issue before them is international law, that is a reference to the whole of international law and not merely the specific treaty before them. And to determine which are the applicable norms of international law applicable to the case, the arbitral tribunal will have to have recourse to the process of treaty interpretation contained in Arts. 31 and 32 of the Vienna Convention.

The fact that the dispute is governed by a treaty and international law does not, of course, exclude the possibility of applying national law and, in particular, host-State law, to other issues in the case, as provided in Art. 42 of the ICSID Convention. Applying national law is not an easy task; it is subject to rigorous requirements which, if they are not complied with, may open the door to annulment proceedings.

Finally, when it comes to referring to past awards, the attitude of commercial arbitrators and investment tribunals is also different. According to the statistics of the International Chamber of Commerce, no more than fifteen percent of its awards cite previous arbitral decisions and most of these citations concern procedural issues and not substantive issues. The situation is different in investment arbitration. While there is no doctrine of precedent per se, investment tribunals concur on the need to take earlier cases into account. This can be easily explained by the fact that in BIT arbitration, one of the parties is a State, it concerns an investment in that State, international law is applicable, the disputes involve to a large extent the same standards (expropriation, fair and equitable treatment, denial of justice, non-discriminatory measures, full protection of security, etc.) and the awards are published and immediately commented on by lawyers coming from all kinds of perspectives. Even if it is not always achieved, consistency is part of the expectations, much more than in commercial cases. It can also be easily tested, which is not the case in commercial arbitration, where the legal and factual parameters are rarely identical. The BIT tribunal will, therefore, for each standard, carefully review the relevant cases and restate them in summary in the award, before applying the results of its analysis to the facts of the dispute and determining whether the conduct of which claimant complains is attributable to the State, taking into consideration the International Law Commission Articles on State Responsibility.

It may be at the end of the process, when the tribunal comes to the stage of determining the damages and the amount of compensation to be awarded to claimant, that the adjudication process offers more similarities with commercial arbitration. Even if the legal source is different (international law or national law or transnational legal principles), the basic principle is that of full compensation, which leads to the application in BIT cases of methods which are well known to commercial arbitrators, such as the discounted cash flow method.

Also, the rules concerning causation applied by commercial and BIT tribunals will often be similar. Indeed, it is generally accepted that international law gives little guidance on the precise test of causation and that, therefore, recourse should be had to private law analyses, in other words, to the general principles of causation recognized by civilized nations (Art. 38 of the International Court of Justice Statute).

IV.   PUBLICISTS AND PRIVATISTS

In conclusion, arbitrating a BIT case or a commercial case are quite different experiences in many respects, as I have tried to demonstrate. Deciding a BIT case is a much more difficult, rigorous, and demanding exercise than deciding a commercial case. But should we go as far to conclude, as apparently some publicists would tend to do, that commercial arbitrators should restrict their work to commercial cases and leave BIT arbitration to genuine public international law specialists?

This reminds me of the time, many years ago, when I was a young assistant professor of law at the Center for International Law at the University of Louvain. There were two sections in the Center, also physically separate: on one side of the corridor, the public international law section and on the other side, the private international law division. They would not easily mix. We could easily feel a sense of superiority of the public international law professors, who were conscious of having expertise and teaching a discipline operating at the level of States, much superior to common matters as the status of immigrants or interstate divorces or choice of law in international contracts. On the other hand, at that time, very few lawyers wanted to specialize in public international law because they did not perceive any possibility to make a reasonable living in that area, while many law graduates choose to specialize in private international law which was supposed to be of everyday use.

Things have changed. In particular, with the development of investment arbitration, public international law has become a field of common practice in international arbitration while private international law nowadays plays a more limited role in commercial cases. On the other hand, publicists and privatists now meet and work together in investment arbitration, and they play a complementary role in the development of the BIT case law. Publicists probably have a better knowledge and feeling for public international law. But being constantly exposed to so many different legal systems, privatists learn fast and they definitely have wide experience in dealing with facts.

I do not agree with the position of certain publicists that discrepancies in BIT awards are attributable to the fact that privatists are more lenient and flexible than the publicists when it comes to treaty interpretation because they import contract interpretation standards. I think that publicists and privatists have a complementary expertise and that their working together in mixed BIT arbitration panels can, and hopefully will, contribute to the development of an harmonious and modern body of international law.

# Comment on the Differing Legal Frameworks of Investment Treaty Arbitration and Commercial Arbitration as Seen Through Precedent, Annulment, and Procedural Rules

*Brooks W. Daly and Fedelma Claire Smith*[*]

| TABLE OF CONTENTS | Page |
|---|---|
| I. Introduction | 151 |
| II. Precedent | 151 |
| III. Award Annulment in Investment Treaty Arbitration and Commercial Arbitration | 155 |
| IV. Is it Feasible to Conduct Treaty Arbitration under Rules That Also Serve in Commercial Disputes, or Do We Need to Generate Additional Sets of Rules, Other than ICSID, Expressly Designed for Investor-State Disputes? | 158 |
| V. Conclusion | 163 |

I. INTRODUCTION

Professor Campbell McLachlan's Report (this volume, pp. 95-145) provides a thorough survey of the differences and convergences of the legal frameworks governing commercial arbitration and investment treaty arbitration. This Comment reflects upon three issues addressed by Professor McLachlan: the importance of precedent in investment treaty arbitration, the annulment of awards in investment treaty and commercial arbitration,[1] and whether existing procedural rules are sufficient for the needs of investment treaty arbitration.

II. PRECEDENT

The use of arbitral precedent to achieve consistency of decisions in arbitral awards is a key indicator that investment treaty arbitration and international commercial arbitration are indeed "different ballgames". While discussion of this topic is muted or absent in modern commercial arbitration discourse, in the last year or so it appears to have

---

[*] At the time of writing, the authors were respectively Deputy Secretary-General and Assistant Legal Counsel at the Permanent Court of Arbitration at The Hague.
[1] For the avoidance of doubt, this comment uses "commercial arbitration" to refer to arbitration between two private parties arising under a contract, while "investment treaty arbitration" refers to arbitration between an investor and a state arising under a bilateral or multilateral treaty for the protection of investment.

become the dominant subject matter for writers on investment treaty arbitration.[2] In international commercial arbitration, disputes often arise from questions of fact, arbitral awards are confidential, and the substantive law applicable to the dispute is the highly developed body of commercial law of a particular jurisdiction. Commercial arbitration awards rarely make interpretations of substantive law that have any impact in other disputes. In contrast, investment treaty disputes often raise similar or identical questions of international law, arbitral awards are published, and the awards themselves serve to elucidate principles of international investment law for future arbitrators.[3]

Because the questions of international law decided by investment treaty tribunals bear upon "sensitive national legislative and regulatory interests",[4] conflicting precedents call the legitimacy of the investment treaty arbitration system into question.[5]

Some commentators are cautiously optimistic that any crisis in the investment treaty system will be averted. Their expectation is that the de facto system of precedent that is emerging will, with the help of diligent arbitrators, lead to a *jurisprudence constante*, and the problem of conflicting precedents will fade over time.[6]

However, for those whom Jan Paulsson has called the "prophets of the apocalypse of conflicting precedents",[7] lack of consistency is a real threat to the current system of investment treaty arbitration. These commentators argue that ad hoc dispute resolution with no *stare decisis*, while appropriate for commercial arbitration, is simply ill-suited to the coherent development of international investment law. The significant potential liability that investment disputes may create for State treasuries requires a system with

---

2. Recent publications containing significant treatment of precedent in investment treaty arbitration include MCLACHLAN, SHORE and WEINIGER, *International Investment Arbitration: Substantive Principles* (Oxford 2007); Special Issue on Precedent in Investment Arbitration, 5 Transnational Dispute Management (May 2008, no. 3) (hereinafter TDM Special Issue on Precedent in Investment Arbitration); Andrea K. BJORKLUND, "Investment Treaty Arbitral Decisions as Jurisprudence Constante" in Colin PICKER, Isabella BUNN and Douglas ARNER, eds., *International Economic Law: the State and Future of the Discipline* (Hart Publishing 2008); Emmanuel GAILLARD and Yas BANIFATEMI, eds., *Precedent in International Arbitration* (Juris Publishing 2008); Karl P. SAUVANT, ed., *Appeals Mechanisms in International Investment Disputes* (Oxford 2008); C. SCHREUER and Matthew WEINIGER, "Precedent" in MUCHLINSKI, ORTINO, SCHREUER, eds., *The Oxford Handbook of International Investment Law* (Oxford 2008).
3. While the discussion of the proper role of arbitral awards among the sources of international law set forth in Art. 38 of the Statute of the International Court of Justice goes on, any reader of the pleadings or attendee at hearings in an investment treaty arbitration today should be persuaded that, de facto, arbitral awards have become a primary source for the establishment of rules of international investment law. See generally, Jan PAULSSON, "International Arbitration and the Generation of Legal Norms" in *International Arbitration 2006: Back to Basics?*, ICCA Congress Series no. 13 (2007).
4. C. BROWER and J. SHARPE, "The Coming Crisis in the Global Adjudication System", 19 Arb. Int. (2003) p. 418.
5. See, e.g., *ibid.*, at pp. 424-428.
6. See, e.g., Gabrielle KAUFMANN-KOHLER, "Arbitral Precedent: Dream, Necessity or Excuse?", 23 Arb. Int. (2007) p. 357, at p. 376.
7. Jan PAULSSON,"'Soft Law' Sources and Impacts in International Arbitration", at the 5th Annual ITA-ASIL Conference, Washington, DC (9 April 2008) remembered by Brooks Daly.

predictable standards that can only be assured through the establishment of a standing court of international investment,[8] or reform of the present regime through introduction of a system of binding precedent.[9] Other commentators have conceived of an interim position whereby a permanent body could give preliminary (and consistent) rulings on points of law, similar to that available at the European Court of Justice, but arbitral tribunals would nevertheless preserve "their basic competence" and the preliminary rulings "would not affect the principle of finality".[10] These proposals appear fanciful from today's perspective, in view of the embryonic stage of the thinking of the commentators[11] as well as the difficult consensus and coordinated effort of States that would be required to reform the existing mechanisms (e.g., amend the ICSID Convention, or align the terms of all bilateral investment treaties (BITs)).[12]

Without taking sides between the optimists and the "prophets of the apocalypse", there is undoubtedly more pressure to reform the investment treaty system today than we have seen in recent decades in the context of commercial arbitration. There has never been a withdrawal from the 1958 New York Convention, but we have seen withdrawal[13]

---

8. "The failings go beyond that of the rogue tribunal or the cowboy arbitrator, in spite of the murmuring of some to this effect. Regardless of how prudently a tribunal acts in an individual case, the system as a whole lacks accountability and openness in fundamental ways, and above all it is open to a perception of bias so long as arbitrators earn appointments by the claim. This can only be remedied [by] moving away from private arbitration and back to the model of public courts."

    Gus VAN HARTEN, *Investment Treaty Arbitration and Public Law* (Oxford University Press 2007) p. 175. For an economic analysis bearing on the question, see William M. LANDES and Richard A. POSNER, "Adjudication as a Private Good", 8 J. Legal Studies, pp. 238-240. The authors posit that systems of adjudication have two functions: (1) dispute resolution and (2) production of rules or precedents. While the market can provide private dispute resolution, production of precedent is a public good and best entrusted to a public body because private actors have little or no incentive to produce precedent.

9. See Marie-Louise M. RODGERS, "Bilateral Investment Treaties and Arbitration: An Argument and a Proposal for the ICSID's Implementation of a System of Binding Precedent" in TDM Special Issue on Precedent in Investment Arbitration, supra fn. 2.

10. C. SCHREUER and M. WEINIGER, "Conversations Across Cases – Is There a Doctrine of Precedent in Investment Arbitration?" in TDM Special Issue on Precedent in Investment Arbitration, supra fn. 2, p. 5.

11. Schreuer and Weiniger leave open the questions of "under what circumstances a tribunal would request a preliminary ruling and whether it would be under an obligation to do so [and] whether these rulings would bind the tribunal or would merely constitute recommendations". *Ibid.*

12. Where an appeals mechanism outside of ICSID is contemplated, it is unlikely that national courts would provide the appropriate venue. Aside from the fact that States imagining themselves as respondents would be reluctant to give the courts of third States jurisdiction to hear appeals on the merits of the award, the courts of some jurisdictions may not allow such appeals to begin with. See Tim TYLER and Archis A. PARASHARAMI, "Finality over Choice: *Hall Street Associates, L.L.C. v. Mattel. Inc.* (US Supreme Court)", 25 JOIA (2008, no. 5) pp. 613-621.

13. On 2 May 2007, Bolivia submitted its notice of withdrawal from the Convention under Art. 71 of the Convention. Pursuant to Art. 71, the withdrawal took effect six months later, on 3 November 2007. In a contemporary interview with Investment Treaty News, Pablo Solon, Bolivia's Chargé d'Affaires for Trade with the Ministry of Foreign Affairs in La Paz, said that Bolivia intends to pursue revisions to its twenty-four BITs in three areas: the definition of

and threatened withdrawal[14] from the ICSID Convention, as well as withdrawal from, and renegotiation of, BITs. This may have nothing to do with concern for consistency, other than the perception that respondent states consistently lose investment treaty arbitration, which does not appear to be supported by the United Nations Conference on Trade and Development's (UNCTAD) statistics, but it does show fragility in the investment treaty arbitration system.[15]

To those who have forgotten that the desire for continuity of jurisprudence was the reason for the collapse of the first permanent multilateral arbitration regime, we would direct attention to this quote:

> "In addition, the court should be able to assure the continuity of jurisprudence. The present court has not gone far in the direction of establishing and developing international law. Each case is isolated, lacking both continuity and connection with the other. A permanent tribunal, deciding cases in relation with each other, would evidently be a means of unifying the law, and therefore claims on this account the attention of the world."[16]

This quote sounds a lot like modern criticism of investment treaty arbitration,[17] but it was uttered in 1907. Its criticism was directed at the Permanent Court of Arbitration (PCA) rather than ICSID. The PCA was created in 1899 for arbitration of disputes

---

investment, performance requirements and dispute resolution. See "Bolivia notifies World Bank of Withdrawal from ICSID, Pursues BIT Revisions", Investment Treaty News, 9 May 2007, available at <www.bilaterals.org/article.php3?id_article=8221>.

14. In April 2007, the Member States of the *Alternativa Bolivariana para la América Latina y El Caribe* (ALBA), namely Bolivia, Cuba, Nicaragua and Venezuela, proclaimed their intention to withdraw from the International Monetary Fund and the World Bank. Yas BANIFATEMI, "Unresolved Issues in Investment Arbitration", Modern Law for Global Commerce, Congress to Celebrate the Fortieth Annual Session of UNCITRAL, Vienna, 9-12 July 2007, at p. 7.

15. In 2007, the total number of known treaty-based arbitrations reached 290. In all, the awards rendered in 2007 did not tilt the overall balance of all cumulative decisions in favor of either party, with overall 42 cases decided in favor of the State, 40 cases decided in favor of the investor, 37 cases settled amicably and 154 pending cases. UNCTAD, "Latest Developments in Investor-State Dispute Settlement", IIA Monitor (1 April 2008, no. 1) at p. 1. UNCTAD, "Latest Developments in Investor-State Dispute Settlement", IIA Monitor (1 April 2008, no. 1) at p. 3, adding that, for seventeen cases that were decided, the decision is not in the public domain.

16. Statement by Mr. Joseph CHOATE, "Proceedings of the Hague Peace Conferences", Conference of 1907, vol. II, First Commission, First Subcommission, Committee of Examination B, first meeting, at p. 595.

17. See, e.g., Barton LEGUM, "Trends and Challenges in Investor-State Arbitration", 19 Arb. Int. (2003) p. 143 at p.147:

> "If the institution of investor-state arbitration is to meet the challenge of its increasing docket, it will have to act more like an institution. If it does not – and if the result of the next few years is a collection of disparate decisions with widely varying and case-specific approaches to the issues presented – states may be tempted to consider replacing the system of *ad hoc* tribunals with a standing one that is perhaps capable of producing more consistent and coherent results."

involving states and its arbitrators were to be "of known competency in matters of international law".[18] Joseph Choate was a Delegate at the 1907 Hague Peace Conference and advocated the creation of a true court as a superior method for the development of international law. At that conference a draft convention was prepared for such an institution. That draft was the basis for the Statute of the Permanent Court of International Justice (PCIJ), adopted by the League of Nations in 1920. The creation of the PCIJ and its successor, the International Court of Justice (ICJ), essentially put the PCA out of business for half a century.

Time will tell whether the early history of the PCA forms a precedent that the investment treaty framework is bound to follow. As the investment treaty system is diverse, constituting arbitration under thousands of BITs, of which many provide arbitration options outside the ICSID system, it is unlikely that any single reform will lead to a fundamental change in the short term. This is particularly true as long as the signature of BITs and ICSID accessions continue to outpace withdrawals from these instruments. Incremental change is more likely, with refinement in the drafting of BIT provisions, such as denial of benefits provisions and most favored nation clauses, which may help prevent parallel proceedings and inconsistent decisions.

III.  AWARD ANNULMENT IN INVESTMENT TREATY ARBITRATION AND COMMERCIAL ARBITRATION

As Professor McLachlan's report tells us, both the ICSID Convention and the UNCITRAL Model Law standards for annulment of awards allow only limited grounds for review and exclude appeals on errors of law. While the ICSID system is self-contained, "[o]utside the framework of ICSID, the review of arbitral awards by national courts may be subject to the vagaries of national laws and judicial approaches at the seat of arbitration".[19] Lately, however, vagaries of the approaches within the ICSID system have come to light. The decision of the *CMS v. Argentina* ad hoc annulment committee has attracted attention for having pointed out what it viewed as numerous errors of law made by the arbitral tribunal, while nevertheless recognizing that its mandate did not allow it to do anything about those errors:

> "Throughout its consideration of the Award, the Committee has identified a series of errors and defects. The Award contained manifest errors of law. It suffered from lacunae and elisions. All this has been identified and underlined by the Committee. However the Committee is conscious that it exercises its jurisdiction under a narrow and limited mandate conferred by Article 52 of the ICSID Convention. The scope of this mandate allows annulment as an option only when

---

18. Art. 23, 1899 Convention for the Pacific Settlement of International Disputes.
19. See Professor Campbell MCLACHLAN's Report, this volume, p. 140.

certain specific conditions exist. As stated already ... in these circumstances the Committee cannot simply substitute its own view of the law and its own appreciation of the facts for those of the Tribunal."[20]

This ad hoc Committee decision has been the subject of significant comment and criticism:

> "on peut se demander si l'insistance sur toutes les erreurs dont, selon le Comité, la sentence serait criblée, est bien conforme à son rôle. Contrairement a une instance d'appel, un comité ad hoc est chargé de s'assurer qu'aucun dysfonctionnement n'a affecté la conduite de la procédure et que la sentence n'est entachée d'aucun vice grave. Il ne doit, par définition, pas se préoccuper du reste.... [L]e comité ne gagne rien a souligner tous les points sur lesquels, a tort ou a raison, il aurait jugé différemment.... Il n'y a aucun avantage ni du point de vue des parties qui voient la sentence maintenue en dépit des erreurs soulignées, ni de celui de la crédibilité de l'institution, à voir les comités ad hoc se comporter non comme de véritables instances d'annulation, mais comme des cours d'appel dépourvues du pouvoir de redresser un mal jugé."[21]

Unlike other ICSID ad hoc Committees that have shown deference to the substantive findings of arbitral tribunals, the *CMS* Committee apparently thought that the interest in the consistent development of international law had to be balanced against the interest in finality of awards: the ad hoc Committee felt compelled to inform us that the arbitral tribunal's award should not be considered good precedent.

It is not necessary to decide whether the *CMS* Committee's approach was the right one to see that the system itself is not ideal if the consistent application of the ICSID Convention's grounds for annulment is the goal. This is because a new annulment Committee is established for each annulment decision under the ICSID Convention, despite the fact that party autonomy is not served by setting up annulment bodies on an ad hoc basis, as the parties do not participate in the selection of the ad hoc Committee members. Here ICSID arbitration could take some inspiration from the commercial arbitration framework. There, although the power to annul is vested in the courts of the place of arbitration, and therefore theoretically spread across hundreds of jurisdictions with disparate approaches to annulment, in practice, a degree of consistency has been achieved through homogenizing legislation (e.g., adoption of the UNCITRAL Model Law) and through the choice of a limited number of places of arbitration where judiciaries are perceived to be consistent in their application of annulment standards. The repeated selection of the same places of arbitration in international commercial

---

20. *CMS Gas Transmission Co. v. Argentine Republic* (ICSID Case No. ARB/01/8) IIC 303 (2007) 25 September 2007, para. 158.
21. Emmanuel GAILLARD, *Chronique des sentences arbitrales*, January, February and March of 2008, at p. 364. Emmanuel Gaillard is also critical of the decision to annul a portion of the award, considering that the ad hoc Committee had evaluated the correctness of the reasons given rather than simply confirming the existence of reasons, the latter being more in conformity with the spirit of Art. 52(1)(e) of the ICSID Convention.

arbitration is reflected in ICC statistics. The place of arbitration in over half of all ICC arbitrations from 2004 to 2006 was England, France, or Switzerland.[22]

It should be recalled that inconsistent application of the public policy grounds for annulment (e.g., "local standard annulment")[23] has been a cause for concern over the years and prompted some to propose a unified system for annulment review of awards in international commercial arbitration.[24] The concentration of the place of arbitration in jurisdictions perceived as reliable responds to that concern and protects parties from erratic annulment decisions. Within these jurisdictions, the organization of the courts promotes consistency. In England, for example, High Court judges receive permanent appointments,[25] and a limited number of judges serving terms of four to six years hear annulment cases at the Court of Appeal in Paris[26] and the Federal Tribunal in Lausanne.[27]

So, the commercial arbitration framework is already seeking to provide consistent application of the annulment standard of review by sending requests for annulment to the same judges; ICSID can achieve the same result by appointing the same people to ad hoc Committees as Professor McLachlan has suggested. A review of the composition of ad hoc Committees reveals that repeat appointments are happening with some frequency, indicating that ICSID is moving in this direction. Thus, the two frameworks are reacting to a similar problem in a similar manner; the problem is just more recent at ICSID than in commercial arbitration.

---

22. ICC Annual Reports, 2004, 2005, 2006. The percentages of ICC arbitrations where the place of arbitration was England, France or Switzerland were: 50.7 percent (2004), 52.1 percent (2005), and 51.9 percent (2006).
23. Jan PAULSSON, "Towards Minimum Standards of Enforcement: Feasibility of a Model Law" in *Improving the Efficiency of Arbitral Agreements and Awards: 40 Years of Application of the New York Convention*, ICCA Congress Series no. 9 (1999) p. 576.
24. See, e.g., Fali NARIMAN discussing the "dream" of Judge Stephen Schwebel and Judge Howard Holtzmann for the "creation of a new international court to resolve disputes that arose over challenges to the validity of international commercial arbitration awards". 20 Arb. Int. (2004, no. 2) pp. 123-137 at p. 128.
25. A High Court Judge holds office during good behavior. See Department for Constitutional Affairs, Outline of Terms and Conditions of Service for High Court Judges (August 2006) at paras. 2 and 9, available at <www.judicialappointments.gov.uk/current/high_ct_judges_outline.htm>. Under the provisions of the Judicial Pensions and Retirement Act 1993, a High Court Judge will be required to vacate his or her office on his or her seventieth birthday (Sect. 26 of the 1993 Act).
26. Art. 3, *Loi organique n°94-100 du 5 février 1994 sur le Conseil supérieur de la magistrature*, version consolidée au 01 juin 2007.
27. See <www.ch.ch/behoerden/00215/00329/00353/index.html?lang=en>.

IV.  IS IT FEASIBLE TO CONDUCT TREATY ARBITRATION UNDER RULES THAT ALSO SERVE IN COMMERCIAL DISPUTES, OR DO WE NEED TO GENERATE ADDITIONAL SETS OF RULES, OTHER THAN ICSID, EXPRESSLY DESIGNED FOR INVESTOR-STATE DISPUTES?

Professor McLachlan's Report responds to the above question that was put to his ICCA Working Group by, among other things, highlighting the divergences between ICSID arbitration and the UNCITRAL Rules and Model Law with respect to transparency of proceedings and the availability of provisional measures. Although he sees a process of convergence on common principles as between the ICSID regime and commercial arbitration procedure, he sees a common understanding as not yet fully realized in practice.

This incomplete convergence has not been the source of much difficulty in practice. It is certainly feasible to conduct treaty arbitration under existing procedural rules that also serve in commercial disputes. No significant impediment to the conduct of BIT arbitration proceedings has arisen because they were conducted under the UNCITRAL Rules or other commercial arbitration rules. One recent study found that more investment treaty arbitrations were being initiated under the UNCITRAL Rules than under the auspices of ICSID, which would confirm the ability of these commercial rules to function in the investment treaty context.[28]

However, it is true that outside of ICSID, none of the most commonly used procedural rules were designed specifically for treaty arbitration, and some modifications could be helpful. In addition to issues of transparency of proceedings and provisional measures discussed by Professor McLachlan, the UNCITRAL Working Group that has undertaken the revision of the UNCITRAL Rules is carefully considering the requirements of investment treaty arbitration as it ponders the possible revision if each article of the 1976 Rules.[29] To begin with, the Working Group has agreed that the reference to "contract" in the first article of the 1976 Rules should be broadened to account for all types of disputes that arise in modern international arbitration. The proposed revision of Article 1(1), set out below, would encompass cases where the parties' dispute arises out of non-contractual relationships, including under a treaty:

"1. Where ~~the~~ parties ~~to a contract~~ have agreed ~~in writing*~~ that disputes ~~in relation to that contract~~ between them in respect of a defined legal relationship,

---

28. Luke Eric PETERSON, "Investment Treaty News: 2006: A Year in Review", Investment Treaty News, 14 December 2007, International Institute for Sustainable Development, <www.iisd.org/pdf/2007/itn_year_review_2006.pdf>, reporting that non-ICSID treaty-based arbitrations eclipse ICSID arbitrations by twenty-one to fifteen for 2006. Of the non-ICSID cases initiated in 2006, eighteen were brought under the UNCITRAL Rules. See also Investment Treaty News, 14 December 2007, <www.iisd.org/pdf/2007/itn_dec14_2007.pdf>.
29. For a summary of the structure and work of the UNCITRAL Working Group, see Judith LEVINE, "Current Trends in International Arbitration as Reflected in the Revision of the UNCITRAL Arbitration Rules", 31 University of New South Wales Law Journal (2008, no. 1) at p. 266.

whether contractual or not shall be referred to arbitration under the UNCITRAL Arbitration Rules, then such disputes shall be settled in accordance with these Rules subject to such modification as the parties may agree ~~in writing~~."[30]

Other issues relating to investment treaty arbitration include:

*1. Consideration of Counterclaims by Respondent States in Investment Treaty Arbitration*

Art. 19(3) of the current rules states that the respondent can bring a counterclaim "arising out of the same contract". The Working Group considered whether this provision was too limited. One aspect of the discussion concerned disputes under treaties and the availability of counterclaims by States.[31] The new language proposed by the Secretariat is:

> "Article 19(3): In ~~his~~ its statement of defence, or at a later stage ... the respondent may make a counter-claim or rely on a claim for the purpose of a set-off [*option 1*: arising out of the same ~~contract~~ legal relationship, whether contractual or not.] [*option 2*: provided that it falls within the scope of an agreement between the parties to arbitrate under these Rules.]"[32]

Option 2 is designed to assure that the new rules do not inadvertently allow States to bring counterclaims where this would not be allowed by the investment treaty pursuant to which the original claim was brought.[33]

---

30. See: "Settlement of Commercial Disputes: Revision of the UNCITRAL Arbitration Rules, Note by the Secretariat", UNCITRAL Working Group II (Arbitration) 47th Sess. (Vienna, 10-14 September 2007) UN Doc A/CN.9/WG.II/WP.147 (2007) at para. 7. Available at <www.uncitral.org/uncitral/en/commission/working_groups/2Arbitration.html>. See also, Jan PAULSSON and Georgios PETROCHILOS, *Revision of the UNCITRAL Arbitration Rules* (2006) paras. 6, 30-31, 35.
31. See, e.g., Jan PAULSSON and Georgios PETROCHILOS, *Revision of the UNCITRAL Arbitration Rules*, para. 174 ("The limitation to contracts is simply inappropriate to arbitrations arising under international treaties."). "Report of the Working Group on Arbitration and Conciliation on the Work of its Forty-Sixth Session" (New York, 5-9 February 2007) UNCITRAL, 46th Sess., UN Doc. /CN.9/619 (20 March 2007) at paras. 157-160. Available at <www.uncitral.org/uncitral/en/commission/working_groups/2Arbitration.html>.
32. "Revision of the UNCITRAL Arbitration Rules – Note by the Secretariat", UNCITRAL Working Group II (Arbitration) 47th Sess. (Vienna, 10-14 September 2007) UN Doc A/CN.9/WG.II/WP.147/Add.1 (2007) at para. 19. Available at <www.uncitral.org/uncitral/en/commission/working_groups/2Arbitration.html>.
33. See, e.g., *Saluka Investments B.V. v. Czech Republic*, Decision on Jurisdiction over the Czech Republic's Counterclaim (UNCITRAL 2004) available at <www.pca-cpa.org/upload/files/SAL-CZ%20Decision%20jurisdiction%20070504.pdf> in which the arbitral tribunal found that it was without jurisdiction to hear the Czech Republic's counterclaim.

2.  *Majority Decisions in the Context of Investment Treaty Arbitration*

Investor-state disputes featured in the context of a debate about the majority rule for awards (Art. 31(1): "When there are three arbitrators, any award or other decision of the arbitral tribunal shall be made by a majority of the arbitrators.") and whether the presiding arbitrator should have the power to issue a casting vote if no majority is possible. In favor of retaining the majority rule, it was argued that it was more appropriate for investor-state disputes, as reflected by ICSID's requirement of a strict majority.[34]

3.  *Silence in Many BITs on Which Version of the UNCITRAL Rules Apply*

Few investment treaties that provide for arbitration under the UNCITRAL Rules foresee an eventual revision of the Rules. They therefore fail to specify which version of the Rules should apply when an arbitration is commenced: i.e., the version in force at the date of the treaty, or the version in force at the date of commencement of the arbitration.[35] The UNCITRAL Rules themselves, never having been amended, also contain no deeming provision about which version of the Rules should apply. The new version of the Rules will need a default rule to avoid confusion if the parties have failed to specify which version should apply. In the course of debate about what that default should be, some States expressed concern about retroactive application of new rules to disputes arising out of treaties that were entered into years or decades ago. The most recent Working Group Report notes that:

> "[A] concern was expressed that [deeming application of rules as at commencement of arbitration] could have unintended retroactive application where the arbitration agreement was formed by the claimant accepting (in a notice of arbitration) an open offer to arbitrate made by the respondent. This concern

---

34. "Report of the Working Group on Arbitration and Conciliation on the work of its forty-seventh session" (Vienna, 10-14 September 2007) UNCITRAL, 47th Sess., UN Doc. A/CN.9/641 (16 June-11 July 2008) para. 70. Available at <www.uncitral.org/uncitral/en/commission/working_groups/2Arbitration.html>. ("It was also suggested that the addition of the presiding arbitrator solution might render the Rules less attractive to States in investor-State disputes. In that respect, it was observed that the Rules of Procedure for Arbitration Proceedings of the International Centre for Settlement of Investment Disputes ('ICSID Rules') operated on the basis of the majority requirement.")
35. "Settlement of Commercial Disputes: Revision of the UNCITRAL Arbitration Rules – Note by the Secretariat", UNCITRAL Working Group II (Arbitration) 45th Sess. (Vienna, 11-15 September 2006) UN Doc. A/CN.9/WG.II/WP.143, para. 9: "The Working Group might wish to note that many investment treaties include a provision on settlement of disputes which refers to the 'arbitration rules of the United Nations Commission on International Trade Law', without determining which version of those Rules would apply in case of revision. Some treaties expressly stipulate that, in the event of a revision of the UNCITRAL Rules, the applicable version will be the one in force at the time that the arbitration is commenced." An exception is the UK Model BIT of 2005, Alternative Art. 8 providing for UNCITRAL Arbitration under the Rules "as then in force" [at the time of commencement of the arbitration].

could arise in arbitration pursuant to a treaty, as well as in certain commercial contexts. It was emphasized that the Rules applicable to such a dispute should be those consented to in the offer to arbitrate (i.e., the treaty or other instrument). It was suggested that a revised version of that provision would be drafted to also make it clear that, 'for agreements or offers to arbitrate made before [date], the parties shall be deemed to have submitted to the previous version of the Rules'. The Working Group generally looked with favor on that proposal recognizing that it had only been proposed during the discussion at this session and might benefit from further refinement." [36]

4. *All Awards Rendered Under the UNCITRAL Rules Are Subject to the Supervisory Jurisdiction of National Courts at the Place of Arbitration*

Because investment treaty arbitration is in the minds of the UNCITRAL Working Group as it proceeds with revision of the Rules, what the Group chooses to preserve in the 1976 Rules may be as relevant as what is changed when seeking to discern the differences in the investment treaty and commercial arbitration frameworks. Specifically, there has been no discussion of changing Art. 1(2), which appears to indicate that mandatory rules of the lex arbitri prevail over the UNCITRAL Rules:

> "These Rules shall govern the arbitration except that where any of these Rules is in conflict with a provision of the law applicable to the arbitration from which the parties cannot derogate, that provision shall prevail."

Nor has there been any discussion of changing the rule that requires the filing of the arbitral award with the courts of the place of arbitration where the law of that country so requires:

> "*Article 32*
> (....)
> 7. If the arbitration law of the country where the award is made requires that the award be filed or registered by the arbitral tribunal, the tribunal shall comply with this requirement within the period of time required by law."

These provisions, taken together with the requirement that the tribunal determine the place of arbitration where the parties have not agreed on it (Art. 16), indicate that there is supervisory jurisdiction of the courts of the place of arbitration over BIT arbitrations under the UNCITRAL Rules. Swiss and English Courts rejected arguments to the contrary in the *Saluka v. Czech Republic* and *Occidental v. Ecuador* annulment proceedings. In *Czech Republic v. Saluka Investments B.V.*, the Czech Republic approached the Swiss

---

36. "Report of the Working Group on Arbitration and Conciliation on the work of its forty-eighth session" (New York, 4-8 February 2008) UNCITRAL 48th Sess., UN Doc. A/CN.9/646 (29 February 2008) para. 76, available at: <www.uncitral.org/uncitral/en/commission/working_groups /2Arbitration.html>.

Federal Court to annul a partial award affirming jurisdiction of the arbitral tribunal, deciding the Czech Republic was in breach of the Dutch-Czech BIT and deferring quantum of compensation to a second award. Saluka argued that such recourse to a national court was excluded by the arbitration clause in the treaty declaring an arbitral award "final and binding" upon the parties. Saluka argued that it was the intent of the parties to the treaty to follow the model as set forth in the ICSID Convention, and thus, by analogy, the contentious treaty provision must be interpreted to the effect that any recourse to national courts has been waived. The Swiss Federal Court found that the arbitration clause could not be construed this way and that there was no express waiver as required by the Swiss Private International Law (Art. 192 (1) PIL).[37] The Federal Court contrasted this to the ICSID Convention which provides for a limited review of arbitral awards in the annulment procedure before an ad hoc committee.[38] In any event, the Federal Court ultimately rejected the annulment request and affirmed the jurisdiction of the arbitral tribunal.[39]

In *Ecuador v. Occidental Exploration and Production Co.*, Ecuador approached the English Courts seeking to set aside an arbitral award rendered under the Ecuador-USA BIT. Occidental opposed the application on the ground that the doctrine of "non-justiciability" applied to prevent the English Court from determining the challenge to an award stemming from a BIT between two other States. The doctrine of non-justiciability establishes a general principle that the municipal courts of England and Wales do not have the competence to adjudicate upon rights arising out of transactions entered into by independent sovereign states between themselves on the plane of international law.[40] Occidental also relied on the principle that the English courts will not interpret treaties that have not been incorporated into English law.[41] Ecuador accepted that the BIT was a treaty governed by public international law and that it had not been made a part of the municipal law of the United Kingdom, but, just because the proposed application under Sect. 67 of the 1996 Act would involve consideration of a non-incorporated treaty between two friendly States, that did not make the matter a "no-go" area for the English Court. In this case, the States parties to the BIT had expressly agreed that disputes between an investor and a State party to the BIT could be determined by arbitration proceedings in States that are parties to the New York Convention 1958. If there was an issue as to the scope of the jurisdiction of the arbitrators who had been appointed by the mechanisms specifically set up by the States parties to the BIT, then it should be justiciable before the court that supervises the arbitral process.[42]

Mr. Justice Aikens held that the court would have to adjudicate upon or enforce rights

---

37. Swiss Federal Court, *Czech Republic v. Saluka Investments B.V.*, Judgment of 7 Sept. 2006 – Challenge to the Award of the UNCITRAL Arbitral Tribunal, Geneva, 17 March 2006, at no. 5.2., IIC 211 (2006), see Norbert HORN, "Current Use of the UNCITRAL Arbitration Rules in the Context of Investment Arbitration", 24 Arb. Int. (2008, no. 4).
38. Swiss Federal Court, as cited, at no.5.4.2.3.
39. Swiss Federal Court, as cited, at no.6.6 and 7.
40. *Ecuador v. Occidental Exploration and Production Co.* [2006] 1 Lloyd's Rep 773 (QB), para. 32.
41. *Ecuador v. Occidental Exploration and Production Co., ibid.*, para. 34.
42. *Ecuador v. Occidental Exploration and Production Co., ibid.*, para. 36.

arising out of transactions entered into by independent sovereign States between themselves on the plane of international law, but that this was not the end of the matter. Although the rights of investors under the BIT had their origin in international law, they were rights that "are intended to be exercised by Municipal law entities in a tribunal that is subject to control under Municipal laws". In this case, Occidental and Ecuador had agreed that rights with their origin in international law would be considered by a tribunal whose procedure was subject to municipal law.[43]

Mr. Justice Aikens was upheld by the Court of Appeal, which addressed the proposition that Occidental was enforcing rights of the United States under the BIT.[44] It rejected this proposition, endorsing the conclusion of Zachary Douglas in his monograph "The Hybrid Foundations of Investment Treaty Arbitration"[45] that "[t]he fundamental assumption underlying the investment treaty regime is clearly that the investor is bringing a cause of action based upon the vindication of its own rights rather than those of its national State".[46] The Court also relied on statements to this effect in a number of recent international arbitration awards. [47]

If Arts. 1(2) and 32(7) of the 1976 Rules remain untouched during a revision process where the UNCITRAL Working Group was aware that the Rules would be used in investment treaty arbitration, then the failed arguments made in *Saluka* and *Occidental* would not appear worth making again in the future; the preservation of Arts. 1(2) and 32(7) in the revised Rules would confirm the intention of the drafters to provide for supervisory jurisdictions of the courts of the place of arbitration in cases under the UNCITRAL Rules. So, from this perspective, the non-ICSID BIT arbitration framework, at least when the case is under the UNCITRAL Rules, looks very much like the international commercial arbitration framework.

V.   CONCLUSION

Concern for the coherent development of international investment law will continue to distinguish investment treaty arbitration from commercial arbitration. While commercial arbitrators will remain focused on resolving disputes in confidential proceedings, the de facto precedent-making role of investment treaty arbitrators will subject them to increasing public scrutiny as new decisions are measured against the ever-growing body of arbitral precedent. Arbitrators will develop practices to better insulate themselves from criticism and States will improve their BIT drafting. Proposals for major reforms or regime change, however, sound far-fetched for the moment.

At the level of annulment, use of a limited number of places of arbitration in

---

43. *Ecuador v. Occidental Exploration and Production Co.*, *ibid.*, para. 73.
44. *Ecuador v. Occidental Exploration and Production Co,* [2005] EWCA Civ 116, IIC 203 (2005) paras. 14-19.
45. Zachary DOUGLAS, "The Hybrid Foundations of Investment Treaty Arbitration", 74 BYIL (2003) p. 151, at p. 169.
46. *Ecuador v. Occidental Exploration and Production Co,* supra fn. 44, para. 20.
47. *Ecuador v. Occidental Exploration and Production Co, ibid.*

commercial and non-ICSID investment treaty arbitration will continue to provide an acceptable level of consistency in the application of annulment standards. ICSID will follow suit, by limiting the pool of individuals appointed to ad hoc annulment committees.

As to procedural rules, it is clear that the UNCITRAL Arbitration Rules (1976) provide a reliable choice for both commercial and investment treaty arbitration. To the extent that anything new is needed, it should be provided by the new UNCITRAL Arbitration Rules expected in 2010, with issues upon which the UNCITRAL Working Group could not reach consensus, e.g. transparency, left to be addressed in treaty provisions.

# Working Group A

# Investment Treaty Arbitration and Commercial Arbitration: Are They Different Ball Games?

## 4. The Actual Conduct

# Investment Treaty Arbitration and Commercial Arbitration: Are They Different Ball Games? The Actual Conduct

*Abby Cohen Smutny*[*]

| TABLE OF CONTENTS | Page |
|---|---|
| I. Introduction | 167 |
| II. Public Nature of the Proceeding | 168 |
| III. Marshaling the Evidence | 172 |
| IV. Interactions Between the International Proceedings and Domestic Court Actions and Law Enforcement Measures | 173 |
| V. Equality of the Parties – A Central Tenet in International Arbitration | 175 |
| VI. Conclusion | 177 |

I. INTRODUCTION

This working group was asked to address the question whether the actual conduct of an investment treaty arbitration is different from commercial arbitration. The short answer is, yes, the actual conduct is different. While individual commercial cases may share various features with investment treaty disputes, the culmination of factors that tends to be present in investment treaty cases creates challenging complexities not typically encountered in commercial disputes.

The differences in the conduct of the arbitration can be seen in each phase of the arbitral process: the various considerations addressed prior to and in the commencement of the arbitration; the actual conduct of the arbitration proceedings themselves; and then following the close of the proceedings, in dealing with an award. Issues relating to the commencement of the arbitration and to drafting the award are discussed by my colleagues.[1] The focus of this paper will be on the conduct of the arbitration itself.

Some of the factors that distinguish investment treaty arbitration (at least in terms of degree) may be seen in considering four issues:

(1) the public nature of the proceedings;
(2) challenges in marshaling the evidence;
(3) interactions between the international nature of the proceedings and domestic laws and proceedings; and
(4) the essential inequality of the parties in an investment treaty arbitration.

---

[*] Partner, White & Case LLP, Washington, DC.
1. See Sarah FRANÇOISE-PONCET and Caline MOUAWAD, "So You Want to Start an Investment Treaty Arbitration? Getting the Notice of Dispute Right", this volume, pp. 178-186 and Toby LANDAU QC, "Reasons for Reasons: The Tribunal's Duty in Investor-State Arbitration", this volume, pp. 187-205.

II.  PUBLIC NATURE OF THE PROCEEDING

It is the nature of investment treaty arbitrations that, in general, they are far more public than commercial arbitrations. As one commentator describes, "[p]ractical developments, both at the institutional level and on the part of individual treaty-based tribunals, have led to a level of publicity unprecedented in the annals of international arbitration…".[2] Many awards and decisions are published. In some cases, most notably in the NAFTA context, the parties' pleadings are published as well.[3] Materials relating to the arbitration are not just published eventually, but in some cases are posted on the internet in near real time. Some cases are conducted with public hearings.[4]

It is not just the subject of the underlying disputes that is widely publicized, but, increasingly, the arguments rehearsed in the case and even the step-by-step procedural developments in the arbitrations are often the subject of all manner of media coverage. Case developments are posted on websites that track case developments, including the ICSID website,[5] and are the subject of numerous e-newsletters. This public access has also made investment treaty arbitrations the subject of daily blogs and chatty list serves. Public information is available not only about the parties to the dispute, but also about the members of the tribunal and counsel, with the result that anyone can easily discover who is sitting on what case and who is appearing as counsel.[6] Investment treaty arbitration proceeds on the public stage and it does so on a scale not comparable to commercial arbitration.

Of course, investment treaty arbitrations are not private disputes. They are disputes about matters of public policy, about legislation, about the conduct of public servants, about national courts, and about the manner in which laws are implemented and regulators regulate. A final award against a State stands as a bill to the taxpayers of a country – and potentially a significant bill at that.[7]

This public component has put a great focus on "transparency" in investment treaty arbitration. As these disputes often revolve around issues such as how a treaty regime should be implemented, the conduct of international economic relations, the legitimacy and effects of a government's governance, and the potentially significant expenditure of

---

2. Noah RUBINS, "Opening the Investment Arbitration Process: At What Cost, for What Benefit?", 3 Transnational Dispute Management (2006, no. 3).
3. For example, many of the pleadings, orders, and hearing transcripts of NAFTA cases involving the United States as a defendant are on the US Department of State website, available at <www.state.gov/s/l/c3741.htm> (last accessed 18 July 2008).
4. These include the NAFTA disputes of *Methanex v. The United States*, *United Parcel Service v. Canada*, *Canfor Corporation v. The United States* (Jurisdiction), *Canadian Cattlemen for Fair Trade v. The United States*, and *Glamis Gold Ltd. v. The United States*.
5. See <www.worldbank.org/icsid>.
6. Trade publications such as Chambers, The American Lawyer, and Global Arbitration Review routinely use this information to "rank" arbitrators, practitioners, and law firms.
7. As one commentator recently observed, "[t]here was a time when a fifty million dollar [investment treaty] case was a big one. It is not uncommon these days to see claims many times that amount." George KAHALE, "A Problem In Investor/State Arbitration", Provisional Issue, Transnational Dispute Management (June 2008).

public funds, a measure of transparency is required for investment treaty arbitration to be accepted.[8] Transparency boosts legitimacy and, arguably, the rule of law – the most essential foundational element for increased capital flows and economic growth and the very reason for investment treaties in the first place. As such, there are good reasons for transparency.

Transparency has consequences, however, and some of these consequences relate to the award. Decisions and awards that are public and that deal with disputes of a most public nature are not consumed by the parties to the dispute alone. Being a matter of public record, they cannot help but have a certain precedential value, which encourages a certain degree of consistency in decision-making.[9]

Rule of law thrives on consistency and predictability, but only so long as decisions are correct, balanced and just. While this dynamic has obvious and important implications for the drafting of the award, it also has implications for parties and counsel who must tailor their advocacy accordingly. To persuade an arbitrator who may be thinking about the precedent perhaps being established, advocates must consider the implications of one's argument beyond the scope of the dispute at hand. All this requires a more rigorous attention to the law and to one's legal reasoning – not only by the arbitrators, but also by the parties – and it calls to mind the tension which may sometimes exist between simply resolving the dispute presented and principled reasoning about the content of the law. As was recently noted:

> "Private, international commercial arbitration tribunals historically have tended to focus almost exclusively on achieving justice in the single case before them. Governments and the public expect an approach to dispute resolution in public law cases that is more consistent and coherent across the full docket of cases. In

---

8. See, e.g., *Methanex v. The United States*, Decision of the Tribunal on Petitions From Third Persons to Intervene as Amici Curiae, dated 15 January 2001, para. 49:

   "There is an undoubtedly public interest in this arbitration. The substantive issues extend far beyond those raised by the usual transnational arbitration between commercial parties. This is not merely because one of the Disputing Parties is a State: there are of course disputes involving States which are of no greater general public importance than a dispute between private persons. The public interest in this arbitration arises from its subject-matter, as powerfully suggested in the Petitions. There is also a broader argument, as suggested by the Respondent and Canada: the Chapter 11 arbitral process could benefit from being perceived as more open or transparent; or conversely be harmed if seen as unduly secretive. In this regard, the Tribunal's willingness to receive *amicus* submissions might support the process in general and this arbitration in particular; whereas a blanket refusal could do positive harm."

   Available at <http://naftaclaims.com/Disputes/USA/Methanex/MethanexDecisionReAuthorityAmicus.pdf>.

9. See, e.g., Gabrielle KAUFMANN-KOHLER, "Arbitral Precedent: Dream, Necessity or Excuse? The 2006 Freshfields Lecture", 23 Arb. Int'l. (2007, no. 3) pp. 357-378; Jeffery P. COMMISSION, "Precedent in Investment Treaty Arbitration: A Citation Analysis of a Developing Jurisprudence", 24 J. Int'l Arb. (2007, no. 2) pp. 129-158.

this sense, what governments and the public expect is for members of tribunals in treaty-based cases to act less like commercial arbitrators and more like judges."[10]

So transparency leads inexorably to a form of precedent; and this, in turn, affects how cases are argued and how they are decided. But can transparency also undermine the dispute resolution process? Transparency, in fact, does present additional challenges.

Prior to the creation of ICSID, the politicization of investment disputes was seen as a significant hindrance to capital flows. As such, one of the main objectives of giving foreign investors direct access to present a treaty claim and, indeed, one of the main goals of ICSID arbitration, was to have a de-politicized method of dispute resolution. Politicized disputes were resolved, if at all, in an expedient manner – and the uncertainties surrounding whether they could or would be resolved was seen as a significant hindrance to investment. The assumption was that, being taken out of the political arena, disputes could be settled by the rule of law, justice more likely would be served promptly, and all would benefit from increased economic growth and cooperation.[11] As one commentator observes:

> "[I]nternational dispute settlement mechanisms are expected to provide a legal and technical – instead of a political – approach to the resolution of disputes regarding foreign investment. By advancing the resolution of disputes through the furtherance of principles of justice rather than political accommodation (which may, of course, be pursued in parallel by other means) private international dispute resolution devices provide a better technical and appropriately depoliticized framework for the development of substantive law and principles regarding foreign investment protection likely to enjoy wide international consensus."[12]

One question that emerges from the intensive transparency that characterizes investment treaty arbitrations today is whether it operates to re-politicize investment disputes, thereby detracting from its effectiveness in resolving disputes in a just and effective manner. Can too much transparency disrupt the dispute resolution process?

Proceeding on a public stage means needing to manage a public relations battlefront to minimize distortion and misinformation. The court of public opinion forms judgment based upon the information available to it. On the claimant side, private parties with claims against the State are sometimes ostracized or harassed; on the respondent side, politicians may be placed under pressures that disrupt a State's presentation of its

---

10. Barton LEGUM, "Trends and Challenges in Investor-State Arbitration", 19 Arb. Int'l (2003, no. 2) p. 143 at p. 146.
11. See Aron BROCHES, in "The Experience of the International Centre for Settlement of Investment Disputes" in Seymour J. RUBIN and Richard W. NELSON, eds., *International Investment Disputes: Avoidance and Settlement* (West 1985) p. 75 at p. 77-78.
12. Horacio A. Grigera NAÓN, "The Settlement of Investment Disputes between States and Private Parties: An Overview from the Perspective of the ICC", 1 J. World Inv. (2000) p. 59 at p. 60. See also Noah RUBINS, *op. cit.*, fn. 2.

defense. While publishing final awards and decisions leads to greater understanding of the system, intensive news coverage of an arbitration can be disruptive to the orderly conduct of the case and can have the effect of frightening off witnesses and of generally disrupting the parties' abilities to marshal the resources and evidence necessary to present their cases.

It is not unusual for a State party to face exorbitant pressures both as to the substance of a case as well as to all aspects of case management. States that have weak institutions and soft rule of law may be less able to manage the effects of so much transparency. What might be managed, for example, by the United States as a respondent without disruption to a case, might wreak havoc on another State's political will and ability to present its defense. Similarly, a claimant's ability to present its case without harassment can be impaired when its claims are subjected to public and political scrutiny before it can be evaluated on its merits. While some claimants seek to use transparency and the political pressure that often follows as another means of pressing their claim against the State, other claimants are aggravated to discover that the arbitration will not remain confidential and the details of their business dealings and perceived failures will be broadcast for public consumption.

This suggests that parties and tribunals need to be mindful of these tendencies so that a proper balance can be found. While there may be some cases well-served by public hearings, there are others that have attracted an intensity of protests, reporters, news cameras, and disruptive media attentions. There is transparency that advances our understanding of the law and there is trial by media. Some situations are best addressed by the parties entering into confidentiality agreements; some tribunals have issued confidentiality orders; and some tribunals have issued provisional measures on issues relating to the release of information outside of the arbitration process.[13]

Another obvious and important factor relating to the public nature of investment treaty arbitration is the potential intervention of third parties. Such interventions are principally justified as being necessary to satisfy concerns about the public nature of the issues in dispute and are usually made by non-governmental organizations, but they might also be made by a party whose rights or interests are in some way the subject of dispute in the arbitration.[14] In some circumstances, it is other States that have

---

13. See *Biwater Gauff (Tanzania) Limited v. United Republic of Tanzania* (ICSID Case No. ARB/05/22), Procedural Order No. 3 dated 29 September 2006, available at <http://ita.law.uvic.ca/>; *The Loewen Group, Inc. and Raymond L. Loewen v. USA* (ICSID Case No. ARB (AF)/98/3), Decision on Hearing of Respondent's Objection to Competence and Jurisdiction dated 5 January 2001, available at <http://ita.law.uvic.ca/>; *Metalclad Corp. v. United States* (ICSID Case No. ARB/(AF)/97/1), Decision on a Request by the Respondent for an Order Prohibiting the Claimant from Revealing Information dated 27 October 1997, available at <www.naftaclaims.com>; *Amco Asia Corp. v. The Republic of Indonesia* (ICSID Case No. ARB/81/1), Decision on Request for Provisional Measures dated 9 December 1983, available at 24 ILM (1985) p. 365.

14. See, e.g., Christina KNAHR, "Transparency, Third Party Participation and Access to Documents in International Investment Arbitration", 23 Arb. Int'l. (2007, no. 2) pp. 327-355; Iain MAXWELL, "Transparency in Investment Arbitration: Are Amici Curiae the Solution?", 3 Asian

intervention rights and those too must be addressed.[15] There is no question that all such interventions increase the cost and complexity of the dispute resolution process, particularly as one or both sides often feel compelled to respond to issues raised in an amicus or other third-party submission.

III. MARSHALING THE EVIDENCE

Gathering and presenting evidence in an investment treaty arbitration can be much more challenging than collecting the evidence relevant to a commercial dispute. One reason for this is the nature of the subject matter and the potentially sweeping scope of claims that can be and often are presented under investment treaties. It is not unusual for claims to be made about the entire life of an investment – its performance history and the course of dealing between the claimant, its related entities and various State agencies and instrumentalities. Disputed facts presented to the tribunal often span a ten-year period of time or more. It is also not unusual for a large number of a respondent State's agencies and instrumentalities to have materials and information that are relevant to the claims presented. The result is an immense amount of material that often needs to be gathered from a wide variety of sources. This relates both to gathering documents and obtaining relevant witness testimony.

State parties facing a wide range of claims typically face particular challenges in gathering documents requested. When responsive documents are called from separate agencies or instrumentalities, obtaining copies of documents may require a State to overcome internal separation of power concerns or issues relating to the independence of the various government branches. There also may be related judicial proceedings to which the executive agency responsible for the State's defense in the arbitration is not a party and therefore does not in fact have ready access, etc. In such circumstances, when documents are difficult to obtain, tribunals must consider carefully whether or not adverse inferences are appropriate or warranted.[16]

State parties also often have to contend with documents subject to executive or crown privileges or that are subject to confidential classifications on the basis of national security. Art. 9(2)(f) of the International Bar Association Rules on the Taking of Evidence recognizes that documents can be excluded from production on the "grounds of special political or institutional sensitivity (including evidence that has been classified as secret by a government or a public international institution)...".[17] Decisions regarding such privileges have reflected the fact-specific context in which they have been presented, with results varying depending upon factors such as whether the tribunal is

---

Int'l Arb. J. (2007, no. 2) pp. 176-186.
15. See NAFTA Art. 1128.
16. See Jeremy K. SHARPE, "Drawing Adverse Inferences from the Non-Production of Evidence", 22 Arb. Int'l (2006, no. 4) pp. 549-571.
17. See Meg N. KINNEAR, Andrea BJORKLUND, and John F.G. HANNAFORD, *Investment Disputes Under NAFTA: An Annotated Guide to NAFTA Chapter 11* (Aspen 2006) pp. 1120:42-1120:45.

persuaded that the cited privilege exists and is applicable and the centrality of the evidence to the proceeding.

Similar issues exist regarding witness testimony. In part due to the typically high turnover of civil servants and the consequent lack of institutional memory, persons with information relevant to the dispute often are outside of either party's control. Former government officials who may be retired or in private practice often have no interest in or incentive to serve as a witness in an arbitration, particularly where their actions are the subject of a public claim. For those witnesses still in government when a claim arises, issues relating to the typically demanding schedules of high government officials often must be addressed. These considerations make obtaining evidence relevant to the claims and defense particularly challenging.

The conduct of investment treaty arbitration also is often significantly affected by an intensive and burdensome need for translation of a vast quantity of material. Due in part to the fact that the parties to an investment treaty arbitration often were not in contractual privity and were not engaged as business partners, documents relating to their interactions often were not translated in advance for the benefit of the foreign investor. That fact, coupled with the wide range of issues that typically characterizes investment treaty claims, often creates a very sizable translation burden for both parties in presenting their case. It is not unusual for thousands of pages of documents to have to be translated. This typically imposes a very significant time and cost burden on the arbitration, including on any process of document production. Translations also often becomes a source of dispute between the parties (as the accuracy of translation is frequently disputed), thus further aggravating the issues in dispute.

Given the nature of investment treaty claims, it also is not unusual for evidence relevant to the issues in dispute to be in the possession and control of third parties. Such circumstances can add a further level of complexity as the tribunal may be confronted with an issue as to which the record presented to it is materially incomplete.

Political motivations can present another significant challenge for a State in marshalling the evidence in a case. While a change in a company's management does not alter a company's economic incentive to present its case, a change in a government's administration can present sensitive political issues, particularly where there might not be the same motivation to defend what may be seen as the misdeeds of political opponents.

IV. INTERACTIONS BETWEEN THE INTERNATIONAL PROCEEDINGS AND DOMESTIC COURT ACTIONS AND LAW ENFORCEMENT MEASURES

As the business of government does not stop with the filing of an investment treaty claim, the subject matter of an investment treaty dispute frequently continues to evolve even while the arbitration proceeds, resulting in a constantly evolving set of facts. Common examples of this often include on-going litigation in the State's courts, sometimes involving third parties to the arbitration, bankruptcy proceedings relating to the claimant's investment vehicle, and investigations by law enforcement agencies of allegations of wrongful conduct.

Such domestic proceedings sometimes lead to applications for a stay of the domestic proceedings and sometimes to a stay of the arbitration.[18] Such further actions also sometimes are themselves the basis of further claims. While on the claimant side, private parties may be concerned about a State taking action to prosecute it as to issues that are the subject of the investment treaty arbitration, States may face the dilemma of trying to avoid aggravating claims presented against it, while not waiving law enforcement rights and obligations. It is not unusual for a State to have to choose between taking no action against the claimant to avoid aggravating investment treaty claims, but thereby potentially waiving rights, especially in the face of domestic statutes of limitation, and taking such further action as it considers appropriate and justified, but then facing applications for provisional measures and other aggravating claims in the arbitration.[19]

Apart from issues surrounding the relationship between a State's law enforcement obligations, States also often have to deal with the fact in many investment treaty cases that the State has a limited ability to raise counterclaims against the claimant, so that any claims a State may have against the claimant must be addressed in domestic court proceedings.[20]

An increasingly common and complex set of factors arise in investment treaty cases when allegations of corruption or other unlawful conduct are made. Such allegations can go both ways – with either the investor alleging that government officials acted in a corrupt manner or the State alleging that the investor obtained its investment through corrupt means.[21]

The issues of proof regarding such claims are challenging.[22] Should the international arbitration be suspended while criminal proceedings are on-going? What if there is a failure to prosecute? To what standard of proof should evidence regarding alleged conduct that would constitute a criminal offense be tested? These can be difficult questions. [23]

While an international tribunal must make decisions based on the evidence presented to it, it is obvious that an international arbitral tribunal is not equipped to function as a

---

18. See, e.g., *Holiday Inns v. Morocco* and *MINE v. Guinea*, as discussed in R. Doak BISHOP, James CRAWFORD, and Michael REISMAN, *Foreign Investment Disputes: Cases, Materials And Commentary* (Kluwer 2005) pp. 387-390; Charles N. BROWER and Ronald E.M. GOODMAN, "Provisional Measures and the Protection of ICSID Jurisdiction Exclusivity Against Municipal Proceedings", 6 ICSID Rev.–Foreign Investment L. J. (1991) pp. 431-461; Richard BOIVIN, "International Arbitration with States: An Overview of the Risks", 19 J. of Int'l Arb. (2002, no. 4) p. 285 at pp. 285-288.
19. See, e.g., *Libananco Holdings Co. Ltd. v. Republic of Turkey* (ICSID Case No. ARB/06/08), Decision on Preliminary Issues dated 23 June 2008, available at <http://ita.law.uvic.ca/>.
20. See, e.g., *Saluka Investments B.V. v. The Czech Republic* (UNCITRAL), Decision on Jurisdiction over the Czech Republic's Counterclaim dated 7 May 2004, available at <http://ita.law.uvic.ca/>.
21. See, e.g., *Inceysa Vallisoletana, S.L. v. Republic of El Salvador* (ICSID Case No. ARB/03/26), Award dated 2 August 2006, available at <www.worldbank.org/icsid>.
22. See Matti S. KURKELA, "Criminal Laws in International Arbitration – the May, the Must, the Should and the Should Not", 26 ASA Bulletin (2008, no. 2) p. 280 at pp. 286-287.
23. See A. Timothy MARTIN, "International Arbitration and Corruption: An Evolving Standard", 1 Transnational Dispute Management (2004, no. 2) p. 1 at p. 6.

criminal court. It cannot compel the production of evidence, particularly not from third parties, and the procedural safeguards that exist in domestic criminal proceedings do not exist in international arbitration. For some investors, however, an international arbitration may provide the only possible recourse in the face of corruption where there might be a lack of political will and/or available resources to ensure domestic law enforcement, and indeed the failure of enforcement can itself be a treaty violation.

V.   EQUALITY OF THE PARTIES – A CENTRAL TENET IN INTERNATIONAL ARBITRATION

The reality in investment treaty arbitration is that the parties are not equal, and indeed they cannot be, as one party is a sovereign nation and the other is an individual or company. The challenge in investment treaty arbitration is to maintain an equal opportunity for each party to present its case notwithstanding the fundamental inequality of the parties.

Some commentators point to the State's "superior" power to influence the law.[24] It is a fact that States legislate, States have the obligation to enforce the laws, State courts must rule on cases before them, and States conclude treaties. These are among the normal functions of a State and are not to be disregarded simply because the State is a party to an arbitration. At the same time, an investment treaty tribunal can appreciate when a State seeks to use its authority solely for the purpose of trying to influence the outcome of an arbitration.

While the position of the State would seem to be "superior" in some ways, the reality in presenting a case in arbitration can be quite different.[25] A State may be saddled by its own internal administrative procedures as an encumbrance to presenting its defense. Its counsel may face the challenge of having a bureaucracy as a client. A State's defense can be hampered by unclear lines of authority and responsibility for the representation of the State or by the lack of a reasonably available person competent to make decisions for the case. Sometimes, multi-agency review must occur before a position in the arbitration can be taken. While States may need time for internal deliberations being concerned about more than just one case, as decisions tend to be precedent-setting and States must be concerned about consistency in such matters, slow decision making can be incompatible with established pleading schedules.

Governments also are usually not well equipped to deal with the process of gathering documents and testimony from throughout the State infrastructure within the short amount of time required by arbitration proceedings. The main reason for this is that different agencies and branches of the government tend to act independently. It is not

---

24. See, e.g., Richard BOIVIN, "International Arbitration with States: An Overview of the Risks", 19 J. of Int'l Arb. (2002, no. 4) pp. 285-300; Charles N. BROWER, "W(h)ither International Commercial Arbitration? – The Goff Lecture 2007", 24 Arb. Int'l (2008, no. 2) p. 181 at pp. 188-190.
25. See George KAHALE, "A Problem in Investor/State Arbitration", Provisional Issue, Transnational Dispute Management (June 2008) p. 1 at pp. 4-5.

unusual for one agency to have to address a formal written request for documents from another, explaining the precise materials requested and the reasons therefor, often with varying degrees of responsiveness. While there may be sound public policy objectives at issue,[26] the time-consuming and inefficient aspects of such an approach to gathering evidence may be at odds with faster pleading schedules sometimes urged by claimants. A lack of coordination among independent agencies also can create significant challenges for a State party seeking to present its defense in a case. The situation is often exacerbated by the highly dispersed nature of the State itself, the fact that the responsible State agency often has minimal experience in dealing with the complexities of an investment treaty arbitration, and the difficulty for many responsible government officials of following a highly complex case conducted in a foreign language.

The transparency with which the business of government is run leaves a State in many respects like a client with many "open doors". While a private party can effectively limit its communications about an on-going case and can effectively focus its communications through counsel, points of contact with a State cannot meaningfully be minimized and can be the source of further evidence or of an admission to be used in the arbitration. A development such as a public parliamentary inquiry into the dispute even as the arbitration proceeds demonstrates the very significant differences between the government and a private litigating party.

A State party often is also encumbered in its ability to present its defense by public procurement rules. Procurement procedures can make it difficult for a State to react quickly to evolving issues that may present themselves in the course of the arbitration.

By contrast, a claimant may be in a more advantageous position. It more likely can be a "nimble" opponent. Claimants more often have all relevant documents centrally organized, may organize evidence and resources in advance of commencing the arbitration, and usually have the benefit of a small number of persons familiar with the entire circumstances of the dispute (and who, likely interacted with many different government representatives each of whom knows little or nothing of the claimant). The claimant's witnesses typically also remain within its control.

Issues involving the inequality of the parties in investment treaty arbitration also may result from disparities in financial resources. While some have observed that "State parties are normally stronger and richer in resources than investors",[27] often, the reverse is true. Some governments face serious budgetary constraints and must defend against claims presented by well-funded claimants. Claimants also may benefit from contingent representation agreements or outside financing for their claims that are not available to respondents.

---

26. See Barton LEGUM, op. cit., fn. 10, at p. 145 ("Governments tend to be almost obsessively concerned with consistency in procedural matters.... Consistency in government serves as an antidote for cronyism. For example, if certain information is available only if a certain form is delivered to a certain office, following that procedure with rigour helps to ensure that the government provides all citizens the same treatment, whether they are wealthy and influential citizens or ordinary folk.").

27. See, e.g., Yoshi KODAMA, "Dispute Settlement under the Draft Multilateral Agreement on Investment – The Quest for an Effective Investment Dispute Settlement Mechanism and its Failure", 16 J. of Int'l Arb. (1999, no. 3) p. 45 at p. 72.

Combined, the inherent and unavoidable inequality of the parties in investment treaty arbitrations presents challenges to the tribunal that must ensure a reasonable equality of opportunity to each party to present its case in arbitration.

VI.  CONCLUSION

One may ask what these various considerations suggest. For arbitrators, these factors present additional challenges to achieving a fair and effective case management that does not impair the rights of either party to present its case and to obtain a just resolution of the dispute at issue. In some cases that might mean imposing some limits on transparency during the course of the arbitration; in some cases it might mean providing realistic time periods for the parties to present their respective cases; in other cases, the tribunal might need to impose an organizational discipline on the parties. In any event, a realistic appreciation of each party's position is critical.

For the parties and the expectations they may bring to the arbitration, although a great deal of emphasis is placed on efficiency in international commercial arbitration to provide a reasonable means of addressing business disputes, in the context of investment treaty arbitration, one might consider the extraordinary nature of the remedy at issue in a different light. Investment treaty arbitration is not a means for resolving business disputes; it is a right to seek compensation from the taxpayers of a State for injury caused by inadequate governance. In that sense, the taxpayers of the State are stakeholders in the process as well. While one may observe that justice delayed is justice denied, the extraordinary nature of the investment treaty remedy suggests that a particularly high premium must be placed upon obtaining a just result that is consistent with the undertakings of the State parties reflected in the treaties.

# So You Want to Start an Investment Treaty Arbitration? Getting the Notice of Dispute Right

*Sarah François-Poncet and Caline Mouawad**

| TABLE OF CONTENTS | Page |
|---|---|
| I. Introduction | 178 |
| II. Form | 179 |
| III. Content | 181 |
| IV. Evidence | 184 |
| V. Language | 185 |
| VI. Service | 185 |
| VII. Conclusion | 186 |

I.  INTRODUCTION

Of the approximately 2,500 bilateral investment treaties (BITs) and the numerous multilateral investment treaties currently in force, a large percentage contain what is commonly referred to as a "cooling off" or consultation period, namely a period of time during which the investor is obliged to seek to resolve the dispute amicably prior to actually commencing the arbitration as a formal matter.[1] Although a few BITs fail altogether to specify the length of any such consultation period,[2] the majority of BITs do provide for a specific consultation period that may range from three months[3] to six months[4] to twelve months[5] or more.[6]

---

* Partner and Counsel, respectively, Salans.
1. Such consultation period usually runs from the date on which a party notifies the other party of a dispute and requests amicable settlement thereof or from the date on which the dispute arises (see, e.g., Art. IX(3) of the Treaty between the Government of the United States of America and the Government of the Republic of Albania Concerning the Encouragement and Reciprocal Protection of Investment dated 11 January 1995). In practical terms, however, the distinction between these two formulations may be merely academic. See *Ronald S. Lauder v. The Czech Republic* (UNCITRAL), Final Award, para. 185 (3 September 2001) (interpreting the phrase "from the date on which the dispute arose" and holding that the waiting period ran from the date on which the State was notified of the breach, not from the date on which the alleged breach occurred).
2. E.g., Art. 12(1) of the Agreement Between the Government of Australia and the Government of the Republic of India on the Promotion and Protection of Investments dated 26 February 1999.
3. E.g., Art. 8(2) of the Agreement on Encouragement and Reciprocal Protection of Investments between the Government of the Kingdom of The Netherlands and the Government of Romania dated 19 April 1994. At the multilateral level, see also Art. 26 of the Energy Charter Treaty and Art. 1119 of the North American Free Trade Agreement (NAFTA).
4. E.g., Art. 11(2) of the Agreement between the Federal Republic of Germany and Ukraine on the Promotion and Mutual Protection of Investments dated 15 February 1993.
5. E.g., Art. 9(2) of the Agreement Between the Government of the Republic of Korea and the

The focus of this paper is to examine how to trigger this consultation period, without which an investor may have difficulties in availing itself of the investor-State dispute resolution mechanism contained in BITs and in seeking to hold the State responsible for breaches of its international obligations. Although this "trigger" is generally considered to be a condition precedent to any investment treaty arbitration[7] – and thus to any action to be brought against a sovereign State – BITs are remarkably silent on the manner in which such "trigger" should be set in motion. Yet this initial phase of the investment treaty arbitral process (or rather, pre-arbitral process) encompasses numerous practical steps that must be undertaken properly so as to avoid potential pitfalls that could give rise to future procedural issues.      Although no definitive or exhaustive checklist can be anticipated – particularly given the absence of arbitral awards having addressed these issues of form, formalities, logistics and procedure – it is these authors' hope that this article will provide a list of the essential practical questions (and even some answers) that arise in connection with launching a BIT arbitration, namely the issuance of a "trigger letter" or, as we will refer to it herein, a "notice of dispute."

II.    FORM

A notice of dispute can take several forms, from a simple one-paragraph letter informing the State that a dispute exists under the relevant BIT to a detailed (and more formal) document setting forth the merits of the investor's claim similar to what a request for arbitration would contain.

The form and corresponding length of such notice will depend on the strategic goals of the investor, its realistic expectations of fruitful settlement discussions and its state of readiness to proceed with the arbitration. If the investor estimates that settlement discussions have a real possibility of success, it may be in the investor's interests to present its case in a complete and forceful manner from the outset so as to impress on the State the importance and merits of the dispute. In turn, this may prompt the State to attempt to work with the investor in good faith to find a negotiated solution. That

---

Government of the Republic of Indonesia Concerning the Promotion and Protection of Investment dated 16 February 1991.

6.  Although outside the scope of this paper, several investment treaty cases have addressed the extent to which an investor may avail itself of a more favorable waiting period before launching an international arbitration through the application of the most favored nation (MFN) clause in a BIT. See, e.g., *Emilio Agustin Maffezini v. the Kingdom of Spain* (ICSID Case No. ARB/97/7), Decision on Jurisdiction (25 January 2000); *Siemens A.G. v. The Argentine Republic* (ICSID Case No. ARB/02/8), Decision on Jurisdiction (3 August 2004); *National Grid plc v. The Argentine Republic* (UNCITRAL), Decision on Jurisdiction (20 June 2006).

7.  That being said, in *Bayindir*, where the claimant failed altogether to submit a formal notice of dispute to the State pursuant to the applicable BIT, the tribunal concluded that the non-fulfillment of this requirement "is not 'fatal to the case of the claimant'". *Bayindir Insaat Turizm Ticaret ve sanayi a.s. v. Islamic Republic of Pakistan* (ICSID Case No. ARB/03/29), Decision on Jurisdiction (14 November 2005), para. 100 (further noting that requiring formal notice would simply mean that the investor would have to file a new request for arbitration and start the proceedings anew, "which would be to no-one's advantage").

being said, the investor may nonetheless wish to reserve some points or arguments in the event that these negotiations were to fail. The investor may also be in a hurry to issue the notice of dispute so as to trigger the consultation period, without taking sufficient time to reflect on or develop the legal bases on which it may wish to rely going forward, and hence may be reluctant to set forth its position in any detail in the notice of dispute.

In short, choosing the right form of the notice of dispute can represent a delicate balance between disclosing enough facts and arguments to demonstrate the merits of the case in the hope of reaching a settlement and not giving advance notice of the entire case which would afford the State additional time in which to mount a defense and/or would compromise the investor's ability to present its case differently once the arbitration starts in earnest. Typically, an investor will adopt a middle-of-the-road approach, setting forth the essentials of its claim in a few pages of a letter with enough information to cause the State to take note of the dispute without divulging all of the nuances and intricacies of the claim.

Another factor that may influence the form of the notice of dispute is the existence of earlier correspondence between the investor and the State concerning the dispute. If the dispute has already been the subject of considerable exchanges between the investor and the State, particularly if the State organ with which such dispute has arisen is the same organ that would be served with the notice of dispute, then there may be less of a need for a longer and more explicit notice of dispute. This may also be the case when there is a contractual relationship between the investor and the State or one of its organs, with the result that there will normally be a chain of correspondence between such parties leading up to the dispute, thus diminishing the need for a detailed notice of dispute.[8]

Finally, it should be recalled that the notice of dispute may be the first document that a future tribunal will read in the file, and thus the manner in which the claim is presented in that initial document may go to the claim's ultimate credibility.

The investor must also decide whether to issue the notice of dispute on its own letterhead or through counsel. Several considerations may factor into this decision. Issuing such a notice through counsel may give the claim a necessary element of gravity and importance, particularly if counsel is influential and/or known to the State locally (although this could also have the reverse effect) and may signal the strength of the investor's resolve to seek redress for the harm suffered. In cases where the investor may have other ongoing business ventures in the State, approaching the State through counsel may also distance the investor from the dispute and permit it to pursue its other businesses in parallel with less concern for drawing attention to its local presence. At the same time, using counsel may also be seen as overly aggressive, putting the State immediately on the defensive and compromising amicable discussions.

---

8. One example of such an approach can be found in *Eureko B.V. v. The Republic of Poland*, where the dispute related to a Share Purchase Agreement between Eureko B.V. and the State Treasury of the Republic of Poland, represented by the Minister of The State Treasury, and as a result, the formal notice was issued following a lengthy correspondence between the parties to such contract and accordingly was only one paragraph long (in contrast to the € 9 billion currently at issue in the quantum phase of that case).

The decisions as to form facing the investor in the BIT context were addressed on the occasion of "Celebrating NAFTA at Ten" in a Statement issued by the Free Trade Commission (FTC) on 7 October 2003 (FTC Statement), wherein the FTC issued a suggested "notice of intent form," which, if properly completed, will satisfy the requirements of Art. 1119 of the North American Free Trade Agreement (NAFTA) for submitting a claim to arbitration[9] and will serve as "the basis for consultations or negotiations between the disputing investor and the competent authorities of a Party".[10] Art. 1119 requires a disputing investor to notify the State in writing of its intention to submit a claim to arbitration at least ninety days before the claim is submitted, and such notice must specify (a) the name and address of the disputing investor, (b) the provisions of NAFTA alleged to have been breached and any other relevant provisions, (c) the issues and factual basis for the claim, and (d) the relief sought and the approximate amount of damages claimed. In turn, the suggested form attached to the FTC Statement spells out the actual information that the investor should submit so as to satisfy the requirements of Art. 1119 and suggests that the investor specify (i) its nationality, (ii) the type of investment made, and (iii) the name of its legal representative (if applicable) and the person to whom correspondence should be directed, together with the documentary support for each of the foregoing.[11] Although the use of this form is not mandatory, it provides much-needed guidance as to both the form and content of notices of dispute, at least in the NAFTA context, as further addressed in the next section.

III.   CONTENT

Intricately intertwined with the form of the notice of dispute adopted is the issue of the actual content of such notice and whether the absence of any specific terms or facts may compromise the triggering of the consultation period.

As a preliminary remark, the *characterization* of the dispute is an issue distinct from the actual *content* of the notice of dispute. Indeed, the framing of the issue at this preliminary stage can be crucial and failure to do so properly may give rise to some future difficulties (even if ultimately surmountable). Thus, for example, if the claim is depicted in the notice of dispute as a dispute arising out of a contract, this may give the State ammunition to argue that the dispute is not a treaty-based dispute but rather a contract-based claim, which could give rise to an objection on jurisdiction and/or admissibility of the claim during the arbitration.[12]

---

9. Statement of the Free Trade Commission on Notices of Intent to Submit a Claim to Arbitration (hereinafter FTC Statement), available at <http://www.ustr.gov/assets/Trade_Agreements/Regional/NAFTA/ asset_upload_file212_3601.pdf>. See also Meg N. KINNEAR, Andrea K. BJORKLUND and John F.G. HANNAFORD, *Investment Disputes under NAFTA: An Annotated Guide to NAFTA Chapter 11* (Kluwer Law International 2006) 1119-6.
10. FTC Statement, supra fn 9, para. 2.
11. FTC Statement, supra fn. 9. See also KINNEAR, et al., supra fn. 9, 1119-7 – 1119-10.
12. This was the case in the *Eureko* arbitration referred to in fn. 8 above, where the State argued, ultimately unsuccessfully, that the dispute arose out of the Share Purchase Agreement and thus should have been heard by the Polish courts pursuant to the exclusive jurisdiction clause set forth

Moreover, the investor must keep in mind that, in a BIT dispute, the State's international responsibility may be engaged only by State conduct, which encompasses conduct attributable to the State. Accordingly, in characterizing the facts underlying its claim, the investor should emphasize the State conduct, and not the conduct of third parties.

Turning to the actual content of a notice of dispute, perhaps the thorniest issue with which an investor and its counsel must wrestle is whether there are any elements required to be contained in such a notice so as to trigger successfully the consultation period, i.e., whether there exists some kind of "check list" of essential elements. Should an investor substantiate its standing as an "investor" or the nature of its "investment" for purposes of BIT protection? How specific should the allegations of BIT breaches be? How much detail should the investor provide about the factual circumstances giving rise to its claim against the State in order to anticipate any objections on these points? Of course, in determining how far to go in this regard, the investor must also be wary of flagging issues that might not otherwise have come to the State's attention.

The failure of BITs to provide any guidance on the content of the notice of dispute is surprising. In contrast, as mentioned above, Art. 1119 of NAFTA, together with the form attached to the FTC Statement, set forth the basic information that must be included in a notice of intent and, as such, highlight precisely the elements upon which the investor must reflect in preparing its notice of dispute in the BIT context as well.

The absence of any guidelines in BITs in this regard can be problematic in particular in deciding whether to enumerate the specific BIT provisions allegedly breached by the State or whether generally to reference a breach of the BIT as a whole. The latter approach risks not being detailed enough to put the State on notice of the substance of the dispute. However, the former approach equally runs the risk of being limitative for the subsequent arbitration, i.e., the failure to cite to a specific treaty provision in the notice of dispute may preclude the investor from seeking relief thereunder in the arbitration (which would have the perverse effect of encouraging investors to issue a laundry list of treaty claims, whether or not substantiated in the given circumstances).

Several tribunals have addressed the issue of the content of the notice of dispute but reached different conclusions. In *Goetz v. Burundi*, pursuant to the notice requirement contained in the relevant BIT, the claimant gave notice to the State with respect to its claims relating to the revocation of a "free trade zone" license, but later sought to expand the scope thereof in its request for arbitration by seeking to include claims regarding taxes and customs paid to the State.[13] The tribunal rejected the supplementary claims as

---

therein. One of the arguments relied upon by the State to this effect was the fact that the short notice of dispute specifically referenced a dispute "over the contract for the sale of shares in PZU and the addenda signed". While the tribunal did not ultimately address this specific argument in its Partial Award on jurisdiction and liability, the presentation of the notice of dispute in this manner gave an additional argument to the State on this point.

13. *Antoine Goetz et al. v. Republic of Burundi* (ICSID ARB/05/3), Award (10 February 1999) paras. 92-93.

inadmissible on the ground that the investor failed to notify and give a detailed description of this claim to the State as required by the BIT.[14]

In contrast, the tribunal in *ADF Group v. United States* addressed this issue in the context of a NAFTA dispute, where the investor-claimant made a claim under Art. 1103 for the first time in its reply memorial rather than in its notice of intent.[15] The United States argued that the tribunal had no jurisdiction to consider such claim because the investor had not raised this provision in its notice of intent and because the State's consent to arbitration was conditioned on compliance with the mandatory provisions of, inter alia, Art. 1119.[16] The tribunal rejected the argument that the consent to arbitration of the United States was conditioned on the provisions set forth in Art. 1119, and held that the investor's failure to set out an exhaustive list of relevant NAFTA provisions in the notice of intent did not strip the tribunal of jurisdiction to consider any unlisted but pertinent NAFTA provisions relating to the dispute.[17] Moreover and in any event, the tribunal held that the respondent had ample opportunity to address this claim in its rejoinder and at the hearing such that it suffered no prejudice from the failure to reference this provision in the notice of intent.[18]

Similarly, in *Generation Ukraine v. Ukraine*, although the claimant's legal case before the tribunal differed from the representations made by the claimant to the State in the course of the consultation period, the tribunal held that

> "[t]he requirement to consult and negotiate, however, does not serve to compel the investor to plead its legal case on multiple occasions. To insist upon a precise congruity in the investor's articulation of its grievances in these different fora would only have a chilling effect on consultation and negotiation between the investor and the host State. There is no doubt that the subject matter of the two mediations was the Claimant's Parkview Project and the conduct of Ukrainian authorities in respect thereto; This is sufficient for the purposes of the requirement in Art. VI(2) of the BIT."[19]

---

14. *Ibid.*, at para. 93. The *CMS* tribunal skirted a similar issue when it found that claimant's additional claim raised after the filing of the request for arbitration was incidental or ancillary to the main claim, which had been properly notified to Argentina and the subject of a six-month consultation period. *CMS Gas Transmission Co. v. The Republic of Argentina* (ICSID Case No. ARB/01/8), Decision on Jurisdiction (17 July 2003) paras. 116-120. Accordingly, the tribunal did not need to decide whether the consultation period was a procedural or jurisdictional requirement since it was clear from the ICSID Arbitration Rules that ancillary claims do not require a new request for arbitration or a new consultation period before the submission of the dispute to arbitration. *Ibid.* at paras. 121-123.
15. *ADF Group Inc. v. United States of America* (ICSID Case No. ARB(AF)/00/1), Award (9 January 2003).
16. *Ibid.*, at paras. 127-129.
17. *Ibid.*, at paras. 133-134.
18. *Ibid.*, at para. 138. The tribunal also considered that the investor's Art. 1103 claim was prompted by a later-issued FTC note of interpretation such that, in failing to mention Art. 1103 in its notice of intent, the investor was not seeking unfairly "to inflict tactical surprise upon the Respondent". *Ibid.*, at para. 136.
19. *Generation Ukraine, Inc. v. Ukraine* (ICSID Case No. ARB/00/9), Award (13 September 2003)

Echoing this approach, the tribunal in *AMTO v. Ukraine*, an Energy Charter Treaty (ECT) case, considered that:

> "A party can request amicable settlement of a dispute without identifying any ECT claims, and an Investor may have good reason not to formulate claims at this stage, in order to avoid taking a position or appearing to threaten the state party with arbitration before bona fide settlement discussions. The purpose of Art. 26(2) – to provide for settlement discussions – requires the avoidance of legal forms, and the facilitation of open communication. The Investor must inform the State of the state of affairs involving disagreement, and request amicable settlement. If the State considers there is insufficient information to initiate discussions then the good faith response is simply to so advise the Investor, and require more detail. In other words, to initiate the type of communications envisaged by Art. 26(2)."[20]

The different result reached in *Goetz v. Burundi* than in the other three aforementioned cases (*ADF Group*, *Generation Ukraine* and *AMTO*) may be explained by the distinction between the factual and the legal bases for the investor's claim. In the former case, the investor failed to notify the State of the *factual* circumstances surrounding his second claim, with the result that no consultation in this regard could have taken place, whereas in the other cases, the investor put the State on notice of the relevant factual circumstances but subsequently ascribed a different *legal characterization* to such facts.[21] Thus, one might conclude from these cases that, where the description of the facts in the notice of dispute covers the factual bases that will subsequently be relied upon (even if not detailed or proven specifically in the notice), this will constitute sufficient notice for BIT consultation periods, regardless of whether such facts are ascribed particular legal consequences in the notice of dispute.

IV.  EVIDENCE

Another practical issue for an investor is the extent of documentary evidence to be submitted in support of its notice of dispute. Whether to submit any attachments or supporting documents together with the notice of dispute and, if so, which ones, must be answered in light of the first two points raised above about the desirable level of detail of such notice in accordance with the strategic goals of the investor. It would seem judicious to submit a copy of the BIT itself (for the avoidance of doubt) as well as a handful of the key documents on which the claim is essentially based. Again,

---

para. 14.5.
20. *AMTO LLC v. Ukraine* (SCC Case No. 080/2005), Final Award (26 March 2008) para. 57.
21. Alternatively, the fact that the relevant BIT in *Goetz* required diplomatic negotiations between the host State and the investor's State of nationality may explain the significance the tribunal accorded to an attempt at amicable settlement. See Christoph H. SCHREUER, "Travelling the BIT Route – Of Waiting Periods, Umbrella Clauses and Forks in the Road", 5 J. W. Inv't & T. (April 2004) p. 231 at p. 237.

substantiating the claim in this manner allows the investor to set the tone of the consultation period and to impress on the State the importance of the claim from the outset, while reserving a more detailed pleading for the arbitral proceedings.

In the NAFTA context, as stated above, the notice of intent form attached to the FTC Statement invites the investor to submit documentary evidence relating to the investor's nationality (e.g., a copy of a passport or a deed of incorporation), the type of investment made (e.g., a copy of a title to property, share certificates or a joint venture agreement), and the name of the investor's legal representative if applicable (e.g., power of attorney of the legal representative).

V. LANGUAGE

Once the notice of dispute is drafted and ready to be issued to the State, the question of the appropriate language of the document arises. Should it be submitted as an original in the language of the State or simply in the language of the investor (or other language specified in the BIT), accompanied by an unsigned translation? Should the documentary evidence attached to such notice of dispute be equally translated into the language of the State? Should any of these translations be certified? If the document is served in both languages, should the investor sign both as originals with equal force?

BITs are again silent on this issue. In practical terms, it may be advisable for the investor to submit the notice of dispute (together with its attachments) in one of the languages of the BIT, together with a translation into the language of the State (if that is not the language already used) so as both to ensure that the notice receives immediate attention and to avoid any future controversies. However, it would appear that this practical precaution need not apply to all of the supporting documents, and need not then set the stage for the future arbitral proceedings being conducted in more than one language.

NAFTA again provides more clarity in this regard. The FTC Statement clearly specifies the language in which the notice of intent should be submitted, namely either as an original in the language of the respondent State (for Canada, this would be either English or French) or as an original in the language of the investor together with a translation thereof (without, however, specifying whether the translation should be certified).[22]

VI. SERVICE

Although BITs require the investor to notify the "Contracting Party involved in the dispute", they do not specify the State organ upon which service of the notice of dispute should be made, much less the contact information for such organ, or the method of notification. In contrast, for purposes of a NAFTA claim, the form notice of intent attached to the FTC Statement expressly designates the State organ for delivery of the

---

22. FTC Statement, supra fn. 9, para. 6. See also KINNEAR, et al., supra fn. 9, 1119-7.

notice and lists the address of the respective office.[23] The failure of BITs to designate the proper authority for service means that the investor must often resort to the State's domestic laws for guidance in this regard and, in case of doubt, err on the side of "over-notifying" the various State organs that might have an interest in or a connection to the dispute. The absence of specific rules in this regard is all the more surprising given the formality that can be required for service of process in commercial matters, for instance through the Hague Convention on the Service Abroad of Judicial and Extra-Judicial Documents in Civil and Commercial Matters.

Neither BITs nor NAFTA references the logistics of actually effectuating service, i.e., in person, by certified mail, courier or facsimile. Moreover, there is no mention of how to obtain proof of service of the notice of dispute in the event it were to be disputed by the State at a later stage. A practical suggestion would be to effect in-person service of the notice of dispute and to bring an additional original thereof for the State to stamp as an acknowledgement of receipt on the date of service. In some cases, it might even be appropriate to have the person effectuating service execute an affidavit to this effect.

VII. CONCLUSION

As seen from the foregoing, BITs offer little guidance on the practical aspects of preparing and serving a notice of dispute so as to trigger the requisite consultation period prior to commencing arbitral proceedings, even though the same recurring issues addressed herein arise in connection with every notice of dispute. The lack of a single form or method to be followed by investor-claimants is both regrettable and fortunate: regrettable because there is no uniformity or consensus as to how a State is best – and most informatively – put on notice of a dispute for the purposes of the consultation period; and fortunate because it affords the future claimant the flexibility to present its claim as appropriate in light of its strategic and local interests. Perhaps this lack of clarity is intentional on the part of Contracting States – which have the ability to specify the acceptable manner of notice either in the BIT or in domestic legislation – but if such is the case, then investor-claimants can hardly be faulted or prejudiced for any so-called deficiencies in their notice of dispute, which this paper has sought to address.

---

23. FTC Statement, supra fn.9. See also KINNEAR, et al., supra fn. 9, 1119-11.

# Reasons for Reasons:
# The Tribunal's Duty in Investor-State Arbitration

*Toby T. Landau QC**

| TABLE OF CONTENTS | Page |
|---|---|
| I. Introduction | 187 |
| II. Court Judgments | 189 |
| III. Commercial Arbitration | 190 |
| IV. Investor-State Treaty Arbitration | 193 |
| V. Common Failures | 202 |
| VI. Conclusions | 204 |

### I. INTRODUCTION

There comes a poignant moment in every arbitration when the parties finally complete their last submission, or despatch their last post-hearing brief and, after months or (more likely) years of endeavour, formally pass the matter over to the tribunal for its determination. The tribunal then withdraws to the privacy of its own deliberations, and may not be heard from again, sometimes for a considerable period, until the publication of its award. The crafting of the decision remains a confidential process, beyond the grasp and scrutiny of all. Yet it is a process at the very heart of the arbitral mandate. Beyond the simple expression of a verdict, it is the tribunal's opportunity to reassure all concerned that they have been both heard and understood; to justify whatever the outcome of the process may be; and to ease the acceptance of its decision, primarily by persuading the losing party of the weaknesses of its case. Indeed, it is the nature and quality of the award itself, as opposed to the actual decision it contains, that will frequently dictate the success or failure of the arbitration as a whole.

It is perhaps surprising, therefore, that awards come in so many shapes and sizes. They may be reasoned or unreasoned; and the reasons themselves – if any – may range from the long to the short; the comprehensive to the incomplete; and the compelling to the bewildering.

Much has been written on the adequacy of reasons in the field of commercial arbitration. Notably, in 1988, in his Freshfields Lecture in London, the Rt Hon Lord Justice Bingham (later Lord Bingham of Cornhill) analyzed why the giving of reasoned judgments has become a standard feature of judicial proceedings; why the provision of

---

\* M.A., B.C.L. (Oxford); LL.M. (Harvard); FCIArb; CArb; Barrister (London); also of the New York State Bar; Essex Court Chambers, London.

full and cogent reasons is essential to a fair process; and why the same standard of decision-making should appertain to commercial arbitration.[1]

Since 1988, the landscape of international dispute resolution has been transformed by the rise of investor-State treaty arbitration. Disputes have become larger, more complex, more public and more sensitive. The interests and issues at stake have broadened. And the arbitral process has been shifted into a new realm of unprecedented political significance. And yet there are still marked fluctuations in the quality of awards in this field.

These variations in quality, and in particular in reasoning, have prompted increasing concerns, and have already been the subject of a few empirical studies.[2] What has so far received little or no attention, however, are the underlying reasons for reasons in this form of arbitration. It is this underlying rationale that must first be analyzed, in order properly to calibrate the appropriate standard of drafting that should apply in this field.

So it is, twenty years on, that the time has come to re-visit Lord Bingham's analysis, and to explore whether the reasons for reasons by national court judges and commercial arbitrators should now be applied in the same way to the determination of investor-State disputes.

As elaborated below, it is suggested that Lord Bingham's analysis is applicable to investor-State treaty arbitration – but the application is fundamentally different as compared to commercial arbitration. Indeed, such is the radically different nature of investor-State arbitration that commercial arbitration is now a false analogy, and new "reasons for reasons" must be addressed.

It is the intention of this paper to highlight these new reasons for reasons, and to urge upon treaty arbitrators a fresh conception of their mandate, divorced from the paradigm of commercial arbitration. The increased responsibility, indeed in some respects unprecedented responsibility, that their role entails brings with it a correlative duty in the crafting of their awards, and the realization of this change in role may ultimately be critical to the very survival of this field of dispute resolution.

The analysis below proceeds in four stages:

(a) a brief restatement of Lord Bingham's "reasons for reasons" in the context of national court judgments;
(b) a review of the "reasons for reasons" by commercial arbitrators; and
(c) consideration of the extent to which (a) and (b) apply – and are sufficient – in the new world of treaty arbitration;
(d) a brief, generalized and "no names" review of some of the more common failures by arbitral tribunals in their approach to reasoning.

---

1. BINGHAM, "Reasons and Reasons for Reasons: Differences Between a Court Judgment and an Arbitral Award", 4 *Arbitration International* (1988) p. 141. Lord Bingham's lecture was written largely by reference to English arbitral practice, and before the promulgation of the English Arbitration Act 1996 which (in Sect. 52(4)) introduced for the first time in English statutory law a requirement that arbitral awards contain reasons.
2. See in particular ALVAREZ and REISMAN, eds., *The Reasons Requirement in International Investment Arbitration*, (Martinus Nijhoff 2008); FAUCHALD, "The Legal Reasoning of ICSID Tribunals – An Empirical Analysis", 19 EJIL (2008) pp. 301-364.

II. COURT JUDGMENTS

In his Freshfields' Lecture, Lord Bingham's starting point was to question why it is customary for judges to give reasoned judgments at all. As he observed, a reasoned judgment, as distinct from a bare decision, is not, after all, a necessary feature of formal dispute resolution. In Lord Bingham's words:

> "... it might well be thought that parties who have endured the tedium and anguish of legal proceedings would wish to be spared yet another journey through country made distasteful by gross over-familiarity".

Lord Bingham then identified five distinct reasons why reasoned judgments have become a standard feature of judicial proceedings. These may be distilled briefly as follows:

(1) *The parties are entitled to be told why they have won or lost.*
It is a basic function of judges not only to resolve disputes, but also to explain to each party why it has won or lost. This reason requires little further explanation. A bare decision, without more, is likely to leave open many issues of fact and law, to which the litigating parties expect answers (just as they expect a final result). Further, there is a therapeutic element: the absence of reasons may well render acceptance of the judgment more difficult for the losing party. Worse still, it may engender resentment or a lack of confidence, and thereby threaten the integrity of the litigation process itself, or at the very least lead to an uncertain peace between the parties. Thus, it is now an accepted element of most court procedures that judgments include a justification for the acceptance of the winning party's position, and (more importantly) discounting the losing party's position.

(2) *A safeguard against arbitrariness.*
The second of Lord Bingham's reasons is closely connected to the first. A requirement that a decision be justified constitutes a safeguard against arbitrariness, private judgment, biased judgment, or "an irrational splitting of the difference" between the parties' respective cases. It is now a principle entrenched in most modern legal systems that a judge must decide disputes by the rational application of principle and authority, and not his or her own personal view of the justice of the case. The provision of reasons is the litigant's guarantee in this regard, and naturally follows from the basic proposition, in Lord Hewart CJ's words, that *"justice should not only be done, but should manifestly and undoubtedly be seen to be done"*.[3]

(3) *A guide to future conduct.*
This reason has two elements.

---

3. R. v. *Sussex Justices, Ex parte McCarthy*, [1924] 1 KB 256.

First, in systems where judicial precedent constitutes a source of law, the provision of reasons may well be essential in order to enable other courts to distinguish a "*ratio decidendi*" from an "*obiter dictum*".

Second, and beyond the technical confines of the doctrine of precedent, wherever conduct is of a kind that may be repeated, the giving of reasons may provide an essential guide both to the immediate and all other interested parties. More often than not, it is the reasons in a judgment, over and above the final result, that provide direction and instruction to those in the same field, and to allow them, as put by Lord Bingham, to "learn from the forensic experience of others".

(4) *Enabling an appellate court to review the decision and decide whether it is subject to reversible error.*
Depending upon the scope of review or appeal that might exist, the giving of reasons in a judgment will often be essential in enabling a higher court to conduct its own review, and to apply whatever standards it has available in deciding whether a decision should be upheld, reversed or varied. As Lord Bingham observed:

> "It is notorious that the worst judgments, namely those in which the findings of fact are most skimpy and the legal rulings most deficient, are often the hardest to challenge. How can the advocate challenge findings of fact when there are none or pinpoint errors of legal reasoning when the judge has eschewed any discussion of legal principle or authority?"

(5) *An intellectual discipline for the decision-maker.*
Lastly, in what he considered a "half reason" for reasons, Lord Bingham identified the intellectual discipline which the requirement of reasons brings to bear upon the decision maker:

> "I cannot, I hope, be the only person who has sat down to write a judgment, having formed the view that A must win, only to find in the course of composition that there are no sustainable grounds for that conclusion and that on any rational analysis B must succeed."

III. COMMERCIAL ARBITRATION

Having identified five reasons for reasons in the context of court judgments, one may next consider the extent to which these apply to commercial arbitral awards.

The starting point here must be the basic proposition that "commercial arbitration" is nothing but an umbrella term for a wide range of different procedures, which may have very little in common, save for the core characteristic that they all involve an agreement to the binding resolution of a dispute by a third party. Just as awards come in all shapes and sizes, so do commercial arbitrations. Historically, a major component in international arbitration has been the simple, one issue, trade disagreement, that requires a speedy answer, where the answer itself is far more important than the reasons. Hence, for example, the so-called "look-sniff" commodity arbitration, in which tribunals are appointed for their skill and experience in commerce, rather than language. Again in Lord Bingham's words: "... tapioca pellets either are, in the experienced judgment of a trade arbitrator, of fair average quality or they are not; whichever way his opinion goes there is probably not much that he can usefully add by way of exegesis".

But this is one end of a rich spectrum. At the other end lies the complex high level international dispute, which requires an extensive investigation, and detailed, sophisticated analysis of fact and law (and often multiple laws).

If one takes a generalized view across this spectrum, it is suggested that four of Lord Bingham's five "reasons for reasons" have an important role to play.

(1) *The parties are entitled to be told why they have won or lost.*
It is sometimes suggested that, if asked, commercial parties would say that the speedy and final determination of the dispute (whichever way this goes) is the most important feature of arbitration, and that a detailed assessment of the merits of each side's case, in contrast, is of little or no importance. This is anecdotal and not easily tested. It also, most likely, reflects a lingering tendency to conceive of commercial arbitration in terms of the (historically important) simple trade dispute. At the other end of the spectrum, however, the assertion is more difficult to accept. International commercial arbitration in its contemporary form is often an extremely elaborate and extensive process, with little connection to its historical roots. It frequently requires the investment of very substantial time and funds by all parties. As the demands – and in particular the costs – of the process increase, so do the expectations of the parties as to the quality and detail of the award. In short, sophisticated parties expending large sums tend to want their money's worth. If in any given case, the parties truly consider a final result more important than the reasons, they remain free to agree to a specially streamlined procedure, including an unreasoned award.

Whatever the precise type of arbitration, the basic proposition remains in all cases that arbitrating parties are entitled to know why they have won and (more importantly) lost. Indeed, given that arbitral awards, unlike court judgments, are generally not self-executing, but require either voluntary performance or separate enforcement action, this factor is of heightened importance here. If the absence of reasons, or adequate reasons, renders acceptance of the award more difficult for the losing party, the success of the arbitration may be directly impugned. Hence, in commercial arbitration, this is much more than a purely "therapeutic" element.

(2) *A safeguard against arbitrariness.*
This second reason applies with equal force to commercial arbitration, in so far as parties have not expressly empowered their tribunal to proceed "ex aequo et bono", by way of "amiable composition", or otherwise in disregard of defined laws or rules of law. The prevailing approach of modern arbitration laws and rules follows Art. 28 of the UNCITRAL Model Law on International Commercial Arbitration (the Model Law), by which arbitral tribunals may only apply broad principles of equity (as distinct from law or rules of law) if the parties have expressly so agreed. It follows therefore, that in the absence of such an agreement, parties are just as much entitled to a safeguard against arbitrariness as litigants before a national court. Indeed, one may argue that parties to a

commercial arbitration have a *greater* right to this safeguard than parties to litigation, given the absence of any appeal in most arbitrations, and the finality of the process.

(3) *A guide to future conduct.*
Lord Bingham's third reason is the one that probably has little role to play in commercial arbitration. Because of the widespread adherence to confidentiality in this field, and because of the absence of any doctrine of precedent, the possible guidance to future conduct that reasons might provide is generally limited to the immediate disputing parties. As such, it is unlikely to be a compelling factor in the crafting of an award – particularly if (as is often the case) the particular facts of the dispute are unlikely to repeat themselves. There are, of course, exceptions, such as the construction of a particular industry standard form contract, or the analysis of an occurrence upon which many disputes depend, but even in these situations the normative value of awards will rarely compare to that of judgments. Certainly, the provision of guidance beyond the immediate disputing parties would be seen by most as squarely beyond the arbitral tribunal's mandate.

(4) *Enabling an appellate court to review the decision and decide whether it is subject to reversible error.*
Lord Bingham's fourth reason has an obvious application to commercial arbitration, albeit that this will vary from forum to forum, depending upon the availability of recourse against awards. In the main, such recourse will comprise either a procedural challenge at the arbitral seat (as per Art. 34 of the Model Law), or the resisting of recognition and enforcement (most likely per Art. V of the 1958 New York Convention 1958). In each case, the provision of reasons may be essential from a court's perspective in order to assess the challenge – and essential from the arbitral tribunal's perspective in order to insulate its award from any such recourse.

(5) *An intellectual discipline for the decision-maker.*
Lastly, Lord Bingham's fifth reason has equal application in the field of commercial arbitration, as many arbitrators would readily admit.

Given these four reasons for reasons, it is little surprise that most modern arbitration laws[4] and rules[5] now impose an obligation upon arbitrators to provide reasons for their awards (in the case of some rules, unless the parties have agreed otherwise). Equally, the issue as to the "adequacy of reasons" has been an abundant source of debate.

Further still, the absence of reasons (or adequate reasons) is a matter that many courts take very seriously. This all the more so when the parties have agreed (e.g., by selecting any Model Law arbitral seat) that awards be reasoned. Indeed, on this basis, a failure to provide adequate reasons could amount to a failure by the arbitral tribunal to comply with the parties' agreement. One recent case has gone a step further. In its decision of

---

4. See, e.g., Art. 31(2) of the Model Law.
5. See, e.g., Art. 25(2) of the ICC Rules; Art. 26.1 of the Rules of the London Court of International Arbitration.

11 March 2008 in *Smart Systems Technologies Inc v. Domotique Secant Inc*,[6] the Quebec Court of Appeal refused to recognize and enforce a foreign arbitral award (which had already been recognized at the seat of arbitration – Albuquerque, New Mexico). It did so on the grounds that the parties having agreed to the application of the Model Law; the award being unreasoned; and the absence of reasons impeding the court's ability to consider the validity of the award and a number of serious errors alleged, the arbitral tribunal's failure to provide any reasons for its award was contrary to public policy (or "*public order as it is understood in international relations*").

IV. INVESTOR-STATE TREATY ARBITRATION

There is then the core question as to what "reasons for reasons" apply in the field of investor-State treaty arbitration. And here there is a persistent view that this form of arbitration may simply be added to the same spectrum of general commercial arbitration identified above. It is accepted by most that there are compelling "reasons for reasons" in this field, and assumed by many that they are the same – if arguably heightened – considerations as apply to any other form of commercial arbitration.

This, it is suggested, is a fundamental misconception. It is based, in turn, on the premise that investor-State arbitration consists simply of commercial arbitration in the context of a treaty – a premise no doubt enhanced by the fact that investor-State tribunals generally comprise the same body of individuals that dominate commercial arbitration, and that these arbitrators, just as the counsel that appear before them, frequently began, and have since spent the bulk of their professional lives, in commercial arbitration.

But commercial arbitration is an incorrect paradigm for this process. Notwithstanding the superficial similarities between the two forms of dispute resolution, and notwithstanding that one system borrows a procedural structure from the other, the two are in truth radically different. When considering the "reasons for reasons", it is imperative that this difference is fully appreciated. This may be elaborated by reference to each of Lord Bingham's five reasons.

(1) *The parties are entitled to be told why they have won or lost.*
There is no doubt that the parties to an investor-State treaty arbitration have an entitlement to be told why they have won or lost. But in this field, they are not the only ones. A broad range of other interests may also have the same entitlement. Further, depending upon the dispute, the nature of the entitlement itself, and the correlative duty upon the tribunal, may well be of a wholly different order to that arising in commercial arbitration.

---

6. *Smart Systems Technologies Inc v. Domotique Secant Inc* [2008] J.Q. No. 1782, 2008 QCCA 444.

These points flow from the peculiar nature of investor-State arbitration. As elaborated in a number of recent studies:[7]

(a) In terms of its positioning and standing, investor-State arbitration as a process is akin to inter-State arbitration (and unlike commercial arbitration) since both the existence and mandate of investor-State tribunals depend upon the consent on the part of two (or more) sovereign states, itself established by a sovereign act (the conclusion of an international treaty). It is, of course, true that investor-State arbitrations also depend upon the consent of investors, but such consent constitutes no more than the pulling of a trigger established by the international agreement of States. By way of setting, this peculiar provenance sets the process apart from a mere private or contractual arrangement.

(b) In terms of its function, investor-State arbitration is more akin to a form of public law adjudication, rather than commercial or contractual dispute resolution. Unlike commercial arbitration, its focus is generally regulatory disputes between individuals and a State (a vertical relationship), as distinct from reciprocal disputes between private parties, or between a private party and a State acting as a commercial entity (a horizontal relationship, in which both disputing parties are equally capable of possessing legal rights and obligations). In other words, BIT disputes, by their very nature, force tribunals to rule on the manner in which States exercise their sovereign discretion, and govern. To this end, they raise broad policy issues that reach far beyond the mutual rights and obligations of parties to a particular contract – issues that may well interact with the lives of ordinary people and the way they are governed. Whether or not this is the intention of such tribunals as they determine the dispute before them, it will frequently and necessarily follow, in so far as one class of individuals is protected by constraining the conduct of governments that continue to represent everyone else. It is this "regulatory" dimension of investor-State arbitration that distinguishes it from the simple determination of contractual rights and obligations – even if one of the parties to a contract is a State.

(c) In the exercise of this function, investor-State tribunals are endowed with powers of review that far exceed those available to national court judges. Given the principles of attribution in customary international law, States are responsible for the acts of each of their constituent elements, including their executive, their legislative and their judiciary. So it is that investor-State tribunals now routinely review, second-guess, and sanction the conduct of governments, parliaments and courts. The ambit of this power would be simply unthinkable in the context of most municipal systems of administrative law, and whilst perfectly understandable as a matter of international law, it is difficult to reconcile with accepted (municipal law) notions of judicial independence, and parliamentary sovereignty.

---

7. See in particular the frequently cited monograph by VAN HARTEN, *Investment Treaty Arbitration and Public Law* (OUP 2007), from which much of this material has been drawn (and greatly oversimplified). See also SUBEDI, *International Investment Law, Reconciling Policy and Principle* (Hart 2008).

(d) Further, investor-State tribunals are mandated to conduct this review by the application of extremely broad, open-textured, standards, as prescribed in BITs (e.g., restrictions on "expropriation"; guarantees of "fair and equitable treatment"; requirements of "non-discrimination" or "national treatment" or "most favoured nation" standards, amongst many others). The language of treaties is often the product of difficult cross-cultural negotiations, and the establishment of a consensus frequently requires the use of generalized and somewhat bland language (which may be susceptible of more than one interpretation).[8] Indeed, in most cases, anything more precise would have been impossible to agree. The result, for investor-State tribunals, is the delegation by States to private arbitrators of a vast discretion in the application of substantive standards to the particular facts of a dispute – a discretion that far exceeds that available to most national court judges who may be empowered to review sovereign conduct.

(e) The lack of guidance in the substantive standards to be applied is further compounded by the absence of any doctrine of *stare decisis* in this field (as is the general position in international law). However detailed previous elaborations of the applicable standards may be, investor-State tribunals do not operate in a hierarchical or unitary system that requires them to follow precedents, or to adopt the conclusions of other courts or tribunals. As succinctly noted by the tribunal in *SGS v. Philippines*:[9]

> "... there is no doctrine of precedent in international law, if by precedent is meant a rule of the binding effect of a single decision. There is no hierarchy of international tribunals, and even if there were, there is no good reason for allowing the first tribunal in time to resolve issues for all later tribunals."

Thus, the discretion of each investor-State tribunal remains, at least in theory, relatively unrestricted.[10]

---

8. See, e.g., *Czech Republic v. European Media Ventures SA* [2008] 1 Lloyd's Rep 186, at para. 19 (Simon J), on the notion of "common intentions", in the context of the interpretation of a BIT in accordance with the Vienna Convention:

    "The proper approach is to interpret the agreed form of words which, objectively and in their proper context, bear an ascertainable meaning. This approach, no doubt reflecting the experience of centuries of diplomacy, leaves open the possibility that the parties might have dissimilar intentions and might wish to put different interpretations on what they had agreed" (and fn. 10: "Mr. Landau referred to the subversive epigram: a treaty is a disagreement reduced into writing").

9. *SGS v. Phlippines*, Decision on Jurisdiction, 29 January 2004, at para. 97.

10. The issue of "precedent" in investor-State arbitration has been the subject of much analysis. See, e.g., the several contributions in BANIFATEMI, ed., *Precedent in International Arbitration*, IAI Series on International Arbitration No. 5 (Juris 2008); and KAUFMANN-KOHLER, "Arbitral Precedent: Dream, Necessity or Excuse?" 23 Arbitration International (2007) p. 357; DI PIETRO, "The Use of Precedents in ICSID Arbitration: Regularity or Certainty?" 10 Int Arb Law Rev (2007) p. 92. See also the extensive analysis of the new positioning and role of arbitral decisions in this field, as compared with the traditional role of treaties, in WÄLDE, *New Aspects of International Investment Law* (Centre for Studies and Research in International Law and International Relations, Hague Academy of International Law 2004) at pp. 63-154.

(f) This extraordinary power of review is coupled with an equally extraordinary power on the part of investor-State tribunals to discipline States by the imposition of damages awards. The scale of these awards may well be very significant indeed. As Van Harten notes by way of one example, in *CME v. Czech Republic* (2001),[11] the tribunal ordered the Czech Republic to pay US$ 353 million to the investor. This amount, according to Van Harten, roughly equated to the Czech Republic's entire health-care budget for the relevant year. If adjusted for population size and gross national income, the award was equivalent to an award of US$19 billion against the United Kingdom; US$ 26 billion against Germany; and US$ 131 billion against the United States.[12] In substance, awards as vast as these constitute material allocations of public funds, which may, in and of themselves, have a direct impact beyond the immediate parties to the dispute. And yet they are allocations effected by private individuals who operate in a sphere completely removed from the limitations, checks and balances that would ordinarily apply to those empowered to make such allocations in a domestic context.

(g) Further still, investor-State tribunals exercise these relatively unstructured and wide-ranging powers in a procedural regime that – again unlike national court judges:

i. lacks any system of substantive appeal;
ii. is often insulated from, or susceptible of only limited, procedural review by national court judges; and
iii. leads in many cases – at last in theory – to compulsory international recognition and enforcement (whether under the Washington Convention 1965, or the 1958 New York Convention).

Against these factors, the simple assertion that "parties are entitled to be told why they have won or lost" will not do. In truth, the position in investor-State arbitration goes much further than this.

First, the investor-State tribunal's audience comprises not only the immediate parties, but all other entities that may be affected by the decision. As explained above, depending on the issues at stake, this could well include broad sections of a given population. A dispute, for example, between a foreign investor and a State over the exercise of the State's emergency powers (e.g., an urgent decision to nationalize a major bank, in order to alleviate a rapid economic slowdown or "credit crunch") could well be as critical for the domestic population as it is for the foreign investor. There may also be other non-parties with a legitimate interest in the substantive matters at stake, such as NGOs, international policy and funding institutions (such as the World Bank) or even other governments. Crafting adequate reasons in order to satisfy such a broad and diverse audience is likely to be a completely different task from simply explaining to the immediate parties why they have won or lost.

Second, the importance, complexity, and political sensitivity of the actual issues themselves (i.e., the exercise by a State of its sovereign discretion) is likely to call for a level of, and care in, reasoning, beyond that required for a commercial transaction. It is

---

11. *CME Czech Republic BV v. Czech Republic*, Award on Damages, 14 March 2003.
12. VAN HARTEN, supra fn. 7 at p. 7.

one thing (for example) to describe the rights and obligations of parties to a commercial sale, or indeed the quality of tapioca pellets. It is quite another thing (for example) to determine the adequacy of an elected government's black empowerment or land distribution policy; or a State's exercise of emergency powers; or (more broadly) its economic or foreign policy; or the activities of an elected legislature; or the determinations of a Supreme Court. This all the more so, if (as is common) the dispute takes place against a backdrop of widespread public debate and activism; if the decision might inflame an already polarized and fragile situation; and if (as suggested earlier) a key function of reasoning is to ease the acceptance of the award.

Third, and leading on from all these points, there is the ever-more critical question of the very legitimacy of the investor-State arbitration process itself. For some time, the system has been under attack from those who argue that it is a process without adequate checks and balances, in which unelected, unrepresentative, and unaccountable individuals wield unjustified power. The rights and wrongs of this debate lie well beyond the scope of this paper. But even if completely misplaced, it is a fact that such criticisms of the process exist, and are gathering pace. It is therefore incumbent on those responsible for operating the system to tailor the arbitral process, in so far as possible, with these pressures in mind. This is not just a broad policy issue regarding the future of BIT dispute resolution as a whole. Rather, it is a concrete matter for each individual case, and each individual tribunal, since to disregard this wider debate may well risk the integrity of the immediate process, and the ultimate award.

One key approach for tribunals is to enhance the transparency of the arbitration, in so far as feasible. Another is to allow the participation of non-parties who may have a legitimate interest in the dispute (whether as third parties or amici curiae), and may require their own "day in court".[13] But the success of all such measures still largely depends on the quality of the final award. There is little to be gained by enhanced transparency, or the inclusion of all interested parties if, at the end of the day, questions remain on the part of those concerned as to precisely how their position was actually taken into account, and why an investor-State tribunal has arrived at the position it has. Indeed, with increased transparency, and increased participation in the process, there is much more pressure on the investor-State tribunal to take into account and reflect all positions in its final determination, and to perfect the presentation of its award.

Once again, these are all dynamics that militate in favour of very carefully and fully reasoned awards. They bear equally on each of Lord Bingham's four other reasons for reasons and, importantly, they are absent in the field of commercial arbitration.

---

13. The issues of (a) "transparency" and (b) the participation of non-parties in investor-State arbitration, have both given rise to passionate debates, and copious analysis. For a useful survey, see DELANEY and MAGRAW, "Procedural Transparency" in MUCHLINSKI, ORTINO and SCHREUER, eds., *The Oxford Handbook of International Investment Law* (OUP 2008) Chap. 19, pp. 721-788.

*(2) A safeguard against arbitrariness.*
In light of the analysis above, Lord Bingham's second reason for reasons has an obvious application in this field. But as with the first reason, it is greatly enhanced here, given the importance and sensitivity of the issues at stake, and the nature of the tribunal's audience.

*(3) A guide to future conduct.*
Unlike the position with commercial arbitration, Lord Bingham's third reason for reasons has an important application to investor-State arbitration, but it requires adaptation in this context. There are two key components here.

*Future "Case Law":* First, there is the need for coherence and stability in what is a nascent but fast-evolving jurisprudence. Unlike commercial arbitration, investor-State arbitral awards are, in the main, public, and indeed widely publicized and debated. In its relatively short life, the field of investor-State arbitration has already generated a huge body of decisions which, in turn, have spawned textbooks, articles, discussion fora, and international conferences. Over and above the numerous BITs themselves, it is the awards of arbitrators that have become the true engine in the development of this field. But this body of decisions has also given rise – already – to marked divergences of approach. There are competing lines of decisions on many key procedural and substantive issues. To name but a few random examples, one may point to the range of approaches on the juridical effect of prescribed preconditions to the commencement of arbitration; to the definition of "investor" and "investment"; to the meaning and effect of "umbrella clauses"; to the analysis and application of "most favoured nation" provisions; to the definition of the components of "fair and equitable treatment" and their relationship with customary international law; and so on.[14] The list, in truth, is now extensive, as reflected in the size of textbook now customarily produced. Some of the inconsistencies involve a single treaty.[15] Some of the inconsistencies involve a single event.[16] Some involve a single dispute.[17] To an extent, these divergences are unsurprising, given the relative youth of the field; the need for doctrine to develop and settle; and the accepted fact that there is no applicable doctrine of precedent or *stare decisis*.[18] Further, (as emphasised, e.g., in the *MOX Plant Case*),[19] identical or similar

---

14. See generally on this issue: GILL, "Inconsistent Decisions: An Issue to be Addressed or a Fact of Life?" in ORTINO, SHEPPARD and WARNER, eds., *Investment Treaty Law – Current Issues*, Vol. 1 (BIICL 2006) at p. 23, and FRANCK, "The Legitimacy Crisis in Investment Treaty Arbitration: Privatising Public International Law Through Inconsistent Decisions", 73 FLR (2005) p. 1521.
15. E.g., the contrast between *Occidental v. Ecuador*, Final Award, 1 July 2004, and *EnCana Corp v. Ecuador*, Award, 3 February 2006.
16. Notably the numerous decisions on Argentina's 2002 emergency legislation.
17. E.g., the now notorious *CME* and *Lauder* cases (*CME Czech Republic B.V. v. Czech Republic*, Partial Award, 13 September 2001, and *Ronald S. Lauder v. Czech Republic*, Final Award, 3 September 2001.
18. The absence of any doctrine of precedent, and the fact that tribunals are free to disregard previous decisions, has become something of an incantation in awards in this field. See, e.g., *Amco v. Indonesia*, Decision on Jurisdiction, 25 September 1983, 1 ICSID Reports 395; *Amco v. Indonesia*,

provisions of different treaties may not necessarily yield the same interpretive results once differences in respective context, objects and purposes, subsequent practice of parties, and *travaux préparatoires* have been taken into account. But, even allowing for this, the overall result remains a growing, and worrying, incoherence, and instability in this area. There is, at least as yet, little predictability, and perfectly understandable concerns when comparable cases lead to very different outcomes. Indeed, as a practical matter, it is currently almost impossible to provide useful advice to disputing parties since, ultimately, so much will depend upon the identity and tastes of the particular arbitrators appointed. All this is welcome fodder for the critics of the system.

Notwithstanding the absence of a doctrine of precedent, there is a common search for consistency. Hence most investor-State tribunals carefully review, and place heavy reliance upon, previous arbitral decisions. As put by the tribunal in *Saipem v. Bangladesh*:[20]

"The Tribunal considers that it is not bound by previous decisions. At the same time, it is of the opinion that it must pay due consideration to earlier decisions of international tribunals. It believes that, subject to compelling contrary grounds, it has a duty to adopt solutions established in a series of consistent cases. It also believes that, subject to the specifics of a given treaty and of the circumstances of the actual case, it has a duty to seek to contribute to the harmonious development of investment law and thereby to meet the legitimate expectations of the community of States and investors towards certainty of the rule of law."[21]

This, it is respectfully suggested, is the correct approach. Unlike commercial arbitration, investor-State tribunals have at least some responsibility beyond the simple resolution of the immediate dispute before them. This is not to be overstated. It is certainly not the case that tribunals must follow previous decisions. Equally, it is not the case that each tribunal has a mandate, or indeed the ability, to make sweeping jurisprudential pronouncements, or to resolve doctrinal debates for all time. As put by one commentator: "There is no multilateral grant of authority over objective

---

Decision on Annulment, 16 May 1986, 1 ICSID Reports 521, at para. 44; *LETCO v. Liberia*, Award, 31 March 1986, 2 ICSID Reports 346, at para. 352; *Feldman v. Mexico*, Award, 16 December 2002, 7 ICSID Reports 341, at para. 107; *SGS v. Philippines*, Decision on Jurisdiction, 29 January 2004, at para. 97; *Enron v. Argentina*, Decision on Jurisdiction (Ancillary Claim), 2 August 2004, 11 ICSID Reports 295, at para. 25; *AES Corp v. Argentina*, Decision on Jurisdiction, 26 April 2005, 12 ICSID Reports 312, at paras. 17-33; *Gas Natural SDG SA v. Argentina*, Decision on Jurisdiction, 17 June 2005, at paras. 36-52. But see fn. 28 below.

19. *The MOX Plant Case (Ireland v. UK)*, Provisional Measure, Order of 3 December 2001, 126 ILR (2005) 260.
20. Decision on Jurisdiction, 21 March 2007, at para. 67.
21. See similarly, *Gas Natural SDG, SA v Argentina*, Decision on Jurisdiction, 17 June 2005, at paras. 36 and 52 (in which the tribunal's conclusions were carefully cross-checked with previous decisions).

interpretation granted to individual tribunals sitting in cases of particular investor-State disputes."[22]

Rather, the collective responsibility of tribunals in this field, at this early stage of its existence, is to pave the way for an orderly development of the law (and even, in so far as possible, to provide momentum for a *"jurisprudence constante"* on key issues). In a system of ad hoc adjudication such as this, and given the absence of a single institution, this can only be done by taking sufficient care in the articulation of awards, such as to render them of use in subsequent cases. Specifically, this entails:

(a) A duty to consider, and to explain departures from, or concurrences with, relevant previous decisions. It bears emphasis that the point here is one of articulation only. There is no difficulty in tribunals refusing to follow earlier relevant decisions. The point, rather, is that such departures should be reasoned. The same is true if previous decisions are to be followed. If little or no regard is paid to previous relevant decisions, and if tribunals look no further than the immediate treaty and the immediate dispute before them, the multiplicity of approaches in this field, and the consequent disorder, will continue.

(b) A duty to elaborate sufficient reasons such as to enable future tribunals to assess the award, and decide whether or not to follow it. This is the correlative of (a) above. If awards are poorly or minimally reasoned, this will impede subsequent tribunals from discharging their duty. There are several dangers here. The poorly reasoned award, which is impenetrable or difficult to analyze, is likely to be ignored by future tribunals, and thereby remain yet another decision isolated from the mainstream of the jurisprudence. Whilst, in Paulsson's conception of a Darwinian "natural selection" amongst awards, such decisions may "flicker and die near-instant deaths",[23] they may also persist, as a testament to the incoherence of the law. Worse still, such decisions may be misunderstood and misused by future parties, tribunals or commentators, in their respective searches for consistency.

*Future Conduct:* As noted, Lord Bingham's third reason for reasons also has a further, quite different, application in this field. To many, the modern law of foreign investment is primarily concerned with promoting the flow of capital into host States, and the protection of aliens' property and interests. There is, however, a broader conception that focuses upon the role of BITs in the development process of host States, and in particular, the imposition by way of treaties of "externally anchored economic reform

---

22. KRISHAN, "A Notion of ICSID Investment" in *Investment Treaty Arbitration: A Debate and Discussion*, Todd Grierson-Weiler, ed. (Juris Publishing 2008 ).
23. PAULSSON, "International Arbitration and the Generation of Legal Norms: Treaty Arbitration and International Law" in *International Arbitration 2006: Back to Basics?*, ICCA Congress Series no. 13 (Kluwer 2007), at p. 881.

and good-governance principles",[24] In short, "top-down" development. As explained by Wälde:

> "... the role of investment treaties is to provide an external anchor for economic policies that are in the long-term sensible for national economies and the global economy, but which are imperilled by forces of, usually short-term, domestic pressures.... External disciplines play a role that can in some aspects be compared to the role of national constitutional law and the prototypes of international constitutional law – as embodied, for example, in WTO and EU law or the European and Latin American Human Rights Conventions.
> (....)
> By providing external disciplines applied by an international adjudicatory process, much like the WTO inter-State trade litigation system, investment treaties provide sanctions for non-compliance in individual cases, but, and perhaps more importantly, they provide a signal for the domestic policy discussion on how economic governance should be....
> The accountability that arises in litigation before an investment tribunal may not be fully immune, but is less subject to political manipulation than any domestic processes – political, administrative or judicial. The prospect of international accountability provides leverage to the good-governance forces within a Government. The prospect of an international sanction and international accountability strengthens the hand of politicians and officials within a national Government who advocate a fair course of dealing rather than yielding too easily to domestic agitation with short-term political advantages and much higher long-term economic and then also political costs usually borne by subsequent Governments."[25]

This external imposition of standards is, thus, not just a matter for treaties. Arbitral awards play a critical role, given that these are the vehicles for detailed interpretation and application of the generic principles set out in treaties. Further, this is not just a question of disciplining host States. As many arbitral awards have now elaborated, there is a key principle of "investor responsibility" that conditions the rights of investors, and just as an investor-State tribunal may set out standards of good governance for a State, so it may also elaborate standards of conduct for investors.

In each case, this is a function beyond the immediate resolution of the dispute, which bears directly upon the quality of reasoning required – and is a factor absent in commercial arbitration.

---

24. Per WÄLDE, in *New Aspects of International Investment Law* (Centre for Studies and Research in International Law and International Relations, Hague Academy of International Law 2004) at pp. 91-120.
25. WÄLDE, *ibid.*, at pp. 104-107.

(4) *Enabling an appellate court to review the decision and decide whether it is subject to reversible error.*
Lord Bingham's fourth reason for reasons has a similar application here as it does to commercial arbitration. Investor-State arbitration may take a number of different forms, each with its own regime for review. BIT arbitrations conducted under the auspices of ICSID will be limited to the ICSID annulment procedure, and insulated from the grasp of national courts. BIT arbitrations conducted under the UNCITRAL Arbitration Rules or other institutional forms of arbitration are likely to be subject to at least a limited procedural review by the courts of the seat. In all cases, there may be further scrutiny at the stage of recognition and enforcement. Just as with commercial arbitration, the provision of reasons is essential not only to facilitate such reviews, but also to insulate awards from undue attacks.

(5) *An intellectual discipline for the decision-maker.*
Lastly, Lord Bingham's fifth reason for reasons is as valid here as in any other adjudicative process.

V. COMMON FAILURES

The question then is whether investor-State tribunals are generally meeting the standard of reasoning that is required of them. Others have already conducted detailed and empirical analyses of particular areas, and particular awards.[26] This lies beyond the scope of this paper. Rather, what is set out below (on a "no names" basis) are three of the more common, general failures by arbitral tribunals in their overall approach to reasoning in this field.

(a) *A Tendency towards Minimalism*
In his Freshfields Lecture, Lord Bingham noted that Common Law courts are often criticized for what he termed a "tendency towards over-elaboration" – a tendency of which he warned commercial arbitrators to be wary. The tendency in investor-State arbitration, it is suggested, veers the other way. It is true that awards in this field tend to be long. More often than not, however, the bulk of the pages comprises an extremely lengthy recitation of the procedural history of the matter, followed by an even more lengthy "cut and paste" from each side's submissions on each point. As one ploughs through this great mass of material, one's expectations may rise as to the analysis to come. And yet, as one finally reaches the promising title "*Analysis*" or "*Conclusions*", one's hopes are frequently shattered, as the award suddenly peters out, and ends, not with a bang but a whimper.[27] In the few pages left between the heading and the dispositive order, very little is often given away as to the tribunal's thinking. The flavour of such awards is one of minimalism – or the expression of no more than is strictly necessary for

---

26. See references in fn. 2 supra.
27. See T.S. ELIOT, "The Hollow Men" (1925) final stanza: "This is the way the world ends / This is the way the world ends / This is the way the world ends / Not with a bang but a whimper."

each proposition, in order to connect the final disposition to at least some of the parties' submissions. In some cases, reasons are given, but by way of short and compressed statements. In others, reasons are pared down in number to the fewest possible propositions. In others, conclusions are given, instead of any reasons at all.

This is a style of drafting that may well have its roots in commercial arbitration. It is motivated by a belief that the tribunal's mandate is simply to resolve the immediate dispute, and in so doing to avoid any possible "hostages to fortune". Hence, even if in deliberations the tribunal has conducted a detailed analysis, the tribunal sees its task in drafting as the pronouncement of its final destination, rather than the voyage by which it arrived there. The overly cynical might also suggest, quite unjustifiably, that this approach also maximizes the role of the tribunal's legal secretary (or juniors in the firm), who may be solely responsible for the drafting of the longest portions of the award.

But this approach fails to address the reasons for reasons set out above. On the basis of these reasons, it is suggested that in the drafting of their awards in this context, it is imperative that tribunals cast off the "commercial arbitration" conception of their role; consider their task afresh; and develop a tendency towards elaboration.

*(b) A Narrow View of "Relevance"*
The second general failure is closely connected to the first. As part of the flawed conception that investor-State arbitration is simply commercial arbitration involving a treaty, and the tendency towards minimalism that this engenders, many tribunals in this field deploy an overly narrow view as to what is a "relevant" issue that needs to be addressed, and what is an "irrelevant" issue that may be ignored. In the context of commercial arbitration, the common approach is to address only those issues that are actually and strictly dispositive of the immediate dispute. In the context of both national courts and commercial arbitration, however, Lord Bingham cautioned against an overly rigorous application of this principle: "[Judges] must not avoid mention of events to which any party reasonably attaches significance even if the significance is not in his view very great."

This is not, of course, a plea that arbitrators (or judges) produce overly long decisions that meander through all points raised, whether or not each is in fact of any consequence to the final result. Clearly, this would be in no parties' interests, and positively dangerous for the integrity of the process itself. Rather, the point is to ensure that all parties leave the process with the sense that the key issues that are of particular importance to them have been taken into account.

In investor-State arbitration, there is a key difference: given the peculiar nature of the process, "relevance" must be tested by reference to all interested entities – not just the immediate parties to the dispute. If, for example, a body of NGOs, or perhaps a wider population in the host State, considers a particular aspect of a dispute of vital significance, the tribunal must at least bear this in mind in its delimitation of "relevant" issues that warrant mention in the award – even if, in the tribunal's own view, and as a matter of strict, cold, logic, a final disposition is possible without any mention of the issue at all.

*(c) A Tendency towards Compilation*
It is argued above that given the nature, and youth, of this field, it is incumbent upon tribunals to advert to previous decisions, whether or not they choose to follow them.

Most tribunals do so, albeit to greatly varying degrees. However, the way in which previous decisions are addressed is very often by way of a somewhat cursory "string citation", frequently in footnotes. Such an approach is unproblematic as long as the "string" is the product of careful consideration by the tribunal. But the creeping and unfortunate tendency here is to substitute mechanical compilation, for a proper analysis of prior reasoning.[28] How often it is that one follows up on a list of references, only to find that the authorities in question in fact contain no support for the proposition for which they have been deployed. Indeed, the emerging phenomenon is the imprecise citation (or string) in one award, which is then unquestioningly adopted and quoted by tribunals in successive decisions. (Once again, the overly cynical observer might, wholly incorrectly, suggest that the tribunal itself did not take responsibility for the offending footnotes in the award).

It is suggested that the standard of reasoning now required in that investor-State arbitration in turn necessitates a more meticulous approach to the evaluation and citation of prior decisions.

## VI.  CONCLUSIONS

There are a number of conclusions that should *not* be drawn from this analysis.

This is not a call for long awards, per se. Nor is it a desire for the production of legal dissertations. Nor is it to encourage tribunals' displays of erudition, for erudition's (or the tribunals') sake. Notwithstanding the reasons for reasons enumerated above, many investor-State arbitrations will be happily and properly resolved by a short and concise piece of work.

Equally, this is not a licence for rambling or overly broad awards. There remain compelling reasons why tribunals in all fields must remain disciplined in the crafting of their decisions, and the selection of matters to be addressed.

Further still, the analysis here must necessarily give way to a range of other factors that may well militate in favour of "less" rather than "more", in the drafting of an award. These include the often complex dynamics within the tribunal and its decision-making process. In particular, there is a real possibility in many cases that all members of the tribunal will be able to agree on the end result, but not on the reasons. In such cases, unanimity may well be more important than a detailed award, and the drafting will then have to be cut back in such a way as to sustain the consensus.[29]

---

28. For some particularly egregious examples, see some of the earlier footnotes in this paper (in particular fn. 18 supra).
29. Cf. in the context of public international law, the debates on the provision of reasons that preceded the First Hague Conference of 1899. At the Committee of Examination's Tenth Meeting on 26 June 1899 (the first reading), the German delegate, Dr. Zorn, requested that there be added a requirement that an award "must state the reasons on which it is based". James Brown Scott's translation of the meeting records:

    "Mr. Martens [whose Draft Plan formed the basis of discussions] recognizes the significance of this proposition. He has on more than one occasion mentioned the advantages that would result from

But these points aside, there is a pressing need for arbitral tribunals in this field to reconsider their approach when drafting awards, and to recognize the duties which this curious form of adjudication imposes.

In particular, it is imperative that tribunals now move away from the commercial arbitration mentality that appears to have infected the practice so far. Given the existing pressures on the system, this is an infection which cannot be left unchecked.

a statement of the reasons upon which the awards of arbitrators are based; especially by this means we would succeed in creating a valuable body of law. But on the other hand he is bound to recognize serious objections which he has met on the part of different arbitrators who are of the highest authority in these matters, and who have called his attention to the fact that in an international conflict arbitrators are not only judges; they are also representatives of their Governments. To require them to state the reasons for their decisions would be to impose upon them one of the most delicate obligations, and perhaps even to embarrass them seriously, if their judicial consciences do not find themselves in accord with the requirements of their Governments or the sensibilities of public opinion in their countries. It is indeed going far to require an impartial arbitrator to condemn his own government. Must we also require him to justify himself expressly and thereby aggravate this condemnation? If the arbitral decision contains only a few sentences all of the arbitrators without regard to their nationality may sign it. Will the result be the same if this award, accompanied by a statement of the reasons on which it is founded, implies a severe criticism of or casts blame upon, one of the parties? It is clear that the arbitrator of the country blamed will be obliged to abstain from voting, and consequently that the decision will have less authority. That is why, in the very interest of the growth of the principle of arbitration, the Russian Government has not gone so far as to provide that arbitral decisions shall be accompanied by a statement of the reasons upon which they are based."

At the second reading on 30 June 1899, Dr. Zorn reintroduced his proposal in the belief "that this addition is necessary to the development of the law of nations". A Mr. Asser was recorded as challenging Mr. Martens, pointing to "a strong guaranty of impartiality in the obligation imposed upon arbitrators to sate the reason for their decision. Thanks to this guarantee the award will never be considered arbitrary." Mr. Martens' objections were defeated, and Dr. Zorn's proposal was eventually passed, and found its way into the final Articles.

# Working Group A

## 5. Remedies in Investment Treaty Arbitration:

## The Bottom Line

# Non-pecuniary Remedies in Investment Treaty and Commercial Arbitration

*Carole Malinvaud*[*]

| TABLE OF CONTENTS | Page |
|---|---|
| I. Introduction | 209 |
| II. Availability of Non-Pecuniary Remedies in State/Investment and Commercial Arbitration? | 210 |
| III. Particularities of Investment Arbitration Limiting the Recourse to Non-Pecuniary Remedies | 226 |
| IV. Conclusion | 230 |

## I. INTRODUCTION

Although commonly described as the bottom line for parties before both arbitral tribunals and State courts, remedies have not always been as closely studied and commented upon as they currently are. The relatively limited considerations dedicated to the issue by some arbitral tribunals in their awards, in combination with recent attempts to infer clear trends from existing case law, invite further study on this topic.

In light of the recent and impressive development of investment arbitration, it is worthwhile examining whether remedies are treated differently in investment arbitration compared to commercial arbitration. There are definitely common grounds, again reinforced by the presence of numerous personalities, whether arbitrators or counsel, acting in both fields.

But what are those commonalities, in particular regarding the availability of non-pecuniary remedies? Are there different sources? Are the standards referred to by the arbitral tribunals the same? Do investment arbitration records show specific or original solutions? Are they two different ball games?

Remedies are defined as "the means of enforcing a right or preventing or redressing a wrong".[1] As a consequence, in a dispute, whether typically commercial or related to an investment, the remedies available to the aggrieved party are not limited to financial compensation, i.e., the monetary equivalent of what the party would have gained, had the breach which gave rise to the dispute never happened.

Thus, commercial arbitration relatively frequently features not only additional financial penalties – such as punitive damages or interests and costs – but also orders for rectification, the adaptation of and filling gaps within contracts, declaratory relief or

---

[*] Partner, Gide Loyrette Nouel A.A.R.P.I. The author wishes to thank Thomas Parigot for his assistance in preparing this contribution.
1. Definition from *Black's Law Dictionary*, 8th edn.

restitution and specific performance. In investment arbitration, available non-pecuniary remedies include the partial or total restitution of property as well as satisfaction.

Nonetheless, the pre-eminence of damages as the almost systematic mode of reparation is clear, notably in investment arbitration.

To some, the situation is deplorable. Indeed, from a certain point of view, damages can appear inadequate when the aggrieved party would rather be reinstated in its rights or obtain the specific performance of the breached obligation instead of being merely compensated by damages equivalent to the value of that to which the party was entitled.

Besides, damages might not always be able to satisfy the aggrieved party for certain aspects of its loss. Such is the case in situations where, for instance, a party suffers moral damage, when the honour or reputation of the party is at stake. Money would probably be less satisfactory than a full apology or public acknowledgment of libel.

The purpose of this study is to determine the reasons behind the near-total lack of recourse to non-pecuniary damages in investment arbitration: whether it is a question of law – such as non-pecuniary damages' availability in the substantive rules applicable to disputes; of the ability of arbitrators to grant forms of relief other than damages (I); or if tribunals' preference for damages can be attributed to reasons of opportunity in consideration of the parties and stakes involved (II).

II. AVAILABILITY OF NON-PECUNIARY REMEDIES IN STATE/INVESTMENT AND COMMERCIAL ARBITRATION ?

The availability of non-pecuniary remedies seems at first glance more established in commercial arbitration (1) than in state/investment arbitration (2).

1. *Non-pecuniary Remedies in Commercial Arbitration*

While faced with a contractual dispute, arbitrators may order specific performance and possibly judicial penalties to facilitate the enforcement of their orders.[2] Whereas frequently used arbitration rules do not impose specific restrictions on the matter,[3] some domestic legislation on arbitration has expressly mentioned the possibility.[4]

---

2. For a detailed study on the subject, see A. MOURRE, "Judicial Penalties and Alternative Remedies in International Arbitration" in L. LEVY and F. DE LY, eds., *Interest, Auxiliary and Alternative Remedies in International Arbitration*, Proceedings of the 27th annual meeting of the ICC Institute of World Business Law, Paris, 26 November 2007.
3. ICC Rules of Arbitration, effective from 1 January 1998; UNCITRAL Model Law on International Commercial Conciliation of the United Nations Commission on International Trade Law (57/18), 19 November 2002; Arbitration Rules of the United Nations Commission on International Trade Law (31/98), 15 December 1976.
4. For example, Sect. 48 of the English Arbitration Act 1996 provides that "[u]nless otherwise agreed by the parties ... [t]he tribunal has the same powers as the [English] court ... to order specific performance of a contract (other than a contract relating to land)".

As a matter of fact, specific performance will be available any time it is provided for by the applicable substantive law (*a*) and the debate shifts to the powers of the arbitrators to order judicial penalties (*b*).

*a. Non-pecuniary remedies provided by the law governing the dispute*

Traditionally, arbitrators will refer to the domestic law designated by the parties and to trade usages and principles to determine whether the substantive rules governing the dispute allow for the recourse to non-pecuniary remedies. The principle of the recourse to non-pecuniary remedies is generally accepted (i) but subject to limitations (ii).

i. Principle[5]

(1) Domestic laws

With regard to compensation, the majority of domestic laws establish, albeit with limitations, the possibility of obtaining restitution in kind or specific performance among the remedies available to aggrieved parties. For example, Art. 1184 of the French Civil Code provides that the party who breaches a contractual obligation can be forced to carry out its duty.[6] Similar provisions exist in Dutch and Swiss law[7] whereas in Germany the Code of Civil Procedure provides that, in the event that the obligation can only be performed by the debtor, the court can fine him if he does not comply as ordered by the decision.[8]

In common law countries, the traditional view is that specific performance can be granted but only at equity and when it appears appropriate in comparison with damages,

---

5. A. MOURRE, "Judicial Penalties and Specific Performance in International Arbitration", *op. cit.*, fn. 2, has been of great help for the preparation of this section.
6. In French law, specific performance of an obligation to give (*obligation de donner*) is not an issue given that it consists of the transfer of property of the goods and that this transfer takes place as soon as each party consents. The question has been more frequently discussed with respect to obligations to do or to abstain from doing something (*obligations de faire et de ne pas faire*). Art. 1142 of the French Civil Code provides: "Any obligation to do or not to do resolves itself into damages, in case of non-performance on the part of the debtor." Nonetheless, case law reduced the scope of this provision and grants specific performance of such obligations when it is still possible, notably on the basis of Art. 1184(2) according to which

    "[a] condition subsequent is one which, when it is fulfilled, brings about the revocation of the obligation, and which puts things back in the same condition as if the obligation had not existed. It does not suspend the fulfilment of the obligation; it only compels the creditor to return what he has received, in the case where the event contemplated by the condition happens."

    Arts. 1143 and 1144 are also used as they allow the destruction of what was made in breach of the agreement or "to have the obligation performed himself, at the debtor's expense". See notably, Gérard LÉGIER, *Répertoire Dalloz, Responsabilité contractuelle*, paras. 207 et seq.; Alain BÉNABENT, *Droit civil, les obligations*, 11th edn. (Montchrestien 2007) paras. 380 et seq.
7. See Art. 3:296 of the Dutch Civil Code and Art. 97 of the Swiss *Code des Obligations*.
8. Art. 888 of the *Zivilprozessordnung*.

the preferred remedy.[9] US case law expressly allows for the recourse to specific performance in arbitration.[10]

(2) Transnational rules

Arbitrators may refer to rules stemming from external sources in addition to domestic laws. For example, international conventions such as the United Nations 1980 Convention on the International Sale of Goods (CISG) may apply and some codified trade usages such as the UNIDROIT Principles or the Principles of European Contract Law (PECL) can be taken into account. These examples do not constitute an exhaustive list of all existing rules but their authority is undisputed and their use in commercial arbitration is widespread.

With respect to the issue of non-pecuniary damages, the CISG explicitly allows a party to seek specific performance[11] (Arts. 28, 46, 62) and the right of an agrieved party to require specific performance is recognized in both the UNIDROIT Principles (Arts. 7.2.2 and 7.2.3)[12] and the PECL.[13]

---

9. *Chitty on Contracts*, vol. I General Principles (2004), Sect. 27-005, p. 1523. See also F. BELLIVIER and R. SEFTON-GREEN, "*Force obligatoire et exécution en nature du contrat en droit français et anglais: bonnes et mauvaises surprises du comparatisme*" in G. GOUBEAUX, et al., eds., *Le Contrat au début du XXIème siècle, Etudes offertes à J. Ghestin,* (LGDJ 2001) p. 91 and T.E. ELDER, "The Case Against Arbitral Awards of Specific Performance in Transnational Commercial Disputes", 13 Arb. Int. (1997, no. 1) pp. 8-11.

10. A. MOURRE, *op. cit.*, fn. 2, p. 12. See *Staklinski [Pyramid Elec. Co.]*, 180 NYS 2d 20 (NY App. Div. 1958), aff'd, 160 NE 2d 78 (NY 1959); *Grayson-Robinson Stores, Inc. [Iris. Constr. Corp.]*, 168 NE 2d 377 (NY 1960).

11. CISG: Art. 28:

    "If, in accordance with the provisions of this Convention, one party is entitled to require performance of any obligation by the other party, a court is not bound to enter a judgement for specific performance unless the court would do so under its own law in respect of similar contracts of sale not governed by this Convention."

    See John FELEMEGAS, "Comparison Between Provisions of the CISG Regarding the Right to Require Specific Performance (Arts. 28, 46 and 62) and the Counterpart Provisions of the UNIDROIT Principles (Arts. 7.2.1-7.2.5)" (2005) <http://cisgw3.law.pace.edu/cisg/biblio/felemegas13.html>.

12. Unlike the CISG, the UNIDROIT Principles distinguish between performance of monetary and non-monetary obligations. Ingeborg SCHWENZER, "Specific Performance and Damages According to the 1994 UNIDROIT Principles of International Commercial Contracts", 1 European Journal of Law reform (1999, no. 3) pp. 289-303. <www.cisg.law.pace.edu/cisg/biblio/schwenzer1.html>.

13. PECL (complete and revised version 1998):

    *Art. 9:102* [Right to Performance: Non-Monetary Obligations]
    "(1) The aggrieved party is entitled to specific performance of an obligation other than one to pay money, including the remedying of a defective performance.
    (2) Specific performance cannot, however, be obtained where:
    (a) performance would be unlawful or impossible; or
    (b) performance would cause the debtor unreasonable effort or expense; or

ii. Traditional limitations

Though accepted in principle, non-pecuniary relief such as specific performance is commonly subject to some limitations. Traditionally, both civil law and common law systems impose two restrictions on non-pecuniary damages: both the nature of the obligation whose performance is sought and the granting of relief itself must be appropriate for the case in question. Specific performance cannot be ordered for obligations that present an intrinsic *intuitu personae*/ strictly personal character. The usual justification for this limitation is the violation of human dignity that results from a person being physically forced to perform an obligation. The classic illustration of this concept is the impossibility of obtaining by force the creation of an intellectual work, such as a painting (ex: UNIDROIT Principles, Art. 7.2.2.).

The relief granted should also be appropriate according to the circumstances of each case.[14] This might not be the case when the breached obligation has consistently been performed over a long period of time. It has been noted in respect of long-term relations that:

> "If, from a certain perspective, the obligation can be considered as a circulating asset, from another point of view one cannot avoid being struck by the ever-

---

(c) the performance consists in the provision of services or work of a personal character or depends upon a personal relationship; or
(d) the aggrieved party may reasonably obtain performance from another source.
(3) The aggrieved party will lose the right to specific performance if it fails to seek it within a reasonable time after it has or ought to have become aware of the non-performance."

*Art. 9:101* [Right to Performance: Monetary Obligations]
"(1) The creditor is entitled to recover money which is due.
(2) Where the creditor has not yet performed its obligation and it is clear that the debtor will be unwilling to receive performance, the creditor may nonetheless proceed with its performance and may recover any sum due under the contract unless:
(a) it could have made a reasonable substitute transaction without significant effort or expense; or
(b) performance would be unreasonable in the circumstances."

*Art. 1:302* [complete and revised version 1998]
"Under these Principles, reasonableness is to be judged by what persons acting in good faith and in the same situation as the parties would consider to be reasonable. In particular, in assessing what is reasonable the nature and purpose of the contract, the circumstances of the case and the usages and practices of the trades or professions involved should be taken into account."

14. Concerning the CISG and the UNIDROIT Principles' provisions, an author has stated that

"In stark contrast to the Convention, the Principles do not treat specific performance as a discretionary remedy which is dependent on domestic law and the rules of the forum, but the Principles expressly provide several exceptions to the general rule on the obligee's right to require performance of non-monetary obligations. These exceptions are based on specific manifestations of the general principle of unreasonableness – *which is also a general principle on which the Convention is based.*"

John FELEMEGAS, *op. cit.*, fn. 11.

increasing phenomenon of the personalization of the contract. We can think here to all those sophisticated agreements (for example agreements for software maintenance) which require from the parties a long-term cooperation, both at the stage of the formation of the contract and at that of its performance, obligations in respect to which the requirements of loyalty, good faith, including contractual solidarity, have been underlined. It can be submitted, without contradiction, that the more a contract is personalized, the more money is an acceptable and satisfactory equivalent in case of non-performance by one of the parties of its obligations. In effect, the more refined and complicated the human relationship, the less reasonable it is to force the parties to be bound thereto against their will."[15]

Although arbitrators' recourse to non-pecuniary damages depends on the availability of such damages in the applied substantive rules, including possible limitations, their power to order such relief is not questioned. Nonetheless, the underlying issue concerning the *imperium juridictio* of the arbitrators remains present with respect to their ability to add a judicial penalty to the relief granted in order to force the execution of the remedy ordered.

b.   *Judicial Penalties – Astreintes*
Although encompassed by the UNIDROIT Principles[16] and looked upon favourably in

---

15. F. BELLIVIER and R. STEFTON-GREEN, *op. cit.*, fn. 9, p. 91 at p. 111.
16. Art. 7.2.4 (Judicial penalty):

"(1) Where the court orders a party to perform, it may also direct that this party pay a penalty if it does not comply with the order.
(2) The penalty shall be paid to the aggrieved party unless mandatory provisions of the law of the forum provide otherwise. Payment of the penalty to the aggrieved party does not exclude any claim for damages."

From Commentary:

"Experience in some legal systems has shown that the threat of a judicially imposed penalty for disobedience is a most effective means of ensuring compliance with judgments ordering the performance of contractual obligations. Other systems, on the contrary, do not provide for such sanctions because they are considered to constitute an inadmissible encroachment upon personal freedom. The present article takes a middle course by providing for monetary but not for other forms of penalties, applicable to all kinds of orders for performance including those for payment of money.
In the case of money judgments, a penalty should be imposed only in exceptional situations, especially where speedy payment is essential for the aggrieved party. The same is true for obligations to deliver goods. Obligations to pay money or to deliver goods can normally be easily enforced by ordinary means of execution. By contrast, in the case of obligations to do or to abstain from doing something, which moreover cannot easily be performed by a third person, enforcement by means of judicial penalties is often the most appropriate solution.
(....)
Since according to Art. 1.11 'court' includes an arbitral tribunal, the question arises of whether

Belgium, France, the Netherlands and Switzerland,[17] it is not common practice for arbitrators to order judicial penalties, and the debate over their application remains quite open.

In most jurisdictions, and in the UNCITRAL instruments, the law is silent on whether arbitrators can grant judicial penalties, but in Sweden, they are expressly excluded from the possible relief granted by arbitral tribunals.[18] Should this silence be construed as excluding the power to order penalties? Should there be a special law authorizing the arbitrator to do so? Under the implied consent theory, parties are deemed to have implicitly consented to arbitrators applying judicial penalties, if such power has not been expressly excluded. Absent any statutory provision, the power of arbitrators to order judicial penalties should be recognized unless the parties have expressly agreed to exclude it.

Like any other form of arbitral relief, judicial penalties are not a measure of enforcement and are therefore not excluded from arbitrability.

French case law has consistently held that the power to issue injunctions and to order penalties in order to ensure their enforcement is part of the jurisdictional powers of an arbitral tribunal.[19]

Under the inherent powers theory, the arbitrators' power to order judicial penalties does not derive from a construction of the arbitration agreement, but from the very nature of their function. In that regard, the Court of Appeals of Paris, in its 24 May 1991 and 7 October 2004 decisions, held that the power to order judicial penalties is "an inherent and necessary extension of the jurisdictional function".[20] Unless stipulated otherwise by the arbitration agreement, arbitrators should be considered to be vested with all the powers that are necessary to fulfil their mission. Thus, the Court of Appeals of Paris even refused to set aside an award where the arbitral tribunal had applied judicial penalties that had not been asked for by the claimant.[21]

---

arbitrators might also be allowed to impose a penalty. While a majority of legal systems seems to deny such a power to arbitrators, some modern legislation and recent court practice have recognised it. This solution, which is in keeping with the increasingly important role of arbitration as an alternative means of dispute resolution, especially in international commerce, is endorsed by the Principles. Since the execution of a penalty imposed by arbitrators can only be effected by, or with the assistance of, a court, appropriate supervision is available to prevent any possible abuse of arbitrators' power."

UNIDROIT, *Principles of International Commercial Contracts 2004*, p. 215, Sects. 1, 2 and 6 under Art. 7.2.4

17. A. MOURRE, *op. cit.*, fn. 2, p. 3.
18. *Ibid.*, p. 5. See the Swedish Arbitration Act of 1999 (SFS 1999:116), Sect. 25: "The arbitrators may not ... impose conditional fines or otherwise use compulsory measures in order to obtain requested evidence."
19. Cass. Civ. 25 July 1882, *DP* 1883, p. 243; Paris, 7 Oct. 2004, JDI (2005) p. 341.
20. Paris, 7 October 2004, *Otor Participations et autres v. Carlyle*, JDI (2005) p. 341, note A. MOURRE and P. PEDONE.
21. Paris, 24 May 1991, Rev. Arb. (1992) p. 636, note J. PELLERIN.

According to professor Pierre Mayer,[22] "the only power which necessarily and directly derives from the arbitral agreement is that of resolving the dispute, in other words the jurisdiction". Any measure stemming from the imperium, such as judicial penalties, requires a statutory provision allowing the arbitrator to order them or the express consent of the parties.

However, professor Charles Jarrosson[23] does not distinguish between *jurisdictio* and *imperium* (since *jurisdictio*, as the power to say how the law should be applied, can be considered part of *imperium*, which encompasses all the powers of the judiciary), but rather between *imperium merum*,[24] the exercise of the power to enforce a penalty (which is not arbitrable) and *imperium mixtum*, the exercise of the power to order a penalty as an ancillary measure meant to ensure the efficacy of a decision taken by the arbitrator to fulfil his mission (which is arbitrable). In this regard, ordering a judicial penalty would be part of *imperium mixtum*.

Despite the fact that, so far, arbitration case law does not provide many illustrations of arbitrators' use of their potential power to order judicial penalties, some awards do show that the practice is not non-existent and that the debate is not purely theoretical.[25]

Thus, in ICC Case No. 7895, the defendant producer requested an injunction to prevent the claimant distributor from selling products that were the subject of an exclusive distribution arrangement; in addition, it requested that the claimant be fined for each product sold in breach of the requested injunction. The arbitral tribunal granted the requested injunction and penalty holding that it had

> "the power, under the ICC Rules, to grant an injunction coupled with a fine, unless a mandatory provision of French procedural law, the procedural law of the place of this arbitration, requires otherwise. In that regard, French courts and French legal authors have found that arbitrators have the power to grant an injunction coupled with a fine."[26]

Although the number of published awards ordering specific performance – possibly coupled with a penalty – is not overwhelming, the practice of granting non-pecuniary remedies in commercial arbitration is indisputable and globally accepted. By contrast, the recourse to these remedies appears far less obvious in investment arbitration.

---

22. P. MAYER, *"Imperium de l'arbitre et mesures provisoires"* in J. HALDRY, J.-M. RAPP, P. FERRARI, eds., *Etudes de procédure et d'arbitrage en l'honneur de Jean-François Poudret* (Lausanne 1999) p. 441.
23. Ch. JARROSSON, *Réflexions sur l'imperium, Etudes offertes à Pierre Bellet* (Litec 1991) p. 245.
24. *Imperium merum* is the power to force a party to comply by exercising a constraint, either directly or through an agent of the State by which the author of the order has the authority to give instructions, Ch. JARROSSON, *ibid.*, pp. 278-279.
25. J.-J. ARNALDEZ, et al., eds., *Collection of ICC Awards*, vol. III (ICC Publishing 1997) p. 429.
26. 11 ICC Court Bulletin (2000, no. 1) p. 67.

2. *Availability but Scarcity of the Recourse to Non-pecuniary Remedies in Arbitrations Involving States*

The recourse to other forms of relief than damages is scarce in investment arbitration, to the extent that one could wonder whether it is actually possible to obtain something other than damages in such circumstances. A logical explanation could be that when the State is the debtor, only financial compensation could be imposed by arbitrators.

An examination of the traditional solutions adopted in inter-State litigation shows that damages are by no means the only possible remedy against a State.

a.  *Common practice of non-pecuniary remedies in inter-state litigation*
Traditionally, the primary remedy granted in case of a state's liability for a wrongful act is not monetary compensation but restitution. The principle is well established as illustrated by the International Law Commission Draft Articles on State Responsibility (ILC Articles);[27] Art. 34 expressly mentions restitution as the first form of reparation before compensation and satisfaction.[28]

i.  Restitution
Art. 35 of the ILC Articles specifies that restitution consists in re-establishing "the situation which existed before the wrongful act was committed". Nonetheless, restitution is not to be ordered automatically and Art. 35 limits its use when it is materially impossible or when restitution would be disproportionate to the wrongful act committed in comparison with the monetary equivalent that would be granted if compensation was chosen.[29]

---

27. The International Law Commission was established by the United Nations General Assembly in 1948 for the "promotion of the progressive development of international law and its codification". The Draft Articles on State Responsibility is one of the achievements of this Commission and the corresponding final text was adopted in August 2001. On 12 December 2001, the United Nations General Assembly adopted Resolution 56/83, which "commended [the articles] to the attention of Governments without prejudice to the question of their future adoption or other appropriate action". The text is published in *Yearbook of the International Law Commission, 2001*, vol. II, Part Two.

28. "*Article 34. Forms of reparation*
Full reparation for the injury caused by the internationally wrongful act shall take the form of restitution, compensation and satisfaction, either singly or in combination, in accordance with the provisions of this chapter."

29. "*Article 35. Restitution*
A State responsible for an internationally wrongful act is under an obligation to make restitution, that is, to re-establish the situation which existed before the wrongful act was committed, provided and to the extent that restitution:
(a) is not materially impossible;
(b) does not involve a burden out of all proportion to the benefit deriving from restitution instead of compensation."

While targeted to protect the interests of a State, these limitations can be compared in their principles with those existing in commercial arbitration.

Public international case law thereafter enacted in the ILC Articles is rich in illustrations of these principles.[30]

(1)   The *Chorzów Factory* case (*Poland v. Germany*, PCIJ, 1926)

The *Chorzów* case is often referred to as it set the standard for compensation in case of wrongful acts committed by States. This decision also reminds us that restitution in kind is the first available remedy, although it is less frequently commented upon for this.

By its judgment rendered on 13 September 1928, the Permanent Court of International Justice stated that the remedy for an international wrong – in that case, an expropriation in violation of a treaty – must "wipe out all the consequences of the illegal act and reestablish the situation which would, in all probability, have existed if that act had not been committed".

Applying that standard to the case at hand, the Court held that the wrongfully dispossessed owners were entitled to "[r]estitution in kind, or, if this is not possible, payment of a sum corresponding to the value which a restitution in kind would bear; the award, if need be, of damages for loss sustained which would not be covered by restitution in kind or payment in place of it – such are the principles which should serve to determine the amount of compensation due for an act contrary to international law".[31]

Moreover, the Court stated that

> "[t]he dispossession of an industrial undertaking – the expropriation of which is prohibited by the Geneva Convention – then involves the obligation to restore the undertaking and, if this be not possible, to pay its value at the time of the indemnification, which value is designed to take the place of restitution which has become impossible".[32]

Because of the circumstances of the case, monetary damages were finally granted but the power of arbitrators to order restitution was not questioned.

---

30. See, e.g., *Chorzów Factory* (*Poland v. Germany*, P.C.I.J.), 1926 Merits, Judgment No. 13, 1928, P.C.I.J., Series A, No. 17, p. 29; *Temple of Preah Vihear* (*Cambodia v. Thailand*, ICJ), Merits, Judgment, I.C.J Reports (1962) p. 6; *United States Diplomatic and Consular Staff in Tehran* (*United States v. Iran*, ICJ, 1980), Order of 12 May 1981, I.C.J. Reports (1981) p. 45; *LaGrand* (*Germany v. United States*, ICJ, 2001) Judgment, I.C.J.Reports (2001) p. 466; *Arrest Warrant of 11 April 2000* (*Democratic Republic of Congo v. Belgium*, ICJ, 2002), I.C.J. Reports (2002) p. 3; *Martini* (*Italy v. Venezuela*, ad hoc, UNRIAA, vol. II (Sales No. 1949.V. 1) (1930) p. 975; *Fonderie Trail* (*United States v. Canada*, ad hoc, 1938, 1941)3 UNRIAA (1949)1939.
31. R.D. BISHOP, J. CRAWFORD and W.M. REISMAN, *Foreign Investment Disputes: Cases, Material and Commentary* (Kluwer 2005) p 1280. *Chorzów*, Judgment No. 13 (Claim for Indemnity – The Merits) of September 13, 1928, P.C.I.J., Series A, No. 17, p. 29, also available at: <www.worldcourts.com/pcij/eng/decisions/1928.09.13_chorzow1/>, p. 47.
32. *Ibid*, pp. 47-48.

(2) The *Rainbow Warrior* case (*France v. New Zealand*, ad hoc, 1990)
As a result of extensive damage caused by two high-explosive devices, the *Rainbow Warrior* – a civilian vessel – was sunk at its moorings in Auckland Harbour, New Zealand on 10 July 1985. Mr. Fernando Pereira, a Dutch citizen, was killed in the incident. The French government recognized that the *Rainbow Warrior* had been sunk by agents of the General Directorate for External Security under French government orders and its readiness to make reparations for the consequences of their actions.

Problems, legal and otherwise, developed over the issue of keeping the French officers on the island and were submitted to arbitration.

The tribunal stated that

> "the authority to issue an order for the cessation or discontinuance of a wrongful act or omission results from the inherent powers of a competent tribunal which is confronted with the continuous breach of an international obligation which is in force and continues to be in force. The delivery of such an order requires, therefore, two essential conditions intimately linked, namely that the wrongful act has a continuing character and that the violated rule is still in force at the time in which the order is issued."[33]

Those two conditions for the availability of specific performance are frequently referred to in subsequent case law.

(3) World Trade Organization Dispute Settlement Body (Uruguay Round, 1995)
Specific performance as the main remedy in inter-state litigation is also illustrated by the World Trade Organization (WTO) dispute settlement system[34] whose primary purpose is to secure the withdrawal of the measure found to be inconsistent with the WTO Agreement. Compensation and countermeasures (the suspension of obligations) are available only as secondary and temporary responses to a contravention of the WTO Agreement (Art. 3.7 of the Dispute Settlement Understanding (DSU). Hence, the dispute settlement system provides a mechanism through which WTO Members can

---

33. *Rainbow Warrior*, R.I.A.A., vol. XX, (1990) p. 217 at p. 270, Sect. 114.
34. The current WTO dispute resolution system, laid out in the Uruguay Round Dispute Settlement Understanding (DSU), has been in force since 1 January 1995. In the event of an alleged breach of a trade agreement by a signatory state, the parties in conflict have a sixty-day consultation period; if no agreement is reached, a Dispute Settlement Body has the power to establish a panel made up of three or five members, who can make recommendations about possible actions for the States to take. These recommendations are not strictly binding; the State may take other avenues to bring itself into compliance. Parties can appeal to the Appellate Body, a panel of three members who can also issue recommendations suggesting how the state in violation can bring itself into compliance. After a "reasonable period" (typically ranging from eight to fifteen months), if the offending State is still in violation, the state seeking relief has the option of instituting retaliatory measures (which must be "equivalent to the level of nullification or impairment", according to DSU Art. 22.4). See generally S. BERMANN, "EC-Hormones and the Case for an Express WTO Postretaliation Procedure", 107 Columbia Law Review (2007) p. 131 and R. HUDECM "Broadening the Scope of Remedies in WTO Dispute Settlement" in F. WEISS and J. WIERS, eds., *Improving WTO Dispute Settlement Procedures* (2000) p. 345.

ensure that their rights under the WTO Agreement can be enforced. It provides primarily for requiring the State to modify its legislation in order to comply with its obligation under WTO.

Thus, in *Canada – Measures affecting the importation of milk and the exportation of dairy products*, upon complaints by the United States and New Zealand (WT/DS103 and WT/DS113),[35] Canada was ordered to modify its regimes for both the importation and exportation of dairy products.

ii. Satisfaction

Another typical non-pecuniary remedy in inter-state litigation is satisfaction, which Art. 37 of the ILC Articles defines as "an acknowledgement of the breach, an expression of regret, a formal apology or another appropriate modality".[36]

This unusual remedy has been used consistently in international law[37] and, according

---

35. WTO Annual Report 2000, p. 72. The Panel and the Appellate Body found that Canada had violated Arts. 3.3 and 8 of the Agreement on Agriculture by providing milk for export at reduced prices (which constituted "export subsidies") and Art. II:1(b) of GATT 1994 by limiting milk.
    In November 1999, Canada agreed to comply with the recommendations of the Dispute Settlement Body (DSB); it agreed with the United States and New Zealand that it would be in full compliance by 31 December 2000, but the time period was later extended to 31 January 2001 (WTO Annual Report 2001, p. 93). When Canada failed to bring itself into compliance by March 2001, New Zealand and the United States requested that the DSB refer the dispute to the original panel and also requested that concessions and other obligations be suspended, pursuant to Art. 22.2 of the DSU. The Panel issued a report on 11 July 2001 declaring that Canada was still out of compliance; the Appellate Body reversed the findings of the Panel in part, and a second compliance panel was established on 17 January 2002. The second compliance panel likewise found that Canada was not in compliance; Canada appealed; the appellate body upheld the Panel's findings (WTO Annual Report 2003, p. 95). Ultimately, the parties resolved the dispute in prolonged consultations, and on 9 May 2003, Canada, New Zealand and the United States informed the DSB that they had agreed upon a solution to the dispute (WTO Annual Report 2004, pp. 50-51).
36. Art. 37 of the ICC Rules reads:

    "1. The State responsible for an internationally wrongful act is under an obligation to give satisfaction for the injury caused by that act insofar as it cannot be made good by restitution or compensation.
    2. Satisfaction may consist in an acknowledgement of the breach, an expression of regret, a formal apology or another appropriate modality.
    3. Satisfaction shall not be out of proportion to the injury and may not take a form humiliating to the responsible State."

37. See the *Rainbow Warrior* case in which the tribunal held that:

    "There is a long established practice of States and international Courts and Tribunals of using satisfaction as a remedy or form of reparation (in the wide sense) for the breach of an international obligation. This practice relates particularly to the case of moral or legal damage done directly to the State, especially as opposed to the case of damage to persons involving international responsibilities."

to James Crawford, most commonly takes the form of either a declaration of the wrongfulness of the act or an apology.[38]

These solutions were developed to deal with the particular situation where a State breaches its international obligations to another State, which makes their transposition to investment cases difficult.

*b.   Scarce and controversial applications of non-pecuniary remedies in investment case law*
As a matter of fact, claimants rarely look for non-pecuniary remedies in their requests for relief and case law on this subject is therefore limited.

Although one could infer that non-pecuniary remedies are unavailable to claimants in investment arbitration, the few available decisions reveal that some arbitral tribunals have considered their use as readily possible if not appropriate.

Besides, it appears that in recent case law this issue was more frequently addressed at early stages of the proceedings when parties seek conservatory measures and those decisions are not necessarily made public.[39]

i.   *Texaco v. Libya* (1997)
To our knowledge,[40] the only illustration of an arbitral tribunal ordering restitution in kind to a State is provided by one of the awards rendered in the cases arising out of the Libyan Government's nationalization of oil concessions in the aftermath of the revolution in 1969.

In *Texaco v. Libya (1977)* the arbitrator ruled that Libyan law did not contain any provision preventing the application of the *restitutio in integrum* principle and ordered restitution in kind.

> "In so doing, the Tribunal does not lose sight of the fact that a resolution using the principle of *restitutio in integrum* must be excluded *if it is absolutely impossible to envisage performance in kind or where an irreversible situation has been created*. In the

---

UNRIAA, vol. XX (Sales No. E/F.93.V.3)(1990) p. 215, para. 122.

38. See comments under the ILC Art. 37 quoting the *Corfu Channel* case in which the tribunal held "[T]o ensure respect for international law, of which it is the organ, the Court must declare that the action of the British Navy constituted a violation of Albanian sovereignty. This declaration is in accordance with the request made by Albania through her Counsel, and is in itself appropriate satisfaction." See *Corfu Channel*, Merits, Judgment, I.C.J. Reports (1949) p .4, at p. 35. Tribunals ordered expressions of regret or apologies in the *"I'm Alone"*, (UNRIAA, vol. III (Sales No. 1949.V.2) (1935) p. 1609) and *Rainbow Warrior* cases; respondent states apologized in the *Consular Relations, Vienna Convention on Consular Relations (Paraguay* v. *United States of America)*, Provisional Measures, Order of 9 April 1998, I.C.J. Reports (1998) p. 248 and *LaGrand* cases *(Germany* v. *United States of America)*, Judgment, I.C.J. Reports (2001) p. 466.

39. See, for example, *City Oriente Ltd v. The Republic of Ecuador* and *Empresa Estatal Petróleos del Ecuador (Petroecuador)* (ICSID Case No. ARB/06/21), Decision on Revocation of Provisional Measures (13 May 2008) and *Occidental Petroleum Corp and Occidental Exploration and Production Co. v. The Republic of Ecuador* (ICSID Case No. ARB/06/11), Decision on Provisional Measures (17 August 2007).

40. In spite of the very interesting wording of Art. 1135 of the NAFTA, no decision rendered on its ground and ordering restitution is listed.

absence of further evidence, *this does not appear to be the case in this instance*. In the Tribunal's best judgment, it seems that the party making the request is alone responsible for fulfilling its obligations and, *in all likelihood, it should be possible for the Libyan Government to take the measures necessary to reestablish the situation logically following from the application of these legal principles*.... These are the reasons, general and specific, for which this Tribunal orders the Libyan Government to fulfill its own obligations in kind."[41] (Emphasis added)

This award was the only one arising out of the Libyan oil nationalization to reach this conclusion. Nevertheless, the parties reached a settlement for damages after the award was rendered and specific performance was never carried out. The arbitrators' reasoning was based strongly in public law due to the circumstances of the case and the particularities of nationalization.

In the other two awards relating to the nationalization of Libyan oil concessions, the sole arbitrators denied BP and LIAMCO specific performance.

Thus, in the award rendered in the *BP v. Libya* case, Judge Lagergen, sole arbitrator, in spite of a well-established rule that *restitutio in integrum* should be applied whenever possible and, although he was of the opinion that the nationalization was unlawful, concluded that:

"the fact that nationalization is de jure an exercise of territorial sovereignty, coupled with the low likelihood that a nationalizing State will reprivatize a nationalized entity, renders the principle of *restitutio in integrum* in effect inapplicable".[42]

In *LIAMCO v. Libya* (1977), the nationalization was considered lawful and consequently damages were the appropriate remedy.

The *Texaco* award was strongly criticized, notably by Professor Brigitte Stern according to whom "Ordering *restitutio in integrum* (specific performance) would be tantamount to denying the sovereign right of a state to nationalize an industry, which is otherwise unambiguously accepted."[43]

This position illustrates how controversial the issue of restitution is, at least in expropriation cases. A review of ICSID case law does not provide a clearer answer.

ii. ICSID case law

ICSID case law does provide illustrations of cases where the power of arbitrators to order non-pecuniary remedies is recognized, but they are scarce and the ordered

---

41. 104 J.D.I. (1977) pp. 350-389 at p. 388, with introduction by J.-F. LALIVE, entitled '*Un grand arbitrage pétrolier entre un Gouvernement et deux sociétés privées étrangères*', ibid. pp. 320-349., English translation: 17 International Legal Materials (1978) pp. 3-37.
42. See quotation of the award in Brigitte STERN, "*Trois Arbitrages, un Même Problème, Trois Solutions: Les nationalisations pétrolières libyennes devant l'arbitrage international*", Rev. Arb.(1980) p. 36.
43. STERN, ibid., pp. 37-38: "*accorder 'la restitutio in integrum', c'est en fait et en droit empêcher l'exercice du droit fondamental de nationaliser qui est proclamé par ailleurs sans ambiguïté*".

remedies were not in fact exercised, revealing reluctance of the arbitrators to impose non-pecuniary remedies.

(1) Doubts as to the power of arbitrators to order non-pecuniary remedies

The *Amco v. Indonesia* case (1984) shows a very prudent position of the arbitrators concerning the possibility to order *restitutio in integrum*.

In 1968, Amco Asia Corporation, a US corporation, submitted an application to the Indonesian Investment Board for the establishment of a "foreign business" incorporated in Indonesia. The Investment Application was approved and an Indonesian subsidiary, P.T. Amco Indonesia was established for the purpose of constructing and operating a hotel in Jakarta. The land on which the hotel was situated was owned by P.T. Wisma Kartika, an Indonesian corporation owned by an Indonesia army cooperative.

Indonesia revoked the license granted to Amco and army troops ousted Amco from the hotel in April 1980.

Consequently, Amco claimed compensation, including for additional capital infusions which it was intending to make and the improved operations which would have resulted therefrom. Amco also claimed that it was entitled to share in hotel profits over a period of thirty years ending in 1999, as provided for in the initial agreement between Amco and P.T. Wisma.

As regards the revocation of the license, Amco invoked violations of due process and the absence of substantive justification. Indonesia's counter-argument relied on the availability of ICSID proceedings as a due process guarantee provided to the investor. The tribunal held in this respect that:

> "It is obvious that this tribunal cannot substitute itself for the Indonesian Government, in order to cancel the revocation and restore the licence: such actions are not even claims, and *it is more than doubtful that this kind of restitution in integrum could be ordered against sovereign states*."[44] (Emphasis added)

(2) Still arguable

In the *Goetz v. Burundi* case (1999), the arbitrators took a more nuanced approach to the issue and chose to leave the restitution option open to the respondent State without imposing such a remedy.

In this case, the claimants requested the annulment of the decision withdrawing the free trade zone certificate previously granted to their Burundi incorporated company and, as a subsidiary claim, that the State be ordered to pay damages.

In an interim award, the arbitrators (Weil (pres.), Bedjaoui, Bredin) invited the parties to agree on monetary compensation or, alternatively, offered Burundi the possibility to opt for retrocession of the certificate:

> "it falls to the Republic of Burundi, in order to establish the conformity with international law of the disputed decision to withdraw the certificate, to give an

---

44. *Amco Asia Corp. v. Republic of Indonesia* (ICSID Case. No. ARB/81/1), Award on the Merits (21 Nov. 1984), para. 202 (available at 24 I.L.M. 1022).

adequate and effective indemnity to the claimants as envisaged in Art. 4 of the Belgium-Burundi investment treaty, *unless it prefers to return the benefit of the free zone regime to them. The choice lies within the sovereign discretion of the Burundian government.* If one of these two measures is not taken within a reasonable period, the Republic of Burundi will have committed an act contrary to international law the consequences of which it would be left to the Tribunal to ascertain."[45] (Emphasis added)

The restoration of the claimants in their right was therefore contemplated by the tribunal as a readily available option but at the discretion of the State.

The parties finally agreed on a settlement according to which Burundi was to reimburse the taxes and customs duties imposed illegally upon the investor as a result of the certificate withdrawal, and to create a new free trade zone regime.

The fact that the award rendered in this case embodies the agreement of the parties and that the two alternatives suggested by the tribunal were conditions to the legality of the expropriation, and not remedies for an illegal expropriation, put the authority of the findings in this case in perspective. When differences later emerged as to whether Burundi was living up to the terms of the settlement agreement, a new, still-pending ICSID arbitration was begun in 2001.

The double feature of an interim award coupled with the option left to the State to perform in kind its obligation is a scenario encountered in subsequent case law. It has the benefit of pragmatism by greatly enhancing the chances of effective performance by the State.

(3)  No doubts as to the power of arbitrators to order non-pecuniary remedies

The position adopted by the tribunal in *Enron v. Argentina* (2007) leaves no doubt that, at least in theory, arbitrators can order non-pecuniary remedies as a sole remedy. Nevertheless, no such relief was granted.

In this case, the dispute arose from the investment made by Enron and its subsidiary, Ponderosa Assets L.P. in Transportadora del Sur (TGS), a gas transportation company. The original, later abandoned claim concerned stamp taxes allegedly imposed by some Argentinean provinces on the investment. The final award deals with an ancillary claim formed by the claimants concerning Argentina's refusal to allow tariff adjustments in

---

45. Decision of 2 September 1998, 15 ICSID Rev. (2000) p. 459, para. 133. See also *CMS Gas Transmission Company v. the Argentine Republic* (ICSID Case No. ARB/01/8), Award (12 May 2005) para. 406:

"Restitution is by far the most reliable choice to make the injured party whole as it aims at the reestablishment of the situation existing prior to the wrongful act. In a situation such as that characterizing this dispute and the complex issues associated with the crisis in Argentina, it would be utterly unrealistic for the Tribunal to order the Respondent to turn back to the regulatory framework existing before the emergency measures were adopted, nor has this been requested. However, as the Tribunal has repeatedly stated in this Award, the crisis cannot be ignored and it has specific consequences on the question of reparation."

accordance with the US Producer Price Index (PPI) and the enactment of a law that nullified PPI adjustments and the calculation of tariffs in US dollars.

In its decision on jurisdiction,[46] the tribunal, composed of Orrego-Vicuña (pres.), Gros Epiell and Tschanz, held that:

> "in addition to declaratory powers, *[the tribunal] has the power to order measures involving performance or injunction of certain acts*. Jurisdiction is therefore also affirmed on this ground. What kinds of measures might or might not be justified, whether the acts complained of meet the standards set out in the *Rainbow Warrior*, and how the issue of implementation that the parties have also discussed would be handled, if appropriate, are all matters that belong to the merits."[47] (Emphasis added)

The generality of the affirmation is significant and the arbitrators' recourse to non-pecuniary remedies appears to be unconditional. Nonetheless, the part of the claim where compensation in kind was requested was later abandoned and in its award on the merits the tribunal framed the restitution as follows:

> "The Treaty does not specify the damages to which the investor is entitled in case of breach of the standards of treatment different from expropriation, i.e., fair and equitable treatment or the breach of the umbrella clause. *Absent an agreed form of restitution by means of renegotiation of contracts or otherwise, the appropriate standard of reparation under international law is compensation for the losses* suffered by the affected party, as was established by the Permanent Court of International Justice in the *Chorzów* Case...."[48] (Emphasis added)

Ultimately, the tribunal decided to grant damages for breach of the Treaty without further reference to restitution in kind which remained a theoretical option in the interim award.

While restitution is the first remedy in inter-State disputes (Draft Articles ILC), it is far from being the first form of relief in investment disputes, which leads to the question of the relevance of the ILC Articles to investor-State disputes. As a matter of fact often referred to, those articles were not primarily meant to address investment disputes. As a matter of example, articles relating to counter-measures or satisfaction are of no application in investor-State disputes.

While they occasionally appear in principle (theoretically possible and affirmed in 2004), non-pecuniary remedies are neither ordered in practice nor enforced. Are there specific features of investment arbitration explaining this phenomenon?

---

46. *Enron v. Argentina* (ICSID Case No. ARB/01/3), Decision on Jurisdiction (14 January 2004).
47. *Ibid.*, para. 81.
48. *Enron v. Argentina*, Award (22 May 2007) para. 359.

III. PARTICULARITIES OF INVESTMENT ARBITRATION LIMITING THE RECOURSE TO NON-PECUNIARY REMEDIES

*1. Possible Restrictions on the Power of Arbitrators to Grant Non-pecuniary Remedies in Instruments Governing Investment Arbitration*

The lack of practical examples of the recourse to non-pecuniary damages in the investment field could be attributed to the absence of provisions dedicated to the subject in the regulations to which arbitrators commonly refer. For example, the 1965 Washington Convention is silent on the subject, prompting a debate on the possibility of granting non-pecuniary relief in the ICSID system. Conversely, the other instruments under examination in this section, notably the North American Free Trade Agreement (NAFTA) and the Energy Charter Treaty (ECT), explicitly contemplate the issue of restitution.

*a.   Washington Convention (1965)*

At first glance, a review of ICSID case law shows the almost systematic use of pecuniary damages to the detriment of other forms of relief (specific performance, injunctions, declaratory relief). This trend prompted questions about whether the ICSID system restricts remedies available to the tribunals and parties in these proceedings.

The text of the Washington Convention and the ICSID Arbitration Rules are of little help as they remains silent on the issue. Furthermore, Art. 54(1) of the Convention (Sect. 6 – Recognition and Enforcement of the Award, Arts. 53-56), which establishes that pecuniary obligations are compulsorily enforceable under the Convention, does not necessarily preclude other forms of relief.

Thus, Art. 54(1) of the Convention provides:

> "Each Contracting State shall recognize an award rendered pursuant to this Convention as binding and enforce the *pecuniary obligations* imposed by that award within its territories as if it were a final judgment of a court in that State."
> (Emphasis added)

Schreuer[49] argues that Art. 54(1) of the Convention should not be construed as restricting the power of the arbitrators to grant non-pecuniary damages.

To buttress his reading of the Convention, Schreuer relies mainly on its drafting history. The restriction to pecuniary obligations was absent from the early drafts but was added when concerns arose about the enforceability of non-pecuniary obligations imposed by awards. Indeed, during the *travaux préparatoires*, the German Executive Director insisted on preserving a possibility to refuse the enforcement of an ICSID award on the basis of the forum's *ordre public*. The question was strongly debated and a compromise was found whereby the obligation to enforce non-pecuniary relief was restricted, but this limitation would not affect the res judicata effect of the obligations

---

49. Christophe SCHREUER, *The ICSID Convention: A Commentary* (2001) p.1115 and "Non-pecuniary Remedies in ICSID Arbitration", 20 Arbitration International (2004, no. 4) pp. 325-332.

imposed by the award.[50] In other words, the award granting specific performance is "res judicata" (Art. 53 of the Convention), however, the State is not obliged to enforce the non-pecuniary obligations imposed by the award.

Therefore, the Convention does not deal with the power of the arbitrators to grant non-pecuniary damages and according to Shreuer "an award could well order the performance of certain acts but all that could be enforced would be the obligation to pay damages for non-compliance with that order".[51]

Nevertheless, the Convention does contain a serious practical restriction on the future enforcement of non-pecuniary awards which limits the parties' interest in claiming such remedy.

*b. Investment treaties*

Recent treaties such as the ECT[52] and the NAFTA[53] mention restitution as an available remedy. Nevertheless, Art. 26(8) of the ECT and Art. 1135 of NAFTA provide that, in the event that restitution is ordered, the award should allow the State to pay damages *in lieu* of the other remedy granted.[54] These provisions, although confirming the availability

---

50. See SCHREUER, *The ICSID Convention: A Commentary*, op. cit., fn. 49, pp. 1124-1130 and BROCHES, "Awards Rendered Pursuant to the ICSID Convention: Binding Force, Finality, Recognition, Enforcement, Execution", 2 ICSID Review (1987) p. 287 at pp. 299-318.
51. *Ibid*, p. 315.
52. Art. 12 of the ECT states:

    "(1) Except where Article 13 applies, an Investor of any Contracting Party which suffers a loss with respect to any Investment in the Area of another Contracting Party owing to war or other armed conflict, state of national emergency, civil disturbance, or other similar event in that Area, shall be accorded by the latter Contracting Party, as regards restitution, indemnification, compensation or other settlement, treatment which is the most favourable of that which that Contracting Party accords to any other Investor, whether its own Investor, the Investor of any other Contracting Party, or the Investor of any third state.
    (2) Without prejudice to paragraph (1), an Investor of a Contracting Party which, in any of the situations referred to in that paragraph, suffers a loss in the Area of another Contracting Party resulting from
    (a) requisitioning of its Investment or part thereof by the latter's forces or authorities; or
    (b) destruction of its Investment or part thereof by the latter's forces or authorities, which was not required by the necessity of the situation, shall be accorded restitution or compensation which in either case shall be prompt, adequate and effective."

53. See Art. 1135.
54. ECT Art. 26(8): Settlement of disputes between an investor and a contracting party.

    "The awards of arbitration, which may include an award of interest, shall be final and binding upon the parties to the dispute. An award of arbitration concerning a measure of a sub-national government or authority of the disputing Contracting Party *shall provide that the Contracting Party may pay monetary damages in lieu of any other remedy granted*. Each Contracting Party shall carry out without delay any such award and shall make provision for the effective enforcement in its Area of such awards." (Emphasis added)

of non-pecuniary remedy in investment arbitration, clearly evidence a reluctance to impose such remedy on a State.

Thus, albeit recognized as a more appropriate means to "wipe out the consequences of the illegal act",[55] restitution is not favoured by the imperative character of these treaties' wording – "shall provide ... for monetary damages in lieu of restitution" – which clearly limits the arbitrator's power. This limitation goes beyond the classical restrictions to restitution when it is materially impossible and imposes a burden out of proportion for the losing party.

This mechanism is also enacted in very recent bilateral treaties such as the free trade Agreements concluded by the United States with Singapore and Chile in 2004 and more generally the Draft updated US Model BIT dated 5 February 2004:

> "Where a tribunal makes a final award against a respondent, the tribunal may award, separately or in combination, only: (a) monetary damages and any applicable interest; and (b) restitution of property, in which case the award shall provide that the respondent may pay monetary damages and any applicable interest in lieu of restitution."[56]

The specific rules applicable to investment arbitration do not exclude the use of non-pecuniary remedies but clearly favour monetary compensation.

2.  *Are Non-pecuniary Remedies Appropriate in Investment Arbitration?*

We have shown a tendency toward the rejection of non-pecuniary remedies in investment arbitration including in ICSID rules or recent treaties; but since this remedy

---

NAFTA Article 1135: Final Award

"1. Where a Tribunal makes a final award against a Party, the Tribunal may award, separately or in combination, only:
(a) monetary damages and any applicable interest;
(b) restitution of property, in which case the award *shall provide that the disputing Party may pay monetary damages and any applicable interest in lieu of restitution.*
A tribunal may also award costs in accordance with the applicable arbitration rules.
2. Subject to paragraph 1, where a claim is made under Article 1117(1):
(a) an award of restitution of property shall provide that restitution be made to the enterprise;
(b) an award of monetary damages and any applicable interest shall provide that the sum be paid to the enterprise; and
(c) the award shall provide that it is made without prejudice to any right that any person may have in the relief under applicable domestic law.
3. A Tribunal may not order a Party to pay punitive damages." (Emphasis added)

55. See commentaries above on the ILC Articles and the *Chorzów* case.
56. See Art. 15.25 of the Free Trade Agreement concluded between the United States and Singapore in force 1 January 2004, Art. 10.25 of the Free Trade Agreement concluded between the United States and Chile in force 1 January 2004 and Art. 34 of the 2004 US Model BIT. Also quoted by C. SCHREUER, "Non-pecuniary remedies in ICSID arbitration", *op. cit.*, fn. 49.

is in theory available, other reasons may be found to explain the scarcity of such awards.

*a.   Non-pecuniary remedies are rarely claimed (as in commercial arbitration)*
Very often, the investor does not even raise the issue. Non-pecuniary remedies either do not necessarily correspond to their expectations or would simply be inapplicable. As a matter of fact, recent cases show that investors naturally find greater interest in seeking non-pecuniary remedy as an interim relief.

*b.   Hardly conceivable in expropriation cases (nature of the goods at stake)*
Since expropriation is a sovereign right (under certain conditions), the issue is often whether there was adequate compensation, not the restoration of the investor's contractual rights.

As a matter of fact, treaties dealing with expropriation focus on monetary compensation as the remedy available for unlawful expropriation and refer in that respect to the "fair market value at the time of expropriation", etc.

What if the missing requirement for the expropriation to be lawful is not the absence of proper compensation but, e.g., the absence of public interest justification as was the case in *BP v. Libya*? Would non-pecuniary remedies be more appropriate in such a case? The answers to this question remain doubtful.

Similarly, the reluctance of investment arbitrators to order restitution in kind seems stronger when it relates to rights over natural resources, where the sovereignty of the State is naturally greater.

Indeed, in *Occidental Petroleum Corporation and Occidental Exploration and Production Company v. Ecuador*, which featured the withdrawal by Ecuador of the investor's rights to exploration and exploitation of hydrocarbons in the Ecuadorian Amazon, the tribunal held that "the Claimants have not established a strongly arguable case that there exists a right to specific performance where a natural resources concession agreement has been terminated or cancelled by a sovereign State".[57]

The tribunal reached this solution after observing that the measures sought by the claimants were not only impossible[58] but would also "constitute a reparation disproportional to its interference with the sovereignty of the State when compared to monetary compensation".[59]

This reasoning which questions the very existence of a right to specific performance seems to be strongly linked to the fact that control of a State over its natural resources was at stake. It remains doubtful whether it could be argued similarly in an investment arbitration relating to services such as public transportation, telecommunication, press, etc.

*c.   Enforcement and State sovereignty*
Another explanation of the scarcity of awards ordering non-pecuniary remedies may lie in the fact that their enforcement necessarily requires the cooperation of the State on its

---

57. ICSID Case No. ARB/06/11, Decision on Provisional Measures (17 August 2007) para. 86.
58. *Ibid.*, paras. 75-82.
59. *Ibid.*, para. 84.

own territory, while damages are enforceable elsewhere and even without the State's cooperation.

These practical considerations are necessarily taken into account by arbitral tribunals willing to preserve the enforceability of their award. For example, it was expressly taken into consideration in the *LETCO v. Liberia* case (1986) where the tribunal decided:

> "LETCO's activities in Liberia were terminated over two years ago. Start-up expenses would be prohibitive and would repeat those already carried out in the initial investment. It is also questionable, given the circumstances, whether LETCO and the Liberian Government would be able to cooperate to successfully recommence the concession. Furthermore, given Liberia's failure to participate in this arbitration, one must doubt whether an injunction by this tribunal would be respected by the Government authorities. Therefore, the tribunal concludes that only reparation in the form of money damages will be adequate in this case."[60]

The same contingency appears in commercial arbitration but may be circumvented by the ordering of a judicial penalty facilitating enforcement of obligation in kind.

IV. CONCLUSION

At this stage of the study, we shall make the following proposition: In investment arbitration, if the conditions provided in the ILC Articles are satisfied, non-pecuniary remedies are available, subject to the State's willingness to abide by the measure ordered, thus offering the State an alternative in a final or interim award.

Provided that the *Chorzów factory* standards for compensation are satisfied, this allows for the State to have the final say on the form of the remedy, striking a reasonable balance between investor and State interests and giving a greater chance of enforcement.

Finally it appears that the application and applicability of non-pecuniary remedies is somehow a dividing line between commercial arbitration and investor-State arbitration.

---

60. *Liberian Eastern Timber Corporation [LETCO] v. Government of Republic of Liberia* (ICSID Case No. ARB/83/2), Final Award (31 March 1986) para. 44.

# Compensation for Unlawful Expropriation, and Other Recent Manifestations of the Principle of Full Reparation in International Investment Law

*Pierre Bienvenu and Martin J. Valasek*[*]

| TABLE OF CONTENTS | Page |
|---|---|
| I. Introduction | 231 |
| II. The Principle of Full Reparation | 232 |
| III. The Principle of Full Reparation Applied to Unlawful Expropriation: Has the Distinction Between Lawful and Unlawful Expropriation Finally Been Accepted? | 241 |
| IV. The Principle of Full Reparation Applied to the Award of Interest and the Apportionment of Arbitration Costs | 261 |
| V. Conclusion | 281 |

## I. INTRODUCTION

One of the bedrock principles in international law is full reparation.

The *locus classicus* of this principle is the *Chorzów Factory*[1] case (see Sect. II of this Report), where the Permanent Court of International Justice (hereinafter PCIJ) stated that

> "reparation must, as far as possible, wipe out all the consequences of the illegal act and re-establish the situation which would, in all probability, have existed if that act had not been committed. Restitution in kind, or, if this is not possible, payment of a sum corresponding to the value which a restitution in kind would bear; the award, if need be, of damages for loss sustained which would not be covered by restitution in kind or payment in place of it – such are the principles which should serve to determine the amount of compensation due for an act contrary to international law."[2]

This principle, and the standard of compensation derived therefrom, have been affirmed on many occasions by both the International Court of Justice (hereinafter ICJ) and various international tribunals.

---

[*] Partners, Ogilvy Renault LLP, Montreal, Canada. We acknowledge the substantial contribution made to this article by Marie Stoyanov, a senior associate who was on secondment to Ogilvy Renault from Gide Loyrette Nouel.
1. *Chorzów Factory (Claim for Indemnity)* (Merits), *Germany v. Poland*, 1928 P.C.I.J. Ser. A., No. 17, Judgment No. 13 (13 September 1928).
2. *Ibid.*, at p. 47.

However, until recently, the implication of *Chorzów Factory* for establishing a different standard of compensation for unlawful as opposed to lawful expropriation seems not to have been fully appreciated by arbitral tribunals in investment cases. Three recent awards – *ADC v. Hungary*,[3] *Siemens v. Argentina*[4] and *Vivendi v. Argentina*[5] – illustrate the significance of departing from the treaty standard of compensation in the case of a breach of the applicable treaty (see Sect. III).

The principle of full reparation has also manifested itself in the debate over interest and costs. This Report looks at these recent manifestations of the principle of full reparation, which have given this bedrock principle new life and meaning (see Sect. IV).

II.   THE PRINCIPLE OF FULL REPARATION

*1.   Chorzów Factory*

The standard of compensation for wrongful acts under customary international law has developed on the basis of the decision of the PCIJ in the *Chorzów Factory* case.[6] It has since been reaffirmed and applied in a number of decisions of the ICJ.[7] In this section, we first

---

3. *ADC Affiliate Limited and ADC & ADMC Management Limited v. the Republic of Hungary* (ICSID Case No. ARB/03/16 (hereinafter *ADC v. Hungary* or *ADC*)), Award of 2 October 2006, (tribunal composed of Charles N. Brower, Albert Jan van den Berg and Neil Kaplan acting as president) available at <http://icsid.worldbank.org>. The authors acted as lead counsel for the investors in *ADC v. Hungary*. See Pierre BIENVENU and Martin J. VALASEK "*ADC v. Hungary*: A Higher Standard of Compensation for an Unlawful Expropriation", 12 IBA Arbitration Newsletter (2007, no. 2) p. 79.
4. *Siemens A.G. v. The Argentine Republic* (ICSID Case No. ARB/02/8 (hereinafter *Siemens*)), Final Award of 6 February 2007, available at <http://ita.law.uvic.ca/documents/Siemens-Argentina-Award.pdf>. The tribunal was composed of Judge Charles N. Brower, Professor Domingo Bello Janeiro and Dr. Andrés Rigo Sureda as President. On 16 July 2007, Argentina applied to the Secretary-General to request annulment of the award. On 19 August 2008, annulment proceedings were suspended as per the parties' request.
5. *Compañía de Aguas del Aconquija S.A. and Vivendi Universal S.A. v. The Argentine Republic* (ICSID Case No. ARB/97/3 (hereinafter *Vivendi v. Argentina* or *Vivendi*)), Award in the Resubmitted Case of 20 August 2007, (tribunal composed of Gabrielle Kaufmann-Kohler, Carlos Bernal Verea and J. William Rowley acting as president), available at <http://ita.law.uvic.ca/documents/VivendiAwardEnglish.pdf>.
6. The Court was composed of Messrs. Anzilotti, Hubner, Lord Finlay (dissenting), Messers. Loder, Nyholm (dissenting), De Bustamante (dissenting in part), Altamira (dissenting in part), Oda, Pessoa, Beichmann, Rabel (concurring with additional observations) and Ehrlich (dissenting).
7. See the Case Concerning Gabcikovo-Nagymaros Project (*Hungary v. Slovakia*), (tribunal composed of Piero Bernardini, Andreas Bucher and Hans Van Houtte acting as president), 1997 I.C.J. 7 (25 Sept.), the LaGrand Case, (*Ger. v. U.S.*) 2001 I.C.J. 466 (27 June), the Arrest Warrants Case, (*Democratic Republic of Congo v. Belgium*), 2001 I.C.J. 3 (14 Feb.), the Case Concerning Avena and other Mexican Nationals, (*Mexico v. U.S.*), 2004 I.C.J. 12 (31 Mar.), and most recently the *Advisory Opinion on the Legal Consequences of the Construction of a Wall in Occupied Palestinian Territory*, 2004 I.C.J. 136 (9 July). Citing these cases, the tribunal in *ADC* observed that "there can be no doubt about the present vitality of the *Chorzów Factory* principle, its full current vigor having been repeatedly attested to by the International Court of Justice" (*ADC, op. cit.*, fn. 3, at para. 493). The

explain the background of the PCIJ's landmark decision (II.*1.a*). We then discuss the rationale behind the decision (II.*1.b*). Finally, we describe the codification of the *Chorzów Factory* standard in the International Law Commission's Draft Articles on Responsibility of States for Internationally Wrongful Acts (hereinafter ILC Draft Articles) (II.*2*).

*a. Background*

*Chorzów Factory* involved the unlawful seizure of a nitrate factory[8] located in Chorzów, in Upper Silesia, which was part of German territory when it was built in 1915.

When Poland regained its independence, after World War I, it was awarded parts of Silesia, including Chorzów. In May 1922, Germany and Poland concluded a Convention concerning Upper Silesia at Geneva (hereinafter the Geneva Convention), whose Arts. 6 through 22 regulated the power of Poland to expropriate certain German assets in Upper Silesia.

According to Art. 7 of the Geneva Convention, Poland was prohibited from expropriating (within the first fifteen years of Poland's sovereignty over Upper Silesia) unless the two following requirements were met:

(i) the measure was considered "*indispensable pour assurer le maintien de l'exploitation*" ("guarantee, in the interest of all parties, the continuity of economic life in Upper Silesia") (Art. 7); and
(ii) the expropriation was in conformity with Arts. 92 and 297 of the Treaty of Versailles (which required Poland to pay equitable compensation to the expropriated owner of the property valued as of the *date of the expropriation/liquidation*) (*ibid.*).

By a ministerial decree dated 24 June 1922, the Polish government unilaterally transferred possession and management of the nitrate factory located in Chorzów to a Polish national. Germany, on behalf of its aggrieved nationals, brought a claim against Poland before the PCIJ under the Geneva Convention.

In Judgment No. 7, concerning the merits of the case, the Court held that Poland's

---

*Chorzów Factory* standard of compensation was also applied by the Iran-U.S. Claims Tribunal in the *Amoco* case, where it was held that "undoubtedly, the first principle established by the Court is that a clear distinction must be made between lawful and unlawful expropriations, since the rules applicable to the compensation to be paid by the expropriating State differ according to the legal characterization of the taking" *(Amoco International Finance Corporation v. The Government of the Islamic Republic of Iran, et. al.*, Partial Award No. 310-56-3 (14 July 1987), reprinted in 15 Iran-U.S. C.T.R. 314, at para. 191). The majority opinion however failed to fully grasp the import of the *Chorzów Factory* decision as regards the calculation of damages (see concurring opinion of Judge Brower). See also, and Martin J. VALASEK, "A Simple Scheme: Exploring the Meaning of *Chorzów Factory* for the Valuation of Opportunistic Expropriation in the BIT Generation", 4 TDM (November 2007, no. 6) at p. 14 et seq.

8. The factory was built in 1915 and managed on behalf of the German government by a German company (Bayerische Stickstoffwerke A.G.). Its ownership was then transferred to yet another German company (Oberschlesische Stickstoffwerke A.G.), with responsibility for management remaining unchanged.

conduct was not in conformity with Art. 6 of the Geneva Convention,[9] which meant that Poland had committed a wrongful act under international law.[10] In Judgment No. 13, concerning the claim for indemnity, the Court observed:

> "It is a principle of international law that the reparation of a wrong may consist in an indemnity corresponding to the damage which the nationals of the injured State have suffered as a result of the act which is contrary to international law. This is even the most usual form of reparation...."[11]

The Court then proceeded to "lay down the guiding principles according to which the amount of compensation due may be determined".[12] The Court started by noting that:

> "The action of Poland which the Court has judged to be contrary to the Geneva Convention is not an expropriation – to render which lawful only the payment of fair compensation would have been wanting; it is a seizure of property, rights and interests which could not be expropriated even against compensation, save under the exceptional conditions fixed by Article 7 of the said Convention. As the Court has expressly declared in Judgment No. 8, reparation is in this case the consequence not of the application of Articles 6 to 22 of the Geneva Convention, but of acts contrary to those articles."[13]

The Court explained why the amount of damages provided for in the Convention was insufficient reparation in the context of "acts contrary" to the same:

> "It follows that the compensation due to the German Government is not necessarily limited to the value of the undertaking at the moment of dispossession, plus interest to the day of payment. This limitation would only be admissible if the Polish Government had had the right to expropriate, and if its wrongful act consisted merely in not having paid to the two Companies the just price of what was expropriated; in the present case, such a limitation might result in placing Germany and the interests protected by the Geneva Convention, on behalf of which interests the German Government is acting, in a situation more unfavourable than that in which Germany and these interests would have been if Poland had respected the said Convention. Such a consequence would not only be

---

9. Art. 6 of the Geneva Convention provides

    "Poland may expropriate in Polish Upper Silesia in conformity with the provisions of Articles 7 to 23 undertakings belonging to the category of major industries including mineral deposits and rural estates. Except as provided in these clauses, the property, rights and interests of German nationals or of companies controlled by German nationals may not be liquidated in Polish Upper Silesia."

10. *Chorzów Factory*, *op. cit.*, fn. 1, at p. 27.
11. *Ibid.*, at pp. 27-28.
12. *Ibid.*, at p. 46.
13. *Ibid.*

unjust, but also and above all incompatible with the aim of Article 6 and following articles of the Convention – that is to say, the prohibition, in principle, of the liquidation of the property, rights and interests of German nationals and of companies controlled by German nationals in Upper Silesia – since it would be tantamount to rendering lawful liquidation and unlawful dispossession indistinguishable in so far as their financial results are concerned."[14]

Finally, in the most often cited passage of its decision, the Court set out the "essential principles" governing the standard of compensation for an illegal act, in this case an unlawful expropriation:

> "The essential principle contained in the actual notion of an illegal act – a principle which seems to be established by international practice and in particular by the decisions of arbitral tribunals – is that reparation must, as far as possible, wipe out all the consequences of the illegal act and re-establish the situation which would, in all probability, have existed if that act had not been committed. Restitution in kind, or, if this is not possible, payment of a sum corresponding to the value which a restitution in kind would bear; the award, if need be, of damages for loss sustained which would not be covered by restitution in kind or payment in place of it – such are the principles which should serve to determine the amount of compensation due for an act contrary to international law."[15]

The Court added:

> "This conclusion particularly applies as regards the Geneva Convention, the object of which is to provide for the maintenance of economic life in Upper Silesia on the basis of respect for the *status quo*. The dispossession of an industrial undertaking – the expropriation of which is prohibited by the Geneva Convention – then involves the obligation to restore the undertaking and, if this is not possible, to pay its value at the time of the indemnification, which value is designed to take the place of restitution which has become impossible. To this obligation, in virtue of the general principles of international law, must be added that of compensating loss sustained as the result of the seizure. The impossibility, on which the Parties are agreed, of restoring the Chorzów Factory could therefore have no other effect but that of substituting payment of the value of the undertaking for restitution; it would not be in conformity either with the principles of law or with the wish of the Parties to infer from that agreement that the question of compensation must henceforth be dealt with as though an expropriation properly so called was involved."[16]

---

14. *Ibid.*, at p. 47.
15. *Ibid.*
16. *Ibid.*, at pp. 47-48.

According to *Chorzów Factory*, the party illegally deprived of an investment by a State is thus entitled, in principle, to *restitutio in integrum*. If that is not possible or practical, the State must pay monetary damages as a substitute for restitution. We refer to such damages as "restitutionary damages". The injured party is also entitled to additional monetary damages for the consequential losses suffered as a result of the unlawful taking, to the extent any such losses are not made good by restitution (or the monetary payment made in lieu of restitution). In any case, the overall goal of this hierarchy of remedies is "full reparation".[17]

b.   *Underlying Rationale for the Standard of Full Reparation*
One may discern in the *Chorzów Factory* judgment two principal reasons underlying the Court's decision.

On the one hand, the judgement makes clear that the preferred means of reparation in international law is *restitution in kind*, which, by definition, occurs at the date of the judgment (at the earliest). It is only where restitution in kind "is not possible"[18] that *indemnification* comes into play. Indemnification in lieu of restitution in kind, however, should equally "wipe out all the consequences of the illegal act and re-establish the situation which would, in all probability, have existed if that act had not been committed".[19] In other words, the satisfaction received by the aggrieved investor in the form of indemnification should be equivalent to restitution in kind.

This is precisely what the Court stated:

> "The dispossession of an industrial undertaking – the expropriation of which is prohibited by the Geneva Convention – then involves the obligation to restore the undertaking and, if this is not possible, to pay its value at the time of the indemnification, *which value is designed to take the place of restitution which has become impossible.*"[20] (Emphasis added)

This rationale for the PCIJ's standard of full reparation has found support in academic writings. For example, Georg Schwarzenberger has written:

> "Illegal confiscation, however, that is to say, expropriation of foreign-owned property in circumstances which amount to a breach of the minimum standard of international law, amounts to an international tort. In this case, compensation

---

17. For the valuation, the Court decided to hold an expert inquiry and referred several questions to the experts. For a discussion on this portion of the judgment and how it was later interpreted by the *Amoco* tribunal, see M. VALASEK, *op. cit.*, fn. 7, at p. 11 et seq.
18. *Chorzów Factory*, *op. cit.*, fn. 1, at p. 47.
19. *Ibid.*
20. *Ibid.*, at pp. 47-48.

serves as a substitute for restitution. Therefore, the value of the property at the time of the indemnification, rather than that of the seizure, may constitute a more appropriate substitute for restitution."[21]

The importance of the date of the decision in terms of valuation of damages under the *Chorzów Factory* standard was also emphasized by Professor Max Sørensen in the following passage of his *Manual of Public International Law*:

"The fact that indemnity presupposes, as the PCIJ stated, the 'payment of a sum corresponding to the value which a restitution in kind would bear' has important effects on its extent. As a consequence of the depreciation of currencies and of delays involved in the administration of justice, the value of a confiscated property may be higher at the time of the judicial decision than at the time of the unlawful act. Since monetary compensation must, as far as possible, resemble restitution, the value at the date when the indemnity is paid must be the criterion."[22]

The second motive underlying the Court's decision in *Chorzów Factory* is the deterrent effect of indemnification in case of unlawful expropriation,[23] which is seen as necessary to distinguish the consequences of lawful and unlawful State conduct and eliminate any perceived advantage or incentive for the expropriating State to act unlawfully. This additional underlying rationale is equally clear from the judgment:

"It follows that the compensation due to the German Government is not necessarily limited to the value of the undertaking at the moment of dispossession, plus interest to the day of payment. This limitation would only be admissible if the Polish Government had had the right to expropriate, and if its wrongful act consisted merely in not having paid to the two Companies the just price of what was expropriated; in the present case, such a limitation might result in placing Germany and the interests protected by the Geneva Convention, on behalf of

---

21. Georg SCHWARZENBERGER, *International Law, International Law as Applied by International Courts and Tribunals*, Vol. 1 (Stevens & Sons Limited, London 1957) at p. 660.
22. Max SØRENSEN, *Manual of Public International Law* (St. Martin's Press, New York 1968) at p. 567, para. 9.18.
23. The importance of this deterrent effect was recently emphasized by Professors Reisman and Sloane:

"Above all, any standard adopted to determine the appropriate date from which to calculate compensation should effectively deter, not reward, consequential and creeping expropriations. In this regard, tribunals seized with cases raising these issues may find it both useful and appropriate to disaggregate the moment of expropriation and the moment of valuation – to distinguish the 'moment of expropriation', which goes to the question of liability (i.e., whether an accretion of measures has ripened into a compensable expropriation) from the 'moment of valuation', which goes to the question of damages."

(W.M. REISMAN and R.D. SLOANE, "Indirect Expropriation and its Valuation in the BIT Generation", 74 *British Yearbook of International Law* (2004) at p. 133).

which interests the German Government is acting, in a situation more unfavourable than that in which Germany and these interests would have been if Poland had respected the said Convention. Such a consequence would not only be unjust, but also and above all incompatible with the aim of Article 6 and following articles of the Convention – that is to say, the prohibition, in principle, of the liquidation of the property, rights and interests of German nationals and of companies controlled by German nationals in Upper Silesia – since it would be tantamount to rendering lawful liquidation and unlawful dispossession indistinguishable so far as their financial results are concerned.[24]

(....)

[I]t would not be in conformity either with the principles of law or with the wish of the Parties to infer from that agreement [that restoring the *Chorzów factory* is impossible] that the question of compensation must henceforth be dealt with as though an expropriation properly so called was involved."[25]

This rationale met with the particular approval of Mr. Rabel, who added the following observation to the Court's judgment:

"It is in fact obvious that the expropriator's responsibility must be increased by the fact that his action is unlawful. Nevertheless, it is in my opinion also obvious that the unlawful character of his action can never place the expropriator in a more favourable position, nor the expropriated Party in a more unfavourable position, either by reducing the indemnity due or by increasing the burden of proof resting upon the Applicant. This point of view, with which the Court in its judgment has not thought fit expressly to deal, appears to me to be in accordance with the general principles of law. It corresponds to the notion which has been very clearly established, for instance in the application of German civil law, namely that the fact that an act is of an unlawful character, in the same way as if it were of a deceptive or defective character – though in principle aggravating the consequences of the act, nevertheless leaves intact, in favour of the injured Party, and to be asserted by him should he choose to do so, the rights to which the act would have given rise if it had been lawful or less culpable."[26]

2. *The Codification of the Chorzów Factory Standard: ILC's Draft Articles on Responsibility of States for Internationally Wrongful Acts*

The general principles established by the PCIJ in the *Chorzów Factory* case have been endorsed by the International Law Commission in accordance with its stated mission of "progressive development of international law and its codification".[27]

---

24. *Chorzów, op. cit.*, fn. 1, at p. 47.
25. *Ibid.*, at p. 48.
26. Observations by Mr. RABEL, *ibid.*, at pp. 66-67.
27. See Art. 1, para. 1, of the Statute of the International Law Commission.

The ILC Draft Articles[28] thus provide:

"*Article 31. Reparation*
1. The responsible State is under an obligation to make full reparation for the injury caused by the internationally wrongful act.
2. Injury includes any damages, whether material or moral, caused by the internationally wrongful act of a State.
(....)

*Article 34. Forms of reparation*
Full reparation for the injury caused by the internationally wrongful act shall take the form of restitution, compensation and satisfaction, either singly or in combination, in accordance with the provisions of this chapter.

*Article 35. Restitution*
A State responsible for an internationally wrongful act is under an obligation to make restitution, that is, to re-establish the situation which existed before the wrongful act was committed, provided and to the extent that restitution:
(a) Is not materially impossible;
(b) Does not involve a burden out of all proportion to the benefit deriving from restitution instead of compensation.

*Article 36. Compensation*
1. The State responsible for an internationally wrongful act is under an obligation to compensate for the damage caused thereby, insofar as such damage is not made good by restitution.
2. The compensation shall cover any financially assessable damage including loss of profits insofar as it is established."

The Commentary on Art. 31 clearly identifies the *Chorzów Factory* case as the source of the "obligation to make full reparation":

"The general principle of the consequences of the commission of an internationally wrongful act was stated by PCIJ in the *Factory at Chorzów* case...."[29]

The Commentary further provides that

"[t]he obligation placed on the responsible State by Art. 31 is to make 'full reparation' in the *Factory at Chorzów* sense. In other words, the responsible State

---

28. Draft Articles on Responsibility of States for Internationally Wrongful Acts, adopted by the ILC at its fifty-third session (2001).
29. James CRAWFORD, *The International Law Commission's Articles on State Responsibility – Introduction, Text and Commentaries* (Cambridge University Press, Cambridge 2002) p. 202 (Commentary (1) on Art. 31).

must endeavour to 'wipe out all the consequences of the illegal act and reestablish the situation which would, in all probability, have existed if that act had not been committed' through the provision of one or more of the forms of reparation set out in chapter II of this part."[30]

The Commentary further notes that reparation is in the form of "restitution or its value, and in addition damages for loss sustained as a result of the wrongful act".[31]

As for the hierarchy between the different forms of reparation, the Commentary on Art. 35 explains that:

> "In accordance with article 34, restitution is the first of the forms of reparation available to a State injured by an internationally wrongful act.[32]
> (....)
> [B]ecause restitution most closely conforms to the general principle that the responsible State is bound to wipe out the legal and material consequences of its wrongful act by re-establishing the situation that would exist if that act had not been committed, it comes first among the forms of reparation. The primacy of restitution was confirmed by the Permanent Court in the *Factory at Chorzów* case...."[33]

The primacy of restitution is however not absolute:

> "[T]here are often situations where restitution is not available or where its value to the injured State is so reduced that other forms of reparation take priority.... quite apart from valid election by the injured State or other entity, the possibility of restitution may be practically excluded, e.g. because the property in question has been destroyed or fundamentally changed in character or the situation cannot be restored to the *status quo ante* for some reason.[34]
> (....)
> Restitution, despite its primacy as a matter of legal principles, is frequently unavailable or inadequate. It may be partially or entirely ruled out either on the basis of the exceptions expressed in article 35, or because the injured State prefers compensation or for other reasons. Even where restitution is made, it may be insufficient to ensure full reparation. The role of compensation is to fill in any gaps so as to ensure full reparation for the damage suffered. As the umpire said in the '*Lusitania*' case:

---

30. Commentary (3) on Art. 31, *ibid.*, at p. 202.
31. Commentary (2) on Art. 31, *ibid.*, at p. 202.
32. Commentary (1) on Art. 35, *ibid.*, at p. 213.
33. Commentary (3) on Art. 35, *ibid.*, at p. 213.
34. Commentary (4) on Art. 34, *ibid.*, at p. 214.

'The fundamental concept of "damages" is ... reparation for a *loss* suffered; a judicially ascertained *compensation* for wrong. The remedy should be commensurate with the loss, so that the injured party may be made whole.'"[35]

As further discussed below (see Sect. III.6), the determination of which (or which combination) among the different means of reparation is most appropriate may prove difficult in some circumstances, for example where the respondent State offers restitution to a claiming party that has asked for compensation instead.

III. THE PRINCIPLE OF FULL REPARATION APPLIED TO UNLAWFUL EXPROPRIATION: HAS THE DISTINCTION BETWEEN LAWFUL AND UNLAWFUL EXPROPRIATION FINALLY BEEN ACCEPTED?

*1. Introduction*

In the previous section, we saw that the *Chorzów Factory* standard is grounded in sound policy, has been applied on numerous occasions by the ICJ, and was codified in the ILC Draft Articles. Nevertheless, it is fair to say that at least in the area of expropriation the full meaning and implication of the *Chorzów Factory* standard have not been uncovered until recently. In a series of ICSID cases, starting with *ADC v. Hungary*, parties and tribunals have awakened to the important distinction between lawful and unlawful expropriation, and to the implications that a finding that an expropriation is unlawful has on the potential damages available to the expropriated party.

In this section, we first survey the arbitral awards that had been held out as supporting the existence of a single "uniform standard" for all types of expropriation, lawful or not. At best, these awards demonstrate that the issue had not been squarely put before a tribunal for decision (III.2). We then briefly describe the cases that have ushered in a new era for *Chorzów Factory*, namely *ADC* (III.3), *Siemens* (III.4) and *Vivendi* (III.5). These cases establish that a treaty standard of compensation that, by its express terms, applies only to lawful expropriation, does not preclude additional damages in the case of unlawful expropriation. Finally, we briefly explore several unresolved issues relating to *Chorzów Factory* (III.6).

*2. The Proper Import of Prior Decisions*

The distinction between lawful and unlawful expropriation seems to have lain dormant for a number of years. This is probably due to the fact that the typical case brought to arbitration did not involve the expropriation of a property whose value had risen after the expropriation.[36]

---

35. Commentary (3) on Art. 36, *ibid.*, at p. 218.
36. This crucial difference was rightly emphasized by the tribunal in *ADC*:

"The present case is almost unique among decided cases concerning the expropriation by States

Indeed, we are aware of no authority in which an arbitral tribunal rejected a claim for a higher standard on the basis that the BIT standard necessarily excluded application of the standard in international customary law for an unlawful taking.

For instance, in *Phillips Petroleum v. Iran*,[37] the issue before the tribunal was not whether a higher standard of compensation should apply in case of unlawful expropriation, but whether a lower standard should apply to lawful expropriation. Although the tribunal decided that the lawful/unlawful distinction was irrelevant under the Treaty of Amity, which it held provided a single standard applying to "the property taken, regardless of whether that taking was lawful or unlawful",[38] it also noted that the claimant did request "no more than the just compensation" based on the single standard of the Treaty.[39]

More importantly, on the basis of the *Chorzów Factory* case, the tribunal stated that the distinction between lawful and unlawful expropriation is

> "relevant only to two possible issues: whether restitution of the property can be awarded and whether compensation can be awarded for any increase in the value of the property between the date of taking and the date of the judicial or arbitral decision awarding compensation. The Chorzów decision provides no basis for any assertion that a lawful taking requires less compensation than that which is equal to the value of the property on the date of taking. In the present case, neither restitution nor compensation for any value other than that on the date of taking is sought by the Claimant, so the Tribunal need not determine whether such remedies would be available with respect to a taking to which the Treaty of Amity applies."[40]

*AAPL v. Republic of Sri Lanka*, in turn, was not a case of expropriation, but one of destruction of property under circumstances not justified by combat action or necessities of the situation, an event expressly provided for under the U.K.-Sri Lanka bilateral

---

of foreign owned property, since the value of the investment after the date of expropriation (1 January 2002) has risen very considerably while other arbitrations that apply the *Chorzów Factory* standard all invariably involve scenarios where there has been a decline in the value of the investment after regulatory interference. It is for this reason that application of the restitution standard by various arbitration tribunals has led to use the date of the expropriation as the date for the valuation of damages."

(*ADC v. Hungary*, op. cit., fn. 3, para. 496).

37. *Phillips Petroleum Co. Iran v. The Islamic Republic of Iran*, The National Iranian Oil Company, Iran-U.S. Claims Tribunal, Award No. 425-39-2 of 29 June 1989 (hereinafter *Phillips Petroleum v. Iran*) 21 Iran-U.S.C.T.R. 79.
38. *Ibid.*, at 121.
39. *Ibid.*, at 122.
40. *Ibid.*

investment treaty (BIT) and to which a different standard of compensation applied.[41]

In *Goetz v. Burundi*,[42] the tribunal never got to the stage of examining whether Burundi's actions were unlawful. After referring to the obligations undertaken by the respondent in relation to expropriation under the applicable bilateral investment treaty,[43] the tribunal noted that the BIT did not require prior compensation. The tribunal concluded that the respondent still had the opportunity to pay such compensation, which would render its measure internationally lawful.[44]

In *Metalclad v. Mexico*, the tribunal decided that the respondent state had indirectly expropriated Metalclad's investment without providing compensation to Metalclad for the expropriation. It held that Mexico violated Art. 1110 of NAFTA.[45] There was, however, no discussion as to the lawful or unlawful character of the expropriation, nor

---

41. See *Asian Agricultural Products Ltd. (AAPL) v. Republic of Sri Lanka* (ICSID Case No. ARB/87/3 (hereinafter *AAPL v. Sri Lanka* or *AAPL*)), Award of 27 June 1990 (tribunal composed of Berthold Goldman, Samuel K.B. Asante and Ahmed Sadek El-Kosheri acting as president) 6 ICSID Rev. – FILJ (1991) p. 526, at para. 88, referring to the rule formulated in 1925 by Max Huber in the *Melilla-Xiat, Ben Kirm* case: *"Le dommage éventuellement remboursable ne pourrait être que le dommage direct, savoir la valeur des marchandises détruites ou disparues"* (*U.N. Reports of International Arbitration Awards*, Vol. II, p. 732). The same standard was interestingly applied in a commercial arbitration conducted under CIETAC Arbitration Rules (unpublished award, summary available at <www.fdi.gov.cn/pub/FDI_EN/Laws/default_anli.jsp>).

42. *Antoine Goetz et Consorts v. République du Burundi* (ICSID Case No. ARB/95/3 (hereinafter *Goetz v. Burundi* or *Goetz*)), Award of 2 September 1998 (tribunal composed of Mohammed Bedjaoui, Jean-Denis Bredin and Prosper Weil acting as chairman) available at <www.worldbank.org/icsid/cases/goetz.pdf>.

43. Namely not to take any expropriatory measure (or measure whose effect would be tantamount thereto), save where justified for public purposes, security or national interests and provided the said measure was taken under due process of law, was not discriminatory or in breach of a particular agreement and was accompanied by provisions ensuring payment of prompt and adequate compensation. Original text:

    "... ne prendre aucune mesure privative ou restrictive de propriété, ni aucune autre mesure ayant un effet similaire à l'égard des investissements situés sur son territoire, si ce n'est lorsque des impératifs d'utilité publique, de sécurité ou d'intérêt national l'exigent exceptionnellement, auquel cas les conditions suivantes doivent être remplies: a) les mesures sont prises selon une procédure légale; b) elles ne sont ni discriminatoires, ni contraires à un accord particulier ... c) elles sont assorties de dispositions prévoyant le paiement d'une indemnité adéquate et effective".

    (*Goetz*, ibid., at para. 124).

44. See *Goetz*, ibid., at para. 131. The tribunal further indicated that it was still open to the respondent to repeal the "expropriatory" measure, which would render the damages issue moot (ibid., at para. 132).

45. *Metalclad Corporation v. The United Mexican States* (ICSID Case No. ARB(AF)/97/1 (NAFTA) (hereinafter *Metalclad v. Mexico* or *Metalclad*)), Award of 30 August 2000, (tribunal composed of Benjamin R. Civiletti, José Luis Siqueiros and Elihu Lauterpacht acting as president) 16 ICSID Rev. – FILJ (2001, no. 1) at p. 197, para. 112.

did Metalclad request that the standard provided under Art. 1110(2) of NAFTA[46] be displaced in favour of the standard provided under customary international law.

In *S.D. Myers v Canada*,[47] Canada was found to have been in breach of its obligations to grant to S.D. Myers "national treatment" and "fair and equitable treatment and full protection and security" (Arts. 1102 and 1105 NAFTA). Although the case was not, therefore, about expropriation, the tribunal nevertheless drew upon the distinction between lawful and unlawful expropriations in discussing the standard of compensation for other breaches:

> "Expropriations that take place in accordance with the framework of Art. 1110 – that is, expropriations that are conducted for a public purpose, on a non-discriminatory basis and in accordance with due process of law – are 'lawful' under Chapter 11 provided that compensation is paid in accordance with the ... *fair market value of the asset* ... formula. Under other provisions of Chapter 11 ... the standard of compensation that an arbitral tribunal should apply may in some cases be influenced by the distinction between compensating for a lawful, as opposed to an unlawful, act. Fixing the fair market value of an asset that is diminished in value may not fairly address the harm done to the investor."[48] (Emphasis in original)

The tribunal then turned to the "authoritative" principle stated in the *Chorzów Factory* case and to the ILC Draft Articles.

In *Middle East Cement Shipping and Handling Co. C.S.A. v. Egypt*,[49] the claimant did not try to displace the BIT standard requiring compensation for expropriation to "amount to the market value of the investment affected immediately before the measures referred to [in the BIT provision on conditions for a lawful expropriation] occurred or became public knowledge".[50]

---

46. Art. 1110(2) of NAFTA provides that

    " [c]ompensation shall be equivalent to the fair market value of the expropriated investment immediately before the expropriation took place ('date of expropriation') and shall not reflect any change in value occurring because the intended expropriation had become known earlier. Valuation criteria shall include going concern value, asset value including declared tax value of tangible property, and other criteria, as appropriate, to determine fair market value".

47. *S.D. Myers, Inc. v. Canada* (NAFTA (UNCITRAL )), Partial Award of 13 November 2000 (tribunal composed of Bryan P. Schwartz, Edward C. Chiasson and J. Martin Hunter acting as president) available at <www.naftaclaims.com/Disputes/Canada/SDMyers/SDMyersMeritsAward.pdf>, at p. 59 et seq., paras. 237 et seq.

48. *S.D. Myers, ibid.*, at para. 308.

49. *Middle East Cement Shipping and Handling Co. C.S.A. v. Egypt* (ICSID Case No. ARB/99/6 (hereinafter *Middle East Cement*)), Award of 12 April 2002 (tribunal composed of Piero Bernardini, Don Wallace, Jr and Karl-Heinz Böcksteigel acting as president) available at <ita.law.uvic.ca/documents/MECement-award.pdf>.

50. *Ibid.*, at p. 36, para. 146.

In *Técnicas Medioambientales Tecmed S.A. v. United Mexican States*,[51] the issue did not revolve around lawful versus unlawful expropriation (which was not pleaded by the claimant and therefore not considered by the tribunal), but around the very definition of expropriation and whether the respondent's actions were proportionate to the claimant's breaches of its obligations. Moreover, the claimant's claim for damages, and the calculation thereof, were based on a specific provision contained in the parties' agreement. The standard of full reparation under customary international law was not therefore presented to the arbitral tribunal.

3.  *ADC v. Hungary*

The decision in *ADC v. Hungary* represents a re-awakening to the important distinction between lawful and unlawful expropriation and to its consequences.

The *ADC* dispute involved contracts awarded in 1994 by a Hungarian state agency to Airport Development Corporation (ADC) to renovate the airport's existing terminal, build a new terminal, and participate in the operation of both terminals over a twelve-year term through a locally incorporated project company. The final agreements were signed in February 1997. The new terminal was commissioned in December 1998, when the project company began to operate the terminals.

The Cypriot investor-companies, whose ultimate beneficial owners were ADC and Aéroports de Montréal, Inc. (ADMC), were incorporated as part of the investment structure: ADC Affiliate Ltd. held the equity in the project company, and ADC & ADMC Management Ltd. collected management fees as terminal manager.

Three years into the successful operation of the airport by the project company, in December 2001, Hungary's Minister of Transport issued a Decree that cancelled the project company's operating rights as well as the terminal manager's management contract and transferred the operation of the airport to a state-owned company, Budapest Airport Rt. The project company was required to vacate its offices within a matter of days, and its employees were pressured to join the new company or leave. No compensation accompanied the Decree, nor was any offer of compensation made in the period following the Decree.

In 2003, the investors commenced arbitration proceedings against Hungary under the BIT between Hungary and Cyprus, claiming compensation for Hungary's breaches of the treaty.

On liability, the tribunal concluded that the Decree effected an unlawful taking of the claimants' investments, and thus constituted a violation of the BIT.[52]

On applicable law, the tribunal had to decide whether the standard of compensation was determined by the treaty or by customary international law, an issue that was vigorously debated by the parties. The answer to this question is of particular importance

---

51. *Técnicas Medioambientales Tecmed S.A. v. United Mexican States* (ICSID Case No. ARB(AF)/00/2 (NAFTA) (hereinafter *Tecmed v. Mexico* or *Tecmed*)), Award of 29 May 2003 (tribunal composed of José Carlos Fernández Rozas, Carlos Bernal Versa and Horacio A. Grigera Naón acting as president), available at <http://icsid.worldbank.org>.
52. See *ADC* Award, *op. cit.*, fn. 3, at Sect. VII.C.

with respect to expropriation, because many BITs set out conditions for a lawful expropriation, including the compensation that must be paid to the expropriated investor, but say nothing about unlawful expropriation. The question that arises therefore is whether the treaty standard should also apply in the case of an unlawful expropriation.

The respondent argued in favour of the application of a uniform standard of compensation, urging the tribunal to reject a differentiated standard based on the distinction between lawful and unlawful expropriation.

In a subsequent article, Audley Sheppard articulated the argument as follows:

> "Where a claim is brought under an investment treaty in respect of an expropriation, and that treaty prescribes a standard of compensation, the question of compliance or non-compliance with the conduct requirements should be immaterial to the standard of compensation and the treaty standard should apply."[53]

It was further argued that the treaty standard should necessarily apply to the exclusion of the standard in customary international law on the basis of the maxim *lex specialis derogat legi generali*.[54]

It was the claimants' submission in *ADC* that Art. 4 of the Hungary-Cyprus BIT[55] is

---

53. Audley SHEPPARD, "The Distinction Between Lawful and Unlawful Expropriation" in Clarisse RIBEIRO, ed., *Investment Arbitration and the Energy Charter Treaty* (Juris Publishing 2006) p. 172. Mr. Sheppard, together with Mr. Beechey, was counsel for the Republic of Hungary in the *ADC* case until 12 August 2005.
54. The rationale of this maxim was explained as early as 1625 by Grotius: "[a]mong agreements which are equal in respect of the qualities mentioned, that should be given preference which is most specific and approaches more nearly to the subject in hand; for special provisions are ordinarily more effective than those that are general" (Hugo GROTIUS, *De jure belli ac pacis*, ii (1925), bk. II, ch. XVI, Sect. XXIX, p. 428). This is generally considered to be a general principle of law, in the meaning of Art. 38 of the Statute of the Permanent Court of International Justice and has been endorsed by the ILC in its Draft Articles: "[t]hese articles do not apply where and to the extent that the conditions for the existence of an internationally wrongful act or the content or implementation of international responsibility of a State are governed by special rules of international law" (Art. 55 of the ILC Draft Articles).
55. Art. 4 of the Hungary-Cyprus BIT provides as follows:

    "1. Neither Contracting Party shall take any measures depriving, directly or indirectly, investors of the other Contracting Party of their investments unless the following conditions are complied with:
    (a) the measures are taken in the public interest and under due process of law;
    (b) the measures are not discriminatory;
    (c) the measures are accompanied by provision for the payment of just compensation.
    2. The amount of compensation must correspond to the market value of the expropriated investments at the moment of the expropriation.
    3. The amount of this compensation may be estimated according to the laws and regulations of the country where the expropriation is made.
    4. The compensation must be paid without undue delay upon completion of the legal

limited to establishing the standard of compensation for a lawful expropriation, and should not be applied to the distinct issue of damages to be granted to the investor for unlawful expropriation.

The claimants first argued that the ordinary meaning of the Treaty's terms limits the scope of Art. 4 to lawful expropriation. Art. 4(1) lists the conduct requirements of a lawful expropriation, which include the payment of "just compensation" by the expropriating State. Claimants contended that the meaning of the term "compensation" in the subsequent provisions of Art. 4, in particular in Art. 4(2), which requires the "amount of compensation" to equal "the market value of the expropriated investments at the moment of expropriation", could not be unrestricted but should be limited to the compensation referred to in the provision immediately preceding it, namely the compensation paid as a condition of a lawful expropriation. The same reasoning applied to Art. 4(3), where the link is reinforced by the insertion of the word "this" before "compensation". Furthermore, it was pointed out that, according to Art. 4(4), the "compensation must be paid without undue delay upon completion of the legal expropriation procedure", which was seen as further evidence that the term "compensation" and its definition only apply to lawful expropriations.

The claimants further submitted that the object and purpose of the BIT militated in favour of affording the potentially higher amount of damages available under customary international law in cases of unlawful takings. The preamble of the BIT states that its object and purpose is the creation of favourable conditions for investment by investors of one Contracting Party in the territory of the other Contracting Party. If a uniform standard of compensation were applied in all instances of expropriation, the state would have no incentive to act lawfully, as no financial consequences would flow from an unlawful expropriation versus a lawful taking (in the particular circumstances where the value of the investment rises after the expropriation).[56]

Finally, it was asserted that restricting compensation to the standard in Art. 4(2) would violate Art. 3(2) of the BIT providing for "full security and protection which in any case shall not be less than that accorded to investments of any third State". A uniform standard of compensation that did not distinguish between lawful and unlawful expropriation would provide less protection under the BIT than the protection afforded to investments from any state with which Hungary had not entered into an investment protection treaty, namely the standard under customary international law.

These arguments were accepted by the *ADC* tribunal, which explicitly rejected Hungary's argument that the BIT should apply as *lex specialis* in the following terms:

---

expropriation procedure, but not later than three months upon completion of this procedure and shall be transferred in the currency in which the investment is made. In the event of delays beyond the three-months' period, the Contracting Party concerned shall be liable to the payment of interest based on prevailing rates."

56. This is generally recognized as being an important purpose of investment treaties. See W.M. REISMAN and R.D. SLOANE, *op. cit.*, fn. 23, p. 115: "[t]o shield investors from illegal expropriation and other arbitrary or discriminatory governmental conduct that threatens to discourage foreign investment remains a vital purpose of BITs".

"There is general authority for the view that a BIT can be considered as a *lex specialis* whose provisions will prevail over rules of customary international law (see, *e.g.,* Phillips Petroleum Co. Iran v. Iran, 21 Iran-U.S. Cl. Trib. Rep. at 121). But in the present case the BIT does not stipulate any rules relating to damages payable in the case of an unlawful expropriation. The BIT only stipulates the standard of compensation that is payable in the case of a lawful expropriation, and these cannot be used to determine the issue of damages payable in the case of an unlawful expropriation since this would be to conflate compensation for a lawful expropriation with damages for an unlawful expropriation. This would have been possible if the BIT expressly provided for such a position, but this does not exist in the present case.

(....)

Since the BIT does not contain any *lex specialis* rules that govern the issue of the standard for assessing damages in the case of an unlawful expropriation, the Tribunal is required to apply the default standard contained in customary international law in the present case."[57]

The tribunal held that the BIT standard of compensation applied only to lawful expropriations. On that basis, and having determined that Hungary's expropriation was unlawful, the tribunal applied the standard articulated by the PCIJ in the *Chorzów Factory* case to indemnify the claimants.

After referencing numerous treaty-arbitration and ICJ cases that affirmed and applied the *Chorzów Factory* standard, the tribunal concluded that "there can be no doubt about the present vitality of the Chorzów Factory principle".[58]

Having accepted the applicability of the *Chorzów Factory* standard, the *ADC* tribunal considered the consequences of its application in the exceptional circumstance of an increase in the value of the investment after the date of expropriation, as opposed to the more typical situation of a decline in value after the expropriation:

"The remaining issue is what consequence does application of this customary international law standard have for the present case. It is clear that actual restitution cannot take place and so it is, in the words of the *Chorzów Factory* decision, '*payment of a sum corresponding to the value which a restitution in kind would bear*', which is the matter to be decided.

---

57. *ADC, op. cit.*, fn. 3, at paras. 481 and 482. This holding may have been misinterpreted in a recent decision, where the tribunal referred to the *ADC* award and held that "there may be a difference between 'compensation' as the consequence of a legal act and 'damages' as the consequences of committing of a wrongful act. This distinction has been noticed by various tribunals. If FMV [fair market value] is not the proper measure of compensation for unlawful expropriation, it is a fortiori not appropriate for breaches of other Treaty standards." (See *LG&E Energy Corp., LG&E Capital Corp. and LG&E International, Inc. v. The Argentine Republic* (hereinafter *LG&E v. Argentina* or *LG&E*), Award of 25 July 2007 (tribunal composed of Francisco Rezek, Albert Jan van den Berg and Tatiana B. de Maekelt acting as president) available at <http://ita.law.uvic.ca/documents/LGEEnglish_003.pdf>, at p. 10, para. 38).
58. *Ibid.*, at para. 493, in fine.

The present case is almost unique among decided cases concerning the expropriation by States of foreign owned property, since the value of the investment after the date of expropriation (1 January 2002) has risen very considerably while other arbitrations that apply the *Chorzów Factory* standard all invariably involve scenarios where there has been a decline in the value of the investment after regulatory interference. It is for this reason that application of the restitution standard by various arbitration tribunals has led to use of the date of the expropriation as the date for the valuation of damages.

However, in the present, *sui generis*, type of case the application of the *Chorzów Factory* standard requires that the date of valuation should be the date of the Award and not the date of expropriation, since this is what is necessary to put the Claimants in the same position as if the expropriation had not been committed."[59] (Italics in original)

The *ADC* tribunal found further support for its application of the *Chorzów Factory* standard, and for its decision that the date of valuation should be the date of the award and not that of the expropriation, in decisions of the European Court of Human Rights (the ECHR).

In particular, in *Papamichalopoulos and Others v. Greece*, the ECHR made a clear distinction between the compensation owed by a State in the case of lawful expropriation and the reparation owed in the case of unlawful dispossession. After having referred to the oft-cited passage of *Chorzów Factory*, the ECHR concluded that the reparation should not be limited to payment of the value of the expropriated properties on the day of their taking but should instead amount to payment of the "current value of the land, increased by the appreciation brought about by the existence of the buildings and the construction costs of the latter".[60]

The *ADC* tribunal also referred to the writings of the former ICJ President, Jiménez de Aréchaga:

"The fact that indemnity presupposes, as the PCIJ stated, the 'payment of a sum corresponding to the value which a restitution in kind would bear', has important effects on its extent. As a consequence of the depreciation of currencies and of delays involved in the administration of justice, the value of a confiscated property may be higher at the time of the judicial decision than at the time of the unlawful act. Since monetary compensation must, as far as possible, resemble restitution, the value at the date when indemnity is paid must be the criterion."[61]

---

59. *Ibid.*, at paras. 496-497.
60. *Papamichalopoulos and Others v. Greece* (Series A, No. 330-B; Application No. 145556/89), European Court of Human Rights (1996) 21 EHRR 439, 31 October 1995, para. 39.
61. JIMÉNEZ DE ARÉCHAGA, "*L'arbitrage entre les États et les Sociétés Privées Étrangères*" in *Mélanges en l'Honneur de Gilbert Gidel*, (1961) p. 367, at p. 375 cited with approval by the sole arbitrator Dupuy in *Texaco Overseas Petroleum Company v. Government of the Libyan Arab Republic*, Award on the Merits of 19 January 1977, 53 I.L.R. 389.

The tribunal in *ADC* therefore concluded that, under the customary international law standard in *Chorzów Factory*, the claimants must be compensated for (a) the estimated value of the claimants' stake in the project company as of the award date (calculated on the basis of the future stream of profits, looking forward from the date of the award), and (b) all unpaid dividends and management fees from the date of expropriation until the date of the award.[62]

The tribunal turned next to the quantum of compensation owed to the claimants. Relying on the discounted cash flow (DCF) method and the analysis presented by the claimants' experts, the tribunal valued the expropriated assets at the date of the award at US$ 76.2 million.[63] This compared to a value of the same assets at the date of expropriation of US$ 64.7 million (including pre-judgment interest).

4.   *Siemens v. Argentina*

The *ADC* award was issued on 2 October 2006. Several months later, the *Chorzów Factory* standard was again applied by an arbitral tribunal sitting in another ICSID case, *Siemens A.G. v. The Argentine Republic*.[64]

This dispute – one of the many cases involving Argentina in the aftermath of its severe economic crisis and the enactment of its "2000 Emergency Law" – arose in connection with a contract for the provision of integrated services related to immigration control, personal identification and electoral information. The contract had been awarded by a 1998 decree to SITS, an Argentinean subsidiary of Siemens.

After completion of the engineering phase, the operation of the immigration control system was halted one day after it had started, in early February 2000, for lack of governmental authorization. Three weeks later Argentina suspended the production, printing and distribution of all new national identity cards because of defects, but prohibited SITS from modifying the process to correct the same.

A special governmental commission, set up to review the contract and propose a way forward, agreed on 10 November 2000 to a proposal submitted by Siemens. This proposal was incorporated into a "Contract Restatement Proposal" later sent by the Argentine government to Siemens. In the meantime, the Argentine Congress had enacted the 2000 Emergency Law, which empowered the President to renegotiate public sector contracts. Under the belief that this would speed up the approval of the Contract Restatement Proposal, Siemens accepted that the contract be included under the provisions of the 2000 Emergency Law. The President of Argentina allegedly promised Siemens that a decree approving the Contract Restatement Proposal would be issued by the end of 2000.

---

62. *ADC*, *op. cit.*, fn. 3, at para. 518. The tribunal developed its reasoning in support of the application and interpretation of the *Chorzów Factory* standard only to the extent necessary. For a more complete discussion of the arguments that were presented to the tribunal in support of its application and interpretation, see Martin VALASEK, *op. cit.*, fn. 7.
63. The award also included an order for costs, which were added to the valuation of the expropriated assets, for a total award of compensation of US$ 83.8 million.
64. *Siemens A.G. v. The Argentine Republic*, *op. cit.*, fn. 4.

No decree had however been issued by March 2001, when the newly appointed Minister of Interior claimed to be unaware of the Contract Restatement Proposal. By May 2001, a new "non-negotiable" draft proposal had been sent to SITS. On 18 May 2001, the contract was terminated by a decree issued under the terms of the 2000 Emergency Law. A subsequent administrative appeal filed by SITS was rejected.

Siemens initiated arbitration, claiming that its investment had been the target of an indirect and creeping expropriation by Argentina for which it had not received any compensation.

With respect to the merits of Siemens' claim for expropriation, the tribunal held that Siemens' investment had indeed been expropriated and that the expropriation was unlawful. In particular, the tribunal found that the expropriation did not meet the requirements of Art. 4(2) of the Treaty, namely, public purpose and compensation. The tribunal found that while the "expropriating decree", as such, could be viewed as having been issued in furtherance of a public purpose against the backdrop of Argentina's financial crisis and the 2000 Emergency Law, it could not be assessed in isolation from the other measures taken by Argentina and the specific circumstances in which it was issued. The tribunal held that

> "Decree 669/01 [the decree expropriating the contract] became a convenient device to continue the process started more than a year earlier long before the onset of the financial crisis. From this perspective, while the public purpose of the 2000 Emergency Law is evident, its application through Decree 669/01 to the specific case of Siemens' investment and the public purpose of same are questionable. In any case, compensation has never been paid on grounds that, as already stated, the Tribunal finds that are lacking in justification. For these reasons, the expropriation did not meet the requirements of Article 4(2) and therefore was unlawful."[65]

As regards the issue of damages, the tribunal had no difficulty rejecting the application of the BIT standard:

> "The law applicable to the determination of compensation for a breach of such Treaty obligations [protection against unlawful expropriation, provision of fair and equitable treatment and full protection and security, protection against arbitrary measures] is customary international law. The Treaty itself only provides for compensation for expropriation in accordance with the terms of the Treaty."[66]

The tribunal then went on to refer to Art. 36 of the ILC Draft Articles and its source, the statement of the PCIJ in the *Chorzów Factory* case. The tribunal explained the importance of this standard in simple, enlightening terms:

---

65. *Ibid.*, at pp. 84-85, para. 273.
66. *Ibid.*, at p. 111, para. 349.

"The key difference between compensation under the Draft Articles and the *Factory at Chorzów* case formula, and Article 4(2) of the Treaty is that under the former, compensation must take into account 'all financially assessable damage' or 'wipe out all the consequences of the illegal act' as opposed to compensation 'equivalent to the value of the expropriated investment' under the Treaty. *Under customary international law, Siemens is entitled not just to the value of its enterprise as of May 18, 2001, the date of expropriation, but also to any greater value that enterprise has gained up to the date of this Award, plus any consequential damages.*[67] (Emphasis added)

Indeed, the tribunal relied for this point, in particular, on the terms of reference devised for the experts by the PCIJ in the *Chorzów Factory* case:

"It is only logical that, if all the consequences of the illegal act need to be wiped out, the value of the investment at the time of this Award be compensated in full. Otherwise, compensation would not cover all the consequences of the illegal act. While the Tribunal has determined that the Treaty does not apply for purposes of determining the compensation due to Siemens, which is governed by customary international law as reflected in *Factory at Chorzów*, it is worth noting that the PCIJ, as the Treaty itself, refers to the value of the investment without qualification. To reach its conclusion, the PCIJ did not need to have 'value' qualified by 'full'. The Tribunal is satisfied that the term 'value' does not need further qualification to mean not less than the full value of the investment."[68]

As for the value of the investment to be compensated, the tribunal noted that it was "the value it [the investment] has now, as of the date of this Award, unless such value is lower than at the date of expropriation, in which event the earlier value would be awarded".[69]

Siemens had based the value of its damages on the book value of its investment, to which it had added *lucrum cessans*. Although the tribunal agreed that the "admittedly unusual approach" followed by claimant had merit in the particular circumstances of the case,[70] it nevertheless rejected the claim for lost profits as it considered that "the amount claimed on account of lost profits [was] very unlikely to have ever materialized".[71]

The tribunal then turned to the claim on account of post-expropriation costs, which it considered "justified in order to wipe out the consequences of the expropriation…".[72]

The tribunal eventually ordered Argentina to pay compensation to Siemens in the amount of nearly US$ 218 million,[73] plus interest and costs.

---

67. *Ibid.*, at p. 112, para. 352.
68. *Ibid.*, at p. 112, para. 353.
69. *Ibid.*, at p. 115, para. 360.
70. *Ibid.*, at p. 114, para. 357.
71. *Ibid.*, at p. 122, para. 379.
72. *Ibid.*, at p. 123, para. 387.
73. Over US$ 208 million for the value of Siemens' investment, US$ 9 million for consequential damages and US$ 200,000 for unpaid bills (*ibid.*, p. 128, at para. 403). It is worth noting in this respect that the tribunal decided that compensation should be paid in dollars in view of the

## 5. Vivendi v. Argentina

The *Chorzów Factory* standard of compensation was also recently applied in the protracted *Vivendi* case.[74]

The case arose out of the privatization of the water and sewage services in the Argentine Province of Tucumán, which was initiated in early 1993 within the broader context of investment liberalization efforts under the Menem presidency. After lengthy negotiations, a concession was eventually granted by the Province, in 1995, to the Consortium of Aguas del Aconquija (CAA).

The privatization process and CAA's tariff structure rapidly became controversial, and the subject of political debate. CAA was subjected to a series of regulatory proceedings related to alleged problems with water quality and invoicing. A public campaign against CAA was launched by several politicians, while the Government publicly announced its intention to rescind the concession agreement. Attempts at finding an amicable solution to the dispute were unsuccessful. CAA finally gave notice that it was rescinding the concession agreement due to breaches by the Province of Tucumán of its obligations.

The Governor of the Province then issued a decree purporting to terminate the concession agreement due to CAA's alleged repeated violations. CAA's ensuing efforts to collect on its outstanding invoices were thwarted by the authorities.

In a first award rendered on 21 November 2000, an arbitral tribunal found that Argentina's federal authorities had not breached the applicable France-Argentina treaty. The tribunal refused to examine the merits of claims under the BIT relating to acts of the provincial authorities, on the ground that in order to do so, it would have to interpret and apply the provisions of a concession agreement that contained a choice-of-forum clause in favour of the administrative courts of Tucumán.

This last part of the award was annulled on 3 July 2002 by a decision of an ad hoc committee, which held that

> "where the 'fundamental basis of the claim' is a treaty laying down an independent standard by which the conduct of the parties is to be judged, the existence of an exclusive jurisdiction clause in a contract between the claimant and the respondent state or one of its subdivisions cannot operate as a bar to the application of the treaty standard. At most, it might be relevant – as municipal law will often be relevant – in assessing whether there has been a breach of the treaty."[75]

Following the annulment procedure, the case was resubmitted by the claimants to a second tribunal.

---

"context of the requirement that the consequences of the illegal act be wiped out" (*ibid.*, at p. 116, para. 361).

74. See *Vivendi v. Argentina, op. cit.*, fn. 5.
75. Decision on Annulment, para. 101, available at <http://ita.law.uvic.ca/documents/vivendi_annulEN.pdf>.

The second tribunal[76] found that the claimants' investment had been indirectly expropriated without compensation:

> "paraphrasing the words of the *Tecmed, CME, Santa Elena,* and *Starrett Housing* tribunals, Claimants were radically deprived of the economic use and enjoyment of their investment, the benefits of which (*ie* the right to be paid for services provided) had been effectively neutralised and rendered useless. Under these circumstances, rescission of the Concession Agreement represented the only rational alternative for Claimants. By leaving Claimants with no other rational choice, we conclude that the Province thus expropriated Claimants' right of use and enjoyment of their investment under the Concession Agreement."[77]

Having found that the damage suffered had indeed been caused by the measures taken in violation of the BIT, the tribunal then turned to the issue of damages per se.

The tribunal first examined the BIT's provisions on expropriation,[78] in relation to which it wrote:

> "the Treaty thus *mandates* that compensation for *lawful* expropriation be based on the *actual value* of the investment, and that interest *shall* be paid from the date of dispossession. However, it does not purport to establish a *lex specialis* governing the standards of compensation for *wrongful* expropriations."[79] (Emphasis in original)

The tribunal then cited the principle of compensation established by the PCIJ at p. 47 of its judgment in the *Chorzów Factory* case, and commented as follows:

> "There can be no doubt about the vitality of this statement of damages standard under customary international law, which has been affirmed and applied by numerous international tribunals as well as the PCIJ's successor, the International

---

76. Composed of Professor Gabrielle Kaufmann-Kohler, Professor Carlos Bernal Verea and J. William Rowley QC, acting as President.
77. *Vivendi*, Award in the Resubmitted Case of 20 August 2007, *op. cit.*, fn. 5, at p. 237, para. 7.5.34 (footnotes omitted).
78. Relevant parts of Art. 5(2) of the BIT provide

    "such measures referred to above [i.e. of expropriation] which could be adopted, shall allow the payment of prompt and adequate compensation, the amount of which, computed on the basis of the actual value of the investments affected, shall be evaluated in relation to the normal economic situation, and prior to any threat of dispossession.... Such compensation, its amount and payment method shall be established, at the latest, on the date of dispossession. Such compensation shall be effectively realizable, paid without delay and freely transferable. It shall bear interest, computed at an appropriate rate, until the date of payment."

79. *Vivendi*, Award in the Resubmitted Case of 20 August 2007, *op. cit.*, fn. 5, at p. 243, para. 8.2.3 (footnotes omitted).

Court of Justice. It is also clear that such a standard permits, if the facts so require, a higher rate of recovery than that prescribed in Article 5(2) for *lawful* expropriations."[80] (Emphasis in original)

Further, referring to Art. 36 of the ILC Draft Articles, the tribunal concluded that

"based on these principles, and absent limiting terms in the relevant treaty, it is generally accepted today that, regardless of the type of investment, and regardless of the nature of the illegitimate measure, the level of damages awarded in international investment arbitration is supposed to be sufficient to compensate the affected party fully and to eliminate the consequences of the state's action".[81]

The *Vivendi* tribunal thus adopted the same line of reasoning as the *ADC* and *Siemens* tribunals on the issue of the applicable standard of compensation.[82]

As regards the actual calculation of damages, the tribunal held that

"[a]t international law, depending on the circumstances arising in a particular case, there are a number of ways of approximating fair market value. The Tribunal accepts, in principle, that fair market value may be determined with reference to future lost profits in an appropriate case. Indeed, theoretically, it may even be the preferred method of calculating damages in cases involving the expropriation of or fundamental impairment of going concerns. However, the net present value provided by a DCF [discounted cash flow] analysis is not always appropriate and becomes less so as the assumptions and projections become increasingly speculative."[83]

In the instant case, the tribunal found that claimants had not established with a sufficient degree of certainty that the concession would have been profitable.[84] The tribunal therefore rejected the claimants' lost profits analysis and turned to alternative methods of evaluating the concession.

Of several possible alternatives (book value, investment value, replacement value or

---

80. *Ibid.* at p. 244, para. 8.2.5 (footnotes omitted).
81. *Ibid.,* at pp. 244-245, para.8.2.7.
82. In a footnote, the tribunal cited the *ADC* award as a "lucid analysis of possible different standards of damages assessment under customary international law and a *lex specialis* established in a BIT" (*ibid.*, fn. 402, at p. 243, para. 8.2.3), but noted that it was issued after the parties submitted their post-hearing briefs and was thus not cited to them.
83. *Ibid.*, at p. 247, para. 8.3.3.
84. *Ibid.*, at p. 248, para. 8.3.5. The tribunal however seemed to lower the standard of proof required in this regard as it was willing to accept, in the absence of a genuine going concern, that likelihood of lost profits be established through "sufficient evidence of its [the claimants'] expertise and proven record of profitability of concessions it (or indeed others) had operated in similar circumstances" (*ibid.*, at p. 248, para. 8.3.4).

liquidation value), the tribunal found that the "'investment value' of the concession appears to offer the closest proxy, if only partial, for compensation sufficient to eliminate the consequences of the Province's actions".[85]

In the end, the tribunal awarded claimants (i) US$ 51 million, representing the investment value of the concession at the date of expropriation, and (ii) US$ 54 million, representing the claimants' additional investment made after that date.

### 6. The Future of the Chorzów Factory Standard

Eighty years after the PCIJ decision in the *Chorzów Factory* case, the distinction between lawful and unlawful expropriation, and the applicability of the customary international law standard of compensation to the latter, have experienced a renaissance.

Based on this venerable doctrine, several tribunals have articulated the view that damages for the unlawful expropriation of an investment are no longer necessarily limited to the value of the investment at the date of the taking, but may also include any subsequent increase in value.

The awards in which this doctrine has received renewed attention are both relatively few in number and relatively recent, and several important issues remain unresolved. For example, future tribunals may well need to address issues such as where to draw the line between lawful and unlawful expropriation, the hierarchy of forms of reparation in specific circumstances, as well as other areas in which the *Chorzów Factory* standard might apply directly or at least be influential. These are addressed briefly below.

*a. Where to draw the line between lawful and unlawful expropriation*

It might be that the core issue in the debate about the applicable standard in cases of unlawful expropriation has now shifted to the question of determining where precisely to draw the line between lawful and unlawful expropriation.

While it is trite law that a state may expropriate property, including a foreign investment, provided it be for a public purpose, in accordance with the law and against payment of compensation,[86] the precise contours of what constitutes a lawful, as opposed to an unlawful expropriation have not yet been clearly and unequivocally established.

The PCIJ itself in the *Chorzów Factory* case expressed views that can be read as conflicting in this regard. The Court suggested, at the outset of its judgment, that the mere failure to pay compensation would be sufficient to render an expropriation unlawful: "The action of Poland which the Court has judged to be contrary to the Geneva Convention is not an expropriation – *to render which lawful only the payment of fair*

---

85. *Ibid.*, at p. 251, para. 8.3.13.
86. Some BITs further require that the expropriation not be undertaken on a discriminatory basis or that judicial review of the expropriatory measure be available. For an in-depth analysis, see Rudolf DOLZER and Margrete STEVENS, *Bilateral Investment Treaties* (Martinus Nijhoff Publishers 1995) at p. 97 et seq. See also Giorgio SACERDOTI, *Bilateral Treaties and Multilateral Investments on Investment Protection*, Collected Courses of the Hague Academy of International Law, Vol. 269 (Martinus Nijhoff Publishers 1998) at p. 379 et seq.

*compensation would have been wanting.*"[87] (Emphasis added) However, the Court then went on to write that limiting the compensation

> "to the value of the undertaking at the moment of dispossession, plus interest to the day of payment ... would only be admissible if the Polish Government had had the right to expropriate and if its wrongful act consisted merely in not having paid to the two Companies the just price of what was expropriated".[88]

The European Court of Human Rights, for its part, seems to be of the opinion that the failure to pay compensation renders an expropriation unlawful, but that the amount of compensation tendered need not always represent "fair market value" or be "full" in order for the expropriation to be lawful. In *Papamichalopoulos v. Greece*, the ECHR held:

> "[T]he act of the Greek Government which the Court held to be contrary to the Convention was not an expropriation that would have been legitimate but for the failure to pay fair compensation.... The unlawfulness of such a dispossession inevitably affects the criteria to be used for determining the reparation owed by the respondent State, since the pecuniary consequences of a lawful expropriation cannot be assimilated to those of an unlawful dispossession. In this connection, international case-law, of courts or arbitration tribunals, affords the Court a precious source of inspiration; although that case-law concerns more particularly the expropriation of industrial and commercial undertakings, the principles identified in that field are valid for situations such as the one at hand."[89]

It later observed that:

> "[T]he taking of property without payment of an amount reasonably related to its value would normally constitute a disproportionate interference which could not be considered justifiable under Article 1 [of the First Protocol]. Article 1 does not, however, guarantee a right to full compensation in all circumstances. Legitimate objectives of public interest, such as pursued in measures of economic reform or measures designed to achieve greater social justice, may call for less than reimbursement of the fair market value."[90]

The arbitral tribunal in the *Siemens* case seems to have taken a different view. According to the *Siemens* tribunal, failure to pay compensation without "justified reasons" could arguably suffice to render an expropriation unlawful and trigger the application of the

---

87. *Chorzów Factory, op. cit.*, fn. 1, at p. 46.
88. *Ibid.*, at p. 47.
89. *Papamichalopoulos and others v. Greece*, 9 ECHR 118, Judgment of 31 October 1995, at para. 36.
90. Judgment of 21 February 1986, ECHR, Series A., No. 98, para. 84.

more favourable standard of reparation set by *Chorzów Factory*.[91] Indeed, having concluded that Argentina's application of the 2000 Emergency Law to Siemens' investment and the purported public purpose for doing so were "questionable",[92] the arbitrators went on to state:

> "In any case, compensation has never been paid on grounds that, as already stated, the Tribunal finds that are lacking in justification. For these reasons, the expropriation did not meet the requirements of Article 4(2) and therefore was unlawful."[93]

Even if this was intended to be a formal holding, it would be of no assistance in determining under what circumstances a State may, in good faith, fail to pay the amount of compensation called for by the treaty provisions or customary international law.

One may nevertheless venture that there would be consensus on the following two propositions:

– The outright refusal by a State to pay compensation without even attempting to justify its position would be considered in bad faith and render the expropriation unlawful;
– The payment of compensation based on the State's substantiated evaluation of the property, even if the amount of the payment is less than the investor's claim, would render the expropriation lawful (as long as the other conditions for a lawful expropriation are satisfied).

The majority of cases most will likely involve situations falling somewhere between these two scenarios, and the outcome in those cases will therefore be more difficult to predict.

A further complication may arise where it can be demonstrated that the respondent State is not in a financial position to pay the amount of compensation required for the expropriation to be lawful. Should the respondent State nevertheless be sanctioned and ordered to pay a higher amount of damages, assuming that the other requirements (for example, public purpose and due process of law) have been met? Or should a defence of necessity be available in appropriate circumstances? The standard for such a defence is demanding, as evidenced by the ILC Draft Articles[94] and recent awards.[95]

---

91. The *Vivendi* tribunal in the resubmitted case might have an even stricter view, as it simply held that "if we conclude that the challenged measures are expropriatory, there will be violation of Article 5(2) of the Treaty, even if the measures might be for a public purpose and non-discriminatory, because no compensation has been paid" (*Vivendi, op. cit.*, fn. 5, at p. 230, para. 7.5.21). One may argue, however, that bad faith was implied in this case of creeping expropriation.
92. *Siemens, op. cit.*, fn. 4, at p. 85, para. 273.
93. *Ibid.*
94. Art. 25 of the ILC Draft Articles provides

> "1. Necessity may not be invoked by a State as a ground for precluding the wrongfulness of an act not in conformity with an international obligation of that State unless the act;
> (*a*) is the only way for the State to safeguard an essential interest against a grave and imminent

### b. Hierarchy of means of reparation

In *Chorzów Factory*, the PCIJ affirmed the primacy of restitution in kind. Damages are only to be awarded, in the Court's own terms, where restitution in kind is "not possible".[96] The Court did not, however, provide guidance as to what would constitute such an impossibility. Nor did it dwell upon Germany's decision to seek compensation instead of restitution, a decision that led one of the dissenting judges to criticize the Court's award of "enhanced" damages.[97] In its Draft Articles, the ILC likewise considers restitution to be the "first of the forms of reparation available",[98] while providing for exceptions to this primacy, namely where restitution is "materially impossible", or involves "a burden out of all proportion to the benefit deriving from restitution instead of compensation".[99]

It remains therefore to be seen how a tribunal would react if a State were to offer restitution instead of damages. Could the investor simply refuse the offer because it "prefers" an award of damages?

Based on our understanding of the *Chorzów Factory* standard, the investor would be entitled to decline an offer of restitution and insist on compensation if the value of its investment at the time the offer were made were significantly lower than the value of the investment at the time of expropriation. But the appropriate solution would be less clear if the State, in compliance with the principle of full reparation, offered damages in addition to restitution, either in a one-time payment, in instalments or through increased returns on the investment (in a concession context, for example). Although this would, in purely financial terms, be equivalent to the damages which might otherwise be awarded, the aggrieved investor could nevertheless have good reasons to resist such a package: loss of confidence in its former partner; unwillingness of its employees to return to a country from which they might have been forcefully expelled; and a preference on the part of its shareholders for less risky investments.

---

peril; and

(*b*) does not seriously impair an essential interest of the State or States towards which the obligations exists, or of the international community as a whole.

2. In any case, necessity may not be invoked by a State as a ground for precluding wrongfulness if:

(*a*) the international obligation in question excludes the possibility of invoking necessity; or

(*b*) the State has contributed to the situation of necessity."

95. See *CMS Gas Transmission Company v. The Argentine Republic* (ICSID Case No. ARB/01/8 (hereinafter *CMS Gas v. Argentina* or *CMS Gas*)), Award of 12 May 2005 (tribunal composed of Marc Lalonde, Francisco Rezek and Francisco Orrego Vicuña acting as president) para. 317 (available at <http://icsid.worldbank.org>: "While the existence of necessity as a ground for precluding wrongfulness under international law is no longer disputed, there is also consensus to the effect that this ground is an exceptional one and has to be addressed in a prudent manner to avoid abuse."

96. *Chorzów Factory*, *op. cit.*, fn. 1, at p. 47. Damages might also be awarded on top of restitution in kind if the latter is insufficient to cover the loss sustained.

97. See Dissenting Opinion by Lord Finlay, *ibid.*, at pp.70-71.

98. Commentary (1) on Art. 35, J. CRAWFORD, *op. cit.*, fn. 29, at p. 213.

99. Art. 35 of the ILC Draft Articles.

It will be interesting to see how future tribunals, if faced with the dilemma, will resolve the tension between the parties' respective choices of means of reparation, especially where each side is able to demonstrate plausible reasons for its choice. We have already listed some of the reasons that might motivate a claimant's preference for compensation. For its part, the respondent State itself may have good reasons to offer restitution in kind: it may be trying to make good some wrongdoing committed under a previous regime; or, faced with the prospect of having to pay damages but lacking the necessary funds to do so, it may wish to avoid further reputational damage, by belatedly complying with its international obligations by the only available means.

Should an arbitral tribunal accord more weight to the burden restitutionary damages would impose on the State than to the preference of the investor?

c.   *New areas of application of the Chorzów Factory standard*

Although the *Chorzów Factory* standard, to the best of our knowledge, has only been applied in the context of treaty arbitration,[100] it may eventually find application in other types of investment arbitration.

One such new context might be an investor's claim against a State party based on the breach of an "internationalized contract".

Under the theory of "internationalized contracts",[101] one may venture that customary international law, including the standard of compensation for unlawful expropriation, could apply under the following circumstances:

— Where the contract contains a stabilization clause or is executed together with a parallel legal stability agreement: such a clause or agreement is ineffective, according to some authors, unless it is governed by international law, as opposed to the host State's legislation, since the State may easily render its commitment ineffective internally;
— Where the parties have agreed on international arbitration to settle their disputes, in particular under the ICSID Convention: one may consider that a truly international tribunal cannot apply domestic law that is contrary to international law (in particular since it has to comply with the objectives of the ICSID Convention, i.e., foster private international investment) and that the parties' intention therefore was for international law to apply;
— Where the contract qualifies as a "foreign investment contract" or an "economic development agreement": one may consider that the international minimum standard of protection should equally apply in such a case, either on the basis of the parties' implied intention or in order to develop a harmonized regime for all such foreign investments, irrespective of their legal framework.

---

100. Since a number of investment arbitrations remain confidential, one may not exclude that the *Chorzów* standard has already been applied in different circumstances.
101. A famous illustration of this theory may be found in the award rendered on 19 January 1977 by sole arbitrator Dupuy in the *Texaco Overseas Petroleum Company – California Asiatic Oil Company v. The Government of the Libyan Arab Republic* case (17 ILM 3 (1978)).

The counter-argument is that the legal risks that an investor accepts to bear when entering into a contract governed by the laws of the host State, in the absence of any BIT, legislation on foreign investment or contractual choice-of-law provision pointing to international law, are accounted for when structuring the investment and the overall bargain, including as regards the anticipated return on investment, the allocation of shares in a project company, etc. Applying international law in such cases might unduly favour the investor and, by leading to unfair results, eventually undermine the legitimacy of international arbitration.

Another context in which the *Chorzów Factory* standard (and other principles of customary international law) might apply is an investor's claim based on the breach of the host State's foreign investment legislation, in which international standards of treatment may be explicitly or implicitly incorporated. Here again, the debate would probably revolve around the need for a uniform regime for all foreign investments *versus* respecting the State's intention when enacting its foreign investment legislation (if different) and the deal the investor has bargained for, all of which may be difficult to reconcile.

Finally, it is possible that the growing acceptance of the *Chorzów Factory* standard (and of the distinction between lawful and unlawful expropriation on which its application depends in treaty arbitration) will influence the development of expropriation law under municipal regimes. The question underlying this last hypothesis is whether the application of a differentiated standard, and the corresponding need to foster compliance by a State with its legal obligations, is limited to the international context, or whether the impunity or limited liability of government authorities should similarly be lifted in the context of a government's relations with its own nationals where the expropriation does not meet the local standards for a lawful expropriation.

IV. THE PRINCIPLE OF FULL REPARATION APPLIED TO THE AWARD OF INTEREST AND THE APPORTIONMENT OF ARBITRATION COSTS

If an aggrieved investor is to be fully compensated for the loss it has suffered as a result of a host State's wrongful act,[102] one may wonder why the principle of full reparation applicable to the investor's substantive claim should not also apply with respect to a claim for interest and arbitration costs.

This was the position taken, to varying degrees, by the tribunals in the *ADC*, *Siemens* and *Vivendi* cases, where the principle of full reparation was applied to the award of interest, and perhaps to some extent the award of costs.

In *Vivendi*, the tribunal held as follows with respect to interest:

"[I]n order 'to wipe-out all the consequences of the illegal act and re-establish the situation which would, in all probability, have existed if the act had not been

---

102. It should be noted that such wrongdoing is not limited to unlawful expropriation, the focus of the previous section of this paper. The standard of full reparation applies to any "internationally wrongful act". See Art. 31(1) of the ILC Draft Articles.

committed' (the *Chorzów* principle), it is necessary for any award of damages in this case to bear interest."[103]

Similarly, in *Siemens*, the tribunal applied the principle of full reparation to the interest rate, the starting date of interest and the decision to award compound interest.[104]

As for the apportionment of costs, the tribunal in *ADC* expressly linked the award of costs to the principle of full reparation:

> "In the present case, the Tribunal can find no reason to depart from the starting point that the successful party should receive reimbursement from the unsuccessful party. This was a complex, difficult, important and lengthy arbitration which clearly justified experienced and expert legal representation as well as the engagement of top quality experts on quantum. The Tribunal is not surprised at the total of the costs incurred by the Claimants. Members of the Tribunal have considerable experience of substantial ICSID cases as well as commercial cases and the amount expended is certainly within the expected range. Were the Claimants not reimbursed their costs in justifying what they alleged to be egregious conduct on the part of Hungary it could not be said that they were being made whole."[105] (Emphasis added)

While most tribunals and authors agree that the principle of full reparation should apply to the awarding of interest (see Sect. IV.*1*), with some discussions remaining as regards the awarding of compound interest (Sect. IV.*1.c*), there still exists a lively debate with respect to the apportionment of costs (Sect. IV.*2*).

1. *The Award of Interest: A Settled Issue?*

When an investor has suffered a loss as a result of the host State's breach of its obligations and when compensation has not been paid voluntarily for the said breach, the investor suffers additional damage as a result of the delay in receiving payment.

It is generally acknowledged that, in order to be "made whole", the investor should also be compensated for this delay, that is, for the period during which he was deprived of monies he could have invested elsewhere as a source of revenue.[106]

---

103. See *Vivendi v. Argentina*, op. cit., fn. 5, at p. 254, para. 8.3.20 (footnotes omitted). See also *LG&E v. Argentina*, op. cit., fn. 57, at p. 18, para. 55: "in the Tribunal's view, interest is part of the 'full' reparation to which the Claimants are entitled to assure that they are made whole".
104. *Siemens*, op. cit., fn. 4, at pp. 126-127, paras. 396-397 and 399-401.
105. *ADC*, op. cit., fn. 3, at p. 101, para. 533. The tribunal finally decided that it would be "*wholly appropriate, as well as just*" to reimburse the claimants the sum of US$ 7,623,693 in respect of their costs and expenses (*ibid.*, at p. 103, para. 542).
106. Interest is an important issue in most arbitrations, and the interest portion of an award may approach or even exceed the actual damages (see *Compañia del Desarrollo de Santa Elena, S.A. v. The Republic of Costa Rica* (ICSID Case No. ARB/96/1 (hereinafter *Santa Elena v. Costa Rica*)), Final Award of 17 February 2000 (tribunal composed of Elihu Lauterpacht, Prosper Weil and L. Yves Fortier acting as president) ICSID Rev. – FILJ , at para. 117, awarding US$ 4 million in damages

The principle of awarding interest in order to ensure full reparation was accepted as early as the 1920s. In the 1926 *Illinois Central RR Co.* case, in adjudicating a claim between Mexico and the United States, and notwithstanding the absence of a specific stipulation in the treaty with respect to the inclusion of interest in pecuniary awards, the tribunal held that arbitral precedents did not appear

> "to be at variance with the principle to which we deem it proper to give effect that *interest must be regarded as a proper element of compensation*. It is the purpose of the Convention of 8 September 1923, to afford the respective nationals of the High Contracting Parties, in the language of the convention 'just and adequate compensation for their losses or damages'. In our opinion *just compensatory damages* in this case would include not only the sum due, as stated in the Memorial, under the aforesaid contract, but compensation for the loss *of the use of that sum during a period within which the payment thereof continues to be withheld.*"[107] (Emphasis added)

The fact that awarding interest contributes to ensuring that the investor receives full reparation also underlies the ILC Draft Articles, Art. 38(1) of which provides:

> "Interest on any principal sum due under this chapter shall be payable when necessary *in order to ensure full reparation*. The interest rate and mode of calculation shall be *set so as to achieve that result.*"[108] (Emphasis added)

As stated in the Commentary under this article,

> "[a]s a general principle, an injured state is entitled to interest on the principal sum representing its loss, if that sum is qualified as at an earlier date than the date of the settlement of, or judgment or award concerning, the claim and to the extent that it is *necessary to ensure full reparation*".[109] (Emphasis added)

It follows that the principle of full reparation should inform all aspects of the issue, i.e., the rate of interest, the date at which interest starts (and stops) accruing, and the application of compound versus simple interest.

Where the parties have agreed these issues, through contract,[110] treaty or investment

---

and US$ 12 million in compound interest).

107. *Illinois Central Railroad Co. (U.S.A.) v. United Mexican States*, Mexico/U.S.A. General Claims Commission, Award of 6 December 1926, *U.N. Reports of International Arbitral Awards*, Vol. IV, at 134-137, 136.

108. The same result is also achieved through the determination of the *dies a quo* and *dies ad quem*: "Interest runs from the date when the principal sum should have been paid until the date the obligation to pay is fulfilled." (Art. 38(2) of the ILC Draft Articles).

109. CRAWFORD, *op. cit.*, fn. 29, Commentary on Art. 38(1), at p. 233.

110. See, e.g., *Autopista Concesionada de Venezuela, C.A. (Aucoven) v. Bolivarian Republic of Venezuela* (ICSID Case No. ARB/00/5 (hereinafter *Aucoven v. Venezuela*)), Award of 23 September 2003 (tribunal composed of Karl-Heinz Böckstiegel, Bernardo M. Cremades and Gabrielle Kaufmann-Kohler acting as president), available at <http://icsid.worldbank.org>. The tribunal applied the

legislation, the tribunal should apply their agreement when awarding damages. However, as noted by several authors, BITs are surprisingly inconsistent in their approach to interest, and often lack sufficiently specific provisions on the question.[111]

*a.   Rate*

Where the rate of interest has not been agreed by the parties, the tribunal is faced with a number of possibilities: the rate that is current in the respondent State, the rate that is current in the investor's State, the rate that is current in the State in whose currency the award is made, one of various available international lending rates, etc. In the absence of any rule of international law fixing the rate of interest,[112] the matter is frequently left for the arbitral tribunal to decide.[113] Arbitral practice does not seem to have settled on any principle in this regard, and most decisions on the rate of interest appear to be fact-driven.

For example, in *Vivendi v. Argentina*, the tribunal rejected the interest rate proposed by the claimants on the grounds that it was "not persuaded that Claimants would have earned 9.7%, compounded, on their respective shares of damages awarded, had such sums been timely paid at the date of Argentina's expropriation of the concession".[114] The tribunal then stated:

> "Having regard to Claimants' business of investing in and operating water concessions, to the anticipated 11.7% rate of return on investment reflected in the Concession Agreement (which the parties had agreed to be appropriate having regard to the nature of the business, the term and the risk involved) and the generally prevailing rates of interest since September 1997, the Tribunal concludes that a 6% interest rate represents a reasonable proxy for the return Claimants could otherwise have earned on the amounts invested and lost in the Tucumán concessions."[115]

---

rate provided for in the contract, which it found not to be prohibited by the law applicable to the merits, namely Venezuelan law (at pp. 102-104, paras. 382-387).

111. See R. DOLZER and M. STEVENS, *op. cit.*, fn. 86, at p. 113. See also G. SACERDOTI, *op. cit.*, fn. 86, at. pp. 403-405.

112. See *Southern Pacific Properties (Middle East) Limited v. Arab Republic of Egypt* (ICSID Case No. ARB/84/3 (hereinafter *SPP v. Egypt*)), Award of 20 May 1992 (tribunal composed of Mohamed Amin El Mahdi, Robert F. Pietrowski and Dr. Eduardo Jimenez de Arechaga) 8 ICSID Rev. – FILJ (1993) p. 390, at para. 222; available at <http://icsid.worldbank.org>.

113. Arbitrators have obviously to take into account the provisions of the applicable law when deciding on the award of interest, in particular where the said law contains a general prohibition of interest. The same law, however, may also provide a way to overcome the prohibition. For example, countries applying the *Shari'a*, under whose general principles the charging of interest is prohibited, in many cases allow legal interest to apply in commercial matters as opposed to civil matters (see Nayla COMAIR-OBEID, "Recovery of Damages for Breach of an Obligation of Payment", in Y. DERAINS and R.H. KREINDLER, eds. *Evaluation of Damages in International Arbitration*, ICC Dossiers (2006) at p. 138 et seq.).

114. *Vivendi, op. cit.*, fn. 5, at pp. 258-259, para. 9.2.7.

115. *Ibid.*, at p. 259, para. 9.2.8.

### b. Date of accrual

With respect to the date of accrual of interest, and in particular the dichotomy between pre- and post-award interest we begin by noting that in cases of unlawful expropriation, where "restitutionary damages" are assessed as from the date of the award, only post-award interest may accrue.[116]

In *AAPL v. Sri Lanka*, the arbitral tribunal found that:

> "The survey of the literature reveals that, in spite of the persisting controversies with regard to cases invoking monetary interest, the case-law elaborated by international arbitral tribunals suggests that in assessing the liability due for losses incurred the interest becomes an integral part of the compensation itself, and should run consequently from the date when the State's international responsibility becomes engaged (cf. R. Lillich, 'Interest in the Law of International Claims', *Essays in Honor of Vade Saario and Toivio Sainio*, (1983), P. 55-56)."[117]

This position met with the approval of the arbitral tribunal in *Metalclad v. Mexico*, which chose among the "*number of factors*" upon which the respondent State's responsibility was founded (denial of a construction permit, administrative and judicial actions, enactment of new regulations), the date it said it was "*reasonable to select*" as the starting date for the accrual of interest.[118]

The award in *Aucuven v. Venezuela*[119] contains a detailed discussion of interest. In that case, the tribunal found that "[i]nterest should generally run from the date on which the principal amount to which it applies became due", which it found to be an approach consistent with both the parties' agreement and the applicable Venezuelan law.[120] As regards the *dies ad quem*, the tribunal in that case dismissed the respondent's argument that claimant was seeking post-award interest on an inflation-adjusted award, which was presumably prohibited under Venezuelan law. The tribunal instead decided that interest should accrue until the day of effective payment:

---

116. See *ADC, op. cit.*, fn. 3, at p. 98, para. 512. Where damages, even for an unlawful taking, are to be properly assessed as of the date of the expropriation (for example, where the expropriated asset loses value after the taking), interest will accrue as from the date of expropriation (see, e.g., *Vivendi, op. cit.*, fn. 5, at p. 257, para. 9.2.3). See also the *Siemens* case, where pre-award interest was granted as from the date each specific loss was suffered.
117. *AAPL v. Sri Lanka, op. cit.*, fn. 41, at p. 571, para. 114.
118. *Metalclad v. Mexico, op. cit.*, fn. 45, at p. 34, para. 128. However, the same tribunal also decided that interest would stop accruing forty-five days from the date on which the award was made, which could either lead to unjust enrichment if Mexico were to pay before that date, or fail to fully compensate Metalclad if Mexico were to pay on a later date. In any case, the requirement of full reparation would not be met. Such a decision is all the more surprising in view of Art. 1110(4) of NAFTA, which provides that "[i]f payment is made in a G7 currency, compensation shall include interest at a commercially reasonable rate for that currency from the date of expropriation until the date of *actual payment*". (Emphasis added)
119. *Op. cit.*, fn.110.
120. *Ibid.* at p. 99, para. 370.

"In the Tribunal's understanding, an 'inflation-adjusted award' bearing the award of *post-award interest* can only be an award indexed for inflation as to the *post-award time*. Indeed, post-award interest is intended to compensate the additional loss incurred from the date of the award to the date of final payment. It bears no relation to the manner in which the Tribunal assesses the damage at the time of the award. From a logical point of view, the fact that the award will take into account the inflation up to the date of the award is irrelevant for the possibility of awarding post-award interest under Venezuelan law."[121] (Emphasis in original)

c.  *Simple v. compound interest*

The most debated issue regarding the award of interest remains the choice between simple and compound interest.

Early tribunals adjudicating claims under public international law generally applied only simple interest. In *Great Britain v. Spain* (Spanish Zone of Morocco), Max Huber observed that :

"*En ce qui concerne le choix entre les intérêts simples et les intérêts composés, le Rapporteur doit tout d'abord constater que la jurisprudence arbitrale en matière de compensations à accorder par un État à un autre pour dommages subis par les ressortissants de celui-ci sur le territoire de celui-là — jurisprudence pourtant particulièrement riche — est* **unanime, pour autant que le Rapporteur le sache, pour écarter les intérêts composés.**"[122] (Emphasis added)

However, he admitted of the possibility of awarding compound interest:

"*Dans ces circonstances, il faudrait des arguments particulièrement forts et de nature toute spéciale pour admettre en l'espèce ce type d'intérêt. Pareils arguments ne sembleraient cependant pas exister, étant donné que les circonstances des réclamations dont le Rapporteur se trouve saisi ne diffèrent pas en principe de celles des cas qui ont donné lieu à la jurisprudence dont il s'agit.*

*Cela est vrai entre autres de certaines éventualités où les intérêts composés sembleraient par ailleurs mieux correspondre à la nature des choses que les intérêts simples, savoir les cas où les biens que les indemnités accordées ont pour but de remplacer s'augmentent par progression géométrique plutôt qu'arithmétique, ce qui arrive par exemple pour les troupeaux de bétail.*"[123]

In an award rendered by an arbitral tribunal established by the governments of France and Peru for the settlement of certain designated claims between the two countries, the arbitral tribunal provided a short explanation for its decision to disallow compound interest: "The capitalization of the interest can result only from a stipulation or from

---

121. *Ibid.* at p. 102, para. 380.
122. *Great Britain v. Spain* (Spanish Zone of Morocco), *U.N. Reports of International Arbitral Awards*, at Vol. II (1924) pp. 615-742, at p. 650.
123. *Ibid.*

circumstances of fact making clear the consent of the debtor to assume such an onerous obligation."[124] This general reluctance to award compound interest, in the absence of special circumstances, was also noted in *R.J. Reynolds Tobacco v. Iran*, where the tribunal failed to find

> "any special reasons for departing from international precedents which normally do not allow the awarding of compound interest. As noted by one authority, '[t]*here are few rules within the scope of the subject of damages in international law that are better settled than the one that compound interest is not allowable....*' Even though the term 'all sums' could be construed to include interest and thereby to allow compound interest, the Tribunal, due to the ambiguity of the language, interprets the clause in the light of the international rule just stated, and thus excludes compound interest."[125] (Emphasis added)

In the *Norwegian Shipowners' Claims* case, the tribunal, while refusing to award compound interest, noted that: "Compound interest has not been granted in previous arbitration cases, and the Tribunal is of the opinion that the claimants have not advanced sufficient reasons why an award of compound interest, in this case, should be made."[126] The tribunal thus implicitly acknowledged that "sufficient reasons" may exist in other cases.[127]

In his concurring opinion in *Starrett Housing*, Holtzmann, J. established a clear link between compound interest and the principle of full reparation:

> "I also believe that in the circumstances of this case interest should be awarded on a compound basis. I reach this conclusion because that is *necessary to make Starrett whole for the actual damage it suffered due to the Respondent's expropriation of its property rights.*"[128] (Emphasis added)

Holtzmann, J. observed:

> "Before the date of taking, the Respondents were fully aware that Starrett was

---

124. SCOTT, The Hague Court Reports (2nd Sect. 1932) p. 32, at p. 35, cited in Marjorie M. WHITEMAN, *Damages in International Law*, Vol. III (United States Government Printing Office, Washington 1943) at p. 2503.
125. *R.J. Reynolds Tobacco Co. v. The Islamic Republic of Iran*, 7 Iran-U.S.C.T.R. (1984) 181, 191-192, citing WHITEMAN, *Damages in International Law*, op. cit., fn. 124.
126. *Norwegian Shipowners' Claims (U.S.A. v. Norway)*, Award of 13 October 1922, *UN Reports of International Arbitral Awards*, Vol. I, 307-346, 341.
127. Some tribunals had in fact awarded compound interest without discussing the appropriateness thereof (see cases referred to in *Santa Elena, S.A. v. The Republic of Costa Rica*, op.cit., fn. 106, in fn. 55 under para. 98, p. 200). Others seem to have applied compound interest without necessarily being aware that they were doing so (see *Sylvania Technical Systems, Inc. v. The Government of the Islamic Republic of Iran*, Award No. 180-64-1 (27 June 1985), reprinted in 8 Iran-U.S.C.T.R. 298).
128. *Starrett Housing Corporation v. The Government of The Islamic Republic of Iran*, Award No. 314-24-1 (14 August 1987), reprinted in 16 Iran-U.S.C.T.R., 112, 251-252.

borrowing money from its U.S. banks on a compound basis in order to finance the Project and provide loans to Shah Goli. Starrett, like most contractors, operated on the basis of back-to-back loans and a substantial line of credit with their banks. It is normal commercial practice that banks customarily charge compound interest to finance such credit facilities."[129]

He further noted that:

"[a]n award of compound interest in this Case would be consistent with international law. The Tribunal has not yet squarely addressed the issue of compound interest. In *R.J. Reynolds Tobacco Co. v. Government of the Islamic Republic of Iran,* Award No. 145-35-3, p. 19011 (6 Aug. 1984), Chamber Three of the Tribunal found that there were no 'special reasons' for departing from international precedents 'which normally do not allow the awarding of compound interest'. The Tribunal relied on a 1943 treatise for the proposition that the rule against compound interest was 'settled'. *Whether or not such a rule existed before 1943, it is no longer appropriate or justifiable."*[130] (Emphasis added)

Holtzmann, J. concluded as follows:

"Modern economic reality, as well as equity, demand that injured parties who have themselves suffered actual compound interest charges be compensated on a compound basis in order to be made whole. International tribunals and respected commentators have come to recognize this principle; it is unfortunate that the Final Award does not."[131]

After Holtzmann, J.'s opinion in *Starrett Housing,* several authors expressed their support for the award of compound interest in light of modern economic conditions. Professor Mann explained:

"In this spirit it is necessary first to take account of modern economic conditions. It is a fact of universal experience that those who have a surplus of funds normally invest them to earn compound interest. On the other hand, many are compelled to borrow from banks and therefore must pay compound interest. This applies, in particular, to business people whose own funds are frequently invested in brick and mortar, machinery and equipment, and whose working capital is obtained by way of loans or overdrafts from banks."[132]

---

129. *Ibid.*
130. *Ibid.*, at p.253.
131. *Ibid.*, at p. 254.
132. F.A. MANN, "Compound Interest as an Item of Damage in International Law", 21 Univ. of California, Davis L.R. (1988, no. 3) p. 577, at p. 585.

Professor Mann also expressly referred to the need to provide *restitutio in integrum* when determining the appropriate amount of interest:

> "If, in accordance with the usual formula, damages are intended to afford *restitutio in integrum* (complete compensation for the wrong suffered) such items of damage should not be excluded. One is not dealing with the payment or repayment of liquidated sums such as the price of goods or a loan or even arrears of agreed interest due in respect of a loan; in such circumstances the general practice of municipal laws or courts does not normally allow the payment of more than simple interest. But as soon as any liability for damages arises, different considerations apply and demand the elimination, by the payment of money, of all foreseeable injuries."[133]

The same position was adopted by Professor Gotanda, who observed that

> "[a]lmost all financing and investment vehicles involve compound interest.... If the Claimant could have received compound interest merely by placing its money in a readily available and commonly used investment vehicle, it is neither logical nor equitable to award the Claimant only simple interest."[134] (Emphasis added)

That awarding interest contributes to fully compensating the investor for its loss was clearly expressed in the *Wena* arbitration. In that case, the arbitral tribunal held that, although capitalized interest is not available under Egyptian law, "compounded interest will best restore the Claimant to a reasonable approximation of the position in which it would have been if the wrongful act had not taken place".[135]

The tribunal, drawing support from both Professor Gotanda's and Professor Mann's opinions, said the following: "This Tribunal believes that an award of compound (as opposed to simple) interest is generally appropriate in most modern, commercial arbitrations."[136] The tribunal's award was challenged in an annulment proceeding. In answer to the specific complaint by Egypt regarding this part of the award,[137] the ad hoc committee reasoned as follows:

---

133. *Ibid.*, at p. 585.
134. John Y. GOTANDA, "Awarding Interest in International Arbitration", 90 Amer. J. Int'l L., (1996) p. 40 at p. 61.
135. *Wena Hotels v. Egypt* (ICSID Case No. ARB/98/4), Award of 8 December 2000 (tribunal composed of Ibrahim Fadlallah, Don Wallace, Jr. and Monroe Leigh acting as president) 41 I.L.M. (2002) 896, at para. 129, citing from *Metalclad v. Mexico*. This solution is to be compared with the tribunal's holding in *SPP v. Egypt*, where compound interest was refused under the contract governed by Egyptian law and awarded under the contract governed by English law (*SPP v. Egypt, op. cit.*, fn. 112, at p. 390, et seq., paras. 220, et seq.).
136. *Wena Hotels v. Egypt, op. cit.*, fn. 135, at para. 129 (footnotes omitted).
137. Egypt argued that in failing to apply Egyptian law to the issue of interest, the tribunal had manifestly failed to apply the applicable law and thus manifestly exceeded its powers.

"Compensation must be, first, 'prompt, adequate and effective' and second, 'compensation shall amount to the market value of the investment expropriated immediately before the expropriation itself'. Although not referring to interest, the provision [of the BIT dealing with expropriation] must be read as including a determination of interest that is compatible with those two principles. In particular, the compensation must not be eroded by the passage of time or by the diminution in the market value. The award of interest that reflects such international business practices meets these two objectives.

The option the Tribunal took was in the view of this Committee within the Tribunal's power. International law and ICSID practice, unlike the Egyptian Civil Code, offer a variety of alternatives that are compatible with those objectives. These alternatives include the compounding of interest in some cases. Whether among the many alternatives available under such practice the Tribunal chose the most appropriate in the circumstances of the case is not for this Committee to say as such matter belongs to the merits of the decision. Moreover, this is a discretionary decision of the Tribunal. Even if it were established that the Tribunal did not rely on the appropriate criteria this in itself would not amount to a manifest excess of power leading to annulment."[138]

In *Santa Elena v. Costa Rica*, the arbitral tribunal observed:

"Even though there is a tendency in international jurisprudence to award only simple interest, this is manifested principally in relation to cases of injury or simple breach of contract. The same considerations do not apply to cases relating to the valuation of property or property rights. In cases such as the present, compound interest is not excluded where it is warranted by the circumstances of the case."[139]

The tribunal justified this statement on the basis of earlier decisions and scholarly writings, and went on to state:

"While simple interest tends to be awarded more frequently than compound, compound interest certainly is not unknown or excluded in international law. No uniform rule of law has emerged from the practice in international arbitration as regards the determination of whether compound or simple interest is appropriate in any given case. Rather, the determination of whether compound or simple interest is a product of the exercise of judgment, taking into account all of the circumstances of the case at hand and especially considerations of fairness which must form part of the law to be applied by this Tribunal.

In particular, where an owner of property has at some earlier time lost the value of his asset but has not received the monetary equivalent that then became

---

138. *Wena Hotels v. Egypt* (ICSID Case No. ARB/98/4), Ad Hoc Committee Decision of 5 February 2002, at paras. 52-53.
139. *Santa Elena v. Costa Rica*, op. cit., fn. 106, at p. 200, para. 97 (footnotes omitted).

due to him, the amount of compensation should reflect, at least in part, the additional sum that his money would have earned, had it, and the income generated by it, been reinvested each year at generally prevailing rates of interest. It is not the purpose of compound interest to attribute blame to, or to punish, anybody for the delay in the payment made to the expropriated owner, it is a mechanism to ensure that the compensation awarded the claimant is appropriate in the circumstances."[140]

Even though the *Santa Elena* case involved extreme circumstances (the investor had not been able to either use or sell its property for almost twenty-two years), the tribunal's decision in that case was nonetheless cited with approval by the arbitral tribunal sitting in *MTD Chile*, which considered that: "Compound interest is more in accordance with the reality of financial transactions and a closer approximation to the actual value lost by an investor."[141] The tribunal in *Azurix v. Argentina* likewise considered that compound interest reflects the reality of financial transactions, and best approximates the value lost by an investor.[142]

In *Tecmed*, the tribunal held that "application of compound interest is justified as part of the integral compensation owed to the Claimant as a result of the loss of its investment".[143]

Even more explicitly, although not dealing with an expropriation, the tribunal in *BG v. Argentina* held that "[t]he standard of 'full reparation' articulated in Section X.A above [citing the *Chorzów Factory* standard, as well as ILC Draft Articles endorsing it] would not be achieved if the award were to deprive Claimant of compound interest."[144]

In the *Aucoven* case, the tribunal first examined the interest issue under Venezuelan

---

140. *Ibid.* at p. 202, paras. 103-104.
141. *MTD Equity San Bhd and MTD Chile SA v. Chile* (ICSID Case No. ARB/01/7 (hereinafter *MTD Chile*)), Award of 25 May 2004 (tribunal composed of Rodrigo Oreamuno, Marc Lalonde and Andrés Rigo Sureda acting as president) at p. 92 para. 251, available at <www.asil.org/ilib/MTDvChile.pdf>. See also *LG&E v. Argentina*, Award of 25 July 2007, *op. cit.*, fn. 57, at p. 29, para. 103: "the Tribunal is of the opinion that compound interest would better compensate the Claimants for the actual damages suffered since it better reflects contemporary financial practice".
142. *Azurix Corp. v. Argentine Republic* (ICSID Case No. ARB/01/12 (hereinafter *Azurix v. Argentina* or *Azurix*)), Award of 14 July 2006 (tribunal composed of Daniel H. Martins, Marc Lalonde and Andrés Rigo Sureda acting as president) available at <http://icsid.worldbank.org>, at p. 157, para. 440.
143. *Tecmed*, *op. cit.*, fn. 51, at p. 79, para. 196. This citation was notably referred to in the recent award rendered on 8 May 2008 in the ICSID Case No. ARB/98/2, *Victor Pey Casado et Fondation Presidente Allende v. Republic of Chile*, (tribunal composed of Mohammed Chemloul, Emmanuel Gaillard and Pierre Lalive acting as president), available at: <http://ita.law.uvic.ca/documents/Peyaward.pdf>, which also awarded compound interest, this time in a case of denial of justice (see p. 227, paras. 715-716).
144. *BG Group plc v. The Republic of Argentina* (UNCITRAL), (tribunal composed of Alejandro M. Garro, Albert Jan van den Berg and Guillermo Aguilar Alvarez acting as president), Final Award of 27 December 2007, available at <http://ita.law.uvic.ca/documents/BG-award_000.pdf>, at p. 135, para. 456.

law and under the relevant contractual provisions (neither of which, the tribunal decided, provided for compound interest). It then examined the issue under international law, upon which the claimant had relied. On the basis of the two cases advanced by the claimant, i.e., *Wena Hotels v. Egypt* and *Santa Elena v. Costa Rica*, the tribunal concluded that:

> "These two ICSID precedents are sufficient in and of themselves to demonstrate that there is no well established principle of international law requiring the award of compound interest in the present case.... Aucoven's submission that international law requires an award of compound interest must thus be rejected."[145]

It is noted that *Aucoven* was a "simple breach of contract" case, not an expropriation case, a distinction which was emphasized by the tribunal in *Santa Elena v. Costa Rica* and expressly cited by the *Aucoven* tribunal.

Although the tribunal in *CME v. Czech Republic* (a case which did involve an expropriation claim) refused to award compound interest, it did so in part because of the already high interest rate that applied under Czech law (ten percent p.a.).[146] The tribunal found that Czech law only allowed an award of simple interest, absent an agreement to the contrary, and further stated that

> "in accord with international law principles and international arbitration practice, the Tribunal does not award compound interest since the purpose of compensation – to 'fully' compensate the damage sustained – in this case does not require the awarding of compound interest, having regard to the generous interest provision of the Czech statute".[147]

It is for these reasons that some commentators submit that the *CME* case supports the position that compound interest should be awarded in cases of expropriation.[148]

The *ADC* tribunal was clearly of the view that it should award compound interest, following the "current trend in investor-State arbitration".[149]

> "As to post-Award interest, contrary to Respondent's submission, the current trend in investor-State arbitration is to award compound interest. Respondent relies on the statement "[t]*here are few rules within the scope of the subject of damages*

---

145. *Aucoven v. Venezuela, op. cit.*, fn. 110, at p. 106, paras. 395-396 (footnotes omitted).
146. *C.M.E. Czech Republic B.V. v. The Czech Republic* (UNCITRAL (hereinafter *CME v. Czech Republic* or *CME*)), Final Award of 14 March 2003 (tribunal composed of Stephen M. Schwebel, Ian Brownlie and Wolfgang Kühn acting as chairman) available at <http://ita.law.uvic.ca/documents/CME-2003-Final_001.pdf>, at p. 158 et seq., paras. 642 et seq.
147. *Ibid.*, at p. 159, para. 643.
148. See C. MCLACHLAN QC, L. SHORE, M. WEINIGER, *International Investment Arbitration: Substantive Principles* (Oxford International Arbitration Series 2007) at p. 345, para. 9.132.
149. *ADC, op. cit.*, fn. 3, at p. 99, para. 522.

in international law that are better settled than the one that compound interest is not allowable" by Marjorie Whiteman in damages in International Law (1943) Vol. III at 1997. While the Iran-U.S. Claims Tribunal echoed Ms. Whiteman's statement, tribunals in investor-State arbitrations in recent times have recognized economic reality by awarding compound interest (see, e.g., *Middle East Cement Shipping Co. S.A. v. Arab Republic of Egypt*, Final Award, 12 April 2002, ICSID Case No. ARB/99/6, at paras. 174-175). In paragraph 104 of the award in *Compañía del Desarrollo de Santa Elena S.A. v. Republic of Costa Rica* (ICSID Case No. ARB/96/1), the Tribunal recognized that the reason for compound interest was not "*to attribute blame to, or punish, anybody for the delay in the payment made to the expropriated owner; it is a mechanism to ensure that the compensation awarded the Claimant is appropriate in the circumstances*". Accordingly, the Tribunal determines that interest is to be compounded on a monthly basis in the present case." (Italics in original)

This was also the position of the tribunal in the *Vivendi* case, which similarly held that "To the extent there has been a tendency of international tribunals to award only simple interest, this is changing, and the award of compound interest is no longer the exception to the rule."[150] Some contemporary authors remain critical of the award of compound interest.[151] However, as noted by others: "If the rule in state-to-state disputes is against compound interest, this is perhaps one area where investment treaty arbitration is developing its own practice. While there is no unanimity, many tribunals have been prepared to award compound interest."[152]

2. *The Apportionment of Arbitration Costs: The Last Frontier?*

a. Introduction

The costs involved in bringing or defending investment claims are substantial and, by all accounts, are only rising over time.

Arbitration costs now effectively comprise an investment in and of themselves, which parties must take into account when deciding whether and how to pursue legal recourses and which they must factor into business plans and budgets. Such is the size of the "investment" in arbitration costs frequently required, and such is the need for external sources of funds by parties to investment disputes, that an entire industry has developed for third-party financing of investment claims.

Nor is this development felt solely by parties. Counsel are pressed to elaborate detailed estimates and budgets, work under contingency fee arrangements and provide

---

150. *Vivendi, op. cit.*, fn. 5, at p. 257, para. 9.2.4. The tribunal notably referred to a review of recent ICSID decisions, which showed that eight granted compound interest, two did not disclose the calculation method used and one did not grant interest (J. GRAY, J. CAIN and W. WILSON, "ICSID Arbitration Awards and Cost", III TDM (December 2006, no. 5)).
151. C.N. BROWER and J.K. SHARPE, "Awards of Compound Interest in International Arbitration: The Aminoil Non-Precedent" in G. AKSEN, et al., eds., *Global Reflections on International Law, Commerce and Dispute Resolution: Liber Amicorum in Honour of Robert Briner* (2005) p. 155, at p. 156.
152. C. MCLACHLAN, QC, L. SHORE, M. WEINIGER, *op. cit.*, fn. 148, at p. 344, para. 9.125.

regular financial updates to their clients and the latter's financiers. And, significantly, arbitrators are expected to consider and determine cost claims with the same care as all other claims in the arbitration – as well they should, given the amounts involved.

In principle, the costs of enforcing or defending legal rights ought not to be an impediment either to an investor wishing to advance meritorious claims against a host State, or to a State required to defend itself, especially against claims it considers spurious. Yet the scale of the costs associated with investment arbitration, and the manner in which such costs are treated by tribunals, may act as just such an impediment.

In this section we examine briefly the treatment of arbitration costs by international tribunals, and explore what is perhaps "the last frontier" remaining to be conquered by the principle of full reparation.

Our argument is that if the concept of full reparation is to have real meaning, there is a solid case to be made for international tribunals to address costs claims on the same basis as they address the parties' substantive claims regarding compensation, that is, with a view to "… as far as possible, wipe out all the consequences of the illegal act and re-establish the situation which would, in all probability, have existed if that act had not been committed".[153] In other words, there is a case for treating the arbitration costs incurred by a claimant who is found to have suffered damages at the hands of a State (or vice versa) as being among the "natural, normal and predictable consequences of the damage inflicted".[154]

Our conclusion is that international tribunals do not generally view the issue in this light, and that even where some form of "loser pays" approach is adopted, full reparation is not, at least not yet, accepted or expressed as the basis for such an allocation of costs. As noted above, there indeed remains "a lively debate" with respect to the issue.

b.   From "No rule" to the "American rule"

Until relatively recently, it was generally understood that there was no established principle discernible in international arbitration theory or practice as regards the apportionment of costs, at least as far as international *commercial* arbitration was concerned.[155] Cloaked in the broad discretion conferred on them by most international

---

153. *Chorzów Factory (Claim for Indemnity)* (Merits), *op. cit.*, fn. 1, at p. 47.
154. G. SCHWARZENBERGER, *op. cit.*, fn. 21, at p. 670.
155. For a detailed analysis, see John Yukio GOTANDA, "Awarding Costs and Attorneys' Fees in International Commercial Arbitration", 21 Michigan Journal of International Law (1999) at pp. 1-50. See also Yves DERAINS and Eric A. SCHWARTZ's analysis of a survey conducted by the ICC Court's Secretariat in 1991: "It can be seen that arbitrators have adopted a variety of approaches in allocating costs in ICC arbitrations, often depending on their own national biases, the substantive outcome of the arbitration and also the behaviour of the parties, e.g., in some cases allowing for honest differences of opinion over difficult issues and in others penalizing bad faith or uncooperative behaviour. Whatever the ultimate decision, however, the arbitrators have normally been expected by the Court to provide reasons for their decisions, in accordance with Article 25(2)." (*A Guide to the ICC Rules of Arbitration*, 2nd edn. (Kluwer Law International 2005) at pp. 373-374). This survey showed that, even in those cases where the claimant won all or most of what he had claimed, and although the respondent was generally ordered to bear all or most of the arbitrators' fees and expenses and the ICC administrative fees, the claimant was only reimbursed its own costs in 50 percent of those cases (*ibid.*, at pp. 371-373).

arbitration statutes or rules (whether the rules of arbitral institutions such as ICSID or the ICC, or ad hoc rules such as the UNCITRAL Arbitration Rules), arbitrators might cite their extensive discretionary authority, refer in the most general terms to the "circumstances of the case", and then decide the matter as they considered "just and reasonable" by applying either the "costs follow the event" approach or the so-called "American rule" under which each party bears its own costs and shares equally the costs of the tribunal and any institution.

As Professor Gotanda observed, as recently as in 1999

> "[i]t is impossible to identify any general practice as to the treatment of costs in international commercial arbitrations. Moreover, the methods used by arbitrators to award costs and fees have led to inconsistent and arbitrary awards. In similar cases, arbitrators have reached different conclusions on whether costs and fees should be awarded and, in cases where they are awarded, there is no consensus on the amount of costs and fees that should be paid to the prevailing party."[156]

Experience in recent years suggests that international tribunals in commercial cases are perhaps less reluctant than previously to apply the "costs follow the event" approach, with some authors now venturing that "in commercial arbitration, it is common for the tribunal to order the losing party to pay the costs incurred by the winning party".[157]

However, this trend – if one can truly be said to exist, which these authors believe remains to be established – clearly has yet to extend to the realm of investment arbitration.

For example, in his Separate Opinion in *Thunderbird v. Mexico*, Professor Thomas Wälde expressed the widely held view that there is

> "a well established NAFTA and ICSID jurisprudence consisting in letting each party, winning or losing, bear its own legal expenses and share the costs of arbitration short of clear evidence of either gross professional misconduct on the part of a party in arbitration or a manifestly spurious claim".[158]

In investment cases, tribunals generally appear still to prefer the American rule, absent

---

156. J.Y. GOTANDA, *op. cit.*, fn. 134, at p. 24, citing A. REDFERN and M. HUNTER, *Law and Practice of International Commercial Arbitration*, 2nd edn. (1991) fn. 134, at p. 407.
157. C. MCLACHLAN QC, L. SHORE, M. WEINIGER, *op. cit.*, fn. 148, at p. 346, para. 9.134.
158. *International Thunderbird Gaming Corporation v. The United Mexican States* (NAFTA (UNCITRAL)) (hereinafter *Thunderbird v. Mexico* or *Thunderbird*), Award of 26 January 2006, (tribunal composed of Agustín Portal Ariosa, Thomas W. Wälde (dissenting as to each party bearing its own costs) and Albert Jan van den Berg acting as president); Professor Wälde's separate opinion is available at <www.naftaclaims.com>, at p. 116. Professor Wälde refers in his opinion to the analysis contained in W. Ben HAMIDA, "Cost Issue in Investor-State Arbitration Decisions Rendered Against the Investor: a Synthetic Table", in 2 TDM (November 2005, no. 5) showing that in nineteen out of twenty-six cases where the investor was the losing party, the arbitrators decided that each party should bear its own costs and that the arbitration costs (including the arbitrators' fees) should be borne in equal parts by each party.

circumstances manifestly justifying a departure from that approach, on the ground that there exists no rule requiring that costs follow the event.[159]

There are, to be sure, political factors at play in investment arbitration – factors that do not exist in commercial cases – which militate against a "loser pays" approach where a State is found to have breached its obligations toward a foreign investor. Among other things, condemning a State to pay the investor's costs can be perceived as a particularly egregious slight, "adding insult to injury", which is delicate where sovereign interests are concerned. Investment arbitration, in particular under the ICSID Convention, has been the target of a number of critics, especially though not exclusively from developing countries.[160] Adding to the potential burden incurred by States when submitting to the jurisdiction of international tribunals could result in turning them against international arbitration altogether. Tribunals can therefore be faced with the difficult task of upholding an investor's rights while evidencing a degree of respectful diplomacy toward the wrongdoer, in part for the sake of the viability of the system as a whole.

There are as well other legitimate policy considerations that militate in favour of something less than a pure "loser pays" (or, "winner takes all") approach to apportioning costs. In his Dissenting Opinion in *S.D. Myers v. Canada*, Professor Bryan P. Schwartz noted that there exist considerations which "to some extent mitigate the application of the principle that the investor should be compensated fully for the losses it has sustained as a direct result of breach of Chapter 11".[161] In Professor Schwartz's words:

> "[i]n many legal systems, such as Canada's, even an entirely successful party does not recover all of its actual legal representation costs. The system provides less than full indemnity for legal costs incurred by a successful party. It aims to encourage even a party that is fully in the right to settle its case, rather than

---

159. See, e.g., *Salini Costruttori S.p.A. and Italstrade S.p.A. v. Kingdom of Morocco* (ICSID Case No. ARB/00/4), Decision on Jurisdiction of 23 July 2001(tribunal composed of Bernardo M. Cremades, Ibrahim Fadlallah and Robert Briner acting as president) 129 JDI (2002) p. 196; *Parkerings-Compagniet AS v. The Republic of Lithuania* (ICSID Case No. ARB/05/8), Award of 11 September 2007 (tribunal composed of Julian D.M. Lew, Marc Lalonde and Laurent Lévy acting as president) available at <http://icsid.worldbank.org>: "There is no rule in international arbitration that costs must follow the event. Thus, the question of costs is within the discretion of the Tribunal with regard, on the one hand, to the outcome of the proceedings and, on the other hand, to other relevant factors." (at p. 95, para. 462).
160. Bolivia's denunciation of the ICSID Convention on 2 May 2007, which it had announced in late April 2007, is only the most dramatic example of these critics and shows that the Calvo doctrine still finds support in some countries. Nicaragua and Venezuela also announced in April 2007 that they could – like Bolivia – denounce the ICSID Convention. Along the same lines, Ecuador notified the Centre, on 4 December 2007, that it does not consent to ICSID jurisdiction for disputes relating to the exploitation of natural resources, such as oil, gas or minerals.
161. *S.D. Myers v. Canada*, op. cit., fn. 47, Final Award on Costs of 30 December 2002, (tribunal composed of Bryan P. Schwartz, Edward C. Chiasson and J. Martin Hunter acting as president) Dissenting Opinion of Professor Schwartz, at p. 6, para. 17.

litigating it to the bitter end. It would seem reasonable for international arbitration panels to adopt this approach generally, including in the context of Chapter 11 cases."[162]

c.   *Potential cracks in the wall: Apportionment of costs in investment arbitration*
Professor Schwartz's dissenting views notwithstanding, in its 2002 Final Award on Costs, the tribunal in *S.D. Myers v. Canada* did depart from the American rule and apportioned costs in part on the basis of "the Majority's perception of the relative 'success', or 'lack of success', of each of the Disputing Parties in the two principal stages of the arbitration".[163]

It did so, however, having expressed the opinion that

> "The purpose of an award of costs is not to punish a respondent for the conduct that made it liable to the claimant. If punishment or dissuasion for that conduct were appropriate, this would be dealt with by an award of damages, not an award in respect of the costs of the proceedings. So far as conduct of the parties may properly be taken into account, the Majority considers that this must be conduct in the initiation of the proceedings, or while they are in progress."[164]

No mention here of *reparation*. Indeed, it would seem that the majority in *SD Meyers* did not consider that reparation (or punishment or dissuasion) plays a role in assessing costs claims, since it found that the only conduct of the parties that may be "properly taken into account" in assessing costs – as opposed to damages – is "conduct in the initiation of the proceedings or while they are in progress".

Similarly, although the majority in *Thunderbird* was fully prepared to depart from the American rule, according to which each party bears its own legal expenses and shares the costs of the arbitration, it did not go so far as to state that the rationale for doing so was to repair any harm:

> "It is also debated whether 'the loser pays' (or 'costs follow the event') rule should be applied in international investment arbitration. It is indeed true that in many cases, notwithstanding the fact that the investor is not the prevailing party, the investor is not condemned to pay the costs of the government. The Tribunal fails to grasp the rationale of this view, except in the case of an investor with limited financial resources where considerations of access to justice may play a role. Barring that, it appears to the Tribunal that the same rules should apply to international investment arbitration as apply in other international arbitration proceedings."[165]

---

162. *Ibid.*, Dissenting Opinion of Professor Schwartz, at p. 6, para. 18.
163. *Ibid.*, Majority Opinion, at p. 17, para. 49; at p. 16, paras. 45-46.
164. *Ibid.*, Majority Opinion, at p. 16, paras. 45-46.
165. *Thunderbird, op. cit.*, fn. 158, at p. 70, para. 214. On that basis, and in view of the fact that Mexico had lost on the issues of jurisdiction and admissibility, the tribunal decided to allocate the costs three-quarters Mexico – one-quarter investor.

That said, in the earlier case of *Azinian v. Mexico*, the tribunal had this to say about the *possibility* of awarding costs against an unsuccessful claimant for reasons of both "reparation" and "dissuasion":

> "The claim has failed in its entirety. The Respondent has been put to considerable inconvenience. In ordinary circumstances it is common in international arbitral proceedings that a losing claimant is ordered to bear the costs of the arbitration, as well as to contribute to the prevailing Respondent's reasonable costs of representation. This practice serves the dual function of reparation and dissuasion."[166]

Nonetheless, after considering a number of circumstances, some truly particular to the case, some arguably not, the *Azinian* tribunal ultimately decided not to make any award of costs.[167]

In *Methanex*, another case in which the claimant was unsuccessful, the tribunal found no reason to depart from the first sentence of Art. 40(1) of the UNCITRAL Rules and accordingly decided that Methanex should bear the costs of the arbitration.[168] As regards the disputing parties' legal costs, the tribunal noted that

---

166. *Robert Azinian, Kenneth Davitian & Ellen Baca v. The United Mexican States* (ICSID Case No. ARB(AF)/497/2 (NAFTA)), Award of 1 November 1999 (tribunal composed of Benjamin R. Civiletti, Claus von Wobeser and Jan Paulsson acting as president), available at <http://ita.law.uvic.ca/documents/Azinian-English.pdf>, at para. 125. It is noted that the tribunal in *S.D. Meyers* opined that for purposes of assessing costs, cases such as *Azinian* in which the claimant is unsuccessful are to be distinguished from those in which the claimant is successful and the State is found to be at fault.

167. Those factors included *"the particular circumstances of the case"*, i.e., the fact that NAFTA is "a new and novel mechanism for the resolution of international investment disputes", and that, as a consequence "the legal constraints on such causes of action were unfamiliar"; that "the respondent may be said to some extent to have invited litigation"; and that "the persons most accountable for the Claimants' wrongful behavior would be the least likely to be affected by an award of costs". (*Ibid.*, at paras. 126-127).

168. *Methanex Corporation v. United States of America* (NAFTA UNCITRAL)) (hereinafter *Methanex v. USA* or *Methanex*)), Final Award of 9 August 2005 (tribunal composed of J. William F. Rowley, W. Michael Reisman and V.V. Veeder acting as president) available at <www.naftaclaims.com>, Part V – Arbitration and Legal Costs, para. 5, p. 2. Art. 40(1) and (2) of the UNCITRAL Rules reads:

> "1. Except as provided in paragraph 2, the costs of arbitration shall in principle be borne by the unsuccessful party. However, the arbitral tribunal may apportion each of such costs between the parties if it determines that apportionment is reasonable, taking into account the circumstances of the case.
> 2. With respect to the costs of legal representation and assistance referred to in Article 38, paragraph (e), the arbitral tribunal, taking into account the circumstances of the case, shall be free to determine which party shall bear such costs or may apportion such costs between the parties if it determines that apportionment is reasonable."

"The practices of international tribunals vary widely. Certain tribunals are reluctant to order the unsuccessful party to pay the costs of the successful party's legal representation unless the successful party has prevailed over a manifestly spurious position taken by the unsuccessful party. Other arbitral tribunals consider that the successful party should not normally be left out of pocket in respect of the legal costs reasonably incurred in enforcing or defending its legal rights.

In the present case, the Tribunal favours the approach taken by the Disputing Parties themselves, namely that as a general principle the successful party should be paid its reasonable legal costs by the unsuccessful party."[169]

Methanex was therefore ordered to pay the United States the amount of its "legal costs reasonably incurred in these arbitration proceedings".[170]

An intermediate approach was adopted by the tribunal in *Azurix v. Argentina*, in 2006, in which Argentina was ordered to bear the arbitration costs while each party bore its own legal costs and fees.[171]

Similarly, in *Vivendi v. Argentina*, the tribunal ordered the parties to share the arbitration costs equally and to bear their own legal and other costs incurred during the *substantive* phase of the proceedings, but ordered the State to reimburse claimants their reasonable legal and other costs incurred during the *jurisdictional* phase of the proceedings.[172]

The decision in *Siemens* provides a further illustration of the lack of consensus among international arbitrators on the correct approach to allocating costs. The majority decided that each party should bear its own legal costs and that seventy-five percent of the fees and expenses of the tribunal and costs of the ICSID Secretariat should be borne by Argentina.[173] However, in his Separate Opinion, Professor Domingo Bello Janeiro stated:

"In my humble opinion always also in agreement with prevailing arbitration practice, I consider that the costs of the proceedings should be allocated equally,

---

169. *Methanex*, op cit., fn. 168, at pp. 3-4, paras. 9-10.
170. *Ibid.*, at p. 4, para. 12. See also (italics in original) *Československa obchodní banka, a.s. v. Slovak Republic* (ICSID Case No. ARB/97/4), Final Award of 29 December 2004, available at <http://ita.law.uvic.ca/ documents/Cesk-Slovakia-AwardDec2004.pdf>, at pp. 126-127, paras. 369-372, another recent case in which the tribunal ordered the Slovak Republic to contribute US$ 10 million to CSOB's costs.
171. *Azurix v. Argentina*, op. cit., fn. 142, at pp. 157-158, para. 441.
172. The tribunal observed that the arguments and issues in dispute were "important, complex and relatively novel". It then referred to the fact that claimants had "succeeded substantially in both the jurisdictional and substantive phases of these proceedings", while respondent had "on a number of occasions sought to reargue jurisdictional issues that had previously been determined by the Tribunal, the Original Tribunal and the ad hoc Committee", which "unnecessarily extended and added considerably to the costs of these proceedings". *Vivendi*, op. cit., fn. 5, at p. 262, para. 10.2.4, at pp. 262-263, para. 10.2.5.
173. *Siemens*, op. cit., fn. 4, at p. 127, para. 402.

unless under exceptional circumstances. In this case, neither Claimant has prevailed in all of its claims, nor have there been exceptional circumstances."[174]

Perhaps the clearest and least equivocal statements by an arbitral tribunal of the link between an award of costs and the principle of full reparation – the high-water mark, as it were – is found in *ADC*. In that case, as noted above, the tribunal held that "*were the Claimants not reimbursed their costs in justifying what they alleged to be egregious conduct on the part of Hungary it could not be said that they were being made whole*".[175] (Emphasis added)

It is noted that the tribunal in ADC reached this conclusion after having observed that "it can be seen from previous awards that ICSID arbitrators do in practice award costs in favour of the successful party and sometimes in large sums (see for example *CSOB v. Slovakia* – US$10 million)". The tribunal also cited "a recent article titled *Treaty Arbitration and Investment Dispute: Adding up the Costs* by M. Weiniger & M. Page, and 2006 1:3 Global Arb. Rev. 44), [in which] the authors state that '*[r]ecently ... some tribunals [in investment arbitration] have adopted a more robust approach, seeing no reason to depart from the principle that the successful party should have its costs paid by the unsuccessful party, as adopted in commercial arbitration*'". (Italics in original)

However, as the foregoing discussion illustrates, many if not most of the "previous awards" of "some tribunals" that have in fact "adopted a more robust approach" and awarded costs "in favour of the successful party", do not in fact explicitly link such awards with the principle of full reparation. As Weiniger and Page accurately summarize, in deciding to allocate costs the motivation frequently expressed most clearly by tribunals in investment arbitrations is the desire to adhere to an approach "adopted in commercial arbitration". Whatever the true intentions of the tribunals in question, allocating costs expressly as a means of ensuring that a damaged party is "made whole" – as in *ADC* – is not the norm among international tribunals in investment cases.

*d. Conclusion*

We began this section by suggesting that the case law indicates that the principle of "full reparation" is not generally accepted by international arbitral tribunals as a basis on which to apportion costs in investment disputes, and that a debate endures in this regard.

One could go further and argue that the case law does not even reveal a consensus as to the appropriateness of the "loser pays" rule; and that even where tribunals do order arbitration costs – including legal costs – to be paid by the unsuccessful party, it is not always clear that they do so motivated by a desire to effect reparation. On the contrary, when it comes to determining the proper grounds for apportioning costs, it appears that there exist almost as many opinions among arbitrators serving on the same tribunal, as among different tribunals.

Whether or not international tribunals ultimately rally around the notion that arbitration costs are among the "natural, normal and predictable consequences" of damage inflicted, that an award of costs "serves the function" of reparation, and that

---

174. *Ibid.*, Separate Opinion of Professor Domingo Bello Janeiro dated 30 January 2007, available at <http://ita.law.uvic.ca/documents/Siemens-Argentina-Opinion.pdf>.
175. *ADC, op. cit.*, fn. 3, at p. 101, para. 533.

absent such an award "it could not be said that [an aggrieved party] were being made whole" remains to be seen.

V. CONCLUSION

We started our discussion by asking whether the differentiated standard articulated by the PCIJ in the *Chorzów Factory* case some eighty years ago had finally been accepted as part of customary international law.

On 24 July 2008, while this paper was being finalized, the arbitral tribunal sitting in the *BGT v. Tanzania* case seemed to take it for granted, as it directly referred to the ILC's "codification of the rules of customary international law on the responsibility of States for their internationally wrongful acts",[176] which it expressed, as regards compensation for unlawful expropriation, as follows:

> "The standard of compensation for unlawful expropriation (being the relevant claim here), includes full reparation for, and consequential losses suffered as a result of, the unlawful expropriation. Full reparation entitles the unlawfully expropriated investor to restitutionary damages which include, but are not limited to, the fair market value of the unlawfully expropriated investment as determined by the application of an appropriate valuation methodology. In addition, the unlawfully expropriated investor is entitled to damages for the consequential losses suffered as a result of the unlawful expropriation. Such losses ordinarily include an entitlement to loss of profits suffered by the investor between the date of expropriation and the award."[177]

---

176. *Biwater Gauff (Tanzania) Ltd. v. United Republic of Tanzania* (ICSID Case No. Arb/05/22), Award (tribunal composed of Gary Born, Toby Landau QC and Bernard Hanotiau acting as president) at para. 773. The reference to the *Chorzów Factory* case was only made explicitly in the context of claims other than expropriation, for which the "broad principle articulated" by the PCIJ (i.e., the need for an award to "'as far as possible wipe-out all the consequences of the illegal act and re-establish the situation which would, in all probability, have existed if that act had not been committed'") was found to be "the common starting point" (*ibid.* at para. 776).
177. *Ibid.* at para. 775. Although the respondent was found to have unlawfully expropriated the claimant's assets, no damages were granted for lack of causation, as the majority found, or because the injury caused had "no quantifiable monetary value", as G. Born stated in his concurring and dissenting opinion (available at <http://icsid.worldbank.org>, at para. 23).

# Working Group A

## 6. The Enforcement of Investment Treaty Awards: Getting to Judgment

# Annulment and Enforcement Review of Treaty Awards: To ICSID or Not to ICSID

*Gaëtan Verhoosel**

TABLE OF CONTENTS | Page
--- | ---
I. The Investor's Choice | 285
II. Annulment Review: How Sharp is the Sword? | 286
III. Enforcement Review: How Strong is the Shield? | 310
IV. Conclusion | 317

I. THE INVESTOR'S CHOICE

A large number of investment treaties in force today offer the investor a choice between two or more procedural options when that investor decides to seek relief through international arbitration under such treaties. Typically the choice will be between a tribunal operating under the ICSID Rules, on the one hand, and a tribunal operating under the Rules of the ICSID Additional Facility, UNCITRAL, the Arbitration Institute of the Stockholm Chamber of Commerce, or the ICC, on the other.

It is trite to say that this right of the investor to make a discretionary choice from among several procedural vehicles is one of the unique features of treaty arbitration. Trite as that observation may be, it is no less an important one. The right to select a body of procedural rules after the dispute has already arisen gives the investor's counsel a strategic opportunity to consider which set of rules best accommodates the specific needs of the client and case at hand.

When we, as counsel, advise clients with respect to this choice, we will explain that the choice should involve consideration of a number of factors. Relevant considerations may include questions of duration, cost, jurisdiction, tribunal composition, applicable law, interim relief, and confidentiality. Our advice will almost invariably – and often prominently – also explain the implications of this choice as to the enforceability of the resulting treaty award. We will tell our client about the "self-contained" enforcement regime of ICSID and the resulting quasi "self-executory" nature of the ICSID award, and contrast it with the non-ICSID alternative of greater state court supervision.

This Report will consider the relevance of the choice between ICSID and non-ICSID alternatives with respect to the ultimate enforceability of the award. The central question then is this: how does the choice "to ICSID or not to ICSID" affect the investor's voyage from an award to a domestic judgment enabling forcible execution? To answer this question, the Report will consider the two possible hurdles on the road to enforcement – annulment review and enforcement review – and consider how these hurdles compare

---

* Partner in the International Arbitration Group, Covington & Burling LLP, London. The invaluable assistance of Ina Popova, Patrick Rohn and Marina Weiss is gratefully acknowledged.

for ICSID and non-ICSID awards. In essence, how sharp is the annulment sword and how strong is the recognition shield for ICSID as compared to non-ICSID awards?

The universe of this inquiry is vast. The Report does not purport to do more than to identify the issues and to examine them in light of anecdotal evidence. The Report will also not address questions of sovereign immunity, invariably the single most important legal hurdle to the actual *execution* of a treaty award. Both within and outside the ICSID system, such questions will be addressed by the execution court in accordance with applicable domestic law.

II. ANNULMENT REVIEW: HOW SHARP IS THE SWORD?

The first threat to the enforceability of a treaty award is the possibility of an annulment or setting aside application. How should the investor assess that risk *ex ante* when choosing between ICSID and non-ICSID alternatives? Is there a basis to conclude that the sword is sharper in one system than in the other?

1. Do the Numbers Tell Us Anything?

The number of annulment and setting aside applications has generally followed the increase in the number of treaty awards issued. By the time the first published non-ICSID treaty award was rendered in 1995, there had already been fifteen published ICSID awards.

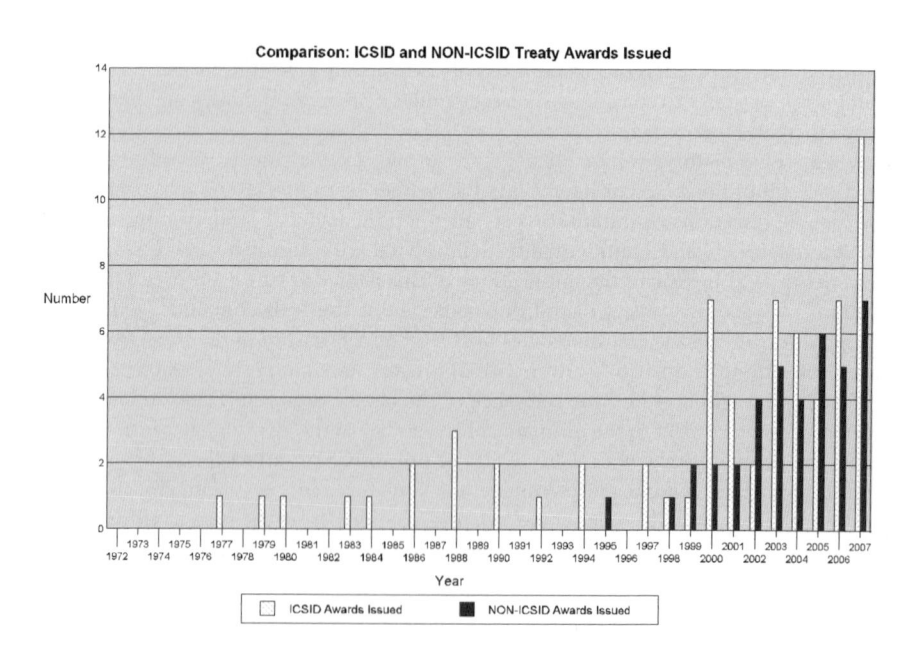

As of April 2008, there were fifteen ICSID ad hoc committee decisions and sixteen non-ICSID set-aside decisions. By 1999, there were five ICSID annulment decisions; the first non-ICSID set-aside decision was issued that year. While ten out of fifteen ICSID ad hoc committee decisions were issued between 2002 and 2008, all sixteen non-ICSID setting aside decisions were issued in the last ten years, by courts in Sweden (four), Canada (four), Switzerland (three), England (two), United States (one), Belgium (one), and Denmark (one).

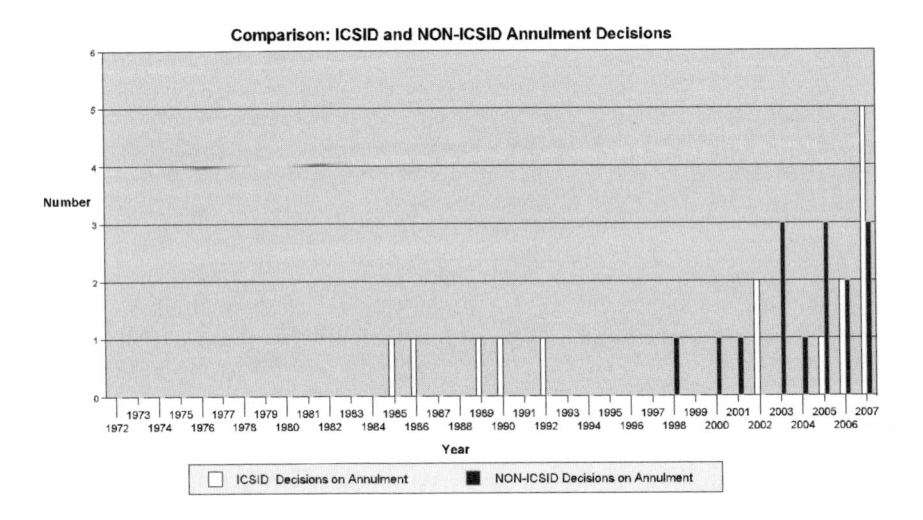

**Comparison: ICSID and NON-ICSID Annulment Decisions**

□ ICSID Decisions on Annulment ■ NON-ICSID Decisions on Annulment

Despite the comparability of populations, the annulment ratio in the case of ICSID awards was significantly higher than the set-aside ratio for non-ICSID treaty awards. Of the fifteen ad hoc committee decisions, forty percent led to annulment: twenty percent annulled the entire award and twenty percent were partial annulments. Of the sixteen court decisions, only one (six percent of the total) led to a set-aside of an award, and even that was only partial.

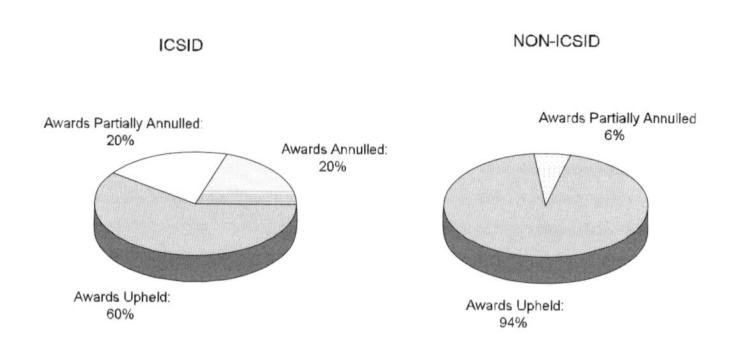

ICSID
- Awards Partially Annulled: 20%
- Awards Annulled: 20%
- Awards Upheld: 60%

NON-ICSID
- Awards Partially Annulled: 6%
- Awards Upheld: 94%

Statistics can prove anything, so the popular saying goes. All the more caution is warranted then where, as here, the population from which the statistics are drawn is limited. For instance, these numbers do not account for the fact that two ICSID decisions that led to total annulment (and were universally criticized for having crossed the line between annulment and appeal) were issued more than twenty years ago. Most commentators agree that the *Vivendi* and *Wena* decisions fifteen years later put the ICSID annulment process again on the right track. When only the decisions rendered in the past ten years are considered, three out of a total of ten ICSID annulment applications eventually led to annulment (two total, one partial), while out of a total of sixteen non-ICSID set-aside applications during the same period, only one led to a partial set-aside. While that still shows a measurable difference, it is not material enough to base any broad conclusions on.

2. *Can Annulment Review Be Avoided Altogether?*

Is there a way for the prospective claimant to avoid the prospect of an annulment proceeding altogether? As shown below, for all practical purposes the answer is most likely no.

a. *Waiver ex ante*
Only a handful of countries allow the parties to enter into an "exclusion agreement"

waiving *ex ante* the right to seek setting aside of an award.[1] Most commentators opine that the Washington Convention precludes *ex ante* waivers on the basis that Art. 52 is not subject to modification by the parties.[2]

The practical importance of this marginal difference between ICSID and non-ICSID awards is in any event limited: in treaty arbitration there will by default exist no submission agreement and the parties will seldom have the opportunity to agree on a waiver *ex ante*. Only in one reported treaty case did the parties expressly agree to waive annulment review on certain grounds in a separate submission agreement. The Swiss Federal Tribunal upheld that waiver.[3] The Federal Tribunal also held in *Saluka*, however, that a bilateral investment treaty (BIT) provision merely confirming the finality of the award is not sufficient to establish a waiver.[4]

*b.    Non-justiciability*

May domestic courts refuse to review treaty awards when such review entails the interpretation of the provisions of a treaty to which the state of the reviewing court is not a party? This was the question presented, under varying guises, in *Occidental* and *Sedelmayer*. Both the English courts (High Court and Court of Appeal) and the Svea Court of Appeal rejected the argument and confirmed their jurisdiction to review, and if necessary annul, treaty awards.

The English High Court and Court of Appeal both held in *Occidental* that English courts were not precluded by the English doctrine of non-justiciability from interpreting provisions of the US-Ecuador BIT to determine whether the tribunal had rightly asserted

---

1. In *Saluka Investments v. Czech Republic,* Swiss Federal Tribunal, Case 4P.114/2006, Decision of 7 September 2006, the Federal Tribunal identified Belgium, Malaysia, Sweden, Switzerland and Tunisia as the only jurisdictions allowing the parties to waive their right to judicial review. As to Switzerland, Art. 192 of the Private International Law Act (PILA) stipulates: "If none of the parties have their domicile, their habitual residence, or a business establishment in Switzerland, they may, by an express statement in the arbitration agreement or by a subsequent written agreement, waive fully the action for annulment or limit it to one or several of the grounds listed in Art. 190(2)." Some have argued that certain grounds for annulment have a public policy aspect and are therefore not at the parties' disposition. See KERAMEUS, "Waiver of Setting-Aside Procedures in International Arbitration", 41 Am. J. Comp. L. (1993) p. 73; DELAUME, "How to Draft an ICSID Arbitration Clause", 7 ICSID Review – FILJ (1992) p. 168; BERGER, "The Modern Trend Towards Exclusion of Recourse Against Transnational Arbitral Awards: A European Perspective", 12 Fordham Int'l L. J. (1989) p. 605; Christoph H. SCHREUER, *The ICSID Convention: A Commentary* (2001) at paras. 57-61 ad Art. p. 52.
2. *Ibid.* SCHREUER, at paras. 53-56 ad Art. 52, opining that Art. 52 "is designed to preserve the integrity of the system of ICSID arbitration and has a public order function".
3. In *France Telecom v. Lebanon,* Swiss Federal Tribunal, Case 4P.98/2005, Decision, 10 November 2005, the investor claimed that the parties had validly waived their right to challenge the award on the ground of lack of jurisdiction. The waiver invoked by the investor was not provided for in the BIT but was agreed in a separate agreement between the parties. The Federal Tribunal agreed that the parties had unambiguously waived the right to challenge the award on the ground of lack of jurisdiction and it concluded that for this reason the jurisdictional objection could not be entertained.
4. See *Saluka,* supra fn. 1.

jurisdiction.[5] The English courts focused on the fact that investors were directly granted rights under BITs and that the reference in the BIT to the New York Convention suggested that the parties to the BIT accepted that state courts may interpret the BIT in the course of annulment and recognition review. In *Sedelmayer*, the Stockholm District Court and the Svea Court of Appeal disposed of a different but analogous argument in the same manner.[6] The requirement in the Germany-Russia BIT that the place of arbitration be in a State Party to the New York Convention was considered indicative of the parties' intention to subject awards to the general rules applicable to international commercial arbitration and to the jurisdiction of domestic courts.[7]

Domestic courts in Canada, Belgium, Switzerland and the United States and have all asserted jurisdiction over challenges of treaty awards. While defendants in future setting aside proceedings in other jurisdictions may try to revive non-justiciability type theories, their prospects of success seem limited.

c.   *(Ir)relevance of labeling*
In each of the jurisdictions reviewed, parties may seek to have interim awards affirming or denying jurisdiction set aside, without awaiting the rendering of a final award.[8] By contrast, under the Washington Convention, while "awards" denying jurisdiction can be the subject of annulment proceedings, mere "preliminary decisions" affirming jurisdiction cannot – at least until they are incorporated in the final award. As a result, when a treaty tribunal affirms jurisdiction in a separate decision, the prospective non-ICSID claimant should anticipate the possibility of immediate setting aside proceedings against the interim award, whereas the prospective ICSID claimant will not face annulment proceedings until after the final award is issued.

Sometimes, however, ICSID tribunals issue a "decision" affirming jurisdiction over certain claims but summarily "dismissing" other claims as a matter of jurisdiction for failure to state a cause of action. In *SGS v. Philippines*, for instance, the Tribunal issued a decision on jurisdiction "dismissing" the expropriation claim and affirming jurisdiction over the fair and equitable treatment and umbrella clause claims (but declaring the latter inadmissible).[9] Similarly, in *Salini* the Tribunal summarily dismissed as a matter of

---

5. *Occidental v. Ecuador*, Court of Appeal, [2005] 2 Lloyd's Rep. 707, upholding the decision of the High Court, Queen's Bench Division, [2005] 2 Lloyd's Rep. 240.
6. *The Russian Federation v. Mr. Franz J. Sedelmayer*, Stockholm District Court, Case Az. T 6-583-98, Judgment, 18 December 2002, excerpted in 2005/2 SIAR 116 et seq.; Svea Court of Appeal No. 525-03, Judgment, 15 June 2005, excerpted in 2005/2 SIAR 132 et seq.
7. See Domenico DI PIETRO, "The Issue of Justiciability of Foreign Investment Arbitral Awards in *Sedelmayer v. Russia* and *OEPC v. Ecuador*", 2005/2 SIAR 136, at pp. 137-138.
8. In Switzerland, for instance, interim and partial awards on jurisdiction and/or liability can be annulled on the grounds of improper constitution of the tribunal and jurisdictional errors (Art. 190(3) of the PILA). In England, a decision on jurisdiction by the arbitrators can be challenged under Sect. 67 of the English Arbitration (International Investment Disputes) Act 1996. Sect. 67(2) explicitly provides that the tribunal may continue the arbitral proceedings and make a further award while an application is pending in relation to a jurisdictional award.
9. *SGS Société Générale de Surveillance S.A. v. Republic of the Philippines*, ICSID Case No. ARB/02/6, IIC (2003) 223.

jurisdiction certain treaty claims for failure to state a cause of action but affirmed jurisdiction over others. Those "decisions" may not be subject to annulment in the ICSID system until they are incorporated in the final award, even though they partly denied jurisdiction.

These ICSID decisions also raise another issue. While they denied jurisdiction over certain claims, what they arguably did was to summarily dismiss those claims on the merits. By labeling the decision as one of jurisdiction, however, such dismissal on the merits may be brought within the purview of annulment on the basis of excess of powers. Moreover, this labeling of summary dismissals as jurisdictional decisions is not limited to the ICSID sphere. A majority of treaty tribunals today appear to treat what are essentially demurrer-type objections as objections of jurisdiction ratione materiae.[10] Domestic courts, however, will not always accept such labeling and re-characterize the point of decision when deemed appropriate.

In *Occidental*, for instance, Ecuador made a preliminary objection that the facts alleged by the claimant could not substantiate an expropriation claim and that the claim should therefore be dismissed at the preliminary stage. The tribunal addressed this objection in its final award as one of "admissibility" and dismissed the expropriation claim. Occidental asked the High Court to set aside this part of the award on the ground that the tribunal had erred on this point as a matter of jurisdiction. The High Court declined, finding that what the tribunal had decided was neither a jurisdictional nor an admissibility issue but plainly a merits issue.[11] The opposite occurred in *Nagel*, where the Svea Court of Appeal accepted the tribunal's characterization of what was plainly a jurisdictional issue as a "substantive" one and refused to review that part of the award for failure to exercise jurisdiction.[12]

---

10. That approach is drawn from the International Court of Justice practice but is not without its critics. See, e.g., J. PAULSSON, "Jurisdiction and Admissibility" in G. AKSEN, et al., eds., *International Law, Commerce, and Dispute Resolution* (2005) at p. 607: "Even if facts are assumed true as pleaded (and there is therefore no resolution of factual controversies), a strike-out application involves a consideration of the merits of the case; the objective of the application is precisely to secure a determination that the legal basis of the claim is meritless."

11. *Occidental v. Ecuador*, High Court, Queen's Bench Division [2005] 2 Lloyd's Rep. 240: "The tribunal decided that, because it was 'so evident that there was no expropriation in this case', therefore it should deal with this claim as a matter of 'admissibility'. English lawyers may find that a curious word to use in the circumstances. But that does not matter. In my view it is evident, looking at the substance of [the section of the Award concerning the expropriation claim], that the Tribunal was making an award on the merits of the expropriation claim. It did not decide it had no jurisdiction to entertain the claim. Accordingly, there is no basis on which OEPC can mount an application to challenge this part of the Award under Sect. 67. OEPC wanted the tribunal to consider the expropriation claim on its merits. In effect it did so, and dismissed the claim."

12. *William Nagel v. Czech Republic*, Svea Court of Appeal, Case T 9059-03, Decision of 26 August 2005. The tribunal had stated at the beginning of its final award that it would decide whether the claimant was an "investor" with an "investment" as part of the "substance" of the matter and not as a preliminary issue. The tribunal later returned to the question and found that the claimant had no "investment" for purposes of the BIT. It then "dismissed" certain claims on that basis. The Svea Court of Appeal rejected claimant's submission that these findings were jurisdictional in nature, holding that instead the tribunal had made it clear they were findings of "substance".

3. *Known Standards Versus Unknown Standards?*

When a prospective claimant chooses arbitration outside the ICSID system, the applicable annulment standards will vary with the seat of the tribunal. Since the prospective claimant in treaty arbitration often has limited control over the choice of the seat, non-ICSID arbitration may seem to entail a degree of uncertainty as to the applicable standards that ICSID arbitration does not. That assumption has to be qualified in at least two ways.

*First*, many tribunals find guidance in the UNCITRAL Notes on Organizing Arbitral Proceedings when determining the seat. As a result, treaty tribunals will typically choose a neutral, arbitration-friendly jurisdiction for the seat. Of close to fifty non-ICSID treaty awards published in the period from 1996 to early 2008, all but one of them was rendered in North American or European jurisdictions that most of us would consider safe havens for arbitration, with Sweden, Canada, Switzerland, the United States and the United Kingdom being the usual suspects.

**Arbitrations held**

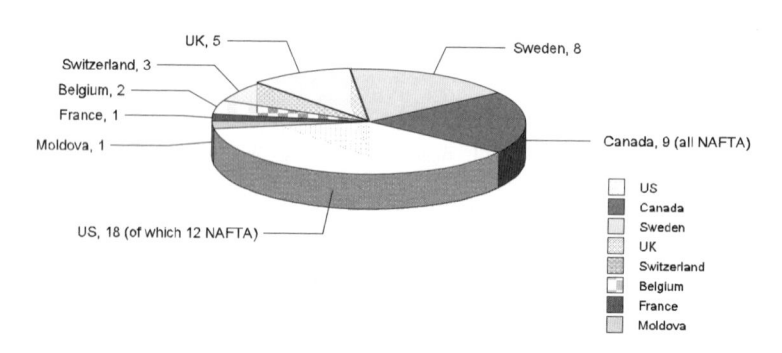

- Sweden, 8
- Canada, 9 (all NAFTA)
- US, 18 (of which 12 NAFTA)
- UK, 5
- Switzerland, 3
- Belgium, 2
- France, 1
- Moldova, 1

While the applicable standards may differ as between these jurisdictions, those differences do not necessarily engender a material degree of uncertainty for the prospective claimant.

*Second*, choosing ICSID does not necessarily mean choosing an established set of well-defined standards. While courts in the above jurisdictions can draw on a wealth of commercial arbitration cases applying the relevant standards, there are only fifteen ICSID annulment decisions to date that may shed light on how the ICSID standards will be applied. As shown below, certain recent annulment decisions suggest that the ground of failure to state reasons, which is not available as a setting aside ground in many of the above jurisdictions, may result in surprising outcomes.

4. *Narrow(ly Applied) Standards Versus Broad(ly Applied) Standards?*

*a. The standards on the books*

The standards as written in the Washington Convention and the domestic laws of major jurisdictions are plainly not identical. They each draw from a different heritage. The grounds for annulment listed in Art. 52(1) of the Washington Convention are modeled on Art. 35 of the International Law Commission's 1958 Model Rules on Arbitral Procedure.[13] Several of the jurisdictions reviewed follow to a greater or lesser extent Art. 34(2) of the UNCITRAL Model Law, which essentially replicates the language of Art. V of the New York Convention.

Of the grounds available under the Washington Convention, only three have really mattered in practice: manifest excess of powers; failure to state reasons; and serious departure from a fundamental rule of procedure. Manifest excess of powers and failure to state reasons were relied upon in equal proportions in three quarters of all decided applications, with the remaining quarter being taken up by allegations of a serious departure from a fundamental rule of procedure. None of the applications based on a serious departure from a fundamental rule of procedure succeeded. Roughly one third of applications based on manifest excess of powers and failure to state reasons did succeed.

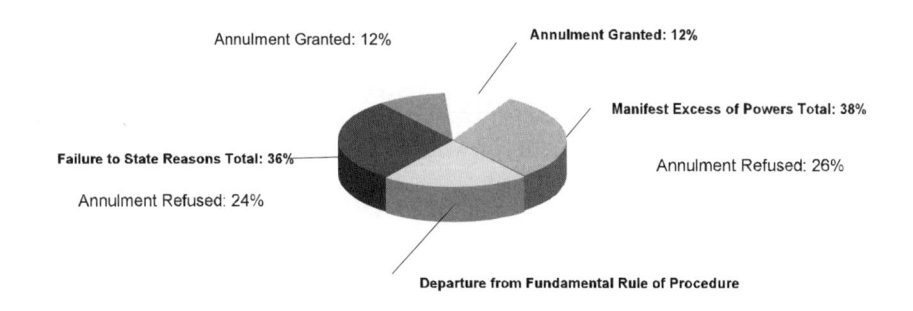

Annulment Granted: 12%

Annulment Granted: 12%

Manifest Excess of Powers Total: 38%

Failure to State Reasons Total: 36%

Annulment Refused: 26%

Annulment Refused: 24%

Departure from Fundamental Rule of Procedure

---

13. YBILC 86 (1958-II).

In the case of non-ICSID treaty awards, almost two thirds of all set-aside applications were based on excess of powers. One quarter relied on public policy, and the remainder was divided between allegations of violation of due process and failure to state reasons. Only one application succeeded partially, on the basis of excess of powers.

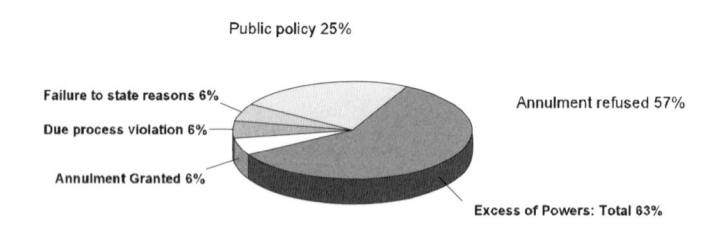

Public policy 25%

Failure to state reasons 6%

Due process violation 6%

Annulment Granted 6%

Annulment refused 57%

Excess of Powers: Total 63%

This asymmetry in terms of the grounds most frequently invoked should not surprise. It is frequent practice in ICSID annulment proceedings to characterize the same alleged flaw in an award as both a manifest excess of powers and a failure to state reasons. Since many of the jurisdictions reviewed expressly or implicitly exclude failure to state reasons as a ground for setting aside, applicants appearing before those courts have less of an incentive to double-dip the way many ICSID applicants do.

b.   *Discretion to annul or set aside*

According to Art. 52(3) of the Washington Convention, an ad hoc committee has "the authority" to annul the award or any part thereof in case any of the grounds set forth in Art. 52(1) is fulfilled. It is now settled law that this provision gives ad hoc committees a measure of discretion to decide whether annulment is warranted when one of the grounds has been met.[14] Art. 34(2) of the UNCITRAL Model Law similarly uses the

---

14. See, e.g., *Compañía de Aguas del Aconquija S.A. and Vivendi Universal S.A. v. Argentine Republic*, ICSID Case No ARB/97/3, Decision on Annulment, 3 July 2002, 19 ICSID Review – FILJ (2004) p. 89, IIC 70 (2002) at para. 66: "[I]t appears to be established that an ad hoc committee has a certain measure of discretion as to whether to annul an award, even if an annullable error is found. Article 52(3) ... has been interpreted as giving committees some flexibility in determining whether annulment is appropriate in the circumstances. Among other things, it is necessary for an *ad hoc* committee to consider the significance of the error relative to the legal rights of the parties"; *CMS Gas Transmission Company v. Argentine Republic*, ICSID Case No. ARB/01/8, Decision on the Application for Annulment, 25 September 2007, IIC (2007) 303, at para. 158, referring to the

permissive "may," giving the court a measure of discretion to set aside the award if one or several of the grounds listed in that provision are fulfilled.[15] With some exceptions,[16] most national provisions replicate this discretionary nature of setting aside review.[17]

c.  *Differently applied standards?*

How do ICSID committees and domestic courts apply the relevant standards? I will address the question with respect to: (i) jurisdictional errors; (ii) failure to apply the proper law of the dispute; (iii) failure to state reasons; and (iv) public policy. Due process violations were alleged in a number of ICSID and non-ICSID cases, but both ICSID committees and domestic courts have set a high bar and no treaty award has been annulled on that basis.[18]

---

narrow and limited scope of its mandate conferred by Art. 52 which "allows annulment as an option only when certain specific conditions exist".

15. See Aron BROCHES, *Commentary on the UNCITRAL Model Law on International Commercial Arbitration* (1990) at para. 5 ad Art. 34.
16. Sect. 34 of the Swedish Arbitration Act stipulates that an award "shall" be wholly or partially set aside if it fulfills one of the grounds listed in that provision. The Swiss arbitration act does not specify whether the court has discretion to annul the award, but the Swiss Federal Tribunal will annul an award if one of the grounds listed in Art. 190(2) of the PILA is fulfilled.
17. See Sect. 10(a) of the United States Federal Arbitration Act (FAA), and Sect. 34(2) of the Canadian Commercial Arbitration Act (CAA). In *The United Mexican States v. Metalclad Corporation* (Reasons for Judgment, 2 May 2001, 5 ICSID Rep., p. 238; Supplementary Reasons for Judgment, 31 October 2001, 6 ICSID Rep., p. 53), the Supreme Court of British Columbia confirmed that Sect. 34(2) of the CAA is permissive in nature. It held that the seriousness of the defect in the arbitral procedure should be considered when the court is deciding whether to exercise its discretion.
18. See, e.g., *Vivendi*, supra fn. 14 (rejecting Vivendi's argument that the tribunal had departed from a fundamental rule of procedure in that its eventual decision, notably as to the dismissal of certain claims, concerned a question not adequately canvassed in argument. The ad hoc committee carefully examined the record of the arbitration and concluded that the parties had a full and fair opportunity to be heard at every stage of the proceedings); *Empresas Lucchetti, S.A. and Lucchetti Peru, S.A. v. Republic of Peru*, ICSID Case No. ARB/03/4, Decision on Annulment, 5 September 2007, IIC 300 (2007) (dismissing claim of departure from fundamental rule of presumption of innocence by deferring in its jurisdictional analysis to Peru's arguments about the motivation for the decrees; finding that not allowing Lucchetti to file a full Memorial on the Merits before the tribunal proceeded to a decision on the Preliminary Objections did not constitute a violation of a fundamental rule of procedure). For examples of non-ICSID Convention awards, see, *Marvin Roy Feldman Karpa v. United Mexican States*, ICSID Case No. ARB(AF)/99/1, (Ontario Superior Court of Justice, Judicial Review, 3 December 2003, 2003 CanLII 34011 (ON S.C.), 8 ICSID Rep. (2005) p. 500 (rejecting Mexico's claim that the tribunal failed to consider Art. 2105 of NAFTA, providing for a law enforcement and privacy carve-out from a party's disclosure obligations, where Mexico had not pled the violation during the arbitration and could have provided the requested information without violating privacy laws)); *Bayview Irrigation District and others v. United Mexican States*, ICSID Case No. ARB(AF)/05/1 (Ontario Superior Court of Justice, Decision of 25 March 2008 (rejecting, after a careful review of the record, the applicant's argument that the tribunal had not afforded it a fair opportunity to present its case)).

i. Jurisdictional error

Applicants frequently allege that the arbitrators improperly exercised, or failed to exercise, jurisdiction as the basis for annulment. In ICSID this will often (but not necessarily exclusively) come under the heading of an alleged manifest excess of powers (Art. 52(1)(b) of the Washington Convention). Under Art. 34(2)(a)(iii) of the UNCITRAL Model Law, an award may be set aside if "the award deals with a dispute not contemplated by or not falling within the terms of the submission to arbitration, or contains decisions on matters beyond the scope of the submission to arbitration...". Similar provisions can be found in most major jurisdictions.[19]

A central question here is: What *standard of review* do committees and courts apply? Both ICSID committees and domestic courts will rightly repeat many times over that they do not sit as courts of appeal on the merits and cannot engage in a de novo review of *the merits*. But that does not say anything about the proper standard of review on matters of *jurisdiction*. If a tribunal either wrongly asserts jurisdiction it does not have or wrongly fails to exercise jurisdiction it does have, it acts contrary to the parties' arbitration agreement. In that sense, one would expect the relevant determination by a reviewing authority to be whether the tribunal was right or wrong in exercising or declining to exercise jurisdiction. The answer is, at least in theory, different for ICSID and non-ICSID awards.

The approach adopted by the courts in Canada, England, Sweden and Switzerland is that of a de novo review of the tribunal's jurisdictional determination. These courts almost invariably consider their task as a binary one: was the tribunal right or wrong in asserting (or refusing to assert) jurisdiction under the treaty as it did? The recent setting aside proceedings in the English High Court in *Occidental Petroleum v. Ecuador* offer a good example. The High Court addressed a challenge by Ecuador under Sect. 67 of the Arbitration Act 1996, alleging that the arbitral tribunal lacked substantive jurisdiction. The High Court formulated the applicable standard of review in unequivocal terms:

> "[I]t is now well-established that a challenge to the jurisdiction of an arbitration panel under section 67 proceeds by way of a re-hearing of the matters before the arbitrators.... [T]he test for the Court is this: was the Tribunal *correct* in its decision on jurisdiction? The test is not: was the Tribunal *entitled* to reach the decision that it did."[20] (Emphasis added)

Following a very careful and detailed review of Ecuador's challenge that the tax exclusion of the BIT had precluded arbitration of a dispute arising out of the denial of VAT refunds, the court dismissed the application.[21]

---

19. See Sect. 10(a)(4) of the FAA; Sects. 67(1) and 68(2)(b) of the English Arbitration Act 1996; Arts. 190(2)(b) and (c) of the PILA; Sect. 34 paras. 1 and 2 of the Swiss Arbitration Act (SAA); and Sect. 34(2)(a)(iv) of the CAA.
20. [2006] 1 Lloyd's Rep. 773, at para.7.
21. The High Court in *European Media Ventures;25;25v. Czech Republic*, [2008] 1 Lloyd's Rep. 186, reiterated the standard of review enounced by the court in *Occidental* and, after a careful and detailed interpretative effort in accordance with the Vienna Convention's interpretation rules,

The same can be seen in the decisions of other courts. While applicants have sought to present a variety of perceived flaws in treaty awards as jurisdictional errors,[22] a recurring theme is that the tribunal was wrong in concluding that there was a qualifying "investment" by a qualifying "investor". While the stated reasons are sometimes terse, especially in the decisions of continental European courts, the courts appear to have engaged each time in a de novo review of that holding of the arbitral award.[23]

---

dismissed the Czech Republic's claim that the tribunal lacked substantive jurisdiction.

22. See, e.g., *Saluka*, supra fn. 1 (when undertaking a de novo review of the applicability of the investment treaty to actions prior to the making of the investment, the Federal Tribunal carefully distinguished between jurisdictional issues and "substantive issues" that were disguised as jurisdictional objections: "The pleadings of the appellant seem to be an attempt to submit the tribunal's judgment on the merits, in disguise of a challenge to the tribunal's jurisdiction, to the full examination of the Federal Tribunal, although the Federal Tribunal's review on the merits is limited to challenges against a final award and to issues of public policy."); *Eureko v. Poland*, Brussels Court of First Instance, Decision of 23 November 2006 (holding that even if the tribunal had asserted jurisdiction in disregard of a forum selection clause, it would still not have acted inconsistently with the arbitration agreement of the parties contained in the BIT).

23. The Federal Court of Canada held in *SD Myers v. Canada*, 2004 FC 38, that the applicable standard of review on that point was "correctness" as regards "pure questions of law," and "reasonableness" as regards "mixed questions of fact and law". The court then engaged in a careful de novo review of the tribunal's reasoning and concluded that the interpretation was correct and the application reasonable. The court made these findings in the alternative, after first holding that Canada could not raise the issue in a setting aside proceeding when it had not properly pleaded the objection to jurisdiction in the arbitration. By contrast, the court held that it had no authority to set aside the award on the basis that the tribunal would have misinterpreted "in like circumstances" in the national treatment standard, but that the tribunal's reasoning was in any event reasonable in that respect.

The Maritime and Commercial Court of Copenhagen in *SwemBalt* addressed Latvia's argument that a vessel could not constitute an investment if the investor had not produced the lease agreement proving title. While noting that "the concept of investment shall be widely interpreted", the court dismissed the application to set aside. *The Republic of Latvia v. SwemBalt Limited*, Case S-22-01, Decision of 7 January 2007.

The Svea Court of Appeal in *Petrobart* dismissed Kyrgyzstan's claim that the investor had made no "investment" within the meaning of the Energy Charter Treaty (ECT). The Svea Court of Appeal dismissed the application after explaining that "the term investment can have different meaning in different international contexts. The meaning of the term as defined in the ECT has a wide scope of application. It is evident from the testimony given ... that when the ECT was negotiated it was an explicit intention to give investment a broad intention." *The Kyrgyz Republic v. Petrobart Limited*, Case No. T 5208-05, Rotel 1602, Judgment 19 January 2007, at p. 8. This stands in contrast to a decision of the Stockholm District Court in *Sedelmayer*, which dismissed Russia's objection that the tribunal had wrongly concluded that Sedelmayer was an "investor" for jurisdictional purposes. The court in that case appeared to accept that Mr. Sedelmayer's claim that he did qualify as an investor was a sufficient basis for the tribunal to assert jurisdiction. According to that court,

"Sedelmayer was already able, by virtue of his claim that he was an investor with a permanent domicile in Germany and was therefore covered by the Convention's investor protection, to turn to an international arbitration court under articles 4 and 10 of the convention to decide the dispute.... How the arbitrators subsequently assessed Sedelmayer's claims are substantive

The Washington Convention would appear to require a different standard of review. Pursuant to Art. 52(2)(b), only a "manifest" excess of powers can justify annulment. This requirement also applies to jurisdictional errors.[24] Different ICSID committees have proposed different interpretations of that qualifier.[25] Many committees and commentators have equated "manifest" with "obvious" or "readily recognizable".[26] The *Lucchetti* committee, for instance, noting that it "is not charged with the task of determining whether one interpretation is 'better' than another, or indeed which among severable interpretations might be considered the 'best' one", concluded that a determination as to jurisdiction is not "manifest" where it is "clearly a tenable one". The *Vivendi* committee on the other hand appears to have taken a different approach, holding that an error as to jurisdiction is "manifest" where "the failure to exercise a jurisdiction is clearly capable of making a difference to the result".[27] That committee would therefore measure the manifest nature of the jurisdictional error by reference to its impact on the outcome. The *Soufraki* committee created yet a third strand of interpretation. In an effort to embrace the approaches of both *Vivendi* and *Lucchetti*, the committee effectively conflated them into a cumulative requirement "that a manifest excess of powers implies that the excess of power should at once be textually obvious and substantively serious".[28]

---

determinations that cannot be subject to review by the District Court."

*Sedelmayer*, supra fn. 6, Stockholm District Court, Judgment, 18 December 2002, at p. 18.

24. As the *Lucchetti* committee noted, the "the wording of Article 52(1)(b) is general and makes no exception for jurisdiction". *Lucchetti*, supra fn. 18, at para. 101.
25. The inclusion of the term "manifestly" can be ascribed to a successful German proposal which was based on the fear that there might be some risk of frustration of awards. The word "manifestly" was not present in the Preliminary Draft of the ICSID Convention and first added in the First Draft; see the drafting history of this ground for annulment in SCHREUER, supra fn. 1, at paras. 137 et seq. ad Art. 52.
26. For instance, the *Wena* committee said that "the excess of power must be self-evident rather than the product of elaborate interpretations one way or another". *Wena Hotels Limited v. The Arab Republic of Egypt*, ICSID Case No. ARB/98/4, Decision on Application for Annulment, 5 February 2002, IIC 274 (2002) at para. 25. Similarly, in *CDC Group v. Seychelles* the committee stated that "even if a Tribunal exceeds its powers, the excess must be plain on its face for annulment to be an available remedy", and that "any excess apparent in a Tribunal's conduct, if susceptible of argument 'one way or the other,' is not manifest". *CDC Group plc v. Republic of Seychelles*, ICSID Case No. ARB/02/14, IIC 48 (2005), Decision on the Application for Annulment, 29 June 2005, at para. 41. The *Lucchetti* committee observed that, "[m]oreover, a request for annulment is not an appeal, which means that there should not be a full review of the tribunal's award"; and that "the word 'manifest' should be given considerable weight also when matters of jurisdiction are concerned". *Lucchetti*, supra fn. 18, at para. 112.
27. *Vivendi*, supra fn. 14, at para. 86. Looking to the "clear and serious implications" of the decision and "the surrounding circumstances", the committee felt obliged to characterize the refusal of jurisdiction as a "manifest" error. The *CMS* committee appears to have taken the same approach when considering Argentina's argument that the tribunal had exceeded its jurisdiction. *CMS*, supra fn. 14.
28. *Hussein Nuaman Soufraki v. United Arab Emirates*, ICSID Case No. ARB/02/7, Decision of the ad hoc Committee on the Application for the Annulment, 5 June 2007, IIC 297 (2007) at para. 40.

Of recent ICSID annulment decisions, only the *Vivendi* decision was based on a manifest jurisdictional error, plainly applying a "correctness" test. Depending on which standard of review ICSID committees will apply in the future, jurisdictional errors may be reviewed differently for ICSID and non-ICSID treaty awards.

ii. Failure to apply the proper law of the dispute

A tribunal's failure to apply the proper law of the dispute may constitute a manifest excess of powers under the Washington Convention and a failure to act in accordance with the arbitration agreement under many domestic laws. Both ICSID committees[29] and domestic courts[30] will typically distinguish between applying the governing law incorrectly and applying the wrong governing law. That line, however, will not always

---

29. As the *Soufraki* committee explained:

> "Misinterpretation or misapplication of the proper law may, in particular cases, be so gross or egregious as substantially to amount to failure to apply the proper law. Such gross and consequential misinterpretation or misapplication of the proper law which no reasonable person (*bon père de famille*') could accept needs to be distinguished from simple error – even a serious error – in the interpretation of the law which in many national jurisdictions may be the subject of ordinary appeal as distinguished from, e.g., an extraordinary writ of certiorari."

Soufraki, supra fn. 28, at para. 86.

30. In *CME v. Czech Republic*, Svea Court of Appeal, Case No. T 8735-01, Decision of 15 May 2003, the Court stated that

> "where it is evident that the arbitrators have applied the law of a different country in violation of such an agreement ... the award may be set aside on the ground that the arbitrators exceeded their mandate. On the other hand ... the Court should not, of course, determine whether the arbitrators erroneously applied the law agreed upon by the parties.... In the opinion of the Court of Appeal, an almost deliberate disregard of the designated law must be involved. There is no excess of mandate where the arbitrators have applied the designated law incorrectly."

In *International Thunderbird Gaming Corp. v. Mexico*, 473 F.Supp.2d 80, the District Court for the District of Columbia dealt with a set-aside application on the ground that the "NAFTA panel acted in 'manifest disregard of the law' by announcing a particular standard for burdens of proof and then failing to apply that standard". The court recalled that to prevail on this point the applicant had to "at least establish that '(1) the arbitrators knew of a governing legal principle yet refused to apply it or ignored it altogether and (2) the law ignored by the arbitrators was well defined, explicit, and clearly applicable to the case'". The court recalled that manifest disregard "means more than error or misunderstanding with respect to the law".

Under Swiss arbitration law, not only the misinterpretation and misapplication of the proper law but even the tribunal's failure to apply the proper law does not constitute a ground for annulment unless it changes the outcome of the arbitration, in which case it can be challenged on the ground of violation of public policy. See Swiss Federal Tribunal, Decision of 14 November 1990, BGE 116 II 634 consid. 4a.

In England, a tribunal exceeds its powers and renders an annullable award under Sect. 68(2)(b) of the Arbitration Act 1996 if the tribunal has applied the wrong system of law to the dispute or particular issues. The court may annul the award if this serious irregularity has caused or will cause substantial injustice to the affected party. Robert MERKIN, *Arbitration Act 1996* (2005) 3rd edn., at p. 171 ad Sect. 68.

be a very clear one and early ICSID committees more than once failed to respect this distinction.[31]

More recent decisions of ICSID committees display greater restraint in determining whether a tribunal went beyond an error of law. They typically place considerable weight on the requirement that the failure to apply the proper law of the dispute must be "manifest". As described below, with the exception of *Mitchell*, ICSID committees in the recent past have refrained from substituting their views of the law for those of tribunals. Instead, they will often state *obiter* how the tribunal did misapply the law but then conclude that this misapplication does not warrant annulment.

Anecdotal evidence suggests that the inquiry by ICSID committees into a tribunal's application of the proper law may at times be more rigorous than that by domestic courts. A side-by-side comparison of the decisions in *MTD* and *CME* serves to illustrate this point. In both *MTD* and *CME*, the applicants argued that the tribunal had failed to apply the proper law of the dispute, under Art. 42(1) of the Washington Convention and Art. 8.6 of the Netherlands-Czech Republic BIT respectively. The ICSID committee in *MTD* and the Svea Court of Appeal in *CME* addressed these similar complaints in a very different fashion.

The ad hoc committee in *MTD* examined whether the tribunal had manifestly not "applied Chilean law to those questions which were necessary for its determination and of which Chilean law was the governing law". The ad hoc committee concluded that it had not but made it clear that it would have annulled the award had it reached the opposite conclusion. The Svea Court of Appeal, by contrast, refused to review "the various sections in the arbitral award ... in order to ascertain which of the sources of law listed in Art. 8.6 of the Treaty have been applied by the arbitral tribunal". Instead, for purposes of its review, the court held that: "it is sufficient to determine whether the arbitral tribunal applied *any* of the sources of law listed in the choice of law clause or whether the tribunal has not based its decision on *any* law at all but, rather, judged in accordance with general reasonableness". Thus, the court was not interested in verifying whether the tribunal had applied the proper law to the right question, but contented itself with verifying that *any* of the laws listed in Art. 8(2) of the BIT had been applied to *any* of the relevant questions.

Closer scrutiny, however, does not necessarily mean a higher likelihood of annulment. Of the last three ICSID decisions annulling all or part of an award, none did so on the basis of a failure to apply the proper law. In *Metalclad*, by contrast, a domestic court plainly did substitute its view of the applicable law for that of the tribunal under the guise of failure to apply the proper law of the dispute. A comparison with the same *MTD* decision illustrates the contrasting approaches.

---

31. *Klöckner Industrie-Anlagen GmbH and others v. United Republic of Cameroon and Société Camerounaise des Engrais*, ICSID Case No. ARB/81/2, Decision on Annulment, 3 May 1985, 2 ICSID Rep. 95, and *Amco Asia Corporation and others v. Republic of Indonesia*, ICSID Case No. ARB/81/1), Decision on the Application for Annulment, 16 May 1986, 1 ICSID Rep., p. 509; see SCHREUER,supra fn. 1, at paras. 167 et seq. ad Art. 52, with reference to further commentators.

Both applicants in those cases had complained that the tribunal had espoused far too broad an interpretation of the fair and equitable treatment clause.[32] Both the *MTD* committee and the British Columbia Court stressed that their task was not to correct any errors of law by the tribunal.[33] The manner in which the committee and the court applied that principle, however, was very different. Finding that the tribunal's interpretation was "defensible," if objectionable, the *MTD* committee refused to annul.[34]

The British Columbia Court, by contrast, developed its own interpretation of fair and equitable treatment and concluded that it contained no transparency obligations. On the basis of its own determination, the Court annulled the award, holding that "the Tribunal did not simply interpret the wording of Art. 1105. Rather, it misstated the applicable law to include transparency obligations and then made its decision on the basis of the concept of transparency".[35]

iii. Failure to state reasons

As shown above, failure to state reasons (Art. 52(2)(e)) is one of the grounds most frequently relied upon in ICSID annulment proceedings. By contrast, none of the arbitration laws reviewed for this paper contain an express provision to the same effect,[36] and courts in those jurisdictions have either positively excluded failure to state reasons as a ground for setting aside,[37] or taken a restrictive approach to it.[38] In the context of

---

32. *MTD Equity Sdn. Bhd. and MTD Chile S.A. v. Republic of Chile*, ICSID Case No. ARB/01/7, Decision on the Application for Annulment, 21 March 2007, IIC 177 (2007) at para. 63 (contending that the tribunal had "misapprehended the standard of fair and equitable treatment under the BIT, applying a standard expressed in a dictum of the TECMED tribunal which in no way represents international law and which cannot be derived from Articles 2(2) and 3(1) of the BIT by any process of interpretation"); *Metalclad*, supra fn. 17, at para. 66 (arguing that tribunal had decided matters beyond the scope of the submission to arbitration by "creating new transparency obligations" in NAFTA under the guise of interpretation of the fair and equitable treatment standard).
33. See *MTD*, supra fn. 32, at paras. 44 et seq., and *Metalclad*, supra fn. 17, at paras. 50 et seq.
34. See *MTD*, supra fn. 32, at paras. 67 et seq.
35. See *Metalclad*, supra fn. 17, at para. 70.
36. As highlighted by the Supreme Court of British Columbia in *Metalclad*, where it tied the obligation to state reasons to the obligation to address all questions,

    "[t]here is a specific provision in the ICSID Convention for annulling an arbitral award when a failure to deal with every question submitted to the tribunal constitutes a failure to state reasons. On the other hand, the only potential basis for setting aside an arbitral award under the International CAA for failure to deal with all questions is S. 34(2)(a)(v) ('the arbitral procedure was not in accordance with the agreement of the parties')."

    *Ibid.* at para. 126.
37. In Switzerland, the Federal Tribunal confirmed on two occasions that the failure to state reasons does neither constitute a violation of the parties' right to be heard nor a violation of public policy. See BGE 116 II 373 consid. 7, and BGE 128 III 234 consid. 4b.
38. In England, an award can be challenged on the ground of "serious irregularity" if the tribunal fails to deal with all the issues that were put to it, but that only applies to a failure to deal with a claim or a distinct defense to a claim advanced before the tribunal and not merely an omission to give

non-ICSID treaty awards, applicants have rarely relied on failure to state reasons as a ground for setting aside.

Given the inherent risk of a slippery slope, ICSID committees routinely caution that a failure to state reasons should not lead lightly to annulment.[39] In addition, several committees have stated that where an award is tainted by a failure to state reasons, the remedy need not be annulment when the committee can reconstruct the reasons.[40] Those notes of caution notwithstanding, however, failure to state reasons has proved to be a relatively fertile ground for ICSID annulment decisions. Two out of three annulments in the past ten years were based on that ground. In *CMS Gas Transmission v. Argentina*, the applicant argued that the tribunal's interpretation of the umbrella clause

---

reasons for the tribunal's conclusion in respect of such claim or defense. Only in those cases in which the award expressed no conclusion as to a specific claim or a specific defense, the award could be said to have failed to deal with an issue. Decision of the Queen's Bench Division (Commercial Court), in *Margulead Ltd. v. Exide Technologies*, [2005] 1 Lloyd's Rep. 324, considering *Hussman (Europe) Ltd. v. Al Ameen Development & Trade Co.*, [2000] 2 Lloyd's Rep. 83 and *Petroships Pte Ltd. v. Petec Trading and Investment Corporation and Others* (The *Petro Ranger*), [2001] 2 Lloyd's Rep. 348.

In Canada, failure to state reasons may only lead to annulment if it reflects a serious defect in the arbitral procedure. In *Metalclad*, supra fn. 17, the Supreme Court of British Columbia stated that "in the absence of an express ground of annulment in the terms of Article 52(1)(e) of the ICSID Convention ... the seriousness of the defect in the arbitral procedure should be considered when this Court is deciding whether to exercise its discretion to either set aside an award ... or to refuse to enforce an award...". *Ibid.* at para. 129.

In the United States, failure to state reasons is not a ground for setting aside and the absence of express reasoning in the award does not imply that the tribunal disregarded the law *Raytheon Co. v. Automated Business Systems, Inc.*, C.A.1 (Mass.) 1989, 882 F.2d 6 ("arbitrators have no obligation ... to give their reasons for an award at all"); *Merill Lynch, Pierce, Fenner & Smith Inc. v. Burke*, N.D.Cal. 1990, 741 F. Supp. 191 ("An arbitrator's award may be made without explanation of the reasons and without a complete record of the proceedings.").

In Belgium, the requirement seems stricter: "[t]he giving of reasons for an arbitral award ... must meet the same standards as judicial decisions: the reasons have to be complete, precise, clear, and adequate"; but "the arbitrator need not respond any more than the judge to a defense that has become irrelevant because of a conclusion in his decision or the resolution he arrives at for the dispute". *Eureko*, supra fn. 22, at para. 1.2.1.

39. The *Vivendi* committee emphasized that "reasons may be stated succinctly or at length, and different legal traditions differ in their modes of expressing reasons". The *Vivendi* committee articulated a dual test: "[F]irst, the failure to state reasons must leave the decision on a particular point essentially lacking in any expressed rationale; and second, that point must itself be necessary to the tribunal's decision." *Vivendi*, supra fn. 14, at para. 65. *See also MTD*, supra fn. 32, at paras. 78 and 92. The same test was adopted in *Lucchetti*, where the tribunal placed special emphasis on the necessity of the determination. *Lucchetti*, supra fn. 18, at para. 128. In his dissenting opinion Sir Franklin Berman professed the view that ICSID tribunals must offer "clear and strong" explanations in the event that they decline jurisdiction over investment treaty claims at the initial stage. Should a tribunal fail to offer "clearly explained and justified" grounds, their ruling might be annullable.

40. The *Wena* committee, for instance, stated: "If the ad hoc committee so concludes, on the basis of the knowledge it has received upon the dispute, the reasons supporting the Tribunal's conclusions can be explained by the ad hoc committee itself." *Wena*, supra fn. 26, at para. 83.

in a US BIT constituted both a manifest excess of powers and a failure to state reasons. In *Mitchell v. Democratic Republic of the Congo*,[41] the applicant argued that the tribunal's interpretation of the term "investment" in Art. 25 of the Washington Convention to include a law firm constituted a manifest excess of powers. In both cases, however, the committees annulled all or part of the award exclusively for failure to state reasons. The *CMS* committee declined, as a matter of judicial economy, to examine whether the award was for the same reason also tainted by a manifest excess of power. The *Mitchell* committee ruled on another ground than the one pleaded by the applicant.

The *CMS* committee addressed Argentina's argument that the tribunal had never explained how CMS could enforce the umbrella clause of the BIT when it was not a party to the underlying contract. The tribunal had dismissed this argument stating that "the Tribunal will not discuss the jurisdictional aspects involved in the Respondent's argument, as these were dealt with in the decision on jurisdiction". As the committee noted, however, the decision on jurisdiction did not address that particular point. The ad hoc committee then went on to consider that an umbrella clause was concerned with "consensual obligations arising independently of the BIT itself" and faulted the tribunal for not stating any basis for its implied conclusion that a claimant who is not the direct beneficiary of such consensual obligations could enforce it using the umbrella clause. While the committee was evidently eager to lay out its own views on the proper construction of the umbrella clause, the partial annulment arguably remained within the boundaries of the standard set for itself by the committee.

The same cannot be said of the *Mitchell* decision. The committee examined the tribunal's finding that the investor's law firm in the Democratic Republic of the Congo (DRC) qualified as an "investment" within the meaning of the BIT and Art. 25 of the Washington Convention. It appears from the excerpts from the unpublished award quoted in the decision that the tribunal had provided clear reasons for its finding that a law firm constitutes an investment within the meaning of both the BIT and the Washington Convention. The tribunal examined the definition of investment in the BIT and concluded that the BIT contains a definition of the notion of investment which is as broad as the concept is used in the ICSID Convention. The tribunal also specifically responded to the DRC's argument that Mr. Mitchell's law firm was not "a long-term operation" or "a significant contribution of resources", as supposedly required by Art. 25 of the Washington Convention.[42]

Some may view the tribunal's interpretation of "investment" as a broad one. The tribunal essentially defined "investment" in Art. 25 of the Washington Convention by reference to the meaning given to that term in the BIT. That approach is not without merit. As the *CMS* committee stated, the task of defining "investment", as that term is used in Art. 25, "was left largely to the terms of bilateral investment treaties or other

---

41. *Patrick Mitchell v. Democratic Republic of the Congo*, ICSID Case No. ARB/99/7, Decision on the Application for Annulment of the Award, 1 November 2006.
42. *Ibid.* para. 24 (quoting excerpts from the unpublished award).

instruments on which jurisdiction is based".[43] But whether the tribunal's conclusion that Mr. Mitchell's law firm constituted an investment was right or wrong is ultimately irrelevant to a determination as to whether the tribunal failed to state reasons. A review of even just the excerpts from the award quoted by the committee makes it clear that the tribunal did provide reasons for its conclusion. It is also clear, however, that the committee disagreed with those reasons:

> "The Award is incomplete and obscure as regards what it considers an investment: it refers to various fragments of the operation, without finally indicating the reasons why it regards it overall as an investment, that is, without providing the slightest explanation as to the relationship between the 'Mitchell & Associates' firm and the DRC. Such an inadequacy of reasons is deemed to be particularly grave, as it seriously affects the coherence of the reasoning and, moreover, as it opens the door to a risk of genuine abuses, to the extent that it boils down to granting the qualification as investor to any legal counseling firm or law firm established in a foreign country, thereby enabling it to take advantage of the special arbitration system of ICSID."[44]

It is hard to follow the committee's reasoning. There was nothing incomplete or obscure about the tribunal's decision. Rather, as the last sentence in the above quote suggests, the committee appeared to have a *policy* concern about the tribunal's broad interpretation of investment and therefore substituted its view of the proper interpretation of that term to that of the tribunal. It is also striking that the committee annulled the award on the basis of a failure to state reasons regarding the question of "investment" when the DRC had sought annulment of the award on the basis of a manifest excess of powers in respect of this question. Even if an ICSID committee has the power to annul an award on the basis of a ground not pleaded provided it does so in relation to the same underlying

---

43. *CMS*, supra fn. 14, at para. 71. See also the Decision on Jurisdiction and Admissibility, 18 April 2008 in *Rompetrol Group N.V. v. Romania*, ICSID Case No. ARB/06/3, IIC 322 (2008), holding in the different but analogous context of interpreting the undefined term "national" in Art. 25:

> "At a deeper level ... the Tribunal is not persuaded that there is anything in the rules of treaty interpretation that would justify giving the ICSID Convention overriding effect for the interpretation of the BIT. It is not as if Article 8(2) of the BIT gave ICSID exclusive jurisdiction over disputes that might arise with an investor, or even gave ICSID primacy by comparison with other forums. On the contrary, in common with most clauses of this kind, Article 8(2) lists several dispute forums, on an equal basis, leaving the choice between them to the absolute discretion of the investor in each particular case.... What then could be the justification for calling in an argument specific to ICSID as a means for controlling the meaning said to have been intended by the Contracting Parties when concluding the BIT? It would be impossible to conceive of the definitions in Article 1 as having one meaning in the context of an ICSID arbitration and another for dispute settlement processes taking place elsewhere."

Ibid. at para. 107.
44. *Mitchell*, supra fn. 41, at para. 40.

defect, the committee's approach does suggest that it was less confident that it could annul the award on the basis of the ground actually pleaded by the DRC.

iv. Public policy

While public policy is not a ground for annulment under the Washington Convention, it is a standard ground for annulment available under most arbitration laws.[45] There is a fair question whether that makes non-ICSID treaty awards more vulnerable than ICSID treaty awards, or whether the ground of public policy proves as fertile as the ground of failure to state reasons in ICSID annulment reviews. The experience thus far suggests it does not. Courts in the jurisdictions reviewed invariably set the public policy bar very high.[46] Since applicants often present as a public policy violation what is in fact simply an alleged failure to apply the proper law or a jurisdictional error, courts easily dismiss such objections.[47]

---

45. The English Arbitration Act 1996 does not mention public policy as a ground. It does permit appeals on points of law, but that does not apply to foreign or international law. *Sanghi;20;20 Polyesters Ltd v. International Investor (KCFC)* [2000] 1 Lloyd's Rep. 480; *Egmatra AG v. Marco Trading Corp* [1999] 1 Lloyd's Rep. 862. In the United States, Sect. 10 of the FAA does not mention public policy as a ground but courts have recognized an award's conflict with public policy as a ground warranting *vacatur*. See, inter alia, *United Food v. Foster Poultry* (US 9th Circuit Court of Appeals), 74 F.3d 169, and *Arizona Electric Power Cooperative, Inc. v. Berkeley*, 59 F.3d 988, 992 (9th Cir. 1995), and *Payne v. Giant Food, Inc.*, D.D.C. 2004, 346 F.Supp.2d 15, *appeal dismissed*, 2005 WL 3695770.

46. *Feldman*, supra fn. 18 (stating at para. 87 that for an award to violate public policy, it "must fundamentally offend the most basic and explicit principles of justice and fairness in Ontario, or evidence intolerable ignorance or corruption on the part of the arbitral Tribunal"); *SD Myers*, supra fn. 23, at para. 56 (objection that the arbitral tribunal had wrongly found that claimant qualified as an "investor" with an "investment" under NAFTA was presented as both an excess of powers and a violation of public policy; the court rejected the public policy argument, holding that "the Tribunal's findings with respect to the two jurisdictional questions ... are not 'patently unreasonable', 'clearly irrational', 'totally lacking in reality', or 'a flagrant denial of justice'"); *France Telecom*, supra fn. 3, at para. 5.2.1 ("for there to be a violation of the principle of *pacta sunt servanda* in violation of public policy, it is necessary that the arbitrators refuse to apply a contractual provision although they established that the parties are bound by it, or vice versa, they apply the contractual provision although they considered that the parties are not bound by it", concluding that Lebanon had not made that showing); *Bayview Irrigation*, supra fn. 18, at para. 64 (rejecting a claim of public policy because "the Tribunal's conduct was not marked by corruption, bribery or fraud or contrary to the essential morality").

47. For example, in *Saar Papier v. Poland*, Case 4P.200/2001, Decision of 1 March 2002, the Swiss Federal Tribunal declined to set aside an award where Saar had argued that the tribunal had incorrectly interpreted the BIT and thereby violated principles of public international law. The Federal Tribunal held that a wrong determination of the facts, or even a manifestly wrong determination of the applicable law, does *not* constitute a violation of public policy. It explained that "a violation of public policy does not occur merely when evidence has been wrongly evaluated or the facts of the case have been wrongly determined or a provision of the law has been clearly violated.... Only the violation of a fundamental principle of law leads to the annulment of an award, provided not only the reasoning but also the result violates public policy." The Federal Tribunal denied that these requirements were met in the case at hand.

v. Conclusion: Different benches, different mindsets

The above survey suggests that, while excesses do occasionally occur both within and outside the ICSID system, at least in the recent past both ad hoc committees and domestic courts have exercised proper restraint when reviewing treaty awards. But while the survey may not suggest significant differences in the ultimate outcome, it does show that there is a real difference in the way ad hoc committees and domestic courts approach their task.

Ad hoc committees in the recent past have often proceeded to a microscopic dissection of the award; identify a number of problems with the award and say what the award should have done; but then conclude that the flaws are not such that they warrant annulment. By contrast, domestic courts will often display much greater deference to the tribunal and engage in what sometimes seems a more high-level review of treaty awards. That is not to say that domestic courts only scratch the surface, but they clearly do not consider it to be their task to undertake the kind of detailed autopsy that ad hoc committees engage in.

This should not surprise, given the different composition of the two benches and the different policy considerations that permeate their respective mindsets. Ad hoc committees are composed of individuals that make up a subculture within the subculture of treaty arbitration within the subculture of international arbitration. Of the roughly forty individuals appointed thus far to ad hoc committees, more than three-quarters had previously sat on ICSID tribunals and more than one-third had previously sat on one or more ad hoc committees. They are invariably distinguished arbitrators and/or distinguished international law scholars who are heavily specialized in the field. By contrast, the bench in the jurisdictions reviewed is composed of a typically sophisticated and experienced judiciary, for whom the review of treaty awards represents only a tiny little portion of the immensely more varied mix of matters that they adjudicate on any given day.

These two very different communities approach their task with a very different mindset. In commercial arbitration hubs like England, Sweden and Switzerland decades of development towards a more arbitration-friendly legal environment have created a judicial culture of sensitivity to and respect for the finality of arbitral awards. That sensitivity seems to be amplified even more when dealing with a highly specialized field of law like treaty arbitration, where courts show considerable deference to the expertise of tribunals. With the exception of *Metalclad*, courts have shown no appetite for second-guessing the legal interpretations developed by those tribunals.

Often composed of professional arbitrators, ad hoc committees will share the concern about finality. But at least some of them are also eager to contribute to the "coherence" of international investment law. Highly specialized and experienced in the field of treaty law, these committee members will seek to correct perceived errors of law in a treaty award without necessarily annulling the award. The result is a phenomenon of "*dictatitis*": that is, frequent and lengthy *obiter dicta* that criticizes the manner in which a tribunal interpreted a treaty provision but which stops short of annulling the award on that basis.

The committee in *MTD*, for instance, said that it would adhere to the "established approach" of restraint displayed by previous committees, but only because, in its view, "Article 52(1) as interpreted by successive committees does give scope for quality control"; and "in the present case, whether one likes the Tribunal's decision or not, it was reached on a rather narrow and specific ground, without systematic implications for controversial issues of the law of investment protection". The committee in *CMS* built on that approach when addressing Argentina's entreaty that the committee give closer scrutiny to the award in view of its implications for the many similar cases against Argentina:

> "As Argentina noted, the present arbitration was the first of a long series relating to the Argentine crisis of 2001-2002. Accordingly, the Committee will seek to clarify certain points of substance on which, in its view, the Tribunal made manifest errors of law."

The committee then proceeded to chastise the tribunal on several points of law.

One can debate whether it is the task of an ad hoc committee to take on the role of such a benign, almost professorial appellate body. After all, its decision will carry no more authority than what the prestige of its members commands in the community. But as long as it is benign and the *dicta* remain no more than that, it matters little for purposes of finality. As illustrated by the *Mitchell* decision, however, once a committee goes down the path of such a de novo review of the tribunal's interpretations of law, the path may turn into a dangerously slippery slope.

5. *Will Enforcement Be Stayed Pending Annulment or Setting Aside Review?*

Under Art. 52(5) of the Washington Convention, an ICSID award will be stayed pending constitution of the committee if the applicant so requests. Once the committee is constituted, the party seeking a stay must request a continuance of the provisional stay, failing which the stay is terminated. The committee has discretion to order a stay or to continue a provisional stay. If a stay is granted, the award cannot be enforced in any ICSID State.

When setting aside is sought of a non-ICSID treaty award, a stay may be granted by the annulment court. In Switzerland, for instance, the court has the power to order a stay upon application of the party seeking annulment or if the circumstances so require.[48] Such a stay is rarely granted and it is subject to the double requirement that the prospect of the application to set aside the award is strong and that immediate enforcement would expose the applicant to serious financial problems or that the amount paid would be very difficult to recover in case the award will be annulled.[49] The stay can be conditioned on the payment of a security if the stay is likely to cause damage to the opposing party.[50] The

---

48. See Art. 103(1) and (3) of the Federal Tribunal Act of Switzerland.
49. See Swiss Federal Tribunal, Decision of 14 December 1993, SZIER 1995, at p. 561.
50. Art. 82(2) of the Federal Civil Procedure Act. See Thomas RUEDE and Reiner HADENFELDT, *Schweizerisches Schiedsgerichtsrecht* (2nd edn. 1993), at p. 374; Jean Francois POUDRET, "Le Projet de Loi sur le Tribunal Federal est-il adapte aux Recours en Matiere d'Arbitrage international?", JDT (2002 I) pp. 5-19 at p. 12.

situation in Sweden is similar.[51] By contrast, in France the enforcement of the award is suspended automatically during setting aside review.[52]

When a party seeks to enforce the award in another jurisdiction pending setting aside review, the enforcement court may stay enforcement in its jurisdiction under Art. V(1)(e) of the New York Convention if the award "... has been set aside or suspended by a competent authority in the country in which, or under the law of which, that award was made".[53] Under a strict reading of this provision the enforcement of the award may only be refused if the award has been suspended by a decision of the competent court of the seat, but not if the enforceability is suspended automatically under the national arbitration law.[54]

While the New York Convention and the UNCITRAL Model Law both provide for the possibility of conditioning a stay of recognition on the provision of suitable security, similar language was rejected by the drafters of the Washington Convention.[55] While several ad hoc committees have required a party seeking annulment to provide a bank

---

51. L. HEUMAN, *Arbitration Law of Sweden: Practice and Procedure* (2003) at p. 656:

    "As regards awards made in Sweden, the Enforcement Authority does not have the power to order a stay of the enforcement. Such an order can only be made by the competent court of appeal in connection with an application for the setting-aside of the arbitral award. In determining such a request for stay of enforcement the Court of Appeal shall consider the likelihood of success in the setting aside proceedings, also taking into account the aim of protecting the final and binding nature of an arbitral award. The court may also take into account the damage that the party requesting the stay would suffer if such a stay is not granted as well as the damage the winning party in the arbitration would suffer if it cannot enforce the award. It has been argued that since the damage suffered by both parties respectively will often be more or less on an equal level, the test will essentially be with regard to the likelihood of the award being set aside. Thus, under Swedish law the initiating of setting aside proceedings does not automatically suspend enforcement proceedings in Sweden."

52. Art. 1506 of the French *Nouveau code de procedure civile* (NCPC).
53. Under Art. VII(1) of the New York Convention domestic rules to the enforcement of awards can be applied in case they are more favorable than those of the Convention. The laws of the Netherlands, Belgium, Luxembourg and France, for instance, differ from Art. V(1)(e) and provide more favorable rules; see the discussion of those provisions in Jean Francois POUDRET and Sebastien BESSON, *Comparative Law of International Arbitration* (2nd edn. 2007) at paras. 926 et seq.
54. See Swedish Supreme Court decision in *Götaverken v. GNMTC*, ICCA *Yearbook Commercial Arbitration* VI (1981) (hereinafter *Yearbook*) p. 133, and the decisions of the Chairman of the Amsterdam Tribunal, *Yearbook* X (1985) p. 490, and the Italian *Corte di Cassazione, Yearbook* XIX (1994) p. 685. However, this distinction has been ignored in *Creighton Limited v. Qatar*, US District Court, *Yearbook* XXI (1996) p. 751.
55. SCHREUER, supra fn. 1, at para. 478 ad Art. 52; New York Convention Art. VI; UNCITRAL Model Law Art. 36(2): "If an application for setting aside or suspension of an award has been made ... the court where recognition or enforcement is sought may, if it considers it proper, adjourn its decision and may also, on the application of the party claiming recognition or enforcement of the award, order the other party to provide appropriate security."

guarantee as a condition for a continued stay,[56] several others have declined to order such security, arguing that the delay occasioned by annulment review is systemic to the ICSID system and can be remedied by the payment of interest.[57]

6. *Appeal and Duration*

While an ICSID committee decision is not subject to appeal, a court decision either upholding or setting aside a treaty award may be subject to appeal in a number of jurisdictions. To date, however, we are not aware of any court decision upholding a treaty award being reversed on appeal. Moreover, notwithstanding the possibility of appeal in the non-ICSID context, the ICSID annulment review process still took on average nearly five months longer than non-ICSID setting aside proceedings. That difference, however, is largely offset by the longer duration of non-ICSID arbitrations.

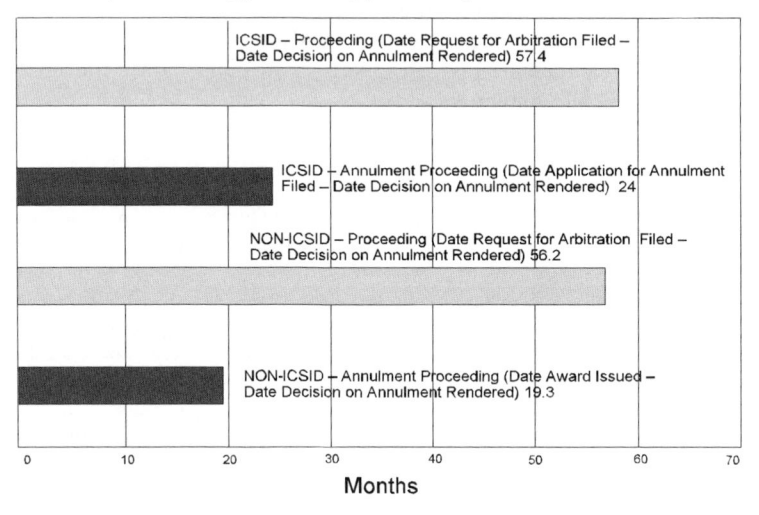

**Average Duration of Proceedings**
**(Not including justiciability proceeding in *OEPC v. Ecuador*)**

| Proceeding | Months |
|---|---|
| ICSID – Proceeding (Date Request for Arbitration Filed – Date Decision on Annulment Rendered) | 57.4 |
| ICSID – Annulment Proceeding (Date Application for Annulment Filed – Date Decision on Annulment Rendered) | 24 |
| NON-ICSID – Proceeding (Date Request for Arbitration Filed – Date Decision on Annulment Rendered) | 56.2 |
| NON-ICSID – Annulment Proceeding (Date Award Issued – Date Decision on Annulment Rendered) | 19.3 |

---

56. *Amco*, supra fn. 31 (First and Second Annulment); *Wena*, supra fn. 26; *CDC Group*, supra fn. 26; *Repsol YPF Ecuador S.A. v. Empresa Estatal Petróleos del Ecuador (Petroecuador)*, ICSID Case No. ARB/01/10.
57. *Maritime International Nominees Establishment v. Republic of Guinea*, ICSID Case No. ARB/84/4, Ad Hoc Committee Decision, 22 December 1989, 4 ICSID Rep., p. 79 at p. 2 (security would place the winning party "in a much more favorable position"); *MTD*, supra fn. 32; *Mitchell*, supra fn. 41; *CMS*, supra fn. 14.

III. ENFORCEMENT REVIEW: HOW STRONG IS THE SHIELD?[58]

The second hurdle that the successful claimant has to take is recognition and enforcement review of the treaty award.[59] The principal questions here are: (i) how automatic is the Washington Convention regime; (ii) how disadvantageous is the New York Convention regime as compared to the ICSID regime; and (iii) are there distinct enforcement advantages of opting out of the ICSID regime?

*1. The Washington Convention Regime: Undeniably Pretty Good*

Art. 54 of the Washington Convention provides for the "full faith and credit" of ICSID awards in any of the ICSID Contracting States. The provision makes a distinction between recognition and enforcement, limiting the obligation to "enforce" (in French and Spanish, *"executer"*, *"ejecutar"*) an ICSID award, "as if it were a final judgment of a court in that State", to the "pecuniary obligations imposed" by the award. Most commentators maintain that non-pecuniary obligations in an award must therefore be enforced through the New York Convention or under domestic law.[60] Various domestic laws implementing the Washington Convention perpetuate this non-applicability of the ICSID enforcement regime to non-pecuniary awards.[61] The only reported cases on the recognition of ICSID awards principally address the distinction between recognition and execution but – albeit sometimes only on appeal – invariably confirm the automaticity of recognition in the ICSID system.[62]

---

58. For recent contributions on the subject, see S. ALEXANDROV, "Enforcement of ICSID Awards: Articles 53 and 54 of the ICSID Convention", and L. CAPLAN, "Post-Annulment Options: Possible Recourse by Investor's Home State", both published on <www.transnational-dispute-management.com>.
59. "Recognition" and "enforcement" are often used interchangeably but have different meanings. "Recognition" consists in acknowledging the legal effect of the foreign award. "Enforcement" relates to the request of various measures of obtaining satisfaction. Recognition and enforcement are almost invariably simultaneously requested and usually precede a request for execution upon the assets of the award debtor.
60. Julian D.M. LEW, Loukas A. MISTELIS and Stefan M. KRÖLL, *Comparative International Commercial Arbitration* (2003) at paras. 28-111; SCHREUER, supra fn. 1, at para. 71 ad Art. 54.
61. Sect. 2 of the English Arbitration Act 1966 provides that once registered, the award will "be of the same force and effect for the purposes of execution as if it had been a judgment of the High Court", but only "as respects the pecuniary obligations which it imposes". Likewise, "proceedings may be taken on the award" and "the High Court shall have ... control over the execution", but only "so far as relates to such pecuniary obligations".
In the United States, 22 U.S.C. Sect. 1650a provides that full faith and credit and the duty to enforce apply only to the pecuniary obligations, all non-pecuniary obligations giving rise only to a "right": *"An award* of an arbitral tribunal rendered pursuant to [the Washington Convention] *shall create a right* arising under a treaty of the United States. *The pecuniary obligations imposed by such an award shall be enforced* and shall be given the same full faith and credit as if the award were a final judgment of a court of general jurisdiction of one of the several States...." (Emphasis added)
62. See *SARL Benvenuti & Bonfant v. People's Republic of the Congo, Cour de Cassation*, 2 July 1987, 1 ICSID Rep. 373; *SOABI v. Senegal, Cour de Cassation*, 11 June 1991, 2 ICSID Rep., p. 337 at p. 341; *LETCO v. Liberia*, US District Court, Southern District of New York, 5 September 1986 and 12

Art. 54(2) of the Washington Convention describes the mechanics, providing that "a party seeking recognition or enforcement in the territories of a Contracting State shall furnish to a competent court or other authority which such State shall have designated for this purpose a copy of the award certified by the Secretary-General". A list of the authorities so designated is available on the ICSID website. While the overwhelming majority of countries have designated a court as the competent authority (and in this case, the recognition and enforcement will often be part of the same process), eight states have designated a non-judicial authority – among them Belgium, Sweden, the Czech Republic and Latvia.[63]

In some of those countries that have designated a non-judicial authority, the implementing legislation clearly lays out the applicable procedure. In Belgium, for instance, the law of 17 July 1970 provides in Art. 3 that the Minister of Foreign Affairs is responsible for the verification of the authenticity of the documents submitted; that the Minister may delegate this responsibility; and that the authenticated documents are then transmitted, by intervention of the Ministry of Justice, to the Clerk of the Brussels Court of Appeal, which grants legal effect to the documents. Sometimes, however, it is less clear what the designated authority will do with the award and what the procedure is. In preparation for this Report, inquiries were made of the designated authorities of one of the above countries, which had not provided for specific procedures in implementation of Art. 54. After a diligent search within three different ministries, the designated authority was unable to answer the inquiry and, with profuse apologies, suggested that we contact ICSID.

2.  *The New York Convention Regime: Not So Bad At All*

The New York Convention allows domestic courts to refuse recognition and enforcement when the applicant establishes one of five grounds: (a) invalidity of the arbitration agreement; (b) lack of due process; (c) excess of mandate by the arbitrators; (d) improper constitution of the tribunal; (e) the award is not binding or has been set aside or suspended in the country where it was rendered. In addition, the court may refuse recognition *sua sponte* on two grounds: (a) non-arbitrability; and (b) public policy of the enforcing state. The drafters envisaged that this list would be exclusive of all other grounds for non-recognition.[64] There are, however, the occasional "judicial casualties".[65]

---

December 1986, US District Court, District of Columbia, 16 April 1987, 2 ICSID Rep., p. 383 at p. 390; *AIG Capital v. Republic of Kazakhstan*, High Court of Justice, Queen's Bench Division, [2006] 1 Lloyd's Rep. 45.

63. The competent authority is the Ministry of Foreign Affairs for Belgium and Sweden, the Ministry of Justice for the Czech Republic, Egypt, Guinea, and Latvia, the Permanent Secretary for Foreign Affairs in Lesotho, and the Ministry of Finance in Sierra Leone.

64. UN Doc. "Recognition and Enforcement of Foreign Arbitral Awards, *Report by the Secretary General and Comments by Governments on ICC Draft*", UN Social and Economic Council, Twenty-first session (31 January 1956) UN Doc. E/2822. (Hereinafter, UN Doc E/2822). Comment by the Swiss delegate:

"This article deals with bilateral or multilateral agreements concluded by the States Parties to the

The authority of courts under Art. V is generally accepted to be discretionary in nature.[66] Countries may restrict that discretion by treaty. Under Art. XI of the European Convention of 1961, for instance, the courts may refuse to recognize and enforce an award that has been annulled in its state of origin only where the annulment was based on the four grounds for annulment listed in the UNCITRAL Model Law. In addition, Art. VII(1) of the New York Convention further restricts the likelihood that an award will be refused enforcement. Often referred to as the "more favorable right" provision, Art. VII(1) of the New York Convention provides, in pertinent part, that "the provisions of the present Convention shall not ... deprive any interested party of any right he may have to avail himself of an arbitral award in the manner and to the extent allowed by the law or the treaties of the country where such award is sought to be relied upon".

---

Convention. Perhaps it should provide that such instruments may be relied on in so far as they stipulate more liberal conditions governing the recognition and enforcement of international arbitral awards in private law but cannot be relied on if they stipulate more stringent conditions."

In response to this suggestion, what is now Art. VII(1) was amended to include the "more-favorable-right" provision.

65. Albert Jan VAN DEN BERG, "Why Are Some Awards Not Enforceable?" in *New Horizons in International Commercial Arbitration and Beyond*, ICCA Congress Series no. 12 (hereinafter *ICCA Congress Series no. 12*) (2005) pp. 291-326 at p. 292. Three cases have been cited as anomalous, due to judicial error (in the case of Italy and Greece) or a deficient implementing legislation (in Australia). *Viceré Livio v. Prodexport*, Yearbook VII (1982) p. 345 (reversing the burden of proof); *Charterer v. Shipowner*, Yearbook XI (1986) p. 500 (requiring the party seeking enforcement to provide provisions Yearbook XI (1986) of New York law showing that the arbitration agreement was valid; *Resort Condominiums International v. Ray Bowell and Resort Condominiums*, Yearbook XXV (2000) p. 628 (applying Sect. 5(8) of International Commercial Arbitration Act 1974 which omits the word "only" in transcribing Art. V of the New York Convention). Of greater concern is the US court decision in *Monde Re*. Monde Re was a Monegasque company which sought to enforce an International Commercial Arbitration Court at the Russian Federation Chamber of Commerce and Industry award made in Moscow against Naftogaz, a Ukrainian corporation. The District Court refused on the ground of forum non conveniens. Monde Re appealed, arguing that forum non conveniens is not a valid ground for refusal of enforcement under Art. V of the New York Convention. Monde Re's appeal was dismissed. The court held that since forum non conveniens is a procedural rule and Art. III allows each country to apply its own procedural rules, as long as the rules applied to foreign awards are not "substantially more onerous" than the procedural rules applied to domestic awards, the Second Circuit Court concluded that Arts. III and V allow dismissal for forum non conveniens. *Monégasque de Reassurances v. Naftogaz and Ukraine*, 311 F.3d 488, 2d Cir. (2002); Yearbook XXVIII (2003) p. 1096. See also *Base Metal Trading Limited (UK) v. OJSC Novokuznetsky Aluminium Factory (Russian Federation)*, Yearbook XXVII (2002) p. 902.

66. See DAVIS, "Unconventional Wisdom: A New Look at Articles V and VII of the New York Convention on the Recognition and Enforcement of Foreign Arbitral Awards", 37 Tex. Int'l L. J. (2002) p. 43, n. 141; UN Doc. E/2822/Add.4, Annex I regarding what was then Art. IV; the Norwegian government commenting that "in view of the fact that it does not impose an obligation on the Contracting Parties, it would probably be better to leave it out altogether", UN Doc. E/2822/Add.5 at 4; UN Doc. E/2822/Add.2 Annex (1956). Part of the debate over the discretionary nature of Art. V is fuelled by a difference in the drafting of the French version. See J. PAULSSON, "*May* or *must* under the New York Convention: An Exercise in Syntax and Linguistics", 14 Arb. Int'l (1998) p.227.

There are no reported decisions refusing recognition or enforcement of non-ICSID treaty awards. A fortiori, there is no evidence to suggest that a court in an enforcement jurisdiction might refuse recognition and enforcement of a treaty award under the New York Convention where a court in the country of origin has already rejected an annulment challenge to the award. If the reported recognition cases in the treaty context offer any guidance for the future, it appears unlikely to occur. In *Sedelmayer v. Russia,* the Svea Court of Appeal and the Swedish Supreme Court had affirmed the lower court's denial of Russia's annulment challenge on the grounds that the tribunal did not have jurisdiction. Sedelmayer then sought recognition in Germany, which was granted by the Berlin Court of Appeal over the same jurisdictional objections by Russia.[67] In *SwemBalt v. Latvia*, Latvia argued the same jurisdictional error before the enforcement court in Sweden and the annulment court in Denmark.[68] Noting that the challenge before the Danish courts was unlikely to succeed, the Swedish courts granted recognition and enforcement.

Recognition is also unlikely to be refused on the basis of Art. IV of the Convention. While this happened in at least two reported commercial cases,[69] it will likely remain an isolated occurrence because of Art. VII, which permits the importation of the more favorable provisions of domestic law.[70] In *Saar Papier v. Poland,* the German

---

67. *Sedelmayer (Germany) v. Russian Federation, Yearbook* XXXI (2006) p. 698. Following recognition by the Berlin court, Sedelmayer was even able to obtain attachment on certain bank accounts of the Russian Embassy that Russia could not prove had been allocated for sovereign purposes: Frankfurt Court of Appeal, 26 September 2002, reported in *Yearbook* XXX (2005) p. 505.
68. *SwemBalt,* Decision of the Svea Court of Appeal, Case No. Ö 7192-01.
69. See, e.g., the Italian *Corte di cassazione* in *Lampart Vegypary (Hungary) v. Campomarzio Impianti (Italy), Yearbook* XXIV (1999) p. 699; Bulgarian Supreme Court in *National Electricity Company AG (Bulgaria) v. ECONERG (Croatia), Yearbook* XXV (2000) p. 678. On the other hand, the Swiss court in *R SA v. A Ltd., Yearbook* XXVI (2001) p. 863, recognized a Chinese award that had not been translated, and the German *Bundesgerichtshof* in *Saar Papier v. Poland,* Case III ZB 43/99, allowed recognition of a Polish award.
70. German law, for instance, does not require the party seeking enforcement to provide a translation of the award or to provide a certified copy of the arbitration agreement, and therefore German courts often apply Art. VII(1) to cure non-compliance with Art. IV of the New York Convention. See, e.g., *Bayern Oberlandesgericht* [Court of Appeal of Bavaria] 11 Aug. 2000, 4 Z SchH5/00, excerpted in *Yearbook* XXVII (2002) pp. 451-454; *Bundesgerichtshof* [Federal Supreme Court] 25 September 2003, No. III ZB 68/02, excerpted in *Yearbook* XXIX (2004) pp. 767-770; *Oberlandesgericht* [Court of Apeal], Schleswig, 15 July 2003, No. 16 Sch 01/03, excerpted in *Yearbook* XXX (2005) pp. 524-527; *Oberlandesgericht* [Court of Appeal] Cologne, 23 April 2004, No. 9 Sch 01-03, excerpted in *ibid.* at pp. 557-562; *Bayerisches Oberstes Landesgericht* [Higher Court of Appeal of Bavaria] 5 July 2004, No. 4Z Sch 09/04, excerpted in *ibid.* at 563-567; *K. Trading Company (Syria) v. Bayerischen Motoren Werke AG (Germany) Bayerisches Oberstes Landesgericht,* 23 September 2004, No. 4Z Sch 005-04, excerpted in *ibid.* at pp. 568-573; *Oberlandesgericht,* Koblenz, 28 July 2005, No. 2 Sch 04/05, excerpted in *Yearbook* XXXI (2006) pp. 673-678; *Oberlandesgericht,* Hamm, 27 September 2005, 29 Sch 1/05, excerpted in *ibid.* at pp. 685-697; *Oberlandesgericht,* Dresden, 2 November 2005, 1 Sch 15/05, excerpted in *ibid.* at pp. 718-719; *Oberlandesgericht,* Dresden, 7 November 2005, 1 Sch 07/04, excerpted in *ibid.* at pp. 720-721; *Oberlandesgericht,* Munich, 28 November 2005, No. 34 Sch 019/05, excerpted in *ibid.* at pp. 722-728.

*Bundesgerichtshof* dismissed an Art. IV objection holding that Art. IV was a mere rule of evidence that is not a reason to refuse recognition where the authenticity of the award is not contested.[71]

3.   *Two Potential Advantages of Opting out of ICSID*

When compared to the Washington Convention, the New York Convention does create an additional risk for the party seeking to enforce a treaty award, even if that risk may not be as material as it would seem at first blush. In addition, the New York Convention also raises the prospect of potentially protracted and costly enforcement litigation, possibly in several jurisdictions at the same time. Those disadvantages are real. But it is often overlooked that opting for a set of rules other than ICSID may also offer some advantages not available under the ICSID system: (i) a non-ICSID treaty award that was previously set aside may still be enforceable in some jurisdictions; and (ii) a claimant in a non-ICSID proceeding may seek a freeze order from domestic courts against the sovereign pending the arbitration.

*a.   Enforcement of a non-ICSID treaty award previously suspended or set aside*
In the ICSID system, once an award has been annulled, it is game over. The only remedy is to resubmit the dispute to another arbitral tribunal. Outside the ICSID context, the notion that a suspended or annulled award could still be enforced has been the subject of considerable controversy.[72] Yet, as controversial as it may be, it is not impossible under the New York Convention, which will almost certainly apply if the award was rendered under the UNCITRAL or ICC rules.

*First*, an award may be granted recognition and enforcement under Art. V(1)(e) of the New York Convention even if it has been "suspended by a competent authority in the country in which, or under the law of which, that award was made". The Svea Court of Appeals, for instance, allowed recognition and enforcement of a treaty award in Sweden even though it was still under annulment review in Denmark, noting that lis pendens was not a valid ground to refuse enforcement.[73]

---

71. *Saar Papier v. Poland*, supra fn. 68. The *Bundesgerichtshof* rejected Poland's objections that the award submitted to the enforcement court was not duly authenticated (see Art. IV(1)(a)) and that the agreement to arbitrate had not been supplied (Art. IV(1)(b)).
72. PETROCHILOS, "Enforcing Awards Annulled in Their State of Origin Under the New York Convention", 48 Int'l & Comp. L. Q. (1999) p. 856 at p. 857.
73. *SwemBalt*, supra fn. 67. However, the suspension of the award in the state of origin was cited by the US court in *Creighton v. Qatar* as reason to refuse enforcement. In that case, the award had been rendered in France and was subject to an automatic *sursis d'exécution* pending appeal by Qatar under Art. 1506 NCPC. *Creighton Ltd. v. Government of the State of Qatar (ministry of Public Works)*, US District Court, District of Columbia, Yearbook XXI (1996) p. 751. See also the decision of the Geneva Court of Appeal in *Continaf B.V. (Netherlands) v. Polycoton S.A. (Switzerland)*, Yearbook XII (1987) p. 505. This conclusion has rightly been criticized on the argument that a suspension should only qualify under Art. V(1)(e) if it has been ordered "by a competent authority" in the state of origin, and not where it results automatically by operation of law. Albert Jan VAN DEN BERG, "New York Convention of 1958 Consolidated Commentary", Yearbook XXI (1996) p. 394 at p. 500; FOUCHARD, GAILLARD, GOLDMAN, *International Commercial Arbitration* (1999) p. 981.

*Second*, annulment in the seat of the arbitration does not constitute a ground to refuse enforcement in a number of jurisdictions, including Belgium, France and Luxembourg. It has been argued that the absence of annulment as a ground for non-recognition creates a more favorable right for the party seeking enforcement in those jurisdictions which the latter can invoke under Art. VII(1) of the Convention. Courts in France[74] and Luxembourg[75] have so held. A US court similarly enforced a previously annulled award in the much-commented *Chromalloy* decision,[76] but subsequent cases have not followed that decision.[77]

---

See also, to this effect, the decisions of the Swedish Supreme Court in *Götaverken,* and the decisions of the Chairman of the Amsterdam Tribunal and the Italian *Corte di Cassazione,* supra fn. 54.

74. The most infamous case in France is *Société Hilmarton v. Société OTV,* in which the *Cour de Cassation* held that Art. VII(1) of the New York Convention permitted the claimant to rely upon the more favorable provisions of the French Civil Code. The court explained that the award (which had been rendered in Switzerland) was an international award, not integrated into the legal system of that state, and therefore remained effective even after having been annulled by the courts of that state. Since there was no basis under French law for refusing to recognize and enforce the award, the court held that the award had to be enforced. The case was followed in four subsequent cases. *Société Hilmarton v. Société OTV,* Cass. 1ière Civ., 10 June 1997, Bull. civ. I, No. 195, 12 Mealey's Int'l Arb. Rep. I-1 (July 1997). See also *Bargues Agro Industrie S.A. (France) v. Young Pecan Company (US), Cour d'appel de Paris,* 10 June 2004, No. 2003/09894, excerpted in *Yearbook* XXX (2005) pp. 499-504; *Directorate General of Civil Aviation of the Emirate of Dubai v. International Bechtel Co. LLC (Panama), Cour d'appel de Paris,* 29 September 2005, No. 2004/07635, excerpted in *Yearbook* XXXI (2006) pp. 629-634.

75. In *Chadmore,* the Luxembourg Court of Appeals affirmed a lower court decision enforcing an award despite the fact that the award was under review in the place of arbitration. The Court relied, among others, on *Hilmarton,* and stressed the importance of allowing a more liberal enforcement régime. *Sovereign Participations International S.A.(Luxembourg) v. Chadmore Developments Ltd. (Ireland) Cour d'appel,* 28 January 1999, excerpted in *Yearbook* XXIVa (1999) pp. 714-723.

76. The US District Court for the District of Columbia enforced an award that had been annulled in Egypt. The court held that, while the Art. V grounds for denial of enforcement were discretionary, Art. VII(1) of the New York Convention was mandatory and required the application of domestic law where it was more favorable. The court enforced the award, citing the fact that Chromalloy was entitled to enforcement under the Federal Arbitration Act, and that the Egyptian judgment of annulment should be refused recognition due to US public policy in favor of enforcing arbitral awards. *In re Chromalloy Aeroservices v. The Arab Republic of Egypt,* 939 F.Supp. 907 (D.D.C. 1996).

77. In *Baker Marine v. Chevron,* the US Court of Appeals for the Second Circuit refused enforcement of an award that had been set aside in Nigeria. The claimant argued that under Art. VII(1) of the New York Convention, the annulment should be disregarded because the grounds on which the award was annulled were not recognized by US domestic law. The court rejected the argument, noting that Nigerian law applied to the arbitration and that there was no reason not to recognize the Nigerian annulment judgment. *Baker Marine, Ltd. v. Chevron, Ltd.,* 191 F.3d 194 (2nd Cir. 1999); see also *Spier v. Calzaturificio Tecnica S.p.A.,* 71 F. Supp.2d 279 (S.D.N.Y. 1999). More recently, in 2007, the US Court of Appeals for the District of Columbia Circuit refused to enforce an award annulled in Colombia. The party seeking enforcement argued that the Colombian judgment annulling the award should not be recognized on the ground that it frustrated US policy in favor of international arbitration. The court rejected the claim holding that "a principal precept of the New York Convention [is that] an arbitration award does not exist to be enforced in other Contracting States if it has been lawfully 'set aside' by a competent authority in the State in which

While courts in many jurisdictions may be unlikely to enforce an award against a sovereign when it has been set aside in the rendering jurisdiction, the possibility that courts in some important jurisdictions may not should not be ignored.

*b.  The availability of interim relief in state courts*

The availability of interim injunctive relief in national courts in anticipation of – in some cases concurrent with – arbitration is a potentially useful tool in treaty cases, where the claimant often understandably fears dissipation of seizable assets by the state pending the arbitration.[78] In the ICSID system, interim relief will almost certainly be only available from the ICSID tribunal, which will take at least several months after the filing of the request for arbitration to be constituted.[79] In *MINE v. Guinea* for example, MINE was even ordered to dissolve the attachments it had obtained in seeking enforcement of a prior non-ICSID award.[80] Moreover, the limited interim relief that an ICSID tribunal may order under Art. 47 does not form part of the final award and thus will not benefit from the Washington Convention's simplified recognition procedure, whereas auxiliary interim relief can be enforced in Europe under Art. 31 of the Brussels Regulation.[81] While the odds of obtaining – and keeping in place – such an order will often be long, its potential should not be ignored.[82]

---

the award was made". *TermoRio S.A. E.S.P*, 487 F.3d 928 (D.C. Cir. 2007).

78. For an excellent survey of the competence of state courts to grant interim relief in support of arbitration in England, Scotland, France, Germany and Switzerland, see V.V. VEEDER, "The Need for Cross-border Enforcement of Interim Measures Ordered by a State Court in Support of the International Arbitral Process", *ICCA Congress Series no. 12* (2005) at pp. 242-271.

79. See SCHREUER, supra fn. 1 at pp. 376-385, and references therein. The French *Cour de Cassation* reached the opposite conclusion in *Atlantic Triton Company Limited v. People's Revolutionary Republic of Guinea*, ICSID Case No. ARB/84/1, Judgment of 18 November 1986, 3 ICSID Rep., p. 3 at p. 10; discussed in FRIEDLAND, "ICSID and Court-Ordered Provisional Measures: An Update", 4 Arb. Int'l (1988) p. 161 at p. 162 et seq. The Court held that Art. 26 of the Washington Convention was *not* intended to preclude conservatory measures in national courts. The decision stands isolated.

80. See *MINE v. Guinea*, supra fn. 57, Decision on Provisional Measures, 4 December 1985 (unpublished), excerpted in Award, 6 January 1988, 4 ICSID Rep., p. 69.

81. Council Regulation 44/2001 on Jurisdiction and Enforcement of Judgments in Civil and Commercial Matters of 22 December 2000 (reproducing Art. 24 of the Brussels Convention); see VEEDER, supra fn. 78, and the decision of the European Court of Justice in *Van Uden v. Deco-Line* [1998] E.C.R. I-7122 et seq.

82. Two recent cases illustrate this. On 27 March 2008 CMS Gas Transmission obtained a temporary freezing order against Argentina pending a hearing on its motion for attachment on Argentine assets, in an attempt to enforce its ICSID award. The order was dissolved several days later as the funds were no longer in New York. By contrast, in February 2008, Exxon sought pre-arbitration conservatory measures from English and Dutch courts in support of an ICC arbitration against PDVSA. Exxon obtained the provisional relief, immobilizing assets worth $12.3 billion, but the freeze was lifted shortly thereafter. Notably, Exxon was at the same time pursuing a parallel ICSID arbitration against the Republic of Venezuela arising out of the same measures.

IV. CONCLUSION

Perhaps predictably, there is no straight answer to the question whether a prospective claimant is better off enforcement-wise with ICSID or other rules.

(a) Statistically, non-ICSID awards have fared better than ICSID awards in annulment proceedings. But the population is too small to base any broad conclusions on this.
(b) For all practical purposes the chances of avoiding annulment review altogether are equally dismal for ICSID and non-ICSID treaty awards.
(c) While the annulment standards applicable to non-ICSID treaty awards will vary with the seat of the tribunal, that uncertainty is mitigated by the prevailing practice of non-ICSID tribunals to pick a "usual suspect" as the jurisdiction of the seat and the guidance provided by a well-developed body of law in those jurisdictions as compared to the handful of ICSID decisions to date.
(d) Domestic courts often appear to display greater deference to treaty awards than ad hoc committees, which increasingly seem to sit as benign appellate bodies. Public policy in domestic laws has thus far not proven to be a black box for annulment purposes, whereas the ground of failure to state reasons may be a slippery slope.
(e) There appears to be no clear advantage in selecting ICSID or other rules in terms of stay of enforcement pending review; security pending stay; or overall duration.
(f) The recognition and enforcement procedures of the Washington Convention are plainly superior to those of the New York Convention by making it easier for the claimant to "smoke out" the sovereign through the pursuit of multiple enforcement actions in little time and with little cost.
(g) That advantage should be weighed against certain enforcement benefits available only with non-ICSID treaty arbitration, including the possibility to seek early interim relief from state courts in aid of execution.

# Defending Investment Treaty Awards: Is There an ICSID Advantage?

*Yas Banifatemi*[*]

TABLE OF CONTENTS | Page
---|---
I. Introduction | 318
II. ICSID Versus Non-ICSID – Varying Factors of Uncertainty | 319
III. Differing Review of the Absence of Reasons for an Award | 321
IV. Limitation of the Review on the Merits | 324

I. INTRODUCTION

Common wisdom has it that, in investment matters, the ICSID system has achieved in the last decade an efficiency outshining, to a certain extent, other international arbitration fora. The question here is not so much ICSID's success and expanding caseload since the late 1990s, in particular as a result of the explosion of the number of bilateral investment treaties (BITs) providing for ICSID arbitration and the investors' recourse to those treaties in their disputes with host States around the world. Rather, it is important to focus on the internal reasons for such proclaimed efficiency that can be found in the ICSID Convention itself.

International arbitration was revolutionized in 1958 by the adoption of the New York Convention laying the grounds for the facilitation of the enforcement mechanism and a limitation of the annulment grounds of international arbitral awards.[1] Fifty years later, the success of the New York Convention is undeniable.[2] In 1965, the ICSID Convention similarly introduced two important innovations in investment matters, by enabling the self-executory nature of arbitral awards and making it an obligation for State parties

---

[*] Partner, member of the International Arbitration practice and Head of the Public International Law practice, Shearman & Sterling LLP, Paris; teacher of investment law and investment arbitration, Panthéon-Sorbonne University (Paris I).
1. New York Convention on the Recognition and Enforcement of Foreign Arbitral Awards, adopted on 10 June 1958 and, as of this writing, binding on 144 States. See Emmanuel GAILLARD and John SAVAGE, eds., *Fouchard Gaillard Goldman On International Commercial Arbitration* (Kluwer Law International 1999) paras. 247 et seq.; Albert Jan VAN DEN BERG, *The New York Convention of 1958 – Towards a Uniform Judicial Interpretation* (Kluwer Law and Taxation Publishers 1981).
2. See in particular Robert BRINER and Virginia HAMILTON, "The Creation of an International Standard to Ensure the Effectiveness of Arbitration Agreements and Foreign Arbitral Awards" in Emmanuel GAILLARD and Domenico DI PIETRO, eds., *Enforcement of Arbitration Agreements and International Arbitral Awards – The New York Convention in Practice* (Cameron May 2008) p. 3 at pp. 19-21; see also Karl-Heinz BÖCKSTIEGEL, "Future Perspectives" in *ibid.*, p. 865.

under Art. 54 to treat arbitral awards as if they were a final judgment of their own courts, and by establishing in Art. 52 a self-contained annulment system.[3]

To what extent have the ICSID rules, in hindsight, achieved greater efficiency such that ICSID arbitration is today the investors' preferred option? To the question whether "to ICSID or not to ICSID", the theme of his Report at this Conference, Gaëtan Verhoosel responds that "there is no straight answer" (this volume, pp. 285-317 at p. 317), an observation that, by itself, seems to challenge the notion of ICSID's pre-eminence in investment arbitration today. This conclusion is based on an in-depth analysis of "the two possible hurdles on the road to enforcement – annulment review and enforcement review – and consider[s] how these hurdles compare for ICSID and non-ICSID awards".[4] My comments will focus on the first aspect of this analysis, namely the comparison between the annulment review of ICSID awards and the setting aside review of non-ICSID awards (often subject to the New York Convention).

II. ICSID VERSUS NON-ICSID: VARYING FACTORS OF UNCERTAINTY

Comparing the respective merits of ICSID and non-ICSID arbitration as regards the review of awards is not as straightforward as it would seem. On the one hand, ICSID establishes a centralized and self-contained review system based on a limited number of specific grounds.[5] On the other hand, non-ICSID investment treaty awards are reviewed by national courts, often at the seat of the arbitration, in what thus constitutes a decentralized system where the grounds for challenge vary from one jurisdiction to the other.

In his final comments, Mr. Verhoosel observes that:

"While the annulment standards applicable to non-ICSID treaty awards will vary with the seat of the tribunal, that uncertainty is mitigated by the prevailing practice of non-ICSID tribunals to pick a 'usual suspect' as the jurisdiction of the

---

3. See Christoph SCHREUER, *The ICSID Convention: A Commentary* (Cambridge University Press 2001) pp. 1098 et seq. and pp. 881 et seq. respectively. Rudolf DOLZER and Christoph SCHREUER, *Principles of International Investment Law* (OUP 2008) p. 279. See also W. Michael REISMAN, *Systems of Control in International Adjudication and Arbitration – Breakdown and Repair* (Duke University Press 1992) pp. 46 et seq.
4. Gaëtan VERHOOSEL, "Annulment and Enforcement Review of Treaty Awards: To ICSID or Not to ICSID", this volume, pp. 285-317 at pp. 317 and 285-286.
5. These grounds are set forth in Art. 52(1) of the ICSID Convention:

"(a) that the Tribunal was not properly constituted;
(b) that the Tribunal has manifestly exceeded its powers;
(c) that there was corruption on the part of a member of the Tribunal;
(d) that there has been a serious departure from a fundamental rule of procedure; or
(e) that the award has failed to state the reasons on which it is based".

seat and the guidance provided by a well-developed body of law in those jurisdictions as compared to the handful of ICSID decisions to date."[6]

Admittedly, regular recourse to such "usual suspects" would reduce the degree of uncertainty for investors who choose to submit the conduct of their dispute to rules other than ICSID. In practice, however, the factors of uncertainty are not necessarily specific to the choice of non-ICSID arbitration over ICSID arbitration.

The existing body of ICSID decisions shows that the variety of the solutions is not specific to national jurisdictions: the decisions rendered by ad hoc committees also vary greatly. The standard of review, for example, was not the same in *Vivendi* and *Wena* as compared to *Patrick Mitchell* and *CMS*.[7] Notwithstanding the integrated nature of the ICSID annulment system and certain ad hoc committees' inspiration to contribute to the "coherence" of international investment law,[8] the fact remains that today, coherence is not achieved and both the method and the solutions adopted may vary from one committee to another.

Even within jurisdictions appearing as "usual suspects", there may be different approaches to the challenge of arbitral awards. The situations, here again, may vary greatly.

At one extreme of the range of options, challenges may be brought before the courts of the respondent State (presumably by the State itself in the event it has lost the arbitration on questions of jurisdiction or on the merits).[9] Considering that, in investment treaty arbitration, the ultimate decision concerns the host State's international responsibility, this situation raises the issue, from a public international law perspective, of the lack of neutrality and lack of independence of the authority deciding the respondent State's challenge to the award, which is an organ of that State itself.

Where the seat of the arbitration is fixed in a neutral forum, the solutions will vary depending on the applicability of the New York Convention and, more generally, a given

---

6. *Ibid.*, p. 317.
7. See infra, para. 9. On the "three generations" of ICSID decisions in annulment proceedings, see Christoph SCHREUER, "Three Generations of ICSID Annulment Proceedings" in Emmanuel GAILLARD and Yas BANIFATEMI, eds., *Annulment of ICSID Award, IAI Series on International Arbitration No. 1* (Juris Publishing 2004) p. 17. The article, however, predates the *Patrick Mitchell* and *CMS* decisions; for critical observations on these decisions, see Emmanuel GAILLARD, "Centre international pour le règlement des différends relatifs aux investissements (C.I.R.D.I.) – Chronique des sentences arbitrages", 134 Journal du droit international (J.D.I.) (2007) p. 359 and 135 J.D.I. (2008) p. 360.
8. On the notion of "precedent" in international arbitration, see Yas BANIFATEMI, ed., *Precedent in International Arbitration, IAI Series on International Arbitration No. 5* (Juris Publishing 2008); see more specifically Gabrielle KAUFMANN-KOHLER, "Is Consistency a Myth?" in *ibid.*, p. 137 at p. 145 et seq. See also infra, p. 323.
9. See, e.g., the setting aside proceeding currently pending before the Czech courts in relation to an UNCITRAL arbitral award whereby the tribunal decided that it had jurisdiction over the dispute between a foreign investor and the Czech Republic: Luke Eric PETERSON, "Czech Republic Continues Efforts to Overturn Confidential Jurisdictional Ruling in BIT Arbitration with German Investor; Prague Court to Hear Arguments as to Incompatibility with EU Law, as Arbitral Proceeding Continues in BIT Dispute", 1 Investment Arbitration Reporter (2008, no. 4) p. 10.

jurisdiction's approach to international arbitration as reflected in the applicable legislation (and whether or not such legislation assumes a modern approach, for example through the adoption of the UNCITRAL Model Law), in the existing body of case law on arbitration, and in the degree of sophistication of the courts in the recognition of the arbitral process. Jurisdictions such as Switzerland and France have, in this respect, adopted the most restrictive standards of review and the highest degree of deference to arbitral awards. The fact that no specific regime exists, in national systems, for investment matters and that the grounds on which an award may be challenged before the courts will be the same in investment arbitration and in commercial arbitration does not alter a given jurisdiction's approach.[10]

The choice of the seat in non-ICSID arbitration is therefore crucial. But this choice normally occurs *after* a decision has been made not to choose the ICSID route and after the choice of one of the other options provided under the applicable treaty.

With this background in mind, it is of particular interest to briefly consider the difference in approach between ICSID and non-ICSID mechanisms as regards two chief grounds for review, namely the failure to state reasons (a ground specific to ICSID arbitration) and the violation of the requirements of public policy (a non-ICSID ground found in the New York Convention and in most arbitration laws).

III. DIFFERING REVIEW OF THE ABSENCE OF REASONS FOR AN AWARD

Although the failure to state reasons is specific to the ICSID Convention under Art. 52(1)(e), this ground for challenge is not necessarily absent in non-ICSID arbitration. A number of arbitration rules provide for the requirement of a reasoned award. For example, Art. 32(3) of the UNCITRAL Rules provides that "[t]he arbitral tribunal shall state the reasons upon which the award is based, unless the parties have agreed that no reasons are to be given". Under Art. 36(1) of the Arbitration Institute of the Stockholm Chamber of Commerce, "[t]he Arbitral Tribunal shall make its award in writing, and, unless otherwise agreed by the parties, shall state the reasons upon which the award is based". Art. 25(2) of the ICC Rules in turn provides that "[t]he Award shall state the reasons upon which it is based". The losing party in an investment arbitration conducted under any of these arbitration rules may therefore attempt to challenge the award for failure to state reasons based on the tribunal's non-compliance with such rules.

---

10. For an example of a challenge to an investment treaty award in the United Kingdom, see *Occidental Exploration and Production Company v. Republic of Ecuador*, Court of Appeal, [2005] 2 Lloyd's Rep. 707, upholding the decision of the High Court, Queen's Bench Division, [2005] 2 Lloyd's Rep. 240. For an example in France, see Paris CA, 25 September 2008, *Czech Republic v. Pren Nreka*, partially reproduced in Alexis MOURRE and Priscille PEDONE, "Sommaires de jurisprudence des cours et tribunaux", in *Les Cahiers de l'arbitrage* (2008, no. 3) p. 36 (Gazette du Palais, 15-16 October 2008). For an example in Switzerland, see Federal Tribunal, 7 September 2006, *Czech Republic v. Saluka Investments BV*, 25 Bull. ASA (2007, no. 1) p. 123. For an example in Sweden, see Svea CA, 15 June 2005, *Russia v. Sedelmayer*, 2 Transnational Dispute Management (Nov. 2005, issue 5).

Under the ordinary rules of international arbitration, the approach taken by domestic courts is often a restrictive one.[11] In France, for example, the approach is very restrictive. The French *Cour de Cassation* has decided that the failure to state reasons is not "in itself contrary to the French understanding of international public policy".[12] Only where the law applicable to the procedure or the arbitration rules stipulate that reasons must be given is non-compliance with such requirement reviewed. The courts then limit their review to the sole *existence* of reasons. No control is exercised on the *correctness* of the reasons.[13]

By contrast, in the ICSID context, the position is not always as clear. There is no consistent case law on the limits assigned to ad hoc committees' review. Practice shows that the degree of review varies from one ad hoc committee to the other. There are in reality three levels of review in ICSID practice.

A number of ad hoc committees have limited their review to the *existence* of reasons for the award. This was notably the approach adopted by the *Vivendi* and the *Wena* committees.[14] In the words of the *Vivendi* committee, the standard of review under Art. 52 is "a failure to state *any* reasons with respect to all or part of an award, not the failure to state correct or convincing reasons", adding that "... [the] correctness [of the reasons] is beside the point".[15]

Other ad hoc committees have extended their review of the award to the *consistency* of its reasoning. In the ICSID context, contradictory reasons amount to a failure to state reasons.[16] Although this standard is not as clear-cut as the verification of the existence of reasons, it has been accepted in practice given that ad hoc committees may restrict their review to the consistency of the reasons without engaging in a review of the correctness of the reasoning.

It is the *correctness* of the reasoning that is the most problematic. Under this standard, the reviewing authority will always engage in an assessment of the adequacy of the reasoning. This was the approach taken in *Klöckner* and *Amco*, the well-known and often

---

11. For examples, see Gaëtan VERHOOSEL, "Annulment and Enforcement Review of Treaty Awards: To ICSID or Not to ICSID", supra fn. 4, at pp. 301-302.
12. French *Cour de Cassation*, 1e civ., 22 November 1966, *Gerstlé v. Merry Hull*, *Juris-Classeur Périodique* [JCP], Ed. G., Pt. II, No. 15,318 (1968), and observations by Henri MOTULSKY; 94 J.D.I. (1967) p. 631, and Berthold GOLDMAN's note; 1967 Revue critique de droit international privé p. 72, and Phocion FRANCESCAKIS' note.
13. The Paris Court of Appeal, for example, decided in 1999 that a challenge based on contradictory reasons would in fact amount to a challenge of the award on its merits, something that is not within the powers of a reviewing court: Paris CA, 26 October 1999, *Patou v. Edipar*, Rev. arb. (1999) p. 811, and Emmanuel GAILLARD's note.
14. See *Vivendi v. Argentina* (ICSID Case No. ARB/97/3), Decision of the Ad hoc Committee on Annulment (3 July 2002) 6 ICSID Rep. (2004) 340; *Wena v. Egypt* (ICSID Case No. ARB/98/4) Decision of the Ad hoc Committee on Application for Annulment (5 February 2002) 6 ICSID Rep. (2004) 129.
15. See *Vivendi v. Argentina*, supra fn. 14, para. 64.
16. See *Klöckner v. Cameroon* (ICSID Case No. ARB/81/2), Decision of the Ad hoc Committee on Annulment (3 May 1985) para. 116, 2 ICSID Rep. (1994) 95; *Amco v. Indonesia* (ICSID Case No. ARB/81/1), Decision of the Ad hoc Committee on Annulment (16 May 1986) 1 ICSID Rep. (1993) 509.

cited test being that the reasons must be "sufficiently relevant" or "reasonably sustainable and capable of providing a basis for the decision".[17] More recently, this was also the approach adopted by the committees in *Patrick Mitchell*[18] and in *CMS*.[19]

To focus only on one of the most recent annulment decisions in *CMS*, it is noteworthy that it was criticized by a number of commentators for *what it does*, namely partially annulling the award for failure to state reasons on the interpretation of an umbrella clause in the applicable BIT giving standing to the claimant as shareholder (whereas, in the committee's view, the License under consideration contained obligations "with regard to investments" enforceable by the company only, not the company's shareholder). The criticism is justified if one considers that the *CMS* committee engaged in an appreciation of the *adequacy* of the tribunal's reasoning with respect to the issue at hand.[20]

The *CMS* decision is even more problematic for *what it does not do* when assessing the adequacy of the tribunal's reasoning. It does not determine the existence of reasons for the award in light of the positions actually taken by the parties before the tribunal. Rather, it reconstructs the reasoning which should have been adopted by the tribunal in light of what the committee deems to be the ideal logic. This clearly flows from a simple sequential reading of the annulment decision:

(1) *what CMS (the claimant) did not say to the tribunal*: para. 91 ("During the hearings, CMS referred to the possibility that an investor might acquire an international law right to compliance with undertakings with regard to investments. But it finally accepted that this was *not the basis of its claim before the Tribunal or of the Tribunal's own reasoning*" (Emphasis added));

(2) *what CMS should have said to the tribunal*: para. 92 ("In the end, CMS relied on a literal interpretation of Art. II(2)(c) ... Although CMS was not entitled as a minority shareholder to invoke those obligations ... the effect of Art. II(2)(c) was to give it standing to invoke them under the BIT");

(3) *what the tribunal said*: para. 93;

(4) *what the tribunal could have said had it had the benefit of CMS's position before the committee*: para. 94 ("It is implicit in this reasoning that the *Tribunal may have accepted the interpretation* of Art. II(2)(c) referred to in para. 92 above ..." (Emphasis added));

(5) *what should have been the reasoning of the tribunal*: para. 95, based on a six-point sequence addressing the "major difficulties" of the tribunal's broad interpretation;

---

17. Klöckner, supra fn. 16, para. 120.
18. See *Patrick Mitchell v. Congo* (ICSID Case No. ARB/99/7), Decision of the Ad hoc Committee on the Application for Annulment of the Award (1 November 2006) referring to reasons that "are so inadequate that the coherence of the reasoning is seriously affected", at para. 21, 21 Int'l Arb. Rep. B1 (Nov. 2006).
19. See *CMS v. Argentina* (ICSID Case No. ARB/01/18), Decision of the Ad hoc Committee for Annulment (25 September 2007) 46 ILM (2007) 1136.
20. On this aspect, see *contra* Gaëtan VERHOOSEL, "Annulment and Enforcement Review of Treaty Awards: To ICSID or Not to ICSID", supra fn. 4 at p. 303, indicating that the committee remained within the boundaries of the standard set.

(6) that not being the tribunal's reasoning, whereas "one would have expected a discussion of the issues of interpretation referred to above", there is a significant lacuna in the Award: paragraphs 96-97;
(7) the award must be partially annulled for failure to state reasons.

This sequence shows that the adequacy of the tribunal's reasoning – presuming that is something that can be reviewed – is not even reviewed against the positions taken by the parties before the tribunal. In other words, the comparison is not between the parties' claims and arguments and the tribunal's decision on that basis. It is an *ex post facto* comparison – in isolation from the parties' positions – between the committee's ideal reasoning and the tribunal's actual reasoning.[21] This method can be contrasted with that of the *Luchetti* committee which emphasized that:

> "it is not part of the Committee's function ... to purport to substitute its own view for that arrived at by the Tribunal.... The Committee is not charged with the task of determining whether one interpretation is 'better' than another, or indeed which among several interpretations might be considered the 'best' one. The Committee is concerned solely with the process by which the Tribunal moved from its premise to its conclusion."[22]

Understandably, the *CMS* committee wanted to create a precedent in light of the issues discussed and the "implications [of its decision] for the many similar cases against Argentina" (namely on the effect of umbrella clauses, and the tribunal's so-called manifest errors of law in making a confusion between measures necessary for the maintenance of public order or the Contracting Parties' essential security interests, and state of necessity under customary international law).[23] The temptation to create a precedent can, however, in no way be a justification for jeopardizing the integrity of the process wanted by the drafters of the ICSID Convention.

IV. LIMITATION OF THE REVIEW ON THE MERITS

By contrast to Art. 52(1)(e), the ground of a manifest excess of powers under Art. 52(1)(b) allows, to a certain degree, a review of the merits of the award on questions such as the exercise of jurisdiction or the application of the proper law by the tribunal. Art. 52, however, limits such review to the situations where such excess of

---

21. See also Emmanuel GAILLARD, "*Centre international pour le règlement des différends relatifs aux investissements (C.I.R.D.I.) – Chronique des sentences arbitrages*", 135 J.D.I. (2008) p. 360 at p. 362.
22. *Lucchetti v. Peru* (ICSID Case No. ARB/03/4), Decision of the Ad hoc Committee on the Application for Annulment of the Award (5 September 2007) para. 112, 22 Int'l Arb. Rep. C1 (Sept. 2007); for a commentary, see Emmanuel GAILLARD, "*Centre international pour le règlement des différends relatifs aux investissements (C.I.R.D.I.) – Chronique des sentences arbitrages*", 135 J.D.I. (2008) p. 349.
23. Gaëtan VERHOOSEL, "Annulment and Enforcement Review of Treaty Awards: To ICSID or not to ICSID", supra fn. 4, at pp. 306-307, referring to *CMS v. Argentina*, supra fn. 19, at para. 45.

powers is *manifest* and ICSID committees have exercised a degree of restraint in this respect.[24]

Under the ordinary rules of international arbitration and outside the ICSID system, an assessment of the award on its merits, which can be exercised on the basis of the public policy ground, can be even more exceptional in some jurisdictions, in particular in the continental tradition.

In France, for example, the *Cour de Cassation* has recently restricted even further the standard of review based on the requirements of international public policy under Arts. 1502.5° and 1504 of the New Code of Civil Procedure,[25] which may concern the arbitral procedure or the merits of the dispute and which has traditionally been exercised very sparingly. This was achieved by a decision rendered recently in the matter of *SNF v. Cytec Industries BV*.[26] The case concerned the question of whether the arbitral tribunal had correctly applied EC law in deciding that the agreement in dispute was null and void as contrary to Art. 81 of the Treaty Establishing the European Community and whether the recognition and enforcement of the award would result in the violation of international public policy. The *Cour de Cassation* decided that any violation of international public policy must be *manifest*:

> "... as regards the violation of international public policy, the recognition and enforcement of the award is reviewed by the annulment court in light of the conformity of its solution with such public policy, a review that is limited to the flagrant, actual and concrete character of the alleged violation".[27]

The control by the French courts of the requirements of international public policy is thus even more restricted today, as it will not go beyond a manifest violation (in this instance, the Court declining to review the correct application of EC law by the arbitral tribunal). Here again, in non-ICSID matters, this shows the importance of the choice of the seat as regards the safeguard of the integrity of the arbitral process.

The brief examination of these two key grounds and the exercise by national courts of a higher degree of self-restraint and deference to arbitral awards[28] provides an

---

24. See Gaëtan VERHOOSEL, "Annulment and Enforcement Review of Treaty Awards: To ICSID or Not to ICSID", this volume, p. 300. Such self-restraint in relation to the manifest excess of powers (Art. 52(1)(b) does not mean, however, that ad hoc committees always avoid engaging in a review of the merits of the award and exercise the same degree of restraint in relation to other grounds, in particular Art. 52(1)(e): see supra, p. 323 and fn. 18 in relation to the *Patrick Mitchell* annulment decision.
25. Under these provisions, an appeal (Art. 1502.5°) or an action to set aside on the same grounds (Art. 1504) may be sought "where the recognition or enforcement is contrary to international public policy".
26. Cass. 1e civ., 4 June 2008, *SNF v. Cytec Industries BV*, Rev. arb. (2008) p. 473, and Ibrahim FADLALLAH's note.
27. Unofficial translation from the French original. For the complete English version of the decision, see ICCA *Yearbook on Commercial Arbitration* XXXIII (2008) p. 489 at p. 493.
28. Gaëtan VERHOOSEL, "Annulment and Enforcement Review of Treaty Awards: To ICSID or Not to ICSID", supra fn. 4, at p. 317.

illustration of the reasons why ICSID's appeal as one of the options available to the parties is increasingly questioned today. If one considers the annulment procedure under Art. 52, the incentive in favor of ICSID arbitration may appear not as strong, given the multiplication of annulment proceedings in recent years, the relatively high proportion of annulled awards[29] and the discrepancy in the standards of review adopted by the ad hoc committees. Yet, the question whether or not ICSID remains the preferred option in investment arbitration no longer primarily depends on the challenge and enforcement mechanisms. Today, the advantages and disadvantages of settling one's dispute within the tried and tested framework of ICSID are almost as significant if one considers the *front end* of the arbitral process (for example, possible questions of jurisdiction, in particular as regards specific requirements under the ICSID Convention)[30] and the *back end* of the arbitral process (namely the challenge and enforcement of the award).

---

29. By the end of 2007, forty percent of the applications for annulment had been successful in the ICSID system, a figure that can be compared with the six-percent percentage provided by Mr. Verhoosel as regards setting aside proceedings before national courts, this volume, at p. 287.
30. On limitations on jurisdiction in the ICSID system, see, e.g., Yas BANIFATEMI, "Unresolved Issues in Investment Arbitration" in *Modern Law for Global Commerce – Proceedings of the UNCITRAL Congress*, 9-12 July 2007, Vienna (forthcoming in 2009).

# Binding Force and Enforcement of ICSID Awards: Untying Articles 53 and 54 of the ICSID Convention

*Guido Santiago Tawil*[*]

TABLE OF CONTENTS | Page
---|---
I. Introduction | 327
II. The Interplay Between Arts. 53 and 54 of the ICSID Convention | 328
III. Conclusion | 336

I. INTRODUCTION

International obligations shall be complied with by States. Failure to do so may amount to an international wrongful act. Arbitral awards related to a State's breach of an international obligation are no exception.[1] Any such decisions are binding upon the parties and, therefore, obligations arising out of them should be properly discharged.

International law provides no general method to enforce decisions issued by international courts or tribunals.[2] However, in most cases, States that consent to a certain international jurisdiction in order to settle disputes generally abide by the resulting decision, whatever its outcome could be.

Referring to the enforcement of judgments from the International Court of Justice (ICJ), it has been said that

> "... generally, the problem of enforcement is not as serious as one might imagine; if a State is willing to accept the jurisdiction of the Court in a specific case, it is usually willing to carry out the Court's judgment; the real difficulty lies in persuading a state to accept the Court's jurisdiction in the first place, or to stick to a commitment to do so made in advance, in the abstract".[3]

---

[*] Co-chair, Arbitration Committee (2009/2010) and Chair, Latin American Forum, International Bar Association; Chair Professor, University of Buenos Aires, Senior Partner, M. & M. Bomchil, Buenos Aires, Argentina. The author would like to acknowledge the assistance of Ignacio J. Minorini Lima in the preparation of this paper. He would also like to disclose his participation as counsel in different cases in which this topic has been addressed. For ethical reasons he will avoid commenting on the particulars of those cases; Member of ICCA.

[1]. As affirmed by Parra in connection with the ICSID system, "For the Contracting State party to the dispute, a failure to abide by and comply with the award is therefore a violation not only of its undertaking to arbitrate, but also of an international treaty obligation." (Antonio PARRA, "The Enforcement of ICSID Arbitral Awards", 24th Joint Colloquium on International Arbitration, Paris, 16 November 2007, p. 7).

[2]. Peter MALANCZUK, *Akehurst's Modern Introduction to International Law*, 7th revised edn. (Routledge, London/New York 1997) p. 275.

[3]. *Ibid.*, p. 289.

Investment awards issued pursuant to the ICSID Convention are subject to a slightly different regime. The general principle remains untouched: an ICSID award is binding and the defeated party must abide by its terms. However, the prominent feature of the Convention lies in its particular enforcement procedure. Besides the availability of diplomatic protection – to be exercised at the discretion of the investor's home State – the Convention establishes an autonomous enforcement mechanism and commits the aid of national jurisdictions to execute pecuniary obligations imposed by awards.[4]

Of course, this does not mean – as it has been erroneously suggested in certain papers and forums – that enforcement constitutes the ordinary way, much less the only available way to obtain compliance. On the contrary, the whole ICSID system's rationale is precisely based on voluntary compliance and the particular enforcement mechanism set out by the ICSID Convention does not displace such principle.

II.  THE INTERPLAY BETWEEN ARTS. 53 AND 54 OF THE ICSID CONVENTION

*1.  Art. 53 Prompts Pacta Sunt Servanda and Res Judicata Under Customary International Law*

Art. 53 of the ICSID Convention reads:

> "(1) The award shall be binding on the parties and shall not be subject to any appeal or to any other remedy except those provided for in this Convention. Each party shall abide by and comply with the terms of the award except to the extent that enforcement shall have been stayed pursuant to the relevant provisions of this Convention.
> (2) For the purposes of this Section, 'award' shall include any decision interpreting, revising or annulling such award pursuant to Articles 50, 51 or 52."

This provision basically deals with the effects of awards on the parties involved in the arbitration proceeding in three aspects:

(i) *finality of an ICSID Award*: no remedy could be sought on the same dispute in any other forum;[5]
(ii) exclusion of external review of an ICSID Award: no court – domestic or international – could subject an award to substantive review;[6] and
(iii) the binding nature of the award between the parties: the losing party must comply with the award.[7]

---

4. Christoph SCHREUER, *The ICSID Convention: A Commentary* (Cambridge 2001) p. 1100 et seq.
5. Rudolf DOLZER and Christoph SCHREUER, *Principles of International Investment Law* (Oxford 2008) p. 287.
6. SCHREUER, *op. cit.*, fn. 4, p. 1084.
7. *Ibid.*, pp. 1086-1087.

Art. 53 reflects customary international law by restating the *pacta sunt servanda* and res judicata principles in the ICSID system.[8] Where an award imposes pecuniary obligations on the defeated party, those obligations shall be honored immediately with no need of further domestic recognition and enforcement process. Compliance with Art. 53 is not subject to any condition other than the possibility of the award being temporarily stayed according to the terms of the ICSID Convention. In particular, it does not make any reference to the need of promoting enforcement proceedings under Art. 54 in order to obtain compliance.[9]

2. *The Enforcement Mechanism Under Art. 54 Is Triggered Upon a Party's Failure to Abide by the Terms of the Award*

It has been recently brought into question whether Arts. 53 and 54 should be jointly construed. Some States parties and scholars have affirmed that compliance with an award against a State is subject to the prior institution of enforcement procedures by the winning party. This position seems not to be in line with the ICSID Convention and its negotiating history.

Art. 54(1) reads:

"Each Contracting State shall recognize an award rendered pursuant to this Convention as binding and enforce the pecuniary obligations imposed by that award within its territories as if it were a final judgment of a court in that State...."

This provision establishes a different obligation than Art. 53. It provides each Contracting State's obligation to collaborate in the recognition and enforcement of awards containing pecuniary obligations pursued by the prevailing party in an ICSID proceeding. Such commitment is substantially different from the main and primary obligation of the parties to an ICSID proceeding to comply with the terms of an award.

While Art. 53 is addressed to the parties in a dispute, Art. 54 is addressed to all Contracting States – not necessarily the host State – in which recognition and/or enforcement could be sought.[10] Only Contracting States – not the investors – bear the obligation established under Art. 54.[11] However, both the host State and the investor are

---

8. As explained by Aron Broches, Art. 53 "... is a restatement of customary international law based on the concepts of *pacta sunt servanda* and res judicata. Article 37 of the Hague Convention for the Pacific Settlement of International Disputes of 1907 expresses the effect of *pacta sunt servanda* as follows: 'Recourse to arbitration implies an engagement to submit in good faith to the award'. And in the *Socobel* case, the Permanent Court of International Justice declared: 'Recognition of an award as res judicata means nothing else than recognition of the fact that the terms of that award are definitive and obligatory." (Aron BROCHES, "Awards Rendered Pursuant to the ICSID Convention: Binding Force, Finality, Recognition, Enforcement, Execution", 2 ICSID Review–FILJ (1987, no. 2) p. 287, at p. 289).
9. Stanimir ALEXANDROV, "Enforcement of ICSID Awards: Articles 53 and 54 of the ICSID Convention", Transnational Dispute Management (September 2008) p. 2.
10. SCHREUER, *op. cit.*, fn. 4, p. 1108; ALEXANDROV, *op. cit.*, fn. 9, p. 2.
11. ALEXANDROV, *op. cit.*, fn. 9, p. 3.

obliged to comply under Art. 53. As explained by Dr. Broches, under Art. 54, the award is "... to be recognized by all Contracting States and not merely by the State party to the dispute".[12]

Therefore, under the ICSID Convention system, the prevailing party does not need to promote enforcement proceedings in order to get an award paid. Nothing in the terms of Art. 53 indicates that the obligation to comply with awards is inextricably related to the enforcement mechanism set out in Art. 54.[13] Triggering enforcement procedures – a right (never an obligation) of the prevailing party against reluctant debtors – presupposes the losing party's default.

The different nature of the obligations arising from Arts. 53 and 54 is confirmed by ICSID negotiating history. In the words of Dr. Broches

> "Article 53 established the principle that the parties were bound to abide by and should comply with the terms of the award. Article 54 set forth the procedure for enforcement of the awards in the courts of the Contracting States, should a party fail to comply with Article 53."[14]

As explained by Professor Schreuer,

> "The obligation to comply [expressed in Art. 53] is independent of any procedural obstacles that may arise in the course of enforcement. Art. 54 refers to the law of the State in which recognition is sought. But any difficulties that may arise under that law in no way affect the obligation of a party to comply with the award. Therefore, a party that successfully resists enforcement of an award before a court ... is in violation of its obligation under Art. 53."[15]

This position has been recently backed by the US Department of State in a letter filed as amicus curiae in an ongoing ICSID annulment proceeding. In the words of the US Government:

> "Article 53(1) of the ICSID Convention addresses a Contracting State party's unequivocal and unconditional obligation to 'abide by and comply with the terms of the award,' subject to a stay of the award pursuant to other relevant provisions

---

12. *History of the ICSID Convention* (1968, reprinted in 2001) Vol. II-1, p. 272.
13. After the 2008 ICCA Conference, the ad hoc Committee in the *Enron v. Argentina* case addressed this question in its decision on the stay of enforcement of the award. Sharing this view, the Committee said: "... nothing in the language of these provisions suggests that these two obligations are related, and in particular, that there is nothing in the language to suggest that the obligation in the second sentence of Art. 53(1) must be read as being subject to an award creditor invoking enforcement mechanisms established pursuant to the obligation in the first sentence of Article 54(1)" (ICSID Case No. ARB/01/3, Decision on the Argentine Republic's Request for a Continued Stay of Enforcement of the Award (Rule 54 of the ICSID Arbitration Rules) 7 October 2008, para. 61).
14. *History of the ICSID Convention* (1968, reprinted in 2001), Vol. II-2, p. 989.
15. SCHREUER, *op. cit.*, fn. 4, p. 1087.

of the Convention. Accordingly, Article 53(1) requires a Contracting State party against which an ICSID award has been entered to satisfy the award once it has been rendered by the Tribunal.

Article 54 does not supersede or condition a Contracting State party's obligation under Article 53 in any way. Rather, Article 54 only applies after the losing State fails to pay an award pursuant to Article 53. In other words, Article 54 simply addresses the obligation of Contracting States to enforce an award in their territories – including where the losing Contracting State has not complied with its Article 53 obligations. The procedural requirements outlined in Article 54 – including enforcement of an award 'as if it were a final judgment of a court in that State' and execution as 'governed by the laws concerning the execution of judgments in force in the State' – certainly do not allow a losing State to avoid its obligation under Article 53 to satisfy an ICSID award in full.

Thus, a State is obligated to abide by and comply with an award rendered against it, irrespective of an investor's enforcement efforts under Article 54. Argentina's position to the contrary is an incorrect interpretation of Articles 53 and 54 of the ICSID Convention."[16]

3. *Art. 54 Was Mainly Introduced as a Means to Deal with Potential Default by Investors*

ICSID negotiating history shows that Art. 54 responds to concerns raised by States as to establishing means to enforce awards against investors.[17] It was understood at that time that States will generally comply with awards as mandated under Art. 53. Drafters were not seriously concerned with non-payment of awards by State parties.[18] As explained by Dr. Broches,

> "The record of compliance by governments with international arbitral awards is very good. Problems have arisen in the past with respect to the implementation of agreements to arbitrate, but the refusal of governments to proceed with arbitration has been based on their contention that the obligation to arbitrate was unenforceable or had been extinguished. If, as has been suggested, the international agreement would remove any doubt as to the legally binding character of an undertaking to arbitrate, there is no reason to believe that governments would not abide by such undertakings."[19]

---

16. Letter dated 1 May 2008, from the International Claims and Investment Disputes Office of the US Department of State submitted in the ICSID annulment proceeding between Siemens A.G. and the Argentine Republic (ICSID Case No. ARB/02/8) available at <http://ita.law.uvic.ca/documents/Siemens-USsubmission.pdf> (footnotes omitted).
17. BROCHES, *op. cit.*, fn. 8, pp. 300-302. See also PARRA, *op. cit.*, fn. 1, p. 8.
18. SCHREUER, *op. cit.*, fn. 4, pp. 1102-1103; ALEXANDROV, *op. cit.*, fn. 9, p. 5.
19. *History of the ICSID Convention*, Vol. II-1, p. 11. Dr. Broches explained as well during the discussion on the ICSID Convention that "… by definition the host State would have undertaken to abide by the award and the problem of enforcement in a third State was not likely to arise" (*ibid.*, p. 428).

In Dr. Broches' opinion, "failure by a State to abide by an award would undoubtedly arouse strong reactions by other States"[20] and "… it was not necessary to provide for forced execution against States under this Convention since the Convention imposed a direct obligation on States to carry out the award".[21]

Default concerns were placed on the investor's side. Capital-importing countries were aware that they would be able to enforce awards against individuals in their own territories, since in general terms assets would be found within their jurisdiction. However, in the understanding that exceptional situations could take place they urged for wider enforceable means.[22] Their concern was that in case an investor did not honor an award and had no assets in their territories, their right to compliance could turn illusory.

Thus, Art. 54 sought to provide assurance to capital-importing countries that "… compliance with an award made in their favor would be just as automatic as it would be if they lost the case".[23] Through this way the ICSID Convention sought to establish "equality not only of rights, but also of obligations, between States and investors".[24]

As explained by Dr. Broches during the consultative meeting of legal experts that took place in Geneva, on 17-22 February 1964,

> "… the question of the enforcement of awards had been included in the draft Convention mainly for the benefit of the developing countries who were thus given a means to enforce awards in their favor against foreign investors".[25]

He further noted that

> "… for the purposes of ensuring compliance with an arbitral award between States, Section 14 [which, as amended, turned out to be Art. 53] would have been sufficient but, since one of the parties to a dispute brought before the Centre would be a private individual, Section 15 which, as amended, turned out to be Article 54 was necessary to give a State the means of enforcing an award in its favor against an individual. The Article had been included with a view to meeting the possible needs of developing countries in disputes with private investors."[26]

---

20. *Ibid.*, p. 430.
21. *Ibid.*, p. 520. He further added that "While the investor was also under an obligation to comply with the award, there was no direct sanction under the Convention for his failure to do so. It was, therefore, provided that where the State was the winning party it could obtain a writ of execution, where-upon the process of execution would run the normal course in the country concerned." (*Ibid.*)
22. *Ibid.*, p. 522.
23. *Ibid.*, p. 427.
24. *Ibid.*, p. 574.
25. *Ibid.*, p. 379.
26. *Ibid.*, p. 424. See also pp. 379 and 425.

During the consultative meeting of legal experts in Santiago, Chile, Professor Andreas Lowenfeld – at that time the US State Department Assistant Legal Adviser for Economic Affairs – noted that draft Art. IV, Sect. 15 (now Art. 54) seemed to cover two distinct matters which should be dealt with separately: on one hand, the enforcement of the award in the host State territory or in the investor's State of origin; on the other hand, the enforcement of the award in a third State. The US delegation was of the view that in the first case sovereign immunity did not need to be maintained. Dr. Broches explained that both cases have been placed on the same level since

> "... the principal purpose of Section 15 (although this was not its only effect) was to give States which had been successful plaintiffs a means to enforce awards against investors who did not have assets within the host State's territories. States would be directly bound by the Convention to comply with awards rendered against them, which could not be void of investors. In the unlikely event that a losing State failed to comply with an award it would be in clear violation of the Convention itself, and the State whose national had failed to obtain satisfaction, could take up his case."[27]

However, the possibility of promoting enforcement proceedings against States, although unusual, was left open under the ICSID Convention. Due to these atypical situations, the existing principles on State immunity from execution were not altered:

> "While those who objected to the principle of State immunity had argued that it ought to be eliminated from the Convention, the majority view was that forced execution should not lie against a State and the rule would, therefore, remain untouched.
> (....)
> In other words the Convention would not change the principles (including the limitations on those principles) applying in Contracting States to enforcement of final judgments against the States."[28]

Art. 55 of the ICSID Convention was introduced to dispel any doubt on this matter.[29] However, it should not be regarded as a right of the State to resist compliance as a "successful invocation of State immunity does not alter the fact that non-compliance with an award is a violation of the Convention".[30]

In the words of the *MINE v. Guinea* ad hoc Committee:

> "State immunity may well afford a legal defense to forcible execution, but it provides neither argument nor excuse for failing to comply with an award. In fact,

---

27. *Ibid.*, pp. 343-344.
28. *Ibid.*, p. 520.
29. SCHREUER, *op. cit.*, fn. 4, pp. 1142-1143.
30. *Ibid.*, p. 1144. See also DOLZER and SCHREUER, *op. cit.*, fn. 5, p. 290.

the issue of State immunity from forcible execution of an award will typically arise if the State party refuses to comply with its treaty obligations."[31]

4.  States Do Generally Voluntarily Comply with Awards

Within the framework of the ICSID Convention negotiating history, the question of enforcement was qualified as "somewhat academic".[32] Such assertion has been proven right.

Voluntary payment under Art. 53 is the ordinary practice in ICSID arbitration.[33] Enforcement proceedings pursuant to Art. 54 are not the rule, but the exception. Publicly available information indicates that only four ICSID awards reached the stage of enforcement before local courts: *Benvenuti & Bonfant v. Congo* – before French courts – *SOABI v. Senegal* – before French courts, *LETCO v. Liberia* – before US courts – and *AIG Capital Partners v. Kazakhstan* – before English courts.[34] Currently, according to public information available within the arbitration world, two countries (the Republic of Seychelles and Argentina) have not yet paid the awards rendered against them in the *CDC* and *CMS* cases, respectively.

Furthermore, under Art. 54(2),[35] most States have designated a court as the competent authority. Only eight States have nominated a non-judicial authority.[36] The practice of appointing judicial courts is consistent with the understanding that they would be called to enforce awards against third parties – a foreign investor or a third State – and not against the State that nominates such an authority and in which the courts are seated. It is assumed that decisions against the host State would be voluntarily complied with.[37]

---

31. *Maritime International Nominees Establishment v. Republic of Guinea*, Interim Order No. 1 (12 August 1988) 4 ICSID Reports, p. 111, at p. 115.
32. *History of the ICSID Convention*, Vol. II-1, p. 304.
33. PARRA, *op. cit.*, fn. 1, pp. 9-12. See also Lucy REED, Jan PAULSSON, Nigel BLACKABY, *Guide to ICSID Arbitration* (Kluwer Law International 2004) p. 107.
34. Edward BALDWIN, Mark KANTOR, Michael NOLAN, "Limits to Enforcement of ICSID Awards", 23 Journal of International Arbitration (2006, no. 1) p. 1, at p. 6; PARRA, *op. cit.*, fn. 1, pp. 3-7.
35. Art. 54(2) further establishes that

    "A party seeking recognition or enforcement in the territories of a Contracting State shall furnish to a competent court or other authority which such State shall have designated for this purpose a copy of the award certified by the Secretary-General. Each Contracting State shall notify the Secretary-General of the designation of the competent court or other authority for this purpose and of any subsequent change in such designation."

36. See chart "Designations of Courts or Other Authorities Competent for the Recognition and Enforcement of Awards Rendered Pursuant to the Convention (Art. 54(2) of the Convention)" available at <http://icsid.worldbank.org>.
37. However, and as noted by Professor Schreuer, the fact that many States have appointed courts or authorities that are competent as well to entertain procedures for recognition and enforcement of foreign judgments and domestic or foreign arbitral awards "… carries the danger of ICSID awards being subjected to the same procedures and standards of review as other awards or foreign

## 5. Additional Reasons that Sustain the Independent Nature of Arts. 53 and 54

### a. Relevance of Art. 27 of the ICSID Convention

The ICSID Convention provides for two available courses of action against recalcitrant State debtors: diplomatic protection under Art. 27 and enforcement procedures pursuant to Art. 54.[38]

To sustain that the recognition and enforcement process set forth under Art. 54 must precede compliance appears as unreasonable as asserting that compliance is dependent upon the exercise of diplomatic protection by the State of the award creditor pursuant to Art. 27.

The text of Art. 27 confirms the independent nature of the obligation set forth under Art. 53 from the one established in Art. 54. Such provision reopens the right to diplomatic protection once Contracting States "have failed to abide by and comply with the award rendered in such dispute". It, thus, repeats the wording of Art. 53 – *to abide by and comply with*.[39]

If the losing party's obligation to comply with an award were to be subject to the recognition and enforcement provisions of Art. 54, Art. 27 should read quite differently. Instead of saying "have failed to abide by and comply with the award", it should have stated "have failed to recognize and enforce the award".[40]

### b. Status of non-pecuniary awards

An ICSID tribunal is not only empowered to award monetary damages. It may well impose an obligation upon any party to perform certain acts or refrain from enforcing specific measures.[41] However, Art. 54 provides for enforcement of pecuniary obligations only.[42]

As explained by Dr. Broches, "…. an award could well order the performance or non-performance of certain acts but all that could be enforced would be the obligation to pay damages if the party did not comply with that order. In the kind of disputes that would

---

judgments, a result that would be inconsistent with the finality and nonreviewability of ICSID awards". (SCHREUER, *op. cit.*, fn. 4, p. 1138).

38. SCHREUER, *ibid.*, pp. 1088-1089; ALEXANDROV, *op. cit.*, fn. 9, p. 5.
39. ALEXANDROV, op. cit., fn. 9, p. 4.
40. *Ibid*. See also *Enron Corporation and Ponderosa Assets, L.P. v. Argentine Republic* (ICSID Case No. ARB/01/3), *op. cit.*, fn. 13, para. 65.
41. Christoph SCHREUER, "Non-Pecuniary Remedies in ICSID Arbitration", 20 Arbitration International (2004, no. 4) p. 325, at p. 326.
42. We share the view expressed by Gaëtan Verhoosel at the 2008 ICCA Conference that non-pecuniary obligations imposed in ICSID awards must be enforced through the New York Convention or under domestic law. (See Gaëtan VERHOOSEL, "Annulment and Enforcement Review of Treaty Awards: To ICSID or Not to ICSID", this volume, pp. 285-317.) As explained by Dolzer and Schreuer, "The obligation to recognize an award extends to any type of obligation under it. By contrast, the obligation to enforce is limited to the pecuniary obligations under the award." (DOLZER and SCHREUER, *op. cit.*, fn. 5, p. 289). See also Campbell McLACHLAN, Laurence SHORE and Matthew WEINIGER, *International Investment Arbitration: Substantive Principles* (Oxford 2007), p. 343.

come before the Centre payment of damages was all that ultimately the parties could expect in the absence of voluntary compliance."[43]

When asked whether limiting enforceability to monetary awards would not weaken the Convention, Dr. Broches denied so. Confirming that the enforcement mechanism under Art. 54 was aimed at States other than the one involved in the dispute, Dr. Broches further stated that "... he could not imagine specific enforcement of provisions of the award, other than its pecuniary provisions, by a third State against the host State".[44] In addition, he expressed that ".... the obligation of a State party to an arbitration proceedings before the Centre was clearly set forth in Article 53 and would not be affected by the proposed language".[45]

In this context, in the event that it was held that the obligation to abide by and comply with the terms of an award under Art. 53 should be necessarily met through the mechanism set out under Art. 54, one would be forced to reach the conclusion that States are not obliged to comply with non-pecuniary awards, which is clearly unacceptable.[46]

III. CONCLUSION

Based on such analysis, one can conclude that:

(i) International obligations shall be voluntarily discharged. ICSID awards are no exception. Art. 53 of the ICSID Convention imposes on the defeated party the obligation to voluntarily comply with the terms of the award.
(ii) Art. 54 imposes the obligation upon all Contracting States to enforce ICSID awards against defaulting parties. Enforcement under Art. 54 (a right of the prevailing party and not its obligation) only comes into play after the host State or the investor failed to abide by the terms of the award.
(iii) The ICSID Convention's negotiating history confirms that Art. 54 should be read separately from Art. 53. In particular, it evidences that such article was introduced to deal with potential default by investors and drafters were not seriously concerned about non-compliance by States.

---

43. *History of the ICSID Convention*, Vol. II-2, p. 991.
44. *Ibid.*, pp. 1019.
45. *Ibid.*
46. ALEXANDROV, *op. cit.*, fn. 9, p. 12. As asserted by the ad hoc Committee in the *Enron* case:

"The Committee further notes that the first sentence of Art. 54(1) of the ICSID Convention is expressed to require Contracting States to enforce only the pecuniary obligations imposed by an award. If the interpretation were accepted that there is no obligation to comply with an award unless and until the judgment creditor avails itself of enforcement mechanisms established pursuant to Art. 54, the result could be that there would never be an obligation to comply with non-pecuniary obligations in an award."

(*Enron Corporation and Ponderosa Assets, L.P. v. Argentine Republic*, *op. cit.*, fn. 13, para. 66).

(iv) State practice confirms that voluntary compliance is the rule and enforcement constitutes the exception.

(v) In case of default, an investor could seek to compel compliance of pecuniary awards by the host State through enforcement under Art. 54 or diplomatic protection pursuant to Art. 27. The wording of Art. 27 confirms that diplomatic protection is available upon refusal by the State to voluntarily comply with the award. To construe that recognition and enforcement under Art. 54 must precede compliance would be as unreasonable as asserting that compliance is dependent upon the exercise of diplomatic protection by the home State of the award creditor.

(vi) Enforcement under Art. 54 is only available for pecuniary awards. The position proposing enforcement as the only way to get an award paid by the host State could lead to the unreasonable conclusion that States are not obliged to comply with non-pecuniary awards.

# Working Group B

# Rules-Based Solutions to Procedural Issues

# Working Group B

# 1. Multi-Party Disputes

# Multi-party Disputes and Joinder of Third Parties

*Nathalie Voser**

TABLE OF CONTENTS | Page
---|---
I. Introduction | 343
II. Advantages of, and Obstacles to, Multi-party Arbitration | 350
III. Arbitration Proceedings Among Multiple Parties to One Agreement with a Uniform Arbitration Clause | 354
IV. Multi-party Arbitration Based on "True" Multi-party Arbitration Clauses | 367
V. Extension of the Arbitration Agreement to Non-signatories | 370
VI. Forms of Participation of Third Parties Other than as a Formal Party | 381
VII. Joinder of Third Parties after the Appointment of Arbitrators | 386
VIII. Current Position of Institutions | 391
IX. The Way Forward: More Provisions on Multi-party Arbitration? | 401
X. Conclusion | 409

## I. INTRODUCTION

*1. General Introductory Remarks*

It is a well-known fact in the field of international arbitration that over the last decade the number of proceedings in which more than two parties are involved has increased rapidly. The reasons for this are common knowledge: the growing international interdependency of commerce and the globalization of today's business world have led to complex contractual relationships which very often involve more than just two parties. As a result, it is safe to say that roughly 40 percent of arbitration cases involve more than two parties.[1]

---

* Litigation and Arbitration partner, Schellenberg Wittmer; Assistant Professor, University of Basel (Switzerland). I would like to thank my colleagues Andrea Meier, Christopher Boog and Patrick Rohn for their review of the draft report and their important contributions, as well as Lars Bauer for his diligent research and editing of the text.
1. A recent statistical analysis of all the challenges brought before the Swiss Federal Supreme Court since the enactment of the 12th Chapter of the Swiss Private International Law Act in 1989 (Swiss PILA), which constitutes the Swiss lex arbitri, revealed that 34 percent of all the challenges (221 cases) were multi-party arbitration disputes. The percentage actually grew, as expected, over time from 25 percent in the early 1990s to 40 percent in 2005. Based on the assumption that it was not the multi-party nature of the proceedings that led to the challenge (for which there is no indication), this statistic can be considered to be reliable. See Felix DASSER, "International Arbitration and Setting Aside Proceedings in Switzerland: A Statistical Analysis", 25 ASA Bull. (2007, no. 3) p. 444 at pp. 461-462. Other publications confirm this number: in 2002 more than 50 percent of the London Court of International Arbitration (LCIA) cases were multi-party proceedings. See Martin PLATTE, "When Should An Arbitrator Join Cases?", 18 Arb. Int'l (2002,

An insider at the ICC International Court of Arbitration has pointed out that the "reality of international commercial disputes has dramatically changed. Before, the great majority of disputes seemed to be bipolar disputes. Presently, an important number of disputes are multiparty and even multi-polar disputes."[2] Consequently, an important distinction should be drawn within multi-party arbitration: on the one hand, there are multi-party arbitrations which are bipolar, meaning that the "parties can normally be divided into two camps: a Claimant camp and a Respondent camp".[3] On the other hand, there are multi-party arbitrations which are multi-polar. This means that there are not just two camps, but more than two diverging interests. It is mainly the latter constellation which today causes difficulties and concerns in the arbitration community.

The issues at stake in multi-party and/or multi-polar arbitration vary greatly. Nevertheless, there are certain types of dispute which typically include more than two parties. Traditionally, such disputes involve construction and major industrial projects (with related sub-contracts),[4] guarantees, defective products, commodities transactions, transactions where the same asset is sold many times,[5] and supply chains[6] or, more generally, back-to-back purchases/sales, where there is an imminent risk that the contractual partner (and thus the party with title to the claim) is not the entity who is the final owner and who suffers the economic damage.[7] In more recent times, other types of dispute have been mentioned, such as shareholders' and joint-venture arbitration,[8] multi-party merger and acquisitions, trust arbitration,[9] insurance and re-insurance

---

no. 1) p. 67 at p. 67. On the other hand, the number of multi-party arbitrations in ICC proceedings is slightly lower, since in 2006 31.7 percent of the new cases filed were multi-party. However, the ICC has also detected a growth tendency in this area. See *"Rapport statistique 2006"*, 18 ICC Ct. Bull. (2007, no. 1) p. 5.

2. Eduardo SILVA-ROMERO, "Brief Report on Counterclaims and Cross-claims: The ICC Perspective", in *Arbitral Procedure at the Dawn of the New Millenium: Reports of the International Colloquium of CEPANI, October 15, 2004* (Bruylant 2005) p. 73 at p. 77.

3. Yves DERAINS and Eric A. SCHWARTZ, *A Guide to the ICC Rules of Arbitration*, 2nd edn. (Kluwer Law International 2005) pp. 70-71.

4. Jane JENKINS and Simon STEBBINGS, *International Construction Arbitration Law* (Kluwer Law International 2006) especially pp. 152-156; Fritz NICKLISCH, "Multi-Party Arbitration and Dispute Resolution in Major Industrial Projects", 11 J. Int'l Arb. (1994, no. 4) p. 57.

5. See Michael E. SCHNEIDER, "Multi-Fora Disputes", 6 Arb. Int'l (1990, no. 2) p. 101 at p. 102 et seq. See also Kristina M. SIIG, "Multi-party Arbitration in International Trade: Problems and Solutions", 1 Int'l J. Liability and Scientific Enquiry (2007, no. 1/2) p. 72 at p. 74, mentioning sub(sub)contractor and commodities transactions.

6. Reinhold GEIMER, *"Dritte als weitere Parteien im Schiedsverfahren"*, in Hans-Eric RASMUSSEN-BONNE, et al., eds., *Balancing of Interests, Liber amicorum Peter Hay zum 70. Geburtstag* (Verlag Recht und Wirtschaft 2005) p. 163 at p. 163.

7. See, e.g., Award on Third Person Notice of 7 April 2004 in ICC Case No. 12171, 23 ASA Bull. (2005, no. 2) p. 270, discussed in Sect. VI.2, below.

8. J. Gillis WETTER, "A Multi-party Arbitration Scheme for International Joint Ventures", 3 Arb. Int'l (1987, no. 1) p. 2.

9. Tina WÜSTEMANN, "Arbitration of Trust Disputes" in Christoph MÜLLER, ed., *New Developments in International Commercial Arbitration 2007* (Schulthess 2007) p. 33 at p. 53.

disputes[10] and sports-related disputes[11] (for example among several sponsors). In such situations, the contracts are interdependent and, quite often, there are back-to-back conditions which call for joint adjudication.

Although multi-party arbitration is of great practical relevance, arbitration as a dispute resolution mechanism is not, in its present state, well-equipped to handle such disputes and there are a number of complex and still unresolved issues. The problems connected to multi-party situations are considered a disadvantage of arbitration[12] and these situations encompass the most complex issues that the international arbitration community faces today. These issues have not only led (and continue to lead) to an abundance of publications,[13] but also to the amending of certain arbitration rules.[14]

This Report shall deal with multi-party proceedings from an overall perspective and address certain specific issues. Before going into a detailed discussion, some of the terms

---

10. K.M. SIIG, *op. cit.*, fn. 5, p. 74; R. GEIMER, *op. cit.*, fn. 6, p. 163.
11. *Ibid.*, p. 163.
12. K.M. SIIG, *op. cit.*, fn. 5, p. 73.
13. Important recent publications include Bernard HANOTIAU, *Complex Arbitrations, Multiparty, Multicontract, Multi-issue and Class Actions* (Kluwer Law International 2005), with an extensive bibliography in fn. 2 at pp. 1-3; Karl-Heinz BÖCKSTIEGEL, Klaus P. BERGER and Jens BREDOW, eds., *Die Beteiligung Dritter an Schiedsverfahren* (Carl Heymanns 2005); Andrea MEIER, *Einbezug Dritter vor internationalen Schiedsgerichten* (Schulthess 2007). See also the following special issues, reports and guidelines: *Complex Arbitrations, Perspectives on their Procedural Implications*, ICC Ct. Bull., Special Supplement 2003; Jean-Louis DELVOLVÉ, "Final Report on Multi-Party Arbitrations, Approved by the ICC's Commission on International Arbitration, submitted to the ICC's executive board on June 14, 1994", 6 ICC Ct. Bull. (1995, no. 1) p. 26; "Chartered Institute of Arbitrators: Guideline on Multi-Party Arbitrations", 72 Arbitration (2006, no. 2) p. 151. Among the vast literature see especially Siegfried H. ELSING, "*Streitverkündung und Schiedsverfahren*", 2 SchiedsVZ (2004, no. 2) p. 88; Serge GRAVEL, "Multiparty Arbitration and Multiple Arbitrations", 7 ICC Ct. Bull. (1996, no. 2) p. 45; Jens KLEINSCHMIDT, "*Die Widerklage gegen einen Dritten im Schiedsverfahren*", 4 SchiedsVZ (2006, no. 3) p. 142; Carolyn B. LAMM and Jocelyn A. AQUA, "Defining the Party – Who is a Proper Party in an International Arbitration Before the American Arbitration Association and Other International Institutions?", 34 Geo. Wash. Int'l L. Rev. (2003) p. 711; Patrice LEVEL, "Joinder of Proceedings, Intervention of Third Parties, and Additional Claims and Counterclaims", 7 ICC Ct. Bull. (1996, no. 2) p. 36; Frank MARTENS, *Wirkungen der Schiedsvereinbarung und des Schiedsverfahrens auf Dritte* (Peter Lang 2005); Konstadinos MASSURAS, *Dogmatische Strukturen der Mehrparteienschiedsgerichtsbarkeit* (Lang 1998); Werner MÜLLER and Annette KEILMANN, "*Beteiligung am Schiedsverfahren wider Willen?*", 5 SchiedsVZ (2007, no. 3) p. 113; M. PLATTE, *op. cit.*, fn. 1; Peter SCHLOSSER, "*Schiedsrichterliches Verfahrensermessen und Beiladung von Nebenparteien*" in Rolf A. SCHÜTZE, ed., *Einheit und Vielfalt des Rechts, Festschrift für Reinhold Geimer zum 65. Geburtstag* (C.H. Beck 2002) p. 947; K.M. SIIG, *op. cit.*, fn. 5; E. SILVA-ROMERO, *op. cit.*, fn. 2; Irene M. TEN CATE, "Multi-party and Multi-contract Arbitrations: Procedural Mechanisms and Interpretation of Arbitration Agreements under U.S. Law", 15 Am. Rev. Int'l Arb. (2004) p. 133; Nathalie VOSER and Andrea MEIER, "Joinder of Parties or the Need to (Sometimes) Be Inefficient" in Christian KLAUSEGGER, et al., eds., *Austrian Arbitration Yearbook 2008* (Manz 2008) p. 115; Reinmar WOLFF, "*Gestaltung einer vertragsübergreifenden Schiedsklausel*", 6 SchiedsVZ (2008, no. 2) p. 59. On the "extension" of the arbitration agreement to non-signatories, see the references in fn. 148 below. The present article is based on sources up to June 2008.
14. Art. 10 of the ICC Rules of Arbitration of 1998 (hereinafter ICC Rules); Art. 4 of the Swiss Rules of International Arbitration of 2004 (hereinafter Swiss Rules).

used in connection with multi-party arbitration should be defined, since it is sometimes difficult to understand the literature due to the differences in nomenclature (see Sub-sect. 2 below). Furthermore, there are important distinctions to be drawn which are relevant for the understanding of the complex issues at stake (see Sub-sects. 3 to 5 below).

The important work done by the Working Group A of the ICCA Congress 2006 in Montréal[15] will not be reiterated here. Instead, the present Report will concentrate on issues which have, so far, been discussed less often in the arbitration community at large. The section on the extension of the arbitration agreement to a non-signatory (see Sect. V below) will be somewhat cursory, and will focus on the Swiss situation; the emphasis will be on the other sections.

There are many other facets of multi-party arbitration which are highly interesting but which this Report does *not* address, such as

– Consolidation of proceedings (see separate Report by Michael Pryles and Jeffrey Waincymer, this volume, pp. 437-499);[16]
– Separate proceedings with the same arbitrators as an alternative to the extension of the arbitration agreement to third parties and/or the joinder of third parties;[17]
– Class-wide arbitrations;[18]
– Amicus curiae briefs.[19]

2. *Important Terms in the Context of Multi-party Arbitration and Joinder*

The term *multi-party arbitration* is an umbrella term, used to reflect the fact that there are more than two parties involved in one arbitration proceeding. As a rule, when speaking about *multi-party arbitration* the focus is not (or is no longer) on who is a party to the arbitration, but rather on the method of appointing the arbitral tribunal and conducting the multi-party arbitration proceedings.

The term *joinder* is commonly used in the context of multi-party arbitration. In more recent literature, the term is limited to situations where a third party is asked to join an

---

15. Albert Jan VAN DEN BERG, ed., *International Arbitration 2006: Back to Basics?*, ICCA Congress Series no. 13 (Kluwer Law International 2007) (hereinafter *ICCA Congress Series no. 13*), Working Group A, 6. Jurisdiction Over Non-signatories: National Contract Law or International Arbitral Practice?, p. 339 et seq.
16. It should be mentioned, however, that with the consolidation of arbitral proceedings with non-identical parties, the same effect as a joinder can be achieved. Thus, some of the results reached in this Report can also be used for the consolidation issue.
17. See also J. KLEINSCHMIDT, *op. cit.*, fn. 13, pp. 142-143, and A. MEIER, *op. cit.*, fn. 13, pp. 119-122.
18. See B. HANOTIAU, *op. cit.*, fn. 13, no. 557 et seq. at p. 257 et seq.; Bernard HANOTIAU, "A New Development in Complex Multiparty-Multicontract Proceedings: Classwide Arbitration", 20 Arb. Int'l (2004, no. 1) p. 39; Samuel ESTREICHER and Michael J. PUMA, "Arbitration and Class Actions after *Bazzle*", 58 Disp. Resol. J. (2003, no. 3) p. 12.
19. See B. HANOTIAU, *op. cit.*, fn. 13, no. 429-436 at pp. 192-196.

already pending arbitral proceeding.[20] More precisely, the term *joinder*, in this Report, covers a situation where a notice of arbitration, which determined the "original" parties to the arbitration, has already been filed. A request for joinder exists when the respondent wants to file a counterclaim either against the claimant and a third party, or solely against a third party (*counterclaim* or *claim against a third party*).[21] A joinder can also cover a situation in which the claimant decides *at a later stage* of the proceedings that a third party should become an *additional* respondent. A joinder is primarily a *procedural issue* and deals with the question of who can participate in a given arbitration. It does not, per se, provide for any answers to the separate issue of whether or not there is a valid arbitration agreement.

Sometimes, the wording used in the context of joinder is not "third party", but *third person*.[22] On the one hand, in a technical sense, this wording is more correct, since the third person to be joined is not yet a party to the arbitral proceedings. On the other hand, if a third person has implicitly consented to the arbitration agreement, it should automatically be a party to the arbitral proceedings. This logic endorses the use of the term "joining of a *third party*", which is more often used than "third person" in the context of joining. This Report will, for reasons of convenience and uniformity, use the term *third party* in connection with joinder.

The term *extension* is most often used in the context of non-signatories to an arbitration agreement. A person or entity may be bound by an arbitration agreement, even though he is not expressly named in the agreement. Thus, the term "extension" always refers to a party who falls within the personal scope of an arbitration agreement.[23] Although some justified criticism has been raised with regard to the concept of extension,[24] for the sake of uniformity this term shall be used in the present Report.

A *claim for recourse* is a claim by the respondent against a third party in order to have recourse should the claimant prevail against the respondent. This claim allows the adjudication of the main claim and the claim for recourse in the same forum. In the terminology used in the United States, the defendant becomes a *third-party plaintiff* and the third party a *third-party defendant*.[25] In contrast to a counterclaim against a third party, a *cross-claim* is a claim made by one respondent against another respondent in the proceedings.[26]

---

20. See, e.g., Bernard HANOTIAU, "Non-signatories in International Arbitration: Lessons from Thirty Years of Case Law", in *ICCA Congress Series no. 13,* p. 341 at p. 341 fn. 2; N. VOSER and A. MEIER, *op. cit.*, fn. 13, p. 115.
21. A. MEIER, *op. cit.*, fn. 13, p. 22 et seq.
22. See, e.g., Award on Third Person Notice of 7 April 2004 in ICC Case No. 12171, 23 ASA Bull. (2005, no. 2) p. 270. One of the rare provisions of an institution which deals with joinder of a third party speaks about a "third person to be joined in the arbitration as a party". Art. 22.1(h) of the LCIA Arbitration Rules of 1998 (hereinafter LCIA Rules).
23. For more details, see Sects. I.3 and V below.
24. B. HANOTIAU, *op. cit.*, fn. 20, p. 343.
25. A. MEIER, *op. cit.*, fn. 13, p. 27.
26. B. HANOTIAU, *op. cit.*, fn. 13, no. 397 at p. 178.

While all these are claims by one party against a third party, the discussion of multi-party arbitration must also look at *intervention*, where a third party wishes to join the arbitral proceedings.[27]

3. *Signatories v. Non-signatories to the Arbitration Agreement*

In light of the fundamental difference between state court proceedings and arbitration regarding the basis for jurisdiction, an important distinction should be drawn between a situation where several parties have signed the arbitration agreement and one where a third party becomes (from the very beginning or later) a party to the arbitral proceedings without having signed the original arbitration agreement. The first situation can be described as arbitral proceedings among multiple signatories to an arbitration agreement and is discussed in Sects. III and IV below. The second situation, which is usually referred to as extension of the arbitration agreement to non-signatories, is more complex, and is covered in Sect. V of this Report.

Two preliminary comments should be made in this context. Firstly, the issue of signatories to an arbitration agreement encompasses different situations. Either multiple parties to an agreement have signed a contract containing an ordinary, uniform bipolar arbitration clause which does not specifically take into account the fact that a multi-party dispute might arise (see Sect. III), or the arbitration clause does indeed anticipate this eventuality and makes special provisions (see Sect. IV). As a second preliminary comment, the difference between multi-party arbitrations among signatories of a mutual arbitration agreement, as compared to the extension to non-signatories, is very important from a practical point of view. As shown below, the arbitration institutions, such as the ICC, also draw important distinctions between these two situations.[28] The fact that the extension to a non-signatory third party means that this third party is considered to be a party to an *existing* arbitration agreement must not be forgotten. In other words, if one accepts the premise that there cannot be arbitration without the consent of all parties involved, there is no methodological difference in principle between these two situations. The legal theories actually all have the same goal: of construing the consent of the third party to the existing arbitration agreement. Following the extensive work by Bernard Hanotiau[29] this is now commonly accepted. One should, however, note that while the above-mentioned premise is correct, the focus on the consent of the third party is not entirely justified. This is because the theory of extension is often understood in a broad sense, and could include, for example, the abuse of rights (which is the basis for the piercing of the corporate veil in some jurisdictions)[30] or the assignment of obligations. There also is an ongoing debate about which theory the arbitration community should adopt for the purposes of extending a written arbitration agreement; some proponents focus on (constructive) consent, others on different theories (such as estoppel or abuse of rights).

---

27. See Sect. III.*4.e* below.
28. See Sect. VIII.*1* below.
29. For a summary, see his ICCA Report: B. HANOTIAU, *op. cit.*, fn. 20.
30. See Sect. V.*2.e* below.

As a final comment, it should be noted that a significant issue that inevitably arises in the context of extension is the form of the arbitration agreement.[31]

4. *Multiple Parties v. Other Forms of Participation in Arbitration Proceedings*

National procedural rules have developed different forms of participation in state court proceedings. A third party either becomes a party based on a claim by one of the existing parties, or based on its own claim. Another variation is when the third party does not become a proper party to the proceedings, but participates nevertheless in order to promote an outcome which is favorable to it, albeit only with limited procedural rights. In Germany, this variation is generally known as a "side intervention" (*Nebenintervention*). France defines it as *intervention volontaire accessoire*. The American system, like the Anglo-Saxon one, does not distinguish between a "side intervention" with limited rights and full party rights of the joining third party.[32]

In the context of this Report, the question arises as to whether international arbitration should also distinguish between different forms of participation and, if so, who should determine these forms. This issue will be discussed in Sect. VI below.

5. *Multiple Parties from the Beginning of the Arbitration vs. Joining of Third Parties After the Constitution of the Arbitral Tribunal*

There is another practically important distinction to be drawn. Whether or not the arbitral tribunal has already been constituted makes an important difference when discussing whether a third party should be joined in the arbitration proceedings. The problems are obvious: Is this possible in the first place? If so, can (or must) the joining party accept the already appointed arbitration panel? Legal doctrine on this issue is scarce. However, when the issue has been addressed, the authors have, at least as a general rule, stated that replacing one or more arbitrators is too burdensome on the existing parties to the arbitral proceedings.[33] It is doubtful that this argument is justified in every situation. Sect. VII will attempt to define some typical situations where the replacement of an arbitrator is justified to allow the third party to be joined, even if this is at the cost of an efficient procedure.[34]

---

31. See Sect. V.3 below.
32. See A. MEIER, *op. cit.*, fn. 13, p. 129.
33. See, e.g., J. KLEINSCHMIDT, *op. cit.*, fn. 13, p. 150.
34. The author has addressed this specific issue recently with Andrea Meier. See N. VOSER and A. MEIER, *op. cit.*, fn. 13, p. 118 et seq.

II. ADVANTAGES OF, AND OBSTACLES TO, MULTI-PARTY ARBITRATIONS

*1. Advantages*

The main advantage of multi-party proceedings versus separate proceedings is that they enhance the efficiency of the dispute resolution, since common issues of fact and/or law may be addressed by the same panel in one proceeding.[35]

There are other good reasons for dealing with related disputes between several parties in one forum, such as avoiding the risk of conflicting awards which can lead to the unjustified loss of a party's claim. This concern is particularly relevant in regard to claims of recourse: if the respondent wishes to take recourse against a third party in a separate proceeding, but the second arbitral tribunal does not honor the findings of the first panel regarding the liability of the respondent, the respondent might face the problem of completely losing its recourse option.[36]

In construction project disputes, other difficulties are encountered; these generally result from the subcontractors and suppliers working together to fulfill the same obligation, namely that of the main contractor.[37] A typical situation involves a claim by the main contractor (claimant) against the owner (respondent), when there is a threat of claims by the subcontractor(s) against the main contractor, even though such claims have not yet been filed. Often, the main contractor cannot claim any damages based on possible claims from the subcontractors, since under many legal systems it is not deemed to have suffered legally relevant damage (in the form of an increase of liabilities) if the claims have not materialized in the form of a judgment against it. Consequently, the main contractor (claimant) risks not being compensated for its potential damages and might still have to pay the subcontractor in *later* proceedings. The situation is even more delicate if the main contractor and the subcontractor concluded a back-to-back agreement, whereby the subcontractor would obtain what the main contractor obtains from the owner. In a two-party arbitration (involving only the owner and the main contractor) this means that no damages can be paid, since there is no legally relevant damage on the claimant's (main contractor's) side. Thus, both the main contractor and the subcontractor end up empty-handed.

*2. Obstacles*

*a. Consensual nature of arbitration*

The main obstacle to multi-party arbitration proceedings stems from the very nature of arbitration as a consensual dispute resolution mechanism.[38] This is also the fundamental difference from state court proceedings: while state courts have authoritative jurisdiction over the parties which is vested in them by the State, in arbitration, the jurisdiction of the arbitral tribunal is derived solely from a common agreement between the parties. While state courts have well-established and predictable rules providing for multi-party

---

35. *Ibid.*, p. 116.
36. *Ibid.*, p. 116.
37. K.M. SIIG, *op. cit.*, fn. 5, p. 74.
38. J. KLEINSCHMIDT, *op. cit.*, fn. 13, p. 142.

proceedings and the joinder of third parties to pending court proceedings, which can be imposed on the parties to the proceedings as well as on third parties, this is not the case in arbitration.

*b.    Arbitration has a two-party (bipolar) setup*

The second main obstacle to multi-party arbitration, which is closely related to the consensual nature of arbitration, is the notion that arbitration is in principle a two-party setup[39] or, as it is sometimes called, a bipolar proceeding.[40] In a bipolar proceeding, the parties are considered to be arbitrating an existing or future dispute amongst themselves. This is well-illustrated by the rules governing the appointment of arbitrators. Although there are exceptions,[41] arbitration codes and institutional rules usually only provide for the appointment mechanism in two-party situations, as per, for example, Arts. 10(2) and 11(3)(a) of the UNCITRAL Model Law on International Commercial Arbitration (the Model Law). Even in those institutional rules which do provide for a multi-party appointment, the standard is that the claimant(s), on the one side, and the respondent(s), on the other side, each jointly appoint one arbitrator.[42]

Although such provisions do provide guidance in certain situations, they are based on a simplified concept that multiple parties can always be divided into two categories, i.e., either claimant or respondent.[43] However, there are many examples in practice, such as chain of delivery, which demonstrate that this view is overly simplistic. Initially, everyone in the chain is united in the interest of proving that there is no defect in the product in question. However, if the final buyer can show that the product was, in fact, defective, the people who were jointly responsible for the delivery – for example, in a case where one party delivered and the other was responsible for the proper transportation and installation – become opponents, since each will try to show that the defect is the other party's responsibility. Another example, where it is more likely that a multi-party arbitration agreement exists, is the situation of claims between two groups of joint venture partners. Here, within the "losing side", it is very likely that each party has separate interests and will want to take recourse against the other partner(s).

*c.    Arbitration is confidential (private)*

A further obstacle to multi-party arbitration which should be mentioned is the confidential nature of arbitration. Confidentiality (or privacy) is often one of the reasons for the parties to choose arbitration as a dispute resolution mechanism, since it allows the dispute, the contract and any business secrets (such as prices or co-operation agreements) to remain undisclosed. Due to the confidential nature of arbitration, it is questionable whether third parties should be allowed to participate in an existing bipolar arbitration.[44]

---

39. K.M. SIIG, *op. cit.*, fn. 5, p. 75.
40. See E. SILVA-ROMERO, *op. cit.*, fn. 2, p. 77.
41. See Art. 1946 of the Dutch Code of Civil Procedure. See K.M. SIIG, *op. cit.*, fn. 5, pp. 76 and 81.
42. See Art. 10(1) of the ICC Rules; Art. 8(4) and 8(5) of the Swiss Rules; Art. 13 of the Arbitration Rules of the German Institution of Arbitration of 1998 (hereinafter DIS Rules).
43. K.M. SIIG, *op. cit.*, fn. 5, p. 75.
44. J. KLEINSCHMIDT, *op. cit.*, fn. 13, p. 144; K.M. SIIG, *op. cit.*, fn. 5, p. 76. See also Loukas A. MISTELIS, "Confidentiality and Third Party Participation: *UPS v. Canada* and *Methanex Corporation v. United States*", 21 Arb. Int'l (2005, no. 2) p. 211.

The issue of confidentiality should not be overemphasized: the parties often have a real interest in joining third parties, who, in such cases are usually familiar with the underlying business transaction. For example, in a situation where a subcontractor and a main contractor are to jointly fulfil the main contractor's obligation toward the owner, the subcontractor is usually aware of the details of the agreement between the owner and the main contractor regarding its own involvement in the relationship and its possible inclusion in the arbitration proceedings.[45] Finally, it is possible to extend the confidentiality to a third party, so that the main purpose of the confidential nature of arbitration, which is not to make confidential information known to the public at large, can still be upheld.[46]

*d. Concerns regarding enforceability and setting aside proceedings*
Concerns regarding enforceability might also be an obstacle to multi-party arbitrations. This is especially the case if additional parties have been brought in based on the "extension" of the arbitration agreement to third parties.[47] The 1958 New York Convention presupposes *an agreement in writing* (see Art. V(1)(*a*), together with Art. II of the New York Convention) and the original of this agreement must be presented to the recognizing court (Art. IV(1)(*b*) of the New York Convention). Consequently, the arbitral tribunal might be reluctant to join third parties who are not signatories to the arbitration agreement. The United States Court of Appeals for the Second Circuit has applied the concept of *arbitrability* from Art. II(2)(*a*) of the New York Convention in order to deny recognition.[48] However, this case has been criticized and seems to illustrate a general difficulty in the United States.[49] Finally, Art. V(1)(*c*) of the New York Convention, which deals with the issue of ultra petita, and Art. V(1)(*d*) of the New York Convention, which deals with the parties' agreement regarding the composition of the arbitral tribunal and the procedure, might be considered stumbling blocks when it comes to the recognition of multi-party awards.[50]

The concern regarding enforceability should not be overemphasized.[51] Legal constructions which lead to the extension of an arbitration agreement to non-signatory third parties do not normally constitute a violation of public policy or lack of arbitrability, which could result in the refusal of recognition under Art. V(2) of the New York Convention.[52] Furthermore, the court seized with the recognition should accept the arbitral tribunal's jurisdiction if it is admissible based on the law chosen by the parties or based on the law of the country where the award was made (Art. V(1)(*a*) of the New

---

45. K.M. SIIG, *op. cit.*, fn. 5, p. 76.
46. According to Art. 3(12) of the IBA Rules on the Taking of Evidence, the arbitral tribunal can unilaterally issue orders to set forth the terms of the confidentiality regarding documents produced in the arbitration. The same should be possible with regard to the joining of a third party.
47. These situations are dealt with under Sect. V below. On the issue of recognition in this specific context, see B. HANOTIAU, *op. cit.*, fn. 20, pp. 345-358.
48. *Sarhank Group v. Oracle Corp.*, 404 F.3d 657 (2d Cir. 2005).
49. See B. HANOTIAU, *op. cit.*, fn. 20, p. 356, who strongly criticizes this decision as being based on an "unusual and stretched theory of arbitrability prevailing in the United States".
50. K.M. SIIG, *op. cit.*, fn. 5, p. 77.
51. *Ibid.*, p. 77.
52. *Ibid.*, p. 79.

York Convention).[53] This opinion assumes that it is possible, or indeed necessary, for the court to respect the findings of the arbitral tribunal's jurisdiction if, based on its own law, it can overcome the form issue. This is the case, for example, in Switzerland, where the Federal Supreme Court held that the form requirement only has to be applied to the original arbitration agreement and that its extension to a non-signatory party is an issue of substantive validity.[54] There are other ways to overcome the form problem, as shown by *Int'l Paper Co. v. Schwabedissen Maschinen & Anlagen GmbH*, where the United States Court of Appeals for the Fourth Circuit held that a party may be precluded (estopped) from claiming that the lack of signature disallowed the recognition if the party relied on the contract by requesting *other* provisions to be enforced to its benefit.[55]

There are further arguments which are not based on the requirements for recognition and which speak against using the issue of enforceability in such a way as to prevent an arbitral tribunal from applying one of the theories used for the extension to non-signatories. Firstly, the place of enforcement is not necessarily known in advance and the level of scrutiny varies considerably from recognition state to recognition state.[56] Secondly, it is commonly known that most parties comply with the awards without the necessity of formal recognition proceedings. Thirdly and finally, the parties should be primarily concerned with the evaluation of the risk of a lack of recognition, and, if they accept such risk for the benefit of the multi-party arbitration, the arbitral tribunal should not interfere.

In sum, although the issue of enforcement should "encourage caution",[57] this problem should not overly influence the decision of the arbitral tribunal: there are many valid arguments for justifying the inclusion of a third (non-signatory) party.

The arguments just discussed regarding enforcement apply analogously to the issue of setting aside within the country where the award had been rendered. In many countries, the same (or very similar) objections which can be argued under the New York Convention also constitute grounds for the vacation of the award.

*e.   Loss of efficiency*

The fifth and final obstacle, loss of efficiency, should also be discussed. Multi-party proceedings can be very cumbersome for purely practical reasons, such as scheduling meetings or hearings. For this reason, it has been suggested that such practical considerations should play a role in deciding the admission of a joinder.[58] This suggestion is not entirely valid. Experienced arbitrators plan the entire proceedings in advance in a provisional timetable. Provided that sufficient time is factored in for unforeseen events, the timetable will typically not change from beginning to end. This means that hearings are scheduled as far as one year in advance. Secondly, the lack of efficiency and the

---

53. See *ibid.*, p. 79.
54. Swiss Federal Supreme Court, 16 October 2003, *X. S.A.L, Y. S.A.L. and A. v. Z. Sàrl and Arbitral Tribunal,* ATF 129 III 727 at p. 736 (cons. 5.3.1) = 22 ASA Bull. (2004, no. 2) p. 364 at p. 387. See also Sect. V.3 below.
55. 206 F.3d 411 (4th Cir. 2000). See B. HANOTIAU, *op. cit.*, fn. 20, p. 358.
56. K.M. SIIG, *op. cit.*, fn. 5, p. 77.
57. B. HANOTIAU, *op. cit.*, fn. 20, p. 355.
58. K.M. SIIG, *op. cit.*, fn. 5, p. 77.

additional need for resources for the party which has to initiate second proceedings are most likely more significant than the practical difficulties in the first arbitration. In fact, the desire to deal with third parties in one proceeding is often dictated by the principle of procedural efficiency, since it is likely to lead to a speedier final adjudication of a complex dispute.[59]

*f.  Conclusion*

In sum, when analyzing the obstacles to multi-party arbitration, the only real obstacles are the consensual nature of the arbitration process and the traditional focus on a bipolar situation in arbitration. Other issues which might be considered obstacles (confidentiality, recognition and loss of efficiency) are less relevant.

III.  ARBITRATION PROCEEDINGS AMONG MULTIPLE PARTIES TO ONE AGREEMENT WITH A UNIFORM ARBITRATION CLAUSE

*1.  Preliminary Remarks*

Multi-party agreements often contain a simple bipolar arbitration clause which does not take into account special situations that might arise, i.e., that the arbitration proceedings will be among multiple parties or even that a multi-polar dispute might occur. This type of multi-party arbitration agreement should be distinguished from a "real" or "true" multi-party arbitration clause which takes into account the fact that there might be multiple parties, either by providing for a specific appointment mechanism and/or by providing for specific rules in case of a multi-polar dispute. This will be dealt with in Sect. IV below.

*2.  Multiple Parties to an Agreement with an Arbitration Clause Is a Sufficient Basis for Multi-party Arbitration Proceedings*

A party who enters into a multi-party agreement containing a uniform arbitration clause is, or should be, aware that multiple disputes may arise out of this relationship and that those disputes may be joined in one and the same proceedings.[60] The question arises as to whether this is sufficient to justify obliging the parties to a multi-party agreement to be joined in one arbitration proceedings if a dispute between several parties to the agreement arises, or whether additional criteria must be met.

Although it might seem entirely self-evident to some that it is admissible to oblige the parties to one agreement to have a single arbitration proceeding, this is not taken for granted by all authors in the field of arbitration. On the contrary, some insist that there also be a special connection between the claims, such as common issues of fact and law

---

59. R. GEIMER, *op. cit.*, fn. 6, p. 164.
60. N. VOSER and A. MEIER, *op. cit.*, fn. 13, p. 115; J. KLEINSCHMIDT, *op. cit.*, fn. 13, p. 146; A. MEIER, *op. cit.*, fn. 13, p. 61.

comparable to what is known in German as *Streitgenossenschaft*.[61] According to other authors, multi-party proceedings are only possible if the parties to the arbitration agreement could have plausibly foreseen that it would not be possible to deal with disputes arising out of their contractual relationship in *bilateral* proceedings.[62]

According to the prevailing view, there is no room for these restrictions in international arbitration. A multi-party agreement with a uniform arbitration clause is a sufficient basis for multi-party arbitration proceedings and the fact of entering into such an agreement must be considered an *implied consent* to multi-party arbitration by each of the parties to the arbitration agreement.[63]

### 3. The Necessity of the Arbitrators' Consent

In the legal literature, the question of whether or not the members of the arbitral tribunal must consent to a multi-party arbitration is a matter of dispute.[64] Clearly, an arbitrator who consents to act as an arbitrator, knowing that there is a multi-party arbitration, has consented to the situation and must act accordingly. A more delicate issue would arise where an arbitrator who, at the time of accepting the mandate, did not know of any potential joinder of a third party. An argument could be made that the joining of a third party changes the arbitrator's mandate and that the arbitrator must therefore consent to a joinder.[65]

An arbitrator who consents to act as an arbitrator based on a multi-party arbitration clause is normally aware of the "risk" of one of the parties in a dispute asking a third signatory to join the proceedings. In such a situation, it is not justified to require the arbitrator's subsequent consent.[66] However, every arbitrator has the right to resign for important reasons, and – in very exceptional cases – the fact that third parties are to be joined can constitute an important reason.[67] This is, for instance, the case if the parties refuse to remunerate the arbitrator for the additional work that will result from such joinder. As a rule, in ad hoc proceedings such a situation will not arise, since the arbitrators and the parties will have provided for remuneration on a time-spent basis or

---

61. Walter J. HABSCHEID, *"Zum Problem der Mehrparteienschiedsgerichtsbarkeit"* in Claude REYMOND, et al., eds., *Schweizer Beiträge zur internationalen Schiedsgerichtsbarkeit* (Schulthess 1984) p. 173 at p. 181; Rainer MARKFORT, *Mehrparteien-Schiedsgerichtsbarkeit im deutschen und ausländischen Recht* (Heymann 1994) p. 114. For further references, see Klaus P. BERGER, *Internationale Wirtschaftsschiedsgerichtsbarkeit, Verfahrens- und materiellrechtliche Grundprobleme im Spiegel moderner Schiedsgesetze und Schiedspraxis* (de Gruyter 1992) p. 209 fn. 489.
62. Peter SCHLOSSER, *Das Recht der internationalen privaten Schiedsgerichtsbarkeit*, 2nd edn. (Mohr 1989) no. 561.
63. R. GEIMER, *op. cit.*, fn. 6, p. 170; N. VOSER and A. MEIER, *op. cit.*, fn. 13, p. 117; Andreas REINER, *Handbuch der ICC-Schiedsgerichtsbarkeit* (Manz 1989) p. 90.
64. See A. MEIER, *op. cit.*, fn. 13, pp. 83-85; Boris NIKLAS, *Die subjektive Reichweite von Schiedsvereinbarungen, Eine systematische Darstellung unter besonderer Berücksichtigung der Mehrparteienschiedsgerichtsbarkeit* (Mohr Siebeck 2008) pp. 250-252.
65. This is the opinion of Thomas RÜEDE and Reimer HADENFELDT, *Schweizerisches Schiedsgerichtsrecht nach Konkordat und IPRG*, 2nd edn. (Schulthess 1993) p. 256 for domestic arbitration in Switzerland.
66. A. MEIER, *op. cit.*, fn. 13, p. 83; B. NIKLAS, *op. cit.*, fn. 64, p. 251.
67. A. MEIER, *op. cit.*, fn. 13, p. 84.

will at least have included some flexibility for unforeseeable additional work. In cases of institutional arbitration, the institutional rules provide for some flexibility to account for any additional work when the fees of the arbitrators are determined.[68]

There could be a practical obstacle to keeping the same arbitrators in the case of a joinder of third parties after the filing of the request or notice of arbitration: a potential new conflict of interest. However, an arbitrator who accepts a nomination is obliged to extend his or her search for potential conflicts of interest beyond the limited scope of the parties and must include potential third parties.[69] This is clearly valid with regard to any third party that is a signatory to the same arbitration clause, but also goes beyond this scope to include affiliates of each party. Therefore, any potential conflict against another signatory should be disclosed, and thus be known, to the parties before the joinder.[70]

### 4. Types of Claims

#### a. Preliminary remarks

The most frequent situation is a claimant alleging that more than one of the signatories to the arbitration agreement is jointly and severally liable. As shown above, each party to a multi-party arbitration clause, as well as the arbitrator who accepts being appointed in the context of a multi-party arbitration clause, is implicitly considered to have accepted multi-party arbitration proceedings. Accordingly, it is recognized that the *claimant* can file its notice for arbitration against several signatories to the arbitration clause.[71]

The more delicate question is whether the *respondent*, upon receipt of the arbitration notice, can do the same. This would mean going beyond a standard counterclaim, and filing a third-party counterclaim or, more generally, a *claim against a third party (Drittwiderklage)* (see Sub-sect. *b* below). A further question is whether it is possible for a claimant or a respondent to file a *claim for recourse* against a third party (Sub-sect. *c*), and if a respondent can bring a cross-claim against a co-respondent (Sub-sect. *d*). Finally, the question of whether the third party can join the arbitration proceedings on its own initiative (*intervention*) shall be addressed (Sub-sect. *e*).

#### b. Claims by the respondent against a third signatory party

While it is accepted that a counterclaim by the respondent against the claimant is possible for connected counterclaims, the issue of whether it is possible to extend the counterclaim to a third person or entity has been debated for some years. In German civil procedure doctrine, this concept is known as *Drittwiderklage*.[72] In principle, the respondent's counterclaim can be directed against the claimant and a third party, or

---

68. J. KLEINSCHMIDT, *op. cit.*, fn. 13, p. 143.
69. See Art. 7 of the IBA Guidelines on Conflicts of Interest in International Arbitration (2004).
70. J. KLEINSCHMIDT, *op. cit.*, fn. 13, p. 149; A. MEIER, *op. cit.*, fn. 13, p. 83.
71. As a rule, the claimant will do so because of the alleged joint and several liability of the various respondents.
72. J. KLEINSCHMIDT, *op. cit.*, fn. 13, p. 142. Under German law, this also includes situations where a respondent wants to just take recourse against a third party (and not also against the claimant). This is commonly known as claim for recourse (*Regressanspruch* oder *Gewährleistungsklage*) and will be dealt with separately (see Sect. III.4.c).

solely against the third party.[73] These two issues can be jointly referred to as *claims by the respondent against a third party*.

The obvious advantage in terms of the efficiency of such claims has already been mentioned.[74] Another important advantage is that the joinder in a single proceeding will guarantee coherent decisions within the same factual or legal disputes.[75]

In recent literature, the possibility of allowing the respondent to file a counterclaim against a third signatory to the same agreement has been recognized. The decisive argument is that any signatory of a common agreement with a common arbitration clause has given its anticipated consent to being included in only one arbitration proceedings.[76]

This view promotes a just approach to arbitration. Firstly, it addresses the equal treatment of the parties. If the claimant is allowed to choose several counterparties, the same right should apply to the respondent.[77] Secondly, in practice, when parties have claims against each other, the issue of which party initiates the arbitration proceedings is often a matter of coincidence. Thus, the allocation of the roles of the parties should not be the decisive factor.[78] Thirdly, in the context of a multi-party arbitration agreement, the refusal of a third party to be joined in a multi-party arbitration amounts to contradictory behavior on the part of this refusing party. According to generally accepted principles, a contradictory behavior cannot be protected and thus the third party is pre-empted from raising any objections to being included in the arbitration proceedings.

c. *Claim for recourse against a third party*

The claim for recourse is an instrument recognized especially in Roman and Anglo-Saxon legal systems. In a claim for recourse, a party to a proceeding can include a third party in the same proceedings in order to raise claims against this party should it lose its case against the original counterparty. The claim for recourse is typically raised by the respondent, although it is also possible for a claimant to do so.[79]

There is no reason to exclude claims for recourse against a third party from the scope of application of claims against third parties, as discussed in the previous section. The only possible reason for excluding a third party who is a signatory to the same agreement and the same arbitration clause would be if one assumed a lack of consent on the part of the individual signatory parties for the adjudication of claims of such types in one arbitration proceeding. Such an assumption, however, is not justified since the

---

73. In Germany, the descriptive term for the first type is *parteierweiternde* or *streitgenössische Drittwiderklage*, and *isolierte Drittwiderklage* for the second type. See *ibid.*, p. 143; A. MEIER, *op. cit.*, fn. 13, p. 21.
74. See Sect. II.*1* above.
75. J. KLEINSCHMIDT, *op. cit.*, fn. 13, p. 143.
76. *Ibid.*, pp. 144-146; A. MEIER, *op. cit.*, fn. 13, p. 67. See also Reinhold GEIMER, "*Beteiligung weiterer Parteien im Schiedsgerichtsverfahren, insbesondere die Drittwiderklage*" in Karl-Heinz BÖCKSTIEGEL, et al., eds., *Die Beteiligung Dritter an Schiedsverfahren* (Carl Heymanns 2005) p. 71 at p. 82, Bernard HANOTIAU, "Complex – Multicontract-Multiparty – Arbitrations", 14 Arb. Int'l (1998, no. 4) p. 369 at p. 384.
77. *Ibid.*, p. 384.
78. J. KLEINSCHMIDT, *op. cit.*, fn. 13, p. 146.
79. A. MEIER, *op. cit.*, fn. 13, pp. 23 and 68.

anticipated consent must extend to all types of claim, including claims for recourse. Therefore, such claims against other signatories should be accepted.[80]

d. *Claims by the respondent against another respondent (cross-claims)*
A respondent's claim against another respondent within the same arbitration proceedings is usually called a *cross-claim*.[81] It should be distinguished from the situations discussed so far, since here there is no joining of a third party. Instead, a new claim is initiated between two existing parties in the ongoing arbitration. A cross-claim will often be a claim in guarantee or in damages, for example, a claim by one subcontractor against another where the main contractor has initiated arbitration proceedings against both.[82]

The arguments in favor of allowing claims against third parties are particularly valid for cross-claims by a respondent against a co-respondent. The signing of a multi-party arbitration clause must be considered an acceptance of multi-party proceedings, extending to all types of claim that might potentially arise among all parties to that agreement. This also applies to the claimant, even though it may have no desire to be involved in a dispute between the two co-respondents.[83]

e. *Claims by third parties (intervention)*
With what is called a *main intervention*, a third party wishes to participate in the proceedings on its own motion, i.e., without being requested to do so by a claimant or a respondent. In Germany and in most parts of Switzerland, in order to become a party, an intervening party must raise claims against both the claimant and the respondent; this leads to new and separate proceedings which, as a rule, are then joined to the existing one.[84] This is typical for the strong bipolar structure of the Germanic system where there are always two parties opposing each other.[85]

Other legal systems do not follow a strictly bipolar structure. In France, the intervention of a third person is possible with the *intervention volontaire principale*, which permits the adjudication of related third-party claims.[86] Similarly, in the United States, it is possible for a third party to join the proceedings by means of a *permissive intervention*, or of an *intervention of right*, in which the third party claims a better right against both the claimant and the respondent.[87]

In view of these different options in the national legal systems, it is not surprising that there is no consensus in international arbitration on the permissibility of an intervention and on what its requirements are; few legal opinions have been expressed with regard to this issue to date. According to Bernard Hanotiau, an intervention is "possible only if

---

80. *Ibid.*, p. 67.
81. B. HANOTIAU, *op. cit.*, fn. 13, no. 397 at p. 178.
82. See *ibid.*
83. For the ICC Court's new practice allowing cross-claims see Sect. VIII.*1* below.
84. A. MEIER, *op. cit.*, fn. 13, p. 17.
85. *Ibid.*, p. 21. Third parties who are neither on the claimant's nor on the respondent's side can only be requested to participate by one of the existing parties if they are called to participate by means of a formal third-party notice (*Streitverkündung*).
86. *Ibid.*, p. 24.
87. *Ibid.*, pp. 28-29.

there is an arbitration agreement between the intervening party and the parties in dispute and they all agree to the intervention".[88] This rule applies to ad hoc arbitration and to cases where the institutional provisions governing the arbitration do not provide for specific rules on this issue.[89]

It is questionable whether, in addition to agreeing to a common arbitration agreement, the parties already in dispute must also agree to the intervention. In the framework of the signatories of a common arbitration agreement, the previously mentioned principle applies: by signing such an agreement, each party to the agreement consents to multi-party proceedings. A third signatory who is not requested to participate by either the claimant or the respondent must be free to decide whether or not it wishes to intervene as an additional party.[90] It is not justified to exclude such a third party from the proceedings (on the grounds of a lack of consent of the parties already in dispute) in the situation of a multi-party arbitration clause. As with the issue of who (the claimant or the respondent) started the proceedings, it can equally be a matter of coincidence whether the specific claimant or the intervening party (both with separate claims against the respondent) started the proceedings. It would thus not be justified to make the intervention dependent on the specific consent of the parties to the arbitration proceedings.

If an intervention is allowed in situations of a multi-party arbitration agreement, it should make no difference if the intervener only has a claim against one of the parties or against both of them. Therefore, the Germanic type of main intervention is permissible.[91]

*f. Conclusion*

It follows from the above that there are no restrictions with regard to the possible claims between multiple parties in arbitration proceedings. In other words, the arbitral tribunal is not bound by the restrictions of the procedural laws of the jurisdiction at the seat of the arbitration. For instance, it would not be justified to deny the possibility of a claim for recourse against another signatory by arguing that the civil procedural rules for court proceedings at the seat of the arbitral tribunal do not recognize these types of claim.[92]

5.  *Decision on the Admissibility of Multiple Parties and the Setting Aside of Such a Decision*

This section covers situations where either the claimant submits a notice of arbitration against multiple signatories to the arbitration agreement, or where the respondent, in its answer to the notice of arbitration, includes not only the claimant but other third

---

88. B. HANOTIAU, *op. cit.*, fn. 13, no. 363 at p. 165. Hanotiau also points out that the Belgian and the Dutch leges arbitrii each contain a specific provision on this issue (*ibid.*, no. 364 at p. 165).
89. *Ibid.*, nos. 363 and 365 at pp. 165-166. The institutional arbitration rules do not, as a rule, provide for any rules on intervention. An exception to this principle is Art. 4(2) of the Swiss Rules; for details regarding this provision, see Sect. VIII.2 below.
90. A. MEIER, *op. cit.*, fn. 13, p. 68.
91. See *ibid.*, p. 68.
92. *Ibid.*, p. 68.

parties who are also signatories to the arbitration agreement.[93] These situations are distinguishable from requests for joinder from parties or the intervention of a third party in an arbitration that has already been commenced.[94]

In ad hoc arbitration, there are only two potentially competent bodies for the decision on joinder: the arbitral tribunal or a court. Until all the members of the arbitral tribunal have been appointed, the arbitral tribunal has not been constituted, and it is thus not possible for it to decide on requests for the joinder of a third party. Where there are difficulties regarding the constitution of the arbitral tribunal, a request to the competent court, asking the court for a decision on the joinder, must be filed. However, because of the principle of *competence-competence*, the court should not make the final decision on this issue, but should leave it up to the arbitral tribunal.[95] Since the principle of *competence-competence* is not one of exclusion, but one of chronological priority, the courts will have the last word on the issue of joinder in setting aside proceedings. After the constitution of the arbitral tribunal, a request by one of the parties to join a third party, or for a third party to intervene, is directed to the arbitral tribunal, and the court has the last word only in setting aside proceedings.

In *institutional arbitration*, the issue is different, since the parties are deemed to have consented to any solution the institutional rules provide regarding multi-party arbitration, such as rules on consolidation or joining of third parties. In this case, the institutional rules prevail and the arbitral tribunal as well as the parties are bound by them.[96] Today, only few institutions provide for special rules on consolidation and joinder. The rules differ as to whether they declare the institution competent to consolidate proceedings or join third parties, or whether they directly address the competence of the arbitral tribunal.[97] If the decision is to be made before the arbitral tribunal is constituted, the institution itself will have to make a prima facie decision as to whether there is a valid arbitration agreement among all parties.[98] In the present context of multiple signatories to arbitration agreements, there can be little doubt that the prima facie test would result in the admissibility of multiple parties. However, the final decision is left to the arbitral tribunal,[99] unless the seat of the arbitral tribunal is in

---

93. See the types of claim explained in Sects. III.4.b to III.4.d) above. It is assumed that the fourth type of claim (intervention by a third party; see Sect. III.4.e), above) necessarily implies that the arbitration proceedings have already commenced.
94. See Sect. VII.1 below.
95. The level of scrutiny depends on the jurisdiction concerned. In Switzerland, for example, the Swiss state court applies Art. 7 of the Swiss PILA, and will only examine the validity of the arbitration agreement on a prima facie basis. In France, however, if the arbitral tribunal has been constituted, the state courts must decline jurisdiction without even examining the validity of the arbitration agreement. Even where the arbitral tribunal has not yet been seized, the state courts must still decline jurisdiction, unless a prima facie examination shows that the arbitration agreement is manifestly null and void (See Art. 1458(1) and (2) of the French New Code on Civil Procedure).
96. The same naturally applies to ad hoc arbitrations if the parties have agreed on a set of ad hoc rules that provide for rules on joinder. See, in particular, Draft Art. 15(4) of the revised UNCITRAL Arbitration Rules. Regarding this provision, see Sect. IX.4.b below.
97. See Art. 22.1(h) of the LCIA Rules; Art. 15 of the Vienna Rules and Art. 4 of the Swiss Rules. For more details see Sect. VIII below.
98. See Art. 6(2) of the ICC Rules; Art. 3(6) of the Swiss Rules.
99. See, e.g., J. KLEINSCHMIDT, *op. cit.*, fn. 13, p. 147 with regard to ICC arbitration.

a jurisdiction where this competence has been withdrawn from the arbitral tribunal and is vested in the state courts, such as in the Netherlands and California.[100]

It is important for all the parties and prospective parties to have a final decision on the admissibility of a third party rendered as early as possible in the arbitration. If the arbitral tribunal wrongly allows third parties to participate, there is a potential for irreparable harm, in that those third parties can obtain confidential information.[101] It is also important for the parties to know whether they may need to initiate separate court or arbitration proceedings in order to stop the expiration of periods of limitation under the law on which they are basing their claim.[102] A decision that comes only at the end of the arbitration proceedings is therefore unsatisfactory. For this reason, the arbitral tribunal will, whenever it is reasonable and practicable, decide on this issue in the form of a preliminary decision. This decision regarding the admissibility of third parties should, in the author's opinion, be qualified as a decision on jurisdiction and not as a procedural decision.[103] With this qualification, many leges arbitrii will allow for setting aside proceedings against the preliminary decision; the parties do not then have to wait for the final award.[104]

There are other potential grounds for setting aside the decision regarding the admission or refusal of multiple parties. Since most institutional rules follow the bipolar approach, the multiple parties on one side might be requested to jointly appoint an arbitrator; if they fail to do so, either all the arbitrators, or at least the arbitrator which one side failed to appoint, will be appointed by the institution. A party to an arbitration clause could be of the opinion that this is against the parties' agreement, and against the relevant rules of the chosen arbitral institution (such as Art. 8(4) of the ICC Rules). Therefore, there could be a claim that the arbitral tribunal has not been properly constituted.[105] Finally, one party could also claim that the right to equal treatment has been violated because, as one of several parties on one side, its influence is much weaker, or diluted, as compared to the opposing side's influence in appointing the arbitrator.[106] Whether or not such grounds for setting aside the decision can be raised before the competent court against a preliminary award of the arbitral tribunal depends on the applicable lex arbitri. Under Swiss law, for example, the claim of improper constitution can be raised against a preliminary award. This is not the case, however, for claims of unequal treatment.[107]

Where the parties have a common arbitration agreement, and based on the analysis above whereby this is sufficient justification for multi-party arbitration, the defense of

---

100. See K.M. SIIG, *op. cit.*, fn. 5, p. 81.
101. R. GEIMER, *op. cit.*, fn. 76, p. 80.
102. If the question is contested and if the issue of prescription is relevant, it might be necessary, for reasons of prudence, to initiate separate proceedings and ask for a stay of the proceedings until the issue of the joinder is finally decided.
103. See R. GEIMER, *op. cit.*, fn. 76, p. 81.
104. See, e.g., Art. 190(3) of the Swiss PILA and Sect. 1040(3) of the German Code of Civil Procedure.
105. See, e.g., Art. 190(2)(a) of the Swiss PILA.
106. See, e.g., Art. 190(2)(d) of the Swiss PILA. This was the situation in the famous *Dutco* decision decided by the French *Cour de Cassation*, see fn. 115 below.
107. See, e.g., Art. 190(3) of the Swiss PILA.

lack of jurisdiction is unlikely to be successful. In such a case, the reasons for an improper constitution and unequal treatment become more important.[108] As will be discussed in the next section, in the context of the appointment of arbitrators, whether or not such a claim is justified in the context of a multi-party arbitration agreement depends primarily on whether multiple parties can be deemed to have identical or at least similar interests as opposed to the interests of the opposing party (or parties). In such cases it appears justified to require them to appoint one arbitrator and, if they fail to do so, to have the institution or the court undertake such an appointment.[109]

6. *Appointment of Arbitrators*

At the beginning of the discussion on multi-party arbitration, the issue of the appointment of arbitrators in multi-party proceedings was considered to be a critical, if not the most difficult, issue.[110] Today, solutions are in place and there is, at least regarding certain questions, a unanimous view on how the issue should be dealt with. A more delicate issue currently is whether or not the bipolar nature of arbitration proceedings, which has been identified as one of the obstacles to multi-party arbitration, should be broadened in multi-polar situations to include the appointment of more than three arbitrators.

*a. The parties have agreed upon the appointment mechanism*
It goes without saying that if the parties have provided for an appointment mechanism in their arbitration clause, this mechanism shall be followed independent of whether the parties have chosen a specific institution or are in an ad hoc arbitration. Furthermore, the parties are free to agree to a different number of arbitrators than one or three. In institutional arbitration, the relevant rules will generally expressly allow the parties to deviate from the two-party concept.[111] Even if this is not the case, since it is based on the parties' mutual agreement, provisions on the number of arbitrators and their appointment should be allowed, as long as the institution feels that it can still provide the service which constitutes the core of the specific institution.

In principle, the parties can also agree on an even number of arbitrators. Such agreements are normally valid.[112] In this case, one of the arbitrators should be empowered to make a tie-breaking decision in order to avoid a potential deadlock and to ensure that a valid award can be issued.[113]

---

108. A. MEIER, *op. cit.*, fn. 13, p. 116.
109. *Ibid.*, p. 92 et seq. and p. 116.
110. Jean-Louis DELVOLVÉ, "*L'arbitrage multipartite en 1992*", 2 ASA Bull. (1992) p. 154 at p. 160.
111. According to Art. 7(6) of the ICC Rules, the parties are expressly allowed to derogate from this provision. This provision is often referred to in multi-party proceedings. See Anne Marie WHITESELL and Eduardo SILVA-ROMERO, "Multiparty and Multicontract Arbitration: Recent ICC Experience", in *Complex Arbitrations, Perspectives on their Procedural Implications*, ICC Ct. Bull., Special Supplement 2003, p. 7 at p. 12.
112. Alan REDFERN and Martin HUNTER, *Law and Practice of International Commercial Arbitration*, 4th edn. (Sweet & Maxwell 2004) no. 4-19 at pp. 185-186.
113. Wolfgang PETER and Thomas LEGLER, Art. 179 Swiss PILA, note 10 in Heinrich HONSELL, et al., eds., *Basler Kommentar, Internationales Privatrecht,* 2nd edn. (Helbing Lichtenhahn 2007).

*b. The multi-party arbitration clause does not provide for an appointment mechanism*
If the arbitration clause provides for a *sole arbitrator*, this raises no specific problems, since all parties must jointly agree on the arbitrator. If such an agreement cannot be reached, the institution or the competent court will effect the appointment.[114]

The issue of appointment of a *three-member arbitration panel* in multi-party arbitrations in *institutional arbitration* is closely associated with the well-known *Dutco* decision rendered by the French *Cour de cassation* in 1992.[115]

Three parties (BKMI, Siemens and Dutco) concluded a consortium for the construction of a cement factory. The arbitration clause provided for ICC arbitration and for a three-member arbitral tribunal. Dutco initiated the proceedings by filing the request for arbitration and appointed its arbitrator. BKMI and Siemens were asked by the ICC Court, following its practice under the old ICC Rules, to appoint one arbitrator. They did so, but under protest. Nevertheless, the arbitral tribunal ruled that it had jurisdiction, and this decision was confirmed by the Paris Court of Appeal. However, this rendering was overturned by the Court of Cassation, which held that a joint appointment violated Siemens' and BKMI's right to equal treatment. It went even further by deciding that the right to equal treatment was part of public policy and, thus, that the right of each party to appoint its arbitrator could not be waived in advance.

This decision has often been commented on and criticized. While the principle was accepted that the right to equal treatment is violated if the interests of the multiple parties who have to nominate one arbitrator are not congruent, prohibiting the parties from waiving their right to appoint their own arbitrator in advance was not considered justified.[116]

In situations such as the *Dutco* case, i.e., where the existence of multiple parties was established before the appointment of the arbitrators,[117] the institutions' answer to the *Dutco* decision was to provide for a mechanism whereby the parties on each side were bound to agree on one arbitrator; if they failed to do so, the institution would appoint the arbitrators and would determine who the presiding arbitrator should be. The first institution to provide for such a rule was the ICC, and others soon followed suit.[118] The rationale behind these rules is obvious: if the institution appoints all the members of the arbitral tribunal, the equal treatment of the parties is ensured. What such provisions do assume, however, is that the *Dutco* decision went too far by holding that the parties could not waive their right to the appointment of an arbitrator in advance, since the choice of

---

114. A. MEIER, *op. cit.*, fn. 13, p. 96.
115. *Siemens AG and BKMI Industrienlagen GmbH v. Dutco Construction Co.*, Cour de cassation (1re Ch. civile), 7 January 1992, Rev. Arb. (1992) p. 470 = ICCA *Yearbook Commercial Arbitration* XVIII (1993) (hereinafter *Yearbook*) p. 140. See also Bernard HANOTIAU, "Joinder of Parties and Joinder of Claims" in François BOHNET, et al., eds., *Mélanges en l'honneur de François Knoepfler* (Helbing & Lichtenhahn 2005) p. 191 at p. 200; Jean-François POUDRET and Sébastien BESSON, *Comparative Law of International Arbitration,* 2nd edn. (Sweet & Maxwell; Schulthess 2007) no. 242 at p. 202.
116. See, e.g., *ibid.*, no. 242 at p. 202.
117. With regard to the appointment/replacement of arbitrators in the situation of a request for joinder after the arbitral tribunal has already been constituted, see Sect. VII.4 below.
118. Art. 10 of the ICC Rules. See also Art. 8 of the LCIA Rules; Art. 8(5) of the Swiss Rules; Sect. 13 of the DIS Rules.

a specific institution containing such a clause must be considered to be an advance waiver.

Interestingly, the institutions differ on how much flexibility they allow themselves when multiple parties on one side cannot agree on one arbitrator. While the ICC Rules (Art. 10(2)) and the Swiss Rules (Art. 8(5)) state that in this case the institution "may" appoint all the members of the panel,[119] others, like the Rules of the London Court of International Arbitration (the LCIA Rules) (Art. 8(1)), the DIS Rules (Sect. 13.2) or the Rules of the Arbitration Institute of the Stockholm Chamber of Commerce (SCC Rules) (Art. 13(4)), formulate this as an obligation of the institution. For the reasons mentioned below in *Category 1,* where the multiple parties have common interests, the institutions should have full flexibility, which includes nominating only the arbitrators on the multiple respondents' side and maintaining the nomination right of the claimant (or the joint nomination by multiple claimants).

What this flexibility entails can be demonstrated by the relevant parts of the standard letter by the Swiss Chambers of Commerce after the filing of a notice of arbitration against several respondents:

> "Pursuant to Article 3, paragraph 8(b) and Article 8, paragraph 4 of the Swiss Rules, the multiple Respondents are invited to designate their arbitrator *within thirty days from the receipt of this letter,* whereupon the presiding arbitrator shall be designated in accordance with Article 8, paragraph 2 of the Swiss Rules.
>
> In case the multiple Respondents fail, within the thirty-day time limit as per the foregoing paragraph, to jointly designate an arbitrator, the Chamber
> – may make the appointment of the wing-arbitrator on behalf of the Respondents, or
> – may
> (i) either proceed to appoint both wing-arbitrators, leaving it to them to designate the presiding arbitrator, or
> (ii) to appoint all three members of the arbitral tribunal,
> it being understood that in both latter cases any previous designation of the arbitrator made by the Claimants shall be disregarded."

In ICC arbitration, the ICC Court has the same flexibility, although the first option is not expressly mentioned in the Rules. However, Art. 10(2) of the ICC Rules is flexible enough to provide for this solution.[120] Indeed, there have been cases in which, despite the respondents' failure to jointly nominate an arbitrator, the ICC Court confirmed the claimant's appointment and only appointed the co-arbitrator for the respondents.[121] The ICC puts the parties on notice that it will resort to Art. 10(2) of the ICC Rules, which quite often leads to the parties agreeing on one arbitrator.[122]

---

119. This is also the solution proposed by the UNCITRAL Working Group in Draft Art. 7*bis*(3) of the revised UNCITRAL Arbitration Rules. See Sect. IX.*4.b* below.
120. W.L. CRAIG, William W. PARK and Jan PAULSSON, *International Chamber of Commerce Arbitration,* 3rd edn. (Oceana Publications 2000) p. 201.
121. See A.M. WHITESELL and E. SILVA-ROMERO, *op. cit.*, fn. 111, p. 12.
122. *Ibid.*, pp. 11-12.

While the various options are thus clear, the institutional rules do not provide the institutions with any guidance regarding how to choose among them if multiple claimants or respondents fail to jointly appoint their arbitrator. Based on the opinions expressed in the arbitration literature, three categories should be distinguished:

*Category 1*
Where the parties on one side (be it multiple respondents or, based on a counterclaim by the respondent, multiple claimants) have *common* interests, but refuse to jointly appoint an arbitrator, it is not justified to disregard the appointment made by the other side.[123] Instead, any opposition to a joint nomination must be considered an attempt to obstruct the smooth commencement of the arbitration. Examples of *identical interests* include a parent company and a subsidiary on one side,[124] or, even more generally, a group of companies (also including sister companies).[125]

*Category 2*
The multiple parties have *similar,* but not identical interests. Here it would also seem to be justified to uphold the appointment of the other side and to apply the same rule as for identical interests. Similar, but not identical, interests exist when the third party is a guarantor of the claim against the respondent, or when the respondent is acting together with a third party, against whom it wants to take recourse in order to defend against the claimant's claim.[126]

*Category 3*
If the parties have *conflicting* interests, i.e., if it is a multi-polar dispute, each of the parties should be able to nominate one arbitrator; if one party fails to do so, the institution should appoint this arbitrator. The nominated or appointed arbitrators designate the chairperson. This may necessitate appointing more than three arbitrators, even if doing so is not based on the consent of all parties. However, this is something which is not possible under most institutional arbitration rules and the normal provision is for the institution to appoint all three arbitrators.

It should be emphasized that the above categorization and its consequences with regard to the appointment of arbitrators is not merely an option, but is in fact mandatory. The fact that each party with distinctly different interests can appoint its own arbitrator has an important psychological effect and improves the chances of the parties accepting the outcome. In addition to this psychologically desirable effect, one should

---

123. Y. DERAINS and E.A. SCHWARTZ, *op. cit.*, fn. 3, p. 184; A. MEIER, *op. cit.*, fn. 13, p. 93; Andreas REINER and Werner JAHNEL, "*ICC-Schiedsordnung*" in Rolf A. SCHÜTZE, ed., *Institutionelle Schiedsgerichtsbarkeit, Kommentar* (Heymann 2006), Art. 10, note 5 (pp. 69-70); Dolf WEBER, "*Wider den Verlust des Bestellungsrechts bei Nichteinigung der Mehrparteiengegenseite auf einen Schiedsrichter*" in Birgit BACHMANN, et al., eds., *Grenzüberschreitungen. Beiträge zum Internationalen Verfahrensrecht und zur Schiedsgerichtsbarkeit, Festschrift für Peter Schlosser zum 70. Geburtstag* (Mohr Siebeck 2005) p. 1063 at p. 1077.
124. A. REINER and W. JAHNEL, *op. cit.*, fn. 123, Art. 10, note 5 (p. 70).
125. W.L. CRAIG, W.W. PARK and J. PAULSSON, *op. cit.*, fn. 120, p. 199.
126. See D. WEBER, *op. cit.*, fn. 123, pp. 1075-1076.

also take into account the fact that, in some jurisdictions, the right to appoint one's own arbitrator has been recognized as being so fundamental that there is a risk of the courts, as seen in the *Dutco* decision, not protecting the limited two-party setup of the institutions.[127] Therefore, the institutions should, in the author's opinion, broaden their view and allow for multi-polar arbitrations.[128] The downside, which is, quite obviously, a lack of efficiency, must be accepted in view of the enhanced procedural fairness and the case law just mentioned. On the other hand, if the interests of two parties are congruent, then letting them appoint one arbitrator each would allow them to align their interest and to obtain a controlling vote in the arbitral tribunal.[129] In such a situation, there is a considerable risk that a court, faced with a motion to set aside or a request for recognition of the award, might allow the objection of an opposing party on grounds of unequal treatment.[130]

Multiple parties in the framework of *ad hoc arbitration* must anticipate that a method of constituting the arbitral tribunal in case of multi-party proceedings may be needed . A critical issue is whether the courts should be permitted to deviate from the parties' agreement that provides for an appointment mechanism and the number of arbitrators. Thus, in a decision rendered in 2001, the Superior Court of Zurich held that a domestic arbitration clause allowing each party to designate an arbitrator was invalid and substituted for it the rule that the parties with a common interest had to appoint one arbitrator. The underlying rationale was the violation of the equal treatment of the parties, which the court considered a mandatory principle of arbitration from which the parties cannot derogate.[131]

If the parties to an ad hoc arbitration have not agreed upon an appointment method, it is necessary for the appointing authority (if such an authority has been nominated) or the competent court to step in and act on behalf of the parties. In so doing, the principles stated above for the three categories of institutional arbitrations should be applied by analogy.[132]

---

127. See, e.g., the case decided by the Superior Court of Zurich, 11 September 2001, reported in 101 Blätter für Zürcherische Rechtsprechung (2002) p. 77, also reported in 20 ASA Bull. (2002, no. 4) p. 694 (with a note by L. HIRSCH, p. 702).

128. See also K.M. SIIG, *op. cit.*, fn. 5, p. 76.

129. Gary B. BORN, *International Commercial Arbitration: Commentary and Materials*, 2nd edn. (Kluwer Law International 2001) p. 677.

130. Such a risk is exemplified by the decision of the Superior Court of Zurich of 11 September 2001, *op. cit.*, fn. 127. Although this decision was rendered in the context of the appointment of the arbitral tribunal, its underlying rationale could also be applied to setting aside or non-recognition.

131. Superior Court of Zurich, 11 September 2001, *op. cit.*, fn. 127. In this case, the common interest of the respondents was not difficult to determine since the underlying dispute was about the request for the dissolution of a company. Under Swiss law, parties to such a claim (on both sides) form what is called a *notwendige Streitgenossenschaft* and have to act together. Thus, it was not difficult for the court to determine that there were indeed parallel interests on the multiple respondents' side.

132. See also N. VOSER and A. MEIER, *op. cit.*, fn. 13, p. 122.

## 7. Costs and Advances on Costs for the Arbitration

The fixing of the *costs* of a given arbitration is left up to the arbitral tribunal at the end of the proceedings and will, as a rule, take into account the outcome. The discretion of the arbitral tribunal is very broad in institutional arbitration,[133] as well as in ad hoc arbitration. The arbitral tribunal is free to go beyond the bipolar setup, and, in a multi-polar dispute among several parties, it can allocate a portion of the costs to each party, depending on the outcome of their respective claims.

It is important in general for the institutions to have broad discretion with regard to the fixing of the *advances on costs* in multi-party proceedings. The basic principle that the claimant bears the final responsibility for the non-payment of the advances on costs if the other parties do not pay their equal shares is not always justified. This is obviously the case if the respondent files a counterclaim against a third party or if one respondent files a cross-claim against another respondent. In terms of advances on costs, the respondent should bear the burden and the consequences of the advance on costs related to the counterclaim or the cross-claim.

True to the bipolar nature of ICC arbitrations, Art. 30(3) of the ICC Rules also applies to situations where there is more than one claimant or more than one respondent.[134] Accordingly, if multiple claimants and/or respondents are involved, in principle, each side must pay half of the advances on costs.[135] The ICC Court is prepared to make exceptions to this rule and has done so in the past; for example, when it was not clear in a multi-polar situation whether the newly joined party was a claimant or a respondent; or, when applying Art. 30(2) of the ICC Rules, where, for example, two respondents raised substantial counterclaims but one of them subsequently refused to pay the separate advances on costs. Here the ICC Court agreed to fix separate advances for the counterclaim of each respondent.[136] According to Silva-Romero, the ICC Court now "may fix separate advances on costs for each of the claims (principal claim, counterclaims, cross-claims), in the spirit of the provisions of Art. 30 of the Rules".[137]

### IV. MULTI-PARTY ARBITRATION BASED ON "TRUE" MULTI-PARTY ARBITRATION CLAUSES

#### 1. Introduction

As mentioned in the introduction (see Sect. I.3 above), a distinction must be drawn between multiple signatories to a standard arbitration clause and signatories to a "real"[138] or "true" multi-party arbitration clause. Only the latter clause provides for special rules taking into account the nature of a multi-party or even multi-polar arbitration.

---

133. See, e.g., Art. 31(3) of the ICC Rules.
134. See Art. 2(ii) of the ICC Rules which specifies that the terms "Claimant" and "Respondent" can include more than one claimant or respondent.
135. A.M. WHITESELL and E. SILVA-ROMERO, *op. cit.*, fn. 111, p. 12.
136. *Ibid.*, p. 14.
137. E. SILVA-ROMERO, *op. cit.*, fn. 2, p. 80.
138. This is a term used by K.M. SIIG, *op. cit.*, fn. 5, p. 78.

Within this category of true multi-party arbitration clauses there are an unlimited number of options. However, two patterns can be distinguished: the first type of multi-party arbitration clause only provides for a special appointment mechanism for the arbitrators (see Sub-sect. 2 below), while the second type is far more complex in that it provides for the joinder of a third party, either directly in one arbitration clause or by linking other related contracts together (see Sub-sect. 3 below).

2.   Provisions Regarding the Appointment of Arbitrators in Multi-party Arbitration Clauses

The ICC Court is regularly faced with the following clause which provides that, if the parties on one side cannot agree to jointly appoint an arbitrator, the proceedings shall be separated:

> "If there are two or more defendants, any nomination of an arbitrator by or on behalf of such defendants must be by joint agreement among them. If such defendants fail, within the time limit specified by the Rules, to agree on such joint nomination, the proceedings against each of them must be separated." [139]

This clause guarantees that respondents who do not have joint interests, and therefore cannot agree on an arbitrator, maintain their right to appoint their arbitrator, albeit in separate proceedings. It goes without saying that, with such a clause, all the advantages of a multi-party arbitration clause are lost in the event that no agreement can be reached among the parties. When the number of potential parties is manageable, and if nominating their own arbitrator is crucial to the parties, the parties should consider providing for the possibility of more than three arbitrators. However, this carries the risk that the respondents' side will refuse to make a joint nomination simply in order for their (common) interests to be overrepresented in the arbitration proceedings. One possible solution might be to provide for a mechanism whereby a third neutral person, or the arbitration institution, is entrusted with deciding the issue of whether the parties actually have joint or separate interests. Depending on this decision, the respondents must either appoint one arbitrator (if they fail to do so, this will be done by the institution) or are allowed to each appoint one arbitrator.

Another clause, found in practice, provides that the institution shall appoint all the arbitrators if the parties on *one* side cannot agree on a joint nomination of their arbitrator.[140] With this type of clause, the appointing authority lacks the flexibility to appoint only one side's arbitrator.[141] This provision guarantees an efficient and speedy start to the arbitration and respects the equality of the parties. However, it has the disadvantage that *both* parties lose the option of choosing their own arbitrator. It also requires a high level of confidence in an institution's choice. If the institution that is acting as the appointing authority has a good selection mechanism and takes into account the nature of the parties and of the dispute, this is not too much of a downside when weighed against the benefit of having multi-polar proceedings before one single body.

---

139. A.M. WHITESELL and E. SILVA-ROMERO, *op. cit.*, fn. 111, p. 12.
140. *Ibid.*, p. 12.
141. See Sect. III.6.*b*.

*3. Provisions Regarding the Joinder of Third Parties in Multi-party Arbitration Clauses*

As mentioned above, it is possible to have all the potential parties sign the same agreement with the same arbitration clause, which provides that each signing party agrees to being joined as an additional party to an arbitration pending between other parties. Based on the above analysis,[142] the fact that a party signed such an agreement should be sufficient to allow for multi-party proceedings. Still, it is useful to expressly provide for this possibility in the agreement, since there are still authors who require additional elements. An alternative option is to include a reference to another arbitration clause in another contract, thereby effectively incorporating it. This method is particularly helpful in a large project, if further parties join the project at a later date. The main contractor can then seek to bind the subcontractor to the arbitration clause contained in the contract between the main contractors and the owner. In this way, it is possible to include the subcontractor in a dispute between the main contractor and the owner.

A particularly helpful example of such a clause is the model clause for joinder and consolidation of the American Arbitration Association in its *Guide to Drafting Alternative Dispute Resolution Clauses for Construction Contracts*:

> "The owner, the contractor, and all subcontractors, specialty contractors, material suppliers, engineers, designers, architects, construction lenders, bonding companies and other parties concerned with the construction of the structure are bound, each to each other, by this arbitration clause, provided that they have signed this contract or a contract that incorporates this contract by reference or signed any other agreement to be bound by this arbitration clause. Each such party agrees that it may be joined as an additional party to an arbitration involving other parties under any such agreement. If more than one arbitration is begun under any such agreement and any party contends that two or more arbitrations are substantially related and that the issues should be heard in one proceeding, the arbitrator(s) selected in the first filed of such proceedings shall determine whether, in the interests of justice and efficiency, the proceedings should be consolidated before that (those) arbitrator(s)."[143]

This clause provides for a useful combination of a signing of the clause and a later adherence to it by reference in another contract. Although it is designed for construction disputes, its approach can be used for any other commercial multi-party situation.

Such clauses (especially if they are combined with a clause on the appointment of arbitrators, as discussed above) would constitute an ideal and predictable solution to multi-party disputes. However, it has repeatedly been noted that they are very rarely

---

142. See Sect. III.2.
143. *The AAA Guide to Drafting Alternative Dispute Resolution Clauses for Construction Contracts*, p. 13. The Guide can be downloaded from the AAA website (<www.adr.org>) after registration. See also A. MEIER, *op. cit.*, fn. 13, p. 59.

used in practice.[144] The reasons for this are unclear but it may be due to a lack of awareness and/or for fear of a substantial loss of the flexibility within the procedure.[145]

## V. EXTENSION OF THE ARBITRATION AGREEMENT TO NON-SIGNATORIES

*1. Introduction*

In the previous sections, the discussion concerned the participation of a third party based on a multi-party arbitration agreement of traditional, bipolar nature (Sect. III), or a "true" multi-party arbitration agreement, which takes into account the multi-party nature of the potential arbitration (Sect. IV). In practice, however, one must assume that many, if not the majority, of the situations in which the issue of multi-party arbitrations arises do not fall under these categories, but occur when there is only a traditional bipolar arbitration agreement between two parties. In such situations, the question arises as to whether third parties who are not mentioned in the arbitration agreement as a party may nevertheless be bound by that agreement.

As a general rule, an arbitration agreement only binds those parties that originally agreed to it.[146] Whether or not a person is a party to the arbitration agreement is primarily a question of the interpretation of the arbitration clause under the applicable rules.[147] The issue of the extension of the arbitration agreement to a third party only comes up if the third party cannot already be considered a party to the arbitration agreement based on the interpretation of the arbitration clause. In such a situation it is necessary to determine if the *personal scope* of the arbitration agreement may be extended to the third party, pursuant to one of the theories developed by arbitral tribunals and courts.

The issue of the extension of the arbitration agreement to non-signatories has engendered a wealth of comments and literature.[148] In the following sections, some of

---

144. K.M. SIIG, *op. cit.*, fn. 5, p. 78; J. KLEINSCHMIDT, *op. cit.*, fn. 13, p. 146; K.P. BERGER, *op. cit.*, fn. 61, p. 290.
145. See *ibid.* p. 209 fn. 490, with reference to Antoine KASSIS, "*L'arbitrage multipartite et les clauses de consolidation*", 14 Droit & Pratique Com. Intern. (1988, no. 2) p. 221.
146. Bernhard BERGER and Franz KELLERHALS, *Internationale und interne Schiedsgerichtsbarkeit in der Schweiz* (Stämpfli 2006) no. 492 at pp. 170-171; Emmanuel GAILLARD and John SAVAGE, eds., *Fouchard, Gaillard, Goldman on International Commercial Arbitration* (Kluwer Law International 1999) (hereinafter *Fouchard, Gaillard, Goldman*) no. 498 at p. 280.
147. In a decision of 22 January 2008 (4A_244/2007), the Swiss Federal Supreme Court ruled that the interpretation based on the principle of good faith led to the affiliate in question being entitled to claim rights under the disputed contract. The arbitration agreement designated the two parent companies "including the affiliates" as parties to the contract.
148. See mainly B. HANOTIAU, *op. cit.*, fn. 13, pp. 7-99, and J.-F. POUDRET and S. BESSON, *op. cit.*, fn. 115, pp. 210-231, both including a comprehensive overview of case law, and the contributions at the ICCA Congress 2006 in Montréal: B. HANOTIAU, *op. cit.*, fn. 20; John M. TOWNSEND, "Non-signatories in International Arbitration: An American Perspective" in *ICCA Congress Series no. 13*, p. 359; Anne Marie WHITESELL, "Non-signatories in ICC Arbitration" in *ICCA Congress Series no. 13*, p. 366; Babak BARIN, "Non-signatories in International Arbitration: Some Thoughts from Canada" in *ICCA Congress Series no. 13*, p. 375. See also Jan-

the theories developed shall be briefly presented with a particular focus on the state of the discussion in Switzerland. However, this Report shall not discuss the special issue of extending an arbitration agreement concluded by a governmental entity to the State,[149] or an extension based on a succession in rights (such as merger or assignment).

The issue under discussion normally falls under the heading "extension of the arbitration agreement to non-signatories". This catchphrase is misleading for two reasons:

Firstly, Hanotiau[150] and others have argued that the term "extension" is misleading because the third party is considered to be bound by the original arbitration agreement. The crucial question is always who can or must be considered to be bound by an arbitration agreement. The answer to this is normally based on the assumed consent of the third party to the underlying contractual relationship, including the related arbitration agreement, or on the third party being estopped from contending that it has not consented to it. Thus, the methodological basis for being bound by an arbitration agreement is, in principle, the same for signatories as for non-signatory third parties.[151] Nevertheless, because the use of this expression has nowadays become commonplace in the world of arbitration, it shall be retained for the purposes of this Report. In addition, as already mentioned, the term "extension" has also been used where a theory was applied which could not be directly linked to the consent (or construed) consent of the parties.[152]

---

Michael AHRENS, *Die subjektive Reichweite internationaler Schiedsvereinbarungen und ihre Erstreckung in der Unternehmensgruppe* (Peter Lang 2001); Marc BLESSING, "Introduction to Arbitration – Swiss and International Perspectives" in Stephen V. BERTI, ed., *International Arbitration in Switzerland, An Introduction to and a Commentary on Articles 176-194 of the Swiss Private International Law Statute* (Helbing & Lichtenhahn and Kluwer 2000) no. 491 et seq. at p. 176 et seq.; Daniel BUSSE, "*Die Bindung Dritter an Schiedsvereinbarungen*", 3 SchiedsVZ (2005, no. 3) p. 118; K. MASSURAS, *op. cit.*, fn. 13, pp. 107-257; B. NIKLAS, *op. cit.*, fn. 64; Jean-François POUDRET, "*L'extension de la clause d'arbitrage: approches française et suisse*", 122 JDI (1995, no. 4) p. 893; Otto SANDROCK, "The Extension of Arbitration Agreements to Non-Signatories: An Enigma still Unresolved" in Theodor BAUMS, et al., eds., *Corporations, Capital Markets and Business in the Law, Liber amicorum Richard M. Buxbaum* (Kluwer Law International 2000) p. 461; Otto SANDROCK, "Arbitration Agreements and Groups of Companies" in Christian DOMINCÉ, et al., eds., *Etudes de droit international en l'honneur de Pierre Lalive* (Helbing & Lichtenhahn 1993) p. 625; James R. SENTNER, "Who is Bound by Arbitration Agreements? Enforcement by and Against Non-Signatories", 6 Bus. L. Int'l (2005, no. 1) p. 55; Stephan WILSKE , Laurence SHORE and Jan-Michael AHRENS, "The 'Group of Companies Doctrine' – Where Is it Heading?", 17 Am. Rev. Int'l Arb. (2006) p. 73; Tobias ZUBERBÜHLER, "Non-Signatories and the Consensus to Arbitrate", 26 ASA Bull. (2008, no. 1) p. 18. See also various contributions in Marc BLESSING, ed., *The Arbitration Agreement – Its Multifold Critical Aspects, A Collection of Reports and Materials Delivered at the ASA Conference held in Basel on 17 June 1994* (ASA Secretariat 1994). With regard to the special issue of the extension of an arbitration agreement to a State, see George ROSENBERG, "State as Party to Arbitration", 20 Arb. Int'l (2004, no. 4) p. 387.

149. See, e.g., B. HANOTIAU, *op. cit.*, fn. 20, pp. 346-347, including some critical comments as to whether this does indeed raise the same issues as the extension of the arbitration agreement from an entity of a group of companies to other entities of the same group.
150. See, e.g., *ibid.*, p. 343.
151. See Sect. I.3 above.
152. See Sect. I.3 above.

Secondly, the emphasis on the signatories is also misleading. In more modern legal codes, other forms of communication which permit the consent to an arbitration agreement to be evidenced by a text have been put on the same footing as signing.[153] In practice, it is nevertheless justified to limit the analysis to signatories, since important commercial contracts will, as a rule, have been specifically negotiated, stated in writing and signed by the parties who are to be bound by them. Assuming that such a contract contains an arbitration clause, it is justified to speak of extension to non-signatories.

The leges arbitrii commonly have a form requirement for the conclusion of an arbitration agreement.[154] The extension of the arbitration agreement inevitably raises the issue of how this form requirement can be reconciled with the extension of the consent to arbitrate to third parties. Finally, the form issue also raises concerns regarding the possibility of recognizing an award when the jurisdiction of the arbitral tribunal is based on an "extended" arbitration agreement, since the New York Convention requires the arbitration agreement to be in writing.[155] The first issue will be addressed below;[156] the second issue has already been discussed in the context of obstacles to multi-party arbitration.[157]

2. *Common Theories for the Extension of the Arbitration Agreement to Non-signatories*

a. *Assumption of consent to arbitrate based on conduct*

One of the most frequent patterns in non-signatory cases is the involvement of a non-signatory third party in the underlying contractual relationship. On several occasions, arbitral tribunals and state courts have held that the conduct of a non-signatory may be considered an expression of its intention to be bound by the arbitration agreement.[158] This occurs with particular frequency in situations among groups of companies.

In the United States, a non-signatory's attempt to enforce an agreement that contains an arbitration clause is regarded as clear evidence that it considers itself bound by the arbitration clause contained therein.[159]

The Swiss Federal Supreme Court upheld an arbitral award that compelled a non-signatory respondent to arbitrate, on the grounds that it had made payments and issued a letter of credit in favor of a party that had expressly entered into the arbitration clause provided for in a work contract. In addition, the third party had also explicitly referred to that contract in several documents.[160] Generally speaking, under Swiss law, a third

---

153. See, e.g., Art. 178(1) of the Swiss PILA.
154. See Art. 7 of the UNCITRAL Model Law and, e.g., Art. 178 of the Swiss PILA.
155. Art. 4(1)(b) of the New York Convention.
156. See Sect. V.3 below.
157. See Sect. II.2.d above.
158. See B. HANOTIAU, *op. cit.*, fn. 13, no. 72-79 at p. 36-39; T. ZUBERBÜHLER, *op. cit.*, fn. 148, pp. 22-24.
159. See *Int'l Paper Co. v. Schwabedissen Maschinen & Anlagen GmbH*, 206 F.3d 411, 418 (4th Cir. 2000); *Nauru Phosphate Royalties, Inc. v. Drago Daic Interests, Inc.*, 138 F.3d 160, 167 (5th Cir. 1998). See also C.B. LAMM and J.A. AQUA, *op. cit.*, fn. 13, pp. 725-726.
160. Swiss Federal Supreme Court, 18 December 2001, 4P.126/2001, *LUKoil-Permnefteorgsintez, LLC v. MIR Construction and Trading Co Inc., Ural Tais Production-Construction Firm and Arbitral Tribunal*, 20 ASA Bull. (2002, no. 3) p. 482 at p. 491 (cons. 3).

party may be bound by an arbitration clause if it played a predominant role in the conclusion and/or the performance of the underlying agreement in a manner that either clearly demonstrated its implied intent to be bound by the arbitration clause, or that, under the principle of good faith or the principle of reliance, could have been understood by the other party (or parties) to mean that the third party intended to be bound by the original arbitration agreement.[161] Consequently, based on the general principles of reliance, a party may not request the application of the arbitration agreement to the non-signatory parent company if it was fully aware, at the time of the conclusion of the contract, that it was dealing only with the subsidiary, and not with the parent company.[162] In such cases, and despite the parent company's involvement in the execution of a contract, the party that seeks to bind the parent company is not counting on the parent company being a party to the arbitration agreement and thus cannot call upon the principles of reliance.

*b.   "Group of companies doctrine"*
The "group of companies doctrine" is probably the most prominent and controversial of the theories on the extension of the arbitration agreement to non-signatories.[163] Until now, the issue of "extension" has been, by and large, reduced to group of companies situations.[164]

The doctrine originated in French arbitration practice in the 1970s. Arguably its most famous formulation was provided in the interim award of 1982 in the *Dow Chemical* case, where the arbitral tribunal stated that

"... the arbitration clause expressly accepted by certain of the companies of the group should bind the other companies which, by virtue of their role in the conclusion, performance, or termination of the contracts containing said clauses, and in accordance with the mutual intention of all parties to the proceedings,

---

161. See also B. BERGER and F. KELLERHALS, *op. cit.*, fn. 146, no. 521 at p. 182, no. 523 at p. 183.
162. *Saudi Butec Ltd et Al Fouzan Trading v. Saudi Arabian Saipem Ltd*, unpublished ICC interim award of 25 October 1994, confirmed by Swiss Federal Supreme Court, 29 January 1996, 14 ASA Bull. (1996, no. 3) p. 496 at p. 500 (cons. 5) and pp. 506-507 (cons. 7).
163. From the vast literature, see especially J.-M. AHRENS, *op. cit.*, fn. 148, p. 128 et seq.; Fouchard, Gaillard, Goldman, *op. cit.*, fn. 146, no. 500-506 at pp. 282-289; Philipp HABEGGER, "Arbitration and Groups of Companies – the Swiss Practice", 3 EBOR (2002, no. 3) p. 517; B. HANOTIAU, *op. cit.*, fn. 13, no. 104-110 at pp. 49-52, and no. 203-208 at pp. 97-98; Sigvard JARVIN, "The Group of Companies Doctrine" in Marc BLESSING, ed., *The Arbitration Agreement – Its Multifold Critical Aspects*, *op. cit.* fn. 148, p. 181; B. NIKLAS, *op. cit.*, fn. 64, p. 218 et seq.; Otto SANDROCK, *"Wirkungen von Schiedsvereinbarungen im Konzern"* in Karl-Heinz BÖCKSTIEGEL, et al., eds., *Die Beteiligung Dritter an Schiedsverfahren* (Carl Heymanns 2005) p. 93; S. WILSKE, L. SHORE and J.-M. AHRENS, *op. cit.*, fn. 148; T. ZUBERBÜHLER, *op. cit.*, fn. 148, pp. 25-27. See also the references in fn. 148 above.
164. B. HANOTIAU, *op. cit.*, fn. 13, no. 105 at pp. 49-50.

appear to have been veritable parties to these contracts or to have been principally concerned by them and the disputes to which they may give rise".[165]

Since this interim award, the formula has been followed in a number of French arbitral awards and court decisions.[166] Some of these have rightly been criticized for being too excessive and for too readily disregarding the separate legal entity of corporations and the fundamental requirement of consent to arbitrate.[167] It should be noted, though, that the formula used in the *Dow Chemical* interim award has already made it clear that the mere existence of a group of companies is not per se sufficient to permit the extension of an arbitration agreement to non-signatory group companies, and that the mutual consent of the parties, whether express or implied by their conduct, is essential.[168] Therefore, it would not be correct to assume from the term "group of companies doctrine" that it suffices for a third party to be a member of the same group of companies as the party that originally concluded the formal arbitration agreement in order to bind it to the arbitration agreement. Finally, it should also be noted that courts and arbitral tribunals in France are increasingly basing their findings on established principles of contract law.[169]

*German* doctrine generally takes a reserved position with regard to extension. The group of companies doctrine is often explicitly rejected as being too general, but German authors and courts have still relied on piercing the corporate veil (*Durchgriff*) or on the existence of apparent authority in order to determine that a non-signatory was bound by an arbitration agreement.[170] In *England*, courts and arbitration practitioners have

---

165. *Dow Chemical v. Isover Saint Gobain*, Interim Award of 23 September 1982 in ICC Case No. 4131, *Yearbook* IX (1984) p. 131 at p. 136 = Rev. arb. (1984) p. 137 at p. 148. The award was confirmed by the Paris Court of Appeal by a judgment of 21 October 1983, Rev. arb. (1984) p. 98.
166. See references with S. WILSKE, L. SHORE and J.-M. AHRENS, *op. cit.*, fn. 148, p. 76, note 11. On French case law see also *Fouchard, Gaillard, Goldman, op. cit.*, fn. 146, no. 502-506 at pp. 286-289; J.-F. POUDRET and S. BESSON, *op. cit.*, fn. 115, no. 255-257 at pp. 217-220; O. SANDROCK, *op. cit.*, fn. 163, pp. 97-99.
167. See, e.g., J.-F. POUDRET and S. BESSON, *op. cit.*, fn. 115, no. 256 at pp. 219-220, and no. 253-254 at pp. 214-216; S. WILSKE , L. SHORE and J.-M. AHRENS, *op. cit.*, fn. 148, pp. 77-78. See also B. HANOTIAU, *op. cit.*, fn. 13, no. 106 at p. 50, who sees "a risk that the formula will be used as a shortcut permitting avoidance of rigorous legal reasoning".
168. See *ibid.*, no. 105-107 at pp. 49-51.
169. S. WILSKE, L. SHORE and J.-M. AHRENS, *op. cit.*, fn. 148, p. 78.
170. See Karl-Heinz BÖCKSTIEGEL, Stefan KRÖLL and Patricia NACIMIENTO, "Germany as a Place for International and Domestic Arbitrations – General Overview" in Karl-Heinz BÖCKSTIEGEL, et al., eds., *Arbitration in Germany, The Model Law in Practice* (Wolters Kluwer 2007) p. 3, no. 60-62 at p. 29; Christian DUVE, "Arbitration of Corporate Law Disputes in Germany" in Karl-Heinz BÖCKSTIEGEL, et al., eds., *Arbitration in Germany, The Model Law in Practice, ibid.*, p. 975, no. 79-80 at p. 1001; Jens-Peter LACHMANN, *Handbuch für die Schiedsgerichtspraxis,* 3rd edn. (Schmidt 2008) no. 509-512; W. MÜLLER and A. KEILMANN, *op. cit.*, fn. 13, pp. 118-119; J.-F. POUDRET and S. BESSON, *op. cit.*, fn. 115, no. 261 at p. 225; O. SANDROCK, *op. cit.*, fn. 163, pp. 107-108.

remained particularly sceptical about the group of companies doctrine.[171] A non-signatory may nevertheless be bound by an arbitration agreement pursuant to other theories such as agency, trust or piercing the corporate veil, although this will generally be harder to achieve than in the French context, due to the importance attributed to the traditional principle of privity of contract and the reluctance to disregard the separate legal entity of companies.[172] Courts and arbitral tribunals in the *United States* have traditionally followed a pragmatic and liberal approach to the problem of including non-signatories in arbitration proceedings. While express references to the group of companies doctrine appear to be relatively infrequent, similar results are achieved by the application of principles such as agency, assumption by conduct, third-party beneficiary, equitable estoppel, fraud, or alter ego/piercing the corporate veil.[173] However, recent case law suggests a trend towards a more restrictive practice, particularly with regard to non-signatory respondents resisting arbitration.[174]

Lastly, in *Switzerland*, legal doctrine and case law are generally restrictive in applying an arbitration agreement to non-signatories, and the group of companies doctrine has met with some scepticism. In the *Boutec* case, the Swiss Federal Supreme Court held that the mere fact that the third party belonged to the same group of companies as the signatory company was not per se sufficient to justify extending an arbitration clause, and that such an extension could only be granted if the third party had created an appearance of being bound by the underlying contract and the arbitration clause, and where the reliance of the other party deserved protection based on the principle of good faith.[175] Thus, under Swiss law the issue of extension does not fall under different rules within a group of companies than outside such groups.[176]

---

171. See especially the decision of the Commercial Court of 4 February 2004 in *Peterson Farms Inc. v. C&M Farming Ltd.*, [2004] EWHC 121 (Comm.), where Langley J held that the doctrine "... forms no part of English law" (para. 59). On this case see John LEADLEY and Liz WILLIAMS, "*Peterson Farms*: There is No Group-of-Companies Doctrine in English Law", 7 Int'l Arb. L. Rev. (2004, no. 4) p. 111; Otto SANDROCK, "The Group of Companies Doctrine Forms No Part of English Law – *Ein bemerkenswertes Urteil der* Queen's Bench", IDR (2005) p. 51; Sarita P. WOOLHOUSE, "Group of Companies Doctrine and English Arbitration Law", 20 Arb. Int'l (2004, no. 4) p. 435.

172. See B. HANOTIAU, *op. cit.*, fn. 20, p. 351; J.-F. POUDRET and S. BESSON, *op. cit.*, fn. 115, no. 262 at pp. 225-226; O. SANDROCK, *op. cit.*, fn. 163, pp. 99-102; S. WILSKE, L. SHORE and J.-M. AHRENS, *op. cit.*, fn. 148, pp. 80-82. See also Olagoke O. OLATAWURA, "The 'Privy to Arbitration' Doctrine: The Withering of the Common-Law Privity of Contract Doctrine in Arbitration Law", 16 Am. Rev. Int'l Arb. (2005) p. 429.

173. See James M. HOSKING, "Non-Signatories and International Arbitration in the United States: the Quest for Consent", 20 Arb. Int'l (2004, no. 3) p. 289 at pp. 290-295; C.B. LAMM and J.A. AQUA, *op. cit.*, fn. 13, pp. 722-728; O. SANDROCK, *op. cit.*, fn. 163, pp. 102-104; S. WILSKE, L. SHORE and J.-M. AHRENS, *op. cit.*, fn. 148, p. 82. See also Alan S. RAU, "Arbitral Jurisdiction and the Dimensions of 'Consent'", 24 Arb. Int'l (2008, no. 2) p. 199 at pp. 213-214, 226-254; J.M. TOWNSEND, *op. cit.*, fn. 148.

174. *Ibid.* at p. 363, 365; T. ZUBERBÜHLER, *op. cit.*, fn. 148, p. 27. See, in particular, *Merill Lynch Investment Managers v. Optibase, Ltd.*, 337 F.3d 125 (2d Cir. 2003); *InterGen N.V. v. Grina*, 344 F.3d 134 (1st Cir. 2003); *Sarhank Group v. Oracle Corp.*, 404 F.3d 657 (2d Cir. 2005).

175. *Saudi Butec Ltd*, *op. cit.*, fn. 162, 14 ASA Bull. (1996, no. 3) p. 496 at p. 506 (cons. 7). On this case see B. HANOTIAU, *op. cit.*, fn. 13, no. 121 at p. 59; J.-F. POUDRET and S. BESSON, *op. cit.*, fn. 115, no. 258 at pp. 223-224; T. ZUBERBÜHLER, *op. cit.*, fn. 148, p. 26.

176. B. BERGER and F. KELLERHALS, *op. cit.*, fn. 146, no. 530-531 at p. 185.

The Swiss Federal Supreme Court's position with regard to group of companies has been approved by the prevailing legal doctrine in Switzerland.[177] As a result, in Switzerland a company within the same group of companies can be subject to an arbitration agreement only if there are circumstances which, under general principles of Swiss law, would lead to the binding of the affiliated company. Some examples of these circumstances include: (i) a subsequent acceptance by the non-signatory company, (ii) agency, (iii) a circumvention of the arbitration agreement which constitutes an abuse of rights, justifying the piercing of the corporate veil or, more generally, (iv) the principle of reliance on good faith.

In sum, the French "group of companies doctrine" does not mean what one might assume from its name, since it is not sufficient for a third party to be part of the same group of companies in order to be bound by an arbitration agreement concluded by another member of the group. Other jurisdictions, while formally declining the French group of companies doctrine, apply more traditional theories of contract law in order to compel non-signatories to arbitrate a dispute stemming from the agreement containing the arbitration clause. The results of these approaches are comparable to the results in France.

*c.    Representation and agency*

Under the principles of representation or agency law, a non-signatory to an arbitration agreement may be considered a principal who is bound to that arbitration agreement if it was entered into by a person acting as its representative or agent.[178] While this argument is often invoked in group of companies situations, the binding effect of representation or agency results from general principles of law.

A preliminary question for the arbitral tribunal is which substantive law determines whether or not a party concluding an arbitration clause validly represented a third party. International arbitral tribunals with their seat in Switzerland should apply the conflict of laws rule provided for in Art. 187(1) of the Swiss PILA in order to determine the law governing the legal capacity to act and the power of representation.[179]

The national agency laws and their application in the context of international arbitration by domestic courts and arbitral tribunals vary, in particular regarding who –

---

177. See M. BLESSING, "Introduction", *op. cit.*, fn. 148, no. 502 at p. 179; J.-F. POUDRET and S. BESSON, *op. cit.*, fn. 115, no. 258-260 at pp. 223-224; B. BERGER and F. KELLERHALS, *op. cit.*, fn. 146, no. 530-531 at p. 185; Werner WENGER, "Article 178 Swiss PILA, note 57" in Stephen V. BERTI, *op. cit.*, fn. 148.

178. See B. BERGER and F. KELLERHALS, *op. cit.*, fn. 146, no. 425-431 at pp. 146-149; B. HANOTIAU, *op. cit.*, fn. 13, no. 18-26 at pp. 10-14; J.-F. POUDRET and S. BESSON, *op. cit.*, fn. 115, no. 274-282 at pp. 236-243; A. REDFERN and M. HUNTER, *op. cit.*, fn. 112, no. 3-35 at pp. 151-152; T. ZUBERBÜHLER, *op. cit.*, fn. 148, pp. 20-22.

179. B. BERGER and F. KELLERHALS, *op. cit.*, fn. 146, no. 426 at p. 146. See, however, Swiss Federal Supreme Court, 8 December 1999, 18 ASA Bull. (2000, no. 3) p. 546 at p. 554 (cons. 2.b/bb), in which the application of the conflict of laws rule provided in Art. 178(2) Swiss PILA was upheld.

the principal, the agent, or both – is compelled or permitted to arbitrate a dispute stemming from the agreement containing the arbitration clause.[180]

In non-signatory cases, the law of agency is often invoked when a party alleges the existence of an undisclosed or apparent mandate in order to (also) include the non-signatory principal (often a parent company of the signatory) in the arbitration. In Switzerland, courts and tribunals will allow the inclusion of a non-signatory only if the facts of the case suggest an agency relationship between signatory and non-signatory and the counterparty's legitimate reliance on this appearance.[181]

*d. Guarantees*

A party may also try to extend an arbitration clause to a non-signatory based on an explicit or implied guarantee by the non-signatory vis-à-vis the requesting party's counterparty, thus attempting to benefit from a "deep pocket".

The mere existence of a guarantee relationship cannot, in general, be considered sufficient grounds for extending the arbitration clause contained in the underlying contract to the non-signatory guarantor.[182] In Switzerland, support for this position can be found in the Federal Supreme Court's reversal of the interim arbitral award on jurisdiction in the well-known *Westland* case. The arbitral tribunal, with its seat in Geneva, held that four non-signatory States were bound to an arbitration agreement entered into by a company they had created and controlled.[183] The arbitrators decided that the States were liable based on implied guarantees in favor of this company. Upon an application to challenge the award brought by one of the States, the Federal Supreme Court set this award aside. It held that the State was not a signatory to the arbitration agreement, and that neither the close control of a state-controlled company by the State nor the close administrative and financial connection existing between them was sufficient to reverse the presumption that the State was not bound by the arbitration agreement concluded by the company as a separate legal entity.[184]

*e. "Piercing the corporate veil"*

In an effort to extend an arbitration agreement to the controlling parent company, parties have also relied on the theory of "piercing the corporate veil".[185] However, this reliance is often vague, since there is no uniform theory of veil piercing, and its prerequisites and legal effects vary between different legal systems.

---

180. For the United States see C.B. LAMM and J.A. AQUA, *op. cit.*, fn. 13, pp. 724-725; J.M. HOSKING, *op. cit.*, fn. 173, p. 293.
181. B. BERGER and F. KELLERHALS, *op. cit.*, fn. 146, no. 427-428 at pp. 147-148; T. ZUBERBÜHLER, *op. cit.*, fn. 148, p. 22.
182. See B. BERGER and F. KELLERHALS, *op. cit.*, fn. 146, no. 508 at pp. 176-177 (Switzerland); J.-P. LACHMANN, *op. cit.*, fn. 170, no. 527 (Germany); C.B. LAMM and J.A. AQUA, *op. cit.*, fn. 13, pp. 727-728 (United States).
183. Interim Award of 5 March 1984 in ICC Case No. 3879, *Yearbook* XI (1986) p. 127.
184. Swiss Federal Supreme Court, 19 July 1988, *Yearbook* XVI (1991) p. 180 = 7 ASA Bull. (1989, no. 1) p. 63, confirming a decision of the *Cour de justice* of Geneva of 3 November 1987, *Yearbook* XVI (1991) p. 175.
185. On "piercing the corporate veil" and related theories see B. HANOTIAU, *op. cit.*, fn. 13, no. 89-99 at pp. 43-47; T. ZUBERBÜHLER, *op. cit.*, fn. 148, pp. 27-30.

In general, "piercing the corporate veil" means disregarding the separate legal entity of a corporation and holding its owners (e.g., a parent company, an individual or a State) legally accountable for the corporation's actions. While the theory is primarily concerned with the liability of the owners, it may also result in them being bound by an arbitration agreement entered into by their corporation.

In most legal systems, piercing the corporate veil is applied only restrictively and is usually limited to situations of abuse of rights or fraud.[186] Under Swiss law, courts and arbitral tribunals generally respect the legal independence of a corporate body and its shareholders, and will apply an arbitration clause to the non-signatory shareholders only in exceptional circumstances. There seems to be only one reported arbitral award, rendered in 1991, where the corporate veil was pierced, and this was under very particular circumstances.[187] In order to succeed, a party requesting the application of the arbitration clause to the controlling shareholders must establish that the shareholders used the company that signed the arbitration agreement only to hide behind the separate legal entity and that such behavior constitutes an evident abuse of rights (see Art. 2(2) of the Swiss Civil Code).[188] Generally, such an abuse of rights is assumed when the company and its owners form a single economic entity and when the corporate structure has been established with the sole purpose of fending off justified claims by creditors or of circumventing statutory or contractual obligations.[189]

It is important to note that, under Swiss law, piercing the corporate veil in a strict sense (called *Durchgriff*) does not result in an *extension* of the contractual obligations including the obligation to arbitrate to an additional party, but leads to a *replacement* of the "sham" company by the shareholder. In this situation the contractual effects have shifted to the controlling entity. Thus, a party requesting the "extension" of the arbitration agreement to a non-signatory on the basis of the theory of piercing the corporate veil may not argue that the "sham" company continues to be bound by the arbitration agreement.[190]

Under Swiss law, these situations of veil piercing in a strict sense must also be distinguished from circumstances where a controlling entity is being held liable for the commitments of a subsidiary based on legal grounds other than the contract containing the arbitration clause (e.g., grounds such as an illegal act, the violation of corporate or

---

186. B. HANOTIAU, *op. cit.*, fn. 13, no. 89-99 at pp. 43-47; C.B. LAMM and J.A. AQUA, *op. cit.*, fn. 13, pp. 722-723.
187. The parent company and sole shareholder had total control over the subsidiary and had stripped the latter of its assets and liquidated it. While the arbitral tribunal refused to extend the arbitration agreement based on the group of companies doctrine, it admitted an abuse of rights and allowed direct action against the parent company. Decision of the ad hoc arbitral tribunal of 1991 in *ALPHA S.A. v. BETA & Co., Société d'Etat de droit ruritanien*, 10 ASA Bull. (1992, no. 2) p. 202. See T. ZUBERBÜHLER, *op. cit.*, fn. 148, pp. 25-26 and p. 29; J.-F. POUDRET and S. BESSON, *op. cit.*, fn. 115, no. 259 at p. 224.
188. See decision of the Swiss Federal Supreme Court in the *Butec* case, 29 January 1996, ASA Bull. (1996, no. 3) p. 496 at pp. 503-504 (cons. 6). See also B. BERGER and F. KELLERHALS, *op. cit.*, fn. 146, no. 526-528 at pp. 184-185.
189. See Swiss Federal Supreme Court, 21 April 1987, *Rinderknecht Administration AG and Rinderknecht & Co. AG v. Galerie Lopes AG*, ATF 113 II 31 at pp. 35-36 (cons. 2). See also Federal Supreme Court, 8 June 1982, *Löwe v. Mazzetta et al.*, ATF 108 II 213 at pp. 214-215 (cons. 6).
190. B. BERGER and F. KELLERHALS, *op. cit.*, fn. 146, no. 528 at pp. 184-185.

group obligations or the principle of good faith). In such circumstances, the controlling entity can only be compelled to arbitrate on the basis of an independent and formally valid declaration of intent to arbitrate.[191]

*3. Issues of Form*

Many jurisdictions have special requirements regarding the form of the arbitration agreement, in order to ensure that the parties are aware of the significant consequences of waiving their fundamental right to take a dispute before a state court.[192] The extension of an arbitration agreement to a third party which has not participated in the conclusion of the agreement therefore raises the question of whether or not the formal requirements have been met.

With regard to the requirements of form, Swiss arbitration law provides in Art. 178(1) of the Swiss PILA that the arbitration agreement be concluded in writing. The parties may use any means of communication which permits the arbitration agreement to be evidenced by text. The parties must be able to prove that they exchanged declarations which are attributable to each party, and which form a binding agreement. The text does not need to bear a signature in order to comply with the requirement of written form.[193] Some scholars take the view that the form requirement applies not only to the initial parties to the arbitration agreement, but also to any third party that is not named as a party in the initial agreement. According to this view, the jurisdiction of the arbitral tribunal with respect to a third party can only be affirmed, if such a submission for arbitration in Switzerland strictly complies with the conditions of form provided for in Art. 178(1) of the Swiss PILA.[194] Other scholars have expressed a more liberal view with regard to this requirement of form.[195]

---

191. See Swiss Federal Supreme Court, 29 January 1996, 14 ASA Bull. (1996, no. 3) p. 496 at pp. 505-506 (cons. 6.b), where the Court held that the case could not be based on the theory of piercing the corporate veil as the (alleged) obligation of the parent company to endow its subsidiary with adequate capitalization could not be based on the contract containing the arbitration clause. See also the decision of the Swiss Federal Supreme Court in the *Westland* case of 19 April 1994, ATF 120 II 155 at pp. 171-172 (cons. 6.d). For these cases, see J.-F. POUDRET and S. BESSON, *op. cit.*, fn. 115, no. 258 at pp. 222-224. See also B. BERGER and F. KELLERHALS, *op. cit.*, fn. 146, no. 524-525 at pp. 183-184. For the situation under German law, see B. NIKLAS, *op. cit.*, fn. 64, pp. 207-215.
192. It has been suggested that one reason for the rather liberal attitude towards extending an arbitration agreement to non-signatory third parties in France is that the French arbitration law does not encompass any formal conditions regarding arbitration agreements. See J.-F. POUDRET and S. BESSON, *op. cit.*, fn. 115, no. 251 at pp. 212-213 and no. 253 at p. 215.
193. B. BERGER and F. KELLERHALS, *op. cit.*, fn. 146, no. 396 at p. 136.
194. See J.-F. POUDRET and S. BESSON, *op. cit.*, fn. 115, no. 258 at p. 221; Jean-François POUDRET, "*Note – Tribunal federal, 1re Cour Civile, 16 octobre 2003, (4P.115/2003); Un statut privilégié pour l'extension de l'arbitrage aux tiers?*", 22 ASA Bull. (2004, no. 2) p. 390 at p. 390.
195. See M. BLESSING, "Introduction", *op. cit.*, fn. 148, no. 504 at p. 180.

In an important decision, on 16 October 2003, the Swiss Federal Supreme Court[196] departed from its previous practice that the form requirement provided for in Art. 178(1) of the Swiss PILA also applied to an agreement where a non-signatory had manifested its intent to be bound by the arbitration agreement.

In this case, a Lebanese construction company had entered into a contract for the construction of a building complex with two other Lebanese companies. The latter were controlled by a Lebanese businessman who had put his wife and his sons on the executive boards of the two companies. He had also provided the financial means by which the two companies operated. The work contract was governed by Lebanese law and provided for arbitration in Switzerland under the ICC Rules of Arbitration. The construction company filed a request for arbitration against the two other companies, as well as against the Lebanese businessman, who was not a formal party to the contract. The respondents contended that the arbitrators lacked jurisdiction over the individual. The arbitral tribunal affirmed its jurisdiction over the Lebanese businessman.

Upon an application to challenge the award, brought by the two companies and the individual, the Federal Supreme Court upheld the arbitrators' decision. In substance, the Federal Supreme Court ruled that the extension of an arbitration clause to a non-signatory was only an issue of the substantive validity of the arbitration clause and was to be determined in accordance with Art. 178(2) of the Swiss PILA. As to the issue of form, the court decided that it was sufficient for the agreement in which the original parties manifested their intention to arbitrate to be evidenced in writing.[197]

This decision was criticized by some authors, who maintained that the submission of the third non-signatory party to the arbitration between the initial parties should, in order to comply with the formal requirements of Art. 178(1) of the Swiss PILA, be derived from documents manifesting the intent of the third party to arbitrate.[198] It was also pointed out that the law contains sufficient mechanisms to overcome the absence of written consent when it appears necessary, for instance, in cases where reliance on such an absence would be an abuse of rights. Furthermore, criticisms have been voiced that this decision creates a special status for non-signatories which is not provided for by legislation, and that it is not appropriate for a third party to lack the same guarantees as the initial parties.[199] Others appreciated the liberal approach and approved of this change by the Swiss Federal Supreme Court, arguing that the requirement of writing merely serves to evidence the existence and contents of the arbitration agreement.[200]

---

196. Swiss Federal Supreme Court, 16 October 2003, *X. S.A.L, Y. S.A.L. and A. v. Z. Sàrl and Arbitral Tribunal*, ATF 129 III 727, also published in 22 ASA Bull. (2004, no. 2) p. 364, with notes by J.-F. POUDRET and P. HABEGGER; Rev. arb. (2004) p. 695, with a note by L. LEVY and B. STUCKY. See also the critical analysis by Otto SANDROCK, "*Die Aufweichung einer Formvorschrift und anderes mehr. Das Schweizer Bundesgericht erlässt ein befremdliches Urteil*", 3 SchiedsVZ (2005, no. 1) p. 1.
197. ATF 129 III 727 at p. 736 (cons. 5.3.1).
198. J.-F. POUDRET and S. BESSON, *op. cit.*, fn. 115, no. 258 at p. 221; J.-F. POUDRET, *op. cit.*, fn. 194, pp. 396-397.
199. J.-F. POUDRET and S. BESSON, *op. cit.*, fn. 115, no. 258 at p. 221. See also J.-F. POUDRET, *op. cit.*, fn. 194; J.-F. POUDRET, *op. cit.*, fn. 148, p. 904.
200. B. BERGER and F. KELLERHALS, *op. cit.*, fn. 146, no. 520 at p. 182, with further references; M. BLESSING, "Introduction", *op. cit.*, fn. 148, no. 504 at p. 180.

The decision of the Federal Supreme Court is certainly courageous, and goes beyond the intentions of the original legislator. This is to be welcomed. Given the fact that arbitration has become the preferred means of dispute resolution in international commerce, it is questionable whether the argument of protecting the parties by certain form requirements is still justified.

## VI. FORMS OF PARTICIPATION OF THIRD PARTIES OTHER THAN AS A FORMAL PARTY

### 1. Introduction

So far, this Report has only dealt with a third party as a *formal party* to the proceedings. This means that this party has its own claim or that a claim is directed against it by one of the other parties in the proceedings. Another form of participation in proceedings occurs when the participating third entity or person does *not* itself raise a claim or defend a claim. For ease of reference (by adapting the descriptive German term *Nebenpartei*), this Report will refer to such a party as a *side party*. A typical situation would be when a respondent intends, in the event that it loses the case, to take recourse against a third entity/person and thus requests this third entity/person to assist it in defending itself against the claimant's claim.

Civil law rules of different jurisdictions have developed a broad variety of different forms of participation in addition to "normal" participation as a formal party. For example, in Germany and most parts of Switzerland, someone becomes a side party either on its own motion as what is called a *side intervener* (*Nebenintervention*) or based on a *third-person notice* (*Streitverkündung*) by one of the formal parties. The side party's role is limited to assisting one of the formal parties. This assistance is important since the outcome of the proceedings is binding on the side party.[201] In the United States, there is a similar system with the *third-party practice* and the common-law-based *vouching-in*. If the participation is to occur on the third party's own motion, this is possible with the *intervention of right*. However, in contrast with the German system, the US system does not distinguish between different types or forms of parties and a party lacking any claims has the same procedural rights in the proceedings as the formal parties.[202] The French system has a mixed approach: if the side party is called against its will, it has an independent procedural position, much like a formal party. If, however, the side party joins on its own motion, it only has limited procedural rights.[203]

### 2. Basic Requirement: Consent of all Parties

In light of the variety of solutions in state court proceedings, it is not surprising that there is no consensus as to whether forms of participation other than as a formal party are admissible in international arbitration. In state court proceedings, a third party can join as a side party even despite the objection of the other party. It is undisputed that this rule

---

201. A. MEIER, *op. cit.*, fn. 13, p. 39; P. SCHLOSSER, *op. cit.*, fn. 13, p. 949.
202. A. MEIER, *op. cit.*, fn. 13, pp. 43 and 129.
203. *Ibid.*, pp. 40 and 129.

for state courts cannot be applied to arbitration proceedings, since arbitration is based on the primacy of party autonomy.

It is accepted that the joining of a side party which is not a party to the arbitration agreement requires the consent of all the formal parties. The justification for this, as put forward by arbitral tribunals and courts, is the confidentiality and privacy of arbitration. In other words, in order to maintain privacy, the parties must agree to the participation of a side party, and by doing so, waive their right to confidentiality and private proceedings.[204]

On 7 April 2004, an ICC Arbitration with its seat in Zurich decided on the circumstances under which a third-person notice was admissible.[205] The background was a dispute between a shipbuilder that had ordered cranes for a vessel which turned out to be defective and the manufacturer. The shipbuilder had sold the vessel to the current ship owner and thus it was the latter who incurred the damage (mainly loss of profit), not the shipbuilder. Very late in the proceedings, the claimant sought the participation of the ship owner while the ship owner himself did not seek participation. The arbitral tribunal qualified this as a third-person notice and determined that, in the absence of any direct or indirect provision agreed upon by the parties on this issue, it was a procedural question which the arbitral tribunal had to determine based on its own discretion under the applicable Swiss lex arbitri. The arbitral tribunal determined that participation of a third person as side intervener or based upon a third-person notice was possible, but required the agreement of all formal parties:

> "Under consideration of the above-mentioned principles of Swiss procedural rules on third persons participation, the following rules govern the issue of third person intervention and third party notice in arbitration proceedings: Since the third person who assists one of the parties as a collateral intervener or based on a third party notice does not become a party to the arbitration proceedings, it is *not* necessary that such third person is a party to the arbitration agreement. However, the conclusion of an arbitration agreement reflects the intention of the parties to be subject to *private and confidential proceedings* that exclude third persons. Therefore, third persons can only be admitted to the arbitration proceedings if all parties to the proceedings agree to this...."[206]

Since the crane constructor had neither explicitly nor implicitly consented to the participation of the ship owner, the request was denied.

In this case, the issue was the participation of a side party with limited procedural rights of assistance. However, the principle that all parties to the arbitration proceedings must agree also applies to side parties with the same procedural rights as the parties.

When public interests are involved, the pressure to have more transparency and to allow participation by third parties, at least in the form of amicus curiae briefs, is

---

204. *Ibid.*, p. 132 with a detailed analysis of the private and public interests involved.
205. Award on Third Person Notice of 7 April 2004 in ICC Case No. 12171, 23 ASA Bull. (2005, no. 2) p. 270.
206. *Ibid.*, p. 273, emphasis added and references omitted.

especially strong. In two famous cases, *Methanex Corporation v. USA*[207] and *United Parcel Service of America v. Canada*,[208] both arbitral tribunals confirmed, under the UNCITRAL Arbitration Rules, that because of the confidential nature of the arbitration proceedings, third parties could neither participate in the hearings (*Methanex* case) nor had standing as a formal party (*United Parcel* case); the tribunals did, however, accept their comments as amicus curiae briefs.[209] This conclusion was reached by qualifying the acceptance of an amicus curiae brief as a procedural issue which, based on Art. 15 of the UNCITRAL Rules, falls within the scope of the arbitral tribunal's jurisdiction.

In practice, a question that is both pertinent and controversial is whether the concluding of a multi-party arbitration agreement (as opposed to a standard bilateral agreement) is sufficient to allow the participation of side parties without the consent of all the formal parties to the arbitration agreement. One line of argument is that if the parties conclude a multi-party arbitration agreement, they are implicitly agreeing to multi-party arbitration proceedings without further requirements.[210] Another argument is that if a party signs an arbitration agreement, it is agreeing to all forms of participation, including participation as a side party with only limited procedural rights and, thus, fewer means of influencing the proceedings. In German legal literature, the prevailing opinion, in principle, favors the latter argument and thus concludes from the multi-party arbitration clause that the parties must accept side parties.[211] The opposing view is based on the argument that an anticipated agreement to include other forms of participation might be accepted for domestic arbitration in a jurisdiction which recognizes the instruments of notice to a third party and intervention, but does not apply in international arbitration, which is based on a claimant-respondent scheme. Moreover, parties coming from different jurisdictions might have very diverging ideas of the role of side parties. While one might accept – and, in the author's opinion should accept – that international arbitration should provide for a mechanism for multi-polar disputes and not be limited to bipolar situations, it is not designed to go beyond the claimant-respondent concept.[212] For all these reasons, and contrary to the opinions voiced primarily in Germany, it cannot be assumed that the multi-party arbitration agreement allows for the participation of other signatories in a form other than as claimant or as respondent. Any other role must thus either be expressly provided for in the arbitration agreement, or agreed upon by all parties including the side party as soon as the issue arises during the proceedings. Whether or not an express agreement by the side party

---

207. *Methanex Corporation v. United States of America*, Decision on Petitions from Third Persons to Intervene as "Amici Curiae", 15 January 2001, at <http://naftaclaims.com/Disputes/USA/Methanex/MethanexDecisionReAuthorityAmicus.pdf> (last accessed 26 May 2008).
208. *United Parcel Service of America v. Government of Canada*, Decision on Petitions for Intervention and Participation as Amici Curiae, 17 October 2001, at <http://naftaclaims.com/Disputes/Canada/UPS/UPSDecisionReParticipationAmiciCuriae.pdf> (last accessed 26 May 2008).
209. See also L.A. MISTELIS, *op. cit.*, fn. 44, p. 224 et seq.; Christina KNAHR, "Transparency, Third Party Participation and Access to Documents in International Investment Arbitration", 23 Arb. Int'l (2007, no. 2) p. 327 at p. 328 et seq.
210. See Sect. III.2 above.
211. See A. MEIER, *op. cit.*, fn. 13, pp. 140-141 with further references.
212. *Ibid.*, p. 141.

should be required is disputed.[213] There is no valid reason not to allow an implied consent, however, if such consent is clear from the circumstances (e.g., if the side party is already participating in the proceedings).[214]

### 3. Example of an Arbitration Clause Providing for Joining of Side Parties

An arbitration clause was recently published in an arbitration journal, reflecting the German approach to the participation of a side party as side intervener (i.e., in order to assist one party).[215] As explained in the article by Wolff, the background of the clause is an M&A transaction where the seller of the target company contractually binds the target company in order to keep the services of this company. This circumstance is reflected in the purchase price. In addition, banks as guarantors are also parties to the M&A transaction, as well as to the service agreement between the seller and the target company. Because of the link between the performance and possible termination of the service agreement and the direct impact this would have on the purchase price between different parties, it is important, if a dispute arises, for all parties to be able to participate in the proceedings, and for the findings of an arbitration to be binding on all parties. The pertinent parts of the proposed clause read as follows:[216]

> "Arbitration Agreement
> (1) [...] ²This present Arbitration Agreement together with the respective clause in the Contract for Services constitutes a uniform dispute resolution mechanism for both this Share Purchase Agreement and the Contract for Services (hereinafter, the Contracts)[...].
> (3) ¹When submitting a request for arbitration hereunder, Claimant(s) shall at the same time send the request by registered mail to all parties to the Contracts who are not named Claimants or Respondents (hereinafter, Invitees). ²The Invitees shall be entitled to join the arbitral proceedings in the role of intervening parties in support of the Claimant(s) or the named Respondent(s). ³No arbitrator shall be appointed before expiration of 30 days from the date when the request has been received by all Invitees. ⁴For the purpose of nominating arbitrators, the Invitees who have joined the arbitral proceedings within said 30 days are deemed to be Co-Claimants or Co-Respondents depending in support of which party they have joined the arbitral proceedings. ⁵Invitees joining after expiration of said term shall not be entitled to participate in the constitution of the arbitral tribunal. ⁶Any arbitral award resulting from such request for arbitration shall be binding upon the Invitees as if they were parties to the arbitral proceedings and regardless of whether they joined the proceedings. ⁷The established material facts and their legal assessment in such award shall be binding upon and between the parties and the Invitees regardless of whether they are favorable.
> [....]"

---

213. S.H. ELSING, op. cit., fn. 13, p. 92.
214. Ibid., p. 92; A. MEIER, op. cit., fn. 13, p. 140.
215. R. WOLFF, op. cit., fn. 13, p. 62.
216. Ibid., p. 62.

This clause includes the issue of the role of an assisting side party – and the effect of such assistance – as well as the impact on the nomination of the arbitrators, and shows that it is possible to draft such clauses in a clear and concise way.

One risk that this clause carries is that one might question whether it *a contrario* excludes the participation of one of the invitees as a formal party (i.e., a party which has its own claims and defenses). In view of the voices which are critical of the participation of signatories as additional formal parties, it might be useful to clarify, in para. (3)(2), that "[t]he Invitees shall be entitled to join the arbitral proceedings in the role *of a formal party or* of intervening parties...". The paragraph dealing with the appointment of the arbitrators would have to be adapted according to one of the methods discussed above.[217]

4. *The Appointment of Arbitrators and the Necessity of Their Consent*

With regard to the appointment of arbitrators, one can assume that (i) either the arbitration clause that provides for the participation of side parties will provide for the appointment mechanism – as is the case in the arbitration clause printed above – or (ii) the parties, when approving the participation of a side party, will discuss, and decide on, the influence of the side party in the appointment process. Since side parties are not formal parties, it is unlikely that they will be accepted as having any rights in this process. On the other hand, any judgment will also have a direct impact on them. The role of the side parties in the appointment process is unclear if there is agreement on the participation but if no consensus can be reached regarding the appointment.[218]

With regard to the arbitrators' position, an arbitrator cannot prevent other *formal* parties from joining the proceedings if all the parties to the proceedings are in agreement, either explicitly or implicitly (e.g., by having concluded a multi-party arbitration agreement).[219] This applies also in the situation of participation as a *side* party where the arbitration clause explicitly provides for such participation.

A delicate and controversial question is what rules should apply if the arbitration agreement does not address this issue. One could argue that the arbitral tribunal can refuse the participation of side parties because, in the absence of any provision in the arbitration agreement, it was not foreseeable and because the agreement to arbitrate binds the arbitrators only to the formal parties to the arbitration.[220] However, the difference from the situation with formal third parties notwithstanding, the arbitrators should not be able to disallow the agreement of the parties, even if they could not foresee the inclusion of side parties at the time of their appointment. Such agreements should be considered to be procedural agreements between the parties which bind the arbitrators under the commonly known lex arbitri or institutional rules.[221] That this is the correct approach is also supported by the arbitrators' inherent right to resign and refusal to continue to act for important reasons.

---

217. See Sect. IV.2.
218. See R. GEIMER, *op. cit.*, fn. 6, p. 167.
219. See Sect. III.3 above.
220. See S.H. ELSING, *op. cit.*, fn. 13, p. 92.
221. A. MEIER, *op. cit.*, fn. 13, p. 142.

## 5. Costs

The parties in arbitration proceedings are legally bound to pay the costs of the proceedings based on the contract between them and the arbitrators and (if there is one) the institution. Side parties are outside such agreements and do not become liable for costs. Any participation of the side parties in the costs of the proceedings must be provided for in internal agreements.[222]

Arbitral tribunals usually have broad discretion in allocating the costs among the parties and can, within this discretion, also decide which of the parties shall bear the additional costs due to the assistance of a side party. In practice, however, the allocation of additional costs will normally not be necessary since the party, who has to agree to the assistance by a side party of its opponent, will most likely make its agreement dependent on the condition that, independent of the outcome of the proceedings, it will not have to bear any additional costs for such assistance.[223]

### VII. JOINDER OF THIRD PARTIES AFTER THE APPOINTMENT OF ARBITRATORS

*1. Introduction and Problem*

What happens if a claimant realizes in the course of the arbitration proceedings that it would be better off if it had directed some of its claims against a party other than the one to whom it directed the notice of arbitration?

Although it is of practical importance, the issue of the joinder of a third party after the arbitral tribunal has been constituted is rarely discussed in detail.[224] It is generally assumed that there is no possibility for a third party to join once the arbitral tribunal has been appointed, since the requirement of equal treatment of the parties cannot be complied with, and thus an award could be set aside. Unless the joining party agrees to accept the already appointed arbitrators, there is only one alternative, and that is to replace the arbitrators by withdrawing the current arbitrators' mandate and constituting a new panel with the participation of the third party. This, even if it is mentioned as a possibility, is not usually seriously contemplated because it is contrary to the goal of procedural efficiency and is considered too burdensome for the party opposing the joinder.[225]

Whether or not a third party joining the proceedings is willing to accept an already appointed tribunal depends on whether it is indeed the joined party who is asking to be joined. However, it is more often the case that a formal party requests the joinder of a third party, against the third party's will, because the requesting party sees this as a means, maybe even the only means, to have its claim satisfied. This can be for

---

222. *Ibid.*, p. 171.
223. *Ibid.*, p. 172.
224. But see B. HANOTIAU, *op. cit.*, fn. 13, no. 367-396 at pp. 166-177; N. VOSER and A. MEIER, *op. cit.*, fn. 13, pp. 115-123; A. MEIER, *op. cit.*, fn. 13, pp. 86-91.
225. R. GEIMER, *op. cit.*, fn. 6, p. 168; N. VOSER and A. MEIER, *op. cit.*, fn. 13, p. 117; A.M. WHITESELL and E. SILVA-ROMERO, *op. cit.*, fn. 111, p. 11.

legal/technical reasons (i.e., if it turns out that it is only the third party that has the standing to be sued), or simply in order to increase the chances of being compensated if there is a positive outcome, i.e., for the purpose of creating a joint liability on a substantive level and with this trying to include the "deep pocket". In this case, the only situation where the third party might be willing to accept an already appointed arbitral tribunal is probably if the prospect of having to defend the claim before the proper forum (be it another arbitral tribunal or state court) seems so daunting that the party would prefer to accept the already constituted arbitral tribunal.

As a final introductory remark, the present author suggests that, for the joining of a third party after the arbitral tribunal has been constituted, it makes no difference whether this third party is bound by the same arbitration agreement,[226] or whether the jurisdiction of the arbitral tribunal over this third party is based on one of the theories allowing an arbitration agreement to be extended to non-signatories.[227]

2. *Competent Body for Decisions on (Late) Joinder Requests*

The basic principles have already been discussed in the context of the discussion of multiple signatories to an arbitration agreement.[228] The fact that the request for joinder may be submitted after the constitution of the arbitral tribunal enables the arbitral tribunal, based on its *competence-competence*, to decide on requests for joinder of a third party, while the state courts will have the last word in setting aside or enforcement proceedings.

In ad hoc arbitration, the arbitral tribunal has full discretion to decide, provided that it does not assume jurisdiction if there is no implied consent of the parties to arbitrate, and provided it respects the parties' right to participate in the appointment of an arbitrator and honors the equal treatment of the parties.

The situation is much more complex in *institutional arbitration*.[229] The role of the institution is very prominent at the beginning of the arbitral proceedings, i.e., until the arbitral tribunal has been constituted. In this phase, institutions will, as a rule, make a prima facie analysis of the admissibility of the joinder.[230] However, the competence regarding such decisions is less clear once the arbitral tribunal has been constituted.

The institution should be competent to undertake the same prima facie test that it would if the arbitral tribunal had not yet been constituted. Under the ICC Rules, for example, applying Art. 6(2) of the ICC Rules, the ICC Court would make the prima facie analysis of the arbitration agreement only if there were an objection to the admissibility of the third party. The reason for making the prima facie analysis even if the arbitral tribunal has already been constituted is that neither the third party that asks to be joined in an already pending proceeding, nor the party to the arbitration requesting the joining of a third party, should benefit from the fact that the arbitral tribunal has already been constituted by not having to undergo the first hurdle which is the ICC

---

226. See Sects. III and IV above.
227. See Sect. V above.
228. See Sect. III.5 above.
229. See B. HANOTIAU, *op. cit.*, fn. 13, no. 368 et seq. at p. 166 et seq.
230. See Sect. III.5 above.

Court's test. The parties opposing the joining should benefit from the same filtering process as at the beginning of the proceedings. This should also be the rule with the other institutions which do not have specific rules on the joining of third parties.[231]

A further issue is how the ICC Court, and other institutions operating under institutional frameworks that provide for rules on joinder and/or consolidation of multiple claims, should handle the relationship between the rules and the powers of the arbitral tribunal. As an example: Art. 4 of the Swiss Rules regulates consolidation and joinder by the Chambers. Does this provision have to be understood as prohibiting, *a contrario*, consolidation or joinder by the arbitral tribunal after its constitution? As a matter of principle, the answer should be "no". An institution cannot render a binding decision on such issues, since this is the prerogative of the arbitral tribunal. Conversely, with regard to the competences of an institution itself to consolidate proceedings at a later stage (as opposed to defining the competences of the institution in relation to the arbitral tribunal), the *a contrario* conclusion seems to be correct.

Once the institutional phase is undergone, it is up to the arbitral tribunal, based on the principle of *competence-competence*, to decide on the joining of a third party. A similar issue arises in the rare cases where the rules provide for the competence of the arbitral tribunal to join a third party "only upon the application of a party". Such a provision can be found in Art. 22.1(h) of the LCIA Rules. Whether this *a contrario* excludes the power of the arbitral tribunal to join a third party upon the third party's own request is debatable.

### 3. Balancing Test

As mentioned in the introduction to this section, the appointment of arbitrators and/or their replacement has been viewed as the crucial stumbling block to the joining of a third party *after* the constitution of the arbitral tribunal. Due to the parties' fundamental right to participate in the nomination of their arbitrator and the prescribed equal treatment of the parties, it is impermissible to force a party to accept an arbitral tribunal whose members have been appointed without that party's participation. Therefore, unless the third party accepts the already nominated members of the arbitral tribunal, claims against the third party must either become the subject of separate arbitral proceedings, or else the members of the arbitral tribunal must be replaced.

The drastic measure of replacing the arbitral tribunal is generally considered unjustified in view of the burden that a replacement would place on the other parties.[232] It has been argued that a replacement would slow down the proceedings, since new arbitrators would have to be elected and relevant steps of the proceedings concerning the third party would have to be repeated before the new tribunal,[233] which would cause additional delays and costs.

---

231. Such as Art. 4(2) of the Swiss Rules and Art. 22.1(h) of the LCIA Rules. Both provisions attribute the competence to decide on the joinder of third parties directly to the arbitral tribunal.
232. See, e.g., J. KLEINSCHMIDT, *op. cit.*, fn. 13, p. 150.
233. *Ibid.*, p. 146.

As with the general issue of joining a party in pending arbitration proceedings, the resulting problem of the necessity to replace one or several arbitrators has, so far, rarely been discussed.[234]

The starting point of the following analysis is a recurring situation in arbitration practice: the claimant files its request for arbitration and obtains a very cursory answer to such request. Subsequently, the arbitral tribunal is constituted and a full statement of claim is submitted. In the answer to the statement of claim, the claimant learns about events which, if had previously been known, would have led the claimant to initiate the arbitration against a third party from the very beginning.

The following are three examples of such a situation:

– As a consequence of a dispute about the termination of a development agreement, the claimant requests certain intellectual property rights from the respondent. In its statement of response, the respondent alleges that these rights are owned by a sister company and not by respondent. The claimant, when filing its request for arbitration, was not aware of, and had no reason to be aware of, this circumstance.
– A claimant raises claims as a result of allegations made, and guarantees given, in the contract negotiation phase. It is under the impression that the negotiating parties are employees of the party that finally signs the agreement. Only after the constitution of the arbitral tribunal does the claimant learn that its negotiating partners were in fact employees of another separate legal entity (which has by now been sold to another group). The claimant wishes to file separate extra-contractual claims against this other entity.
– On respondent's side, a similar issue can arise if, for example, respondent learns in the course of the proceedings that it is not the claimant, but an affiliate of claimant, who has fulfilled the contractual duties of the claimant which gave rise to a counterclaim and has thus assumed the position of a de facto party in the execution of the contract.

The common denominator in these cases is the fact that the claimant is not at fault in *not* including the third party *before* the constitution of the arbitral tribunal. In such a situation, and especially if the counterparty is responsible for the fact that the claimant did not extend its claim to the third party from the beginning, there should, *as a rule*, be sufficient justification for the joinder of the third party even at the cost of having to replace members of the arbitral tribunal. The emphasis is on "as a rule", since the method submitted is a *balancing test,* in which there are other factors which should be taken into account, such as the stage of the proceedings and how much of the proceedings – in particular the taking of evidence – would have to be repeated, and whether it is necessary to replace one or two arbitrators or whether, under the applicable rules, it is possible to simply add an additional arbitrator.[235]

---

234. But see N. VOSER and A. MEIER, *op. cit.*, fn. 13; A. MEIER, *op. cit.*, fn. 13, p. 87. See also B. BERGER and F. KELLERHALS, *op. cit.*, fn. 146, no. 776 at p. 276, who at least implicitly affirm the possibility of replacing the arbitrators since they are suggesting ways of newly constituting the tribunal should a respondent wish to file a claim for recourse against a third party.
235. N. VOSER and A. MEIER, *op. cit.*, fn. 13, pp. 120-121.

If, on the other hand, the necessity to join a third party could have been established at the outset, a joinder after the constitution of the arbitral tribunal should only be allowed if it does not seriously change the course of the arbitration proceedings, except, of course, for the fact that all parties agree to the joining, primarily in order to avoid separate claims. In other words, situations where the need to join a third party at a late stage is caused by the fact that the requesting party has been careless or too slow in reviewing all the documents available to it, or in interviewing all persons involved, cannot be remedied by allowing the joinder of a third party in the arbitration proceedings.

4. *Replacement of Arbitrators*

Once the arbitral tribunal has decided that the request for a joinder should be allowed, it will try to make the new party accept the appointed tribunal. However, for reasons already mentioned, the third party cannot be forced to accept an arbitral tribunal in whose nomination it did not participate. In following the principles established above for the nomination of arbitrators,[236] three categories must be distinguished: In Category 1 and 2, one of the parties (or several parties) and the joining party have identical or similar interests, while in Category 3, the interests are different, i.e., it is a multi-polar dispute:

*Category 1 and 2*
It is sufficient, following the previously given rationale, to replace only the arbitrator appointed by the party sharing the interest with the new party, and to ask them to make a new joint appointment, failing which the court (in ad hoc proceedings) or the institution (in institutional arbitration) must make the appointment. The position of an already appointed chairperson is delicate. If the chairperson has been appointed directly by the parties, he or she must also be replaced. If, however, the chairperson has been appointed by the party-appointed arbitrators, the limited, indirect impact that the parties have on the nomination does not justify the replacement of the chairperson.[237]

*Category 3*
Here the need to maintain equality between the parties requires that *both* party-appointed arbitrators be replaced and nominated by the institution or the competent court. The proposed method of replacement corresponds to the principles laid out in Art. 10(2) of the ICC Rules; this rule should also apply, by analogy, outside the framework of ICC arbitrations.[238] However, in a slight variation of this rule, the chairperson would not have to be replaced if he or she was appointed by the co-arbitrators (and not directly by the parties).[239] If the applicable institutional rules provide for multiple arbitrators, this would also be applicable in the case of a late joinder. In

---

236. See Sect. III.6.*b* above.
237. N. VOSER and A. MEIER, *op. cit.*, fn. 13, p. 121.
238. *Ibid.*, p. 122.
239. *Ibid.*, p. 122.

other words, it would be possible to add to the arbitral tribunal one arbitrator nominated by the joined party.

5.  *Application of Relevant Rules for the Amendment of the Claim in the Course of Pending Arbitration Proceedings*

As a rule, in *institutional* arbitration, there will be a provision limiting the possibility of changing claims and/or adding new claims. According to Art. 19 of the ICC Rules, for example, the authorization of the arbitral tribunal is necessary in order to add new claims outside the limits of the terms of reference.

According to Derains, the request to join a third party in order to raise claims against this party must be qualified as a new claim pursuant to Art. 19 of the ICC Rules.[240]

The requirements of Art. 19 of the ICC Rules regarding new claims, arguably, do not usually present an extra hurdle. If a replacement of the arbitral tribunal is justified, the same factors that would justify this will also justify the proceedings being extended to cover a new claim.[241] In both cases, a balancing test must show whether the interests of a party requesting the third-party joinder or those of the joining party, if it requests to join on its own motion, outweigh the interests of the other party or of both parties in the proceedings, to reach a conclusion of the arbitration proceedings, as quickly as possible.

In ad hoc arbitration, there are no similar express rules, unless it is an ad hoc arbitration under the UNCITRAL Arbitration Rules. Art. 20 of the UNCITRAL Arbitration Rules provides the framework for amending claims and defences. In practice, ad hoc arbitral tribunals have decided on the joining of third parties by applying this provision.[242]

VIII.  CURRENT POSITION OF INSTITUTIONS

In this section, the positions of some of the arbitration institutions regarding the issues discussed above shall be presented. The selected institutions are of special interest to the arbitration community, either because they are very frequently used or because they contain special provisions regarding multi-party arbitration which go beyond the mechanism for the appointment of arbitrators and address the possibilities of joining a third party.

---

240. Yves DERAINS, "The Limits of the Arbitration Agreement in Contracts Involving More than Two Parties" in *Complex Arbitrations, Perspectives on their Procedural Implications*, ICC Ct. Bull., Special Supplement 2003, p. 25 at p. 33.
241. When deciding on the admission of a new claim within the framework of ICC proceedings, the arbitral tribunal will consider factors such as the possibility of undue delay resulting from the new claim or of prejudice to one of the parties. K.P. BERGER, *op. cit.*, fn. 61, p. 329. If the request to join a party is also accepted in light of Art. 19 of the ICC Rules, new Terms of References must be drawn up and signed by all parties (i.e., including the new party) and arbitrators (including any new and/or replaced arbitrator). For the practical issue of how to formalize this, see Sect. VIII.*1*.
242. See cases mentioned in B. HANOTIAU, *op. cit.*, fn. 13, no. 369-371 at pp. 166-168.

The discussion below comes with the caveat that it has so far not been discussed with, or confirmed by, the institutions themselves, but relies on material that can be found in the legal literature.

*1. ICC Rules*

In the aftermath of the *Dutco* decision, the ICC established a Working Group on multi-party arbitration under the chairmanship of Jean-Louis Delvolvé, which submitted its final report to the ICC's Executive Board in 1994.[243] The recommendations led to the new provision of Art. 10 of the ICC Rules regarding the appointment of arbitrators in multi-party arbitration in the revised Rules of 1998.[244]

The revised ICC Rules have not departed from the bipolar concept. This clearly follows from Art. 2(2) of the ICC Rules, which requires each party to be placed either on the claimant's or on the respondent's side. Art. 10 of the ICC Rules regarding the appointment of arbitrators is also based on this concept. By now, this provision is well-established and its application is clear in the context of

– one claimant filing a request for arbitration against multiple respondents;
– multiple claimants filing a request for arbitration against one respondent; or
– multiple claimants filing a request for arbitration against multiple respondents.[245]

However, the ICC Rules do not provide answers as to whether the respondent can, in its response to the request for arbitration, file a counterclaim against a third party or a cross-claim against another respondent. For this reason, the ICC Court's traditional position as of 1998 was not to allow such claims unless all parties had agreed otherwise.[246] It was the clear understanding of the authors of the ICC Rules that the ICC had a bipolar approach.[247] This strict position was already being criticized in 1998. It was argued that the sole right of the claimant to choose the parties violated the parties' right to equal treatment.[248]

Under pressure from the growing number of both multi-party and multi-polar disputes, the position of the ICC Court has changed. The ICC Court decided that it could deviate, to a certain extent, from the strict reading of the ICC Rules. Fortunately, the new practice of the ICC Court has been repeatedly reported in recent years[249] and thus has become predictable. The current position of the ICC Court is briefly summarized as follows:

---

243. See J.-L. DELVOLVÉ, *op. cit.*, fn. 13, p. 26.
244. Y. DERAINS and E.A. SCHWARTZ, *op. cit.*, fn. 3, p. 181.
245. See *ibid.*, p. 181 et seq. See also Sect. III.6.b above.
246. E. SILVA-ROMERO, *op. cit.*, fn. 2, p. 76.
247. See *ibid.*, pp. 75-77.
248. See Yves DERAINS and Eric A. SCHWARTZ, *A Guide to the New ICC Rules of Arbitration* (Kluwer Law International 1998) p. 74; E. SILVA-ROMERO, *op. cit.*, fn. 2, pp. 77-78.
249. See A.M. WHITESELL and E. SILVA-ROMERO, *op. cit.*, fn. 111, p. 7, E. SILVA-ROMERO, *op. cit.*, fn. 2, p. 73 and A.M. WHITESELL, *op. cit.*, fn. 148, p. 366. For a detailed report on the position of the ICC, see also B. HANOTIAU, *op. cit.*, fn. 13, no. 375-390 at pp. 169-175.

— If a *request for arbitration is filed against multiple respondents*, the ICC Court – in applying Art. 6(2) of the ICC Rules – will apply different theories in order to decide on a prima facie basis whether the arbitration can proceed against the multiple respondents even if one or several of them are *not* signatories to the arbitration agreement. The theories applied by the ICC Court include agency, assignment, succession of companies, group of companies or alter ego, or participation in the conclusion, performance or termination of the contract containing the arbitration agreement.[250]

— If a *request for arbitration is filed by several claimants*, the ICC Court's traditional view was to rule that the whole matter could *not* proceed if it found that the proceedings could not continue with regard to only one of the claimants. According to the reports of Whitesell and Silva-Romero, the ICC Court seems to have changed this position: it now does allow an arbitration to continue after having made a negative Art. 6(2) decision against one (or more), but not all, of the claimant parties after respondent filed jurisdictional objections against one (or more) of them.[251]

— According to the ICC Court's current practice, and with the proviso that the parties have not agreed to the joinder of a third party, it will allow a *third party to be joined upon request of the respondent* if three conditions are met:[252]

(1) The third party must have signed the arbitration agreement on the basis of which the arbitration agreement has been filed;
(2) The respondent must introduce either a counterclaim or a cross-claim. This means that the ICC Court now allows respondents to file cross-claims;
(3) The request for joinder of the third party must be made before the arbitrators have been appointed or confirmed. According to the ICC Court, the purpose of this condition is to ensure that all parties to arbitration have the same opportunity to participate in the nomination of the arbitral tribunal.[253]

This practice invites several comments:

First of all, it shows that the ICC Court is open to endorsing the theories explained above with regard to the *inclusion of non-signatories* to an arbitration agreement when applying the provision of Art. 6(2) of the ICC Rules. However, the mere fact that a third party to be joined belongs to the same group of companies does not appear to qualify it for inclusion as a formal party. Instead, there must be additional factors, such as participation in the negotiations or execution of the contract.[254] This is to be welcomed, since the basic principle of arbitration as a consensual procedure must be upheld.

The practice of issuing *negative decisions under Art. 6(2) of the ICC Rules* against only one or more claimant(s) out of a group of claimants is justified and to be welcomed since

---

250. A.M. WHITESELL and E. SILVA-ROMERO, *op. cit.*, fn. 111, p. 8.
251. *Ibid.*, p. 10; A.M. WHITESELL, *op. cit.*, fn. 148, p. 367 fn. 2.
252. E. SILVA-ROMERO, *op. cit.*, fn. 2, p. 80; A.M. WHITESELL and E. SILVA-ROMERO, *op. cit.*, fn. 111, p. 11.
253. *Ibid.*, p. 11; E. SILVA-ROMERO, *op. cit.*, fn. 2, p. 80.
254. See decision of the ICC Court reported by A.M. WHITESELL and E. SILVA-ROMERO, *op. cit.*, fn. 111, p. 10 (first case on this page).

otherwise any claimant(s) with a valid prima facie claim would have to re-institute new ICC proceedings.

The ICC Court has *partly departed from its traditional preferential treatment of the claimant*, since it now permits the respondent to join third parties in its answer to the request for arbitration. However, the requirements still represent substantial discrimination against respondent. Since the ICC Court requires the third party to be a signatory to the arbitration agreement, it would appear not to allow the joinder of a third party upon request of the respondent to be based on the same theories justifying the extension of the arbitration agreement which are available to the claimant. There is no apparent justification for this distinction. If the ICC Court, in principle, allows the inclusion of third parties upon the request of the respondent, the theories applied should mirror those applied to the claimant's request to include further respondents outside the scope of the signatories to the arbitration agreement. In the author's opinion, the ICC Court should relinquish its restrictive practice which limits the joining of third parties upon request of the respondent to signatories of the arbitration agreement.

The ICC Court's requirements apply to situations where the parties to a multi-party arbitration agreement are aware from the outset that they wish to include further parties. However, based on requirement No. (3) above, it appears that the ICC Court would not allow a respondent to join a third party after the constitution of the arbitral tribunal. As explained above,[255] there are situations where a replacement is the correct way to proceed and, therefore, should, in the author's opinion, be accepted by the ICC Court.

Another issue that the arbitral tribunal faces in connection with the late joinder of a third party, is the *signed terms of reference,* as provided for in Art. 18 of the ICC Rules. If, after the commencement of the arbitral proceedings, a third party is joined, the fact that this third party has not signed the terms of reference raises a problem. A practical solution to this issue has been proposed by Derains, and consists of an amendment of the original terms of reference. If one of the parties refuses to sign the *amended* terms of reference, these are submitted to the ICC Court for approval pursuant to Art. 18(3) of the ICC Rules.[256] The necessary adaptation of the terms of reference could be made even simpler by creating a *separate addendum* to the original terms of reference, rather than recreating new terms of reference which must be signed by all the parties, including the newly joined party.[257]

Finally, it should be pointed out that the ICC Court does not deal with requests to *join a party other than as a formal party*. This follows from its practice of requiring respondent to file a counterclaim or a cross-claim in order to join a third party. In the past, the ICC Court has refused to add a new party if no claims have been raised against it by the respondent.[258] This approach is correct, since institutions, in principle, should deal with

---

255. See Sect. VII.4 above.
256. Y. DERAINS, *op. cit.*, fn. 240, p. 33.
257. See A. MEIER, *op. cit.*, fn. 13, p. 90.
258. A.M. WHITESELL and E. SILVA-ROMERO, *op. cit.*, fn. 111, p. 8. In the same report another case is mentioned in connection with cost issues where it was not clear whether "the new party could ... be considered as either a claimant or a respondent since it was not making any claims itself and the claimant was not raising any claims against it". *Ibid.*, p. 14. It must be assumed that in this case the parties had agreed to the participation of the third party in some form other than as a formal party.

disputes and *claims* between parties in an efficient way. Furthermore, as has been shown above, the joinder of a third party as side party requires the agreement of all formal parties.[259] If, however, such an agreement already exists, a decision of the ICC Court is not required.

2. *Swiss Rules*

Unlike the ICC Rules, the Swiss Rules provide a specific provision regarding the joining of a third party. Art. 4(2) of the Swiss Rules provides as follows:

> "(2) Where a third party requests to participate in arbitral proceedings already pending under these Rules or where a party to arbitral proceedings under these Rules intends to cause a third party to participate in the arbitration, the arbitral tribunal shall decide on such request, after consulting with all parties, taking into account all circumstances it deems relevant and applicable."

The Swiss Rules are based on the UNCITRAL Arbitration Rules and have been adapted to match what the drafters considered to be the current best practice. Apart from the introduction of an expedited procedure for amounts in disputes of less than 1 million Swiss francs (Art. 42(2) of the Swiss Rules), Art. 4(2) is the most prominent example of the authors' endeavours to put the Swiss Rules in line with the current best practice in arbitral proceedings.

This provision has been received with mixed reactions and has been criticized. The concern is that it grants the arbitral tribunal the competence to allow a joinder without the consent of the party to be joined (if the request comes from one of the parties to the proceedings) or the parties to the proceedings (if the joinder request comes from a third party). In other words, the worry is that the mere fact that all parties have concluded an arbitration agreement providing for arbitration under the Swiss Rules could cause them to be joined together.[260] To follow this interpretation would have a severe impact on the third party's right to participate in the appointment of the arbitrators. It also raises the issue of whether any party who accepts a Swiss Rules arbitration clause is deemed to have consented to being joined in pending proceedings, and, likewise, whether the existing parties must accept the joining. The question is whether this clashes with the parties' justified expectations, in the absence of any arbitration agreement, of having private bilateral proceedings.

At least one commentator has interpreted Art. 4(2) of the Swiss Rules as giving the arbitral tribunal the power to disregard the consent of the third party to be joined, as well as to disregard the consent of one of the parties to the arbitration.[261] However, this

---

259. See Sect. VI.2 above.
260. J. KLEINSCHMIDT, *op. cit.*, fn. 13, p. 148.
261. Philippe GILLIÉRON and Luc PITTET, Article 4 Swiss Rules, notes 11-12 in Tobias ZUBERBÜHLER, et al., eds., *Swiss Rules of International Arbitration, Commentary* (Schulthess 2005); N. VOSER and A. MEIER, *op. cit.*, fn. 13, p. 120.

interpretation is not imperative.[262] It is perfectly possible to read this provision primarily as a *declaratory norm* intended to point to competences that the arbitral tribunal already has and, more importantly, to make the parties aware of these competences. In other words, the open wording cannot be a substitute for the consent of the parties to the arbitration and the third party.[263] Instead, it provides a necessary basis from which to take into account future developments and best practices in this complex and changing area. In the author's opinion, Art. 4(2) of the Swiss Rules allows the arbitral tribunal to join third parties without the consent of the existing parties and/or the third party only if, in view of all the circumstances, the *balance of interest between the party refusing and the party requesting joinder is clearly in favor of the requesting party*. The authors of this provision intended to grant the arbitral tribunal the broadest possible flexibility in deciding on joinder requests by either a party to the arbitration or a third party, taking into account each individual case.[264] In view of the consensual nature of arbitration, arbitral tribunals should always seek to rely on the consent of all the parties involved and, therefore, should be restrictive in ignoring a lack of consent.

Such a narrow interpretation of Art. 4(2) of the Swiss Rules is also justified since the arbitral tribunal must avoid the possibility of setting aside or lack of recognition of the award on the grounds that a party can claim that the tribunal had no jurisdiction and/or that the party's right to participate in the nomination was violated. Another indication for this interpretation is to be found in Art. 4(2) of the Swiss Rules. This provision does

---

262. It should be noted that the authors who have suggested that Art. 4(2) of the Swiss Rules should be understood to grant the arbitral tribunal the competence to join a third party without the consent of all participants were only referring to Julian D. M. LEW, Loukas A. MISTELIS and Stefan M. KRÖLL, *Comparative International Commercial Arbitration* (Kluwer Law International 2003) no. 16-42 at p. 390 (see P. GILLIÉRON and L. PITTET, *op. cit.*, fn. 261, Article 4, notes 11-12). However, Lew, Mistelis and Kröll do *not* express an opinion on Art. 4 of the Swiss Rules but refer more generally to institutional rules that allow for joinder and intervention. Beyond this, the connection to the next paragraph, where Art. 22.1(h) of the LCIA Rules is mentioned (LEW, MISTELIS and KRÖLL, no. 16-43 at p. 390), makes it clear that the statement in no. 16-42 should be taken to refer to institutional rules which explicitly allow for the joinder and intervention without the consent of all parties. Lastly, when LEW, MISTELIS and KRÖLL published their textbook on international arbitration (in 2003), the Swiss Rules were not yet in force. See also the more cautious statement by J. KLEINSCHMIDT, *op. cit.*, fn. 13, p. 148; according to him only future practice will show whether or not Art. 4(2) of the Swiss Rules will be used to join third parties based merely on the fact that this third party has concluded a Swiss Rules arbitration clause with one of the parties.
263. See also A. MEIER, *op. cit.*, fn. 13, p. 107.
264. Wolfgang PETER, "*Die neue Schweizerische Schiedsordnung – Anmerkungen für die Praxis*", 2 SchiedsVZ (2004, no. 2) p. 57 at p. 60, and similarly Wolfgang PETER, "Some Observations on the New Swiss Rules of International Arbitration", Jusletter of 12 July 2004, note 18 at <http://www.weblaw.ch/de/content_edition/jusletter/Artikel.asp?ArticleNr=3242> (last accessed 23 May 2008) who states:

"As it was not considered practicable to set out in the Swiss Rules a comprehensive designation of all conceivable scenarios, the drafters preferred to simply indicate that consolidation of arbitral proceedings and the participation of third parties may be ordered, thus affording the appropriate bodies (the Chamber, or the Arbitral Tribunal, as applicable) the necessary flexibility in deciding on each individual case."

not provide for an explicit waiver of the joining party regarding the designation of its arbitrator, as this is the case in Art. 4(1) of the Swiss Rules. Art. 4(1) addresses the consolidation of a new proceeding with an existing one where the parties to the new proceedings are not identical with the parties to the already pending proceedings. Had Art. 4(2) of the Swiss Rules intended to disregard the parties' right to the nomination of the arbitral tribunal, this would have been included as well. Finally, it may be assumed that if the authors of the Swiss Rules had wanted, in general, to allow a joinder without the consent of the participants, this would have been explicitly stated since it would be such a far-reaching and unexpected provision.

Although it carries a certain risk, in light of the arbitral tribunal's theoretically broad competences, such a provision has several advantages:

— The arbitral tribunal will be able to join other parties to an arbitration agreement not only based on their implied consent,[265] but also based on Art. 4(2) of the Swiss Rules. Although Art. 4(2) of the Swiss Rules is not strictly necessary for this effect,[266] it facilitates the situation and might satisfy parties who did not anticipate being drawn into a pending proceeding, even if they should have been aware of such a possibility.
— One consideration worth noting is that this flexible provision enables the joining of recourse claims of one party (typically the respondent) in the same proceeding, without the specific consent of the other party, i.e., based on the mere fact that the Swiss Rules have been chosen as the applicable arbitration rules (this fits with a narrow reading of Art. 22.1(h) of the LCIA Rules).[267]
— Art. 4(2) of the Swiss Rules clearly allocates the competence for such a decision to the arbitral tribunal and not to the Chamber. This is valid according to the principle of *competence-competence*.
— The parties are made aware of the possibility of joinder at the time of the conclusion of the arbitration agreement, which might prompt them to provide for specific rules on multi-party arbitration if the context of the arbitration clause calls for this. Such rules might also entail that the parties explicitly agree to the joining of third parties after the commencement of the arbitration.
— Art. 4(2) of the Swiss Rules resolves the potential difficulties which other institutions could have regarding the question of whether, by negative implication, any joinder after the beginning of the arbitral proceedings should be excluded.
— Finally, it allows for future developments to be encompassed in this very dynamic area of international arbitration.

## 3. *LCIA Rules*

The London Court of International Arbitration Rules (LCIA Rules) are another set of institutional rules which provide for the joining of a third party. Art. 22.1(h) of the LCIA Rules provides, under the heading of additional powers of the arbitral tribunal, as follows:

---

265. See Sect. III.*2* above.
266. A. MEIER, *op. cit.*, fn. 13, p. 105.
267. See Sect. VIII.*3* below.

"Unless the parties at any time agree otherwise in writing, the Arbitral Tribunal shall have the power, on the application of any party or of its own motion, but in either case only after giving the parties a reasonable opportunity to state their views:
(....)
(h) to allow, only upon the application of a party, one or more third persons to be joined in the arbitration as a party provided any such third person and the applicant party have consented thereto in writing, and thereafter to make a single final award, or separate awards, in respect of all parties so implicated in the arbitration."

This clause makes it clear that the competence to decide on joinder requests lies with the arbitral tribunal. However, it limits this competence with regard to an application by one party, and, one must assume, excludes *a contrario* applications by the third party.

It is noteworthy that under the LCIA Rules it is sufficient for the applying party and the third person to have concluded an agreement in writing: the consent of the other party does not appear to be necessary. Since it is (still) questionable whether the parties would expect a provision that provides for an anticipated consent to arbitrate in the arbitration rules they have chosen, it is not surprising that this provision is one of the most disputed.[268]

One interpretation of this provision is that it does indeed assume the anticipated consent of one of the parties to the arbitration by agreeing to the LCIA Rules.[269] According to another, narrower reading of Art. 22.1(h) of the LCIA Rules, the provision does not anticipate consent to an arbitration agreement between the non-requesting party and the third party. Instead, it is assumed that by means of the written agreement between the applying party and the third party, the arbitration is only expanded to the additional dispute between these two parties. It is further assumed that there is no new arbitration agreement between the non-applying party and the third party. In other words, the provision allows a related dispute between the applicant party and the third party (typically a claim for recourse in chain contracts) to be decided by the same tribunal.[270] The consent assumed in this interpretation implies consent to the arbitral tribunal being competent to make a *procedural* order allowing claims against the third party to be decided together with the pending proceedings. It further encompasses a consent to waive, to the extent necessary, the right to confidentiality provided for in Art. 30 of the LCIA Rules. The provision would not, however, assume a competence of the arbitral tribunal to issue an award in which the third party is obliged towards the non-consenting party or *vice versa*.

The fact that previous versions of the LCIA Rules (of 1926 and 1932) contained a provision for the consolidation of a dispute between one of the parties to the arbitration

---

268. Volker TRIEBEL and Robert HUNTER, *"LCIA-Schiedsregeln"* in Rolf A. SCHÜTZE, ed., *Institutionelle Schiedsgerichtsbarkeit, Kommentar* (Heymann 2006) Art. 22, note 10, p. 404.
269. J.D.M. LEW, L.A. MISTELIS and S.M. KRÖLL, *op. cit.*, fn. 262, no. 16-44 at p. 390.
270. Anthony DIAMOND, "The New (1998) LCIA Rules, Multi-Party Arbitrations – Formation of and Vacancies in the Tribunal – The Removal of Arbitrators – Truncated Tribunals" in: London Court of International Arbitration, New Arbitration Rules 1998, Centre of Construction Law and Management Conference at King's College London, 5 June 1998, p. 2.

and a third party, and the controversy regarding the issue that evolved in the context of the 1998 amendment,[271] might raise questions regarding the validity of this narrow reading.[272] However, others (especially the LCIA itself) are better suited to make a final decision on this. In any event, Art. 22.1(h) is very rarely applied, and only one case has been reported where the joinder was in fact accepted against the wishes of one of the parties to the proceedings.[273]

Interestingly, while the Swiss Rules provision in Art. 4(2) is sometimes considered to be a threat, Art. 22.1(h) of the LCIA Rules has been considered one of the advantages of LCIA arbitration in the context of chain contracts.[274]

4. *Vienna Rules*

The Vienna International Arbitration Centre (VIAC) of the Austrian Federal Chamber of Commerce recently revised its arbitration rules. The revised Vienna Rules entered into force on 1 July 2006.[275] The amendments were substantial and were prompted by the new Austrian Arbitration Act, which also entered into effect on 1 July 2006.

The old Vienna Rules already contained, in Art. 10, a complex provision regarding the prerequisites of multi-party arbitration. The revised Art. 15 of the Vienna Rules goes beyond this provision and now reads as follows:

> "*Multiparty Proceedings*
> *Article 15*
> 1. A claim against two or more Respondents shall be admissible only if the Centre has jurisdiction for all of the Respondents, and, in the case of proceedings before an arbitral tribunal, if all Claimants have nominated the same arbitrator, and:
> a) If the applicable law positively provides that the claim is to be directed against several persons; or
> b) If all Respondents are by the applicable law in legal accord or are bound by the same facts or are joint and severally bound; or
> c) If the admissibility of multiparty proceedings has been agreed upon; or
> d) If all Respondents submit to multiparty proceedings and, in the case of proceedings before an arbitral tribunal, all Respondents nominate the same arbitrator; or
> e) If one or more of the Respondents on whom the claim was served fails or fail to provide the particulars mentioned in Article 10 paragraph 2, b) and c) within the thirty-day time-limit (Article 10 paragraph 1)."

---

271. V. TRIEBEL and R. HUNTER, *op. cit.*, fn. 268, Art. 22, notes 11-12, pp. 404-405.
272. See also Marc BLESSING, "*Die LCIA Rules – aus der Sicht des Praktikers*", 1 SchiedsVZ (2003, no. 5) p. 198 at p. 203, who states that this provision "very reluctantly" provides for the joining of third parties to LCIA arbitration proceedings.
273. V. TRIEBEL and R. HUNTER, *op. cit.*, fn. 268, Art. 22, notes 18-19, p. 406.
274. *Ibid.*, Art. 22, note 19, p. 406.
275. English Version available at <http://portal.wko.at/wk/format_detail.wk?angid=1&stid=323813&dstid=8459&opennavid=0> (last accessed 26 May 2008).

The requirement that the respondents are to be bound by the same arbitration agreement (as was provided for in Art. 10 of the former Vienna Rules) is no longer a possible alternative.[276] Instead, the new provision goes beyond the same arbitration agreement and allows, under alternative (b), joint arbitration proceedings against all respondents if they are "in legal accord" or if they are liable on the same factual grounds or because they are jointly and severally liable. The first requirement of "legal accord" (*Rechtsgemeinschaft*) is particularly challenging to understand. It appears that the explicit consent of the respondents to be joined together in single arbitration proceedings can be disregarded and that the consent to the Vienna Rules can be considered as an anticipated consent to arbitration.

It should be noted that this provision is one-sided, since it only allows the claimant to file a claim against multiple respondents. It also has no bearing on the joining of respondents after the commencement of the arbitration proceedings since it only provides for a mechanism for doing so if the initial claim has been filed against multiple respondents. However, in this situation the provision goes beyond the consent of the respondent and permits a multi-party arbitration in the situations mentioned in Art. 15(1) of the Vienna Rules.

### 5. SIAC Rules

The Arbitration Rules of the Singapore International Arbitration Centre (SIAC Rules) were revised in 2007.[277]

Rule 8 contains provisions for the appointment of the arbitrator(s) in multi-party settings. If the parties fail to agree on the procedure for appointment of arbitrators or if the agreed procedure fails, the Chairman of the Centre (see Rule 1.2 SIAC Rules) is given the authority to appoint the co-arbitrator(s).

With regard to the joinder of additional parties, Rule 24(b) SIAC Rules contains a notable provision. It gives the arbitral tribunal the power "to allow other parties to be joined in the arbitration with their express consent, and to make a single final award determining all disputes among the parties to the arbitration". Although this is a crucial issue, it is not entirely clear whether the reference to "their" consent means the consent of all the parties or only of the "other" parties.

It is also of interest that, in contrast to the LCIA Rules, the arbitral tribunal is not limited to considering requests by one of the existing parties, but can also consider requests for intervention from a third party.

---

276. Franz T. SCHWARZ and Christian W. KONRAD, "The New Vienna Rules", 23 Arb. Int'l (2007, no. 4) p. 601 at p. 617.
277. Arbitration Rules of the Singapore International Arbitration Centre (SIAC Rules), 3rd edn., 1 July 2007.

IX. THE WAY FORWARD: MORE PROVISIONS ON MULTI-PARTY ARBITRATION?

*1. Introduction*

The growing number of multi-party arbitration proceedings calls for rules applicable to situations where a multitude of entities are involved in a transaction, or, in a broader sense, in a project that may at some point engender a dispute to be resolved by arbitration. Based on the increasing interdependence of commerce, one must assume that the need to join third parties will grow further in the future.[278] Thus, the premise for the following discussion is that there is a clear need for additional guidance and rules in this area.

Specific rules for multi-party arbitration are necessary primarily in two areas: firstly, to provide rules regarding the appointment of arbitrators in multi-party situations and, secondly, to provide rules that address the issue of joining third parties at the beginning, but also at a later stage of the proceedings. In the following discussion of provisions offering solutions to multi-party situations, the focus shall be on the latter, since the first issue is one of equal treatment of all parties, which is easier to resolve.

In the context of international arbitration, there are three levels where such provisions can be envisioned:

– the arbitration agreement itself;
– institutional arbitration rules or rules chosen for ad hoc proceedings such as the UNCITRAL Arbitration Rules; or
– the applicable arbitration laws.

*2. Specific Provisions Agreed by the Parties*

It has been explained that the main obstacle to multi-party arbitration is the consensual nature of arbitration.[279] As has been correctly stated recently in one of the many publications on the issue of multi-party arbitration, the core feature of arbitration is also its Achilles heel.[280] With regard to joinder, the consensual nature of arbitration means that neither the claimant nor the respondent has to accept a third person joining the arbitration proceedings and filing claims against one or both of the existing parties to the arbitral proceedings. The consensual nature of arbitration goes beyond this in that, even if there is a valid arbitration agreement between one of the parties and the third (joining) party, the other party can refuse the joining of such party since each arbitration clause is independent and separate. This means that the consent given when agreeing to an arbitration clause is limited to future arbitration proceedings involving the exact same parties to the arbitration agreement (or their successors in title).[281]

Any solution to the problem beyond the arbitration agreement itself is not in line with the consensual nature of arbitration and should be applied only secondarily. In the

---

278. A. MEIER, *op. cit.*, fn. 13, p. 232.
279. See Sect. II.2.a above.
280. K.M. SIIG, *op. cit.*, fn. 5, p. 73.
281. R. GEIMER, *op. cit.*, fn. 6, p. 170.

author's opinion, this is also true, although to a lesser extent, for solutions based on construed or anticipated consent of the parties. In other words, problems connected to potential or actual multi-party arbitration are best resolved by achieving agreement between all parties involved.[282] This requires all the parties and the lawyers advising the parties in the conclusion of contracts (which could potentially entail a multi-party dispute situation), to be aware of the issues and their possible solutions. The arbitration institutions, in turn, should provide assistance for this by drafting standard arbitration clauses for the joinder of third parties.[283]

One could stop here and assert that any attempt to provide for rules in arbitration laws and institutional rules regarding the joinder of third parties are only "second best" and should not be attempted in the first place.[284] However, in the overall interest of arbitration as a fair and effective dispute resolution mechanism, there should be some minimum default rules in the event that the parties have not themselves provided for the multi-party issue in their arbitration agreement.[285]

The first question is: which of the two remaining levels (statutory provisions in the applicable arbitration law or rules of the arbitration institutions) should be favored to optimally provide such fallback rules? This issue will be discussed in the following sections.

3.   Rules in the Applicable Arbitration Laws

Only the applicable arbitration law can disregard the consensual nature of arbitration or, rather, replace the consent of the parties by a statutory rule. If it seems desirable to exceed the limitations of the consensual process of arbitration, only a solution on the statutory level, involving adapting the lex arbitri, is possible.

Until now, arbitration laws have not normally included provisions dealing with multi-party arbitration in general or with the joinder of third parties. However, there are exceptions to this rule:

– According to Art. 1045 of the Dutch Code of Civil Procedure, the arbitral tribunal may allow a third party to intervene, or may allow one of the parties to join a third party in a pending arbitration, if it has an interest in the case. However, this provision is purely declaratory in nature, since the intervention or the joinder will only be allowed if all parties agree to it in writing.[286]
– The revised Austrian arbitration law contains a provision which allows the court to appoint the arbitral tribunal if multiple parties, who have to jointly appoint one or

---

282. The same conclusion was reached in the "Guideline on Multi-Party Arbitrations" issued by the Chartered Institute of Arbitrators, 72 Arbitration (2006, no. 2) p. 151 at pp. 154-155.
283. A. MEIER, *op. cit.*, fn. 13, pp. 232-233.
284. See *ibid.*, p. 232.
285. For arguments in favour of adding specific rules on consolidation and joinder, see also K.M. SIIG, *op. cit.*, fn. 5, p. 82.
286. *Ibid.*, p. 81.

several arbitrators, do not reach an agreement within four weeks.[287] This provision is limited to the issue of appointing arbitrators in multi-party proceedings.
– According to the Italian Code of Civil Procedure, as amended in 2006, a party to an arbitration agreement can ask a third party to join the proceedings.[288] The required conditions are that all parties must be bound by the same arbitration agreement *and* that the appointment of the arbitrators must be agreed upon by the parties, i.e., the arbitration agreement (i) defers to a third party for the appointment of the arbitrators, or (ii) the arbitrators are appointed by agreement of all parties or (iii) the other parties, following the appointment by the first party of an arbitrator or the arbitrators, appoint by common agreement an equal number of arbitrators or entrust their appointment to a third party. This provision has been qualified as unique in comparative law.[289] It does indeed seem to be the only legal provision which renounces the requirement of specific consent of all parties involved to the joinder. However, it does not go beyond what has been proposed above as the effect of a common arbitration agreement in general.[290]

The reason why arbitration laws do not generally provide for the joinder of a third party lies in the inherent conflict between the consensual nature of arbitration and a statutory joinder not based on consent.[291] Another reason, which is more relevant in practice, is that the same effect can be reached by consolidating the proceedings if the parties to the two proceedings are *not* identical. Thus, there are provisions, e.g., in US State law, where the consolidation issue also, in part at least, covers the joinder issue.[292]

This reluctance on the part of the legislature is justified. As shown in the discussion regarding mandatory third-law provisions,[293] it is valid to question whether the parties to arbitration must give up their extensive rights in order to accommodate the overriding interests of maintaining the States' protection of arbitration as a preferred means of international business dispute resolution. However, the issue of joinder of third parties is not primarily about overriding public interests, but about the interests of the parties to a specific arbitration, and possibly of a third party to join this arbitration. In the context of the private interests of parties (vs. the overriding public interest), it is justified to uphold the consensual nature of the arbitration as a true alternative to state court proceedings. Thus, the legislature should be extremely reluctant to impose rules which disregard this consensual nature of arbitration.

Another downside of statutory provisions is that any provision would be limited to the territory where the arbitration law is applicable, which creates an unacceptable patchwork of international arbitration.

---

287. Sect. 587(5) of the Austrian Code of Civil Procedure.
288. Art. 816*quater* of the Italian Code of Civil Procedure, as amended by Legislative Decree of 2 February 2006, English translation available at <http://www.camera-arbitrale.it/show.jsp?page=169949>. For a summary, see *Yearbook* XXXI (2006) p. 502.
289. J.-F. POUDRET and S. BESSON, *op. cit.*, fn. 115, no. 244 at p. 204.
290. See Sect. III.2 above.
291. J.D.M. LEW, L.A. MISTELIS and S.M. KRÖLL, *op. cit.*, fn. 262, no. 16-47 at p. 391.
292. See, e.g., Dutch and Californian laws mentioned by K.M. SIIG, *op. cit.*, fn. 5, p. 81.
293. See, e.g., Nathalie VOSER, "Mandatory Rules of Law as a Limitation on the Law Applicable in International Commercial Arbitration", 7 Am. Rev. Int'l Arb. (1996, no. 3/4) p. 319.

As shown above, legislators should not intervene in the consensual process and provide for rules on joinder. They also should not provide for declaratory provisions, as is the case in the Netherlands and in Italy, since there is a considerable risk of thereby raising difficult questions, for instance regarding what the powers of the arbitral tribunal are outside the scope of the provision in question.

4. *Provisions in Institutional Arbitration Rules or Ad Hoc Arbitration Rules*

a. *Are such rules desirable and, if so, what are their basic principles?*
The important difference between provisions on multi-party arbitration in arbitration laws, on the one hand, and similar provisions in institutional arbitration rules (or rules for ad hoc arbitration such as the UNCITRAL Arbitration Rules), on the other, is that the latter, if the arbitration takes place under these rules, are consensual in nature, since they were chosen by the parties. Thus, such provisions are within the realm of the consent of the parties, even though the parties might not in every case be aware of them.

With regard to the issue of the *appointment of arbitrators*, there is no doubt that in the aftermath of the *Dutco* case the arbitration institutions had to provide more sophisticated appointment mechanisms for multi-party situations. The solutions are now well established and can be exemplified by many of the provisions introduced in the latest revisions of the institutional rules.[294] What remains unresolved and open to dispute is whether, if one side fails to appoint its arbitrator, the institution should automatically appoint all arbitrators, or, as is argued in this Report,[295] the institution should have full discretion to appoint only the defaulting side's arbitrator.

With regard to the *joinder issue*, it is obvious that in institutional arbitration it is impossible to rule on third parties that have never submitted to the relevant institutional rules. It is, therefore, impossible to require a third party, against whom one of the parties of a pending arbitration has, for example, a claim of recourse, to participate in the pending proceedings.[296]

It has already been established that, generally speaking, it is necessary to provide for fallback rules in case the parties fail to do so in their arbitration agreement. When deciding on the issue of whether such fallback rules in institutional rules are desirable, the critical question is whether such provisions contradict the legitimate expectations of the parties who rely on the consensual and separate nature of the arbitral proceedings with the party with whom they have established an arbitration clause.

Today the issue of joinder of third parties has reached a level of discussion in international arbitration where all individuals involved in international arbitration and advising the parties must be aware of such special provisions in the institutional rules. This is particularly the case in light of the trend for providing for such rules in institutional arbitration, as illustrated in some of the latest revisions of the Swiss Rules, the Vienna Rules, and the SIAC Rules, as well as the ongoing discussion regarding the

---

294. See Art. 10(2) of the ICC Rules, Art. 8(5) of the Swiss Rules, Art. 8(1) of the LCIA Rules, Sect. 13.2 of the DIS Rules, Art. 13(4) of the SCC Rules, and Rule 3.2 of the SIAC Rules.
295. See Sect. III.6.*b* above.
296. K.M. SIIG, *op. cit.*, fn. 5, pp. 80-81.

revision of the UNCITRAL Arbitration Rules.[297] It is to be expected that this trend will increase and thus that the awareness of the parties will improve. In addition, one should not forget that institutional arbitration rules are not only used by the "inner circle" of arbitration practitioners, but also by parties and their representatives, who are less experienced. In these situations one cannot assume that the arbitration agreement will be as sophisticated as the complexity of the matter may require. It is important, therefore, for the arbitration rules to be user friendly and to provide for solutions to issues that are highly relevant in practice. For these reasons, the present author would suggest that institutional rules *can* and indeed *should* provide for rules regarding joinder of third parties.

An even more delicate question is whether such rules should be narrow and specific in order to clearly delineate the competence of the arbitral tribunal (as is the case for Art. 22.1(h) of the LCIA Rules), or whether the provisions should be broader, thereby granting maximum flexibility to the arbitral tribunal (as the solution of Art. 4(2) of the Swiss Rules).

The first type of rule enhances the predictability for the parties, but entails loss of flexibility on the part of the arbitral tribunal to provide for a joinder where a situation calls for it but is not provided for in the rules. For example, what if a third party claims to have a better right to an object in dispute between two parties, such as when there is a dispute about looted art? According to some theories a party may, under certain circumstances, be prohibited from withholding its consent to arbitrate. In such cases, a flexible provision like Art. 4(2) of the Swiss Rules could be useful. More generally, the interest of one party to be limited to a dispute with the other party to the arbitration agreement might have to be set aside in favor of the interest of the other party to include a third party, since the disadvantages for the former are less significant than the (potential) downside for the latter. Provisions providing for a narrow joinder of a third party and requiring the consent of this party will exclude, based on an *a contrario* argument, the joinder/intervention of third parties in situations where the balancing test would call for a joinder.

Giving the arbitral tribunal a broader and more flexible competence is a sensitive topic since the parties are rightly concerned that the very nature of arbitration proceedings, an agreement to arbitrate with specific parties in private proceedings, is at risk. If arbitration is to be a real alternative to court proceedings, this nature must be upheld, and no arbitrator should be given a "tool" to disregard the necessity of the consent of all parties. One could also add that the parties had the option to provide for a solution on the multi-party situation in the arbitration agreement. Such solutions could also include the "silent" participation of a third party in the proceedings, in order to support the party in the defence of the claims.[298] On the other hand, as previously explained in view of the broad and flexible clause of Art. 4(2) of the Swiss Rules, there are good arguments for including a provision regarding joinder in the rules.[299]

---

297. See discussion in Sect. IX.*4.b* below.
298. See the useful solutions proposed by Michel DUBISSON, "Arbitration in Subcontracts for International Projects", 1 J. Int'l Arb. (1984, no. 3) p. 197 at p. 210 et seq. and the sample clause in Annex 2 for the relationship between main contractor and subcontractor.
299. See Sect. VIII.*2* above.

The balance is very difficult to strike, and there is no right or wrong. Each institution must decide individually where it wants to position itself in the arbitration market, i.e., whether it wants to be viewed as assisting (certain) parties needing a joinder who have not provided for the necessary contractual solution, and/or as assisting a third party wishing to intervene; finally, it must decide, how it wishes to assist (i.e., by means of very narrow rules or a rule giving the arbitral tribunal a broad flexibility). At the end of the day, the best outcome will be if all institutions do not reach the same conclusion, since this will help differentiate between the institutions and will allow the parties to make a real choice between the different options.

Even if no final solution on the provision on joinder is reached in this Report, the preparatory analysis and research shows that, with regard to the appointment of arbitrators and/or the joinder of third parties, the institutions should make sure that the following aspects are taken into account:

*Appointment of arbitrator(s)*
In order to prevent one side with multiple parties from obstructing the arbitration proceedings, the institution shall be at liberty only to appoint the defaulting side's arbitrator and shall respect the appointment made by the other side in situations where the defaulting side has identical or similar interests.

*Position of respondent*
Respondent should be put on an equal footing with claimant in the rules in terms of its options to include further parties in its answer to the notice of arbitration.

*Joining of third parties after the constitution of the arbitral tribunal*
Institutional rules should make it clear that any provisions on consolidation and/or joinder with reference to the competence of the institution prior to the constitution of the arbitral tribunal do not exclude the competence of the arbitral tribunal, once it has been constituted, to decide on a consolidation and/or joinder request.

A procedure should be put into place which guarantees that the same (i.e., not stricter) preliminary analysis (such as the prima facie test) will be made if a third party is joined after the constitution of the arbitral tribunal.

b.   *Proposed revision of the UNCITRAL Arbitration Rules*
The UNCITRAL Arbitrations Rules of 1976 are based on a bipolar model of arbitration and do not expressly deal with the specific problems of multi-party arbitrations. In light of the developments in the last three decades – both with regard to the complexity of business transactions and the recent adaptations of institutional arbitration rules – the UNCITRAL Working Group II has decided that the ongoing revision of the UNCITRAL Arbitration Rules should be used to also address multi-party arbitrations.[300]

---

300. Reports and other documents of the Working Group are available at <http://www.uncitral.org/uncitral/en/commission/working_groups/2Arbitration.html>. For an overview of the revision's history, see, e.g., Markus WIRTH, "The Current Revision of the UNCITRAL Arbitration Rules" in Christoph MÜLLER, ed., *New Developments in International Commercial Arbitration 2007* (Schulthess 2007) p. 1 at p. 2.

The most remarkable modifications in this respect include the proposals for new articles dealing with the appointment of arbitrators in multi-party arbitrations (Draft Art. 7*bis*),[301] and for the joinder of third persons to pending arbitration proceedings (Draft Art. 15(4)).[302]

Regarding the *appointment of arbitrators*, the present version of Draft Art. 7*bis*(2) requires multiple claimants and/or respondents to jointly appoint an arbitrator. In the event of a failure to constitute the arbitral tribunal, Draft Art. 7*bis*(3) gives the appointing authority, at the request of any party, the discretion to either make a default appointment of the joint arbitrator or to revoke any prior appointment and appoint all three arbitrators itself.

The discretion granted to the appointing authority regarding appointment corresponds to Art. 10(2) of the ICC Rules and Art. 8(5) of the Swiss Rules, but is in contrast to Art. 8.1 of the LCIA Rules. As already discussed, this discretion is to be welcomed.[303]

The latest version of Draft Art. 15(4) regarding the *joinder of third persons* reads as follows:

> "The arbitral tribunal may, on the application of any party, allow one or more third persons to be joined in the arbitration as a party and, provided such a third person and the applicant party have consented, make an award in respect of all parties involved in the arbitration." [304]

The UNCITRAL Working Group considered this draft article in a first reading at its 46th session in February 2007.[305] Its members agreed that the provision would constitute a major modification to the Rules and expressed diverging views on its details and even on its necessity. While some supported the inclusion of a provision allowing the joinder of third persons even against the objection of the other party, others insisted on the necessity of consent by all parties, or at least the inclusion of an opt-in or opt-out

---

301. See "Settlement of commercial disputes: Revision of the UNCITRAL Arbitration Rules, Note by the Secretariat", UNCITRAL Working Group II (Arbitration), forty-seventh session (Vienna, 10-14 September 2007), UN Doc. A/CN.9/WG.II/WP.147 (3 August 2007) para. 41.
302. Initially, Draft Art. 15(4) was sub-divided into sub-para. (a), dealing with the consolidation of different claims between the parties to an arbitration, and sub-para. (b), containing the present text of para. (4) on joinder of third persons. The Working Group, however, agreed that an express provision on consolidation might not be necessary in the revised UNCITRAL Arbitration Rules and deleted sub-para. (a). See "Report of the Working Group on Arbitration and Conciliation on the work of its forty-sixth session", (New York, 5-9 February 2007) UNCITRAL, 40th Sess., UN Doc. A/CN.9/619 (25 June-12 July 2007) (hereinafter Working Group Report 619) para. 120; "Settlement of commercial disputes: Revision of the UNCITRAL Arbitration Rules, Note by the Secretariat", UNCITRAL Working Group II (Arbitration), forty-seventh session (Vienna, 10-14 September 2007), UN Doc. A/CN.9/WG.II/WP.147/Add.1 (3 August 2007) (hereinafter Secretariat Note 147/Add.1) para. 7.
303. See Sect. III.6.*b* above.
304. See, Secretariat Note 147/Add.1, *op. cit.*, fn. 302, para. 5.
305. See "Working Group Report 619", *op. cit.*, fn. 302, paras. 121-126.

proviso.[306] The Working Group decided to consider the matter at a future session.[307] In the meantime, it has requested, and received, comments from several arbitration institutions on the frequency and practical relevance of joinder in arbitration.[308]

In light of the diverging views represented in the Working Group, it remains to be seen whether, and if so, with what modifications, Draft Art. 15(4) will make it into the final version of the revised UNCITRAL Arbitration Rules. Therefore, only a few remarks shall be made regarding the current draft.

As argued above, *institutions* should provide for provisions on joinder.[309] However, with regard to rules for ad hoc arbitration, the situation is different. For institutions, there is at least a common jurisdiction of the institution (in a non-technical sense) over all the parties which have chosen such institution; ad hoc arbitration rules are not under the umbrella of a commonly chosen institution. This makes it less appropriate for providing rules on joinder. Furthermore, the fact that the parties have not chosen an institution should make them more aware of the need to provide for certain situations in their agreement. This speaks against the inclusion of a rule on joinder in the UNCITRAL Arbitration Rules.

If the working group nevertheless decides to go forward, the following should be taken into account in future drafts:

(1) According to the Working Group, Draft Art. 15(4) is inspired by Art. 22.1(h) of the LCIA Rules.[310] Like the latter provision, Draft Art. 15(4) makes the rendering of an award with regard to *all* parties dependent on the application of one of the existing parties. There is no room for a third person intervening on its own motion. The wording of the draft article seems to suggest that the consent of the non-applicant party is not a necessary precondition for joining the third party, but that the arbitral tribunal may also allow a joinder against the express objection of the other party to the arbitration. This also seems to be the interpretation of the Working Group.[311] It seems that, in drafting this provision, the authors wanted to allow for the possibility of the arbitral tribunal

---

306. *Ibid.*, para. 122.
307. *Ibid.*, para. 126. This will most probably take place at the Working Group's 49th session in September 2008 or its 50th session in February 2009.
308. See Secretariate Note 147/Add.1, *op. cit.*, fn. 302, para. 8, along with a summary of the comments provided by the International Court of Arbitration of the ICC, the LCIA and the Swiss Arbitration Association (ASA).
309. See Sect. IX.*4.a* above.
310. "Settlement of commercial disputes: Revision of the UNCITRAL Arbitration Rules, Note by the Secretariat", UNCITRAL Working Group II (Arbitration), forty-sixth session (New York, 5-9 February 2007), UN Doc. A/CN.9/WG.II/WP.145/Add.1 (6 December 2006) p. 3; "Working Group Report 619", *op. cit.*, fn. 302, para. 121. The Paulsson/Petrochilos-Report proposed in Rule 15(8) a wording that was nearly identical to Art. 22.1(h) of the LCIA Rules. See Jan PAULSSON and Georgios PETROCHILOS, "Revision of the UNCITRAL Arbitration Rules. A Report" (2006), paras. 138-139, available at <http://www.uncitral.org/pdf/english/news/arbrules_report.pdf> (last accessed 25 May 2008). On the LCIA Rules, see Sect. VIII.*3* above.
311. "Working Group Report 619", *op. cit.*, fn. 302, para. 122. See also M. WIRTH, *op. cit.*, fn. 300, p. 12. In contrast, the Paulsson/Petrochilos-Report considered "the consent of the parties to the main claim as well as that of the third party" as a necessary requirement for a joinder. J. PAULSSON and G. PETROCHILOS, *op. cit.*, fn. 310, para. 138.

rendering awards which would include claims between the non-consenting party and the third party.[312] However, with reference to the discussion under the LCIA Rules, where it was explained that either a broader or a more narrow reading is possible,[313] it is not entirely clear from the wording what the competences of the arbitral tribunal shall be. It is recommended that this be clarified in the provision itself.

(2) Regarding the consent of a third party to be joined, the wording of Draft Art. 15(4) differs remarkably from that in Art. 22.1(h) of the LCIA Rules. The wording of the latter provision makes clear by the word "provided" that consent (expressed in writing) between the applicant party and the third person is necessary for the joinder itself. The wording of Draft Art. 15(4) of the revised UNCITRAL Rules mentions the consent requirement only in connection with the arbitral tribunal's authority to render a single award in respect of all parties involved in the arbitration. Because of the word "and", a literal understanding of this provision suggests that the arbitral tribunal has the power to join one or more parties to the arbitration even if there is no consent by the third party, but without the possibility of making an award with respect to all parties. It is not clear from the published materials what reasons led to this change in the wording and if the drafters actually intended any substantive deviation from the LCIA Rules. It is also not clear what the consequences would be, and whether the intention is to include the possibility of rendering an award between the requesting party and the third party against the objection of the third party and the other party to the proceedings. This is an issue which needs further clarification.

## X. CONCLUSION

Based on the analysis in this report, the following theses are presented as conclusions:

*Thesis 1*
Because of the consensual nature of arbitration, the best way of resolving multi-party and multi-polar disputes using arbitration as a dispute resolution mechanism is to provide for rules regarding the joinder of third parties and the appointment of arbitrators in the case of multi-party arbitration in the arbitration agreement.

For this purpose,

— lawyers who advise parties entering into an agreement where there are commercially-related third entities should improve their command and knowledge of the issues at stake and of the various options, and
— arbitration institutions should draft standard arbitration clauses for (complex) multi-party contracts.

---

312. See M. WIRTH, *op. cit.*, fn. 300, p. 12 who refers to an award "with effect between the employer and the sub-contractor" rendered after the application of the contractor in proceedings initiated by the employer.
313. See Sect. VIII.*3* above.

*Thesis 2*
National arbitration laws should not provide for rules on the joinder of third parties.

*Thesis 3*
There are good arguments for and against the inclusion of specific provisions on joinder in institutional rules, in the event that the parties have not provided for rules in their arbitration agreement. Nevertheless, when balancing these arguments, the present author concludes that the institutions should indeed provide for pertinent provisions on joinder.

*Thesis 4*
If an institution wishes to provide for rules on joinder, a decision needs to be reached on the principle of whether the rules should provide for the specific situations where this is possible, or whether the arbitral tribunal should have full discretion. Again, there are valid arguments for and against each solution.

*Thesis 5*
Arbitration institutions should not provide for any default rules regarding participation in any form other than as formal party.

*Thesis 6*
Ad hoc arbitration rules should not provide for rules on joinder.

# Multi-party Arbitration and Rule-making: Same Issues, Contrasting Approaches

*Cristián Conejero Roos**

TABLE OF CONTENTS | Page
--- | ---
I. Introduction | 411
II. The Assumptions | 411
III. The Issues | 413
IV. Joinder of Third Parties (Particularly Late Joinder) | 419
V. The Overall Assessment | 431
VI. Conclusions | 433

I. INTRODUCTION

The Report prepared by Nathalie Voser provides a thorough, in-depth and overarching review of the most challenging issues concerning multi-party disputes in current international arbitral practice.[1]

My comments are limited to specific issues raised in Ms. Voser's Report. Sect. II states basic assumptions before dealing with the relevant issues. Sect. III addresses the regulation of multi-party arbitration through national laws and arbitration rules. Sect. IV deals with the joinder of third parties and identifies the different solutions embodied so far in arbitration rules governing this matter. Finally, Sect. V provides a general assessment and describes certain practical and theoretical considerations.

II. THE ASSUMPTIONS

This Comment is based on a number of premises, which allows us to narrow down the discussion to specific multi-party arbitration issues. The assumptions are as follows:

*1. Procedural Focus*

Multi-party arbitration is a concept broad enough to encompass both substantive and procedural issues. In a multi-party scenario, the core question of whether some or all of the parties have consented to arbitration may be relevant, particularly if non-signatory parties are involved and objections have been raised as to their lack of consent to submit to arbitration. This question could involve procedural issues, such as whether joinder of

---

* Counsel, International Arbitration, Cuatrecasas (Paris and Madrid). Lecturer on international arbitration, ESSEC (Paris) and Universidad Autonóma de Madrid.
1. Nathalie VOSER, "Multi-Party Disputes and Joinder of Third Parties", this volume, p. 343-410.

these non-signatory parties is admissible if there is no express agreement, or how the multiple parties are to constitute the arbitral tribunal. Conversely, doctrines allowing a non-signatory party to be deemed a party to the arbitration agreement relate to the substantive question of whether that party has consented to arbitration.[2]

The situations examined below relate only to procedural aspects of multi-party arbitration, particularly the regulation of the joinder of third parties to ongoing proceedings, the different approaches taken, and their advantages and disadvantages.

*2. International Commercial Arbitrations and Multi-Party Disputes*

With the extraordinary parallel development of investment arbitration, procedural issues concerning multi-party disputes have also become hot issues in this field of dispute resolution. However, the experiences drawn and conclusions reached here relate exclusively to international commercial arbitration. Even if many of the issues discussed in this Comment may also be relevant in multi-party investment arbitrations, there are some special features of investment arbitrations that call for a different approach. Accordingly, Ms. Voser's Report deliberately excludes them.

This means that highly debated issues in investment arbitration such as third party or non-party participation, particularly in the form of *amicus curiae*, are not addressed here.

*3. Multipolar Scenarios*

Many of the issues that this Comment addresses relate to cases in which the common denominator is not only the existence of multiple parties on each side, but the existence of multiple and divergent interests.

There are multi-party arbitrations in which the multiple claimants or respondents act as if they were a single party, due to a common interest. These cases do not necessarily give rise to multi-party procedural issues. This is particularly the case regarding the constitution of the arbitral tribunal when there are multiple parties on each side who, due to their lack of divergent or opposing interests, have no problems agreeing on the arbitrators. On the contrary, if the multiple parties on the same side (either the claimants or respondents) have different or conflicting interests, it is more likely that multi-party issues may arise.[3]

---

2. See, for a thorough analysis of these issues, Bernard HANOTIAU, *Complex Arbitrations: Multiparty, Multicontract, Multi-issue and Class Action* (Kluwer Law 2005) and "Problems Raised by Complex Arbitrations Involving Multiple Contracts – Parties-Issues – An Analysis", 18 Journal of International Arbitration, (2001, no. 3) pp. 255-297; *Complex Arbitrations, Perspectives on their Procedural Implications*, ICC Ct. Bull., Special Supplement 2003 (hereinafter *ICC Special Supplement on Complex Arbitrations*; and Nathalie VOSER, *op. cit.*, fn. 1, this volume, at pp. 372-379.
3. Jean-Louis DEVOLVÉ, "Final Report on Multi-Party Arbitrations", 6 ICC CT. BULL. (1993, no. 1) p. 30.

III. THE ISSUES

This section addresses the so-called philosophical question posed by the Report as to whether there is a need to regulate multi-party issues, and then examines whether such regulation should be achieved through national laws or arbitration rules.

1. *Regulation of Multi-Party Arbitration Issues: Is It Desirable?*

I start by sharing an anecdote. During my graduate legal studies, I approached a learned arbitration practitioner and professor to ask him whether he saw any interest in an article about joinder of third parties, and his short answer was: "Joinder of third parties? It is not an issue. Either you agree or you don't."[4] Unsurprisingly, he is not alone. Some months ago, during the assessment of the ten years of the current ICC Rules for Arbitration, and particularly of some issues concerning joinder and multi-party arbitration, another reputed specialist complained bitterly about the dangerous path being taken by arbitral institutions in making specific regulations on these matters, without express agreement of the parties. Thus, the issue obviously begs an answer.

There is a position favoring the restriction of rule-making when it comes to complex multi-party issues and, particularly, joinder. The arguments that militate in favor of that position are inter alia that

(1) regulation of joinder, consolidation, intervention or the like should lie with the parties in light of the principle of party autonomy;
(2) parties in international arbitration seek predictability, and regulation of these issues through national laws or arbitration rules defeat that purpose, as it puts the parties in uncertain and unforeseen scenarios; in other words, greater predictability comes with less or no regulation; and
(3) applying mechanisms for joinder that do not result from the consent of the parties may give rise to obstacles or problems at the enforcement stage of the arbitral award.

Perhaps because of my experience as counsel at the ICC International Court of Arbitration, I take the opposite view, as I can clearly see the benefits of regulating multi-party issues. I believe that regulation of multi-party issues

(1) should not be exclusively left to the parties' arbitration agreement;
(2) does not conflict with the principle of autonomy of the parties; and
(3) should not cause enforcement problems and may even protect the enforcement of the award.

---

4. See Julian LEW, Loukas MISTELIS and Stefan KRÖLL, *Comparative International Commercial Arbitration* (2003) p. 388 (The authors note: "Generally joinder is only possible if all parties involved consent.").

*a. Multi-party issues should not be exclusively left to the parties' arbitration agreement*
I agree with John Gardiner's position that, in principle, it is for the parties to foresee multi-party issues and anticipate them by crafting tailored arbitration clauses. However, it is not realistic to expect that in every case. Empirical data reveals an important increase in multi-party arbitrations,[5] and yet one sees few specific tailored multi-party arbitration clauses.[6] Hence, this common-sense advice is still of limited application in practice.[7]

This is consistent with the fact that there are no perfect draftsmen, and complex multi-party issues such as possibilities for joinder to ongoing arbitral proceedings, consolidation of claims involving several parties arising out of different contracts, or third-party voluntary intervention are not within the legal knowledge of the average lawyer, let alone laymen. But, even if they were, negotiators may still prefer not to raise them up front when negotiating the arbitration clause, either for strategic reasons or to avoid losing flexibility in the arbitration clause.[8] Strategically speaking, bringing up these issues might reveal certain intentions to play procedural cards that are better saved for the battlefield, if necessary. In terms of flexibility, parties may prefer to keep the drafting of the arbitration clause simple and straight-forward to avoid further discussions or delays, both when negotiating and enforcing it.

I also dare to take issue with the argument that parties do not like multi-party regulation because, under multi-party regulation, they would be placed in unforeseen scenarios. Empirical data suggests that the parties have expressed major concerns about not having solutions for multi-party issues such as joinder,[9] which the parties did not initially consider when agreeing to arbitrate. On the other hand, that one did not foresee multi-party issues in the arbitration clause does not mean that their regulation, through national laws or arbitration rules, should always come as a surprise. In reality, regulation creates the burden of understanding the consequences of choosing such arbitration rules or national laws before accepting them. Specific provisions might shed light on the conditions under which issues such as joinder or consolidation may proceed, which would help anticipate, and even control, potential outcomes when the parties have not agreed on solutions under the arbitration clause.

---

5. Yves DERAINS and Eric SCHWARTZ, *A Guide to the ICC Rules of Arbitration*, 2nd edn. (2005) p. 28 ("Indeed, in recent years, there has been a significant increase in the number of multi-party arbitrations administered by the ICC.").
6. Julian LEW, Loukas MISTELIS and S. KRÖLL, *op. cit.*, fn. 3, p. 391.
7. Nathalie VOSER, *op. cit.*, fn. 1, this volume, p. 369 ("Such clauses (especially if they are combined with a clause on the appointment of arbitrators, as discussed above) would constitute an ideal and predictable solution to multi-party disputes. However, it has repeatedly been stated that they are very rarely used in practice.").
8. Eric SCHWARTZ, "Choosing between Broad Clauses and Detailed Blueprints" in *Improving the Efficiency of Arbitration Agreements and Awards: 40 Years of Application of the New York Convention*, ICCA Congress Series no. 9 (1999) p. 105.
9. See Price Waterhouse Report, "International Arbitration: Corporate Attitudes and Practices" (2006) p. 7 ("Other concerns associated with international arbitration include ... the difficulty of joining third parties to proceedings.").

b.  *Rules for multi-party disputes do not conflict with the parties' autonomy. They help reinforce it*

Rules on multi-party disputes do not run counter to the principle of party autonomy. One may argue that when the parties opt for a specific lex arbitri or for arbitration rules providing solutions to these issues, they are exercising and enforcing this principle. Ultimately, it is for the parties to choose these bodies of rules and laws, which may contain multi-party provisions, and to incorporate them into their own arbitration agreement. A reputed practitioner once said that arbitration clauses do not exist in a vacuum and that they are completed by the rules chosen by the parties.[10] This is particularly the case for multi-party issues governed by those rules.

Moreover, regulating multi-party disputes might actually help enforce the parties' agreement. If, for example, claimant A files an arbitration against respondent B, and respondent B counterclaims against claimant A and third party C, who happens to be a signatory party to the agreement containing the arbitration clause, the decision to join party C to the proceedings, even in spite of objections from claimant A or party C itself, will help enforce the agreement to arbitrate among the parties to the agreement. Without a mechanism allowing an arbitral institution or an arbitral tribunal to take that decision, respondent B would be forced to litigate its claims only against claimant A, and file a separate arbitration against party C. Leaving aside arguments of efficiency, it is clear that such a result would be inconsistent with the parties' own arbitration agreement. Hence, multi-party regulation helps protect the core basis of the arbitration proceedings against strategic behavior from the parties, that is, the arbitration agreement itself.[11]

c.  *Multi-party regulation should not give rise to enforcement problems and may protect the enforcement of the award*

The argument that multi-party regulation risks the unenforceability of the arbitral award needs to be clarified: Exactly which multi-party issues and what multi-party regulations?

Multi-party issues can entail various situations. Some of the recurring examples are

(1) when one or more claimants file an arbitration against one or more respondents, some of whom are not signatories to the arbitration agreement and have allegedly not consented to arbitrate;
(2) problems with the constitution of the arbitral tribunal, when the multiple parties on one or both sides are unable to agree on a party-appointed arbitrator; and

---

10. Jan PAULSSON, "Vicarious Hypochondria and Institutional Arbitration", 6 Arb. Int. (1990, no. 3) p. 226.
11. I do not agree with the argument that "[B]ecause of the contractual and confidential nature of arbitration, as a general rule, neither voluntary nor compulsory intervention may be envisaged unless provided for by a specific clause," Jean-Louis DEVOLVÉ, *op. cit.*, fn. 3, p. 34. If such joinder or intervention refers to a party to the arbitration agreement, there would not be any breach of the contractual nature of the arbitration.

(3) questions of joinder, when one or more respondents seek the joinder of a third party to ongoing arbitral proceedings based on the same contract on which the principal claims are based, or additional or different contracts.

The question is: what multi-party regulations concerning these issues could give rise to enforcement problems?

Except for the question of jurisdiction, which in any case calls for a decision with res judicata effect, it seems that these issues are procedural, and the arbitration rules and laws are to help make the arbitral procedure efficient and effective, while respecting the boundaries of party autonomy.

Provisions dealing with the constitution of the arbitral tribunal in a multipolar scenario, in which the multiple parties are unable to agree on an arbitrator, have been established to avoid, and not to create, enforcement problems.

Provisions permitting arbitral institutions to step into the proceedings to exclude some of the multiple claimants or multiple respondents on a prima facie basis, such as Art. 6(2) of the ICC Arbitration Rules, do not seem to present any enforcement problems, as that decision is not a jurisdictional finding taken in the form of an award that might require subsequent enforcement. It is merely an administrative decision by virtue of which an arbitral body, such as the ICC Court, decides whether an agreement among all the parties involved in the arbitration may exist to refer their disputes to a set of arbitration rules.

Finally, the frequently criticized joinder regulation does not seem to create enforcement problems *per se*, provided it respects the agreement to arbitrate and the equal treatment of the parties. Whether arbitration may be commenced by multiple claimants or against multiple respondents, even with non-signatories, based on one or multiple contracts, is no longer an issue. But, if the parties object, then the arbitral tribunal must decide in light of the *kompetenz-kompetenz* principle. Such decision generally embodied in an arbitral award, if taken in violation of the parties' arbitration agreement, may subsequently be exposed to challenges to the arbitral award or to defenses to resist its enforcement.

From a purely procedural perspective, the joinder ultimately seeks the same purpose as a request filed against multiple respondents: i.e., to bring a third party, even if non-signatory, to the arbitration agreement, and based on one or more contracts, to an arbitral proceeding at the respondent's – instead of the claimant's – request. I fail to see any reason why this opportunity should not be afforded to the respondent(s). And I also fail to see why and how this possibility would give grounds to enforcement problems, except when the joinder is so broad that it may infringe the limits of the parties' consent to arbitrate, or when the joinder is accepted after the constitution of the arbitral tribunal and without having given the third party joined to the proceedings equal treatment in the constitution of the arbitral tribunal. Both situations, which are dealt with below, are exceptional and are not an excuse to accept a general unenforceability argument against joinder regulation. Finally, other multi-party issues such as whether a non-signatory party may be deemed a party to the arbitration agreement are common to multi-party arbitrations in general, and not to joinder in particular. These objections, if raised by the parties, will ultimately be decided by the arbitral tribunal in the form of an arbitral award. Any enforcement problems would be related to the arbitral award itself and not the multi-party regulation.

Last, but not least, under certain circumstances, provisions on multi-party disputes might even protect the enforcement of the arbitral award. The typical case is found in provisions allowing the constitution of the arbitral tribunal in a multi-party scenario, in which the parties were unable to agree on the appointment of the arbitrators.[12] Rules ensuring the constitution of the tribunal, while respecting the parties' equal treatment, would clearly protect the subsequent enforcement of an arbitral award.

In short, rule-making is not damaging per se. It simply shifts the burden to the parties who need to be aware of the scope and consequences of choosing a given set of provisions under national laws or arbitration rules, and exercise the duty to choose them wisely. Therefore, I concur with the views expressed in the Report that rule-making in multi-party arbitration is, in principle, desirable.

2. *Is the Same Goal Achieved Through Regulation by Either National Laws or Arbitration Rules?*

I would draw a line between arbitration laws and rules. In my view, national laws should not deal with multi-party issues, except for the isolated case of fallback solutions to constitute the arbitral tribunal in a multi-party context.[13] The Report justifies this conservative approach,[14] and I agree, with some additional grounds.

*First*, the parties' degree of knowledge and awareness is important. Parties should be aware of the consequences of choosing specific arbitration rules and national laws. However, although parties agree on arbitration rules in the arbitration clause, they seldom choose a national law as governing the arbitral procedure. Generally, this is a consequence of having chosen a certain city as the place of arbitration or, even worse, of the fixing of such place by an arbitral institution or the arbitral tribunal. Further, as the most-often-used sets of rules used in international arbitration are limited to only a handful of institutions, arbitration practitioners are generally well versed in their scope, contents and application. The same does not necessarily happen with national arbitration laws, which are more numerous and sometimes offer drastic differences in approaches and content.

*Second*, rules on multi-party issues under national laws often vest the national courts with the powers to decide the multi-party issues.[15] Because of the nature of international

---

12. See, inter alia, Art. 10(2) of ICC Rules, Art. 8 of the Rules of the London Court of International Arbitration (LCIA), Art. 6(5) of the Rules of the International Center for Dispute Resolution, Art. 13(4) of the Stockholm Chamber of Commerce Rules (SCC), and Art. 8(3) to 8(5) of the Swiss Rules of International Arbitration.
13. See, for example, Art. 587(5) of the Austrian Arbitration Act (Federal Gazette 2006/7), Art. 15(2)(b) second paragraph of the Spanish Arbitration Act (Law No. 60/2003), Art. 23(c) to (e) of the Peruvian Arbitration Act (Legislative Decree No. 1071/2008).
14. Nathalie VOSER, *op. cit.*, fn. 1, this volume, p. 402.
15. See, for example, Arts. 1045 and 1046 of the Dutch Arbitration Act, allowing Dutch courts to intervene in issues of consolidation and joinder, and Chap. II, Title II, Arts. 149 and 150 of the Colombian Arbitration Act (Decree No. 1818/1998).

arbitration, which calls for expert knowledge of the field, parties are generally better off entrusting arbitral institutions or arbitrators to decide these questions. National courts, which are not specialized in arbitration and often have backlogs of cases, might not be well equipped to deal with these issues. Further, parties go to arbitration to avoid litigation before courts, and regulations leaving the solution of multi-party issues in the hands of national courts would go against that aim.[16]

*Third*, provisions of national laws often run the risk of mirroring prevailing multi-party rules in a litigation context. Thus, the scope of the powers vested in the courts might be too broad,[17] or the rules might simply reflect the treatment of third parties in court litigation procedures, as in the case of Colombia[18] or Italy.[19] The temptation to replicate court practices in civil litigation is clear because it is generally easier to find procedural rules dealing with third party joinder in national court proceedings.[20]

The Report recommends that national laws should not regulate multi-party issues, with the exception of rules to constitute the arbitral tribunal. I fully agree with this.

---

16. That might explain why, in the Netherlands, parties often exercise their right to opt out of the provision allowing Dutch courts to take decisions on consolidation, which proves that parties prefer to remain outside the scope of action of courts when dealing with complex procedural issues.
17. See, for example, Art. 1045 of the Dutch Arbitration Act, which calls for a broad discretion for national courts to decide on consolidation of parallel arbitral proceedings. From what I understand from Dutch arbitration practitioners, this has led the parties to often exercise their right to opt out of this provision.
18. In Colombia, for example, under Art. 149 of the Colombian Arbitration Act (Decree No. 1818/1998), if, due to the legal nature of the issues to be decided in the arbitration, the arbitral award affects the rights of a third party that did not sign the arbitration clause, the arbitral tribunal must order that the third party be notified, so that it can adhere to arbitration. If the third party decides not to adhere, the arbitration must be terminated. The third party intervention will be governed by the rules applicable to third parties under the Colombian Code of Civil Procedure (Art. 150).
19. Art. 816-*quater*, last paragraph of the Italian Code of Civil Procedure, provides: "If the situation contemplated by the first paragraph does not occur [joinder of third parties] and if the joining of parties to the proceedings be necessary by law (*litisconsorzio necessario*), the arbitration cannot proceed." As some Italian commentators note with regards to the amendments introduced in 2006 to the Italian Code of Civil Procedure: "The effect of the reforms involves a risk of making arbitration too similar to civil proceedings. Moreover, the excessively formal and legalistic character of the new legislation has the potential to influence negatively the effectiveness and speed of the proceedings," Daniele CUTOLO and Antonio ESPOSITO, "The Reform of the Italian Arbitration Law", 24 J. Int'l Arb. (2007, no. 1) p. 49.
20. Nathalie VOSER, *op. cit.*, fn. 1, this volume, p. 350. ("While state courts have well-established and predictable rules providing for multi-party proceedings and the joinder of third parties to pending court proceedings, which can be imposed on the parties to the proceedings as well as to third parties, this is not the case in arbitration.").

IV. JOINDER OF THIRD PARTIES (PARTICULARLY LATE JOINDER)

At the core of the debate on multi-party arbitration lies the question of whether the joinder of third parties to ongoing arbitral proceedings should be accepted. We will briefly examine this issue from the perspective of rule-making, by examining the different approaches already taken by law- and rule-makers.

An assessment of the different regulations, under existing national laws or arbitration rules on the question of joinder concludes that the topic does not have a uniform solution. There are divergent approaches to deal with the same basic question, that is, whether a joinder request should be admitted and under which conditions. From reviewing the rules containing provisions on joinder, it appears that there are at least four factors that may affect its outcome. *First*, whether the chosen rules include a provision on joinder. *Second*, if there is a provision, whether it requires the parties to agree to the joinder to proceed. *Third*, whether the provision is narrow and specific, or broad and general. *Fourth*, whether the provision admits a joinder only before the constitution of the Arbitral Tribunal, or also afterwards.

1.  *To Regulate or Not to Regulate?*

From a rule-making perspective, the first question revolves around the necessity to have provisions regulating joinder. There are two approaches: the "hands-off approach", or the lack of any specific regulation, and the "hands-on approach", which is reflected in the establishment of express provisions.

*a. The "hands-off approach"*

Under this policy, there are no express provisions dealing with joinder of third parties. This is the case under the 1976 UNCITRAL Arbitration Rules, most institutional and ad hoc arbitration rules, and national arbitration laws, which, save for the exceptions examined below, do not contain provisions on joinder.[21]

This approach questions what happens if there is a joinder request. Does the silence mean that the joinder cannot be accepted? It could be argued that if there is no express agreement from the parties or regulation from the chosen rules, joinder should not proceed. Interestingly, the lack of express regulation has not necessarily been construed as barring a joinder request. According to some practitioners, there would still be room to accept a joinder under the broad discretionary powers vested upon the arbitrators to conduct the proceedings under provisions such as Art. 15 of the 1976 UNCITRAL Arbitration Rules.[22]

---

21. See examples provided under fns. 14, 15 and 16. However, in general this is not the approach taken under national laws, which are much more cautious on this issue. Some authors rightly note that "... the different arbitration laws in general do not contain provisions dealing with the joinder of third parties or their intervention" (see, Julian LEW, Loukas MISTELIS and S. KRÖLL, *op. cit.*, fn. 4, p. 390).
22. See, Report of the Working Group on Arbitration on the Work of its Forty-Fifth Session (Vienna, 11-15 September 2006) UNCITRAL, 45th Sess., UN Doc. A/CN.9/614 (25 June-12 July 2007) p. 18 ("It was observed that practice showed that third parties were able to join arbitral

Nevertheless, from the end-users' perspective, the main problem with the "hands-off approach" is that it does not provide predictability or certainty on whether the joinder would proceed and, if so, what the conditions would be. Because there are no specific provisions laid down under the rules, the parties lose all their ability to predict, let alone control, the joinder outcome.

b.   *The "Hands-on Approach"*
The other approach is to establish express procedural rules dealing with joinder. This provides the benefit of indicating this possibility to the parties and eventually giving them the power to control, or at least predict, the outcome of a joinder request. In short, it provides greater certainty and predictability and, in some cases, also greater control. However, achieving these goals depends on the nature and scope of the joinder regulation.

2.   *To Agree or Not to Agree?*

In current joinder regulation, the first relevant question is whether the joinder acceptance depends on the parties' agreement. In other words, the parties' ability to control the joinder of a third party will vary, depending on whether the joinder rule requires an agreement to join. I have identified at least three different approaches under arbitration rules to answer this question:

a.   *The "full agreement approach"*
Under this approach, certain national laws and arbitration rules allow the joinder and reflect this acceptance through an explicit provision. Nonetheless, for the joinder equation to be successful, it is necessary for (a) the parties to the arbitral proceedings to agree; (b) the third party (or party requesting or seeking to be joined) to agree ; and (c) the arbitral tribunal to give it authorization.

The Netherlands Arbitration Act and the Belgian Judicial Code have both taken this approach. Art. 1045 of the Netherlands Code of Civil Procedure provides:

> "(1) At the written request of a third party who has an interest in the outcome of the arbitral proceedings, the arbitral tribunal may permit such party to join the proceedings, or to intervene therein. The arbitral tribunal shall send without delay a copy of the request to the parties.
> (2) A party who claims to be indemnified by a third party may serve a notice of joinder on such a party. A copy of this notice shall be sent without delay to the arbitral tribunal and the other party.
> (3) The joinder, intervention or joinder for the claim of indemnity may only be permitted by the arbitral tribunal, having heard the parties, if the third party

---

proceedings under the UNCITRAL Arbitration Rules and the Working Group agreed that there might not be a need to include an express provision on that matter in a revised version of the UNCITRAL Arbitration Rules.").

accedes by agreement in writing between him and the parties to the arbitration agreement.

(4) On the grant of a request for joinder, intervention, or joinder for the claim of indemnity, the third party becomes a party to the arbitral proceedings. Unless the parties have agreed thereon, the arbitral tribunal shall determine the further conduct of the proceedings."[23]

More recently, Art. 1696 *bis* of the Belgian Judicial Code has included a similar provision:

"1. Any affected third party may request the arbitral tribunal to intervene in the proceedings
2. A party may serve a notice of joinder on a third party.
3. In any event, in order to be admitted, the intervention of a third party requires an arbitration agreement between the third party and the parties in dispute. Furthermore, it is subject to the unanimous consent of the arbitral tribunal."[24]

On the level of arbitration rules, a good example of this policy is found in Art. 41(4) of the rules of the Netherlands Arbitration Institute (NAI):

"The joinder, intervention or joinder for the claim of indemnity may only be permitted by the arbitral tribunal, having heard the parties and the third party, if the third party accedes to the arbitration agreement by an agreement in writing between him and the parties to the arbitration agreement. On the grant of request for joinder, intervention or joinder for the claim of indemnity, the third party becomes a party to the arbitral proceedings."

A slightly more flexible variation of this approach is to accept the joinder if there is consent from the third party and no objection from the original parties to the ongoing proceedings. That is the case of Art. 26 of the 1997 Iranian International Commercial Arbitration Act, which seems to refer to the case of third parties who are strangers to the arbitration agreement, as it requires them to accept the arbitration agreement and rules and the arbitrator.[25]

Such provisions are particularly useful when the purpose is to admit the joinder of third parties who are foreign to the arbitration agreement, i.e., parties that did not originally consent to arbitrate. In these circumstances, the need for a global agreement would make sense as it would create a new arbitration agreement among the parties and the third party to be joined.

The problem is that these rules generally do not draw any line in the sand as to whether they refer only to joinder of third parties foreign to the arbitration agreement or to any joinder of third parties. Consequently, their practical benefit is limited because

---

23. English translation available at <www.kluwerarbitration.com> (subscription required).
24. English translation available at <www.kluwerarbitration.com> (subscription required).
25. Full text of the Iranian Law available at 15 J. Int'l Arb. (1998, no. 3) p. 42.

the parties can achieve the same result without a specific rule recognizing their ability to do so.[26] As one author states about the Dutch provision, this rule "brings criticism in that it does not distinguish the situations, notably the cases of joinder pursuant to the arbitration agreement of a party which remains a third party to the proceedings and of joinder of 'absolute third parties'", that is, parties who are not bound by the arbitration agreement".[27]

Additionally, in the case of third parties to the proceedings who wish or are sought to be joined and are truly parties to the arbitration agreement, this provision leads to what I believe is an unfair situation. While a claimant can always file arbitration against any of the parties bound by the arbitration agreement without the need for their consent, respondents would only be afforded this opportunity if both the arbitral tribunal and all the parties involved agree. In other words, the party that shoots first would obtain a clear procedural advantage.[28]

More importantly, because the truly complex cases of joinder are not those in which all the parties agree, but those in which the parties disagree on whether the joinder should proceed, such provisions are useless to solve these situations.

b. *The "partial agreement approach"*

Under this regime, the joinder may proceed if there is an agreement of one the parties to the arbitral proceedings and the third party sought to be joined.

Unlike the *full agreement approach*, this approach is more efficient as it may allow a joinder to proceed even if one of the parties to the proceedings objects to it, because it does not require the agreement of all the parties. Thus, the parties lose in terms of control of the joinder outcome, because the objection of one party is not enough to defeat the joinder request.

However, it still needs the agreement of the third party sought to be joined, which may frustrate the joinder when there are clear elements to suggest that this party is indeed a party to the arbitration agreement, but it refuses to participate in the proceedings for strategic or other reasons.

---

26. See Thomas BEVILACQUA, "Voluntary Intervention and Other Participation of Third Parties in Ongoing International Arbitrations: A Survey of the Current State of Play", 1 World Arbitration and Mediation Review (2006, no. 4) pp. 507-538 ("As such, these laws do not go beyond what would in any event likely have been the result achieved by the parties without the modified legislation.").
27. Alexis MOURRE, "*L'Intervention des Tiers à l'Arbitrage*", Gazette du Palais, (2001, no. 123) p. 27.
28. A similar objection was made within the Working Group discussing the revision of the 1976 UNCITRAL Arbitration Rules in connection to the current draft provision on joinder (see fn. 26). It was noted that the requirement of consent to join "would not be necessary as the provision already requires that the party to be joined should be a party to the arbitration agreement. The agreement of parties to apply UNCITRAL Arbitration Rules would imply their consent to the application of the joinder provision and to the possibility of the arbitral tribunal being constituted without their consent. Requiring additional agreement by the party to be joined would provide that party with a veto right, which may not be justified." Report of the Working Group on Arbitration on the work of its forty-ninth session (Vienna, 15-19 September 2008) UNCITRAL, 49th Sess., UN Doc. A/CN.9/665, pp. 24-25.

There are two salient examples of this approach, with substantial differences between them. The first is found under the LCIA Arbitration Rules and the second is Art. 15(4) of the Draft Revised UNCITRAL Arbitration Rules.

Art. 22.1.h of the LCIA Rules provides:

"1. Unless the parties at any time agree otherwise in writing, the Arbitral Tribunal shall have the power, on the application of one party or on its own motion, but in either case only after giving the parties a reasonable opportunity to state their views:

...

(h) to allow, only upon the application of a party, one or more third persons to be joined in the arbitration as a party provided any such third person and the applicant party have consented thereto in writing, and thereafter to make a single final award, or separate awards, in respect of all parties so implicated in the arbitration."

Art. 15(4) of the Draft Revised UNCITRAL Arbitration Rules provides:

"4. The arbitral tribunal may, on the application of any party, allow one or more third persons to be joined in the arbitration as a party provided such person is a party to the arbitration agreement and has consented to be joined. The arbitral tribunal may make an award in respect of all parties so involved in the arbitration."[29]

The common feature in both provisions is that they do not require the consent of all the parties to the arbitration, but they do require the consent of at least the party making the application and of the party or parties who are to be joined in the proceedings.[30]

The main difference, however, is that while the provision under the Draft UNCITRAL Arbitration Rules limits the joinder possibility to a "*party to the arbitration agreement*", the LCIA Rules remain silent on this issue. The consequence might not be trivial. Arguably, under the LCIA provisions, a party could bring into ongoing proceedings a third party foreign to the arbitration agreement, despite the objections of the opposing party in the arbitral proceedings on this same ground. This could cause problems with enforcing an arbitral award, due to the lack of an arbitration agreement among the parties to the proceedings and the third party joined.

---

29. "Settlement of commercial disputes: Revision of the UNCITRAL Arbitration Rules", Note by the Secretariat, UNCITRAL Working Group II (Arbitration) 49th Sess." (Vienna, 15-19 September 2008) UN Doc. A/CN.9/WG. II/WP. 151, p. 15. For the status of this proposed provision, see Nathalie VOSER, *op. cit.*, fn. 1, this volume, pp. 406-409.
30. Alan REDFERN, Martin HUNTER, Nigel BLACKABY and Constantine Partasides, *Law and Practice of International Commercial Arbitration* (2004) p. 32 (commenting on the LCIA provision in particular).

## c. The "no agreement approach"

Under this regime, there is no need for an agreement, full or partial, to join a third party to ongoing arbitral proceedings, which means that the party requesting the joinder of a third party to the arbitral proceedings may succeed, even if there are objections from (i) the opposing party, and (ii) the third party itself. The decision depends on the arbitral institution or the arbitral tribunal.

Interestingly, based on the same premise, there are contrasting approaches, such as the ICC current joinder practice, which has been labeled "conservative", on the one hand, and the Swiss Arbitration Rules, which have probably taken the most liberal approach on joinder, on the other.

The ICC current practice[31] is to admit the joinder of third parties where three conditions are met. First, the party or parties to be joined must have signed the arbitration agreement that is the basis for the arbitration. Second, the respondent must have claims against the party that it seeks to have joined. Third, the request for joinder must be made before any arbitrators have been appointed or confirmed by the Court, to ensure that the parties have had an equal opportunity to participate in the constitution of the arbitral tribunal and so as not to prevent the operation of Art. 10 of the Rules.[32]

On the other end, there are broad provisions that leave ample discretion to the arbitral institution or the arbitrators to decide whether the joinder should proceed. An illustrative example is found under Art. 4(2) of the Swiss Arbitration Rules:

> "Where a third party requests to participate in arbitral proceedings already pending under these Rules or where a party to arbitral proceedings under these Rules intends to cause a third party to participate in the arbitration, the arbitral tribunal shall decide on such request, after consulting with all parties, taking into account all circumstances it deems relevant and applicable."

Like the ICC approach, the Swiss Rules do not require the parties' agreement for a joinder to be admitted. Nevertheless, the Swiss provision does not specify requirements for the joinder to be accepted, but leaves the decision to the discretion of the arbitral tribunal.[33]

---

31. Until recently, the Court's approach to the issues raised in this regard was very restrictive. Unless the parties otherwise agreed, the Court did not permit respondents to join new parties to the arbitration proceedings (see Anne Marie WHITESELL and Eduardo SILVA ROMERO, "Multiparty and Multicontract Arbitration: Recent ICC Experience" in *ICC Special Supplement on Complex Arbitrations*, op. cit., fn. 2, pp.10-11; and Yves DERAINS and Eric SCHWARTZ, op. cit., fn. 5, p. 69). A full explanation of the ICC Court's past practice is found in J.L. DEVOLVÉ, "Final Report on Multi-Party Arbitrations", op. cit., fn. 3, pp. 41-43.
32. Yves DERAINS and Eric SCHWARTZ, op. cit., fn. 5, p. 72.
33. A similar approach has recently been taken by the new Arbitration Rules of the Madrid Court of Arbitration, in force since 1 January 2009. Art. 9(2) of these Rules provides: "The arbitrators may, at the request of any party and after hearing all of them, allow the appearance of one or more third parties as parties to the arbitration."

## 3. Narrow and Specific, or Broad and General Provisions?

Another factor that plays a critical role in the outcome of a joinder request is whether the regulation is narrow and specific, by establishing strict requirements for the joinder to be admitted, or broad and general, leaving a great degree of discretion to the body called to decide on this issue (arbitral institution or tribunal).

The ICC approach is clearly narrow in its scope and treatment of joinder. It only permits the joinder of signatory parties to the arbitration agreement on which the arbitration is based. This would, in principle, exclude parties foreign to the arbitration agreement and even non-signatory parties (which are allegedly bound by the arbitration agreement), as well as individuals or entities who are signatories in a different capacity than that of a party (i.e., guarantor).[34] Additionally, joinder may proceed only at the request of one of the Respondents and the request must be based on specific claims that are asserted against the third party. This requirement leaves out joinder at the third party's voluntary request, or joinder of a third party for reasons other than the existence of specific claims against it (i.e., to provide evidence, to defend the respondents' position). In principle, joinder is barred if it is sought once the arbitral tribunal has been constituted.

In contrast, there is a broad provision under the Swiss Rules, which, instead of setting forth conditions for the joinder, vest the arbitrators with the power to decide on such request, provided that the parties are previously heard on their position, and the arbitral tribunal assesses all other relevant circumstances. Further, the request may be made by the parties to the ongoing arbitral proceedings or by the third party.

The current proposal under the Draft Revised UNCITRAL Arbitration Rules is probably half-way between both solutions, as it leaves the arbitrators discretion to decide on the joinder. However, at the same time, it requires the consent of the third party joined and expressly limits the joinder to third parties who are parties to the arbitration agreement.[35]

From the end-users' perspective, a narrow and specific provision makes it easier to predict the outcome of the joinder. The ICC practice, leaving aside possible critics of the legitimacy of the three conditions and the unequal position in which it puts respondents,[36] already tells the parties that certain joinder requests (e.g., joinder of a party who is not a party to the arbitration agreement, a joinder request without asserting claims, or a joinder once the arbitral tribunal has been constituted) will not be

---

34. Although recent (still unpublished) cases seem to show a relaxation of this first condition as the ICC Court has been prepared to accept joinder of parties who signed an agreement related to the contract containing the arbitration clause (MOU, for example) or are otherwise mentioned or identified in the arbitration clause, or of parties who are successors-in-interest of the signatory parties to the arbitration agreement, or of guarantors provided that the scope of the arbitration agreement is broad enough so as to encompass disputes related to the guarantees (Simon GREENBERG, Presentation Delivered at ICC Young Arbitrators Colloquium, Paris, 19 January 2009).
35. In contrast, the LCIA Rules are arguably broader in that they accept the joinder of parties who are or might be strangers to the arbitration agreement.
36. Nathalie VOSER, *op. cit.*, fn. 1, this volume, pp. 392-393.

considered. Parties may not like it, but at least they can expect a certain outcome. A broad and general provision that leaves the decision to the arbitrators and does not provide specific requirements for the joinder makes it harder to predict the outcome.

4.     Ex-ante or Ex-post Joinder?

The impact of joinder regulation depends on whether it allows the joinder to proceed only before the constitution of the arbitral tribunal (*ex-ante* joinder) or whether it can also take place afterwards (*ex-post* joinder). In an *ex-ante* joinder, the third party joined still has the opportunity to participate in the constitution of the arbitral tribunal in the same way as the original parties to the proceedings, but in an *ex-post* joinder, this is not possible, in principle, because the arbitral tribunal is already in place.

A late joinder in which the third party has not been given the opportunity to participate in the constitution of the arbitral tribunal could give rise to an allegation of prejudice or unequal treatment to challenge the arbitral award or its enforcement.[37] Hence, for its relevance, we focus on this *ex-post* scenario in particular.

5.     Considerations on the Question of Late Joinder

In the case of a late joinder, it has been argued that the requirement for equality between the parties in the constitution of the arbitral tribunal could be compromised. That requirement would not be met where the third party is obliged to accept the arbitrators chosen by the original parties to the arbitration.[38] Nevertheless, it is important to identify in which cases the protection of such a requirement would be at risk as this does not always appear to be the case. Moreover, in situations in which this principle is exposed, it is important to assess possible solutions to eliminate or at least reduce the risks associated with the joinder.

*a.     Cases where the late joinder endangers the enforcement of the arbitral award*
Where the parties to the proceedings were given the right to participate in the constitution of the arbitral tribunal, and the third party that joined the proceedings late was deprived of this right, there might be an allegation of unequal treatment. However, there are some situations in which this does not happen.

In cases where the original parties to the proceedings were unable to agree on the sole arbitrator or the members of the arbitral tribunal (e.g., in multi-party cases) and, as a result, the arbitral tribunal was fully constituted by an arbitral institution or a national court, the third party could not raise an allegation of unequal treatment. The same goes

---

37. Clyde CROFT SC, Christopher KEE, William HO, "Report on Forty-Ninth Session of the UNCITRAL Working Group II (Arbitration)", Asian Pacific Regional Arbitration Group, available at <www.aprag.org> p. 67 ("More precisely, concern was expressed at the potential prejudice to a subsequently joined 'third party' who had not been able to take part in the constitution of the arbitral tribunal.").
38. Philippe FOUCHARD, Emmanuel GAILLARD and Bertrand GOLDMAN, *International Commercial Arbitration* (1999) p. 662.

for cases in which the parties to the arbitration agreement had already agreed on the arbitrators in the arbitration clause (although these are rare in international arbitration),[39] provided that the third party joined is also a party to the arbitration agreement.

That said, it is true that in most cases the original parties to the proceedings do participate – in one way or another – in the constitution of the arbitral tribunal. Does this automatically mean that third parties joined later in the proceedings would be put in an unequal position? Not necessarily. There are some solutions to avoid that a late joinder gives rise to enforcement problems due to this ground.

b.   *Possible solutions*

i.   First solution: No joinder after constitution of the arbitral tribunal

One way to avoid problems with late joinder is not to accept it: that is, for the joinder to proceed, it must always be requested before the arbitral tribunal is constituted. The rationale behind this is clear: the absence of consent from the joined party may lead to the arbitral award being challenged on grounds of irregularities in the constitution of the arbitral tribunal or unequal treatment of the third party. So far, this is the position the ICC has adopted.

Nevertheless, the main problem is that a party may only learn about facts causing it to want to join a third party, or the third party itself may learn about the arbitration and request its voluntary joinder, after the arbitral tribunal has been constituted. In this solution, the joinder would no longer be available.

ii.  Second solution: Joinder only if there is an agreement, or at least no objections (particularly from the third party), to the constitution of the arbitral tribunal

This solution would limit the possibilities of joinder to situations where all the parties concerned, that is, the parties to the proceedings and the third parties joined, agree on the constitution of the arbitral tribunal. However, there would be no risk of an allegation of unequal treatment.[40]

In a more flexible variation, the parties' non-objection would act as a waiver to any challenges to the arbitral award based on the grounds that the third party did not participate in constituting the arbitral tribunal. Even the original parties to the proceedings may have objections if, for example, as a result of the joinder of the third party, independence or impartiality issues affect one or more of the arbitrators, or the claims related to the third parties have special features that require an arbitrator with different expertise and skills. Therefore, while it appears that this should only concern the third party, it might affect any of the parties.

---

39. Alexis MOURRE, *op. cit.*, fn. 27, p. 31.
40. As noted during the discussions within the Working Group revising the UNCITRAL Arbitration Rules: "An alternative approach ... was a suggestion that once the arbitral tribunal had been constituted general consideration of prejudice safeguards by the arbitral tribunal would not be sufficient to protect the third party sought to be joined and, consequently, the consent of that party should be required," Clyde CROFT SC, Christopher KEE, William HO, *op. cit.*, fn. 37, p. 67.

The problem with this approach is that, if there is no agreement on the constitution of the arbitral tribunal, or one of the parties raises objections, there is no fallback solution allowing the joinder to proceed.

iii. Third solution: Joinder subject to the arbitral tribunal's discretion after considering the risks of accepting it

Some modern arbitration rules such as the Swiss Rules or, more recently, the Court of Madrid Arbitration Rules, grant the arbitrators the power to decide on the joinder. In doing so, the arbitrators will assess the risks of accepting the joinder, such as possible allegations of unequal treatment by the third party sought to be joined. This solution is also supported by the ongoing discussions on the revision of the UNCITRAL Arbitration Rules.[41]

Under this approach, the arbitrators would decide whether, even when faced with objections from parties, there would be a question of unequal treatment that could compromise the validity of the arbitral proceedings and, ultimately, of the arbitral award.

In other words, merely asserting an objection or lack of agreement on the constitution of the arbitral tribunal would not suffice to reject a joinder request, except when the arbitral tribunal considers its acceptance detrimental to the proceedings.

iv. Fourth solution: Replacing the arbitrators and reconstituting the arbitral tribunal

Another solution that has been endorsed mostly as a fallback position is that when, upon a joinder request, the parties do not agree on the constitution of the arbitral tribunal, they may replace the arbitrators and constitute a new arbitral tribunal. Ms. Voser proposes this alternative as part of a "balance test" that allows recourse to this exceptional remedy *"where the counterparty is responsible for the fact that the Claimant did not extend its claims to the third party from the beginning"*.[42] She further distinguishes whether the third party joined has the same or divergent interests as one of the original parties to the proceedings, to determine if only one co-arbitrator or both of them should be replaced.

This view is supported by the ICC Report on Multi-party Arbitrations, which notes that when the arrival of a new party in the dispute raises the problem of the arbitrator's independence and neutrality, or his or her intellectual or professional ability to deal with the matter, this *"could be resolved, for example, simply by following the ordinary procedure applying for the replacement of arbitrators"*.[43]

While this formula might seem inefficient, as Ms. Voser acknowledges, it offers a compromise to allow a joinder filed late because one of the parties concealed relevant information to identify the parties against which the claims should have been asserted. The problem, in my view, is who should make that finding. If the arbitral tribunal has

---

41. "Support was also expressed for a provision being included in paragraph (4) of Article 15, expressly requiring the arbitral tribunal to hear the views of the parties and assess any prejudice which may occur as a result of the joinder." Clyde CROFT SC, Christopher KEE, William HO, *op. cit.*, fn. 37, p. 67.
42. Nathalie VOSER, *op. cit.*, fn. 1, this volume, p. 389.
43. J.L. DEVOLVÉ, *op. cit.* fn. 3, p. 38.

to rule on this question, it will be placed in an uncomfortable situation, having to decide an issue that could automatically lead to its own replacement. Would not this prevent the arbitrators from taking action? Conversely, if an arbitral institution has to intervene, it is unlikely that it would be well equipped and entitled to make that finding. Hence, while I accept the assumption suggested in Ms. Voser's Report, I feel it would be difficult to implement in practice.

6.  *Conclusion: Agreement to Join or Agreement to Arbitrate?*

The review above shows that the joinder regulation is far from being harmonized and, as a result, the outcomes may vary substantially. However, we can draw general conclusions.

First, a hands-off approach offers no *predictability* on whether a joinder may proceed without agreement of the parties, and on the outcome of a joinder request. In contrast, the hands-on approach offers, to a greater or lesser extent, some predictability as to the outcome.

Second, depending on the approach taken, the parties have more or less *control* over the outcome of a joinder request made by one of them. The closer we get to a full-agreement approach, the greater the degree of control that the parties retain over the joinder outcome. However, the closer we get to a no-agreement approach, the lesser the degree of control the parties have. The reason is simple: Under the rules requiring the parties' agreement, they will always retain some degree of control over whether the joinder can proceed, whereas, under the no-agreement approach, the parties lose complete control over the outcome, the decision depending solely on the arbitral institution or the arbitrators.

Why are there rules that require the parties' agreement to accept the joinder?[44] This requirement seems necessary because the joinder alters the way the proceedings have been structured so far, and this needs the parties' agreement. I do not share this position. While the claimant has the right to file claims against several respondents that are parties to the arbitration agreement, without seeking their permission, the same principle should apply for respondents who wish to file counterclaims not only against the claimant, but also or exclusively against third parties who are parties to the arbitration agreement. As the Report mentions, this is a matter of equal treatment.[45] In exceptional circumstances, however, express consent to join might amount to new consent to arbitrate if the joinder relates to a party that is foreign to the arbitration agreement binding the original parties.

Thus, the threshold question should not be whether the parties or the third party agree to the joinder, but whether they have agreed to arbitrate.

This means that if there were objections to the joinder, either from one of the parties or from the third party sought to be joined, the arbitrators would have to decide the core issue of whether the third party is a party to the arbitration agreement. The problem is that certain rules do not require the arbitrators to go through this analysis. As Ms. Voser

---

44. Both the full-agreement approach and the partial-agreement approach require that the parties (at least some of them) and the arbitrators agree on the joinder.
45. Nathalie VOSER, *op. cit.*, fn. 1, this volume, p. 357.

puts it, "it might be that provisions which regulate the issue of joinder not only override the lack of consent to joint proceedings but also the lack of consent to arbitrate with the parties to the original arbitration". In this respect, I find provisions allowing the joinder of a third party who is not necessarily a party to the arbitration agreement risky, particularly if the joinder of a stranger or foreign third party is accepted despite objections from one of the parties to the ongoing arbitral proceedings. For the same reason, it is best for regulations admitting the joinder of a party who is foreign to the arbitration agreement to adopt a full agreement's approach, so that such subsequent consent may be deemed a new agreement to arbitrate among the parties to the ongoing proceedings and the third party.

Third, the impact of this multi-party regulating trend is yet to be seen. Some have suggested that it will lead to a proliferation of joinder of third parties. Although conclusions at this point would be speculative, I doubt it. During my time at the ICC, I experienced the ICC's shifting policy from a "full-agreement approach" to a "no-agreement approach" for acceptance of joinder of third parties. While the number of joinder requests increased over those years, as the multi-party arbitrations increased, the increase was not dramatic and, more importantly, cases in which there was a clear abuse of this device remain the exception. Policy decisions on whether joinder rules should be implemented must consider the general needs and potential risks associated with them, and not the exceptional cases and pathological situations. Abusive joinder requests are still part of the exceptional and pathological members of the arbitration family.

In addition, there are a number of other control mechanisms to avoid abuses. If there is a narrow and specific joinder rule, the control is provided by the requirements set out by the rule itself. If there is a broad and general provision, the control should be ensured by the quality of the arbitral institution and the arbitrators, who should avoid reaching results inconsistent with what the parties could have expected when agreeing to arbitrate. If the arbitrators are good enough to repel frivolous claims, dismantle dilatory fishing expeditions or counter unjustified anti-arbitration injunctions, I believe they can also do well in taking measures to deter groundless or abusive requests for joinder.

Finally, I fully agree with Ms. Voser in that there are no perfect solutions and each rule owes its scope to a particular policy or approach.[46] However, I have particular sympathy for a no-agreement approach limited to parties who are bound by the arbitration agreement, as it respects the basic principle of party autonomy and provides for greater efficiency because the joinder outcome does not depend on the agreement of all or some of the parties involved in the proceedings.[47] In my view, the core question

---

46. Nathalie VOSER, *op. cit.*, fn. 1, this volume, p. 406. ("The balance is very difficult to strike and there is no right or wrong. Each institution has to decide for itself where it wants to be positioned in the arbitration market.").
47. A full-agreement approach might prove an interesting solution for joining third parties to an ongoing arbitration (i.e., parties who are not parties to the underlying arbitration agreement). This approach would, under those circumstances, amount to a new arbitration agreement between the parties to the arbitration and the third party. For this to happen, it is not necessary to have a provision establishing this solution, but parties can always achieve this result.

should not be whether there is an agreement to join the third party, but whether there is an agreement to arbitrate.[48]

## V. THE OVERALL ASSESSMENT

### 1. Practical Considerations

We have seen that there is a fundamental *"whether"* question, i.e., whether regulation is desirable. I believe it is. On a purely practical level, the lessons are clear: draft the arbitration clause carefully and choose the arbitration rules (and the seat of arbitration) wisely. Drafting the arbitration clause to foresee solutions to multi-party issues is undoubtedly the best and most predictable way to tackle potential problems. Rule-making should always remain a default solution to help parties who, out of ignorance or a deliberate strategy, have not agreed to solve these issues from the outset. As mentioned earlier, the arbitration clause does not exist in a vacuum.

Then, we face the *"who"* question, i.e., accepting that regulation is necessary, who should make the decisions on issues such as joinder or prima facie acceptance of a multi-party request for arbitration? From a practical level, it would be most efficient to vest these powers in arbitral institutions and arbitrators rather than in national courts.

Finally, there is the *"how"* question. As the market for international arbitration becomes more diversified and the offer in terms of arbitration laws and rules expands, the users should be aware of the potential consequences of choosing a given set of provisions, either under national laws or arbitration rules. Our brief review shows that there are divergent approaches to deal with similar issues, giving different, often contrasting, results. Knowledge and understanding of the clients' needs and risks in a potential arbitration will help with choosing the appropriate set of rules to predict how to achieve, or to avoid, issues such as joinder or consolidation in arbitral proceedings. If, for example, there is a risk of having to litigate against non-signatories to the arbitration agreement and your client might be placed in a respondent's position, then enquiring about joinder possibilities under the arbitration rules is a necessary exercise in the arbitral due diligence process.

### 2. Theoretical Considerations

On a more philosophical level, current issues in multi-party disputes show that core principles in arbitration are not fully aligned, which creates underlying tensions when developing international arbitration.

*First*, when discussing the *constitution of the arbitral tribunal*, tension seems to appear between due process and the party's right to appoint the arbitrator of its choice. Due

---

48. As noted by de Boisesson, "one party of the proceedings, claimant or defendant, is always entitled to request other parties to participate in the proceedings, as long as it can prove that they are indeed parties, not to the proceedings, but to the arbitration agreement", Matthieu DE BOISESSON, *Le Droit Francais de l'Arbitrage* (1990) p. 534.

process is the safeguarding of the parties' equal treatment and, if multiple parties on one side have conflicting interests, solutions enabling an institution or a national court to constitute the whole arbitral tribunal might be warranted. But when equal treatment is not an issue, why should an arbitral institution sacrifice the party's right to appoint the arbitrator he or she best sees fit? As the Report concludes, a balance test should be struck to avoid defeating the parties' autonomy in the name of due process, when no due process is compromised.[49]

*Second*, when it comes to joinder of third parties, there seems to be tension between efficiency and fair administration of justice,[50] on the one hand, and party autonomy,[51] on the other. Most of the advantages in favor of joinder of third parties refer to a more efficient procedure. However, these principles cannot be used to go beyond the limits imposed by the parties' consent. Again, a balance test might favor joinder without infringing the boundaries of party autonomy, when the joinder is admitted without requiring an agreement to join, but simply an agreement to arbitrate.[52] For the same reason, joinder of third parties foreign to the arbitration agreement would require a subsequent agreement of all parties involved to respect the parties' consent.

Finally, confidentiality and privacy have been underscored as one of the main advantages of international commercial arbitration and particularly valued by end-users.[53] However, recent developments in arbitral practice show that issues such as third-party intervention in arbitrations involving states create tension between transparency, on the one hand, and confidentiality, on the other.[54] In the context of investment arbitration, there is a movement towards greater transparency that might be at odds with the principle of confidentiality, but it may still permeate into the more general field of international arbitration involving state parties.

In short, the current state of rule-making shows that there are different approaches to the most recurring issues in a multi-party context, which have different outcomes. One may wonder to what extent the policies behind these are influenced by the priority

---

49. I believe that solutions calling for some degree of discretion, such as ICC or LCIA or Draft Revised UNCITRAL Rules, establishing that the institution "may" as opposed to "shall" appoint all the members of the arbitral tribunal, should be preferred to those establishing a mandatory duty to constitute the whole tribunal, such as those found under German Institution of Arbitration, Netherlands Arbitration Institute or SCC Rules.
50. Nathalie VOSER, *op. cit.*, fn. 1, this volume, p. 350.
51. Nathalie VOSER, *ibid*, p. 351.
52. Emmanuel GAILLARD, "The Consolidation of Arbitral Proceedings and Court Proceedings" in *ICC Special Supplement on Complex Arbitrations, op. cit.*, fn. 2.
53. Price Waterhouse Report, "International Arbitration. Corporate Attitudes and Practices" (2006) p. 7.
54. Nathalie VOSER, *op. cit.*, fn. 1, this volume, pp. 351 and 382. See, also, L. Yves FORTIER and Stephen DRYMER, "Third Party Intervention and Document Discovery", 4 Journal of World Investment, (June 2003, no. 3) p. 473; Andrew TWEEDDALE, "Confidentiality in Arbitration and the Public Interest Exception", 21 Arb. Int. (2005, no. 1) p. 59; and "Confidentiality and Third Party Participation: *UPS v. Canada* and *Methanex Corporation v. United States*", 21 Arb. Int. (2005, no. 2) p. 211.

rule-makers give to some of these principles. As long as these tensions remain in place, the same issues will find different, or even contrasting, approaches and solutions.

VI.   CONCLUSIONS

Rule-making is an evolving process that must keep pace with the new realities that international arbitration faces. Multi-party disputes are undoubtedly one of them. Only a decade ago, there were hardly any rules dealing with joinder, consolidation and third-party intervention. Thus, experience is recent, and we are still testing the results and identifying the right policies.

In a seminal paper on this topic called "Multi-partite Arbitrations: An Agenda for Law-makers," Lord Mustill, referring to consolidation in general terms, said:

> "The theoretical difficulties of consolidation are manifold and the topic can become very complex if approached *a prior*. Might there not be something to be said for approaching the problem from the other end, by collecting and collating those instances where consolidation has been attempted in practice; the means adopted; the practical success or otherwise of the exercise; the occurrence and outcome of any proceedings to challenge or to enforce the consolidation order and the resulting award? This will permit the identification of practical needs, and set the enquiry on the road to reliable and useful solutions – even if on a modest scale."

Lord Mustill can be satisfied that what we sought at the ICCA Conference in Dublin, under the guidance of an extraordinary report, was to enquire *"about reliable and useful solutions, even if on a modest scale"*.[55]

---

55. Lord MUSTILL, "Multi-Partite Arbitrations: An Agenda for Law-Makers", 7 Arb. Int. (1991, no. 4) pp. 401-402.

# Working Group B

## 2. Consolidation of Claims

# Multiple Claims in Arbitration Between the Same Parties

*Michael Pryles\* and Jeffrey Waincymer\*\**

| TABLE OF CONTENTS | Page |
| --- | --- |
| I. Introduction | 437 |
| II. General Principles of Jurisdiction | 439 |
| III. Claimant's Claims | 443 |
| IV. Respondent's Claims | 448 |
| V. Consolidation | 463 |
| VI. Addition of New Claims | 470 |
| VII. Synthesis and Analysis | 474 |
| VIII. Avenues of Management | 494 |
| IX. Conclusions | 497 |

## I. INTRODUCTION

When a dispute arises between parties there may be a multitude of claims which are made. In part this is because international commercial relations are becoming ever more complex. Often there are long-term relationships involved, perhaps with framework and ancillary contracts. More than one might give rise to disputes. At times there are differing contracts relating to trade and investment on the one hand and payment and guarantees on the other. Within any contract there may also be multiple claims flowing backwards and forwards as to the performance of each party.[1] At times these may be non-contractual claims that nevertheless relate to the central transaction. Where the parties have agreed to arbitrate disputes a question therefore arises as to whether all the claims between them, or only some, can be referred to the arbitral tribunal which has been constituted. It is thus of fundamental importance to consider how arbitration can or should deal with the entire range of multiple claims that might be brought between the same parties.

These questions are interesting and complex and not yet fully explored on a comprehensive basis, with the bulk of the analysis to date relating to specific sub-

---

\* Immediate past President of the Australian Centre for International Commercial Arbitration and the Asia Pacific Regional Arbitration Group; former Court member of LCIA and ICC; Member of ICCA.

\*\* Professor of International Trade Law, Monash University; Australian government-nominated ICSID arbitral panelist; World Trade Organization Panelist.

1. Some commentators describe claims flowing in both directions between claimant and respondent as "cross-claims". We refrain from using this term as others limit it to the quite discrete question of whether one respondent is able to bring separate claims as against other existing respondents or third parties. See for example Eduardo SILVA-ROMERO, "Brief Report on Counterclaims and Cross-Claims: The ICC Perspective" in *Arbitral Procedure at the Dawn of the New Millennium: Reports of the International Colloquium of CEPANI*, 15 October 2004, p. 73.

elements such as counterclaims, set-off, consolidation or the proper treatment of ensemble contracts. These discrete but related questions should be distinguished from the problems posed by multi-party arbitrations, which have attracted more attention in the literature. This Report is confined to multiple claims in arbitrations between the same parties. This conference has a parallel publication in relation to multi-party arbitration.[2] While we are not exploring those issues, it is ultimately important to consider whether the same principles or challenges apply in that context.[3] We thus invite readers to consider whether there is or ought to be consistency of approach in the treatment of each distinct topic.

When an arbitration is commenced between two parties a number of discrete questions can therefore arise:

(i) Which claims can be put forward by the claimant?
(ii) Which claims can be put forward by the respondent?
(iii) Can the claimant and the respondent subsequently add new claims?
(iv) If separate proceedings are commenced between the same parties (a second arbitration or litigation), can the two proceedings be consolidated or otherwise harmonized?

The questions posed presume that the parties are not in agreement, as they may of course agree between themselves to allow or bar claims or consolidated tribunal hearings. Where instead arbitrators are asked to decide on such disputed preliminary questions, there is a need to identify the principles by which such determinations should be made. At times, arbitrators are given some discretionary leeway, in which case they will naturally consider the practical ramifications of their decisions. It is immediately obvious that if not all claims are dealt with in one arbitration between the two parties, and if two or more proceedings are commenced, there may be much less efficiency in terms of expense and time as well as the risk of inconsistent decisions. On the other hand, if distinct claims are brought together against the wishes of one party, this might offend against the very foundations of consent as the basis of arbitration. It may also lead to a tribunal dealing with an issue in situations better suited to a differently constituted tribunal.

Even if the different claims ought to be heard before different dispute resolution bodies, each tribunal might then have additional procedural decisions it must make in

---

2. Nathalie VOSER, "Multi-party Disputes and Joinder of Third Parties", this volume, pp. 343-410.
3. We note for example that Bernard Hanotiau, who has done significant work on the topic of multi-party arbitration, footnoted a major article by saying that while that problem area is generally referred to as multi-party arbitration, his work "adopts a slightly different perspective in as much as it examines the various problems raised by the resolution of disputes originating from a network of contracts". In his view, "(t)he subject is more general, as well as being more specific": Bernard HANOTIAU, "Complex Arbitrations: Multi-Party, Multi-Contract, Multi-Issue and Class Actions", 14 Arbitration International (1998) p. 369, fn. 1. He has also written a book on the subject: Bernard HANOTIAU, *Complex Arbitrations Multiparty, Multicontract, Multi-issue and Class Actions* (2005). Similarly, the Committee on International Commercial Arbitration of the International Law Association considered all of these issues under the heading of "Complex Arbitrations".

order to promote the greatest fairness and efficiency between the matter before it and the parallel or sequential proceedings. At the very least, each tribunal cannot ignore as a matter of course, the existence and procedural implications of parallel proceedings.

While we have identified a number of discrete questions for consideration, our methodology seeks to combine general and specific analysis. We begin by examining principles of jurisdiction in general as a precursor to the examination of the discrete questions. We then address the existing rules, cases and scholarly opinions which have in the past addressed each distinct issue. We then seek to bring the various discrete questions together to see if it is possible to identify broad policy considerations which should guide answers to each of these questions and then consider the various solutions which may be adopted. We then draw attention to some of the proposals for revised arbitral rules to resolve these questions which various institutions and groups, in particular the UNCITRAL Working Group on International Arbitration and Conciliation, are being asked to consider. The Report also briefly addresses some procedural choices that tribunals might face, both where multiple claims are allowed and where they are denied.

In aiming to discern whether there are some common principles that might apply, we have sought to identify the various methods and criteria that have been applied in the case law or which are recommended by commentators to resolve the approach which should be taken to multiple claims. We note that some authors follow a *conflicts* methodology; some are primarily concerned with identifying *efficient* solutions; while others are concerned to limit themselves to questions of *consent*. Our overall thesis is that while there are a number of theories that are relevant, the starting point should always be a question of consent. What did the parties agree to? Conflicts and efficiency analyses should best be seen as elements of a determination of consent rather than alternative paradigms. We will also seek to show why better guidance is needed from the parties themselves, either via the drafting of their arbitration clause or via selection of institutional rules that carefully articulate admissibility criteria.

II.  GENERAL PRINCIPLES OF JURISDICTION

Leaving aside the special case of arbitrations mandated by treaty or legislation, it is a trite principle that arbitration is dependent on the existence of an agreement between the disputant parties, and that the terms of the arbitration agreement define and therefore limit arbitral jurisdiction. This is a reflection of the role of consent as the basis of arbitration. Because of the potential importance of questions of consent to our topic, we feel that before examining the admissibility of claims, counterclaims, set-off and the possible consolidation of multiple proceedings, it will be useful to recall general principles of jurisdiction which limit and will therefore guide questions of claim admissibility.

There are in fact two separate questions:

— Which matters can be or must be referred to arbitration? and
— Following the commencement of an arbitration, which matters have been properly referred to that arbitration?

The two questions are separate and should not be confused. Generally an arbitration agreement provides for the arbitration of future disputes which may arise between the parties and is included in their substantive contract. In other cases, an arbitration agreement is sometimes entered into after a dispute has arisen and is solely confined to the arbitration of that identified dispute (submission). In the more common case of an arbitration agreement covering future disputes, it will apply to disputes which arise between the parties during the currency of their contract and sometimes after the contract has terminated. In some cases, it can deal with disputes about precontractual negotiations. In each of these situations, the clause is a continuing one which is capable of application to more than one dispute which may arise between the parties.

On the other hand once a dispute has arisen and a tribunal has been appointed, that tribunal is authorized to resolve the matter referred to it but not necessarily any matter which may subsequently arise between the parties even if it is encompassed within the arbitration agreement. An arbitral tribunal is not a standing body empowered to hear any dispute which arises between parties during the currency of a contract but is empowered to hear a particular dispute or disputes.

In relation to the first question, we first turn to a consideration of the scope of matters that may be referred to arbitration under the arbitration agreement.

*1. Scope of Arbitration Agreement*

If the primary way to consider the admissibility of multiple claims is through the paradigm of consent, it is natural to turn to the arbitration agreement itself which is the gateway to consent to arbitrate. Thus, rather than working from particular instances such as claims, counterclaims, set-off and applications for consolidation, one might instead naturally begin by identifying the scope of the arbitration agreement to try and see what if anything can be discerned about the parties' intent as to multiple claims.[4]

It is rare for an arbitration agreement to provide for the arbitration of any disputes which may arise between the parties without any further qualification. Typically the agreement will provide for the arbitration of disputes arising from a particular relationship, usually the substantive contract in which it is embedded. Indeed the definition of an arbitration agreement contained in Art. II(1) of the Convention on the Recognition and Enforcement of Foreign Arbitral Awards 1958 (the New York Convention) refers to an agreement in writing under which the parties undertake to submit to arbitration all or any differences which have arisen or which may arise between them "in respect of a defined legal relationship, whether contractual or not...". Art. 7(1) of the UNCITRAL Model Law on International Commercial Arbitration (the Model Law) is in similar terms. Thus an arbitration agreement providing for the arbitration of disputes "arising under this contract" would not, prima facie, appear to apply to the arbitration of disputes relating to another contract. At one time it was thought that such an agreement would not apply to the arbitration of ex-contractual claims such as those

---

4. Indeed Poudret and Besson address "the particular case of set off" in the section of their work dealing with the scope of the arbitration agreement ratione materiae: Jean-Francois POUDRET and Sebastien BESSON, *Comparative Law of International Arbitration*, 2nd edn. (2007).

based on tort or founded on statute. However now it is accepted that such claims fall within an arbitration clause provided that they bear a sufficient nexus to the contractual relationship established between the parties. Similarly, earlier views that an arbitral tribunal cannot determine the initial validity of a contract have now largely been abandoned.[5]

When interpreting the scope of an arbitration agreement, it will often be necessary to consider the applicable law, including the proper approaches to interpretation. It has long been recognized that under the doctrine of separability, an arbitration agreement may have a different applicable law to the balance of any contract within which it is found. Mark Blessing has noted nine possible laws that could apply in such circumstances.[6] Some scholars suggest that the normal position is to apply the lex arbitri. This might be justified on the basis that this is the law expressly referred to in Art. V(1)(*a*) of the New York Convention in the context of one of the discretionary bases for refusing enforcement. Another possible justification is that the place most closely connected to an agreement to arbitrate would be the seat of arbitration, where such a closest-connection conflicts rule is seen as most applicable. Others such as Lew, Mistelis and Kroll[7] and Redfern and Hunter[8] suggest that the law governing the subject matter might best apply, an option provided for by Art. 178(2) of the Swiss statute on Private International Law.[9]

At the very least, we should be aware that problematic questions of consent in determining the scope of an arbitration agreement will often be bound up with equally complex conflict of laws questions. For example, complexities may arise if a potential set-off emanates from a different arbitration agreement which in turn could call for a different applicable law. Even where the set-off emanates from the same agreement, if the conflict approach adopted is to look for the law most closely connected to the individual claim, that may differ between claims and various forms of counterclaims. Some legal systems draw a distinction between counterclaim and set-off and link the substantive law of the set-off to the law of the primary claim on the basis that the law of a defence should follow the law of the claim. We address this further below in Sects. IV.*2* and IV.*3*. At this stage we merely wish to highlight the potential interplay between conflicts methodology and determinations of the scope of the arbitration agreement.

Others eschew a strict conflicts approach, preferring a broader-ranging factual analysis. Blessing invites a consideration of all salient factors with a view to determining

---

5. See, for example, Emmanuel GAILLARD and John SAVAGE, eds., *Fouchard, Gaillard Goldman on International Commercial Arbitration* (1999) pp. 210-211 (hereinafter *Fouchard Gaillard Goldman*).
6. Marc BLESSING, "The Law Applicable to the Arbitral Clause and Arbitrability" in *Improving the Efficiency of Arbitration Agreements and Awards: 40 Years of Application of the New York Convention*, ICCA Congress Series no. 9 (1999) p. 168.
7. Julian LEW, Loukas MISTELIS and Stefan KRÖLL, *Comparative International Commercial Arbitration* (2003) p. 121.
8. Alan REDFERN, Martin HUNTER, Nigel BLACKABY and Constantine PARTASIDES, *Law and Practice of International Commercial Arbitration*, 4th edn. (2004) pp. 124-125.
9. Federal Code on Private International Law of 18 December 1987.

what is "objectively fair and subjectively reasonable" in all the circumstances.[10] We return to consider these alternative methodologies in our concluding analysis.

2. *Particular Reference*

Once a dispute falling within the terms of the arbitration agreement arises, a party may refer it to arbitration. The tribunal, once constituted, is not empowered to continue indefinitely, or at least for the duration of the contract, and hear any and all disputes which arise throughout the duration of the contract. The jurisdiction conferred on the arbitrator is dependent on the matters referred to him or her for decision.

Mustill and Boyd[11] state that an arbitrator has no jurisdiction over disputes which were not in existence when the appointment was made.[12] However it does not logically follow that an arbitrator has jurisdiction over all disputes which exist at the time of his or her appointment. The parties may only refer one or some of the disputes to the arbitrator and not others.[13]

In an ad hoc arbitration the dispute will generally be that identified in the notice of arbitration served by the claimant, although it is arguable that the respondent's response or defence is also relevant in clarifying the ambit of the dispute.

In an ad hoc arbitration under the UNCITRAL Arbitration Rules, the arbitration is commenced by a Notice of Arbitration. The Notice of Arbitration may but does not have to contain the statement of claim.[14] If it does not, it would still seem that the Notice of Arbitration would have to give some details of the dispute to be referred to arbitration. It would unlikely be adequate for a Notice of Arbitration simply to refer existing disputes that have arisen to arbitration. In this regard it should be noted that Art. 21 of the UNCITRAL Model Law states that:

> "Unless otherwise agreed by the parties, the arbitral proceedings in respect of a particular dispute commence on the date on which a request for that dispute to be referred to arbitration is received by the respondent."

The reference to "that dispute" suggests a specified and identified dispute.

In an International Chamber of Commerce (ICC) arbitration the claimant initiates the proceedings by filing a Request for Arbitration under Art. 4 of the ICC Rules of Arbitration with the Secretariat of the ICC International Court of Arbitration. The

---

10. BLESSING, above fn. 6.
11. Michael MUSTILL and Stewart BOYD, *The Law and Practice of Commercial Arbitration in England*, 2nd edn. (1989) p. 129.
12. It could of course be possible to expressly authorize an arbitrator to have such jurisdiction, for example through nominating a particular construction referee to deal with allowances claims. That may not be desirable if the unavailability of the arbitrator could render the agreement pathological: *Ibid.*
13. The need to define a dispute for the purposes of determining the arbitrator's jurisdiction is well recognized in the English cases. See for example *Kawasaki Kisen Kaisha, Ltd v. Government of Ceylon*, [1962] 1 Lloyd's Rep 424.
14. UNCITRAL Arbitration Rules, Art. 18(1).

Request must contain, inter alia, "a description of the nature and circumstances of the dispute giving rise to the claim(s)" and "a statement of the relief sought". The respondent is then required to file an Answer which may contain counterclaims. This is done prior to the constitution and establishment of the tribunal. It is certainly arguable, therefore, that in ICC arbitrations the initial ambit of the dispute is determined by both the Request for Arbitration and the Answer to the Request, and the claimant's reply to any counterclaim filed in accordance with Art. 5(6) of the ICC Rules of Arbitration. Thereafter the ambit of the dispute referred to arbitration is more particularly defined in the Terms of Reference, made in accordance with Art. 18 of the ICC Rules, and which might be seen as constituting a new arbitration agreement at least if signed by both parties.[15] Other leading institutional rules would lead to similar conclusions.

The Report now proceeds to examine the existing nature, rules and differences in view as to each particular type of claim; those of the claimant, counterclaims and set-offs by respondent and the related question of consolidation of proceedings.

III. CLAIMANT'S CLAIMS

It is, of course, for the claimant to formulate the claims which it seeks to put forward in an arbitration. The claimant will be limited by the terms of the arbitration agreement which will define matters which the parties have agreed can be referred to arbitration. This usually can be done by reference to a particular contract and by specifying the relationship which the claims must possess to that legal relationship.

Even if the claims bear the necessary connection with the defined legal relationship and therefore prima facie fall within the jurisdiction of the tribunal, it is sometimes contended that the claims cannot be put forward because there is no "dispute" between the parties. The English texts generally refer to the need for a dispute and define the arbitrators' jurisdiction in terms of the dispute which has been referred to him or her. In the opinion of Mustill and Boyd[16] the need for a dispute is not a rule of law but arises simply because in the great majority of cases that is what the arbitration agreement says. For example if a claim is made for payment of monies due under a contract and it is clear that the respondent has no defence and seeks to raise no defence other than its impecuniosity, is there a "dispute" which can be referred to arbitration? In our opinion there is a dispute because the claim has been made and has not been satisfied. In any event such esoteric arguments can be avoided by drafting an arbitration clause to include a "claim" and a "difference" as well as a "dispute". Well-drafted clauses allow for all disputes which could conceivably flow from the contract between the parties. Nothing should turn on the distinction between terms such as "dispute" and "difference".[17]

It might also be contended that an arbitrator has no jurisdiction with respect to a claim concerning a difference of opinion as to the future performance of a contract. However we submit that a sufficiently widely drawn arbitration agreement should enable a party

---

15. *Commonwealth Development Corporation v. Montague*, [2000] QCA 252.
16. MUSTILL and BOYD, above fn. 11.
17. *Fouchard Gaillard Goldman*, above fn. 5, p. 299 (fn. 248).

to seek a declaration as to the meaning of a contract which is relevant for its future performance.

The more significant limitation to the jurisdiction of an arbitral tribunal, and the claims which can be put forward, is by reference to the subject matter of the claim. It is to this matter that we now turn.

Until recently English courts adopted a pedantic approach to the construction of an arbitration agreement. They focused on the words employed and drew fine distinctions between the terms used. Thus some judges took the view that a clause referring disputes "arising under" a contract was narrower than a clause referring disputes "arising out of" a contract[18] and it was commonly accepted that a clause referring disputes "in relation to" or "in connection with" a contract was broader and therefore conferred a more extensive jurisdiction on the arbitral tribunal. These fine distinctions were particularly relevant in relation to the question of whether an arbitral tribunal had jurisdiction to hear disputes concerning pre-contractual representations,[19] rectification[20] and claims founded on statute for misleading and deceptive conduct or for breach of competition law.[21]

In contrast to the strict and pedantic construction of arbitration clauses adopted in many common law jurisdictions, civil law jurisdictions are often more liberal and tend to construe arbitration agreements in a broader way. However it seems that the difference between the classic common law approach and the more liberal civil law approaches may now have disappeared. The recent decision of the House of Lords in *Premium Nafta Products Limited v. Fili Shipping Company Limited*[22] marks a change in the position adopted in the United Kingdom. In that case the House was concerned with arbitration clauses in eight charterparties. The relevant clause gave each party an election to refer "any dispute arising under this charter..." to arbitration in London. One of the questions for determination was whether the clause was, as a matter of construction, broad enough to cover the question of whether the contract was procured by bribery. Lord Hoffmann observed:

> "Both of these defences raise the same fundamental question about the attitude of the courts to arbitration. Arbitration is consensual. It depends upon the intention of the parties as expressed in their agreement. Only the agreement can tell you what kind of disputes they intended to submit to arbitration. But the meaning

---

18. *Heyman v. Darwins Ltd*, [1942] AC 359, 399.
19. See the decision of the Supreme Court of South Australia in *Main Electrical Pty Ltd v. Civil & Civic Pty Ltd*, [1978] 19 SASR 34.
20. See *Printing Machinery Co Ltd v. Linotype and Machinery Ltd*, [1912] 1Ch 566.
21. There are many Australian cases examining whether claims under the Trade Practices Act 1974 (Cth) are arbitrable. See for example the early decisions in *White Industries v. Trammel* (1983) 51 ALR 779 and *Allergan Pharmaceuticals Inc v. Bausch and Lombe Inc* (1985) ATPR 40-636. Compare the more recent approach in *Comandate Marine Corp v. Pan Australia Shipping Pty Ltd* (2006) 238 ALR 457. As to claims involving breach of competition laws see the liberal decisions of the United States Supreme Court in *Mitsubishi Motors Corp v. Soler Chrysler-Plymouth Inc*, 473 US 614 (1984) and the decision of the High Court of New Zealand in *Attorney-General v. Mobil Oil NZ Ltd*, [1989] 2 NZLR 649 which are instructive.
22. [2007] UKHL 40.

which parties intended to express by the words which they used will be affected by the commercial background and the reader's understanding of the purpose for which the agreement was made. Businessmen in particular are assumed to have entered into agreements to achieve some rational commercial purpose and an understanding of this purpose will influence the way in which one interprets their language.
(....)
If one accepts that this is the purpose of an arbitration clause, its construction must be influenced by whether the parties, as rational businessmen, were likely to have intended that only some of the questions arising out of their relationship were to be submitted to arbitration and others were to be decided by national courts. Could they have intended that the question of whether the contract was repudiated should be decided by arbitration but the question of whether it was induced by misrepresentation should be decided by a court? If, as appears to be generally accepted, there is no rational basis upon which businessmen would be likely to wish to have questions of the validity or enforceability of the contract decided by one tribunal and questions about its performance decided by another, one would need to find very clear language before deciding that they must have had such an intention."

Having regard to these considerations, Lord Hoffmann said that the court was required to give effect, so far as the language used by the parties would permit, to the commercial purpose of the arbitration clause. He then referred to earlier English decisions and further observed, with considerable frankness, that the fine distinctions drawn in these cases "reflect no credit upon English commercial law". He then stated the new approach which should henceforth be adopted:

"In my opinion the construction of an arbitration clause should start from the assumption that the parties, as rational businessmen, are likely to have intended any dispute arising out of the relationship into which they have entered or purported to enter to be decided by the same tribunal. The clause should be construed in accordance with this presumption unless the language makes it clear that certain questions were intended to be excluded from the arbitrator's jurisdiction."

Lord Hoffmann concluded that the language of the arbitration clause contained nothing to exclude disputes about the validity of the contract, whether on the grounds that it was procured by fraud, bribery, misrepresentation or anything else.
In summary, an appropriately drafted arbitration clause will enable a claimant to put forward claims concerning the contract itself and in respect of pre-contractual representations, associated claims in tort and statutory claims (including competition law matters) concerning the conduct attendant upon the negotiations and conclusion of the contract and its effect.
An interesting question which has arisen is whether a claimant is confined to putting forward claims with respect to the contract that is referred to in the arbitration agreement or can also put forward claims with respect to other contracts. This matter

445

has been analyzed, primarily from the perspective of French law, in an interesting and informative article by Philippe Leboulanger.[23] This matter is also addressed by Bernard Hanotiau in a very detailed article published in 2001, and a subsequent manuscript.[24] We briefly address their comments in the context of additional claims of claimant but return to the question of multiple contracts in a discrete section below (Sect. VII.4) where we examine the rationale for allowing both claims and counterclaims from distinct contracts. We examine competing justifications based on consent, efficiency and conflicts methodology. At this stage we analyze the issue in the context of the claimant's claims alone.

Accordingly to Leboulanger, the classic theory of contract holds that each individual agreement within a group of contracts is a completely independent agreement. But he goes on to say that this traditional notion does not correspond to current contractual practice. He says that whenever there is an economic link between contracts, ensuing from the contracts' nature and mutual function, these agreements should not be regarded as autonomous agreements but should be analyzed together with all the other related contracts. He makes reference to French doctrine and case law and also to decisions of certain arbitral tribunals. As an example he refers to the ICSID award delivered in *Klockner v. Cameroon*.[25] There the tribunal adopted a "commercial reality" analysis and, applying the law of the Republic of Cameroon, considered that the reciprocal obligations constituted a single legal relationship despite the existence of separate and successive instruments governing the rights and obligations of the parties. In another arbitration[26] an arbitral tribunal, applying the law of Luxembourg, came to a different conclusion on the facts and did not consider two agreements as a single legal relationship because "both the intentions of the parties and the language of the relevant legal instruments do not permit such an application".

Leboulanger proceeds to provide guidelines for determining whether multi-contract situations should be treated as a whole. The first criterion is to see whether the agreements make up one single business transaction in the sense that the obligations are undertaken for the accomplishment of a single goal and are economically interdependent. A second criterion is the wording of the contracts concerned. He says that agreements may be considered to be interrelated when they were concluded on the same date, for the same duration, for the same purpose. Another indication of interrelationship is the presence of a master agreement outlining the obligations undertaken by the parties which are more particularly described in ancillary agreements. Sometimes the recitals to an agreement will refer to other agreements and thereby establish their interdependence. Essentially, Leboulanger is addressing the evidentiary

---

23. Phillipe LEBOULANGER, "Multi-contract Arbitration", 13 Journal of International Arbitration (1996) p. 43.
24. Bernard HANOTIAU, "Problems Raised by Complex Arbitrations Involving Multiple Contracts, Parties and Issues: An Analysis", 18 Journal of International Arbitration (2001) p. 253; Bernard HANOTIAU, *Complex Arbitrations Multiparty, Multicontract, Multi-issue and Class Actions*, op. cit., fn. 3.
25. Award of 21 October 1983, 2 ICSID Reports (1986) 9.
26. ICC Award in Case No. 6829 of 1992.

factors in light of which a tribunal might accept that there was consent to multiple claims. One possibility is an inference of consent to arbitrate disputes based on one contract under an arbitration agreement in another contract. Alternatively, there might be a finding of consent to add disputes under the contract without an arbitration agreement, to disputes raised under the contract with such an agreement.

Hanotiau examines a number of French cases where the courts have uniformly considered that if two agreements between the same parties are closely connected and one finds its origin in the other or is the complement or implementation of the other, the absence of an arbitration clause in one of the contracts does not prevent disputes arising from the two agreements being submitted to an arbitral tribunal and being decided together.

The question is then if the two contracts are interconnected and may be regarded as forming one legal relationship, when can a claimant put forward claims with respect to each of the contracts in the one arbitration proceeding? In this regard it is necessary to distinguish a number of situations. The first case is where one contract contains an arbitration agreement and the second contract does not contain any dispute resolution agreement. In this situation French theory would appear to hold that the claimant may put forward claims founded on both contracts in the one arbitration. The lack of an arbitration agreement in the other contract is presumably seen as more of an oversight or explained on the basis that repetition was unnecessary given the intended closeness of the contracts, rather than evidence that the parties prefer litigation over arbitration for disputes arising under it.

If each contract contains an arbitration clause in identical terms the traditional view is that the claimant can commence an arbitration and put forward claims based on both agreements in the one arbitration. Leboulanger says that it is reasonable to infer that the parties' intention was to consider the two agreements as one unified and indivisible transaction "and this is the reason why the arbitration clause was repeated, in identical terms, in each one of the agreements".[27]

Where the two agreements contain differing arbitration or jurisdictional clauses the traditional view is that it is unlikely that claims founded on both agreements can be put forward in the same arbitration.[28] The practice of the ICC International Court of Arbitration is explained by Anne-Marie Whitesell and Eduardo Silva-Romero in a recent paper.[29] Whitesell and Silva-Romero observe that for the ICC Court to decide that a single arbitration shall proceed on the basis of multiple contracts, three criteria must be fulfilled. The first is that all contracts must have been signed by the same parties. The second is that all contracts must relate to the same economic transaction. Thirdly the dispute resolution clauses contained in the contracts must be compatible. The authors referred to a recent case where the Court decided that a single arbitration would not

---

27. LEBOULANGER, above fn. 23, p. 77.
28. HANOTIAU, "Problems Raised by Complex Arbitrations Involving Multiple Contracts, Parties and Issues: An Analysis", above fn. 24, p. 329.
29. Anne Marie WHITESELL and Eduardo SILVA-ROMERO, "Multiparty and Multi-contract Arbitration: Recent ICC Experience" in *ICC International Commercial Arbitration Bulletin Special Supplement* (2003) p. 7.

proceed on the basis of two contracts, given that one of the contracts contained an ICC arbitration clause and the other submitted disputes to the jurisdiction of the Paris courts. In another case the Court decided that a single arbitration would not proceed on the basis of two arbitration agreements contained in different contracts, one of which referred to Paris and the other to Geneva as the place of arbitration. The Court also decided that a single arbitration could not proceed on the basis of two arbitration agreements referring to different methods for constituting the arbitral tribunal. The authors explain that when making such decisions the Court endeavours to respect and follow the parties' intentions as expressed in their arbitration agreements. They note that there was one arbitration which the court allowed to proceed on the basis of multiple contracts, despite the fact that the contracts provided for different applicable substantive laws.

A more expansive approach might be based on a view that where there are differing dispute resolution clauses, it is at least arguable that the intent of each was simply to explain what to do with *single* claims but not multiple claims. Clear evidence that the parties want single disputes to be in different fora is not necessarily conclusive evidence that they would not want that matter raised in a different forum as a joint claim. We do not seek to refute the traditional presumption, but instead point to the desirability of a more nuanced analysis. We address this further in a section below (Sect. VII.4) dealing more comprehensively with multi-contract situations.

IV.  RESPONDENT'S CLAIMS

*1.  Introduction to Claims by Respondents*

We address the treatment of respondent's claims by first separately considering counterclaims and set-off defences. We then seek to integrate that analysis with the consideration of claimant's claims and consolidation of multiple hearings with a view to determining whether common principles might apply to each.

A *counterclaim* is usually seen as a claim brought by a respondent in a civil suit against the claimant that is independent of the primary claim. The term is used in contradistinction to a *set-off* which is seen as a defence to the primary claim. Because it is not simply a defence, a counterclaim leads to a separate judgment which may be in excess of the judgment under the primary claim. Furthermore, the counterclaim remains alive even if the initial claim is withdrawn. Thus it is truly a reverse claim and not a defence as such. Because a counterclaim remains alive even if the primary claim is withdrawn or invalid, it must be based on its own independent evidence of consent. As always, such consent should be found to emanate from the arbitration agreement itself, either directly or through a lex arbitri that expressly allows for counterclaims. Even then the counterclaim should be linked to the original arbitration agreement. Numerous scholars support this view.[30]

---

30.  Vladimir PAVIĆ, *Counterclaim and Set-Off in International Commercial Arbitration* (2006) p. 104; Gary BORN, *International Commercial Arbitration*, 2nd edn. (2001) p. 298; *Fouchard Gaillard Goldman*, above fn. 5, pp. 660-661; REDFERN, et al., above fn. 8, p. 295.

While a counterclaim is normally a distinct action, at times it might be raised on a conditional basis, that is to say, the tribunal might only be asked to consider it should it find prima facie liability under the primary claim.[31] This would not alter its distinct nature, however.

Civilian systems describe set-off claims in differing ways, the essential meaning of which is *compensation*.[32] The case of set-off in international economic arbitration was comprehensively analyzed by Klaus Peter Berger in 1999.[33] As his important contribution shows, the proper treatment of set-off claims is far more complex and controversial than that of counterclaims. Berger notes the particular problem facing international commercial arbitration. On the one hand, given that there is no harmonized view as to the nature and ambit of set-off within domestic legal systems, arbitral rules would be reluctant to be too prescriptive. On the other hand, these very complexities together with the lack of prescription forces arbitrators to try to find a justifiable methodology for the treatment of such claims.

For our purposes, the distinction between set-off and counterclaim is important in terms of finding evidence of consent to admissibility. As we will discuss below in Sect. IV.3 in relation to set-off defences, the consent-based logic that some commentators employ is to the effect that parties must have intended that all relevant defences can be raised against claims. It is suggested that a contrary position would offend against the most fundamental principles of justice, due process and fairness. Thus there is a presumption in allowing set-off defences to be admissible.

While we explain below why we believe that those presumptions need more careful consideration, a different analysis is required with counterclaims. It is to this that we now turn.

*2. Counterclaims*

*a. Admissibility of counterclaims*

As noted, a counterclaim must find a jurisdictional basis within the arbitration agreement that supported the primary claim, although that could emanate from a finding that multiple contracts, only some of which contain arbitration clauses, are sufficiently connected to allow this to occur.

A properly drawn agreement would allow for both claims and counterclaims under the contract that contains the arbitration clause. It is the connection to the contract and not who makes the claim that matters, although there can still be consent issues as to the constitution of the tribunal which should hear the case. We noted at the outset that tribunals are not standing dispute settlement bodies. Thus a counterclaim that only arises

---

31. Final Award in ICC Case No. 7314 of 1995, ICCA *Yearbook Commercial Arbitration* XXIII (1998) (hereinafter *Yearbook*) p. 49.
32. Descriptions in other languages include *compensación, compensazione, Aufrechnung, Verrechnung* and *verrekening*.
33. Klaus Peter BERGER, "Setoff in International Economic Arbitration", 15 Arbitration International (1999) p. 53.

after a tribunal is constituted would not fit within the particular reference to arbitration, unless permitted under the arbitration agreement or the institutional rules.[34]

Even where the events giving rise to the counterclaim arose before the constitution of the tribunal, there may still be fairness considerations, particularly as to tribunal composition and particularly as counterclaims under some procedural systems do not need to be notified prior to tribunal composition. In such circumstances if one party's concern is raised as a claim, the other party sees the contention in the Notice of Arbitration and can select an arbitrator with the issues in dispute in mind. Conversely, where a counterclaim is notified after the constitution of the tribunal, there can be a legitimate question as to whether the parties have consented to *that* tribunal hearing a reverse claim that was unknown to at least one of the parties when the initial arbitration was commenced. This issue might not be a problem where the clause expressly refers to counterclaims, as parties may consent to that imbalanced situation.

There are other strategic concerns. Most commentators also see a counterclaim as one that can only be brought by a respondent as against the claimant. Thus a respondent cannot raise claims against other respondents or against third parties under any express permission to raise counterclaims.[35] Critics point to the strategic corollary that this leaves the claimant with the sole right to designate the parties to the arbitration. Not only does that suggest some due process imbalance, but this may also be an economic incentive to bring claims so as to take the preferred position as claimant.[36]

There are a number of other permutations that arise in multi-contract situations. The simplest question concerns a counterclaim arising under the same arbitration agreement. Another would be a counterclaim based on a different arbitration agreement. A third is a counterclaim on a matter on which there is no arbitration agreement. A fourth possibility is a counterclaim on a matter subject to a forum agreement.[37] The permutations were already alluded to in the previous section on claimant's claims and arise again in the context of set-off. We have noted that we will deal with these permutations in Sect. VII.4 below that considers the interplay between differing contracts and dispute settlement clauses as they might apply to all of the claims and reverse claims covered in this article.

Before leaving this question, however, we again wish to point out the complex consent questions that these permutations throw up and caution against simplistic presumptions. There are a number of possible ways of dealing with these scenarios, with different presumptions of consent. As noted above, the strict view is that different clauses show an intent to have the other disputes only heard in the other place. Hence the first tribunal rejects the counterclaim. A second option is to not consider the

---

34. Cf. Art. 19 ICC Rules.
35. If claims between respondents or joinder of third parties can be allowed under the notion of counterclaims, this would raise significant problems in terms of consent overall and in terms of key logistical questions such as appointment of the tribunal: Michael BÜHLER and Thomas WEBSTER, *Handbook of ICC Arbitration*, 1st edn. (2005) p. 77. These and other challenging issues in multi-party arbitration are dealt with in the parallel Report by Nathalie VOSER, op. cit., fn. 2, this volume, pp. 343-410.
36. BÜHLER and WEBSTER, above fn. 35.
37. *Ibid.*

counterclaim but wait until the outcome of the other forum to decide whether there is indeed a net amount that should be ordered to be paid between one party and the other.

An alternative approach might be to interpret the second dispute settlement clause to see if it was showing *exclusive* intent about disputes regardless of whether they arose by way of claim or counterclaim, or instead, whether the only intent was in relation to *primary* claims. The latter argument suggests that where parties say that certain claims will be brought in one forum, they are only speaking of the obligations of the *claimant* in commencing an action. Such clauses, the argument proceeds, say nothing about when and why that same issue could instead be brought as a counterclaim in a matter already brought elsewhere. Even if this view is appealing, it does not presume that there is automatic jurisdiction to hear the counterclaim under the first clause. All it says is there is no presumptive evidence of a lack of intent to allow this to occur.

As always, the parties could resolve these ambiguities by carefully delineating in their arbitration agreement which counterclaims, if any, are permitted. In the absence of a clear delineation in their agreement, guidance may be found within the arbitral rules which might apply. It is to this that we now turn.

*b.   Counterclaims and arbitral rules*
In the absence of express agreement by the parties in their arbitration clause to the allowance of counterclaims, the next possibility is that they have indicated a similar choice through their selection of a seat and its attendant lex arbitri and/or their selection of arbitral rules.

The various lex arbitri and procedural models fall into two broad categories. One group simply states that counterclaims may be brought or identifies the time limits within which they can be brought. This category does not seek to identify the degree of connection required for the counterclaim to be admissible. An example of this arises in Art. 9 of the Swiss Rules of International Arbitration (the Swiss Rules).[38] Within this category a distinction should also be drawn between rules expressed in the form of the Swiss Rules and those which, while not defining the degree of connection required for a counterclaim to be admissible, refer to "*any* counterclaim" (emphasis added) brought by a respondent. Rules which provide for counterclaim in this way include the following: Art. 4(1) of the Singapore International Arbitration Centre (SIAC) Rules,[39] Art. 5(3) of the Australian Centre for International Commercial Arbitration (ACICA) Rules,[40] Art. 13(1) of the China International Economic and Trade Arbitration Commission (CIETAC) Rules,[41] Art. 2(b) of the London Court of International Arbitration (LCIA)

---

38. "Any counterclaim or set-off defence shall in principle be raised with the Respondent's Answer to the Notice of Arbitration."
39. "The Respondent shall send a Response within 14 days of receipt of the Notice of Arbitration which shall contain:... (b) a brief statement of the nature, circumstances and quantification, if any, of any *envisaged* counterclaims...." (Emphasis added)
40. "The Answer to Notice of Arbitration may also include: any counterclaim...."
41. "Within forty-five (45) days from the date of receipt of the Notice of Arbitration, the Respondent shall file with the CIETAC its counterclaim in writing, if any."

Rules,[42] Art. 36(b) of the World Intellectual Property Organization (WIPO) Expedited Arbitration Rules,[43] and Art. 5(b) of the Hong Kong International Arbitration Centre Short Form Arbitration Rules.[44] Whether the use of the word "any" instead of "a" to qualify the class of counterclaim has the significance of broadening the class of admissible counterclaims is a matter for further consideration, although in our view that is unlikely to have been the clear intention of the drafters of those rules.

A similar general reference is provided by Art. 2(f) of the UNCITRAL Model Law which simply states that the provisions of the law apply to a counterclaim.[45] An indirect reference is found in ICC Rule 30(5) which clarifies the inclusion of counterclaim and set-off amounts in the advance on costs.[46]

Other rules seek to define the linkage required for admissibility. One group takes a conservative approach, limiting admissibility to counterclaims from the same contract. For example, UNICTRAL Arbitration Rules (UAR) Art. 19(2) and (3) speak of counterclaims "arising out of the same contract". Under UAR, if it is from the same contract, the accepted view is that it does not need to be limited to contractual claims. The test might be broader if it referred to counterclaims "relating to" the same contract, a view alluded to by Christopher Kee in his article addressing this topic.[47] There is no equivalent in the UNCITRAL Model Law although the Working Group suggested the Model Law should be interpreted with a similar restrictiveness to UAR.[48] Art. 22(3) of the ACICA Rules is worded to give effect to a broader formulation: "… the Respondent may in its Statement of Defence … make a counterclaim or claim for the purpose of a set-off, *arising out of, relating to or in connection with* the contract". (Emphasis added)

---

42. "Within 30 days of service of the Request on the Respondent, (or such lesser period fixed by the LCIA Court), the Respondent shall send to the Registrar a written response to the Request (the Response), containing or accompanied by:… (b) a brief statement describing the nature and circumstances of any counterclaims advanced by the Respondent against the Claimant."
43. "Any counter-claim or set-off by the Respondent shall be made or asserted in the Statement of Defense.…"
44. "Within 14 days of receipt of the Claimant's Statement of Claim case file, the Respondent shall submit to the Arbitrator and to the Claimant a Statement of Defence containing:… (b) any counterclaim, together with a brief statement of the remedies sought.…" However, the purview of the WIPO Rules generally may be understood to envisage a wider scope for the arbitrability of counterclaims when provisions allowing for counterclaim are read alongside Art. 70(d) of the Arbitration Rules: "Where the amount of the counter-claim greatly exceeds the amount of the claim or *involves the examination of significantly different matters* … the Center in its discretion may establish two separate deposits on account of claim and counter-claim." (Emphasis added)
45. "For the purposes of this Law: … *(f)* where a provision of this Law, other than in articles 25*(a)* and 32(2)*(a)*, refers to a claim, it also applies to a counter-claim, and where it refers to a defence, it also applies to a defence to such counter-claim."
46. "If one of the parties claims a right to a set-off with regard to either claims or counterclaims, such set-off shall be taken into account in determining the advance to cover the costs of arbitration in the same way as a separate claim insofar as it may require the Arbitral Tribunal to consider additional matters."
47. Christopher KEE, "Setoff in International Arbitration – What Can the Asian Region Learn?", 1 Asian International Arbitration Journal (2005, no. 2) p. 148.
48. BERGER, above fn. 33, p. 64.

Another group takes a different approach to the linkage test and draws attention to the same *arbitration agreement* or the same *relationship* rather than the contract per se. See for example Art. 3(2) of the National Arbitration Rules of the American Arbitration Association (AAA) and Art. 7(a) of the Rules of Arbitration and Conciliation of the International Arbitral Centre of the Austrian Federal Economic Chamber (Vienna Rules). Similarly the AAA International Arbitration Rules provide that "a respondent may make counterclaims or assert set-offs as to any claim *covered by the agreement to arbitrate*",[49] and that "[a] party may not amend or supplement a claim or counterclaim if the amendment or supplement would *fall outside the scope of the agreement to arbitrate*".[50] (Emphasis added) This is shared to a degree by the ICSID Rules of Arbitration, Art. 40(1) of which provides that "a party may present an incidental or additional claim or counter-claim arising directly out of the subject-matter of the dispute, provided that such ancillary claim is within the scope of the consent of the parties and is otherwise within the jurisdiction of [ICSID]".[51]

c.   *Theories with respect to counterclaims*
There does not appear to be controversy with respect to the need for distinct consent to underlie a counterclaim. The key difference in view is based on the evidentiary standards and methods of determining consent. This will either involve interpretation of the arbitration agreement or the lex arbitri and procedural rules. The more broadly the terms are drafted, the easier it is to allow a counterclaim. The biggest problem is with rules that simply allude to the procedural steps required, without attempting to define an admissibility standard. Even rules that have attempted such a definition have rarely dealt with the question with enough precision to guarantee certainty and consistency.

A "same relationship" test obviously allows for at least some multi-contract situations but is also likely to lead to differing responses from tribunals, with some looking to an expansive interpretation, while others might take a more circumspect approach to controversial fact situations.

Even with a broader formulation, admissibility under multi-contract situations would still need to be linked back to an agreement to arbitrate found within one contract that, because of the integrated nature of the various contracts, is held to be broad enough to encompass claims under distinct contracts.

3.   Set-off

a.   *Introduction to set-off*
As noted above, the term counterclaim is used to describe an independent claim that is not in the nature of a defence. Set-off, on the other hand, is seen as a defence.

If the set-off is allowed and established, it has a number of implications. Because the set-off is limited in amount to the totality of the original claim, there can be no monetary award in favour of a person raising it. Furthermore there is no need for separate awards

---

49. AAA International Arbitration Rules, Art. 3(2).
50. AAA International Arbitration Rules, Art. 4.
51. ICSID Rules of Procedure for Arbitration Disputes, Art. 40(1).

on claim and set-off defence. The other corollary of this is that if the claim is not made out or is withdrawn, there is no need to adjudicate upon the set-off. A set-off merely provides a defence to the claim. Hence it operates "as a shield, not as a sword".[52]

From the time that an adjudicator finds in favour of the set-off right, it will either operate retrospectively or prospectively depending upon whether the applicable law provides for automatic application or application from the time of the notice or perhaps even the time of judgment. This can affect rights to interest and measurement of damages. It might also often have different costs implications to counterclaims, although costs will of course be a discretionary matter. By way of example, if a set-off is a full defence, a tribunal might order costs in favour of a respondent who has succeeded in entirely blocking the claim. On the other hand, a successful set-off that only partially reduces the primary claim, might still see the claimant successful on costs to the extent of the net amount. Conversely, where both a claim and counterclaim are successful, each successful party might anticipate costs on their successful element.

While a set-off is normally raised by a respondent, it could also be raised by a claimant against a counterclaim brought by a respondent.[53] On the other hand, one set-off cannot be brought as against another set-off.

While these propositions are clear, much of the law of set-off is contentious and varies greatly between different legal families. This makes it difficult to determine what the general treatment of sef-offs should be under international arbitration. For this reason, we turn now to a consideration of the differences in views between legal families as to the nature of set-off in the context of considering admissibility factors within international arbitration.

b.     *The nature of set-off*
For an arbitrator, there are both procedural questions as to admissibility, and substantive questions as to the inherent nature of set-off. One of the complexities in dealing with set-off is that some legal systems treat it as substantive while others treat it as procedural. Even within some legal systems different types of set-off fall into each category.[54] Berger notes that the long-standing dispute as to whether set-off was procedural or substantive in nature under civil law was decided in favour of the latter view.[55] For the purposes of this Report the more it is seen as substantive, the more it might be argued to inherently undermine the claim and hence be admissible. The more it is procedural, the more it is seen as an efficiency measure that simply aims to reduce total transaction costs in resolving multiple claims.[56]

---

52. *Stooke v. Taylor*, [1880] 5 QB 569, 575 as cited in BERGER, above fn. 33, p. 60.
53. See for example ICC Award in Case No. 3540 of 1980, reprinted in Michel JARVIS and Yves DERAINS, eds., *Collection of ICC Arbitral Awards (1974-1985)* (1990) pp. 105, 112, 399, 402.
54. BERGER, above fn. 33, p. 54.
55. *Ibid.*, p. 55.
56. In some domestic legal systems efficiency arguments even mean that some counterclaims, where sufficiently linked to the primary claim, must be pleased or they will be lost under principles of res judicata, e.g., Rule 13 of the United States Federal Rules of Civil Procedure (2007) which distinguishes between compulsory and permissive counterclaims. Aeberli notes that the distinction in arbitration has become blurred because it emanated from domestic legal systems but has been

As is discussed below, even this distinction does not necessarily lead to differing outcomes as many see efficiency factors as key guides to implied consent. As we suggest below, efficiency arguments are more justifiable when linked to consent. Efficiency factors might then apply indiscriminately to both procedural and substantive reverse claims. This concern to discern the intent of the parties on a case-by-case basis cautions against automatic transplanting of domestic litigation notions of set-off into the field of international commercial arbitration. The aim of avoiding multiplicity of litigation underlying common law allowance of set-off rights is in the main about efficient use of the courts and allocation of taxpayers' money, not about the original intent of the litigants.[57] The point is simply that the consent logic differs greatly depending on which view of set-off we begin with.

As noted above, Professor Klaus Peter Berger has made a major study of set-off in international arbitration.[58] As to substantive issues, Professor Berger has also noted and analyzed a recent attempt to articulate harmonized principles of set-off through the 2004 edition of the UNIDROIT Principles of International Commercial Contracts (UPICC).[59] Art. 8.1 UPICC states:

> "(1) Where two parties owe each other money or other performances of the same kind, either of them ('the first party') may set off this obligation against that of its obliger ('the other party') if at the time of set-off,
> (a) the first party is entitled to perform its obligation;
> (b) the other party's obligation is ascertained as to its existence and amount and performance is due.
> (2) If the obligations of both parties arise from the same contract, the first party may also set off its obligation against an obligation of the other party which is not ascertained as to its existence or to its amount."[60]

---

reduced in significance in some jurisdictions because of procedural reforms: Peter AEBERLI, "Abatements, Setoff and Counterclaims in Arbitration Proceedings", 3 Arbitration and Dispute Resolution Law Journal (1992, no. 1) p. 2.

57. The history of the establishment of statutory set-off shows other reasons why it has little direct relevance for arbitral matters. Aeberli notes that the legislation sought to remove the potential injustice if a defendant might be imprisoned for non-payment of debts when in fact money was owed in the other direction: Ibid., p. 4, citing *Stoke v. Taylor* (1880) 5 QBD 569; *Green v. Farmer* (1786) 4 BURR 2214. A statutory remedy was required to deal with this as equity had only established set-off rights for connected transactions.

58. BERGER, above fn. 33, p. 53.

59. Klaus Peter BERGER, "Set-off" in *ICC International Commercial Arbitration Bulletin Special Supplement* (2005) p. 17.

60. Principles of European Contract Law, reprinted in O. LANDO, E. CLIVE, A. PRÜM and R. ZIMMERMANN, eds., *Principles of European Contract Law* (2003) Arts. 13:101 and 13:102(1). Similar principles have been articulated by arbitral tribunals.

There are also similar rules on set-off in Part III of the Principles of European Contract Law (PECL) published in 2003.[61] Case law has articulated similar principles. For example ICC Award in Case No. 3540 suggested that:

> "according to the general principles of law, non-contractual set-off is subject to four cumulative conditions: similarity and reciprocity of the subjects, performances of an identical nature, the claims should be certain and liquid, and finally maturity of the claims (i.e., not subject to a time limit)".

Like most harmonization exercises, the UNIDROIT draft or such arbitral articulations of principle must either express a preference for the views of one legal family over others, or find some compromise point between each. Compromises are often suboptimal, often papering over remaining differences in view between negotiators. Such negotiating fora might seek a compromise simply in order to further the cause of harmonization, leaving it to later jurisprudence to make some key refinements.

In such instances, arbitrators stating a preference for one theory of set-off might do so because they see a preferred uniform policy position or because they adopt a conflicts methodology and follow this to the legal family from which particular principles are identified. The purpose of this Report is not to analyze set-off per se via a consideration of all of these factors. It is instead to determine the admissibility of multiple claims between parties within the field of international commercial arbitration. Hence a comparative analysis of differences between legal systems and the principles articulated by UNIDROIT should be looked at primarily in helping us decide whether set-off should be allowed as of right and if not, by what other principle should admissibility be determined on a case-by-case basis.

Berger suggests rightly that the historical perspective may help us understand the different concepts of set-off. In most contentious issues of legal policy, we are faced with potential conflicts between fairness and efficiency and the subsidiary elements of certainty versus flexibility. Hence, Roman law saw the establishment of the right of set-off as an exception to the historical procedural formalism of classical Roman law which did not initially even allow reverse claims arising from the same contract.[62] From an early equitable basis, the right expanded to claims arising out of the same contract to then encompass claims outside of that contract. That progression in Roman law led civilian legal systems to develop the right using notions contemplating either set-off or the alternative description, compensation.[63] Where the common law is concerned, it also began with the notion of equitable set-off in relation to claims that were sufficiently connected.

Perhaps the fundamental difference in the development of the laws of set-off in different legal families is between those that see set-off as not simply a reverse claim but instead as a means of performance. On this view, where a claim is made and a respondent declares a set-off, the respondent is saying that even if the primary claim is

---

61. *Ibid.*, p. 59 et seq.
62. BERGER, above fn. 33, p. 55.
63. *Compensation, compensación, compensazione, Aufrechnung, Verrechnung, verrekening.*

made out, it has fully performed its obligations as a result of the declared set-off. When articulated in that manner it can be argued to be a direct response to the claim and hence an integral part of an assessment of the continuing validity of that claim by the tribunal. In our view, one of the difficulties with this analysis is that it puts all set-off defences within the one category, regardless of the degree to which the facts truly relate to the primary claim. A contrary argument might be to the effect that the only important commercial issue is whether the respondent truly owes money to the claimant. While that may be so in a purely economic sense, it cannot be the only way to deal with arbitration where jurisdiction must depend on some logical consent. Hence a perspective that treats all set-off claims as performance may not be an ideal way to resolve arbitration jurisdiction questions as it does not concern itself with the degree to which those facts might come within the original arbitration clause.

The second conceptual problem is that this doctrinal perspective fails to distinguish adequately between the *establishment* by a tribunal of contested legal rights and the determination of the *remedies* that flow from breach of those rights. For example, if a contested claim is fully made out in law at the same time as a set-off is made out on unrelated facts, one could argue conceptually that the set-off merely explains why there will be no remedy by way of an order of payment of money. One could still say that the primary claim is discretely made out in full. Different legal cultures have certainly taken different views on this issue. Once again we are not seeking to criticize the domestic developments within any legal family or to recommend harmonized principles of substantive set-off law. We are instead concerned with the different articulations and theoretical opinions on set-off and their impact upon a consent-based approach to admissibility questions. In doing so, we further explore some aspects of the law of set-off and then return to the question of presumptions as to consent.[64]

There are a number of different factual permutations that deserve separate analysis. Where debts are connected, a cross-entitlement is often a pure defence and does not even need to be treated as a set-off. Consider for example, a case of a buyer and seller who have an ongoing two-way commercial relationship with regular two-way payment obligations. The supplier sues the buyer for outstanding payment but the buyer says the claim fails to take into account agreed allowances for faulty goods. This need not be separately pleaded as a set-off if the claimant is only entitled to a net amount under their agreement. It is simply an allegation that the net position as claimed is wrong. This is at times described as contractual set-off. If it is expressly or impliedly agreed to in this way it would easily fall within any arbitration agreement covering the primary claim.

c.   *Liquidated and unliquidated claims and rights to set-off*
In most legal systems, more general set-off is not available for unliquidated damages. It essentially deals with mutual debts. That already raises an issue for us as arbitration agreements are not so limited. PECL has moved away from other legal systems on this

---

64. For a more detailed analysis of the comparative position see BERGER, above fn. 33, p. 55; Philip WOOD, *English and International Setoff* (1989); S. Rory DERHAM, *Setoff*, 2nd edn. (1996); PAVIĆ, above fn. 30, p. 101.

issue by not requiring that the set-off must be ascertained as to existence and amount.[65] Art. 13:102(1) PECL provides adjudicators with discretion to allow a set-off of an unascertained amount where it "will not prejudice the interests of the other party". Such a test begs the question before us as to arbitral jurisdiction, as admissibility in the face of objections would at least be argued to be such prejudice. On the other hand, if admissibility is justifiable via consent, then such an argument should not succeed as it is *initial* consent that matters, not consent at the time of the dispute.

The common law has also seen a tempering of this rule as to unliquidated damages. *Hanak v. Green*[66] saw the English Court of Appeal allow an unliquidated claim by way of equitable set-off against a damages claim for defective workmanship. There might also be situations where the reverse claim, while unascertained, is sufficiently high so that one can be certain that it exceeds the principal claim. In these circumstances it would be sufficiently ascertained to support set-off of the entire claim.[67]

Berger suggests that the requirement of an ascertained and existing cross-obligation "can be explained by the function of set-off as a means of private enforcement of the cross-claim of the party declaring the set-off".[68] Unfortunately, this policy justification would also not resolve the issue of arbitral treatment. If that is the essence of the right then it is more in the nature of a distinct remedy rather than a true defence to the original claim. Furthermore, to describe it as a means of private enforcement says nothing about the appropriate dispute resolution forum for determining whether such private enforcement was valid or not.

d.   *Automatic application versus claims as to set-off*

There is also the distinct question as to whether a set-off operates automatically (ipso iure) or whether it requires a declaration by one of the parties. The latter distinction would have little relevance to arbitration. If the entitlement is not within the reference and is not pleaded it cannot be dealt with by a tribunal.[69] Berger indeed criticizes the development of the ipso iure effect of set-off. Arts. 8.3 and 8.4 UPICC now indicate that set-off is effected by notice and does not operate automatically. We agree with Berger that this solution better accords with the legal certainty that is of particular importance in international business.[70] Yet this arguably removes some of the strength in the argument in favour of automatic admissibility of set-off. The more it applies automatically to undermine a claim, the more one could argue that it is an inherent element of a just determination of the ambit and validity of such a claim. Conversely, if it is a unilateral right of self-execution, the ability to legally evaluate the validity of that purported self-execution still must be based on mutual consent if the forum is to be an arbitral one.

---

65. BERGER, above fn. 59, p. 20.
66. [1958] 2 QB 9.
67. BERGER, above fn. 59, p. 20.
68. *Ibid*.
69. Berger also notes that in litigation the same procedural issue applies. BERGER, above fn. 33, p. 56.
70. BERGER, above fn. 59, p. 21.

*e.    Independent and equitable set-off*

In different legal systems, it is further classified into independent or equitable set-off. In our view, this distinction is particularly important for the purposes of this Report as it alludes to the degree of factual connection between the claim and set-off. If the first and perhaps essential question as to admissibility is consent, then the degree of connection between primary claim and set-off defence may be relevant to that determination.

An independent set-off at common law is allowed for where it is capable of being ascertained with suitable precision, described as liquidated. This would also include some damages claims, for example, where they arise out of an express contractual provision setting up a damages formula, such as in the case of late performance in construction contracts.

Such an independent set-off need not arise out of related transactions and is seen as purely procedural, requiring the imprimatur of legal proceedings. As such it cannot be invoked unilaterally. It is sometimes described as statutory set-off.[71] Aeberli provides a strong argument that statutory set-off never acquired the characteristics of a substantive defence and criticizes the contrary assertion by Mustill and Boyd.[72]

Conversely, Berger notes that where equitable or transaction set-off is concerned it operates as "a true, substantive defence against the respondent's liability to pay a debt otherwise due. It may be invoked independently of the order of a court or arbitral tribunal."[73] To be characterized as an equitable set-off the cross-claims must be "inseparably connected with the transaction giving rise to the claim so that the title of the plaintiff at law to prosecute his demand is impeached".[74] The cases suggest that the set-off need not necessarily arise out of the same contract. Aeberli also argues that at common law, an equitable set-off has the characteristics of a substantive rather than a procedural defence. He takes issue with the suggestion by Mustill and Boyd that equitable set-off is a procedural defence and must therefore come within an express submission to arbitration.[75]

Aeberli notes a number of older common law cases which dealt with unliquidated damages and which appear to have held that the only matter to establish for equitable set-off is the simple fact whether the reverse claim was inseparably connected with the dealings and transactions which gave rise to the primary claim. After criticizing those cases, Aeberli suggests that equitable set-off in common law should be seen as applicable "where the cross-claim alleges matters which can be identified as depriving the defendant

---

71. DERHAM, above fn. 64, p. 56. Aeberli notes and criticizes an English Court of Appeal decision that a statutory set-off can be raised against a claim for specific performance. He supports the dissenting judgment of Kerr LJ that at most the cross-debt is relevant to the equity of granting specific performance. AEBERLI, above fn. 56, p. 5 citing *Bicc v. Burndy*, [1985] 1 All ER 417.
72. AEBERLI, above fn. 56, p. 6 citing MUSTILL and BOYD, above fn. 11, p. 130.
73. BERGER, above fn. 33, p. 58 citing *AWA Ltd v. Exicom Australia Pty Ltd*, [1990] NSWLR 705 and "*The Kostas Melas*", [1981] 1 Lloyd's Rep 18.
74. *The Angelic Grace*, [1981] 1 Lloyd's Rep 288. See also *National Westminster Bank Plc v. Skelton*, [1993] 1 WLR 72.
75. MUSTILL and BOYD, above fn. 11, p. 130.

of the benefit for which the plaintiff was demanding payment, or hinder or prejudice the defendant in enjoyment of that benefit".[76]

Even if this is an accurate reflection of the position at common law, it does not give a clear indication of how a tribunal should proceed. If the test is that it needs to be so inseparably connected so as to impeach the title of the plaintiff, how else could this be so if the cross-claim does not otherwise come within the arbitration agreement or is otherwise founded on the consent of the parties? Even if it arises out of the same contract, if it is not within the initial reference to arbitration, by what principles of consent ought it to be nevertheless included? In our view, this is the nub of the question where set-off admissibility is concerned. Because it is so complex and uncertain it is unfortunately the case that whichever way a tribunal goes on these issues, there might be challenges to its determination and/or enforcement.

Even under the common law, an equitable set-off does not apply automatically. Its equitable basis simply means that it is unconscionable for the creditor to consider the debtor being in default where an equitable set-off is sufficient to counter the primary claim.[77] Thus in *Aires Tanker Corporation v. Total Transport Ltd* the House of Lords considered that a set-off which had been previously notified, but which was not pleaded in any suit within a statutory time period, was lost and did not negate the primary claim.

An alternative view of the nature of substantive set-off under the common law is provided by Wood.[78] He describes equitable or transaction set-off as a "self-help" remedy. A debtor might unilaterally rely on the remedy or alternatively, may exercise the right by relying on it as a defence in judicial proceedings. In the latter case the judgment has a retroactive effect from the point in time at which it accrued. Derham takes issue with this formulation[79] although it is not necessary for our purposes to resolve that doctrinal debate. As suggested throughout, differences between legal families and doctrinal differences within those families are unlikely to be a sensible gateway for arbitrators to resolve these questions.

Derham also notes situations where a truly substantive set-off defence may have other significant contractual consequences for the claimant's rights. He cites examples where one party is entitled to take a particular course of action only where the other party fails to make a payment as and when due. If, however, the latter has an equitable basis for refusing to make the payment, then the express options provided for the benefit of the creditor should not be seen as coming into play.[80]

In his article on set-off under UPICC, Berger suggests that "[s]et-off is based on the idea that performance of claims existing reciprocally between two parties must be simplified and that therefore, whenever equity ... requires, the setting off of mutual claims should be allowed".[81] It is suggested that it would be against good faith to ask each party to perform its obligations separately. One could readily envisage circumstances

---

76. AEBERLI, above fn. 56, p. 10.
77. DERHAM, above fn. 64, pp. 57-58.
78. WOOD, above fn. 64, pp. 111-112.
79. DERHAM, above fn. 64, pp. 57-58.
80. *Ibid.*, pp. 62-63.
81. BERGER, above fn. 59, p. 18.

where that would be so, but much is dependent on the facts of each case and whether the set-off has merit or not or is instead used as a delaying tactic. There is also no inherent logical link between saying that it is not in good faith to claim money when you know you have an equal payment obligation in reverse and in then saying that such logic must always impose itself upon the claimant no matter what permutation of dispute resolution clauses apply in relation to each. Most importantly, good faith notions ought to apply differently depending on the degree to which the claimant is either aware of the set-off or accepts its validity. If the claimant does not believe that the cross-claim has merit, then the good-faith-based initial premise simply does not hold. Thus we are again suggesting that determining admissibility based on some *inherent* notion of set-off as a distinct legal concept, particularly when this varies so much between legal families, is not an ideal way for the arbitral world to move forward on this issue.

Berger also notes a number of authors who find great similarity between set-off and counterclaim where as is usual in international commercial arbitration, money claims are at stake.[82] For example, Bühler and Webster find the distinction between counterclaims and set-off to be "difficult to see".[83] They argue that in most systems, the adjudicator must find a claim in a certain amount and that it arose in a context where a party is entitled to a set-off. They suggest that if this is an accurate assessment of the law, the first step is really demonstrating that there is a counterclaim of some nature while the second step shows that it has a sufficient connection to the primary claim. On the other hand, Berger also suggests that in spite of similarities, set-off and counterclaims "have to be distinguished sharply from each other".[84]

We return to these questions in our concluding sections where we try to consider the consent framework in the context of all types of claims concurrently. At this stage we merely wish to reiterate that there is no simple solution to the question of admissibility of set-off claims. It should not automatically be allowed simply because all legal families entitle them as "defences". A conflicts methodology that simply leads to this position is less than ideal although we explore this further below. From a consent logic, there are at most a priori presumptions either way which will be affected by variations in facts on a case-by-case basis. As with counterclaims, one important question is whether the set-off arises under a different contract with its own dispute resolution clause. As noted, we also address these permutations more fully in a section below.

Finally, as we discuss below, even if a tribunal considers that a set-off cannot be brought before it, the mere presence of such a claim may be relevant to the tribunal's decisions on the timing of the proceedings and application of the award and other procedural matters. Parties could be presumed to intend that arbitrators make such discretionary decisions with an eye to all relevant surrounding circumstances and not treat the instant dispute as occurring in a vacuum. On the other hand, arbitrators should not seek to resolve the *implications* of those external circumstances unless they are directly within jurisdiction.

---

82. BERGER, above fn. 33, p. 58.
83. BÜHLER and WEBSTER, above fn. 35, p. 76.
84. BERGER, above fn. 33, p. 59.

## f. Procedural rules dealing with set-off

Similar to the spread of procedural arbitration rules with respect to counterclaims, rules allowing for set-off fall into a number of different permutations in terms of wording, and by implication, in terms of variations in the broadness/narrowness of the conditions for admissibility of claims of set-off.

Art. 19(3) of the UNCITRAL Arbitration Rules provides for a similarly narrow scope as its counterclaim provision, contingent on a connection with the same contract as the one forming the basis of the original claim. A respondent may thus "rely on a claim arising out of the same contract for the purpose of a set-off".

The ICC Rules of Arbitration provision on set-off is contained in Art. 30(5), the same provision which allows for counterclaims to be made by a respondent. That is, as with its provision for counterclaim, the admissibility of set-off per se is acknowledged; however, *conditions* of admissibility are not articulated any further.

Art. 42(3) of the WIPO Arbitration Rules[85] falls into the category of provisions which provide for set-off by the use of the word "any", and as discussed with reference to counterclaim provisions, the attendant implications of this wording might distinguish such rules from a rule which provides for "*a*" claim of set-off, which could designate a narrower category for the purposes of admissibility, although we again question whether this is the clear intent behind the use of the word "any".

The Swiss Rules constitute yet another formulation for the admissibility of claims of set-off. Art. 21(5) provides that "[t]he arbitral tribunal shall have jurisdiction to hear a set-off defence even when the relationship out of which this defence is said to arise is not within the scope of the arbitration clause or is the object of another arbitration agreement or forum-selection clause". As such, this clause unreservedly provides for the widest ambit of admissible set-off claims. Schedule 2.1 of these rules, dealing with the calculation of the value of the dispute's claims further provides that "[t]he value in dispute is further increased by the amount of set-off defences of *non-connected claims* to be evaluated by the Arbitral Tribunal."[86]

---

85. "Any counter-claim or set-off by the Respondent shall be made or asserted in the Statement of Defense or, in exceptional circumstances, at a later stage in the arbitral proceedings if so determined by the Tribunal. Any such counter-claim or set-off shall contain the same particulars as those specified in Article 41(b) and (c)."

86. The SIAC Arbitration Rules fall into a category which provides no explicit acknowledgment of set-off claims. Whether the wording of Art. 24 implicitly provides a right to make set-off claims should be the subject of further analysis. SIAC Rules, Art. 24:

"In addition and not in derogation of the powers conferred by any applicable law of the arbitration, the Tribunal shall have the power to:....
(b) allow other parties to be joined in the arbitration with their express consent, and make a single final award *determining all disputes* among the parties to the arbitration...." (Emphasis added)

## V. CONSOLIDATION

Sometimes, after an arbitration has been commenced, a party to that arbitration will seek to start a second arbitration concerning the same or a related contract or legal relationship. It may be the respondent in the first arbitration who seeks to put forward a claim in a second arbitration rather than by way of a counterclaim in the first arbitration. Alternatively the claimant in the first arbitration may, for various reasons, put forward additional claims in a second arbitration. A question which then arises is whether the two sets of proceedings are desirable or whether they can and should be consolidated.

Consolidation can always occur if the parties agree to do so. But this is unlikely because one of the parties has taken a deliberate decision to commence a second arbitration. However, consolidation may be possible if authorized by the relevant arbitral rules or if provided for by the lex arbitri.

Turning first to arbitration rules, Art. 4(6) of the ICC Rules of Arbitration provide for consolidation as follows:

> "When a party submits a Request in connection with a legal relationship in respect of which arbitration proceedings between the same parties are already pending under these Rules, the Court may, at the request of a party, decide to include the claims contained in the Request in the pending proceedings provided that the Terms of Reference have not been signed or approved by the Court. Once the Terms of Reference have been signed or approved by the Court, claims may only be included in the pending proceedings subject to the provisions of Article 19."

Schäfer, Verbist and Imhoos suggest that the discretion to consolidate goes against the principle of party autonomy but argue nevertheless that where there is a "genuine connection" between the cases, consolidation will result in more effective proceedings and avoid the risk divergent decisions.[87] In our view, if the parties have expressly selected the ICC Rules and if one concentrates on consent at the outset, one cannot necessarily view a decision by the ICC Court to consolidate as going against party autonomy.

There is also a debate as to whether the court has the sole power to rule on consolidation or whether in cases where the terms of reference have already been signed or approved, indirect joinder can be effected by a tribunal under Art. 19, dealing with acceptance of late claims. On its plain meaning, Art. 19 allows for such a discretion. A converse argument would be that such an application is in essence a consolidation application which should have been dealt with solely under Art. 4(6). Schäfer, Verbist and Imhoos suggest that the tribunal might make a decision under Art. 19 and then convey the decision to the parties and the court for the latter to rule on the matter.[88] It is not clear how that procedure can easily be derived from the express rules. If the tribunal does not have the power under Art. 19, then all the court would be doing is

---

87. Erik SCHÄFER, Herman VERBIST and Christophe IMHOOS, *ICC Arbitration in Practice* (Kluwer Law Intenational 2005) p. 34.
88. *Ibid.*

determining that the tribunal has improperly applied Art. 19. If it does have that power, there is no express jurisdiction for the court to have supervisory jurisdiction over the tribunal's determination.

Hanotiau suggests that rather than considering the timing of the terms of reference as the key deadline, a better solution, if compatible with the rules, would be to allow consolidation as long as the case has not gone beyond the pleading stage.[89]

Some rules provide for a discretion but give little guidance on the relevant factors. For example, Art. 12 of the Belgian Centre for Arbitration and Mediation (CEPANI) Rules states:

> "When several contracts containing the CEPANI arbitration clause give rise to disputes that are closely related or indivisible, the Appointments Committee or the Chairman of CEPANI is empowered to order the joinder of the arbitration proceedings. The Committee appoints the tribunal and may increase the number of arbitrators to a maximum of five."

Art. 4 of the Swiss Rules provides that consolidation may occur so long as in making their decision, the relevant Chambers and the Special Committee consult with the parties. Art. 4, however, provides little guidance as to what must be considered by these bodies, save noting that the link between the cases in respect of which consolidation is proposed must be the subject of deliberation, as well as calling for consideration of "all circumstances" surrounding the disputes.[90]

A unique provision on consolidation is contained in the NAFTA. The decision on consolidation is not taken by an administering body but by a separate tribunal established under Art. 1126 to decide consolidation. Art. 1126(2) of the NAFTA provides:

> "2. Where a Tribunal established under this Article is satisfied that claims have been submitted to arbitration under Article 1120 that have a question of law or fact in common, the Tribunal may, in the interests of fair and efficient resolution of the claims, and after hearing the disputing parties, by order:
> (a) assume jurisdiction over, and hear and determine together, all or part of the claims; or
> (b) assume jurisdiction over, and hear and determine one or more of the claims, the determination of which it believes would assist in the resolution of the others."

---

89. HANOTIAU, above fn. 3, p. 379.
90. "Where a Notice of Arbitration is submitted between parties already involved in other arbitral proceedings pending under these Rules, the Chambers may decide, after consulting with the parties to all proceedings and the Special Committee, that the new case shall be referred to the arbitral tribunal already constituted for the existing proceedings. The Chambers may proceed likewise where a Notice of Arbitration is submitted between parties that are not identical to the parties in the existing arbitral proceedings. When rendering their decision, the Chambers shall take into account all circumstances, including the links between the two cases and the progress already made in the existing proceedings."

If a Tribunal established under Art. 1126 assumes jurisdiction then other Tribunals previously established under Art. 1120 cease to have jurisdiction with respect to the claim or part of the claim over which the Art. 1126 Tribunal has established jurisdiction. The Art. 1120 Tribunal will ordinarily adjourn its proceedings or they can be stayed by order of the Art. 1126 Tribunal.

In addition to consolidation provided for in arbitral rules, the lex arbitri may make provision for consolidation either by court order or by the tribunal. An example of the latter is Sect. 24 of the International Arbitration Act 1974 of Australia. It provides as follows:

> "1. A party to the arbitral proceedings before an arbitral tribunal may apply to the tribunal for an order under this section in relation to those proceedings and other arbitral proceedings (whether before that tribunal or another tribunal or other tribunals) on the ground that:
> (a) a common question of law or fact arises in all those proceedings;
> (b) the rights to relief claimed in all those proceedings are in respect of, or arise out of, the same transaction or series of transactions; or
> (c) for some other reason specified in the application, it is desirable that an order be made under this section.
> 2. The following orders may be made under this section in relation to 2 or more arbitral proceedings:
> (a) that the proceedings be consolidated on terms specified in the order;
> (b) that the proceedings be heard at the same time or in a sequence specified in the order;
> (c) that any of the proceedings be stayed pending the determination of any other of the proceedings."

The operation of this provision is quite limited. In the first place Sect. 24 is part of Division 3 of Part III of the International Arbitration Act. Part III gives effect, in Australia, to the UNCITRAL Model Law. Division 3 contains certain additional provisions which are optional. Division 3 only applies if the parties to the arbitration agreement have agreed that the division applies. Moreover if there is more than one tribunal appointed, both tribunals must agree to the consolidation or else the application lapses.[91]

In Australia, the Uniform Commercial Arbitration Acts of the States and Territories govern those arbitrations which are not governed by the International Arbitration Act 1974. These are generally domestic arbitrations, however parties to international arbitrations can agree to have their arbitration governed by the domestic regime by excluding the Model Law. Consolidation is dealt with in Sect. 26 of the Commercial Arbitration Acts which requires that:

> "(3) An order or a provisional order may not be made under this section unless it appears—

---

91. Sect. 24(7).

(*a*) that some common question of law or fact arises in all of the arbitration proceedings;
(*b*) that the rights to relief claimed in all of the proceedings are in respect of or arise out of the same transaction or series of transactions; or
(*c*) that for some other reason it is desirable to make the order or provisional order.
(4) When arbitration proceedings are to be consolidated under this section, the arbitrator or umpire for the consolidated proceedings shall be the person agreed on for the purpose by all the parties to the individual proceedings, but, failing any such agreement, the Court may appoint an arbitrator or umpire for the consolidated proceedings."

Sect. 26(2) empowers arbitral tribunals to order consolidation of arbitral proceedings which satisfy the broad criteria set out in Sub-sect. (3). Sects. 26(2)(*d*) and (*e*) and Sect. 26(4) provide for court oversight of the consolidation process. The power of consolidation under the Commercial Arbitration Acts is broader than that provided for under the International Arbitration Act 1974 as the Commercial Arbitration Acts do not require both tribunals to agree to the consolidation. Rather, Sect. 26(2)(*e*) allows the court to intervene where the tribunals make inconsistent orders.

In Hong Kong consolidation in domestic arbitrations is dealt with in Sect. 6B of the Arbitration Ordinance (Cap. 341). Sect. 6B empowers the court to order consolidation in circumstances similar to those set out in Sect. 26(3) of the Uniform Commercial Arbitration Acts of Australia, which are discussed above.

Another law which empowers the court to order consolidation is Art. 1046 of the Netherlands Arbitration Act. This article allows the President of the District Court of Amsterdam to order consolidation upon request of any of the parties to the arbitrations. However unlike the Australian and Hong Kong provisions, this article does not set out criteria to be satisfied, other than that the subject matter of the arbitrations must be "connected".

In the United States, para. 1281.3 of the California Code of Civil Procedure provides for consolidation of domestic arbitrations. However the criteria that must be satisfied before the court will order consolidation are stricter than those discussed above, as the disputes must arise from the same transactions or series of transactions, *and* there must be common issues of law or fact creating the possibility of conflicting rulings by the different tribunals.

Many of the institutional rules are silent on the issue of consolidation,[92] others providing only implicit references to its possibility. The SIAC Arbitration Rules may provide the tribunal with a power to consolidate proceedings, but only on a broad interpretation of the wording of Art. 24:

"In addition and not in derogation of the powers conferred by any applicable law of the arbitration, the Tribunal shall have the power to:...

---

92. For example, the ACICA Rules, the AAA International Arbitration Rules.

(b) allow other parties to be joined in the arbitration with their express consent, and make a single final award determining *all disputes among the parties* to the arbitration." (Emphasis added)

The provisions discussed above can be compared with other regimes which require all parties to consent before the court will order consolidation. The courts in New York had, until recently, allowed the possibility of court-ordered consolidation of separate arbitral proceedings where they raised the same issues of law or fact. However in 1993 the position changed and consent is now necessary for consolidation. In *Government of the United Kingdom of Great Britain v. The Boeing Company*,[93] the Court of Appeals for the Second Circuit held that a District Court cannot order consolidation of arbitration proceedings arising from separate arbitration agreements, even where the proceedings involve the same questions of fact and law, unless the parties have consented to such consolidation. The requirement that all parties consent before consolidation will be ordered is also found in para. 684.12 of the Florida International Arbitration Act and Sect. 27(2) of the International Commercial Arbitration Act of British Columbia, Canada.

In the United Kingdom, the Parliamentary Advisory Committee to the revised Arbitration Act considered that granting a statutory power for consolidation to a tribunal or a court would negate party autonomy.

Section 35 of the Arbitration Act 1996 (UK) now provides:

"35.–(1) The parties are free to agree –
(a) that the arbitral proceedings shall be consolidated with other arbitral proceedings, or
(b) that concurrent hearings shall be held,
on such terms as may be agreed.
(2) Unless the parties agree to confer such power on the tribunal, the tribunal has no power to order consolidation of proceedings or concurrent hearings."

UNCITRAL is currently considering revision of its Arbitration Rules. One proposal raised but not pursued was to include a provision on consolidation of cases. The Working Group on International Arbitration and Conciliation, at its 45th session in Vienna, 11-15 September 2006, was divided on the desirability of including such a provision. Paras. 79 and 80 of its report stated as follows:

"79. The Working Group was informed that, in some cases, under the Rules, consolidation of cases was only possible where the parties specifically so agreed and proceeded to consider whether additional provisions on that matter should be added to the Rules. Some support was expressed for inclusion of such provisions based, for example, on the approach taken in Art. 4 (6) of the ICC Rules, which allowed consolidation when all proceedings related to the same 'legal relationship'

---

93. 998 F.2d 68 (1993).

and subject to the consent of the parties to submit to rules that permitted such consolidation.

80. However, doubts were expressed as to the workability of such a provision given that the Rules often applied in non-administered cases. It was suggested that a number of issues raised by consolidation might be dealt with by other procedures such as set-off or joinder. In that respect, reference was made to Art. 22.1(h) of the LCIA Arbitration Rules."

A draft Art. 15(4)(a) was prepared which provided:

"The arbitral tribunal may, on the application of any party:
(a) assume jurisdiction over any claim involving the same parties and arising out of the same legal relationship, provided that such claims are subject to arbitration under these Rules and that the arbitration proceedings in relation to those claims have not yet commenced[.]"

It will be noted that this provision, if it had been adopted, would have contained a number of qualifications. Under this proposal, consolidation could only be ordered where

— the parties are the same;
— the claims arise out of the same legal relationship;
— the consolidated claims are subject to arbitration under the UNCITRAL Rules; and
— proceedings in relation to the consolidated claims have not yet commenced.

The penultimate qualification might conceivably be met even though the consolidated claims arise under another, but interrelated contract, and do not contain an UNCITRAL arbitration clause provided that the tribunal is of the opinion that the two contracts together can be considered as one.

Even if these conditions for consolidation were applicable and were fulfilled, the tribunal would still possess a discretion and would not have to order consolidation. No indication is given as to the criteria or circumstances which the tribunal may have regard to in exercising such a discretion.

At its 46th session held in New York on 5-9 February 2007, the Working Group on Arbitration and Conciliation again expressed conflicting views as to the desirability of such a provision. Its report states:

"116. The Working Group noted that, in some cases, under the Rules, consolidation of cases was only possible where the parties specifically so agreed and proceeded to consider whether a provision on that matter should be added to the Rules, as proposed under document A/CN.9/WG.II/WP.145/Add.1.

117. Some support was expressed for inclusion of such a provision. It was said that such a provision could be useful in situations where several distinct disputes arose between the same parties under separate contracts (e.g., related contracts or a chain of contracts) containing separate arbitration clauses or to avoid a situation where a party initiated a separate arbitration in respect of a distinct claim

under the same contract in order to gain a tactical advantage. Consolidation in such situations might provide an efficient resolution of the disputes between the parties, and also might reduce the possibility of inconsistent awards in parallel arbitrations.

118. It was said however that such a provision should be carefully drafted in order to clarify that consolidation would only be possible if either the claim was already subject to UNCITRAL Arbitration Rules, or the parties expressly agreed that the claim should be subject to consolidation.

119. However, doubts were expressed as to the workability of such a provision particularly when the Rules applied in non-administered cases. As well, it was said that either the provision was intended to deal with new claims under the same contract, and that situation would be better dealt with under provisions on amendment of the statement of claim, or that provision was intended to cover several distinct disputes arising between the same parties under separate contracts containing separate arbitration clauses. In that latter situation, the application of the provision might subject parties to arbitration proceedings under terms, which differed from those, agreed in their arbitration agreement. It was said that that situation raised complex issues, and might result in unfair solutions.

120. After discussion, the Working Group agreed that it might not be necessary to provide for consolidation under the Rules and deleted subparagraph (a) (see below, paragraphs 157-160)."

As noted, the Working Group did not pursue this suggestion, although its criteria might influence decision makers who have a discretion. The rule- and legislative-based provisions on consolidation are predicated on the desirability of promoting efficiency and preventing incompatible results which could flow from separate proceedings. As noted above, some commentators and the UK Parliamentary Advisory Committee criticize consolidation on the basis that it impairs party autonomy and the right of the party to commence a separate arbitration. That would certainly be so where there is a mandatory law that applies irrespective of the parties' agreement. However, in our view, where the ability to consolidate arises under arbitral rules or a lex arbitri chosen by the parties, it is difficult to see that party autonomy is infringed by applying a provision agreed to by the parties, directly or indirectly.

In most cases any power to order consolidation is discretionary. Many matters could be considered in the exercise of the discretion including:

— The degree to which the second case can be linked to the connecting test within the first arbitration agreement. Stated another way, to what extent could the separate action have instead been brought as an element of the primary claim.
— The desire for efficiency and the avoidance of inconsistent results.
— The nature of the two disputes and whether efficiency would in fact be served by hearing them together (for example if one dispute is much more complex then the other).
— Whether the parties have provided for arbitration in different venues.
— Whether the lex arbitri and/or the lex causae in the two matters differ.

VI. ADDITION OF NEW CLAIMS

*1. Introduction*

After the arbitration has commenced, and the claimant and the respondent have put forward their respective claims, can the parties subsequently add new claims? Whether new claims can be introduced during the course of an arbitration is dependent on the ambit of the matters referred to the existing arbitration. The relevant arbitral rules and the lex arbitri may also be relevant.

A distinction should, however, be made between late claims where there is a debate as to whether they are within jurisdiction and late claims where a tribunal might nevertheless reject an otherwise valid claim simply because of the problems caused by its lateness. Where the latter is concerned, tribunals will give consideration to such factors as the reasons for lateness, the importance of the issues, the degree to which they are related to the primary claims, the implication of addressing new claims and facts at the later stage and whether it might undermine the utility of earlier findings. For example, if the new claims are put forward towards the conclusion of the first arbitration and, possibly, after the hearing has taken place, the introduction of new claims at this late stage could itself be regarded as inefficient and indeed unfair. For the purposes of this Report the first category is of more significance as it raises primary jurisdictional questions.

As was noted at the outset, there are two distinct questions. Is the claim capable of being brought within the arbitration agreement and is it within the scope of the actual reference to arbitration? Thus the fact that the new claims fall within the ambit of the arbitration agreement is not necessarily sufficient. It may be contended that the new claims go beyond the dispute or difference referred to the arbitration already commenced and thereby require the commencement of a new arbitration.

If consent is the determining factor, insufficient guidance is given by most procedural rules. This is because most arbitral rules simply refer to counterclaims and set-off in a procedural timing sense rather a jurisdictional sense. In our view, procedural issues can also be confused with consent issues. Note should be made of ICC Case No. 7237/1993[94] where a counterclaim was allowed even though the deadline stipulated in ICC Rule 5(5) was not complied with. If the only evidence of consent to counterclaims and set-off is because of the adoption of a particular set of rules which mandates them within certain procedural time limits, how does a tribunal presume that there was an intent to even allow counterclaims where the procedural stipulations were not complied with? If consent is simply based on the adoption of a particular procedural model and it stipulates exact time limits, then a claim made outside of those limits cannot be presumed to have been consented to, although the matter is more complicated if the tribunal is expressly given a discretion to allow late claims.

Aeberli suggests that when counterclaims are raised for the first time after the submission to arbitration there is no jurisdiction to hear them unless expressly referred

---

94. 8 ICC Bulletin (May 1997) p. 65.

to in the submission to arbitration.[95] That will depend, however, on the applicable rules as these are part of that express agreement.

Questions of timing can also be impacted upon by the type of claim. For example, can a set-off be raised if the events on which it is based only come about after the Notice of Arbitration? The argument against would be that it is not a true set-off. A set-off is something that normally exists prior to the claim, the existence of which explains why all of the sum demanded was inaccurate. A set-off entitlement which arises afterwards is instead a new counterclaim.

2. *Arbitral Rules and New Claims*

We turn now to an examination of general procedural rules about amendments and late claims. Art. 23(2) of the UNCITRAL Model Law provides:

> "Unless otherwise agreed by the parties, either party may amend or supplement his claim or defence during the course of the arbitral proceedings, unless the arbitral tribunal considers it inappropriate to allow such amendment having regard to the delay in making it."

This article is based on, but is not identical to, Art. 20 of the UNCITRAL Arbitration Rules. The latter provides:

> "During the course of the arbitral proceedings either party may amend or supplement his claim or defence unless the arbitral tribunal considers it inappropriate to allow such amendment having regard to the delay in making it or prejudice to the other party or any other circumstances. However, a claim may not be amended in such a manner that the amended claim falls outside the scope of the arbitration clause or separate arbitration agreement."

The differences between Art. 23(2) of the UNCITRAL Model Law and Art. 20 of the UNCITRAL Arbitration Rules concern the limits to the amendments permitted. Art. 23(2) of the Model Law confines the arbitral tribunal's discretion to disallow an amendment or supplement to circumstances where it considers it "inappropriate to allow such amendment having regard to the delay in making it". The limitations prescribed by Art. 20 of the UNCITRAL Arbitration Rules extend beyond delay and include "prejudice to the other party or any other circumstances". Art. 23(2) of the UNCITRAL Model Law is non-mandatory[96] and thus Art. 20 of the UNCITRAL Arbitration Rules would prevail if the parties had provided for arbitration under those rules.

A second difference between the two sets of provisions is the express inclusion in Art. 20 of the UNCITRAL Arbitration Rules of the limitation that "a claim may not be

---

95. AEBERLI, above fn. 56, p. 13.
96. Howard HOLTZMANN and Joseph NEUHAUS, *A Guide to the UNCITRAL Model Law on International Commercial Arbitration* (1989) p. 648; Peter BINDER, *International Commercial Arbitration and Conciliation in UNCITRAL Model Law Jurisdictions* (2005) p. 209.

amended in such a manner that the amended claim falls outside the scope of the arbitration clause or separate arbitration agreement". Holtzmann and Neuhaus consider that this limitation also applies under the UNCITRAL Model Law, although it is not expressly stated.[97] Such a position should be inferred in any event as jurisdiction under the Model Law is linked to disputes within the relevant arbitration agreement. If a party challenges a claim under a Model Law arbitration, the tribunal must rule upon it. If the parties agree to allow the new claim, then it is a new agreed submission to arbitrate the point, although this could not technically bind the tribunal because it only entered into a contract to arbitrate the original dispute. An interesting question is also whether the phrase "amend or supplement" is broad enough to encompass "new" claims or whether it simply alludes to variations of *existing* claims.

The last sentence of Art. 20 of the UNCITRAL Arbitration Rules is a reference to the scope of the arbitration clause. It does not refer to the particular disputes or differences which were referred to arbitration. In relation to this latter point, there are two possible constructions of the UNCITRAL provisions. One would allow a new claim, even if it does not fall within the disputes or differences referred to arbitration at the outset. A second, more restrictive construction would confine the making of an amendment to a claim which does fall within the dispute or differences referred to arbitration.

Even if the latter view were taken, the parties can by agreement expand the jurisdiction of the tribunal. They can confer broader jurisdiction than that prescribed in the arbitration clause and they can also expand or extend the disputes referred to a particular tribunal. In this regard Art. 4 of the UNCITRAL Model Law is relevant. It provides:

> "A party who knows that any provision of this Law from which the parties may derogate or any requirement under the arbitration agreement has not been complied with and yet proceeds with the arbitration without stating his objection to such non-compliance without undue delay or, if a time-limit is provided therefor, within such period of time, shall be deemed to have waived his right to object."

Thus, in referring to the scope of the arbitration agreement, Holtzmann and Neuhaus observe:

> "It should be noted, however, that the parties may expand the scope of the arbitration agreement under Article 7(2) by failing to raise a timely objection to the lack of an arbitration agreement. Thus, if a claimant amends its statement of claim to include a new claim that is otherwise outside the scope of the existing arbitration agreement, it may be that the respondent, by failing to object to the expansion in an amendment to its statement of defense, will thereby accede to the creation of a new arbitration agreement covering the expanded dispute."[98]

---

97. *Ibid.*, p. 649.
98. *Ibid.*

In our view, this would only be an accurate statement if the tribunal accepts that such behaviour equals consent. The more problematic question is to decide whether unintentional actions which would nevertheless fit within concepts of estoppel and waiver in some legal systems, should be treated as akin to consent for the purposes of arbitral jurisdiction. We leave such questions for further discussion in our concluding remarks.

The ICC Rules of Arbitration also contain an express provision concerning new claims. Art. 19 provides:

> "After the Terms of Reference have been signed or approved by the Court, no party shall make new claims or counterclaims which fall outside the limits of the Terms of Reference unless it has been authorized to do so by the Arbitral Tribunal, which shall consider the nature of such new claims or counterclaims, the stage of the arbitration and other relevant circumstances."

This provision freezes the parties' claims and counterclaims as stated in the Terms of Reference. However new claims are permitted with the authority of the arbitral tribunal. It would seem, therefore, that an amendment to a claim or counterclaim does not require the consent of the arbitral tribunal unless it constitutes a new claim or counterclaim. It seems that in the past arbitral tribunals have taken differing approaches as to what constitutes a new claim. Derains and Schwartz state:

> "Nevertheless, because of the different treatment reserved under Art. 19, as under Article 16 of the former Rules, to claims falling inside or outside 'the limits fixed by the Terms of Reference', the Arbitral Tribunal will be required to make a determination in this regard whenever a party wishes to introduce a new claim in the arbitration. Over the years, this is a matter as to which ICC Arbitral Tribunals have adopted widely varying approaches, depending on the circumstances, the meaning given to the word 'claim' and the arbitrators' different conceptions of what falls 'within the limits of' the Terms of Reference. Thus, for example, certain arbitrators have construed very expansively the Terms of Reference's scope so as to include any new claim based on the same facts or, if based on different facts, for the same relief, or otherwise 'linked' directly or indirectly to the claims already before the Arbitral Tribunal. Other Tribunals, meanwhile, have taken a more restrictive approach and have, thus, treated as new claims outside the limits of the Terms of Reference claims based on the same facts, but on different legal grounds, or claims for the same relief, but based on different facts."[99]

For example, in ICC Case No. 7047 (1994), a principle was propounded whereby a claim would only be seen as being new and not within the limits of Art. 16 of the former ICC Rules if it raised issues of fact and of law which are completely new compared with

---

99. Yves DERAINS and Eric SCHWARTZ, *A Guide to the ICC Rules of Arbitration*, 2nd edn. (2005) pp. 268-269.

the issue in dispute so far. If it is, however, a claim subsequently based on different reasoning, but still on the same facts, it is within the limits of Art. 16 of the ICC Rules.[100]

It might be contended that Art. 19 only permits new claims to be made with the authorization of the arbitral tribunal if these fall within the dispute or difference referred to arbitration. The wording of Art. 19 suggests no basis for such a restrictive interpretation and confers authority on the arbitral tribunal to authorize new claims and counterclaims. However as a safeguard the arbitral tribunal is given a broad discretion and can disallow new claims having regard to the stage of the arbitration and other relevant circumstances. Once again, we see these issues being best resolved within a consent paradigm.

VII. SYNTHESIS AND ANALYSIS

1. *Policy Reasons Behind Admissibility*

In previous sections we have outlined the nature, rules and key doctrinal debates about the different forms of inter-party claims, including synthesis of claims by way of consolidation. This section brings these categories back together to see what, if any, are the common principles and criteria that should be used to determine admissibility.

From a policy perspective key general reasons to allow multiple claims include efficiency (including cost savings), speed and the desirability of avoiding conflicting decisions or conflicting evidence and the avoidance of some of the pitfalls flowing from the composition of multiple tribunals where overlap may raise questions of prejudice or undue influence. Arguments against allowing multiple claims include the possibility that there was lack of real consent and the consequent negative implications for enforceability and the encouragement of spurious reverse claims to add to the costs of the initial hearing with a view to promoting more favourable settlement. In addition it cannot be presumed in all cases that involve multiple claims that consolidation will indeed be speedy and more efficient.

Scholars and practitioners have tended to either caution against multiple claims or advocate broad inclusion. Rather than contending for one school of thought over the other in terms of expansive versus restrictive admissibility, we aim instead to look at the kinds of factors and methods that should guide the analysis on a case-by-case basis. We have noted that procedural challenges in dispute resolution are inevitably about balancing certainty against flexibility and fairness against efficiency. We aspire to all four values but they will inevitably conflict. Hence trade-offs need to be made, ideally on some coherent and logical basis.

In terms of a logical approach, the differing methodologies that have been applied are a conflicts approach, an efficiency-based approach or an approach based on a broad analysis of actual and implied consent. Our working hypothesis is to consider whether consistency would best be promoted by first analyzing the issue as a question of consent. In this way, flexibility is allowed for by eschewing any strong evidentiary presumptions

---

100. See also ICC Case No. 6223 (1991), 8 ICC International Arbitration Bulletin (1997, no. 2) p. 70.

one way or another. A tribunal would instead look at all factors in any individual case to see how confident it can truly be as to the express or implied consent to admissibility. Consideration of questions of fairness and efficiency should in our view be seen as merely means by which consent can be implied, rather than a justification for a tribunal to ignore what it should at times accept as contradictory evidence of intent.

Before doing so, however, we first consider whether admissibility questions might instead best be resolved via a conflicts paradigm. Those supporting a conflicts approach are often seeking a scientific methodology that would hopefully lead to more consistent and predictable outcomes, always a laudatory goal, in and of itself. As we seek to show in the next section, however, this is not likely to be the case where admissibility of multiple claims is concerned.

2.  *Choice of Law Approaches to Admissibility*

Fouchard, Gaillard and Goldman[101] point to authors advocating a choice of law method for determining arbitral validity. A choice of law method would lead to interpretation of the arbitration agreement under the laws governing its existence and validity.[102] On the other hand, courts and tribunals will often analyze the scope of an arbitration agreement without any reference to national laws, relying instead on transnational rules and trade usages. Fouchard, Gaillard and Goldman note the approach of the French courts to that effect.[103] The authors argue that it is preferable to apply such generally accepted principles and for courts to employ the rules they deem best suited to assess validity.[104] Both Fouchard, Gaillard and Goldman[105] and Poudret and Besson[106] also consider that general principles of interpretation are sufficiently similar under different national laws, so that determination of applicable law will often not play a vital role in interpretation.

For the purposes of this Report it is worth considering one example of how a contrary choice of law approach might apply to see whether the results would be more scientific, certain and fair. We consider the particularly difficult question of set-off. This is an ideal test example as the differences between legal families are significant and hence a conflicts methodology might be one means of making choices between alternatives. Given that different legal families treat set-off either as procedural or substantive and also have differing views about the extent to which a set-off defence is inextricably linked to a claim and hence more likely to be within the claim's jurisdictional ambit, the question is whether determinations as to admissibility might simply flow from the answers given by the law determined to be applicable to the set-off itself.

Here different legal systems diverge as to the proper law that should apply, in part as a result of differences in view about its essential nature as a defence. For example, should

---

101. *Fouchard Gaillard Goldman*, above fn. 5, pp. 308-309.
102. *Ibid.*, pp. 255-257 (fn. 68).
103. *Ibid.* (fn. 71 et seq.).
104. *Ibid.*, pp. 308-309 (fn. 285).
105. *Ibid.*, pp. 255-256.
106. *Ibid.*, p. 152.

the law of the set-off follow the law of the primary claim, on the basis that it inherently undermines it, or should it be found to have its own governing law based upon the connecting factors to its own essential factual elements? Should these questions depend upon the timing of the claim for set-off? For example, where the set-off predates the claim, it might be thought to have some level of intrinsic merit based on the likely applicable law as and when it arose, although the level is not determined until dispute settlement. Yet even that is complicated. If the question is whether set-off is permissible or not in terms of whether the set-off entitlement is already due, that would normally be a question to be determined under the law applicable to that claim, which is normally the law applicable to the contract.[107] This is to be compared with the contrary view that the law of the set-off as a defence to the primary claim should follow the law of that claim.

These questions also raise issues of procedural justice. If the applicable law of a set-off follows the law of the primary claim and if the respondent could choose instead to raise its entitlement by way of a separate claim rather than as a set-off defence, it gives the respondent an effective choice over governing law, depending on where it seeks to raise the issue. Similar strategic questions might apply to the claimant if the law of set-off follows the law of the claim. Thus if a claimant could either sue in tort or contract in relation to a commercial joint venture where a respondent has a separate contractual set-off and if the proper law of the tortious and contractual primary actions would be different, should the claimant's choice of how it frames its case affect the law applying to the set-off?

Berger notes that in France and Belgium a different conflicts principle is applied. He refers to a cumulative theory under which the set-off is only justified if both the personal laws of the debtor and creditor would declare it admissible.[108] Applying this rule to arbitration would make successful applications for admissibility stronger and more clearly anticipated by both parties. On the other hand, it would deny admissibility to potentially meritorious claims.

Berger suggests that this cumulative approach is also followed by arbitrators to add persuasiveness to their decisions where they would be justified under a range of applicable laws. In our view that is quite different to the more restrictive domestic approach that he identified. On the latter view, unless the set-off satisfies *both* laws it cannot be considered. Under the more traditional approach to cumulation by arbitrators, they are simply looking to be able to say that the more the same outcome would be mandated under alternative applicable laws, the more they are confident that their suggested outcome is a just one. More often than not, a cumulative approach is utilized to identify a false conflict and indicate that the same substantive principles will apply no matter what choice of law is made. In ICC Case No. 5971, after considering that set-offs under related contracts were admissible, the tribunal turned to the governing law. The tribunal adopted a comparative approach with a view to seeing that if the various laws

---

107. Berger notes Art. 10(1)(b) Rome Convention which indicates that the law applicable to the contract governs all issues relating to the performance of the contract: BERGER, above fn. 59, p. 22.
108. BERGER, above fn. 33, p. 63.

were essentially harmonized it might not be necessary to discuss the conflicts of laws principles which might apply.[109] The tribunal did find comparable principles under each of the potential legal systems that would apply under a conflicts methodology.

On balance, the dual-compliance cumulative approach to set-off admissibility referred to by Berger ought not to be preferred in international arbitration as such a restrictive approach is unlikely to be consistent with presumed intent. Berger notes that the approach emanates from different domestic considerations, namely as a corollary of the *ex lege* effect of the *compensation légale* which historically did not call for a declaration by either party.[110]

Another question is whether an express selection by the parties of a broad substantive law which expressly allows for set-off, resolves the admissibility question in arbitration. Thus if parties agree to arbitrate claims under procedural rules which do not provide any indication of which set-offs may be allowed, but have their contractual arrangement subject to PECL, could the express right to set-off within that contract law regime be the basis of a finding of consent to jurisdiction? Could such an argument be supported by Art. 13:107(a) PECL which provides that the parties can agree to exclude a right to set-off, thus suggesting that it is an opt-out substantive law rather than an opt-in model? This might readily apply in simple cases but other problems arise when UPICC tries to deal with a set-off in the face of multiple claims or conversely, multiple reverse claims against an individual claim. How should the set-off be allocated in each case? Art. 8.4 provides discretion to the party declaring the set-off where it has more than one reverse claim. UPICC does not directly address the converse situation, although Art. 13:105(2) PECL indicates that a set-off in response to multiple claims also allows for some choice.

Any articulation of substantive law rights as between parties in their business dealings does not necessarily reflect consent to provide similar choices in allocating set-off rights to different dispute settlement fora. If the set-off facts come within the arbitration clause, this would be easy in any event. If they do not, at most this selection of substantive law is valuable evidence pointing in the opposite direction to the clause itself, but it is once again a decision forced on a tribunal based on inadequate drafting.

If a conflicts methodology is to be used under a consent paradigm, a number of domestic principles might appear to be ill-suited to arbitration. For example in some countries it is not possible to set off claims made in different currencies. This does not seem to be a sensible presumption in the field of international commercial arbitration where in most cases, the two parties to the dispute naturally deal in different currencies. UPICC has also sought to temper this rule. Art. 8.2 UPICC indicates that set-off may be exercised if both currencies are freely convertible and there is no stipulation that the payment by the party claiming set-off must be in a specified currency.[111]

It might even be the case that the mutuality of claims called for under Art. 8.1 of UPICC which encapsulate the established principle that reciprocal claims owing by separate corporate personalities are not generally eligible for set-off, should not

---

109. Para. 138.
110. BERGER, above fn. 33, pp. 63-64.
111. The stricter position in common law has also been criticized.

automatically apply in arbitration. The consent-based paradigm at least allows for a group of companies theory to provide for jurisdiction in some circumstances at least.[112]

If a conflicts approach is utilized, the following list of questions might be a guide:

1. There are two distinct questions. Firstly, is the set-off allowed to be raised as a reverse claim? Secondly, if so, has it been made out? We are only concerned with the first question.
2. In considering admissibility there are four conflicts options to consider:

(a) the lex causae of the primary claim on the theory that it is a substantive defence;
(b) the lex arbitri on the basis that admissibility is a procedural issue;
(c) the personal laws of either or both of the parties;
(d) the law of closest connection, however that is to be determined.

This Report does not seek to resolve these conflicts issues as to set-off, a major topic in its own right. Instead it has used this complex example to show problems with undue reliance on conflicts approaches. There is no consensus as to which conflicts rule to apply and no guarantee that this would lead either to consistent results or results that would meet the parties' legitimate expectations. Those advocating a conflicts approach might wish to consider how they would deal with the following example. Let us assume that two parties have selected a substantive law that sees a set-off as an inherent defence that need not be separately declared. At the same time, they have selected a set of arbitral rules and/or an arbitration agreement that expressly denies a set-off right. Which element of the parties' consent should prevail, the clear denial of the set-off right or the indirect inclusion via the choice of substantive law? Once again we are not advocating one view over another. Instead we see this example as showing how there can be potentially conflicting but important aspects of consent that a tribunal should seek to reconcile on a case-by-case basis.

For the purpose of this Report, we merely need to note that a conflicts methodology under current domestic approaches will not solve our problems in a way that would be beyond debate. Given that tribunals are given broad discretions as to which conflicts rules to apply and given the extreme differences in approaches of domestic regimes, the outcome would not be clear and consistent and would often lead to substantive principles applying which are ill-suited to international arbitration.

3. *Resolving Admissibility via a Consent-based Paradigm*

Many of the differences in view as to admissibility of multiple claims can in our view be explained by differences in approach to a determination of consent. A tribunal that works from a strong albeit rebuttable presumption that parties would always want an efficient resolution of their disputes is likely to find that admissibility is justified in most

---

112. See the parallel session on Multi-party Disputes (this volume, pp. 341-433).

instances.[113] Conversely, a tribunal that wants to see some express provision allowing for admissibility within the arbitration clause, the lex arbitri or the procedural rules selected by the parties would be less inclined to find admissibility in most instances. Between the extremes, different arbitrators might wish to see differing levels of direct or indirect evidence of actual intent before making conclusions either way.

An earlier section (Sect. II under *1* and *2*) distinguished between disputes which *may* be brought, which involves an analysis of the scope of the arbitration agreement and the separate question as to which disputes *have* been brought, involving an analysis of the particular reference to arbitration. Each involves questions of intent, which in the event of disagreement between the parties, involves questions of construction by the tribunal. Such a process of construction is itself a determination as to the consent of the parties.

This Report does not seek to resolve these questions per se, as the question of consent in arbitration and how it is to be determined is a broader question and may best be answered after an inductive analysis of all contentious aspects of arbitration where consent is in issue. This would include cases where there is a dispute as to whether there was in fact any agreement to arbitrate or disputes about the meaning of potentially pathological arbitration clauses. Our aim is to illuminate the issues and provide a stepping stone on the way to such an inductive analysis.[114]

*a.   Interpretation of the arbitration agreement*
In any consent paradigm, the starting position should be the words of the arbitration agreement itself. If there is more than one contract and arbitral clause, the interplay between each must also be considered.

At times the words of the arbitration agreement should be supplanted with the lex arbitri and arbitral rules derived through that agreement. This draws attention to the express comments made by the parties on the issue. Unfortunately in many instances, the drafting is less than perfect. It is important to understand that determinations of intent based solely on ambiguous drafting are dangerous. While this is an obvious proposition, it is particularly important when considering multi-contract situations and the interplay between differing permutations of dispute settlement provisions. We deal with this scenario in a separate section (Sect. VII.*4*) below.

Fouchard, Gaillard and Goldman analyze a number of principles of interpretation that ought to be considered by any tribunal when interpreting agreements to arbitrate. The first is the principle of interpretation in good faith. We agree that this principle should always apply but also agree with the authors' caution against misapplying it. They note that merely challenging the validity or ambit of an arbitration clause is not presumptively an act of bad faith.

---

113. This is the purpose behind the express mandate to bringing set-off claims under the Swiss Arbitration Rules, Art. 21(5).

114. "Because the basis for arbitration is the will of the parties, arbitrators can only hear disputes over issues which the parties have agreed to put before them." *Fouchard Gaillard Goldman*, above fn. 5, p. 298 (fns. 243-245). "Without the agreement of all the parties, [an arbitrator] has no jurisdiction to consider other matters in dispute between the parties, even if this makes commercial sense or one of the parties wishes him to widen the reference." AEBERLI, above fn. 56, p. 2.

This principle of interpretation invites the tribunal to look behind the declared intention for what could have been the true intention at the time of entering the arbitration agreement. This can be particularly relevant where multiple claims are concerned. At the time of negotiation of the arbitration agreement, parties hope that there will not be disputes, would usually not be aware whether they would be claimant or respondent in the event of any dispute and could in good faith be presumed to want their disputes resolved efficiently and amicably. Once a dispute has arisen, however, parties tend to think of their own best interests, which could include looking for the most tactically advantageous dispute settlement process. It is the initial intent and not the latter, which should be determinative.

Fouchard, Gaillard and Goldman go on to derive more specific rules of interpretation flowing from the obligation to interpret contracts in good faith. The tribunal must look for intention in context, taking into account the consequences which the parties reasonably and legitimately envisage.[115] The authors also suggest that the attitude of the parties after signature and up until the time of the dispute arising should be taken into account as subsequent conduct confirming their original perceptions. They note that this is sometimes referred to as "practical and quasi-authentic interpretation" or "contemporary practical interpretation", commonly applied in arbitral case law.[116] The authors also note that this leads to a requirement that the agreement must be interpreted as a whole. For our purposes, while certainly an appropriate suggestion, it will still pose challenges of circularity. For example, in group-of-contract situations, what is the "whole" to be interpreted? The authors do see this as appropriate to such circumstances.

The authors then turn to the principle of effective interpretation. They note that this is a recognized element of most legal systems, sometimes described under the maxim *ut res magis valeat quam pereat*. It has also commonly been used in international law interpretation.[117] While Fouchard, Gaillard and Goldman treat it separately to the principle of interpretation in good faith, both the International Court of Justice and the International Law Commission have in fact seen it as a subset of that concept.[118]

The principle applies readily to pathological clause situations but in our view, not necessarily so to multiple claims. Where pathological clauses are concerned the principle of effective interpretation salvages the true intent which was "distorted by the parties' ignorance of the mechanics of arbitration".[119] No persons can be presumed in good faith to have wanted to expressly provide for arbitration in an ineffective manner. Hence it is natural to add meaning to shift somewhere from the inadequate express clause, filling the gaps where possible or treating it as a nullity where the faults are irreparable. In multiple claims cases, however, there may not be a gap that needs filling, but instead

---

115. *Fouchard Gaillard Goldman*, above fn. 5, pp. 256-258.
116. *Ibid.*, p. 258 (fn. 79).
117. See for example *Corfu Channel Case*, [1949] ICJ Reports 24.
118. *Ambatielof*, [1953] ICJ Reports 10; *Case Concerning Rights of United States Nationals in Morocco*, [1952] ICJ Reports 196; *Yearbook of the International Law Commission* (1966-II) p. 219 as cited in Ian SINCLAIR, *The Vienna Convention on the Law of Treaties* (1984) p. 118.
119. *Fouchard Gaillard Goldman*, above fn. 5, pp. 266-268.

simply limited evidence of the ambit of consent. Parties can often intend separate proceedings. The question is to properly determine when that is the case.

Fouchard, Gaillard and Goldman then draw attention to the principle of interpretation *contra proferentem*. At first sight this would appear to be an unusual principle to apply to the determination of the *common* intent of two parties, given that it directs a preference against the drafter of an arbitration clause. The authors direct attention to it in a more limited sense, namely that "the party responsible for drafting the ambiguous or obscure text should not be entitled to rely on that ambiguity or obscurity (in claiming, for example, that a particular disputed matter is not covered)...".[120] It would be rare for this to apply to multiple claim cases. Most institutional clauses do not clearly deal with multiple claims, hence a party arguing for a limited coverage on the basis that all cross-claims must be sufficiently connected to the primary contract is hardly relying improperly on their own creation of ambiguities.

Fouchard, Gaillard and Goldman then proceed to reject two other potential and extreme principles. The first is that a strict interpretation would demand the clearest evidence of consent. Some have asserted that an arbitration agreement should be interpreted restrictively on the basis that parties should not lightly be seen to have given away their rights to national court jurisdiction. Examples include ICC Award in Case No. 2138,[121] and ICC Award in Case No. 2321.[122] At the other extreme is the principle of *in favorem validitatis* which equates to a presumption in favour of arbitration, as for example has been applied by an American court in *Moses H. Cone Memorial Hospital v. Mercury Construction Corp.*[123] We agree with their rejection of those two extreme presumptions. A principle of strict interpretation would imply that there could never be cross-claims flowing from a second contract with a distinct arbitration clause. *In favorem validitatis* would promote a contrary presumption. Strict interpretation of arbitration clauses is outmoded and hopefully died out alongside judicial paternalism and distrust of arbitration. The contrary presumption may well be still be supported by some in appropriate circumstances[124] but in our view it does not apply to multiple claims. It could certainly be appropriate when determining the law governing the validity of the arbitration agreement. If the agreement would be valid under some laws but not others, that might well colour the tribunal's discretion as to applicable law. The authors point out however that interpreting consent is a different question.

All of our concerns with *effete utile* presumptions as stated above, apply even more strongly with *in favorem validitatis*. Presumptions of validity are in our view misapplied in multiple claim circumstances. Here it is not about validity of a particular agreement. It is about its scope. Such considerations are simply subsets of the overall approach to determination of the scope of arbitration agreements which may involve many questions besides that of multiple claims. In all cases the question is interpreting the intention of

---

120. *Ibid.*, p. 259-260.
121. JDI 1975, p. 934.
122. JDI 1975, p. 938.
123. 460 US 1, 24-25, 1983, cited in POUDRET and BESSON, above fn. 4, para. 304.
124. For example Art. 178(2) of the Swiss statute on Private International Law which provides for interpretation of the arbitration agreement *in favorem validitatis*.

the parties. For the purposes of multiple claims, too expansive an interpretation would go against the true intent of the parties. Too narrow an interpretation would lead to additional proceedings and costs and the potential of contradictory judgments. None of the principles or presumptions can be looked at in isolation. They all are simply guides to determining the ultimate question, namely the intent of the parties.

*b.     Procedural rules as guides to consent*

We have previously noted that if the primary question is that of consent, one must begin with the arbitration agreement as supplanted by the lex arbitri and any procedural rules agreed upon. Where the latter expressly deals with the admissibility question and where the parties have consented to those rules applying, evidence of consent is clear.[125]

Unfortunately, if consent is the determining factor, insufficient guidance is given by most procedural rules. As noted above, this is because most arbitral rules simply refer to counterclaims and set-off in a procedural timing sense rather than identify the typology of cross-claims that can be brought.

We also note that the consent logic flowing from express references in the lex arbitri, varies significantly if an appointing authority selects the seat rather than the parties, as this is one step removed from the parties' actual or implied consent. Even here, if the likely choices by the institution or tribunal would be known, inferences as to the parties' legitimate expectations can still be contended for.

At times the choices made may have a fundamental impact on admissibility. For example, an appointing authority has a particular challenge where it has the discretion to nominate a seat and where it is aware that a party wishes to bring a set-off defence. Should one select a seat that is favourable to such cross-claims?

Finally, even where procedural rules are not clear, consent might be found through waiver or acquiescence for example, via a claimant not objecting to a claim by the respondent when it is pleaded. Consent could also be inferred if a party objects to a matter being raised in court on the basis of an allegation that it is subject to an arbitration clause. A tribunal already invested with jurisdiction under that clause might then consider that the assertion in court is effectively evidence of an agreement to arbitrate.[126]

*c.     Implied consent to the raising of any and all defences*

As noted above, many commentators and tribunals have tended to differentiate between counterclaims and set-off on the basis that the latter is considered to be a defence. It is suggested that it flows as a fundamental principle of justice that a respondent should be able to raise any available defence. In our view this approach can too easily fail to distinguish between different types of defences. It also fails to consider the way the concept and justification fit within a consent based arbitration paradigm.

Our previous analysis suggested that there is a significant difference between different forms of set-off. The mere description of all as "defences" fails to address the degree of

---

125. Parties can also always agree to modifications, and tribunals sometimes will invite agreement but cannot force it. An example of such an invitation was in the *Sofidis* case. Interim Award No. 2 in ICC Case No. 5124 (unpublished) cited BERGER, above fn. 33, p. 65 (fn. 88).
126. ICC Case No. 7453 of 1994, 124 JDI (1997) p. 107.

connection between the set-off claim and primary claim, which we believe to be the key to deciding on the treatment of set-off within a consent paradigm.

There is also the problem of the interplay between the arbitration agreement, procedural rules and the nature of the set-off in an individual case. In looking at set-off, Berger invites separate consideration of the lex loci arbitri and the scope and interpretation of the arbitration agreement in deciding on procedural admissibility of a set-off defence. While these are certainly two distinct sources of relevant principles, these are both evidentiary aspects of consent. If the parties have expressly selected a seat that either expands or contracts the ability to plead such defences, they have provided express evidence in that regard. The same is true if they have selected arbitral rules that address the issue, or if they expressly cover the matter in their contractual arbitral agreement.

Thus we believe that the mere nature of set-off claims as defences does not resolve the issue without broader consideration of all circumstances. Nevertheless, for the purposes of analysis it is appropriate to consider when and why a defence should be admitted as of right, absent any other factors that add to or detract from a finding of consent between the parties. In this context, we believe that it is important to consider different categories of defences. The first category involves defences that are inherent in the particular dispute and which any sophisticated legal system would say are part of the process by which the ultimate rights and obligations of the parties must be determined. Examples of such defences in the sphere of commercial contracts include the duty to mitigate loss and the obviation of damages in the face of force majeure or frustration. Other examples of the first category that permeate other areas of law include contributory negligence and abuse of rights under civilian principles.

All such defences go to tempering the ramifications of the claim within the four walls of its own fact situation. They directly relate to the claim as such and should therefore be included under any view of justice. In civil cases the proper measure of damages can only be identified after the claimant has set up its gross damages entitlement under the applicable law which will usually look at issues of foreseeability and causation. That figure then needs to be tempered in light of the above-mentioned defences if and when they are made out.[127] Because they are inextricably linked to the facts of the claim, they will also have identical links to the relevant court or tribunal's jurisdictional mandate. There could not even be questions of statute of limitations or out of date counterclaims of this nature. It would also be highly unusual if the tribunal which had been selected as appropriately expert to deal with the primary claim, was not similarly expert to deal with the defence.[128]

---

127. Another simple situation that does not call for complex admissibility determinations is where a breach causes both benefit and detriment to the claimant and hence the damages caused are only the net amount: BERGER, above fn. 33, p. 53 (fn. 1).
128. In the rare cases where this was not so, the respondent can at least consider these issues when recommending its choice of arbitrator, although we have noted that it is undesirable to allow for notification of defences after tribunal composition where this would disadvantage the claimant at the selection stage.

The same logic should apply to other similar defences which may vary in title and content from jurisdiction to jurisdiction.[129]

At the other extreme are differences which do not affect the legal entitlement of the primary claim but deal instead with issues of cash flow and duplication. They are premised on the understanding that even if the claimant can make out its primary claim, the respondent has an equal or greater entitlement under a distinct right, which means that the claimant has no *net* right to any legal remedy.

A key policy reason underlying this aspect of the domestic law of set-off is in cases of potential insolvency. Treating the set-off as a means of identifying the true net figure, if any, to be passed between the parties, shields the respondent from the normal position of an unsecured creditor. Otherwise the respondent might be required to pay the full amount of the claim to a liquidator and then find that its set-off amount places it in a long list of unsecured creditors. Yet most legal systems provide separate rules for insolvency set-off and this category is not included in UPICC or PECL, so this cannot be a key factor for arbitrators deciding *a priori* intent.

The distinction between inherent defences and cash-flow situations does not mean that the second category should never be seen as admissible in arbitral proceedings. It is simply that where consent is used as a key to determining admissibility, the consent logic in the context of cash-flow and duplication concerns inevitably differs significantly to the consent logic when one is discussing a defence integral to identifying the validity of the claim. Even that statement is contentious as we again acknowledge that in some legal systems and conflicts theories, there is no inherent bright-line distinction between these two categories. At the very least, however, the fact that a particular domestic legal system describes such an entitlement as a defence should not be determinative in an

---

129. Craig, Park and Paulsson note the related doctrine of *exceptio non adimpleti contractus*. Under this doctrine, one party's performance is excusable because of the failure of the other. The authors suggest that there is evidence that it is an autonomous rule of international arbitration. ICC Case No. 2583 of 1976, 1 ICC Awards p. 304; Case No. 3540 of 1980, 1 ICC Awards 105, 399. While Craig, Park and Paulsson define *exceptio* broadly, *Black's Law Dictionary*, for example, defines it in narrower terms: "An exception in a contract action involving mutual duties or obligations to the effect that the plaintiff may not sue if the plaintiff's own obligations have not been performed." Bryan GARDNER, ed., *Black's Law Dictionary*, 8th edn. (2004) p. 603. ICC Case No. 3540, Award made 3 October 1980 (JDI (1981, no. 4) p. 914) described the *exceptio* doctrine as meaning that the plaintiff is not entitled to relief "because he has not performed his own part of the agreement". It also considered that this principle was part of the general principles of law which form the *lex mercatoria*, which was the law they had chosen to apply when expressly empowered as *amiables compositeurs*. Another example is that a right to claim *abatement* was initially an exception to the common law rule that counterclaims could not be raised as defences to an action but instead needed to be brought in separate proceedings (AEBERLI, above fn. 56, p. 3). Abatement at common law, akin to Art. 50 of the CISG, flows from a doctrine of partial failure of consideration based on an allegation that fault of the plaintiff has led the to value of goods or services supplied being less than was contracted for (*Ibid.*, citing *Allen v. Cameron* (1833) 1 Cr & M 832; *Mondel v. Steel* (1841) 8 M & W 858). If the primary claim is for failure to pay for the goods, then a claim as to abatement is obviously a direct substantive defence which would inevitably come within the four walls of the initial arbitration agreement.

arbitral situation.[130] Such a domestic legislative policy often aims to minimize duplicate proceedings and save taxpayers costs. Again these are factors which might help a tribunal identify a presumed intent, but a mandatory rule of a government seeking to save its own court expenses is based on a quite distinct logic.[131]

We have thus suggested that it is important to distinguish between different types of defences; on the one hand those that are truly inherent as responses to the primary claim and those which are more in the nature of defences to the cash-flow implications of a final order in favour of the claimant. Because some set-off claims fit the first category but most do not, it does not advance the appropriate consideration of their place in arbitral proceedings by simply acknowledging that they are treated as defences in domestic litigation systems.

In our view, the ultimate question in all cases is whether the parties intended at the outset for there to be cross-performance of these obligations and whether there is a single dispute resolution body intended to analyze both elements of that cross-performance. Inherent defences would fall within the arbitration agreement in any event. Cash-flow defences call for additional presumptions as to intended efficiency to be justifiable and it is to this factor that we now turn.

d.   *Efficiency and implied consent*
There are two important points we believe should be made. The first is that efficiency should simply be one of a range of factors to be considered by tribunals that are faced with uncertain guidance from the arbitration agreement and the rules themselves. Secondly, it is important to understand how it should be utilized. It is right for tribunals to consider efficiency factors as a means of identifying a good faith *a priori* intent of the parties. It should not simply be that tribunals look at efficiency per se from their own post-dispute perspective, regardless of other evidence of parties' intent.

Where tribunals are properly using efficiency as one element of likely intent of the parties, this will inevitably need to be integrated with a range of other factors that we believe need to be taken into account. As we have noted, arguments in favour of admissibility or consolidation include general efficiency, reducing the transaction costs of parallel proceedings, overall timeliness, and the avoidance of some of the pitfalls flowing from the composition of multiple tribunals where overlap may raise questions of prejudice or undue influence. Countervailing factors include the concern that reverse claims might be brought on spurious grounds to actually delay proceedings, frighten the claimant into settlement and add immediate financial burdens through the arbitral advance on costs. In addition, admissibility or consolidation may raise questions as to the suitability of the tribunal to deal with all of the multiple claims and might provide undesirable tactical advantages in tribunal selection to the respondent. Presumptions

---

130. US domestic civil procedure at times even demands that a set-off be raised lest this be lost for good.
131. Whether something constitutes a defence may also be relevant under the applicable law of assignment. Under common law for example, an assignee of a debt generally takes subject to defences available to the debtor as against the assignor where they arose prior to the debtor receiving a notice of the assignment. (DERHAM, above fn. 64, p. 3.)

based on general efficiency alone are only a small part of a commercially realistic response to all of these competing factors.

All of these other elements, when considered in the context of the circumstances that existed between parties at the time they first agreed to arbitrate, may also lead to diverse inferences. While some authors and practitioners work from a presumption that business people intended to have efficient proceedings and efficient solutions to any jurisdictional questions (a reasonable presumption in and of itself), that will at best be a rebuttable presumption.[132] To the extent that a tribunal is interested in considering subjective evidence, the presumption is weaker as it presumes certain objective features of the parties that may not be evident in the instant case. Even if the entire analysis is to be limited to objective evidence and inferences, our key point is that an efficiency paradigm might be more complex than would at first appear to be the case. For example, would all parties simply wish to allow counterclaims and set-off on the basis of efficient resolution of the disputes between all parties and as a bar to duplicity of proceedings? One countervailing criterion is that by accepting a counterclaim or set-off, the amount in dispute and hence the costs of arbitration will increase. Most rule systems will add the amount of the claim and cross-claims together to determine the advance on costs unless they truly overlap in substance. This can be a particular concern if it is foreseeable that at times there will be inflated counterclaims that are tactically aimed at frightening the claimant into taking a reduced settlement. Berger notes the use of counterclaims as delaying tactics or as retaliatory devices. Ulmer notes the practical inspiration for many counterclaims to have something to bargain with and set parameters for arbitrators who might try and find mid-position solutions.[133] Craig, Park and Paulsson point out that the requirement to include this in the advance of costs can act as a deterrent to such strategic claims[134] although in our view, if there is enough in dispute, a costs advance obligation would have little deterrent effect, particularly where this might provide for differential hardship in cases where the parties are in vastly differing financial circumstances.

In addition to the costs implications of multiple claims there is also the question of tribunal composition, an issue we have alluded to throughout. Consider an extreme example where the primary claim is essentially about complex questions of law where the parties have selected a tribunal that is expert on such issues. Now envisage reverse claims that deal only with challenges as to the quality of professional building or engineering activities. The parties might prefer different experts for the latter claims. In some cases preferred arbitrators for the second dispute might be professional engineers, builders or architects who are not legally trained and thus may be unsuitable for the first

---

132. For example, if an arbitration clause provides that claims are to be brought in an arbitration where the respondent's country is to be the seat, should a cross-claim also have that seat or was the intent to have any defender of a claim to be at "home" during proceedings? PAVIĆ, above fn. 30, p. 105.

133. Nicholas ULMER, "Winning the Opening Stages of an ICC-Arbitration", 8 Journal of International Arbitration (1991) p. 33, at p. 42; Léonard FLETCHER, "Unrealised Expectations – The Root of Procedural Confusion of International Arbitrations", 2 Journal of International Arbitration (1985, no. 3) pp. 7-14.

134. Laurence CRAIG, William PARK and Jan PAULSSON, International Chamber of Commerce Arbitration, 3rd edn. (2000) p. 150.

dispute. While this is not necessarily so, the example simply highlights the fact that one cannot necessarily presume that the wish to bring finality to all disputes between the parties and the wish to avoid duplication in costs will necessarily mean that an existing tribunal formed in response to the first dispute, can confidently presume implied intent to allow it to claim a mandate over a broad category of claims.

A realistic assessment of the likely thinking of the parties at the outset might raise some counter-intuitive hypotheses. Parties do not hope to have disputes from the outset. More often than not, if an individual party envisages the possibility of a future dispute it would most likely be envisaged as either one brought on reasonable grounds by it or one brought on unreasonable grounds by the other contracting party. This is because if the other party's claim was reasonable, the first party would believe it would honour it without the need for an adjudicated dispute. The contentious case, therefore, is to consider how each might have wished at the outset to defend against claims they do not agree with. In this event, there is at least a possible hypothesis that they might be presumed from the outset to want whatever strategic advantage that may be permissible to a defendant, subject to ethical and good-faith duties. As Hanotiau has pointed out in the context of multi-contract multi-party arbitrations, "(t)he absence of co-ordination of dispute resolution clauses, therefore, is not necessarily pathological. It is sometimes intended deliberately. The same goes for the possible refusal to consolidate the proceedings."[135]

Tribunals should thus be particularly careful not to stretch existing principles to try and promote efficiency in the face of some of arbitration's more intractable problems. Those problem areas may well be a small but important group of cases where parties might genuinely prefer litigation over arbitration or where these matters have to be raised and dealt with carefully in the parties' agreement to arbitrate, particularly in multi-contract circumstances. It is naturally the case that courts have greater opportunity to allow counterclaims, consolidation or joinder than is the case for tribunals. That perspective, suggested by Leboulanger[136] is supported by Poudret and Besson.[137]

Having said this, much can be gained from a consideration of efficiency perspectives. Parties can certainly be presumed to want an efficient resolution of meritorious disputes from the outset. Even if some business people would not want this, arbitration ought to be built on good-faith approaches. Hence if a party is trying to destabilize proceedings or promote inefficiency, perhaps in order to frustrate a claimant, such tactical endeavours in the face of a dispute should not colour the determination of implied good faith consent from the outset.

We have said that attention should be focused on *a priori* implied consent rather than behaviour after the dispute has arisen, although the latter may help our understanding of ambiguous original intent. Where subsequent behaviour is concerned, in some legal systems there will be a further need to consider whether there has been an abuse of rights through a party either blocking or relying on an extension of the powers to cover multiple claims. Tribunals should not be quick to reach such conclusions. Many tactical

---

135. HANOTIAU, above fn. 3, p. 371.
136. LEBOULANGER, above fn. 23, p. 43.
137. POUDRET and BESSON, above fn. 4, para. 312.

considerations are perfectly reasonable and would not offend against notions of good faith.

Converse presumptions of intent include that if set-offs are not readily allowed, there may be additional expense, delay and even financial disaster for a party truly entitled to a net benefit in circumstances where they had paid out on one claim and the other party is insolvent before they can be forced to pay on the reverse claim. Craig Park and Paulsson also note that in these circumstances there may be increased pressure on the respondent to settle for less than a reasonable amount.[138]

Thus we support a concern to supplant the interpretation of the arbitration agreement, where necessary, with a careful assessment of all factors that might help a tribunal draw conclusions as to the likely *a priori* intent of the parties. Implied intent to promote efficient solutions is an important working hypothesis, as long as it is seen as one factor that needs to be looked at alongside others and within the paradigm of consent, not tribunal paternalism. We noted that integrating the terms of the agreement and efficiency and other presumptions of intent is particularly challenging where multiple contracts are involved and it is to this topic that we now turn.

### 4. Admissibility Under Related Contracts

At times tribunals are asked to consider whether an arbitration clause in one contract can encompass a range of other contracts because the subject matter and the underlying facts are sufficiently similar to make it appropriate to do so. Similar arguments arise if claims are brought under contracts other than those expressly referred to in the Terms of Reference where the latter are utilized.[139]

These issues were first addressed in the context of claimant's claims and were touched on again in the context of respondent's claims. In this section we combine the analysis but separate out the various permutations; namely where one contract with an arbitration clause is argued to be closely related to other contracts with no dispute resolution clauses; secondly where different contracts have identical arbitration clauses; thirdly where different contracts have differing arbitration clauses; and finally where different contracts have arbitration clauses in some cases and choice of forum clauses in others. We have divided the analysis in this way so that we can consider the implications as to consent in each of these permutations and then see how that would impact upon the treatment of discrete claims and counterclaims as well as consolidation applications.

We believe that in addition to considering whether all claims should be allowed, tribunals must also consider how to conduct proceedings even if some claims are rejected. They must still consider the appropriate elements of due process within each arbitral process, at least with an eye to what is happening with the other. In either circumstance tribunals also have to consider the potential impact on enforceability of their decisions as to admissibility.[140]

---

138. CRAIG, Park and Paulsson, above fn. 134, p. 647.
139. See for example ICC Case No. 7184.
140. *Fouchard Gaillard Goldman*, above fn. 5, pp. 303-304 (fn. 262).

*a. Claims under closely related contracts without their own dispute settlement clauses*
Poudret and Besson note the developments in French law allowing extension of an arbitration agreement to a dispute arising from a group of contracts if there are sufficient economic links between the various agreements and also if the aspects of the dispute are "inseparable", although the authors question whether the courts which articulated this standard were truly faced with facts that would ground such a test.[141]

Where attention is given to the closeness of the relationship, this draws attention to principles such as *ensemble économique* and *ensemble légale*. Here there are again a number of permutations depending upon whether the second contract has its own dispute settlement clause or not and if so, whether it is arbitral- or court-based. In this section, we are presuming that there are no such clauses in the other contracts.

Where there is one overriding agreement, (a framework agreement or heads of agreement), which contains an arbitration clause and where there is no arbitration clause in related contracts emanating from the first, most would agree that the most likely intent was to cover all disputes under the one arbitration agreement.[142] An example is the award of 1 October 1980.[143] In this case a set-off under a loan agreement was accepted in a claim under a sales contract that alone had an arbitration clause.

Similar issues are raised in multi-party situations where an arbitration agreement entered into by one member of a company group might be held to encompass other members of that group. While this is outside the scope of this Report, one situation raises questions as to whether we are dealing with multi-party or mere multi-contract situations. Groups of companies only raise questions of significance when they are separate legal entities. If one is merely a branch of another, it will come within an arbitration agreement entered into by the corporate entity.[144] Even where there are technically distinct legal entities, Fouchard, Gaillard and Goldman suggest that "the question is whether and to what extent the legal fiction of corporate personality must give way to the realities of human conduct and should no longer protect those who hide behind the corporate veil in order to promote their own interests at the expense of those who have dealt with the corporation".[145]

Another complex situation is where amendments are made from time to time to extend contracts. Are these variations of the original agreement, perhaps undermining an original arbitration clause; or are they separate promises not subject to an arbitration agreement; or are they merely contemplated steps to be taken in performance of the original contract and hence subject to its dispute settlement provisions? This should again be a question of determining *a priori* intent after a consideration of all relevant circumstances.

---

141. POUDRET and BESSON, above fn. 4, para. 309.
142. *Fouchard Gaillard Goldman*, above fn. 5, pp. 301-306 (fns. 264-267). *Isover v. Dow Chemical Co*, Rev de l'Arb (1984) p. 137. It is also the basis for extending arbitration agreements from a legally independent state-owned entity to the state itself as per the *Pyramids* case. See *Fouchard Gaillard Goldman*, above fn. 5, pp. 292-294 (fn. 225).
143. *Yearbook* XII (1987) p. 84.
144. *Fouchard Gaillard Goldman*, above fn. 5, pp. 282-283.
145. *Ibid.*, pp. 284-286. See also *Isover v. Dow Chemical Co*, above fn. 142, p. 137.

b.  *Admissibility of claims subject to contracts each with their own identical dispute settlement clause*

Many commentators work from the presumption that if the same parties have two contracts with arbitration clauses in identical terms, they can be presumed from the outset to have wanted a global settlement of mutual claims. However, Fouchard, Gaillard and Goldman correctly note that "the answer depends on the interpretation of the parties' intention at the outset". Nevertheless, they suggest that it is "generally legitimate to presume" that the identical clauses signify an intent to submit the entire operation to a single tribunal.[146] Even here such a presumption might readily be rebutted. Hanotiau cites ICC Award in Case No. 5989[147] where the parties signed two related contracts on the same day. Conversely he notes the case of *Abu Dhabi Gas Liquefaction Co Ltd v. Eastern Bechtel Corporation*.[148]

One reason why the parties might nevertheless wish to have different tribunals under identical arbitration clauses relates to composition, a matter we have addressed above and which is simply a countervailing factor to a blanket efficiency presumption. For example, if the claimant was unaware of the potential respondent's claim at the time of constituting the first tribunal and believed that it would have picked a different expert if that claim was known, from its perspective at least, there is no necessary intent to have the same tribunal deal with both. At most it is a question of the trade-off between efficiency and duplication on the one hand, against optimal tribunal composition on the other. If composition is a problem, the best solution might not be rejection of admissibility but instead, requirement of early notification of reverse claims to allow this to be taken into account at the time of tribunal selection as is the case with a number of institutional rules.

c.  *Admissibility of claims subject to contracts each with similar but not identical dispute settlement clauses*

This category deals with cases where the arbitration clauses are identical in most respects, but have some key differences. Examples might be differing seats for each and/or differing number of arbitrators. In such circumstances Hanotiau suggests that separate proceedings must be initiated. "Mere concern for the good administration of justice cannot prevail over the intent of the parties."[149] Even here is it logical to presume *conclusively* that they would not have wanted consolidation in the event that claims and reverse claims were both brought? The parties' identification of different seats may have been relevant on the presumption that there was only one claim, but the clause might still be capable of being interpreted to the effect that they have not given any indication of the preferred seat if there were multiple claims. For example, in a construction contract with a side loan agreement the parties might have selected a neutral and

---

146. *Fouchard Gaillard Goldman*, above fn. 5, pp. 302-304 (fn. 255).
147. *Yearbook* XV (1990) p. 74.
148. Rev de l'Arb (1983) p. 119. See also PAULSSON and VEEDER's comments on *"The Vimiera"* in Arbitration International (1986, no. 2) p. 310; HANOTIAU, above fn. 3, pp. 274-275 (fns. 22, 23).
149. HANOTIAU above fn. 3, p. 375.

conveniently located seat for loan disputes but a different seat under the construction contract, being where the building work is taking place. This might have been simply to make it cheaper for the arbitrators to take a view of the physical building where appropriate or because that is the seat that is demanded by the host State of the building works. Even with such provisions, they may still have preferred from the outset that a claim under the loan would simply piggyback on the construction seat in the event of concurrent disputes. Our suggestion is not that arbitrators should always accept this logic but simply that irrebuttable presumptions to the contrary from inadequately drafted clauses make little sense within a consent paradigm.

Similarly if the two contracts call for differing numbers of arbitrators, perhaps because disputes under one were presumed to be likely to be dealing with bigger amounts than under the other, it might still be cheaper to consolidate the smaller claim in front of the panel of three rather than force one three-person hearing and a separate single-person hearing. This will not always be the case but to again presume a lack of consent as a matter of course flowing from a separate arbitration agreement would not be a presumption that one could confidently predict to be commercially sound in all circumstances. If consolidation would clearly save time and money and if the party arguing against consolidation cannot articulate any fairness or efficiency factors in its favour, that may be telling.

It is also possible to envisage cases where parties would not have intended differing arbitration clauses to automatically block reverse claims on essentially related matters. For example, differing clauses cannot wholly overcome the policy arguments in relation to true defences. Arguably the second clause is only a promise about what to do with respect to *primary* claims and not a waiver of a right to raise true defences as and when needed. As Fouchard, Gaillard and Goldman note, where cross-claims are not allowed, fairness and efficiency arguments would also be complicated if a party in one arbitration claims that it refused to perform its obligations because of a breach by the other party in the matter being considered under a second arbitration. The same logic may apply with ensemble contracts where claims under one contract still fit within the wording of different arbitration agreements in other contracts.[150]

---

150. For example, in ICC Case No. 5971 a tribunal concluded that three separate agreements with differing arbitration clauses nevertheless all referred to the same purpose of the construction and operation of a new facility to be operated as a joint venture. They therefore formed a "*unité économique*". As such, set-off claims arising in relation to the separate agreements could nevertheless come to be directly covered under the broad scope of the joint venture agreement. The only challenging conceptual question was in relation to set-off claims that exclusively arose from the other agreements. The tribunal considered that because of the close interrelatedness of the three agreements, set-off claims arising under either one must be heard and considered by the tribunal under the principle *le juge de l'action est le juge de l'exception*. The tribunal did not pass on the conclusion it would have drawn if the set-off claims originated from a more "distant" contract. Because of the closeness, the tribunal felt it would have needed a clear indication that the parties had the real intention to keep the three agreements totally separate from each other if it was to rule against set-off claims.

*d. Reverse claims with contracts combining arbitration clauses and jurisdiction clauses*
While most authors treat the situation of differing arbitration clauses and jurisdiction clauses together, they need to be considered separately under an intent paradigm. We have suggested above that any presumptions flowing from differences in arbitration clauses should be rebuttable at most. The situation is different where arbitration and forum clauses are brought together. A separate contract with a jurisdiction clause indicates an intent to litigate and not arbitrate such disputes. The parties may simply be saying that for that type of dispute they want a completely different type of adjudicator, with a differing conflicts methodology and a different procedural model. For example, ICC Case No. 4392 refused to extend an arbitration clause to a related agreement that had a jurisdiction clause.

5.  Harmonization

If a second arbitration is instituted, and it is not possible to consolidate the two arbitrations, is some form of harmonization or co-ordination between the two sets of proceedings possible and desirable?

The most obvious way of achieving a degree of harmony between the two proceedings is to appoint the same persons to both tribunals. Philippe Leboulanger[151] describes this as "de facto consolidation". By way of illustration he refers to the decision of the English Court of Appeal which avoided the risk of contradicting awards by appointing the same arbitrator in two parallel proceedings. In *Abu Dhabi v. Eastern Bechtel*[152] the parties referred to court the question of whether separate arbitrators or the same arbitrator should be appointed to the two arbitrations. The Court of Appeal held that it had power to appoint the same arbitrator to both arbitrations.

While this elegant solution largely avoids the risk of inconsistent decisions, it is still not as efficient as consolidating the arbitrations in one proceeding. However the tribunal can, by appropriate orders, direct that hearings be held sequentially and therefore manage costs. In some cases courts may have the authority to order that proceedings in two arbitrations be heard together.[153]

In order to have the same personnel on two tribunals it is necessary for the parties, and sometimes the administering authority, to make identical appointments. This does not always happen. The second tribunal may consist of different personnel or there may be some overlap of personnel between the two tribunals but not a complete identity. Anne-Marie Whitesell and Eduardo Silva-Romero[154] discuss ICC practice. They say that where the parties have not agreed to have the same tribunal in parallel proceedings and one side decides to nominate an arbitrator already acting in a related matter, to which the opposing party objects, the Court must decide whether to confirm that arbitrator. The Court takes into account various factors including whether the parties, counsel and the issues to be decided are identical and the stage that the arbitral proceedings have

---

151. LEBOULANGER, above fn. 23, p. 60.
152. [1982] 2 Lloyds Law Reports 425.
153. LEBOULANGER, above fn. 23, citing the former Arbitration Ordinance 1982 of Hong Kong.
154. WHITESELL and SILVA-ROMERO, above fn. 29.

reached. They say that the Court assesses whether the arbitrator would have access to information that would not be available to other members of the arbitral tribunal and also considers whether a decision has been rendered in one of the matters that might cause the arbitrator to prejudge the related case. Each case is evaluated separately and decisions can therefore go either way depending on the circumstances.

Whitesell and Silva-Romero give as an example a case where the respondent nominated an arbitrator acting in a related case and the claimant objected on the ground that the arbitrator would have access to information not available to other members of the arbitral tribunal. Counsel in both cases were the same, the claimants were the same and the respondents were related companies. No award had been rendered in the related case and there were no overlapping issues. The Court decided to confirm the co-arbitrator. In consequence the claimant changed its mind and decided to nominate the same co-arbitrator in the second case.

However in two more recent cases the Court decided not to confirm a co-arbitrator even though the parties and counsel were the same. The Court was influenced by the advanced stage of the first proceedings and the possibility the co-arbitrator could obtain privileged information in the second proceedings.

Leboulanger[155] raises a question of good faith. He asks whether a party can be considered in good faith when, on the basis of the existence of two distinct but identical arbitration clauses contained in two inter-related agreements, it seeks the constitution of two distinct arbitral panels and thereby increases the costs and creates the risk of contradicting awards. He says that an arbitration clause is nothing but one of the clauses of an agreement and the principle of good faith should apply to the constitution of the arbitral tribunal, which corresponds to the performance of the obligations assumed under the arbitration clause. In his view a party who refuses to designate the same arbitrator in parallel arbitral proceedings might be considered in violation of its obligation to perform, in good faith, its undertakings assumed under the arbitration clause.

Where the two tribunals are not identical, the risk of inconsistent decisions may be reduced if there is an exchange of information or documentation between the two arbitrations. In one situation there were parallel ICSID and ICC arbitrations. The respondent in both cases was the same but the claimants differed. The claimant in the ICSID case was a shareholder of the claimant in the ICC case. The two tribunals were different and there was no common member. The tribunal in the ICSID case ordered the respondent to produce all the documentation in the ICC case. The ICC tribunal issued a corresponding order requiring the respondent to produce all the documentation in the ICSID case.

The exchange of documentation in parallel arbitrations may raise questions of confidentiality, particularly where the parties in the two arbitrations are not identical. Even where the parties are the same, but the tribunals differ and contain a common member, an interesting question may arise. Can the common arbitrator refer to or otherwise have regard to a document produced in arbitration A in arbitration B? If the arbitrator discloses it, is it a breach of a duty of confidentiality? As confidentiality belongs to the parties and as the parties are the same in both proceedings, it might be thought

---

155. LEBOULANGER, above fn. 23, pp. 90-91.

that there was no breach. But disclosure is being made to the other members of the tribunal. Bernard Hanotiau[156] says that the principle of neutrality, independence and impartiality of the arbitrator is of paramount concern and the duty of confidentiality will lead the arbitrator in some cases to reach the conclusion that it is no longer possible to fulfil the arbitrator's duties in total independence or impartiality and that he may have to resign. However in other cases the arbitrator may simply make a full disclosure of the problem to the co-arbitrators and the parties.

VIII. AVENUES OF MANAGEMENT

We have noted that if the parties are in agreement at the outset, they can articulate the desired treatment of multiple claims in their arbitration agreement. For example the Model Arbitration Clause of the Netherlands Arbitration Institute encompasses "all disputes arising in connection with the present contract and further contracts resulting therefrom".[157] Where there are multiple contracts with differing dispute resolution clauses, another possible approach is to provide for a clear hierarchy between them.[158] If the arbitration clause does not cover this but they are in agreement at the time of the dispute, they can express agreement by way of a distinct *compromis* which would itself be a revised agreement to arbitrate.

The situation is quite different where an institutional or rule-based solution is proposed. The difficulty with any solution in institutional rules is that the solution must be drafted before disputes have arisen. Thus it must be of a general nature and be able to deal fairly and efficiently with all permutations of facts. Here the difficulty is that the drafter must consider what trade-offs would be appropriate between flexibility and certainty.

If issues of consent are to be resolved by express provisions either in statutes establishing the lex arbitri or institutional or ad hoc rules, there are three broad possibilities. The rules could be drafted on an opt-in basis. They could indicate that the tribunal may deal with certain issues where the parties expressly agree. Such a provision adds nothing in terms of initial consent and would prevent inclusion if the parties could not agree once a dispute arose. A second approach would be to express the view that set-off and counterclaim rights would never be mandatory save where they are truly dealing with inherent defences central to the initial claim, in which case they fall within the arbitration agreement which underpins the initial claim. Hence they would in all other cases be subject to distinct consent of the parties on a case-by-case basis.

An alternative approach is an opt-out provision which allows the tribunal to consider set-off and counterclaim except where the parties agree otherwise. Even if an opt-out approach is adopted there is a need to consider just how to define counterclaims and set-off that are presumptively included. Should it be any form of counterclaim or set-off

---

156. HANOTIAU, above fn. 24, p. 350.
157. That may raise semantic debates about the difference between a contract that "relates" to another or which "results" from another.
158. POUDRET and BESSON, above fn. 4, para. 268.

recognized by the applicable law or should it expressly be limited to claims that could be brought within the original arbitration agreement? Even in the latter event, should the tribunal be given a discretion not to include the reverse claim where the circumstances of the case suggest that the benefits of separate proceedings outweigh the savings of a consolidated hearing? Examples alluded to above would be where the tribunal as initially constituted may not have appropriate expertise to deal with the multiplicity of claims. Perhaps counterclaims or set-off rights should be notified prior to the composition of the tribunal so the claimant can turn its mind to similar considerations to the respondent in selecting the tribunal. Actual pleadings can be left to differing time limits. Respondents who refrain from giving such notification to try to gain tactical advantages would in most cases be found out in terms of when the likely counterclaim and set-off came to their attention.

At the other extreme, the rules might allow for the broadest category of reverse claims. An example is Art. 21(5) of the Swiss Rules of International Arbitration which states:

> "The arbitral tribunal shall have jurisdiction to hear a set-off defence where the relationship out of which this defence is said to arise is not within the scope of the arbitration clause or is the object of another arbitration agreement or forum-selection clause."[159]

Pavić suggests that the drafters had procedural economy as their prime consideration.[160] Wolfgang Peter suggests instead that the justification for Art. 21(5) is the right to defence.[161]

One can readily note various advantages and disadvantages with an approach such as Art. 21(5) of the Swiss Rules. An express rule of that nature removes most of the uncertainty and potential for costly debate about the admissibility or otherwise of set-off defences. That alone should reduce transaction costs significantly. In most cases it will further reduce transaction costs by removing a multiplicity of actions. A concern to find the appropriate net figure that a claimant is entitled to will remove problems arising from mutual payment obligations with attendant timing, cash-flow and in extreme cases insolvency problems. For those who would see certain types of set-off at least as inherent elements in identifying the true net amount payable between the parties, rules providing for set-off defences might thus be seen as an inherent part of a just legal system.

Conversely disadvantages of such a rule include its blanket nature, encompassing both set-offs that are described above as true defences, primarily equitable set-off, and those that are simply relating to cash-flow issues. Such a clear-cut rule does not help to

---

159. As from January 2004 arbitral institutions in Basel, Bern, Geneva, Lausanne, Lugano and Zurich adopted uniform rules to deal with international arbitration.
160. Pavić implies that this at first glance goes against the will of the parties but it depends whether the express agreement to arbitrate under the Swiss Rules provides the necessary consent per medium of the article itself: PAVIĆ, above fn. 30, p. 108.
161. Wolfgang PETER, "Some Observations on the New Swiss Rules of International Arbitration", 22 ASA Special Series (2004) p. 1 at p. 9.

distinguish between these categories to the extent that one believes there are conceptual and policy reasons for doing so. It also does not help distinguish between valid and bona fide set-off claims on the one hand and those which are instead aimed at delaying payment and/or pressuring a claimant into settling for a reduced amount.

The articulation of the law in the Swiss Rules also does not make it clear whether a tribunal has a discretion to consider these matters when a set-off defence is raised. For example, while the rule stipulates that the tribunal "shall" have jurisdiction over such set-off defences, where these are not part of the original arbitration agreement it is not clear whether the tribunal must consider the defence or whether it instead has a discretion whether or not to do so.[162] To the extent that it is unclear whether the discretion exists, this will add transaction costs in individual disputes where this has to be debated. Because it is a fundamental procedural and jurisdictional question, uncertainty as to the tribunal's powers may be grounds for challenge of the award or enforcement proceedings.[163] If there is no discretion, then the problems alluded to above from a blanket rule point to costs as well as benefits from such an initiative. If the rules do contain a discretion, there is a question as to whether different tribunals are likely to be able to apply such a discretion in a fair and consistent manner.

Even though the inclusionary power seems clear, there still may be uncertainty where there are clashes between contracts, particularly as this may give rise to interpretative challenges for the tribunal and complex questions of the interplay between courts and tribunals in some circumstances at least. As to the first, if two separate arbitrations were commenced, each with an Art. 21(5) equivalent, could set-off from one be raised under the other? Could the provisions be used as a basis for seeking consolidation? Could a tribunal say that the contract later in time is intended to take precedence over the former one as the most recent indication of the intent of the parties? What if instead, an earlier contract referred to arbitration subject to Art. 21(5) and a later related contract has a choice of forum clause? Would it be held to be a variation of the Art. 21(5) entitlements because it is later in time? The tribunals might have to unravel issues of *lis pendens*, good faith and abuse of rights. What would happen if one contract referred to the Swiss Rules including Art. 21(5) but a related contract expressly indicated that there are no rights to bring set-off defences? What if the second contract was earlier in time, concurrent or subsequent to the first contract? What if two institutions had a 21(5) equivalent and separate cases were brought to each? Hopefully in most circumstances, the order of the procedural steps taken by the parties should indicate what would be a fair procedural determination in the circumstances.

At the very least, in a world where commercial entities can choose between different arbitral centres, it is a valuable option and indeed experiment to have a highly respected arbitral venue offering such a model.

At the extreme, a rule might also allow for all cross-claims including unrelated counterclaims on the grounds of an efficient resolution of all inter-party claims. Thus Pierre Karrer has even suggested that Art. 21(5) could be applied to counterclaims

---

162. PAVIĆ, above fn. 30, p. 108.
163. *Ibid.*, p. 109.

notwithstanding that it only expressly refers to set-off.[164] Our observations above would also apply to such an initiative.


IX. CONCLUSIONS

After beginning with an elaboration of the importance of looking to the agreement of the parties, we have traversed the discrete issues of claims by claimant, claims by respondent and consolidation applications. We then tied these topics together to see whether they could all be dealt with systematically under various paradigms, namely, a conflicts methodology, efficiency-based logic, enforceability and an analysis of *a priori* consent.

We suggest the following broad principles.

(1) The starting point in discerning consent to multiple claims is always the arbitration agreement before the initial tribunal, together with the lex arbitri and the procedural rules if any, agreed to by the parties.
(2) Assuming there is only one contract involved, it is obviously the case that if it expressly provides for or denies the opportunity for additional claims, this is the end of the matter.
(3) The corollary of this is that in all other cases, the tribunal will be dealing with a dispute between the parties as to the admissibility of some of the claims. The tribunal is forced to analyze the agreement and applicable law and rules to discern what the parties truly intended at the outset, in the circumstances that have in due course arisen. It is a question of construction and not a discretionary matter, unless an express discretionary power has been granted via the rules.
(4) Where claimant's initial claims are concerned, when considering the type of claims that can be brought, it is a question of construction of the arbitration agreement alone as initial jurisdiction flows from that agreement.
(5) If instead it is an attempt by claimant to add a new claim after the arbitration has commenced, the arbitration agreement is still the gateway. Rules such as Art. 19 ICC Rules deal with timing issues and provide a discretion as to late acceptance of new claims after the Terms of Reference have been drawn, but this would still be provided the claims otherwise fall within the subject matter of the agreement to arbitrate.
(6) However, even if a late claim is within the agreement, the lex arbitri or procedural rules agreed to may place time limits on additional claims and/or may add a discretion to deny otherwise admissible claims.
(7) Difficulties may arise with late claims in ad hoc arbitrations without any guidance in any rules.
(8) Turning to respondent's claims, because a counterclaim remains alive even if the primary claim is withdrawn or invalid, it must be based on its own independent evidence of consent. As always, such consent should be found to emanate from the arbitration

---

164. Pierre KARRER, "Arbitration Under the Swiss Rules of Arbitration in Switzerland and Elsewhere" (Paper presented at the 12th Croatian Arbitration Day, Zagreb, 2 December 2004), cited in PAVIĆ, above fn. 30, p. 111 (fn. 35).

agreement itself, either directly or through a lex arbitri or rules that expressly allow for counterclaims.

(9) The rules vary from those which give no guidance as to the type of counterclaims that may be brought to those defining the linkage. Defined linkages are either to the contract of the arbitration agreement or the same relationship. Even then it is important to construe these rules alongside the arbitration agreement as there may be variances between the two. For example, if the arbitration agreement expressly allowed for a broader range of counterclaims than the rules, most would consider that the express reference was the better indication of the true intent of the parties. The same would hold if the arbitration agreement was expressed to be narrower.

(10) Where set-off is concerned, we are not comfortable with the view that being defences, all set-offs must be admissible on the basis that justice demands that any defence must be allowed. They are seen as defences in domestic systems. These systems display very different approaches to the treatment of set-off even if all describe them as defences. Furthermore, domestic litigation treatment is built on many policy considerations not relevant to arbitration.

(11) For arbitration, we suggest that a similar approach should be taken to counterclaims. Is the set-off within the agreement and/or the applicable lex arbitri and rules. If so it should be permitted. If not, for example an independent set-off in an ad hoc arbitration, the mere description as a defence does not in our view suffice. All additional claims need to be sufficiently linked to the primary arbitration clause under which they are sought to be introduced. Merely calling some or all of them "defences", particularly as that term is viewed in domestic legal systems, or defining them as substantive as opposed to procedural rights, should not replace a careful analysis of the sufficiency of the linkage to the consent to arbitration.

(12) If parties agree on rules which expressly address an issue, this is again clear evidence of consent. For example, adoption of the Swiss Rules and Art. 21(5) is clear consent to allow a broad range of set-offs.

(13) Turning to multiple contract situations and respondent's claims, it is reasonable to start with the view that identical clauses can lead to multiple claims being brought together and differences in clauses constitutes evidence to the contrary. Nevertheless, we observe that, as to the first, some cases may raise legitimate procedural justice concerns as to composition even where clauses are identical. Where there are different clauses, being a matter of construction of both in context, it is at least arguable that such clauses may say nothing more than that *isolated* claims must go to different places. They may give no clear indication of what was intended for *concurrent* reverse claims. In these circumstances, tribunals should analyze all of the factors in construing intent.

(14) In any event, admissibility of counterclaims under multi-contract situations would still need to be linked back to an agreement to arbitrate found within one contract that, because of the integrated nature of the various contracts, is held to be broad enough to encompass claims under distinct contracts.

(15) Additional counterclaims and set-offs after the initial stages again draw attention to the rules selected and the potential for time-limits and/or express discretionary powers in an institution or tribunal.

(16) Principles of consolidation build upon similar issues. In most cases the decision to order consolidation is discretionary.

(17) Where discretions are expressly provided for additional claims or consolidations, many matters could be considered in the exercise of the discretion including:

– How closely are the two disputes linked in terms of their facts? Obviously if they are sufficiently linked, then the entitlement comes about directly under the arbitration clause and not via discretion of a tribunal; but even circumstances that do not fit directly into the agreement can have various degrees of connection to the primary claim.
– In terms of efficiency, are there clear transaction-cost savings to be made by having one tribunal?
– Are there questions of evidence that would best be heard by a single tribunal, either to prevent inconsistency or to promote confidentiality?
– Do the facts show that it would be both fair and efficient to try to find the net payment obligations if any between the parties rather than to separate these out through more than one tribunal hearing? Alternatively, could cash-flow issues simply be dealt with via awards that are timed to allow netting out mutual payment obligations?
– Is the tribunal composition adequate to deal with each of the matters both in terms of expertise and in terms of cost benefit as to number of arbitrators?

Finally, a question arises as to how to resolve those multiple claims disputes where an analysis of the agreement and rules leaves a tribunal in doubt. Some suggest a conflicts approach; some suggest that efficiency considerations are the best evidence of the presumed intent of the parties.

As to the latter, a contentious question would be whether all or any of the aforementioned factors relevant to express discretions, can also be considered in determining the likely intent of the parties in cases not clearly resolved by the agreement and rules.

In such circumstances we support a concern to supplant the interpretation of the arbitration agreement, where necessary, with a careful assessment of all factors that might help a tribunal draw conclusions as to the likely *a priori* intent of the parties. Implied intent to promote efficient solutions is an important working hypothesis, as long as it is seen as one factor that needs to be looked at alongside others.

As we have noted, arguments in favour of admissibility or consolidation include general efficiency, reducing the transaction costs of parallel proceedings, overall timeliness, and the avoidance of some of the pitfalls flowing from the composition of multiple tribunals where overlap may raise questions of prejudice or undue influence. Countervailing factors include the concern that reverse claims might be brought on spurious grounds to actually delay proceedings, frighten the claimant into settlement and add immediate financial burdens through the arbitral advance on costs. In addition, admissibility or consolidation may raise questions as to the suitability of the tribunal to deal with all of the multiple claims and might provide undesirable tactical advantages in tribunal selection Presumptions based on general efficiency alone are only a small part of a commercially realistic analysis of likely intent in the hopefully small number of troublesome cases where the agreement and rules are still ambiguous.

# Consolidation and Joinder in Arbitration – The Arab Middle Eastern Approach

*Nayla Comair-Obeid**

| TABLE OF CONTENTS | Page |
|---|---|
| I. Introduction | 500 |
| II. Current Middle Eastern Approach on Consolidation and Joinder | 501 |
| III. Meeting the Challenges of the Construction Industry in the Middle East in Relation to Multi-party Disputes | 506 |
| IV. Conclusion | 509 |

## I. INTRODUCTION

The question of consolidation and joinder, previously only an issue for court proceedings, has now become a hot topic in arbitration and has given rise to controversial opinions among scholars as well as in case law. The UNCITRAL Working Group II on International Arbitration and Conciliation is considering a provision that would stipulate a single determination of related claims arising under separate contractual instruments.[1]

Michael Pryles and Jeffrey Waincymer dealt in their survey with the possible ways to address such questions of consolidation which are related to single determination of related claims arising under separate contractual instruments between the same parties.[2]

---

\* Partner, Obeid law firm (Beirut); Professor of International Arbitration, Lebanese University; Member of Council, Institute of World Business Law, ICC; Chairman, Lebanese Branch, Chartered Institute of Arbitrators.

1. At its thirty-ninth session (New York, 19 June-7 July 2006), the United Nations Commission on International Trade Law (UNCITRAL) agreed that, in respect of future work of the Working Group, priority shall be given to a revision of the UNCITRAL Arbitration Rules (1976) (the UNCITRAL Arbitration Rules or the Rules). At its forty-fifth session (Vienna, 11-15 September 2006), Working Group II undertook to identify areas where a revision of the UNCITRAL Arbitration Rules might be useful. In this respect, a provision on consolidation of cases was added to Art. 15, which provided that "the arbitral tribunal may, on the application of any party, assume jurisdiction over any claim involving the same parties and arising out of the same legal relationship, provided that such claims are subject to arbitration under these Rules and that the arbitration proceedings in relation to those claims have not yet commenced". It may be recalled that the Working Group considered that it might not be necessary to provide for consolidation under the Rules ("Report of Working Group on Arbitration on the work of its forty-sixth session" (New York, 5-9 February 2007) UNCITRAL, 40th Sess., UN Doc. A/CN.9/619 (25 June-12 July 2007) para. 120).
2. Michael PRYLES and Jeffrey WAINCYMER, "Multiple Claims Between the Same Parties", this volume, pp. 437-499 at p. 437.

He considered how arbitration can or should deal with the entire range of multiple claims that might be brought between the same parties and focused on the need to identify the general principle of jurisdiction which limits and guides questions of a claim's admissibility.

In his study, a number of questions have been analyzed in order to assert how such single determination shall be decided, taking into consideration the basis of arbitration – which is the parties' consent, reflected in the parties' agreement – and doing this on a case-by-case basis. In his view, several factors need to be considered by arbitral tribunals when identifying the parties' intention, including efficiency and fair arbitral proceedings in terms of expense, time and avoidance of the risk of inconsistent decisions.

He suggested a uniform methodology to discern the parties' intention in view of a possible consolidation of claims between the same parties if the arbitration agreement is not clear and if the institutional arbitration rules do not provide for consolidation.

Nathalie Voser addressed the issue of complex arbitration arising in multi-party disputes, especially with respect to the joinder of a third party after the arbitration has commenced, and of the possible inclusion of a third party in the arbitration proceedings in the typical situation of construction projects.[3]

The question we pose concerning the Middle Eastern countries is whether consolidation is acceptable in a proceeding with a non-signatory third party, in relation to separate but connected contractual instruments, and if the joinder of a third party is possible. A critical issue is also to be considered in the construction industry in the Middle East, especially due to the construction boom in the Gulf area, leading us to propose a provision on consolidation.

In the first part of this Comment, we shall address those issues in the Arab Middle Eastern countries and focus on current legislation and precedents in these countries. In the second part we shall examine the challenges that complex disputes in the construction industry are facing in this region.

II. CURRENT MIDDLE EASTERN APPROACH ON CONSOLIDATION AND JOINDER

*1. Legislation*

The legislation of Arab countries pertaining to arbitration is fairly recent. These countries are divided into three categories. The first category includes the countries which reformed their legislation on arbitration, based on the UNCITRAL Model Law on International Commercial Arbitration (the Model Law), with or without

---

3. Nathalie VOSER, "Multi-Party Disputes and Joinder of Third Party", this volume, pp. 343-410.

modifications: this is the case in Bahrain,[4] Egypt,[5] Jordan,[6] Oman,[7] Syria[8] and Tunisia.[9] The second category includes the countries inspired by the French arbitration model, such as Lebanon,[10] Libya,[11] Morocco[12] and Algeria.[13] The third category comprises countries that still do not have any modern legislation on arbitration. It is to be noted that the United Arab Emirates (UAE)[14] and Qatar[15] are currently reforming their legislation, that Saudi Arabia[16] and Kuwait[17] have their own specific legislation on arbitration, and finally that Iraq,[18] according to a 2007 US Department of State Report,

---

4. In Bahrain arbitration is governed by two laws: the first one, specific to international commercial arbitration, is Decree Law No. 9/1994, and the second one, specific to domestic arbitration, is Decree Law No. 12/1971 incorporated in the Code of Civil and Commercial Procedure (Arts. 233-243).
5. Egypt promulgated Law No. 27 (the Arbitration Law) in 1994.
6. The Jordanian Law of Arbitration No. 18 was promulgated in 1953 and was subsequently amended in 1962. In 2001 it was superseded by Law No. 31.
7. On 28 July 1997 Oman enacted the Law on Arbitration in Civil and Commercial Disputes by Sultani Decree No. 47.
8. The Syrian Arbitration Rules were promulgated by Law No. 4 of 2008.
9. Tunis promulgated its Arbitration Code in Law No. 42/1993, dated 26 April 1993.
10. The Lebanese Rules on Domestic and International Arbitration are incorporated in the Lebanese Code of Civil Procedure, promulgated by the Decree Law No. 90/1983. These Rules were amended in 2002 by Law No. 440/2002 (Arts. 762-821).
11. In 1953 Libya amended its Code of Civil and Commercial Procedure, Chapter 4 of which included provisions on arbitration which resembled the old Egyptian provisions; those related to arbitration were amended several times: in 1970, 1972, 1973 and 1975.
12. In Morocco arbitration is covered by the provisions of the Code of Civil and Commercial Procedure.
13. On 25 April 1993, in an effort to modernize its laws, Algeria enacted Decree No. 9/1993, which amended the Procedural Law (Sect. 4) to include provisions on international commercial arbitration.
14. The UAE Arbitration Rules are incorporated in the UAE Code of Civil Procedure, Federal Law No. (11) of 1992 (Arts. 203-218). These rules are currently subject to revision, based on the UNCITRAL Model Law.
15. The rules relating to arbitration are incorporated in the Qatari Code of Civil and Commercial Procedure No. 13/1990 (Arts. 190-210).
16. The Kingdom of Saudi Arabia enacted legislation on arbitration in the Royal Decree No. M/46, dated 12 March 1983.
17. In 1980, Kuwait passed Law No. 38/1980 on Civil and Commercial Procedure which includes, in Arts. 173-188, provisions concerning voluntary arbitration. Although modern by Gulf standards, these provisions do not include modern arbitration principles such as *Kompetenz-Kompetenz* or the principle of severability of the arbitration clause in a contract. They also vest the judiciary with considerable powers to intervene in arbitrations. For these reasons, there is pressure in Kuwait to enact a new legislation on domestic arbitration, adopting the principles of the UNCITRAL Model Law. Kuwait also has a system of "judicial arbitration" pursuant to Law No. 11/1995 under which parties may voluntarily submit disputes in writing to panels consisting of three judges and two members who have relevant expertise.
18. In 1969, a new Code of Civil and Commercial Procedure was enacted in Iraq, Chapter II of Volume Three of which deals with arbitration (Arts. 251-276). On the international front, although US advisors are urging it to do so, Iraq has not yet become a signatory to the 1958 New

"has not yet signed or adopted the two most important legal instruments for international commercial arbitration, namely the New York Convention and the attendant rules and procedures of the UNCITRAL".

Most of these three categories did not provide any provision in relation to consolidation and joinder, either in their national laws or in the rules of their arbitration centers.

*a. National laws*

Almost all the national laws of Middle Eastern countries dealing with arbitration do not provide for consolidation of claims or joinder of a third party. However, an exception is to be noted in the Lebanese Code of Civil Procedure, which provides only for the joinder of a third party in its Art. 786, stipulating that a third party could be joined to an arbitral proceeding only if all the parties to the arbitral proceeding agreed thereto.

The fact that these national laws adopt the classical approach is understandable and justified, since this approach is based on the general principles governing arbitration, namely the privity of the arbitration agreement and the parties' autonomy.

In Arab countries, a third party could only be joined to an arbitral proceeding if all the parties to the arbitral proceeding and the third party agreed thereto. In addition, if a party wishes to join a third person to the arbitral proceeding but could not obtain the consent of the other party, it could only initiate a distinct arbitral proceeding against it. In that case, we will be facing a complex situation where two related proceedings with different parties are dealt with by different arbitral tribunals.[19] The Middle Eastern arbitration centers adopted a similar approach.

*b. Arbitration centers*

The Middle Eastern arbitration centers,[20] even the most pioneering ones,[21] did not adopt a provision on consolidation or joinder.

---

York Convention or the ICSID Convention. At present, no mechanism exists for the enforcement of foreign arbitral awards other than by obtaining a local judgment into which they are incorporated.

19. Hamzeh HADDAD, *Arbitration in the Arab Legislation*, Part I, 1st edn. (Al-Halabi Legal Publications 2007) p. 315.
20. Bahrain Center for International Commercial Arbitration, Jordanian Law and Arbitration Center, Oman Commercial Arbitration Center, Qatar International Center of Arbitration, Kingdom of Saudi Arabia (KSA) Commercial Arbitration Center, Tunis Center for Conciliation and Arbitration, Yemen Center for Conciliation and Arbitration.
21. Dubai International Arbitration Center (DIAC): New Rules for DIAC were issued by Decree No. 11/2007 and entered into effect on 7 May 2007, upon their approval by H.H. the Ruler of Dubai, on 6 May 2007, and their issuance in the Official Gazette No. 321 on 7 May 2007. These new DIAC Rules replaced the previously applicable Rules of Commercial Conciliation and Arbitration of Dubai Chamber and Industry No. 2 of 1994.

The Cairo Regional Center for International Commercial Arbitration (CRCICA), which is an international organization operating in Egypt since 1979, adopted the UNCITRAL Arbitration Rules and applied these Rules with minor amendments made successfully in 1998, 2000, 2002 and 2006. They became effective as of 1 January 1998, 1 October 2000, 21 November 2002 and October 2006, respectively.

However, one exception is found in the Rules of Conciliation and Arbitration of the Lebanese Arbitration Center of the Beirut Chamber of Commerce and Industry (CCIB),[22] in Art. 8 of Appendix II on the consolidation of claims (inspired by Art. 4(6) of the ICC Rules in its pre-January 1998 version), which provided the following:

> "When the party presents a Request for Arbitration in connection with a legal relationship already submitted to arbitration proceedings by the same parties and pending before the Court of Arbitration, the Court may decide to include that claim in the existing proceedings, subject to the provisions of Article 16 of the Beirut Chamber of Commerce and Industry Rules of Arbitration."

In this respect, the Court of Arbitration could, under the Rules of the Lebanese Arbitration Center of the CCIB, consolidate several pending proceedings if:

(1) consolidation is requested by a party;
(2) the arbitration proceedings are between the same parties; and
(3) the arbitration proceedings are in connection with the same legal relationship.

To my knowledge, there is no precedent with respect to consolidation by virtue of the above provision.

2.   *Case Law*

Having researched the precedents in the Arab countries dealing with consolidation or joinder, I found one (unpublished) case involving joinder under the Rules of the Cairo Regional Center for International Commercial Arbitration.

This case is related to a distribution agreement between A, a manufacturer of water heaters in Egypt, and B, a distributor of the electrical water heaters in the Egyptian market. A terminated this agreement on the grounds that B failed to place firm orders for the year 2007.

Alleging a wrongful termination of the distribution agreement by A, B presented a Request for Arbitration. A requested C, the supplier of components for the water heaters, to join the arbitration proceedings based on several elements: in the first place C and B were partners, as C was owned and controlled by individuals who were shareholders of B; secondly, C and A were bound by a supply agreement which is related to the distribution agreement, both agreements having been signed on the same day and containing the same terms as per the arbitration clause; and finally, C was liable to indemnify A, as C failed to supply components that were necessary for the production of the water heaters.

C commenced a parallel proceeding against A under the supply agreement (an issue of consolidation arises).

---

22. The Lebanese Chamber of Commerce and Industry was created on 8 May 1995.

The tribunal dismissed the request for joinder on the grounds that it exceeded the scope of its jurisdiction under the distribution agreement and thus potentially would expose its final award to annulment for the following reasons:

(1) The parties did not consent to joinder and A and C were "*separate legal persons*".
(2) The arbitration agreement did not expressly provide the arbitral tribunal with the power to join a third party to an arbitral proceeding and "*a specific provision on joinder would be required to override the need for privity in an arbitration agreement*". Furthermore, this tribunal was not able to read the arbitration clause of the distribution agreement as creating personal jurisdiction over a non-signatory party to this agreement; especially as C did not sign the distribution agreement.
(3) The Cairo Regional Center Rules and the Egyptian 1994 national law No. 27 do not contain any provision on joinder or consolidation.

> "The group of contracts and group of companies doctrines may be valid in other legal systems, but they do not seem to have been recognized in Egyptian law, at any rate for the present jurisdictional purposes and on the facts of this case."

Concerning the consolidation issue, the arbitral tribunal considered that the

> "economic considerations and inconsistent outcomes are valid considerations, but the tribunal has no power to join and these considerations cannot of themselves create it. The tribunal trusts that the C v. B arbitral tribunal will give the appropriate weight to any factual findings made by this Tribunal that may be relevant to the matters before the other tribunal."

The position adopted by this arbitral tribunal is an expression of the classical approach and is in line with current Arab legislation and with the precedents of the Arab State courts. This approach applies to consolidation and joinder alike. In fact, on several occasions, the Lebanese[23] and Syrian State courts[24] reiterated their positions on the non-admissibility of the request for joinder of a third party to an arbitral proceeding, and considered that such request shall be dismissed unless all the parties to the arbitral proceeding and the third party agreed to the joinder.

The upholding of this conservative approach in the Arab countries is not in line with the French approach, which now opts for a much more modern approach in relation to connected contracts or groups of contracts.

---

23. Lebanese Supreme Court, 5th Chamber, 19 February 2002, Decision No. 21/2002, The Lebanese Review of Arab and International Arbitration (2002, no. 22) p. 66.
   Beirut Appeal Court, 3rd Chamber, 19 February 2004, Decision No. 300/2004, The Lebanese Review of Arab and International Arbitration (2004, no. 29) p. 50.
24. Syrian Supreme Court, Decision No. 71/494, 1998, Al-Alousy, Rule 73.

Effectively, the French Supreme Court admits the transmission of the arbitration agreement in a chain of contracts to a non-signatory party[25] and, recently, adopted a much advanced position in its decision dated 27 March 2007[26] where it confirmed the automatic transmission of these clauses by adopting the direct method, stating that "in a chain of contracts transferring property, the arbitration clause is automatically transferred as (it is) an accessory of the right to act, which in itself is an accessory of the substantive right transmitted; the homogenous or heterogeneous nature of that chain has no impact thereon".

This new trend has to be taken into consideration by practitioners, courts and arbitral tribunals in the Arab Middle Eastern countries, due to the high frequency of complex transactions (construction, finance, etc.) concluded in these countries consequent to the important cash flow generated from the latest surge in oil prices.

III. MEETING THE CHALLENGES OF THE CONSTRUCTION INDUSTRY IN THE MIDDLE EAST IN RELATION TO MULTI-PARTY DISPUTES

Every year, millions of business contracts are entered into which provide for arbitration as a means of resolving conflicts.

What distinguishes a construction dispute from other disputes is the number of parties that are usually involved therein. Unlike a shipping contract, for instance, which is customarily between three parties – or an insurance contract – a construction contract may involve a significant number of parties: namely, the employer, designer(s), engineer(s), supervisor(s), contractors(s), subcontractor(s), suppliers(s), etc.

The Middle East in general, and more specifically the Gulf region, has witnessed an unprecedented boom in the construction industry, the like of which – in terms of speed and volume – has never been witnessed, save in post-World War II Europe.

The construction sector in the Gulf Cooperation Council, which comprises Bahrain, Kuwait, Oman, Qatar, and Saudi Arabia and the UAE, has witnessed a great boom with projects estimated at hundreds of billions of dollars, a significant part of which is being spent on the UAE's large projects. The projection for the coming decade is that the sector will continue to grow, thanks to the unprecedented increase in oil revenues, which resulted in the accumulation of great surpluses.

The numbers below speak for themselves:

– In the Emirate of Dubai, for instance, the construction sector GDP has increased by 166 percent during the period 2000-2004, and has grown with an annual average growth

---

25. French Supreme Court (*Cour de Cassation*), 1st Civil Chamber, 6 February 2001, Rev. Arb. (2001) p. 765.
26. French Supreme Court (*Cour de Cassation*), 1st Civil Chamber, 27 March 2007, Rev. Arb. (2007) p. 785.

rate of 27.7 percent during the same period. This is reflected in the number of active construction companies in the Emirate, around 6,000 companies.[27]

— In 2006, there were over 2,100 projects either planned or underway in the Gulf region, with a total value of a staggering US$ 1 trillion, of which the UAE and Saudi Arabia made up 29 percent and 20 percent, respectively. By May 2007, the total project value had surged to US$ 1.47 trillion.[28]

— Of the world's 125,000 construction cranes in operation, Dubai accounts for 20 percent, i.e., 25,000 cranes.[29]

— The construction boom witnessed in the UAE and Saudi Arabia has not only caused a shortage of material, but also of manpower. In addition to US and European construction services providers, companies from China, Indonesia, Japan, Korea, Malaysia and Singapore, as well as Egypt, Jordan and Lebanon, are striving to increase their presence.

— The UAE currently has the tallest high-rises (higher than 300 meters) in the world. It is home to two Guinness records (the tallest building, the Burj Tower, and the biggest shopping mall, the Dubai Mall).[30]

Where there are multiple parties with disputes arising from the same transaction, complications may often be reduced by the consolidation of all disputes. Parties can provide for the consolidation of two or more separate arbitrations into a single proceeding or permit the intervention of a third party in arbitration. In a construction dispute, consolidated proceedings may eliminate the need for duplicative presentations of claims and avoid the possibility of conflicting rulings from different panels of arbitrators. Conversely, consolidating claims might be a source of delay and expense.

*1. Potential Challenges*

A common problem that frequently arises in major construction projects involving many parties is when a dispute between the employer and the main contractor is referred to arbitration and the main contractor wishes to join the subcontractor in the proceedings, on the basis that if there is any liability, the main contractor wishes to pass some or all of that liability on to the subcontractor. The question to be posed is whether a third party (contractor, subcontractor, suppliers, etc.) could be joined and whether related arbitrations could be consolidated.

In staged and long-term projects involving many parties, the problem is further accentuated, as is shown in the following scenario involving one single contract with more than two parties and related contracts between the same or different parties:

---

27. "Dubai Construction Sector: Facts and Figures", 7 February 2006, at <www.zawya.com/story.cfm/sidZAWYA20060206091719> (last accessed 2 June 2008).
28. Hong Kong Trade Development Council, "Construction Boom in UAE and Saudi Arabia: Opportunities for Hong Kong", 2 August 2007, Executive Summary, <www.hktdc.com/econforum/tdc/tdc070801.htm> (last accessed 2 June 2008).
29. *Ibid.*
30. *Ibid.*, under 1. Backdrop.

*Scenario:*
Owner A, entered into three separate contracts with three different contractors, namely B, C and D, to perform works on different sections of a 110-storey tower.

Contractor B was assigned excavation and earth-moving works; Contractor C was assigned civil works, including cladding and finishing works; Contractor D was assigned electro-mechanical works.

Most of the contracts are UAE model contracts based on FIDIC (International Federation of Consulting Engineers) 1987, reprinted in 1992. All of these contracts contain an ICC arbitration clause. A prerequisite before going to arbitration is provided for in the respective contracts, namely, that amicable settlement of any dispute that may arise should be attempted, and such attempts are to be led "by the director of each company on behalf of each contractor with a director on behalf of the Owner".

The arbitration clause refers to UAE law as the applicable law, the seat of arbitration being Dubai.

Each of the aforementioned main contractors entered into a series of back-to-back sub-contracts with subcontractors, namely (B1, B2, B3, C1, C2, C3, D1, D2 and D3).

Here we have a project with a critical path, involving thirteen parties. The nature of the project entails that certain works cannot commence before, and are conditional upon, the completion of certain other works on the project. In other words for example, if subcontractor B2 is delayed, subcontractors C3 and D1 are automatically delayed as they cannot start performing their tasks under their respective contracts with the main contractors before B2 completes the execution of the works assigned to him.

Subcontractor C2, responsible for the design and execution of the cladding works on the project, went through a phase of insolvency, and was subsequently forced to file for bankruptcy. Such an event, in all likelihood, is bound to affect the entire critical path of such a gigantic project, and it did.

Contractor C strived to salvage the project by undertaking the responsibility to perform the unexecuted cladding works and tried to achieve it in the program float. However, this delay in the cladding delayed the other subcontractors with respect to fit-out, thus resulting in the issuing of variation orders for the other subcontractors and a request for an extension of time.

Here we have a situation where Owner A is not in a position to sue (or be sued) in relation to any of the contracts entered into between the three main contractors and the nine subcontractors, albeit all of which are connected to the same project that forms the subject matter of his contract with the three main contractors. In this connection, it is worth noting that a dispute arose in respect of delays and disruptions to most of the contracts.

Such a hypothetical scenario does not belong to the realm of fiction, but is rather experienced in a number of "staged" and complex projects around the world, and is becoming very frequent across the Middle East, due to the large number of complex projects that are springing up across the region.

It is hereby submitted that in projects of such nature, magnitude and complexity, the absence of consolidation and joinder clauses in the series of contracts between the owner and all those involved in the execution of the project – be they contractors, subcontractors, designers, suppliers, etc. – is bound to continue to lead to such an impasse, whereby the various parties to a series of contracts dealing with a single project cannot be brought within the ambit of the arbitration proceedings due to the absence of the above-mentioned clause.

## 2. Proposed Consolidation Clause

It is hereby submitted that for a consolidation clause to serve its intended purposes, it must pursue the following prerequisites:

– The consolidation clauses contained in the various contracts pertaining to the same project must be drafted in an identical manner, so as to remove any doubt as to the intention of the parties and to provide the relevant arbitrator with clear guidance when determining consolidation: i.e., the same scope, same institution, same governing law and same seat.
– They should unequivocally state the criteria for consolidation of the proceeding: arising from the same transaction, or raising common questions of fact and law, etc.
– They should determine the time limit (or the cut-off time) within which a request for consolidation or joinder shall be submitted.
– They should determine any other matter that is pertinent to the specific case in hand.

Lawyers, when drafting construction contracts, need to endeavour to ensure that a provision for consolidation is provided for. Such a clause could take any number of forms with the main focus being on the automatic and unfettered transmission of the arbitration clause and consolidation of arbitrations arising out of the same economic enterprise. One such example of a clause leading to an automatic transmission of the arbitration clause is presented hereunder:

> "Owners, all contractors, subcontractors, suppliers, engineers, architects, designers, and all other parties involved in the construction of this project, including but not limited to parent company guarantors and assignees, are bound, each to each other, by this arbitration clause, provided such party has signed this contract, or has signed a contract which incorporates this contract by reference, or signs any other agreement appertaining in any shape or form to this project to be bound by this arbitration clause."

## IV. CONCLUSION

As has been shown above, multi-party arbitration raises a number of key challenges to all those involved in the field of arbitration. The fast-paced developments witnessed the world over and the ever-increasing complexities of contractual obligations make it incumbent upon us to attempt to devise creative and ingenious remedies to the obstacles and hurdles encountered in our quest for a timely and fair resolution of disputes.

Two key areas stand out and are readily discernable, namely:

— The consolidation of related arbitrations; and
— The joinder of a third party who is not a signatory to the arbitration agreement.

These are serious issues and are key problems facing arbitration today. The Middle East, probably more than any other region, is in serious need of a solution due to the lack of adequate provisions on consolidation and joinder in the legislation and the rules of their arbitration centers.

The parties' consent still remains the basis of any possible solution to remedy these problems. I am of the opinion that lawyers can play a very important role in guiding the parties when drafting the dispute settlement clause, by contemplating a provision for consolidation or joinder, taking into consideration the nature of the transaction, its specificity and complexity.

Recommendations for possible solutions are:

— Incorporate in the institutional rules the relevant provisions, as per the ICC, London Court of International Arbitration, American Arbitration Association, Singapore International Arbitration Centre, Stockholm Chamber of Commerce, etc.). This can resolve some, but not all, of the problems.
— Provide guidance at the drafting stage, trying to put the agreement in the context of the whole transaction/ project, and viewing it as a mere link in a chain comprising many links.
— Contemplate a model clause for all parties that might be involved in a construction project, akin to the arbitration clause for FIDIC or similar standard forms of contract.
— Similarly, contemplate an optional provision under the UNCITRAL Arbitration Rules.

Michael Pryles and Jeffrey Waincymer favor that any modification to arbitration rules should be discretionary, as opposed to mandatory; I totally agree with him. I also submit that any changes to arbitral rules allowing for consolidation and joinder of third parties should provide the parties with an "exit" or an "opt-out" clause, if they so desire. The challenge before us is to strike the right balance between the desires to reach effective resolution of disputes while, at the same time, upholding the sacrosanct right of party autonomy.

# Working Group B

# 3. Summary Disposition

# Applications for the Early Disposition of Claims in Arbitration Proceedings

*Judith Gill QC*[*]

TABLE OF CONTENTS | Page
---|---
I. Introduction | 513
II. The Acceptable Face of Early Disposition | 513
III. Disposition of Issues on an Expedited and Summary Basis | 516
IV. The ICSID Approach | 517
V. Investment Treaty Provisions | 519
VI. Where Should Tribunals Draw the Line? | 520
VII. Use of the Tools Currently Available | 521
VIII. The Way Forward | 524

## I. INTRODUCTION

This paper will address the scope for and use of applications of early disposition of claims in arbitration proceedings. However, any consideration of this topic needs to begin with consideration of what we mean by applications for the *"early disposition"* of claims. In particular it is important to distinguish between sequential and summary disposition – on the one hand, a tribunal simply being asked to dispose of one or more issues in the normal way but before other issues are dealt with, e.g., addressing liability before quantum, and on the other hand a tribunal deciding issues on an expedited, summary basis.

In the former case, which I shall call the *"acceptable face of early disposition"*, the arbitration will proceed by way of a full airing of the issues in question (including if appropriate a full evidential hearing on that particular issue or claim), even if other issues may remain to be dealt with at a later stage. In the latter case, where issues are decided on an expedited, summary basis, the tribunal will reach its conclusion on more limited information and evidence. This distinction is at the heart of why early disposition of claims can be viewed by some as an everyday occurrence in international arbitration, but by others as highly contentious and arguably improper.

## II. THE ACCEPTABLE FACE OF EARLY DISPOSITION

It is not at all uncommon for an arbitration tribunal to conclude that it will deal first with particular issues, rather than hearing the entire case all at once. Such an approach is perfectly acceptable where the relevant rules subject to which the arbitration is being

---

[*] Partner and Head of International Arbitration Group, Allen & Overy LLP.

conducted so permit, whether they be institutional or other arbitration rules or national legislation.

Such permission is implicit in the ability of a tribunal to make more than one award and of course many institutional and other arbitration rules contemplate that the tribunal may make partial or interim awards rather than confining the tribunal to a single final award: see for example Art. 26.7 of the Rules of the London Court of International Arbitration (LCIA): "The Arbitral Tribunal may make separate awards on different issues at different times. Such awards shall have the same status and effect as any other award made by the Arbitral Tribunal." Similarly Art. 32(1) of the UNCITRAL Rules provides: "In addition to making a final award, the arbitral tribunal shall be entitled to make interim, interlocutory, or partial awards." The definition of "Award" in Art. 2(iii) of the ICC Rules includes an interim, partial or final award, and Art. 38 of the Stockholm Chamber of Commerce Rules provides that the tribunal "may decide a separate issue or part of the dispute in a separate award".

Similarly national legislation may specifically contemplate the making of more than one award. For example Art. 1049 of the Arbitration Act 1986 of the Netherlands permits a tribunal to render a final award, a partial final award, or an interim award. Art. 188 of the Swiss Private International Law Act 1987 provides that, unless the parties otherwise agree, the tribunal may make partial awards and under Sect. 47 of the Arbitration Act 1996 the tribunal may, subject to agreement otherwise by the parties, make more than one award at different times on different aspects of the matters to be determined. Sect. 47 also makes clear that the tribunal may, in particular, make an award relating to an issue affecting the whole claim.

So it seems the power to make awards on different issues exists, but when is its exercise appropriate? Each case will turn on its own particular facts but, for example, the making of awards on different issues may be appropriate:

(1) Where the determination of a particular issue or claim at an early stage will save time or costs or both in relation to the future conduct of the reference. This may be the case, for example, where there is a dispute as to the law applicable to the substantive issues in the case and an early determination of the issue will save the parties from having to present their cases on the basis of each of the alternative laws that the tribunal might ultimately determine are applicable.

(2) Where the determination of a particular issue or claim is likely to be decisive of the whole or a significant part of the dispute. Thus it may be expedient to deal with issues of liability before those relating to quantum or to resolve defences based on limitation periods said to be applicable at an early stage. It may also be appropriate to deal first with a number of principal issues or claims which the parties believe will assist in resolving the remaining matters in dispute between them. This is particularly so in large, complex cases where issues may be selected for early decision which will be commercially, even if not legally, determinative of the case in the sense that a decision on them is likely to help the parties resolve their other differences without the need for further proceedings. In its February 1996 report on the Bill which became the English Arbitration Act 1996,

the Departmental Advisory Committee emphasized the importance of a tribunal being empowered to take such an approach in order to save time and money.[1]

(3) Where there is no dispute between the parties that at least a certain sum is due from one party to the other, notwithstanding that there may be further sums in dispute or further claims or cross-claims which may give rise to liability. The tribunal can in these circumstances issue an award for the sum that is indisputably due.

(4) Where there is an ongoing loss or cause of action and the tribunal is persuaded that it should issue an award for losses incurred to a certain date, leaving open the option of a further award or awards for future losses.

(5) Where the proceedings are of a size and complexity that from a managerial perspective the only practical course is to deal with the issues or groups of issues in stages.

Tribunals also of course often issue awards dealing solely with a challenge to their jurisdiction and again the applicable rules or national legislation may specifically contemplate this.[2]

Even in the context of this type of early disposition of issues or claims caution must be exercised as there are potential downsides to a tribunal determining particular issues in advance of others. In particular, by dealing with the case in a piecemeal fashion, there may be a danger that resolution of the dispute as a whole will take longer than it otherwise would have done and the parties may be put to additional overall expense. The decision to deal with particular issues first is often based on the fact that, if resolved a certain way, those issues will be determinative – commercially or legally – of the case. However the tribunal cannot know how the issues will be decided and it may be that either the decision does not achieve that result or – arguably even more frustrating for the parties – having heard evidence and argument on particular issues the tribunal then declines to determine them in advance and proceeds with the case as a whole. The likelihood of increased costs and delay in these circumstances is obvious. Or perhaps, where the decision to make an award on a particular issue or issues is made at an early stage of the proceedings, it may subsequently prove to be less determinative, legally or commercially, than originally envisaged because the case turns out to be rather more complex than originally thought.

The tribunal must always therefore consider carefully whether there is any real advantage to the parties – and that means all of them – in proceeding with the case on a sequential basis, or whether it will simply add to the overall costs of the reference and cause unnecessary delay.

---

1. See paras. 226 to 230 of the Departmental Advisory Committee Report.
2. See e.g. Art. 186(3) of the Swiss Private International Law Act 1987, Section 31(4)(a) of the English Arbitration Act 1996 and Art. 16(3) of the UNCITRAL Model Law.

III.  DISPOSITION OF ISSUES ON AN EXPEDITED AND SUMMARY BASIS

Turning to the question of summary disposition, it is uncontroversial to suggest that tribunals generally do not possess the powers of summary disposition conferred on national courts. For example under Rule 56 of the US Federal Rules of Civil Procedure application may be made for summary judgment by a claimant or defending party "with or without supporting affidavits" and may be granted by US courts where there is "no genuine issue as to any material fact and ... the moving party is entitled to judgment as a matter of law". If summary judgment is not given on the whole case and a trial of some or all aspects of the case is necessary, on the summary judgment motion the court "shall if practicable" ascertain what material facts are actually and in good faith controverted, and those which are not, and direct "such further proceedings in the action as are just". At trial, the uncontroverted facts are deemed established.

Similarly in England Civil Procedure Rule 24 and the accompanying Practice Direction allow the court to give summary judgment on the whole claim or a particular issue if it considers that that claimant has no real prospect of succeeding on it or the defendant has no real prospect of successfully defending it. The application may be based on a point of law (including a question of construction of a document), or the evidence (or lack of it) which can reasonably be expected to be available at the trial or a combination of these and the parties are entitled to serve written evidence in support of or in opposition to the application. The court can give judgment on the claim, strike it out or dismiss it, refuse the application for summary judgment or, if it thinks the claim or defence may succeed but is unlikely to do so, make a conditional order requiring payment of a sum of money into court or the taking of a specified step as a condition of the claim or defence being allowed to proceed.

The important feature of these types of processes for present purposes is that although either or both parties may serve written evidence or affidavits, there is no full exploration of all the evidence in relation to the particular issue or claim being dealt with. Rather the matter is dealt with by submission and by reference to pleadings and other documents on file as well as such abridged evidence as the parties advance in order to persuade the court that there are, or are not, real prospects of success or genuine issues of material fact.

Policy reasons dictate why national courts need such powers, including the effective management of the State's resources for dispute resolution. The same considerations do not apply to arbitrators who are selected (and paid) to deal with the particular dispute. Further such a process is arguably incompatible with the right of parties to an arbitration to have their case heard and to deal with the case against them.

That said, there is widespread recognition of the need for efficiency in the arbitration process and in some quarters at least that has manifested itself in a decision to confer on tribunals express powers of early disposition. In particular there do exist arbitration rules that confer specific authority on tribunals to decide particular issues on an expedited basis and of course the parties can specifically agree fast-track procedures such as the "Short Form Arbitration Rules" of the Hong Kong International Arbitration Centre.

## IV. THE ICSID APPROACH

Art. 41(5) of the ICSID Arbitration Rules perhaps requires special attention in this context. It was introduced by the April 2006 amendments to the ICSID Arbitration Rules and introduced a new provision that:

> "Unless the parties have agreed to another expedited procedure for making preliminary objections, a party may, no later than 30 days after the constitution of the Tribunal, and in any event before the first session of the Tribunal, file an objection that a claim is manifestly without legal merit. The party shall specify as precisely as possible the basis for the objection. The Tribunal, after giving the parties the opportunity to present their observations on the objection, shall, at its first session or promptly thereafter, notify the parties of its decision on the objection."

The section goes on to make clear that the decision of the tribunal is without prejudice to the right of a party to file an objection to jurisdiction under Art. 41(1) or to object, in the course of the proceeding, that a claim lacks legal merit. Art. 41(6) goes on to state that if the tribunal decides that *"all claims are manifestly without legal merit"*, it shall render an award to that effect. Presumably, therefore, unless the tribunal concludes that the entirety of the claims brought are manifestly without legal merit, their decision must be given in a form other than an award, which of course has ramifications as regards enforcement.

The ICSID Additional Facility Rules, which apply where one or more of the jurisdictional requirements for ICSID arbitration are not met, have similar provisions at Art. 45(6) and (7).

What then was the intention behind the ICSID rule? In its Working Paper of 12 May 2005 on Suggested Changes to the ICSID Rules and Regulations ICSID noted that the Secretary-General's power to screen Requests for Arbitration did not extend to the merits of the dispute. The new powers under Art. 41(5) and (6) were intended in part at least to address this by allowing a party to ask the tribunal to look at the merits on an expedited basis at a very early stage and if appropriate issue an award dismissing the case. Interestingly however, the draft text being considered at that stage referred to claims being "manifestly without merit". The word "legal" was added subsequently.

In "The Development of the Regulations and Rules of the International Centre for Settlement of Investment Disputes",[3] ICSID's then Deputy Secretary-General Antonio Parra again emphasized that the Secretariat's power to refuse registration of a Request for Arbitration only arose where it disclosed a manifest lack of jurisdiction. He went on:

> "The Secretariat is powerless to prevent the initiation of proceedings that clear this jurisdictional threshold, but are frivolous as to the merits.... One of the amendments to the ICSID Arbitration Rules made in 2006 was to introduce a

---

3. 41 Int. Law. (2007) p. 47.

procedure, in Rule 41, for the early dismissal by arbitral Tribunals of patently unmeritorious claims."

Similarly Aurélia Antonietti, also formerly with ICSID, has described the rationale of Art. 41(5) as being to offer the possibility to a respondent of raising an objection based on the claim manifestly lacking legal merit once it has been registered. She notes that as the Secretary-General is required to register the Request for Arbitration unless he finds on the basis of the information contained in the Request that the dispute is manifestly outside the jurisdiction of the Centre, "this leaves no room for considerations of the merits of the dispute at the stage of the registration process".[4]

As Ms. Antonietti explains:

"The introduction of the new paragraph (5) allows a party to request the tribunal, at an early stage in the proceeding, to dismiss all or part of a claim on an expedited basis. The expedited objection can be a jurisdictional objection and/or an objection related to the merits." .... "It is not envisaged that an ICSID tribunal renders a summary award or partial award. Indeed, the current ICSID framework does not recognise the concept of partial awards. If a tribunal finds one claim to be without legal merits, but cannot pronounce itself as to the other claims (for example because further development of the factual record is needed), it is expected that the proceeding will continue. In practice, this might significantly reduce the actual interest in Rule 41(5). It is hoped, in any event, that the use of Rule 41(5) will be exceptional and circumscribed to frivolous claims only."

Whatever ICSID's intention in introducing Art. 41(5) and (6), the precise scope and meaning of the expression *"manifestly without legal merit"* is likely to be developed by the tribunals required to apply it. The term *"manifestly"* suggests something that is plain and obvious, which is consistent with the short time limits applied for both objections and their determination by the tribunal, but the precise standard to be applied will no doubt need to be developed. Similarly the scope of what is meant by *"without legal merit"* is potentially subject to different interpretations. Is the tribunal confined to considering simply whether the claim is sustainable as a matter of law without any consideration of the factual circumstances in which it is said to arise? In her article Ms. Antonietti commented that the insertion of the word "legal" before "merits" was "to avoid inappropriate discussions of the facts of the case at that stage". But does the legal merit of a claim have to take into account, to some extent at least, its factual context and whether the facts alleged are capable of amounting to a claim with legal merit? The commentaries referred to above suggest that Art. 41(5) and (6) were not intended to be confined purely to questions of law, but rather to apply more broadly to *"patently unmeritorious claims"*. However, given the time limits contemplated by Art. 41(5) a factual investigation of any substance would seem impractical. So presumably the tribunal will largely have to treat the factual allegations of the claimant as true for the purposes of the

---

4. "The 2006 Amendments to the ICSID Rules and regulations and the Additional Facility Rules", 21 ICSID Review – Foreign Inv. L.J. (2006) p. 427, at p. 439.

application. If that is right, it may be therefore that on its true construction Art. 41(5) is in fact doing no more than requiring the tribunal, once objection is raised, to consider at this early stage whether the claim is sustainable as a matter of law. If so, it is perhaps a less adventurous provision than might at first blush be thought.

Quite how Art. 41(5) and (6) will come to be interpreted by ICSID tribunals is not yet known. There has been one decision, reported in the arbitration press but not publicly available,[5] where a tribunal ruled that a US$ 700 million arbitration against Jordan by US company TransGlobal over an oil concession in the Dead Sea should continue, after an attempt to use Art. 41(5) to challenge the claim proved unsuccessful.[6] It is of course only when this or other similar decisions are available that jurisprudence will develop as to how tribunals will resolve the scope of application of these articles.

V.   INVESTMENT TREATY PROVISIONS

There are interesting provisions to be found in the investment treaty and free trade agreement context also.

For example both Art. 28.4 of the 2004 United States Model Bilateral Investment Treaty (BIT) and Art. 10.20.4 of the Central America-Dominican Republic-United States Free Trade Agreement (CAFTA) provide that:

> "Without prejudice to a Tribunal's authority to address other objections as a preliminary question, a Tribunal shall address and decide as a preliminary question any objection by the respondent that, as a matter of law, a claim submitted is not a claim for which an award in favor of the claimant may be made under [Article 34 of the US Model BIT and Article 10.26 of CAFTA]."

Both then set out elaborate provisions on how the objection is to be dealt with by the tribunal. In particular, the objection has to be submitted to the tribunal as soon as possible after the tribunal is constituted, and in no event later than the date the tribunal fixes for the respondent to submit its counter-memorial. On receipt of an objection the tribunal has to ("*shall*") suspend any proceedings on the merits, establish a schedule for considering the objection, and issue a decision or award on the objection, with reasons. In deciding the objection, the tribunal assumes that the claimant's factual allegations in support of its claim are true.

These provisions of the model BIT and CAFTA do not contemplate a summary disposition of the case. Rather they focus on whether as a matter of law the claim is one for which an award may be made pursuant to the relevant provisions dealing with awards. A very narrow reading of these provisions might suggest that the enquiry is limited to whether as a matter of law the type of relief is contemplated in the provisions dealing with awards. That would seem to be unnecessarily restrictive and the inclusion

---

5. Since this article was written the decision has been made available on the ICSID website, <http://icsid.worldbank.org>.
6. *Trans-Global Petroleum Inc v Hashemite Kingdom of Jordan* (ICSID Case No. ARB/07/25).

of an elaborate process of determining the objection perhaps warrants a broader interpretation, encompassing objections that no award can be made because the claim must fail as a matter of law.

The provisions mandate the tribunal to determine whether as a matter of law the claim is one for which an award may be made as soon as the objection is raised and before proceeding with the case on the merits. Such an exercise is essentially determining a particular issue, namely the question whether the claim can proceed as a matter of law, and so arguably falls within what I have termed the acceptable face of early disposition. The provisions are therefore formalizing what many would consider an approach that represents good practice in any event. However the express inclusion of such provisions might be thought to indicate the existence of a perceived need to encourage tribunals to deal with claims lacking in legal merit at an early stage. In that sense it might be seen as another example of rule makers sending a signal to arbitration tribunals that they can and should be willing to tackle such issues at an early stage of the proceedings.

VI. WHERE SHOULD TRIBUNALS DRAW THE LINE?

It is perhaps inevitable given the developments outlined above and the revision currently being undertaken of the UNCITRAL Rules that the question arises whether other rule makers should follow the ICSID model of introducing specific provision requiring tribunals to consider early disposition of particular issues. To what extent can there really be said to be a need for them to do so? To answer that, perhaps a closer look is needed at where the line is to be drawn between what is, and what is not, acceptable from a jurisdictional perspective. However, given the apparent perception by some at least of a need to encourage tribunals to exercise their powers, we should perhaps also consider the willingness of tribunals to use the tools currently available to them when faced with a case where early determination of particular issues or indeed the whole claim might be beneficial.

There is of course nothing inherently objectionable about a procedure that falls short of a full evidentiary hearing and of course the applicable procedural law or arbitration rules may in any event restrict the right of a party to insist upon this. One has simply to consider document-only arbitrations to reinforce that conclusion.[7] But how far can a tribunal go down the path of curtailing the process or the evidence? Guidance will usually be given in the provisions of the applicable arbitration rules or national laws which contain the tribunal's obligation to act in accordance with the requirements of due process or natural justice. Typically this takes the form of a requirement that the tribunal act fairly as between the parties and allows each an opportunity to present its case and to deal with that of the other party or parties.

The precise formulation may vary: c.f. Art. 15(1) of the UNCITRAL rules which provides that "the arbitral Tribunal may conduct the arbitration in such manner as it considers appropriate, provided that the parties are treated with equality and that at any stage of the proceedings each party is given a *full* opportunity of presenting his case"

---

7. Art. 20(6) of the ICC Rules reinforces this.

(emphasis added). See also Art. 18 of the Model Law which provides that "The parties shall be treated with equality and each party shall be given a full opportunity of presenting his case."

By way of contrast, Art. 15(2) of the ICC Rules requires the tribunal to "act fairly and impartially and ensure that each party has a *reasonable* opportunity to present its case". Similarly Art. 14.1(i) of the LCIA Rules imposes on the tribunal a general duty at all times "to act fairly and impartially as between all parties, giving each a *reasonable* opportunity of putting its case and dealing with that of its opponent". Likewise Art. 16(1) of the Rules American Arbitration Association (AAA) requires that "the parties are treated with equality and that each party has the right to be heard and is given a *fair* opportunity to present its case". (Again emphasis added in each case)

Whatever the precise test to be applied in the particular case, it is the need to comply with the applicable standard of natural justice or due process which provides the yardstick of what a tribunal can and cannot do. The difficulty in practice of course is applying these broad statements of principle to the particular circumstances of the case. It is not difficult to understand why a tribunal might take a conservative approach when it knows that, the more borderline the case, the greater the likelihood that its decision will fall to be scrutinized by a national court judge who may or may not adopt a 'pro-arbitration' attitude to such matters.

But is having a *"reasonable"* or *"fair"* opportunity of putting your case and dealing with that of your opponent necessarily inconsistent with the notion of summary disposition of a claim or issue? Perhaps so if it is stipulated that a *"full"* opportunity must be given, but surely what is *"reasonable"* or *"fair"* must depend on the particular circumstances?

VII.  USE OF THE TOOLS CURRENTLY AVAILABLE

On one level the conservatism of tribunals with regard to early disposition of issues is entirely understandable, and there are a number of reasons to which a tribunal might legitimately refer as grounds for concluding that allowing the arbitration to run its normal course is the right approach. At its most basic, a successful party would feel understandably aggrieved if the result of a tribunal taking a bold stance on early disposition of issues was to bring into question the validity of the award.

However tribunals also have obligations imposed under arbitration rules and procedural laws to manage cases efficiently and, though the bar may be set at a low level, a failure to do so can itself render an award vulnerable. Under the LCIA Rules for example, Art. 14.1 records the tribunal's general duty: "to adopt procedures suitable to the circumstances of the arbitration, avoiding unnecessary delay or expense, so as to provide a fair and efficient means for the final resolution of the parties' dispute".

Furthermore, there is a perception in some quarters that it is a failing of arbitration that parties cannot achieve the speed of resolution of their dispute which the case demands. Why should a party be allowed to pursue an utterly hopeless claim or defence through possibly years of proceedings, simply because they inserted an arbitration agreement into their contract rather than providing for the jurisdiction of the national courts? The problem is perhaps particularly acute in certain sectors such as the banking industry where the mindset tends to be enforcement of rights rather than resolution of disputes. Arguably however the problem is more widespread and arbitration may be failing the business community generally by not embracing the early resolution of claims or issues in an appropriate case.

As mentioned, an important question to be addressed in this context is whether tribunals are making the most of the tools currently available to them. Dealing with issues sequentially, particularly if some are or may be determinative, has already been discussed. But even if the applicable institutional or other rules contain no express provision akin to that of Art. 41(5) of ICSID and the parties' reference to arbitration contains no specific guidance such as that in the 2004 US Model BIT or CAFTA, tribunals may still have power to entertain such applications for early disposition of cases lacking in legal substantiation. Justification for such an approach can be found within the certain rules themselves. For example:

*AAA*: Art. 16.3 of the International Arbitration Rules provides that "The Tribunal may in its discretion ... direct the parties to focus their presentations on issues the decision of which could dispose of all or part of the case."

*LCIA*: Art. 14.2 provides that "Unless otherwise agreed by the parties under Article 14.1, the Arbitral Tribunal shall have the widest discretion to discharge its duties allowed under such law(s) or rules of law as the Arbitral Tribunal may determine to be applicable; and at all times the parties shall do everything necessary for the fair, efficient and expeditious conduct of the arbitration." See also Art. 14.1, referred to above, which records the Tribunal's general duty: "to adopt procedures suitable to the circumstances of the arbitration, avoiding unnecessary delay or expense, so as to provide a fair and efficient means for the final resolution of the parties' dispute".

*ICC*: The ICC Rules are less explicit than many others but nevertheless, as mentioned above, specifically contemplate a tribunal issuing a partial award. Additionally, Art. 20(1) provides the general duty that the tribunal "shall proceed within as short a time as possible to establish the facts of the case by all appropriate means". Art. 20(2) states that "After studying the written submissions of the parties and all documents relied upon, the Arbitral Tribunal shall hear the parties together in person if any of them so requests or, failing such a request, it may of its own motion decide to hear them." Art. 20(6) provides that the tribunal "may decide the case solely on the documents submitted by the parties unless any of the parties requests a hearing". Art. 32(1) provides that the time limits set out in the Rules may be shortened by the tribunal, but this requires the consent of the parties. These provisions also therefore provide considerable flexibility for the tribunal to tackle specific issues on an efficient basis.

*UNCITRAL Rules*: Art. 15.2 provides "If either party so requests at any stage of the proceedings, the arbitral tribunal shall hold hearings for the presentation of evidence by witnesses, including expert witnesses, or for oral argument. In the absence of such a request, the arbitral tribunal shall decide whether to hold such hearings or whether the proceedings shall be conducted on the basis of documents and other materials". See also Art. 15(1) of the UNCITRAL Rules referred to above requiring equal treatment and a full opportunity to the present case.

These provisions would seem to provide considerable opportunity for tribunals to be creative in their approach to the early disposition of issues or claims which are legally unsustainable. Indeed there are undoubtedly examples where tribunals have done precisely that and taken a firm, proactive approach. Equally, and though definitive empirical evidence is not available, experience suggests that there is a tendency amongst tribunals to allow parties and their advisers to proceed down the well-trodden procedural path of a typical arbitration. Even where a party seeks to challenge this approach, there is a tendency to adopt what is no doubt a "safe" course but which arguably fails to rise to the challenge of providing an efficient and effective dispute resolution mechanism. Why then might the tools available not be utilized to the maximum extent? Possible reasons include:

– The tribunal may have concerns about the likelihood of a challenge to any award in national courts or its enforcement (based on arguments of a failure of due process/natural justice).
– The tribunal may also be concerned at the impression given to the parties and their representatives by it taking what might be seen as shortcuts in the procedure (i.e., that the parties will feel shortchanged by the process).
– The tribunal may not be fully engaged in the case on the merits until its later stages. In those circumstances it may not feel confident exploring issues for early determination on its own initiative or even ruling on such matters where they are raised by one of the parties. No tribunal wants to be put in the position of discovering subsequently that what seemed like an appropriate decision to deal with particular issues turns out to be unhelpful or impossible, or worse still that earlier decisions on such issues turn out to have been in error.
– The tribunal may be concerned about the utility of tackling issues on a piecemeal basis; as mentioned above, this has the potential to add to the overall expense of the arbitration and to delay the proceedings.
– Though undoubtedly not an overriding factor for the vast majority of arbitrators, it is not of course necessarily in the arbitrator's own best interests to bring about the early disposition of the case, thereby bringing his or her income stream to an end.

There are genuine issues – or mostly so – but nevertheless there clearly are cases where issues arise that are capable of being resolved on an expedited basis and perhaps without a full airing of all the evidence pertaining to them. The focus of ICSID Rule 41(5) and the provisions of the US Model BIT and CAFTA suggest this is particularly so where there is a question of law at issue between the parties which is potentially determinative of the dispute. To take two recent examples where this occurred:

*CDC v. Republic of Seychelles* – In this ICSID case (which pre-dated Rule 41(5)), the sole arbitrator acceded to the claimant's request that the case should proceed first with the determination of whether the respondent's defences to claims under certain loan agreements and related sovereign guarantees were capable in law of amounting to a good defence, even if all the underlying facts were, for these purposes only, accepted as true. After receiving the respondent's counter-nemorial, the claimants wrote to the tribunal requesting that it suspend the procedural calendar in order to resolve these preliminary issues of law prior to the claimant filing its reply, so that the claimant would not incur unnecessary costs and expense responding to matters which the claimant contended had no place in the proceedings. The hearing proceeded on the basis that it was confined to determining only this preliminary question. Accordingly, the claimant did not produce any factual or expert witness evidence at the hearing. However the respondent did do so, and the claimant cross-examined those witnesses. The award found against the respondent, holding that the various defences put forward by it were not capable at law of constituting a defence to the claims.[8]

The respondent sought to annul the award on various of the grounds including the improper treatment of evidence, bias and impartiality on the part of the arbitrator, defective deliberation and a failure to answer questions put to the tribunal. None of these were successful.[9]

*An ad hoc insurance arbitration* – In an ad hoc arbitration in London of an insurance coverage case, the claimant alleged that the basis of the defence to coverage advanced by the respondent insurers was unsustainable as a matter of the applicable substantive law. Immediately following the initial exchange of pleadings the claimant made an application to the tribunal for this issue to be determined. The application was based in part at least upon the potential saving in time and costs that would result from having the issue resolved at an early stage of the arbitration. In the circumstances the tribunal declined to determine the issue, but hived it off to be dealt with if and when necessary following the determination of the other issues in the case. Subsequently, following an award on those other issues, the question whether the defence was sustainable became live once more and the claimant again applied to the tribunal for it to be determined as a matter of law without the need for factual or expert evidence. The case settled before the tribunal ruled on that application, but it is noteworthy that the arguments advanced by the respondent insurers on both occasions included that it would be procedurally unfair to resolve the issue without disclosure of documents and witness evidence. This was notwithstanding the claimant's acceptance that for purposes of the application the tribunal should assume all factual allegations made by the respondent were well-founded. This example perhaps demonstrates a certain mindset, which practitioners need to overcome.

VIII. THE WAY FORWARD

The revisions to the UNCITRAL Arbitration Rules currently proposed do not introduce a provision similar to Art. 41(5) of the ICSID Rules. Nevertheless, as mentioned above, the UNCITRAL revisions are likely to prompt a review of the various sets of institutional rules, so this is an opportune moment to reflect on whether it would be helpful to broaden or to emphasize the powers of tribunals in relation to early disposition of claims or issues.

---

8. *CDC Group plc v. Republic of Seychelles* (ICSID Case No. ARB/02/14), Award (17 December 2003) available at <http://icsid.worldbank.org>.
9. *CDC Group plc v. Republic of Seychelles* (ICSID Case No. ARB/02/14), Decision on Annulment (29 June 2005) available at <http://ita.law.uvic.ca>.

Interestingly, the question of summary disposition was considered by an ICC Task Force on Arbitrating Competition Issues. Their report "Evidence, Procedure and Burden of Proof" concluded it was "likely a summary judgment vehicle would not work in the ICC context and culture" and recommended that the ICC Rules should not be amended to allow for summary judgment.

There does not seem to be a strong call for arbitration rules generally to adopt powers similar to those of national courts enabling *summary* disposition of issues or claims. It is perhaps more a question of the existing powers being fully utilized in appropriate cases so as to bring about the *expedited* resolution of issues or claims in an appropriate case.

This suggests that whilst widespread rule changes may not be necessary, there is scope for an increased focus on developing a culture among arbitrators in which the use of their powers for disposing of issues or claims at an early stage in the proceedings is more readily adopted both to encourage consideration of sequential determination of issues and to deal with cases which are unsustainable legally.

How can this be done? It is perhaps an area where the rule-makers – or rule-revisers – do have a role to play by providing greater encouragement and guidance to both tribunals and parties on the early determination of dispositive issues or claims. For example, tribunals might be specifically required to consider whether the case involves issues or claims that are suitable for early or sequential determination, whether on the basis that there is an objection based on lack of legal merit or because they are or may be determinative. A similar obligation might be imposed on the parties. That need not detract from the current case management obligations imposed but arguably would reinforce them by imposing a positive requirement for tribunals and parties specifically to address their minds to the topic. Ultimately this is perhaps a cultural issue. If tribunals become accustomed to the fact that it is part of their role to consider using the tools at their disposal for the early disposition of issues in appropriate cases in the same way as they consider matters such as jurisdiction and applicable law, that might of itself go some way to addressing the concerns raised by the business community. If nothing else, the failure to adopt such a course more often might be more acceptable if seen to be the result of a considered assessment, as opposed to mere conservatism or tribunals simply defaulting to the traditional long form procedure.

# Comments on Judith Gill's Report on Applications for the Early Disposition of Arbitration Proceedings

*Teresa Giovannini*[*]

TABLE OF CONTENTS | Page
---|---
I. Introduction | 526
II. Desirability of Statutory Changes | 527
III. Are There Desirable Early, Expedited Determinations? | 529
IV. How to Address Early, Expedited Determination? | 530
V. Conclusion | 531

I. INTRODUCTION

Judith Gill addressed the two existing ends of the spectrum, namely the determination of one or more issues before others (e.g., liability before quantum) on the one hand, and the early expedited and summary determination of these issues on the other hand (this volume, pp. 513-525).

Ms. Gill recalled that the possibility of early determination of certain issues is admitted in most arbitration rules[1] as well as in national legislations.[2]

My comments will focus on three issues:

(a) Are regulatory changes desirable?
(b) Are there desirable early, expedited determinations?
(c) How to address early, expedited determination?

---

[*] Attorney at Law, Partner, Lalive, Geneva, Switzerland.
1. London Court of International Arbitration Rules (LCIA Rules), Art. 26.7; also Swiss Rules of International Arbitration (Swiss Rules), Art. 32.1 which provides that: "In addition to making a final award, the arbitral tribunal shall be entitled to make interim, interlocutory, or partial awards"; Chamber of National and International Arbitration of Milan, Arbitration Rules, Art. 37.1 and 37.2 that state that "The Arbitral Tribunal may render a partial award when it settles only one or some of the issues of the dispute" and that "the Arbitral Tribunal may render an interim award to settle one or more ... substantive issues"; Stockholm Chamber of Commerce Arbitration Rules of 2007 (SCC Rules), Art. 38 provides that "The Arbitral Tribunal may decide a separate issue or part of the dispute in a separate award."
2. English Arbitration Act 1996, Sect. 47; similarly, the Swiss Private International Law Act (PIL Act), Art. 188 that states that: "Unless the parties have agreed otherwise, the arbitral tribunal may render partial awards"; in Italy, indirectly admitted by Art. 820(c) of the Code of Civil Procedure (2006).

## II. DESIRABILITY OF STATUTORY CHANGES

Ms. Gill suggests that there is no "strong call for arbitration rules generally to adopt powers ... enabling *summary* disposition of issues or claims".[3] (Emphasis in original) I would generally agree with such a statement, with one exception only: namely the insertion of a rule permitting the tribunal to issue a preliminary, expedited decision on the payment of the advance on costs clearly and unambiguously.

Most arbitration rules indeed provide for the parties to the arbitration proceedings to pay the advance on arbitration costs equally or proportionally.[4] However, practice shows that more frequently than not, respondent parties default on their obligation to advance their share of the costs,[5] thereby obliging the claimant to pay the second half of the advance on arbitration costs if it wants the arbitration to proceed.[6] While in some cases, the respondent party may have legitimate reasons for its default,[7] in the majority of the cases, the refusal to pay the advance is perceived as a manoeuvre to delay the proceedings and to render the prosecution of the claim more difficult for the claimant.[8]

Independently of the question as to whether the defaulting party has good and valid reasons to refuse paying its share, the issue here is whether the arbitral tribunal is

---

3. See this volume, p. 525
4. Thus and for example, the Arbitration Rules of the International Chamber of Commerce International Court of Arbitration (ICC Rules), Art. 30(3) provides that "The advance on costs fixed by the Court shall be payable in equal shares by the Claimant and the Respondent"; Milan Chamber of Commerce, Arbitration Rules, Art. 41(4) provides that the advance payments required by the Secretariat: "shall be requested of all parties in equal parts ... or shall be requested of the parties in different proportions on the basis of the value of their respective claims"; Swiss Rules, Art. 41(1) states that "The arbitral tribunal, on its establishment, shall request each party to deposit an equal amount as an advance for costs [of arbitration]..."; LCIA Rules, Art. 24.1 provides that: "[t]he LCIA Court may direct the parties, in such proportions as it thinks appropriate, to make one or several interim or final payments on account of the costs of the arbitration"; UNCITRAL Arbitration Rules (UNCITRAL Rules), Art. 41(1) provides that "[t]he arbitral tribunal, on its establishment, may request each party to deposit an equal amount as an advance for the costs [of the arbitration]".
5. See Sigvard JARVIN, "*Wenn die beklagte Partei ihren Anteil des Kostenvorschusses nicht bezahlt: Folgen der Nichtzahlung aus Sicht der ICC-Verfahrensordnung, schwedischen und schweizerischen*" in Alain PLANTEY, Karl-Heinz BOCKSTIEGEL and Jens BREDOW, eds., *Festschrift für Ottoarndt Glossner zum 70. Geburtsag*, (Verlag Recht und Wirtschaft GmbH 1994) pp. 155-164; Pierre KARRER, "Arbitration saves! Costs: Poker and Hide-and-Seek", 3 Journal of International Arbitration (1986, no. 1) pp. 35-46, fn. 13.
6. See in this regard ICC Rules, Art. 30(4) which provides for the suspension or automatic withdrawal of the proceedings in case the advance is not fully paid; see also, Swiss Rules, Art. 41.4 that sets out the same rule in providing that "[i]f the required deposits are not paid in full ... the arbitral tribunal may order the suspension or termination of the arbitral proceedings"; Art. 41(4) of the UNCITRAL Arbitration Rules that states that "[i]f the required deposits are not paid in full ... the arbitral tribunal may order the suspension or termination of the arbitral proceedings".
7. For example, due to an inability to meet costs; alleged lack of jurisdiction; insolvency of the claimant.
8. See Micha BÜHLER, "Non-payment of the Advance on Costs by the Respondent Party – Is There Really a Remedy?", note to ICC Case No.12491 in 24 ASA Bulletin (2006, no. 2) pp. 290-301.

empowered to take a decision on this point – in other words, whether it has jurisdiction or not to issue a preliminary, expedited award ordering (or refusing to order for good and valid reasons) the respondent to pay its share of the advance on arbitration costs.

While arbitration rules generally provide that the reference to given rules implies full adherence to and acceptance of these rules[9] and logically therefore of the rule under scrutiny here, practice shows that there is substantial discrepancy among practitioners on the question of whether the arbitral tribunal has jurisdiction to address this very issue that clearly must be dealt with in an early and expedited manner to make sense.

The problem has been addressed by learned authors and in particular in various ICC decisions. A number of them follow the "contractual approach" and therefore hold that the parties' obligation to pay equally or proportionally the advance required is binding upon them.[10] Thus and for example, the tribunal in ICC Case No. 10526 declared that "the obligation to pay half of the advance, as provided by the Rules, must be regarded as a contractual obligation, and any dispute relating thereto is a 'dispute arising out of the present contract' within the meaning of the arbitration clause".[11]

An assertion to the contrary is based on the proposition that there is a distinction in the ICC Rules between financial aspects of arbitration for which the arbitral tribunal is competent and those for which the institution (for example the ICC Court) is competent. Accordingly, the parties are deemed not to be contractually bound (each towards the other) to pay their share of the advance on costs.[12] As a consequence (not always followed by arbitral tribunals that quite strangely sometimes resolve the issue through an interim measure of protection)[13], the arbitral tribunal logically could not make a decision dealing with the advance on costs.[14]

The issue is more than sensitive and is of such a nature to considerably help respondent parties to obstruct the arbitration process and even to result in this process sometimes being artificially stopped for lack of sufficient additional funds on the claimant's side.

To avoid such dilatory tactics used and abused too often, and in line with the principle adopted in the LCIA Rules (Art. 24.3) that "the party paying the substitute payment shall be entitled to recover that amount as a debt immediately due from the defaulting party", I would strongly suggest the insertion in the arbitration rules of the provision contained in Art. 45(4) of the new Arbitration Rules of the Stockholm Chamber of Commerce that provides, with regard to the advance on costs, that "[i]f a party fails to make a required

---

9. See ICC Rules, Art. 6(1); Swiss Rules, Art. 1(1); Milan Chamber of Commerce Arbitration Rules, Art. 1(1); UNCITRAL Arbitration Rules, Art. 1(1).
10. E.g., W. Laurence CRAIG, William W. PARK and Jan PAULSSON, *International Chamber of Commerce Arbitration*, 3rd edn. (Oceana Publications, Inc. 2000) p. 268; Partial Award of 2 December 2000 in ICC Case No. 10526, J.D.I. (2001) 1179 (Annot. S. JARVIN).
11. ICC Case No. 10526, Partial Award of 2 December 2000, supra, fn. 10.
12. See Matthew SECOMB, "Awards and Orders Dealing with the Advance on Costs in ICC Arbitration: Theoretical Questions and Practical Problems", 14 ICC ICArb. Bull (2003, no.1) pp. 59-70, paras. 23-31.
13. *Ibid.*, para. 25, p. 64.
14. See in this respect, ICC Case No. 12491, Partial Award No. 2 of 1 June 2004, in 24 ASA Bulletin (2006 no. 2) pp. 281-289.

payment, the Secretariat shall give the other party an opportunity to do so within a specified period of time.... *If the other party makes the required payment, the Arbitral Tribunal may, at the request of such party, make a separate award for reimbursement of the payment.*"[15] (Emphasis added)

In addition to putting an end to the long-running debate as to the jurisdiction of the arbitral tribunal with respect to this specific issue of advance on arbitration costs, such a provision would considerably – in the author's view – increase the efficiency of the arbitration process by avoiding both the problems of a claimant party having to face unbearable financial charges at the outset of the dispute and the loss of time triggered by a respondent's passive attitude with respect to the payment of its share of arbitration costs. Such a provision might also discourage respondent parties' dilatory tactics.

III. ARE THERE DESIRABLE EARLY, EXPEDITED DETERMINATIONS?

I would also like to recall here that an evidentiary hearing or an oral hearing is not a constitutive element of the right to be heard.[16] As set forth by the Swiss Supreme Court (free translation):

> "The arbitral tribunal can refuse to proceed to the taking of evidence without violating the right to be heard if the evidence offered is not suitable to be the basis for [the tribunal's] conviction, if the fact to prove is already established, if it is irrelevant or if the tribunal, in proceeding to an anticipated evaluation of the evidence, reaches the conclusion that its conviction is already formed and that *the result of the evidentiary measure sought cannot* modify it its conviction."[17] (Emphasis added)

Besides the traditional and widely known bifurcation between liability and quantum damages – a bifurcation that might be held disastrous in terms of costs and efficiency if

---

15. On the subject, see José ROSELL, "*Le nouveau Règlement de la Chambre de Commerce de Stockholm de 2007: vers un certain alignement sur le Règlement de la CCI*" in *Les Cahiers de l'Arbitrage*, (2008, no. 1) pp. 29 et seq., at p. 31, with reference to Kaj HOBÉR and William MCKECHNIE, "New Rules of the Arbitration Institute of the Stockholm Chamber of Commerce", 23 Arbitration International (2007, no. 2), p. 273.
16. E.g., in Switzerland: the right to be heard embodied in Art. 190(2) of the PIL Act does not cover a mere violation of an agreed procedural rule. The tribunal is entitled to proceed to an anticipated evaluation of evidence: Swiss Supreme Court, decision of 1 July 2004, 4P.93/2004, in 23 ASA Bulletin (2005, no. 1) pp. 139-144; confirmation of the rule that the right to be heard does not include the right to oral argument in Supreme Court, decision of 5 January 2007 4P.240/2006, available at <www.bger.ch> (last accessed 21 July 2008). As recalled in ATF 121 III 331, cons.3b p. 333, "the right [to be heard] is violated when, by mistake or misunderstanding, the arbitral tribunal does not take into consideration ... arguments, evidence ... submitted by one of the parties and *relevant for the decision to be made*", available at <www.bger.ch> (last accessed 21 July 2008).
17. Swiss Supreme Court, decision of 21 September 2007, 4A.220/2007, available at <www.bger.ch> (last accessed 21 July 2008).

not decided very early in the proceedings, or the preliminary decisions on the law applicable to the merits of the disputes – various other issues can, in the author's view, be advantageously decided upon on an expedited, summary basis without putting the arbitral tribunal at risk of potentially contradictory or regrettably premature decisions.

Such issues can consist for example in:

(1) *Prescription*: such an objection can generally easily be dealt with at the very beginning of the proceedings in a summary, expedited manner. The early decision of the arbitral tribunal on this issue can substantially clean up, and maybe even put an end to part of the claims or counterclaims;

(2) *Set-off*: it sometimes occurs that a party alleges that the contract at stake or the law applicable prohibits any set off, with the consequence for example that the price of the goods delivered is due, independent of the defects in the goods eventually alleged by the debtor. The issue is important, since it can trigger the shifting of the burden of proof from one party to the other;

(3) Preliminary legal issues that can be possibly decided upon before any decisions on the claims. Examples can be found in the definition of the contractual obligations, conformity of supplies to the specifications, time frame of performance, applicability and definition of rates.[18]

Addressing these issues at an early stage of the proceedings obviously requires that the arbitral tribunal engages immediately on the merits, a characteristic rarely found in practice, as underscored by Ms. Gill. But even if it does engage immediately in the proceedings, how can the arbitral tribunal address early, expedited determination?

IV.   HOW TO ADDRESS EARLY, EXPEDITED DETERMINATION?

An early determination obviously requires a proactive attitude of the arbitral tribunal. Such a proactive attitude is already generally suggested in the UNCITRAL Notes on Organizing Arbitral Proceedings which set out the concept that the arbitral tribunal "in considering the parties' allegations and arguments ... may come to the conclusion that it would be useful for it or for the parties to prepare, for analytical purpose and for ease of discussion, a list of the points at issue as opposed to those that are undisputed", specifying that "such an identification of points at issue might help to concentrate on the essential matters, to reduce the number of points at issue by agreement of the parties, and to select the best and most economical process for resolving the dispute".[19] The

---

18. See Michael SCHNEIDER, "Lean Arbitration: Cost Control and Efficiency Through Progressive Identification of Issues and Separate Pricing of Arbitration Services", 10 Arbitration International (1994, no. 2) pp. 119-140.
19. UNCITRAL Notes on Organizing Arbitral Proceedings, Sect. 11 "*Defining points at issue; order of deciding issues; defining relief or remedy sought*", para. 43, available at <www.uncitral.org/pdf/english/texts/arbitration/arb-notes/arb-notes-e.pdf> (last accessed 21 July 2008).

Notes also address the question of early decision by the arbitral tribunal on given issues as follows:

> "[i]f the arbitral tribunal has adopted a particular order of deciding points at issue, it might consider it appropriate to issue a decision on one of the points earlier than on the other ones. This might be done, for example, when a discrete part of a claim is ready for decision while the other parts still require extensive consideration, or when it is expected that after deciding certain issues the parties might be more inclined to settle the remaining ones.... Questions that might be the subject of such decisions are, for example, jurisdiction of the arbitral tribunal ... or the liability of a party."[20]

The arbitral tribunal might, therefore, be proactive in the following ways:

(a) By drawing the parties' attention at the preliminary hearing as to the legal possibility of issuing partial awards;
(b) By explaining the interest of addressing in a preliminary, expedited manner, issues that are central to the decision on the damages claimed;
(c) By inviting the parties to identify at the outset (i.e, in the statement of claim and in the answer) the issues that – in their respective views – could be addressed in a preliminary, expedite manner to make the arbitration process more efficient. In this process, the arbitral tribunal must obviously carefully avoid suggesting issues – such as interest rates or prescription (if not already addressed by them) to the parties;
(d) By explaining that such issues – to be efficiently and expeditiously addressed – shall be decided upon documentary evidence only;
(e) By explaining that – should the parties consider that witness hearings are necessary to address these issues – the arbitral tribunal can decide not to hold such hearings in a process of anticipated evaluation of evidence, if such process is admissible under the applicable law (procedural or substantive).

Upon receipt of the briefs, the arbitral tribunal would then set up the list of identified issues of substance and invite the parties to address their comments on the possibility of addressing them in a preliminary, expedited decision.

## V.   CONCLUSION

Be it through the tools mentioned or others, the fact remains that it is indeed urgent that our community pursue all possible efforts to ensure that the arbitration process be as efficient as practicable and shorter than it is at present. The credibility and the long-term survival of the institution of arbitration are at stake.

---

20. *Ibid.*, para. 45.

# Summary Disposition in International Arbitration

*Michael M. Collins S.C.*[*]

TABLE OF CONTENTS

| | Page |
|---|---|
| I. A Subtle Shift | 532 |
| II. Witness Statements | 533 |

I. A SUBTLE SHIFT

Considering the virtues of efficiency, speed and cost-saving which arbitration is supposed to represent, it is somewhat surprising that some commentators treat summary disposition in arbitrations rather like Dr. Johnson's dog walking on its hind legs; it is not done well but one is surprised to find it done at all. And yet, the incisive cutting to the chase, the throwing aside of lawyers' technicalities, the arbitrator's fearless courage in the face of the moribund quagmire of litigation procedure, are the very stuff of our arbitral dreams. With one bound of jurisprudential verve, our hero is free, truth and justice are established, and even the disappointed losers, like the enemy ranks of Tuscany watching Horatio swim the Tiber to freedom can "scare forbear to cheer".

Well, real life, of course, is not much like that as most of us know to our cost. Arbitration is, or at least can be, as prone to as lengthy delays, costs, irrationality and unfairness as litigation, and generally without the remedy of an appeal. It may therefore appear somewhat odd that the familiar litigation procedures of seeking to strike out a claim at an early stage on a preliminary issue or on the basis that the claimant's case, even if factually true, affords the claimant no relief should provoke such hesitancy among the arbitration community.

The reasons for this are well known and most of them revolve around some version of due process or as we refer to it in Ireland, natural or constitutional justice. By definition, a summary disposition involves a truncated hearing where a decision, possibly a final decision, is made without hearing all the available evidence. Hence the significance of one of the issues touched upon by Judith Gill (this volume pp. 513-525) namely the extent to which the rules governing the arbitration require that each party be afforded a full or merely a reasonable opportunity of presenting their case. I think a subtle shift is discernible in the proposed revisions to the UNCITRAL Arbitration Rules towards greater case management by the arbitrator and a corresponding greater degree of flexibility in what the arbitrator can do. Thus, while the old Art. 15(1) of the UNCITRAL Rules required that "at any stage of the proceedings each party is given a full opportunity of presenting his case" (emphasis added), the proposed amended version reads "and at an appropriate stage of the proceedings, each party is given an opportunity of presenting its case" (emphasis added). There is a subtle change here: "any stage" has

---

[*] Chairman, Bar Council of Ireland.

been changed to "appropriate stage" and the requirement for a "full" opportunity to present the party's case is replaced simply by a requirement for "an opportunity". This seems to provide support for the notion that the arbitrator can readily entertain applications for summary disposition, a notion underpinned by the final sentence of the proposed amended Art. 15(1):

> "The Arbitral Tribunal, in exercising its discretion, shall conduct the proceedings with a view to avoiding unnecessary delay and expense and to provide a fair and efficient process for resolving the parties' dispute."

Certainly, the courts of the United States have had little difficulty in concluding that arbitrators have jurisdiction to grant motions for summary disposition despite the fact that there is no such express authority under the Federal Arbitration Act though it should be noted that the Revised Uniform Arbitration Act introduced in 2000 does give arbitrators an express power to deal with a motion for summary disposition based exclusively on documentation. Such explicit authorization is also to be found in the Comprehensive Arbitration Rules of JAMS (Judicial Arbitration and Mediation Services). The Commercial Arbitration Rules of the American Arbitration Association (AAA) do not, so far as I understand it, expressly authorize summary disposition but do not prohibit it and in language which echoes Art. 15(1) of the UNCITRAL Rules, the AAA Rules give a wide discretion to the arbitrator to expedite the resolution of the dispute. American courts have, for the most part, focussed on the combination of the absence of a prohibition on summary disposition and the wide discretion given to an arbitrator as to how to conduct the proceedings to find that arbitrators under these various systems do have the power to grant motions for summary disposition.

## II. WITNESS STATEMENTS

There is just one aspect of the due process/natural justice debate that I want to focus on in this context and it concerns the use of written witness statements in lieu of or in partial substitution for oral testimony given by the plaintiff's witnesses as evidence in chief. One traditional objection to summary disposition is that the nature and quality of the claimant's case may change by virtue of the evidence that is tendered on behalf of the claimant particularly where there may be issues of credibility involved. That objection is sometimes met by the arbitrator assessing the application on the assumption that all of the facts alleged by the claimant in the pleadings will be established in evidence. If, taking the claimant's case at its height in this way, it is manifest that the claimant cannot establish any cause of action or any wrongdoing recognized under the relevant law or cannot be awarded any meaningful relief, then the arbitrator should be able to strike out the claim without any great fear of doing an injustice. However, this is not, in itself, a complete answer. Arbitrators, like courts, remain slow to take this step because of a natural unwillingness to resolve a case without being seen to give both sides a full opportunity to argue their point. Arbitrators, contrary to popular illusion, are human and are frequently unwilling to run the risk of having their award set aside on the grounds of some procedural unfairness with what they may perceive as a consequential risk of damage to their own reputation as arbitrators. Summary disposition motions therefore represent professional banana skins for an arbitrator.

Of course, some comfort can be found from the decision of the European Court of Human Rights in *Z. v. United Kingdom* (2001) 34 ECHR 97 where the Court effectively sanctioned a striking out procedure as compatible with Art. 6 of the Convention for the Protection of Human Rights and Fundamental Freedoms and held that such a procedure did not deprive a claimant of his right of access to the Court. Nonetheless, this only means that summary disposition is not by its nature a breach of fair procedures so that the banana skin remains an integral part of the respondent's seductive invitation to the quick fix.

These risks may be significantly lessened where the arbitrator has the benefit not merely of the pleadings or written legal submissions or skeleton arguments from the parties, but also written witness statements from the witnesses proposed to be called on behalf of the claimant (and perhaps the respondent also). Whether a summary disposition should be granted now no longer depends quite so much on the extent to which the pleadings reveal a sustainable case or defence which may after all be ultimately an adjudication on the skill or absence thereof of the lawyer in drafting the pleadings. The arbitrator can now engage in a much more meaningful way with the substance of the dispute and the risk of complaint from the disappointed claimant that he or she did not have an adequate opportunity to present his or her case is correspondingly less.

Whether written witness statements are a proper or adequate substitute for oral evidence in chief is, in itself, a significant topic. For example, where credibility is an important issue, it may be that hearing the witness give his or her evidence in chief is almost as important as the cross-examination where a written witness statement will inevitably have been filtered and pampered by the loving hands of the parties' lawyers. One of the most famous of all Irish barristers, Niall McCarthy S.C., who subsequently became a Supreme Court judge, once tellingly remarked that in his view the ability to extract a plaintiff's own story in evidence in chief without the luxury of leading questions was a greater and more difficult skill for an advocate than the more vulgar skill of cross-examination.

The significance of witness statements to a summary disposition application becomes more complex if the witness statements are not full witness statements i.e. are not intended as a comprehensive substitute for evidence in chief but are in the nature of summary statements or precis of the evidence the witness will give orally. Such summaries or precis should cover the essential points of the witnesses' testimony but will not necessary go into all the detail. Inevitably, the arbitrator will be met with the argument that he or she cannot strike out the claim or the defence in such circumstances because he does not have the full story.

As luck would have it, that particular situation has arisen in a long court trial in which I am currently involved and where the judge's solution is not, I think, in any way atypical of how courts and arbitrators face up to these issues. The plaintiff is a property developer whose business is bankrupt and where he owes the bank around € 30 million. However, he has sued the bank and the receiver appointed by the bank on the basis that the bank engaged in a fraudulent conspiracy when it lent him the money. This novel claim rests on the theory that the bank was worried about the enforceability of its security on the initial loan. It therefore agreed to lend him a further sum, repayable on demand, without any (it is alleged) real intention of permitting him to utilize the money but only for the purpose of taking fresh security to remedy a perceived defect in the earlier security. Once the fresh security was in place, the bank called in the loans at the first sign of trouble and appointed a receiver, actions which the plaintiff says were in furtherance of fraud on the part of the bank.

Under the direction of the court, the parties exchanged witness statements which were directed to be merely summaries or précis of the evidence which would be given but which in practice closely resembled full witness statements. At the close of the opening argument on behalf of the plaintiff, the bank brought an application that the court should forthwith dismiss the fraud case against the bank on the grounds that nothing in the witness statements allied to the legal submissions made in opening argument could warrant the court in ever making a finding of fraud against the bank. Part of the plaintiff's argument was that he should not be denied the opportunity to cross-examine the relevant witnesses from the bank because in its nature, fraud and conspiracy are hidden wrongdoings which a plaintiff cannot be expected to demonstrate solely on the basis of discovered documentation. The bank replied that the burden of proof lay on the plaintiff and there was no reason to suppose that the bank witnesses would ever have to be called to give evidence notwithstanding the written summaries of their intended evidence if they were called.[1]

Despite the extremely tenuous evidence in support of the fraud allegation, the court declined to strike out the claim, primarily on the basis that the claim was formulated in the alternative on the grounds of negligence and misrepresentation so that more or less the same evidence was going to have to be called even if the fraud claim was struck out. Since there would therefore be little or no saving in time or costs by striking out the fraud claim, the court reasoned that the balance of justice favoured permitting the plaintiff to maintain its case without prejudice to the bank's right to renew its application to strike out the claim at the close of the plaintiff's case i.e. after the plaintiff had called his witnesses and they had been subjected to cross-examination.[2]

Such a realpolitik solution will be familiar to everybody in this room. But what will be equally familiar is the fact that such motions are sometimes brought, not with any particular expectation that they will be successful, but with a view to instilling in the arbitrator from a very early stage the notion that the claimant's case (or defence as the case may be) is inherently weak, should be viewed with suspicion and that the arbitrator should be alert to the first opportunity to dismiss the claim. Furthermore, such an application may have the not inconsiderable benefit (as it did in the litigation to which I have just referred) of significantly narrowing the issues which are truly in dispute. Through the process of simply arguing the application for summary disposition, the claimant's lawyer may be forced to concede that there are certain aspects of the claim as

---

1. It is advisable for an arbitrator to bring clarity to the status of witness statements i.e. whether they are treated as documents in evidence or only so if and when the author of the statement is called to give sworn evidence.
2. The curious may note that the bank subsequently made such an application at the close of the plaintiff's evidence and was successful in having the case dismissed. *Cunningham v. First Active*, High Court of Ireland, unreported, 15 December 2008.

pleaded which cannot be stood up or that he or she is no longer pursuing some particular issue. Such narrowing of the issues with the consequential saving in costs is frequently in itself well worth the trouble of even an unsuccessful summary disposition motion.

# Working Group B

# 4. Provisional Measures

# Interim Measures – Ongoing Regulation and Practices (A View from the UNCITRAL Arbitration Regime)

*Luis Enrique Graham*[*]

| TABLE OF CONTENTS | Page |
|---|---|
| I. Introduction | 539 |
| II. The UNCITRAL Model Law Provisions On Interim Measures | 540 |
| III. Approach by the UNCITRAL Working Group in Considering the Incorporation of New Provisions Regarding Interim Measures in the UNCITRAL Arbitration Rules | 560 |
| IV. Overview Of Interim Measures Issued By An Arbitral Tribunal | 562 |
| V. Conclusions | 567 |
| Annex I: Status of the Working Group Regarding the Revision of the UNCITRAL Arbitration Rules | 570 |
| Annex II: Examples of Interim Measures Issued by an Arbitral Tribunal | 575 |
| Annex III: Anti-suit Injunctions | 578 |
| Annex IV: Provisions in Rules, Legislation and Case Law that Balance Convenience and the Likelihood of Success by the Requesting Party | 580 |

I. INTRODUCTION

The regulation and practice on interim measures of protection within the field of arbitration have been a subject of debate for many years. This applies to the international as well as the domestic arena. Although most of the content of this Report can be applied to arbitration in general, and the distinction between the international and domestic fields can be put aside for the purpose of an analysis of the topics covered herein, the guiding path is the regulation and practice in international arbitration. Some of the topics for elaboration deal exclusively with the context of international arbitration. This is particularly the case for the UNCITRAL system (notwithstanding that some national states have enacted the UNCITRAL system for their domestic arbitration regime as well) and for matters of enforcement within the framework of the 1958 New York Convention on the Recognition and Enforcement of Foreign Arbitral Awards (the New York Convention).

As arbitration has increasingly become the common dispute resolution method for many areas within the commercial world, the regulatory development and practice of interim measures have become more sophisticated. Any arbitration practitioner knows that interim measures are *the* issue in an increasing number of commercial disputes. Moreover, arbitration practitioners have developed a very dynamic set of interim measure tools to make arbitration an effective means of dispute resolution.

---

[*] Partner, Chadbourne & Parke, LLP; President, Mexican Bar Association.

The regulation and practice of interim measures in arbitration have evolved within the perception of two premises. On the one hand, there has been an idea that the broad powers conferred upon an arbitrator for the conduct of the proceedings necessarily embrace the power to issue an interim measure related to the dispute. On the other hand, there has been the demand to develop a system that not only confirms the availability of those powers but also fulfils two complementary purposes: (a) the need to count on an interim measures regulation system that illustrates the different choices of interim measures available for the users of international arbitration, and (b) the convenience of creating a system which helps achieve a balance between the needs of the party requesting the interim measure and those of the party affected by that measure. The arbitration community has been very sensitive to the importance of creating and maintaining equilibrium in this common scenario in which a conflicting interest appears: the requesting party's need of an interim measure to make arbitration an effective tool and the need for safeguards for the party affected by the issuance of the interim measure. These have been some of the most relevant underlying concepts within the construction of the UNCITRAL system.

II. THE UNCITRAL MODEL LAW PROVISIONS ON INTERIM MEASURES

*1. The Original Text of the Model Law (Its Contribution and Limitations)*

The drafters of the original text of the UNCITRAL Model Law on International Commercial Arbitration (the Model Law) included a regime for interim measures which dealt with some of the matters demanded by the arbitration community at that time,[1] and was intended to be acceptable to national legislatures. The original approach was very useful, even though nowadays it might be seen as a very modest contribution to arbitration practice.

In brief, the original system could be described as one that stated that the arbitral tribunal was empowered to order interim measures, unless the parties agreed otherwise (opt out), as well as to determine appropriate security in connection with the measure (Art. 17).[2] Likewise, the Model Law established a dual, compatible formula regarding

---

1. The UNCITRAL Model Law on International Commercial Arbitration was issued in 1985.
2. "The legislative history of article 17 reflects the Working Group's resolution of several fundamental issues of policy. First, differing views were expressed ... over whether the power of the arbitral tribunal to order interim measures should be deemed to be implied.... Second, the Working Group addressed several times the scope of this implied power. There was some sentiment for specifically limiting the measures that could be taken ... but ultimately a broader power was approved.... A third question of policy that was addressed was the question of the arbitral tribunal's power to enforce an interim measure it orders.... The Working Group ultimately decided not to address this question because it touched on matters dealt with in laws of national procedure and court competence and would probably be unacceptable to many States."

Howard HOLTZMANN and Joseph NEUHAUS, *A Guide to the UNCITRAL Model Law on International Commercial Arbitration: Legislative History and Commentary* (Kluwer, The Hague 1989) pp. 530-531.

the roles of the arbitral tribunal and the courts: the competence of one did not exclude the other (Art. 9).[3]

In a period of approximately fifteen years after the adoption of the Model Law, the users of arbitration became very familiar with and attracted to the use of interim measures in support of arbitration. Arbitration practitioners, as reported in a document reflecting the UNCITRAL deliberations, requested taking additional steps in favor of the interim measures regime.[4]

Among the areas in which the UNCITRAL regime for interim measures was considered to present some problems and limitations were the following:

a. *The interpretation of the correct meaning of the expression "the subject-matter of the dispute" (original text of Art. 17 of the Model Law)*

The purpose of an interim measure was confined to *"the subject-matter of the dispute"*. The provision in Art. 17 of the Model Law originally stated as follows:

> "... the arbitral tribunal may, at the request of a party, order any party to take such interim measure of protection as the arbitral tribunal may consider necessary in respect of the subject-matter of the dispute...".

This wording created some complications because on many occasions the restriction was imposed on the request that it had to be related, literally, to the *"subject-matter of the dispute"*. This certainly was an undesired and a limited approach to the intention of an interim measures regime. The wording was incorporated, essentially, from Art. 26(1) of the UNCITRAL Arbitration Rules (the UNCITRAL Rules), which still sets forth the following:

> "At the request of either party, the arbitral tribunal may take any interim measures it deems necessary in respect of the subject-matter of the dispute, including measures for the conservation of the goods forming the subject-matter in dispute, such as ordering their deposit with a third person or the sale of perishable goods."

Some interpreters reached an undesirable understanding of the original Model Law text by misreading the UNCITRAL Rules provision (which was the antecedent used by the drafters of the Model Law). The problem was caused by a restrictive understanding of the Model Law provision along with the introductory phrase of the provision still contained in the UNCITRAL Rules. The Model Law established that the interim measure had to be *"in respect of the subject-matter of the dispute"*. And, when a party in a dispute faced the need for an interim measure aside from a mere securing of goods, the party against

---

3. As Howard Holtzmann and Joseph Neuhaus said in the first Working Group report of 23 March 1982 (A/CN.9/216), "The Working Group agreed that interim measures by a national court were compatible with arbitration." HOLTZMANN and NEUHAUS, *op. cit.*, fn. 2, pp. 332-336.
4. "Possible future work in the area of international commercial arbitration, Note by the Secretariat", UNCITRAL Working Group II (Arbitration) 32nd Sess. (Vienna, 17 May-4 June 1999) UN Doc. A/CN.9/460 (6 April 1999).

whom the measure was to be granted raised the argument that a request for a measure that was not confined to a tangible "*subject-matter of the dispute*" exceeded the purpose of an interim measure. That interpretation relied upon the literality of the wording used in Art. 17 of the Model Law, and endorsed, as suggested, by the example set by Art. 26(1) of the UNCITRAL Rules. It was argued that the latter served as an illustration of the nature of an interim measure within an arbitral proceeding: that is to say, its use was limited to goods related to the subject-matter of the dispute.

The original text of the Model Law was not intended to restrict the use of interim measures only to those pertaining to a tangible subject matter of the dispute.[5] The opposite argument, when raised in arbitrations, was a contentious position based upon a misleading literal reading of a provision and did not correspond with the intention of the drafters and the good-faith needs of commercial arbitration.

b.     *Absence of guidelines in connection with the assessment of the request*
The original Model Law regime was silent as to the criteria to be used when judging a request for an interim measure. This scenario could be seen in two ways that are not only different, but opposite to each other.

One suggested that a silent regime on the matter of assessment of the petition was the best system, considering the flexibility needed in commercial arbitration. Following this line of analysis, this method was optimal, considering the broad range of possible scenarios that the arbitrator and the parties face when dealing with a request for interim measures. It was said that a casuistic catalogue was not only impossible to obtain, but more importantly, inconvenient to introduce.

The other suggested that, even recognizing the complexity of the issue and the unimaginable range of scenarios dealing with requests for interim measures, it was advisable to design a regime which fulfills two complementary needs: flexibility and guidance for both the parties and the arbitrator when facing the request and assessment of an interim measure.

c.     *Absence of a regime for modification of an interim measure*
Given that the world of interim measures is, by definition, necessarily surrounded by changing circumstances, it was highlighted that a provision for the modification of such measures was advisable. There was some reason in arguing that such a provision was superfluous, since it was part of the powers implicitly conferred upon the arbitral tribunal. In principle, it was unquestionable that since the arbitral tribunal had the power to issue an interim measure, for many reasons it was evident that it also had the power to modify it. Nevertheless, some guidance as to how to proceed when dealing with a need for modification of such a measure was advisable and, certainly, a confirmation of the implicit powers conferred on the arbitral tribunal could not hurt the system.

---

5. "Settlement of Commercial Disputes – Preparation of uniform provisions on interim measures of protection, Note by the Secretariat", UNCITRAL Working Group II (Arbitration) 36th Sess. (New York, 4-8 March 2002) UN Doc. A/CN.9/WG.II/WP.119 (30 January 2002) (hereinafter Secretariat Note 119) p. 12.

*d. Absence of provisions for the enforcement of interim measures*

There was a vacuum in connection with a regime for the enforcement of interim measures. That was the cause of various relevant complications. The first was the debate as to whether interim measures should be enforceable. The second was the question as to the safeguards that should be implemented in favor of the party against whom the interim measure is issued.

This was an area in which the national legislations adopted very diverse systems. The picture was very unfavorable for an international arbitration regime seeking harmonization. The landscape included some systems which expressly prohibited the enforcement of interim measures, and others which meticulously regulated the procedure and safeguards for their enforcement. During the work of UNCITRAL when drafting the Model Law, there was the impression that, at that time, a uniform system acceptable to national legislations was unattainable due to the national procedural regimes which, in many cases, lead to concerns on public policy matters.[6]

*2. The Target for UNCITRAL in 1999*

The steps envisioned by UNCITRAL were the following:[7]

— to regulate with certainty in connection with the variety of available interim measures;[8]
— to establish a set of guidelines for the arbitral tribunal when facing a request to issue

---

6. Sundaresh MENON and Elaine CHAO, "Reforming the Model Law Provisions on Interim Measures of Protection", 2 Asian International Arbitration Journal (2006, no. 1) p. 1.
7. The matter of interim measures has received a great deal of attention from the arbitration community around the world.
    As an example of this assertion, it is relevant to note that the International Centre for Settlement of Investment Disputes (ICSID) discussed (during 2004 and 2005) an amendment to its interim measures regime, specifically to Art. 37 of the Rules of Procedure for Arbitration Proceedings (Arbitration Rules). The proposed changes entered into force in April, 2006. For reference see "Possible Improvements of the Framework for ICSID arbitration", ICSID Secretariat Discussion Paper, 22 October 2004 pp. 5-7; and "Suggested Changes to the ICSID Rules and Regulations", ICSID Secretariat Working Paper, 12 May 2005, p. 6.
    Within the significant changes in the area of interim measures, the "emergency arbitrator" must be mentioned; this role was introduced in the International and Commercial Arbitration Rules of the American Arbitration Association and the International Centre for Dispute Resolution in the reforms that also came into force in 2006. The introduction of the "emergency arbitrator" creates an expedited regime to handle requests for interim measures before the arbitral tribunal is constituted.
8. For the purpose of this article, the expression "interim measures" is used to cover not only interim measures scenarios, but also those regarding preliminary orders, unless a specific mention is made or the opposite should be the logical conclusion of the circumstances described therein. The distinction of interim measures and preliminary orders, and their reciprocal relationship, is contained, mainly, in Sects. 2 and 3 of the Model Law, as amended in 2006. A more detailed commentary of those sections is included below (Sect.II.4.e.).

an interim measure of protection; to create a set of grounds for modification, suspension or termination of an interim measure (that is to say, criteria for the "administration" of an interim measure);
—to create a set of provisions to enable the enforcement of an interim measure on the basis of a harmonized approach.

It must be added that one of the general principles that UNCITRAL'S Working Group II on International Arbitration and Conciliation (the Working Group) had in mind from the beginning of its deliberations was to maintain an arbitral tribunal's flexibility when handling a request for an interim measure.[9]

The Working Group devoted a significant amount of time to the discussion of the amendment concerning a new interim measures regime. The first Working Group session which covered this topic was held in 2000. The final text was approved in the Working Group session held in January 2006, and was approved by the Commission in July 2006.

A brief description of the UNCITRAL work in this process of amending the Model Law regime for interim measures could be depicted as *"many battles and one war"*. Needless to point out that those battles and that war were conducted with the highest standards of expertise and candidness and a very clear commitment: to create a regime consistent with the dynamics of international commerce and acceptable to national legislatures. As usual in UNCITRAL, the debate was exhaustive, seeking the fine-tuning of every single word. And this is no exaggeration.

All the debates on interim measures were aimed at fine-tuning a general underlying concept of the regime needed for the Model Law. The debates were aimed at creating the right provisions but, generally speaking, with no significant doubts as to what result UNCITRAL was looking for. Metaphorically speaking, those deliberations dealt with the right ship to take, not the right port to sail towards. This statement applies, for instance, to the guidelines for the arbitral tribunal in assessing the request, to the non-exhaustive approach to the inventory of interim measures that the Model Law should set forth, to the discretionary powers of the arbitral tribunal in determining the appropriateness of security in connection with the measure, among other items of the regime.

3. *The Debate on Ex Parte Interim Measures (A "Which Port to Sail Towards" Debate)*

As stated above, there was one discussion which, indeed, following the metaphorical language, dealt with "which was the right port to sail towards". This was the case of the ex parte interim measures.

---

9. "Experience has demonstrated that a maximum of party autonomy and flexibility coupled with a minimum of rules of law and formalities are needed in order for arbitrators or conciliators to be able to act, in each case, in accordance with the particularities of the case." José María ABASCAL ZAMORA, "Barcelona Afterthoughts", 20 Journal of International Arbitration (2003 no. 1) pp. 111-119.

The deliberations regarding the pros and cons of creating a regime for ex parte interim measures began, and they continued in various UNCITRAL sessions, with a serious concern regarding the suitability of this regime.

The topic of discussion was twofold: whether an ex parte formula had a place in arbitration and, particularly, in a body of rules drafted with the aspiration to be a Model Law for further enactment in national legislations; and if an ex parte measures regime was to be integrated in the Model Law, whether such measures were eligible for court enforcement. Henceforth, the deliberations were particularly intense, and because of the publication of the working papers produced by UNCITRAL the debate reached the world arbitration community. Various conferences were organized around the world to discuss the suitability of an ex parte interim measures regime.

One of the initial objections against an ex parte regime tried to be grounded in the nature of a Model Law. Some considered it a very ambitious step in the regulation of international arbitration and a very sensitive matter to include in a body of uniform legislation. Some expressed the idea that should an ex parte system be stimulated, it was an assignment to be undertaken when drafting provisions for arbitration rules.

Furthermore, there were some opponents who alleged that these sorts of measures were more the result of theoretical exercises than actual needs in arbitration practice.

Another argument, which was raised within the debate in the arbitration community, was that ex parte communications (implicit in an ex parte regime) would open an undesirable opportunity for one party to introduce allegations on the merits of the case with no involvement of the counterparty.

*a.     Too aggressive an innovation?*

Innovation will always be a challenge and this task for UNCITRAL was no exception. The goal was to create a system that would satisfy the concern for adequate safeguards and at the same time provide an effective means to make arbitration as effective as arbitration users demanded. Moreover, the implementation of such a system would be more successful if done at a legislative level. Despite the fact that the arbitral framework is governed by the autonomy of the parties (which encompasses the applicability of arbitral rules), and therefore any regime could be designed within the provisions of arbitral rules, such an approach is undesirable from the perspective of harmonization. Precisely for that reason the best approach was to create a model law regime. The last decades are witness to the positive impact of harmonization within the arbitration culture. It is fair to assert that had it not been for the harmonization process surrounding the evolution of arbitration worldwide, arbitration would not have achieved the level of acceptance and effectiveness within the international commercial arena. In this context, the notion of harmonization is used not only to address a product in the form of model legislation, but also in relation to other sets of regulations that have played an astounding role in searching for a uniform system for arbitration in general; such is the case, for instance, with the New York Convention and other international treaties (many of them drafted along the lines of the New York Convention) and some arbitration rules which, de facto, have served as a source of imitation (or at least of inspiration, in some cases) for families of arbitration rules. However, for the purpose of supporting this argument, it is fair to say that, since the Model Law "formula" was so successful in promoting the use of arbitration and its effectiveness, the best option was to make the ex parte interim measures regime part of the Model Law.

b.   *Only a need to stimulate academic debate?*
Some suggested that the need for ex parte interim measures was the result of the fabrication of a theoretical model which had no justification in the real world of commerce and arbitration. That was inaccurate. Certainly, for a practitioner, a request for an ex parte interim measure is not an everyday situation. But that does not destroy the real need for it. In arbitration, as in many other legal institutions, occasional needs should also be taken into account. An example from the arbitration world confirms this. Ex aequo et bono arbitrations are not common in arbitration; however, such a system exists and works when used. There is a virtue in having those institutions as part of the arbitration regulation.

I acted as sole arbitrator in an ICC arbitration, in which I wish an ex parte interim measure system had already been in effect. One party contacted me, on a truly urgent basis, in writing (not copying to the counterparty), to inform me that the counterparty had just obtained a court order to request payment and enforce a garnishment resolution if payment was not immediately made. The origin of that court order (within "*summary commercial proceedings*") was a dispute concerning a matter which was part of the merits of the arbitration. The party affected by that court order requested an interim measure from the arbitrator in order to stop the imminent enforcement of the court order. Since no ex parte regime applied to the arbitral process, before any other activity I had to inform the other party of the request being submitted by copying the brief which contained the request, in compliance with Art. 3(1) of the ICC Rules.[10] Had it been an ex parte regime, the arbitrator would have issued a preliminary order directing the party not to obtain the enforcement of the court order before the interim measure request was examined (this would be acting in accordance with Art. 17B of the Model Law). The corollary of this is that the rarity of experiences dealing with ex parte interim measures is the consequence of not having such regime. As one delegate said in the UNCITRAL Working Group, "*in order to have violin concerts, first you need to have a violin*", so, no argument should be grounded on the basis of an absence of violin concerts.

c.   *A dangerous ingredient of ex parte allegations?*
The risk of ex parte allegations, as a component of ex parte interim measures, was also an issue of discussion. The argument suggested that such a measure would be translated

---

10. The ICC Rules (Art. 3(1)) state the following in connection with the obligation to provide a copy of all communications to the counterparty (as well as the arbitral tribunal and the Secretariat):

    "All pleadings and other written communications submitted by any party, as well as all documents annexed thereto, shall be supplied in a number of copies sufficient to provide one copy for each party, plus one for each arbitrator, and one for the Secretariat. A copy of any communication from the Arbitral Tribunal to the parties shall be sent to the Secretariat."

into a questionable opportunity for the requesting party to undertake an ex parte approach to the arbitrator in order to argue the merits of the case. This objection is not sustainable for the following reasons.

The principle of equal treatment of the parties doubtlessly is one of the imperative elements of arbitration, and that principle can be applied in the event of limited access to the arbitrator on an ex parte basis. Although the requesting party has access to the arbitrator without the counterparty's knowledge before it receives notice of the "preliminary order" granted (or denied), that requesting party is confronted with the fact that all communication produced within the ex parte stage (including oral communications) shall be disclosed to the counterparty as soon as the arbitral tribunal issues a decision concerning the preliminary order (the notion of preliminary order is used within the precise meaning and effects attributed by Chapter IV.A of the Model Law). This procedure allows the affected party to reply as soon as he is informed of the arguments in favor of the petitions and the terms under which the order was dictated. In fact, the Model Law states that this obligation on the arbitrator (to communicate all information as received) is in effect "immediately after the arbitral tribunal has made a determination in respect of an application for a preliminary order". This allows the affected party to react within a very short period of time after the ex parte allegation has been produced and, as part of such reaction, to reply to the requesting party's arguments in support of the application.

Should the arbitrator fail to disclose all communications received from the requesting party, including oral communications, the arbitrator would indeed be violating the principle of equal treatment of the parties (and the rules of procedure in general). Nevertheless, if such was the case, the violation would not be the result of an ex parte order in itself, but rather of a breach of procedural duty imposed upon the arbitrator. In other words, the undesirable scenario (a non-disclosed ex parte allegation) would be the consequence of a deviation from the guidelines which regulate ex parte orders, but not a consequence of the ex parte application itself. This is true even before the fact that the request shall, inevitably, include arguments on the merits to the extent that the arbitrator shall analyze such arguments as part of the preliminary "assessment" of the case surrounding the requested measure. The party affected by the order, will be able to react in greater detail with respect to the information and allegations submitted by the requesting party.

*4.    Highlights of the Current UNCITRAL Interim Measures Regime*

In July 2006, UNCITRAL approved the latest amendments to the Model Law. Such amendments included the insertion of an entire chapter (Chapter IV.A) that regulates, comprehensively, the whole regime of interim measures issued by an arbitral tribunal. Art. 9 (included in Chapter II. Arbitration agreement), which deals with the role of courts in interim measures, remains untouched. Next, some aspects of the new regulation are highlighted.

*a.    The regime is an "opt out" system*
The entire regime is an "opt out" formula (for interim measures as well as preliminary orders).

The Working Group and the arbitration world thoroughly discussed the type of system that was more suitable to the needs of arbitration users regarding interim measures.

During the debate, many voices were heard in support of either an opt-in or opt-out system, respectively. The focus of the analysis was a philosophical one, as it corresponds to the issue of what the right default formula should be. It was extremely relevant to pay attention to the real-life arbitration world, as any practitioner knows that in a great majority of the disputes he has taken part in as counsel, the drafting of the arbitration clause was not done by arbitration experts.[11] In the best of cases, it could be affirmed that the clause might have been drafted by an expert, but whoever decided to copy that clause (taken from another contract) was not an expert. Therefore, it is unrealistic to expect that a regime would be effective if the drafters of arbitration clauses decided, in each case, which interim measures system would be best for satisfying the needs and expectations of the parties to that contract. Experience leads us to foresee that the sort of interim measures regime to be included (or excluded) in a particular arbitration clause is fully dependent on the format of the arbitration clause available (to the contract drafter) at the time the contract is prepared. In summary, arbitration clauses, in a tremendous number of cases, are not drafted by arbitration experts and a legislative default rule must assume such a landscape.

For the reasons expressed above, though perfectly possible in theory, it was unrealistic that an opt-in formula was going to do any good for commercial arbitration. On the contrary, the prevailing view was that, should the regime be conceived as an effective tool in favor of the effective use of commercial arbitration, the regime had to be designed on the basis of a default rule that would contain the complete set of rules for interim measures unless otherwise agreed by the parties. Thus, with this system, if the drafter decides that the interim measures regime, as regulated in the Model Law, does not meet the needs of the parties to the contract, he is free to *opt out* of such regime. Should the interim measures regime be designed as an opt-in formula, it would be a poor contribution for the users of arbitration.

The debate on the type of default system to select was particularly intense regarding ex parte interim measures (in Sect. II.4.e below are references to the ex parte system which, in fact, includes no interim measures, but only preliminary orders). Nevertheless, the opt-out approach was also accepted.[12] Moreover, because of the consensus solution

---

11. Informal non-official "pools" (conducted in coffee-breaks during arbitration conferences) reveal that a vast majority of the arbitral clauses seen in arbitration controversies present problems. Some of those problems come in the form of unnecessary procedural complications, others as the cause of frustration of the arbitration. Most of the time when an arbitration expert is asked to propose an arbitration clause, he follows the easy, safe and effective solution, which consists in literally "copying" a Model Law clause. Every time I see an arbitral clause with more than five lines, I become suspicious that procedural trouble is just around the corner.
12. "29. A widely shared view of the Working Group at its thirty-seventh session was that, if ex parte measures were included, then the provision should indicate that such measures only be granted in exceptional circumstances (A/CN.9/523, para. 17). The words 'in exceptional circumstances' have been included after the words 'the arbitral tribunal may'. The Working Group agreed that paragraph (4) (a) of the United States proposal should be revised to take into account the views

adopted by UNCITRAL, which was the result of careful safeguards included in the new regulation, it is reasonable to expect that national legislatures will embrace the Model Law for this regime.

b. *The flexible nature of the form of the interim measure*

An interim measure is relevant not only because it has binding effect for the parties within the arbitral process, but also because an interim measure can be subject to an external effect: the enforcement of such measure by a court. And it is precisely the binding effect in the outside world that gives importance to the formal nature that the interim measure ruling takes.

UNCITRAL adopted a liberal and wise approach: to establish the same effect for an interim measure regardless of whether or not it takes the form of an award or another form.[13]

This is not an issue of semantics. It is well known that many jurisdictions are extremely grounded in formalistic conceptions of legal institutions, and this might have a negative effect on certain decisions subject to further requests for recognition or enforcement by the courts. Such an assertion is primarily true if, among other considerations, the framework of the New York Convention applies.

There is extensive case law, throughout many national jurisdictions, which demonstrates that assertion regarding the effectiveness of an arbitral decision with respect to its formal denomination, particularly when the umbrella of the New York Convention is sought. Despite the fact that the legal nature of the decision corresponds to its content and effects, and the denomination with which it is labeled should be irrelevant, or at least a matter of secondary importance, some courts may possibly deny the recognition or enforcement of an interim measure because it is not an award.

However, at the same time, it is important that the arbitral tribunal has the power to decide whether an interim measure should be issued in a different form (not an award). A good example that reveals the helpfulness of this dual approach is the case of arbitrations governed by rules which establish additional steps for the issuance of an award, which results in a longer period of time for the arbitral tribunal to issue a measure. Such is the case, for instance, in ICC arbitration which compels the arbitrator

---

and concerns expressed by the Working Group and, in particular, to recognize the parties' freedom of contract by allowing them to contract out of the provision giving the tribunal the power to grant an ex parte interim measure of protection (A/CN.9/523, para. 31). To make this decision effective, paragraph (7) (a) of the revised draft includes the phrase 'by the parties' after the opening phrase, 'Unless otherwise agreed' as suggested at the thirty-seventh session of the Working Group (A/CN.9/523, para. 54)."

"Settlement of Commercial Disputes – Preparation of uniform provisions on interim measures of protection, Note by the Secretariat", UNCITRAL Working Group II (Arbitration) 38th Sess. (New York, 12-16 May 2003) UN Doc. A/CN.9/WG.II/WP.123 (hereinafter Secretariat Note 123) para. 29.

13. Art. 17(2) (Model Law). "An interim measure is any temporary measure, whether in the form of an award or in another form, by which...."

to submit any award to the "scrutiny" of the ICC Court.[14] This time-saving issue becomes of the essence in most of the requests for interim measures. The issuance of the interim measure, if justified, must be expedited; otherwise it might turn out to be absolutely ineffective. For these reasons, it is not uncommon (and this is precisely the Model Law approach) that the arbitral tribunal grants an interim measure by means of a "procedural order" or a resolution identified by a similar expression.

c.  *The inventory of interim measures is exhaustive, but generic*
The Model Law contains a list of interim measures which, though exhaustive, encompasses in four categories all possible generic scenarios which provide the basis for issuing an interim measure.

The intention of the Working Group was not to create an exhaustive and lengthy list of interim measures. Such a list would face the common scenario in which either the counsel's or the arbitral tribunal's creativity would be constrained by a list prepared by less-imaginative legislative drafters.

From the beginning of the deliberations, the general intention was to create a provision which permits flexibility for the arbitrator as well as the parties in finding the appropriate measure for each specific need. The methodology adopted for that type of regulation was to identify the generic categories to cover the possible scenarios for a request for interim measures. In doing so, the Working Group formulated a list of generic descriptions of activities (active and passive) which encompasses all conceivable orders that a party might be directed to observe. This methodology resulted in the following provisions:

> "*Art. 17(2) Model Law*
> An interim measure is any temporary measure, whether in the form of an award or in another form, by which, at any time prior to the issuance of the award by which the dispute is finally decided, the arbitral tribunal orders a party to:
> (a) Maintain or restore the status quo pending determination of the dispute;
> (b) Take action that would prevent, or refrain from taking action that is likely to cause, current or imminent harm or prejudice to the arbitral process itself;
> (c) Provide a means of preserving assets out of which a subsequent award may be satisfied; or
> (d) Preserve evidence that may be relevant and material to the resolution of the dispute."

d.  *The assessment of the request for an interim measure*
UNCITRAL considered that the assessment of the request for an interim measure should

---

14. The scrutiny of the award is regulated in Art. 27 of the ICC Rules:

    "Before signing any Award, the Arbitral Tribunal shall submit it in draft form to the Court. The Court may lay down modifications as to the form of the Award and, without affecting the Arbitral Tribunal's liberty of decision, may also draw its attention to points of substance. No Award shall be rendered by the Arbitral Tribunal until it has been approved by the Court as to its form."

be undertaken by the arbitral tribunal following a few general guidelines, but maintaining the flexibility in the use of the tribunal's powers as a hallmark of the arbitration procedure (and which the Model Law has incorporated within its regulatory framework).

The purpose was to design an assessment tool which allows the arbitral tribunal to consider a balance of two variables.[15] In this train of thought, the Model Law sets forth that the arbitral tribunal should undertake an analysis which combines the following assessment tools:

(a) a foreseeable harm not adequately reparable by monetary compensation and a kind of harm that has a greater impact than the possible harm affecting the party against whom the measure is granted; and
(b) a preliminary evaluation of the requesting party's position as to the merits of the dispute.[16]

These two assessment criteria apply solely to the interim measures which fall within the following generic categories: maintenance of the status quo, prevention of an action that would negatively affect the arbitral process, and preservation of assets (included in Art. 17(2)(a), (b) and (c)). Such criteria will only apply to interim measures aiming at the preservation of evidence (as set forth in Art. 17(2)(d)), only if the arbitral tribunal deems it appropriate.[17] The more accessible requirement applicable to interim measures for

---

15. "70. The following is the Commentary on the Rules:

   ... The latter term corresponds to the common-law concept of 'balance of equities'. Considerations of fairness include the strength of the merits of the applicant's claim, the urgency of the need for a provisional remedy, and the practical burdens that may result from granting the remedy...."

   Secretariat Note 119, *op. cit.*, fn. 5, para. 70.

16. "... and that reasonableness and proportionality apply in the case of ex parte measures" (Secretariat Note 123, *op. cit.*, fn. 12, para. 30).

17. The assessment guidelines to grant an interim measure are described in Art. 17A of the Model Law:

   "(1) The party requesting an interim measure under article 17(2)(a), (b) and (c) shall satisfy the arbitral tribunal that:
   (a) Harm not adequately reparable by an award of damages is likely to result if the measure is not ordered, and such harm substantially outweighs the harm that is likely to result to the party against whom the measure is directed if the measure is granted; and
   (b) There is a reasonable possibility that the requesting party will succeed on the merits of the claim. The determination on this possibility shall not affect the discretion of the arbitral tribunal in making any subsequent determination.
   (2) With regard to a request for an interim measure under article 17(2)(d), the requirements in paragraphs (1)(a) and (b) of this article shall apply only to the extent the arbitral tribunal considers appropriate."

preservation of evidence is plausible;[18] in most cases, it is very difficult for preservation of evidence to cause harm. An exception could be if, for instance, the evidence consists of disputed goods whose sale is part of the regular course of business of the party against whom the measure is intended. In a situation like this, an arbitrator would likely move in the direction of assuring the means to conduct whatever test or inspection is needed in connection with the disputed goods, but avoiding what, in fact, would turn out to be an order to freeze assets (in the form of an interim measure).

A few details must be pointed out in connection with the preliminary evaluation of the merits of the dispute (as to the position of the requesting party). The arbitrator is expected to undertake his duty in such a way that he will not be prejudiced in making a decision on the merits of the case. Either an arbitrator or a court, in most cases, when dealing with a request for an interim measure has to undertake a fast preliminary analysis of the merits surrounding the dispute. He has to take a "bird's-eye view" of the merits of the controversy. The following reasons ought to be highlighted.

First, this is not an uncommon situation exclusive to the matter of interim measures. For example, an arbitrator undertakes a preliminary analysis of the case when deciding on the admission of certain evidence to the record; in doing so, he may assess a likely impact that the process of production of the evidence (i.e., a report on accounting records) might have on one of the parties vis à vis the position of the party (seeking that evidence) on the aspect of the merits related to the piece of evidence being considered for admission.

Secondly, the regime has two important caveats. One of them is contained in Art. 17A(1)(b) which sets forth that "The determination on this possibility [that the requesting party will succeed on the merits of the claim] shall not affect the discretion of the arbitral tribunal in making any subsequent determination." The other has to do with the arbitral tribunal's power to modify its interim measure decision, as stated in Art. 17D. Therefore, should the arbitral tribunal come into contact with elements that lead it to have a different impression of the merits of the dispute, it will have the chance (and duty, in some cases) to "modify, suspend or terminate an interim measure or a preliminary order". The Working Group was very strong in its intention to ensure broad powers for the arbitral tribunal when evaluating a modification, suspension or termination of the measure (or the preliminary order as well).[19]

---

18. "... [T]he obligation on the requesting party to satisfy a tribunal of the balance of convenience and reasonable possibility of success on the merits of the claim would be 'only to the extent the arbitral tribunal considers appropriate'. Therefore, where a request is made for an interim measure for the preservation of evidence, a less onerous burden of proof may be placed on the requesting party where appropriate."

    Sundaresh MENON and Elaine CHAO, op. cit., fn. 6, p. 18.
19. The Working Group had the following view regarding the convenience of assuring broad powers in favor of the arbitral tribunal when assessing a modification, suspension or termination of a measure or a preliminary order.

    "20. At the thirty-seventh session of the Working Group, it was said that the discretion to modify or terminate an interim measure should not be limited. It was observed that, given the

What UNCITRAL did was incorporate in the new regime a set of guidelines that has been in use in other procedural frameworks, which have been built upon the need to take into consideration the balance of convenience and the likelihood of success by the requesting party.[20] This is not only positive due to the proved experience of the formula, but also because of the familiarity of national legal systems with such a system and, therefore, sympathy with it at the time of enactment in a national legislation.

*e. The UNCITRAL dual system: preliminary orders and interim measures (the ex parte dilemma)*

The ex parte regime and its applications and issues are dealt with below. The sole purpose of this section is to depict the highlights of the system "created" by UNCITRAL for ex parte "interim measures", which as a result of the system, strictly speaking, and according to the text and the clear intention of the Working Group, turn out to be that there are no ex parte interim measures, but only ex parte preliminary orders.

The dual system of the Model Law could be summarized as follows. The Model Law does not allow ex parte interim measures. However, the Model Law does regulate an ex parte regime for preliminary orders. The system works as follows.[21] The underlying

---

extraordinary nature of such measures, if a tribunal had the power to grant such measures then it should also have the power to modify or terminate them. The Working Group may wish to consider whether the text currently included in square brackets being 'in light of additional information or a change of circumstances', originally used in the Secretariat proposal (see A/CN.9/508, paras. 88-89) should be included to avoid establishing an arbitrary discretion."

Secretariat Note 123, *op. cit.*, fn. 12, para. 20). Consistent with this view, as expressed in this UNCITRAL document, the final text omitted the language originally placed between brackets.

20. Arbitration rules, legislation and court case law, created around the world, contain provisions that follow these principles. Annex IV contains a non-exhaustive list with samples of such provisions.

21. The Model Law ex parte system is explicitly contained in "Section 2. Preliminary orders", and implicitly in other sections. Sect. 2 includes Arts. 17B and 17C, which state the following:

*"Article 17B. Applications for preliminary orders and conditions for granting preliminary orders*
(1) Unless otherwise agreed by the parties, a party may, without notice to any other party, make a request for an interim measure together with an application for a preliminary order directing a party not to frustrate the purpose of the interim measure requested.
(2) The arbitral tribunal may grant a preliminary order provided it considers that prior disclosure of the request for the interim measure to the party against whom it is directed risks frustrating the purpose of the measure.
(3) The conditions defined under article 17A apply to any preliminary order, provided that the harm to be assessed under article 17A(1)(*a*), is the harm likely to result from the order being granted or not.

*Article 17C. Specific regime for preliminary orders*
(1) Immediately after the arbitral tribunal has made a determination in respect of an application for a preliminary order, the arbitral tribunal shall give notice to all parties of the request for the interim measure, the application for the preliminary order, the preliminary order, if any, and all other communications, including by indicating the content of any oral communication, between any party and the arbitral tribunal in relation thereto.

assumption (which has to be "assumed" by the arbitrator) is that a prior disclosure of the petition to the counterparty jeopardizes the objective of the measure. That being the case, a party submits a dual petition before the arbitrator: an application for a "preliminary order" and a request for an "interim measure". The counterparty receives no notice of the petition. If the arbitral tribunal considers that it is justified not to give notice of the petition to the counterparty, the arbitral tribunal issues a "preliminary order" and informs the parties of it together with any document or communication (including oral communications) as provided by the petitioner of the "order/measure". Afterwards, the affected party is entitled to argue in connection with the counterparty's petition.[22] Finally, the arbitral tribunal issues a decision either terminating the preliminary order, or confirming or modifying its terms and incorporating such terms (the original or the modified terms) in an interim measure.

The main distinction between a preliminary order and an interim measure is that only the latter is eligible for court enforcement. Although a preliminary order is binding upon the parties, it cannot be taken before a court for its enforcement.

Whereas the interim measure is conceived as the means to ensure the effectiveness of the award, the preliminary order is to make the interim measure effective.[23]

As for the timing framework for the issuance and the effect of the preliminary order, it can be said that the objective was to create a mechanism ensuring the arbitral tribunal's ability to dictate a preliminary order, but at the same time, to limit the time in which the order remains in effect. For this reason, an additional very important safeguard in the ex parte system is that the preliminary order is in effect for only twenty days.

A final aspect to point out is that Art. 17C(5) of the Model Law indicates that a preliminary order does not constitute an award. This is to ensure that the arbitral

---

(2) At the same time, the arbitral tribunal shall give an opportunity to any party against whom a preliminary order is directed to present its case at the earliest practicable time.
(3) The arbitral tribunal shall decide promptly on any objection to the preliminary order.
(4) A preliminary order shall expire after twenty days from the date on which it was issued by the arbitral tribunal. However, the arbitral tribunal may issue an interim measure adopting or modifying the preliminary order, after the party against whom the preliminary order is directed has been given notice and an opportunity to present its case.
(5) A preliminary order shall be binding on the parties but shall not be subject to enforcement by a court. Such a preliminary order does not constitute an award."

22. The following UNCITRAL working paper illustrates the scope of the opportunity to "present its case".

"40. It is recalled that, at its thirty-ninth session, the Working Group agreed that the words 'opportunity to be heard' should be replaced by 'opportunity to present its case', in order to encompass both a hearing of the responding party and a written submission from that party...."

"Settlement of Commercial Disputes – Preparation of uniform provisions on interim measures of protection, Note by the Secretariat", UNCITRAL Working Group II (Arbitration) 41st Sess. (Vienna, 13-17 September 2004) UN Doc. A/CN.9WG.II/WP.131.

23. Pilar PERALES VIESCASILLAS, "*Medidas cautelares en el arbitraje comercial internacional: modificación de la ley modelo de la CNUDMI*", Revista Jurídica de Catalunya, (2007, no. 2) p. 422.

tribunal's decision is not subject to court enforcement while the affected party has not received an opportunity to present its case before the arbitral tribunal.

*f.  Provisions on security, disclosure and liability matters*

Three other elements of the new Model Law regime for interim measures are the regulation of security, disclosure and liability.

One of the most effective safeguards when dealing with interim measures is the provision of security for potential damages that might result from the measure. The Model Law includes a set of stipulations on that matter (Art. 17E).[24] The Model Law grants discretionary powers for the arbitral tribunal to request a provision of security as a condition to grant an interim measure or a preliminary order. Although in both cases (interim measures and preliminary orders) the powers of the arbitral tribunal are discretionary, the language used in the Model Law suggests, intentionally, that the matter of security should receive greater attention in the case of preliminary orders. Whereas in the event of interim measures the Model Law states that "the arbitral tribunal may require ... to provide appropriate security", in the case of preliminary orders the Model Law indicates that "The arbitral tribunal shall require ... to provide security ... unless the arbitral tribunal considers it inappropriate or unnecessary to do so." Hence, though in both cases the arbitral tribunal can dispense the provision of security, the wording of the Model Law suggests a stricter approach by the arbitral tribunal when considering dispensing the provision of security in the case of a preliminary order. The reason for that difference in approach is simple and justifiable: in the preliminary-order stage there is no one to speak for the party against whom the order might be granted.

The regulation incorporated in the Model Law establishes a duty of full and frank disclosure for any party in connection with the interim measure. Such a framework indicates that the arbitral tribunal may request any party to disclose any material change related to the interim measure and the surrounding circumstances under which such measure was granted. Moreover, in the case of a preliminary order, the applicant party must reveal such information to the arbitral tribunal and this obligation will remain in force until the party against whom the order has been requested has had the opportunity to present its case.[25]

---

24. The Model Law contains the following rules in connection with security:

    "(1) The arbitral tribunal may require the party requesting an interim measure to provide appropriate security in connection with the measure.
    (2) The arbitral tribunal shall require the party applying for a preliminary order to provide security in connection with the order unless the arbitral tribunal considers it inappropriate or unnecessary to do so."

25. The Model Law contains the following rules in connection with the duty of disclosure:

    "(1) The arbitral tribunal may require any party promptly to disclose any material change in the circumstances on the basis of which the measure was requested or granted.
    (2) The party applying for a preliminary order shall disclose to the arbitral tribunal all circumstances that are likely to be relevant to the arbitral tribunal's determination whether to grant or maintain the order, and such obligation shall continue until the party against whom the

The issue of liability for costs and damages caused by an interim measure was a matter intensely debated by the Working Group. In principle, it might be considered appropriate for this matter to be dealt with by national laws and their liability regimes. Nevertheless, the intention of the Working Group was to ensure, at the level of the Model Law, a strict regime which establishes a clear and unquestionable liability on the party who requested the measure for those costs and damages arising from such measure, should the arbitral tribunal later find that the measure should not have been granted. And in order to obtain that result, the Model Law sets forth a very direct cause-and-effect scheme. It points out that liability applies "for any costs and damages caused by the measure or order to any party" if later the interim measure is found inappropriate.[26]

By following this system, the Model Law ensures that a liability regime be in effect with the sole enactment of the Model Law by national states and, likewise, that a cause-and-effect scheme is observed; liability will occur if the interim measure causes negative financial consequences and the measure is found to be unjustified. This approach makes the intrusion of a liability regime less onerous for the party requesting the interim measure more difficult, particularly if a general regime in the domestic legislation opens the possibility to invoke the privilege of certain exceptions for liability in analogous cases. After deliberations, the Working Group decided that the provision dealing with liability should clearly state its application for interim measures as well as preliminary orders.[27]

---

order has been requested has had an opportunity to present its case. Thereafter, paragraph (1) of this article shall apply."

26. The Model Law contains the following rules in connection with liability for costs and damages:

"*Article 17 G. Costs and damages*
The party requesting an interim measure or applying for a preliminary order shall be liable for any costs and damages caused by the measure or the order to any party if the arbitral tribunal later determines that, in the circumstances, the measure or the order should not have been granted. The arbitral tribunal may award such costs and damages at any point during the proceedings."

It must be pointed out that the Working Group was clear that the expression "proceedings" should be read as "arbitral proceedings".

"28. It was also agreed that any explanatory material accompanying paragraph (6 bis) should clarify that the reference to 'proceedings' referred to the arbitral proceedings and not to the proceedings relating to the interim measure...."

"Settlement of Commercial Disputes – Preparation of uniform provisions on interim measures of protection, Note by the Secretariat", UNCITRAL Working Group II (Arbitration) 43rd Sess. (Vienna, 3-7 October 2005) UN Doc. A/CN.9/WG.II/WP.138, para. 28.

27. "26. In order to assist deliberations on paragraph (6 bis), the Secretariat had prepared a note (A/CN.9/WG.II/WP.127) containing information received from States on the liability regimes that applied under their national laws in respect of interim measures of protection. It was observed that, of the legislation contained therein, the national laws did not distinguish between inter partes and ex parte measures in relation to the liability regimes that applied. It was suggested that, for that reason, the square brackets around that paragraph should be deleted and the Working Group should consider possible improvements to the text."

Another relevant aspect of the liability regime is to determine whether a strict link exists between the final decision on the merits of the dispute and the justification of the measure granted. The clear direction adopted by the Working Group was that there is no strict direct link on this matter. Or, stated from the opposite angle, an adverse decision on the merits should not necessarily imply an adverse decision on the liability issue related to the interim measure.[28] Although the two concepts should be evaluated in their entirety and in their interaction, the decision of the arbitral tribunal can take separate roads.

*g.   Enforceability of interim measures*

The Working Group's analysis was guided by the regime established in the Model Law for the enforcement of awards. Nevertheless, from the beginning of the deliberations it was clear that interim measures and awards are different, notwithstanding that they share some similarities. With that in mind, the Working Group envisioned the creation of a set of provisions which would incorporate the regime contained in the Model Law (Chapter VIII) for the recognition and enforcement of awards and adapt it to the specific features of the nature and scope of interim measures.

One of the arguments in favor of using the Model Law regime for the enforcement of awards was that this regime has been effectively used for many decades. Among other considerations to point out, is that it has been positively tested in various legal systems. The main aspects of the recognition and enforcement of the interim measures regime are as follows:

(a) The arbitral tribunal may not authorize the enforcement of the interim measure if it considers it to be inappropriate in the light of the circumstances of the interim measure in particular, and the overall dispute in general. To this purpose, the Model Law incorporated the opt-out approach in favor of the tribunal (*"unless otherwise provided by the arbitral tribunal"*; Art. 17H(1).

(b) The party who was granted the interim measure must inform the court of any modification regarding the terms of the interim measure.

(c) The court may order the requesting party to provide security.

(d) The grounds for refusing a petition for recognition or enforcement are the following:

(d.1) Those contained in provisions included in Art. 36 of the Model Law.[29] With regard

---

*Ibid.*, para. 26.

28. "27. ... final decision on the merits should not be an essential element in determining whether the interim measure was justified or not". *Ibid.*, para. 27.

29. The provisions referred to in Art. 17I(1)(a)(I) (with respect to the regime for refusal of enforcement of an award, as established in the Model Law) state the following:

"(1) Recognition or enforcement of an arbitral award, irrespective of the country in which it was made, may be refused only:
(a) at the request of the party against whom it is invoked, if that party furnishes to the competent court where recognition or enforcement is sought proof that:
(I) a party to the arbitration agreement referred to in article 7 was under some incapacity; or the said agreement is not valid under the law to which the parties have subjected it or, failing any

to the ground set forth in Art. 36(1)(a)(v) (an award not binding on the parties or set aside or suspended by a court), such hypothesis was adapted to the nature of an interim measure and transported to Art. 17I(1)(a)(iii), which states a ground for refusal when "The interim measure has been terminated or suspended by the arbitral tribunal or, where so empowered, by the court of the State in which the arbitration takes place or under the law of which that interim measure was granted."

(d.2) Incompatibility of the interim measure with the powers conferred upon the court, though it is set forth that such court can adapt ("reformulate") it in order to ensure compliance with its own powers, but with no modification of its substance.

(e) The scope of the court's role is limited to examining the application regarding the interim measure. Additionally, the Model Law is clear that ".... The court where recognition or enforcement is sought shall not, in making that determination, undertake a review of the substance of the interim measure." (Art. 17I(2)). The clear intention, and wording, of the Model Law is to ensure that, at the stage of enforcement of an interim measure, the court's intervention is not extended to the substance of the matter which is within the jurisdiction of the arbitral tribunal. Moreover, this restriction guarantees that the determination of the court will not be decisive with regard to a further application for recognition or enforcement of an award, should the court receive new elements for consideration that might result in a different conclusion from that issued when the interim measure was tested.

It is of the essence to bear in mind, as pointed out above, that only interim measures are eligible for court enforcement. Preliminary orders (which are granted ex parte), though binding upon the parties, cannot be subject to court enforcement.

h. *Interim measures issued by a court*
One of the relevant innovations in the Model Law's new interim measures regime is the provision which deals with court-ordered interim measures. Prior to the 2006 amendment, the Model Law had a very conservative approach to the matter of powers of the courts requested to grant an interim measure.

---

indication thereon, under the law of the country where the award was made; or
(ii) the party against whom the award is invoked was not given proper notice of the appointment of an arbitrator or of the arbitral proceedings or was otherwise unable to present his case; or
(iii) the award deals with a dispute not contemplated by or not falling within the terms of the submission to arbitration, or it contains decisions on matters beyond the scope of the submission to arbitration, provided that, if the decisions on matters submitted to arbitration can be separated from those not so submitted, that part of the award which contains decisions on matters submitted to arbitration may be recognized and enforced; or
(iv) the composition of the arbitral tribunal or the arbitral procedure was not in accordance with the agreement of the parties or, failing such agreement, was not in accordance with the law of the country where the arbitration took place; ...."

The aspect of court powers is a very challenging one. UNCITRAL has been extremely careful when dealing with matters that fall within the functioning of the national court systems. Indeed, this is a very sensitive subject. It has to do with the structure and traditions of the court system, and not just with a catalogue (whether broad or restrictive) of measures available to the courts of a given judicial system.

For these reasons, the original text of the Model Law was silent on the matter of interim measures that a court can decree in connection with an arbitration. However, the new Art. 17J contains some broad yet very useful guidelines. The recent provision states the following guiding principles:

(a) Court jurisdiction is not limited to those interim measures issued by an arbitral tribunal seated within its jurisdiction. This is particularly relevant in international commercial arbitration. There are many occasions in which there is need for court assistance within a jurisdiction other than the seat of the arbitration but maintaining a point of contact with the territory in which an interim measure is to be enforced.
(b) The Model Law does not set out an inventory of interim measures available to the courts. Rather, it sets the principle that the means available to the courts are the same as those applicable in court proceedings. In following this system, the Model Law ensures that there is no collision with the court's procedural and substantive framework. Additionally, the Model Law recognizes the applicability of the court's procedural regulation.
(c) Likewise, this regulation establishes a very relevant guideline as to the court's role when deciding on an issue regarding an interim measure. Such a guideline relies on the statement that the court shall take into consideration "the specific features of international arbitration". This is, certainly, an essential tool to promote the harmonization of the interim measures regime, and it is consistent with and supportive of the mandate in favor of the uniform application of the law as set forth in Art. 2A of the Model Law.[30]

---

30. Such uniform application principle is stated in Art. 2A. (Model Law):

"*Article 2A. International origin and general principles*
(1) In the interpretation of this Law, regard is to be had to its international origin and to the need to promote uniformity in its application and the observance of good faith.
(2) Questions concerning matters governed by this Law which are not expressly settled in it are to be settled in conformity with the general principles on which this Law is based."

III. APPROACH BY THE UNCITRAL WORKING GROUP IN CONSIDERING THE INCORPORATION OF NEW PROVISIONS REGARDING INTERIM MEASURES IN THE UNCITRAL ARBITRATION RULES

1. *Conceptual-philosophical Perspective Taken by the Working Group in the Suggested Changes to Art. 26 of the UNCITRAL Arbitration Rules*

As soon as UNCITRAL finished the amendment to the Model Law on the matter of the form of the arbitral agreement and the interim measures regime, it decided to undertake a revision of its Arbitration Rules.

The Rules currently contain one provision regulating "Interim Measures of Protection", in Art. 26. It states the following:

> "(1) At the request of either party, the arbitral tribunal may take any interim measures it deems necessary in respect of the subject-matter of the dispute, including measures for the conservation of the goods forming the subject-matter in dispute, such as ordering their deposit with a third person or the sale of perishable goods.
> (2) Such interim measures may be established in the form of an interim award. The arbitral tribunal shall be entitled to require security for the costs of such measures.
> (3) A request for interim measures addressed by any party to a judicial authority shall not be deemed incompatible with the agreement to arbitrate, or as a waiver of that agreement."

From the initial deliberations within UNCITRAL, the prevalent orientation adopted by the Working Group was in line with the following concepts:

(a) To consider the integration of the new interim measures regime established in Chapter IV.A of the Model Law.[31]
(b) To maintain, to the extent possible, the structure and wording style as currently contained in the Rules, as well as to preserve the flexible system under which the Rules are structured. This was pointed out along with the argument, which is certainly true,

---

31. "The Working Group was generally of the view that Art. 26 should be revised to take account of that new chapter [of the amended UNCITRAL Model Law]." "Report of the Working Group on Arbitration and Conciliation on the work of its forty-fifth session" (Vienna, 11-15 September 2006) UNCITRAL, 45th Sess., UN Doc. A/CN.9/614 (25 June-12 July 2007) (hereinafter Working Group Report 614) "Support was expressed for the proposed updating of article 26 based on the most recently adopted international standard on interim measures." "Report of the Working Group on Arbitration and Conciliation on the work of its forty-seventh session" (Vienna, 10-14 September 2007) UNCITRAL, 47th Sess., UN Doc. A/CN.9/641 (16 June-11 July 2008) (hereinafter Working Group Report 641) para. 47.

that due to the success and prestige of the Rules (which have even lead to those Rules being "adopted" as a dispute resolution system by international treaties) modifications should not be undertaken as if acting in a vacuum.[32]

(c) To follow the content of Chapter IV.A of the Model Law for provisions to be integrated into the Rules. Deviations from the language of the Model Law's new regime should be avoided.[33]

(d) To omit provisions which, though appropriate and effective in a Model Law, would not be suitable for a set of rules, since rules are an extension of party autonomy. One of the categories of provisions falling under this concept is that of the enforcement regime for interim measures.[34]

2. *Specific Highlights of the Working Group's Perspective on the Review of Art. 26 of the UNCITRAL Arbitration Rules*

The Working Group has already prepared a Draft to revise the current Art. 26 of the Rules.[35] In doing so, it has followed the general approach described in the preceding

---

32. ".... In recognition of the success and status of the UNCITRAL Arbitration Rules, the Commission was generally of the view that any revision of the Rules should not alter the structure of the text, its spirit or its drafting style, and should respect the flexibility of the text rather than make it more complex...." "Report of the United Nations Commission on International Trade Law on the work of its fortieth session" (Vienna, 25 June-12 July 2007) UN Doc. A/62/17 (Part I); (para. 172) (July 2007).

33. The following is a good example of the Working Group's intention is to stay with the language of the Model Law and of the reasons in support of such concern: Working Group Report 641, *op. cit.*, fn. 31.

    "48. A proposal was made that paragraph (2) (c) should be amended expressly to refer to security for costs through an addition of the words 'or securing funds' after the word 'assets'. Opposition was expressed to that proposal as it could connote that the corresponding provision in the UNCITRAL Arbitration Model Law was insufficient to provide for security for costs. The Working Group agreed that security for costs was encompassed by the words 'preserving assets out of which a subsequent award may be satisfied'."

34. "... [T]he Working Group agreed that, given the nature of the Rules, a number of provisions contained in Chapter IV A should not be replicated, such as provisions on the enforcement of interim measures. The view was expressed that the provisions of Chapter IV A [Chapter IV A. Interim measures and preliminary orders] that were of a contentious nature and had previously given rise to diverging views in the Working Group should not be included in the UNCITRAL Arbitration Rules, in order not to endanger their wide acceptability."

    Working Group Report 614, *op. cit.*, fn. 31, para. 105.

35. At the time of this writing, the latest draft is in the UNCITRAL document A/CN.9/WG.II/WP.149.

    Some arbitral institutions initiated the endeavor to review their rules in order to incorporate the Model Law regime for interim measures. For instance, Canaco already did. Canaco incorporated the entire Model Law new regime. It integrated the provisions contained in Sects. 1 through 3. The only sections not adopted are Sects. 4 and 5 which, evidently, fall outside the nature of a body of rules (Sects. 4 and 5 deal with "*Recognition and enforcement of interim measures*"

section, "Conceptual-philosophical Perspective Taken by the Working Group"), but it has also considered some specific adjustments vis à vis the amended Art. 17 of the Model Law. The main changes envisioned by the Working Group are analyzed in Annex I.

IV.   OVERVIEW OF INTERIM MEASURES ISSUED BY AN ARBITRAL TRIBUNAL

Throughout the evolution and practice of commercial arbitration there has been a great variety of opinions as to the nature of interim measures and their suitability for arbitration. The discussion has included the matter of the effectiveness of interim measures ordered by an arbitral tribunal. Any practitioner knows that the purpose of obtaining an arbitral ruling is for it to be effective (and not only valid). An interim measure decision is not obtained in order to be framed and hung on a wall.[36]

The debate has followed different angles. One important angle of analysis is the effectiveness of the arbitrator's powers vis à vis arbitration jurisdictions. Likewise, the analysis can also be undertaken in the form of a question: *"How important is the court enforcement element in interim measures?"*

1.   *Effectiveness of Interim Measures in Commercial Arbitration: Arbitration Jurisdiction vis à vis Court Jurisdiction*

The following elements have to be considered when reviewing the effectiveness of interim measures in commercial arbitration.

There is an advantage in having one single entity deal with all the matters of the dispute. However, there are situations in which it is certainly not feasible, or convenient, to rely solely on the powers of the arbitral tribunal to preserve the subject matter of the arbitration. In such circumstances the state courts' intervention is advisable. Nevertheless, the best scenario is one that allows the parties to have all the disputes in connection with their controversy resolved in one single framework; this includes the disputes on the merits and the ancillary matters, as well as those regarding the need to preserve the final determination of the claims.

The use of an ongoing arbitration as the vehicle to obtain interim measures is also something that has to be understood on the grounds of the effectiveness of the court system. This assertion should not be understood as a suggestion that recourse to interim measures within the arbitration scheme is a consequence of a negative perception of the courts' aid. The advantages of the arbitral tribunal's assistance on this matter are also relevant when a supportive and effective court platform is present. However, recourse to an arbitral tribunal in order to obtain an interim measure is commonly sought because of the difficulty of obtaining access to a particular court jurisdiction or because of the limited effectiveness of interim measure resources available at that court. The former occurs when the issue of territorial or substantive jurisdiction arises and a complicated

---

and *"Court-ordered interim measures"*).
36. For a list with examples of different types of interim measures, see Annex II. A more detailed review of anti-suit injunctions is in Annex III.

procedural battle takes place before a court admits the request for an interim measure. The latter takes place when the law of the court does not include a flexible, dynamic and expeditious regime to handle requests for interim measures and their consequent complications and challenges. In many jurisdictions the evolution of interim measures in arbitration legislation has been faster, and a more sensitive approach has been taken, with respect to the needs in support of commercial transactions (in which flexibility, dynamism and speed are of the essence).

2. *How Important Is the Court Enforcement Element in Interim Measures?*

The importance of the enforcement element could seem an obvious point, and in some way it is. As a first approach to the enforcement matter, it is valid to say that a provision of law which is impossible to enforce is useless. This assertion applies not only to the issue of interim measures, but to law in general. That is one of the elementary reasons why the Model Law includes a section on enforcement (and recognition) of interim measures.[37] Nevertheless, from the practitioner's point of view, the evaluation of which road to take in order to obtain an interim measure is one that requires a broader analysis.

There is no single element that might provide guidance as to whether to go before the arbitral tribunal or the court in order to obtain an interim measure. Rather, the correct analysis, and consequently, the correct decision, should consider the following aspects in connection with the specific features of the facts that give rise to the need for an interim measure.

*a. Risk of insolvency and the need to preserve assets out of which an award may be enforced*
There are disputes in which a party is confident that it will prevail on the merits, but it is also aware that some time will have to elapse before having an award and, consequently, the opportunity to enforce its rights. By that time, there will probably be no assets out of which the award may be enforced. Other considerations aside, the wise thing to do is to go to the courts and obtain an interim measure. By doing so, the same entity will issue the interim measure and enforce it: two steps in one.

On the other hand, sometimes immediate enforcement is not of the essence. This occurs, for example, when the counterparty is a solvent company or individual. In such case, all of the counsel's energy and creativity are focused on the substance of the interim measure he is requesting and not on its enforcement. Sufficient assets will be waiting for him should he prevail in the arbitration. In these circumstances, although consideration of the issue of enforceability of the interim measure is something that does not hurt, in the balance of the analysis the party may choose to keep the "entire case" within the jurisdiction of the arbitral tribunal due to the advantages already described (see this section above, under "*1.* Effectiveness of Interim Measures in Commercial Arbitration: Arbitration Jurisdiction vis à vis Court Jurisdiction").

---

37. Sect. 4 of Chapter IVA of the Model Law, "*Recognition and enforcement of interim measures*".

*b.   Availability of court assistance: a supportive and effective court? An effective legal framework?*

In many jurisdictions the court system has a very restrictive regulation of interim measures, either because of the text of the law or because of the way in which tradition has understood the role and scope of interim measures, or a combination of both. In some jurisdictions the procedural court law (and its interpretation) has not evolved at the pace of arbitration law.

Art. 9 of the Model Law offers a good example on this matter. This article sets forth a broad statement as to the jurisdiction of courts with regard to interim measures.[38] Some interpreters consider that in the absence of an express provision restricting the powers of the court, the article should be interpreted as a recognition in favor of the court granting interim measures with no fewer powers than those granted (expressly or implicitly) in favor of an arbitral tribunal. In contrast, others consider that a court is bound by its general regime for interim measures, as regulated in other sections of the law (applicable to commercial disputes other than arbitration) or other laws, as might be the case depending on the legal structure of each jurisdiction. Within this analytical framework, the Mexican jurisdiction is a good example of this issue. Mexico enacted the Model Law in its original text (the 2006 amendments are in the process of being enacted by Congress). This could be the basis for a broad interpretation as to the powers of arbitral tribunals to grant interim measures. However, the procedural commercial court regime contains very limited options for interim measures (an extremely restricted inventory).[39] Therefore, though not expressly restricted in the commercial legislation, it is highly likely that a court will refuse to issue an interim measure that falls outside the catalogue of measures it is entitled to take when dealing with commercial disputes in

---

38. Art. 9 of the Model Law states the following:

*"Arbitration agreement and interim measures by court*
It is not incompatible with an arbitration agreement for a party to request, before or during arbitral proceedings, from a court an interim measure of protection and for a court to grant such measure."

This article is part of the original text of the Model Law and remained after the 2006 amendment. Nowadays, Art. 17J of the Model Law offers additional guidance as to the role of the courts in issuing interim measures. Art. 17J of the Model Law indicates that:

*"Court-ordered interim measures*
A court shall have the same power of issuing an interim measure in relation to arbitration proceedings, irrespective of whether their place is in the territory of this State, as it has in relation to proceedings in courts. The court shall exercise such power in accordance with its own procedures in consideration of the specific features of international arbitration."

39. Mexican commercial legislation considers only the following inventory of interim measures:

(a) Order not to leave the jurisdiction, for persons only.
(b) Seizure of goods/Attachment prior to judgment, which courts rarely grant, due to the difficulty to prove the hypotheses set by the legislation.

general. The Mexican case is just one example of the many national states whose procedural laws provide very restricted options for interim measures. In cases like these, the party in need of an interim measure will certainly opt for filing a request before the arbitral tribunal.

c.   *The issue of choice of court forum*
In some cases the intention of going to a court in order to obtain an interim measure encounters the issue of identifying the appropriate court jurisdiction for that purpose. This is particularly common when there is an international dispute and various jurisdictions have a point of connection with it. Likewise, in the specific case of interim measures, this issue is aggravated when the subject matter of the dispute is not easily located, or when it is not tangible. The latter, for example, is the case in the appointment of a neutral temporary administrator of a company with offices and operations in many countries.

These surrounding elements are more or less complicated depending on the rules of jurisdiction of the court from which the interim measure is requested. Whereas some court systems are more flexible in having rules of minimum contact to assign jurisdiction, others have very casuistic sets of conflict of law rules that, in most of the cases, prove not to be flexible or inclusive to handle the complexities of the factual and legal scenarios of many types of disputes, especially where the international component arises. Any of these two systems frequently gives rise to highly creative arguments when a party challenges the jurisdiction of the court that receives the request for the interim measure.

In contrast, a request filed before an arbitral tribunal does not give rise to this kind of discussion. This is particularly true with regard to the territorial component of jurisdiction, since the performance of the arbitral tribunal is not confined to a particular territory but rather to a particular dispute (the notion of the seat of the arbitration does not result in issues of territorial jurisdiction).

d.   *The importance of the expertise of the arbitrator*
The focus of this article is not to elaborate in detail as to the features of arbitration in general or the qualifications expected from an arbitral tribunal. For the purpose of the topic covered here, it is sufficient to mention that the appointment of an arbitrator, if adequately made, results in the right expertise for the particular dispute. Thus, it is reasonable to assume that the individual or group of individuals who have received a mandate to hear that dispute will have the expertise required to handle the technicalities involved in the interim measure requested.

e.   *The enormous power vested in the arbitral tribunal to make adverse inferences*
Probably, one of the most important powers that an arbitral tribunal has is that of drawing adverse inferences from the procedural conduct of the parties. Although the concept of adverse inference is widely accepted throughout many national jurisdictions, I have found that it is particularly powerful in arbitration. This assertion relies on a fact, and not on a theory. The fact is that the arbitrators have the unique position of close and direct contact with the dispute and the parties, mainly because of the much smaller number of cases submitted before an arbitrator, especially if such a number is compared

with the number that any court faces. Any arbitration practitioner is sensitive to this power and fact, and grants a great deal of importance to it. Henceforth, the analysis of a court vis à vis an arbitral tribunal granting an interim measure takes another direction.

The restriction for arbitrators regarding compulsory enforcement (included in the handling of interim measures) is viewed from a different angle.

The party requesting an interim measure may not be seeking the enforcement of the measure as a primary objective. That party knows that should the counterparty not comply with the interim measure, as ruled by the arbitrator, it could have a devastating effect on that counterparty in the form of provoking the arbitral tribunal to make adverse inferences from his procedural conduct. This becomes a tremendously powerful tool available to the arbitrator and, indirectly, for the requesting party. With this understanding, it is very likely that counsel for the party requesting an interim measure will not be very concerned about arbitrators' limited powers of enforcement. An adverse inference in his favor might be much more powerful than a compulsory enforcement ordered by a court. These comments apply to interim measures as well as to preliminary orders; the latter are also binding upon the parties (Model Law Art. 17C(5)).[40]

*f.    Interim measures and their recognition and enforcement under the New York Convention*
The enforcement of interim awards is relevant in the context of the scope of application of the New York Convention. One of the various elements to define the scope of application of the New York Convention is the nature of the decision to be enforced. The main component of such a treaty is that it creates an international legal framework for the enforcement of arbitral awards. Art. I(1) of the Convention states, among other criteria, that its application is obtained from an arbitral award for which recognition and enforcement are requested. Art. I(2) contains an inclusive description, rather than a definition, of what is an "arbitral award". The inclusive provision establishes that such awards are those issued by arbitrators appointed for each case as well as those issued by permanent arbitral bodies. Thus, the text of the Convention has no express guidelines as to how to identify an arbitral award.

The drafters of the New York Convention were wise. Fifty years of successful application and interpretation have demonstrated this. And one of the hallmarks of such wisdom is that the Convention omits definitions of the key institutions it deals with. In this line of thought, it is noticeable that the Convention deals with, but does not define, aspects such as contractual and non-contractual relationships, presentation of the case, binding award, public policy and many others. The drafters decided to leave the definition and scope of key elements of the Convention to the interpreter. The evolution, practice and dynamism of international arbitration have proceeded at such a pace that should the Convention have included a "definitions system", it would have encountered many obstacles a couple of years after its entry into force. It is highly likely that a treaty based on definitions would have resulted in many usages and practices falling outside the scope of its grounds for application.

When testing the New York Convention with regard to various types of awards and requests for recognition and enforcement, the interpreter must undertake an analysis as

---

40. See Pilar PERALES VIESCASILLAS, *op. cit.*, fn. 23, p. 442.

to the intention and purpose of the Convention. They were not aimed at creating a formalistic crossword in which the text is of the essence (as if it were the ritual of a sacred text). Of course, any interpretation exercise has to take the text into account; but to reach conclusions on the sole grounds of what the text says and what the text does not say is the perfect method to undermine the Convention regime.

Some court decisions have touched on the issue of the enforcement of "interim awards", "partial awards", and the like. For instance, in one decision, the Colombian Supreme Court of Justice ruled that an award on jurisdiction is not eligible for recognition under the New York Convention as it does not resolve the merits of the dispute.[41] In the same vein, that court concluded that the expression, "arbitral award" refers only to a decision that ends the subject matter of the dispute. In another case, the State Council of Colombia stated that the issue of validity of the arbitral agreement is something that falls outside the jurisdiction of the court since such matter shall be included in the final award and court involvement shall come in the event such award is challenged.[42] These two decisions would fall within the grounds of Art. 17(2)(b) of the Model Law. Reflecting the opposite trend is a US District of Columbia court decision that, implicitly, admitted the possibility of determining jurisdiction in a partial award in an ICC arbitration which had decided, in final terms, some of the issues within the merits of the controversy.[43]

There is no restriction on applying the New York Convention to the recognition and enforcement of interim awards. Recognition or enforcement may not be granted on the grounds of the examination undertaken by the court and taking into consideration the particularities of the case; nevertheless, what cannot be accepted is to deny such a request on the mere grounds that it is an interim award. The purpose of the New York Convention was to ensure certainty and effectiveness of the agreement of the parties to arbitrate and of the resolutions issued by an arbitral tribunal as a consequence of such agreement. This is the true core purpose of the Convention. The Convention does not set limits as to the nature of awards to be recognized and enforced. Therefore, the interpreter should not impose them.

V.  CONCLUSIONS

The use of interim measures in arbitration has experienced a significant growth among practitioners and it has created an intense debate as to the appropriate regime to regulate them. The core of the topic has always been the concern of having a regime that

---

41. *Merck & Co. Inc., et al. v. Tecnoquímicas SA*, ICCA *Yearbook Commercial Arbitration* XXVI (2001) (hereinafter *Yearbook*) pp. 755-766 (Colombia no. 3).
42. *Empresa Colombiana de Vías Férreas (Ferrovías) v. Drummond Ltd.*, *Yearbook* XXIX (2004) pp. 643-656 (Colombia no. 4).
43. *Telcordia Technologies, Inc. v. Telkom SA, Limited*, *Yearbook* XXX (2005), pp. 762-770 (US no. 484).

maintains a balance between two ends that often conflict: the requesting party's need for an interim measure to make arbitration an effective tool, and the need for safeguards for the party affected by the issuance of the interim measure.

The original 1985 text of the Model Law contained a regime to regulate the use and application of interim measures. Some believed that as this was a broad regime, which essentially stated the availability of interim measures, there was no need to seek a detailed set of rules. However, there were sound reasons in favor of resolving some issues for which, frequently, the Model Law text offered no clear answers: for example, the appropriate meaning of the expression "the subject-matter of the dispute", the absence of guidelines in connection with the assessment of the petition, the lack of a regime for modification of an interim measure, and the absence of provisions for the enforcement of interim measures. These were some of the issues that led the arbitration community to demand guidelines and safeguards in order to make interim measures a more effective tool. That was the aim of UNCITRAL's Working Group on Arbitration.

One of the very useful provisions within the new UNCITRAL regime is the "inventory" of interim measures. It must be pointed out, though, that with the clear objective of not deviating from the flexibility that arbitration practice demands, UNCITRAL created, a set of generic categories to cover the possible scenarios for interim measures rather than a specific and exhaustive catalogue. That purpose was fulfilled by Art. 17(2) of the Model Law. Thus, though exhaustive, it was generic.

The most sensitive deliberations within the Working Group took place when the subject of ex parte "measures" was addressed. At the end of the debates, the result was a well-balanced set of provisions which established, in few words, the possibility of seeking interim protection before the other party is heard but with no possibility for enforcing it in the courts (those are the Preliminary Orders). The right of court enforcement was reserved for those measures issued only after the counterparty has had the opportunity to be heard (Interim Measures). Thus, there are no ex-parte interim measures but only ex-parte preliminary orders that are not eligible for court enforcement.

Interim measures are indeed an effective tool in arbitration. This assertion can be as true as that, sometimes, the result obtained by means of an interim measure might be as relevant as the decision on the merits of the dispute. For this reason, it is crucial to consider the grounds for effectiveness of the interim measure.

The first element of the effectiveness equation to take into account is the power of the arbitral tribunal. Any sophisticated arbitration practitioner knows that an arbitrator will consider it an act of bad faith, in terms of procedural conduct, if a party disobeys an order for an interim measure. Here is one of the scenarios in which the arbitral tribunal can make use of a very effective power: the power of making adverse inferences. Therefore, on many occasions the fact that the arbitral tribunal is not vested with coercive powers to ensure the complete effectiveness of an interim measure is not a matter of concern for the arbitral tribunal itself or for the party requesting the measure. In the same vein, it may be advisable to maintain the case (the merits as well as the interim measure application) within one single jurisdiction – the arbitral tribunal's. Nevertheless, notwithstanding the advantage of having one single entity dealing with all matters of the dispute, there are circumstances in which it is necessary to obtain court assistance, either in the form of enforcement of the interim measure issued by the arbitral tribunal or in the form of a court-ordered interim measure. The decision as to where to go to request an interim measure has many angles. There is no closed catalogue of recipes to assess this matter. Each scenario must be assessed on the basis of the essence of timing, as well as the approach of the local court regarding interim measures vis à vis that of the arbitral tribunal.

Moreover, this line of analysis raises the relevance of the New York Convention. Some discussion has arisen concerning the applicability of the New York Convention to the enforcement of interim awards dealing with interim measures. There is no restriction to applying the New York Convention to the recognition and enforcement of interim awards. The interpreter must observe that the intention of the New York Convention was to ensure certainty and effectiveness of the agreement of the parties to arbitrate and of the resolutions issued by an arbitral tribunal in consequence of that agreement. Within that framework, the Convention does not impose limits on the basis of the nature of an award. Therefore, the New York Convention must apply to requests for enforcement of interim awards containing an interim measure.

# ANNEX I

## Status of the Working Group Regarding the Revision of the UNCITRAL Arbitration Rules

This Annex I describes the direction that the Working Group envisions towards a new interim measures regime for the UNCITRAL Arbitration Rules.

(a) *No need for confirmation that interim measure can take the form of an award*
Whereas the Model Law includes a provision stating that an interim measure might be *"in the form of an award or in another form"* (Art. 17(2) of the Model Law), it has been suggested that such a provision is unnecessary in the Rules.[44]

This is one of the changes suggested in light of the nature of a set of rules. The modification introduced in the Draft, rather than deviating from the Model Law, works as an adaptation of the Rules consistent with their role and that of the Model Law.

The Model Law, as indicated above, does contain a system which allows the enforcement of an interim measure regardless of the form it takes. It was no longer necessary to establish a "permissive message" with the intention of assuring the enforcement of the award; at least not in the Rules.

(b) *Eliminate the implicit restriction that the interim measure is related to "the subject-matter of the dispute"*
It was viewed, with sound reasons, that the current wording of Art. 26(1) of the Rules was unnecessarily restrictive by prescribing that the interim measure shall be granted in connection with *"the subject-matter of the dispute"*. This wording was criticized when the Working Group was deliberating on the amendments to the Model Law (the old Model Law wording was adopted from the current text of Art. 26(1) of the Rules). For this reason, there has been consensus that the Rules should also state that there was no intention to limit, in such manner, the scope and nature of interim measures.[45]

---

44. "After discussion, the Working Group agreed that it would be preferable to maintain the text of Art. 26 as contained in A/CN.9/WG.II/WP.145/Add.1. In that context, it was considered desirable to avoid unnecessary departure from the provisions on interim measures as contained in chapter IV A of the UNCITRAL Arbitration Model Law. It was observed that the words 'whether in the form of an award or another form' which appeared in Art. 17(2) of the UNCITRAL Arbitration Model Law had been deleted from the corresponding article in the revised Rules (Art. 26(2)). It was explained that, while in the past some practitioners might have used the form of an award for interim measures with a view to enhancing their enforceability, this no longer had much purpose given that the UNCITRAL Arbitration Model Law now contained provisions permitting enforcement of interim measures regardless of the form in which they were issued."

Working Group Report 641, *op. cit.*, fn. 31, para. 51.

45. "... For instance, the words '*in respect of the subject-matter of the dispute*', which were deleted from the equivalent provisions in Chapter IV A, could also be deleted from Art. 26 for being overly restrictive". *Ibid.*, para. 53.

*(c) The debate as to the adoption of the ex parte regime ("preliminary orders")*

Once the concept of the ex parte regime was raised during the deliberations of the Working Group a major conceptual struggle was reinitiated.[46] The debate focused on the following considerations, among others.

The opponents of the inclusion of an ex parte regime argued the following points. The first objection was purportedly based on the distinction of the role of the two bodies of regulations.[47] This premise is unquestionable (there is a distinct role), though the conclusion is incorrect. Certainly the two instruments fulfil a different function; nevertheless, that does not automatically make the ex parte regime unsuitable for inclusion in the Rules.

The following possible scenario surrounding an arbitration must be recognized. It is the case in which the lex arbitri is not a Model Law legislation but the Rules are applicable due to the agreement of the parties. In such event, should the Rules contain an ex parte regime, such regime would be plainly effective as part of the parties' agreement. The only event in which the ex parte regime contained in the rules could not be valid would be if the law (unlike the Model Law) prohibits the parties from entering into an ex parte regime. This is an extremely unlikely scenario. In conclusion, such a regime being included in the Rules could not harm and, contrary to the purported argument based on the different roles of the two instruments, could play a very helpful role in the absence of a Model Law legislation within a given jurisdiction.

The second objection was under the assumption that, due to sensitivities regarding the ex parte system, a less receptive attitude by states may be foreseen when dealing with issues of investment arbitration in which the Rules apply.[48] Interestingly, one of the issues of concern as to the suitability of including the preliminary orders in the Rules was related to the lengthy and detailed formula included in the Model Law. A regulation must be judged in terms of its clarity and consistency as well as the result it creates, not in terms of the length of its text.[49]

---

46. "... The Working Group considered whether provisions on preliminary orders, as contained in section 2 of chapter IV A of the UNCITRAL Arbitration Model Law should be included in the Rules. Diverging views were expressed." Working Group Report 614, *op. cit.*, fn. 31, para. 104.
47. "Against the inclusion of such provisions, it was stated that the Rules and the UNCITRAL Arbitration Model Law had different purposes in that the Rules were directed to parties, whereas the UNCITRAL Arbitration Model Law was directed to legislators.... It was further clarified by those opposing inclusion of provisions on preliminary orders in the Rules that the intention was not to reject the corresponding provisions in the UNCITRAL Arbitration Model Law, but rather to acknowledge the difference in nature and function between the two instruments."

    Working Group Report 641, *op. cit.*, fn. 31, para. 54.
48. "55. It was also stated that introducing such provisions in the Rules could undermine their acceptability, particularly by States in the context of investor-State dispute...." *Ibid.*, para. 55.
49. During the progress of the Working Group sessions, indeed some criticism was raised on the grounds of the length of Art. 17 as amended. Nevertheless, it is fair to say that the increase in length was, mainly, in proportion to the details on the safeguards integrated into the new regime. The article is well structured and interpreter-friendly regarding the scope and application as well as specific guidelines in connection with preliminary orders (as the key piece of the ex parte regime). UNCITRAL commented the following; "57. ... the length of the provision should not

There were also arguments supporting the inclusion of the ex parte system within the text of the Rules. Those considerations were, summarily, the following.

The set of provisions for the ex parte regime, as included in the Model Law, was the result of a very careful and thorough analysis. It can fairly be said that the deliberation process was not only confined to UNCITRAL but in fact was taken to the attention and debate of the international arbitration community. The set of provisions created by UNCITRAL ensured a well-structured system with a balance between effectiveness of the measure and safeguards for the affected party.[50] Furthermore, it must not be forgotten that the proposed regime for inclusion in the Rules is maintained along the lines of confirming that this (and any other regime) is confined to the limits imposed by the parties as they wish.[51]

The inclusion of the ex parte regime within the Rules (and consistent with the Model Law structure) would foster the harmonization process. One of the implicit guidelines in UNCITRAL work can be stated as follows: if in doubt, go in favor of harmonization. Thus, those who express concerns as to the suitability of the inclusion of such a regime in the Rules should consider the important benefits of continuing with the harmonization process in international arbitration. Harmonization is, no doubt, one of the main reasons behind the effectiveness and broad use of arbitration in the commercial world.

*(d) Ongoing status of the Working Group regarding a proposal for Art. 26 and its direction*
UNCITRAL is working on a draft to amend Art. 26 of the Rules (A/CN.9/WG.II/WP.149).[52] Along with the "conceptual-philosophical perspective" and the "specific

---

constitute an argument against their inclusion in the Rules". *Ibid.*, para. 57.
50. "In favour of the inclusion of provisions on preliminary orders, it was said that the text formed part of an accepted compromise package which enabled the arbitral tribunal to prevent a party from frustrating the purpose of an interim measure, subject to carefully crafted safeguards ... and would therefore contribute to harmonization of international commercial arbitral practice in relation to the granting of preliminary orders." *Ibid.*, para. 56.
51. "It was stated that, since the Rules would apply pursuant to an agreement of the parties, provisions in the Rules that would bestow on the arbitral tribunal the power to issue preliminary orders would not come as a surprise but as the result of a conscious decision of the parties to opt into such a legal regime." *Ibid.*, para. 58.
52. At the time of this writing, the latest draft for an amendment to Art. 26 of the Rules (Secretariat Note 149, *op. cit.*, fn. 35) states the following:

"1. The arbitral tribunal may, at the request of a party, grant interim measures.
2. An interim measure is any temporary measure by which, at any time prior to the issuance of the award by which the dispute is finally decided, the arbitral tribunal orders a party to:
(a) Maintain or restore the status quo pending determination of the dispute;
(b) Take action that would prevent, or refrain from taking action that is likely to cause, current or imminent harm or prejudice to the arbitral process itself;
(c) Provide a means of preserving assets out of which a subsequent award may be satisfied; or
(d) Preserve evidence that may be relevant and material to the resolution of the dispute.
3. The party requesting an interim measure under paragraph 2 (a), (b) and (c) shall satisfy the arbitral tribunal that:
(a) Harm not adequately reparable by an award of damages is likely to result if the measure is not ordered, and such harm substantially outweighs the harm that is likely to result to the party against

highlights" referred to above (Sects. III.*1* and *2*), it is relevant to point out that the latest draft for amendment, and the line of thought by UNCITRAL delegates, is consistent with the system designed and approved for the Model Law in its Chapter IV.A.

The modifications observed in the current draft for discussion vis à vis the amended Model Law regime are just a few. The proposed changes are aimed at adjusting those provisions that need a different treatment in accordance with the nature of a set of Rules, in contrast to that of a Model Law. Likewise, some proposed deviations from the language of the Model Law text originate in the clear intention to follow, as much as possible, the structural language of the Rules as currently in effect.

*(d.1) The "opt-out" system*

The Draft does not contain an opt-out formula (the Model Law does have it for access to the entire interim measures regime in general, and to the ex parte preliminary orders in particular). Because of the consensual nature of arbitration, some might argue that non-inclusion of an opt-out mechanism is irrelevant, since the parties can opt out (in

---

whom the measure is directed if the measure is granted; and

(b) There is a reasonable possibility that the requesting party will succeed on the merits of the claim. The determination on this possibility shall not affect the discretion of the arbitral tribunal in making any subsequent determination.

4. With regard to a request for an interim measure under paragraph 2 (d), the requirements in paragraph 3 (a) and (b) shall apply only to the extent the arbitral tribunal considers appropriate.

5. If the arbitral tribunal determines that disclosure of a request for an interim measure to the party against whom it is directed risks frustrating that measure's purpose, nothing in these Rules prevents the tribunal, when it gives notice of such request to that party, from temporarily ordering that the party not frustrate the purpose of the requested measure. The arbitral tribunal shall give that party the earliest practicable opportunity to present its case and then determine whether to grant the request.

6. The arbitral tribunal may modify, suspend or terminate an interim measure or an order referred to in paragraph 5 it has granted, upon application of any party or, in exceptional circumstances and upon prior notice to the parties, on the arbitral tribunal's own initiative.

7. The arbitral tribunal may require the party requesting an interim measure or applying for an order referred to in paragraph 5 to provide appropriate security in connection with the measure or the order.

8. The arbitral tribunal may require any party promptly to disclose any material change in the circumstances on the basis of which the interim measure or the order referred to in paragraph 5 was requested or granted.

9. The party requesting an interim measure or applying for an order referred to in paragraph 5 shall be liable for any costs and damages caused by the measure or the order to any party if the arbitral tribunal later determines that, in the circumstances, the measure or the order should not have been granted. The arbitral tribunal may award such costs and damages at any point during the proceedings.

10. A request for interim measures or an application for an order referred to in paragraph 5 addressed by any party to a judicial authority shall not be deemed incompatible with the agreement to arbitrate, or as a waiver of that agreement."

general terms; of course, this consensual system has limits) of the provisions contained in the Rules. However, two aspects are to be underlined concerning this opt-out mechanism.

On one hand, some national courts do concede a great deal of importance to opt-out regulations, in as much as such courts see the opt out as the necessary recognition of a permissive scenario in favor of party autonomy. Briefly, those national laws accept that the parties modify or exclude a certain provision only if such provision expressly recognizes the right to opt out. Nevertheless, some voices are raised in support of the view that the situation is different when dealing with rules (arbitration rules) as opposed to a law (either model law or its desired next step in the form of national enacted law). And such voices rely on the fact that since a set of arbitration rules is a piece of a contractual relationship, the parties are free to opt out with no need for express permission. This is consistent with the fundamental notions and consequences of party autonomy as one of the essential ingredients (and, probably, "the" essential ingredient) of commercial arbitration.

On the other hand, what UNCITRAL is attempting to do is to stick to the language of the current Rules unless there is an absolute need to justify a deviation from such language. The Rules, in their current text, do not contain the opt-out mechanism for interim measures, though they follow a "the tribunal may" approach. The Draft preserves the expression "the tribunal may".

*(d.2) Just "Orders", not "Preliminary Orders"*
The prevalent view is to incorporate an ex parte system in the Rules (for the reasons stated above, among others). Nevertheless, it was suggested that this system, though consistent with the Model Law, should avoid using a notion that needs to be defined in terms of its requirements, scope and administration, such as the notion of "*preliminary order*" (which is used in the Model Law and deals with these consequential issues).[53]

The Draft recognizes the possibility that the arbitral tribunal issues a temporary order with no prior disclosure to the party against whom the order is granted until such party receives notice of the request for such order (Art. 26(5) of the Draft). In general terms, it can be said that the Draft system is consistent with the Model Law regime; however, the Draft does not deal with some of the detailed aspects of the ex parte regime. What the Draft essentially does is recognize the power of the arbitral tribunal to order a party not to frustrate the purpose of the requested measure, so that time does not play an adverse role in the opportunity for the arbitral tribunal to gather sufficient information in order to determine the suitability of the measure requested.

---

53. "60. A number of delegations expressed their willingness to continue the discussion at future sessions about the possible replication in the Rules of the provisions of the UNCITRAL Arbitration Model Law dealing with preliminary orders. The Working Group requested the Secretariat to prepare for consideration at a future session a short draft sentence expressing the notion that the arbitral tribunal was entitled to take appropriate measures to prevent the frustration of an interim measure ordered by the arbitral tribunal. It was suggested that such a sentence should avoid terminology such as 'preliminary order' to avoid having to define that term."

Working Group Report 641, *op. cit.*, fn. 31, para. 60.

# ANNEX II

# Examples of Interim Measures Issued by an Arbitral Tribunal

This Annex II lists some of the most representative types of interim measures in the context of commercial arbitration. The list is non-exhaustive and the grouping criterion is arbitrary.

*a. Miscellaneous*
(1) Abstention from disclosing to third parties privileged or sensitive information; this involves, i.e., trade and technology secrets,[54] and information to which a party has had access during the regular course of business.
(2) Abstention from using a trademark.
(3) Abstention from manufacturing and selling goods related to a dispute on intellectual property rights.
(4) Selling perishable goods and placing the proceeds of the sale in the custody of a third party.
(5) Undertaking an inspection before the regular course of business obstructs the possibility of conducting an effective inspection, i.e., when the application of an industrial manufacturing process is done in a manner in which the requesting party argues non-fulfillment of the counterparty's obligations.
(6) Undertaking any proactive action in order to preserve a right; this could include payment of a duty or bringing a claim in order to interrupt the statute of limitations.
(7) Continuance in the supply of products necessary for one of the parties to continue with his regular course of business. This is the case of a distribution agreement in which the beneficiary of the order will be able to continue to supply the products to the final customer for such products, and also in the case in which the products are a relevant input of the production process of such beneficiary.
(8) Avoidance of disposal of goods which constitute the tangible subject matter of the merits of the arbitration, such as in those claims known as *actio in rem*. A variety of the implementation of this measure is the placement of goods in custody with a third party. On occasion, the suitable measure could be one that orders the delivery of disputed goods to one of the parties, subject to placement of security. A variant of this measure results from the order to stop from moving an asset out of a certain territorial jurisdiction.
(9) Prohibition on easily drawing on a letter of credit or documents easily liquidated.

---

54. This one of the examples of express concern that UNCITRAL wanted to include in the Model Law as one being covered by the hypothesis of Art. 17 such law, "Summary Record of the 316th Meeting" (Vienna, June 1985), UNCITRAL, 18th Session (Vienna, 3-21 June 1985), UN Doc. A/CN.9/SR.316 (DATE OF DOC) para. 40, and "Report of the United Nations Commission on International Trade Law on the working of its 18th Session" (Vienna 1985) 40th Session Supplement No. 17, UN Doc. A/40/17, para. 167.

### b. Order pertaining to liquid assets

(1) Separation of a sum of money in order to secure payment of a monetary claim. This measure has to be analyzed by the arbitral tribunal particularly in the event of an imminent insolvency (as one of the scenarios in which to grant this measure). The requesting party should not only demonstrate the basis of his claim, but additionally, the insolvency position threatening the debtor. Moreover, in as much as this interim measure is being considered, there are insolvency provisions that vary depending on a particular jurisdiction and may be relevant in connection with the effectiveness of such segregation of assets should an insolvency procedure arise. Likewise, this matter has to be faced by taking into consideration the fact that some insolvency provisions establish some safeguards in favor of third parties (creditors) as a matter of public policy. Thus, the interim measure granting a petition for separation of a sum of money might be subject to the restrictions imposed by insolvency legislation.

(2) Placement of a deposit, or separation of a sum of money by other means, in order to secure a party's legal costs. This is subject to specific regulation in some arbitral rules.[55]

### c. Construction Industry

(1) Preservation of evidence relevant to the arbitration. For instance, in the construction industry, the following types of interim measures are commonly issued:

(i) To prevent a party from sealing/covering the works that will be subject to a dispute.
(ii) To order a party to provide samples of materials whose quality/adequacy is disputed.
(iii) To order a party to allow experts of the other party to access and inspect the site in connection with a dispute over the conditions of the soil or other circumstances, so that

---

55. Among the arbitral rules which deal with the matter of security for legal costs, are the following:

Art. 25.2 of the London Court of International Arbitration Rules:

"The Arbitral Tribunal shall have the power, upon the application of a party, to order any claiming or counterclaiming party to provide security for the legal or other costs of any other party by way of deposit or bank guarantee or in any other manner and upon such terms as the Arbitral Tribunal considers appropriate. Such terms may include the provision by that other party of a cross-indemnity, itself secured in such manner as the Arbitral Tribunal considers appropriate, for any costs and losses incurred by such claimant or counterclaimant in providing security. The amount of any costs and losses payable under such cross-indemnity may be determined by the Arbitral Tribunal in one or more awards. In the event that a claiming or counterclaiming party does not comply with any order to provide security, the Arbitral Tribunal may stay that party's claims or counterclaims or dismiss them in an award"

Art. 46 b of the World Intellectual Property Organization Arbitration Rules:

"Interim Measures of Protection and Security for Claims and Costs
....
(b) At the request of a party, the Tribunal may, if it considers it to be required by exceptional circumstances, order the other party to provide security, in a form to be determined by the Tribunal, for the claim or counter-claim, as well as for costs referred to in Article 72."

experts can undertake an analysis in the most efficient manner (some technical tests become very expensive to conduct once a certain progress in the works is achieved).

(2) Request for payment of a "work order", despite it being contested by the owner, when the involved amount would have a significant impact on the cash flow needs of the project.

d. *Corporate management and damage control in ongoing business relationships*
(1) Delivery of codes of access to specialized software needed to run the business.
(2) Access to routine records in order to supervise the company's management and performance.
(3) Establishment of joint signatures for drawing checks.
(4) Abstention from undertaking certain activities which do not correspond to the regular course of business, or from engaging in some business activities which, though consistent with the normal course of business, should not be undertaken unless some duties are imposed upon the party against whom the measure is decreed. In the case of a dispute dealing with shareholders' rights (particularly if minority rights), it is common for one of the parties to request an interim measure that will require the managing party to report on some transactions, either before or after the transaction takes place (and in some cases both).
(5) Appointment of a neutral manager for some or all of the company's activities.
(6) Abstention from executing a corporate resolution.
(7) Appointment of counsel for representation of the company's interest (different from conflicting parties' respective counsel).

e. *Anti-Suit Injunctions*
Annex III (pp. 578-579) includes overall comments regarding Anti-Suit Injunctions.

# ANNEX III

## Anti-suit Injunctions

Anti-suit injunctions fall within the hypothesis set forth in Art. 17(2)(b) of the Model Law (the only type of anti-suit injunctions discussed here are those issued by an arbitral tribunal).

This is an area in which many procedural challenges arise. Such challenges are due to the collision of jurisdictions or, at least, the confrontation between jurisdictions which, in the opinion of one of the parties, should hear the case. And, possibly, the main ingredient of complexity results from the fact that there is no directly superior court empowered to rule as to which tribunal (arbitral or judiciary) is the one appropriate to hear the case.

An arbitral tribunal is only entitled to rule on its jurisdiction, but not in such a way as to deprive a court of the jurisdiction pertaining to it (and the same can be stated in regard to another arbitral tribunal). Thus, the arbitral tribunal's powers are constrained, on this matter, to rule whether the subject matter of the controversy falls within the scope of its jurisdiction. If one of the parties attempts to take the case (or actually takes it) before a court, the arbitral tribunal will order him to avoid causing harm or prejudice to the arbitral process. This "harm or prejudice" (words used by the Model Law) takes place when parallel proceedings occur as a result of the filing of a claim before a court, notwithstanding that an arbitral tribunal is clearly empowered to hear the case.

As in many areas of arbitration, the arbitrator (and the party requesting the anti-suit injunction) must be aware of the jurisdictional rules of the court handling the parallel claim and, certainly, the jurisdictional rules and "access to justice" criteria of the court which will later receive the request for recognition or enforcement of the award. With this in mind, the arbitral tribunal will design the appropriate anti-suit injunction that fits the needs of the specific case.

There is no universal recipe for the terms and conditions that an anti-suit injunction should include. Occasionally, the arbitral tribunal issues a ruling ordering a party to request a stay of court proceedings. Whether the arbitral tribunal should go further, ordering a party to withdraw its court filing, is a question that must be adequately assessed, ensuring that it is not considered, at a later stage, a restriction to the right of access to justice.

A safe criterion commonly used by arbitral tribunals is to order the parties, at the request of one of them, to refrain from pursuing court proceedings that breach their duty to submit a dispute to arbitration and that will result in harm or prejudice to the arbitral process itself or to the decisions to be ruled within such arbitral process. Of course, this general "formula" must be adapted to the particular features of each case. By following this approach, the arbitral tribunal places the initial burden of deciding the specific scope of the measure upon the party against whom the measure is granted. Such party must comply in good faith with the request of the arbitral tribunal. It is very likely that at some point, in a later stage, the issue of compliance or non-compliance with the measure will reappear before the arbitral tribunal. Should this occur, the arbitral tribunal shall at least take into account the procedural conduct of such party at the time of examining the merits of the dispute.

Some practitioners argue as to the feasibility of granting an award of damages in case a party breaches an anti-suit injunction.[56] In connection with this matter, it is of the essence to bear in mind that one of the principles of contract law is that the parties not only want the covenants included in the agreement, but also the consequences of such agreement, which are the result of good faith and fair dealing. And, it is precisely within this context that a party is not only expected to submit its case to arbitration should a dispute arise, but also to avoid recourse to a court for that case. The natural objective of an arbitral clause is to set the grounds for handling the case in an orderly and efficient manner and this cannot be achieved if one of the parties resorts to a state court. The necessary corollary of this principle is that the breach of a duty implies the burden to compensate for damages caused to the other party.

An aspect to consider when analyzing the issue of compensation for damages is the fact that, as with any compensation, it is limited by its nature of restitution, and therefore it cannot result in a profit for the affected party. For this reason, it is necessary to bear in mind the compensation that the court may grant, and the scope of such compensation.

The arbitral tribunal must take these two aspects into account when addressing the matter of compensation for breach of an anti-suit injunction. And, certainly, the same analysis must be undertaken by the court with regard to the arbitral tribunal's compensation decision.

Nevertheless, what certainly is a straightforward cause-and-effect analysis is the notion that the arbitral tribunal should grant compensation for those damages resulting from the costs associated with the issues related, within the arbitration, to the court proceedings that were unduly initiated.

A final but highly relevant aspect that the arbitral tribunal must consider is the following: the arbitral tribunal must ensure that the injunction does not collide with legitimate party rights. Such is the case when a particular remedy is not available before the arbitral tribunal's jurisdiction, or when there is the need to preserve a right, faced with the risk of a limitation period.

---

56. For a brief reference on that argument see Laurent LÉVY, "Anti-Suit Injunctions Issued by Arbitrators" in Emmanuel GAILLARD, ed., *Anti-Suit Injunctions in International Arbitration* (IAI Seminar Paris, Juris Publishing Inc. 2003) p. 120.

# ANNEX IV

# Provisions in Rules, Legislation and Case Law That Balance Convenience and the Likelihood of Success by the Requesting Party

EXAMPLES OF RULES

*Hong Kong (Rules of the Hong Kong International Arbitration Centre)*

These Rules contain a provision that enables the arbitrator to decree an interim payment if such arbitrator considers that it is undoubtedly due:

> "*Article 11. Powers and Jurisdiction of the Arbitrator*
> ....
> (m) Order the making by one party to another of an interim payment of monies alleged to be due where, in the opinion of the Arbitrator, payment is undoubtedly due...."

*Australia (Rules of the Australian Centre for International Commercial Arbitration)*

> "*28. Interim Measures of Protection*
> ....
> 28.3 Before the Arbitral Tribunal orders any interim measure, the party requesting it shall satisfy the Arbitral Tribunal that:
> (a) *irreparable harm is likely to result if the measure is not ordered;*
> (b) such harm substantially outweighs the harm that is likely to result to the party affected by the measure if the measure is granted; and
> (c) *there is a reasonable possibility that the requesting party will succeed on the merits,* provided that any determination on this possibility shall not affect the liberty of decision of the Arbitral Tribunal in making any subsequent determination."
> (Emphasis added)

*Mexico (Rules of Canaco; Cámara Nacional de Comercio)*

> "*Article 31 A. Conditions for Granting Interim Measures*
> 1. The party requesting an interim measure under paragraph a), b) or c) of paragraph 2 of article 31 shall satisfy the arbitral tribunal that:
> a) *Harm not adequately reparable by an award of damages* is likely to result if the measure is not ordered, and such harm substantially outweighs the harm that is likely to result to the party against whom the measure is directed if the measure is granted; and
> b) *There is a reasonable possibility that the requesting party will succeed on the merits* of the claim. The determination on this possibility shall not affect the discretion of

the arbitral tribunal in making any subsequent determination.
....." (Emphasis added)

*United States (Optional arbitration rules of the American Arbitration Association (AAA))*

"O-4. Interim Award
If after consideration the emergency arbitrator is satisfied that the party seeking the emergency relief has shown that immediate and irreparable loss or damage will result in the absence of emergency relief, and that such party is entitled to such relief, the emergency arbitrator may enter an interim award granting the relief and stating the reasons therefore."

EXAMPLES OF LEGISLATIVE PROVISIONS

In addition to the arbitration rules, procedural codes also provide that interim or protective measures shall be granted only if the likelihood of success and the dangerous delay are proved:

*Argentina*

Several articles of the Argentinean Procedural Code establish that the damages caused by an unjustified delay shall be proven before the court grants an interim measure.
For example, Art. 210 states:

"Attachment prior to judgment can be requested by:
1) the co-heir, the apartment owner or a company partner *if he is able to prove the likelihood of success and the dangerous delay*." (Emphasis added)

*France*

The French New Code of Civil Procedure provides in its Art. 809 as follows:

"The president may, at any time, even where confronted with serious objections, provide by way of summary interlocutory proceedings for such protective measures or such measures as to keep the status quo of the matters as required, either *to protect from an impending damage, or to abate a nuisance manifestly illegal*.
Where liability resultant from an obligation cannot be seriously challenged, he may award an interim payment to the creditor or order the mandatory performance of the obligation even where it shall be in the nature of an obligation to perform." (Emphasis added)

EXAMPLE OF COURT CASE LAW

Mexican federal courts, and the Mexican Supreme Court, have supported in many decisions that those principles should be satisfied in order to obtain protective measures.

> "The preliminary injunction (*suspension*) against the attachment prior to judgment of bank accounts, shall be granted for the purpose of allowing free access to the owner (*quejoso*) as long as no tax is owed.
> (....)
> According to the principles of the likelihood of success (*apariencia de buen derecho*) and the dangerous delay (*peligro en la demora*), on which every protective or interim measure relies, when those principles are proved, it is possible to give positive effects to an interim measure; ... this is to allow the exercise of rights paralyzed by an official governmental action..." which is being challenged by the *amparo* proceedings."[57]

---

57. Unanimous decision of the 15th Administrative Tribunal of the First Circuit (*Décimo Quinto Tribunal Colegiado en Materia Administrativa del Primer Circuito*); request for suspension (*revisión*) no. 359/2007, Register no. 170801, published in XXVI Semanario Judicial de la Federación y su Gaceta, December 2007, p. 1702.

# Interim Measures in International Commercial Arbitration: A Commentary on the Report by Luis Enrique Graham

*Nael G. Bunni**

| TABLE OF CONTENTS | Page |
|---|---|
| I. Synopsis | 583 |
| II. General | 583 |
| III. Art. 26 of the UNCITRAL Arbitration Rules | 586 |
| IV. Interim Measures in Construction Arbitration | 588 |
| V. Concluding Remarks | 605 |

I. SYNOPSIS

Mr. Luis Graham has provided us with an all-encompassing Report on a number of aspects relating to interim measures, including amongst others, the background to the changes made to Art. 17 of the UNCITRAL Model Law on International Commercial Arbitration (the Model Law); the approach taken by the Working Group on revising Art. 26 of the UNCITRAL Arbitration Rules on interim measures; an overview of interim measures issued by an arbitral tribunal; its use in practice; and many others.[1] My task is to comment on that Report and in doing so, to assess the impact of the revisions to Art. 26; propose best practices for arbitrators considering applications for provisional measures; and consider the most effective use of such applications for parties seeking relief. I have concentrated, for the reasons outlined below under II. General, on areas relating to construction and engineering arbitration, as they have a very unique place in the field of arbitration. In that area, to which I will refer simply as "construction arbitration", the debate on ex parte interim measures forms an essential element.

II. GENERAL

As in litigation, interim protection in international commercial arbitration is there to ensure that the status quo between the parties is not affected throughout the arbitral proceedings. Interim measures of protection are temporary in nature, designed to

---

\* Senior Director, Bunni & Associates; Chartered Engineer, Conciliator & Registered Chartered Arbitrator; Visiting Professor in Construction Law and Contract Administration, Trinity College Dublin; Member of ICCA.
1. "Interim Measures – Ongoing Regulations and Practices (A View from the UNCITRAL Arbitration Regime)", this volume, pp. 539-582. In this commentary, I have adopted Mr. Graham's definition of "interim measures" to cover not only scenarios of interim measures, but also those regarding preliminary orders, unless a specific mention is made or the opposite should be the result of a logical placement of the circumstances described therein.

"preserve a factual or legal situation so as to safeguard rights the recognition of which is sought from the court having jurisdiction as to the substance of the case".[2] The purpose behind them is to ensure that either party to an arbitration agreement suffers minimum damage throughout the arbitral proceedings, through the final settlement of the dispute and the ultimate enforcement of the award. In carrying out the research for this Commentary, I found that whilst there is significant literature on the topic of interim measures, none of it is specifically related to construction arbitration. Contracts for construction and engineering projects and the disputes that arise out of, or in their connection, are quite unique and very different from those for other commercial transactions.[3] Essentially, arbitration cases resulting from such contracts are complex; and they involve large sums of money with a multiplicity of disputes where conflict has resulted from various aspects of fact, law and quantum. The facts are generally related to events or circumstances that eventuated on, or off, the site of the project and in many cases involve highly technical issues. The legal issues usually involve not only principles related to contract law, but also some that are mainly related to provisions attached to the parties' agreement that form a very special area of the law, which requires special expertise in the areas relevant to that contract. The quantum issues will always relate to complex mathematical calculations requiring specific capability and expertise, including the use of computerized programming and relevant software. Therefore, with the belief that no assessment of the impact of the revisions to Art. 26, nor any proposal for best practice or most effective use of interim measures could be complete without a special reference to construction cases, I decided that I should focus on, and examine the interim measures that would most often be sought in such arbitration cases.

Generally, however, with the steady growth of arbitration as the main international dispute resolution mechanism, interim measures, and the role they play in arbitral proceedings, have become increasingly important. Statistics show that the number of interim measures applied for has been comparatively low, although rapidly increasing.[4]

---

2. *Van Uden Maritime BV (t/a Van Uden Africa Line) v. Kommanditgesellschaft in Firma Deco-Line*, (C-391/95) [1998] ECR I-7091, at 7133.
3. See in this connection two references by the author: Nael G. BUNNI, *The FIDIC Forms of Contract*, 3rd edn. (Blackwell Publishing, Oxford 2005) Chapter 7 for the inherent characteristics of the construction contract and Chapters 13 and 16 for some of the unique obligations contained in it; also Nael G. BUNNI, *Risk and Insurance in Construction*, 2nd edn. (Spon Press, London 2003) pp. 187-190.
4. At the 2006 ICCA Congress in Montreal, Neil Kaplan gave certain figures in relation to the number of interim measures that were actually applied for within the London Court of International Arbitration (LCIA). Between 1st January 2004 and May 2006, a total of 245 arbitration proceedings were commenced, with 16 applications for expedited proceedings, out of which 8 asked for interim measures. Neil KAPLAN, "Interim Measures – A Practical Experience" in A.J. VAN DEN BERG, ed., *International Arbitration 2006: Back to Basics?* ICCA Congress Series no. 13 (hereinafter *ICCA Congress Series no. 13*) (Kluwer 2007) p. 771. Also, Kaj Hobér noted that requests for interim measures are not very frequent on the basis of the statistics that he gave in his Report "Interim Measures by Arbitrators" in *ICCA Congress Series no. 13*, pp. 721-750. Julian Lew gave the figures that from 1985 to 2000 there were only 75 International Chamber of Commerce (ICC) cases in which some form of interim relief had been sought. See Julian LEW, "Control of Jurisdiction by Injunctions Issued by National Courts" in *ICCA Congress Series no. 13*, pp. 185-220.

A large proportion of these applications are found in construction arbitration, particularly in the form of anti-suit injunctions, as will be discussed below. An arbitral tribunal will normally have the power to grant interim measures, unless the parties to the dispute specifically provide otherwise. Most, if not all, of the institutional rules that govern arbitration contain, and have contained, for some considerable time, provisions that give power to the arbitral tribunal to grant interim measures.[5] Mr. Graham deals with the various rules in Sect. II.4.d and Annex IV of his Report.[6]

Moving from the rules to the law of arbitration, whilst it is widely accepted that arbitral tribunals have the requisite authority to grant interim measures, there are exceptions. For example, in England, an arbitral tribunal only has this authority if it has been specifically bestowed upon it by the parties.[7]

However, one of the major problems with an interim measure granted by an arbitral tribunal is enforcement. Because interim measures are not final, in the sense that they deal mainly with procedural matters and are generally temporary in nature, they are not automatically regarded as an arbitral award.[8] Further, they may require the involvement of third parties, over whom an arbitral tribunal does not have authority to make orders. This follows from the fundamental principle that the jurisdiction of an arbitral tribunal is based upon the consent of the parties to the arbitration agreement.

With this in mind, the UNCITRAL Working Group on International Commercial Arbitration considered the matter and decided that the need for an enforcement mechanism is greatest for measures to facilitate subsequent recognition and enforcement of the award, and to a lesser extent measures intended to preserve the status quo between the parties. Art. 17 of the Model Law as revised in July 2006 defined interim measures as follows:

> "An interim measure is any temporary measure, whether in the form of an award or in another form by which at any time, prior to the issuance of the award by which the dispute is finally decided, the arbitral tribunal orders a party to:

---

5. See this volume, pp. 553 and 580-582. For example, the ICC Rules which date back to 1922 have all contained such provisions with the exception of the 1927 Rules, which were silent on interim measures.
6. Some institutional rules and the relevant articles within them are set out here as examples. American Arbitration Association: Art. 34; International Centre for Dispute Resolution: Art. 21; ICC: Art. 21, Art. 23; ICSID: Rule 39 ; Swiss Rules of International Arbitration: Art. 26; LCIA: Art. 25; Arbitration Institute of the Stockholm Chamber of Commerce: Art. 31; Dubai International Arbitration Centre: Art. 31.
7. Under Sect. 38(1) of the 1996 Arbitration Act the parties are empowered to determine the arbitrator's interlocutory powers, but there are default powers conferred upon the arbitrator under Sect. 38(c), which relate to security for costs and evidence.
8. The issue of interim measures differs greatly from State to State. For example, in Italy the power to grant interim measures is one that belongs solely to the national courts, whereas in Switzerland, in the absence of an agreement to the contrary, the parties are to apply initially to the arbitral tribunal, rather than to the courts, for *"provisional or protective measures"*. As referred to in fn. 7 above, England, it seems, is between these two extremes in that under the 1996 Arbitration Act, unless otherwise agreed between the parties, the arbitral tribunal has the power to order certain interim measures that are specified within the Act.

(a) Maintain or restore the status quo pending determination of the dispute;
(b) Take action that would prevent, or refrain from taking action that is likely to cause, current or imminent harm or prejudice to the arbitral process itself;
(c) Provide a means of preserving assets out of which a subsequent award may be satisfied; or
(d) Preserve evidence that may be relevant and material to the resolution of the dispute."

The conceptual and philosophical perspectives taken by the Working Group in suggesting changes to Art. 26 of the UNCITRAL Arbitration Rules are described in Sect. III.*1* of Mr. Graham's Report.[9] To follow these changes, a revision of Art. 26 of the UNCITRAL Arbitration Rules is now necessary and is being undertaken by the Working Group to coincide with the revised Art. 17 of the Model Law.

III. ART. 26 OF THE UNCITRAL ARBITRATION RULES

As stated above, the proposed amendments to Art. 26 of the UNCITRAL Arbitration Rules reflect the changes that were made to Art. 17 of the Model Law. The controversial change envisaged by the amendment is the question of ex parte orders and whether or not provisions for these orders should be included. As discussed below, this is particularly important for construction arbitration. It is worth repeating here the presently proposed amendments to Art. 26 of the UNCITRAL Rules of Arbitration, which reads as follows against the text of the existing Art. 26, which is set out in the footnotes:

"1. The arbitral tribunal may, at the request of a party, grant interim measures.[10]
2. An interim measure is any temporary measure by which, at any time prior to the issuance of the award by which the dispute is finally decided, the arbitral tribunal orders a party to:
(a) Maintain or restore the status quo pending determination of the dispute;
(b) Take action that would prevent, or refrain from taking action that is likely to cause, current or imminent harm or prejudice to the arbitral process itself;
(c) Provide a means of preserving assets out of which a subsequent award may be satisfied; or

---

9. See this volume, pp. 560-561.
10. The original version of Art. 26 states:

"At the request of either party, the arbitral tribunal may take any interim measures it deems necessary in respect of the subject matter of the dispute, including measures for the conservation of the goods forming the subject matter in dispute, such as ordering their deposit with a third person or the sale of perishable goods."

(d) Preserve evidence that may be relevant and material to the resolution of the dispute.[11]

3. The party requesting an interim measure under paragraph 2 (a), (b) and (c) shall satisfy the arbitral tribunal that:

(a) Harm not adequately reparable by an award of damages is likely to result if the measure is not ordered, and such harm substantially outweighs the harm that is likely to result to the party against whom the measure is directed if the measure is granted; and

(b) There is a reasonable possibility that the requesting party will succeed on the merits of the claim. The determination on this possibility shall not affect the discretion of the arbitral tribunal in making any subsequent determination.

4. With regard to a request for an interim measure under paragraph 2 (d), the requirements in paragraph 3 (a) and (b) shall apply only to the extent the arbitral tribunal considers appropriate.

5. If the arbitral tribunal determines that disclosure of a request for an interim measure to the party against whom it is directed risks frustrating that measure's purpose, nothing in these Rules prevents the tribunal, when it gives notice of such request to that party, from temporarily ordering that the party not frustrate the purpose of the requested measure. The arbitral tribunal shall give that party the earliest practicable opportunity to present its case and then determine whether to grant that request.

6. The arbitral tribunal may modify, suspend or terminate an interim measure or an order referred to in paragraph 5 it has granted, upon application of any party or, in exceptional circumstances and upon prior notice to the parties, on the arbitral tribunal's own initiative.

7. The arbitral tribunal may require the party requesting an interim measure or applying for an order referred to in paragraph 5 to provide appropriate security in connection with the measure or the order.

8. The arbitral tribunal may require any party promptly to disclose any material change in the circumstances on the basis of which the interim measure or the order referred to in paragraph 5 was requested or granted.

9. The party requesting an interim measure or applying for an order referred to in paragraph 5 shall be liable for any costs and damages caused by the measure or the order to any party if the arbitral tribunal later determines that, in the circumstances, the measure or the order should not have been granted. The arbitral tribunal may award such costs and damages at any point during the proceedings.

10. A request for an interim measure or an application for an order referred to in paragraph 5 addressed by any party to a judicial authority shall not be deemed incompatible with the agreement to arbitrate, or as a waiver of that agreement."[12]

---

11. The original version of Art. 26 states: "Such interim measures may be established in the form of an interim award. The arbitral tribunal shall be entitled to require security for the costs of such measures."
12. Originally Art. 26(3), with some minor amendments.

The proposed amended version of Art. 26 of the UNCITRAL Arbitration Rules goes into considerably more detail than the current provisions. As stated above, the most controversial proposed amendment is Sub-sect. 5, quoted above, which provides the power of an arbitral tribunal to award ex parte interim measures. In his Report at Sect. II, Mr. Graham outlines the debate that took place and the case for and against that type of an interim measure.[13] In this regard, it is important to note that in assessing whether or not it is wise to include, in the Rules, an application for a preliminary order from the tribunal, the applicant must ensure that such application includes not only arguments in favour of the application, but also arguments that speak against the granting of such preliminary orders. This corresponds to the obligation counsel have in ex parte matters before the courts, i.e. that the party making the application has a duty of utmost good faith to the court to disclose all facts as known at the time of the application, whether they be in support of the application being made or not. The Court of Appeal of England and Wales established in *Brink's MAT Ltd v. Elcombe* that: [14]

> "(i) the duty of the applicant is to make a 'full and fair disclosure of all the material facts'....
> (ii) The material facts are those which it is material for the judge to know in dealing with the application as made; materiality is to be decided by the court and not by the assessment of the applicant or his legal advisors....
> (iii) The applicant must make proper enquiries before making the application...."

IV.  INTERIM MEASURES IN CONSTRUCTION ARBITRATION

Before considering the changes that are being proposed to Art. 26 of the UNCITRAL Arbitration Rules, I shall first deal with the type of interim measures that are frequently sought in construction arbitration. Many of these interim measures are of a procedural nature only and, as such, they are intended to regulate the relationship between the parties and the tribunal at some time during the arbitration proceedings. I have selected from my own construction arbitration files a number of different forms in which such measures were sought. These are set out in Sect. IV.1 below:

1.   *Different Forms in Which Interim Measures Are Sought*

– Anti-suit injunctions
– Order to continue or to stop certain works, including the covering up of work already executed which is the subject of a dispute and thus, its inspection would be necessary for the purpose of resolving the dispute;
– Order not to call on a bank guarantee;
– Order to refrain from having a press conference or press release;

---

13. See this volume, pp. 540-559.
14. *Brink's MAT Ltd v. Elcombe*, [1988] 3 ALL ER 188 at 193.

— Order not to make public certain information or not to break the confidentiality of a previously held amicable dispute resolution forum;
— Order not to dispose of or relocate certain assets;
— Order not to dispose of or relocate certain evidence;
— Order for inspection of site or certain manufacturing unit, including an order to allow experts of the counterparty to have access to the site;
— Order for inspection and/or testing of certain item or machinery, including the provision of samples for such testing;
— Order to comply with certain provisions of the contract that require payment such as a decision of a dispute adjudication board, which is temporarily binding on the parties;
— Order to continue sales for distribution;
— Order to appoint an expert; and
— Order for Security for Costs.

Specific examples of some of the above interim measures are set out in Sects. IV.3 to IV.5 below. It is appropriate to mention however, that other than the last two orders referred to above, all would be sought in the form of an application for an injunction, be it a mandatory or prohibitive in nature. I will, therefore, deal first with Injunctions in Sect. IV.2 below, leaving the orders for appointment of a tribunal expert and for Security for Costs to follow.

2.  *The Requirements for Injunctive Relief*

In the seminal Irish case of *Campus Oil Ltd. v. Ministry for Industry and Energy (No. 2)*,[15] which dealt directly with the granting of an interlocutory injunction, the court laid down the following criteria that a court must follow in determining whether an interlocutory injunction should be granted or not.

> "Interlocutory relief is granted to an applicant where what he complains of is continuing and is causing him harm or injury which may be irreparable in the sense that it may not be possible to compensate him fairly or properly by an award of damages. Such relief is given because a period must necessarily elapse before the action can come for trial and for the purpose of keeping matters in status quo until the hearing.... Not only will the court have regard to what is complained of and whether damages would be an appropriate remedy but it will consider what inconvenience loss and damage might be caused to the other party, and will enquire whether the applicant has shown that the balance of convenience is in his favour."

The court based its finding on the decision of the Court of Appeal of England and Wales in the decision of *American Cyanimid v. Ethicon Ltd.*[16]

---

15. *Campus Oil Ltd. v. Ministry for Industry and Energy (No. 2)*, [1983] IR 88.
16. *American Cyanimid v. Ethicon Ltd.*, [1975] AC 396.

Therefore, it can be taken from the above, that in looking at this issue, and whether or not to issue an interim order directing a party to do or to refrain from doing something, the arbitral tribunal must have regard to the following:

– The tribunal must ensure that the application being made is not an attempt by the applicant to have the tribunal decide the ultimate issue in the arbitral proceedings summarily, without the applicant having proven its case and similarly, before the respondent can effectively defend itself.
– The tribunal must firstly be satisfied that the applicant has shown that irreparable harm, which cannot be adequately compensated for by damages, would be suffered.
– Conversely, it should also satisfy itself that if the respondent is successful in defending the overall claim, that it can be adequately compensated by damages if an injunction were to be granted.
– The tribunal must question whether the damages that could potentially be awarded outweigh the irreparable harm that the respondent would suffer if an injunction were to be granted, and were it ultimately found that it should not have been.
– The tribunal must bear in mind that the ultimate purpose in granting an injunction is to preserve the *status quo* that exists between the parties, and then go on to determine where the balance of convenience lies in terms of whether or not to grant the injunction.

The requirements that must be met, as set down above, are reflected in the proposed amendment to Art. 26 of the Rules, specifically Sub-sect. 2 which sets down the purpose and intention of interim measures of protection.

In this connection, it is useful to quote from the proceedings of the Institute for Transnational Arbitration's 16th Annual International Commercial Arbitration Workshop entitled "The Art of Arbitrating",[17] held on 16 June 2005, where an extremely useful debate took place during a mock scenario whereby an application, under the LCIA Rules, for an interim measure before an arbitral tribunal was being made. Mr. John Beechey, acting on behalf of the respondents in the exercise, stated as follows:

> "... they [the Applicant] want you to decide that our ... product is not up to their standards, and ... [we] should be prevented from selling it.... We've heard Mr. King argue for this. He says it's all justified by their terminating our licensing agreement. That's their argument. But this tribunal cannot decide if [the Applicant's] reputation is being harmed, without deciding the merits. And at this stage in the proceedings, I suggest that that's inappropriate.
> (....)
> Well, Mr. Chairman, the tribunal has the authority to grant interim relief under the LCIA Rules. That's clear. But it shouldn't exercise its discretion to grant interim relief when the applicant hasn't shown why such relief is necessary, much less why the relief is needed to preserve the status quo and to prevent irreparable harm. What the LCIA Rules do not contemplate is the grant of interim relief as

---

17. As documented in 23 Arbitration International (2007, no. 2).

a casual measure to be implemented upon the whim of a party. And further, if the tribunal were to grant some portion of [the Applicant's] request, an award is not necessary. A simple order or directive or recommendation from the tribunal should be sufficient."

Therefore, in order to allow an arbitral tribunal to reach a fully informed decision on the matter, one must assess what is important and relevant to be presented to an arbitral tribunal. In my opinion, at the very least, the following should be opened to the tribunal:

– More than bare allegations or assertions;
– Some form of statement of the grounds upon which the Applicant is relying in support of its application; and
– Affidavits or even oral testimony bearing in mind the serious consequences of such an application.

It will also be open to the tribunal to apply a particular standard in determining whether the applicant has met its case. In this regard, it is important to bear in mind that before a tribunal is minded to grant an interim measure of this nature, some element of urgency must be before the tribunal (i.e. if the tribunal does not act now, some kind of irreparable harm is imminent). The granting of an injunction is of course a discretionary remedy, and will depend on the circumstances of the particular case before the tribunal.

3. *Examples of Applications for Injunctions*

The following are detailed examples of some of the applications for injunctions, arranged in the order given in Sect. IV.*1* above.

*a.    Anti-suit injunctions*

One important injunction that keeps appearing in construction arbitration cases is the anti-suit injunction. The power of an arbitrator to issue an anti-suit injunction in these cases is one that has long been recognized in international commercial arbitration. It is generally granted where there is a need to ensure that neither party attempts to aggravate or delay the arbitral process by bringing the dispute, which is covered by an arbitration agreement, before a court that has no jurisdiction, usually a national court. From this, it can be taken that the powers of an arbitral tribunal are therefore not limited to the resolution of the dispute, but also include the power to rule on its own jurisdiction to hear the parties' arguments in relation to the dispute, the *competence-competence* principle. This type of injunction was sought in the High Court of England and Wales (Commercial Court) decision in *Republic of Ecuador v. Occidental Exploration & Production*,[18] in which a tribunal award ordering the claimant to stop bringing claims in relation to the arbitration to the Ecuadorian courts was upheld. In the decision, Judge Aikens held that

---

18. *Republic of Ecuador v. Occidental Exploration & Production*, 2nd March 2006, [2006] EWHC 345 (Comm.).

"the tribunal must have the power to make orders that are intended to give the proper effect to its primary order granting [the investor] monetary compensation. (....)

It is an order which is consequential to the order granting [the investor] monetary compensation, and is made so as to endure that [the investor] does not obtain a double recovery."[19]

As this topic is being dealt with by another speaker, I will only make two remarks, which relate to construction and engineering arbitration cases:

– The first is to highlight the fact that such an injunction does not have to be a proactive one, i.e. it could be used not only where the tribunal renders an injunctive order, but it could simply be a passive one by the tribunal proceeding with the arbitration notwithstanding any interference from a court without jurisdiction. In a paper presented by Emmanuel Gaillard on the topic of interim measures, he noted the following:

"As early as 1970, a sole arbitrator, Pierre Lalive, in ICC Case No. 1512, chose to continue the arbitral proceeding in the face of simultaneous national court proceedings, although, in appearance, he had not been requested to (and so did not) issue an anti-suit injunction. The dispute was between an Indian cement company and a Pakistani bank. It arose in connection with a guarantee agreement, containing an ICC arbitration clause, that the bank had offered to the cement company in relation to the obligations of a manufacturer to deliver a certain amount of cement to the cement company. When the manufacturer failed to deliver the cement, the cement company initiated ICC arbitration against the bank to enforce guarantee. The arbitration took place in Geneva. In a second preliminary Award, dated 14 January 1970, the sole arbitrator addressed an argument by the Pakistani bank that the arbitrator lacked jurisdiction because the Pakistani cement manufacturer had brought an action (after the initiation of the arbitral proceeding) against the bank in a Pakistani court. In addition, the bank had brought suit against the Indian cement company and the Pakistani cement manufacturer in the High Court of West Pakistan, which then issued an injunction restraining the Indian cement company from pursuing the arbitration.

In upholding his jurisdiction, the sole arbitrator found that 'the defendant's decision to institute the national lawsuits was another tactical move to gain time and to slow down the arbitration proceedings'. Noting that the parties had agreed to international arbitration outside Pakistan according to the ICC Rules, the arbitrator declared that there was a widely held principle that 'once the parties have chosen a law to govern the arbitration proceedings, there is no room for the laws of the country of the parties'.
(....)

---

19. *Ibid.*, paras. 125 to 127.

Thus, the arbitrator made clear that he would exercise jurisdiction despite the Pakistani court proceedings."[20]

– The second comment is related to the frequency of these measures. Emmanuel Gaillard referred to five cases which fall into the category of anti-suit injunctions. Most of these cases were in the construction field, but that list was not exhaustive, as it did not include at least five ICC cases where this author was involved, either as chairman or member of the tribunal or sole arbitrator: These were ICC cases No. 6798 and No. 7799, both of which involved the Pakistani courts (as is the case cited in the previous point); ICC Case No. 7748, which involved the courts in Yemen; ICC Case No. 10623, which involved the courts in Ethiopia; and ICC Case No. 11396, which involved the courts in India. These facts highlight the importance of this type of interim measures in construction arbitration. Judgments were reported in at least two of these five cases,[21] and are referred to below.

– In ICC Case No. 6798, the First Partial Award was published which was unfavourable to the claimants in that it effectively eliminated the majority of the claimants' monetary claims. Following the publication of the First Partial Award, the claimants made an application to the District Court at Sheikhupura for orders that the First Partial Award rendered by the tribunal be filed under the provisions of the Pakistani Arbitration Act 1940. Following this, the claimants made a separate application to the International Court of Arbitration of the ICC for the removal of the tribunal. The tribunal accepted that it was open to the International Court of Arbitration of the ICC to remove the tribunal if it saw fit to do so and stated that it would abide by that Court's decision. However, the International Court of Arbitration of the ICC rejected the claimants' application. The claimants, being dissatisfied with the decision of the International Court of Arbitration of the ICC, made a further application to the District Court in Pakistan for the removal of the tribunal. They also challenged the tribunal's First Partial Award and contended that the curial law of this arbitration was Pakistani Law. In support of their contention, they intended to show that the parties had agreed that the curial law of any arbitration between them was that of Pakistan. None of these matters were previously argued or raised by either of the parties before the tribunal. Subsequently, a witness summons was issued to the tribunal, directing its members to appear before the Pakistani court on a given date. Having heard the parties on the issue, the arbitral tribunal rendered a decision in which it declined to appear before the Pakistani Court and stated, inter alia;

> "The Arbitrators presently consider that since, pursuant to the Arbitration Agreement, the Parties have subjected themselves to the procedural law of England and since these proceedings have commenced in London and continued

---

20. Emmanuel Gaillard, "Anti-suit Injunctions Issued by Arbitrators" in *ICCA Congress Series no. 13*, pp. 235-266, at p. 252.
21. *Hitachi Ltd v. Rupali Polyester*, (1998 SCMR 1618); and *Companie d'Entreprises CFE, SA (Belgium) v. The Government of the Republic of Yemen, comprising inter alia the former Government of the People's Democratic Republic of Yemen*, 17 Mealey's International Arbitration Report (October 2002, no. 10).

in London until the issue of the First Partial Award and beyond, the seat of the Arbitration is England and the governing procedural law is that of England and only the Courts of England have jurisdiction over the Arbitration, the Arbitrators and any award they render."

The respondent had requested a limited stay of the proceedings whilst the claimant, on the other hand, wished the proceedings to go forward as scheduled. The tribunal however, stated that, in the absence of agreement between the parties, it would only be prepared to proceed if the claimants were either to:

"(1) Withdraw the Pakistani proceedings, or
(2) Undertake to bring the subject matter of these proceedings before the English Courts as the Courts applying the curial law and exercising the supervisory power over this Arbitration."

The District Court in Pakistan, in a fully reasoned judgment, declined supervisory jurisdiction of the arbitration and dismissed the claimant's application. This decision was appealed to the Supreme Court, and again the tribunal declined to enter an appearance as ordered. In a statement to the court the tribunal reiterated its position and pointed out that

"...any suggestion that a court has jurisdiction to hear submissions on or to set aside a foreign award based on the use of its country's substantive law in the foreign arbitration ignores the nature of the international arbitral concept. This concept is based on the principle that the competent authority for exercising supervisory powers and entertaining any application in any matter relating to a properly constituted international arbitration is the court of the Seat of the Arbitration. The Arbitrators wish to add that in their experience, this concept is of supreme importance in the minds of those entering into agreements or providing finance in international commerce. Furthermore, it is these parties' confirmed belief that any dispute arising from such commercial activities must be resolved in an entirely neutral forum, even when applying the substantive law of a contracting state."

– In light of the statements issued above, the tribunal continued on to proceed with the arbitration on the basis that the relevant authority to exercise any supervisory jurisdiction in relation to the arbitral proceedings was the courts within the Seat of the Arbitration. One of the reasons behind the tribunal's decision was that any dispute between the parties must be decided in an independent impartial forum and in accordance with the Rules of Natural Justice.
– In ICC Arbitration, Case No. 11396, after the Terms of Reference were agreed and signed by the parties, a provisional timetable was drawn up for the whole arbitral proceedings, which catered for certain substantive preliminary issues to be determined first. The arbitrator, having held a comprehensive hearing where he heard extensive factual evidence and legal arguments relating to the preliminary issues, rendered a partial award in which he largely vindicated the position of the claimant. Upon receiving the

partial award, the respondent resorted to the local court challenging and attaining the annulment of that partial award. In the meantime, the local court issued a temporary injunction restraining the arbitrator from proceeding further in the arbitration until a decision was reached by that court in respect of the respondent's application. However, the arbitrator, having heard the parties in that connection, took the decision to proceed with the arbitration. In the arbitral proceedings that followed, the claimant submitted its witness statements of fact and expertise and its legal arguments regarding the substantive issues, but despite repeated requests from the arbitrator, the respondent did not submit its own. Furthermore, although the respondent was duly notified, it did not appear at the full hearing and the arbitration was subsequently concluded with a final award in favour of the claimant. The respondent instituted proceedings at the place of arbitration, Cyprus, to set aside the final award. In a judgment of considerable detail, the court rejected the application with costs to the claimant.

b.  *Order not to dispose of or relocate certain evidence*
This situation arose in an international arbitration where one of the disputes related to the construction of a bridge deck on the construction of a fly-over over a five-lane super-highway. During the steel reinforcement fixing operations of the flyover there was a clash between certain reinforcement bars and the ducts for the stressing tendons. When the framework was struck it was discovered that there were major defects in the poured sections of the structure, including large voids that were evident below the ducts in the mid-span regions. Consequently, the engineer ordered that this section of the bridge be demolished and rebuilt. An arbitration commenced and one of the major disputes between the parties was the delay and disruption caused to the project as a result of this problem. It emerged that certain parts of the demolished bridge had been kept by the contractor. The employer therefore sought an order from the arbitral tribunal directing the contractor to preserve as evidence, the sections of the demolished bridge for inspection by the tribunal. This order was duly granted.

c.  *Order to comply with a certain provision of the contract that requires payment*
For contracts using the 1999 FIDIC (International Federation of Consulting Engineers) Forms of Contract for major works, the second step in its dispute resolution clause, Clause 20, provides for disputes to be referred to a dispute adjudication board "DAB". Clause 20 incorporates the Rules of Arbitration of the International Chamber of Commerce. The fourth paragraph of Sub-Clause 20.4 provides as follows:

> *"The decision* [of the DAB] *shall be binding on both Parties, who shall promptly give effect to it unless and until it should be revised in an amicable settlement or an arbitral award as described below."* (Emphasis added)

Under these contracts, the decision of the DAB can be either temporarily binding (i.e. where one of the parties is dissatisfied with the decision) or final and binding when neither party has given a notice of dissatisfaction. A party who is dissatisfied with the decision has to give a notice of dissatisfaction with the decision pursuant to Sub-Clause 20.4. When a decision of the DAB has not become final and binding, and the party against whom the decision was made fails to comply with it, Sub-Clause 20.7 of these contracts permits the party who wishes to enforce the DAB's decision to immediately commence arbitration proceedings under Sub-Clause 20.6, requesting the tribunal, once appointed, to order that, as an interim or conservatory measure, the non-compliant party comply with the DAB's decision.[22]

d.   Order to appoint an expert

Where the parties' experts are employed to provide authoritative impartial and independent professional opinions regarding a specific area of expertise, but have not provided the level of expertise demanded, it is sometimes necessary for the tribunal to appoint its own expert. Two possible trends are set out in Sect. IV.4 below.

e.   Order for security for costs

Many examples exist under this category in both domestic and international arbitration, as can be seen in Sect. IV.5 below.

4.   The Appointment of Experts

One of the main types of interim measures that a tribunal may decide to invoke in construction arbitration cases is the appointment of its own expert on a matter of technical nature pertinent to the arbitral proceedings. This will most likely occur in two modes:

— Where the respondent does not, whether partially or fully, participate in the expertise procedure ordered by the tribunal, which normally relates to matters of an intricate and complex nature. Such reluctance could be for various reasons, including the cost of such expertise and the contention that it was up to the claimant to prove its case and it was not for the respondent to help the claimant do so; and
— When the experts appointed by the parties do not act in the required spirit of independence and impartiality which results in their reports being diametrically opposite in nature and consequence. In such a situation, unless the answer to the problem is truly black or white, which is rare, these reports are a waste of time and money and do not further the resolution of the dispute.

It is then, either through a request from one of the parties or the desire of the tribunal that an order is issued for the appointment of a tribunal expert.

An example of the first mode has occurred in one international arbitration where the tribunal was concerned with a consideration of the quantification of the contractor's claim based on variations that had to be made, and were made, to the project; and whether the calculations were to be determined at one or more of the rules enunciated in the case of *Henry Boot Construction Ltd v. Alstom Combined Cycles Ltd.*, i.e. whether billed

---

22. In this connection, Art. 23(1) of the ICC Rules provided for in Sub-Clause 20.6, states, in part, as follows: "... as soon as the file has been transmitted to it, the Arbitral Tribunal may, at the request of a party, order any interim or conservatory measure it deems appropriate".

rates, rates based on billed rates or on a fair valuation.[23] In doing so, the tribunal had to consider the re-designed and varied works and the conditions under which the project was executed by the contractor. The tribunal found that the respondent's engineer and its experts had taken too narrow a view of the facts that were set out in the arbitration, which was more than likely the result of a mandate that was limited. Furthermore, the tribunal found the respondent's evidence in this regard unsatisfactory and unpersuasive and in relation to the issue of quantum, the tribunal had to refer to the parties' appointed experts. However, there was a failure by both experts to reach any meaningful agreement in relation to quantum. Subsequently, and as a direct consequence of the inability of these experts to provide a fully impartial and independent report, the tribunal issued, what was intended to be its final award in the form of a partial award, and appointed its own independent expert to examine and report to it on the valuation of the claimant's claim. Thus, in this case, the tribunal had to appoint its own expert as a result of one party's expert being prevented from carrying out his function effectively by virtue of the limited and restrictive mandate given to him by his client.

The second mode of appointment of an expert by the tribunal occurs where the experts of both parties, either owing to instructions from their own clients or of their own volition, fail in their duty and obligation to give the tribunal a full, independent and impartial expert opinion on a particular technical issue.

In cases of the second mode, an issue of expertise would be before a tribunal whose members might not have the requisite knowledge to adjudicate upon it. However, in other cases a member of the tribunal may be capable of adjudicating on the relevant issues involved, but in such a case, unless that member is the chairman, the parties and the other tribunal members need to endorse such adjudication. Even then, the usual problem faced is one of time, availability and cost. Consequently, a tribunal may conclude that it requires an independent expert to provide the requisite advice on the particular technical or specific issue(s).

Under most, if not all, arbitration rules, a tribunal has the power to appoint an expert if it so decides. However, it is vital that the authority to appoint an expert is not construed as a licence to delegate the arbitrators' decision-making authority to the expert. This being said, it is also vital to note that a tribunal should only ever deviate from the expert's opinion if by applying its own reasoned judgment in respect of the relevant issue, it finds a more appropriate answer. In such a situation, the tribunal should provide its reasoning in the award. Of course, it should also be borne in mind that this may not necessarily be the most prudent thing to do in light of the lack of knowledge or

---

23. *Henry Boot Construction Ltd v. Alstom Combined Cycles Ltd.*, [1999] BLR 123. In this case, there were three rules for valuation of variations, namely:

   Rule 1: where work is of similar character and executed under similar conditions to work priced in the bill of quantities it shall be valued at the rates and prices contained therein;
   Rule 2: where work is not of a similar character or is not executed under similar conditions, the rates and prices in the bill of quantities shall be used as the basis for valuation so far as may be reasonable; and
   Rule 3: failing which a fair valuation shall be made.

understanding of the relevant complicated technical issues that would arise in such cases, which was the reason for appointing the expert in the first place.[24] Therefore, whenever this happens, the tribunal should inform the expert of its decision and seeks his or her comments to avoid a misunderstanding of the technical issues involved.

In international commercial arbitrations, for reasons of confidentiality that covers the majority of arbitral awards and procedural orders, it is difficult to determine how often, or even if, a tribunal has appointed its own expert and what issues have arisen as a result.

5. *Security for Costs*

It is appropriate to note that some arbitration rules expressly provide power for the tribunal to grant security for costs.[25] Some others do so through the provisions of the interim measures, and so, for example, the wording of Art. 23 of the 1998 ICC Rules of Arbitration is broad enough to encompass an application by a party for, and the issuing of, a decision by the arbitral tribunal on, security for costs.[26] An interim measure for security for costs demands its own mechanisms and requirements and it is of two types, the first is dealt with in Sect. IV.5.*a* and the second is dealt with in Sect. IV.5.*b* below:

a.   *An interim measure for security from a claimant sought by a respondent*
More often than not, owing to the intricacies of a construction arbitration and the considerable amount of money that inevitably is involved in disputes relating to it, an application for security for costs would ordinarily be made by a respondent where there was credible evidence to show that there was reason to believe that the claimant would be unable to pay the costs of the respondent if it was successful in defending the case. In such a case, the arbitral tribunal could require sufficient security to be given for those costs, including the arbitral tribunal's fees and any costs incidental thereto and further, could stay all proceedings until the security was provided. It is important to bear in mind that in all applications where a respondent seeks security for costs, the burden will always be on the respondent to prove the facts that it alleges in support of its application. One of the main things that a tribunal will have to consider is whether or not, in granting an order for security for costs, it would essentially be depriving the claimant of its right

---

24. Nael G. BUNNI, "Some Thoughts from Experiences in Construction Arbitrations" in *ICCA Congress Series no. 13*, pp. 789-794.
25. Art. 25 of the LCIA Rules, effective as of 1998, ICCA *Yearbook Commercial Arbitration* XXIII (1998) (hereinafter *Yearbook*) p. 369; Art . 37 of the Arbitration Rules of the Netherlands Arbitration Institute (NAI Rules), effective as of 1998, *Yearbook* XXIIII (1998) p. 394. Art. 46(b) of the Rules of the World Intellectual Property Organization (WIPO) provides as follows: "At the request of a party, the Tribunal may, if it considers it to be required by exceptional circumstances, order the other party to provide security in a form to be determined by the Tribunal, for the claim or counter-claim, as well as for costs referred to in Article 72."
26. Marc BLESSING, *The ICC Arbitral Procedure under the 1998 ICC Rules – What Has Changed?*, 8 ICC Bull. (1998, no. 2) p. 30. See also, Yves DERAINS and Eric A. SCHWARTZ, *A Guide to the New ICC Rules of Arbitration,* (Kluwer 1999) pp. 273-274; and W. Laurence CRAIG, William W. PARK and Jan PAULSSON, *Annotated Guide to the 1998 ICC Arbitration Rules,* (Oceana/ICC Books 1998) p. 138.

to take the case forward and proceed with the arbitration. It is worth mentioning in this connection that in *Parkinson & Co., v. Triplan Ltd.*,[27] a landmark decision on this type of security was handed down in the England and Wales Court of Appeal by the then Master of the Rolls, Lord Denning MR, which provided useful criteria for whether or not such an order should be made. The decision has provided the following criteria in construction cases:

(1) Is the claimant's claim bona fide and not a sham?
(2) Has the claimant a reasonably good prospect of success?
(3) Is there an admission by the respondent on the pleadings or elsewhere that liability of the respondent exists? This includes a payment into "court" of a substantial sum of money, which had not been merely to get rid of a nuisance claim?
(4) Was the application for security for costs being used oppressively so as to try to stifle a genuine claim?
(5) Has the claimant's poor financial circumstances been brought about by any conduct by the respondent, such as a delay in payment or a delay in doing its own part of the contractual arrangements? In construction arbitration, this question could extend to the General Conditions that are normally attached to the Contract Agreement.[28]

i. Assessment and equitable principles

However, it is clear from looking at these questions that there is no hard and fast rule to be applied in assessing the issue of whether or not to grant such applications for security for costs. The arbitrator must apply certain equitable principles, including looking at the facts of the case and deciding whether or not the interests of justice lie in favour of granting or denying the application. This is exactly what the court did, in the case of *Aquila Design (GRP Products) Ltd. v. Cornhill Insurance plc*,[29] when it declined to order security for costs. Whilst accepting that the plaintiff's claim was made *bona fide* and had an even chance of success, the court concluded nonetheless that, although if the defendant succeeded they would be out of pocket. To order security for costs would effectively prevent the plaintiffs from pursuing their claim. Similarly, in the case of *Peppard & Co Limited v. Bogoff*,[30] the court found that two special circumstances existed that warranted its refusal to grant an order for security for costs: "The financial position of the plaintiff may, if he substantiates his case, be due to the very actions of the defendants for which they are sued and there is a co-plaintiff within the jurisdiction to whom the defendants may look for payment of their costs." A similar finding was made in the Irish decision of *SEE Company Ltd v. Public Lighting Services Limited*.[31]

---

27. *Parkinson & Co., v. Triplan Ltd*, [1973] 1 QB 609.
28. *Parkinson & Co., v. Triplan Ltd.*, [1973] 1 QB609, at page 626.
29. *Aquila Design (GRP Products) Ltd. v. Cornhill Insurance plc*, [1988] BCLC 134.
30. *Peppard & Co Limited v. Bogoff*, [1962] IR 180.
31. *SEE Company Ltd v. Public Lighting Services Ltd*, [1987] ILRM 255.

ii. Examples in international construction

In the international construction scene there could be many reasons for an application for security for costs. In one particular case of note, the parties involved were of two different nationalities; and pursuant to an article similar to Art. 30 of the ICC Rules, an "advance on costs" was fixed by the relevant administering institution.[32] The respondent, despite having filed a counterclaim, refused to pay its share of the advance on costs. The claimant thus sought to have the advance on costs apportioned as between its claim on the one hand and the respondent's counterclaim on the other. The respondent, however, then withdrew its counterclaim and the claimant was left to pay the remaining amount outstanding in respect of the respondent's share of the advance on costs. Subsequently, the respondent made an application to the tribunal for security for costs and further, for a stay of the arbitral proceedings pending the provision of such security. The respondent's grounds for such an application were: firstly, enforcement of arbitral awards in the claimant's jurisdiction were particularly difficult and secondly, the claimant had little or no assets in that jurisdiction or any other jurisdiction that would meet any obligations under an arbitral award. The claimant responded to the application by pointing out that if an order for security was granted, it would be precluded from proceeding with its claim, particularly in light of the fact that the respondent had refused to pay the advance on costs. The claimant submitted that the respondent could not be allowed to claim against the impecuniosity of the claimant when, it was alleged, the respondent had caused the claimant's impecuniosity in the first place. Having considered the submissions of both parties in this regard, the tribunal rendered a decision in the following terms: First, the respondent had known that it was contracting with a company of the claimant's nationality at the formation of the contract and should have investigated and ascertained the position in relation to the enforcement of potential awards at the beginning of the contract, if it were so concerned. Secondly, the tribunal found that the fact the advance on costs was paid in full by the claimant was relevant since if it had not been able to do so it would not have been able to proceed with the claim. The tribunal held in this regard that the respondent could not derive any advantage from its own wrongdoing. Finally, the tribunal, having considered the injustice to the claimant if ordered to provide security for costs, against the injustice to the respondent if the claimant was not so ordered, found that the injustice to the claimant would be more serious. On this basis, the tribunal decided that it would not be equitable to order the sought security. In light of the facts of this case, and where arbitration rules similar to the ICC Rules apply, it is of particular interest to note the comments of Craig, Park and Paulsson in their book on the ICC Rules. They state as follows:

---

32. Art. 30(3) of the ICC Rules states that

> "The advance on costs fixed by the Court shall be payable in equal shares by the Claimant and the Respondent. Any provisional advance paid on the basis of Article 30(1) will be considered as a partial payment thereof. However, any party shall be free to pay the whole of the advance on costs in respect of the principle claim or the counterclaim should the other party fail to pay its shares. When the Court has set separate advances on costs in accordance with Article 30(2), each of the parties shall pay the advance on costs corresponding to its claims."

"One of the reasons for not specifying security for costs as an interim measure is that many considered it undesirable to call attention to its availability or to suggest that it was a normal interim measure. The remedy is considered by many to be inappropriate in most circumstances for ICC arbitration, where specific provisions are made for the funding of arbitration costs by advances to be made by the parties in equal shares. This expression of the contractual intent of the parties should be given effect and it may be said arguably to exclude additional measures to secure a party from the possibility that its adversary would not be able to pay a costs order made against it in a final award. In order for a claimant to pursue its claim in arbitration it will have already had to advance a substantial amount as fixed by the Secretariat or the ICC Court. It is not as if the claimant will not have been willing or required to make a substantial arbitration costs investment in the prosecution of its claim. The ICC practice of advances on costs offers a certain guarantee against abusive and extravagant claims...."[33]

iii.   Other examples

Another reason for an application for security for costs could be where funds recovered cannot be effectively transferred out of the jurisdiction due to exchange-control legislation. A further reason could be a devaluation of the currency of the country of residence of the party against whom costs might eventually be awarded. This latter aspect was considered in a procedural order in ICC Case No.10032, dated 9 November 1999. However, it was considered insufficient under the particular circumstances of the case. In this connection, a paper by Pierre A. Karrer and Marcus Desax, provided some guidelines.[34] The arbitral tribunal stated that the discretion to order security for costs should be exercised with "*considerable restraint*". The tribunal described the scope of its power as follows:

"Accordingly, the Arbitral Tribunal, in the light of the circumstances of the present case, holds that it would be appropriate for it to exercise its discretion to make an order for security for costs.
(i) if the Respondent, which has requested that such an order be addressed to the Claimants, can show:
(a) that the factual situation at the present time is substantially different from that which existed at the time the parties entered into their arbitration convention, and
(b) that the present situation is of such a nature as to render it highly unfair to require it to conduct the arbitration proceedings without the benefit of such security;

---

33. W. Laurence CRAIG, William W. PARK and Jan PAULSSON, *International Chamber of Commerce Arbitration*, 3rd edn. (Oceana 2000) pp. 468-469.
34. Pierre A. KARRER and Marcus DESAX, "Security for Costs in International Arbitration, Why, When, and What If..." in Robert BRINER, et al., eds., *Law of International Business and Dispute Settlement in the 21st Century, Liber Amicorum Böckstiegel* (Heymann 2001) pp. 339-353.

(ii) unless the Claimants, which oppose the making of an order for security for costs, can show:
(a) that the making of such order for security for costs would in effect deny their right of access to arbitration for reasons not attributable to them, and
(b) that, after having weighed the parties respective interests considering both the subject matter of the dispute and the circumstances giving rise to the request for an order for security for costs, the making of such order would appear to be highly unfair to Claimants."

*b.   Security for costs from a party seeking an interim measure*
Security may also be required at an interlocutory stage when a party seeks an interim measure. Such security might be requested from the party that is seeking the interim measure with the objective of providing an effective safeguard to the party against whom the measure is sought should it transpire that the interim measure was unjustified. In such a situation, if the security is not provided, more often than not, the interim measure would not be ordered. In Art. 17(E), the Model Law grants discretionary powers for the arbitral tribunal to request security as a condition for granting an interim measure.[35]

*6.   The Assessment of a Request for an Interim Measure*

The interim measures set out in Sects. IV.*1* to IV.*4* above come within the list of the four categories of generic scenarios contained in the new Art. 17(2) of the Model Law and thus provide the basis for rendering the measures described.[36] Art. 17(2) of the Model Law prescribes the form in which the measure is to be rendered and continues to

---

35. "*Art. 17 Sexies. Provision of security*
    (1) The arbitral tribunal may require the party requesting an interim measure to provide appropriate security in connection with the measure.
    (2) The arbitral tribunal shall require the party applying for a preliminary order to provide security in connection with the order unless the arbitral tribunal considers it inappropriate or unnecessary to do so."

36. The assessment guidelines to grant an interim measure are described in Art. 17(A) of the Model Law:

    "*Article 17 Bis. Conditions for granting interim measures*
    (1) The party requesting an interim measure under article 17(2)(a), (b) and (c) shall satisfy the arbitral tribunal that:
    (a) Harm not adequately reparable by an award of damages is likely to result if the measure is not ordered, and such harm substantially outweighs the harm that is likely to result to the party against whom the measure is directed if the measure is granted; and
    (b) There is a reasonable possibility that the requesting party will succeed on the merits of the claim, provided that any determination on this possibility shall not affect the discretion of the arbitral tribunal in making any subsequent determination.
    (2) With regard to a request for an interim measure under article 17(2)(d), the requirements in paragraphs (1)(a) and (b) of this article shall apply only to the extent the arbitral tribunal considers appropriate."

describe the four categories of an interim measure.[37] The assessment of security for costs is more difficult as it has to take into account many other factors, as described in Sect. IV.5 above.

It can therefore be concluded that Sub-sects. 1 to 4 of the proposed provisions of Art. 26 of the UNCITRAL Arbitration Rules are necessary and compatible with the Model Law.

However, whilst I agree with Mr. Graham that Sub-sect. 5 is compatible with the new provisions of Art. 17 of the UNCITRAL Model Law on Arbitration, I beg to differ with him on its suitability for inclusion in the UNCITRAL Arbitration Rules. I do suggest here that it would not be advisable for a set of Rules, that is intended for universal adoption and use, to include such a controversial provision as the ex parte provision. I say this for the following three reasons:

– For jurisdictions that have not adopted the UNCITRAL Model Law on Arbitration or for those that have, but without the ex parte provision (such as Austria), a rule as controversial as this, would most likely exclude the rules from being used intact in that jurisdiction.[38]
– The number of objections to the ex parte provision as a matter of principle has far greater weight than the advantages it might provide. This is particularly important in view of the fact that statistically the number of interim measures sought is low and only a small percentage of them would benefit from such a provision. The disadvantages might be disastrous for arbitration.
– In a complex arbitration, such as in construction, it would be extremely difficult for a party requesting an order to properly include the counter argument in the necessary completeness required, as discussed in the last paragraph of Sect. III above.

Whilst there are some who support the idea of an arbitral tribunal having the power to grant ex parte interim measures, there is a significant number who remain in

---

37. Art. 17(2) of the Model Law:

"An interim measure is any temporary measure, whether in the form of an award or in another form, by which, at any time prior to the issuance of the award by which the dispute is finally decided, the arbitral tribunal orders a party to:
(a) Maintain or restore the status quo pending determination of the dispute;
(b) Take action that would prevent, or refrain from taking action that is likely to cause, current or imminent harm or prejudice to the arbitral process itself;
(c) Provide a means of preserving assets out of which a subsequent award may be satisfied; or
(d) Preserve evidence that may be relevant and material to the resolution of the dispute."

38. In the amendment to its Civil Procedural Rules on Arbitration, Austria has adopted some of the provisions contained in the 2006 UNCITRAL Model Law relating to interim measures. However, as can be seen from Sect. 593, this was done without conferring on arbitral tribunals the authority to issue ex parte preliminary orders. See also Hansjörg STUTZER, "Interim Measures in Arbitration – An Update", Arbitration Newsetter Switzerland (27 October 2006).

opposition to the whole idea. In a lucid and well argued paper Professor van Houtte[39] summarized the conditions that must apply before an arbitrator could issue such an interim measure. Due to their relevance to the assessment of ex parte measures, these conditions are quoted below.

> "(a) there should be an urgent need for the measure;
> (b) the irreparable harm that would result from not ordering the measure should outweigh the harm that would result to the other party if the measure were ordered;
> (c) there should be a substantial likelihood that the requesting party would succeed on the merits of the dispute;
> (d) the arbitral tribunal should be convinced that the interim measure would only be effective if taken ex parte;
> (e) the ex parte measure should only be effective for no more than 20 days unless the other party would be heard;
> (f) the requesting party should have to inform the arbitral tribunal of all relevant material and circumstances in order to allow it to assess whether the conditions have been met and remain fulfilled;
> (g) an appropriate security may be requested, if the tribunal deems this proper."

Professor van Houtte went on to set down ten reasons why ex parte measures should not be awarded in arbitration. In this connection, but with respect to the UNCITRAL Arbitration Rules, the most important of these reasons could be summarized as follows:

– Interim measures are incompatible with the consensual nature of arbitration;
– Interim measures are incompatible with the principle of *"the right to be heard"*;
– The granting of an interim measure may lead to prejudiced arbitrators;
– Interim measures may create a conflict of interest of some sort with a party-appointed arbitrator;
– Certain types of interim measures that may be granted by a tribunal are irreversible;
– There is a difficulty in upholding and implementing the "full and frank" disclosure requirements; and
– The granting of an interim measure incorrectly could expose the tribunal to certain liabilities.

There are a number of additional reasons against the concept of ex parte interim measures:

– By virtue of the urgency that normally lies behind the application, it would require a tribunal to be available on very short notice to decide the application. At the best of times this would be extremely difficult;

---

39. Professor Dr. Hans VAN HOUTTE, "Ten Reasons Against a Proposal for Ex Parte Interim Measures of Protection in Arbitration", 20 Arbitration International (Kluwer Law International 2004, no. 1), pp. 85-95.

– Ex parte applications should only be granted where notice of the application would bring about the harm, which is sought to be prevented. Otherwise, there is no justification for what amounts to an intrusion into the right to a fair hearing; and
– A court is generally in a better position to control such an application, ensure that proper safeguards are in place, enforce non-compliance and sanction abuse as well as afford a party, against whom an ex parte order has been granted, speedy redress. A tribunal, however, might have difficulty with such control.

For the above reasons, it is my view that the power to order ex parte interim measures of protection should be reserved for the courts alone. I am also of the opinion that to implement such a provision would be in direct contravention of Art. 18 of the Model Law of Arbitration, which states that "The parties shall be treated with equality and each party shall be given a full opportunity to present his case."

V. CONCLUDING REMARKS

In conclusion, I provide some points to note:

– Whilst an arbitral tribunal is in a position to grant interim measures and, if the need arises, to be able to issue preliminary orders on an ex parte basis, such measures and orders do add an additional layer of complexity and uncertainty to the arbitral process.
– The work that has been carried out by the UNCITRAL Working Group in respect of Art. 17 of the Model Law is really very impressive. My concern is that with the proposed inclusion of ex parte provisions in the amendments to Art. 26 of the UNCITRAL Arbitration Rules, are we going a step too far? Is such a provision too much of a dramatic change that might necessarily prevent some States from adopting and implementing such rules, even if they had adopted the new provisions of the Model Law?

The proposed amendments to Art. 26 of the UNCITRAL Arbitration Rules are necessary to harmonize the varying approaches under different jurisdictions, but particular care must be exercised to ensure reality and practicality in procedures, particularly in the field of construction arbitration.

# Provisional Measures

*Yang Ing Loong*[*]

| TABLE OF CONTENTS | Page |
|---|---|
| I. Revision to Art. 26 of the UNCITRAL Arbitration Rules | 606 |
| II. Impact of the Proposed Revisions to the UNCITRAL Arbitration Rules | 607 |
| III. Best Practices for Arbitrators Considering Applications for Provisional Measures | 608 |
| IV. A Survey of Two Asian Jurisdictions in Relation to Interim Measures | 609 |

I.   REVISION TO ART. 26 OF THE UNCITRAL ARBITRATION RULES

Art. 26 of the UNCITRAL Arbitration Rules (the Rules) specifically empowers a tribunal operating under the Rules to "take any interim measures it deems necessary in respect of the subject-matter of the dispute".

Art. 26 reads as follows:

> "1. At the request of either party, the arbitral tribunal may take any interim measures it deems necessary in respect of the subject-matter of the dispute, including measures for the conservation of the goods forming the subject-matter in dispute, such as ordering their deposit with a third person or the sale of perishable goods.
> 2. Such interim measures may be established in the form of an interim award. The arbitral tribunal shall be entitled to require security for the costs of such measures.
> 3. A request for interim measures addressed by any party to a judicial authority shall not be deemed incompatible with the agreement to arbitrate, or as a waiver of that agreement."

The latest draft (as of June 2008) for an amendment to Art. 26 (CN.9/WG.II/WP.149) was tabled at the session of the Working Group II on Arbitration (the Working Group) at its 4-5 February 2008 meeting. The proposed amended Art. 26 is substantially longer than the current Art. 26 and is closely modeled on the provisions on interim measures contained in Chapter IVA, Art. 17 of the UNCITRAL Model Law on International Commercial Arbitration, which was adopted by the Commission in 2006.[1]

The difference between the Model Law and the Rules is, of course, that the former, once enacted, becomes the law of the State whereas the latter is basically a set of rules that parties may wish to adopt for their arbitrations. Thus, views have been expressed

---

[*] Partner, Sidley Austin LLP, Singapore.
[1] The latest proposed draft of Art. 26 (as of this writing) can be found in Nael G. BUNNI, "Interim Measures in International Commercial Arbitration: A Commentary on the Report by Luis Enrique Graham", this volume, pp. 583-605 at pp. 586-587.

to the effect that the Rules should not slavishly mirror the Model Law. However, there is much to be said for uniformity between the Rules and the Model Law if the objective is to ensure the universal application of the Rules, especially in the context of ad hoc arbitrations.

II.  IMPACT OF THE PROPOSED REVISIONS TO THE UNCITRAL ARBITRATION RULES

First, the proposed Rules introduce a more clearly defined scope of what constitutes "interim measures" and removes the reference to "subject-matter of the dispute". This is a laudable move as it removes the limitation that the measure has to be referable to the subject-matter of the dispute which, it is submitted, is too narrow.

The proposed Rule also introduces a clear threshold for granting an interim measure. First, it is premised on damages not being an adequate remedy. Second, it requires the applying party to demonstrate at least a prima facie prospect of success on the merits. When a party applies for the preservation of evidence (under the draft Art. 26(d)), the tribunal has the discretion as to whether the applicant has to satisfy the aforesaid two requirements.

Third, while the proposed Rule requires the applying party to notify the tribunal of a material change of circumstances (thus imposing, by implication, a continuing obligation to make full and frank disclosure), one questions whether the Rule should clearly spell out the obligation on the applying party to make full and frank disclosure at the time of making the application (a yardstick used at common law). The writer's concern is that if such an obligation is not expressly stated, the right to apply for an interim measure might be subject to abuse. On the other hand, there is no harm in making it clear that the applying party should fully and frankly disclose to the tribunal all relevant and material facts in support of its application (which it ought to do in any event), as this will be in accordance with the standards of justice and integrity that are expected in international arbitrations.

An important innovation of the proposed Rule is that it allows for an ex parte application for interim relief. This is, understandably, a fiercely debated issue and has not been finally settled. Proponents of this innovation say, inter alia, that the element of surprise is sometimes necessary and justified in order to ensure that the respondent does not take steps to frustrate the object of the arbitration. They also argue that if proper safeguards are in place, there is no conceivable reason why an arbitral tribunal should not be able to grant ex parte interim relief. The proposed Rule seeks to address some of these safeguards by requiring, for instance, the tribunal to afford the party against whom an order is made the right to be heard at the earliest practicable opportunity. The proposed Rule also empowers the tribunal to impose security on the applying party and the discretion to discharge the order, either upon application by the adversely affected party or on its own initiative.

The opponents of this innovation argue that granting the right to make an ex parte application is not consistent with the consensual nature of arbitration. They also raise the argument that it deprives the parties equal access to the tribunal – a bedrock of the consensual nature of international arbitrations.

The verdict is still out on which camp will prevail, but clearly there are many who see the need to have such an innovation in place in order to make international arbitration an even greater success than it already is at the moment. It is submitted that should this proposal be adopted, it will whittle down even further the limited role that the courts already have in international arbitrations (at least in Model Law countries) and that would surely be a welcome move to the great majority of arbitration users and practitioners.

However, the all-important question that remains unanswered is – even if all are agreed that ex parte orders should be part and parcel of international arbitration, are such orders enforceable in court? It is submitted that enforceability should logically follow the adoption of the ex parte principle, otherwise the object of having such a principle under the Rules would be rendered meaningless and nugatory.

III. BEST PRACTICES FOR ARBITRATORS CONSIDERING APPLICATIONS FOR PROVISIONAL MEASURES

In the writer's opinion, the ultimate objective of the Working Group in coming up with the draft is to reflect best practices, which revolves round the concept of ensuring that the tribunal's discretion is exercised fairly and with a view to safeguarding the arbitral process.

How should the tribunal deal with ex parte applications? In line with the principle in international arbitrations of equal access to the tribunal, a tribunal should exercise great care in the event of an ex parte application made to him. On the one hand, the tribunal has to ensure that such an application is not an abuse of the arbitral process to gain an unfair advantage over the adversary. On the other hand, the tribunal has to be vigilant not to let the object of the arbitration be frustrated by the other party taking steps to evade its obligations by, for example, dissipating assets or destroying evidence.

The tribunal has to "balance the degree of harm suffered by the applicant if the interim measure was not granted against the degree of harm suffered by the party opposing the measure if that measure was granted".[2]

Until there is a consensus on the amended Rules, the status quo is that the tribunal should give the party against whom an order for provisional measure is sought an opportunity to be heard and fully present its response to the application. The tribunal ought also to ensure that the party making the application has made full and frank disclosure and provide an undertaking as to costs and damages.

It is instructive to consider the approach of the Iran-US Claims Tribunal, which has been instrumental in interpreting and applying the Rules including the provision granting the tribunal authority to take interim measures.

In considering requests for interim measures, the Iran-US Claims Tribunal laid down the following requirements:

---

2. "Settlement of Commercial Disputes – Preparation of uniform provisions on interim measures of protection, Note by the Secretariat", UNCITRAL Working Group II (Arbitration) 43rd Sess. (Vienna, 3-7 October 2005) UN Doc. A/CN.9/WG.II/WP.138, para. 16, available at: <http://www.uncitral.org/uncitral/en/ecommission/working_groups/2Arbitration.html>.

(a) the Tribunal will consider whether it has prima facie jurisdiction to support an order for interim measures;
(b) interim measures will be ordered when "necessary", which encapsulates "the notions that the party requesting the measure is facing harm to rights it is pursuing in the arbitration and that the harm is so imminent that it cannot await the tribunal's final decisions on the merits";
(c) the Tribunal may also consider the impact of interim measures of protection on the final award. Thus, such measures will be withheld in the event that they would render the claim moot or otherwise prejudge the claim.

## IV. A SURVEY OF TWO ASIAN JURISDICTIONS IN RELATION TO INTERIM MEASURES

It is instructive to compare and contrast two different Asian jurisdictions to see the approach and attitude each has towards court support of interim measures in arbitrations.

### 1. Singapore

The Singapore legal regime is supportive of arbitration, including the aspect of interim measures. Recent court decisions in Singapore reiterate the principle that once the parties have agreed to arbitration as a means of dispute resolution, their first port of call — in terms of seeking interim relief — should be the arbitral tribunal, not the courts.

In the Singapore Court of Appeal decision in *NCC International AB v. Alliance Concrete Singapore Pte Ltd* [2008] SGCA 5, the court made it clear that its powers to make interim orders should only be used in support of arbitration. From a practitioner's point of view, this means that the court will consider that its processes are not to be used to bypass the arbitral tribunal or abused to gain a procedural advantage.[3]

The court explained that the primary source for interim relief should be the arbitral tribunal. Accordingly, help from the courts should only be sought when "arbitration is inappropriate, ineffective, or incapable of securing the particular form of relief sought". Such situations include the following:

(a) where third parties over whom the arbitral tribunal has no jurisdiction are involved;
(b) where matters are very urgent; or
(c) where the court's coercive powers of enforcement are required.

A common example of a situation where all three factors are likely to be involved will be the grant of an injunction to freeze the respondent's assets.

There are two other interesting decisions in Singapore that touch on the court's powers to grant interim relief in support of foreign arbitrations (i.e., arbitrations not seated in Singapore).

---

3. "... under the IAA regime, although the court has concurrent jurisdiction with the arbitral tribunal to order interim measures, the court will nevertheless scrupulously avoid usurping the functions of the arbitral tribunal in exercising such jurisdiction and will only order interim relief where this will aid, promote and support arbitration proceedings": per V.K. RAJAH, J.A.

In *Swift-Fortune Ltd v. Magnifica Marine SA* [2007] 1 SLR 629; [2006] SGCA 42, the High Court held that Sect. 12(7) of the International Arbitration Act was intended to only apply to arbitrations where Singapore was stipulated as the seat of the arbitration and did not apply to arbitrations which had arisen out of an international arbitration agreement but which did not stipulate Singapore as the seat of the arbitration.

On appeal, the Singapore Court of Appeal upheld the decision of the High Court.

Shortly after the *Swift-Fortune* decision, a different High Court Judge in *Front Carriers Ltd v. Atlantic & Orient Shipping Corp* [2006] 3 SLR 854 held that the court did have jurisdiction to assist a foreign arbitration.

The Singapore Court of Appeal, in hearing the *Swift-Fortune* appeal, made it clear that it was not deciding on the merits of the decision in the *Front Carriers* case and left open the question whether the plaintiffs in *Front Carriers* could succeed under Sect. 4(10) of the Civil Law Act, if two preconditions were satisfied:

(a) the plaintiff has a recognizable cause of action under Singapore law; and
(b) the court has personal jurisdiction over the defendant.

In summary, therefore, it would appear that a party to an arbitration should, as a general rule, apply to the arbitral tribunal for interim measures unless it is a situation falling within the exceptions laid down by the Court of Appeal in *NCC International*. That decision of the Court of Appeal can only serve to promote international arbitration in Singapore.

2. *People's Republic of China (PRC)*

In contrast with the position under the UNCITRAL Model Law, China's arbitral institutions have no power to order interim measures which are exclusively within the purview of the Chinese courts. Moreover, there are only two categories of interim measures expressly enumerated, namely, protection of evidence or preservation of property which can be sought by the parties. These two significant features form the overall uniqueness of interim measures in the Chinese arbitral system which is different from the Model Law or any other major non-Chinese institutional rules.

As to preservation of property in foreign-related arbitration, Art. 256 of the PRC Civil Procedural Law states:

> "If a party has applied for taking measures of protection, the foreign-related arbitration institution of the People's Republic of China shall submit the party's application for a decision thereupon to the intermediate people's court in the place where the party to whom the measures of protection are directed has his domicile or where his property is located."

As to preservation of evidence in foreign-related arbitration, Art. 68 of the PRC Arbitration Law provides:

> "If a party to a foreign-related arbitration applies for taking interim measures of protection of evidence, the foreign-related arbitration commission shall submit his

application to the intermediate People's Court in the place where the evidence is located."

These provisions indicate expressly that the competent courts to issue interim measures to applications forwarded by arbitral institutions are the Chinese Intermediate Courts.

The arbitration rules of the PRC's most well-known arbitral institution, China International Economic and Trade Arbitration Commission (CIETAC), do not confer on the arbitral tribunal the power to grant interim measures. There are two articles in the CIETAC Rules that are relevant to the issue of interim measures: Arts. 17 (Preservation of Property) and 18 (Protection of Evidence).

Art. 17 of the CIETAC Rules provides:

"When any party applies for the preservation of property, the CIETAC shall forward the party's application for a ruling to the competent court at the place where the domicile of the party against whom the preservation of property is sought is located or where the property of the said party is located."

Art. 18 of the CIETAC Rules provides:

"When a party applies for the protection of evidence, the CIETAC shall forward the party's application for a ruling to the competent court at the place where the evidence is located."

The CIETAC Rules are silent on other provisional measures, such as "orders preserving the *status quo*" and "temporary prohibiting orders". However, following the same logic as with the preservation of property and evidence protection, the answer to whether the arbitrator has the power to issue provisional measures is still likely to be no.[4]

This begs the question whether a party can simply go directly to the court to obtain interim relief. The position appears to be that a party could not apply for an interim injunction before a suit is filed in court.[5] The party seeking to apply is therefore caught in a "Catch 22" scenario. In order to get interim relief, he needs to go to court. However, he cannot go to the court directly because he has an arbitration agreement with the counterparty and any legal action that he commences in court will be stayed in favor of arbitration, so he needs to commence arbitration and apply for interim relief through the arbitral commission. However, even if the requesting party could go to court, PRC law relating to injunctions and other preliminary relief is unclear. The real difficulty that a party seeking provisional relief in China would face is that as a matter of

---

4. The arbitration rules of the Beijing Arbitration Commission (BAC) are similar: see Art. 54 of the BAC Rules.
5. In a Judicial Interpretation entitled "Opinion on several Questions concerning Application of the Civil Procedure Law" dated July 1992, the Supreme People's Court appears to have held that non-preservation injunctive relief is not available prior to filing suit. However, Art. 93 of the Civil Procedure Law allows a party to apply for property preservation orders before commencement of the court action, provided that he brings a lawsuit within thirty days (see Art. 250 of the Civil Procedure Law).

practice, Chinese courts typically will not grant provisional injunctive relief even in respect of domestic court proceedings (other than IP infringement cases).

The current position in the PRC, therefore, is that a party who wishes to apply for interim relief should, in the first instance, apply to the arbitral commission and let the arbitral commission refer the matter to the competent court for a ruling. The caveat here is that the powers of the PRC courts to grant interim measures are relatively weak and this, coupled with the protectionist proclivities of the courts and the weak enforcement regime, makes it a real challenge for a party in a PRC arbitration to effectively protect its rights prior to the rendering of the award.

Practically speaking, this very restricted regime for application of interim measures in the PRC gives impetus to contracting parties in foreign-related contracts[6] to press for arbitration outside of the PRC, as that will give the parties an opportunity to apply for interim measures to the arbitral tribunal. There still remains a stumbling block: if the arbitral tribunal orders the preservation of property in China, or protection of evidence in China, ultimately the body with the teeth to enforce such orders is the Chinese courts and one encounters all the problems associated with enforcement in China.

It is probably unrealistic to expect the PRC Arbitration Law to be amended any time soon to allow interim measures to be ordered by arbitral tribunals. Chinese judges will probably be reluctant to embrace the concept that an interim or procedural order made by an arbitral commission or an arbitral tribunal could be of equal force as one issued by a court, as the autonomy of the arbitration procedure is compromised in various ways by the residual powers of the Chinese courts to interfere in the arbitration process.

Perhaps one radical alternative (albeit more realistic) approach is to abandon the "postman" role of the arbitration institutions and have the application for interim measures directly submitted to the competent Chinese courts. Although this will reduce even further the role of the arbitral institutions or tribunals in this area, it would at least address the problem of unnecessary delays that can be caused by transmission of the application through the arbitration institutions. Such delays can substantially affect the efficacy of the arbitral process.

---

6. I refer to foreign-related contracts here, because if a contract is made between two purely domestic PRC entities (and this includes foreign-invested enterprises set up in China), arguably the parties can only designate CIETAC or a local arbitration commission to arbitrate their disputes.

# Working Group B

## 5. The UNCITRAL Rules Revision: An Assessment

# Round Table on the Assessment of the Revision of the UNCITRAL Rules on International Commercial Arbitration

*David D. Caron, Moderator**

| TABLE OF CONTENTS | Page |
| --- | --- |
| I. Introduction | 615 |
| II. Understanding and Critiquing the Revision Process | 616 |
| III. Implications of Revision for the Use of the UNICTRAL Rules in Treaty Settings | 625 |
| IV. Making the Administration of an Ad Hoc Arbitration Run Smoother | 626 |

I. INTRODUCTION

*David D. Caron*: "This discussion concerns an assessment of the ongoing revision of the United Nations Commission on International Trade Law (UNCITRAL) Rules. Let me set a few ground rules and describe what we are going to do. We have three main topics to discuss. At the end of each topic, we will take two questions.

Our topic is change: the change of the UNCITRAL Rules adopted by the UNCITRAL in 1976 and recommended for use by the General Assembly also in 1976. Those rules have grown in use and significance, as we know, in part because they were used by the Iran-U.S. Claims Tribunal and the procedural orders of that body are in the public domain. Similarly, as we know, the Rules are widely named in bilateral investment treaties (BITs) and the North American Free Trade Agreement (NAFTA) as an option for the investor to choose, and they are also used in NAFTA. Thus, we have had public sources available to find out how the Rules have been employed.

Although we are talking about change we have to realize the Rules have been changing already over these years. We know they have been adopted by a variety of arbitral centers. The Hong Kong International Arbitration Centre, for example, uses the UNCITRAL Rules, adjusting them slightly to the Centre. Similarly, when the UNCITRAL Model Law came along, buried in it are essentially the UNCITRAL Rules but updated by our experience with the Rules. And finally and more recently, the Swiss

---

\* University of California at Berkeley.
The Participants in this Round Table are:

James E. Castello, Partner, King & Spalding;
Georgios Petrochilos, Partner, Freshfields Bruckhaus Deringer;
Michael E. Schneider, Partner, Lalive & Partners; Chair of UNCITRAL Working Group II on International Arbitration and Conciliation.
Josefa Sicard-Mirabal, International Court of Arbitration;
William K. Slate, President, American Arbitration Association and International Center for Dispute Resolution;
Christopher To, Secretary-General, Hong Kong International Arbitration Centre.

Rules of International Arbitration from 2006 were based on the UNCITRAL Rules but depart rather dramatically with the changes and additions reflecting modern practice. This first revision of the Rules by UNCITRAL is often traced to a long time-member and founder of the International Council for Commercial Arbitration (ICCA), Pieter Sanders, who in 2004 suggested such an effort in an article.[1] In 2006, Georgios Petrochilos did an unofficial report for UNCITRAL on that possible revision. That sequence brings us to the present revision effort nearing completion.

To discuss this change we have six persons actively involved with the revision process with us today. As a disclaimer for the group, their comments are made in their individual capacities and not as representatives of any organization."

II. UNDERSTANDING AND CRITIQUING THE REVISION PROCESS

*David D. Caron*: "Our first of three topics is 'understanding and critiquing the revision process'. What is this process? How is the product being made? Let us look at how, as we say, the sausage is made. My first question goes to Michael Schneider of Lalive & Partners in Geneva. He has chaired the Working Group on International Arbitration and Conciliation since its September 2006 session, but he is speaking in his own capacity today. Michael, there have been four sessions so far. Please, describe the process. Is it a governmental, diplomatic, or a technical process? How is this done?"

*Michael E. Schneider*: "First, I should describe the composition of the group. You have in the Working Group a mirror of the Commission itself – the sixty members. You have sixty member governments, observer governments, NGOs, IGOs: a wide range of participants. Among the governments some just send a member of the local missions in New York or Vienna, but many governments take this process very seriously and send excellent specialists. Those specialists are sometimes from the ministries, but often are from the academic or practical community. Thus, you have a very experienced group. One very interesting and perhaps unusual feature of the work in UNCITRAL in general and of this group in particular, is the de facto equality to speak. Anybody who has something to say, be it an arbitration association or the most important government, is given an opportunity to speak. This makes for a very knowledgeable discussion and a discussion which brings out very lively debate.

You have, to some extent, different sensitivities. Sometimes there may be a feeling that some governments are a bit more reserved, but that is very rare. Basically, there is a spirit of working together. There is perhaps one exception. In some other working groups of UNCITRAL I heard that sometimes delegations may seek to achieve a specific objective, may have an 'agenda'. In our Working Group I have not noticed such an 'agenda' by delegations; so everybody is there to make the process work and have a satisfactory product.

---

1. Pieter SANDERS, "Has the Moment Come to Revise the Arbitration Rules of UNCITRAL?", 20 Arb Int'l (2004) p. 243.

As to the evolution of the work, you have heard at the start that the Commission had discussed the possibility of revision for some time already and that the impetus came from Pieter Sanders and Georgios Petrochilos.

Then, we had four sessions, starting not with the Rules but with the identification of areas that would be useful to look at. That was in one session in September 2006 in Vienna. The Secretariat had prepared a document, which is still useful to read, influenced by the Petrochilos Report which then was the basis on which the Working Group identified subjects we would look into further. Next, we had a first draft prepared by the Secretariat and then we started looking into the second draft which is what we have now.

A few words on the process. The discussions start in the Assembly among all the distinguished delegates. This is at a first level, just opinions. Then, a very important part of the process is the consultation breaks, networking, building up of an opinion in a way that is more productive than a discussion in a large group. Out of these discussions, some points for the Secretariat to work on are raised. I mentioned the drafts already. I should mention here that the Secretariat has done an exceptionally good job in preparing the work and summarizing the outcome at the end of the discussion.

And then there is consultation outside of the Working Group with the arbitration community in a number of conferences. Today's conference is one of the particular important ones to get feedback from the arbitration community.

A few words on the principles of the revision. The basic rule is that the revision of the UNCITRAL Rules should not alter the structure of the text, its spirit, or its drafting style and should reflect the flexibility of the text rather than making it more complex. This is something that we repeat every time and it is really respected, with all participants making a great effort at keeping the Rules as they are. The relation to the Model Law is something that is on our mind because the Rules must work in the context of the Model Law. But there is no rule of necessary identity because we want to assure that the Rules also work in non-Model Law countries. There are a number of provisions where the Rules differ from the Model Law, such as the writing requirement. The Model Law preserves the writing requirement. In the Working Group, we've decided not to keep this requirement because some countries do not require that the arbitration agreement be in writing. We felt it was necessary that we ensure that the Rules also work in those countries. That shows you the interface with the Model Law.

There is another very important principle in the work. That is, we have looked at the use of the Rules and came to the conclusion, supported by the Commission itself, that it is important to keep the generic nature of the Rules. These are commercial Rules that are intended to apply to all kinds of disputes and we have tried to resist the attempt to have them tailor-made for specific purposes. What is also important is that we do not build in mechanics that make them difficult to use in certain situations. For instance, thinking of the treaty context we took out 'contract' and changed it to 'relationship' with this purpose in mind. Another principle is that we don't want to degrade the present version of the Rules.

Finally, some words about the difficulties. You can imagine that with a group of such size and diversity it is not very easy to run the process, in particular since there are five languages often in translations. Many delegations speak in English but there are some that require translations. Another difficulty is that there are so many learned people with so many different views on the subject. There are no votes in the Working Group: you have to get to consensus. An example, is that the Model Law and the present rules speak of the place of arbitration. One very learned member of a distinguished delegation said 'place' is not the right word; we should use seat. You can image that in this group if someone brings up the difference between 'seat' and 'place', we spent a very long time on terminology. We have not reached consensus yet whether to use 'seat' or 'place'. That is the downside of having so many learned people in the group.

I want to close by saying one important thing. There are many revolutionary, intelligent ideas. We have to be modest, however, and make sure that we have an instrument that works. The final product might not be the cutting edge, but our objective is for it to work and to work without an institution."

*David D. Caron*: "Thank you, Michael. A follow up point – you mentioned that the governments speak but when you go down the list of people involved, you see people with institutions such as the International Chamber of Commerce (ICC). What does it mean to say the governments speak?"

*Michael E. Schneider*: "There are some issues where members, the government representatives consult with their governments. It is perhaps less frequent than in other working groups, but as I said, governments in a number of cases pick arbitration specialists and sometimes they are civil servants with no specific arbitration expertise or relationship. You have the full range, and sometimes you get the delegation that has no idea about arbitration. The majority of the governments, however, I would say, pick people that are familiar with arbitration."

*David D. Caron*: "Thank you. Let me now turn to Josefa Sicard-Mirabal from the ICC. Josefa, the ICC is in the beginning stage of revision of its rules. As you hear the description of the UNCITRAL process, how do you react? How do you think about what the ICC would do? Is it a different process?"

*Josefa Sicard-Mirabal*: "It is not very dissimilar but there are some differences. The ICC Commission, which is the legislative arm of the ICC, is the one that starts the process. I will compare it to what we are doing now.

The process has started. The recommendation to revise the ICC Rules was sent out to the national committees. The ICC Commission has, up to date, ninety different member countries, which is similar to sixty members of governments, as referred to by Michael. The national committees are from different regions of the world. Member countries are represented by renowned arbitrators of each country.

The ICC Commission sent out to the national committees a request to consider whether it is useful or necessary to revise the Rules. It is also asking the community to refer to which parts it thinks should be amended and provide a draft language. All of that is being done right now and all of the national committees have until 30 June to provide such draft language.

Thereafter, the ICC also has conferences, which you also mentioned [Michael], to engage in a discussion and receive suggestions. All of those comments are noted and recorded. Thereafter, we encourage the national committees to seek business community feedback. Thus, we get comments from the national committees, the conferences, the business community and we also seek comments from the ICC Court of Arbitration as well as its Secretariat.

The ICC Commission will then establish a task force, which will be composed of different members of the different national committees. They will review all comments and may provide their own suggestions. A report is prepared and presented to the ICC Commission at large, where we may have more than ninety countries represented. Then it is discussed. Bear in mind that the ninety different countries represented means many different languages as well as all the different legal systems represented.

Finally, the ICC Commission presents a final report, which will then be taken by consensus in the ICC Commission as a whole and presented for final approval to the governing body of the ICC. Thus, the process is similar and different."

*David D. Caron*: "Thank you. Now, let's go to William Slate. Bill, you are the President of both the American Arbitration Association (AAA) and the International Centre for Dispute Resolution (ICDR) and an observer in this revision process. How do the observers get their views heard? Does it seem effective? What is the interaction between the institutions and the UNCITRAL process?"

*William Slate*: "It is a privilege to be a part of the Working Group process. The input that comes into the process from institutions and individuals comes into different ways and I'd like to supplement some of Michael's comments in that regard. The process in the UNCITRAL is an interactive process where a given subject is discussed over several sessions. Michael told us what happened in those sessions. What is also interesting is that between those sessions the delegates are talking about what's going on, giving speeches, meeting with bar groups and other institutions and having a discussion about the work in progress. This makes for a very rich ultimate contribution when the Working Group meets and, as it was suggested, the input was incredibly diverse. The governments sometimes provide a governmental and political input. In addition, we have academics, institutions and NGOs. The newest NGO group is a group of corporate counsel, a major user. Additionally, and a more direct response to your question, with respect to our own delegation to UNCITRAL, we have a practice of rotating the membership of the delegation on a regular basis, looking particularly to geography and subject matter expertise, recently involving a delegation from Great Britain, Canada, Switzerland and the United States. In the future, there will be individuals from other countries as well. Thus, there is both a cultural and legal perspective that enables the process to be quite right.

With regard to whether we feel that we are able to make a contribution there – I think that the answer is unequivocally, yes. Again, as Michael said, everyone there has an opportunity for equal voice and I think, it is fair to say that we feel we made some valuable contribution to a quite contentious issue that went on at some length having to do with Art. 17 of the UNCITRAL Model Law. We felt like we were able to make a contribution of some value to that issue."

*David D. Caron*: "Thank you, Bill. Let me turn to Christopher To. Chris, you are the Secretary-General of the Hong Kong International Arbitration Centre. That Centre uses the UNCITRAL Rules with some adjustment to adapt them to the Centre. First, are you involved in this process? Are you waiting for these Rules to arrive? Are you going to substitute them? How do you think the various centers will deal with this?"

*Christopher To*: "Thank you, David. Our Centre has been using these Rules for more than twenty-four years. We actually recommend them. And as Michael mentioned, they are very generic. You can't cater for every single country around the world. I think, you have to be more generic. You have to look at different issues. Different countries have to adopt those Rules and modify them to suit their own region.

In terms of how we are consulted, we did write to UNCITRAL asking whether we can get involved. UNCITRAL wrote a very nice letter back to us and said there are too many bodies involved. We suggested to send one representative of the twenty-four arbitration bodies in Asia. They very positively agreed. If you look at the website, there are two reports with a lot of Asian input. It does not mean that every center around the world has to sit in the UNCITRAL process, but at least, if we all work together and have a unified proposal, UNCITRAL can hear the voice of Asia. In terms of what Michael said about searching for a generic set of rules, I can give you an example. An example is the writing requirement. In Hong Kong we have an electronic transaction act which says that anything done in electronic means is covered in writing as well. Thus, being generic helps.

Another issue is that we have to adapt this type of rules because we have certain things we have to supplement. One area is challenge. If you look at the UNCITRAL Arbitration Rules, they do not give you much substance as to how to manage the procedure of challenge. Thus, if you go to our website, we supplemented that with certain procedures because more and more people are now challenging arbitrators. We see more and more of this happening because people are becoming more sophisticated.

Whether or not we adopt the UNCITRAL Rules after they are modified depends on what they will have to offer. Currently, our Centre is trying to draft some new rules based on the Swiss Arbitration Rules. The Swiss Arbitration Rules, as you know, are based on the UNCITRAL Rules as well. You can see that we are actually heading in a different direction. It does not mean that we are not going to adopt or recommend the UNCITRAL Rules when they come out. We just feel that we should have an all-encompassing package for someone who wants to choose our Rules. For the ones who want to use the UNCITRAL Rules, they can still choose to do so and our Centre will still administer the process."

*William Slate*: "If I might quickly add one other institution's deference to the UNCITRAL process. At ICDR, we have been working for over a year now with an international task force to develop a rule or a set of guidelines dealing with document production. That is how we restrain, if you will, in fair and balanced ways such evils as interrogatories and depositions. We have a guideline which we think is quite good. I say guideline because one of the decisions whether this was to be a rule or a guideline had to do with the present work of UNCITRAL and the wish of the institutions to not frequently amend their rules. Thus, we have produced this guideline in which we say in due course this will be a rule. This will be folded into the ICDR rules but we are waiting until the UNCITRAL finishes its work."

*Georgios Petrochilos*: "I have no difficulty understanding and realizing that the changes to the UNCITRAL Rules that were described are improvements, because they are technical improvements. What I have not been able yet to see and I would appreciate their views on that, is how these changes are country-specific, region-specific. That I think will be a very useful insight for our audience and for me."

*David D. Caron*: "So, Chris, I think the question to you is how are they context-specific, how are they specific to Asia, to Hong Kong. How are the Rules more like the Swiss Rules in updating to modern practices?"

*Christopher To*: "I think, we are not trying to modify the UNCITRAL Rules drastically *per se* because as I mentioned earlier, we have been using them for twenty-four years and I personally find them very user-friendly. The issue is, for example, what about the challenge area? How do you go about it? Are there any set guidelines about the arbitration bodies having a challenge procedure? When I first wrote a letter to all the bodies around the region no one had any challenge procedures. We had to sit down and draft our own challenge procedures to cater for the Hong Kong context as well as the Asia context. Another area that the UNCITRAL Rules don't really cater for is language. The arbitral tribunal, once it is appointed can decide on the language, whether it should be English or Chinese. What about, for example, if the contract says that English and Chinese shall prevail concurrently? If the parties don't agree what language to use, do we use Chinese or English? Which one prevails? These are the issues we find, for example, could be solved if we had developed procedures that are more flexible and supplement the UNCITRAL Rules. Thus, the UNCITRAL Rules are there and they are very generic, as Michael mentioned. However, in terms of different regions we have to look at ourselves and see where we are, and we can supplement it. We talk about arbitrating being flexible, cost-effective and quick. We have to actually adapt and see how to change this process to make it more effective."

*David D. Caron*: "Let me go back to Georgios. Georgios, as I mentioned already, you were on the earlier study before this process started and even then these Rules were changing in local application in different ways. They were already being modified. Why did you think revisions were necessary? Have the goals you sought been achieved, have they been satisfied?"

*Georgios Petrochilos*: "Certainly. Thank you for your question. The purpose of the Report that Jan Paulsson and I prepared was straightforward. The first aim was to make a comprehensive case for revision. In part this was because the Rules had not been revised since 1976. For those who have been interested in arbitral archeology, they were based on rules from 1966 that two bodies of the General Assembly of the United Nations had drawn up for regional disputes. Thus, that was the first aim. The secondary aim was to frame the debate in terms that would be as specific as possible in respect of both the scope and the direction of the revision. We drew up that report which had two parts. One part was generic and that was the shortest part – it had an introduction, a summary and the main directions. Then, there was an article-by-article, provision-by-provision section where we proposed specific changes. Those changes fell in three categories.

There were some changes that practice had shown were absolutely necessary because the Rules had gaps and difficulties that have the potential to paralyze them. Now, we all agree here that we are far from making any suggestion or any critique of the Rules that might lead people who use the current version to think that the Rules are dangerous. They are not. They are a testament to the wisdom and the experience of their drafters. However, there were some areas, for example multi-party arbitration, which had not been thought of. They were completely unknown. Thus, that was the first kind of change that we proposed.

The second kind of change we proposed was to codify best practice. There we looked at the practice – of course, of the Iran-U.S. Claims Tribunal, regional rules like the Cairo Rules, the Hong Kong Rules and so on. We also looked at rules of other institutions that have very different rules, such as the ICC Rules, and so on. There, we tried to codify best practice. One prime example is the codification of what we thought was best practice in respect of truncated tribunals.

The third area includes those changes that are desirable. We again are codifying best practice but also looking at additional issues. Joinder and consolidation are such points.

You asked me what I think, and perhaps what Jan Paulsson thinks, we have achieved. Again, the primary aim was to make the case for revision. In 2004, Professor Sanders had written his groundbreaking article and in 2006 in Vienna he said in a keynote speech that the Rules were very successful, but that the time had come for a face-lift – these were his words.[2] I think, what we have achieved is that we have indicated the breadth of the possible revision. I believe this was very useful because it has focused the attention and it has persuaded the UNCITRAL Member States and the Secretariat to embark on that process.

The secondary aim is to look at specific changes and to commend those changes to the wider audience and provoke thought reaction and further consideration. I will tell you honestly that when we drew up our report we were very pleased with our suggestions and we were rather happy with ourselves. With some of our changes we still are. And, perhaps surprisingly for all who know us, very reluctantly we have now come to accept that intelligent critique of and change to our Report are within human grasp. More seriously, our changes and specific wording were not at all intended to be carved in stone. One of the things that really gave us a lot of pause and provoked some debate with a number of colleagues externally and internally was this. These are ad hoc rules; this is an unusual element. They thus are an unusual beast. They are not supervised, except when the parties agree to do so. In principle, they are not supposed to be supervised. That creates its own dynamic. Also, they are supposed to operate, as everybody has said and rightly so, in every place in the world, in a very wide spectrum of disputes. So, the comprehensiveness of the Rules was something that really exercised our minds."

*David D. Caron:* "Thank you. Let me go to James Castello. He is with King & Spalding in Paris. James, you have been on the UNCITRAL Working Group for fifteen sessions.

---

2. Delivered at the Joint UNCITRAL/International Arbitral Centre of the Austrian Federal Economic Chamber (VIAC) Conference on 30 Years UNCITRAL Arbitration Rules (Vienna, 6-7 April 2006).

From that perspective, what are your reactions to this process and to what you have heard so far?"

*James Castello*: "Well, I think one lesson that we learned from the revision of the Model Law and are seeking probably to apply to the revision of the Rules is this: try not to take five years doing it! I would just like to add one or two details to the very good overview that our Chairman Michael Schneider just gave, one of which is that we never have votes in the UNCITRAL Working Group. We try to reach a point where there is more or less a consensus in the room. That is a very delicate task because, of course, everyone has the right to speak as Michael said, but on the other hand, you do want to have some mechanism whereby you reach a point where everyone agrees. That is one of the things that makes it take time.

Regarding consultation breaks, I think that an edict went out at the U.N. at one point that there have been too many coffee breaks. But since there must be some breaks, they were renamed consultation breaks. One always hopes that the Chairman drinks plentifully and declares these consultation breaks, which do serve this very useful purpose of coalescing a consensus. I agree with that.

I think more substantively, there are a couple of areas where what we have done in revising the Model Law has had an influence on our current work on the Rules. One of them, on which, actually, I might have a slightly different take than Michael did, is the writing requirement. I think this is an area in which what we did in the Model Law has guided what we seem to be doing in the Rules. There was a requirement in Art. 7 of the Model Law which pretty closely tracked the language in Art. V of the 1958 New York Convention. It said that, in order for an arbitration agreement to be enforceable, it had to meet certain requirements as to written form, such as being embodied in an exchange of letters or a signed document. There was a very strong feeling in the Working Group during the revision of the Model Law that this was very outdated. But the question we faced was: How far into the future do we want to modernize? In the end, unusually, we could not reach complete agreement, no matter how many consultation breaks we had. So, what we did was actually to put two options in the Model Law that state legislators can decide to adopt. One of them, as Michael said, was to keep the language that the arbitration agreement had to be in writing because that did track the language in the New York Convention. We simply redefined 'in writing' very broadly so that a much broader range of agreements will satisfy that definition. We hoped that we might encourage courts to take a more liberal view of the New York Convention without actually having to reopen it.

At the same time, there was a much more forward-looking 'futuristic' proposal, which was to do away with the writing requirement altogether. So, we put that in as a second option. When we came to the Rules and we were confronted with this requirement that parties had to adopt the Rules in writing, I think the feeling was that we had to get rid of that because there will be some countries that will take up our invitation in the Model Law's second option to do away with the writing requirement altogether. Interestingly, there were a number of delegations who resisted that and said that the Rules are actually serving a different purpose here and maybe we should think of the Rules as trying to encourage parties to a best practice. It might not be a good idea for the UNCITRAL Rules to seem to be encouraging people not to have a written agreement because it just invites a great deal of disagreement over what the terms of the agreement are. But at the end of the day, we thought it was too much to have a formality requirement in the Rules, which might not be tracked in the national law.

The other substantive influence I would note is in the area of interim measures and, as Michael mentioned, we have a very extensive chapter in the Model Law which I am sure many of you have seen. Some people have asked why we have to be so detailed on this particular aspect of arbitral procedure in the Model Law. The Working Group did think long and hard about that. Ultimately, I think we concluded that our principal goal was to try to create a regime for court enforcement of arbitral interim measures. And the more we thought about that and examined that issue, the more we worried that courts might be reluctant to enforce all interim measures issued by tribunals. And we then worried that legislatures might be reluctant to pass laws requiring courts to do that unless we gave them more guidance and unless we were clear about what kinds of powers arbitrators had to issue interim measures. So, we ended up in the revised Model Law with a fairly detailed description of what kinds of measures can be issued by tribunals and what the conditions for issuing them are. I think, turning now to the Rules, that obviously we can't really have any provisions about court enforcement in the Rules, so it will be a shorter provision for that reason. However, I think the inclination has otherwise been to track the Rules to be consistent with the interim measures provisions from the Model Law."

*David D. Caron*: "Thank you, we will take one question from the floor."

*Gerold Herrmann*: "Thank you. As a former Secretary of the UNCITRAL, I have two words to explain remarks made by James Castello. The first is on the five years of the Model Law. What is normally not seen by outsiders (I am not saying you are one, James), is that there are in fact two processes going on when UNCITRAL works towards a law, not rules. First, you need to agree on the rule, on the provisions of the law, but more importantly you have to inform and educate the people from the ministries, the government representatives whom you need. I will give you a concrete example from an area, which is my second language, insolvency. When we did the law on insolvency there was a very good example already by the International Bar Association (IBA). An excellent law in my view. However, I told them from the beginning, and I did not become very popular in the beginning, that no state will ever adopt it. It will not be considered by any government because there was no ministry involvement from the beginning. That is a process that one has to take into account in terms of looking at the time it takes.

Second point, the consultation breaks. I invented them when I was Secretary of the UNCITRAL and the reason is very simple. There is always, as you know, one conference officer sitting in the room. One of his tasks is to put down exactly when you start the proceedings and when you finish. The time that you don't use the conference facility, the interpreters is possibly counted against you later. That includes coffee breaks when it comes to giving priority to meetings at certain times. So, I said, let us rename them. They are consultation breaks and they are not counted for that purpose. And that is the reason we call it that."

III. IMPLICATIONS OF REVISION FOR THE USE OF THE UNICTRAL RULES IN TREATY SETTINGS

*David D. Caron*: "Let me turn to our second topic this morning. As Michael mentioned, there is a drive to have a set of rules that are generic, a set of rules that fit all situations. Therefore, you have to set to the side at the moment the idea that there is some modification to the Rules for investment treaties. That is out of our discussion. Nonetheless, there is knowledge in the Working Group that these Rules are used in treaty arbitration. And there are some implications that follow from that. I was wondering if we can go to Michael and if you can just comment very quickly on what these implications are. Particularly, I would ask that you transition to the question of retroactivity and how that question in a way has come out of this context."

*Michael E. Schneider*: "The new Rules will apply only to agreements that have been concluded after their adoption. The retroactivity rule, which we are discussing will apply only in the next change. So we have not had the courage which some institutions have had to introduce retroactivity. Of course this type of situation is easier to handle if you have an institution.

The problem that came up then is what happens in treaty arbitration where a treaty, let us say, of the year 2000 provides for UNCITRAL arbitration and the investment arbitration commences, let us say, in 2012. In one of the constructions at least, the commencement of an arbitration by the investor is construed as acceptance of an offer to arbitrate, so the arbitration agreement is concluded then only in 2012. Thus, if you have a state making an offer to arbitrate in 2000 with certain rules in mind which then is accepted in 2012 when the new rules have been adopted, you have a problem. We had to redraft that rule to make the effectiveness of the agreement clear, that it remained the version that was offered even though the agreement to arbitrate was concluded after the new rules had been adopted.

Here is an example of how we are trying to not create additional problems or avoid problems even though we are not specifically regulating investment arbitration. Indeed such a situation can arise in the commercial context, as in tender proceedings or in competition agreements."

*David D. Caron*: "Thank you. It is significant that the implication of what Michael just said is that actually two sets of Rules will continue for quite some time."

*James Castello*: "There are a number of other issues that I think are raised by having an investor-State application of the Rules, so it is not just the transparency issue. I think we have been taking those up as we go along."

*Michael E. Schneider*: "James is right. One of the concerns is that in some circles the investor-State treaty arbitration is limited to certain issues, whereas what is important and a large part of the Working Group had this opinion, is if you discuss investor-State arbitration you should discuss all issues that arise in this context."

## IV. MAKING THE ADMINISTRATION OF AN AD HOC ARBITRATION RUN SMOOTHER

*David D. Caron*: "It is interesting that one of the original motivations for the first set of Rules was that they be able to be administered without an institution, administered by the parties. At the same time, this intervening period has shown some problems with the system that was put in place and so, a third theme is how to make that party administration run smoother. Here I would like to turn back to Georgios. As I understand it, Georgios, one proposed revision will give the Permanent Court of Arbitration (PCA), which at present has a rather limited role of merely designating the appointing authority, more of a role. This is something that you think the PCA is ready for, I gather."

*Georgios Petrochilos*: "I have very unwisely accepted to introduce the proposition for your reflection and for comments by my friends on either side. Perhaps I could say a few introductory words to lay a foundation for the proposition that I am to defend.

The first point – and it is a narrow and technical point – is that the PCA can be designated as the appointing authority and has been designated as the appointing authority in a number of large commercial contracts and in a number of BITs. I will come to that point in a minute. The second point is that the PCA will not designate itself as the appointing authority. The practice is that this is considered by the PCA to be against the spirit of the Rules. Therefore, the PCA will not act as the appointing authority unless both parties agree on that. Now, again by way of foundation, today under the present Rules and as in any system of non-administered arbitration, non-institutional arbitration, it is imperative that there be an appointing authority to exercise the selection functions for the tribunal and the quasi-judicial functions relating to the replacement and challenge of arbitrators. I suppose all of us counseling those consulting us would immediately recommend to parties that they choose their appointing authority in the arbitration agreements. However, many do not. They are prompted to do so by the model arbitration clause in the Rules but sometimes parties will not turn to that point, or there would be no prospect of an agreement within reach. For those cases, the Rules intend to have a mechanism to have an appointing authority in place – and I am sorry to be exploring ground that is known to everyone here, but it is good to have some foundation.

The PCA, that is the Secretary-General of the PCA, supported now by the International Bureau which comprises twenty-five or so members of professional staff, will act as the designating authority of another entity, which is called the appointing authority. That will happen only in two cases: when the parties are unable to agree on their appointing authority directly or when the agreed-upon appointing authority fails or refuses to act. That is the test. That is important because the process now of designation comprises four steps. For those who have had the pleasure of going through those four steps, I am saying nothing new. But many have not, so let me outline those pleasurable steps.

First, one has to identify a need for an appointing authority. Under the present system an appointing authority will only be designated if there is a need for an appointment to be made. Then, that interested party has to make an application to the Secretary-General of the PCA and that application needs to be accompanied by documentation – that is, the notice of arbitration, the contract or a separate arbitration agreement, proof of service of the notice of arbitration, indication of the nationalities of the parties, indication of any persons or institutions that the parties might have considered, power of attorney under the authority of which the applicant is making the request to the Secretary-General and a payment of € 750. That is the first step.

Second step. The PCA now has to consider the relevant factors, which include comments by the parties, nationalities of the parties, the nature of the dispute, the place of arbitration, the language of the arbitration, the complexity and magnitude of the case, the fees charged by potential appointing authorities and the anticipated reaction time of the possible appointing authorities. And it would not have failed to receive your attention that steps one and two will be the very same steps, the very same intellectual process that the appointing authorities and the parties will go through after an appointing authority has been designated.

Step three: Inquiries to be made of possible appointing authorities to see if there is any risk of bias or potential problem of independence, and so on.

And finally, step four, the designation. Then, if the appointing authority so designated fails to make an appointment within the time-period specified, which is thirty or sixty days depending on the appointment, the matter comes back to the Secretary-General of the PCA.

Having completed that description by way of foundation, I think here we will be saying nothing new in suggesting that this process is not a model of streamlined efficiency. That had been noted by a number of delegations. Notably Belgium, France, Germany and the United Kingdom said it would be better to have the PCA make the appointment directly, be the appointing authority by default. No strong objection was then raised, although some objections were raised to the PCA as the designating authority at a very early stage. We can go through those objections, as I am sure we will because my friends will probably take them up and rightly so. However, the reason that proposal was not accepted was that the Secretary-General of the PCA had indicated that the organization was not then willing or able to undertake that task. Thirty years later, I think, that is no longer the case and I have some interesting statistics.

The Secretariat of the PCA, called the International Bureau, has, as I said 25 professional staff, and since 1976 it has received 311 requests to designate an appointing authority, act as an appointing authority or make decisions on challenges. In actual fact, the PCA has needed to take action under those requests. In the past three-and-a-half years, sixty-one designations and appointments have been made by the PCA. As I said before, the PCA has been named as the appointing authority directly in twenty BITs and the Energy Charter Treaty. The PCA has also already designated twenty individuals and twenty-five institutions as the appointing authority.

In light of that evolution of the PCA – which in 1976 had conducted three cases in thirty years and today that no longer the case – the question is asked, Can we now cut the middle step and have the PCA as the appointing authority by default? That is, except if either party objects to that, or the PCA, in light of the circumstances of the case – for example, a very particular technical character of the dispute – decides to make the designation rather than undertake the task of the appointing authority. I think the idea commends itself for further discussion which, I think, it will receive in the Working Group in September. For now, it is simply an idea. And there is of course opposition, all of which is loyal, and you will hear from the opposition. For my part, what I should like to hear from the opposition is a response in three points.

First, if one can streamline the process in that way, is it not the only conceivable objection to the proposal that the PCA does not have the requisite experience or expertise? I have some difficulties seeing how that can be demonstrated. The second point is that it is difficult, for me at least, to see how it can be said that designating an appointing authority involves a lesser or different responsibility than making an appointment directly. One has to remember that under the current system, when the PCA has made the designation the matter is out of its hands. The appointing authority can be removed only if it fails or if it refuses to act. If the parties do not like it, so be it. The last question is this. There is a view that the current system caters for regionalism but there have only been twenty-five designations of institutions out of the hundreds of institutions that exist. That is for good reasons. Not all institutions are equally experienced or perhaps equally to be trusted. They do not have the same track record. I am not sure how leaving matters as they are would enhance regionalism. I would like to hear on those points. Thank you for you patience."

*David D. Caron*: "Thank you, Georgios. I would like to turn, not labeling them as opposition but as representatives of institutions and centers, to Bill, Josefa and Chris. You can respond to any of the three questions or the other question which was, can we now cut out the middle step."

*William Slate*: "Well, I would answer those questions. There is a certain allure when you say four steps. I think they are probably two. You go to the PCA and the PCA, if appropriate, will designate an appointing authority, simplified. However, I think that only makes sense as long as the end product is a knowledgeable, informed and qualitative decision. I put a question to you as I discuss further: is it possible for one entity in the entire world to have in-depth knowledge about every possible neutral who might be appointed. I think that is a substantial challenge.

To place this a little further in context, unless we fall into some slumber, if you will, as to the significance of the arbitration appointment segment as a part of the overall arbitration process, somehow relegating this in our minds to some kind of parenthetical ministerial footnote is not good. Recall that two of the five reasons set out in Art. V of the New York Convention as to why recognition and enforcement of an award may be refused, directly touch upon the appointment of the arbitrator. As to the current discussion, it is important to be said as well that this is a discussion about process and about opinions, as Georgios said, and about best practice ultimately.

Now, we have some statistics which I think are helpful. I thought in anticipation of this session I will collect a few statistics myself. So, I went to seven institutions and I asked them to answer three questions. These institutions were resident in Latin America, Asia, Africa, North America and Europe. Of course of the seven, three were appropriately from Europe. I asked each of the institutions these questions. How many times over the last three years has your institution been designated as the appointing authority under the PCA? What fee, if any, is charged for the service by your institution? And lastly, do you have any opinion respecting the change in the process to permit worldwide appointments from one entity or any feelings about the matter of local institutional involvement in the process?

As to the first question – how often was your institution designated by the PCA as an appointing authority over the past three years – of the seven institutions, four said not at all and the other three were appointed eleven times collectively. So, some variation there with respect to the answer to that question.

As to the second question – what fee do you charge – they range from zero (no charge) by one institution for acting as a designated appointing authority to a low US$ 500 at one end to a high of US$ 2,000. So, an average of about US$ 1,100 for the fee for that service. The PCA's € 750 is around US$ 1000, to keep it in one dollar fee. So, again some variations. It should be noted that these are very modest amounts and there are very small case numbers.

As to question three – do you have any opinion respecting the change in the process to permit worldwide appointments from one entity or any feelings about the matter of local institutional involvement in the process – there were no variations from the seven institutions. They shared an expressed belief as to the significant contribution of the appointing process by local or regional institutions, specific references being made to experience and knowledge of neutrals and their respective variance. This is what institutions do. They train, engage with, observe and know the quality of their neutrals and the fit of a given neutral for a given subject dispute. One institution said, we know who is who, their experience. Another said, it's unthinkable not to have this important element. No one sees this as a burden but rather as an essential value-added to the appointment practice."

*Josefa Sicard-Mirabal*: "I am going to address the questions you raised, Georgios, and it is requisite expertise and experience. I will dovetail with what Bill has mentioned but also go back to your reference. You said that the PCA has twenty-five members in the Secretariat as opposed to the sixty members that the ICC has in the Secretariat. The ICC also has an outreach to 90 different countries – 92 in terms of national committees – and 126 court members from where it can glean well-known learned arbitrators. So, we have a wide spread, as you had also mentioned, Bill, from where we can designate. Now that I have mentioned the word "designation", the ICC Rules refer to lack of independence as viewed in the eyes of the parties, which is a subjective standard for appointment or confirmation of arbitrators, and the UNCITRAL Rules refer to independence and impartiality. ICC Rules are much broader which aids in limiting the number of challenges that may come. So, I would say that the PCA may very well acquire the expertise and experience, but as compared to the ICC right now, I think that it falls short."

*Christopher To*: "I agree with my colleague from the ICC. One of the areas of concern is about the cost and the speed of arbitration. Now, the PCA does have the expertise and experience, but Bill mentioned, for example, local expertise or neutrals. They don't really know, for example, who the people are in the region. I think that is one thing they really need to brush up on in terms of wanting to be capable of doing a global appointment of arbitration on neutrals. They really have to know about the local scene and who the people want.

Another thing is, for example, the language. James mentioned there are six languages. What happens if they submit some of the documents in Chinese? Would the PCA have to get someone to translate those documents into English in order to make an appointment? Lastly, there may be a hidden cost that no one has thought about. What about people from Brazil who submit documents there as well? That is another issue. An additional issue is liability. What happens if the PCA appoints the wrong arbitrator and the arbitrator did not do a very good job? Would the parties take recourse against the PCA? Currently now, in Hong Kong, we are immune from prosecution if we do things properly. If we are not dishonest, we are ok. Basically, that is a thing that the PCA has to think about. In saying that, I think the PCA has the experience. It is just a matter of time. If they address all these issues, I would put my hand on my heart and say let's do it. However, if they don't address these issues, I will be cautious. That is my viewpoint."

*Michael E. Schneider:* "Just two points. The subject has been extensively discussed. In the minutes of the meeting in February 2007, the prevailing view was that the proposal constituted a major unnecessary departure. The existing mechanism should be preserved. The objections that were raised against the proposal were not, as you may think from the discussion this morning, from the institutions alone. This was an issue on which I have felt a particularly strong objection: perhaps, not always rational, but a very strong objection. One other point that needs to be brought into the discussion is that, we have expanded the role of the appointing authority and have streamlined the procedure. In particular, as Georgios said, the process of designating an appointing authority can start at any time during the arbitration process. Thus, if there is a problem it has been diminished. That explains the scope of the debate."

*David D. Caron:* "Relating to another change, we will go to the last question I have, which is to James. James, there is a proposal that the fees will be reviewed in some manner by the Secretary-General of the PCA. An example of the proposed text is as follows:

'*Article 39 – Costs*
1. The fees of the arbitral tribunal shall be reasonable in amount, taking into account the amount in dispute, the complexity of the subject matter, the time spent by the arbitrators and any other relevant circumstances of the case.
2. If an appointing authority has been agreed upon by the parties or designated by the Secretary-General of the Permanent Court of Arbitration at The Hague, and if that authority has issued a schedule of fees for arbitrators in international cases which it administers, the arbitral tribunal in fixing its fees shall take that schedule of fees into account to the extent that it considers appropriate in the circumstances of the case.
3. The arbitral tribunal shall make a proposal setting out the principles according to which its fees are to be fixed, and shall subsequently specify the amounts established by applying those principles. At any stage, (a) the arbitral tribunal, or (b) any party, no later than 15 days after the proposal was made, may ask that the principles or the amounts of the fees, and, if applicable, the deposit, be established by the appointing authority or, if no appointing authority has been agreed upon or if the agreed appointing authority does not decide within thirty days of a party's

request, by the Secretary-General of the Permanent Court of Arbitration at The Hague.'

Perhaps you can just describe what the Working Group is doing here."

*James Castello*: "One thing that has been recognized as a disadvantage of having non-administered arbitration is that there have been some reports over the years of some problems in setting arbitrators' fees. Obviously, if you have a non-administered arbitration then the arbitrators set their own fees in consultation with the parties. There have been certain circumstances where some arbitrators took an unfair advantage of the situation. In particular, in the middle of a case, having already established one basis for fees, the arbitrators might say that the case seemed more difficult and the fees should actually be higher. The question is what kind of control parties can have over this problem. The Rules currently do say that if there is already an appointing authority and that appointing authority has published a schedule of fees, the arbitrators should take that into account in fixing their own fees. However, the proposed revision now under discussion would go further and say that, if you have a specific complaint as a party about either the basis for or the calculation of fees, you can go the appointing authority. If there is no appointing authority or one refuses to act, then you can go to the PCA Secretary-General. The Secretary-General has graciously agreed to serve this rather thankless job of actually stepping in and making sure that the fees of the arbitrators are reasonable."

*David D. Caron*: "Thank you. There is time for two questions."

*Richard Kreindler*: "I would like to go back to the very beginning of our discussion where we talked about the logistics, the efforts to include a wide variety of views with respect to whether the UNCITRAL Rules, the ICC rules, the efforts that the ICDR has been engaged in with respect to document production. It may be of interest and not entirely inappropriate to mention in this group that in respect to taking of evidence, the IBA has launched a recent initiative, which is just in the starting blocks, to revisit the IBA Rules on the Taking of Evidence in International Commercial Arbitration which are about to celebrate their tenth anniversary next year. I have been asked to chair that initiative. It has not been called a task force, it has not been called a working group, although we are obviously tapping into the expertise and the input from the prior working group from about ten years ago. It has been very interesting to learn from what you have observed and what you have remarked about the lessons learned from trying to include a wide disparate set of views. Anyone who is interested in engaging in this effort with respect to the IBA rules should certainly be welcome to contact me."

*Ronald Bettauer*: "Just on the question of the PCA, I wonder why there was no comment that the head of the PCA is typically a Dutch diplomat, not necessarily with any expertise in arbitration to start. While the professional staff is superb and while when I was with the government we saw the PCA as an excellent institution for our state-to-state disputes, it strikes me as a bit odd to think of relegating to the Dutch Foreign Ministry the task of deciding who the person is who will be the appointing authority. Any comment on that?"

*Georgios Petrochilos:* "That is a very fair question, of course. The custom to date has been that the Secretary-General is a Dutch diplomat, or a Dutch retired official or a Dutch academic or a Dutch jurist. The job, however – and I went to the internal bylaws of the PCA to check that point – is one of an international civil servant. Although the Administrative Council to which the Secretary-General has to report is headed by the Foreign Minister of the Netherlands, all of the Member States – now 109 – of the PCA do have a say in that. That is, I think, a point worth mentioning, in the sense that the process of appointing an arbitrator will be a task for which the Secretary-General would be answerable to the entire constituency of Member States. That would give, I suppose, some comfort to the forty percent of states or state entities that are typically involved in cases before the PCA. I am not sure that what you just mentioned is, in fact, a con. I would tend to think that it may be a pro."

# Working Group B

## 6. Recent Developments in International Arbitration

# Quo Vadis Arbitration?

*A lively discussion under the guidance of Catherine Kessedjian* and William W. Park**

Arbitration is a trust business. However, voices are heard to the effect that arbitration is taking a direction which is not entirely satisfactory. The participants discussed what is wrong or right with the direction taken and, if wrong, what ought to be changed. They also discussed whether we need to go back to a so-called "Golden Age".

*Fali Nariman, India* : "Let me just say how I see arbitration generally going. I think in this age of instant communication there is much greater awareness of what different people in different parts of the world are doing and that's sometimes a good thing and sometimes not such a good thing. We are past the stage when Cedric Barclay used to say, "What's the use of writing reasons for awards? They're not meant for posterity, they're meant for the two parties." But I'm afraid with all the publications that have cropped up we get into the situation of too many awards, too much publicity of awards, much commentary of awards. I am not entirely certain it is a good thing. Of course, the plus side is that we can assess how well a particular decision has been reasoned (or "motivated"). The dark side is that we are sacrificing the main goal of arbitration – which has always been intended as a resolution of disputes. That is already much – and we are probably not gaining much in transforming arbitration into something else."

*Jim Carter, United States*: "I am struck by the fact that users have the same complaints all the time. Whether they're thinking of a bygone Golden Age or not, they always say: 'Well why can't you make it cheaper and more efficient and faster?' and 'Maybe I don't need reasons for my awards, or maybe I do.' But they're always operating on the basis of the last bad thing that happened to them. Hence, my conclusion is that, while we need to try to listen to the users, of course, most users don't know that much because most of them are sporadic users. I would guess this was true in the bygone Golden Age as well. There are regular users of commercial arbitration who have a regular docket all the time; but that's a very limited universe and they have certain needs and certain perceptions as to what they want. They may very well want quick decisions and no reasoning and very flexible rules -- or not. They may want something else. But to start off by saying let's get some users together and see what they think is wrong with arbitration, will lead, as it always has, to a variety of diverse perspectives on it reducible to: (1) we're not perfectly happy; (2) we lost too many cases; (3) it costs too much. So I don't think much has changed from the bygone Golden Age."

*Tony de Fina, Australia*: "I listened carefully to what Fali said about the publication of awards and the fact that many awards now enter into the public arena. Certainly it seems

---

\* Professor, Université Panthéon-Assas Paris II.
\*\* Professor of Law, Boston University; Member of ICCA.

to fly in the face of the Golden Age of arbitration where everything in relation to arbitration was confidential, unless the parties had agreed otherwise. At that time, awards were not precedents in the common law meaning of the concept. That has changed. More and more awards are published. But more importantly those awards that are published have elements or some elements which may be influential on international public law and international private law, because of the constant expansion of arbitrability. I would pose that publication of seminal awards which have great international legal significance is meritorious."

*John Townsend, United States*: "This is an arbitration conference, and here we are deep in philosophy. I thought the enlightenment had pretty well done in the Greek concept of falling away from a Golden Age and had replaced it with the concept of progress; and then Darwin came along and explained to us all that we were engaged in a battle for survival. I think that's probably a more accurate way to look at the world of arbitration. Arbitration offers a means to an end, and the end is the resolution of disputes. I wouldn't pretend to hold out an end as lofty as the achievement of justice. If you want people to use your way of resolving disputes, you have to be prepared to offer alternatives to competing means of doing so. We don't want arbitration to respond to competition from the court system by trying to imitate it or duplicate it. There has been a real trend over the years to get away from some of the informality of arbitration. And going right to the heart of the matter that I think Mr. Nariman may have been referring to, to a more heavily procedural, heavily litigated, heavily documented process. The result is that we have reached the point that much arbitration now resembles court process except that the arbitrators don't wear black robes – or not yet. That is a mistake. We need to pull back from that trend and at least try to achieve the goals Jim [Carter] was talking about and which all of our clients tell us they want, which is a more economical and faster process. I commend to you for reading the ICDR's new set of guidelines which was just adopted, effective as of the beginning of this month [June 2008]. These guidelines are intended to provide guidance for arbitrators in administering exchanges of information. They constitute a very strong admonition to arbitrators to remember that they have the primary responsibility for making the process more economical and faster than litigation, for restraining the parties from duplicating the process that Americans call discovery and the rest of the world uses unprintable words to describe. They address in some detail, case by case, what arbitrators should strive to achieve in managing exchanges of documents, in telling the parties that they're not going to have depositions; that they're not going to have interrogatories, and that if they want electronic documents, they're going to get them in the form most convenient for the party that has them and they may have to pay for the privilege. I hope you will find this is a pulling back from the attempt to imitate litigation and an attempt to keep arbitration something different and more workable."

*Françoise Lefèvre, Belgium*: "I would like to offer another view on the issue of consulting users. I agree that some users are not really familiar with what happens in arbitration and with all the issues we have been discussing for the last few days. But many are quite sophisticated users of arbitration and may offer very constructive views beyond speed, cost and other traditional issues. Maybe it would be interesting to have a meeting like this, with a subject like this one, with clients present, with users of arbitration telling us what they think we should be doing. It might be useful to have direct contact, direct discussion, with sophisticated and unsophisticated users of arbitration as well. I heard you say that arbitration is a world apart. But it should not be completely detached from reality. And the reality is not only the legal questions we discuss among ourselves in conferences such as this one; but reality is what the clients ultimately want, because that's what our job is all about."

*Mauro Rubino Samartano, Italy*: "I preside the European Court of Arbitration. In view of the importance of the subject I'm not expressing my own views but I speak on behalf of this body. There have been two main developments in recent years. First, there is a large increase in arbitration. As for many other things, this trend has good and bad sides. The good side is more work for many of us. Also, people have a hope that we do a better job than courts. The negative aspect is that a lot of new people come aboard and not many of them know the rules of the game. Others who know the rules of the game are too busy. It may be difficult, as Fali Nariman suggested, to go back to the Golden Age because the time of justice under the oak tree is gone. Nevertheless there's no future if you don't look back. Users need few simple things. They need a good decision to be made very quickly. Well, at least one of them wants it very quickly, while the other one wants it as late as possible!

Some arbitrators imitate judges. This to me is a mistake. People come to us arbitrators because they want something different from court proceedings – and better. So anyone who imitates a judge is, in my view, on the wrong track. Our purpose is to serve, not to magnify ourselves, not to become rich. At least in America, an arbitrator earns much less than counsel.

I repeat, we arbitrators are there to serve."

*Phillip Capper, United Kingdom*: "Probably the largest industry in the world creates infrastructure -- construction, engineering, oil and gas, highways transport. Those infrastructure projects routinely and typically have used arbitration as their only means of final dispute resolution. The practitioners are specialists but even the users are repeat users, perhaps not by choice but it's the nature of the industry. Therefore knowing what the decisions contain and seeing how one can deal with these matters is essential to the good functioning of the industry. Those projects are document-heavy. They may be electronic-document-heavy now, but they are still document-heavy. I think it's a tribute to the specialist practitioners in that kind of arbitration that we've actually seen practices which are at the forefront. For example, experts are routinely required to meet in advance to agree as many issues as can be agreed, so as to converge on questions before the hearing. Witness conferencing, particularly of experts, is very typical in that field. I think we need to recognize that there are these different sectors which call for different kinds of proceedings."

*Max Abrahamson, Ireland*: "I have the big advantage that I'm old enough to have practiced far back in the Golden Age. Business people have always sought a paradise lost and they have defined paradise as a world without lawyers! We should accept the starting point according to which clients know their own business best. I absolutely disagree with the

637

view that we should proceed under the assumption that clients really don't know what they want, and that we know better than they do. I practice in the construction industry. It is a very complex industry which triggers disputes, of course. However, there is also a parallel industry that I call the 'claims industry'. We need to focus on what the construction industry wants, not what the claims industry wants. We have to go back to the essential feature of arbitration: that it is not intended to be an adversarial process. I would describe it as an interactive investigation. It's investigatory. The arbitrator is entitled to say to all those who appear, including the lawyers, 'Your role is to help me interactively because you are representing your client, but you interact with me and I interact with you and it's not purely adversarial.'

My final point is as follows: I've been involved in arbitrations where you have discovery -- full common law discovery -- and systems where you don't. I find it odd that the procedure which seems to be curtailed is discovery, whereas by comparison I think discovery -- interactively ordered and carried out -- is probably one of the most important processes for getting at what I have no hesitation in calling justice in arbitration."

*Fathi Kemicha, Tunisia*: "I have to say that arbitration is becoming far from being a perfect world. We have a real problem with access to arbitration. It is normally really international. However, the actors, the counsels, are coming mostly from one region. The techniques involved nowadays in arbitration are much more inspired by English or American cultures and by English or American law firms. This very strong feature prevents a great number of users from contributing or participating in the arbitration process.

We have to reflect on two aspects. The first one is the way we are conducting arbitrations. Even in civil law countries (my region is a good example), I see large English law firms come in, imposing common law proceedings and appointing arbitrators from their legal system. Personally I'm happy with this because it is easy for me to work with these techniques and legal cultures. But I do know my colleagues have difficulties to do so and to represent their clients properly. This is particularly true for small firms, sole practitioners. This is why I say we need to think about access to arbitration.

The second aspect concerns transmission of arbitration skills. In this Conference we have a large number of people attending. How many are coming from the developing world? How many can afford to attend when they are working as sole practitioners or in small law firms? Therefore, how many get the opportunity to obtain the proper education in the field? We have to do something about all of that."

*Vera van Houtte, Belgium*: "I would like to come back for a minute to the user. We use the word all the time and we are assuming that the 'User' wants a quick and a good decision and he or she wants it in as cheap a way as possible. Now who is the user? I would say to many of us here, the users are lawyers. The users, to a large extent, are also the counsels. It is counsel who very often advises the client to write an arbitration clause in his contract, and it is counsel who ultimately is going to participate in the arbitration proceedings. So when you're asking what the user wants, we have to think of both the counsel and the ultimate client. My question is whether the ultimate client and the counsel indeed always want the same thing at all times of an arbitral proceeding.

Someone said before that one party wants a quick decision and the other party does not want a quick decision. Let's look at that for a minute. The party who does not want a quick decision is assumed to be the party who is likely to lose. Now, are we certain that the party who is likely to lose really wants to know that or to receive the 'bad' award as late as possible? Has that client been told by its counsel that the later the decision is going to come, the more costs it may have to pay ultimately? Has that client been told by its counsel that the later the decision comes, the more interest it may have to pay on the principal amount? These are questions which I think we, as arbitration practitioners, have to address very urgently and we must be certain that the clients know of these aspects of the arbitration as well. Otherwise, we fail in our role as advisors of our clients. And these questions have to be asked over and over again, not only at the beginning of the procedure, not only when you are writing the arbitration clause into the contract, but throughout the arbitration proceeding: to reconsider at all times whether the proper time has come for a settlement."

*Dushyante Dave, India*: "I think everyone of us would agree that the Golden Age of arbitration has to be restored. But there is another angle to it. What may appear today to be a purely private dispute between two parties, more often than not involves very substantial public interest. It may be a simple dispute about construction, but it may involve construction of a dam which may affect millions of people in a particular country. By allowing these kinds of disputes to be determined in the private chambers of arbitral tribunals and ignoring the parties ultimately affected, the public, sooner or later we will lose focus and we will lose the confidence amongst the majority of people. And that's why today large numbers of amicus briefs are being filed in arbitral tribunals. Some of the tribunals have taken extremely positive steps to accept those briefs and hear the parties who are going to be affected. My question to every one of us here is should the arbitral process really neglect these vital public interests in deciding what may appear to be ostensibly private interests of the parties, but actually affecting millions of people?"

*Kap-You (Kevin) Kim, Korea*: "I'd like to indicate some sort of perspective of what Europeans call the Far East (Korea, Japan and China), which are civil law countries in the Asian culture. There we conduct many arbitration cases every year. I'll say that at least in Korea the Golden Age has not yet come. Nowadays we have so many arbitration conferences in Asia and all over the world. In the case of investment arbitration, there are probably more conferences than actual cases.

Nonetheless, my experience shows that there is a kind of happy middle ground between civil and common law traditions which works well. Also, new technologies, for example witness conferencing, are very helpful to bridge the gap between different types of players. Another useful tool is post-hearing submissions rather than oral presentations. Our clients are all happy with that procedural tool. As far as evidence is concerned, the IBA Guidelines and Evidence Rules are very useful. However, we still face difficulties with privilege issues. Indeed the civil law/common law divide remains very deep in that respect. Korean clients, for one, have no idea how to protect their documents under the attorney-client privilege. But it is very difficult for us to persuade arbitrators or practitioners on the other side to accept our concept of attorney-client privilege. We still need some international harmonization on these issues.

Turning now to the issues of time and cost: portraying arbitration as a speedier and cheaper process than court proceedings is a serious misrepresentation nowadays -- somewhat fraudulent. Cost is a real threat to clients. In some cases, clients have decided to revert to litigation after they have had a long and difficult arbitration. I learned many tactics during my experience, and some inexperienced arbitration practitioners have some very odd attitudes. We do encounter people who, as Michael Hwang expresses it, are 'arbitration gangsters' (or other people would speak of an 'arbitration wannabe' level of inexperience). All of them cause a lot of problems. That is one of the threats to the current field of arbitration that we need to overcome."

*David Brynmor Thomas, United Kingdom*: "I have two observations. First, I'm struck: we have been talking about a Golden Age and some past Golden Age. I'm struck by the observation that those who forget the lessons of history are bound to repeat it. I don't want to hark back to a Golden Age but to English legal history. England started out with common law. Issues arose in relation to the common law which became highly codified and sclerotic, and so in parallel to that developed the system of the Chancery courts. The Chancery courts in turn became highly formalized and sclerotic. Interesting issues then arose in relation to the parallel jurisdictions between the Chancery and the Kings Bench courts. That was addressed by the Judicature Act in England. In parallel, if you talk to legal historians, the concept of precedent in English common law started out essentially as something personal to the judges. It was almost a res judicata issue. The judge was bound to determine the same case the same way. The concept of precedent, the concept of *stare decisis* in English law, started to arise with effective law reporting in the nineteenth century. So where does this take us in arbitration? I'm concerned that in the short period of time that I've been involved in this community, we have got more and more bits of soft law. We've got guidelines on evidence, and they're important. We cite them to tribunals. There are guidelines on arbitrators' disclosure and conflicts of interest. So many things are now being promulgated that arbitration practice may very well ossify, will solidify in the way that English common law did. We will end up with precedent not because we choose to do so, but simply because we will repeat what English common law did in the nineteenth century. We will end up with precedent available and we will regard it as binding.

The second observation goes to the fact that much of this process is normative. We end up with 'there is a way to do something'. This was Fathi Kemicha's observation. And I suggest that that is actually the wrong approach for us to take. If arbitration is viewed as an economic phenomenon, as a market, the strange thing that we are doing nowadays is that we are taking the product and we're making it a very uniform product in terms of what the users can acquire. In another panel, this morning, we discussed amendments to the UNCITRAL Model Law. Various institutions all around the world endorse, recommend and use variations of the UNCITRAL Rules. There are in fact similarities between the UNCITRAL Rules and the ICC Rules or, at least conceptually, the LCIA Rules and all sorts of other rules. Competition in arbitration does exist because it is a market place, at least regionally speaking. Institutions know people who are locally based, and who have the language skills and expertise in some industry, for example, the construction industry and the like. There is no economic competition so to speak."

*Marc Blessing, Switzerland*: "I suggest that we should take Fathi Kemicha's intervention very seriously and I propose that his topic would be the central topic for ICCA in Rio: that is to say, how can you make sure that the developing world is happy with the system of arbitration? This is my preliminary remark and suggestion.

I have two comments on procedure. Reflecting on Vera [van Houtte]'s comment, I very much regret that there is not enough stimulus and invitation to the actual clients for their participation in the proceedings. Clients tend to leave the arbitration process to their counsel, and will refrain from mentioning an issue or sharing their impressions on the issues before the arbitral tribunal. I suggest that this is entirely wrong. Whenever I can, I strongly invite the parties themselves to be present during the proceedings. If possible, I even invite their senior executive members to participate. I can recall so many arbitrations which had a very good outcome only because at least one of the CEOs participated at least in part of the hearings. They were listening to their own counsel and were able to step back and take a look at the merits of their own case, and in most of those cases, the CEOs and the managers were able to settle the dispute.

My second brief remark as to the proceedings goes to the fact that arbitrators should focus on the needs of the parties as to the future of their relationship, instead of focusing on past difficulties, the wrongdoings committed by them. Most parties in our world do not realize that they will meet again in the marketplace. They have common interests and it is a much better service we render to them when we call their attention to options which will facilitate the future. Hence, I am struck by the lack of enthusiasm from arbitrators to make all possible attempts to solve a dispute by settlement, by negotiated settlement. There are too many arbitrators that refrain from being proactive, from having an interactive role and seeing to it that parties have a much better solution than a hard, fast and cold arbitral award. I suggest that we should overcome hesitations, particularly in the United Kingdom, and maybe also in Ireland, where an arbitrator is almost accused of misconduct if he or she paves the way for a settlement."

*Edna Sussman, United States*: "I want to add to the remarks that were made by the last two speakers, that we need to think not only about arbitration but also about alternative dispute resolution as a whole. It's our job to help the parties resolve their dispute. Conciliation is a tradition in many parts of the world as part of arbitration. In China, for example, the arbitrators are expected to try to conciliate the parties. If conciliation fails, then they continue with arbitration. In South America, most countries accept the same. As you know, there has been an explosion of mediation in the United States, the EU directive on Mediation is coming along. So conciliation and mediation are very much the wave of the future, and I think we need to do a lot more work on how we can incorporate it into our practices. For example, we need to look closely at how significant the due process issues are. If the arbitrator caucuses separately with the parties, would it really jeopardize the enforcement of the award on due process grounds? Can such objections not be knowingly waived by the parties? The entire subject of how to integrate mediation into the arbitration process needs a serious examination. Some of the institutions suggest mediation to the parties as a step in the arbitration but with a second neutral who has no role in the arbitration. Is this the only way to go about it? How should we, or the institutions, propose mediation to the parties Are there legal questions that must be addressed from existing applicable legal frameworks? These are all questions that need to be studied with care, but it is essential that a broader menu of alternative dispute resolution choices be made readily available to the parties, even within an arbitration."

*Matthieu de Boissëson, France*: "I was extremely impressed by the statement made by our friend David Brynmor about the danger of normalization. I fully agree with him. However, I would like to make a few additional observations because this is one of the main problems we are facing for the future of arbitration. In order to do so, we need to recognize the difference between harmonization and uniformity. Harmonization has been a phenomenon which was extremely helpful during the last thirty years, in order to create a world in which an international award may be enforced, and the procedures of international arbitration may be approached by different people coming from different cultures. But now we are providing a product with a lot of guidelines and we run the risk of fossilizing or solidifying the product, and this is a danger. We have to recognize the fact that the motivations of the users are very varied. There are big differences in the arbitration world. For instance, a company in France, an international company like Total or Lafarge, has recourse to arbitration because it knows that the courts, in the civil law world, cannot afford to provide the same services as international arbitrators do. They do not have the means to go into a difficult case in depth, to organize witness testimony, experts, conferencing, hearings, long hearings, and long oral presentations. The motivation for a company in the United States or England may be different because the recourse to arbitration there may mean a more flexible procedure.

We also have to recognize that arbitrators have to respect the differences between counsel and between the parties to the arbitration. This is extremely important. In my view, this is one of the responses to be given to the problem expressed by Fathi Kemicha. Some arbitrators are obsessed by what they call the 'state of the art'. They are obsessed with managing the procedure; they apply all kinds of preconceived and ready-made sets of rules. This is a danger. It is very important to understand and take into account the fact that users may have different styles, may have different approaches and to try to respect these cultural differences. This is the first duty of the arbitrator in international arbitration.

Finally, we should not dream about a Golden Age but perhaps we should go back to some fundamentals in arbitration. The first fundamental is the will of the parties, the intent of the parties. The parties can choose among a wide range of possibilities to resolve their dispute: mediation, mini-trial, conciliation, arbitration, state court proceedings, etc. They have to scrutinize these means with their counsel and choose the one that best fits their needs. If time and cost are of the essence for them, they should choose fast-track proceedings. They work very well and are a real success in arbitration services. Again, I insist that there is a real danger of normalization. We should tailor the proceedings to each case. If we do that, then I am very optimistic about the future of arbitration."

*Charles Molineaux, United States*: "I was recently at one of these conferences but it was not called an arbitration conference, it was a dispute resolution conference. As it happened, Day One was really run by FIDIC and Day Two by the ICC. Day One showed that there is tremendous success in the use of dispute review boards in construction contracts, which are largely run and conducted by engineers. The tremendous success of these dispute review boards is a gigantic rebuke to arbitration and the expense and time involved in arbitration. This is why I agree with Vera van Houtte's comment. The users come first. We are not an institution. We are an instrument of justice. Let's think of the users."

*Bill Slate, United States*: "It is fine to reflect on how we conduct our profession. This is not specific to arbitration professionals but is quite common in all professions. We should acknowledge that we are not always doing things in the right way. However, I would refrain from concluding that all is lost. Indeed, it isn't. I think there is a quite long list of standards enhancing our activities. For example, it has become quite obvious that we have more serious scholarship in this field than anytime ever before. This has contributed, and continues to contribute, in very significant ways to how we do our work. There's a growth in technology, particularly among institutions but also among practitioners to make us more aligned with the users. There is phenomenal growth in this field. If we're not doing a great deal that's right there wouldn't be so many people turning to these processes for resolution. In my capacity as head of an institution, I can say that for every letter I get (and I get a lot -- people are not shy about writing E-mails and sending letters at the conclusion of a case and saying how they feel about it) expressing concern about cost and delay, I get at least eight or nine letters from people who say, 'This really worked.' And often they didn't win, but they said, 'This is a legitimate process.' The list goes on. I think the refinement of rules is a great contribution here. So there's much that we are doing to be proud of and I see in the short time I've been in this field (fifteen years -- who's counting) the standards are being raised consistently for individuals and for institutions. So please let's not despair in the midst of all these fine suggestions about what we might do. What we must do: we must give serious inquiry to the subject of the cost, the accessibility issue of arbitration and the impact of culture on conflict management -- a very serious issue that's residing largely under the table but has to be embraced and seriously considered. And lastly, we must figure out a way to collect serious data. We've all heard that 'comparisons are odious'; but we have to know how we're doing, how do we compare with others and what the other options are. We have virtually no data in this field. This must be addressed among institutions and ad hoc providers for us to really understand how long does it take? What does it cost? Who is using what? Who is not using it and why? And how we can enhance the delivery of these services?"

*Diana Droulers, Venezuela*: "The growth in the number of institutions proposing arbitration services around the world these days is simply staggering. We need to understand how much local institutions influence international arbitration and vice-versa. We can only benefit from the fact that ICCA meets in Rio in 2010, that the IBA this year [2008] will be in Latin America and that many networks are being set up throughout the world. In Latin America, we have an ADR network which is made up of local centers which are conducting research in the area. The network is financed by the Inter-American Development Bank in order to produce studies of the different processes existing in the region. Of course, I can only speak of Latin America because it's my region. But I understand that this is happening in various regions of the world. So the

643

Golden Age created by those who had the privilege of setting up the system and giving us the tools with which we are working nowadays, the Golden Age hasn't arrived in all the regions of the world. And it might just be getting there. All of you who did live through the Golden Age gave us the appropriate tools, and the institutions are doing a lot to make those tools work better and to make the right guidelines and to help everyone to climb on board to this way of solving conflicts."

*Ian Murray, Scotland*: "My first observation is a plea: Can we please move towards simplicity! Guidelines, regulations and so on tend to make the process more and more complex. This is counterproductive particularly for the people who are doing the one-off arbitration for their clients, particularly the small firms. These people want simplicity. So do the local arbitrators who may not have been accustomed to doing it on the North American or European scales. I am currently involved in a project where three or four Anglophone countries in Africa are seeking to set up one single arbitral panel which will be available for disputes throughout that region. One cry comes up all the time in this endeavor: please let us have simple rules so that everyone can understand them, particularly the people who are first-time users of arbitration.

This brings me to my second point. I wish to express my entire concurrence with what Fathi [Kemicha] said. It is embarrassing, and it has happened to me on more than one occasion, to be involved in an arbitration with a 'small' firm from a developing country on one side and the mighty New York law firm who does this every week on the other side. How far can arbitrators go to make sure that the balance is reasonably fair in the way the matter is conducted? I would answer that the tribunal has to be fairly proactive. People may dislike management but that has been my solution.

Finally, I would like you to think about the following portrayal of the Golden Age. My family name is Murray. Five centuries ago in a large chunk of Perth of Scotland there was a panel of seven people called Murray, and all disputes involving Murrays either as claimants or defendants were dealt with by that panel. I would like to see that restored but I fear it is not practical."

*Jingzhou Tao, People's Republic of China*: "Arbitration has really become a business. We talk about the user all the time, but we are really discussing among ourselves. We also should not forget the post-award phase. What are we doing to foster dialogue with the judges who are going to decide whether the party will get the real benefit from the award? This is why I wonder whether ICCA as an institution should have more dialogue with the judiciary, especially in countries which are not as arbitration-friendly, so that we can have more enforcement of awards throughout the globe."

*Frank Murphy, Ireland*: "First, I take away from the discussion we just had that we must not fall into the trap of becoming too cumbersome with documentation, with rules and procedures. We must try and get over what each and every one of us feels when we sit as arbitrators: that is, the fear of being overturned. The fear that somebody will say our decision is rubbish. We've got to be interactive, not so much concerned with how we are going to be perceived, because we will have plenty of time to work that out when the dispute is resolved. If we put our energies and our efforts into bringing the parties together they will in fact at the end of the day resolve the dispute by themselves.

Second, I would like to voice a disagreement with those among us who have talked about confidentiality as a cornerstone of arbitration. Let's be realistic. There is no such thing as confidentiality anymore. You can Google anybody anywhere about anything. This is why we've got to be very careful, we've got to keep everything on record because somebody, some day, will find out about it."

*François Dessemontet, Switzerland*: "It is difficult to speak about 'arbitration' in general. In reality, we should distinguish different kinds of arbitration proceedings. There are arbitrations online, arbitrations with consumers, arbitrations under the auspices of World Trade Organization or investment arbitrations. And, of course, there is inter-state arbitration with specific traditions. We should look at each of these types with different spectacles. We should be concerned with all these different users and not only with the very large companies. We may have one model in mind, but we should be flexible enough to adapt that model to the specific needs of each kind of arbitration."

# Plenary Session

# The New York Convention at 50

# Hypothetical Draft Convention on the International Enforcement of Arbitration Agreements and Awards

## Explanatory Note

*Albert Jan van den Berg*[*]

| TABLE OF CONTENTS | Page |
|---|---|
| General Considerations | 649 |
| Title | 651 |
| Article 1 – Field of Application | 651 |
| Article 2 – Enforcement of Arbitration Agreement | 653 |
| Article 3 – Enforcement of Award – General | 656 |
| Article 4 – Request for Enforcement | 658 |
| Article 5 – Grounds for Refusal of Enforcement | 660 |
| Article 6 – Action for Setting Aside Pending in Country of Origin | 664 |
| Article 7 – More Favorable Right | 665 |
| Article 8 – General Clauses | 666 |
| Annex I: Text of the Hypothetical Draft Convention on the International Enforcement of Arbitration Agreements and Awards | 667 |
| Annex II: Comparison of Texts: Proposal for Revisions to the 1958 New York Convention | 670 |

GENERAL CONSIDERATIONS

1. After fifty years in existence, the Convention on the Recognition and Enforcement of Foreign Arbitral Awards, New York, 10 June 1958 (the New York Convention) is in need of modernization:

(a) A number of provisions need to be added (for example, a definition of the scope of application with respect to agreements that fall under the referral provisions of Art. II(3); a waiver of a party to rely on a ground for refusal of enforcement; a reference to the arbitration agreement in the more-favorable-right provision of Art. VII(1));
(b) A number of provisions need to be revised (for example, the written form as required by Art. II(2) for the arbitration agreement is stricter than almost any national law; the refusal of enforcement on the ground of a setting aside on any ground in the country of origin may import parochial annulment);

---

[*] Hanotiau & van den Berg, Brussels; Member of Amsterdam and Brussels (EU) Bar; President, Netherlands Arbitration Institute (NAI); Professor of law (International Arbitration) Erasmus University, Rotterdam; Member of ICCA.

(c) A number of provisions are unclear (for example, the notion of an award "not considered as domestic" in Art. I(1); the expression "duly authenticated original award" in Art. IV(1)(a); the word "may" in the English text of Art. V(1); the words "terms of submission" and "scope of submission" to arbitration in Art. V(1)(c); the notion of a "suspended" award in Art. V(1)(e); the reference to "any interested party" in Art. VII(1));

(d) A number of provisions are outdated (for example, the reference to "permanent arbitral bodies" in Art. I(2); the reference to the law under which the award was made in Art. V(1)(e)); and

(e) A number of provisions need to be aligned with prevailing judicial interpretation (for example, the public policy referred to in Art. V(2) means international public policy).

2. The Preliminary Draft Convention on International Enforcement of Arbitration Agreements and Awards (the Draft Convention, se this volume, pp. 000-000) is intended to achieve the above modernization. The Draft Convention is also intended to be readily understandable by practitioners and judges in many countries. To achieve that goal, the text is kept at a bare minimum and the solutions offered are clear and simple, and are based on what is current practice.

3. The above shortcomings in the New York Convention cannot be remedied by the UNCITRAL Model Law on International Commercial Arbitration of 1985 (the UNCITRAL Model Law), as revised in 2006. The reason is that the provisions relating to enforcement of an arbitral award as set forth in the UNCITRAL Model Law are almost the same as those contained in Arts. III-VI of the New York Convention (Art. 35), because of the policy decision taken in 1985 to follow as closely as possible the New York Convention.

4. Nor can the New York Convention's shortcomings be remedied adequately and comprehensively by a "Recommendation regarding the interpretation" issued by international bodies such as UNCITRAL in 2006 regarding Arts. II(2) and VII(1). The mechanism of guidance notes in interpreting an international convention is useful for texts that can be subject to various interpretations, but its value is limited if a text is lacking or if the guidance contradicts an existing text.

5. It is expected that the time required for adherence by States to the Draft Convention is less than for the New York Convention, since the Draft Convention builds on the structure and concepts of the New York Convention. Thus, Arts. 1 to 7 of the Draft Convention deal with matters that are similar to those contained in Art. I to VII of the New York Convention. Furthermore, it will be readily understood that the Draft Convention constitutes a necessary update of the New York Convention which has matured after fifty years of existence.

6. The object and purpose of the Draft Convention are the same as for the New York Convention: to facilitate the enforcement of the arbitration agreement and arbitral award as much as possible. However, the Draft Convention is clearer in that the object and purpose aim specifically at international arbitration.

TITLE

7. The title of the Draft Convention reflects what is covered by it: the enforcement of the arbitration agreement (i.e., the referral of the dispute to arbitration) and the enforcement of the arbitral award. The title of the Draft Convention also makes clear that the Draft Convention is intended to serve international arbitration.

8. In contrast to the New York Convention, the Draft Convention's title no longer refers to the enforcement of "foreign" arbitral awards, but rather to the "international" enforcement of arbitral awards. The word "foreign" is omitted since, insofar as its field of application is concerned, the Draft Convention does not distinguish between an award made abroad and an award made within the country in which enforcement of the award is sought (see Art. 1). Instead, the Draft Convention's applicability is dependent on whether the agreement or award is international according to the criteria set forth in Art. 1(1).

ARTICLE 1 – FIELD OF APPLICATION

*Paragraph 1 – Arbitration Agreement*

9. As mentioned, the New York Convention does not contain a definition of which arbitration agreements fall under the referral provisions of its Art. II(3). That lacuna is filled by the definition given in the first paragraph of Art. 1 of the Draft Convention.

10. The definition requires in essence that the arbitration agreement concerns international arbitration. The broad criteria for determining international arbitration as set forth in Art. 1(1) of the Draft Convention are a condensed version of the definition set forth in Art. 1 of the UNCITRAL Model Law. It therefore should be assumed that an arbitration agreement is international for the purposes of the Draft Convention unless the parties have their place of business or residence in the same State and all other elements relevant to the dispute referred to in the agreement are connected only with that State.

11. The court shall refer the dispute to arbitration under the provisions of Art. 2 irrespective of whether the place of arbitration is within or outside the country where the agreement is invoked. The agreement providing for international arbitration as defined in Art. 1(1) is not limited to an agreement providing for arbitration in a country other than the country where the agreement is invoked (which is one of the limited interpretations under Art. II(3) of the New York Convention).

*Paragraph 2 – Arbitral Award*

12. With respect to the enforcement of the arbitral award, according to its Art. I(1), the New York Convention applies to the enforcement of an arbitral award made in another (Contracting) State in any event (first criterion). The New York Convention further applies to the enforcement of an arbitral award that is not considered as a domestic award in the State where the enforcement is sought (second criterion).

13. The first criterion also applies to the enforcement of a purely domestic award under the New York Convention if such an award was made in another (Contracting) State. In contrast, the first criterion excludes an award resulting from an international arbitration that was made in the State where enforcement is sought.

14. The applicability of the second criterion, on the other hand, depends on whether the State where enforcement is sought considers certain awards as non-domestic awards. The drafters of the New York Convention had in mind an arbitral award resulting from an arbitration governed by an arbitration law that is different from the arbitration law of the place of arbitration. The legislation implementing the New York Convention in the United States, as interpreted by the courts, applies the second criterion to arbitral awards that result from an international arbitration in the United States governed by federal law.

15. The uncertainties inherent in the applicability of the New York Convention are resolved by the definition given in para. 2 of Art. 1 of the Draft Convention. According to that definition, the Draft Convention applies to the enforcement of any arbitral award that concerns international arbitration, irrespective of the place where the award was made. The criteria according to which an arbitral award is international are the same as those for the arbitration agreement set forth in para. 1 of the Draft Convention.

16. Under this approach, the same arbitration is treated in a uniform manner for the purposes of the Draft Convention's field of application. This remedies another shortcoming of the New York Convention under which it can happen with respect to the same arbitration that the arbitration agreement is deemed to fall under the referral provisions of Art. II(3), whilst the arbitral award does not come within the New York Convention's definition of its field of application (e.g., the award is made within the country where enforcement is sought).

17. The clear choice for international arbitration also comports with the reference to international public policy in connection with the referral to arbitration (Art. 2(2)(c)) and the enforcement of the award (Art. 5(3)(h)).

18. The definition of the Draft Convention's scope means that the arbitration law of the place of arbitration (which is also the place where the award was or will be made) does not determine the Convention's applicability. On the other hand, the arbitration law of the place of arbitration and award can be relevant under the Convention in a number of other respects (validity of the arbitration agreement, Arts. 2(2)(b) and 5(3)(b); composition of the arbitral tribunal, Art. 5(3)(d); arbitral procedure, Art. 5(3)(e); binding force of the award, Art. 5(3)(f); setting aside of the award, Art. 5(3)(g); (see also para. 94 below)). In this respect too, the Draft Convention complies with the UNCITRAL Model Law whose field of application is in essence territorial.

19. A consequence of the Draft Convention's field of application to the enforcement of any award resulting from an international arbitration is that the references in its text to "the country where the award was made" in Art. 5(3) may include the country where enforcement of the award is sought under the Draft Convention.

*Paragraph 3 – Recognition*

20. Para. 3 provides that the provisions of the Draft Convention apply to the recognition of the arbitral award accordingly. A separate provision regarding recognition is inserted

for reasons of drafting so that the Draft Convention's provisions are not unduly burdened by recurring references to the recognition of the award, as is the case in the New York Convention.

*No Reservations*

21. Unlike Art. I(3) of the New York Convention, the Draft Convention does not offer States the possibility to adopt a reciprocity reservation or a commercial reservation. With respect to the reciprocity reservation, the Draft Convention is premised on the more modern principle of universal applicability of treaties. As regards the commercial reservation, that reservation has not played any significant role in the interpretation and application by the courts of the New York Convention.

ARTICLE 2 – ENFORCEMENT OF ARBITRATION AGREEMENT

22. Art. 2 is an elaboration of Art. II(3) of the New York Convention.

*Paragraph 1 – General Obligation to Refer*

23. Para. 1 sets forth the general obligation of the courts in the Contracting States to enforce arbitration agreements by means of referral to arbitration.

24. The obligation concerns arbitration agreements that fall under the Draft Convention as defined in Art. 1(1). See paras. 9-10 above.

25. The term "refer ... to arbitration" is retained from Art. II(3) of the New York Convention. It includes other forms of enforcing arbitration agreements as practiced in a number of countries (such as the "stay of court proceedings" in favor of arbitration).

26. The text mentions referral of a "dispute" to arbitration, which language is considered to be semantically more correct than referral of the "parties" to arbitration as stated in Art. II(3) of the New York Convention.

27. The language is mandatory ("shall", see also para. 2) and, as is the case under the New York Convention, a court does not have a discretionary power whether or not to refer.

28. The text of para. 1 is concerned with the situation of a dispute having been brought before a national court, as is the case in Art. II(3) of the New York Convention. However, it should not be taken to exclude other types of court proceedings in relation to the arbitration agreement, such as a specific action to compel arbitration.

29. It is not incompatible with the arbitration agreement to which Art. 2 applies for a party to request, before or during the arbitral proceedings, from a court an interim measure of protection, and for a court to grant such measure (cf. Arts. 9 and 17 J of the UNCITRAL Model Law).

*Paragraph 2 – Grounds for Refusal of Referral*

30. Para. 2 of Art. 2 contains a limitative list of circumstances under which a court shall not refer the dispute to arbitration. Referral may not be refused on any other ground.

31. The introductory sentence of para. 2 makes clear that the grounds for non-referral are to be asserted and proven by the party against whom the arbitration agreement is invoked in the court proceedings. Such an express provision is lacking in the New York Convention. It corresponds to the provision in Art. 5(3) of the Draft Convention (built on Art. V(1) of the New York Convention) that the party against whom enforcement of an arbitral award is sought has to assert and prove the grounds for refusal of enforcement of the arbitral award.

*Ground (a) – Arbitration Agreement Not Invoked In Limine Litis*
32. Ground (a) of para. 2 is to the effect that the arbitration agreement is to be invoked before submission of a statement on the substance of the dispute (in ordinary cases, it is the defendant who makes the submission). This is another provision that is lacking in the New York Convention but can be found in a number of arbitration laws (e.g., Art. 8(1) of the UNCITRAL Model Law).

*Ground (b) – Lack of Valid Arbitration Agreement*
33. Ground (b) of para. 2 addresses a major problem under the New York Convention. Art. II(1) of the New York Convention requires the written form for an arbitration agreement, which is defined in Art. II(2) as including "an arbitral clause in a contract or an arbitration agreement, signed by the parties or contained in an exchange of letters or telegrams". The requirement of the written form is more stringent than is imposed by virtually all modern arbitration laws. It prompted UNCITRAL to issue a "Recommendation regarding the interpretation" in 2006, in which it suggested applying Art. II(2) "recognizing that the circumstances described therein are not exhaustive". The interpretation, however, has its limits as the text of Art. II(2) requires either a signed contract or an exchange, which excludes less formal ways of acceptance.

34. It is submitted that requirements for the form of the arbitration agreement are no longer needed. Actually, modern arbitration laws are gradually abandoning the requirement of the written form, treating the arbitration clause on the same footing as other clauses in a contract (see the recent discussion at UNCITRAL, resulting in alternative options for the definition and form of the arbitration agreement in Art. 7 of the UNCITRAL Model Law, at the thirty-ninth session in 2006). The Draft Convention follows this trend by no longer imposing an internationally required written form. Rather, as is the case under the New York Convention in other respects regarding the arbitration agreement, the Draft Convention refers to the applicable law for questions concerning the validity of the arbitration agreement. The applicable law may include provisions similar to the revised Art. 7 of the UNCITRAL Model Law.

35. The New York Convention does not contain a rule of conflict of laws for determining the law applicable to the arbitration agreement at the stage of referral to arbitration. The absence of conflict rules has given rise to diverging judicial interpretations, ranging from the law of the forum to the law where the award will be made or will likely be made. The Draft Convention retains the latter conflict rule since it will lead to the same law governing the arbitration agreement at the stage of enforcement of the arbitral award (see Art. 5(3)(a)). This option is supported by the experience in practice that, whilst a number of laws are potential candidates for governing an arbitration agreement, the law of the place of arbitration is held to be the

governing law in most cases. Furthermore, the applicability of the law of the place of arbitration to the validity of the arbitration agreement has the advantage that a choice by the parties (or arbitral institution) for a favorable place of arbitration implies a choice for a law that is probably also favorable to the validity of the arbitration agreement.

36. Ground (c) mentions the place where the award will be made. The country where the award will be made is the same as the place of arbitration (cf. UNCITRAL Model Law, Art. 31(3)).

37. It will frequently happen that the place of arbitration is known at the time the validity of the arbitration agreement is to be determined under Art. 2 of the Draft Convention. Unlike fifty years ago, parties are now well aware of the legal significance of choosing the place of arbitration, as it entails the applicability of the arbitration law of the place of arbitration, and that it is not to be confused with the place of arbitration in the physical sense (cf. UNCITRAL Model Law, Arts. 1(2) and 20(2); see also para. 94 below). In many cases, the parties have fixed a place of arbitration in their arbitration agreement or have agreed on arbitration rules under which the arbitral institution or the arbitral tribunal determines the place in the absence of an agreement of the parties.

38. In those rare cases in which the place of arbitration is not yet known at that time or any indication is lacking where the award will likely be made, one has to fall back on the arbitration law of the country where the arbitration agreement is invoked.

39. It may be recalled that most arbitration laws adopt the doctrine of the separability of the arbitration agreement, that is, the invalidity of the main contract in which the arbitration agreement (clause) is included or to which the arbitration agreement relates does not affect the validity of the arbitration agreement (e.g., UNCITRAL Model Law, Art. 16(1)). A logical consequence of the separability doctrine is that the law applicable to the contract is not necessarily the same as the law governing the arbitration agreement (clause).

40. Questions regarding validity of the arbitration agreement should be broadly understood. They include capacity, existence, formation, scope and contents. In practice, most cases concern the scope of the arbitration agreement, i.e., whether a dispute is covered by the wording of the arbitration agreement (in the United States also referred to as "arbitrability"). With respect to contents, that matter too is to be determined under the applicable law. The sole exception is public policy (see para. 44 below).

41. There is no need to include in the Draft Convention language such as that which appears in Art. II(1) of the New York Convention ("an agreement in writing under which the parties undertake to submit to arbitration all or any differences which have arisen or which may arise between them in respect of a defined legal relationship, whether contractual or not") as these matters are almost always dealt with by the applicable law (e.g., UNCITRAL Model Law, Art. 7, Option I and II).

42. Ground (b) of para. 2 allows a court to examine the validity of the arbitration agreement on a prima facie basis only in the context of dealing with a request to refer the dispute to arbitration under Art. 2 of the Draft Convention. The reasons for such a limited examination are that the referral should be decided expeditiously by the court, and that that arbitral tribunal is the first instance to conduct a full review of an objection to the validity of the arbitration agreement, subject to eventual subsequent court control in an action for setting aside or enforcement of the arbitral award.

*Ground (c) — Violation of Public Policy*

43. Ground (c) of para. 2 corresponds to the terminal proviso of Art. II(1) of the New York Convention ("concerning a subject matter capable of settlement by arbitration"). There are three differences. First, the ground is listed as a ground for refusal of referral of the dispute to arbitration that is to be asserted and proved by the party against whom the arbitration agreement is invoked (with the possibility of the court relying on it on its own motion pursuant to para. 3). Second, the matter of arbitrability forms part of public policy. Arbitrability, therefore, is not expressed as a separate ground for refusal of referral to arbitration, but is subsumed in the public policy ground. Third, the public policy ground is limited to the narrower category of international public policy as developed by courts in many countries in relation to public policy, including arbitrability, under the New York Convention.

44. Ground (c) of para. 2 concerning public policy also means that it can constitute an exception to the applicability of the law of the place of arbitration for determining the validity of the arbitration agreement as provided in para. 2(b). The exception will occur if the place of arbitration is in a country other than the country where the agreement is invoked. In that case, all questions regarding the validity of the arbitration agreement are to be determined under the law of the place of arbitration, with the exception of questions regarding public policy, in particular arbitrability in the sense of the dispute being capable of settlement by arbitration. These questions are to be judged under the rules of international public policy of the country where the agreement is invoked.

*Paragraph 3 — Application of Public Policy by Court on Its Own Motion*

45. Para. 3 is to be viewed in light of the fact that the New York Convention provides that a court can apply the public policy exception on its own motion with respect to the arbitral award (Art. V(2)). If the Draft Convention expressly allows a court to rely on its own motion on public policy in relation to the arbitral award (see Art. 5(4)), a court should also be allowed to rely on public policy on its own motion in relation to the arbitration agreement. Although — to the extent that it could be researched — a court has never applied the public policy defense on its own motion, that provision is repeated in the Draft Convention for reasons of its acceptability.

ARTICLE 3 — ENFORCEMENT OF AWARD — GENERAL

46. The sequence of the articles concerning enforcement of the arbitral award is the same as under the New York Convention: Art. 3 concerns enforcement in general; Art. 4 deals with the matters that the party seeking enforcement has to accomplish; Art. 5 contains the grounds for refusal of enforcement to be asserted and proven by the party against whom enforcement is sought or to be applied by a court on its own motion; and Art. 6 addresses the situation where the action for setting aside is pending in the country of origin. Within that sequence, a number of redundancies, obstacles and uncertainties created by the New York Convention are dealt with in the Draft Convention.

47. The obligation to enforce awards concerns arbitral awards that fall under the Draft Convention as defined in Art. 1(2). See paras. 12-21 above.

48. Art. 3 no longer contains the New York Convention Art. III language "Each Contracting State shall recognize arbitral awards as binding and", as this language has not proven to be necessary in practice. Rather, like the other provisions of the Draft Convention, Art. 3 specifies that it is to be applied by the courts in the Contracting States.

*Paragraph 1 – Conditions for Enforcement*

49. Para. 1 expresses what is the generally accepted interpretation under the New York Convention: the conditions for enforcement are those set forth in the Convention only. Contracting States are not allowed to add, delete or amend conditions. For example, if an arbitral award comes within the scope of Art. 1(2) of the Draft Convention, an enforcement court is not allowed to impose other requirements as to jurisdiction in respect of a request for enforcement. Para. 1 applies only to awards the enforcement of which is sought under the Draft Convention (see Art. 7 concerning the more favorable right to enforce on another basis).

*Paragraph 2 – Procedure for Enforcement*

50. Para. 2 is also similar to the New York Convention. The Draft Convention does not specify the procedure for enforcement of an arbitral award, which procedure is left to the law of the country where enforcement is sought (subject to the provisions of paras. 3 and 4). In light of the grounds for refusal of enforcement set forth in Art. 5 of the Draft Convention, the procedure implies that the party against whom the award is invoked is afforded the opportunity to present its case. Hence, the procedure is not ex parte.

51. The procedure under the law of the forum cannot be such that it affects in some manner the conditions of enforcement mentioned in the Draft Convention. Accordingly, the Draft Convention's conditions for enforcement referred to in para. 1 prevail over the domestic rules of procedure of enforcement referred to in para. 2 if they conflict with each other.

*Paragraph 3 – No Onerous Requirements*

52. Para. 3 comes in lieu of the second sentence of Art. III of the New York Convention ("There shall not be imposed substantially more onerous conditions or higher fees or charges on the recognition or enforcement of arbitral awards to which this Convention applies than are imposed on the recognition or enforcement of domestic arbitral awards").

53. The language is changed from "conditions" in Art. III of the New York Convention to "requirements on the procedure" in order to make clear the difference between para. 1 (conditions for enforcement are exclusively governed by the Convention) and para. 2 (procedure for enforcement is governed by the law of the country where enforcement is sought). Furthermore, the comparison with the enforcement procedure of domestic awards is abandoned so that a harmonized "light" international standard for the enforcement procedure can be achieved. The change in language should also be viewed in light of the requirement of para. 4.

*Paragraph 4 – Court to Act Expeditiously*

54. Para. 4 addresses a serious problem under the New York Convention: in a number of Contracting States, the procedure for enforcement of Convention awards is unacceptably slow. The Draft Convention stipulates that the courts must act expeditiously on a request for enforcement. Corollary to that obligation is the obligation of the parties to assist the enforcement court in fulfilling the obligation. It is left to the legislature and judiciary in the Contracting States how the enforcement proceedings can be expedited in terms of procedure.

55. Para. 4 prevails over the provisions of para. 3 if and to the extent that the procedure under the law of the country where enforcement is sought has the effect of an unacceptably slow enforcement procedure for an award falling under the Draft Convention.

*Provisions Not Included in the Draft Convention*

56. A counterclaim in enforcement proceedings would in principle be incompatible with the Draft Convention, and in particular paras. 3 and 4 of Art. 3.

57. The Draft Convention does not contain provisions on the periods of limitation for the enforcement of an arbitral award. It is to be noted that these periods vary considerably. For example, the period is six months in People's Republic of China, three years in the United States, six years in England, and twenty years in The Netherlands.

58. Nor does the Draft Convention contain provisions on the awarding of post-judgment interest by the enforcement court. That faculty is granted to courts in some Common Law countries, but unknown in many other countries. There is no need to include provisions on interest in the Draft Convention as interest until the date of payment is usually granted in international awards, provided that a party has specifically sought an award of such interest.

ARTICLE 4 – REQUEST FOR ENFORCEMENT

59. Art. 4 deals with the conditions that a party seeking enforcement of an award within the scope of the Convention should comply with.

*Paragraph 1 – Conditions Entitling Leave for Enforcement*

60. Para. 1 makes clear that the conditions set forth in Art. 4 are the only conditions that need to be met. Once the party seeking enforcement of the award has fulfilled them, that party is entitled to a leave for enforcement on the award, unless the party against whom the award is invoked asserts and proves one of the grounds for refusal of enforcement set forth in Art. 5(3), or the enforcement court finds that enforcement of the award would violate its international public policy under Art. 5(3)(h) in conjunction with Art. 5(4).

61. Para. 1 further specifies that the presence of grounds for refusal of enforcement can be found by a court "under the conditions of Arts. 5 and 6", which include: the principles set out in Art. 5(1)-(2) (grounds for refusal of enforcement are exclusive and

to be applied in manifest cases only); Art. 5(5) (waiver of right to invoke a ground for refusal of enforcement); and Art. 6 (setting aside action pending in country of origin, i.e., country where award was made).

*Paragraph 2 – Original Award*

62. Para. 2 requires a party seeking enforcement of an award to submit the original of the award. Para. 3 adds that instead of the original of the award, a certified copy can be supplied.

63. Art. IV(1)(a) of the New York Convention requires the submission of "the duly authenticated original award or a duly certified copy thereof". In practice, a party seeking enforcement either submits the original of the award, without any authentication, or a certified copy. The text of para. 2 of Art. 4 of the Draft Convention conforms to that practice.

*Paragraph 3 – Copy of the Award*

64. Para. 3 allows a party seeking enforcement to submit a certified copy. Under the New York Convention, most courts accept a certification by a variety of authorities (the administrator of a reputed arbitral institution; a notary public; a consular service) and do not impose formalistic requirements. That practice is carried forward in para. 3 by providing that the certification should be in such form as directed by the court before which enforcement is sought.

*Paragraph 4 – Translation*

65. Para. 4 is also less formal than Art. IV(2) of the New York Convention which prescribes a translation that in all cases is certified by "an official or sworn translator or by a diplomatic or consular agent". A number of courts no longer require the translation of documents if they are familiar with the foreign language in question (notably English). The main reason for this attitude is to avoid unnecessary costs, as it is commonly known that the translation of an arbitral award can be expensive. Para. 4 reflects that practice.

*No Submission of Arbitration Agreement*

66. Unlike Art. IV(1)(b) of the New York Convention, Art. 4 of the Draft Convention does not oblige the party seeking enforcement of the award to supply (a copy of) the arbitration agreement. The abandonment of this requirement follows the liberalization of the formal requirements regarding the arbitration agreement in the Draft Convention (see para. 33 above).

67. An identical amendment was made with respect to the UNCITRAL Model Law in 2006, in which the presentation of a copy of the arbitration agreement is no longer required under Art. 35(2) for enforcement of the award irrespective of the country of origin.

68. Moreover, certain courts interpret Art. IV(1)(b) of the New York Convention as requiring the party seeking enforcement to prove the validity of the arbitration

agreement, which is contrary to one of the main features of the Convention that the party against whom the enforcement is sought has the burden to prove the invalidity of the arbitration agreement. That main feature is retained in the Draft Convention (Art. 5(3)(a)).

69. The arbitration agreement on which the arbitral award is based is almost always referenced in the arbitral award so that no uncertainty will exist regarding the agreement on which the award is based.

*Other Provisions Not Included in the Draft Convention*

70. The phrase "at the time of the application" as appearing in Art. IV(1) of the New York Convention has not been retained either. The phrase has led to refusals of enforcement by some courts on formalistic grounds. By omitting the phrase in the Draft Convention, courts are offered more flexibility to determine the latest moment at which a party can submit the original or certified copy of the arbitral award in the proceedings (or rectify an incorrect filing).

ARTICLE 5 — GROUNDS FOR REFUSAL OF ENFORCEMENT

71. Art. 5 is modeled on Art. V of the New York Convention with a number of clarifications and adjustments.

*Paragraph 1 — Grounds Are Limitative*

72. Para. 1 provides that the grounds for refusal of enforcement are listed limitatively. No other grounds may be applied. In particular, the review of the merits of an arbitral award is not one of the grounds for refusal of enforcement set forth in Art. 5.

*Paragraph 2 — In Manifest Cases Only*

73. Para. 2 addresses an issue under the New York Convention: does an enforcement court have a residual power to enforce an award notwithstanding the presence of a ground for refusal of enforcement? The answer to the question is given in para. 2 by providing that enforcement shall be refused in manifest cases only. In manifest cases, there is no room for the application of a residual power.

74. Para. 2 comports with the underlying rationale that enforcement should be refused solely in serious cases. See also Art. 5(5) (waiver of right to invoke ground for refusal).

*Paragraph 3 — Ground for Refusal of Enforcement*

75. Paras. 2 and 5 of Art. 5 combined alleviate the need to deal with the question under Art. V(1) of the New York Convention whether the introductory language of the grounds for refusal of enforcement should be permissive ("enforcement may be refused") or mandatory ("enforcement shall be refused"). Having both provisions in the Draft

Convention, the introductory language of para. 3 can be unambiguous by being mandatory.

76. The introductory language of para. 3 is also clearer than Art. V(1) of the New York Convention in respect of the distinction between an assertion and proof for the assertion.

*Ground (a) – Lack of Valid Arbitration Agreement*
77. Ground (a) of Art. 5(3) is a simplified version of Art. V(1)(a) of the New York Convention. First, as the Draft Convention no longer imposes requirements for the form of the arbitration agreement, there is no reference to a corresponding provision in the Convention (comp. Art. V(1)(a) of the New York Convention: "the agreement referred to in Art. II"). Second, all questions regarding the validity of the arbitration agreement are deemed to be covered by the expression "no valid arbitration agreement". Third, the conflict rules are reduced to one simple rule: the law of the country where the award was made. That country is synonymous with the place of arbitration. See paras. 33-40 above; see also para. 66 above.

78. The uniform and simple conflict rule applies also to questions regarding the capacity of the parties to conclude the arbitration agreement. It therefore is not necessary to include in ground (a) an express reference to the incapacity of a party as is made in Art. V(1)(a) of the New York Convention ("under the law applicable, were under some incapacity").

*Ground (b) – Violation of Due Process*
79. Ground (b) of Art. 5(3) is a modernized version of Art. V(1)(b) of the New York Convention. It embodies the fundamental due process rights as set forth in current arbitration legislation (e.g., UNCITRAL Model Law, Art. 18, the difference being that "full opportunity" is replaced by "reasonable opportunity" in the Draft Convention).

*Ground (c) – Excess of Authority*
80. Ground (c) of Art. 5(3) is a simplified version of Art. V(1(c) of the New York Convention, whose language, moreover, is unclear (see para. 1(c) above).

81. Ground (c) applies if the arbitral tribunal has granted more than the relief sought (*extra petita*). In that case, enforcement can still be granted for that part of the relief granted that is within the relief sought, provided that the two can be severed.

82. The matter of the relief granted outside the relief sought (*extra petita*) must be distinguished from the relief granted outside the scope of the arbitration agreement but within the relief sought. In such a case, ground (a) of Art. 5(3) (invalid arbitration agreement) applies, and not ground (c).

*Grounds (d) and (e) – Irregular Composition of Arbitral Tribunal or Arbitral Procedure*
83. Grounds (d) and (e) of Art. 5(3) are similar to ground (d) of Art. V(1) of the New York Convention. For reasons of clarity, they are presented in separate grounds.

84. If and to the extent that there is an agreement of the parties on the composition of the arbitral tribunal or the arbitral procedure, the arbitration law of the country where the award was made (i.e., the place of arbitration) does not come into play insofar as grounds (d) and (e) of Art. 5(3) of the Draft Convention are concerned. Under the

present text of Art. V(1)(d) of the New York Convention, that rule has given rise to the question whether an agreement of the parties on those matters can also deviate from the mandatory rules of the arbitration law of the place of arbitration (e.g., an agreement on an even number of arbitrators in a country where an uneven number is mandatorily prescribed by the law). The text of Art. 5(3)(d)-(e) does not allow refusal of enforcement on the basis of such a contravention. In that case, an aggrieved party should seek the setting aside of the award in the country of origin and, if successful, seek the refusal of enforcement on ground (g), i.e., the award has been set aside in the country where it was made. The same solution is offered by the UNCITRAL Model Law (comp. Art. 34(2)(a)(iv) with Art. 36(1)(a)(iv)).

85. As mentioned before, the expression "the law of the country where the award was made" can refer to the country where enforcement of the award is sought (see para. 18 above).

*Ground (f) – Award Not Binding*
86. Ground (f) of Art. 5(3) corresponds to Art. V(1)(e) of the New York Convention inasmuch as it concerns the expression "the award has not yet become binding on the parties". The word "binding" had been inserted in the New York Convention in lieu of the word "final" as it appeared in the Geneva Convention of 1927 in order to denote that a leave for enforcement on the award granted by a court in the country of origin is no longer required for enforcement abroad (the system of the so-called "double exequatur").

87. The word "binding" in the New York Convention, however, has given rise to differing interpretations. The Draft Convention retains the prevailing interpretation that the word "binding" means that an award is not binding if it is still open to appeal on the merits before an appeal arbitral tribunal or a court in the country of origin. Appeal arbitration is allowed in a number of countries and specifically agreed to, in particular, in commodity arbitration. An appeal on the merits before a court is rare nowadays. The possibility of a setting aside or annulment of an arbitral award in the country of origin is not equivalent to an appeal on the merits. Consequently, in most cases an arbitral award can be enforced under the Draft Convention as soon as it is rendered.

*Ground (g) – Award Set Aside in Country of Origin*
88. The action to set aside (annul, vacate) an arbitral award is contemplated by virtually all arbitration laws. The competence to consider and decide on the setting aside of an arbitral award belongs exclusively to the courts of the country where the award was made (the country of origin, which is equivalent to the place of arbitration). Setting aside is to be distinguished from enforcement which can be considered and decided by courts of any country insofar as it concerns the courts' (territorial) jurisdiction.

89. Ground (g) adopts the solution offered by Art. IX(2) of the European Convention on International Commercial Arbitration of 1961. Accordingly, the refusal of enforcement is limited to cases where the award has been set aside on grounds equivalent to grounds (a) to (e) of Art. 5(3) of the Draft Convention. Grounds (a) to (e) of Art. 5(3) correspond in turn to generally recognized grounds for setting aside an arbitral award resulting from international arbitration (see Art. 34(2)(a) of the UNCITRAL Model Law).

90. The term "equivalent" is chosen since the wording of the grounds for setting aside may differ under domestic law. The expression refers to grounds that may be semantically different but are comparable in content and scope.

91. The solution proposed in ground (g) of Art. 5(3) of the Draft Convention means, in particular, that a setting aside on (domestic) public policy or parochial grounds in the country of origin is not a ground for refusal of enforcement under the Draft Convention.

92. Ground (g) offers a solution between two extreme positions. On the one hand, Art. V(1)(e) of the New York Convention provides as a ground for refusal of enforcement an award that has been set aside on any ground in the country of origin. On the other, according to French courts, the setting aside of the award in the country of origin is no ground for refusal of enforcement at all in France. The French courts take that position outside an application of the New York Convention.

93. Ground (g) concerns the situation that the award has been set aside in the country of origin. If an action for setting aside the award is pending in the country of origin, the provisions of Art. 6 apply.

94. Ground (g) does not include the expression "under the law of which" the award was made, as is the case for Art. V(1)(e) of the New York Convention. Having regard to the observations made in para. 36 above, the reference to the country where the award was made suffices. In practice, parties almost never agree to the applicability of arbitration law other than the law of the place of arbitration.

*Ground (h) – Violation of Public Policy*
95. Ground (h) corresponds to Art. V(2) of the New York Convention. As is the case for the referral to arbitration (see para. 43 above), there are three differences. First, the ground is listed as a ground for refusal of enforcement that is to be asserted and proven by the party against whom enforcement of the award is sought (with the possibility of the court relying on it on its own motion pursuant to para. 4). Second, the matter of arbitrability forms part of public policy. Arbitrability, therefore, is not mentioned as a separate ground for refusal of enforcement, but is subsumed under the public policy ground. Third, public policy is limited to the narrower category of international public policy as developed by courts in many countries in relation to public policy, including arbitrability, under the New York Convention.

Suspension of Award
96. The grounds for refusal of enforcement of an award under the Draft Convention do not include a suspension of the award in the country of origin. Art. V(1)(e) of the New York Convention contains such a ground, which has caused uncertainty in practice. Courts interpret the ground to mean that it refers to a suspension of enforcement. The courts are divided whether it contemplates a suspension of enforcement specifically ordered by a court only or also a suspension by operation of law (which occurs in some countries when an application for setting aside is made). As matters regarding enforcement in the country of origin, including suspension of enforcement, are limited to that country, there is no need to address this in the Draft Convention.

*Paragraph 4 — Application of Public Policy by Court on Its Own Motion*

97. Para. 4 is explained in para. 45 above.

*Paragraph 5 — Waiver of the Right to Invoke a Ground for Refusal of Enforcement*

98. With respect to para. 5, the New York Convention does not contain an express provision on the waiver of a right to invoke a ground for refusal of enforcement. Some courts have interpreted the New York Convention as implying a discretionary power not to refuse enforcement if a party can be held to have waived the right to rely on a ground for refusal of enforcement, but this is not an established interpretation. The interpretation is mainly based on the permissive expression "enforcement may be refused" in the opening proviso in Art. V(1) of the New York Convention in its English text. The Draft Convention, however, employs the mandatory expression "enforcement shall be refused", which would no longer permit the interpretation (see para. 75 above).

99. For those reasons, the Draft Convention contains express provisions on the waiver of the right to invoke a ground for refusal of enforcement in para. 5 of Art. 5. The provisions are based on Art. 4 of the UNCITRAL Model Law.

100. The provisions of para. 5 apply in the enforcement proceedings under the Draft Convention irrespective of whether or not the arbitration law of the place of arbitration contains similar waiver provisions. In this manner, a better uniform treatment of the enforcement of awards can be achieved.

101. The waiver is limited to grounds (a) to (e) of Art. 5(3). Grounds (f) and (g) are not matters that can be the subject of a waiver since they occur subsequent to the arbitration (i.e., binding force of the award and setting aside of the award, respectively). Ground (h) is not a matter for a waiver in the arbitration either, since it concerns international public policy of the country where the enforcement is sought.

ARTICLE 6 — ACTION FOR SETTING ASIDE PENDING IN COUNTRY OF ORIGIN

102. Art. 6 is similar to Art. VI of the New York Convention.

*Paragraph 1 — Adjournment*

103. Para. 1 codifies the prevailing interpretation by the courts under the New York Convention that an enforcement court has the discretionary power to adjourn the decision on enforcement. In order to preserve a broad power of the enforcement courts in that respect, the Draft Convention does not codify the test regularly used by the enforcement courts when considering an application to adjourn, which is the likelihood of success of the setting aside action in the country of origin.

104. It is not deemed necessary to specify in the text of para. 1 that the expression "pending" refers not only to a pending setting aside action in first instance, but also to an appeal, including the period for lodging the appeal, unless a party has validly renounced the appeal.

*Paragraph 2 – Security*

105. Para. 2 expands the terminal proviso in Art. VI of the New York Convention ("and may also, on the application of the party claiming enforcement, order the other party to give suitable security").

106. If the decision on enforcement is adjourned, the enforcement court may, at the request of the party seeking enforcement, order the party against whom enforcement is sought to provide suitable security for the event that the application for setting aside is rejected in the country of origin.

107. On the other hand, if the decision on enforcement is not adjourned, the enforcement court may, at the request of the party against whom enforcement is sought, order the party seeking enforcement to provide suitable security for the event that, subsequent to enforcement, the award is set aside in the country of origin. The justification for the latter case is that the party against whom the award is enforced should be able to recover what it has paid to the other party in the enforcement action. However, courts will likely exercise more restraint in ordering security to be provided by a party seeking enforcement of an award since the Draft Convention's goal is to facilitate enforcement.

108. The form of "suitable security" is also left to the discretion of the enforcement court. It is customary in many countries to order the relevant party to provide an appropriate bank guarantee or to pay the amount in question into an escrow account.


ARTICLE 7 – MORE FAVORABLE RIGHT

109. Art. 7 contains a more-favorable-right provision that is based on Art. VII(1) of the New York Convention. It forms part of the Draft Convention's goal to facilitate enforcement in as large a number of cases as possible. The Draft Convention is conceived as imposing minimum requirements only and a Contracting State may be less demanding than the Convention by offering a more liberal legal regime.

110. The text of Art. VII(1) of the New York Convention applies to the enforcement of the arbitral award only and does not mention the arbitration agreement. UNCITRAL suggests in its "Recommendation regarding the interpretation" of 2006 that Art. VII(1) "should be applied to allow any interested party to avail itself of the rights it may have, under the law or treaties of the country where an arbitration agreement is sought to be relied upon, to seek recognition of the validity of such an arbitration agreement". That interpretation is codified in Art. 7 which expressly refers to both the arbitration agreement and the arbitral award.

111. Art. VII(1) of the New York Convention is drafted in an indirect manner: the provisions of the New York Convention shall not "deprive any interested party of any right he may have to avail himself of an arbitral award in the manner and to the extent allowed by the law or treaties of the country where the award is relied upon". Art. 7 is clearer by referring to enforcement on a legal basis other than the Draft Convention in the country where the agreement or award is relied upon.

112. The "legal basis" mentioned in Art. 7 can be another treaty, domestic statute law or case law concerning the enforcement of arbitration agreements or arbitral awards in

international arbitration. Such law and treaties may be applicable in particular to the referral of a dispute to international arbitration outside the court's jurisdiction and the enforcement of arbitral awards rendered abroad in an international arbitration.

113. Art. 7 implies a fork in the road with respect to the legal basis on which enforcement is sought. If the party seeking enforcement has elected another legal basis for enforcement, that basis applies to the exclusion of the Convention. If the legal basis were a combination of the Draft Convention and another legal basis, a party seeking enforcement could select a combination that deprives the other party of its rights to defenses under the Draft Convention. That would be inconsistent with the balanced scheme for the defenses offered by the Draft Convention, and, hence, constitute a violation of due process.

114. Conversely, a party against whom enforcement is sought is not allowed to rely on another basis for its defenses to enforcement, unless and until the party seeking enforcement has elected another legal basis. It would be incompatible with the Draft Convention if a party seeks enforcement on the basis of the Convention, but the other party is allowed to invoke in whole or in part defenses originating from another legal basis.

115. In practice, however, it is expected that in almost all cases the party seeking enforcement will rely on the legal regime of the Draft Convention since it is rather favorable to enforcement.

116. Art. VII(1) of the New York Convention also contains a so-called "compatibility provision", i.e., the New York Convention does not affect the validity of other multilateral or bilateral treaties concerning enforcement. The compatibility provision is one of the provisions that is possibly to be inserted as part of the General Clauses since it is a typical treaty provision.

ARTICLE 8 – GENERAL CLAUSES

117. The General Clauses are to be considered and possibly included in the Draft Convention. They include amongst others:

(a) Designation of Competent Enforcement Court
(b) Interpretation
(c) Relationship with the New York Convention
(d) References to the New York Convention in other treaties
(e) Compatibility with other treaties
(f) [No] reservations
(g) General reciprocity (see also para. 21 above)
(h) Applicability of the Draft Convention to territories and in federal states
(i) Signature, ratification and accession, and deposit
(j) Entry into force
(k) Retroactive [in]applicability; transitional clauses
(l) Denunciation
(m) Notifications
(n) Language of authentic texts.

# ANNEX I

# Text of the Hypothetical Draft Convention on the International Enforcement of Arbitration Agreements and Awards

*Article 1 — Field of Application*
1. This Convention applies to the enforcement of an arbitration agreement if:

(a) the parties to the arbitration agreement have, at the time of the conclusion of that agreement, their place of business or residence in different States, or
(b) the subject matter of the arbitration agreement relates to more than one State.

    2. This Convention applies also to the enforcement of an arbitral award based on an arbitration agreement referred to in paragraph 1.
    3. Where this Convention refers to the enforcement of an arbitral award, it comprises the recognition of an arbitral award.

*Article 2 — Enforcement of Arbitration Agreement*
1. If a dispute is brought before a court of a Contracting State which the parties have agreed to submit to arbitration, the court shall, at the request of a party, refer the dispute to arbitration, subject to the conditions set forth in this article.
    2. The court shall not refer the dispute to arbitration if the party against whom the arbitration agreement is invoked asserts and proves that:

(a) the other party has requested the referral subsequent to the submission of its first statement on the substance of the dispute in the court proceedings; or
(b) there is prima facie no valid arbitration agreement under the law of the country where the award will be made; or
(c) arbitration of the dispute would violate international public policy as prevailing in the country where the agreement is invoked.

    3. The court may on its own motion refuse to refer the dispute to arbitration on ground (c) mentioned in paragraph 2.

*Article 3 — Enforcement of Award — General*
1. An arbitral award shall be enforced exclusively on the basis of the conditions set forth in this Convention.
    2. The law of the country where enforcement is sought shall govern the procedure for enforcement of the award.
    3. There shall not be imposed onerous requirements on the procedure for enforcement nor substantial fees or charges.
    4. Courts shall act expeditiously on a request for enforcement of an arbitral award.

*Article 4 – Request for Enforcement*
1. Fulfillment of the conditions set forth in this article entitles the party seeking enforcement to be granted enforcement of the arbitral award, unless the court finds that a ground for refusal is present under the conditions set forth in articles 5 and 6.
2. The party seeking enforcement shall supply to the court the original of the arbitral award.
3. Instead of an original of the arbitral award, the party seeking enforcement may submit a copy certified as conforming to the original. The certification shall be in such form as directed by the court.
4. If the arbitral award is not in an official language of the court before which enforcement is sought, the party seeking enforcement shall, at the request of the other party or the court, submit a translation. The translation shall be in such form as directed by the court.

*Article 5 – Grounds for Refusal of Enforcement*
1. Enforcement of an arbitral award shall not be refused on any ground other than the grounds expressly set forth in this article.
2. Enforcement shall be refused on the grounds set forth in this article in manifest cases only.
3. Enforcement of an arbitral award shall be refused if, at the request of the party against whom the award is invoked, that party asserts and proves that:

(a) there is no valid arbitration agreement under the law of the country where the award was made; or
(b) the party against whom the award is invoked was not treated with equality or was not given a reasonable opportunity of presenting its case; or
(c) the relief granted in the award is more than, or different from, the relief sought in the arbitration and such relief cannot be severed from the relief sought and granted; or
(d) the composition of the arbitral tribunal was not in accordance with the agreement of the parties, or in the absence of such an agreement, not in accordance with the law of the country where the award was made; or
(e) the arbitral procedure was not in accordance with the agreement of the parties, or in the absence of such an agreement, not in accordance with the law of the country where the award was made; or
(f) the award is subject to appeal on the merits before an arbitral appeal tribunal or a court in the country where the award was made; or
(g) the award has been set aside by the court in the country where the award was made on grounds equivalent to grounds (a) to (e) of this paragraph; or
(h) enforcement of the award would violate international public policy as prevailing in the country where enforcement is sought.

4. The court may on its own motion refuse enforcement of an arbitral award on ground (h) of paragraph 3.
5. The party against whom the award is invoked cannot rely on grounds (a) to (e) of paragraph 3 if that party has not raised them in the arbitration without undue delay after the moment when the existence of the ground became known to that party.

*Article 6 – Action for Setting Aside Pending in Country of Origin*
1. If the application for setting aside the award referred to in article 5(3)(g) is pending in the country where the award was made, the court before which the enforcement of the award is sought under this Convention has the discretion to adjourn the decision on the enforcement.

2. When deciding on the adjournment, the court may, at the request of a party, require suitable security from the party seeking enforcement or the party against whom the award is invoked.

*Article 7 – More Favorable Right*
If an arbitration agreement or arbitral award can be enforced on a legal basis other than this Convention in the country where the agreement or award is invoked, a party seeking enforcement is allowed to rely on such basis.

*Article 8 – General Clauses*
The General Clauses to be considered and possibly included in the Draft Convention include amongst others:

(a) Designation of Competent Enforcement Court
(b) Interpretation
(c) Relationship with the New York Convention
(d) References to the New York Convention in other treaties
(e) Compatibility with other treaties
(f) [No] reservations
(g) General reciprocity
(h) Applicability of the Draft Convention to territories and in federal states
(i) Signature, ratification and accession, and deposit
(j) Entry into force
(k) Retroactive [in]applicability; transitional clauses
(l) Denunciation
(m) Notifications
(n) Language of authentic texts.

# ANNEX II

# Comparison of Texts:
# Proposal for Revisions to the 1958 New York Convention

| NEW YORK CONVENTION 1958 | HYPOTHETICAL DRAFT CONVENTION 2008 |
| --- | --- |
| *Article I* | *Article 1 – Field of Application* |
| [No comparable provision] | 1. This Convention applies to the enforcement of an arbitration agreement if:<br>(a) the parties to the arbitration agreement have, at the time of the conclusion of that agreement, their place of business or residence in different States, or<br>(b) the subject matter of the arbitration agreement relates to more than one State. |
| 1. This Convention shall apply to the recognition and enforcement of arbitral awards made in the territory of a State other than the State where the recognition and enforcement of such awards are sought, and arising out of differences between persons, whether physical or legal. It shall also apply to arbitral awards not considered as domestic awards in the State where their recognition and enforcement are sought. | 2. This Convention applies also to the enforcement of an arbitral award based on an arbitration agreement referred to in paragraph 1. |
| [Passim] | 3. Where this Convention refers to the enforcement of an arbitral award, it comprises the recognition of an arbitral award. |
| 2. The term "arbitral awards" shall include not only awards made by arbitrators appointed for each case but also those made by permanent arbitral bodies to which the parties have submitted. | [Deleted] |

| NEW YORK CONVENTION 1958 | HYPOTHETICAL DRAFT CONVENTION 2008 |
|---|---|
| 3. When signing, ratifying or acceding to this Convention, or notifying extension under article X hereof, any State may on the basis of reciprocity declare that it will apply the Convention to the recognition and enforcement of awards made only in the territory of another Contracting State. It may also declare that it will apply the Convention only to differences arising out of legal relationships, whether contractual or not, which are considered as commercial under the national law of the State making such declaration. | *[See Article 8 - General Clauses below]* |
| *Article II* | *Article 2 – Enforcement of Arbitration Agreement* |
| 1. Each Contracting State shall recognize an agreement in writing under which the parties undertake to submit to arbitration all or any differences which have arisen or which may arise between them in respect of a defined legal relationship, whether contractual or not, concerning a subject matter capable of settlement by arbitration. | *[Deleted in part; see paragraph 3(c)]* |
| 2. The term "agreement in writing" shall include an arbitral clause in a contract or an arbitration agreement, signed by the parties or contained in an exchange of letters or telegrams. | *[Deleted]* |
| 3. The court of a Contracting State, when seized of an action in a matter in respect of which the parties have made an agreement within the meaning of this article, shall, at the request of one of the parties, refer the parties to arbitration, unless it finds that the said agreement is null and void, inoperative or incapable of being performed. | 1. If a dispute is brought before a court of a Contracting State which the parties have agreed to submit to arbitration, the court shall, at the request of a party, refer the dispute to arbitration, subject to the conditions set forth in this article. |

| NEW YORK CONVENTION 1958 | HYPOTHETICAL DRAFT CONVENTION 2008 |
|---|---|
| *[See in part paragraph 3 above]* | 2. The court shall not refer the dispute to arbitration if the party against whom the arbitration agreement is invoked asserts and proves that: |
| *[No comparable provision]* | (a) the other party has requested the referral subsequent to the submission of its first statement on the substance of the dispute in the court proceedings; or |
| *[See paragraph 3]* | (b) there is *prima facie* no valid arbitration agreement under the law of the country where the award will be made; or |
| *[See paragraph 1 in fine]* | (c) arbitration of the dispute would violate international public policy as prevailing in the country where the agreement is invoked. |
| *[No comparable provision]* | 3. The court may on its own motion refuse to refer the dispute to arbitration on ground (c) mentioned in paragraph 2. |
| **Article III** | ***Article 3 – Enforcement of Award – General*** |
| Each Contracting State shall recognize arbitral awards as binding and enforce them in accordance with the rules of procedure of the territory where the award is relied upon, under the conditions laid down in the following articles. There shall not be imposed substantially more onerous conditions or higher fees or charges on the recognition or enforcement of arbitral awards to which this Convention applies than are imposed on the recognition or enforcement of domestic arbitral awards. | 1. An arbitral award shall be enforced exclusively on the basis of the conditions set forth in this Convention. |
| | 2. The law of the country where enforcement is sought shall govern the procedure for enforcement of the award. |
| | 3. There shall not be imposed onerous requirements on the procedure for enforcement nor substantial fees or charges. |

| NEW YORK CONVENTION 1958 | HYPOTHETICAL DRAFT CONVENTION 2008 |
|---|---|
| *[No comparable provision]* | 4. Courts shall act expeditiously on a request for enforcement of an arbitral award. |
| **Article IV** | **Article 4 – *Request for Enforcement*** |
| *[No comparable provision]* | 1. Fulfillment of the conditions set forth in this article entitles the party seeking enforcement to be granted enforcement of the arbitral award, unless the court finds that a ground for refusal is present under the conditions set forth in articles 5 and 6. |
| 1. To obtain the recognition and enforcement mentioned in the preceding article, the party applying for recognition and enforcement shall, at the time of the application, supply:<br>(a) The duly authenticated original award or a duly certified copy thereof; | 2. The party seeking enforcement shall supply to the court the original of the arbitral award. |
| *[See paragraph 1(a)]* | 3. Instead of an original of the arbitral award, the party seeking enforcement may submit a copy certified as conforming to the original. The certification shall be in such form as directed by the court. |
| (b) The original agreement referred to in article II or a duly certified copy thereof. | *[Deleted]* |
| 2. If the said award or agreement is not made in an official language of the country in which the award is relied upon, the party applying for recognition and enforcement of the award shall produce a translation of these documents into such language. The translation shall be certified by an official or sworn translator or by a diplomatic or consular agent. | 4. If the arbitral award is not in an official language of the court before which enforcement is sought, the party seeking enforcement shall, at the request of the other party or the court, submit a translation. The translation shall be in such form as directed by the court. |

| NEW YORK CONVENTION 1958 | HYPOTHETICAL DRAFT CONVENTION 2008 |
|---|---|
| *Article V* | *Article 5 – Grounds for Refusal of Enforcement* |
| [No comparable provision] | 1. Enforcement of an arbitral award shall not be refused on any ground other than the grounds expressly set forth in this article. |
| [No comparable provision] | 2. Enforcement shall be refused on the grounds set forth in this article in manifest cases only. |
| 1. Recognition and enforcement of the award may be refused, at the request of the party against whom it is invoked, only if that party furnishes to the competent authority where the recognition and enforcement is sought, proof that: | 3. Enforcement of an arbitral award shall be refused if, at the request of the party against whom the award is invoked, that party asserts and proves that: |
| (a) The parties to the agreement referred to in article II were, under the law applicable to them, under some incapacity, or the said agreement is not valid under the law to which the parties have subjected it or, failing any indication thereon, under the law of the country where the award was made; or | (a) there is no valid arbitration agreement under the law of the country where the award was made; or |
| (b) The party against whom the award is invoked was not given proper notice of the appointment of the arbitrator or of the arbitration proceedings or was otherwise unable to present his case; or | (b) the party against whom the award is invoked was not treated with equality or was not given a reasonable opportunity of presenting its case; or |

| NEW YORK CONVENTION 1958 | HYPOTHETICAL DRAFT CONVENTION 2008 |
|---|---|
| (c) The award deals with a difference not contemplated by or not falling within the terms of the submission to arbitration, or it contains decisions on matters beyond the scope of the submission to arbitration, provided that, if the decisions on matters submitted to arbitration can be separated from those not so submitted, that part of the award which contains decisions on matters submitted to arbitration may be recognized and enforced; or | (c) the relief granted in the award is more than, or different from, the relief sought in the arbitration and such relief cannot be severed from the relief sought and granted; or |
| (d) The composition of the arbitral authority or the arbitral procedure was not in accordance with the agreement of the parties, or, failing such agreement, was not in accordance with the law of the country where the arbitration took place; or | (d) the composition of the arbitral tribunal was not in accordance with the agreement of the parties, or in the absence of such an agreement, not in accordance with the law of the country where the award was made; or |
| [See paragraph 1(d)] | (e) the arbitral procedure was not in accordance with the agreement of the parties, or in the absence of such an agreement, not in accordance with the law of the country where the award was made; or |
| (e) The award has not yet become binding on the parties, or has been set aside or suspended by a competent authority of the country in which, or under the law of which, that award was made. | (f) the award is subject to appeal on the merits before an arbitral appeal tribunal or a court in the country where the award was made; or |

| NEW YORK CONVENTION 1958 | HYPOTHETICAL DRAFT CONVENTION 2008 |
|---|---|
| *[See paragraph 1(e)]* | (g) the award has been set aside by the court in the country where the award was made on grounds equivalent to grounds (a) to (e) of this paragraph; or |
| 2. Recognition and enforcement of an arbitral award may also be refused if the competent authority in the country where recognition and enforcement is sought finds that: | *[See paragraph 4 below]* |
| (a) The subject matter of the difference is not capable of settlement by arbitration under the law of that country; or | *[Subsumed in ground (h) below]* |
| (b) The recognition or enforcement of the award would be contrary to the public policy of that country. | (h) enforcement of the award would violate international public policy as prevailing in the country where enforcement is sought. |
|  | 4. The court may on its own motion refuse enforcement of an arbitral award on ground (h) of paragraph 3. |
| *[No comparable provision]* | 5. The party against whom the award is invoked cannot rely on grounds (a) to (e) of paragraph 3 if that party has not raised them in the arbitration without undue delay after the moment when the existence of the ground became known to that party. |
| **Article VI** | *Article 6 – Action for Setting Aside Pending in Country of Origin* |
| If an application for the setting aside or suspension of the award has been made to a competent authority referred to in article V(1)(e), the authority before which the award is sought to be relied upon may, if it considers it proper, adjourn the decision on the | 1. If the application for setting aside the award referred to in article 5(3)(g) is pending in the country where the award was made, the court before which the enforcement of the award is sought under this Convention has the discretion to adjourn the decision on the enforcement. |

| NEW YORK CONVENTION 1958 | HYPOTHETICAL DRAFT CONVENTION 2008 |
|---|---|
| enforcement of the award and may also, on the application of the party claiming enforcement of the award, order the other party to give suitable security. | |
| | 2. When deciding on the adjournment, the court may, at the request of a party, require suitable security from the party seeking enforcement or the party against whom the award is invoked. |
| *Article VII(1)* | *Article 7 – More-Favourable-Right* |
| 1. The provisions of the present Convention shall not affect the validity of multilateral or bilateral agreements concerning the recognition and enforcement of arbitral awards entered into by the Contracting States nor deprive any interested party of any right he may have to avail himself of an arbitral award in the manner and to the extent allowed by the law or the treaties of the country where such award is sought to be relied upon. | If an arbitration agreement or arbitral award can be enforced on a legal basis other than this Convention in the country where the agreement or award is invoked, a party seeking enforcement is allowed to rely on such basis. |
| *Articles VII(2) - XVI* | *Article 8 - General Clauses* |
| | The General Clauses to be considered and possibly included in the Draft Convention include amongst others: |
| [No comparable provision] | (a) Designation of Competent Enforcement Court |
| [No comparable provision] | (b) Interpretation |
| Article VII(2) | (c) Relationship with the New York Convention |

| NEW YORK CONVENTION 1958 | HYPOTHETICAL DRAFT CONVENTION 2008 |
|---|---|
| *[No comparable provision]* | (d) References to the New York Convention in other treaties |
| *Article VII(1)* | (e) Compatibility with other treaties |
| *Article I(3)* | (f) [No] reservations |
| *Article XIV* | (g) General reciprocity |
| *Articles X - XI* | (h) Applicability of the Draft Convention to territories and in federal states |
| *Articles VIII - IX* | (i) Signature, ratification and accession, and deposit |
| *Article XII* | (j) Entry into force |
| *[No comparable provision]* | (k) Retroactive [in]applicability; transitional clauses |
| *Article XIII* | (l) Denunciation |
| *Article XV* | (m) Notifications |
| *Article XVI* | (n) Language of authentic texts. |

# Celebrating the Fiftieth Anniversary of the New York Convention

*Teresa Cheng, BBS, SC, JP**

| TABLE OF CONTENTS | Page |
|---|---|
| I. Introduction | 679 |
| II. Wording | 679 |
| III. Public International Law | 681 |
| IV. English Courts' Power to Direct Arbitrators to Re-make an Award | 682 |
| V. Judicial Approaches to the New York Convention | 683 |
| VI. What Remedy? | 684 |
| VII. Conclusion | 687 |

I. INTRODUCTION

The 1958 New York Convention has been one of the most successful conventions. It laid the foundation for the success of international commercial arbitration. On its fiftieth anniversary, it is apt to review the success or otherwise of the application of the New York Convention and to consider, as Albert Jan van den Berg puts it, whether it will survive the next fifty years. The beauty of the New York Convention is its simplicity. The spirit and intent of the New York Convention is trite, namely to enforce arbitration agreements and arbitral awards without prejudice to the rights and protection the State has already afforded to the parties under its laws or other treaties. Yet it is also the brevity of its wording that may have caused the problems parties encounter in seeking to enforce arbitration agreements or awards under the New York Convention.

The question for consideration is whether it is desirable to have a new convention that addresses some of the problems that have surfaced over the years. Given that the issue is discussed in Dublin, one may pose the question as: Should we have a Dublin Convention in place of the New York Convention?

Before embarking on the details of the draft Convention, one must identify the cause of the problems before deciding what remedy is to be applied. Furthermore, the pros and cons of working from a fifty-year-old convention as opposed to a newly drafted one should also be considered.

II. WORDING

As alluded to above, the wording of the New York Convention, whilst simple and direct, nonetheless creates room for development, in the right as well as the wrong way. The

---

* Barrister; Deputy President for 2007 and President for 2008, Chartered Institute of Arbitrators; Vice Chairperson, Hong Kong International Arbitration Centre; Adjunct Professor, School of Law, City University of Hong Kong; Member of ICCA.

concept of what amounts to a written agreement has changed from its archaic form. "In writing" and "written agreement" in many jurisdictions have either been interpreted or legislated in such a way to meet the modern business world. For instance, in Hong Kong, under Sect. 2AC of the Arbitration Ordinance, the definition of what amounts to a written agreement is expanded beyond the traditional forms. The gist of the definition is that "in writing" amounts to the agreement being recorded in some written forms. It codifies the court decisions that have been made but also provides a broad definition with a view to precluding the unmeritorious arguments on whether or not the agreement is in writing.

The discretionary nature of Art. V is now well accepted internationally. There is no longer any argument, or any sustainable argument, that would suggest that the word "may" in Art. V should mean anything other than a discretionary "may" as opposed to a mandatory "shall".[1] However, this residual discretion given to the enforcing court to still enforce the award even if a ground is made out under Art. V still has a fundamental and conceptually difficult question to overcome. This relates to the effect of annulment on enforcement. Where an award has been annulled in its supervisory jurisdiction, some argue that there is no longer, conceptually, any award to enforce and therefore the discretion conferred in the opening words of Art. V could not apply in such situations. In other jurisdictions, such as Hong Kong, the discretion is still maintained.[2]

It is trite and well recognized that the grounds upon which parties can rely to resist enforcement have been exhaustively listed in Art. V. Yet, resourceful litigants and their legal representatives have attempted to raise what would otherwise clearly be outside these exhaustive grounds as a basis to resist and to delay the enforcement of arbitral awards. Attempts to broaden the scope of public policy by self-induced circumstances, such as to create a situation whereby the award could no longer be enforced, should not be condoned nor even entertained. Such attempts include the creation of a situation of impossibility to perform, thereby inviting the enforcing court to refuse to even recognize the award as a court judgment on the ground of public policy. Impossibility was a ground that was raised by a party seeking to resist enforcement of a CIETAC arbitral award in Hong Kong. It was couched in the terms of "contrary to public policy", contending that enforcement of the award directing the parties to continue to perform the contract as ordered by the arbitral tribunal would be contrary to public policy because not all the steps and obligations set out in the agreement of the parties could be complied with. The Hong Kong Court of First Instance rejected the plea of impossibility and the Court of Appeal dismissed the appeal.[3]

---

1. See, for instance, *China Nanhai Oil Joint Service Corporation Shenzhen Branch v. Gee Tai Holdings Co. Ltd.*, HKLR (1995) at p. 215.
2. *Karaha Bodas Co. LLC v. Persusahaan Pertambangan Minyak Dan Gas Bumi Negara (No. 2)*, 4 HKC (2003) at p. 488; *Hebei Import & Export Corp. v. Polytek Engineering Co. Ltd.*, 2 HKC (1999) at p. 205.
3. *Xiamen Xinjingdi Group Ltd. v. Eton Properties Ltd.*, 4 HKLRD (2008) at p. 972. The Court of Appeal dismissed the appeal of the two respondents in the arbitration on 22 May 2009, CACV 106/2008 and CACV 197/2008, Hon Rogers VP, Le Pichon and Hartmann JJA, 11 June 2009.

III. PUBLIC INTERNATIONAL LAW

The more prevailing and real difficulty in the application of the New York Convention arises where the issues involve questions of private international law and public international law. The problem often arises when enforcement is sought against States or State-owned companies. One is not looking at what has been described as hometown justice. The question is the effect of the legitimate public international law doctrine of State immunity on the New York Convention.

Courts in various jurisdictions recognize, as in the Hong Kong and Spanish courts,[4] that enforcement is comprised of two phases: the first of registration or recognition – that is, conversion of the award into a court judgment – and the second in the form of execution. The conversion of an award of the arbitral tribunal into a judgment of the enforcing court, enforceable by execution, requiring the losing party to pay the winning party, say, is manifestly an exercise by the enforcing court of its adjudicative jurisdiction. This is the effect of the registration of an award under the New York Convention. The proceedings to register an award under the New York Convention relate to the parties' agreement to use arbitration as the dispute resolution process. It does not relate to the underlying transaction. The adjudicative jurisdiction of the enforcing court invoked relates to, and solely to, the regularity of the award under the exhaustive grounds listed in the New York Convention.

The recognition stage is similar in nature to the registering of a foreign court judgment in the national court, which is an act *jure imperii* rather than an act *jure gestionis*: e.g., *AIC Ltd v. Federal Government of Nigeria & Anor*;[5] see also *Svenska Petroleum Exploration AB v. Government of the Republic of Lithuania & Anor. (No. 2)*.[6]

By analogy, following these two English court decisions, in an application to recognize an arbitral award under the New York Convention, a State may well be entitled to rely on immunity from suit notwithstanding the commercial nature of the underlying transaction dealt with in the arbitration. The recognition of an arbitral award by which the court grants leave to convert the award into a court judgment does not yet interfere with the rights of the property of a State. The question of immunity from execution does not arise.

Hence, irrespective of the enforcing court's view in relation to the issue of that State's position on sovereign immunity, the court may conclude that there is immunity from jurisdiction albeit subject to the question of waiver. Only if the enforcing court has jurisdiction over the State could the substantive application to enforce under the New York Convention be made.

At the execution stage, the question of immunity from execution will arise. The considerations in this aspect therefore would not arise if there is immunity from jurisdiction such that the arbitral award would not even be recognized before this court. It will have to be considered, however, if the court comes to the conclusion that there

---

4. *Saroc, S.p.A (Italy) v. Sahece, S.A. (Spain)*, ICCA Yearbook Commercial Arbitration XXXII (2007) p. 571.
5. [2003] EWHC 1357 (QB) at paras. 24-28.
6. [2007] QB 886 at para. 137.

is a waiver of immunity from jurisdiction and therefore grants leave to recognize the arbitral award so that execution measures may subsequently be undertaken.

It is well established that waiver of immunity from jurisdiction does not constitute waiver from execution. The factors to be considered in relation to any waiver of immunity from execution tend to be more narrowly construed, and the international law and practice on this is less settled and not entirely uniform. The approaches to be adopted will be deferred to discussion on another day.

It is respectfully submitted that unless and until the 2004 United Nations Convention on Jurisdictional Immunities of States and Their Property is fully ratified and come into effect, this problem cannot be resolved through any modifications of the New York Convention alone. These overarching problems involving States and their property from which State immunity is normally attached are matters that can only be addressed through diplomatic channels and discussions in the United Nations in the context of public international law.

IV.   ENGLISH COURTS' POWER TO DIRECT ARBITRATORS TO RE-MAKE AN AWARD

There are at the moment three systems in which recourse against awards can be made. In the first, those jurisdictions which follow the UNCITRAL Model Law, recourse is only by way of setting aside under Art. 34. The second system is the English approach, whereby under the English Arbitration Act international arbitration awards may be challenged by way of leave to appeal on points of law, remittance on certain situations, as well as set-aside procedures for procedural irregularity. Under the English Arbitration Act, the court, when dealing with an appeal on a point of law, can remit the award back to the tribunal for its consideration, vary the award with that of the court's own judgment and then direct the tribunal to render a new "award" in accordance with its direction. Lastly there are jurisdictions which follow the UNCITRAL Model Law in so far as international arbitrations are concerned, but for domestic arbitrations follow the English system.

The question arises as to whether a new "award" which was rendered at the direction of the court with no deliberation or discussion on the part of the arbitral tribunal should be treated as an award within the meaning of the New York Convention. The initial reaction would be a resounding yes; but upon reflection as to the scheme in which the New York Convention was developed in the international community, one wonders whether that was what was envisaged. A national court judgment does not have the same benefit as a New York Convention award, and one wonders whether by domestic legislation allowing the national court to replace the decision of the arbitral tribunal one could allow the judgment of the national court to effectively enjoy the same protection and effect of an international arbitration award intended to be protected by the New York Convention. This is a question that requires further reflection.

## V. JUDICIAL APPROACHES TO THE NEW YORK CONVENTION

The matters discussed above affect the successful and effective implementation of the New York Convention. Yet they do not really turn on the wordings of the Convention.[7] They relate to judicial approaches to the New York Convention. The real problem that has to be addressed is the application of the New York Convention by various national courts.

The interpretation of the articles of the Convention is not always uniform, and the way in which discretion is exercised is also diverse. Decisions are not always fully reasoned or published, due to the different judicial systems in various jurisdictions and their practices.

Procedures in which enforcement proceedings are taken are not always transparent and are often diverse. In some jurisdictions, such as Hong Kong, the procedures are straightforward: permission is granted for an award to be converted into a court judgment by way of an ex parte, paper-only application. The parties seeking to resist enforcement may then take out an inter-partes summons so as to set aside the ex parte order that has been granted. In some other jurisdictions, the enforcement procedures are cumbersome and time-consuming as they require the party seeking enforcement to take out a summons whereby the matter would first have to be argued between the parties before it is converted into a court judgment. This creates room for recalcitrant losing parties to delay the enforcement measures especially if courts are receptive to applications for adjournments when sought. In most cases, it is the execution stage where the problems manifest themselves, resulting in the failure or inability of the winning party to recover against the losing party.

Given the fact that the award can be enforced in all the New York Convention States, there are occasions whereby inconsistent results in enforcing the same award arise in different jurisdictions. Again, this is not unreasonable given that each jurisdiction must adjudicate upon the matter before it without preference for or defiance of decisions made in other national courts carrying out the same or similar function. Yet, it is these problems that have caused the concerns on the part of the litigants and their legal representatives when seeking to enforce an arbitral award.

The major issue in relation to the application of the New York Convention is the inconsistent ways different national courts would apply the ground of public policy to refuse enforcement. Different cultural, social and economic values in divergent societies inevitably result in, understandably, different concepts of public policy. Whilst there is a strong reason for promoting one international public policy, it is perhaps too ambitious to impose that on all the jurisdictions that have different social, religious and cultural norms from those of other jurisdictions that promote the adoption of international or transnational public policy. It has to be borne in mind that even in the common law world, there are different judicial pronouncements as to what amounts to public policy[8]

---

7. Except the issue involving State immunity and that relating to the English Arbitration Act.
8. E.g., violation of the most basic notions of morality and justice; so fundamentally offensive to [the jurisdiction's] notions of justice; such a grave departure from basic concepts of justice as applied by the [jurisdiction's] court.

but none has attempted to definitively demarcate and particularize the term. There is very good reason for that. It is important to keep this preclusionary tool available to address situations not yet envisaged by the current commercial world but which judges, with their judicial independence and wisdom, would be able to identify. Public policy has been described as the unruly horse, a bit like an elephant, effectively something which could not be fully defined but, as it is often said, a judge would know it when he sees it. There is no doubt that there are some universally adopted concepts of what is contrary to public policy, such as that of fraud. There may be other notions so basic to a particular jurisdiction's morality that may be manifested in a form of public policy that is unique to that jurisdiction. This will particularly be so in the context of religious or social norms peculiar to that jurisdiction. To what extent the international community can fairly impose on those jurisdictions what it considers as the norm to be adopted is something that has yet to be seen.

Judicial approaches to public policy are fundamental, and I respectfully refer to a paper delivered by High Court Judge of Hong Kong, Stone J. at the "50th Anniversary of the New York Convention: Challenges for the Judiciary" Conference in December 2008 in Beijing in celebration of the fiftieth anniversary of the New York Convention, which sets out the Hong Kong judiciary's approach to public policy.[9]

VI. WHAT REMEDY?

All of the above difficulties in the application of the New York Convention emanate not, it is submitted, from the wordings but from the interpretation of the wordings and the approaches adopted by the judiciary in the various enforcing jurisdictions. The freedom of the judiciary to properly interpret and enlarge the meaning of the wordings so as to adhere to and foster the spirit and intent of the New York Convention is, in my respectful submission, more important than tying down the hands of the judges and thereby limiting the way the New York Convention can be developed to meet the changing international commercial world. The question is, how to ensure that countries in both civil law and common law jurisdictions participate in this process.

More importantly, the remedy to address the inconsistent approaches in the application of New York Convention through the introduction of a draft Dublin Convention brings with it the following risks. There are States which may no longer be willing to participate in the revised Convention and there is no method by which the international community can ensure that all the 144 States will sign up to the new Dublin Convention.

Secondly, transitional arrangements will have to be put in place; this, by its own very nature, creates confusion and inconsistencies. A lacuna may arise, thereby putting awards at risk.

Ultimately and importantly, a new line of authorities will be developed on the new wordings. At the end of the day, resourceful and ingenious lawyers would still be able

---

9. "The Judicial Approach to Public Policy in the Context of Enforcement of Convention Awards: A Hong Kong Perspective".

to devise arguments in light of the new wordings, notwithstanding that these wordings are generally accepted as clear and unambiguous. The judges in some jurisdictions may be led astray and thereby create a jurisprudence inconsistent with the intention of the new Convention. The current jurisprudence, subject to the question of public policy and the effect of annulment on enforcement, is more or less universally adopted and reasonably well developed. Practitioners know what grounds will be successful and when they would be pushing through an open door. These risks and problems that will have to be addressed through the introduction of an improved convention must be assessed. Ultimately, it is a question of balancing. There may be a time when the only remedy or enhancement is to amend the Convention, but is now the time? Probably not.

One asks rhetorically, is it not a more pragmatic and realistic approach to address the problems by first taking these steps before modifying the instrument itself:

— facilitate development of consistent jurisprudence for adoption by national courts;
— establish a judicial forum for exchanges of experience on the application of the New York Convention;
— establish objective criteria for assessment of States' compliance with the New York Convention.

*1. Development of Consistent Jurisprudence*

At the moment, generally speaking, each Convention State develops its own jurisprudence through its own judicial system, whether by way of judicial precedents or directions from the higher courts or the legislature. This "internal" development could be enhanced through the development of something with an international perspective.

It is trite that in interpreting an international treaty, following the Vienna Convention, judgments from various jurisdictions should be used to provide and develop a consistent jurisprudence internationally. That, it seems, is no longer adequate. This may be a result of the deliberate omission or lack of competence on the part of practitioners who fail to draw to the attention of the national court the decisions from various jurisdictions regarding the New York Convention and thereby hinder the proper development of jurisprudence in this area.

It is therefore suggested that judgments from all the jurisdictions be collated and analyzed by an international body or working group so as to create a "judicial direction" that can be promulgated for use by judiciaries of all the New York Convention States. This "judicial direction" has to be updated regularly, preferably in line with the suggestion below.

UNCITRAL has used recommendations on the interpretation of the articles of the UNCITRAL Model Law on International Commercial Arbitration for adoption by practitioners and judiciaries. There is no reason why such a "recommendation" cannot similarly be created by a body of internationally renowned arbitration practitioners through analysis of the judgments that have been promulgated in various jurisdictions. ICCA's *Yearbook Commercial Arbitration* is the primary source of such data, and it is therefore probably most appropriate that ICCA should take the lead in forming such a working group.

## 2. Judicial Forum

Practitioners attend international conferences to learn about practices in other jurisdictions as well as to exchange ideas. Judges do the same in other areas, and it would therefore be useful if a biennial conference of judges within a region, or internationally, could be held to enable judges to exchange views. The format could be a day for a series of plenary sessions with judges and practitioners, followed if necessary by a half day of closed-door discussions whereby views can be frankly exchanged and problems experienced in one's own jurisdiction shared and discussed with others. The closed-door session amongst judges may provide a platform for constructive exchanges and sharing of experiences and ideas amongst judiciaries in a region. Judges could be exposed to practices in the region, and hopefully later internationally, and receive updates from fellow judges on the latest developments. Sustainable development will be achieved.

It is to be hoped that the systematic approach to ensure that judges are kept abreast of the latest developments internationally will eliminate the occasional "judicial casualties". Remarks based on anecdotal evidence of a "bad" judgment from a jurisdiction which are made in seminars tend to create resentment which is not beneficial to the sustainable development of international arbitration in the long term. A systematic "exchange of views" together with the use of the "judicial direction" will ultimately enable a consistent jurisprudence to be developed for the benefit of the users of arbitration in the long term.

Yet, this may not be enough. The qualitative enhancement has to be quantified. As the former Secretary of the UNCITRAL Mr. Jernej Sekolec said at the VIAC Conference in March 2008, some objective criteria should be established.

## 3. Objective Assessment

Whether the obligation to observe the New York Convention is honoured is not easy to measure objectively in the light of the different judicial systems and procedures. Yet just as the financial viability and performance of a country or government is assessed by some objective standards, the inability or refusal of a country to comply with its treaty obligations should similarly be measured against some objective criteria. The extent to which a judicial system respects its international treaty obligations reflects the commercial risk a foreign entity will have to take when investing in that jurisdiction. The global economy is such that foreign investment becomes a norm. To ensure a level playing field such that the foreign investment would not be unfairly or unjustly treated, there ought to be ways in which one can assess the extent to which national courts would respect the international treaty obligations. The way to assess it ought to be based on some objective criteria whilst taking into account the economic development of the jurisdictions.

Anecdotal comments may merely represent the occasional judicial casualties that every jurisdiction every now and then encounters. Such comments tend not to be constructive. They only present part of the facts and therefore create resentment. The compliance of a jurisdiction with its international obligation to honour the New York Convention should not be judged by such anecdotal comments or judicial casualties. There ought to be something more objective and general.

The exact criteria to be adopted and the way they are to be monitored or measured is a matter for further discussion, if pursued. At this stage, I would venture to suggest some of the criteria that may be considered for inclusion for providing a standard. These criteria can include:

— The simplicity or otherwise of procedures in applying to enforce an award, such as whether it is first by way of ex parte application in writing or by taking out some inter partes summons;
— Whether any special procedures need to be complied with, such as to obtain translations or certified awards, to meet the local procedural requirements;
— The average timing of processing the different stages of enforcement up to the date of the judgment;
— The simplicity or otherwise of procedures governing how evidence is to be received and argument dealt with;
— Whether the judicial approach adopted generally reflects the spirit and intent of the New York Convention: for instance, who bears the burden of proof in establishing the grounds set out in Art. V, whether this requirement is reflected in the procedures or in the precedents, etc.;
— Is there a specialist list or are a few designated judges to handle New York Convention applications;
— The number of applications under the New York Convention, the number where enforcement is granted, the number where enforcement is refused;
— Whether reasons for refusing to enforce an award are given;
— Whether the reasons refer to the New York Convention;
— Whether the reasons accord with the international judicial direction or jurisprudence on the New York Convention.

If the criteria can be objectively framed, they should be able to be objectively measured by a group of independent practitioners who review these regularly. An index can then be prepared and the extent to which each jurisdiction honours its New York Convention treaty obligations can then be viewed at a glance as opposed to judged against the anecdotal evidence repeated in every seminar as if that represents the overall performance of that jurisdiction.

It is respectfully submitted that this objective-criteria approach not only benefits the enhancement of the exchange of judicial experience, as suggested in the previous section, it also provides international companies guidance on the risk they have to assess and price for when investing in various jurisdictions. Importantly, it will enable various jurisdictions of the New York Convention States to themselves reflect on how they have been complying with the treaty obligations, and for the government and the judiciary then to fully reflect and implement the spirit and intent of the Convention itself.

VII. CONCLUSION

In summary, I would respectfully submit that before one embarks on re-drafting the New York Convention, it is more harmonious and constructive to first attempt to carry out the three steps set out above because they would address the fundamental problems that underlie the successful application of the New York Convention itself. If these approaches set out above are able to address the concerns and remove the anomalies that appear every now and then, it is best left to the judiciary of the 144 Convention States, and hopefully more in the future, to develop the jurisprudence that will allow the New York Convention to take its place firmly and strongly in the world of international commercial arbitration.

# The Urgency of Not Revising the New York Convention

*Emmanuel Gaillard*[*]

| TABLE OF CONTENTS | Page |
|---|---|
| I. Introduction | 689 |
| II. Is There a Need to Revise the New York Convention? | 690 |
| III. Should a Revision Be Nevertheless Contemplated, It Should Strike a Different Balance | 693 |

## I. INTRODUCTION

As with its fortieth anniversary, the celebration of the fiftieth anniversary of the 1958 New York Convention on the Recognition and Enforcement of Foreign Arbitral Awards has justifiably given rise to questions as to the necessity and/or feasibility of the Convention's revision. To date, the majority view has been in favor of not opening such an avenue.[1] Today, however, important scholars have suggested that the Convention has aged in such a way and has given rise to a sufficiently large number of unsatisfactory decisions that the time has come to initiate a revision process.[2] A preliminary draft has been put forward to stimulate reflection on the subject.[3]

---

[*] Professor of Law, University of Paris XII; Head of the International Arbitration practice, Shearman & Sterling LLP; Member of ICCA.

1. See for example G. HERMANN, "The 1958 New York Convention: Its Objectives and Its Future" in *Improving the Efficiency of Arbitration Agreements and Awards: 40 Years of Application of the New York Convention*, ICCA Congress Series no. 9 (1999) (hereinafter *ICCA Congress Series no. 9*) p. 15; A.J. VAN DEN BERG, "The Application of the New York Convention by the Courts" in *ICCA Congress Series no. 9*, p. 34; A.J. VAN DEN BERG, "Striving for Uniform Interpretation" in *Enforcing Arbitration Awards Under the New York Convention: Experience and Prospects* (United Nations Publication 1999) p. 42; W. MELIS, "Considering the Advisability of Preparing an Additional Convention, complementary to the New York Convention" in *ibid.*, p. 44; P. SANDERS, "A Twenty Year's Review of the Convention on the Recognition and Enforcement of Foreign Arbitral Awards", 13 The International Lawyer (1979) p. 269 et seq.; J. PAULSSON, "L'exécution des sentences arbitrales dans le monde de demain", Rev. arb. (1998) pp. 637-652; J. PAULSSON, "Towards Minimum Standards of Enforcement: Feasibility of a Model Law" in *ICCA Congress Series no. 9*, p. 575.

2. See, in particular, A.J. VAN DEN BERG's Explanatory Note, this volume, pp. 649-666. See also *11th IBA International Arbitration Day, The New York Convention: 50 Years*, 1 February 2008 at <www.uncitral.org/pdf/uncitral/NYarbday-programme.pdf> (last accessed 21 August 2008). For a comprehensive review of the case law generated on the basis of the Convention, see E. GAILLARD and D. DI PIETRO, eds., *Enforcement of Arbitration Agreements and International Arbitral Awards* (Cameron May 2008).

3. See the text of the Hypothetical Draft Convention proposed by A.J. VAN DEN BERG, this volume, pp. 667-669.

Although its language is at times dated and certain of its provisions could be modernized,[4] the New York Convention continues, on the whole, to fulfill its purpose in a satisfactory manner and there would be, in my opinion, more to lose than to gain in embarking upon a revision process. Should a revision nevertheless be considered by the States parties to the New York Convention, it could not simply embrace the suggestions found in the Hypothetical Draft prepared for the purposes of this Conference.

II. IS THERE A NEED TO REVISE THE NEW YORK CONVENTION?

The reason why I strongly believe that the New York Convention should be left alone is threefold. It can be summarized by what I call the "three NOs": there is no need, no hope and no danger.

*1. There is No Need to Revise the New York Convention*

The sole fact that the language of the Convention is at times outdated and that some of its provisions could be fine-tuned does not warrant embarking upon a revision of an instrument binding on 144 States at the time of this writing. Such a massive undertaking would be justified only if one were to identify serious flaws in the enforcement process and ascertain that those flaws can be cured by a mere modification of the language used in the instrument.[5]

Put in perspective, there are only two serious issues regarding the enforcement of awards, none of which can be fixed by a revision. The first difficulty stems from recurring instances of bias in favor of local companies, in particular State-owned companies, by the courts in certain jurisdictions at the place of enforcement. However, what revision would prevent the Russian courts (which have shown little evidence of independence in the recent Yukos or TNK-BP sagas) from refusing to enforce an award affecting the interests of a State-owned company of the Russian State itself on the ground

---

4. For example, Art. II(3) could be clarified in that courts confronted with a dispute covered by an arbitration agreement should limit their determination of whether the arbitration agreement is "null and void, inoperative or incapable of being performed" to a prima facie review. Art. V, which sets forth the grounds for refusing recognition or enforcement of an award, is somewhat convoluted. It could be both simplified and modernized in the following manner: first, the reference to the "law of the country where the award was made" with respect to the validity of the arbitration agreement (Art. V(1)(*a*)) or with respect to the composition of the arbitral tribunal (Art. V(1)(*d*)) is outdated; second, Art. V(1)(*e*), which provides that the recognition or enforcement of an award can be refused if "the award has not yet become binding on the parties, or has been set aside or suspended by a competent authority of the country in which, or under the law of which, [it] was made", should be removed or, at the very minimum, limited in scope. Finally, the issue of arbitrability under Art. II(1) and Art. V(2)(*a*) could also be modernized.
5. The 2008 PricewaterhouseCoopers report on *International Arbitration: Corporate Attitudes and Practices* does not suggest any such difficulties. It reveals, in relation to recognition and enforcement of arbitral awards, that "[t]he majority of [surveyed] corporations that had enforced awards reported that they had not encountered major difficulties in doing so", at <www.pwc.co.uk/pdf/PwC_International_Arbitration _2008.pdf?utr=1> (last accessed 21 August 2008) p. 6.

of an alleged violation of public policy?[6] The public policy exception will always be present and the courts of the place of enforcement will always be in a position to manipulate that ground to refuse enforcement.

The second and very serious problem is that of States that conclude arbitration agreements, lose in the arbitration and never satisfy the award. The *SEEE v. Yugoslavia* award, for example, took twenty-eight years to be enforced.[7] The *Noga* case provides another striking example of the losing State's abusive resistance to enforcement.[8] These difficulties have no relation whatsoever with the New York Convention but result solely from the State's ability to invoke its immunity from execution to resist enforcement. They could effectively be resolved through an international instrument. Yet, no significant progress was made in this respect in the 2004 United Nations Convention on Jurisdictional Immunities of States and their Property.[9]

---

6. See the Report of the Committee on Legal Affairs and Human Rights, "The Circumstances surrounding the Arrest and Prosecution of Leading Yukos Executives", S. LEUTHEUSSER-SCHNARRENBERGER, Parliamentary Assembly, Council of Europe (November 2004, doc. 10368); Report on Economic Affairs and Development, "Europe's Interest in the Continued Economic Development of Russia", K. SASI, Parliamentary Assembly, Council of Europe (September 2006, doc. 11026) para. 57; E. S. BERGER, "Corruption in Russia's *Arbitrazh* Courts", 14 BNA'S Eastern Europe Reporter (2004, no. 12); E. S. BERGER, "Corruption in the Russian *Arbitrazh* Courts: Will there be Significant Progress in the Near Term?", 38 The International Lawyer (2004, no. 1); "The Judicial System of the Russian Federation: a System-Crisis of Independence", Report of the NGO RUSSIAN AXIS (2004).
7. Award of 2 July 1956, 25 Int'l L. Rep. (1957) p. 761. For a Swiss decision, see Trib. Vaud, 12 February 1957 (*Société Européenne d'Etudes et d'Enterprises v. République Fédérative de Yougoslavie*), Rev. Crit. Dr. Int. Pr. (1958) p. 359; for a Dutch decision, see *Hoge Raad*, 26 October 1973, as translated by G. GAJA, 5 International Commercial Arbitration (1978) p. 18; for a French decision, see *Cour de cassation*, 1st Civil Chamber, 18 November 1986 (*Etat français v. Société européenne d'études et d'entreprises (S.E.E.E.) et autres*), 26 International Legal Materials (1987) p. 373. See also, G. R. DELAUME, "*SEEE v. Yugoslavia*: Epitaph or Interlude?", 4 Journal of International Arbitration (1987, no. 3) p. 25.
8. *Ambassade de la Fédération de Russie en France et al. v. Compagnie Noga d'Importation et d'Exportation*, Rev. arb. (2001) p. 116; Court of Appeal, Paris 1st Civil Chamber, 22 March 2001, Rev. arb. (2001) p. 607; United States Court of Appeals, Second Circuit, 16 March 2004 (*Compagnie Noga d'Importation et d'Exportation S.A. v. The Russian Federation*) ICCA Yearbook Commercial Arbitration XXIX (2004) pp. 1227-1250. For an overview of the *Noga* arbitration and litigation in French and American courts, see N.B. TURCK, "French and US Courts Define Limits of Sovereign Immunity in Execution and Enforcement of Arbitral Awards", 17 Arbitration International (2001, no. 3) p. 327 et seq.
9. See General Assembly Resolution 59/38, annex, *Official Records of the General Assembly, Fifty-ninth Session, Supplement No. 49* (A/59/49), 2004. See also H. FOX, "State Immunity and the New York Convention" in E. GAILLARD and D. DI PIETRO, eds., *op. cit.*, fn. 2, p. 829; E. GAILLARD, "Effectiveness of Arbitral Awards, State Immunity from Execution and Autonomy of State Entities, Three Incompatible Principles" in E. GAILLARD and J. YOUNAN, eds., *State Entities In International Arbitration, IAI Series on International Arbitration No. 4* (Juris Publishing 2008) p. 179.

2. *There is No Hope to Achieve a Better Instrument Than the Existing Convention*

There is no hope, in the current environment, that a significant number of the 144 States parties to the Convention (at the time of this writing) would agree to make the enforcement process more efficient.

The pro-arbitration bias which has been the prevailing state of mind in a number of States in the past decades has been somewhat undermined by the dramatic development of arbitrations based on investment protection treaties. States being, by definition, in the position of a defendant in such arbitrations, they have tended to develop a defendant mindset.[10] In this context, it is doubtful whether a large number of States, which are increasingly in a position to resist enforcement of awards, would be genuinely willing to enhance the effectiveness of the enforcement process. Against that background, it is not even certain that the degree of liberalism achieved in 1958 could be attained today.

3. *There is No Danger in Leaving the Current Instrument Untouched*

On the other hand, there is no danger in leaving the New York Convention in its current state. The genius of the Convention is to have foreseen the evolution of arbitration law. As per its Art. VII, the Convention sets only a minimum standard. States can always be more liberal. By definition, the Convention cannot freeze the development of arbitration law. Thus, there is no danger in leaving it untouched.

The assessment of the efficiency of the enforcement of awards in today's world cannot be made by considering solely the New York Convention case law. In some of the most pro-arbitration jurisdictions such as France, the number of cases referring to the New York Convention is scarce precisely because the ordinary rules governing enforcement of awards in France are more liberal than those of the Convention and are routinely applied without any need to refer to the Convention.[11] The Convention is there as a safeguard. It does not need to be used, but it does no harm.

---

10. See, for example, S. SCHWEBEL, "The United States 2004 Model Bilateral Investment Treaty: An Exercise in the Regressive Development of International Law" in *Global Reflections on International Law, Commerce and Dispute Resolution* (ICC Publishing 2005) p. 815 et seq. The regression of the pro-arbitration bias in the United States is also evidenced by the legislative progress of the Arbitration Fairness Act of 2007 [A bill to amend chapter 1 of title 9 of United States Code with respect to arbitration], which restricts significantly the arbitrability of a number of matters, including pre-dispute arbitration agreements to arbitrate disputes "arising under any statute intended ... to regulate contracts or transactions between parties of unequal bargaining power", as well as the principle of the autonomy of the arbitration agreement and that of competence-competence. At the time of writing, the Bill had been introduced into the Senate (12 July 2007) and undergone hearings in the Committee on the Judiciary Subcommittee on the Constitution (12 December 2007); see, Sect.4.2, Fairness Arbitration Act of 2007, Library of Congress, at <http://thomas.loc.gov/cgi-bin/bdquery/z?d110:s.01782:> (last accessed 21 August 2008).

11. *Cour de cassation*, 1st Civil Chamber, 29 June 2007 (*Société Putrabali Adyarnulia v. Société Rena Holding et Société Mnogutia Est Espices*) Rev. arb. (2007) p. 507; *Cour de cassation*, 1st Civil Chamber, 23 March 1994, Rev. arb. (1994) p. 327, note Ch. JARROSSON, p. 328.

Should one conclude that it would be useful to modernize the grounds for the review of awards by national courts, the first candidate for a revision would be Art. 34 of the UNCITRAL Model Law on International Commercial Arbitration which sets out the grounds for the setting aside of awards. In 1985, the drafters of the Model Law chose not to revisit the annulment grounds in Art. 34 but simply track those found in Art. V of the New York Convention. Presumably, some progress in the drafting of those grounds – which correspond to the grounds to refuse enforcement in the Convention – could be achieved. The modernization of those grounds in Art. 34 would enable States to adopt a new set of standards regarding the setting aside of awards, which could easily be transposed for the purposes of the recognition and enforcement of awards pursuant to each jurisdiction's ordinary rules, while keeping the New York Convention as a minimum standard. In so doing, one could achieve modernization of the grounds for the review of awards without jeopardizing the delicate balance struck in the New York Convention.

III. SHOULD A REVISION BE NEVERTHELESS CONTEMPLATED, IT SHOULD STRIKE A DIFFERENT BALANCE

The Hypothetical Draft Convention proposed for the purposes of discussion in this Conference is clearly thoughtful and internally consistent. In my opinion, however, it does not achieve the desired balance.

The title itself is telling: it is a proposed convention on the "international enforcement of arbitral awards", whereas it should be a convention on the "enforcement of international arbitral awards". What is "international" is the award, not the enforcement.

More fundamentally, the gist of the Hypothetical Draft Convention is to adopt a purely traditional choice of law approach, which consists in allocating the issues which may arise in the context of the enforcement of an arbitration agreement or an arbitral award essentially between the law of the seat and the law of the place of enforcement. The law of the seat is mentioned seven times in the Hypothetical Draft Convention. It would essentially govern the arbitration agreement and, on a subsidiary basis, the composition of the arbitral tribunal and the arbitral procedure. The law of the place of enforcement is mentioned three times and, understandably, would govern international public policy, including arbitrability.

This systematic use of a choice of law approach is highly problematic. The least one would expect from a convention elaborated at the beginning of the twenty-first century – whose purpose is to facilitate the enforcement of arbitration agreements and arbitral awards – is to develop internationally acceptable standards and not merely distribute matters between the law of the seat and that of the place of enforcement, irrespective of their content, degree of liberalism or sophistication.

Such a criticism equally applies to the proposed rules regarding the arbitration agreement and those regarding the recognition of the award.

## 1. The Arbitration Agreement

According to the Hypothetical Draft Convention, the courts seized of a dispute should refer such dispute to arbitration if "there is *prima facie* no valid arbitration agreement under the law of the country where the award will be made".[12] I concur whole-heartedly with the *prima facie* test, which I have long advocated. That is the whole idea of the negative effect of competence-competence.[13]

However, the reference to the law of the seat as the governing law of the arbitration agreement is misplaced. It is not a good connecting factor for the arbitration agreement. Further, it takes away most of the benefit of the limitation of the assessment of the existence and validity of the arbitration agreement to a *prima facie* test.

One can easily anticipate the difficulties associated with the use of a *prima facie* test in a system based on a choice of law approach. The question arises in situations in which one of the parties engaged in a dispute before a court invokes an arbitration agreement while the other party opposes the reference of the dispute to arbitration. That court must determine *prima facie* if the arbitration agreement is valid and binding on the relevant parties. If, following the proposed Hypothetical Draft Convention, the court has to apply to this issue the law of the seat of the arbitration, it may find itself in an impasse in all cases in which the seat has not been selected at that stage. Presuming the seat has been selected, either in the arbitration agreement or pursuant to the mechanisms contemplated in the relevant arbitration rules, the matter is still significantly complicated by the requirement of resorting to the law of the seat. In many instances, that law will be foreign to the court seized of the matter and may well have to be evidenced by way of expert witnesses. In all likelihood, each party will present experts with diverging views. Lengthy expert testimonies may ensue and it is easy to predict that the simplest arbitration clause will give rise to convoluted discussions based on alleged theories found only in the law of the seat.

In reality, *prima facie* means *prima facie*. The court seized of the matter can assess the arbitration agreement on its face. It can determine if the agreement exists as between the parties and has been entered into in circumstances which are not manifestly aberrational. Nothing further is required and any argument going beyond such a simple assessment on the basis of generally accepted practices should be left to the arbitrators to decide in the first instance. This is why *prima facie* and the requirement of reasoning in choice of law terms are hardly compatible.

## 2. The Arbitral Award

In 1958, the tension between those who wanted to deal with "international" awards (which calls for a substantive rules methodology) and not with the "foreign" awards

---

12. Art. II(2)(b) of the Hypothetical Draft convention, this volume, pp. 667-669.
13. See, for example, E. GAILLARD and Y. BANIFATEMI, "Negative Effect of Competence-Competence, The Rule of Priority in Favour of the Arbitrators" in E. GAILLARD and D. DI PIETRO, eds., *op. cit.*, fn. 2, p. 257, and references cited therein.

(which calls for a choice of law approach) resulted in a compromise.[14] This compromise consisted, as far as the validity of the arbitration agreement, the composition of the arbitral tribunal and the arbitral procedure are concerned in the context of the enforcement of the award, in downgrading the law of the seat of the arbitration to a subsidiary position applicable only absent an agreement between the parties. This was a major step as compared to the mandatory application of the law of the seat found in the Geneva Conventions of 1923 and 1927. The Hypothetical Draft Convention does not entail any progress in this respect. The progress would be to remove the reference to the law of the seat. What is at stake are "international" awards, not "Swiss" or "Indian" awards.

As to the difficult issue of the enforcement of an award set aside in the country in which the arbitration took place, the Hypothetical Draft does not achieve any significant progress either. To permit the recognition of awards set aside by the courts of the seat of the arbitration on the basis of grounds other than those which are generally accepted and found in the Convention is not going to solve the problem of awards conveniently set aside for the benefit of the local party, often the State or a State-owned entity (as in *TermoRio* in Colombia or *Bechtel* in Dubai).[15] If the Hypothetical Draft Convention were to be adopted, parties seeking to exploit the fact that the arbitration took place in their own country and to have their courts annul the award with a view to resist enforcement elsewhere would simply have to become a little more savvy. They would have to seek the annulment of the award on the basis of an accepted ground, but since those grounds necessarily include the violation of due process or international public policy, their task would not be too difficult. They would simply have to argue that, in the case at hand, such a violation took place. If successful, for good or bad reasons, the net result of the Hypothetical Draft Convention would be to give an international effect to such decisions even if they are designed to rescue the local party. The impact of parochial decisions would not have been taken care of, quite to the contrary.

One has to recognize that a court wanting to favor the local party can not only use a ground to set aside which is not generally accepted (for instance, in *Chromolloy*, the fact that the award allegedly misapplied administrative law)[16] but also misapply in a much more subtle way grounds which are generally accepted (due process and international public policy being the easiest to manipulate). Why should the court where the money

---

14. On the negotiating history of the New York Convention, see, e.g., Robert BRINER and Virginia HAMILTON, "The History and General Purpose of the Convention. The Creation of an International Standard to Ensure the Effectiveness of Arbitration Agreements and Foreign Arbitral Awards" in E. GAILLARD and D. DI PIETRO, eds., *op.cit.*, fn. 2, p. 3.
15. *Consejo de Estado de Colombia, Sala de lo Contencioso Administrativo, Sección Tercera*, 1 August 2002 (*Electrificadora del Atlántico S.A. E.S.P. v. Termorío S.A. E.S.P*) expte. 11001-03-25-000-2001-004601 (21041); Dubai Court of Cassation, 15 May 2004 (*Int'l Bechtel Co. Ltd. v. Dep't of Civil Aviation of Gov't of Dubai*) (*Bechtel*). For decisions relating to *Bechtel* in American and French Courts, see, *In re Arbitration Between Intern. Bechtel Co., Ltd. and Department of Civil Aviation of the Government of Dubai*, 360 F.Supp.2d 136 (DDC 2005) and Paris Court of Appeal, 29 September 2005 (*Bechtel*), Rev. arb. (2006) p. 695, note H. MUIR-WATT.
16. Cairo Court of Appeal, 5 December 1995 (*Ministry of Defence v. Chromalloy Aero Services Company*), Rev. arb. (1998) p. 723, note Ph. LEBOULANGER.

is attached defer to the decision of the court in which the arbitration took place, especially when this place is the home country of one of the litigants? The Hypothetical Draft Convention simply fails to address this crucial problem.

In short, the issues raised by a potential revision of the New York Convention are much more intricate and likely to be highly controversial than one would expect at first sight. Against that background, the inescapable conclusion is that it is absolutely urgent to do nothing.

# Comments on the Proposal to Amend the New York Convention

*Carolyn B. Lamm*[*]

| TABLE OF CONTENTS | Page |
|---|---|
| I. Introduction | 697 |
| II. Albert Jan van den Berg's Hypothetical Draft Convention | 705 |
| III. Conclusion | 707 |

I. INTRODUCTION

I support Albert Jan van den Berg's proposal to amend the 1958 New York Convention, recognizing of course that achieving such an amendment would face significant political and practical challenges. These challenges include the following:

— Reaching agreement among the 144 States parties to the New York Convention (at the time of this writing) on its amendment;
— Each of the State parties may need to enact implementing legislation;
— The need for a transition period while some States will have implemented the changes but others have not, in order to permit the adequate functioning of the system in the interim. During this transition it will be a challenge to work with different parallel regimes.

I would like to start my analysis by looking back at the negotiating history of the New York Convention and specifically a marvelous summary that Albert Jan van den Berg included in his Pace Law Review article.[1] I want to quote just one or two things from the history that set out what objectives were identified as the most important. Then I want to test whether that is where we are in terms of the developing jurisprudence.

The Summary Records of the United Nations Conference on International Commercial Arbitration held in New York in May and June 1958[2] indicate what the negotiators sought, for example:

---

[*] Partner, White & Case LLP, Washington, D.C.
1. Albert Jan VAN DEN BERG, "When is an Arbitral Award Nondomestic Under the New York Convention of 1958?", 6 Pace L. Rev. (1985) p. 25 at p. 36.
2. The *travaux préparatoires* of the New York Convention, including the Summary Records of the New York Convention of May and June 1958 and the preceding work of the United Nations Economic and Social Council and United Nations Secretariat, are reprinted in G. GAJA, ed., *International Commercial Arbitration: New York Convention*, Binder 1 (1985). They are also available on the Internet at: <www.uncitral.org/uncitral/en/uncitral_texts/arbitration/NYConvention_travaux.html>.

"… the best solution would be for the internal laws of countries to be standardized by the adoption of a uniform law…".[3]

I don't think we have seen that happen, despite the fact that (at the time of this writing) 70 domestic legislatures have enacted legislation based on the UNCITRAL Model Law on International Commercial Arbitration (the Model Law).[4] Secondly, it was considered

"… most important that each signatory State should know exactly what the other States were undertaking to do".[5]

I am not sure we have that. And, third, it was thought to be

"… essential that an absolutely clear criterion, incapable of divergent interpretations, should be established".[6]

I will prove we do not have that.

Indeed, the Convention is not "absolutely clear" nor is it "incapable of divergent interpretations". In various cases, many lawyers have spent thousands of pages and even more hours arguing to the courts and litigating certain issues under the provisions of the existing Convention. Some of those issues are the following:

(1) The meaning of the word "may" under Art. V(1): How much discretion does it confer to the court to refuse recognition and enforcement? What is the extent of what the court may do?

(2) Whether, under the specific language of an arbitration clause, the enforcement forum must respect the decision to set aside the award of the forum "in which, or under the law of which, that award was made" given a complete divergence of views as to the meaning – and application – of the words "in which" and "under the law of which" under Art. V(1)(e).

(3) The meaning of "contrary to the public policy of that country" under Art. V(2)(b): As one examines the decisions rendered by national courts under the provisions of the existing New York Convention, it is difficult to discern whether the inconsistency is, as Teresa Cheng noted, due to differences in the courts' approach.[7] A review of the decisions, admittedly, reveals a good deal of confusion – if not incompetence – on the part of many national courts. Inconsistencies may, however, also be due to a parochial approach by national courts seeking to protect domestic interests. I think we have all

---

3. U.N. Doc. E/CONF.26/SR.6 (12 Sept. 1958) p. 9 (summarizing the statement of the Colombian delegate).
4. For updates on the status of enactment of the UNCITRAL Model Law, see: <www.uncitral.org/uncitral/en/uncitral_texts/arbitration/1985Model_arbitration_status.html>.
5. U.N. Doc. E/CONF.26/SR.6 (12 Sept. 1958) p. 9 (summarizing the statement of the Colombian delegate).
6. Ibid.
7. "Celebrating the Fiftieth Anniversary of the New York Convention", this volume p. 679-688, at pp. 683-684.

seen that in decisions, and in litigation. Or is it confusion by counsel as to what the appropriate words mean? Or is it just aggressive advocacy arguing for individual advantage, as Emmanuel Gaillard suggests?[8]

I would now like to examine the real inconsistency among court decisions in various jurisdictions that have taken diametrically opposed positions as to whether an arbitral award that has been set aside in its country of origin may be enforced elsewhere.

We are all familiar with some of the cases decided in favor of enforcing a vacated award. I will discuss some of these first, before turning to cases in which courts declined to enforce a vacated award.

Thus, in *Pabalk v. Norsolor*,[9] the French *Cour de Cassation* ruled that an ICC award annulled at the arbitral seat (in Vienna) may be enforceable in France because Art. VII allowed the award creditor to avail itself of the award to the extent allowed by the laws of the enforcement forum, and French civil procedure allowed for such enforcement.[10] The *Cour de Cassation* went on to state that the French court "had a duty to determine, even *ex officio*, if French law would not allow [the award creditor] to avail itself of the award at stake".[11]

Ten years later, the proceedings in the courts of France, Switzerland and the United Kingdom in the well-known *Hilmarton* case highlighted the problem that can result from the enforcement of an arbitral award that has been set aside in its country of origin, as well as the lack of consistency in interpreting and applying the same language ("public policy") of the New York Convention. The dispute in that case centered on the claim of Hilmarton Ltd., a UK consulting firm, against the French company Omnium de Traitement et de Valorisation (OTV) for payment of consultancy fees. Having lost in its ICC arbitration in Geneva against OTV in 1988, Hilmarton successfully applied to the Geneva Court of Appeal to have the arbitral award annulled.[12] OTV appealed to the Swiss Federal Tribunal and, in addition, sought enforcement of the annulled award in Paris. Before the Swiss Federal Tribunal ruled on OTV's appeal (which it later rejected), the Paris Tribunal of First Instance granted OTV's request for enforcement. Upon appeal, the Paris Court of Appeal upheld the enforcement decision,[13] and Hilmarton appealed further to the French *Cour de Cassation*.

In the meantime, the Swiss Federal Tribunal had rejected OTV's appeal and affirmed the Geneva court's annulment of the award.[14] Hilmarton thereupon instituted a second ICC arbitration against OTV in Geneva, which resulted in an award in Hilmarton's favor in 1992. Hilmarton then sought to enforce in France both the second ICC award and the

---

8. "The Urgency of Not Revising the New York Convention", this volume, pp. 689-696.
9. *Pabalk Ticaret Limited Sirketi v. Norsolor S.A.*, *Cour de Cassation*, France (9 Oct. 1984), reported in ICCA *Yearbook Commercial Arbitration* XI (1986) (hereinafter *Yearbook*) p. 484.
10. *Ibid.*, at p. 489.
11. *Ibid.*, at pp. 489, 491.
12. *Hilmarton v. Omnium de Traitement et de Valorisation*, *Cour de Justice du Canton de Genève* (17 Nov. 1989), reported in *Yearbook* XIX (1994) pp. 214, 215, 218.
13. *Hilmarton Ltd. v. Omnium de Traitement et de Valorisation*, *Cour d'Appel*, Paris (19 Dec. 1991), reported in *Yearbook* XIX (1994) p. 655.
14. *Omnium de Traitement et de Valorisation v. Hilmarton*, *Tribunal Fédéral*, Switzerland (17 Apr. 1990), reported in *Yearbook* XIX (1994) pp. 214, 219, 221.

Swiss Federal Tribunal's decision annulling the first award. The Court of First Instance of Nanterre granted both requests for enforcement in 1993,[15] and OTV appealed to the Court of Appeal of Versailles.

In the still pending appellate proceeding before the French *Cour de Cassation* concerning enforcement of the first (annulled) ICC award, Hilmarton argued, among other grounds, that the court should refuse to recognize and enforce that award as a matter of public policy under Art. V(1)(e) of the New York Convention given that it had been set aside in its country of origin. In its decision of 23 March 1994, the *Cour de Cassation*, however, disagreed finding that under Art. VII of the New York Convention, OTV could invoke the more favorable provision of Art. 1502 of the French New Code of Civil Procedure, which did not include the ground of Art. V(1)(e) among the grounds for an appeal against a decision granting recognition and enforcement.[16] The *Cour de Cassation* also held that the first ICC award was "an international award which is not integrated in the legal system of [Switzerland], so that it remains in existence even if set aside [in Switzerland] and its recognition in France is not contrary to international public policy".[17]

Notwithstanding this final decision of the highest French court, the Court of Appeal of Versailles, more than one year later, reached essentially the opposite conclusion, rejecting OTV's appeals and thus affirming the Nanterre court's decisions to recognize and enforce both the second ICC award and the Swiss Federal Tribunal's decision to set aside the first ICC award.[18] On further appeal, the *Cour de Cassation* in 1997 reversed the decisions of the Versailles Court of Appeal holding that "a final French decision bearing on the same subject between the same parties creates an obstacle to any recognition in France of court decisions or arbitral awards rendered abroad which are incompatible with it".[19]

Having exhausted its remedies in France, Hilmarton then turned to the English courts and there obtained recognition and enforcement of the second ICC award in 1999.[20] Of note, the English High Court rejected OTV's argument that enforcement of the award would be contrary to public policy, finding that "of course only ... English public policy" (not international public policy) was relevant.[21] As Pierre Mayer succinctly summarized the outcome: "The current situation is thus the following: France recognises only the first

---

15. *Hilmarton Ltd. v. Omnium de Traitement et de Valorisation*, *Tribunal de Grande Instance*, Nanterre (22 Sept. 1993), reported in *Yearbook* XX (1995) p. 194.
16. *Hilmarton Ltd. v. Omnium de Traitement et de Valorisation*, *Cour de Cassation*, France (23 Mar. 1994), reported in *Yearbook* XX (1995) pp. 663, 664-665.
17. *Ibid.*, at p. 665.
18. *Omnium de Traitement et de Valorisation v. Hilmarton Ltd.*, *Cour d'Appel*, Versailles (29 June 1995), reported in *Yearbook* XXI (1996) p. 524.
19. *Omnium de Traitement et de Valorisation v. Hilmarton Ltd.*, *Cour de Cassation* (10 June 1997), reported in *Yearbook* XXII (1997) p. 696 at p. 697.
20. *Omnium de Traitement et de Valorisation S.A. v. Hilmarton*, High Court of Justice, Queen's Bench Division (Commercial Court) (24 May 1999), reported in *Yearbook* XXIVa (1999), p. 777.
21. *Ibid.*, at p. 779.

award, rendered in favour of the French company; England recognises only the second award, rendered in favour of the English company."[22]

In the United States, we have the *Chromalloy* case,[23] where the United States District Court for the District of Columbia enforced an arbitral award made in Egypt and under Egyptian law, although the Egyptian Court of Appeal had set aside the award. The US court based its decision on the grounds that Art. V makes refusal to enforce only discretionary and that Art. VII[24] enables a secondary jurisdiction to enforce because recognizing the decision of the Egyptian court would violate clear US public policy in favor of final and binding arbitration of commercial disputes.[25] Specifically, the court found that Art. VII allowed the award creditor to maintain all rights to recognition and enforcement that the creditor would have under domestic law if the Convention did not exist.[26] Finding that Art. VII "mandates that this Court *must* consider [Chromalloy's] claims under applicable US law",[27] the court then analyzed the award under the US Federal Arbitration Act and concluded that no ground for setting aside the award existed under the Act, and the award therefore was proper under U.S. law.[28] The court rejected Egypt's argument that the court should grant res judicata effect to the decision of the Egyptian Court of Appeal on the ground that doing so would violate the United States' "emphatic federal policy in favor of arbitral dispute resolution".[29]

I note that this was a case of first impression before the United States District Court for the District of Columbia, and the *Chromalloy* court's decision does not show that the court had any knowledge of the earlier decisions of the French courts, or of any other non-US courts, interpreting the New York Convention.[30]

Incidentally, as Chromalloy also brought enforcement proceedings in France, the Paris Court of Appeal reached the same conclusion as the US court, confirming the position that it had adopted, and that the *Cour de Cassation* had affirmed, earlier in the *Hilmarton* case. As in *Hilmarton*, the court found that under Art. VII of the New York Convention, Chromalloy was entitled to rely on the narrower scope of grounds for refusal of recognition and enforcement under the French New Code of Civil Procedure.[31]

---

22. Pierre MAYER, "Revisiting *Hilmarton* and *Chromalloy*" in *International Arbitration and National Courts: The Never Ending Story*, ICCA Congress Series no. 10 (2000) p. 165 at p. 168.
23. *Chromalloy Aeroservices v. Arab Republic of Egypt*, 939 F.Supp. 907 (D.D.C. 1996), also reported in *Yearbook* XXII (1997) p. 1001.
24. Art. VII(1) of the New York Convention provides in relevant part:

    "The provisions of the present Convention shall not ... deprive any interested party of any right he may have to avail himself of an arbitral award in the manner and to the extent allowed by the law or the treaties of the country where such award is sought to be relied upon."

25. 939 F. Supp. 907 (D.D.C. 1996) at pp. 909-910.
26. *Ibid.*, at p. 910.
27. *Ibid.*, at p. 914.
28. *Ibid.*, at p. 911.
29. *Ibid.*, at p. 913 (quoting *Mitsubishi v. Soler Chrysler-Plymouth*, 473 U.S. 614, 631 (1985)).
30. *Ibid.*, at 907 et seq.
31. *The Arab Republic of Egypt v. Chromalloy Aeroservices, Inc.*, *Cour d'Appel*, Paris (14 Jan. 1997), reported in *Yearbook* XXII (1997) p. 691 at p. 692-693.

Moreover, the court found that "the award rendered in Egypt was an international award which, by definition, is not integrated in the legal system of [Egypt]", with the consequence that the court felt free to disregard the Egyptian annulment decision.[32]

Turning back to the United States, I should mention the *KBC v. Pertamina* case, where the United States District Court for the Southern District of Texas, in Houston, and the United States Court of Appeals for the Fifth Circuit recognized and enforced an arbitral award despite the fact that the award had been set aside in Indonesia,[33] which in that case was the country "under the laws of which" the award was made. Nonetheless, the Fifth Circuit vacated the Houston Court's injunction of the Indonesian set-aside proceeding.[34] In so doing, the Fifth Circuit avoided addressing the issue of whether the Indonesian court was the proper forum for annulment under the New York Convention.[35] Instead, citing to the District of Columbia decision in *Chromalloy*,[36] the Fifth Circuit found that Art. VI of the New York Convention "grants the enforcement court discretion to enforce an award even though annulment proceedings may be taking place elsewhere".[37] The Fifth Circuit's observations highlight the court's dilemma under the existing Convention:

> "By allowing concurrent enforcement and annulment actions, as well as simultaneous enforcement actions in third countries, the Convention necessarily envisions multiple proceedings that address the same substantive challenges to an arbitral award.... In short, multiple judicial proceedings on the same legal issues are characteristic of the confirmation and enforcement of international arbitral awards under the Convention.
> 
> (....)
> 
> By its silence on the matter, the Convention does not restrict the grounds on which primary jurisdiction courts may annul an award, thereby leaving to a primary jurisdiction's local law the decision whether to set aside an award. Consequently, even though courts of a primary jurisdiction may apply their own domestic law when evaluating an attempt to annul or set aside an arbitral award, courts in countries of secondary jurisdiction may refuse enforcement only on the limited grounds specified in Article V."[38]

---

32. *Ibid.*, at p. 693.
33. *Karaha Bodas Co. v. Perusahaan Pertambangan Minyak Dan Gas Bumi Negara (Pertamina)*, 190 F.Supp.2d 936 (S.D. Tex. 2001), also reported in *Yearbook* XXVII (2002) p. 814. In the interest of full disclosure, I note that I acted for the Republic of Indonesia in that case and in related proceedings in other courts.
34. *Karaha Bodas Co. v. Perusahaan Pertambangan Minyak Dan Gas Bumi Negara (Pertamina)*, 335 F.3d 357, 360 (5th Cir. 2003), also reported in *Yearbook* XXVIII (2003) p. 908.
35. 335 F.3d at p. 366.
36. *Ibid.*, at p. 369, fn.52.
37. *Ibid.*, at p. 367, fn.42 (quoting Leonard V. QUIGLEY, "Accession by the United States to the United Nations Convention on the Recognition and Enforcement of Foreign Arbitral Awards", 70 Yale L.J. (1961) p. 1049 at p. 1071 ("explaining that as a 'reasonable complement to Article V(1)(e)' Article VI is 'wholly discretionary, and the enforcing State is free to refuse adjournment and to enforce the award, nullification proceedings in the rendering State notwithstanding'")).
38. 335 F.3d at pp. 367-368.

Albert Jan van den Berg's Draft goes a long way to protect against that, and I will address that below.

Other courts, including in France and the United States, have taken the opposite view, deciding not to enforce a vacated award.

It is interesting to note that in a decision preceding the *Norsolor*, *Hilmarton* and *Chromalloy* cases, the Paris Court of Appeal interpreted Art. V(1)(e) of the New York Convention as mandating refusal of enforcement and accordingly refused enforcement of a Swiss award, which the Swiss court had vacated as "arbitrary".[39] The later decisions of the Paris Court of Appeal and the French *Cour de Cassation* in *Hilmarton* and *Chromalloy* presumably have reduced the authoritative value of that decision.

Subsequent to *Chromalloy*, a number of US court decisions have distinguished that case and refused enforcement of awards set aside at the seat of the arbitration.

In *Baker Marine (Nig.) v. Chevron (Nig.)*, the United States Court of Appeals for the Second Circuit affirmed a decision of the United States District Court for the Northern District of New York denying petitions of Baker Marine to enforce two Nigerian awards, which had been set aside by a Nigerian court.[40] Relying on *Chromalloy*, Baker Marine argued that under Art. VII of the New York Convention it was nonetheless entitled to avail itself of the awards because US law (i.e., the law of the enforcement forum) did not recognize the grounds on which the Nigerian court had set aside the awards. The court rejected that argument on the grounds that the parties' arbitration agreement was governed by Nigerian law and made no reference to US law, and that Baker Marine had not asserted any violation by the Nigerian court of Nigerian law.[41] The court explained that,

> "as a practical matter, mechanical application of domestic arbitral law to foreign awards under the Convention would seriously undermine finality and regularly produce conflicting judgments. If a party whose arbitration award has been vacated at the site of the award can automatically obtain enforcement of the awards [sic] under the domestic laws of other nations, a losing party will have every reason to pursue its adversary 'with enforcement actions from country to country until a court is found, if any, which grants the enforcement'."[42]

Baker Marine also argued that Art. V(1)(e) gave the court discretion not to enforce an award that had been set aside in its country of origin. The court rejected that argument finding that Baker Marine had not shown any "adequate reason for refusing to recognize the judgments of the Nigerian court".[43] In so doing, the court distinguished

---

39. *Clair v. Berardi*, Court of Appeal, Paris (20 June 1980), reported in *Yearbook* VII (1982) p. 319 at p. 321.
40. *Baker Marine (Nig.) Ltd. v. Chevron (Nig.) Ltd.*, 191 F.3d 194 (2nd Cir. 1999), also reported in *Yearbook* XXIV (1999) p. 909.
41. 191 F.3d at pp. 196-197.
42. *Ibid.*, at p. 197, fn.2 (quoting Albert Jan VAN DEN BERG, *The New York Arbitration Convention of 1958: Towards a Uniform Judicial Interpretation* (1981) p. 355).
43. *Ibid.*, at p. 197.

*Chromalloy* on its facts, pointing out that in *Chromalloy* the parties had expressly waived any appeal or other recourse against the arbitral award.[44]

Following *Baker Marine*, the United States District Court for the Southern District of New York, in *Spier v. Calzaturificio Tecnica*, for the same reasons refused to enforce an Italian award that had been set aside in Italy.[45]

More recently, in 2007, the United States Court of Appeals for the District of Columbia joined this trend to limit the effects of *Chromalloy*, in *TermoRio v. Electranta*.[46] The court expressly "subscribed to the reasoning of the Second Circuit in *Baker Marine*" and distinguished *Chromalloy* on its facts.[47]

Distinguished legal writers also have taken diametrically opposed positions on the issue as to whether an arbitral award that was vacated in its country of origin may be enforced elsewhere. Emmanuel Gaillard has taken the position that enforcement is permissible, emphasizing the "strength of the connecting factors between the dispute and each of the states involved":

> "The French conception of state review of awards rests on the idea that the state of the place of enforcement is as well positioned as the state of the seat to assess whether an award should be recognized and enforced.... The state of enforcement ... has a very real interest in ensuring that the award meets the standards of what it considers to be a decision worthy of public support. On a very basic level, between the state of the seat, which provides hotel rooms and conference centers for an arbitration, and the state of enforcement which permits the seizure and sale of assets in its territory, there can be little doubt but that the latter has the stronger interest in reviewing the award. This view is perfectly consistent with the New York Convention, which permits the state of enforcement to apply its own conception of public policy and its own standards concerning the arbitrability of the dispute in all cases. The fact that the state of the seat may also be the place or one of the places of enforcement of the award does not alter this analysis."[48]

Based on a textual analysis, Jan Paulsson has taken the position that Art. V(1) of the New York Convention allows enforcement of an award set aside in its country of origin.[49] He also has advocated a differentiated approach under which the enforcement forum should give effect to an annulment in the country of origin only where the ground for annulment was included in the first four paragraphs of Art. V(1) of the New York Convention and Art. 36(1)(a) of the UNCITRAL Model Law and thus constituted an "international standard annulment". Conversely, under this approach, the enforcement

---

44. *Ibid.*, at p. 197, fn.3.
45. *Spier v. Calzaturificio Tecnica, S.p.A.*, 71 F.Supp.2d 279 (S.D.N.Y. 1999).
46. *Termorio S.A. E.S.P. v. Electranta S.P.*, 487 F.3d 928 (D.C. Cir. 2007), also reported in *Yearbook* XXXIII (2008) p. 955.
47. 487 F.3d at pp. 935, 937.
48. Emmanuel GAILLARD, "The Enforcement of Awards Set Aside in the Country of Origin", 14 ICSID Rev. – FILJ (1999) p. 16 at pp. 44-45 (referring to Art. V(2) of the New York Convention).
49. Jan PAULSSON, "*May* or *Must* Under the New York Convention: An Exercise in Syntax and Linguistics", 14 Arb. Int'l (1998) p. 227.

forum should be free to disregard the annulment if it was based only on "local standards" (i.e., a "local standard annulment", based on standards not included in the first four paragraphs of Art. V(1) of the New York Convention and Art. 36(1)(a) of the UNCITRAL Model Law).[50] In Jan Paulsson's view, this approach would create "incentives for national courts to conform to internationally accepted standards".[51]

Eminent writers also have expressed the contrary view. Thus, Michael Reisman stated:

> "nullificatory consequences of decisions in primary jurisdictions have a universal effect. In terms of the dynamic of the convention, once an award has been set aside in a primary jurisdiction, it is not supposed to be enforceable anywhere else.
>
> Once a venue or a governing law is selected, the convention gives to it a primacy with regard to the validity of the award. If an award is rendered, let us say, in Switzerland and is nullified under Swiss law, nothing should be enforceable in any other jurisdiction."[52]

Albert Jan van den Berg similarly wrote: "If the arbitral award has been set aside in the country of origin, foreign courts are bound by that decision. In that case, they must refuse recognition and enforcement of the award".[53]

The literature thus provides clear evidence of a significant conflict. As Pierre Mayer pointed out "when the award was set aside in the country of the seat, the lack of uniform reaction among the foreign countries can be disastrous".[54] As a solution, he suggested drafting a new convention, additional to the New York Convention, that would enter into force only once a large number of States ratifies it.[55] With this, I turn now to Albert Jan van den Berg's proposed revision of the New York Convention.

II.   ALBERT JAN VAN DEN BERG'S HYPOTHETICAL DRAFT CONVENTION

I think it is with elegant simplicity and clarity of language that Albert Jan van den Berg's Draft gives us an approach that eliminates much of the textual ambiguity that gave rise to the litigation and the inconsistency of results discussed above.
(1) In its Art. 5(3)(g), using the word "shall" instead of "may", the Draft makes clear,

> "Enforcement of an arbitral award *shall* be refused if, at the request of the party against whom the award is invoked, that party asserts and proves that ... the award has been set aside by the court in the country where the award was made

---

50. Jan PAULSSON, "Enforcing Arbitral Awards Notwithstanding a Local Standard Annulment (LSA)", The International Court of Arbitration Bulletin (1988, no. 1) p. 14 at p.29.
51. *Ibid.*, at p. 31.
52. W.M. REISMAN, *Systems of Control in International Adjudication and Arbitration* (1992) p. 114.
53. *Op. cit.*, fn. 1, pp. 41-42.
54. Pierre MAYER, *op. cit.*, fn. 22, at p. 172.
55. *Ibid.*, at p. 175.

on *grounds substantially equivalent to grounds (a) to (e) of this paragraph.*" (Emphasis added)

"Shall be refused" is a welcome clarification: It requires refusal of enforcement where the award has been set aside based on specified grounds ((*a*)-(*e*)); it strengthens primary jurisdiction; it avoids contradictory results; promotes greater harmonization of set-aside standards; and leads to greater predictability and less litigation in the post-award process.
(2) Referring to the country of origin of the award, the Draft no longer contains the two criteria of the present Convention's Art. V(1)(*e*): the situs where the award was made or the situs of the law under which the award was made. Instead, Art. 5(3)(g) of the Draft focuses exclusively on the country "where the award was made". Although, as Albert Jan van den Berg explains,[56] it is rare for parties to select an arbitration law other than the law of the place of arbitration, such cases do arise.[57] For those cases, the Draft provides a more predictable approach that also will be less prone to litigation.
(3) Art. 5(3)(g) of the Draft specifies that a set-aside in the country of origin must be respected elsewhere if it is premised "on grounds substantially equivalent to grounds (a) to (e) of this paragraph". In contrast, Art. V(1)(*e*) of the existing Convention is silent with respect to the grounds for annulment. The Draft thus limits the grounds for setting aside an award to grounds "substantially equivalent" to those contained in the UNCITRAL Model Law in order for the set-aside to have universal effect[58] and permits discretion for domestic law grounds that go beyond. As Jan Paulsson has said,[59] this approach may increase harmonization of recognized set-aside grounds and reduce litigation.
(4) Turning to public policy: Under the New York Convention, Art. V(2)(*b*), the public policy exception, has been interpreted to include the domestic public policy of the forum, as we have seen in some of the cases discussed above. As mentioned, in the *Hilmarton* case, the English High Court found that "of course only ... English public policy" (not international public policy) was relevant.[60] In the view of the High Court of Delhi, the court in *Cosid Inc. v. Steel Authority of India Ltd.*, the enforcing court was simply to apply the notions of public policy of the country of enforcement: "... the expression 'public policy' in ... Art. V(2)(*b*) of the New York Convention refers to the *public policy of the country where enforcement is sought*, i.e., India".[61] Similarly, the Hong Kong Court of Final Appeal found that "international public policy" referred not to "some standard common to all civilised nations" but rather to "those elements of a state's own public

---

56. Explanatory Note at 23 (this volume, pp. 649-666).
57. *See, e.g.*, *Karaha Bodas Co. v. Perusahaan Pertambangan Minyak Dan Gas Bumi Negara (Pertamina)*, 335 F.3d 357, 363 (5th Cir. 2003), also reported in *Yearbook* XXVIII (2003) p. 908 (where the arbitration agreement provided for arbitration in Geneva and referenced Indonesian procedural law, the Indonesian court found that it had primary jurisdiction to annul an award made in Switzerland).
58. See Explanatory Note at 35-36 (this volume, pp. 654-655).
59. *Op cit.*, fn. 49, p. 31.
60. *Omnium de Traitement et de Valorisation S.A. v. Hilmarton*, High Court of Justice, Queen's Bench Division (Commercial Court) (24 May 1999), reported in *Yearbook* XXIV (1999) p. 777, at p. 779.
61. *Cosid Inc. v. Steel Authority of India Ltd.*, High Court of Delhi (12 July 1985), reported in *Yearbook* XI (1986) p. 502 at p. 507 (emphasis added).

policy which are so fundamental to its notions of justice that its courts feel obliged to apply the same not only to purely internal matters but even to matters with a foreign element by which other states are affected".[62]

This has been a source of great mischief in some jurisdictions and was in fact the subject of an International Law Association interim report which found, "Uncertainty and inconsistencies concerning the interpretation and application of public policy by State courts encourage the losing party to rely on public policy to resist, or at least delay, enforcement."[63] As Audley Sheppard stated, "[p]ublic policy is often regarded as a vague concept which is impossible to define, which varies from State to State. This leads to uncertainty and unpredictability, which encourages the unsuccessful party in the arbitration to resist enforcement of the award on grounds of public policy."[64]

Albert Jan van den Berg's Draft Art. 5(3)(h) makes clear that the only predicate to denying enforcement is "international public policy prevailing in the country where enforcement is sought".[65] The Draft thus clarifies that this exception is limited to international public policy, and thus promotes greater harmonization and predictability. By limiting the application of international public policy to the extent it *prevails* in the enforcement forum, Art. 5(3)(h) also defers to some extent to the enforcement forum's laws, perhaps thereby making the transition more palatable to those countries that so far have applied exclusively domestic public policy.

III. CONCLUSION

The Draft addresses many of the problems that we have encountered in interpreting the New York Convention over the past fifty years. An examination of the national courts' decisions and scholarly writings fully supports the need for the change and simplification reflected in the Draft Convention. Although the effort required to amend the New York Convention will be great, if the Draft Convention is adopted, fifty years from now we will look back to conclude that it was worth the effort.

---

62. *Hebei Import and Export Corp. v. Polytek Engineering Co. Ltd.*, [1999] 1 HKLRD 665, 674, per Bokhary PJ, also reported in *Yearbook* XXIV (1999) p. 652.
63. International Law Association, "Interim Report on Public Policy as a Bar to Enforcement of International Arbitral Awards", London Conference (2000), in International Law Association, *Report of the Sixty-Ninth Conference* (2000) p. 340 at p. 374.
64. Audley SHEPPARD, "Public Policy and the Enforcement of Arbitral Awards: Should there be a Global Standard?", 1 Oil, Gas & Energy Law Intelligence (March 2003, no. 2).
65. See "The Text of the Hypothetical Draft Convention", this volume, pp. 667-669.

# Comments on a New York Convention for the Next Fifty Years

*Rory Brady SC**

| TABLE OF CONTENTS | Page |
| --- | --- |
| I. Introduction | 708 |
| II. Empirical Evidence | 709 |
| III. Art. 3(4) Expedition | 710 |
| IV. Art. V(3)(a) – Valid Arbitration | 711 |
| V. Conclusion | 711 |

I.   INTRODUCTION

The risk of conflicting or deficient judicial interpretations of international conventions or laws giving effect to them is a fact of life. Whether these varying and indeed at times conflicting results can, in the future, be avoided is the real challenge facing those looking at the next fifty years of the 1958 New York Convention. The twin goals of efficiency and uniformity in the enforcement of international arbitration awards are probably shared by everybody. But the critical issue, it seems to me, that faces the participants in today's debate is whether a new convention is both necessary and a practicable objective. Ultimately those who need to be convinced are not legal practitioners but decision makers and legislators. Hence, the case for change, if it is to be sustained, must be made at a variety of levels, political, economic and legal. A one dimensional legal perspective does not reveal the entire canvas for the operation of the New York Convention.

There are I believe a number of aspects of the draft proposal that will create real and substantial problems in achieving the objective of a new convention being adopted. Firstly, what looks like a rather innocuous clause requiring the expedition of proceedings to which the New York Convention applies might carry a latent financial burden. Secondly, the validity of an arbitration agreement being determined by the place where the award is made may not, in reality, reflect the real intentions of the parties to the agreement.

I do not believe that there will be any real political impetus behind the proposed changes unless and until it is demonstrated that all possible solutions, to what are accepted and acknowledged deficiencies, are exhausted. In other words it is only at a point in time when it is recognized that the New York Convention is in a state of crisis and its ultimate objective is being thereby subverted that change will follow. The task of promoting that change requires convincing the international community of 144 States (at the time of this writing) who are parties to the New York Convention of the necessity for such change. That is a gargantuan task and one, I suspect, that will not be readily achieved. In this world there are too many other priorities attracting the attention of policy makers, decision makers and legislators. Those who promote change are in

---

*   Senior Counsel in practice at the Irish Bar.

competition for the time and attention of those who can make the changes. There are many other more urgent tasks facing the international community.

Before referring to some specific subject matter I think it is necessary to look at the actual practical results of the operation of the last fifty years of the New York Convention. Does the empirical evidence point relentlessly towards a need for change?

II.  EMPIRICAL EVIDENCE

There are I believe two fundamental questions. Firstly, what has been the actual success rate of the New York Convention in the enforcement of arbitration awards and agreements? Secondly, what have been the bases for refusals of applications made in domestic courts pursuant to the New York Convention?

The *Year Book Commercial Arbitration* records approximately 1,400 court decisions, throughout the world, on the interpretation and application of the New York Convention. Approximately half of these cover decisions concerning enforcement of awards. As is pointed out by its distinguished editor of the seven hundred or so enforcement decisions refusal has occurred in some seventy cases. This is a ten percent failure rate when viewed from one perspective. It does not, on its face, demonstrate and manifest a systemic deficiency in the implementation of the New York Convention throughout the world. But of course statistics are never the full story. To have been one of those seventy applicants who failed means that for that litigant the New York Convention has failed their cause: Or has it?

When one comes to take a broad view of problems in procuring enforcement of awards it is necessary to draw a dichotomy between problems that are soluble and those that are not soluble. In the latter category I refer to situations where the paper work or the proofs are simply not in order. Accordingly, there is a failure to comply with the requirements of the New York Convention and/or domestic legislation. In addition because of defects in the arbitral process an award is not enforced. These are not problems caused by the New York Convention. They stem from different problems. Amending the New York Convention will not provide an antidote to those problems. Where, however, there is some scope for change is in relation to the process of interpretation of the domestic laws and the New York Convention. Here, of course, it is necessary to keep in mind the different monist and the dualist legal systems. When one comes to interpret domestic legislation, implementing the New York Convention, the greatest scope for inconsistency with the objective of the New York Convention arises. However, the problem that thereby arises is one of interpretation and that is an inherent risk of the interpretation of domestic laws implementing any international convention. Thus, even if the New York Convention is amended to reflect the proposals advanced here today the risk of misapplication and misinterpretation, at domestic level, will continue to subsist. No matter how carefully crafted the words of a new convention will be the problems will not be eliminated.

I believe that there is a compelling case for greater judicial interaction among different jurisdictions. The provisions of the Treaty of The European Union address the necessity for closer judicial co-operation. Law Reform Commissions throughout the world consult with each other. International lawyers regularly meet to address the knotty issues of the day. Through this process of exchange of ideas and experiences I believe one can evolve an acceptable set of general principles to influence the judicial approach to the New York Convention. One simple principle comes to mind. It should be accepted, readily, that when one comes to interpret domestic laws (in a dualist system) that the domestic legislation should be interpreted in a manner consistent with the New York Convention. A second proposition that merits consideration is according a status to publications by groups of jurists on the interpretation of the New York Convention. While each court system and judiciary respect its own independence and sovereignty closer judicial cooperation will not derogate from those principles. Instead they will facilitate a more harmonious approach to solving the problems arising from the New York Convention. I certainly believe that as a project one would have to exhaust this possible option as an antidote to the deficiencies that arise before one could convince the international community of the necessity for the new Convention.

But there are other factors that in my view are not conducive to a happy welcome to today's proposal. I shall address them now.

III. ART. 3(4) EXPEDITION

At first blush the duty to act expeditiously should be universally attractive. There are few litigants and even fewer lawyers who do not want their case heard quickly. The noble aspiration of an early trial date and finality is a shared value. But the real issue that we have to address here today is whether that aspiration (if expressed in a new Convention) could possibly carry a price tag? Let me explain.

The European Court of Human Rights has evolved a jurisprudence (a rather curious one, some say) whereby a financial liability can apply to a State because of litigation delays in its court system. Ireland has been subject to fines by the European Court of Human Rights. The latest one was of the magnitude of € 15,000. The omission to have in place a system to secure the timely progress of litigation has been the basis of that financial liability. I suspect the principle, as it has developed, is not attractive to Ministers for Finance of the member States of the Council of Europe. This is a judge-made law. The question we have to address is whether there is a real risk that a convention that imposes a duty of expedition could give rise to a financial liability.

My concern relates to dualist legal systems and, specifically, to common law jurisdiction. To insert into a statute a duty of expedition may carry with it the risk of a judicial interpretation that this amounts to a statutory duty. Moreover, in so far as there is concern with civil obligations what scope is there in applying the European Convention on Human Rights jurisprudence to evolving a domestic law remedy for delay. I do not know the answers to these questions. However, I think one would need to reflect long and hard on the risk that such a provision could be perceived as creating a financial liability. If so that would be the death knell of any proposal. It may also give rise to public law remedies. It may well be legislative draftsmen can find a solution that excludes any risk of a financial consequence of a failure to comply with a duty of expedition. So be it. But that is not the real issue. The question is the degree to which there is a risk of a judicial sanction on the State deriving from a new convention and a new law.

## IV. ART. V(3)(A) — VALID ARBITRATION

Determining validity by reference to the country where the award is made creates, for me, a philosophical problem. The word "validity" is intended to have a wide ambit. It contains within its purview all of the grounds of challenge currently addressed in Art. V(1)(a) of the New York Convention. However, with the New York Convention the primary law is the law to which the parties have subjected their agreement. Fundamentally arbitration is a consensual process. It is because the parties have agreed to submit to the decision of an arbitrator that the courts step back from the process. I cannot see any compelling reason to depart from the normal rule that the choice of the parties to a contract should prevail. While it is, of course, the case that where parties agree to an arbitration that they are thereby on notice of the applicable legal system that creates its own problems. We all proceed on the assumption that the arbitration clause is, so to speak, an independent bargain. Where the parties choose a proper law under the contract with an arbitration clause it is all part of the same commercial bargain. As lawyers we have created the legal fiction of the stand-alone and independent arbitration clause that survives fundamental breaches of contract, rescission and so on and so forth. But this fiction should not be extended too far. If the parties wish to have issues such as validity determined by their choice of law that is a decision that should be respected. It achieves legal certainty in exactly the same way as the proposal in Art. 5(3)(a).

## V. CONCLUSION

I am grateful to Albert Jan van den Berg for his thought-provoking and thorough analysis of the problems with the New York Convention (this volume, pp. 649-666). I, unfortunately, remain a sceptic as to the necessity for change. Moreover I do not believe the case for change will be convincing until we have exhausted all other options.

# ICCA DUBLIN CONFERENCE LIST OF PARTICIPANTS

**Argentina**

Tawil, Guido Santiago
Member of ICCA
M & M Bomchil
Suipacha 268, 12th Floor
C1008AAF Buenos Aires

Yaryura, Cintia
Office of the Republic of Argentina
Posadas 1641
1112 Buenos Aires

**Australia**

Bonnell, Max
Mallesons Stephen Jaques
Governor Phillip Tower, Level 53
1 Farrer Place
Sydney, NSW 2000

Brown, Neil Anthony
Murdoch University
PO Box 2140, St. Kilda West
Melbourne, Victoria 3182

Creer, James
GPO Box 563
Sydney, NSW 2001

De Fina, Antonino Albert
de Fina Consultants
55 Capella Crescent
Moorabbin, Victoria 3189

Easton, Graham
G. R. Easton Pty. Ltd.
73 Carlotta Street
Greenwich
Sydney, NSW 2065

Griffith, Gavan, QC
205 William Street
Melbourne, Victoria 3000

Handley, Kenneth
Court of Appeal NSW Australia
2/38 Milson Road
Cremorne
Sydney, NSW 2090

Herbon, Alice
University of Tasmania
Hobart Campus
Private Bag 89
Hobart, Tasmania 7001

Jones, Douglas
Clayton Utz
No. 1 O'Connell Street
Sydney, NSW 2000

Kay Hoyle, Jonathan
Mallesons Stephen Jaques
Governor Phillip Tower, Level 61
1 Farrer Place
Sydney, NSW 2000

Lees, Amanda
Blake Dawson
Level 35, Grosvenor Place
225 George Street
Sydney, NSW 2000

Megens, Peter
Mallesons Stephen Jaques
Bourke Place, Level 50
600 Bourke Street,
Melbourne, Victoria 3000

Stephenson, Andrew
Clayton Utz
333 Collins Street, Level 18
Melbourne, Victoria 3000

Waincymer, Jeffrey
Monash University
Wellington Road
Clayton
Melbourne, Victoria 3800

**Austria**

Baier, Anton
Baier Boehm Attorneys at Law
Kärntner Ring 12
1010 Vienna

Haugeneder, Florian
Wolf Theiss

713

Schubertring 6
1010 Vienna

Herrmann, Gerold
President of ICCA
Reimersgasse 16 B2
1190 Vienna

Kremslehner, Florian
Dorda Brugger Jordis Rechtsanwaelte GmbH
Dr Karl Lueper Ring 10
1010 Vienna

Melis, Werner
Honorary Vice President of ICCA
International Arbitration Centre of the
Austrian Federal Economic Chamber
Wiedner Haupstrasse 63
1045 Vienna

Montineri, Corinne
United Nations
Vienna International Centre
PO Box 500, Room E0450
1400 Vienna

Pitkowitz, Nikolaus
Graf & Pitkowitz Rechtsanwaelte GmbH
Stadiongasse 2
1010 Vienna

Reiner, Andreas
ARP Andreas Reiner & Partners
Freyung 6/12
Vienna 1010

Steindl, Barbara
Torggler Attorneys at Law
Dr. Karl Lueger Ring 10/5
1010 Vienna

## Bahrain

Ajaji, Khaled
Ministry of Justice
Diplomatic Area, 3rd Floor
Manama

Al Boainain, Abdulla
Heclaya Building
Diplomatic Area, 4th Floor
Manama

Al Khalifa, Khaled
Ministry of Justice
Diplomatic Area, 3rd Floor
Manama

Hussein, Ahmed
Ministry of Justice
Diplomatic Area, 3rd Floor
Manama

Khalaf, Yousif
Economic Development Board
Seef Tower
PO Box 11299
Manama

MacPherson, James
Government of Bahrain
Ministry of Justice
Diplomatic Area, 3rd Floor
Manama

## Belgium

Baldew, Marike
Hanotiau & van den Berg
IT Tower, 9th Floor
Avenue Louise 480 B9
1050 Brussels

Hanotiau, Bernard
Member of ICCA
Hanotiau & van den Berg
IT Tower, 9th Floor
Avenue Louise 480 B9
1050 Brussels

Lefevre, Francoise
Linklaters
Rue Bredenode 13
1000 Bruxelles

Van den Berg, Albert Jan
Member of ICCA
Hanotiau & van den Berg
IT Tower, 9th Floor
Avenue Louise 480
1050 Brussels

Van Houtte, Hans
Faculty of Law

Tiensestraat 41
3000 Leuven

Van Houtte, Vera
Ioxsumstraat 25
1000 Brussels

**Bermuda**

Elkinson, Jeffrey
Conyers Dill & Pearman
1 Church Street
HM11 Hamilton

**Brazil**

Batista Martins, Pedro
Rua Timoteo da Costa
371 Apto. 301 Lebion
Rio de Janeiro 22450-130

Birenbaum, Gustavo
Ferro, Castro Neves, Daltro & Gomide
Advogados
Avenida Rio Branco, No. 85
Centro, 13th floor
Rio de Janeiro 20040-004

Braghetta, Adriana
L.O. Baptista Advogados
Avenida Paulista, No. 1294, 8th Floor
Cerqueira Cesar
Sao Paulo 01310-100

Chateaubriand Martins, Andre
Sergio Bermudes Law Office
Praça XI de Novembro 20, 8th Floor
Rio de Janeiro 20010-010

Consentino, Antonella
Sergio Bermudes Law Office
Praça XV de Novembro 20, 8th floor
Rio de Janeiro 20010-010

Fernandes de Andrade, Gustavo
Sergio Bermudes Law Office
Praça XV de Novembro 20, 8th Floor
Rio de Janeiro 20010-010

Ferro, Marcelo
Ferro, Castro Neves, Daltro & Gomide

Advogados
Avenida Rio Branco, No. 85
Centro, 13th Floor
Rio de Janeiro 20040-004

Fichtner, José Antonio
Andrade & Fichter Advogados
Avenida Almirante Barroso, 139, 4th Floor
Rio de Janeiro 20031-005

Fragata, Octavio
Barbosa, Mussnich & Aragao Advogados
Avenida Almirante Barroso 52, 32 Floor
Rio de Janeiro 20031-000

Franco, Alice
Ferro, Castro Neves, Daltro & Gorride
Advogados
Avenida Rio Branco, No. 85
Centro, 13th Floor
Rio de Janeiro 20040-004

Garcia de Fonseca, Rodrigo
Wald e Associados Advogados
Avenida Almirante Barroso 52, 8th Floor
Rio de Janeiro 20031-000

Giusti, Gilberto
Pinheiro Neto Advogados
Rua Hungria 1100
Sao Paulo 01455-000

Goncalves, Eduardo Damiao
Barretto Ferreira, Kujawski, Brancher e
Goncalves Society de Advogados
R Dr Eduardo de Souza Aranha
V.N. Conceicao, No. 387, 15th Floor
Sao Paulo 04543-121

Lee, Joao Bosco
Castro & Lee Sociedade de Advogados
Avenida Nossa Senhora da Luz, 1755
Hugo Lange
Curitiba 82520-060

Mussnich, Francisco
Barbosa, Mussnich & Aragao Advogados
Avenida Almirante Barroso 52, 32nd Floor
Rio de Janeiro 20031-000

Nanni, Giovanni Ettore
TozziniFreire Advogados

Rua Borges Lagoa, No. 1328
Sao Paulo 04038-034

Nehring Netto, Carlos
Member of ICCA
Nehring e Associados Advocacia
Avenida Paulista 1294, 12th Floor
01310-915 Sao Paulo-SP

Noemi Pucci, Adriana
Veirano Advogados
Avenida das Nações Unidas 12.995
18th Floor
Sao Paulo 04578-000

Pecoraro, Eduardo
Ferro, Castro Neves, Daltro & Gomide
Advogados
Rua Ramos Batista 198, conjunto 92
Sao Paulo 04552-020

Pinto, José Emilio
José Emilio Nunes Pinto Advogades
Avenida Presidente Juscelino Kubitschek 28
9th Floor
Sao Paulo 04543-000

Prado, Mauricio
L.O. Baptista Advogados
Avenida Paulista, No. 1294, 8th Floor
Cerqueira Cesar
Sao Paulo 01310-100

Robalinho Cavalcanti, Fabiano
Sergio Bermudes Law Office
Praça XV de Novembro 20, 8th Floor
Rio de Janeiro 20010-010

Rocha da Silva, Fabricio
Sergio Bermudes Law Office
Rua Frei Caneca, No. 1380, 5th Floor
Sao Paulo 01307-002

Seabra, Andre
Ferro, Castro Neves, Daltro & Gomide
Advogados
Avenida Rio Branca, No. 85
Centro, 13th Floor
Rio de Janeiro 20040-004

Tepedino, Gustavo
Gustavo Tepedino Advogados

Rua da Assembleia 58
Centro, 10th Floor
Rio de Janeiro 21011-000

Tepedino, Ricardo
Sergio Bermudes Law Office
Rua Frei Caneca, No. 1380, 5th Floor
Sao Paulo 01307-002

Vieira Souto Costa Ferreira, Marcio
Sergio Bermudes Law Office
Praça XV de Novembro 20, 8th Floor
Rio de Janeiro 20010-010

**Bulgaria**

Ganev, Angel
Djingov, Gouginski, Kyutchukov & Velichkov
10 Tsar Osvoboditel Blvd
1000 Sofia

**Canada**

Andrighetti, Vikki
BCF
1100 René-Lévesque Boulevard West
Montréal PQ H3B 5C9

Barin, Babak
BCF
1100 René-Lévesque Boulevard West
Montréal PQ H3B 5C9

Bienvenu, Pierre
Ogilvy Renault
1981 avenue McGill Collège, Suite 1100
Montréal PQ H3A 3C1

Cadieux, Rene
Fasken Martineau DuMoulin
The Stock Exchange Tower
800 Victoria Square, 34th Floor
Montréal PQ H4Z 1E9

Davidson, Paul
Carleton University
Department of Law
1125 Colonol By Drive
Ottawa ON K1S 5B6

## LIST OF PARTICIPANTS

Elliot, David
Fraser Milner Casgrain
1420 – 99 Bank Street
Ottawa ON K1P 1H4

Fortier, Yves
Member of ICCA
Ogilvy Renault
1981 avenue McGill Collège, Suite 1100
Montréal PQ H3A 3C1

Grierson-Weiler, Todd
19 – 2014 Valley Run Boulevard
London ON N6G 5N8

Judge, John A.M.
Stikeman Elliott
5300 Commerce Court West
199 Bay Street
Toronto ON M5L 1B9

Lalonde, Marc
Advisory Member of ICCA
Stikeman Elliott
1155 René-Lévesque Boulevard West
33rd Floor
Montréal PQ H3B 3V2

Laurin, Marc
Stikeman Elliott
1155 René-Lévesque Boulevard West
40th Floor
Montréal PQ H3B 3V2

Leon, Barry
Torys
TD Centre
79 Wellington Street W, Suite 3000
Toronto ON M5K 1N2

McLaren, Richard
The University of Western Ontario
300 Dundee Street
London ON N6B 1T6

Ouimet, Eric
BCF
1100 René-Levesque Boulevard West
25th Floor
Montréal PQ H3B 5C9

Rosen, Howard
LECG Canada Ltd.

55 University Avenue, Suite 1000
Toronto ON M5J 2H7

Rowley, J. William
McMillan Binch Mendelsohn
181 Bay Street, Suite 4400
Toronto ON M5J 2T3

Vlavianos, George
Bennett Jones
4500, 855 – 2nd Street SW
Calgary AB T2P 4K7

Walker, Janet
Osgoode Hall Law School
4700 Keele Street
Toronto ON M3J 1P3

### Chile

Jana, Andres
Alvarez Hinzpeter Jana
Avenida Andres Bello 2711, 8th Floor
Las Condes 7550006

Orrego Vicuña, Francisco
Member of ICCA
Francisco Orrego Vicuna Y Compania
Avenida El Golf No. 40, 6th Floor
Santiago 7550107

### China (Mainland)

Chen, Jian
China International Economic & Trade
Arbitration Commission
6/F Golden Land Building
32 Liang Ma Qiao Road
Chaoyang District
100016 Beijing

Fang, Jian
Beijing Arbitration Commission
16/F China Merchants Tower
No. 118, Jian Gua Road
Chaoyang District
100022 Beijing

Gao, Fei
China International Economic & Trade
Arbitration Commission

6/F Golden Land Building
32 Liang Ma Qiao Road
Chaoyang District
100016 Beijing

Houzhi, Tang
Advisory Member of ICCA
China International Economic & Trade
Arbitration Commission
6/F Golden Land Building
32 Liang Ma Qiao Road
Chaoyang District
100016 Beijing

Tao, Jing Zhou
Jones Day Beijing Office
China World Tower 1, 32nd Floor
1 Jian Guo Men Wai Avenue
100084 Beijing

Wang, Ruichen
China International Economic & Trade
Arbitration Commission
6/F Golden Land Building
32 Liang Ma Qiao Road
Chaoyang District
100016 Beijing

Wang, Xi Lian
Beijing Arbitration Commission
16/F China Merchants Tower, No. 118
Jian Gua Road
Chaoyang District
100022 Beijing

Yao, Junyi
China International Economic & Trade
Arbitration Commission
6/F Golden Land Building
32 Liang Ma Qiao Road
Chaoyang District
100016 Beijing

Yu, Jianlong
China International Economic & Trade
Arbitration Commission
6/F Golden Land Building
32 Liang Ma Qiao Road
Chaoyang District
100016 Beijing

**Croatia**

Sikiric, Hrvoje
Faculty of Law
Trg Marsala Tita 14, 3rd Floor
Zagreb 10000

**Czech Republic**

Horacek, Vit
Glatzova & Co.
Husova 5
11000 Prague

Klein, Bohuslav
Arbitration Court Prague
c/o Economic Chamber of the Czech
Republic and Agricultural Chamber of the
Czech Republic
Dlouha 13
11000 Prague 1

Mares, Alexandr
Mares Partners
Betlemske Namesti 6
11000 Prague

Pohunek, Milos
Arbitration Court
c/o Economic Chamber of the Czech
Republic and Agricultural Chamber of the
Czech Republic
Dlouha 13
11000 Prague 1

**Denmark**

Dalgaard-Knudsen, Frants
Plesner
Amerika Plads 37
2100 Copenhagen

Korsgaard Petersen, Maiken
Danders & More
Lautrupsgade 7
2100 Copenhagen

Spiermann, Ole
University of Copenhagen
Skt. Peders Straede 19
1453 Copenhagen K

Terkildsen, Dan
Danders & More
Lautrupsgade 7
2100 Copenhagen

## Egypt

El Kosheri, Ahmed Sadek
Member of ICCA
Kosheri, Rashed & Riad Law Firm
16 Maamal El Sokkar Street
Garden City
11451 Cairo

Hafez, Karim
Hafez
5 Ibrahim Naguib Street
Garden City
11451 Cairo

Khalifa, Amani
Hafez
5 Ibrahim Naguib Street
Garden City
11451 Cairo

Nassar, Nagla
Nassar Law
37 Kasr el Nil Street
Cairo 11211

## Finland

Jarvinen, Antti
Hannes Snellman Attorneys at Law Ltd.
Etelaranta 8
00130 Helsinki

Möller, Gustaf
Arbitration Institute of the Central
Chamber of Commerce of Finland
World Trade Center
Aleksanterinkatu 17
00101 Helsinki

Palmroos, Anna-Maria
Castren & Snellman Attorneys Ltd.
PO Box 233
00131 Helsinki

Savola, Mika
Hannes Snellman Attorneys at Law Ltd.
Etelaranta 8
00130 Helsinki

Zykov, Roman
Hannes Snellman Attorneys at Law Ltd.
Etelaranta 8
00130 Helsinki

## France

Banifatemi, Yas
Shearman & Sterling
114, avenue des Champs-Eluseés
Paris 75008

Barbet, Jerome
Clifford Chance
9, place Vendome
75038 Paris

Betto, Jean-Georges
Lovells
6, avenue Kléber
75116 Paris

Blumrosen, Alexander
Bernard-Hertz-Bejot
8, rue Murillo
75008 Paris

Bond, Stephen
White & Case
11, Boulevard de la Madeleine
75001 Paris

Bonnard, Sebastien
Gide Loyrette Nouel AARPI
26, Cours Albert 1er
75008 Paris

Bouckaert, Christian
Bopslaw
47, rue Dumont d'Urville
75116 Paris

Bouzols-Breton, Mireille
Technip
6-8, allée de L'Arche
92400 Courbevoie

Buehler, Michael
Jones Day
120, rue du Faubourg Saint Honoré
75008 Paris

Carducci, Guido
Carducci
29, rue Montagne de l'Esperou
75015 Paris

Castello, James
Dewey & LeBoeuf
51, avenue Pierre Charron
75008 Paris

Charlton, Anthony
Deloitte Finance
185, avenue Charles de Gaulle
92524 Neuilly Sur Seine

Colaiuta, Virginie
Hughes Hubbard & Reed
47, avenue Georges Mandel
75116 Paris

Craig, William Laurence
Orrick
31, avenue Pierre 1er de Serbie
75782 Paris

Davis, Frederick T.
Debevoise & Plimpton
21, avenue George V
75008 Paris

De Boisséson, Matthieu
Darrois Villey Maillot Brochier
69, avenue Victor Hugo
75783 Paris

Degos, Louis
Frère Cholmeley Eversheds
8, Place d'Iéna
75116 Paris

Derains, Yves
Member of ICCA
SCP Derains & Associes

167 bis, avenue Victor Hugo
75116 Paris

Duprey, Pierre
Darrois Villey Maillot Brochier
69, avenue Victor Hugo
75783 Paris

Firby, Michael
Limic Limited
2, Boulevard des Champeaux
95160 Montmorency Val d'Oise

Flower, Andrew
Deloitte Finance
185, avenue Charles de Gaulle
92524 Neuilly Sur Seine

Franc-Menget, Laurence
Gide Loyrette Nouel AARPI
26, Cours Albert 1er
75008 Paris

Francois-Poncet, Sarah
Salans
9, rue Boissy d'Anglas
75008 Paris

Fry, Jason
ICC International Court of Arbitration
38, cours Albert 1er
75008 Paris

Gaillard, Emmanuel
Member of ICCA
Shearman & Sterling
114, avenue des Champs-Elysées
75008 Paris

Gouiffès, Laurent
Allen & Overy
26, Boulevard des Capucines
75009 Paris

Hammoud, Lara
International Chamber of Commerce
38, cours Albert 1er
75008 Paris

Heitzmann, Pierre
Jones Day
120, rue du Faubourg Saint Honoré
75008 Paris

LIST OF PARTICIPANTS

Henry, Marc
Lovells
6, Avenue Kléber
Paris 75116

Hertzfeld, Jeffrey
Salans
9, rue Boissy d'Anglas
75008 Paris

Honlet, Jean-Christophe
Salans
9, rue Boissy d'Anglas
75008 Paris

Horrigan, Brenda
Salans
9, rue Boissy d'Anglas
75008 Paris

Kaplan, Charles
Herbert Smith
20, Rue Quentin Bauchart
75008 Paris

Kessedjian, Catherine
Université Panthéon-Assas Paris II
12, Place du Panthéon
75005 Paris

Kiffer, Laurence
Teynier, Pic & Associes
56, rue de Londres
75008 Paris

Kirby, Jennifer
Herbert Smith
20, Rue Quentin Bauchart
75008 Paris

Legum, Barton
Salans
9, rue Boissy d'Anglas
75008 Paris

Leleu-Knobil, Nanou
International Arbitration Institute
c/o Shearman & Sterling LLP
114 avenue des Champs-Elysées
75008 Paris

Lemaire, Gillian
Dewey & LeBoeuf
51, rue Pierre Chanon
75008 Paris

Leurent, Bruno
Winston & Strawn
25, avenue Marceau
75116 Paris

Lyonnet, Geoffroy
Curtis, Mallet-Prevost, Colt & Mosle
6, avenue Velasquez
75008 Paris

Malintoppi, Loretta
Frere Cholmeley Eversheds
8, Place d'Iéna
75116 Paris

Malinvaud, Carole
Gide Loyrette Nouel AARPI
26, Cours Albert 1er
75008 Paris

Mantilla-Serrano, Fernando
Shearman & Sterling
114, avenue des Champs-Elysées
75008 Paris

Mares, Patrick
Fleury Quentin Marès Delvolvé Rouche
1-3, rue de Caumartin
75009 Paris

Mayer, Pierre
Dechert
32, rue de Monceau
75008 Paris

McDougall, Andrew
White & Case
11, Boulevard de la Madeleine
75001 Paris

McNeill, Mark
Shearman & Sterling
114, avenue des Champs-Elysées
75008 Paris

Meese, Richard
Cabinet Meese
24, Place du Général Catroux
75017 Paris

Michou, Isabelle
Herbert Smith
20, rue Quentin Bauchart
75008 Paris

Mohtashami, Reza
Freshfields Bruckhaus Deringer
2, rue Paul Cezanne
75008 Paris

Mourre, Alexis
Castaldi Mourre & Partners
73, Boulevard Haussmann
75008 Paris

Nairac, Charles
White & Case
11, Boulevard de la Madeleine
75001 Paris

Ostrove, Michael
Debevoise & Plimpton
21, avenue George V
75008 Paris

Paris, Laurent
Cournot Association d'Avocats
91, rue du Faubourg Saint Honoré
75008 Paris

Paulsson, Jan
Member of ICCA
Freshfields Bruckhaus Deringer
2, rue Paul Cezanne
75008 Paris

Perez, José Maria
Bredin Prat
130, rue de Faubourg Saint-Honoré
75008 Paris

Peterson, Patricia
Linklaters
25, rue de Marignan
75008 Paris

Petrochilos, Georgios
Freshfields Bruckhaus Deringer
2, rue Paul Cezanne
75008 Paris

Philippe, Mireze
International Chamber of Commerce

38, cours Albert 1er
75008 Paris

Pinsolle, Philippe
Shearman & Sterling
114, avenue des Champs-Elysées
75008 Paris

Polkinghorne, Michael
White & Case
11, Boulevard de la Madeleine
75001 Paris

Portwood, Tim
Bredin Prat
130, avenue du Faubourg Saint-Honoré
75008 Paris

Raoul-Duval, Pierre
Gide Loyrette Nouel AARPI
26, Cours Albert 1er
Paris 75008

Rosell, José
Hughes Hubbard & Reed
47, avenue Georges Mandel
75116 Paris

Rosher, Peter
Clifford Chance
9, place Vendome
75038 Paris

Rouche, Jean
Fleury Quentin Marès Delvolvé Rouche
1-3, rue Caumartin
75009 Paris

Silva Romero, Eduardo
Dechert
32, rue de Monceau
75008 Paris

Stern, Brigitte
Université Paris 1
7, rue Pierre Nicole
75005 Paris

Tercier, Pierre
Member of ICCA
International Chamber of Commerce
38, cours Albert 1er
75008 Paris

LIST OF PARTICIPANTS

Turner, Peter
Freshfields Bruckhaus Deringer
2, rue Paul Cezanne
75008 Paris

Van Leeuwen, Melanie
Loyens Loeff Selafa
1, avenue Franklin D. Roosevelt
75008 Paris

Vermal, Ana
Proskauer Rose
374, rue Saint-Honoré
75001 Paris

Wetmore, Todd
Shearman & Sterling
114, avenue des Champs-Elysées
75008 Paris

Whitesell, Anne-Marie
Dechert
32, rue de Monceau
75008 Paris

Young, Michael
Herbert Smith
20, rue Quentin Bauchart
75008 Paris

Ziade, Roland
Cleary Gottlieb Steen & Hamilton
12, rue de Tilsitt
75008 Paris

**Germany**

Böckstiegel, Karl-Heinz
Member of ICCA
Parkstrasse 38
51427 Bergisch-Gladbach

Bredow, Jens
German Institute of Arbitration
Beethovenstrasse 5-13
50674 Cologne

Busse, Daniel
Lovells
Untermainanlage 1
60329 Frankfurt am Main

Dolzer, Rudolf
Institut für Völkerrecht
Adenauerallee 24-42
53113 Bonn

Elsing, Siegfried H
Hoelters & Elsing
Immermannstrasse 40
40210 Düsseldorf

Friedrich, Bettina
Friedrich Korch Hanefeld
Feldbergstrasse 23
60323 Frankfurt

Hanefeld, Inka
Friedrich Korch Hanefeld
Chilehaus A
Fischertwiete 2
20095 Hamburg

Heeg-Stelldinger, Christine
Brodermann & Jahn Rechtsanwaltsgesellschaft
Neuer Wall 71
20354 Hamburg

Hennecke, Rudolf
Freshfields Bruckhaus Deringer
Heumarkt 14
50667 Cologne

Kratzsch, Suzanne
Thuemmel Schuetze & Partner
Urbaustrasse 7
70182 Stuttgart

Kreindler, Richard H.
Shearman & Sterling
Gervinusstrasse 17
60322 Frankfurt

Kröll, Stefan
Merlinweg 97
50997 Cologne

Kühn, Wolfgang
Heuking Kühn Lüer Wojtek
Cecilienallee 5
40474 Düsseldorf

Lörcher, Torsten
Kranhaus 1

Im Zollhafen 18
50678 Cologne

Nacimiento, Patricia
White & Case LLP
Bockenheimer Landstraße 20
60323 Frankfurt am Main

Raeschke-Kessler, Hilmar
Raeschke-Kessler & Waclawik
Am Oickhäuterplatz 18
76275 Karlsruhe-Ettlingen

Sachs, Klaus
CMS Hasche Sigle
Brienner Strasse 11/V
80333 Munich

Schaefer, Erik
Cohausz & Florack
Bleichstrasse 14
40211 Düsseldorf

Schaefer, Jan K.
Allen & Overy
Taunstor 2
60311 Frankfurt am Main

Schuetz, Christina
Shearman & Sterling
Gervinusstrasse 17
60322 Frankfurt

Triebel, Volker
Rechtsanwalt & Barrister
c/o Lovells
Kennedydamm 17
40476 Düsseldorf

Umbeck, Elke
Freshfields Bruckhaus Deringer
Alsterarkaden 27
20354 Hamburg

Von Schlabrendorff, Fabian
Clifford Chance
Mainzer Landstrasse 46
60596 Frankfurt

Weimann, Thomas
Clifford Chance
Königsallee 59
40215 Düsseldorf

Witz, Wolfgang
Allen & Overy
Taunstor 2
60311 Frankfurt am Main

**Greece**

Dimolitsa, Antonias
Antonias Dimolitsa & Associates
12 Milioni Street
10673 Athens

Vassardanis, Ioannis
Alexander Vassardanis & Partners
30 Vassilissis Olgas Street
151 24 Maroussi, Athens

**Hong Kong SAR**

Aglionby, Andrew
Baker & McKenzie
14/F Hutchison House
10 Harcourt Road
Central

Cheng, Teresa Yeuk Wah
Member of ICCA
Des Voeux Chambers
10 Des Voeux Road
Central

Fohlin, Paulo
Vinge
2003 Hutchison House
10 Harcourt Road
Central

Jamison, Jim
Clifford Chance
Jardine House, 28th Floor
One Connaught Place
Central

Lin, Mark
Lovells
One Pacific Place
88 Queensway, 11th Floor
009023

Moser, Michael J.
Hong Kong International Arbitration Centre

AIG Tower
38/F Two Exchange Square
8 Connaught Place
Central

Schwedt, Kirstin
Linklaters
Alexandra House, 10th Floor
18 Chater Road
Central

To, Christopher
Hong Kong International Arbitration Centre
38/F Two Exchange Square
8 Connaught Place
Central

Wall, Colin John
Commercial Mediation & Arbitration
Services Ltd.
Workingview Commercial Building, Suite 1206
21 Yiu Wa Street
Causeway Bay

## Hungary

Kecskes, Laszlo
Arbitration Court
Hungarian Chamber of Commerce & Industry
Kossuth Lajos tér 6-8
1055 Budapest

Szász, Iván
Vice President of ICCA
Eros Ugyvedi Iroda
Squire, Sanders & Dempsey
Roosevelt tér 7-8
1051 Budapest

## India

Dave, Dushyant
Member of ICCA
43 Prithviraj Road
110011 New Delhi

Dholakia, Shishir
97 Lawyers Chambers
Supreme Court of India

Tilak Marg
110001 New Delhi

Nariman, Fali Sam
Honorary President of ICCA
F-21/22 Hauz Khas Enclave
110016 New Delhi

Parikh, Devan
501-502 Shilip, near Navrang Pura
Municipal Market, C G Road
380009 Gujarat Ahmedabap

Tiwari, Mamta
Fox Mandal Little & Co.
A-9, Sector 9
201 301 Uttar Pradesh

## Ireland

Abrahamson, Max
McCann Fitzgerald
Riverside One
Sir John Rogerson's Quay
Dublin 2

Agnew, Dennis
BCM Hanby Wallace
88 Harcourt Street
Dublin 2

Appel, Mark
International Centre for Dispute Resolution
14 Merrion Square
Dublin 2

Aylmer, William
Eugene F. Collins Solicitors
Temple Chambers
3 Burlington Road
Dublin 4

Black, Declan
Mason Hayes & Curran
South Bank House
Barrow Street
Dublin 4

Bourke, Roddy
Law Society of Ireland
Blackhall Place
Dublin 7

Brady, Rory
Suite 2.43.2
Distillery Building
145/151 Church Street
Dublin 7

Bridgeman, James
Law Library
Four Courts
Dublin 7

Brown, Andrew
Deloitte & Touche
Deloitte & Touche House
Earlsfort Terrace
Dublin 2

Bunni, Nael
Member of ICCA
Bunni & Associates
Bearna
42 Thormanby Road
Howth, County Dublin

Butler, Edmund
LK Shields Solicitors
39/40 Upper Mount Street
Dublin 2

Byrne, Gary
BCM Hanby Wallace
88 Harcourt Street
Dublin 2

Carey, Gearoid
Matheson Ormbsy Prentice
70 Sir John Rogerson's Quay
Dublin 2

Carrigan, Michael W.
Eugene F. Collins Solicitors
Temple Chambers
3 Burlington Road
Dublin 4

Carroll, Jerry
Bar Council
Four Courts
Dublin 7

Casey, Rachel
Law Library

Four Courts
Dublin 7

Clarke, Brian
A&L Goodbody
IFSC
North Wall Quay
Dublin 1

Collins, Michael
Law Library
Four Courts
Dublin 7

Connolly, James
Law Library
Four Courts
Dublin 7

Daly, Sharon
Matheson Ormbsy Prentice
70 Sir John Rogerson's Quay
Dublin 2

Devitt, Lea
Dillon Eustace
33 Sir John Rogerson's Quay
Dublin 2

Doherty, Alan
Law Library
Church Street
Dublin 7

Doyle, John
Dillon Eustace
33 Sir John Rogerson's Quay
Dublin 2

Dunne, Donal
Eugene F. Collins Solicitors
Temple Chambers
3 Burlington Road
Dublin 4

Dunne, John
Chambers
61-63 Dame Street
Dublin 2
Dublin

Fahey, Siobhan
Siobhan Fahey Consultant

LIST OF PARTICIPANTS

Gold Coast Road
Dungarvan
Waterford

Fahy, Ciaran
66 Eglinton Road
Donnybrook
Dublin 4

Fenelon, Larry
Leman Solicitors
10 Herbert Lane
Dublin 2

Ferriter, Cian
Law Library
Four Courts
Dublin 7

Finlay Geoghegan, Mary
Judge of the High Court of Ireland
Four Courts
Ground Floor (East Wing)
Inns Quay
Dublin 7

Fitzgerald, Norman
O'Donnell Sweeney Eversheds
1 Earlsfort Centre
Earlsfort Terrace
Dublin 2

Fogarty, Kenneth
Four Courts
Inns Quay
Dublin 7

Foley, Isabel
Arthur Cox
Earlsfort Centre
Earlsfort Terrace
Dublin 2

Gaffney, John
O'Flynn Exhams
58 South Mall
Cork

Gallagher, Hon. Paul
Attorney General of Ireland
Dublin

Gardiner, Paul
Law Library
Four Courts
Dublin 7

Gaughan, Aoife
A&L Goodbody
IFSC
North Wall Quay
Dublin 1

Gayer, Sasha
Law Library
Church Street Building
158-159 Church Street
Dublin 7

Gibson, Emily
Bar Council of Ireland
Law Library
Four Courts
Dublin 7

Glynn, Greg
Arthur Cox
Earlsfort Centre
Earlsfort Terrace
Dublin 2

Gogarty, Bernard
Law Society of Ireland
Blackhall Place
Dublin 7

Gordon, John
2 Arran Square
Arran Quay
Dublin 7

Greene, Michael
A&L Goodbody
IFSC
North Wall Quay
Dublin 1

Harrington, Eamon
Law Society of Ireland
Blackhall Place
Dublin 7

Heneghan, Jarleth
William Fry

Fitzwilton House
Wilton Place
Dublin 2

Hunt, Patrick
Law Library
Church Street Building
158-159 Church Street
Dublin 7

Hussey, Anthony
Law Society of Ireland
Blackhall Place
Dublin 7

Hutchinson, Brian
UCD School of Law
University College
Belfield
Dublin 4

Kelly, Joseph
A&L Goodbody
IFSC
North Wall Quay
Dublin 1

Kelly, Peter
Judge of the High Court of Ireland
Dublin

Kennedy, Liam
A&L Goodbody
IFSC
North Wall Quay
Dublin 1

Keogh, Damien
Matheson Ormsby Prentice
70 Sir John Rogerson's Quay
Dublin 2

Kirrane, Rory
Mason Hayes & Curran
South Bank House
Barrow Street
Dublin 4

Lehane, Darren
Law Library
Four Courts
Dublin 7

Lenny, Andrew
Arthur Cox
Earlsfort Centre
Earlsfort Terrace
Dublin 2

MacCann, Lyndon
1 Arran Square
Arran Quay
Dublin 7

MacGuill, James
Law Society of Ireland
Blackhall Place
Dublin 7

MacMahon, Noel
Law Library
Four Courts
Dublin

Maguire, Conor
Law Library
Four Courts
Dublin 7

Maguire, Elizabeth
Law Library
Four Courts
Dublin 7

Maguire, Roderick
Bar Council of Ireland
Law Library
Four Courts
Dublin 7

Marray, Eamon
15 Maretimo Villas
Blackrock
County Dublin

McCullough, Eoin
1 Arran Square
Arran Quay
Dublin 7

McDonald, Denis
Law Library
Four Courts
Dublin 7

LIST OF PARTICIPANTS

McDonnell, Conor
Arthur Cox
Earlsfort Centre

Earlsfort Terrace
Dublin 2

McDonnell, Petria
Judge of the Circuit Court of Ireland
15/24 Phoenix Street North
Smithfield, Dublin

McEvoy, Dermot
O'Donnell Sweeney Eversheds
1 Earlsfort Centre
Earlsfort Terrace
Dublin 2

McGarry, Paul
Distillery Building
145-151 Church Street
Dublin 7

McGennis, Paul
BCM Hanby Wallace
88 Harcourt Street
Dublin 2

McGovern, Aedan
Law Library
Four Courts
Dublin 7

McGovern, Brian
High Court of Ireland
Four Courts
Ground Floor (East Wing)
Inns Quay
Dublin 7

McPhillips, Oonagh
Department of Justice
Pinebrook House
71-74 Harcourt Street
Dublin 2

Meehan, Gerard
Law Library
Four Courts
Dublin 7

Moore, Anthony
Law Library
Four Courts
Dublin 7

Moran, Michael M.
Deloitte & Touche
Deloitte & Touche House
Earlsfort Terrace
Dublin 2

Mulcahy, Kieran
Deloitte & Touche
Deloitte & Touche House
Earlsfort Terrace
Dublin 2

Mulcahy, Rowena
Mulcahy Robinson
Fitzwilliam Hall
Fitzwilliam Place
Dublin 2

Munnelly, Brid
Matheson Ormsby Prentice
70 Sir John Rogerson's Quay
Dublin 2

Murphy, David
McCann Fitzgerald
Riverside One
Sir John Rogerson's Quay
Dublin 2

Murphy, Frank
Law Society of Ireland
Blackhall Place
Dublin 7

Murphy, Roderick
Judge of the High Court of Ireland
Four Courts
Ground Floor (East Wing)
Inns Quay
Dublin 7

Murray, Brian
Law Library
Four Courts
Dublin

Nolan, David
Law Library
Four Courts
Dublin 7

Nolan, Karen
Law Library
Four Courts
Dublin 7

O hOisin, Colm
Law Library
Four Courts
Dublin 7

O'Beirne, Fiona
McCann Fitzgerald
Riverside One
Sir John Rogerson's Quay
Dublin 2

O'Brien, Patricia
Department of Foreign Affairs
80 St Stephen's Green
Dublin 2

O'Callaghan, Jim
Law Library
145-151 Church Street
Dublin 7

O'Connell, Jennifer
Law Library
Four Courts
Dublin 7

O'Donohoe, David
Arthur Cox
Earlsfort Centre
Earlsfort Terrace
Dublin 2

O'Donnell, Turlough
Bar Council
Distillery Building
145-151 Church Street
Dublin 7

O'Donoghue, James
Bluett & O'Donoghue Architects
1 Chancery Street
Dublin 7

O'Higgins, Paul
Law Library
Four Courts
Dublin 7

O'Keeffe, Terence
Dublin City Council
Civic Offices
Wood Quay
Dublin 8

O'Neill, Bairbre
Bar Council of Ireland
Law Library
Four Courts
Dublin 7

O'Reilly, James
Law Library
Four Courts
Dublin 7

O'Sullivan, Owen
William Fry
Fitzwilton House
Wilton Place
Dublin 2

Phelan, Maurice
Mason Hayes & Curran
South Bank House
Barrow Street
Dublin 4

Quinn, Michael
William Fry
Fitzwilton House
Wilton Place
Dublin 2

Reichert, Klaus
145-151 Church Street
Four Courts
Dublin 7

Scanlon, Daniel
Matheson Ormbsy Prentice
70 Sir John Rogerson's Quay
Dublin 2

Shanley, Peter
Suite 311
The Capel Building
Mary's Abbey
Dublin 7

Shaw, George
Department of the Taoiseach

Government Building
Dublin 2

Sills, Martin
Permanent TSB
56/59 St. Stephen's Green
Dublin 2

Simms, Daniel
Distillery Building
145-151 Church Street
Dublin 7

Solan, Dudley
A&L Goodbody
IFSC
North Wall Quay
Dublin 1

Stapleton, Peter
Dillon Eustace
33 Sir John Rogerson's Quay
Dublin 2

Steen, Neil
Law Library
145-151 Church Street
Dublin 7

Stewart, Ercus
Distillery Building
145-151 Church Street
Dublin 7

Terry, Regina
Department of Justice
Pinebrook House
71-74 Harcourt Street
Dublin 2

Trainor, John
Law Library
Four Courts
Dublin 7

Trueick, Jim
O'Donnell Sweeney Eversheds
1 Earlsfort Centre
Earlsfort Terrace
Dublin 2

**Italy**

Armandola, Maria Elena
Pavia e Ansaldo
Via del Lauro 7
20121 Milan

Azzali, Stefano
Chamber of Arbitration of Milan
Palatto Turati
Via Meravigli 9/B
20123 Milan

Bernardini, Piero
Member of ICCA
Studio Legale Ughi e Nunziante
Via Vente Settembre 1
00187 Rome

Bortolotti, Fabio
Buffa, Bortolotti & Mathis
Studio Legali Associati
Via Alfieri 19
10121 Torino

Cicogna, Michelangelo
De Berti Jacchia Franchini Forlani
Via San Paolo 7
20121 Milan

Crespi Reghizzi, Gabriele
Lombardi Molinari e Associati
Via Andegari 4/A
20121 Milan

De Berti, Giovanni
De Berti Jacchia Franchini Forlani
Via San Paolo 7
20121 Milan

Di Pietro, Domenico
Chiomenti Studio Legale
Via XXIV Maggio 43
00187 Rome

Fumagalli, Luigi
University of Milan
Facoltà di Giurisprudenza
Via Festa del Perdono 7
20122 Milan

Henke, Albert
Clifford Chance Studio Legale
Piazzetta M Bossi 3
20121 Milan

Radicati de Brozolo, Luca G.
Bonelli Erede Pappalardo
Via Barozzi, No. 1
20122 Milan

Rubino-Sammaranto, Mauro
Lawfed Rubino-Sammartano e Associati
Viale Cassiodoro 3
20145 Milan

## Japan

Kodama, Masafumi
Kitahama Partners
1-8-16, Kitahama
Chuo-ku
Osaka 541-0041

Lewis, Harriet Yoshida
Nagashima Ohno & Tsunematsu
Kioicho Building
3-12, Kioicho
Chiyoda-ku
Tokyo 102-0094

Nakamura, Tatsuya
The Japan Commercial
Arbitration Association
3rd Floor, Hirose Building
3-17, Kanda Nishiki-cho
Chiyoda-ku
Tokyo 101-0054

Nishimura, Toshiyuki
3rd Floor, Hirose Building
3-17, Kanda Nishiki-cho
Chiyoda-ku
Tokyo 101-0054

Oghigian, Haig
Baker & McKenzie
Tokyo Aoyamo Aoki Korna Law Office
The Prudential Tower
2-13-10, Nagatacho
Tokyo 100-0014

Onuki, Masaharu
The Japan Commercial
Arbitration Association
Osaka Office
The OCCI Building, 2-8, Honmachibashi
Chuoku
Osaka 540-0029

Sawai, Akira
Osaka Prefecture University
1-1, Gakuen-cho, Nakaku
Sakai
Osaka 599-8531

Taniguchi, Yasuhei
Member of ICCA
Matsuo & Kosugi
Fukoku-Seimei Building
18th Floor
2-2, Uchisaiwai-cho
Chiyoda-ku
Tokyo 100-0011

Tezuka, Hiroyuki
Nishimura & Asahi
Ark Mori Building
1-12-32 Anasaka
Minato-ku
Tokyo 107-6029

Yamashita, Rieko
Tokyo University
5-28-20, Hakusan
Bunkyo-ku
Tokyo 112-8606

Yanase, Shuji
Nagashima Ohno & Tsunematsu
Kioicho Building
3-12, Kioicho
Chiyoda-ku
Tokyo 102-0003

## Kenya

Wako, Hon. S. Amos
Member of ICCA
Attorney General
PO Box 15053
Langata
Nairobi

LIST OF PARTICIPANTS

**Korea**

Bang, John
Bae, Kim & Lee
647-15 Yoksam-dong
Gangnam-gu
135-723 Seoul

Kim, Jae Hyun
The Korean Commercial Arbitration Board
Room No. 4303
Korea World Trade Centre
Samsung-dong, Gangnam-gu
135-729 Seoul

Kim, Kap-you
Member of ICCA
Bae, Kim & Lee
647-15 Yoksam-dong
Gangnam-gu
135-723 Seoul

Lee, Jae Woo
The Korean Commercial Arbitration Board
Room No. 4303
Korea World Trade Centre
Samsung-dong, Gangnam-gu
135-729 Seoul

Park, Eun-Young
Kim & Chang
Seyang Building
223 Naeja-ding, Jongno-gu
110-720 Seoul

Yoon, Byung-Chol
Kim & Chang
Seyang Building
223 Naeja-dong
Jongno-gu
110-720 Seoul

**Lebanon**

Comair-Obeid, Nayla
Obeid Law Firm
Makarem Building
Sami El Solh Avenue
BP 116/2234 Law Courts
Beirut 1109 2020

**Malaysia**

Abraham, Cecil
Member of ICCA
Zul Rafique & Partners
Suite 17.01, 17th Floor
Menara PanGlobal
8 Lorong P. Ramlee
50250 Kuala Lumpur

Abraham, Sunil
Zul Rafique & Partners
Suite 17.01, 17th Floor
Menara PanGlobal
8 Lorong P. Ramlee
50250 Kuala Lumpur

Gomez, Rodney
Messrs Shearn Delamore & Co.
Wismz Hamzah-Kwong Hing
7th Floor, No. 1 Leboh Ampang
50100 Kuala Lumpur

**Mexico**

Alvarez Avila, Gabriela
Curtis, Mallet-Prevost, Colt & Mosle SC
Ruben Dario No 281, 9th Floor
11580 Mexico City

González de Cossío, Francisco
González de Cossío Abogados SC
Bosque de Acacias 61 B
Bosques de las Lomas
11700 Mexico City

Graham, Luis Enrique
Chadbourne & Parke
Paseo de Tamarindos 400 - B, 22nd Floor
Col. Bosques de las Lomas
05120 Mexico City

Montserrat, Manzano
Von Wobeser Y Sierra S.C.
Guillermo Gonzalez Camarena 1100
7th Floor
Santa Fe Centro de Cuidad
01210 Mexico City

733

## Netherlands

Borelli, Silvia
Managing Editor, ICCA Publications
Permanent Court of Arbitration
Peace Palace, Carnegieplein 2
2517 KJ The Hague

Braat, Jurriaan
Omni Bridgeway
Tobias Asserlaan 5
2517 KC Den Haag

Brower, Charles N.
Iran-United States Claims Tribunal
Parkweg 13
2585 JH The Hague

Brunetti, Maurizio
Permanent Court of Arbitration
Peace Palace, Carnegieplein 2
2517 KJ The Hague

Daly, Brooks
Permanent Court of Arbitration
Peace Palace, Carnegieplein 2
2517 KJ The Hague

De Boer, Margriet
De Brauw Blackstone Westbroek
Zuid-Hollandlaan 7
2596 AL The Hague

De Groot, Diederik
DLA Piper Netherland NV
PO Box 75258
1070 AG Amsterdam

De Ly, Filip
Erasmus University Rotterdam
Johan Buziaulaan 33
3584 ZT Utrecht

De Vries, Gwen
Kluwer Law International
Zuidpoolsingel 2
2408 ZE Alphen a/d Rijn

Grimmer, Sarah-Jane
Permanent Court of Arbitration
Peace Palace, Carnegieplein 2
2517 KJ The Hague

Koedoot, Mirjam
De Brauw Blackstone Westbroek
Zuid-Hollandlaan 7
2596 AL The Hague

Leijten, Marnix
De Brauw Blackstone
WestbroekZuid-Hollandlaan 7
2596 AL The Hague

O'Malley, Nathan
Conway Stendahl
1132 Otto Reuchlinweg
3007 KC Rotterdam

Ouwehand, Jeroen
Clifford Chance
Droogbak 1a
1013 GE Amsterdam

Remmerswaal, Walter
Omni Bridgeway
Tobias Asserlaan 5
2517 KC Den Haag

Siegel, Alice
ICCA Publications
Permanent Court of Arbitration
Peace Palace, Carnegieplein 2
2517 KJ The Hague

Smith, Tamela
Denneweg 2
2514 CG The Hague

Van Baren, Willem
Allen & Overy
Apollolaan 15
1077 AB Amsterdam

Van den Bosch, Thabiso
Conway Stendahl
Otto Reuchlinweg 1132
3072 MD Rotterdam

Van der Bend, Gerhardus
De Brauw Blackstone Westbroek
Zuid-Hollandlaan 7
2596 AL The Hague

Van Haersolte-van Hof, Jacomijn
HaersolteHof

LIST OF PARTICIPANTS

Delistraat 27
2585 VX The Hague

Van Maanen, Charlotte
Netherlands Arbitration Institute
Aert Van Nesstraat 25 J/K
3012 CA Rotterdam

Verschoor, Vincent
Kluwer Law International
Zuidpoolsingel 2
2408 ZE Alphen a/d Rijn

Von Hombracht-Brinkman, Fredy
Netherlands Arbitration Institute
Aert van Nesstraat 25 J/K
3012 CA Rotterdam

Ynzonides, Marc
De Brauw Blackstone Westbroek
Zuid-Hollandlaan 7
2596 AL The Hague

**New Zealand**

McLachlan, Campbell, QC
Victoria University of Wellington Law School
PO Box 600
6140 Wellington

Williams, David
Member of ICCA
David A R Williams QC
PO Box 405
Shortland Street
1140 Auckland

**Nigeria**

Busari, Olatunde
Akinwunmi & Busari
163/165 Broad Street
Old Niger House, 2nd Floor
Lagos

Fubara Anga, Lawrence
Aelex
Marble House, 7th Floor
1 Kingsway Road
Ikoyi
234 Lagos

Ojo, Bayo
Bayo Ojo & Co.
4th Floor, ITF Building, No. 6
Adetokunbo Ademola Crescent
Wuse 2
Abuja

Oyekunle, Tinuade
Honorary Vice President of ICCA
Tinuade Oyekunle and Company
Sonotina Chambers
17 Olujobi Street
Gbagada Phase 1
G.P.O. 9433, Lagos

**Pakistan**

Ali Khan, M. Makhdoom
Fazle Ghani Advocates
F-72/1, Block 8
KDA 5, Clifton
Karachi 75600

**Poland**

Boruc, Marcin
Chadbourne & Parke
Emilii Plater 53
00-113 Warsaw

Gessel, Beata
Polska Konfederacja Pracodawcow
Prywatnych Lewiatan
Klonowa 6
00-591 Warsaw

Hartung, Monika
Wardynski & Partners
Aleje Ujazdowskie 10
00-478 Warsaw

Kos, Rafak
Kubas, Kos, Gaertner
Adwokaci SP.P.
Rakowicka 7
31-511 Krakow

Laszczuk, Maciej
Laszczuk I Wspolnicy Sp K
Pl. Pilsudskiego 2
00-073 Warsaw

735

Nowaczyk, Piotr
Court of Arbitration at the
Polish Chamber of Commerce
Trebacka 4
02-798 Warsaw

Okolski, Jozef
Court of Arbitration at the
Polish Chamber of Commerce
Trebacka 4
02-798 Warsaw

Pieckowski, Sylwester
Polskie Stowarzyszenie
Sadownictwa Polubownego
Klonowa 6
00-591 Warsaw

Szumanski, Andrzej
Polska Konfederacja Pracodawcow
Prywatnych Lewiatan
Klonowa 6
00-591 Warsaw

Szurski, Tadeusz
Advisory Member of ICCA
Court of Arbitration at the
Polish Chamber of Commerce
Trebacka 4
02-798 Warsaw

Wardynski, Tomasz
Wardynski & Partners
Aleje Ujazdowskie 10
00-478 Warsaw

Wisniewski, Andrezej
Polska Konfederacja Pracodawcow
Prywatnych Lewiatan
Klonowa 6
00-591 Warsaw

Zbiegien, Tomasz
Chadbourne & Parke
Emilii Plater 53
00-113 Warsaw

**Portugal**

Alves Pereira, José
Alves Pereira, Teixeira de Sousa & Associados

Avenida da Liberdade 38-3
1250-145 Lisbon

Judice, José Miguel
PLMJ
Avenida do Leberdade 224
1250-148 Lisbon

**Romania**

Fruth-Oprisan, Despina
Romanian Court of International Commercial
Arbitration
Chamber of Commerce & Industry of
Romania
030595 Bucharest

**Russia**

Khvalei, Vladimir
Baker & McKenzie
Sadovaya Plaza, 11 Floor
7 Dolgorukovskaya Street 7
127006 Moscow

Komarov, Alexander
Member of ICCA
International Commercial Arbitration Court
Chamber of Commerce and Industry of the
Russian Federation
6 Ilyinka Street
109012 Moscow

Kurochkin, Dmitry
Herbert Smith CIS
10 Ulitsa Nikolskaya
109012 Moscow

Lebedev, Sergei
Honorary Vice President of ICCA
Maritime Arbitration Commission
Chamber of Commerce and Industry of the
Russian Federation
6 Ilyinka Street
109012 Moscow

Pellew, Dominic
Lovells
5th Floor Usadba Centre
22 Voznesensky, Pereulok
125009 Moscow

## Singapore

Cooke, Timothy
Baker & McKenzie, Wong & Leow
27-01 Millenia Tower
1 Temasek Avenue
039192 Singapore

Hwang, Michael
Vice President of ICCA
Michael Hwang S.C.
1 Marina Boulevard, No. 25-01
018989 Singapore

Koh, Swee Yen
Wong Partnership
1 George Street, No. 20-01
049145 Singapore

Lau, Christopher
Alban Tay Mahtani & de Silva
Singapore & Verulam Building
39 Robinson Road
No. 07-01, Robinson Point
068911 Singapore

Pryles, Michael
Member of ICCA
32 Maxwell Road
069115 Singapore

Spooner, Guy
Norton Rose (Asia)
31-01 North Tower
1 Raffles Quay
048583 Singapore

Tan, Chuan Thye
Baker & McKenzie, Wong & Leow
27-01 Millenia Tower
1 Temasek Avenue
039192 Singapore

Tan, Richard
Lovells Lee & Lee
80 Raffles Place
No, 54-01 UOB Plaza 1
048624 Singapore

Tay, Yu-Jin
Shearman & Sterling
6 Battery Road, No. 25-03
049909 Singapore

Yang, Ing-Loong
Sidley Austin LLP
6 Battery Road
Suite 40-01
Singapore 049909

## Spain

Arias, David
Perez-Llorca
Alcalá, 61
28014 Madrid

Armesto, Juan
Armesto & Asociados
General Pardiñas, 102, 8th Floor
28006 Madrid

Bonelli, Emilio
CIMA
Calle de Hermosilla, 8
28001 Madrid

Bonnin, Victor
Garrigues
Calle de Hermosilla, 3
28003 Madrid

Cairns, David J.A.
B Cremades y Asociados
Calle Goya, 18, 2nd Floor
28001 Madrid

Calvo, Juan
CIMA
Calle de Hermosilla, 8
28001 Madrid

Claros, Pedro
Cuatrecasas Abogados
Passeig Gràcia 111
08008 Barcelona

Conejero Roos, Cristian
Cuatrescasas SRL
Velazquez, 63
28001 Madrid

Cremades, Bernardo
Member of ICCA
B Cremades y Asociados

Calle de Goya, 18, 2nd Floor
28001 Madrid

Fernández-Armesto, Juan
Armesto & Asociados
General Pardiñas, 102, 8th Floor
28006 Madrid

Fernández Ballesteros, Miguel Angel
Fernández Ballesteros & Asociados
Calle de Serrano, 22
28001 Madrid

Fortun, Alberto
Cuatrecasas Abogados
Paseo de Gracia, 111
08008 Barcelona

Fröhlingsdorf, Josef
Fröhlingsdorf Abogados Asociados SL
Calle de Nuria 36, 1° 4
28034 Madrid

Gomez-Acebo, Alfonso
Garrigues
Calle de Hermosilla, 3
28003 Madrid

Gutierrez, Elena
CEO 40
Amado Nervo, 12
28007 Madrid

Hamilton, Calvin
Hamilton Abogados
Espalter, 15, 1st Floor
28014 Madrid

Hendel, Clifford J.
Araoz & Rueda
Paseo de la Castelllana, 164
28046 Madrid

Hierro, Antonio
Cuatrecasas Abogados
Paseo de Gracia, 111
08008 Barcelona

Lopez de Argumedo, Alvaro
Uria Menendez Abogados SLP
Principe de Vergara, 187
28002 Madrid

Montero, Felix José
Perez-Llorca
Alcalá, 61
28014 Madrid

Moscardo, Miguel
Garrigues
Calle de Hermosilla, 3
28003 Madrid

Pantaleon, Fernando
Garrigues
Calle de Hermosilla, 3
28003 Madrid

Perez Pardo de Vera, Angel
Uria Menendez Abogados SLP
Principe de Vergara, 187
28002 Madrid

Soto, Margarita
Garrigues
Calle de Hermosilla, 3
28003 Madrid

Venegas Grau, Carmen
Perez-Llorca
Alcalá, 61
28014 Madrid

Villanua, Deva
Armesto & Asociados
General Pardiñas, 102, 8th Floor
28006 Madrid

**Sweden**

Andersson, Fredrik
Mannheimer Swartling Advokatbyrå AB
Östra Hamngatan 16
40314 Göteborg

Bagner, Hans
Advokatfirman Vinge KB
Smålandsgatan 20
11187 Stockholm

Bendrik, Mats
Advokatfirman Nordenson Law
Grev Turegatan 13A
11446 Stockholm

## LIST OF PARTICIPANTS

Bessman, Stefan
Baker & McKenzie
PO Box 5719
11487 Stockholm

Dahlberg, Hans
Setterwalls
Arsenalsgatan 6
10139 Stockholm

Dhuner, Karl J.
Dhuner Jarvengren
Riddargatan 7A
11435 Stockholm

Eliasson, Nils
Mannheimer Swartling Advokatbyrå AB
PO Box 1711
11187 Stockholm

Eriksson, Andreas
Advokatfirman Vinge KB
Smålandsgatan 20
11187 Stockholm

Franke, Ulf
Honorary Secretary General of ICCA
Arbitration Institute of the Stockholm
Chamber of Commerce
PO Box 160 50
10321 Stockholm

Gernandt, Johan
Advokatfirman Vinge KB
Smålandsgatan 20
11187 Stockholm

Heuman, Lars
Department of Law
Stockholm University
4th Floor, Universitetvaegen 10C
10691 Stockholm

Hobér, Kaj
Mannheimer Swartling Advokatbyrå AB
PO Box 1711
11187 Stockholm

Johansson, Tom
Nilsson & Co. KB
PO Box 7761
10396 Stockholm

Johnsson, Bengt Åke
White & Case Advokat AB
PO Box 5573
11485 Stockholm

Lundblad, Claes
Mannheimer Swartling Advokatbyrå AB
PO Box 1711
11187 Stockholm

Madsen, Finn
Advokatfirman Vinge KB
PO Box 4255
20313 Malmö

Magnusson, Annette
Mannheimer Swartling Advokatbyrå AB
PO Box 1711
11187 Stockholm

Nilsson, Bo G. H.
RydinCarlsten Advokatbyrå AB
PO Box 1766
11187 Stockholm

Nordenson, Harald
Setterwalls
Arsenalsgatan 6
10139 Stockholm

Ohrstrom, Marie
PO Box 16050
10321 Stockholm

Oldenstam, Robin
Mannheimer Swartling Advokatbyrå AB
Oestra Hamngatan 16
40314 Göteborg

Ragnwaldh, Jakob
Mannheimer Swartling Advokatbyrå AB
PO Box 1711
11187 Stockholm

Shaughnessy, Patricia
Department of Law
Stockholm University
4th Floor, Universitetvaegen 10C
10691 Stockholm

Söderlund, Christer
Advokatfirman Vinge KB

PO Box 1703
11187 Stockholm

Vargo, Daniel
Advokatfirman Nilsson & Co.
PO Box 7761
10395 Stockholm

Wennerholm, Fred
Setterwalls Advokatbyrå
Arsenalsgatan 6
11147 Stockholm

Wiwen-Nilsson, Tore
Mannheimer Swartling Advokatbyrå AB
Sodergatan 22
20314 Malmö

## Switzerland

Arfazadeh, Homayoon
Phython & Peter
Rue Firmin-Massot 9
1207 Geneva

Baertsch, Philippe
Schellenberg Wittmer
15 bis, rue des Alpes
1211 Geneve

Baizeau, Domitille
Lalive Attorneys-at-Law
Rue de la Mairie 35
1207 Geneva

Besson, Sebastian
Python & Peter
Rue Firmin-Massot 9
1206 Geneva

Blessing, Marc
Bär & Karrer
Brandschenkestrasse 90
8027 Zurich

Briner, Robert
Advisory Member of ICCA
Lenz & Staehelin
Route de Chêne 30
1211 Geneva 17

Brown, Jamar
Lenz & Staehelin
Route de Chêne 30
1211 Geneva 17

Brown-Berset, Dominique
Lalive Attorneys-at-Law
Rue de la Mairie 35
1207 Geneva

Brunner, Christoph
Python & Peter
Laupenstrasse 47
3008 Bern

Burkhardt, Martin
Lenz & Staehelin
Bleicherweg 58
8027 Zurich

Casserly, David
Court of Arbitration for Sport
Avenue de Beaumont 2
1012 Lausanne

Dasser, Felix
Homburger AG
Weinbergstrasse 56/58
8006 Zurich

Dessemontet, François
University of Lausanne
Chemin des Fleurettes 21
1007 Lausanne

Favre-Bulle, Xavier
Lenz & Staehelin
Route de Chêne 30
1211 Geneva 17

Genton, Pierre Michel
PMG
Rue du Centre 72
1025 Lausanne St. Sulpice

Giovannini, Teresa
Lalive Attorneys-at-Law
Rue de la Mairie 35
1207 Geneva

740

LIST OF PARTICIPANTS

Gregoire, Nicolas
SGS Societe Generale de Surveillance
1 Place des Alpes
1211 Geneva 1

Gunter, Pierre-Yves
Python & Peter
Rue François-Bellot 6
1206 Geneva

Habegger, Philipp
Walder Wyss & Partners
PO Box 1236
8034 Zurich

Hehenberger, Patrick
PMG
Rue du Centre 72
1025 Lausanne St. Sulpice

Heiskanen, Veijo
Lalive Attorneys-at-Law
Rue de la Mairie 35
1207 Geneva

Hoffmann, Anne Kristin
Python & Peter
Rue Firmin-Massot 9
1206 Geneva

Johnson Wilcke, Alexandra
Schellenberg Wittmer
15 bis, rue des Alpes
1211 Geneva

Jolles, Alexander
Schellenberg Wittner
Löwenstrasse 19
8021 Zurich

Kaelin-Nauer, Claudia
Lavaterstrasse 98
8002 Zurich

Karrer, Pierre A.
Karrer Arbitration
Lavaterstrasse 58
8002 Zurich

Kaufmann-Kohler, Gabrielle
Member of ICCA
Schellenberg Wittmer

15 bis, rue des Alpes
1211 Geneva

Lalive, Pierre
Advisory Member of ICCA
Lalive Attorneys-at-Law
Rue de la Mairie 35
1207 Geneva

Lustenberger, Urs
Lustenberger Glaus & Partner
PO Box 1073
8032 Zurich

Marzolini, Paolo
Lenz & Staehelin
Route de Chêne 30
1211 Geneva

Nater-Bass, Gabrielle
Homburger
Weinbergstrasse 56/8
8006 Zurich

Oetiker, Christian
Vischer
Aeschenvorstadt 4
4010 Basel

Palay, Marc
Winston & Strawn
Rue de Rhone 43
1204 Geneva

Patocchi, Paolo Michele
Lenz & Staehelin
Route de Chêne 30
1211 Geneva

Peter, Wolfgang
Python & Peter
Rue Firmin-Massot 9
1206 Geneva

Preti, Philippe
Baker & McKenzie
Rue Pedro-Meylan 5
1208 Geneva

Reichert, Douglas
1 rue Etienne Dumont
Case Postale 5327
1211 Geneve

Roney, David
Schellenberg Wittmer
15 bis, rue des Alpes
1211 Geneva

Schlaepfer, Anne-Veronique
Schellenberg Wittmer
15 bis, rue des Alpes
1211 Geneva

Schneider, Michael E
Lalive Attorneys-at-Law
Rue de la Mairie 35
1207 Geneva

Schwenzer, Ingeborg
University of Basel
Peter Merian Weg 8
4002 Basel

Spoorenberg, Frank
Tavernier Tschanz
11 bis, rue Toepffer
1206 Geneva

Triebold, Claudius
Schmid Eversheds
Stadelhoferstrasse 22
8001 Zurich

Veit, Marc
Walder Wyes & Partners
PO Box 1236
8034 Zurich

Vock, Dominik
Meyer Mueller Eckert Partners
Kreuzstrasse 42
8008 Zurich

Von Segesser, Georg
Schellenberg Wittmer
Löwenstrasse 19
8021 Zurich

Voser, Nathalie
Schellenberg Wittmer
Löwenstrasse 19
8021 Zurich

Wiebecke, Martin
Anwaltsbüro Wiebecke

Kohlrainstrasse 10
8700 Küsnacht/Zurich

Wühler, Norbert
International Organization for Migration
Route des Morillons 17
1211 Geneva

Yasseen, Rabab
Mentha & Partners
Rue de l'Athénée 4
1205 Geneva

## Thailand

Henderson, Alastair
Herbert Smith (Thailand) Ltd.
1403 Abdulrahim Place
990 Rama IV Road
10500 Bangkok

## Tunisia

Houerbi, Sami
c/o ICC
Centre Misk, Bloc B, Apt. B19
1073 Montplaisir-Tunis

Kemicha, Fathi
Member of ICCA
Kemicha Legal Consulting KLC
PO Box 27
Les Berges du Lac
1053 Tunis

## Turkey

Cosar, Utku
Cosar Attorneys at Law
Inonv Cad No. 18/2
Taksim
Istanbul 34437

## Ukraine

Alyoshin, Oleg
Vasil Kisil & Partners
17/52A Bogdana Khmelnitskogo
01030 Kiev

LIST OF PARTICIPANTS

Glukhovska, Olga
Magisters
38 Volodymyrska
01034 Kiev

Slipachuk, Tatyana
Vasil Kisil & Partners
17/52A Bogdana Khmelnitskogo
01030 Kiev

**United Arab Emirates**

Bourke, Patrick
Norton Rose (Middle East)
Gate Precinct Building 3, DIFC
PO Box 103474
Dubai

**United Kingdom**

Abdullah, Hayley
O'Melveny & Myers
Warwick Court
5 Paternoster Square
London EC4M 7DX

Aeberli, Peter
3 Paper Buildings
London EC3Y 7EU

Ashford, Peter
Cripps Harries Hall
Wallside House
12 Mount Ephraim Road
Tunbridge Wells, Kent TN1 1EG

Barrington, Louise
Centre of Construction Law
King's College London
Old Watch House
Kings College, Strand
London WC2R 2LS

Beechey, John
Clifford Chance
10 Upper Bank Street
London E14 5JJ

Bellhouse, John
White & Case

5 Old Broad Street
London EC2N 1DW

Benson, Cyrus
Gibson Dunn & Crutcher
Telephone House
2-4 Temple Avenue
London EC4Y 0HB

Bhattacharyya, Gautam
Reed Smith
Beaufort House
15 St. Botolph Street
London EC3A 7EE

Boyd, Stewart
Essex Court Chambers
24 Lincoln's Inn Fields
London WC2A 3EG

Brekoulakis, Stavros
School of International Arbitration
Queen Mary University London
67-69 Lincoln's Inn Fields
London WC2A 3JB

Brynmor, Thomas David
Herbert Smith
Exchange House
Primrose Street
London EC2A 2HS

Bueno, Antonio, QC
Equity House
Blackbrook Park Avenue
Taunton TA1 2PX

Burn, George
Salans – London
Millennium Bridge House
2 Lambeth Hill
London EC4V 4AJ

Byrne, Louise
Debevoise & Plimpton
Tower 42, Old Broad Street
London EC2N 1HQ

Cameron, Peter
CEPMLP
University of Dundee
Carnegie Building
Dundee DD1 4HN

743

Capper, Phillip
White & Case
5 Old Broad Street
London EC2N 1DW

Clarke, Andrew
Exxon Mobile International Ltd.
Ermyn Way
Leatherhead, Surrey KT22 8UX

Clarke, Lara
Debevoise & Plimpton
Tower 42, Old Broad Street
London EC2N 1HQ

Cotran, Eugene
Dean & Dean Solicitors
32 Gloucester Road
London W3 8PD

Cowan, Paul
White & Case
5 Old Broad Street
London EC2N 1DW

D'Agostino, Justin
Herbert Smith
Exchange House
Primrose Street
London EC2A 2HS

Davison, Michael
Lovells
Altantic House
Holborn Viaduct
London EC1A 2FG

De Lacy, Richard, QC
3 Stone Buildings
Lincoln's Inn
London WC2A 3XL

De Navacelle, Stephane
Debevoise & Plimpton
Tower 42, Old Broad Street
London EC2N 1HQ

Dervaird, John
4 Moray Place
Edinburgh EH3 6DS

Desplats, Maxime
Debevoise & Plimpton
Tower 42, Old Broad Street
London EC2N 1HQ

Doyle, Camilla
PricewaterhouseCoopers
Plumtree Court
London EC4A 4HT

Dufetre, Anne-Sophie
Debevoise & Plimpton
Tower 42, Old Broad Street
London EC2N 1HQ

Dundas, Hew R.
Suite 410, 83 Victoria Street
London SW1H 0HW

Dutson, Stuart
Eversheds
Senator House
85 Queen Victoria Street
London EC4V 4JL

Edwards, David
O'Melveny & Myers
Warwick Court
5 Paternoster Square
London EC4M 7DX

Escobar, Alejandro
Baker Botts (UK) Ltd.
41 Lothbury, 3rd Floor
London EC2R 7HF

Farren, Ania
Baker Botts (UK) Ltd.
41 Lothbury, 3rd Floor
London EC2R 7HF

Finizio, Steven
Wilmer Cutler Pickering Hale & Dorr
4 Carlton Gardens
London SW1Y 5AA

Flannery, Louis
Howes Percival
252 Upper Third Street
Milton Keynes MK9 1DZ

Fleuriet, Kenneth
King & Spalding
25 Cannon Street
London EC4M 5SE

LIST OF PARTICIPANTS

Foster, David
O'Melveny & Myers
Warwick Court
5 Paternoster Square
London EC4M 7DX

Foyle, Andrew
1 Essex Court
Temple
London C4Y 9AR

Frangeskides, Maria
Orrick, Herrington & Sutcliffe
Level 35, Tower 42
25 Old Broad Street
London EC2N 1HQ

Fraser, David
Baker & McKenzie
100 New Bridge Street
London EC4V 6JA

Friedman, Mark W.
Debevoise & Plimpton
Tower 42, Old Broad Street
London EC2N 1HQ

Friel, Steven
Davies Arnold Cooper
6-8 Bouverie Street
London EC4Y 8DD

Gal, Daniel
Dewey & LeBoeuf
1 Minster Court
Mincing Lane
London EC3R 7YL

Gearing, Matthew
Allen & Overy
One Bishops Square
London E1 6AD

Gill, Judith
Allen & Overy
One Bishops Square
London E1 6AD

Goldberg, David
SJ Berwin
10 Queen Street Place
London EC4R 1BE

Goldsmith, Peter
Debevoise & Plimpton
Tower 42, Old Broad Street
London EC2N 1HQ

Greenwood, Christopher
London School of Economics
Houghton Street
London WC2A 2AE

Griffin, Peter
31 Minister Road
London NW2 3SH

Guether, Thomas
Dewey & LeBoeuf
1 Minster Court
Mincing Lane
London EC3E 7YL

Hannon, Paul
47/E Lennox Gardens
London SW1X 0DF

Heilbron, Hilary
Brick Court Chambers
7-8 Essex Street
London WC2R 3LD

Heneghan, Patrick
Skadden, Arps, Slate, Meagher & Flom (UK)
40 Bank Street
Canary Wharf
London E14 5DS

Herlihy, David
Skadden, Arps, Slate, Meagher & Flom (UK)
40 Bank Street
Canary Wharf
London E14 5DS

Hill, Richard
Fulbright & Jaworski International
85 Fleet Street
London EC4Y 1AE

Hodges, Paula
Herbert Smith
Exchange House
Primrose Street
London EC2A 2HS

745

Hopkinson, Raichel
Denton Wilde Sapte
1 Fleet Place
London EC4M 7WS

Hudson, James
K & L Gates
110 Cannon Street
London EC4N 6AR

Hunter, Ian
Essex Court Chambers
24 Lincoln's Inn Fields
London WC2A 3EG

Hunter, J. Martin
Member of ICCA
Essex Court Chambers
24 Lincoln's Inn Fields
London WC2A 3EG

Inglis, William
Deloitte & Touche
Stonecutter Court
1 Stonecutter Street
London EC4A 4TR

Jagusch, Stephen
Allen & Overy
One Bishops Square
London E1 6AD

Joseph, David
Essex Court Chambers
24 Lincoln's Inn Fields
London WC2A 3EG

Neil Kaplan CBE QC
Member of ICCA
Pine House
The Square
Stow-on-the-Wold GL54 1AF

Kavanagh, David
O'Melveny & Myers
Warwick Court
5 Paternoster Square
London EC4M 7DX

Key, Paul
Essex Court Chambers
24 Lincoln's Inn Fields
London WC2A 3EG

Knox, Susan
Kroll Ontrack
12 Farringdon Road
Cardinal Tower
London EC1M 3HS

Knutson, Robert
95 Woodwarde Road
London SE22 8UL

Lagerberg, Gerry
PricewaterhouseCoopers
Plumtree Court
London EC4A 4HT

Landau, Toby, QC
Essex Court Chambers
24 Lincoln's Inn Fields
London WC2A 3EG

Lane, Patrick
39 Essex Street
London WC2R 3AT

Lawton, Charles
26 Abingdon Villas
London W8 6BX

Leaver, Peter
1 Essex Court
Temple
London EC4Y 9AR

Lee, Michael
20 Essex Street
London WC2R 3AL

Lennon Jr., Michael P.
Baker Botts (UK) Ltd.
41 Lothbury, 3rd Floor
London EC2R 7HF

Levy, Mark
Allen & Overy
One Bishops Square
London E1 6AD

Luker, Jo
Practical Law Company
19 Hatfields
London SE1 8DJ

LIST OF PARTICIPANTS

Macaulay, Bruce
Skadden, Arps, Slate, Meagher & Flom (UK)
40 Bank Street
Canary Wharf
London E14 5DS

MacLeod, David
4, 2F2 Barclay Terrace
Edinburgh EH10 4HP

Madden, Penelope
Skadden, Arps, Slate, Meagher & Flom (UK)
40 Bank Street
Canary Wharf
London E14 5DS

Maher, Patrick
Deloitte & Touche
Hill House
1 Little New Street
London EC4A 3TR

Marchili, Silvia
King & Spalding
25 Cannon Street
London EC4M 5SE

Marriott, Arthur
Member of ICCA
Dewey & LeBoeuf
1 Minster Court
Mincing Lane
London EC3R 7YL

Mash, Jeremy
Olswang
90 High Holborn
London WC1V 6XX

Meredith, Ian
K & L Gates
110 Cannon Street
London EC4N 6AR

Michaelson, Justin
SJ Berwin
10 Queen Street Place
London EC4R 1BE

Miles, Wendy
Wilmer Cutler Pickering Hale & Dorr
4 Carlton Gardens
London SW1Y 5AA

Milsom, Amanda
Practical Law Company
19 Hatfields
London SE1 8DJ

Mistelis, Loukas
School of International Arbitration
Queen Mary University of London
67-69 Lincoln's Inn Fields
London WC2A 3JB

Mitchard, Paul
Skadden, Arps, Slate, Meagher & Flom (UK)
40 Bank Street
Canary Wharf
London E14 5DS

Morgan, Simon
Simmons & Simmons
CityPoint
1 Ropemaker Street
London EC2Y 9SS

Moyler, Ian
Brick Court Chambers
7-8 Essex Street
London WC2R 3LD

Nadar, Aisha
Queen Mary University of London
London SW1A 1NH

Nairn, Karyl
Skadden, Arps, Slate, Meagher & Flom (UK)
40 Bank Street
Canary Wharf
London E14 5DS

Nesbitt, Simon
Lovells
Atlantic House
Holborn Viaduct
London EC1A 2FG

Oda, Hiroshi
Herbert Smith
Exchange House
Primrose Street
London EC2A 2HS

Page, Joanna
Allen & Overy

One Bishops Square
London E1 6AD

Paisley, Kathleen
White & Case
5 Old Broad Street
London EC2N 1DW

Parratt, David
Faculty of Advocates
Advocates Library, Parliament House
High Street
Edinburgh EH14 1AY

Rawding, Nigel
Freshfields Bruckhaus Deringer
65 Fleet Street
London EC4Y 1HS

Ray, Aloke
White & Case
5 Old Broad Street
London EC2N 1DW

Redfern, Alan
1 Essex Court
Temple
London EC4Y 9AR

Reid, Greg
Linklaters
1 Silk Street
London EC2Y 8HQ

Rohn, Patrick
Debevoise & Plimpton
Tower 42, Old Broad Street
London EC2N 1HQ

Rowland, John
4 Pump Court Chambers
4 Pump Court
Temple
London EC4Y 7AN

Ruff, Deborah
Dewey & LeBoeuf
1 Minster Court
Mincing Lane
London EC3R 7YL

Runeland, Per
SJ Berwin

10 Queen Street Place
London EC4R 1BE

Schwarz, Franz
Wilmer Cutler Pickering Hale & Dorr
4 Carlton Gardens
London SW1Y 5AA

Seeger, Karolos
Debevoise & Plimpton
Tower 42, Old Broad Street
London EC2N 1HQ

Shackleton, Stewart
Eversheds
Senator House
85 Queen Victoria Street
London EC4V 4JL

Shankland, Matthew
Weil, Gotshal & Manges
1 South Place
London EC2M 2WG

Sheppard, Audley
Clifford Chance
10 Upper Bank Street
London E14 5JJ

Sinclair, Anthony
Allen & Overy
One Bishops Square
London E1 6AD

Sindler, Michelle
Olswang
90 High Holborn
London WC1V 6XX

Smith, Michael Forbes
Chartered Institute of Arbitrators
12-14 Bloomsbury Square
London WC1A 2LP

Snodgrass, Elizabeth
Freshfields Bruckhaus Deringer
65 Fleet Street
London EC4Y 1HS

Stackpool-Moore, Ruth
Debevoise & Plimpton
Tower 42, Old Broad Street
London EC2N 1HQ

LIST OF PARTICIPANTS

Stockford, Claire
Crowell & Moring
11 Pilgrim Street
London EC4V 6RN

Style, Christopher
Linklaters
1 Silk Street
London EC2Y 8HQ

Sutcliffe, Jonathan
Fulbright & Jaworski International
85 Fleet Street
London EC4Y 1AE

Taylor, Eleanor
Kluwer Law International
250 Waterloo Road
First Floor
London SE1 8RD

Taylor, Tim
SJ Berwin
10 Queen Street Place
London EC4R 1BE

Temmink, Robert-Jan
Outer Temple Chambers
222 Strand
London WC2R 1BA

Tevendale, Craig
Herbert Smith
Exchange House
Primrose Street
London EC2A 2HS

Tirado, Joseph
Norton Rose
3 More London Riverside
London SE1 2AQ

Vagenheim, Alexandre
Essex Court Chambers
24 Lincoln's Inn Fields
London WC2A 3EG

Veeder, V.V.
Member of ICCA
Essex Court Chambers
24 Lincoln's Inn Fields
London WC2A 3EG

Verhoosel, Gaëtan
Covington and Burly
265 Strand
London WC2R 0

Wade, Shai
Reed Smith Richards Butler
Beaufort House
15 St. Botolph Street
London EC3A 7EE

Walsh, Simon
O'Melveny & Myers
Warwick Court
5 Paternoster Square
London EC4M 7DX

Warne, David
Reed Smith
Beaufort House
15 St. Botolph Street
London EC3A 7EE

Welsh, Angeline
Allen & Overy
One Bishops Square
London E1 6AD

Wessel, Jane
Crowell & Moring
11 Pilgrim Street
London EC4V 6RN

Winstanley, Adrian
LCIA
70 Fleet Street
London EC4Y 1EU

Woolhouse, Sarita
Fenners Chambers
19 Rustat Road
Cambridge CA1 3QR

Wordsworth, Samuel
Essex Court Chambers
24 Lincoln's Inn Fields
London WC2A 3EG

York, Stephen
Reed Smith Richards Butler
Beaufort House
15 St. Botolph Street
London EC3A 7EE

**United State of America**

Abrahamson, Laura
Occidental Petroleum Corporation
10889 Wilshire Blvd
Los Angeles, CA 90024

Aguilar-Alvarez, Guillermo
Member of ICCA
Weil, Gotshal & Manges
767 Fifth Avenue
New York, NY 10153

Alexander, Jay
Baker Botts
1299 Pennsylvania Avenue, NW
Washington, DC 20004-2400

Alwyn, Ken
Office of Ken Alwyn
160 San Pablo Avenue
San Francisco, CA 94127

Amirfar, Catherine
Debevoise & Plimpton
919 Third Avenue
New York, NY 10022

Andreeva, Yulia
Debevoise & Plimpton
919 Third Avenue
New York, NY 10022

Arif, Ali
Crowell and Moring
1001 Pennsylvania Avenue, NW
Washington, DC 20004

Arkin, Harry
Arkin and Associates
1660 Lincoln Street, Suite 2830
Denver, CO 80264

Armas, Oliver
Chadbourne & Parke
30 Rockefeller Plaza
New York, NY 10112

Ashman, Vivienne
Simpson Thacher & Bartlett
425 Lexington Avenue
New York, NY 10017-3954

Astigarraga, José
Astigarraga Davis
701 Brickell Avenue, 16th Floor
Miami, FL 33131

Barkett, John
Shook, Hardy & Bacon
201 S. Biscayne Blvd, Suite 2400
Miami, FL 33131

Barnes, Stacey
Hanszen Laporte
4309 Yoakum Road
Houston, TX 77006

Battle, Thomas
The Battle Law Firm
38 Redbud Ridge PL
The Woodlands, TX 77380

Bedard, Julie
Skadden, Arps, Slate, Meagher & Flom
Four Times Square, Room 47-108
New York, NY 10036-6522

Berghoff, Ethan
Baker & McKenzie
1 Prudential Place
Chicago, IL 60001

Bettauer, Ronald
George Washington University Law School
1518 Highwood Drive
McLean, VA 22101-5800

Bishop, Raymond Doak
King & Spalding
1100 Louisiana, Suite 4000
Houston, TX 77002-5213

Boccuzzi, Carmine
Cleary Gottlieb Steen & Hamilton
1 Liberty Plaza
New York, NY 10006

LIST OF PARTICIPANTS

Bowman, John
King & Spalding
1100 Louisiana Street, Suite 4100
Houston, TX 77002

Boykin, James
Hughes Hubbard & Reed
1775, 1 Street, NW
Washington, DC 20006

Bray, Daina
Freshfields Bruckhaus Deringer
520 Madison Avenue
New York, NY 10022

Brennan, Lorraine
International Institute for
Conflict Prevention & Resolution
575 Lexington Avenue
New York, NY 10022

Cann, Frederic
Cann Lawyers
1300 SW Fifth Avenue, Suite 2750
Portland, OR 97201-5617

Caron, David
University of California
Berkeley School of Law
Boalt Hall 445
Berkeley, CA 94720-7210

Carter, James
Sullivan & Cromwell
125 Broad Street, 32nd Floor
New York, NY 10004-2498

Coe, Jack
Pepperdine Law School
24255 Pacific Coast Highway
Malibu, CA 90263

Collins, Michael
Crandall, Hanscom & Collins
10 School Street
Rockland, ME 04848

Dagar, Bina
Ameya Consulting
25 Cedar Parkway North
Livingston, NJ 07039

De By, Robert A.
Dewey & LeBoeuf
1301 Avenue of the Americas
New York, NY 10019

Dolenz-Extale, Nicole
Baker & McKenzie
1114 Avenue of the Americas
New York, NY 10036

Donovan, Donald Francis
Vice President of ICCA
Debevoise & Plimpton
919 Third Avenue
New York, NY 10022

Elul, Hagit
Hughes Hubbard & Reed
One Battery Park Plaza
New York, NY 10004

Enix-Ross, Deborah
Debevoise & Plimpton
919 Third Avenue
New York, NY 10022

Febish, Chrystal
Juris Publishing Inc.
71 New Street
Huntington, NY 11743

Freedberg, Judith
3530 Coral Way, Apt. 516
Miami, FL 33145

Freyer, Dana
Skadden, Arps, Slate, Meagher & Flom
Four Times Square
New York, NY 10036-6522

Gardiner, John
Skadden, Arps, Slate, Meagher & Flom

Four Times Square
New York, NY 10036-6522

Garfinkel, Barry H.
Skadden, Arps, Slate, Meagher & Flom
Four Times Square
New York, NY 10036-6522

Goldstein, Marc
Marc J. Goldstein Law Offices
7 Arbitration Chambers
1230 Avenue of the Americas, 7th Floor
New York, NY 10024

Gusy, Martin
Wuersch & Gerling
100 Wall Street, 21st Floor
New York, NY 10005

Hanessian, Grant
Baker & McKenzie
1114 Avenue of the Americas
New York, NY 10036

Haridi, Samaa
Crowell and Moring
1001 Pennsylvania Avenue, NW
Washington, DC 20004

Hayden, Donald
Baker & McKenzie
1111 Brickell Avenue, Suite 1700
Miami, FL 33131

Hellmann, Elizabeth
Skadden, Arps, Slate, Meagher & Flom
Four Times Square
New York, NY 10036-6522

Hennike, Toni
Exxon Mobil Corporation
800 Bell Street
EMB 1707-C
Houston, TX 77002

Hinchey, John
King & Spalding

1180 Peachtree Street
Atlanta, GA 30309

Holtzmann, Howard
Honorary Vice President of ICCA
630 Fifth Avenue
Suite 2000
New York, NY 10011

Hosking, James
Clifford Chance US
31 West 52nd Street
New York, NY 10019

Kehoe, Edward
King & Spalding
1185 Avenue of the Americas, 35th Floor
New York, NY 10036

Kerr, John
Simpson Thacher & Bartlett
425 Lexington Avenue
New York, NY 10017-3954

Kingsbury, Benedict
New York University School of Law
40 Washington Square South, 314
New York, NY 10012

Kitzen, Michael
Juris Publishing Inc
71 New Street
Huntington, NY 11743

Kuck, Lea
Skadden, Arps, Slate, Meagher & Flom
Four Times Square, Room 40-302
New York, NY 10036-6522

Lake, Jennifer
333 Seventh Avenue, 14th Floor
New York, NY 10001

Lamm, Carolyn
White & Case
701, 13th Street, NW
Washington, DC 20005

LIST OF PARTICIPANTS

Landsman, Kim
Patterson Belknap Webb & Tyler
1133 Avenue of the Americas
New York, NY 10036-6710

Leader, Jordan
Proskauer Rose
1585 Broadway
New York, NY 10036

Leatzow, Jim
Leatzow & Associates Inc
1265 Pine Isle Road
Three Lakes, WI 54562

Lindsey, David
Clifford Chance US
31 West 52nd Street
New York, NY 10019

Menaker, Andrea
White & Case
701 13th Street, NW
Washington, DC 20005

Mentz, Barbara
Barbara A. Mentz Attorney
140 West 66th Street, Suite 2B
New York, NY 10024

Miles, Craig
King & Spalding
1100 Louisiana Street, Suite 4100
Houston, TX 77002

Molineaux, Charles
Construction Arbitration Worldwide
1660 International Drive, Suite 400
McLean, VA 22102

Moses, Margaret
Loyola University
Chicago School of Law
25 East Pearson
Chicago, IL 60611

Naimark, Richard
American Arbitration Association
1633 Broadway, 10th Floor
New York, NY 10019-6708

Nelson, Timothy
Skadden, Arps, Slate, Meagher & Flom
Four Times Square
New York, NY 10036-6522

Newman, Lawrence
Baker & McKenzie
1114 Avenue of the Americas
New York, NY 10036

Ordway, Eric
Weil, Gotshal & Manges
767 Fifth Avenue
New York, NY 10153

Park, William
Member of ICCA
Boston University Law Faculty
765 Commonwealth Avenue
Boston, MA 02215

Parra, Antonio
Honorary Secretary General of ICCA
International Center for Settlement of
Investment Disputes
The World Bank
1818 H Street NW
Washington, DC 20433

Pearsall, Patrick
Office of the Legal Adviser
Suite 203, South Building
2430 E Street, NW
Washington D.C. 20037-2851
United States

Pierce, John V. H.
Wilmer Cutler Pickering Hale & Dorr
399 Park Avenue
New York, NY 10028

Port, Nicola
Debevoise & Plimpton
919 Third Avenue
New York, NY 10022

Prager, Dietmar
Debevoise & Plimpton
919 Third Avenue
New York, NY 10022

Price, Jennifer
King & Spalding
1100 Louisiana Street, Suite 4100
Houston, TX 77002

Reed, Lucy
Freshfields Bruckhaus Deringer
520 Madison Avenue, 34th Floor
New York, NY 10022

Reisenfeld, Kenneth B.
King & Spalding
1700 Pennsylvania Avenue, NW
Washington, DC 20006

Rivkin, David W.
Debevoise & Plimpton
919 Third Avenue
New York, NY 10022

Roesser, John
Proskauer Rose
1585 Broadway
New York, NY 10036

Rovine, Arthur W.
Fordham Law School
1114 Avenue of the Americas
New York, NY 10036

Santens, Ank
White & Case
1155 Avenue of the Americas
New York, NY 10036

Schnabl, Marco
Skadden, Arps, Slate, Meagher & Flom
Four Times Square 47-416
New York, NY 10036-6522

Schorr, Edward
Lovells
590 Madison Avenue
New York, NY 10022

Sentner, Robert
Nixon Peabody
437 Madison Avenue
New York, NY 10022

Sherwin, Peter
Proskauer Rose
1585 Broadway
New York, NY 10036

Sicard-Mirabel, Josefa
ICC International Court of Arbitration
1212 Avenue of the Americas, 21st Floor
New York, NY 10036

Simmons, Beth
Harvard University
1737 Cambridge Street
Cambridge, MA 02138

Skinazi, Heather
Occidental Petroleum Corporation
10889 Wilshire Blvd.
Los Angeles, CA 90024

Slate II, William K.
Member of ICCA
American Arbitration Association
1776, 1 Street, NW, Suite 850
Washington, DC 20006

Smith, Reginald
King & Spalding
1100 Louisiana Street, Suite 4100
Houston, TX 77002

LIST OF PARTICIPANTS

Smutny, Abby Cohen
White & Case
701, 13th Street NW
Washington, DC 20005

Stevens, Margrete
King & Spalding
1700 Pennsylvania Avenue, NW, Suite 200
Washington, DC 20006

Sussman, Alexander
Fried, Frank, Harris, Shriver & Jacobson
1 New York Plaza
New York, NY 10004

Sussman, Edna
Hoguet Newman Regal & Kenney
10 East 40th Street
New York, NY 10583

Tahbaz, Christopher
Debevoise & Plimpton
919 Third Avenue
New York, NY 10022

Torterola, Ignacio
Embassy of Argentina
Procuracion del Tesoro de la Nacion
1600 New Hampshire Avenue
Washington, DC 20009

Townsend, John
Hughes Hubbard & Reed
1775, 1 Street, NW
Washington, DC 20006

Vasani, Sarah
King & Spalding
1100 Louisiana Street, Suite 4100
Houston, TX 77002

Vicien-Milburn, Maria
United Nations
42nd Street and First Avenue
New York, NY 10017

Ziade, Nassib
International Centre for Settlement of
Investment Disputes
Room No. U3-171
The World Bank Group
Washington, DC 20433

**Venezuela**

Droulers, Diana
Arbitration Centre, Caracas Chambers
PO Box 2831
1010 Caracas

# INTERNATIONAL COUNCIL FOR COMMERCIAL ARBITRATION (ICCA)

*Correspondence address:*
Mr. Antonio R. Parra
Secretary General ICCA
c/o International Centre for Settlement of Investment Disputes
1818 H Street, NW
Washington, DC 20433
USA
Phone:+1-202 744 8801
Fax:+1-202 522 2615
E-mail: arparra@earthlink.net

LIST OF OFFICERS AND MEMBERS

July 2009

OFFICERS

*Honorary Presidents*

THE HON. GIORGIO BERNINI (Bologna, Italy)
Former Minister of Foreign Trade and Member of Parliament; Former Member, Italian Antitrust Authority; Professor, University of Bologna, Chair of Arbitration and International Commercial Law; President, Association for the Teaching and Study of Arbitration and International Trade Law (AISA); Member, Executive Committee, Italian Arbitration Association; Senior Partner, Studio Bernini e Associati

MR. FALI S. NARIMAN (New Delhi, India)
President, Bar Association of India; Honorary Member, International Commission of Jurists; Past President, Law Association for Asia and the Pacific (LAW ASIA); Member, Court of the LCIA; Past Vice Chairman, International Court of Arbitration of the International Chamber of Commerce (ICC); Past Co-Chair, Human Rights

Institute of the International Bar Association (IBA); Senior Advocate, Supreme Court of India

PROF. PIETER SANDERS (Schiedam, The Netherlands)
Honorary President, Netherlands Arbitration Institute; Professor Emeritus, Faculty of Law, Erasmus University, Rotterdam

*President*

DR. GEROLD HERRMANN (Vienna, Austria)
Former Secretary, United Nations Commission on International Trade Law (UNCITRAL); Honorary Professor, University of Vienna

*Honorary Vice Presidents*

JUDGE HOWARD M. HOLTZMANN (New York, USA)
Honorary Chairman of the Board, American Arbitration Association (AAA); Substitute Judge, Iran-United States Claims Tribunal, The Hague

PROF. SERGEI LEBEDEV (Moscow, Russian Federation)
President, Maritime Arbitration Commission; Member of the Presidium, International Commercial Arbitration Court of the Russian Federation Chamber of Commerce and Industry; Professor, Moscow Institute of International Relations (University); Former Commissioner, UN Compensation Commission; Member, UNCITRAL Working Group on Arbitration

DDR. WERNER MELIS (Vienna, Austria)
President, International Arbitral Centre of the Austrian Federal Economic Chamber, Vienna; Past Vice President, LCIA

MS. TINUADE OYEKUNLE (Lagos, Nigeria)
Member, Association of Arbitrators of Nigeria; Fellow, Chartered Institute of Arbitrators, London; Member, Arbitration Committee of the Lagos Chamber of Commerce; Chartered Arbitrator; Chairman, Education & Training Committee of the Chartered Institute of Arbitrators; Member, Board of Management of the Chartered Institute of Arbitrators, London; Regional Representative for Promotion of Arbitration in the West African Region; Past Chairman, Chartered Institute of Arbitrators, Nigeria Branch; former Member, London Court of International

Arbitration (LCIA); Correspondent of UNIDROIT; Barrister and Solicitor of the Supreme Court of Nigeria, Arbitrator and Notary Public

*Vice Presidents*

MR. DONALD FRANCIS DONOVAN (New York, USA)
Adjunct Professor, New York University School of Law; Vice President, American Society of International Law; Immediate Past Chair, Institute for Transnational Arbitration; Former Chair, U.S. National Committee International Chamber of Commerce (ICC), International Court of Arbitration; Board of Directors, Human Rights First

MR. MICHAEL HWANG, SC (Singapore)
Former Vice Chair, Committee D, International Bar Association; Member, Permanent Court of Arbitration; Vice-Chair, International Court of Arbitration of the International Chamber of Commerce (ICC); Exco Member, Institute of Transnational Arbitration; Member, LCIA; Member, International Council of Arbitrators for Sport (ICAS); Former Acting High Court Judge, Singapore; Adjunct Professor, National University of Singapore; Deputy Chief Justice, Dubai International Financial Centre; Chartered Arbitrator; President, Law Society of Singapore; Advocate and Solicitor, Singapore

PROF. DR. IVÁN SZÁSZ (Budapest, Hungary)
Professor of Law, University of Economic Sciences, Budapest; Honorary President, Legal Commission at the Hungarian Chamber of Commerce; Past Ambassador of Hungary to the European Communities; Member, International Court of Arbitration of the International Chamber of Commerce (ICC); Attorney-at-law, Squire Sanders & Dempsey

*Honorary Secretary General*

MR. ULF FRANKE (Stockholm, Sweden)
Past Secretary General, ICCA; Secretary General, Arbitration Institute of the Stockholm Chamber of Commerce; President, International Federation of Commercial Arbitration Institutions (IFCAI)

*Secretary General*

MR. ANTONIO R. PARRA (Washington, DC, USA)
Past Deputy Secretary-General and Legal Adviser, International Centre for Settlement of Investment Disputes (ICSID); Visiting Professor, University College London Faculty of Laws; Fellow, Chartered Institute of Arbitrators; Consultant, World Bank

MEMBERS

MR. CECIL ABRAHAM (Negeri Sembilan, Malaysia)
Fellow, Chartered Institute of Arbitrators; Fellow, Malaysian Institute of Arbitrators; Past Member, LCIA Court; Past President, Inter-Pacific Bar Association; Vice President, Asia Pacific Regional Arbitration Group (APRAG)

MR. GUILLERMO AGUILAR-ALVAREZ (New York, USA)
Past General Counsel, International Court of Arbitration of the International Chamber of Commerce (ICC); Principal Legal Counsel for the Government of Mexico for the Negotiation and Implementation of NAFTA; Partner, Weil Gotshal & Manges

PROF. DR. ALBERT JAN VAN DEN BERG (The Netherlands)
General Editor, ICCA *Yearbook Commercial Arbitration*; President, Netherlands Arbitration Institute; Professor of Arbitration Law, Erasmus University, Rotterdam; Attorney

PROF. DR. PIERO BERNARDINI (Rome, Italy)
Past Professor of Arbitration Law, LUISS University, Rome; Vice-President, Italian Arbitration Association; Past Vice-President, International Court of Arbitration of the International Chamber of Commerce (ICC)

PROF. DR. KARL-HEINZ BÖCKSTIEGEL (Bergisch-Gladbach, Germany)
Professor Emeritus of International Business Law, University of Cologne; Chairman, German Institution of Arbitration (DIS); Patron, Chartered Institute of Arbitrators; Past President, International Law Association; Past President, LCIA; Past President, Iran-United States Claims Tribunal, The Hague

PROF. DR. NAEL G. BUNNI (Dublin, Ireland)
Past President, The Chartered Institute of Arbitrators; Past Board Member, LCIA; Visiting Professor in Construction Law & Contract Administration, Trinity College, Dublin; Chartered Engineer and Chartered Registered Arbitrator; Member, Board of Trustees, and Chairman, Executive Committee, Dubai International Arbitration Centre

MS. TERESA CHENG, BBS, SC, JP (Hong Kong)
Deputy President for 2007 and President for 2008, Chartered Institute of Arbitrators; Vice Chairperson, Hong Kong International Arbitration Centre; Adjunct Professor, School of Law at the City University of Hong Kong; Chartered Engineer; Barrister

PROF. BERNARDO M. CREMADES (Madrid, Spain)
Professor, Faculty of Law, Madrid University; Member of the Madrid Bar

MR. DUSHYANT DAVE (New Delhi, India)
Senior Advocate, Supreme Court of India; Member, National Legal Services Authority of India; President, Asia Pacific Users' Council, LCIA; Member, LCIA Court; Member, Board of the American Arbitration Association (AAA); Vice-Chair, Arbitration Committee, International Bar Association (IBA)

M$^E$ YVES DERAINS (Paris, France)
Past Secretary General, International Court of Arbitration of the International Chamber of Commerce (ICC); Chairman, *Comité Français de l'Arbitrage*; Member of the Paris Bar

MR. L. YVES FORTIER, CC, QC (Montréal, Canada)
Chair, Hong Kong International Arbitration Court; Former Ambassador and Permanent Representative of Canada to the United Nations; Chairman and Senior Partner Ogilvie Renault Montréal; Former President and Honorary Vice President, LCIA; Judge ad hoc, International Court of Justice

PROF. DR. EMMANUEL GAILLARD (Paris, France)
Professor of Law, University of Paris XII; Past Member, LCIA Court; Chairman, International Arbitration Institute; Past Chairman, International Arbitration Committee, International Law Association

PROF. DR. BERNARD HANOTIAU (Brussels, Belgium)
Professor of International Dispute Resolution, University of Louvain; Vice-President, London Court of International Arbitration; Vice-President, Institute of Transnational Arbitration; Vice-President, CEPANI (Belgium); Member, Brussels and Paris Bars


PROF. J. MARTIN H. HUNTER (London, United Kingdom)
Professor of International Dispute Resolution, Nottingham Trent University; Visiting Professor, King's College London University; Chairman, Dubai International Arbitration Centre; Honorary Dean of Postgraduate Studies, T.M.C. Asser Instituut, The Hague; Barrister


MR. NEIL KAPLAN, CBE, QC (Gloucestershire, United Kingdom)
Former Judge, High Court, Hong Kong; Chairman, Hong Kong International Arbitration Centre 1991-2004; Honorary Professor, City University of Hong Kong; Past President, The Chartered Institute of Arbitrators


PROF.DR. GABRIELLE KAUFMANN-KOHLER (Geneva, Switzerland)
Professor, Private International Law and International Dispute Resolution, Geneva University Law School; Honorary President, Swiss Arbitration Association (ASA); Attorney, Partner, Lévy Kaufmann-Kohler


DR. FATHI KEMICHA (Tunis, Tunisia)
Member, International Law Commission of the United Nations; Member, World Bank Group Sanctions Board; Member, Board of Trustees and Executive Committee, Dubai International Arbitration Centre; First appointed Secretary General, Constitutional Court of the Kingdom of Bahrain (January 2003 – December 2005); Former Vice President, London Court of International Arbitration (LCIA); *Avocat à la Cour*, Member of the Paris and Tunisia Bars


MR. KAP-YOU (KEVIN) KIM
Senior Advisor, Korea Commercial Arbitration Board (KCAB); Vice President, Korean Council for International Arbitration( KOCIA); Member, ICC International Court of Arbitration; Member, London Court of International Arbitration (LCIA); Board Member, American Arbitration Association (AAA); Vice Chair, IBA Arbitration Committee; Member, Drafting Subcommittee for the revision of ICC Rules; Member, Subcommittee on revision of IBA Rules on Taking Evidences; Panel of Arbitrators, ICSID; Adjunct Professor of Law, Seoul National University

PROF. ALEXANDER S. KOMAROV (Moscow, Russian Federation)
Chairman, International Chamber of Commerce (ICC) Russian National Committee, Arbitration Commission; Professor, Russian Academy of Foreign Trade; President, International Commercial Arbitration Court at the Russian Federation Chamber of Commerce and Industry

PROF. AHMED S. EL-KOSHERI (Cairo, Egypt)
Professor of International Economic Law and Former President, International University for African Development (Alexandria); Member, *l'Institut de Droit International*; Partner, Kosheri, Rashed & Riad Law Firm

MR. ARTHUR MARRIOTT, QC (London, United Kingdom)
Board Member, Hong Kong International Arbitration Centre; Solicitor

M<sup>E</sup> CARLOS NEHRING NETTO (São Paulo, Brazil)
Former Member, International Court of Arbitration of the International Chamber of Commerce (ICC); Member, LCIA

PROF. FRANCISCO ORREGO VICUÑA (Santiago, Chile)
Professor of Law, University of Chile and first Director of the LL.M. on Investments, Trade and Arbitration offered jointly with the University of Heidelberg and the Max Planck Institute; Judge and former President, Administrative Tribunal of the World Bank; Member, Chairman's List of ICSID Arbitrators; former Vice President, London Court of International Arbitration; Member, Latin American Committee of Arbitrators of the ICC

PROF. WILLIAM W. PARK (Cohasset, USA)
Professor of Law, Boston University; General Editor, Arbitration International; Vice President, London Court of International Arbitration; Past Chairman, American Bar Association Committee on International Commercial Dispute Resolution

PROF. JAN PAULSSON (Paris, France)
General Editor, ICCA *International Handbook on Commercial Arbitration*; President, LCIA; President, World Bank Administrative Tribunal; President, European Bank for Reconstruction and Development Administrative Tribunal

PROF. DR. MICHAEL PRYLES (Melbourne, Australia)
President, Australian Centre for International Commercial Arbitration; Member, LCIA Court; Co-Chairman, ICC Asia Pacific Arbitration Commission; Former

Commissioner, United Nations Compensation Commission; Former Commissioner, Australian Law Reform Commission; Former Henry Bournes Higgins Professor of Law, Monash University, Melbourne; Visiting Professor of Law, University of Queensland, Bond University, Murdoch University; Consultant, Clayton Utz

MR. WILLIAM K. SLATE II (Washington, DC, USA)
President and Chief Executive Officer, American Arbitration Association (AAA); Founder, Global Center for Dispute Resolution Research; Member, Arbitrator and Mediator, Panels of the International Court of Sport (Switzerland); Member, International Commercial Arbitration Court at the Ukraine Chamber of Commerce and Industry; Member, China International Economic and Trade Arbitration Commission (CIETAC)

PROF. YASUHEI TANIGUCHI (Tokyo, Japan)
Professor Emeritus, Kyoto University; Professor, Senshu University Law School; President, Japan Association of Arbitrators; Special Advisor to the Japan Commercial Arbitration Association (JCAA); Former Member, Appellate Body of the World Trade Organization (WTO); Of Counsel, Matsuo & Kosugi

PROF. DR. GUIDO SANTIAGO TAWIL (Buenos Aires, Argentina)
Professor, University of Buenos Aires School of Law; Senior Vice Chair, IBA Arbitration Committee; Member, London Court of International Arbitration (LCIA); Attorney at Law, Partner, M. & M. Bomchil

PROF. DR. DR. HC. PIERRE TERCIER (Fribourg, Switzerland)
Professor, Faculty of Law, University of Fribourg; Chairman, International Court of Arbitration of the International Chamber of Commerce (ICC); Visiting Professor of the Universities of Paris II and Torino; Former Chairman, Swiss Antitrust Commission

MR. V.V. VEEDER, QC (London, United Kingdom)
Vice President, London Court of International Arbitration; Council Member, ICC Institute of World Business Law and of the Arbitration Institute of the Stockholm Chamber of Commerce; Visiting Professor on Investment Arbitration, King's College, University of London; Chairman, ARIAS (UK)

THE HON. S. AMOS WAKO, F.C.I.ARB, SC (Nairobi, Kenya)
Attorney General, Republic of Kenya; Former Chairman, Arbitration Tribunal, Kenya Chamber of Commerce and Industry; Former Vice President, LCIA – Africa Region; Arbitrator, Vienna Convention on Law of Treaties, Centre for Settlement

of International Disputes; Former Chairman, Law Society of Kenya; Former Member, International Advisory Committee of WIPO Centre for Settlement of Disputes; Former Commission Member, International Commission of Jurists; Former Deputy Secretary General, International Bar Association (IBA); Former Secretary General, African Bar Association; Former President, Asian-African Legal Consultative Organisation; Member, International Law Commission (2007 - 2011)

DR. WANG SHENG CHANG (Beijing, People's Republic of China)
Vice Chairman and Secretary General, China International Economic and Trade Arbitration Commission (CIETAC); Vice Chairman, China Maritime Arbitration Commission (CMAC); Vice Chairman, Asia Pacific Region Arbitration Group (ARPAG); Professor of Law, University of International Economics and Business, Beijing

MR. DAVID A. R. WILLIAMS, QC (Auckland, New Zealand)
Former Judge of the High Court of New Zealand; Chief Justice of the Cook Islands; Judge, Court of Dubai International Financial Centre; Past President, Arbitrators and Mediators Institute of New Zealand; Member, Board of Directors, American Arbitration Association; Former Member, ICC Court of International Arbitration; Former Member, LCIA

*Advisory Members*

DR. ROBERT BRINER (Geneva, Switzerland)
Past Chairman (now Honorary Chairman), International Court of Arbitration of the International Chamber of Commerce (ICC); Past President, Iran-United States Claims Tribunal, The Hague

MR. ROBERT COULSON (Riverside, USA)
Former President, American Arbitration Association (AAA)

PROF. DR. RADOMIR DJUROVIČ (Belgrade, Serbia)
Former President, Arbitration Court of Yugoslavia; Professor of International Commercial Law, Belgrade University

DR. DR. OTTOARNDT GLOSSNER (Kronberg, Germany)
Past Chairman, International Chamber of Commerce (ICC) Commission on International Arbitration; Honorary President, German Institution of Arbitration (DIS) Cologne/Berlin; Attorney-at-law

PROF. DR. PIERRE LALIVE (Geneva, Switzerland)
*Président d'honneur*, Swiss Arbitration Association (ASA); Professor Emeritus, Geneva University; Honorary Chairman, Institute of International Business Law and Practice (ICC); Member (Former President), *l'Institut de Droit International*; Attorney-at-Law, Lalive, Geneva


THE HON. MARC LALONDE (Montréal, Canada)
Former ad-hoc Judge, International Court of Justice; Former Minister of Justice and Attorney General; Former Minister of Energy, Mines and Resources; Former Minister of Finance; Former President, LCIA North American Users Committee; Member, Institute of International Business Law and Practice


MR. MARK LITTMAN, QC (London, United Kingdom)
Barrister


MR. ALAIN PLANTEY (Paris, France)
Former Member of the *Conseil d'État*; Member and Former President, *Institut de France*; Member and Former President, Academy of Moral and Political Sciences (*Institut de France*); Former Ambassador of France; Former Professor of Law, University of Paris I; *Président d'honneur*, International Court of Arbitration of the International Chamber of Commerce (ICC)


THE HON. ANDREW JOHN ROGERS, QC (Sydney, Australia)
Former Chief Judge, Commercial Division, Supreme Court of New South Wales; Chairman, National Dispute Centre, Sydney; Adjunct Professor, University of Technology, Sydney


DR. JOSÉ LUIS SIQUEIROS (Mexico City, Mexico)
Past President, Mexican Academy of International Commercial Arbitration; Past President, Inter-American Bar Association; Past Chairman, Inter-American Juridical Committee (OAS)


DR. HABIL. TADEUSZ SZURSKI (Warsaw, Poland)
Past President, Court of Arbitration at the Polish Chamber of Commerce; Vice President, Polish Arbitration Association; Member, Polish Bar; Member of the Scientific Council of the Institute of International Law, Warsaw University; Honorary President of the Court of Arbitration at the Polish Confederation of Private Employers as well as of the Court of Arbitration of the Polish Chamber of Commerce

PROF. TANG HOUZHI (Beijing, People's Republic of China)
Honorary Vice Chairman, China International Economic and Trade Arbitration Commission (CIETAC); Vice Chairman, CCPIT/CCOIC Beijing Conciliation Centre; Professor, Law School of the People's University of China; Visiting Professor, Amoy University School of Law; Arbitration Adviser, UN International Trade Centre; Fellow and Chartered Arbitrator, The Chartered Institute of Arbitrators; Former Court Member, LCIA; Honorary Professor, Hong Kong City University School of Law; Vice President, International Federation of Commercial Arbitration Institutions (IFCAI)